D0894416

ENCYCLOPEDIA OF RELIGIOUS AND SPIRITUAL DEVELOPMENT

ENCYCLOPEDIA OF RELIGIOUS AND SPIRITUAL DEVELOPMENT

EDITORS

ELIZABETH M. DOWLING

ImagineNations Group

W. GEORGE SCARLETT

Tufts University

A SAGE Reference Publication

For information:

Sage Publications, Inc.
2455 Teller Road
Thousand Oaks, California 91320
E-mail: order@sagepub.com

Sage Publications Ltd.
1 Oliver's Yard
55 City Road
London EC1Y 1SP
United Kingdom

Sage Publications India Pvt. Ltd.
B-42, Panchsheel Enclave
Post Box 4109
New Delhi 110 017 India

Printed in the United States of America on acid-free paper

Library of Congress Cataloging-in-Publication data

Encyclopedia of religious and spiritual development / editors, Elizabeth M. Dowling, W. George Scarlett.
p. cm. — (Sage program on applied developmental science)
"A SAGE reference publication."
Includes bibliographical references and index.
ISBN 0-7619-2883-9 (hardcover)
1. Youth—Religious life—Encyclopedias. 2. Faith development—Encyclopedias.
3. Youth psychology—Encyclopedias. I. Dowling, Elizabeth Meredith.
II. Scarlett, W. George. III. Title. IV. Series.
BV4571.3.E53 2005
200′.83′03—dc22 2005012704

06 07 08 09 10 9 8 7 6 5 4 3 2 1

Acquiring Editor: Jim Brace-Thompson
Editorial Assistant: Karen Ehrmann
Typesetter: C&M Digitals (P) Ltd.
Indexer: Teri Greenberg
Cover Designer: Janet Foulger

Contents

Advisory Board

List of Entries

Reader's Guide

The distinction between that which is religious and that which is spiritual is far from clear-cut and far from being an either-or type of distinction. For example, the Dalai Lama is both a religious figure and a spiritual exemplar. We have therefore purposely kept the concepts of religious and spiritual together in organizing the encyclopedia's Reader's Guide. We have also placed each entry into a category that best defines its relationship to the religious and/or spiritual. However, given that some entries are representative of more than one category, we have placed in parentheses the name of the category to which the entry also closely applies. We hope this Reader's Guide provides some sense of the scope and range of the characteristics and contexts that are involved in religious and spiritual development. We also hope that this Reader's Guide helps to frame what might be missing from this encyclopedia—as explained in the Introduction—as well as where the study of religious and spiritual development may turn in the future.

THE ARTS

Angelou, Maya (see also Exemplars)
Crashaw, Richard (see also Exemplars)
Dance
Dance Festivals, Latvian
Donne, John (see also Exemplars)
Drama
Film
Gospel Music
Herbert, George (see also Exemplars)
Islamic Art
L'Engle, Madeleine (see also Exemplars)
Lewis, C. S. (see also Exemplars)
Literature, Children's
Literature, Moral Development in
Music
Myth
Narrative
Siqueiros, David Alfaro
Spirituals, African American
Vaughan, Henry (see also Exemplars)

CONCEPTS, RELIGIOUS AND SPIRITUAL

Angels
Apocalypse
Attitudinal Dimension
Awe and Wonder
Body
Child's God
Childhood Experiences
Christian Spirituality
Conversion (see also Practices, Religious and Spiritual)
Devil
Doubt
Eschatology
Evil
Faith
Fundamentalism
God
God, Hindu View of (see also Practices, Religious and Spiritual)
Grace
Happiness
Heaven
Hell
Hinduism, Supreme Being of, the Hindu Trinity
Kingdom of God
Krishna
Mindfulness (see also Practices, Religious and Spiritual)
Mysticism
Mysticism, Jewish

HEALTH

LEADING RELIGIOUS AND SPIRITUAL FIGURES

Central Religious Figures

Exemplars and Influential Figures

SCHOLARS

NATURE

Crop Circles
Ecology
Environmental Ethics
Gaia Hypothesis
Mother Earth
Naturalism
Nature (see also Places, Religious and Spiritual)
Nature, the Sacred in
Wilderness (see also Places, Religious and Spiritual)

ORGANIZATIONS

Educational Organizations (see also Supports/Contexts)
Faith-based Service Organizations (see also Supports/Contexts)
InterVarsity
Jesuit Volunteer Corps
Save the Children
Search Institute
Sierra Club
Teen Challenge
UNESCO
UNICEF
United Nations
World Youth Day
YMCA
Young Life
YouthBuild

PLACES, RELIGIOUS AND SPIRITUAL

Altars
Churches
Delphi
Mecca
Meherabad
Mosque
Nature (see also Wilderness)
Retreats
Sistine Chapel
Stonehenge
Tower of David
Western Wall
Wilderness (see also Nature)

PRACTICES, RELIGIOUS AND SPIRITUAL

Alchemy
Asceticism
Astrology
Buddhism, Socially Engaged
Conversion (see also Concepts, Religious and Spiritual)
Cults (see also Supports/Contexts)
Dance
Dialogue, Inter-Religious
Discernment
Eucharist
Fasting
Forgiveness
God, Hindu View of (see also Concepts, Religious and Spiritual)
Gospel Music (see also Art)
Health and Medicine (see also Health)
Islam, Five Pillars of
Karma, Law of
Lord's Prayer
Magic
Meditation
Mindfulness (see also Concepts, Religious and Spiritual)
Native American Spirituality, Practices of
Neo-paganism
Objectivism
Pluralism (see also Concepts, Religious and Spiritual)
Pluralism, Hindu (see also Concepts, Religious and Spiritual)
Prayer
Psychological Prayer
Ritual
Sacraments
Sacrifice (see also Concepts, Religious and Spiritual)
Service
Speech, Ethical
Spirituals, African American (See also Art)
St. Ignatius, Spiritual Exercises of
Tarot
Vodun (Voodoo)
Volunteerism
Wicca and Witchcraft
Witches, Popular Culture
Worship
Yoga

SUPPORTS/CONTEXTS

Assets, Developmental
Belief and Affiliation, Contextual Impacts on
Child and Youth Care
Communities, Intentional Spiritual
Cults
Education, Christian Religion
Education, Spiritual Development in
Educational organizations (see also Organizations)
Faith-based Service Organizations (see also Organizations)
Human Rights
Parental Influence on Adolescent Religiosity
Peer and Friend Influences on Adolescent Faith Development
Politics and Religion in the American Presidency
Quaker Education
Religious Diversity in North America

TEXTS

Apocrypha/Deuterocanonical Books
Bhagavad Gita
Bible
Bible, Christian
Bible, Jewish
Book of Mormon
Confessions of St. Augustine
Dead Sea Scrolls
Dhammapada
Enoch, Book of
Gnostic Gospels
Qur'an
Torah

THEORY

Differences between Religion and Spirituality in Youth
End of Life, Lifespan Approach
Faith Maturity (see also Health)
Object Relations
Positive Youth Development (see also Health)
Psychoanalytic Perspective
Psychological Type (see also Health)
Psychopathology, Personality, and Religion (see also Health)
Relational Consciousness
Religious Theory, Developmental Systems View
Religious Transformation
Science and Religion
Semiotics
Stage-Structural Approach to Religious Development

TRADITIONS

Aboriginal
Baptists
Buddhism
Catholicism
Christianity
Christianity, Orthodox
Confucianism
Daoism
Episcopal Church
Hinduism
Islam
Judaism, Conservative
Judaism, Orthodox
Judaism, Reconstructionist
Judaism, Reform
Mexican American Religion and Spirituality
Mormonism
Native American Spirituality
Presbyterian
Rosicrucianism
Shamanism
Spirituality, Australian
Zoroastrianism

About the Editors

Elizabeth M. Dowling., Ph.D, is the director of research for The ImagineNations Group. Elizabeth works closely with local, national, regional, and international research partners to design and implement effective and sustainable research practices for ImagineNations and oversees information transfer to all members of the ImagineNations staff. She graduated from Haverford College in 1991 with a B.A. in psychology and received a M.Ed. from Lesley University in 1994 in early childhood education. She received her doctorate in child development from Tufts University. Elizabeth is the author of numerous publications in leading journals and handbooks of human development.

W. George Scarlett is an assistant professor and deputy chair of the Eliot-Pearson Department of Child Development at Tufts University. Professor Scarlett received a B.A. from Yale University, an M.Div. from the Episcopal Divinity School, and a Ph.D. (in developmental psychology) from Clark University. He has published extensively in the areas of religious and spiritual development, children's play, and approaches to children's problem behavior. In addition to his writing, teaching, and administrative work, he has been a long-time consultant for Head Start and the director of a residential camp for emotionally disturbed children.

Contributors

Abercrombie, Eric N.
Case Western Reserve University

Alberts, Amy E.
Tufts University

Altman, Penny F.
Sharon, Massachusetts

Allen, Wm. Loyd
McAfee School of Theology

Al-Solaim, Lamis
Royal Holloway University of London

Anderson, Pamela M.
Tufts University

Antonucci, Toni C.
University of Michigan

Barrett, Justin L.
Douglas County Young Life

Baughman, Michael J.
Princeton Theological Seminary

Beit-Hallahmi, Benjamin
University of Haifa

Bell, David
Emory University

Berndtson, Annie
Tufts University

Blakeney, Charles David
University of Fribourg

Blakeney, Ronnie Frankel
University of Fribourg

Bobek, Deborah L.
Tufts University

Bornstein, Marc H.
National Institute of Child Health and Human Development

Bosacki, Sandra
Brock University

Boyatzis, Chris J.
Bucknell University

Brady, Richard
Sidwell Friends School

Bridgers, Lynn
Emory University

Brotter, Jake Jurkowitz
Tufts University

Brown, Edna
University of Michigan

Cain, Clifford Chalmers
Franklin College

Charlesworth, William R.
University of Minnesota

Chartrand-Burke, Tony
York University

Cheek, Dennis William
John Templeton Foundation

Chilton, Bruce
Bard College

Chirban, John T.
Harvard Medical School
Hellenic College

Chu, Pamela
Harvard Graduate School of Education

Clendenen, Avis
Saint Xavier University

Clinton, Boruch
Ottawa Torah Institute

Coggan, Sharon L.
University of Colorado at Denver

Crawford, Cory
Harvard University

Cutting, Christopher
Wilfrid Laurier University

Delgado, Grace Peña
California State University, Long Beach

Dillon, James
State University of West Georgia

Dowling, Elizabeth M.
ImagineNations Group

Duffy, Timothy John
College of the Holy Cross

Duns, Ryan Gerard
John Carroll University

Fernsler, Christine
Sidwell Friends School

Fiori, Katherine L.
University of Michigan

Flick, Jr., Hugh M.
Yale University

Forman, Jed Daniel
Tufts University

Fountain-Harris, Chantal
Tufts University

Francis, Leslie J.
University of Wales, Bangor

Galarneau, Charlene A.
Tufts University

Gearon, Liam
University of Surrey Roehampton

Gilmore, Christopher
The Holistic Education Foundation

Glickman-Simon, Richard
Tufts University

Gold, Genevie
Tufts University

Goździak, Elżbieta M.
Georgetown University

Grainger, Teresa
Canterbury Christ Church University College

Gross, Zehavit
Bar Ilan University

Gubbay Helfer, Sharon
Concordia University

Halstead, J. Mark
University of Plymouth

Haselhoff, Eltjo H.
Dutch Centre for Crop Circle Research

Holcomb, Gay L.
Asbury College

Hooker, Charles
Emory University

Jindra, Ines Wenger
Spring Arbor University

Johnson, Baylor
St. Lawrence University

Johnson, Mark C.
YMCA of the USA

Johnson, Troy
California State University

Johnson-Miller, Beverly C.
Asbury Theological Seminary

Kasimow, Harold
Grinnell College

Kendall-Seatter, Sue
Canterbury Christ Church University College

Kibble, David G.
Huntington School

Kiesling, Chris
Asbury Theological Seminary

King, Pamela Ebstyne
Fuller Theological Seminary

Kirchner, Sandra R.
Miami University

Klassen, Chris
York University

Knaster, Mirka
Oakland, California

Lakeou, Lula
Tufts University

Lawton, Jane E.
Santa Fe, New Mexico

Lerner, Richard M.
Tufts University

Leslie, Anne
YouthBuild USA

Lindemann, Evie
Yale University School of Nursing

Lodish, Richard
Sidwell Friends School

Mackenzie, Elizabeth
Boston College

McClellan, Ian
Tufts University

Massey, Karen G.
Mercer University

Michaels, Cathleen
East Bay Conservation Corps Charter School

Molleur, Joseph
Cornell College

Morrissey, Taryn W.
Cornell University

Mueller, Ross A.
Fuller Theological Seminary

Najmi, Danyal
Tufts University

Neufeld, Dietmar
University of British Columbia

Nikolajev, Olga
Ottawa, Ontario

Oberholtzer, Edward C.
Tufts University

O'Leary, David M.
Tufts University

Osborn, Peter
Tufts University

Poe, Gary R.
Palm Beach Atlantic University

Posner, Meredith
Tufts University

Raman, Varadaraja V.
Rochester Institute of Technology

Redditt, Paul L.
Georgetown College

Reich, K. Helmut
University of Fribourg

Richert, Rebekah
Harvard University

Roehlkepartain, Eugene C.
Search Institute

Rutman, Lori Ellen
Stanford University School of Medicine

Rymarz, Richard
Australian Catholic University Limited

Scarlett, W. George
Tufts University

Schliesser, Christine Cochlovius
Tübingen University

Schuldenfrei, Brian
Sinai Temple, Los Angeles

Schwartz, Kelly Dean
Nazarene University College

Schweitzer, Friedrich
Universität Tübingen

Scott, Daniel G.
University of Victoria

Semetsky, Inna
Monash University

Shenton, Andrew
Boston University

Sinkin, Amelia
Tufts University

Snarey, John
Emory University

Sniegocki, John
Xavier University

Spitzer, Lee B.
American Baptist Churches of New Jersey

Stavros, George
The Danielsen Institute

Steorts, Mitchael C.
Tufts University

Stoneman, Dorothy
YouthBuild USA

Streib, Heinz
University of Bielefeld

Thomas, Trudelle
Xavier University

Thuesen, Peter J.
Tufts University

Trousdale, Ann M.
Louisiana State University

Van Slyke, James A.
Fuller Theological Seminary

Varnish, Amanda
Brock University

Verni, Kevin
Tufts University

Walser, Joseph
Tufts University

Watkins, Greg
Stanford University

Webster, Jane S.
Barton College

White, David F.
Emory University

Wieland-Robbescheuten, Julie
Wilfrid Laurier University

Wilson, Melanie
New England Network for Child, Youth & Family Services

Wong, Ping Ho
The Hong Kong Institute of Education

Worthington, Jr., Everett L.
Virginia Commonwealth University

Wright, Brian L.
Tufts University

Acknowledgments

The editors would like to thank our editorial assistant, Jennifer Davison of the Institute of Applied Research in Youth Development (IARYD) at Tufts University. With true patience and a bright sense of humor and spirit, Jennifer kept authors and editors in line and on task. We would also like to thank Richard M. Lerner and the faculty, students, and staff at IARYD for the support and time that they willingly gave us during this project. We have greatly benefited from the guidance of our editors at Sage Publications, most especially Jim Brace-Thompson, Sanford Robinson, and Karen Ehrmann. Finally, we would like to thank our families and friends—and all those who have inspired our own religious and spiritual development. Your kindness, love, and faith contributed to the creation and development of this encyclopedia.

Introduction

In the 18th and 19th centuries, religion and spirituality were supposed to be replaced by science and reason—or so many thought. But that did not happen, and today, religion and spirituality play a major role in people's lives and in determining world affairs. So to be informed about today's world requires being informed about matters pertaining to religion and spirituality. This is especially the case in a pluralistic global society that is growing increasingly "connected." No longer are different religious groups found only in far-away places, to be experienced only in books or through word of mouth. Instead, we now live in communities and nations where multiple religions and multiple spiritualities are practiced. Furthermore, many of us have access to radio, television, newsprint, and the worldwide Web, allowing us, with the turn of a knob or the click of a switch, to immerse ourselves in other cultures. We now are brought face-to-face with religious and spiritual diversity.

Despite the world becoming a global village, religion and spirituality still elicit negative stereotypes and foster fear, hatred, and even war. And yet, religion and spirituality also foster peace and unity. Today, then, perhaps more than ever, it is especially important that we understand one another by understanding one another's faith traditions and equally critical that we understand positive, healthy, religious and spiritual development. We must seek to bridge divides, counteract negative stereotypes, and explode destructive myths so as to set the conditions that connect us to all our fellow humans.

This encyclopedia joins a recent trend in research and scholarship aimed at better understanding the similarities and differences between world religions and spiritualities, between expressions of the divine and between experiences of the transcendent. It does so, however, with a focus on the *development* of religiosity and spirituality.

Spiritual development and religious development are about identity development and how, across the human life span, one sees oneself in relation to that which is considered divine or transcendent. While religious development is usually about identifying oneself with a particular religious tradition, its practices and beliefs, spiritual development is about becoming a whole person, someone who stands for something that defines and gives meaning to being human. The two may overlap–so that what is spiritual is also religious–but they need not. There is religion without spirituality and spirituality without religion.

Due to the work and contributions of scholars and academics, much has been learned about what it means to be human and about the process of human development. We have learned that individual development involves the interplay of multiple contexts, contexts that interact in dynamic ways across the life span. No two people share the same biology or the same combination of contexts and experiences, so every person has a unique developmental history. The same is true for religious and spiritual development. Owing to the innumerable contexts that influence individual development throughout the life span, religious and spiritual development must be understood as different for each person.

Furthermore, given that the contexts that affect religious and spiritual development are innumerable, it is impossible to capture the entirety of their expressions or influence within one encyclopedia. In deciding, then, on what entries to collect, we narrowed down a seemingly endless list of possible entries to present a sample of contexts and experiences that are central for at least some people, in some parts of the world, some of the time. We *do not* assume that all people are equally affected by or touched by the same contexts. We *do* assume that people of different ages, genders, faiths, and ethnicities are more or less affected by the contexts discussed in this encyclopedia at different times in their lives. Therefore, we cannot reiterate enough that the entries collected in this encyclopedia are offered as a collection of contexts that potentially impact individual and group religious and spiritual development. We were intentional in making the selections we did. Their diversity represents the diversity in religious and spiritual development.

This encyclopedia covers a wide range of topics—from ideas, to places, to people. Furthermore, the topics come in all sizes—from small topics, such as particular cultic practices, to large topics, such as major religions. Some will say that we have included that which should be excluded and excluded that which should be included—and to a certain extent, they may be right. However, once again, our intent was not to achieve a perfectly balanced and representative sample of entries, because it is difficult to say what such a sample would look like and, most certainly, each reader will have his or her own interests and definition of a balanced and representative sample. Rather, our intent was to provide a sample of entries to help the reader become better informed about the complexity of factors involved in religious and spiritual development, so as to become better able to function in a pluralistic society and better able to support personal spiritual growth.

With a recent heightened level of interest in the study of religious and spiritual development, we imagine that in the future we will come to learn more about the individual and shared characteristics and contexts that influence the development of spirituality and religiosity. As such, a future reference work on this topic may have a very different list of entries than the collection we present. We welcome this change and look forward to what further research will contribute to the study and practice of healthy religious and spiritual development.

This encyclopedia does not, then, teach all there is to know about religious and spiritual development, but it can help point the reader in the right directions, so that the reader can become better informed. We hope the reader will use this encyclopedia that way—as a pointer, or, to change the metaphor, as a window into the many fascinating and complex phenomena and people that figure centrally in discussions of the development of religiousness and spirituality. We also hope the reader will use this encyclopedia for personal growth, to help answer those personal questions that, if left unanswered, can stunt or arrest spiritual growth.

—Elizabeth M. Dowling and W. George Scarlett

ABORIGINAL SPIRITUALITY, AUSTRALIAN

The spirituality of Aboriginal people in Australia is traditionally associated with specific tracts of land in diverse ways. The ancestral spirits permeate social life, and individuals within each group develop a genuine sense of belonging with the spiritual and physical landscapes. Within individual regions, various social groups possess certain traits in addition to their spiritual beliefs. They have a shared language or dialect and economic system, and particular songs and ceremonies that belong to their specific clan. Descent groups occupy particular environments and come to be associated with specific territories. Children at birth are taught which descent group they belong to and what part of the land is theirs to be part of and protect. They are taught songs and told stories about their ancestors.

There have been perhaps 300 language groups in Aboriginal Australia. Today, many of those languages no longer exist. There are approximately 20 languages still spoken by more than a few people. As none of the languages were written, many have been lost forever. Clans or other descent-based groups comprised the social frameworks within each. Descent groups acted as guardians of the land inherited from their ancestors. By belonging to a clan, individuals are provided with a birthright, a passport to a portion of the land, shared customs, and the obligation to comply with the rigorous rules of the social structure that accompany clan membership. All children learn these rules at an early age. At each stage of development, they are expected to know and behave in certain ways in relationship to their own family, the land, and their spiritual relationship to both.

Clans consist of men, women, and children who are considered to be descendants of the same ancestor or ancestors, but whom at any one time, are scattered throughout a number of different lands. All clan members within a language group are related, even if distantly, and all relationships are recognized and respected. Unwritten rules govern how people are addressed by one another and what behaviors are appropriate for each relationship and each age group. These social relationships and rules are all part of the laws of the Dreaming.

At birth, children possess their own spiritual presence, and the rest of the group already knows their kinship ties. They are given a special name at a ceremony. From their earliest days, children live within their kin structure and are gradually taught how to behave toward other people. They have special kinship terms and relationships. For example, it is common for the mother's brother to occupy the most important place in the life of a male child, guiding the young boy along the early steps towards initiation and manhood.

An extended family usually lives at the same camp and moves about the territory as a group. Kinship is a crucial element in the structuring of social and spiritual relationships in Aboriginal societies. Kinship is of prime importance throughout Aboriginal Australia, and is applied to all people inclusively. It is part of the spiritual relationship to the land and their ancestors.

In traditional societies, everyone with whom an Aboriginal person comes into social contact is likely to be recognized as some kind of relative. Every individual is connected to everyone else by descent, marriage, or some other form of affiliation. To an outsider, the network of relationships and obligations might seem complex. Nobody remains outside the kinship system, and all are required to carry out their obligations and responsibilities toward others and the land. No one is forgotten. If children are left orphaned or adults widowed, they are incorporated into the kinship system. This in turn connects all to a spiritual life. In its simplest form, the notion of kin is based on the idea that a man calls his brother's children son and daughter. In turn, they address him as father as they do their biological father. A man's sister's children are considered son and daughter.

Traditionally, spiritual beliefs permeate every aspect of life. The spirit helps the individual pass through a series of important life events or rites of passage. The laws are laid down in the Dreaming. The Dreaming is a term used to describe the spiritual, natural, and moral order of the cosmos. Each life segment brings with it a set of rights and obligations.

Children spend a lot of their time in the company of other youngsters and various adults, especially members of the extended family. They enjoy great freedom as long as their actions do not harm anyone and they obey instructions such as staying clear of dangerous and sacred places. Proper respect to elders and family is to be shown at all times. Many of the proper ways of behaving are conveyed to children through stories and songs around the campfire. These stories vary from region to region and are passed on orally. The stories have several levels. The first stories were for children and all community members. The same story may vary in information for different ages and contain sacred information. Art and drawings are also used to convey spiritual information linking always to the land.

Creation stories follow a general pattern, all related to the land and landscape. Before creation, the land now called Australia was a barren place, devoid of all human life. In the Dreamtime, Ancestral Beings came down from the stars and rose from the earth. They moved across the land, singing into existence an intricate network of rivers, deserts, mountains, forest, animals, and birds. They stretched to the sun announcing; "I am Ant!" "I am Snake!" "I am Kangaroo!" "I am Emu!" As they called out the names they created sacred songs that brought aspects of the land into being. Each region would be influenced by several powerful figures and those Ancestral Beings would then continue to support and resource the communities living within that area. When their work was done, the Ancestral Beings sank into the earth or returned to the sky, ready to be called upon by prescribed ritual.

Australian Aboriginals understand that they act as custodians of the land, and are therefore responsible for protecting the world of the spirit beings that created the land and still live in mountains, waterholes, trees, rocks, and sky. The Ancestral Beings are honored and called to protect the land by prescribed rituals of the elders. The places on the earth where Ancestral Beings brought forth life are still known as sacred sites.

The all-pervasive powers of the Ancestral Beings of the Dreaming are present in the land and natural species, and reside within individuals. Particular groups, tribes, or clans fulfill their responsibilities, working within a highly complex structure that incorporates spiritual belief, sacred law, ceremonies, kinship, and places in a particular area with which they have been associated for many thousands of years. It is associated with their day-to-day survival in provision of food and medicines, ritual songs, objects, and graphic designs.

One of the best-known sacred sites in Australia is Uluru (Ayers Rock), on the land of the Pitjantjatjara people, which is of particular significance to the Mala (Wallaby) and Kunia (Carpet Snake) clans. There are many other sacred sites throughout Australia. In simple terms, sacred sites are like churches. Each site has particular meaning and significance and special ceremonies and ways of behaving associated with it. Often their location and significance are closely guarded secrets and cannot be shared with outsiders. It is not proper to discuss sacred sites with everyone, as some sites are only to be shared by men and some sites are only for women. Men's and women's business are scrupulously segregated, but of equal power and importance in traditional societies.

Land represents the mainspring of the psyche and well-being of the people who inhabit a certain territory. Communities and individuals are still directly responsible for the protection of the land under their guardianship. This responsibility or custodianship forms the basis of much of the conflict that continues to exist between Aborigines and those who operate in a way that abuses the sacred obligations placed on those who inhabit the land. Land can never be sold or traded, as it represents a sacred bequest from the Ancestral Beings and the Dreaming.

Specialized knowledge of any territory, such as details of ritual and the more intimate details of the particular relationship of any community to their traditional lands, is jealously guarded. It is considered sacrilegious to share privileged information with outsiders. From an early age children are taught relationships and knowledge about their role in learning and passing on rituals and information belonging to their particular family group.

Aboriginal law is very sacred and complex. Ceremonial objects used in rituals to do with the law are revered, and kept in the possession of either the "clever man" or "clever woman." It is a serious transgression of the law to look upon them, even by accident. Aboriginal elders are "wise men and clever women" who have the sacred responsibility of acting as guardians of the land and the sites created by the Ancestral Beings. They believe that disturbance of a sacred site by entering without the appropriate ceremony represents a violation of that trust that has been handed down for hundreds of generations, long before Australia was settled by others. All children are taught to show respect to their elders.

The Ancestral Beings are still relevant today. Day-to-day activities are carried out within the framework of that original structure created many thousands of years ago. They continue to inspire, protect, support, and govern daily life of traditional Aboriginal people, and are recognized by all Aborigines, even those who have grown up in cities. The Dreaming has deep and sacred meanings. It is inaccurate to refer to Dreaming stories as fables or folklore, as the Dreaming is not fictitious to many Aboriginal people.

This traditional and complex culture was in no way prepared to encounter white explorers and settlers from alien cultures with a vastly different belief system. The colonizers believed that Australia was an empty continent, or *terra nullius*, which is Latin for "a land belonging to no-one." It was established as a concept in European international law in the age of European colonization. Nyoongar elder Yongar Mungan tells the story of Aboriginal leader Yellagonga who, when greeted by Captain James Stirling in the southwest of Western Australia, "*He* bowed and offered his country and resources to the settler." It was thought the settlers were countrymen who had returned from the spirit world.

Today, many Aboriginal people in Australia still honor their traditions. All people in Australia know that to the first people of Australia the land was filled with an intricate web of Dreaming. "We walk together on sacred ground. Black feet, white feet, footprints, soft upon the land. The Tjukurpa (Pitjantjatjara word for Dreaming) moves beneath our feet. The landscape is alive."—Anon.

—*Jane E. Lawton*

FURTHER READING

Horton, D. (1994). *The encyclopedia of Aboriginal Australia.* Canberra, Australia: Australian Institute of Aboriginal and Torres Strait Islander Studies.

Jacob, T. (1991). *In the beginning: A perspective on traditional Aboriginal societies.* Perth, Western Australia: Ministry of Education.

Caruana, W. (1996). *Aboriginal art.* New York: Thames and Hudson.

Australian Institute of Aboriginal and Torres Strait Islander Studies. Retrieved February 5, 2005, from www.aiatsis.gov.au

ADVERSITY, OVERCOMING

Adversity refers to hardship and misfortune. Although what constitutes hardship and misfortune may vary from one person to another, there are general stressors considered by most to be conditions defining hardship and misfortune. Stressors come in two types: acute and chronic. Acute stressors are major life events such as the loss of a loved one, a divorce, and a major accident causing bodily harm. Chronic stressors include long-term neglect (by parents, peers, others in general), poverty, and permanent physical and mental disabilities. Religion often serves as a means to cope with such adversity.

The research on coping distinguishes between three types, namely, *self-directing, deferring,* and *collaborative* types. The self-directing type refers to when people rely mostly on themselves to cope; the deferring type refers to when people take control by giving control over to God; the collaborative type refers to when people collaborate with God, that is, see both themselves and God as actively participating in the coping process.

The self-directing type of coping is associated with a greater sense of personal control and higher self-esteem. An example of self-directing coping is having a sense that God will support one's decisions on how to cope, but the decisions themselves are one's own. The deferring type of coping is associated with lower self-esteem, less planning and problem solving, and greater intolerance for the differences found in others. An example of the deferring type is when individuals pray for God to do something miraculous. The collaborative type of coping is similar to the self-directing type in that it too is associated with greater sense of personal control and greater self esteem. However, with the collaborative type, there is an active give-and-take between the individual and God. For example, an individual may pray for support and strength needed to solve certain problems defining his or her adverse situation.

No matter what type of coping, all follow similar steps. First, there is a major life event, followed by an appraisal and then some coping activity that focuses either on fixing a problem or on improving some emotional-psychological condition. Appraisal plays a central role in the coping process. In making an appraisal of their adverse circumstances, individuals can see the same circumstances very differently. For example, when told they have a cancerous tumor, individuals can appraise their situation as a challenge to take on or as a hopeless situation that they have to accept. These different appraisals determine what strategies will follow.

Religion can play an integral role in coping with adversity. Indeed, after tragic events, sometimes turning to religion can seem the only way to cope. Religious coping activities are numerous, and include cultivating relationships with members of a faith community, including the clergy, as well as cultivating a relationship with God. They include cognitive change, such as finding a lesson or meaning in adversity; emotional change, such as feeling dependent on God; behavioral change, such as leading a more caring life; and social change, such as investing energy in social causes. It is difficult to determine how many people turn to religion in order to cope with adversity. However, research has shown that for many people in adverse circumstances, religion is indeed relied on for coping.

—Meredith Posner

See also Coping in Youth

FURTHER READING

Pargament, K. I. (1997). *The psychology of religion and coping.* New York: Guilford Press.

Pargament. K I. (1990). God help me: Toward a theoretical framework of coping for the psychology of religion. *Research in the Social-Scientfic Study of Religion, 2,* 195–224.

Smith, C., & Carlson, B. (1997). *Stress, coping, and resilience in children and youth.* Chicago: University of Chicago Press.

ALCHEMY

The word *alchemy* is itself of Arabic origin, although its original significance is lost. Forms of alchemy have been practiced over many hundreds of years by the Greeks, Egyptians, Chinese, Indians, and Arabs, but in Europe it reached the peak of its popularity with a proliferation of new texts on the subject in the 16th and 17th centuries. It was practiced by figures as diverse as John Dee, Francis Bacon, Thomas Vaughan, Robert Boyle, and Isaac Newton. The popular image of alchemists was of secret brotherhoods and individual fraudsters (Ben Jonson's satirical play *The Alchemist* and Pieter Bruegel the Elder's drawing of the same name illustrate this), but it was not until the growth of modern science in the 18th century (to which alchemy had itself made no small contribution) that interest began to decline.

The Swiss psychoanalyst Carl Jung introduced a new approach to alchemy in the 20th century. He noted a close correspondence between the dreams and fantasies of his patients and the writings of alchemists, particularly in terms of recurrent symbols and images (such as sun and moon, king and queen, toad, dragon, eagle, and rose). He considered that alchemical literature could be explained in psychological terms, and he viewed the symbols as manifestations of a "collective unconscious." Although Jung's own life and work were profoundly influenced by his contact with alchemy, the impact on psychoanalytical theory has so far been limited.

Alchemy, sometimes known simply as "The Art," is an esoteric mixture of ancient wisdom and quasi-scientific experimentation. Essentially it is about transformation, particularly the purification and perfection of base, unrefined materials. The transformation may be at a physical or spiritual level. At a physical level, it is usually expressed in terms of the attempt to transform base metals into gold, and it involves complex procedures in the laboratory. It may also be about transformation from sickness to health, or from old age to youth. At the spiritual level, the various alchemical processes in spiritual transformation may be symbolic of the attempt to perfect base human nature; the transformation and purification occur as a result of the spiritual experiences encountered on the journey through life.

Many key alchemical terms have meaning on the physical and spiritual levels simultaneously. For example, conjunction (sometimes called the alchemical marriage) refers in the laboratory to the fusing of mercury and sulphur, but at a spiritual level (especially in the writing of a Christian alchemist like Jakob Boehme) it refers to the soul's union with God; it is variously symbolized by the marriage of a king and queen, by sexual union, by astrological conjunction (e.g., of the sun and the moon) and by the figure of the hermaphrodite.

The goal of the "sacred philosophy" of the alchemists was to produce the Philosopher's Stone, which could then be used as the agent of all kinds of transformation, including turning base metals into gold, prolonging life, and curing the sick. The Stone could take a variety of forms, including powder or liquid, and was also known as the Elixir or Tincture. The alchemical process was thus to turn the *prima materia* ("ordinary matter"—although of course there was much debate about what was the best substance to start with) into the Philosopher's Stone by separating it into its components, purging its impurities, and reconstituting it in perfect proportion in its refined form. There was no precise formula for achieving this result. The alchemist had to create a model of the universe (or of human consciousness) within a sealed, preferably egg-shaped, glass vessel or flask. Through a complicated succession of gradual heating and distillation, the transformation of the *prima materia* could take place. The transformation required the "death" of the body or original substance, the ascension of the "soul," the reuniting of the two in a new way and the fixing of the volatile elements thus generated.

The sequence of 12 stages of the laboratory process are described by the 15th-century English alchemist, Canon George Ripley, as calcination, solution, separation, conjunction, putrefaction, congelation, cibation, sublimation, fermentation, exaltation, multiplication, and finally projection (i.e., the use of the Stone for transformation). The whole operation is described in the symbolic language of birth, marriage, death, resurrection, battles, dragons, birds, and celestial bodies.

In a spiritual sense, the *prima materia* on which the alchemist works is himself, and (at least from a Christian perspective) Christ is the perfect Philosopher's Stone. When the alchemist seeks to free the soul (mercury) and spirit (sulphur) from the body (salt) and to reunite them in a purified form, he is seeking to purge himself of the impurity of sin, so that he can be made again in Christ's image. The alchemical process thus helps an understanding of God's will and purpose in creation. Many 17th-century Christian writers and poets use images drawn from alchemy to convey deep spiritual truths. George Herbert, for example, in his poem "The Elixir," claims to have found in the principle of doing every action as if for God "the famous stone that turneth all to gold."

—J. Mark Halstead

See also Art, Visual; Herbert, George; Jung, Carl and Post-Jungians

FURTHER READING

Burland, C. A. (1967). *The arts of the alchemists.* London: Weidenfeld and Nicolson.

Gilchrist, C. (1984). *Alchemy: the great work.* Wellingborough: Aquarian Press.

ALTARS

The *Oxford English Dictionary* defines *altar* as a block, pile, table, stand, or other raised structure, with a plain top, on which to place or sacrifice offerings to a deity. The altar can be a place where incense is burned in worship. Nearly all world religions and faiths have use of an altar. The classical Hebrew sense of the altar is as the meeting place between heaven and earth. The physical altar becomes the place of meeting between the Creator and humanity. It is the place of sacrifice and of communion. The altar is always a very special place of devotion and deepest respect.

In many religions, the altar began as the place of sacrifice. This altar would have been temporary and erected for the moment. Offerings were made to a deity, including fruits, vegetables, animals, and even humans (in some societies and times). Once a faith tradition or religion became a bit more permanent, the altar was eventually turned into a very permanent structure located inside a sacred building, temple, or church. Only the ritually trained were allowed to come to the altar. Barriers and railings were set up to keep out those not fully trained to minister at the altar.

Christianity sees the altar on many levels. The altar is where simple gifts of bread and wine are placed for Eucharistic worship. The altar becomes the table of the Lord. The Last Supper of Jesus sees a meal becoming a time for theology. The altar and/or table now takes on deeper meaning. Just like in any family, a special meal with family gathered takes on a deeper meaning. The table indeed becomes an altar. Great care is taken to set the table/altar, special vessels are used on the table/altar, and stories are shared (sacred scriptures are proclaimed). Once at the table, people tend to stay there. Being allowed at the big persons' table is seen as an initiation into adulthood. The meal is more than just a sharing of food. Even though one may take great pride in a beautifully set table/altar, it is the experience of communion with one another that is of prime importance. After Jesus' resurrection from the dead, it was at table that he revealed himself to his followers, in the breaking of the bread. Again, it is the table/altar that becomes a place of action and of convergence between believers and the deity.

More recently, a split in understanding of the altar has developed. The altar has become a place for meals, remembrance, and community. The older idea of altar as the place of sacrifice is fading away in some circles of believers. The altar is now seen as the table of the Lord where the community gathers. Some communities try to hold on to the multiple ideas of altar. Some would see the altar as the place of sacrifice, the Lord's Table, and a place of nourishment and strength for the community gathered. The altar can be a table of joy, a place of communion and peace, and a source of unity and friendship.

There is one final aspect of altar that is slowly being forgotten. The altar has also been a place of memorial for a person who died for the faith or the deity. The graves of special people had altars erected on them in some religious faiths. The purpose of this altar was to be a memorial of the martyr's death. In fact, in most Roman Catholic churches, altars have to have a relic (an object of a saint) placed into the altar. Some ancient churches are built over the remains of an early believer (e.g., the central church of Roman Catholicism, the Vatican in Rome, is built on Saint Peter's remains).

Today, most communities would see the altar as a place of gathering of the believers. It is a place where the mystery of God's gift unfolds, and the community is nourished and fed. The altar should be seen as a place where all are welcomed, where the poor find justice, victims of oppression find freedom, and the whole of humanity is reunited with its Creator.

—Rev. David M. O'Leary

See also Christianity; Churches; Eucharist; Judaism; Sacrifice

ANGELOU, MAYA

I Know Why the Caged Bird Sings (1969) is a powerful, inspirational childhood autobiography by Maya Angelou, the well-known literary, artistic, and spiritual figure. The book spans her early childhood through adolescence, most of it spent in the South in the 1930s and 1940s. The author's voice is primarily the first-person vantage point of a child. The opening scene is Easter Sunday in church, with young Maya squirming in the children's section; spiritual and religious issues permeate the book. Angelou captures many common paradoxes of living, and explores the role of faith and spirituality in reconciling these tensions. Pervasive through the book are influences of race, gender, socioeconomic status, geographical region, and historical era. This autobiography contextualizes spiritual development. Every page speaks a human voice, and thus captures the authenticity of the personal and institutional in a child's spirituality.

Throughout the book, Angelou illustrates how children's many social contexts—family, church, school, peers, neighborhood, and so on—all influence spiritual development. Spirituality's life-affirming role in the African-American community is made particularly evident in Maya's childhood during which she lived in a small, segregated town in Arkansas. The values, worldviews, and disciplines in the faithful communities of which she is a part uphold her spiritual journey. However, other communities (such as Maya's time in St. Louis with her mother) are lacking in spiritual grounding, and Maya's development suffers. In both communities, Maya's spirituality is crucial in her resilience against tough odds.

A crucial figure in Maya's life is her maternal grandmother, Momma, who raises Maya and her older brother in Stamps, Arkansas, after the children's negligent parents in California sent them packing. Momma shares her theology in verbal assertions, such as God "never gives us more than we can bear" (p. 132) and

"God is love. Just worry about whether you're being a good girl then he will love you" (p. 47). Momma's authoritarian behavior, demands for cleanliness and obedience in the name of God, and her own daily spiritual disciplines provide a powerful model for Maya's observational learning of spirituality. Momma begins each day with morning prayer and she regularly invokes God to cope with stressors. A traumatic incident occurred when unkempt, impudent white girls approached Momma to mock her, a display of disrespect that Momma would never tolerate from her own family. Young Maya watched helplessly as her grandmother stood her ground, and did not defend herself but instead quietly uttered under her breath. Maya, the young spiritual apprentice observing her grandmother's faith in action, could hear her elder singing, "Bread of heaven, bread of heaven, feed me til I want no more." Maya saw that faith serves as a shield against the slings and arrows of a hard life, and she concluded that "whatever the contest had been out front, I knew Momma had won" (p. 27). This indelible experience, witnessing how faith allows one to endure suffering and enables one to salvage spiritual victory from the jaws of defeat, gave Maya a deep metaphor to grasp the essential theme of death and resurrection.

While Momma provides spiritual discipline and strength, Maya's older brother, Bailey, provides an unconditional love that creates in Maya a more balanced, healthy spirituality. Bailey is Maya's companion and supporter. In a most eloquent passage (p. 19), Maya writes: "Of all the needs . . . a lonely child has, the one that must be satisfied, if there is going to be hope and a hope of wholeness, is the unshaking need for an unshakable God. My pretty Black brother was my Kingdom Come." While Momma embodies God's omnipotence and absoluteness, Bailey incarnates God's unconditional, loving acceptance. Others, too, contribute to Maya's spirituality, such as Louise, Maya's first childhood friend, and Mrs. Flowers, the aristocrat of Black Stamps who makes Maya "proud to be Negro" (p. 79).

Angelou's journey illustrates developmental trends in faith development (e.g., Fowler). In middle childhood, Angelou has a "mythic-literal" faith "absorbed" from her family; Deuteronomy with its rigid laws is her favorite book of the Bible. Later in childhood, Maya experiences growing skepticism and questioning about her community's faith norms. As Maya approaches adolescence, a revival meeting (chapter 18) generates doubt in her, as she is confused by worshipping God in a tent with a dirt floor, and she wondered, "Would God the Father allow His only Son to mix with this crowd of cotton pickers and maids, washerwomen and handymen?" The book is a window into the child's soulful struggles with the worth of herself and her people in God's eyes. The book continues through adolescent struggles, and a more personal "individuative-reflective" orientation begins to emerge as she wrestles with sexuality, vocation, self-esteem, and changing interpersonal relations.

This wonderful autobiography is a study of resilience, of the child's capacity to not only survive but even thrive amid adversity. Maya's spirituality, shaped by many forces, is the fertile soil in which this resilience grows. This is a superb book for a mature adolescent group, although sections describing Maya's sexual abuse as a child and her adolescent sexual explorations will disturb some. Boyatzis and Braxton, among other sources, may help educators, parents, or youth ministers use Angelou's book. Childhood autobiographies have become popular, and many emphasize spiritual themes, including Kimmel, Scot, and Hampl. Each eloquently depicts the inextricable links between childhood and adolescent spirituality, and the family, church, community, and time and place in the American landscape. Amidst this fine literature, Angelou's book is perhaps the finest case study of spiritual development.

—Chris J. Boyatzis

FURTHER READING

Angelou, M. (1969). *I know why the caged bird sings.* New York: Bantam.

Boyatzis, C. J. (1992). Let the caged bird sing: Using literature to teach developmental psychology. *Teaching of Psychology, 19,* 221–222.

Braxton, J. M. (Ed.). (1999). *I know why the caged bird sings: A casebook.* New York: Oxford University Press.

Hampl, P. (1992). *Virgin time.* New York: Ballantine.

Kimmel, H. (2001). *A girl named Zippy: Growing up small in Mooreland, Indiana.* New York: Doubleday.

Scot, B. J. (1995). *Prairie reunion.* New York: Riverhead.

ANGELS

In English, the word "angel" comes from the Greek word *angelos* meaning messenger. In Christian, Islam, and Jewish beliefs, angels are said to be supernatural beings above ordinary mankind, or citizens of inner space. As messengers from God, their function is to praise and to serve God and mankind, helping in many different ways those in harmony with them. Also known as Prets, Devas, Bhuts, and Devtas, angels are believed to be everywhere, although they have never been known to incarnate in human form. They remain mostly invisible, and are sexless by nature. Without apparent feelings, through their service they express love and compassion for humans in distress. In watching over virtually every aspect of human activity, there are also records of them being on hand in order to help the creative progress of activities that are serving a spiritual purpose. This especially applies to those on earth ready to become more conscious and responsible for their own spiritual development.

"Angel" is a generic name for a vast host of invisible beings said to populate the seven heavens. Some people express angels as thoughts of God. There is no one correct way of perceiving angels or beings of light. In so far as they reflect and amplify our own condition, they can appear in as many ways and in many colors. Most are said to be so dazzling that their forms look as if weaved out of fluid light beams. Although some of the Higher Beings have been seen to be as tall as the sky, angels are said to be in the same line of evolution as earth's nature spirits of the fairy kingdom. To define elusive angel forms could be said to be as difficult as defining electrons is for the quantum physicist. Better to experience them directly.

In the first centuries of the Christian era, many known as heretics called on angels for help, just as pre-Christian "pagans" had been blamed for calling on the many gods of the old religion, paganism. In Latin *religio paganorum* means "peasants' religion." Thus, for centuries the Church forbade the "ignorant" faithful to give the angels names. From its religious rites it also banned anything that could evoke them, preserving only the names of the four main archangels familiar to Jews, Christians, and Muslims. Although their names Michael, Gabriel, Raphael and Uriel are male, most commentators see all angels as having no specific human gender. And virtually all the world's systems of religious belief include celestial beings in their cosmologies, their scriptures containing references of angelic interventions.

Moving down from the Supreme Creator or God, angels are organized in a celestial hierarchy, by means of classifications generally accepted by commentators of many faiths including the Cabbalists and angel historians. Not all traditional institutions or academics have agreed on the order and content of these hierarchies and, indeed, the spelling in English of many angels often varies. However, Dionysius the Areopagite, a disciple of Saint Paul in the sixth century, described three categories or spheres of angels, with three orders in each. Using this model of nine orders of service, angels who serve as heavenly counselors are in the first sphere and contain the seraphim, cherubim and thrones, all of which contemplate God's goodness and reflect his glory. A brief description of the nine orders of angelic beings follows.

1. **Seraphim**: Singing the music of the spheres, these angels are among the most wise and dedicated in their love of God. Although remote from human experience, they are said to help regulate the movement of the heavens. The heavenly hosts might seem to work in graded ranks. However, it is more helpful to see them all working as one so that the seraphim, who seem furthest removed from us on earth, also work with the God in each human being. For example, Isaiah in his vision saw the six-winged seraphim above the throne of God, and one of them carried a burning coal to his mouth to purge his sin.

2. **Cherubim**: Contemplating God's Laws, cherubim are the guardians of light. No matter how remote they seem, their light, as from the stars, filters down from the heavens and touches our lives on earth. Some astrologers claim that there are 72 angels, in groups of 18. These control all four elements, each angel governing 5 degrees of the Zodiac. Overseeing the element of *Fire,* 18 angels control action, illumination, and transformation. Eighteen angels control the element of *Water,* expressed as emotion, love, desire, and passion. For the element of *Air,* another 18 angels oversee practical intelligence and communication. Helping human prosperity, security, and abundance, 18 angels oversee the element of *Earth.* As for birth, the single word *cherub,* portrayed as a winged baby with a chubby, rosy face, is mentioned in the Christian bible, Genesis 3:24.

3. **Thrones:** Thrones represent the first order in the third sphere. Think of these angels as celestial solicitors. They implement the laws mentioned above. In dark days, it is good to remember that, as well as being companion angels with each of

the planets, the Earth angel, guardian of this world, can be especially solicitous to those in spiritual need.

4. **Dominions:** These heavenly beings govern the activities of all angelic groupings below them. They also integrate the spiritual and material worlds. Although they serve the laws and orders of God and thereby prescribe action, they rarely contact individual souls. Nonetheless, their service is very much in tune with the constraints of physical reality.

5. **Virtues:** From the Divine Source, essential energies come from good deeds. Thus, those who work with these beings can become infused with great spiritual energies necessary at this time for our present home planet, Earth. Virtues are beyond and before powers (see next category).

6. **Powers:** These beings are the keepers of collective consciousness and cosmic history, as well as bearers of the conscience of all humanity. The angels of birth and death are therefore included here. Like the leaves of a tree draw down the powers of sunlight into the soil, so these light beings draw down the energies of the divine plan. Multifaith in service, they work with and for all that exists, holistically, without fear or favor. Their intention is to help the spiritual evolution of this planet. Thus, they govern the operations engaged in by both the Thrones and the Dominions.

7. **Principalities:** In medieval angelology, these were known as guardian angels, not of human individuals, but of large groups such as nations and the welfare of their cities. Even today's multinationals, as in worldwide corporations, have such protection as appropriate to their consciousness and spiritual development.

8. **Archangels:** Many religions tell of spiritual beings that have never incarnated. Those most mentioned are the archangels. They oversee the actions of human leaders. The four main archangels familiar to Jews, Christians, and Muslims follow:

   - Michael, the messenger of divine judgment, usually depicted with a sword to subdue Satan (represented sometimes as a dragon), to cut away evil. As the Guardian of Peace, he also holds a pair of scales suggesting, perhaps, that balance in all matters is the ultimate wisdom.
   - Gabriel, the messenger of divine mercy and Revelation is often depicted holding a lily to represent at the Annunciation, purity, and truth. Sometimes seen with an ink well and quill, his function is as the heavenly communicator of the Word of God. Not only did he visit the Virgin Mary in the form of a man, Gabriel also visited Mohammed as he slept, with the angel's feet astride the horizon in order to dictate the Koran.
   - Raphael is the bringer of divine healing, his right forefinger pointing toward heaven. Often he is shown as a pilgrim with a gourd. In front of him leaps a curative fish. By way of saving a suicide, such a fish has been known to leap out of water when some unfortunate—but blessed—soul on a riverbank is thinking of drowning himself. Raphael also holds a staff or caduceus entwined with a snake to symbolize healing.
   - Uriel, as the radiant regent of the sun, is the bearer of the fire of God, and is seen with a flame in his open hand. He rules over thunder and terror so that, like lightning, the knowledge of God can be delivered to the people of the earth. Helping to interpret and decode our inner voice, prophecy and wisdom are also his domain. He can appear holding a scroll, or with a book at his feet that he gave to Adam with all the medicinal herbs in it.
   - The Recording Angels are often referred to by those who wish to consider that all deeds on earth are seen and accountable. Metatron might be considered the most earthly of archangels. Taken up to heaven as a wise and virtuous man, he is now depicted holding a pen or quill while recording human deeds in the Book of Life.

9. **Angels:** As indicated above, angels can appear in many forms and have many different functions. In India, for example, they are known as *pitarah.* Although dealing less with individuals these household deities are perceived to protect families against illness, famine, drought, and other disasters. To the Australian aboriginal, the *wajima* represents the spirit of an ancestor. For the Pueblo peoples of the American Southwest, the *kachina* is known as a guiding, beneficent life spirit.

In Kabbalism, the Tree of Life contains a complete system expressing angelology, the nature of humanity's origins and relationship to God, including the doctrine of reincarnation. In the Jewish Kabbalah (or Qabalah), this traditional mystic map represents physical creation. Increasingly today, it is also used in relationship to Tarot cards and to astrology.

In the study of astrology, 18 angels are said to control the element of Earth. Eighteen more angels control Fire (indicating action, illumination, and transformation). Eighteen control Water (indicating emotions, love, desire, and passion). Eighteen control the element of Air (indicating practical intelligence and communication). Those interested in the symbolism of numbers, as in numerology, will notice that reduced to their lowest denominators, all the numbers mentioned here boil down to a nine. Since multiples of nine always reproduce themselves, as in $9 \times 2 = 18$; $1 + 8 = 9$, this divine number represents eternity. Given that the unnumbered hosts of angels are said to be beyond human calculation, perhaps one of the best known accounts of angels concerns Jacob and his ladder teeming with these light-filled angelic beings. However, not all angels have stayed heaven bound.

Fallen Angels: The line between a good angel and a bad angel, or demon, can seem unclear. For example, the angel Samael has been seen as a force for good in one era and as a devil in the next. This could depend on how their supernatural "power" is perceived. Lucifer, after all, has been called the Angel of Light as well as the Devil. As personified powers mediating between the divine and the human, fallen angels are those who chose no longer to obey the laws of God. But perhaps not all is lost. William Blake, the poet-philosopher and mystic artist, states that Lucifer will return to God's throne once "the soul emerges from the illusion of evil..."

Guardian Angels: Children of all ages and through all civilizations have been aware of their guardian angels. Intimate as unseen breath, they watch over our spiritual growth throughout our lives until enlightenment is eventually achieved through all the light and heavy lessons to be encountered on earth. Unconditionally, they love and cherish, guide and protect us. Alert always to our needs, they are especially helpful in the moments we open ourselves in relaxed acceptance of their divine presence. The guardian angel of youth carries bow and arrows and a slingshot to indicate athletic prowess. A fun-loving and positive approach to life is thus encouraged, celebrating youthful qualities that can thrive in all those who stay young at heart throughout their entire lives.

All loving beings in this world who help others, even starving animals in the wild who do not attack good people, can be said to be "angels." In terms of human service to the suffering, consider Florence Nightingale. Nursing dying soldiers during the Crimean war, she was known as an angel of mercy, a title that relates to nursing staff even today. She was certain that not just war wounds eventually kill, but that lack of hygiene in living conditions caused fatal diseases. Further, she stated that when the human spirit is in a state of dis-ease, it is because the laws of God are not being obeyed.

> 'Angel aides' says William Blake
> 'Gently help Seekers for God's sake.'
> In light beams they bask
> Unseen till we ask.
> Best blessings let each human make.

—Christopher Gilmore

FURTHER READING

Ambika, W. (1995). *The angel oracle.* London: Connections.

Corten, T. (1992). *Discovering angels.* Oxfordshire, UK: Caer Sidi Publications.

Daniel, A., Wyllie, T., & Ramer, A. (1992). *Ask your angels.* London: Piatkus.

Watson, D. (1993). *A dictionary of mind and spirit.* London: Optima.

Harvey, C. L. (2002). An Angel for the new education. *Soul Educator, 9* (25), 4.

Twitchell, P. (1977). *Letters to Gail (Vol. II).* Menlo Park, CA: Illuminated Way Press.

APOCALYPSE

In popular usage, the word *apocalypse* refers to a cataclysmic event that results in the devastation or utter destruction of humanity. However, the technical use of the term is reserved for a genre (or type) of literature found in the biblically based religious traditions (Judaism, Christianity, and Islam). Examples of this literature surface in times of anxiety, when a community is experiencing great change or persecution.

The authors use evocative imagery and stock literary techniques to encourage their readers to remain true to the faith as the day will soon come when God will intervene and restore order. On that day the faithful will be rewarded, and the wicked will be punished.

Apocalypses receive their name from the Revelation (*apokalypsis* in Greek) of John, found in the Christian New Testament. However, the Revelation of John is not the only apocalypse, nor is it the first. Scholars who seek the origins of apocalyptic literature look to the writings of two sixth-century B.C.E. Jewish prophets: Ezekiel and Zechariah. Writing at the time of the Babylonian Exile (587–538 B.C.E.), when the Jerusalem Temple had been destroyed and many of the residents of Judah (southern Israel) had been deported to Babylon, the authors of these texts describe ecstatic visions in which they are transported to the throne of God and shown that the current tribulations will end and Israel will be restored to peace and prosperity. The Judahites were indeed returned to their homeland.

In the second century B.C.E., writers drew upon the techniques of Ezekiel and Zechariah to describe new visions to provide hope for their readers. The book of Daniel and the noncanonical *1 Enoch,* both written in response to attacks on Jewish culture by the Syrian king Antiochus IV Epiphanes (ca. 175–164 B.C.E.), are the first true apocalypses. These texts are similar in form to Ezekiel and Zechariah but include additional literary techniques that are used in later apocalyptic texts such as Revelation. These techniques include pseudonymous authorship (the visionary, and thus the narrator of the text is a legendary figure of the past); an other-worldly journey (the visionary is taken on a journey through the heavens and/or to the throne of God); an overview of history (from the beginning of time to the period of the visionary, followed by detailed "prophecies" of the recent past from the visionary's time to the time of the book's composition, and then a set of ambiguous prophecies of the real author's own future); eschatology (descriptions of the "end time" when God will destroy the author's and his community's enemies and bring about a new age of peace and prosperity); elaborate imagery (angels and demons proliferate, and various kings and kingdoms are represented symbolically as composite beasts); and a promise of personal salvation (those among the community who have died will be rewarded for their faith in the afterlife). All of these techniques, though often misunderstood by modern readers, can be found in other literature of antiquity. Their general use, then, ensured that readers of the time would be able to "de-code" an apocalypse, and see in it a plea to remain faithful until the time when God will bring an end to the current tribulation.

The influence of apocalyptic literature extended into the first-century C.E. when several charismatic preachers called on God to rid Judea (formerly Judah) of its latest rulers: the Romans. One such preacher was John the Baptist who, the New Testament gospels tell us, criticized the Judean aristocracy and warned of a "wrath to come" (Matthew 3:7; Luke 3:7). John was executed, but before his death he was able to groom an apparent successor in Jesus of Nazareth who, borrowing imagery from Daniel, spoke about "the Son of Man coming in clouds" (Mark 13:26) at the end of the age.

The apocalypticism of the Jesus movement carried over into letters written by the apostle Paul (ca. 50–65 C.E.). In these letters, Paul describes the resurrection of Jesus as the "first fruits" of a general end-time resurrection of the faithful.

Apocalytic literature continued to develop in Judaism after the beginnings of the Jesus movement. Texts found among the Dead Sea scrolls, such as the *War Rule,* provide evidence of first-century Jewish apocalyptic thought.

As Christianity gradually separated from Judaism, Christians encountered persecution and martyrdom for their beliefs and actions. Faced with the possibility of losing adherents, Christian writers employed the apocalyptic genre to strengthen the faith of their community. Revelation, for example, is believed to be a response to the persecution of Christians under the emperor Domitian, and the noncanonical *Apocalypse of Peter,* with its gruesome tour of Hell, was written, most likely, to prevent Christians from joining the Jewish revolt of 135–137 C.E.

Apocalyptic expectations temporarily waned after the persecution of Christians ceased in the fourth century. But Muhammad, the seventh-century founder of Islam, drew upon apocalyptic motifs when he warned the citizens of the Arabian city of Mecca that their behavior would be punished on the forthcoming Day of Judgment. Shi'i Muslim groups make particular use of apocalyptic ideas. Seeing themselves as the object of persecution by the Sunni majority, Shi'i Muslims wrote that the rightful leader of the Muslim community will return to establish universal justice and usher in the Day of Judgment.

Even though apocalypses focus on events close to the time that the text was composed, many contemporary readers continue to see in them indications of the coming "apocalypse." Such apocalyptic expectation reached its height during the Cold War. At that time, anxieties about worldwide nuclear destruction led Christian preachers and authors (such as Hal Lindsey, *The Late Great Planet Earth,* 1977) to seek relief in apocalyptic texts, and inspired filmmakers to draw upon and transform apocalyptic motifs to craft biblically based horror films (such as *The Omen* series).

When anxieties about the Cold War ceased, apocalyptic ideas receded, although today some Christian denominations—most notably Jehovah's Witnesses, Seventh-Day Adventists, the Church of Jesus Christ of Latter-Day Saints (Mormons), and the Worldwide Church of God—retain a strongly apocalyptic worldview, as do the occasional radical apocalyptic (or "millennial") groups such as the Branch Davidians of Waco, Texas. However, these groups have always been in the minority. The norm has always been to create or focus on apocalyptic literature as the need arises, in response to times that challenge a community's capacity to hope.

—Tony Chartrand-Burke

See also Dead Sea Scrolls; Eschatology; Jesus; Muhammad

FURTHER READING

Boyer, P. (1994). *When time shall be no more: Prophecy belief in modern American culture.* Cambridge: Harvard University Press.

Collins, J. J. (1998). *The apocalyptic imagination: An introduction to the Jewish matrix of Christianity* (Rev. ed.). Grand Rapids, MI: Eerdmans.

Himmelfarb, M. (1983). *Tours of hell: An apocalyptic form in Jewish and Christian literature.* Philadelphia: University of Pennsylvania Press.

McGinn, B. (1979). *Visions of the end: apocalyptic traditions in the Middle Ages.* New York: Columbia University Press.

APOCRYPHA/ DEUTEROCANONICAL BOOKS

The 16 extra books found in the Greek translation of the Hebrew Bible are known as the Deuterocanonical Books by Catholic and Orthodox traditions and as the Apocrypha (meaning "hidden") in Protestant traditions. Originally written in Hebrew, Greek, and Aramaic, this collection includes the history books of the Maccabees, which outline the successful rebellion of the Jews against their Greek (Seleucid) overlords, the establishment of a sovereign Jewish political and religious state under the Hasmoneans, and its eventual demise under Rome in 63 B.C.E. They also include wisdom books similar to Proverbs (the Wisdom of Solomon and Sirach), stories such as Tobit, Judith, Susanna, Bel and the Dragon, an extra psalm (Psalm 151), and the Prayer of Manasseh. These books reflect Jewish life and theology from approximately 300 B.C.E. to 70 C.E.

—Jane S. Webster

See also Bible, Jewish; Catholicism; Christianity, Orthodox

FURTHER READING

Bandstra, B. L. (2003). *Reading the Old Testament: An introduction to the Hebrew Bible.* Belmont, CA: Wadsworth.

Harris, S. L. (2003). *Understanding the Bible.* Boston, MA: McGraw-Hill.

AQUINAS, THOMAS

Thomas Aquinas is a towering figure in the history of the Dominican Order of friars in theology and philosophy. The exact date of his birth is not known, but most sources state that the year was 1225, and the place was the castle of Rocca Secca, midway between Rome and Naples. Early in life, he planned to join the Order of Preachers, the Dominican friars. This did not please his family, who conspired to keep him from joining the Dominicans. They even kidnapped him and locked him in a castle tower for over a year. Thomas Aquinas was still drawn by the Order's intellectual apostolate and the mendicant way of life. In 1244, he joined the Order. The rest of his brief life was divided between Paris and Italy, studying, lecturing, and writing. He did this until his death at age 49, in 1274. His greatest writing was the *Summa Theologica*, completed in 1266. This massive work fills five volumes and addresses Aquinas's very mature thought on all the Christian mysteries. The format consists of questions, objections, and authoritative replies in each article, providing a very concise summary of his view on the matter under discussion. His *Summa Theologica* became the model and standard theological text in many schools and universities.

The *Summa Theologica* was written as a systematic exposition of theology. It is divided into three parts, of which the second is further subdivided into two. The first part deals with the reality of God and creation. It also includes a treatment on human nature and the intellectual life. Aquinas strongly maintained the primacy of the intellect over the will. The second part deals with the moral life, considering the final end of humankind and the general moral themes of virtues and vices. The final section concerns Jesus the Christ, and the sacraments of the Roman Catholic Church.

Aquinas was very adept at using Aristotle's and Plato's philosophical insights, patristic writings, and clear reasoning. His oral teachings and his writings on theology, philosophy, and scripture were equal to the work of several people in his day. Sources state that he dictated to four or five secretaries at the same time. Throughout his life he was always very modest and unassuming. A man of deep prayer and spiritual insight, he saw himself as devoting his life to God through theological scholarship. Yet, he also lent his intellect to helping the everyday believer. He wrote commentaries for the average person on the basic prayers, including the Creed, the Our Father, and the Hail Mary.

He was canonized a saint of the Roman Catholic Church in 1323. A later honor was bestowed on him in 1567, being declared a doctor of the Church, because of his writings, and is now known as the "angelic doctor" because of one of his writings on angels.

In his day, his writings were not immediately or universally accepted. A commission was appointed to examine his writings, as his use of Aristotle was suspect. Aristotelianism was seen as radical and unorthodox. The use of non-Christian philosophers like Aristotle and Plato brought the attention of Church authorities. Three years after Aquinas's death, 21 theses of Aquinas were condemned as in error by the bishop of Paris. Yet, through the centuries, the Roman Catholic Church has embraced his writings, theology, and liturgical music as accurately relaying the true faith. His *Summa Theologia* was the greatest monument of the age. It was one of only three reference works laid on the table of the assembly at the Council of Trent, the other two books being the Bible and the pontifical decrees. In the revised calendar of feasts in the Roman Catholic Church, the Thomas Aquinas feast day is celebrated on January 28.

—Rev. David M. O'Leary

ART, ISLAMIC

Islamic art does not mean art with a specifically Islamic subject matter, but rather art produced by Muslims. There is nothing in Islam that corresponds to Christian iconography. Indeed, there is a conscious avoidance of painting with a religious theme, whether portraits of the Prophet Muhammad, his companions, or his wives, or incidents from the Qur'an or the life of the Prophet. Human figures do not feature at all in the decoration of religious buildings or in copies of the Qur'an, mainly because there, in particular, they might distract worshippers from the true object of their prayers and spiritual meditations. However, none of this should be taken to imply that Islamic art is not religious, or that it does not derive its inspiration from the Qur'an. On the contrary, beauty is perceived as a divine quality in Islam, and art opens up a pathway to contemplative knowledge whose ultimate object is divine beauty. A *hadith* (saying of the Prophet) reminds Muslims that, "Allah is beautiful and he loves beauty." Artistic creativity (when given expression within the boundaries permitted by Islamic law) is considered a God-given skill that should be used to celebrate His greatness.

However, these are not the only differences between Western and Islamic art. In Islam, a work of art is not judged in terms of its assumed originality, for continuity of style and imitation of predecessors are equally important. Little attention is normally paid to the individual genius of the artist or his personality, mood, or psychological state. Indeed, these things are as far as they could be from the spirit of Islamic art. The most important thing about a work of art is not who produced it, but what spiritual values it conveys, or what spiritual vision it embodies.

Indeed, the whole conception of art in Islam differs from Western conceptions. Figurative painting (whether on wood, canvas, or wall), print-making, and sculpture are generally not valued, because they tend to imitate nature, whereas Islamic art is more concerned to represent the meaning and spiritual quality of things rather than their physical and material form. For this reason, Islamic art has rarely valued perspective or three-dimensional work, and has preferred, rather than reproduce natural forms, to transmute or transfigure them into something more abstract or stylized. There is no distinction of worth in Islam between fine art and applied art. The three most valued forms of art are

1. Calligraphy (particularly Arabic words from the *Qur'an*
2. Architecture
3. Decorative arts and crafts (particularly wood and stone carving, pottery, glassware, mosaics, metalwork, carpets, and bookbinding, and the illumination and illustration of books, especially in the Safavid and Ottoman traditions)

Every object from the religious building to the humble household utensil has to be endowed with some beauty. Apart from calligraphy, the two most common forms of ornamental decoration are the arabesque (ornamental leaf and branch designs) and complex geometrical patterns. The unending repetition of these patterns reflects Allah's infinite nature and the interrelatedness of all His creation. The study of Islamic art has often traditionally been considered the best way to understand the spiritual dimension of the Islamic culture as a whole. This is perhaps because its balance, harmony, and unity convey an inner truth without requiring complex rational evaluation or explanation. The incorporation of Western values into contemporary Islamic art has diminished its distinctive identity and has sometimes been lamented as leading to a loss of spirituality.

—J. Mark Halstead

See also Islam; Qur'an

FURTHER READING

Burckhardt, T. (1976). *Art of Islam: language and meaning.* London: World of Islam Festival Publishing Co.

Nasr, S. H. (1987). *Islamic art and spirituality.* Ipswich: Golgonooza Press.

ART, VISUAL

Virtually all cultures have used art for religious purposes. The drawings in Paleolithic caves seem to have served a spiritual purpose. Some of the animals depicted are drawn with exaggerated features that make them take on a supernatural power, which suggests, for the artists, that the animals had religious meaning. The ancient Egyptians used art to please their gods and to ensure long life. Since ancient times, indigenous cultures and religious traditions everywhere have used artistic objects and images in rituals and in transmitting the stories that express their faith. Art, then, has been a central means for expressing all things religious.

However, art carrying religious themes has not always expressed or conveyed what might be called spiritual meaning, while art without religious themes has often done so. The distinction rests on whether the artist and viewer experience in art what is commonly referred to as *transcendence*—a higher power or insight into a deeper meaning of life. An example of art expressing spiritual feelings without any specific religious meaning is the images drawn of daily work in a field and of everyday life in general—as can be shown in many of the French impressionists' paintings. For many, these images take on spiritual meaning.

For religious purposes, art has been used for religious rituals, for teaching, and for expressing spiritual feelings. Art used to enhance the ritual aspects of religion can be found almost anywhere. For centuries, vessels and jewelry have been made for use in religious rituals. The Ijebu of Yoruba use ritualistic containers in the form of animals to exhibit particular animals' strengths. More cultures than can be named use masks in religious ceremonies that may represent sacred animals, gods, or goddesses. During religious ceremonies, some cultures have individuals put on masks representing gods or goddesses to assume their spiritual powers.

In preliterate societies, art has been an important way to teach. For example, at the height of the Renaissance, images were made to teach illiterate persons about the characters, events, and stories in the Bible. Another favorite subject was that of saints, who were often depicted on triptychs for use as personal altars. This was a time when the only art that was commissioned was about religion, and so much of the art from this period was religious without expressing something spiritual.

Art in places of worship is often intended to elicit feelings of awe and reverence. For example, in the Sistine Chapel, the viewer looks up at a huge mural on the ceiling that is obviously meant to overwhelm the viewer with its image of a very powerful God.

Many cultures use art to tell stories central to their religion and to commemorate various gods. A walk through any museum collection of African or Aztec art is apt to show artifacts and images on bowls depicting such stories with religious themes.

Religious symbols are often carried around in everyday life as people wear a symbol of their faith in their jewelry. These visual representations allow people to hold their religion close to them wherever they go. Art, then, provides concrete, visible, and even portable manifestations of a person's faith.

Despite the distinction between religious and spiritual art, the intent behind most religious art is both. Tibetan sand paintings are among the clearest and most consistent examples of art that is both religious and spiritual. The images, which are made by a mosaic of tiny bits of colored sand carefully placed over many days, include typical Tibetan iconography. After the sand painting is finished, it is swept up and placed in the river, a spiritual act symbolizing life's impermanence, one of the central messages in Buddhism.

In the 20th century, the emphasis in art has been less on the religious and more on the spiritual. Spiritual art becomes personal, and relies more on the viewer's internal experience. When religious icons are removed from art, spirituality may actually be more accessible and more easily communicated across faiths and cultures. Wassily Kandinsky talks about art that is essentially timeless in its spiritual meaning. For Kandinsky, the successful spiritual artwork is internal and timeless.

Religious art and art with spiritual meaning has played and still plays an essential role in the faith of both communities and individuals. The images and objects may change, and the balance between religious and spiritual may change as well. However, what remains constant is the central importance of art as a means for expressing transcendence and life's meaning.

—Chantal Fountain-Harris

FURTHER READING

Barzun, J. (1973). *The use and abuse of art.* Princeton, NJ: Princeton University Press.

Lipsey, R. (1988). *An art of our own: The spiritual in twentieth-century art.* Boston: Shambhala.

ASCETICISM

Asceticism is a lifestyle of rigorous self-discipline, often using some form of self-denial and/or simple living as the means for spiritual improvement and development. The word itself is rooted in the Greek word *ascesis,* emphasizing a disciplined lifestyle. The ancient Greeks used it in reference to both athletes and philosophers. Athletes were ascetic in the sense that they were disciplined to train hard every day in preparation for competition. The term was used of philosophers when discussing those who, for the sake of wisdom, spent more time in contemplation, and avoided what were considered more worldly pursuits, for the purpose of developing character and virtue.

While the practice of asceticism is generally equated with healthy religious and/or spiritual development by those who practice and preach it, throughout history there are many stories of asceticism gone awry wherein, for example, with the hopes of achieving a closer relation to that which is considered divine, an individual or group took the practice of asceticism to the extreme, risking good health. As such, the practice of asceticism and the benefits that come with it are often debated and disputed.

One example of a Greek philosopher who emphasized the ascetic life was Pythagoras, a Greek who sought to instill virtue in his followers through a very disciplined lifestyle. The hope was that as persons gave up their illogical pursuit of passions, they gained character and wisdom and no longer sought after more worldly pursuits. Both Stoics and Cynics were also considered ascetic as they emphasized a disciplined lifestyle in which one progressed in virtue and moved away from a variety of vices because of a disciplined lifestyle. Ascetic discipline continued to be a theme in many Greek philosophical circles well into the second and third centuries C.E.

Asceticism has long been a part of most major religious traditions as well. Most religions have groups who seek spiritual wisdom through some form of self-discipline and self-denial. In Hinduism, Brahmins have long emphasized the ascetic lifestyle Some of their practices were extremely rigorous including the practices of rolling on the ground for hours at a time, and standing on tiptoes throughout the day, as well as remaining exposed to the extremes of weather for long periods with little or no clothing. Judaism has had various groups that practiced forms of asceticism through very austere lifestyles. Most notable were the Nazarites who were noted for their separation from the rest of society, avoidance of wine and any by-products, and never cutting their hair. Buddhism also has an ascetic emphasis, but in a more communal setting than the Brahmins. For the Buddhists, there is not necessarily the desire to progress toward God or some other spiritual being, but to reach the state of nirvana through a lifestyle that emphasizes chastity, honesty, and the avoidance of intoxicating drinks.

In early Christianity, ascetic practices were often seen as preparation for martyrdom. In the Roman world of the first through the third centuries, Christians faced the very real possibility that they would be martyred for their faith. Therefore, the Church wanted all believers to be ready in both body and spirit for their coming test. Ascetic disciplines such as fasting, celibacy, and prayer were all thought to be ways that one could unite body and soul with God.

As the prospects for persecution dimmed with the rise of Constantine in the early fourth century, another approach to the ascetic life developed. Ascetics began to move out into the deserts of Egypt and the wilderness of Syria seeking God. Again these men and women sought God's wisdom through a very disciplined life, unencumbered with the day-to-day routines of life in the more inhabited regions of their world. Anthony of Egypt is the first literary figure of this Christian movement. He was a young Alexandrian who, upon hearing a sermon to give up all he had and follow God, dispersed his family's wealth and went to live the ascetic life in the Egyptian desert at the end of the third and beginning of the fourth century. His life is chronicled in the *Life of Anthony* penned by Athanasius, the bishop of Alexandria, Egypt during that time.

Asceticism in Christianity began to move in a more communal direction with the coming of the Middle Ages. Especially with the formation of religious orders in the West, the ascetic life became somewhat institutionalized, particularly in Benedict of Nursia's *Rule* of the sixth century.

Asceticism has almost always involved self-denial and a very austere life, but has also served as an equalizer in many traditions. Persons from all socioeconomic groups have heard its call. In Christianity in particular, it has given women an avenue for leadership, as there have been many exemplary women ascetics in the Christian tradition. Asceticism continues in most religious traditions through the present age, and continues to serve as a trigger of religious and/or spiritual development.

—Gary R. Poe

FURTHER READING

Brown, P. R. (1971). The rise and function of the holy man in late antiquity. *Journal of Roman Studies, 61,* 80–101.

Chakroborti, H. (1993). *Asceticism in ancient India: In Brahmanical, Buddhist, Jaina and Ajivika societies.* Columbia, MO: South Asia Books.

Harpham, G. (1987). *Ascetic imperative in culture and criticism.* Chicago: University of Chicago Press.

Wimbush, V., & Valantasis, R. (Eds.). (2002). *Asceticism.* New York: Oxford University Press.

ASSETS, DEVELOPMENTAL

Although there is increasing evidence that religion and spirituality can protect young people from problem behaviors, increase resilience, and promote thriving, the mechanisms underlying this association are unclear. The developmental assets framework offers a tool for exploring these links. Developed by Search Institute in the 1990s as a synthesis of research in adolescent development, prevention, resilience, and related fields, the framework identifies 40 experiences, relationships, opportunities, skills, and other qualities that form a foundation for healthy development (Table 1).

Studies of adolescents across North America show that developmental assets are a powerful predictor of their health and well-being, regardless of their race or ethnicity, socioeconomic status, or gender. The more assets that young people have, the less likely they are to engage in a wide range of high-risk behaviors (e.g., substance use, violence, and antisocial behavior), and the more likely they are to engage in thriving behaviors (e.g., valuing diversity, exhibiting leadership, and serving others). In addition, developmental assets are associated with religious and spiritual development on conceptual, empirical, and application levels.

CONCEPTUAL

In addition to the obvious connection to the religious community asset (#19), the connections between developmental assets and spiritual development are evident when one recognizes spiritual development as involving a search for connectedness, meaning, purpose, and contribution. Explicitly relevant assets include (see Table 1 service to others (9), caring (26), equality and social justice (27), sense of purpose (39), and positive view of personal future (40).

EMPIRICAL

Religious adolescents report consistently higher access to developmental assets, engage in fewer risk behaviors, and report higher levels of thriving indicators. Adolescents who are active in a faith community have, on average, five more developmental assets than those who are not active. In addition, the more assets that young people experience, the greater the likelihood that they are to participate in religious community and to place high importance on religion and spirituality. It is likely that developmental assets mediate the influence of religion. This role may be explained in part by the consistent expectations to contribute and to maintain a positive moral lifestyle that are embedded within religious traditions and communities, the intergenerational and peer support that young people experience, and the sense of meaning and purpose that shape a positive identity and spiritual life.

Table 1 Search Institute's 40 Developmental Assets

External Assets	*Internal Assets*
Support	**Commitment to Learning**
1. Family support	21. Achievement motivation
2. Positive family communication	22. School engagement
3. Other adult relationships	23. Homework
4. Caring neighborhood	24. Bonding to school
5. Caring school climate	25. Reading for pleasure
6. Parent involvement in schooling	
Empowerment	**Positive Values**
7. Community values youth	26. Caring
8. Youth as resources	27. Equality and social justice
9. Service to others	28. Integrity
10. Safety	29. Honesty
	30. Responsibility
	31. Restraint
Boundaries and Expectations	**Social Competencies**
11. Family boundaries	32. Planning and decision making
12. School boundaries	33. Interpersonal competence
13. Neighborhood boundaries	34. Cultural competence
14. Adult role models	35. Resistance skills
15. Positive peer influence	36. Peaceful conflict resolution
16. High expectations	
Constructive Use of Time	**Positive Identity**
17. Creative activities	37. Personal power
18. Youth programs	38. Self-esteem
19. Religious community	39. Sense of purpose
20. Time at home	40. Positive view of personal future

SOURCE: Search Institute. Copyright © 1997 by Search Institute, Minneapolis, MN 55413 (www.search-institute.org). Used with permission.

APPLICATION

In addition to its role in examining the relationship between religion and spirituality and overall healthy development, the asset framework has been widely adopted as a tool to assist faith communities in understanding and strengthening their roles in nurturing young people's faith and spiritual lives in the context of overall healthy development. In addition to the pilot projects and resources developed by Search Institute to promote this application, a number of other organizations, such as the U.S. Conference of Catholic Bishops, have utilized the asset framework as a tool for strengthening their engagement with children, youth, and families.

—*Eugene C. Roehlkepartain*

See also Search Institute

FURTHER READING

National Conference of Catholic Bishops. (1997). *Renewing the vision: A framework for Catholic youth ministry.* Washington, DC: United States Catholic Conference.

Roehlkepartain, E. C. (1998). *Building assets in congregations: A practical guide to helping youth grow up healthy.* Minneapolis, MN: Search Institute.

Roehlkepartain, E. C. (2003). Building strengths, deepening faith: Understanding and enhancing youth development in Protestant congregations. In R. M. Lerner, F. Jacobs, & D. Wertlieb (Eds.). *Handbook of Applied Developmental Science: Vol. 3, Promoting Positive Youth and Family Development* (pp. 515–534). Thousand Oaks, CA: Sage.

Scales, P.C., & Leffert, N. (2004). *Developmental assets: A synthesis of the scientific research on adolescent development* (2nd ed.). Minneapolis, MN: Search Institute.

Wagener, L. M., Furrow, J. L., King, P. E., Leffert, N., & Benson, P. (2003). Religion and developmental resources. *Review of Religious Research, 44*(3), 271–284.

ASTROLOGY

Astrology has long been a controversial subject. As a method of predicting the future and dictating personality traits based on an individual's time and place of birth, it was long ago discarded in favor of modern science. As long as astrology is approached from a literalistic viewpoint, it carries too many contradictions for the modern scientific consciousness to accept. Any example can be cited of two very different people born at precisely the same time, as thousands are across the world every moment, and this seems to be enough to disqualify astrology as any kind of meaningful concept.

But a literalistic perspective is not the only possible approach. The subject is of interest to historians, mythographers, and others for academic reasons, and it still appeals to millions of aficionados around the world for the insight it can bring to the ever-popular quest for self-discovery. Due to this alone, astrology is relevant to the subject of modern spirituality.

HISTORY

Mythographer Joseph Campbell suggests that the original awareness of the cosmos, arrayed with its diamond patterns of starlight, came as a result of the adoption of agriculture as a lifestyle at the dawn of the Neolithic era, at approximately 7000 B.C.E. Attention to the marvelously regular patterns of the stars helped to fix the best timing for planting and harvesting. Past this handy practicality, it was only a matter of time before the mythic imagination began to project familiar images onto the sky, connecting the dots in a grand vision that remade the stars into god carriers. Thus, the ancient art of astrology was developed in nearly every developed civilization of the ancient world, including Egypt, the Middle East, Persia, India, China, and the empires of Mesoamerica. There is possibly no more graphic example of the erection of a sphere of psychic protection in what the sociologist Peter Berger entitled the "Sacred Canopy." The pretty star patterns of the night sky came to represent a glorious sacred canopy of dancing gods, leaping beasts, and fleeing enemies, helping to demarcate a people's all-important sense of place in the world.

The Western system of astrology was inherited from the Babylonians, and later embellished by the Greeks and Latins. Each of the planets was named after a prominent god, and as such, their titles were bequeathed to us to this day. Originally called the "zodiakos," or "circle of animals," the ancient system merged with many currents of influence in the Hellenistic era in a process often referred to as "syncretism," as myriad sources mingled to produce an array of new systems including astrology, alchemy, Tarot, Kabbalah, hermetic arts, and many more.

Emerging Christianity was certainly not immune from this phenomenon of syncretism. As historian Jean Seznec details, the early Church both adopted aspects of astrology, such as the prominent role played by the star of Bethlehem in leading astrologers from the east to the birth of their savior, but also repudiated it. Astrology embodied the concept of unalterable fate, which went against their concepts of free will and irresistible grace. Still, astrology continued to enjoy extreme popularity through the Renaissance, as popes, kings, and great ladies such as Catherine de Medici employed professional astrologers, and all the major universities hosted chairs in astrology. In Seznec's words, this demonstrates well "to what extent the church yielded to the prevailing superstition." How else can we explain, he asks, the role played by the constellations of the zodiac in the decorations at the Vatican?

If Christianity leveled some of the original blows at astrology, the rationalism and empirical sciences of the early modern era seemed to finish it as any kind of viable explanation for one's fate and place in the world. But the 20th century witnessed a revival of interest in mythic forms, along with the introduction of metaphorical and symbolic methodologies, such as those featured in many perspectives from the New Age movement, to the revival of neopaganism, to the symbolic interpretations of the psychologists. Jungian archetypal theory has played an especially significant role in the revival of interest in astrology and other symbol systems of the ancient world, for the archetypal expressions they contain, rather than for any literal influence on day-to-day life.

And in 20th-century currents of thought, not even the literal applications of astrology can be so easily dismissed anymore, now that quantum physics has uncovered a whole new world of correspondences among particles, gravitational currents, and the strange influence of thought. In an era when we can easily document the gravitational pull of the moon, we can no longer summarily dismiss what might be more subtle, but no less genuine, gravitational and wave patterns emanating from various spatial bodies and sectors of the sky. The new paradigm pictures our world as permanently bathed in a very real cascade of cosmic forces, affecting every inhabitant of the globe. Although of course the specific understandings are quite different, still, this vision might not be so drastically removed from the sacred canopies of the ancients who imagined the same globe as bathed in a continual stream of cosmic influences.

Twentieth-century astrologers, such as Walter Koch, Dane Rudhyar, Michel Gauquelin, Marc Edmund Jones, Evangeline Adams, Lois Rodden, and Noel Tyl have passed the ancient art of astrology down to the contemporary era. The current practice of astrology is carried out with extreme mathematical sophistication, as every minute measurement and aspect of the interactive dance of the stars is scrutinized to produce untold thousands of lines of analysis. The resulting system is a hybrid phenomenon, as classical deities are merged with images drawn on the sky. But typically, astrologers do not receive an education in classical mythology, nor do most mythographers and classicists turn their attention to the "superstition" of astrology. Hence, astrologers are not always in a position to recognize the appropriate deities involved in their art.

THE SYSTEM

An individual's "sun sign," that is, the position of the sun relative to the earth on one side and the constellation along the ecliptic behind it, is only the most basic identifying marker in astrology. To obtain the full picture, a zodiacal "chart" is constructed for each individual, and for specific events, by diagramming the precise positions in the sky of all the constellations and planets at a given moment. Special significance is attached to certain sectors of the sky for the moment of birth, especially the "ascendant" or "rising sign," the constellation on the eastern horizon, and the "midheaven," the zenith point directly above. Whatever sign or planets that happened to be in these sensitive sectors at the moment of birth will be read as having an important influence on that individual's life and character. Also, astrologers are not always aware of their blind spot. All the planets are "read" for their significance except one—the earth, the planet we are riding on while projecting our fanciful images onto the sky. The sun sign is *opposite* to the placement of the earth, so each sign's opposite, the "earth sign," must also be taken into consideration to yield thorough results in an astrological reading. Similarly, individuals born "on the cusp," between two signs, need to have both those signs' qualities applied in order to see the special combination that person represents.

Signs and Planets, Houses and Elements

The system's orienting point is the date of the vernal equinox, around March 20, when the sun annually enters the constellation Aries, the Ram. This is the first sign, then, and considered the first "house" or sector in the universal system, on which all other charts are then superimposed. Each house will be assigned specific aspects of life. In the case of the first house, these include personality itself and physical appearance. Each constellation along the ecliptic is associated with a specific deity, and through that god's personality elements, a complex of factors is identified. In this way, the first house, Aries, is ruled by Mars, god of war; hence the "warlike" qualities of the Aries personality such as the enthrallment of battle, debate, argument, and competition, and the powerful nature of the Aries in general. Aries is considered a fire sign, as each constellation is correlated with one of the four elements. Fire signs include Aries, Leo, and Sagittarius; earth: Taurus, Virgo, and Capricorn; air: Gemini, Libra, and Aquarius; and water: Cancer, Scorpio, and Pisces.

The second "house" is Taurus, the Bull, ruled by Venus, goddess of love. As an earth sign, Taureans will have a strong connection to the earth, and the qualities of fertility, sexuality, and sensuality. They are practical and "down to earth," but they can get bogged down, as if "stuck in the mud." The concerns of the second house include physical comfort, money, finances, and support systems. In this sign, the hybrid nature of the astrological system can be seen. The sign is ruled by Venus. But when the image of the bull is added, an entirely different deity emerges, the bull-god, Dionysus, or Osiris of ancient Egypt. This god's complex symbolism must be included for thorough assessment of this type.

The third house is the realm of Gemini, the Twins, ruled by Mercury. Among many other things, this god is a trickster and a thief, lending many Geminis a fascination with the shady side of life. The third house is said to rule over the area of communication of all types, media, short trips, and so on. The image of the Twins adds the characteristic of a dual nature. The sign's air nature links it to the world of intellect and ideas, and shows the connection to birds, flitting about from branch to branch, from subject to subject, as Geminis will often feature the famous short attention span.

The fourth house is Cancer, the Crab, ruled by the Moon goddess, whose phases lend Cancerians a moody, changeable, unpredictable nature. Nurturing, parenting, and issues of home life are the characteristic areas ruled by this house. The crab demonstrates the Cancer's love of hoarding and hiding things, especially feelings. Cancers will typically hate to have anyone else invade this inner sanctum of secrets, trampling on the soft inner parts inside the crab's protective shell.

The fifth house is Leo, the Lion, king of the jungle, ruled by the Sun god, Apollo in Greek myth, though since there is no planet with this title in our solar system, he is another unrecognized mythic presence in astrology. As children of Apollo, discus thrower, Leos are typically very athletic, active, ambitious, and driven. This sector rules over children and childhood, as if to eternalize the era when we all played in the sun with a carefree, fun-loving attitude. The famous sunny personality of the Leo will be the result. As their regal connections hint, Leo can believe he or she is, or should be, the center of attention.

The sixth house is Virgo, the Virgin, demure and shy, yet feeling the need to be of some real service to others. The sixth house rules over this concept of service, the actual workplace, and also health, making nursing and healthcare professionals among its classic exponents. Virgos' classic defining characteristic is their busybody nature and attention to tiny details, making them efficient and organized, but often considered picky by others.

The seventh house is occupied by Libra, the Scales of Justice. This is the domain of relationships of all sorts, friendship, love, and also enemies. Libra is refined, and fascinated by the works of civilization, especially its art forms and the elegance of language. The sign's air nature will lend the native a tendency to want to keep it light. Ruled by Venus, goddess of beauty, the Libran will have a highly developed aesthetic sensibility, sometimes tending toward vanity. But here is another missing presence, as the image of the scales carries a totally different deity, Athena, goddess of justice. The keen Athenian interests in political affairs and dedication to fairness and justice are often overlooked. Many Librans are lawyers or judges, as the scales of justice represent their domain.

The constellation of Scorpio, the Scorpion, is next. Its eighth house placement correlates it to issues of life, death, and rebirth, as this is the season of the death of the plant life. As such it is ruled by Pluto, god of death. Scorpio natives are the most intense of all the signs. They can fly into a rage and are known by their scorpion's sting of cutting words and uncensored truth-telling. Yet they bear the profound wisdom of the crone goddess of the underworld, Hecate. Before Pluto was discovered in 1930, astrology assigned rulership of this sign to Ares, based on the concept of the war god's forceful personality and ruthless nature.

The Scorpionic heaviness gives way to the soaring ambitions of Sagittarius, the Centaur, occupying the ninth house. This sector rules over matters relating to philosophy, religion, law, writing, publishing, and travel to faraway places. The Sagittarius is the great wanderer and adventurer. Ruled by Jupiter, the native expresses the buoyant optimism, jovial nature, and commanding presence of this grandest of the planets. Sagittarius' inquisitive nature and eternal search for truth will lead them to explore many interests, but their pronounced impatience and lack of discipline will make starting things very easy, but finishing anything a life-long quest.

Capricorn, the Goat, resides in the 10th house, the realm associated with career, ambition, society, and authority of all kinds. The Capricorn native is serious and dedicated to duty and service toward society. The concept of the work ethic could have been designed with the Capricorn in mind; noses always to the grindstone, they do not always know how to loosen up and enjoy life. Work and duty keep them insulated and in control, protecting them from having to feel. This type can be plagued by a sense of unworthiness, as they continually seek approval from others. The sign is traditionally ruled by Saturn, who represents the boundaries and restrictions, and the very principle of discipline that Jupiter seeks to escape. Capricorn's children are the functionaries and protectors of the social order.

Again a different deity is hidden when the particulars of the zodiacal image are added: it is a hybrid goat and fish symbol, and named for the cornucopia, the horn of plenty. Capricorn natives might be glad to find out that this complex of mythic references points to a much more fun-loving god than Saturn, namely Pan, the woodland goat god. Pan rules over the whole pastoral lifestyle, which included herding, hunting, and fishing; hence the fusion of goat and fish. Saturn's ancient connection to agriculture adds yet another dimension of complexity to the sign of Capricorn. It is the great father of the zodiac, working hard to provide nourishment and serving as the authority figure for all his children.

As we move to the 11th house, Aquarius, we move out to the faraway planet Uranus, another more recent discovery of the 18th century. Ancient astrology assigned its rulership to Saturn, suggesting an aged quality to this sign. Here the traditional aspects of the Saturnine personality are merged with the revolutionary spirit of Uranus, as the forces of tradition and innovation combine. An air sign, Aquarius, the Water Bearer, represents the development of the higher mind and the refined products of civilization, in this case, science and technology. The Aquarian spirit is inventive, innovative, futuristic, and infused with the grand optimism and promise of science. The 11th house is considered to rule over the vast masses of society, one's country, neighborhood, and circle of friends. The great humanitarians of history are so often Aquarians, caring for the generalized masses, but sometimes unable to fulfill needs in ordinary life and truly offer love to an individual person.

The 12th house is Pisces, the Fish, two entwined swimmers, one pointing up toward higher consciousness, the other downward into the vast, unfathomable unconscious. The Piscean is plunged into the sea, at home in the deep unconscious. In fact, many of Neptune's children prefer that dreamy environment to the harsh light of day in the physical world. Natives will be subject to the mood swings, glassy complacency, and sudden, irrational tempests of the sea. The 12th house stands for the collective realm, the vast universe. As such, the Piscean native will be characterized by a pronounced need to experience the transcendental. Neptune's soft tones and soothing rhythms lead the native to prefer to live in a fantasy realm, and to never remove their rose-colored glasses. As such their downfall is their tendency toward dependencies of all types, such as drug and alcohol addiction.

Aspects, Transits, and More

Many patterns and correlations between planets and signs emerge as their interactive dance is charted. The signs sharing an element, earth, air, fire, or water, measure as "trine" in relation to each other, the most harmonious of all relationships. Planets and signs that fall at 90-degree angles to each other are "squares" and are considered the toughest relationships. "Oppositions" are 180-degree angles, which are difficult but uncanny in carrying a combination of opposites. These angle measurements, or "aspects," can be applied to relationships between people and also within a person's own character. If the sign on the ascendant is a square to the position of one's sun, the result is a person somehow in inner conflict. A chart featuring many trines will mark a fortunate person who faces little opposition in life. Prominent positioning of the planets will lead some to be ruled by the darker or more violent planets, called "malefics," including Mars, Saturn, and Uranus, whereas others can count themselves lucky to be ruled by the milder sensibilities of the "benefics," especially Venus and Jupiter.

The details of the work involve charting "transits," as the current movements of the planets always affect or "touch off" aspects related to the placement of the planets and signs in one's natal chart. Progressions must also be taken into consideration, as the complex puzzle construction never ends. Compelling questions engage astrologers, such as the issue of "generational astrology," as the very slow-moving outer planets visit one constellation for decades, binding entire generations together in values and personality aspects. With work enough to challenge many schooled intellects for centuries to come, it is only to be regretted that such a fascinating and useful field as astrology should have to suffer from a social stigma that views it as illegitimate. Consideration of the symbolic significance alone of the myriad elements involved, makes it a subject most worthy of serious attention by reflective, educated students.

—Sharon L. Coggan

See also Neo-paganism

FURTHER READING

Berger, P. (1967). *The sacred canopy: Elements of a sociological theory of religion.* New York: Doubleday & Co.

Campbell, J. (1974). *The mythic image.* Princeton, NJ: Princeton University Press.

Jung, C. G. (1962). *Man and his symbols.* New York: Dell Publications.

Rudhyar, D. (1936). *The astrology of personality.* New York: Doubleday.

Seznec, J. (1953). *The survival of the pagan gods: The mythological tradition and its place in Renaissance humanism and art.* New York: Pantheon Books.

Tyl, N. (1998). *Synthesis and counseling in astrology: The professional manual.* St. Paul, MN: Llewellyn Press.

ATTACHMENT FORMATION

Understanding the impact of the parent–child relationship awakens our deepest concern, for we intuitively perceive that initial bonds with others affect who we are for our entire life. Our physical, emotional, and spiritual connections constitute what is called *attachment.* Attachments are enduring emotional bonds whose existence provides the cornerstone for the development of trust and intimacy in human relationships throughout life.

These early bonds can also affect our ability and capacity to trust God and have faith. The dynamics in our earliest bonding experiences provide the template upon which we build intimate connections with all others—God included. Our former relationships establish the foundation for our current relationships.

The relationship between attachment theory and faith is not definitive; however, one's ability to develop trust in God is driven by one's early attachment experiences. The healthy dependency that we feel toward our parents can develop into a more general healthy feeling of dependency on God. Just as children perceive their parents as good caretakers who they want to know and love, as adults God is experienced in a personal way as this symbol of the good. That transfer of trust is the result of healthy attachment in early childhood. To understand that process, it is important to first understand attachment in a child's first years.

Attachments first occur between the child and his or her primary caregiver, whether parent or caretaker, that is, whomever the child is exposed to most often. Research in child development demonstrates that without successful bonding during the first 2 years of childhood, the child's personality can be harmed. Children deprived of nurturance, who have not formed personal, human bonds during the first 2 years of life, show permanent difficulty establishing meaningful relationships in later childhood and throughout their adult lives. In other words, the quality of care provided in the first 2 years has a significant effect on the child's relationships for the duration of his or her life. Of course, this fact does not diminish the importance of continued care throughout childhood and adolescence for the full development of a person.

The substantial literature called "attachment theory" explains how the relationship between a dependent individual—the *attached person*—evolves between one or more nurturing providers, or the attached figures. Based on the newborn's bonding experience, three attachment styles have been characterized that extend into childhood and well beyond: secure attachment, avoidant attachment, and ambivalent attachment.

In general, the securely attached child's caretaker is warm and sensitively attached, producing a secure adult who usually has securely attached children; the avoidantly attached child's caretaker is emotionally unavailable or rejecting, developing into a dismissive adult, and usually has avoidantly attached children; the ambivalently attached child's caretaker is unpredictable or chaotic, growing into a preoccupied adult, and usually has ambivalently attached children.

The lack of nurturing experiences early in life gives rise to both damaged emotional developments and the reenactment of dysfunctional homes. Poor attachments lead to a spectrum of behaviors described as "attachment disorders"—from shyness to antisocial behaviors, which often create a "snowball effect" as poor child care often leads to the child becoming a neglectful parent for his or her own children. Emotionally paralyzed children often become parents of emotionally paralyzed children, as they seek to care for their children in the same way that they were not cared for.

Studies show that children who have spent most of infancy in an environment lacking human partners or sufficient conditions for sustained human attachment later demonstrated measurable impairment in three areas: attachment to parental figures, intellectual functioning, and impulse control—particularly control of aggression. Therefore, there is a connection between attachment and both how personalities form and how early struggles with caretakers resurface in later relationships.

To nurture healthy attachment, children must feel that the world is a positive place and that they have value and importance in that world. Parents must successfully form a deep connection with the child and convey their presence. They must demonstrate through their actions (1) their attention to the child's significance and value, (2) their recognition of the child's needs and wants, and (3) their love and its unconditional quality.

The quality of the parent–child relationship launches a series of developmental experiences that become visible at the various stages of development in childhood and adolescence. Boys and girls may have different developmental experiences, and as a result acquire skills differently through their particular interactions. As children grow, their maturation becomes focused. Between ages 6 and 12, children generate a strong sense of self, develop defense mechanisms against stress, and explore their growing intellectual capacities. In the absence of a strong bond, restrictions occur in both play and attentive behavior. The inability to express the self gets transferred to social situations and often leads to social isolation, antisocial behavior, or unrealistic expectations of others.

During the changes of adolescence, ages 13 to 21, identity formation is enhanced by identification with others. The range of emotionality and confusion about self and others is expressed through the quality of interactions with others. Transitions occur dramatically and often in the multiple spheres of development; the maturation of self shows distinct growth in biological, intellectual, moral, emotional, sexual, social, and spiritual spheres. The adolescent feels engaged with many but often committed to none. Emotionally deprived teenage girls may act out their fantasies of having a baby and become pregnant. They vicariously identify with the baby's need for love and nurturance. Many often reinvolve their own mothers in caring for their babies, in an effort to receive the care from their own mother that they missed in childhood.

Studies indicate that most infants form attachments to both parents at about the same time, but that by the second year of life, boys, in fact, prefer to interact with their fathers. They begin to seek out and imitate the father's activities and behaviors as expressing identification. Findings show that mothers and fathers generally represent different types of experiences for infants, suggestive of the fact that both parents have simultaneously independent and interrelated influences on infant development.

Research about attachment formation has made clear that relationships with childhood caretakers influence religious behavior and our relationship with God. Those with secure attachments to God, defining the relationship as comfortable and providing happiness and satisfaction, experience greater life satisfaction, less anxiety, depression, and physical illness than those with anxious attachments to God that are characterized as experiencing God as inconsistent or unresponsive to needs. Those with anxious attachment to God or avoidant relationships tend to display emotion-based religiosity, marked by relatively sudden religious change, compensating for insecure relationships by becoming more religious or finding a new relationship with God. Avoidant attachment sufferers find God impersonal, distant, and having little intent in the person.

In secure attachment, God provides a secure base through a relationship supporting confidence and strength to face the challenges of daily life, in addition to being a counsel, offering care at times of crisis. While we do not know the processes by which attachments influence health, inevitably the reduced perception that resources outweigh pressures appears as an advantage.

When parents acknowledge their child's importance and abilities, they in turn recognize the child's "true self," and those intrinsic gifts that cultivate dignity, identity, and direction. By introducing children to their own innate qualities of the "true self" (spontaneity, reasoning, free will, creativity, spirituality, discernment, and love) and guiding them as they deepen their critical connections (their evolving relationships with self, others, and God), a child becomes equipped with resources necessary for healthy attachment in later life.

Promoting early attachment helps transition children positively into mature adults who are capable of engaging in caring and supportive relationships. Strong attachment also provides solid foundations upon which children can build healthy spiritual relationships with God. Nurturing spirituality through prayer and participating in a spiritual community are useful ways for establishing links as well as transitioning between parental bonds and spiritual bonds, these links of attachment are important for healthy relationships with self, others, and God.

—John T. Chirban

FURTHER READING

Bowlby, J. (1969). *Attachment and loss: Vol. I, Attachment.* New York: Basic.

Cassidy, J., Shaver, P. R. (Eds.). (1999). *Handbook of attachment: Theory, research, and clinical applications.* New York: Guilford.

Chirban, J. T. (2004). *True coming of age: A dynamic process that leads to emotional well-being, spiritual growth, and meaningful relationships.* New York: McGraw-Hill.

Rowatt, W. C., & Kirkpatrick, L. A. (2002). Two dimensions of attachment to God and their relation to affect, religiosity, and personality constructs. *Journal for the Scientific Study of Religion, 41*(4): 637–665.

Winnicott, D.W. (1965). *The maturational processes and the facilitating environment: Studies in the field of emotional development.* London: Hogarth.

ATTITUDINAL DIMENSION OF RELIGION

The scientific study of religious development during childhood and adolescence has helped to sharpen the understanding of religion as a multidimensional concept. The attitudinal dimension of religion has emerged from such research as a particularly powerful and important key to understanding the influence of religion and spirituality on the development and formation of young people.

Since the late 1920s, attitudes have been of central concern to several streams within social psychology. Although there is no unanimity among social scientists regarding the way in which attitude should be defined, the main consensus is to regard attitudes as concerned with affect rather than with cognition or behavior. Attitudes are concerned with how people feel about things, rather than with what they believe about things or with what they actually do in relation to things.

Furthermore, attitudes are understood to be fundamental, deep-seated, and covert predispositions. Attitudes are hidden below the surface. In that sense they cannot be seen with the naked eye but have to be inferred from the stable patterns of behaviors and opinions that they help to shape.

Attitudes are often shaped and formed below the level of the young person's consciousness. Attitudes are shaped by experience, beliefs, and actions. As covert predispositions, once shaped, attitudes may be quite difficult to reformulate. Unless consciously and critically examined, attitudes shaped during childhood and adolescence may persist for much of adult life. It is wise, therefore, for those concerned with the religious and spiritual development of children and adolescents to take attitude development seriously.

In understanding the attitudinal dimension of religion, it is helpful to distinguish this dimension from three other dimensions generally referred to in discussion of religious development during childhood and adolescence: affiliation, belief, and practice. The dimension of religious affiliation refers to the religious group with which the young person identifies either at the level of faith group (say, Hindu or Sikh) or at the level of denomination within a faith group (say, Baptist or Catholic). The dimension of religious belief refers to what the young person believes, either in terms of content (say, life after death), or in terms of style (say, conservative or liberal). The dimension of religious practice refers to what the young person does, either publicly (say, attend church or synagogue) or privately (say, perform prayers or read the scriptures).

In comparison with these other three dimensions (affiliation, belief, practice), the attitudinal dimension is able to get to the heart of the young person's religion and spirituality. Affiliation is to some extent socially shaped by family of origin and may say little about the young person's personal choice. Beliefs are shaped by different traditions and live in the mind rather than in the heart. Religious groups may be divided by beliefs, but united by attitudes. Practices (especially public practices) are shaped by many external pressures: One young person may attend church in response to parental pressure, while another may stay away from church in response to peer group pressure. Attitudes (an affective response for or against religion) are personal and special to the individual young person).

The measurement and assessment of attitudes was significantly shaped by two pioneering psychologists around 1930, L. L. Thurstone and R. A. Likert. Subsequently, others have refined the science, and psychologists of religion have benefited from this general development in social psychology.

In the 1970s, Leslie J. Francis initiated a research program concerned with the assessment of attitude toward Christianity during childhood and adolescence, employing the Francis Scale of Attitude Toward Christianity. This research began in the United Kingdom, and has since been extended by others in Australia, Canada, France, Germany, Hong Kong, Netherlands, Norway, South Africa, United States, and elsewhere. More recently, similar instruments have been developed to assess attitudes within other faith traditions, including the Katz-Francis Scale of Attitude Toward Judaism, the Sahin-Francis Scale of Attitude Toward Islam, and the Santosh-Francis Scale of Attitude Toward Hinduism. These instruments enable studies originally conceived in a Christian context to be replicated and extended in other faith contexts. Cumulatively, these studies have illustrated the centrality of the attitudinal dimensions of religion in shaping a wide range of aspects of the personal and social development of children and adolescents.

This research has examined the factors that can promote or inhibit the development of positive attitudes toward religion during childhood and adolescence, including parental religious practice, socioeconomic status, contact with church, type of school attended, friendship networks, patterns of television viewing, pop culture, and basic factors like gender, age, and personality. This program of research has also examined the factors that can be influenced and shaped by positive and negative attitudes toward religion, including issues like abortion, altruism, beliefs about the world, conservatism, evolutionary theory, gender orientation, intelligence, mental health, moral values, pro-social values, purpose in life, scientism, self-actualization, self-esteem, and suicidal ideation.

The empirical evidence from this research demonstrates that a positive attitude toward religion plays an important role in youth/human development. In turn a range of personal and contextual factors play an important role in shaping an individual's attitude toward religion.

The attitudinal dimension of religion has therefore proved to be an important key to understanding the influence of religion and spirituality on the development and formation of young people. Those who care for and hope to better understand the religious development of young people and/or the healthy development of young people need to take seriously the attitudinal dimension of religion.

—Leslie J. Francis

FURTHER READING

Kay, W. K., & Francis, L. J. (1996). *Drift from the churches: Attitude toward Christianity during childhood and adolescence*. Cardiff: University of Wales Press.

AUTISM

Autism is a developmental disability that is usually diagnosed in early childhood. There is a spectrum of autistic disorders ranging from classical autism to the higher-functioning pervasive developmental disorder. These disorders are characterized by (1) impairments in the ability and desire to form basic social relationships, (2) abnormal communication and language skills, and (3) limited or nonexistent imagination, and rigid patterns of behavior with a desire for sameness. Although the exact cause of autism remains a puzzle to researchers, many scholars claim that there is a genetic component to the disorder.

Similar to the complex phenomenon of autism, the concept of spirituality also remains a challenge to define. The experience of spirituality remains dependent on individual experience. That is, spirituality can mean different things to different people. Spirituality can involve belief of a higher power, or a way of life defined by a particular religion. It can also involve a feeling of being one with the environment and others, or a guiding sense of meaning or value in life. For some, it may include a desire to understand and express their purpose in life, and understand their place in a greater spectrum. It can include the experience of love, joy, pain, sorrow, peace, contentment, and wonder about life's experiences, and to care about and respect all living things.

Overall, both autism and spirituality are multifaceted concepts that remain relatively unexplored within the disciplines of social sciences and education. Even less understood is the concept of spirituality as it relates to autistic children and their caregivers. This lack of definition leads to further questions regarding how researchers and educators can address these issues in children. It is important to explore the connections between the two concepts as a better understanding of the spiritual experience for autistic children may provide insight into the inner worlds of these children and assist them in developing a sense of spirituality.

The study of spirituality and autism is particularly difficult due to the nature of the disorder. Autism is a disability that involves impairment in psychological connection and affective engagement with others, the skills necessary for spiritual awareness with others. Since most spiritual experiences involve relating, how can autistic children participate in spiritual activities? Furthermore, autistic children have language impairments, making it difficult for them to communicate. These communicative deficits present a problem for those children attempting to participate in spiritual activities where many of the teachings are explained through written texts, such as the Bible.

Another challenge in experiencing spirituality for autistic children is their difficulty with understanding and representing abstract concepts. Much religion is based on theological principles. Since they are unable to think in abstract terms, religion may seem imposed by an institution detached from their own reality. This experience can be frustrating, as one autistic individual described religious experience as being like "an outsider looking in." If a concept of spirituality is to exist for autistic children, it must respect the culture of those who cannot understand the concepts of universality and abstraction easily.

Although there are many challenges for autistic children's experience of spirituality, several forms of therapy aimed at increasing the autistic child's emotional responsiveness are used today, and may in turn foster their ability to experience spirituality. For example, music therapy has been shown to greatly improve autistic children's communication, and may help to promote a sense of spirituality. Music is a form of expression to most people to varying degrees. It is comparable to verbal language in its variety, subtlety, and power to affect communication in the emotional realm. It is particularly useful with nonverbal individuals as it does not require the use of language. By aiding in their communicative abilities, it may assist autistic children to express themselves and their spirituality.

Therapy with animals such as dogs or dolphins has also been used to assist autistic children. Animal therapy has been useful in encouraging pro-social behaviors, by decreasing self-absorption, and making autistic children more aware of their social environment. By improving children's social, communication, and emotional skills, autistic children may be better equipped to experience and express spirituality.

A sense of spirituality can be very enriching to the life of an autistic child. Based on the developmental challenges the autistic child faces, it is important that it be considered in terms of the context of the individual's emotional, cognitive, and spiritual environments. Spirituality must also be rooted in their personal, cultural, and religious experiences. If this can be accomplished, then spirituality can play a positive role in the lives of autistic children.

—*Amanda Varnish and Sandra Bosacki*

FURTHER READING

Isanon, A. (2001). *Spirituality and the autism spectrum: Of falling sparrows.* Philadelphia: Jessica Kingsley Publishers.

Morris, L. (2001). Autism and spirituality. In J. Erricker, C. Ota, and C. Erricker (Eds.), *Spiritual education: cultural, religious, and social differences: New perspectives for the 21st century* (pp. 234–247). Portland: Sussex Academic Press.

Redefer, L. A., & Goodman, J. F. (1989). Pet facilitated therapy with autistic children. *Journal of Autism and Developmental Disabilities, 19*(3): 461–467.

Turry, A., & Marcus, D. (2003). Using the Nordoff-Robbins approach to music therapy with adults diagnosed with autism. In Daniel J. Wiener, & Linda K. Oxford (Eds.), *Action therapy with families and groups: Using creative arts improvisation in clinical practice* (pp. 197–228). Washington, DC: American Psychological Association.

AWE AND WONDER

There is wide agreement that awe and wonder occupy a central place within spirituality, particularly the spirituality of young children. The two terms capture something important about their curiosity and fascination with things, their extraordinary capacity to enter into fantasy and exercise their imagination, their intense awareness of immediate experiences and emotions, and their innocent raising of profound questions about the meaning of life. Yet the terms themselves are far from straightforward. It is not immediately clear what sort of responses they describe, whether these responses are natural or learned, whether they are essentially religious concepts, or what educational value, if any, they have. It is not even clear whether the two terms are synonymous.

Of the two terms, perhaps "wonder" is the more straightforward. It refers to a feeling of surprise and admiration, evoked by an experience that is in some way inexplicable or that surpasses expectation. We wonder at things that go beyond our finite selves, and the emotion thus reminds us that there is more to life than those things we can easily understand. We feel wonder not only when we are confronted with something exceptional or spectacular (like one of the "seven wonders of the world"), but also when we experience something of the mystery of life or when we suddenly achieve fresh insights into familiar things (like the color of a flower or the awareness of love). By reminding us of our own limitations, wonder may lead to humility, reverence, and an appreciation of things that are greater than ourselves. But it can also evoke curiosity and a desire to learn. Wonder may therefore be a starting point for both scientific and philosophical investigations, a point made by Aristotle in his *Metaphysics.*

Like wonder, the concept of awe includes feelings of solemn admiration and reverence, whether directed towards a superior or divine being or in response to something vast or splendid in the natural world. But in the case of awe, these feelings may also involve a sense of fear, especially the fear of something vaster than oneself that may impinge on one's life and leave one helpless. The intimate connection between fear and awe is illustrated by the fact that in many languages, including Hebrew and Greek, the same word is used for both concepts; recent English translations of the Bible (such as the Revised Standard Version) often use the term "awe" in preference to the Authorized Version's "fear" to describe the appropriate human response to God (e.g., 1 Chron. 16:25; Matt. 17:6; Heb. 12:28). Awesome fear may also be a response to the ravages of nature, to wanton destruction, or to death, loss, suffering, separation, and despair, especially where these are experienced by the innocent and the helpless.

At first glance, therefore, it may seem possible to construct a continuum of feeling in which "awe" occupies a central place, with "admiration" and "wonder" on one side and "fear" and "dread" on the other. But closer examination reveals awe as a more complex concept, inspiring wonder and fear, admiration and terror, at the same time. The experience of awe thus provides spiritual insights into the precarious nature of human life, human insignificance, and powerlessness, and the fact that our destiny does not lie entirely in our own hands. By providing a deeper understanding of the potential and limitations of the human condition, the emotion of awe contributes to our spiritual development.

For some people, such feelings may be shadows of the awe that is felt in the presence of God, the awe that inspired Carl Boberg to write

> O Lord my God, when I in awesome wonder
> Consider all the works Thy Hand hath made,
> I see the stars, I hear the mighty thunder,
> Thy pow'r throughout the universe displayed;
> Then sings my soul, my Saviour God, to Thee:
> How great Thou art, how great Thou art!
>
> *(Translation by S. K. Hine)*

This emphasis on the importance of wonder, reverence, and awe as a response to the divine is particularly seen in the work of the theologian Rudolf Otto (1869–1937). He claims that all humans can experience a nonrational aspect of religion (the "holy") as a result of their innate capacity to respond to the "numinous" (or divine mystery).

If the emotions of awe and wonder contribute to our understanding of the place of humans in the broader scheme of things, they clearly have educational value. It is easy to encourage young children to be aware of jewels in a raindrop or the vastness of the night sky, to use fantasy techniques to become a bird soaring in the sky, or to see a flower as if for the first time. The telescope and the microscope both open up a range of experiences to which young children will naturally respond with awe and wonder. As they grow older, awe may also be inspired by an awareness of evil and suffering and the capriciousness of fate, and the study of tragedy (which according to Aristotle evokes awe and pity) is one example of a way of using this awareness to promote spiritual, emotional, and moral growth. Perhaps our current overuse of words like "wonderful" and "awesome" indicates a hunger for a certain kind of human emotion, a craving to probe deeper into the beauty, pain, and mystery of the human condition.

—*J. Mark Halstead*

B

BAPTISM

Baptism is a Christian ritual that involves washing water over the head or entire body of someone who is publicly entering the church. Whether the baptism is done by dunking someone entirely under the water (a practice common among Baptists) or sprinkling water on someone's forehead (a practice common in the Roman Catholic Church), water is important because of its presence in the baptism of Jesus and because of its symbolic qualities.

The ritual is rooted in the practices of John the Baptist who used baptism as a way to help people seek forgiveness from their sins (Matthew 3:1–12, Luke 3:1–14) and in Jesus' own baptism at the hands of John the Baptist (Matthew 3:13–17, Mark 1:9–11, Luke 3:15–17). The church continues the practice not only in imitation of Jesus' life and ministry, but also in fulfillment of Jesus' final command in Matthew 28:18–20 to "[g]o therefore and make disciples of all nations, baptizing them in the name of the Father and of the Son and of the Holy Spirit, teaching them to observe all that I have commanded you; and lo, I am with you always, to the end of the age."

Baptisms are almost exclusively performed by ordained clergy. Although the details of a baptism vary a lot across denominations, the clergy will somehow put water upon the person's head (by sprinkling, pouring, etc.) or whole body (by dunking). The vast majority of clergy will then say, "I baptize you in the name of the Father and of the Son and of the Holy Spirit." While baptizing in the name of the Trinity is the most common and most historically practiced method, some denominations baptize "in the name of Jesus," and some pastors baptize in the name of the "Creator, Sustainer, Redeemer" or other alternative formulas. After baptizing a person or group of people, the congregation will then make a pledge to welcome the baptized into their community and help that person grow in his or her faith.

Baptism is an important part of Christian life. It is considered a sacrament in all churches that have sacraments, and is therefore a "means of grace," or process through which God's grace is given to a person. In some churches, only adults or persons considered old enough to make decisions for themselves (usually this means that they must be an adolescent) are eligible for baptism because it is a life-long commitment to live a Christ-like life and be a part of the church. In their tradition, baptism is something that should be remembered and understood before it is done. Adult baptism is most common in what are generally considered to be "conservative" or "evangelical" traditions, such as Baptists, Church of God, or Pentecostal. In other churches, infants may be baptized as well as adults. In these traditions, baptism is understood to be a life-long commitment to live a Christ-like life and to be a part of the church; however, they feel that this is a promise that a parent can make on behalf of a child. In these traditions, which tend to be considered "liberal," "mainline," or "sacramental," a person is given the chance later in life to go through a process called "confirmation" in which they confirm the vows made for them at their baptism. Churches that do not baptize infants will generally have a "commissioning service" in which the baby is presented to a congregation who then promise to raise the child in the faith.

Christians draw meaning from the properties in water as they understand baptism. Water is used to wash—similarly, baptism is understood as a cleansing of one's soul from the marks of sin. Water is life-giving—similarly, baptism is understood to be a life-giving ritual. Through baptism, people are permanently brought into the community of faith that will help them lead a more fulfilling life. Water is also dangerous, and people cannot breathe under water. Because of this, in Scripture (i.e., Rom. 6) and the church tradition, baptism is seen as a death with an immediate new life. Baptism, therefore, is an enormous commitment. Through baptism, a person loses her or his own life, and the life then belongs to God and the church.

—Rev. Michael J. Baughman

See also Christianity; Grace; Sacraments

FURTHER READING

Coppenger, M. (2001). *First person: What should a Baptist make of other baptisms?* Retrieved May 15, 2003, from www.bpnews.net/printerfriendly.asp?ID=10486.

Riggs, J. W. (2002). *Baptism in the Reformed tradition*. Louisville, KY: Westminster John Knox Press.

The United Methodist Church. (2000). *By water and the spirit: A United Methodist understanding of baptism*. Retrieved May 15, 2003, from www.gbod.org/worship/ articles/water_spirit/.

Vatican Archive. "Baptism," Roman Catholic Catechism. Retrieved May 15, 2003, from www.vatican.va/archive/ccc_css/archive/catechism/p2s2c1a1.htm.

Witaker, E. C. (1960). *Documents of the Baptismal liturgy*. London: Athenaeum.

BAPTISTS

Baptists are one of the largest Protestant groups in Christianity. Defining Baptists is a difficult task because one of the hallmarks of Baptists is their diversity. Baptists in the United States alone are divided into some 50-plus major groups with a total membership of well over 20 million people. They are divided by such concerns as ethnicity, theology, and cultural issues. Divided as they are, they share a common heritage as well as practices and beliefs. The Baptist religion represents well the diversity of contexts that are potentially involved in the origin and development of a religion.

HISTORY

Baptist beginnings are associated with John Smyth (1554–1612), a Separatist Puritan minister in England. As a Separatist, Smyth was convinced that the Church should be separate from the English Crown. As a Puritan, he believed that the Church of England needed further purification from the remaining vestiges of Catholicism. His views were contrary to the Anglican Church of that time, and rather than face persecution, he fled to Holland with his London congregation. While there, he was influenced by Mennonites, who converted him to their view of believer's baptism. Believer's baptism is the belief that infant baptism is not biblical, and therefore should be discontinued. In its place they argued for what they believed was the biblical model for baptism in which a new convert first professed his or her new faith and then was baptized. In practice, this meant that usually only adults or teens would be baptized, never infants. This was a radical notion since infant baptism had been practiced almost exclusively for at least a thousand years. Smyth is responsible for articulating two core Baptist principles—this idea of believer's baptism, and the idea of religious liberty. He also founded the first Baptist church while in Holland.

Thomas Helwys (1550–1616), another minister who fled to Holland with Smyth, helped in the founding of the first Baptist church. When Smyth decided to join this Baptist church with the Mennonites, Helwys decided that he did not want to participate and wanted to remain separate. So, in 1611, Helwys returned to England where he founded the first Baptist Church in East London. In 1612, his work *A Short Declaration of the Mystery of Iniquity* was published. In this work Helwys articulates the first claim in English for absolute religious freedom. He stated that King James had no authority over the spiritual matter of persons' souls. Because of his views, Helwys was eventually imprisoned where he died in 1616. His associate John Murton continued the work of Helwys, and by 1644 there were forty-seven Baptist churches in England preaching believer's baptism and religious liberty.

Henry Jacob began another strain of Baptist life (1563–1624) in 1616. Jacob was pastor of a Puritan church. He did not want to completely separate from the Anglican Church, but he did begin to embrace believer's baptism. His theological background, like that of many Puritans, was greatly influenced by the theology of John Calvin. Referred to as Reformed theology, these Puritans embraced such theological ideas as predestination (all human destinies, in this life and the next, are predetermined by God) and limited atonement (the atoning work of Christ is limited to only the elect, those predetermined before the beginning of time). These views were not acceptable to the earlier Baptist churches started by Smyth and Helwys, who were more influenced by Arminian theology (named after Jacob Arminius who argued against Calvinism and for the place of human free will). This disagreement over free will or predestination is the first division among Baptists. While they agreed on such things as religious liberty, and especially on believer's baptism, they disagreed about the idea of free will and how deterministic God was.

Baptists in the Smyth-Helwys tradition came to be known as General Baptists, arguing that the atoning work of Christ was a general atonement available to all people who would accept it. Baptists in the Henry Jacob tradition came to be known as Particular Baptists, arguing that Christ's atoning work was only for a particular group, those elected predetermined before the beginning of time. This tension between the General Baptists and the Particular Baptists still exists today.

Early Baptists were more concerned with the theology of baptism and the spiritual state of the one being baptized than they were with the actual practice. By 1640, Richard Blunt, who was in the Particular Baptist vein, became convinced that total immersion of the new convert was the correct biblical symbol of remembering the burial and resurrection of Jesus. By 1641, baptism by immersion was the standard practice in several Baptist churches in the London area.

A Baptist presence arrived in North America at about this time in the person of Roger Williams (1603–1683). Williams was a Cambridge-educated Puritan chaplain who came to Boston in 1631. He began preaching a message of separation of church and state in the nonseparating Massachusetts Bay Colony. By 1635, he was banished from the colony for what were termed "erroneous views," such as supporting the Native Americans' rights as owners of the land, that Anglican ministers should not be listened to, and that civil magistrates' power extended only to "the outward states of men."

Williams left Massachusetts in 1636, and sought and received a Royal Charter to found the Rhode Island colony in 1644. This colony, founded on the ideal of religious freedom, was the home of the first Baptist church in North America, founded in 1639 in Providence. He continued to debate the issue of religious liberty with John Cotton of the Massachusetts Bay Colony, most notably in his *The Bloudy Tenet of Persecution*, written in 1644. Williams welcomed all persons to Rhode Island, believing that people should be free to worship whomever and however they wanted, or to choose not to worship at all. Because of his insistence on religious liberty, the first Jewish synagogue in North America was founded in Providence, Rhode Island as well. By 1700, there were approximately 10 churches with around 300 members in the New England colonies. New Baptist churches continued to develop in both England and the North American colonies. As more churches were established, Baptists began to join together in associations of churches. General and Particular Baptists continued to feud in England, with the resulting establishment of a variety of associations and confessional statements.

The Baptist experience in North America was similar to that in the British Isles during this period. The first organization of Baptist churches in North America came in 1707 with the Philadelphia Baptist Association. This association was formed by five churches in Philadelphia, and eventually produced the Philadelphia Confession of Faith in 1742, based almost solely on the Second London Confession. This Association and Confession was very influential in Baptist life in North America for years to come. Baptists in North America also struggled with the debate between the more Arminian-minded and the more Calvinistic churches. The Great Awakening in the middle of the 18th century served to polarize the issues between these two groups. As in most other groups, such as the Anglicans and the Presbyterians, there were supporters of the Great Awakening and those opposed to its efforts. This led to splits in most of these groups, and the Baptists were no different.

The more revivalistic Baptists, those favoring the Great Awakening, came to be known as the Separate Baptists. They were more Arminian in their beliefs, and placed a strong emphasis on evangelism, while believing that humans could respond to the preaching of the Gospel. They were the equivalent of the General Baptists in England. Those opposing the Awakening and its revivals were known as Regular Baptists. They were more Calvinistic in their beliefs and argued that no human efforts could lead one to salvation. They were like the Particular Baptists in England who argued that humans were incapable of making such decisions because all humanity inherited the sin initiated by Adam and Eve. God had preordained before the beginning of time those chosen for heaven and those left behind. No amount of human efforts, evangelistic or otherwise, could change that eternal decree. Baptist Churches began organizing Associations according to these theological differences.

Two of the most influential Associations after Philadelphia were formed in the South. William Screven, who had strong connections with the Calvinistic Baptists of the Philadelphia Association, started the first Baptist church in the South. He founded a Baptist church in Charleston, South Carolina in the early 1690s. By 1751, a Charleston Association of Baptist churches was formed. This "Charleston tradition" as it came to be called, was the source of Calvinistic thought in Baptist churches in the South well into the 20th century. In 1758, the Sandy Creek Association of Baptist churches was formed in Sandy Creek, North Carolina. This Association was initiated with the preaching of two preachers, Shubal Stearns (1706–1771) and Daniel Marshall (1706–1784), both of whom had been influenced by the Great Awakenings in the New England and middle colonies. Eventually these two traditions would set aside their theological differences to organize around the purposes of missions, evangelism, education, and the formation of the Southern Baptist Convention in the mid-19th century.

Baptists continued to grow from that point on with a strong emphasis on global missions. There were always tensions over issues like the Arminian/Calvinist debates, but most Baptists decided that the call to send missionaries was greater than the debates that separated them. This foreign missionary emphasis derived from the work of Luther Rice (1783–1836) and Adoniram Judson (1788–1850), who originally went to India in 1812 as missionaries of the Congregationalists from the New England area. While in the field they came to accept the idea of believer's baptism by immersion and decided to become Baptists. Judson went on to Burma, and Rice returned to the United States to seek funding for their efforts from the Baptists. In the process, he toured the country seeking financial support for their work, and under his leadership started the "Baptist Society for the Propagation of the Gospel in India and other Foreign Parts." This became the root of what became a national organization of Baptist churches in 1814 called "The General Missionary Convention of the Baptist Denomination in the United States of America for Foreign Mission." It was also known by its shorter name, "The Triennial Convention," because it would meet for business every three years.

The work of Baptists continued to grow and thrive both in the United States, and around the world in the 19th century. From 1814 to 1844, Baptists increased 360%, while the U.S. population as a whole only increased 140%. In 1845, the Triennial Convention became the American Baptist Missionary Union.

All of this came to a halt with a great split in the mid-19th century over the issue of slavery. All denominations faced splits during this time, but most were reconciled later. Not so with the Baptists. As tensions rose between North and South, Baptist bodies, both North and South, took sides. Finally, in 1845, Baptists in the South split from those in the North, forming the Southern Baptist Convention. With this move, the Baptists' two largest bodies were formed out of the split of the main group, and Baptists were left with the Southern Baptist Convention and the Northern Baptists. Unlike the Methodists and Presbyterians who split over slavery but eventually reunited, these two Baptist bodies have never rejoined. To this day, there is still a Southern Baptist Convention, the largest body of Baptists, and the American Baptists, which was once the Northern Baptists. In addition, there are still some 50-plus other Baptist groups in the country, as well as national Baptist groups in countries all around the world.

BELIEFS AND PRACTICES

Baptists can be identified by their unique beliefs, organizational structures, and worship practices. Two major beliefs have dominated Baptist thought through the years. Believer's baptism and the separation of church and state are two key components to a Baptist identity. Primarily, Baptists have always been motivated by the concern for all of humanity to become baptized believers. Through efforts of evangelism, foreign missionaries, and educational institutions, Baptists have sought to find ways to emphasize conversion to their understanding of Christianity. This understanding is a rejection of infant baptism emphasized in most mainline denominations, and an emphasis on bringing persons to a crisis point where they accept the atoning work of Jesus on their behalf, and then publicly profess this through the initiatory act of baptism. In Baptist theology, it is not the baptism itself that works conversion, but the individual's profession that she or he now accept the atoning work of Jesus. Baptism is a symbolic and obedient act that publicly confirms the interior spiritual condition of the one being baptized.

Growing out of the Separatist tradition in England, and having faced persecution both in England and the North American colonies, Baptists have always argued for the separation of church and state. This was not important as a political principle for Baptists, but has always been a theological point for Baptists. As Roger Williams argued in colonial Massachusetts and based on the New Testament, the state does not have a role in the spiritual well-being of its citizens. The best thing that the state can do is to create the environment where all faiths are free to worship and accept new members, without aid or deterrence from the state. Baptists have often argued that people should be free to worship however they want, or not to worship at all. Any faith dependent on the state is not truly dependent on God, and therefore is not true to the essence of Christianity.

Baptists claim that the only authority outside of God is the Bible. They are a highly biblical people when it comes to religious authority. They often claim as their mantra, "no creed but the Bible." By this they seek to refute long-standing traditions and a more hierarchical authority structure such as popes and bishops. They developed confessional statements, but they were always tempered by a high regard for Scripture.

Baptists are organized around a congregational form of ecclesiology or church government. This is in reference to their recognition that all members of a congregation are equal, and no one individual requires special authority to serve in a leadership role. The term that they developed for this is "soul liberty," or what others call the "priesthood of the believer." The idea here is that each individual Christian is equal in the eyes of God and requires no priestly intermediary. Therefore, clergy are usually not dressed in any liturgical vestments, and many members of a church can be involved in the leadership of a church. Additionally, each Baptist church is an independent and autonomous entity. There is no bishop or board outside of the church body that makes decisions or provides leadership. Each church is independent and free to call their own pastors, to work with other churches or not, and generally to establish their own ministry patterns.

Baptist worship follows what is generally referred to as "low church." There is no set liturgy, and churches are free to structure their worship however they see fit. Early in their history, spontaneity was often an ideal in Baptist worship services. Ideally, anyone can preach and preside over the serving of what Baptists usually call the Lord's Supper. This is in place of Communion or the Holy Eucharist in other traditions. Since Baptists do not believe that there are any sacraments, their understandings of the practices in the church are somewhat different than other traditions. There are two ordinances, baptism and the Lord's Supper, but they are both described in more symbolic terms.

There are differences here among Baptists in both understanding and practice, but for the most part, Baptists hold to a more symbolic and less sacramental view of these worship activities. Neither of these practices is considered essential for the salvation of the individual Christian, and their place in the church is often described more as a memorial to past events, than having any present-day spiritual efficacy.

Because of their strong missionary vigor beginning in the late 18th century, Baptists today can be found around the globe. Baptists continue to be the largest Protestant group in the United States, and continue to send missionaries around the world. Yet they continue in their various sectarian ways, split still over issues like the Calvinistic-Arminian debates that have haunted them through the centuries. Baptists continue to emphasize believer's baptism, and many still call for the separation of church and state. Divided as they are, though, they still continue in the tradition from which they came, and they continue to spread to all parts of the globe.

—Gary R. Poe

See also Baptism; Baptist Youth, Religious Development in; Presbyterian

FURTHER READING

Brackney, W. H. (1988). *The Baptists.* New York: Greenwood Press.

Brackeny, W. H. (Ed.). (1983). *Baptist life and thought: 1600–1980.* Valley Forge, PA: Judson Press.

Freeman, C., McClendon, J. W, Jr., & Velloso da Silva, C. R. (Eds.). (1999). *Baptist roots: A reader in the theology of a Christian people.* Valley Forge, PA: Judson Press.

Furr, G. A. & Freeman, C. (Eds.). (1994). *Ties that bind: Life together in the Baptist vision.* Macon, GA: Smyth & Helwys.

Goodwin, E. C. (Ed.). *Baptists in the balance: The tension between freedom and responsibility.* Valley Forge, PA: Judson Press.

Leonard, B. J. (2003). *Baptist ways: A history.* Valley Forge, PA: Judson Press.

Leonard, B. J. (Ed.). (1994). *Dictionary of Baptists in America.* Downer's Grove, IL: Intervarsity Press.

McBeth, H. L. (1987). *The Baptist heritage.* Nashville, TN: Broadman.

McBeth, H. L. (1990). *A sourcebook for Baptist heritage.* Nashville, TN: Broadman.

Torbet, R. G. (1973). *A history of the Baptists.* Valley Forge, PA: Judson Press.

Tull, J. (1972). *Shapers of Baptist thought.* Valley Forge, PA: Judson Press.

White, B. (1996). *The English Baptists of the seventeenth century.* Didcot, England: Baptist Historical Society.

BAPTIST YOUTH, RELIGIOUS DEVELOPMENT IN

The Baptist family of churches arose out of the Protestant Reformation and Anabaptist movements of the 16th century. The first Baptist churches were founded in Holland (1609) and England (1611). In the United States, the First Baptist Church in America was established in Providence, Rhode Island by Roger Williams in 1638–1639. In the first decade of the 21st century, Baptist denominations have more than 37 million adherents who live throughout the world.

Although a noncreedal and individualistic people, Baptists have nevertheless upheld certain defining values, including separation of church and state (religious liberty), soul freedom (the right and obligation of the individual to express his/her own understanding of the Christian life), the autonomy or self-governance of the local church, a commitment to live according to the standards of the New Testament, regenerate church membership (only those who can testify to a personal saving experience may join the church as a member), and believer's baptism by immersion. These defining features have influenced how Baptists have sought to promote the spiritual formation and development of children under their care.

Translating these concepts to the arena of childhood spiritual formation, Baptists have developed and practiced four core principles that facilitate the spiritual development of youth. Baptist spiritual formation encourages the individual child to seek and encounter God for himself/herself, to read and learn from the Scriptures, and apply its insights on a personal level, to join with others in order to journey faithfully, and to accept God's call as expressed through Christian service.

THE INDIVIDUAL'S ENCOUNTER AND JOURNEY WITH GOD

The Baptist adherence to the principles of separation of church and state, autonomy of the local church, and soul freedom create a religious environment that encourages the individual person to take responsibility for his/her spiritual development. Coercion from governmental (secular), ecclesiastical (denominational), or even familial sources is vehemently opposed by Baptists. In terms of spiritual formation in youth, Baptists therefore seek to provide maximum freedom for children to grow in their understanding of the Christian life. Specifically, this entails a tension between being encouraged to commit one's life to Christ on one hand, and being protected from premature commitments to God or the church on the other.

The Baptist faith emphasizes the need to confront one's sinfulness and to accept forgiveness of those sins by acknowledging Jesus Christ as one's Savior and Lord. Baptists do not speak in terms of original sin (an innate sinfulness passed down through generations), but instead emphasize that each person inevitably succumbs to temptation and falls short of God's standards of holiness. Once children reach "the age of accountability" (defined as knowing the difference between right and wrong, or the beginnings of conscience), they are considered morally responsible for their behavior. This is a psychospiritual awakening or development, and thus not strictly chronological. In practice, most Baptists would say this transition takes place between the ages of 4 to 6. Prior to reaching the age of accountability, children are considered innocents, and are not held liable, in spiritual terms, for their actions.

Baptists therefore believe that infants and very young children who die are granted eternal life in heaven without the need for expressing a personal faith commitment to God (which they are too young to do), or for undergoing church rituals such as infant baptism. In place of infant baptism, Baptists practice a ceremony variously called infant/child or parental dedication. Inspired by the Biblical dedications of Samuel and Jesus, infant/child or parental dedication involves the parents presenting their infant or child to God and to the church during a worship service. The parents declare that they will raise their child in the Christian faith by personally modeling its values and by encouraging their family to be active in the life and witness of the local congregation. Although the focus is on the child's spiritual future, the onus of responsibility is placed on the adults. The congregation also commits itself to providing for the spiritual nurture of the child. Prayers are then offered for both parents and child.

As the child grows in spiritual awareness, it is hoped that he/she will decide to make a personal commitment to God through Jesus Christ. The church's ministries (Sunday School, children's sermons, and worship services) are mobilized to encourage the development of a sensitive conscience and a desire to seek God's presence in their lives. Grace, mercy, and forgiveness represent the offer of God's love and care, in response to the message that God expects humanity, both individually and corporately, to embrace justice and righteousness.

Baptists are perhaps most famous for their practice of baptism by immersion as the symbol of embracing the Christian journey and identifying with Jesus' death and resurrection. For Baptists, baptism is a public act of personal faith in which a person declares the intention to become a disciple of Jesus Christ and to live out the Christian journey by joining with other believers (by becoming a member of a specific church). In most Baptist churches, children are encouraged to take this step when they are able to articulate their commitment to Christ and understanding of the basics of Christian beliefs and practices. In practice, this usually is reserved for those who are in their early teens, but some congregations will permit younger children who display a more precocious grasp of the faith to be baptized as well.

BECOMING A STUDENT OF THE SCRIPTURES

As a Biblicist movement, Baptists have historically emphasized the authority and centrality of the Scriptures for informing how believers should live out the Gospel of Jesus Christ. In 1824, Baptists created the Baptist General Tract Society, which later was renamed the American Baptist Education Society, and helped create the American and Foreign Bible Society in 1837. Baptists are avid and dedicated students of the Scriptures, and seek from it principles for spirituality and morality.

Children as well as adults are expected to engage in ongoing Bible study in order to further their spiritual formation and development. Baptists have placed particular stress on the promotion of Sunday Schools, youth group programs, Bible clubs, and summer vacation Bible schools. The goal of this educational emphasis is not merely intellectual knowledge, but the gaining of wisdom and the deepening of spiritual commitment. Baptists read and study the Bible in the pursuit of personal application of timeless Scriptural truths so that ongoing spiritual transformation may take place. Recounting the stories of Biblical role models is a favored teaching methodology in Baptist youth classes because it encourages youth to emulate the faithfulness of the spiritual giants of the Bible. Although less prominent in the Baptist tradition, non-Biblical sources can also be used to educate youth about the spiritual life. John Bunyan's classic allegory of the Christian journey, *The Pilgrim's Progress,* is a well-known text (Bunyan was a Baptist minister who lived between 1628 and 1688).

JOINING WITH OTHERS TO JOURNEY FAITHFULLY

Baptism, as a symbol of the individual's desire to journey in the Christian way, also serves as the individual's official incorporation into the community of believers. In the Baptist tradition, the emphasis on the individual's relationship with God is counterbalanced by the recognition that one needs the companionship of others to negotiate the challenges of the spiritual life, and this is why participation in congregational life becomes an integral aspect of Baptist spirituality.

The Baptist practice of prayer serves as a case in point. On the one hand, each Baptist member is expected to develop, cultivate, and maintain a personal prayer discipline. On the other hand, conversational prayer in the presence of others—the Baptist prayer meeting—is a core feature of classic Baptist church life. In contrast to the more contemplative forms of prayer, Baptist prayer experiences tend to emphasize a spontaneous conversational style in which members take turns praying for the needs of one another. Children are introduced to this form of prayer at an early age, and are expected to practice it as soon as they begin talking.

ACCEPTING GOD'S CALL TO SERVE

The Baptist emphasis on personal spiritual development also incorporates the dimension of sacrificial service. To follow Christ as a disciple entails serving the world even as Jesus served others. In the Baptist tradition, therefore, ministry is not just the fruit of a positive spiritual life. It is a vital aspect of it.

This ministry can take many forms. It may involve evangelism, worship leadership, teaching, hospitality, and various forms of community involvement and social action. In Baptist churches, children are expected and encouraged to express the notion of the "priesthood of all believers" by testing their gifts and talents in the service of others. Inviting others to church and to a consideration of the claims of the Baptist faith, singing in the choir or playing musical instruments, helping to disciple younger children, and sharing their testimonies at their baptism are just some of the ways Baptist youth are encouraged to unite faith with deeds. Such activities are considered both ends in themselves as well as aspects of an ongoing spiritual formation in anticipation of serving the church and the world as adults.

—Rev. Dr. Lee B. Spitzer

See also Baptism; Baptists

FURTHER READING

Bunyan, J. (1998). *The pilgrim's progress.* Oxford: Oxford University Press, 1998.

Goodwin, E. C. (2002). *Down by the riverside: a brief history of the Baptist faith.* Valley Forge, PA: Judson Press.

Goodwin, E. C. (1995). *The new Hiscox guide for Baptist churches.* Valley Forge, PA: Judson Press.

Wardin, Albert W. (Ed.). (1995). *Baptists around the world: A comprehensive handbook.* Nashville: Broadman and Holman Publishers.

BARTLETT, PHOEBE

Phoebe Bartlett (1731–1805) experienced an emotional religious conversion at age 4. She became the most famous exemplar of childhood piety in late Puritan New England after the colonial minister Jonathan Edwards described her transformation in a popular treatise. Her conversion occurred amid the religious revivals in western Massachusetts led by Edwards (1703–1758), early America's most important Calvinist theologian and pastor of the First Congregational Church of Northampton. Bartlett and a young woman, Abigail Hutchinson, were Edwards's (1738) principal case studies in *A Faithful Narrative of the Surprising Work of God,* which provided a model script for later evangelical Protestant revivalists.

Four-year-old Phoebe's story began in the spring of 1735, when she took a keen interest in the religious talk of her 11-year-old brother, who had recently experienced the life-changing conversion that New England Puritans demanded as evidence of a person's election to salvation. Soon Phoebe was retreating five or six times a day to her closet for secret prayer. During one of these sessions, her mother overheard her begging the Lord for forgiveness of her sins. Emerging from the closet in uncontrollable weeping, Phoebe resisted her mother's efforts to comfort her until suddenly she stopped crying and exclaimed, "Mother, the kingdom of heaven is come to me!" (Goen, 1972: 200). In the months that followed, she continued to grow in holiness, strictly observing the Sabbath and counseling other children in spiritual matters. She also showed great love toward her pastor, as Edwards himself reported. His account does not describe her adult life, although parish records indicate that she was not admitted to full communion until shortly before her marriage in 1754, a common practice among adults in Puritan New England.

Edwards's narrative of Phoebe Bartlet's conversion reflects the ambivalence toward children's religious experience in late Puritan culture. On the one hand, Edwards and other orthodox clergy believed that children and adults inherited Adam's sin, and thus deserved eternal punishment. In sermons preached to special meetings of children, Edwards emphasized God's anger at their sins and warned them of the danger of dying in childhood before being born again in Christ. On the other hand, Edwards saw children as capable of genuine saving faith and took their spirituality seriously. During the 1734–1735 revivals he admitted 20 children under the age of 14 to full communion, a practice shunned by earlier ministers.

Edwards's views of children have had a similarly mixed influence on later Protestant culture. On the one hand, his writings provided subsequent evangelicals with a weapon against the Enlightenment's rejection of original sin and other Augustinian doctrines. On the other hand, his idealization of childhood (and female) piety ironically paved the way for Victorian

Protestantism's sentimental views of human nature and domestic piety.

—*Peter J. Thuesen*

See also Narrative; Christianity

FURTHER READING

Brekus, C. A. (2001). Children of wrath, children of grace: Jonathan Edwards and the Puritan culture of child rearing. In M. J. Bunge (Ed.), *The child in Christian thought* (pp. 300–328). Grand Rapids, MI: Eerdmans.

Goen, C. C. (Ed.). (1972). *The works of Jonathan Edwards: Vol. 4. The Great Awakening.* New Haven, CT: Yale University Press.

Lambert, F. (1999). *Inventing the "Great Awakening."* Princeton, NJ: Princeton University Press.

BELIEF AND AFFILIATION, CONTEXTUAL IMPACTS ON

In any human life, many factors help to determine the multiple contexts that influence one's religious affiliation and beliefs. Certainly, one's religious affiliation will impact one's religious beliefs, as will one's beliefs influence decisions made throughout life about religious affiliation. To better understand the impact of context on religious affiliation and beliefs in childhood and adolescence, it is important to also consider how contexts interact with individual developmental characteristics. A person's age, gender, ethnicity, nationality, and family background all help to form all interact with a young person's context to define issues of religious development and identity.

It is also important to consider that adolescence can be a time of religious doubt, a time when young people pull away (often for just a short while) from affiliating themselves with the religious beliefs and tradition of their family, or indeed any religious tradition and/or beliefs at all. The experiences and interactions that one has with the contexts which influence religious affiliation and beliefs will have a significant impact on if and how doubt affects a young person's religiosity. A few of these contexts which can influence religious affiliation and belief are considered below.

Young people typically identify/affiliate with the context of those closest to them (e.g., the religion of their parents) and share their religious beliefs. Participating in the religious traditions and beliefs of one's parents involves young people growing up in religious communities and peer groups—all of which influence a young person's connection to that tradition. Some young people are brought up in families where religious beliefs are strong and where participation in religious worship and practice is part of family life. In other families, religious beliefs may be weak and attendance at a place of worship will be rare or nonexistent. Some young people may be part of families and religious traditions that present a positive image of God and others may be exposed to a more authoritarian and punishing image of God. These environmental or contextual experiences are just a few examples of the many that might impact a young person's religious affiliation and beliefs.

Contexts that impact religious affiliation are broader than one's immediate familial environment. Some young people are brought up in an environment where everyone around them belongs to a single religious community. Others are brought up in a society where there are a range of religious communities and beliefs: as a result they will likely meet people from different religious communities who hold different beliefs and attitudes to their own. Some young people grow up in a society or culture where religious belief is strong. In other societies and cultures belief in religion may be weak. Some young people are educated in schools where one single religion is taught. Some are educated in schools where a variety of religions are taught. Others attend schools where religion is not taught at all.

An example of the differences in religious belief and affiliation that can be found within a country is identified and explained in research that finds that young people living in Great Britain who are from families that originally came from the Indian subcontinent are likely to have a stronger religious affiliation than a Caucasian young person in Great Britain. Hence, it is not surprising that most young Muslim Asians in Great Britain seek out and become involved in religious practice and traditions (e.g., attending a religious school—a mosque school—where they learn Arabic, the Qur'an, and about Muslim religious traditions) more so than their white peers.

When looking at differences in religious belief and affiliation across countries, it is helpful to compare the experiences of young people in Great Britain with their same-aged peers in the United States and, as well, with their peers in Jordan, a predominantly Muslim country in the Middle East. A survey carried out in Great Britain in 2000 examined the strength of young people's religious beliefs. Twenty-nine percent of young people in state schools said that they believed that God existed. Forty-four percent said that they did not know whether God existed, while 28% said that they did not believe in God at all. Only 8% of those young people believed that it was good to follow a religion seriously, while 77% said that it might be good to follow some elements of a religion.

In the United States, religious belief among the population is stronger than in Great Britain, and this is reflected in a stronger religious belief and church attendance among young people. In 1999, 43% of American teenagers said that they thought that "having a deep religious faith" was very important to them; only 23% said that they thought it unimportant. In 1996, a survey showed that around 53% of American young people attended church at least once a month, while 38% attended at least weekly. There has been, over the past thirty years, a decline in the numbers of young people attending church in the United States, but the decline has not been as rapid as that seen in Great Britain. These differences in religiosity in young people in the two nations might be partly explained by the fact that churches in the United States are often more of a focus for the local community. They run activities for young people and have staff members whose role it is to work with them. As a result, in 1996 a survey showed that 56% of young people had been involved in a church-based youth group.

Jordan, a country in the Middle East, presents us with a different picture. Here most families are practicing Muslims. In a survey carried out in 2000, 94% of young people at two schools in Jordan said that they believed in God. Only 2% said that God did not exist. More than 70% of the Jordanian students said that it was good to follow a religion seriously and the vast majority—over three quarters—said that they tried to follow some of the religious rules and practices of the Muslim religion.

There is a potentially endless list of contexts that influence an individual's religious affiliation and beliefs across one's life time. To better understand and support the healthy development of religious affiliation and belief in childhood and adolescence, it is critical that a contextual view of religious development is taken.

—David G. Kibble

See also Parental Influence on Adolescent Religiousness; Peer and Friend Influences on Adolescent Faith Development; Transformation, Religious

FURTHER READING

Brierley, P. (2000). *The tide is running out, London.* London: Christian Research.

Kibble, D. G., Hamdi, N., and Shuker, A. Abu al. (2001). Young People in Britain and Jordan: a Comparison of East and West. *Theology, 104,* 335–344.

Smith, C., Denton, M. L., Faris, R., and Regenerus, M. (2002). Mapping American adolescent religious participation. *Journal for the Scientific Study of Religion, 41*(4), 597–612.

BENSON, PETER L.

Some scholars spend a whole career focusing on specific dimensions of religion or spirituality. Others seek to understand other dimensions of human development and rarely acknowledge the spiritual or religious dimension. Social psychologist Peter L. Benson has both contributed significantly to the broad field of applied human development, and to understanding religious and spiritual development. Thus, his work is an important resource for integrating an understanding of spiritual development as a core dimension of human development.

Benson was born on May 2, 1946, in Duluth, Minnesota, and spent portions of his childhood and adolescence in several towns and cities in Kansas and Illinois. He then attended Augustana College, Rock Island, Illinois, where he earned a double major in psychology and religion. He then attended Yale University, where he earned an M.A. in psychology of religion (1970), followed by studies at the University of Denver, where he earned another M.A. (1972) and a Ph.D. (1973) in experimental social psychology.

After several years in academia, Benson moved to Minneapolis-based Search Institute in 1978, and became its president in 1985. In addition to a range of research studies in prevention and youth development, Benson led significant studies on the role of religion in society and in adolescent development. This growing body of work led to his receipt in 1989 of the William James Award from the American Psychology Association for career contributions to the psychology of religion.

In 2003, Benson launched a new initiative on spiritual development in childhood and adolescence with support of the John Templeton Foundation. Designed to be international, multidisciplinary, and multifaith in scope, the initiative will seek to contribute to an increased recognition of spiritual development as an integral component of human development, while also providing insights and tools that equip practitioners to nurture the spirit in young people.

As this work continues, it will inevitably reflect the themes that have shaped Benson's work to date: respect for multiple ways of learning and knowing, the relationship between person and society and culture, a commitment to both the inner journey and social change, a desire to promote the common good, and integration of science and practice. Its scope and breadth, although daunting to some, offers a unique opportunity for Benson's expansive vision and integrative scholarship to add important new insights and understanding for both science and practice.

—Eugene C. Roehlkepartain

FURTHER READING

Benson, P. L., Donahue, M. J., & Erickson, J. A. (1993). The faith maturity scale: Conceptualization, measurement, and empirical validation. In M. L. Lynn & D. O. Moberg (Eds.), *Research in the social scientific study of religion* (Vol. 5, pp. 1–26). Greenwich, CT: JAI Press.

Benson, P. L., Masters, K. S., & Larson, D. B. (1997). Religious influences on child and adolescent development. In N. E. Alessi (Ed.), *Handbook of child and adolescent psychiatry: Vol. 4. Varieties of development* (pp. 206–219). New York: Wiley.

Benson, P. L., Roehlkepartain, E. C., & Rude, S. P. (2003). Spiritual development in childhood and adolescence: Toward a field of inquiry. *Applied Developmental Science, 7*(3), 204–212.

Benson, P. L., Scales, P. C., Sesma, A. Jr., & Roehlkepartain, E. C. (2005). Adolescent spirituality. In K. A. Moore and L. Lippman (Eds.), *What do children need to flourish? Conceptualizing and measuring indicators of positive development.* New York: Kluwer Academic/Plenum Publishers.

Benson, P. L., & Williams, D. L. (1982). *Religion on Capitol Hill: Myths & realities.* San Francisco: Harper & Row.

BHAGAVAD GITA

The Bhagavad Gita is the most revered and best-known sacred work in the Hindu world. It contains the essential doctrines of mainstream Hinduism. It is in the format of a dialogue in which the divine Krishna expounds spiritual truths to the hero Arjuna in the context of an impending war. The work appears in the Hindu epic known as *Mahabharata.*

Its eighteen chapters are divided into three sections. The first deals with the practice of yoga, stresses the importance of asceticism for the spiritual aspirant, and affirms divine omnipresence. Soul and transmigration are also explained. The second expounds Vedanta which is central to Hindu philosophy. Here Krishna reveals his cosmic aspect (Vishvarupa) of dazzling radiance. Arjuna was dazzled by a direct encounter with the Divine which can be blinding. In the last section, the *purusha-prakriti* duality is explained. Human consciousness (*purusha*) is more basic than the phenomenal world (*prakriti*). Without it, the clockwork of a mechanical world would be as irrelevant as libraries buried in the sea. The physical universe takes on significance only in the context of an experiencing observer (*purusha*).

Like other great works of perennial significance, the value of the Gita lies in the insights that may be adapted from age to age to draw contextual nourishment. Scholars and commentators have written voluminously on the interpretations of the Gita, which have also touched people beyond the Hindu tradition.

The Gita speaks of an unchanging principle spanning the ever-changing world of fleeting impressions. As spectators of a show we may laugh at the comedy and shed tears at the tragedy. But we must never forget that what we are witnessing is only a show, and that there is a real world outside. Likewise, even in the triumphs and tribulations of life, we must bear in mind that beneath all transient experiences, there is something more permanent, more durable, more intrinsically real.

Another teaching of the Gita relates to our attitudes to work: While engaged in a task, we should not be preoccupied with the fruits of our actions. We must undertake only *desireless action* (*nish-kama karma*): In any undertaking, our commitment should be total and selfless. The aim should be completion of the task and not reaping the fruits that might accrue. Exertion in a spirit of total detachment enhances efficiency.

Desireless action becomes relevant in public involvements. Temptations of personal gains can only spell disaster. The Gita suggests that in our commitments to community, in our campaigns for a just cause, in political actions and social services, we must dedicate ourselves without any thought of self-interest.

The Gita stresses the importance of different paths (*margas*) that people follow: intellectual, activist, and spiritual-aesthetic. It is more dangerous to try to do another's mode (*paradharma*) perfectly than to try to execute, however inadequately, one's own *(svadharma*). *Svadharma* is what one can and must do with one's talents and tendencies. We must realize our potential and recognize our limitations. Our work and aspirations must be determined by these, and not by what others may achieve. Often people wreck their lives because of envy and ambition.

The Gita also gives a message of historical optimism to the effect that whenever and wherever injustice and oppression arise, an appropriate leader will emerge to reinstate justice and righteousness.

The Gita can stand alone, but it appears in the middle of a Hindu epic, suggesting that its truths become particularly relevant in the context of Indian culture.

The Gita is presented as a dialogue with the brilliant Arjuna in a state of utter confusion. This reflects the predicament of the keenest intellects in the face of social, moral, and spiritual dilemmas. Scholarship and intelligence cannot tackle questions pertaining to life and God. In moments of deep despair, at the crossroads of spiritual anguish, we should seek counsel from the enlightened.

The Gita expounds the highest philosophies on a battlefield. This reminds us that the deeper problems of existence are not to be relegated to hours of leisure and retirement. Ethical and religious considerations must be in our minds at every heartbeat of life's activities, in the center of the storm as well as in the quiet of the countryside.

Problems pertaining to war and peace are complex, as are conflicts of everyday life. Who can assert categorically what is right and what is wrong, what is punishment and what is forgiving? It is not by conventional rules and common perceptions that we can arrive at correct decisions. Events in the world, where we may play a major or a minor part, often have far deeper significance than we might imagine; their grander purpose in the scheme of things may not always be clear to our imperfect understandings.

The Bhagavad Gita is glorious music. When we hear it chanted in its traditional rhythm and immerse ourselves in its serene melody, we experience an inner peace such as only the loftiest expressions of the human spirit can afford. The piously simple and the profoundly sensitive are moved by it. Throughout India's history, many thinkers, great and modest, lay and religious, have been touched by this work. Thinkers outside of the Hindu tradition have also found meaning and message in the Gita.

The Gita combines poetry and philosophy, music and religious solace. It kindles subtle thoughts, and calls for decisive actions. It consoles the bereaved and uplifts the dejected. It thrills the soul and illumines the mind. Few other works have accomplished so much for over a millennium of human history. The Bhagavad Gita has been translated, fully or partially, into more than seventy languages, and commented upon by countless scholars.

—Varadaraja V. Raman

FURTHER READING

Edwin, A. (1885). *The song divine.* Wheaton, IL: Theosophical Publishing House.

Edgerton, F. (1944). *The Bhagavad Gita.* Cambridge, MA: Harvard University Press.

Prabhupada, A. C. B. S. (1972). *Bhagavad-Gita as it is.* Los Angeles: Bhaktivedanta Book Trust.

Radhakrishnan, S. (1948). *The Bhagavad Gita.* London: George Allen & Unwin.

Raman, V. V. (1997). *Nuggets from the Gita.* Bombay: Bharatiya Vidya Bhavan.

BIBLE

The Bible refers to a collection of 66 to 80 books, usually in a single volume, understood to represent the stories and teachings about the God of the Jewish and Christian traditions. The word "bible" comes from the Greek word meaning "book." Jews and Christians (Catholics, Orthodox, and Protestant) all use different collections, but for each, these books authoritatively define and inform their tradition and culture. The Bible is thus also known as "Scripture," "the word of God," "sacred," and "holy." Those who follow the words of the Bible literally, or with attention to exact details, are known as literalists or fundamentalists; those who follow them in principle, adopting the ethics to their own time and place, are known as liberals. Fundamentalists and liberals thus invest a different degree of authority in the Bible.

Different translations of the ancient manuscripts are referred to as "versions," the more familiar ones being the Jewish Publication Society Tanakh, the King James Version (KJV), the New Revised Standard Version (NRSV), and the New International Version (NIV). Some versions, such as the Living Bible, are paraphrases into simplified English.

Because it has profoundly affected the development of Western culture, it is important to be familiar with the Bible in order to interpret its cultural products (film, literature, politics, history, etc.).

—*Jane S. Webster*

See also Apocrypha/Deuterocanonical Books; Bible, Christian; Bible, Jewish; Catholicism; Christianity, Fundamentalist; Judaism

FURTHER READING

Achtemeier, P. J. (Series Ed.). (1996). *HarperCollins Bible dictionary.* San Francisco: HarperSanFrancisco.

Meeks, W. (Series Ed.). (1993). *The HarperCollins study bible.* San Francisco: HarperCollins.

White, J. B. & Wilson, W. T. (2001). *From Adam to Armageddon: A survey of the Bible* (4th ed.). Belmont, CA: Wadsworth Thomson Learning.

BIBLE, CHRISTIAN

The Christian Bible is revered as the most important book of the Christians. It combines the Hebrew Bible, known to Christians as the Old Testament (OT), and the New Testament (NT). Catholic and Orthodox Bibles also include the Deuterocanonical Books. Like the OT, the NT was written over time (from about 50–150 C.E.) by a number of authors. It contains 27 books (4 gospels; 1 history book, 21 letters, and an apocalypse), and continues themes introduced in the OT, such as the intervention of God in history, promises (covenants) made to Israel, and the role of the Jews in the world. Focus centers on the life and meaning of Jesus, a man understood to be the messiah (which means "anointed") and the son of God.

The four gospels recount the life, death, and resurrection of Jesus. The first three gospels are very similar and so are known as the Synoptic Gospels ("seen together"). Most scholars accept that Mark was likely written first (ca. 65–70 C.E.); Luke and Matthew (both after 70 C.E.) use the narrative framework of Mark but insert some unique material (called "M" and "L," respectively). They also both insert a large number of sayings of Jesus and a few additional narratives—collectively known as the hypothetical source Q (for *Quelle,* the German for "source")—although these materials are used differently by Matthew and Luke. Although tradition claims that the disciples, or those close to Jesus' disciples, wrote the gospels, this source theory suggests that the authors were not eyewitnesses to all of the events they report. The fourth gospel, John, is unlike the Synoptic Gospels. It includes some unique stories (e.g., Samaritan Woman, miracle of changing of the water into wine) and many long speeches by Jesus. All four gospels describe Jesus as one who led an exemplary life, taught his disciples (apostles), and performed many miracles. He died willingly "for the sake of the world," then rose from the dead after three days and was seen by many witnesses. He now reigns in heaven, but will return on the last day of the world to judge people based on their behavior.

The second volume of Luke, the Acts of the Apostles, describes the response of Jesus' followers to his death and resurrection, especially Peter, John, and Paul. The apostles, filled with the power of the Holy Spirit, do miracles and the news about Jesus spreads from Jerusalem to Rome.

The NT contains many letters. Thirteen of them are attributed to Paul. At first, Paul persecuted the new Christians. On the road to Damascus, Paul met the resurrected Jesus and became a Christian himself. He spent the rest of his life traveling throughout the northeastern Mediterranean area, teaching people about Jesus and starting churches. These letters represent some of the correspondence that was preserved between Paul and the churches and people he met. Paul's letters are divided into three groups. The undisputed letters, most probably written by Paul, include 1 Thessalonians, 1–2 Corinthians, Philippians, Philemon, Galatians, and Romans. The disputed letters include the Deutero-Pauline letters (Ephesians, Colossians, and 2 Thessalonians) and the Pastoral Epistles (1–2 Timothy, Titus). Although all claim to be written by Paul, changes in vocabulary, style, and the understanding of Jesus and appropriate Christian behavior differ significantly.

Other letters are attributed to James and Jude (brothers of Jesus) and Peter. Three letters (1–3 John) are so similar to the Gospel of John that they are attributed to the same person, although the author of the letters is identified as "the elder." Topics of the NT letters include reflections on the purpose and effect of the life and resurrection of Jesus, especially as he relates to Jewish traditions (the law, circumcision, ethical behavior, food laws, etc.). They instruct churches (or individuals) on leadership, worship practice, behavior codes, identifying false teachers, the return of Jesus, and suffering. Some personal information is also shared. Although the book of Hebrews is usually included in the list of letters, and at one time had been attributed to Paul, it does not follow the typical letter form nor is it similar in style and content to the other NT letters. Hebrews describes Jesus as superior to the prophets, angels, Moses, Joshua, and the priests; he is a superior sacrifice made once for all time.

The final book of the NT is the Book of Revelation, an apocalypse ("revelation") given to John (unlikely the author of the Gospel and Letters of John) in a mystical journey to heaven. John uses symbolic language to describe heaven and the events that occur there which, in turn, affect the events experienced on earth. He describes a battle between the forces of good (God, the lamb who was slain [i.e., Jesus], the angels) and the forces of evil (Satan, the devil, the beast); good ultimately wins. People on earth may experience persecution and cosmic upheaval, but those who are faithful will prevail.

The undisputed letters of Paul were likely written first, followed by the gospels, and the other letters from 70–120 C.E. The various NT documents were gathered together in their present form by the fourth century. The earliest existing manuscripts date to the early second century.

—Jane S. Webster

See also Apocrypha/Deuterocanonical Books; Bible; Bible, Jewish; Jesus

FURTHER READING

Harris, S. L. (2002). *The New Testament: A student's introduction* (4th ed.). New York, NY: McGraw-Hill.

White, J. B. & Wilson, W. T. (2001). *From Adam to Armageddon: A survey of the Bible* (4th ed.). Belmont, CA: Wadsworth Thomson Learning.

BIBLE, JEWISH

The Jewish Bible is revered as the most important book of the Jews. It contains thirty-nine books and is divided into three sections: the Law (also known as the Torah or the Pentateuch), the Prophets (Nebi'im) and the Writings (Ketubim). The first letters of the Hebrew titles are combined for the alternate name, the TanNaKh. Because it was written in Hebrew (some parts are in Aramaic), it is also known as the Hebrew Bible, or the Masoretic Text (MT). Christians refer to the Hebrew Bible as the Old Testament.

TORAH

The first and most important section, called the Torah ("the way" in Hebrew) or the Law, contains five books (Genesis, Exodus, Leviticus, Numbers, Deuteronomy), and thus is sometimes called the Pentateuch, meaning "five tools or vessels." These five books trace the history of Israel from creation (Adam and Eve), through the patriarchs (Abraham, Isaac, Jacob [known also as Israel, from whence comes the name of the nation of Israel], and his 12 sons), through their enslavement in Egypt and their deliverance by Moses 400 years later, and their journeys in the wilderness where they received instructions on how to live when they returned to the Promised Land (modern Israel). The narrative ends with the death of Moses.

Although authorship is traditionally ascribed to Moses (c. 1250 B.C.E.), most modern scholars accept the validity of the documentary hypothesis, which claims that the Torah was composed of four intertwined documents. The narratives combine two sources that are identified as the "Yahwist" and the "Eloist" sources because of the term used to refer to God (Yahweh and Elohim, respectively). These sources were likely compiled between 1000 and 700 B.C.E. A third source, known as the Priestly source, contributed the interspersed genealogies, and the descriptions of religious practices, festivals, and regulations. A fourth source, the Deuteronomist, provided most of the Book of Deuteronomy (long speeches by Moses), and likely had a hand in the overall editing of the collection during the Babylonian exile in the sixth century B.C.E.

PROPHETS

The Book of the Prophets is divided into two main sections: the Former Prophets and the Latter Prophets. Though they are mainly narrative in form, the Former Prophets get their name from the stories of prophets contained therein. The first book, Joshua, recounts the military conquest of the Promised Land led by Joshua. Judges describes the chaos which followed the conquest, and the sequence of "judges" (prophets or military leaders) who took leadership. Samson and Gideon are the most memorable examples. The double volumes of Samuel and Kings trace the transition from the temporary rule of the judges to the permanent but precarious rule by the monarchy. Samuel, the judge, anoints first Saul and then David as king. Solomon, known as the wise king, succeeds him. During the reign of Rehoboam, a civil uprising leads to a division of the kingdom into Israel in the North and Judah in the South. 1 and 2 Kings tell the stories of these kings until the destruction and dispersion of Israel by Assyria in the eighth century, and the exile of Judah to Babylon in the sixth century B.C.E. Prophets, such as Samuel, Nathan, Elijah, and Elisha, convey messages from God to the kings, usually challenging their behavior. The Former Prophets recount the history of Israel from the conquest to the exile. Most scholars agree that the Former Prophets were written during the exile in order to explain why the people no longer lived in the land that had been promised to them by God.

The Latter Prophets, with only a few short narratives, mainly represent the words "spoken from God to the prophet." The Major Prophets, so designated by their length, are Isaiah, Jeremiah, and Ezekiel. The Minor Prophets, also known as the Book of the Twelve, include such shorter texts as Joel, Micah, and Hosea. The books are ordered roughly by chronology. Dating is often distinguished as pre-exilic (eighth century, such as Amos and Micah), exilic (sixth century, such as Ezekiel and Jeremiah), and post-exilic (fourth to fifth centuries, such as Haggai), and are determined by their internal references to historical events, ruling powers, and major concerns. Many books have been adjusted by later editors. The prophets explain what God is doing in the life of Israel and why.

WRITINGS

The third major section of the Hebrew Bible is called the Writings. These books are drawn mainly from the post-exilic and reconstruction period (fourth to fifth centuries). Ezra and Nehemiah recount the stories of Judah's return from Babylon after the exile and the reconstruction of the temple and the holy city of Jerusalem. The people became known as "Jews" at that time. The longest book in the Bible, the Psalms, is found in this section and represents the song book (Psalter). These psalms, numbering 150 in all and written over 1,000 years, include a diverse collection of community or individual laments (appeals for help), thanksgivings, praise, wisdom (teaching), and royal psalms. The Book of Proverbs is a collection of the poetic wise sayings (wisdom literature), supposedly written by King Solomon (10th century B.C.E.), but more likely composed from the eighth to the fifth centuries and collected and edited by the intellectual elite (government officials and teachers) in the exilic and post-exilic period. They give advice on such things as proper etiquette, appropriate speech, and choosing a mate, but all advice is undergirded by "fear of the law." The Song of Solomon is a love poem. Ruth, Esther, and Daniel tell stories of faithful individuals.

CANONIZATION

The collection of the books of the Bible came together gradually, mainly during the exile, but some books were not yet in their final form by the first century C.E. The books were written and preserved by priests, royal officials, prophets, and teachers (sages). The legendary *Letter of Aristeas* (which is not included in the Bible) describes how the Bible was miraculously translated by 70 scholars into Greek, producing the Septuagint (meaning "seventy," hence the Roman numeral designation LXX). In wide use by the first century C.E., the Septuagint contained about 16 more books or additions than the Hebrew Bible; these 16 books are known collectively as the Apocrypha or Deuterocanonical Books by Christians. Because the early Christian church claimed the Greek Septuagint as their Bible, the Jews decided that only words written originally in Hebrew (or Aramaic) up to the time of Ezra were to be included in their Bible. The oldest existing manuscripts of the Hebrew Bible were found among the Dead Sea Scrolls.

—Jane S. Webster

See also Apocrypha/Deuterocanonical Books; Bible; Bible, Christian; Dead Sea Scrolls; Judaism; Moses

FURTHER READING

Bandstra, B. L. (2003). *Reading the Old Testament: An introduction to the Hebrew Bible.* Belmont, CA: Wadsworth.

Harris, S. L. (2003). *Understanding the Bible.* Boston, MA: McGraw-Hill.

BIOLOGICAL AND CULTURAL PERSPECTIVES

Spirituality is present in every known culture; it plays a significant role in the lives of a great many humans, and despite constituting a gentle part of human nature, has the paradoxical power to transform lives and even world events. The problem with extending our inquiry to children is that modern science has not advanced very far into explaining how spirituality actually originates and develops in individuals. Studies of the early lives of great spiritual figures such as St. Teresa of Avila or a Dalai Lama shed some light on how spirituality emerges and develops in the young child. However, life history accounts of spiritual leaders are relatively few in number and usually not systematic and objective enough to allow for valid generalizations. As for spirituality in other species, we know nothing (should we even ask the question?), although comparative psychologists do have information on consciousness in animals, consciousness being a precondition for spirituality to exist in a living being.

At its minimum, the term "spiritual" implies awareness of an entity that surpasses one's immediate senses. It is more than seeing a landscape or hearing beautiful music. Experiencing this entity can charge us with feelings of peace and excitement as well as motivate us to pursue such an entity further. Obviously, religion also entails some degree of spirituality, but religion usually requires attention to sacred texts, doctrines, public worship, codified rituals, and formal methods of education. A spiritual person can, if desired, go through life without support from any of these more communal offerings. The term "spiritualism" itself usually has a more restricted meaning denoting a belief in a world of spirits that can be contacted through a medium.

Traditional approaches to understanding spirituality are usually cultural in nature—that is, defined as those customs, language forms, rules of conduct, thoughts, and beliefs that constitute the way of life of a group of like-minded people. Noncultural approaches to spirituality such as the biological approach are very rare perhaps because for many biologically oriented scientists they may appear irrelevant. Body and mind are usually conceived of as having totally different properties—as scholars have debated for centuries. But there is no need to ignore examining both within the same context.

BIOLOGY

Adopting the biological approach is based on the premise that all properties of human nature have a physical or material dimension to them. Hence spirituality, as any other human property, should be viewed in terms of genes and their associated brain mechanisms and their possible evolutionary histories. However, genes and brains are only part of the story. The environments of both invariably have to be considered—all living organisms need to be nurtured by outside sources. Not only is a favorable environment essential for survival and growth but for reproduction as well. The capacities to perform all life functions—organic, behavioral, and psychological—have to be transmitted across generations via genes. But this can only be achieved if genes and their products are exposed to favorable environments. Cultural practices are also transmitted from one generation to another not by genes, of course, but by various forms of learning—providing such learning can take place in a supportive environment offered by family, community, and society in general.

The present approach, then, is based on two assumptions—first, that all humans have an evolutionary history which, while antedating each individual's own existence, nevertheless exerts some form of causal influence upon the individual. Second, that from the moment of conception until death the genes and environment interact to have an impact (minute or colossal) on virtually everything the individual does, feels, thinks, and believes. That is the way it is and will be for all living things.

Tracking the evolutionary origins and cultural development of such a complex, often elusive subjective phenomenon as spirituality has to largely rely upon intuition, common knowledge, and a thin smattering of scientific knowledge. Tracking religion, however, is different. Scientific knowledge of religion—because it is so well-expressed in terms of easily observed behavioral practices and written documents—has been accumulating for over a century.

GENES

We now know for certain that at conception each human (with the exception of identical twins) has a unique combination of genes. Part of this combination is shared with other species, and a much larger part is shared with all other humans. Recent studies of adults reveal that religiosity, as a stable individual trait, has a small but not insignificant genetic component to it. This finding is of twofold interest—it accounts in part for the universal presence of spirituality in individuals living in different cultures, as well as for the fact that individuals raised in the same culture differ in the strength of their biological propensity for spirituality.

Even when life circumstances are similar, some individuals will respond to spiritual teaching with great enthusiasm, others will ignore it, and still others will reject it with a passion.

THE BRAIN AND CONSCIOUSNESS

The human brain is a biological structure whose origins are in species-specific genes that have millions of years of evolutionary history behind them. The brain's development in each species' member, however, as already intimated, is influenced by each member's everyday interactions with the world. The fact that the brain is the physical locus of consciousness means it is also the locus of spirituality; no brain, no spirituality—at least as we commonly use the term spirituality. That the spiritual may take on another form, as expressed by the soul, for example, is viewed by most scientists as falling outside the realm of scientific inquiry.

The fact that spirituality's locus is the brain implies for some that it can be explained by brain neurochemistry rather than by nonphysical causes. But such an implication is not convincing. While it is true the brain operates according to physical laws, it does not follow that consciousness is a gas-like product of brain activity that follows similar laws and can therefore be observed and analyzed into elements. Even the best of current brain technology does not allow us to view subjective events. For example, experimental subjects seeing a particular brain locus turn orange during a brain scan while they are thinking of a tree will not see a tree on the monitor. They will see what looks like a neurological correlate of a tree. The gap between the orange locus and the actual subjective experience of a tree is unbridgeable for now, and probably will be forever.

While we may know our own thoughts with certainty, we know with less certainty the thoughts of others—unless they tell us. Being told by others is, however, not the only clue we rely on to determine whether they are having thoughts. Nonverbal behaviors and their accompanying stimulus situations also help us infer that thinking is taking place in another person—or in animals, as pet lovers like to tell us.

Nevertheless, what we do know for certain about such radically different entities as brain and mind is that they causally interact. Physical acts such as chewing and swallowing food reduce the conscious experience of hunger pangs. Being informed that a pill one takes will eliminate a physical ailment (even though the pill is an experimental placebo) can result in the disappearance of the ailment. Body affects mind, and mind affects body—the causal arrow works in both directions.

EVOLUTION

One of the most challenging questions facing scientists today is how the genes that contribute to building brain proteins, which in turn make thinking possible, came into existence. Evolutionary psychologists hypothesize that behavioral and psychological properties of organisms serving vital functions are products of eons of genetic evolution. According to evolutionary theory, genes that produce brains that in turn produce consciousness have evolved because consciousness serves critical life functions. For example, consciousness allows for awareness of resources necessary for survival as well as of the presence of predators or dangerous situations. Conceivably, then, protohumans having consciousness-producing brains and who took appropriate actions have survived long enough to pass on the genes for these brains to their offspring. In evolutionary terms, "consciousness genes" are adaptive, and adaptive traits are genetically transmittable across generations. The same could conceivably be true for a trait like spirituality.

Evolutionists also have a second evolutionary explanation for the origins of spirituality, one resting on species comparisons. Comparing humans with other species (primates in particular) reveals many similarities ranging from genes and anatomy to quite a few behaviors as well as to some basic psychological functions. Charles Darwin's report on his dog (he called it "a very sensible animal") is a classic example. On a slightly breezy day, his dog growled and barked when an open parasol beside him moved. In interpreting the dog's reaction, Darwin noted that he "reasoned to himself in a rapid and unconscious manner, that movement without any apparent causes indicated the presence of some strange living agent, and that no stranger had a right to be on his territory." Such an explanation may seem a bit stretched, but it is not implausible. Darwin was an excellent observer and very cautious about making unwarranted speculations. He also had a big theory to back him up.

As of today, we know nothing about spiritual evolution in nonhuman species. A baboon staring quietly at a sunset may be engaging in baboon spirituality. Or it may not. Most likely, we will never know. Humans staring at a sunset can tell us what they are experiencing, and we can judge from there whether their experience qualifies as spiritual or not.

CULTURE

There have been no controlled studies of what specific cultural factors have a *causal* effect on spiritual development in children. Of course, in most cultures children are taught to pray and think about God or spirits, but the causal connection between what they are taught and their spiritual development is far from understood. A cursory search of the research literature on religious beliefs reveals that there are some connections between such variables as parental values, social class, intelligence, and educational level on the one hand, and their children's religiosity and level of moral development on the other. However, all of this research is correlational in nature, which means that we cannot ascribe with any certainty causal connections between these factors and religiosity.

Additionally, there appear to be no systematic scientific studies of spirituality per se in early childhood. Anecdotal accounts of spirituality in children exist, but they are not sufficiently rigorous or systematic enough to give them status above what parents, clergy, teachers, and interested lay persons can already tell us.

EARLY DEVELOPMENT

No matter how seriously we emphasize genes, evolution, and basic human brain functioning (all factors that precede in time the creation of the individual), and no matter how we emphasize the powerful roles of culture and environment (factors outside the individual), a person's life comes about through the dynamic interaction of all these factors. This is a mouthful. But it is true. And it poses one of the biggest problems for all sciences. One can make a good argument for the case that studying the developing human is more difficult than studying the formation of the universe. Major elements of the universe are in every human, but put together in such a complex (one could say miraculous) way, it is possible we will never know completely how humans come to be what they are. Fortunately, psychologists such as Piaget and Erikson have contributed valuable ideas and observations on how religious ideas (not necessarily spirituality) develop over time. Their insights as well as those of William James and Fowler are among the first to investigate the true nature of this dynamic interaction.

We assume that this interaction begins in the first days of life. At present, we cannot say for certain, however, when a child first becomes spiritual. Most newborns appear conscious of persistent or sudden, novel stimulation such as gastrointestinal pain or a loud noise. Some months after birth, the repeated speech sounds and behavior made by others appear to have a cumulative impact upon the infant's consciousness as indicated by observable signs of awareness and expectation in the infant.

During toddlerhood, children begin talking about unseen entities (monsters, ghosts, scary people), entities that they have probably heard about from adults and siblings. It is conceivable that these experiences are the developmental forerunners of later beliefs in spiritual beings. As for possible general cognitive mechanisms responsible for such experiences, child psychologists agree that toddler and preschooler assimilate what they hear from others to their own thoughts. Young children often talk about God and ghosts, say prayers with gusto, and not infrequently ask questions about things not seen.

LATER CHILDHOOD

Developmental psychologists have discovered that the thought of school-age children rapidly becomes enriched as a result of both formal instruction and everyday experience. With age, moral and religious beliefs become more cognitively elaborated and abstract. While cognitive growth during the school years is directly affected by outside influences, children also react on the basis of personal preferences and experiences—some listen eagerly to religious talk, some not at all; and some distort whatever is said to them. As many adults, children tend both to absorb what they hear and read by way of their preferences and recently acquired idiosyncratic filters. Unlike many adults, though, they also tend to faithfully mimic the words and behavior of those around them. They can often memorize prayers and perform simple religious rituals seemingly without effort. Whether spiritual thoughts and feelings accompany such behavior is another matter.

ADOLESCENCE

For certain, spirituality in late adolescence and early adulthood is influenced greatly by education and by religious and spiritual models. For many adolescents (at least in most Western cultures), questioning religious and moral norms is frequently undertaken in earnest. Many seek more elaborate reasons about why they should believe or not believe what they have learned when they were younger. Once again reactions to these answers are contingent not only on earlier cultural experiences, but also on the child's innate as well as learned interests and prejudices.

As for factors related to spiritual development per se, psychologists generally agree that the average child's religious and moral development progresses along a series of what appear to be universal stages, starting with individual predilections and culminating in abstract principles that apply to all peoples at all times. Such stages parallel cognitive growth in general. However, until wider and deeper sampling across non-Western societies is conducted, the question of the universality of such a series still remains open.

It is during adolescence that many youth seek spiritual guidance to what they feel (and perhaps already know in a less sophisticated fashion) to be a transcendent entity. Such guidance may be supplied by teachers of religions practiced in cultures other than their own or by charismatic figures that have made an emotional impression on them. And this impression can be very strong, as we can see from the powerfully motivated, often self-sacrificial, behavior of many young religious adults politically active today on the world's scene.

CONCLUSIONS

In-depth and representative studies covering life-span development of spirituality in individuals still have to be done. Surely many clergy, spiritual masters, teachers, and parents interested in children's spiritual life possess a wealth of information that could aid us in better understanding such development. But this wealth of information has not yet been systematically documented and collated for scholarly examination.

Whatever understanding we now have, there is no question that spirituality has most likely been part of the human condition for as long as humans have existed. We can infer this from prehistorical burial remains and cave paintings. Despite the demanding physical conditions of Pleistocene life, our distant ancestors still managed to be concerned with things unseen. A good example of this is burial customs in which valuable material goods are placed in the graves of the deceased. The widespread existence of such customs is remarkable given that our primitive ancestors must have surely been aware of the fact that burial costs entail valuable resources and time, all of which have to be borne by members of their group. However, perhaps just because the world at the time was so demanding and perilous for early humans, imagining and hoping for a better life in some other place may well have made suffering and death more bearable.

Clearly, wanting to make contact with the unseen and exploring the possibility of life after death—activities that net no known material advantage—has a unique place in a world dominated by material concerns. The universal presence of spirituality attests to a rather peculiar power inherent in the human mind, one which materialists can not wholly deny and which sages, saints, and seers have long known as a given of human nature. With care, this power could be cultivated (one would hope) into something of great value for individuals as well as for communities whose members share the same religious beliefs. While we have little evidence at present to justify hope for a successful cultivation of spirituality in all humans, we know for certain that spiritual insights can create inner peace (many saints and masters), help moderate social conflict (Gandhi), and, by virtue of the asceticism associated with them (St. Francis of Assisi), help preserve the physical world. One could argue that precisely because spiritual experiences strengthen human communities and do not exhaust the world's resources, spiritually guided families will increase in number and their genes will spread throughout increasingly more of humanity. If this happens at a widespread enough level, the world could become a more habitable place for everyone.

—William R. Charlesworth

FURTHER READING

Higgins, J. J. (1973). *Thomas Merton on prayer.* New York: Doubleday.

Ridley, M. (2003). *Nature via nurture: Genes, experience, and what makes us human.* New York: Harper Collins.

Stone, R. (1956). *The mystic Bible.* Beas, India: Shri R. D. Ahluwalia, Radha Swami Satsang.

Swinburne, R. (1997). *The evolution of the soul* (Rev. ed.). Oxford: Clarendon Press.

Underhill, E. (1919). *Mysticism: A study in the nature and development of man's spiritual consciousness* (8th ed.). London: Methuen.

BODY

At the level of physical sensations, the human body is nonsectarian and morally neutral. The nostrils that feel air pass in and out are not Jain, Catholic, or Muslim. The hands that touch another person's body cannot tell whether it is Jewish, Shinto, or Baha'i. Vibrations in the throat that give rise to speech and song are not good or bad. Yet every religious culture envisions and interprets the body through a specific worldview. That perspective is not monolithic but a complex mixture of beliefs and attitudes that have varied through the centuries.

The body may be the object of fear, distrust, loathing, condemnation, hostility, and even harsh punishment. Conversely, it may be the object of gratitude, respect, blessing, mindfulness, and tender care. Different traditions may appreciate the body as a gift from God, a holy temple, or a vehicle through which to know absolute reality—they seek liberation *in* the body. Others may consider it a prison or tomb of the soul, a snare that impedes spiritual progress, or an enemy to be conquered—they seek liberation *from* the body.

Dualistic thinking has given rise to such divergent views. For example, Western philosophical and theological schools generally have explained the human body as inferior in contradistinction to the superior soul, spirit, or mind. Some describe body and soul as not only separate but also antagonistic. Others explain body and soul as both discrete *and* integral aspects of a whole human being. Dualism consequently shows up as a series of polarities between sacred and secular, spirit and flesh, asceticism and voluptuousness, male and female. There is spirituality that is vertical, ascending, "up there," puritanical, disembodied, and transcendent, versus spirituality that is horizontal, descending, "down here," sensuous, and based in the everyday world.

Eastern traditions generally see the human being as consisting not only of a material body but also of subtle energy "bodies"—a kind of meta-anatomy and physiology. Hindus, for example, distinguish various "sheaths" or "envelopes" (*koshas*)—physical and psychic layers of graduated refinement that clothe the spirit. Certain techniques involve addressing the centers and channels of these "bodies." *Yoga* (Sanskrit for "yoke") is more than a set of postures for physical benefits; it is a means for seeking spiritual emancipation and communion with the Divine. Special breath control techniques called *pranayama* (Sanskrit *prana,* "life energy") can help awaken *kundalini* (Sanskrit for "coiled") energy at the base of the spine and move it up through all seven energy centers or "wheels" (*chakras*) that sit in alignment down the middle of the body. Each one operates on a subtle sensory level related to states of consciousness.

Historically, in Christianity there has been great ambivalence toward the body in general and sexuality in particular. Negative impressions of the body led to painful practices. Ascetics engaged in wearing hair shirts, flagellating themselves, and performing other mortifications to subdue the body's passions. The early church father Origen even castrated himself. St. Francis of Assisi called the body "Brother Ass" and believed that it should be frequently whipped. St. Augustine and St. Thomas of Aquinas were exceptions, asserting that the body is not a prison but reveals the goodness of the Creator. This is a prominent teaching found in the Hebrew Bible.

It is also consistent with prehistoric Goddess-centered, Earth-based traditions as well. While many texts of patriarchal religions denigrated the female body as a decided threat to a man's spiritual effort, these earlier traditions considered both the body of a woman and the whole planet sacred. Women, such as the *devadasis* ("female servants of the deity"), were not barred from sacred rituals because of their bodies, but served in them and enjoyed religious prestige. The *devadasis* dedicated their lives to song and dance in the temples of India. They married the deity rather than any mortal man. The Hindu worldview understood both erotic and reproductive sexuality as a reflection of the divine, to be channeled in the spirit of transcendence. The contemporary women's spirituality movement has resurrected the sacred feminine and its association with the natural world.

Another contrast to ascetic spirituality is an approach to the body that calls for moderation and balance. This is what the Buddha proposed after years of carrying out severe austerities popular among wandering sages in what is now Nepal and India. He realized that starvation and other deprivations did not lead to enlightenment any more than an excess of sensual pleasures did when he was a prince. The result is a path known as "the Middle Way." Mindfulness of the body is central to the Buddha's instructions. He taught that it is possible to know everything about the world through the body and eventually attain spiritual freedom.

Whatever a tradition's perception, the body is at the heart of all spiritual teachings, for embodiment is the ground of human experience. Physical existence offers an unparalleled opportunity to participate in spiritual unfolding—what Buddhists call "this precious human birth." All parts of the body, all the senses, and all the postures are put into the service of God, the Great Spirit, Allah, the Great Mother, Enlightenment, the Tao, or the Divine Source. There is also the understanding that a person cannot comprehend or practice the teachings when certain mental or bodily impairments are present.

Some practices for deepening spirituality help build up and sustain the body in a healthy condition. Without such strength it is difficult, if not impossible, to pray, meditate, make pilgrimages, sing, chant, or dance. Tibetan Buddhists follow a rigorous routine of doing prostrations—a minimum of 100,000—to activate the body and its inner energy channels, purify any blockages, imprint wholesome patterns, and build up merit. In the process of moving from a standing position to full-length prostration, practitioners incorporate reflections, prayers, and visualizations. Prostrations are one of four foundational or preliminary practices that prepare them to realize higher insights.

The objective of doing prostrations and other movements impeccably, not mechanically, is for a genuine transformation to occur. All traditions acknowledge reciprocity between external postures and gestures and internal states. Moving or maintaining body parts in a balanced and harmonious way has an impact on the innermost dimension of being. It is the reason for being meticulous and precise in such activities as ritual prayer or meditation. For example, each stage of Islamic worship—from standing with both hands a bit in front and to the sides of the head to full prostration with the forehead on the ground or floor—enacts an aspect of relationship between Creator and creation.

Similarly, inner states are "fleshed out" through the body. *Panim,* the Hebrew word for face, is related to *penim,* for "inside, interior, within." The *Zohar,* a Kabbalistic text, states that what is in a person's heart and mind is visible in the face. When Moses came down from Mount Sinai after speaking with God, the skin of his face was luminous (Exodus 34:29). After Jesus went up on a mountain with Peter, James, and John, his face was as radiant as the sun (Matthew 17:1–2). On the other hand, the Dalai Lama has pointed out that even people who are handsome look ugly when their faces turn livid with anger.

Intimate physical activities also can serve spiritual purposes. The Jewish tradition, which sees the body as neither intrinsically sacred nor evil, sanctifies every bodily act through blessings—upon seeing a rainbow, washing, engaging in conjugal sex, defecating, and so on. Reciting a blessing is a moment in which to consider, acknowledge, and appreciate God's role in providing everything—eyes that witness beauty or organs that absorb nutrients and eliminate waste. One rabbi said that, when done properly, eating is as much of a gateway to unification with God as prayer is.

Thus, all the senses and body parts participate in spiritual practice. Ears listen to sacred music and song, the ringing of church bells, and the cries of *muezzins* in the minarets of mosques calling the faithful to prayer five times a day. Noses smell the smoke of incense. Mouths savor the taste of wine and good food to fulfill the *mitzvah* (Hebrew for "commandment") of enjoying and honoring the Sabbath and festivals. Hands cross the body, sprinkle or pour holy water to baptize, anoint with oil, and perform *mudrās* (Sanskrit for "sign"), ritual gestures that convey spiritual ideas. Feet stamp the ground in traditional Native American ceremonies and spin Mevlevī Sūfīs ("whirling" dervishes) around and around their leader in ecstatic dance to seek mystical union with the Divine.

As the Jewish liturgical poem *Nishmat kol hai* ("The soul of all living") teaches, every limb, every fiber of a human being is to be used in praise of the holy. Without the concrete reality of the body, there would be no access to the experience of ultimate peace and happiness, to the realization of any tradition's spiritual goals.

—Mirka Knaster

FURTHER READING

Bishop, C. (1996). *Sex and spirit.* New York: Little, Brown.

Kasulia, T. P. (Ed.), with Ames, R. T. & Dissanayake, W. (1993). *Self as body in Asian theory and practice.* Albany: State University of New York Press.

Law, J. M. (Ed.). (1995). *Religious reflections on the human body.* Bloomington: Indiana University Press.

Rayburn, C. A. (1995). The body in religious experience. In R. W. Hood, Jr. (Ed.), *Handbook of religious experience* (pp. 476–494). Birmingham, AL: Religious Education Press.

Synnott, A. (1992). Tomb, temple, machine and self: The social construction of the body." *British Journal of Sociology, 40*(1): 79–110.

Religion. (1989). [Articles on the body in various spiritual traditions] *19*, July.

BODY IMAGE AND EATING DISORDERS, WOMEN'S

There is a long history between religion and eating. In the sixth century B.C.E., Eastern religions used fasting to release the soul from the material world. In later centuries, "holy fasting" occurred when many women fasted for spiritual self-redemption, purification of the soul, or to participate in the suffering of Christ (Bynum, 1987). Even today, contemporary eating problems are also sometimes framed in religious and spiritual language and imagery (Lelwica, 1999). There is reason to believe that in some cases, religion has a positive role in one's body image and eating behavior, whereas in other instances it has a negative role.

Studies of diagnosed patients in clinics have found that women with eating disorders often suffer from overall feelings of spiritual unworthiness and have negative God images and fear of abandonment by God. In one case, a woman invoked religious symbols of light and dark to describe her abnormal eating. Eating was impure and defiling to her and thus consistent with a Satanic meaning of night's darkness, so she ate only at night. In such cases, women used religious language and symbols to justify disordered eating and endow it with some grander meaning (Banks, 1996). Two-thirds of a sample of young patients with eating disorders received Communion less often in order to consume fewer calories. Together, these cases show that links between religion and eating can be complex. In some cases, women use religion to motivate and perpetuate their disordered eating, whereas in others women have used their disorder to restrict their involvement in religious practices.

Treatment studies also reveal complex links between religion and eating behavior. One study found that inpatient women who improved in spiritual well-being during treatment also improved in body image and eating attitudes. Some African-American churches have used successful weight-loss programs based on the structure and spiritual themes of Alcoholics Anonymous, and Orthodox Jewish teenagers with eating disorders often involved rabbinic authorities in their treatment. Thus, eating disorders can be related to religious issues and may be treated within those social contexts and worldviews. Indeed, various religious denominations have employed spiritual dimensions in treating disordered eating.

Research has examined different religious groups. In one mixed-age sample of clinic patients, higher proportions of Roman Catholics and Jews and lower proportions of Protestants had eating disorders relative to the general population. In one study of adolescents in England, disordered eating was more common in Muslim than Hindu youth. Poor body image and eating are often due to pathological family relations. In one study of American college women, intrinsic religiosity was a buffer against unhealthy family influence. That is, the more the women integrated their faith into their lives, the less their body image was harmed by pathological dynamics in the family. Recent studies have found that for teenage girls with a history of being sexually abused, higher religiosity was a protective factor against the later development of eating disorders. Collectively, these studies suggest that religion and spirituality are linked to improvement or protection from disordered eating.

A series of recent studies by Boyatzis and colleagues have studied links between religion, eating, and body image in normal samples of nondiagnosed American females. One study of teenage girls (average age 16 years) found that while girls' overall self-esteem was the strongest predictor of how girls felt about their weight and appearance, girls' belief in God predicted significant additional variance in the girls' body image; thus, the stronger girls believed in God, the higher their body image, even above and beyond what their overall self-esteem contributed to their body image. In a series of studies on college women, those with healthier body image and eating also prayed more often, had a closer and more loving relationship with God, had an intrinsic faith orientation that integrated their religion with their life, and were more likely to view their bodies as holy and sacred. In another sample, women higher in quest orientation—who value doubt and are open to change in their religious beliefs—had lower body image scores. In college men, religiosity did not predict their body image or eating disorder scores as well as their existential well-being did (i.e., their sense of meaning and purpose in life).

Unfortunately, all of this research had correlational designs, making it impossible to know if religion actually affects body image. Fortunately, a new study by Boyatzis et al. (2005a) avoided this problem in an experimental design. College women took a pretest on their body image and then were randomly assigned, in a later testing session, to read different kinds of "body affirmations." The groups had been balanced on the basis of their pretest body image scores and their ratings of how important religion was to them. One group of women read religious messages about their bodies (e.g., "God created my body, and I am able to see the divine perfection in my body"); in another condition, women read spiritual statements that did not mention God (e.g., "I wish to see my body only as whole and perfect"). Comparing their scores before and after reading these statements, women who read the religious and spiritual affirmations improved significantly more than did women in a control group who did not read body affirmations. In conclusion, across this series of studies on normal college women, there is virtually no evidence that higher religiosity is related to feeling worse about one's body or to have unhealthy eating practices. To the contrary, this series of studies show that in young women without eating disorders, being religious and spiritual is related to more positive body image and healthier eating.

Together, the work described above confirms that for many women, religious and spiritual issues are intertwined deeply with their body image and eating. For some, religion can be a source of self-loathing; for others, religion may be their saving grace. For this latter group, religion could offer a framework of meaning that emphasizes deep and permanent qualities as more important than the superficial features of appearance, weight, and eating habits. Because women with eating disorders commonly have negative thoughts about their bodies and fears of losing control around food, religion may provide "a sense of ultimate control through the sacred when life seems out of control" (Pargament, 1997: 310). Women who are more religious may be motivated to try to have a healthier body, or they may view their bodies and eating in a more self-forgiving or accepting light, or both. In one study (Boyatzis et al., 2003b), a college woman wrote on a survey, "God doesn't care how big my butt is." An important conclusion from all of this work is that scholars and practitioners could better understand young people's body image and eating problems by considering their spiritual and religious beliefs and practices.

—*Chris J. Boyatzis*

FURTHER READING

Ahmad, S., Waller, G., & Verduyn, C. (1994). Eating attitudes and body satisfaction among Asian and Caucasian adolescents. *Journal of Adolescence, 17,* 461–470.

Banks, C. G. (1996). "There is no fat in heaven": Religious asceticism and the meaning of anorexia nervosa. *Ethos, 24,* 107–135.

Bemporad, J. R. (1996). Self-starvation through the ages: Reflections on the pre-history of anorexia nervosa. *International Journal of Eating Disorders, 19,* 217–237.

Bemporad, J. R. (1997). Cultural and historical aspects of eating disorders. *Theoretical Medicine, 18,* 401–420.

Boyatzis, C. J., O'Connell, S., Manning, A. E., Backof, S., Bender, L., & Hall, A. F. (2005a). *Effects of religious and spiritual affirmations on women's body image.* Manuscript submitted for publication.

Boyatzis, C. J., & McConnell, K. M. (2002). *Females' religious and spiritual well-being, body esteem, and eating disorders.* Paper presented at the meeting of the American Psychological Association, Chicago, August.

Boyatzis, C. J., & McConnell, K. M. (2005b). *Quest orientation in young women: Age trends and relations to body image and disordered eating.* Manuscript submitted for publication.

Boyatzis, C. J., McConnell, K. M., Baranik, L., Pietrocarlo, K., Walsh, J., & Zuluaga, A. (2003a). *Women's sanctification of the body and eating disorders: Viewing the body as a sacred "gift from God."* Paper presented at the Mid-Winter Meeting on Religion and Spirituality, Baltimore, MD, March.

Boyatzis, C. J., McConnell, K. M., Baranik, L., Pietrocarlo, K., Walsh, J., & Zuluaga, A. (2003b). *In their own words: Women describe how their religious and spiritual beliefs influence their body image and eating behavior.* Paper presented at the Mid-Winter Meeting on Religion and Spirituality, Baltimore, MD, March.

Boyatzis, C. J., & Walsh, J. (2005c). *Adolescent girls' body image in relation to self-esteem and religiosity.* Manuscript submitted for publication.

Brumberg, J. J. (1988). *Fasting girls: A history of anorexia nervosa.* Cambridge, MA: Harvard University Press.

Bynum, C. W. (1987). *Holy feast and holy fast: The religious significance of food to medieval women.* Berkeley: University of California Press.

Chandy, J. M., Blum, R. W., & Resnick, M. D. (1996). Gender-specific outcomes for sexually abused adolescents. *Child Abuse and Neglect, 20,* 1219–1231.

Dancyger, I., Fornari, V., Fisher, M., Schneider, M., Frank, S., Wisotsky, W., Sison, C., & Charitou, M. (2002). Cultural factors in orthodox Jewish adolescents treated in a day program for eating disorders. *International Journal of Adolescent Medicine and Health, 14,* 317–328.

Davis, N. L., Clance, P. R., & Gailis, A. T. (1999). Treatment approaches for obese and overweight African American women: A consideration of cultural dimensions. *Psychotherapy: Theory, Research, Practice, Training, 36,* 27–35.

Forthun, L. F., Pidcock, B. W., & Fischer, J. L. (2003). Religiousness and disordered eating: Does religiousness modify family risk? *Eating Behaviors, 4,* 7–26.

Graham, M.A., Spencer, W., & Andersen, A. E. (1991). Altered religious practice in patients with eating disorders. *International Journal of Eating Disorders, 10,* 239–243.

Joughin, N., Crisp, A. H., Halek, C., & Humphrey, H. (1992). Religious belief and anorexia nervosa. *International Journal of Eating Disorders, 12,* 397–406.

Kumanyika, S. K., & Charleston, J. B. (1992). Lose Weight and Win: A church-based weight loss program for blood pressure control among Black women. *Patient Education and Counseling, 19,* 19–32.

Lelwica, M. M. (1999). *Starving for salvation: The spiritual dimensions of eating problems among American girls and women.* New York: Oxford University.

Manning, A. E., & Boyatzis, C. J. (2005). *College men's body image in relation to their religiosity and existential well-being.* Manuscript in preparation.

Miles, M. R. (1995). Religion and food: The case of eating disorders. *Journal of the American Academy of Religion, 63,* 549–564.

Morgan, J. F., Marsden, P., & Lacey, J. H. (2000). "Spiritual starvation?": A case series concerning Christianity and eating disorders. *International Journal of Eating Disorders, 28,* 476–480.

Pargament, K. I. (1997). *The psychology of religion and coping.* New York: Guilford.

Richards, P. S., Hardman, R. K., Frost, H. A., Berrett, M. E., Clark-Sly, J. B., & Anderson, D. K. (1997). Spiritual issues and interventions in the treatment of patients with eating disorders. *Eating Disorders: The Journal of Treatment and Prevention, 5,* 261–279.

Smith, F. T., Hardman, R. K., Richards, P. S., & Fischer, L. (2003). Intrinsic religiousness and spiritual well-being as predictors of treatment outcome among women with eating disorders. *Eating Disorders: The Journal of Treatment and Prevention, 11,* 15–26.

Sykes, D. K., Leuser, B., Melia, M., & Gross, M. (1988). A demographic analysis of 252 patients with anorexia nervosa and bulimia. *International Journal for Psychosomatics, 35,* 5–9.

BONHOEFFER, DIETRICH

Dietrich Bonhoeffer (1906–1945) is best known as a martyr, theologian, and political conspirator. The diversity represented by these attributes is reflective of Bonhoeffer's brief life, cut short at the age of 39 by Nazi gallows. Despite the brevity of his life, Bonhoeffer left behind a rich written legacy, comprised of 16 volumes of theological and spiritual thoughts and insights, letters, papers, sermons, and poems. Two of his best-known works rank as spiritual classics: *Discipleship* (also known as *Cost of Discipleship*) and *Life Together.* Bonhoeffer's legacy has left an imprint on the spiritual and religious lives of many who read his works and study his theological perspective, and his own life serves as a model of religious and spiritual development across the human life span.

BIOGRAPHICAL INFORMATION

A person's work cannot be separated from his or her life, without, however, reducing one to the other. This is especially true with Dietrich Bonhoeffer. He was born into an upper-middle class family in 1906, a few years before the outbreak of World War I. His father was a well-respected professor of psychiatry at the University of Berlin in Germany, where Bonhoeffer would eventually teach as well. Much to the surprise of his family—who had little religious background—Bonhoeffer chose to study theology. After completing his first dissertation titled *Sanctorum Communio*—hailed by Karl Barth as a "theological miracle"—at the age of 21, Bonhoeffer lived for a year in Barcelona, Spain, serving as an assistant pastor to a German congregation.

Before starting his career as a professor of theology at Berlin University, Bonhoeffer spent a year at Union Theological Seminary in New York for postdoctoral studies. This year was marked by two friendships that proved to be very influential for Bonhoeffer's theological and spiritual development. One of the friendships was with the French pacifist, Jean Lasserre, who impressed Bonhoeffer by taking the Sermon on the Mount literally. The other, an African American by the name of Frank Fisher, opened Bonhoeffer's eyes to the pervading racism against African Americans and their struggle against such injustices. Marked by these friendships, Bonhoeffer returned to Germany and became increasingly aware of and opposed to the rise of Nazism and its radical discrimination against Jews. Bonhoeffer refused cooperation with the Nazi regime, and was thus forced into underground work, agreeing to serve as the head of an illegal seminary for the "Confessing Church."

Understanding that war was becoming not only a likely possibility but a desired goal of the Nazi regime, Bonhoeffer became actively engaged in international ecumenical efforts for peace, and was scorned at home by Nazi supporters and labeled as "anti-German." As his awareness grew about the manifold atrocities committed by the Nazis—primarily against the Jews, but also against other dissenting groups and individuals in politics, religion, and society at large—Bonhoeffer decided to participate in a political conspiracy to assassinate Hitler. His group was discovered, however, and after spending two years in a Nazi jail, Bonhoeffer was executed in 1945, only days before the arrival of the Allied troops.

BONHOEFFER'S THEOLOGICAL AND SPIRITUAL LEGACY

Bonhoeffer has influenced and inspired generations of theologians and laypeople around the world with his theological and spiritual insights, as well as his life. A variety of thinkers, even those in opposition, have used Bonhoeffer to support their work. These differences in understanding and using Bonhoeffer are primarily due to the unfinished nature of Bonhoeffer's final and most controversial writings: *Ethics* and *Letters and Papers From Prison.*

Bonhoeffer's earlier works, however, are quite different in nature. His two dissertations in particular, *Sanctorum Communio* and *Act and Being,* are highly academic, rather abstract treatises of various topics in theology and little known beyond theological circles. Geared toward a wider audience is Bonhoeffer's little booklet about Christian community, *Life Together*, which summarizes his experiences with the illegal seminary of the Confessing Church. *Life Together* explores various facets of Christian community and spirituality. In this booklet, Bonhoeffer also seeks to reintroduce spiritual disciplines often neglected in Protestant Christianity, such as confession and meditation.

Around the same time, Bonhoeffer wrote his second "spiritual classic": *Discipleship.* Famous for its radical critique of "cheap grace," that is, grace and forgiveness without repentance and discipleship, *Discipleship* argues for "costly grace" instead. Here, Bonhoeffer draws from the Sermon on the Mount to give concrete and practical advice on what it means to be a disciple of Christ. Followers of Christ need to renounce themselves and be transformed into the image of the incarnate, crucified, and resurrected Christ. Published in 1937, with the Nazis in full power, *Discipleship* offers the attentive reader a practical message about the implications of the Sermon on the Mount for everyday Christian life.

Given the context of Bonhoeffer's participation in political conspiracy, his book *Ethics* appears quite different in language and content. Designed as an academic work, its terminology as well as train of thought presupposes more theological training in its readers than Bonhoeffer's previous two books. Bonhoeffer was never able to finish *Ethics.* The various manuscripts comprising this work—only parts of which had been reworked by Bonhoeffer—were published posthumously and show clear signs of their unfinished nature. Despite the difficulties present in this work, the reader willing to engage it will find rich rewards, for invigorating and thought-provoking new insights emerge from its pages. Bonhoeffer engages here in nothing less than a radical deconstruction of the common ethical endeavor that starts with the questions of what is good and how to be good.

Instead, Bonhoeffer proposes within the pages of the manuscripts that the starting point ought to be the inquiry into *who* is good. For Bonhoeffer, the answer is clear: Christ alone proves an adequate beginning for all ethical thought. Christ as the good also becomes synonymous with reality itself, for after the Fall, humans have only a distorted view of reality. Based on these premises, Bonhoeffer moves on to explicate his understanding of the responsible life, structured by the following two factors: obligation (to God and other humans) and freedom. Bonhoeffer examines obligation from the perspectives of *Stellvertretung* (vicarious representative action or deputyship) and accordance with reality. Freedom takes concrete shape in the accountability for one's life and action, and the venture of the concrete decision. The latter includes for Bonhoeffer also the necessity to accept guilt for the sake of another person.

Even more heatedly debated among Bonhoeffer's readers than his *Ethics* is his final work, *Letters and Papers From Prison.* Smuggled out of prison and published only after his death, this exchange of letters, papers, and poems with his close friend Eberhard Bethge comprises revolutionary new ideas for theology and spirituality. Here we read about "a religionless Christianity" in "a world come of age" that needs a different, namely a "nonreligious interpretation" of biblical and theological concepts. Bonhoeffer holds that due to the advances in science and the experiences in two world wars, people can no longer be "religious" in the traditional sense of the word. Religion, for Bonhoeffer, thus comes to stand for the imprisonment of Christianity, and we as readers become witnesses of Bonhoeffer's struggle of how to speak concretely and without using religious language about Christ and the Church in a manner relevant to his contemporaries. He finds a starting point in "prayer and righteous action." The Church itself comes to be understood as the true one only "when it exists for others."

BONHOEFFER IN A NUTSHELL

Being faced with the almost overwhelming variety and wealth of Bonhoeffer's theological and spiritual legacy, one can justifiably ask whether a common thread connects his works and his legacy. This unifying element is found in Bonhoeffer's consistent Christocentrism. Bonhoeffer's unwavering focus on Christ as the center of his theology and spirituality is perceptible throughout both his works and his own life journey, stations of which included being a pastor and a professor of theology, as well as being a double agent conspiring against the Nazi regime, resulting in his execution. His work and his life will undoubtedly continue to influence and trigger religious and spiritual development for years to come.

—Christine Cochlovius Schliesser

FURTHER READING

Bonhoeffer, D. (1937, 2001). *Discipleship.* G. B. Kelly, & J. D. Godsey (Eds.). B. Green, & R. Krauss (Trans.). Minneapolis: Fortress Press.

Bonhoeffer, D. (1949, 2005). *Ethics.* C. J. Green (Ed.). R. Krauss, Ch. C. West, and D. W. Stott (Trans.). Minneapolis: Fortress Press.

Bonhoeffer, D. (1939, 1995). *Life together.* In G. B. Kelly (Ed.). D. W. Bloesch (Trans.). Minneapolis: Fortress Press.

Bonhoeffer, D. (1951, 1997). *Letters and papers from prison.* E. Bethge (Ed.). R. Fuller, F. Clark, et al. (Trans.). New York: Simon & Schuster.

Bethge, E. (1967, 2000). *Dietrich Bonhoeffer: A biography.* In V. J. Barnett (Ed., Rev.). Minneapolis: Fortress Press.

Kelly, G. B., & Nelson, F. B. (2003). *The cost of moral leadership—The spirituality of Dietrich Bonhoeffer.* Grand Rapids/Cambridge: Eerdmans.

BOOK OF MORMON

The Book of Mormon is a compilation of Scripture considered sacred, along with the Bible, by members of the Church of Jesus Christ of Latter-Day Saints (LDS). It contains the writings of ancient prophets who documented their revelations from God concerning the spiritual well-being of their people. Members of the LDS faith have inherited the nickname "Mormons" because of their belief that this book is additional Scripture existing alongside the Bible. It forms the foundation of Latter-Day Saint doctrine, and constitutes for Mormons, along with the Old and New Testaments, another witness to the divinity of Jesus Christ.

ORIGINS OF THE BOOK OF MORMON

In 1823 the young Joseph Smith, founder and first prophet of the Mormon faith, reported visitations by heavenly beings, who told him of the whereabouts of metal plates buried in upstate New York. Etched onto these gold plates were the writings of prophets who lived on the American continents more than a thousand years before. Smith was instructed by the heavenly beings to unearth the plates and translate them into English. Once he obtained the plates, Smith dictated the translation to one of a number of scribes. According to those who witnessed the process, when resuming translation after a hiatus of any length, he resumed where he left off from the previous session without repetitions or gaps. After the translation was finished, the angelic messenger took back the plates, although not until they had been shown to 11 men and 1 woman. Their witness can be read in the opening pages of modern editions of the Book of Mormon as "The Testimony of the Three Witnesses" and "The Testimony of the Eight Witnesses."

In 1830, Grandin published the first edition of the Book of Mormon in Palmyra, New York. Since then, the book has been issued in numerous editions and has been translated from English into more than 100 languages.

CONTENT OF THE BOOK OF MORMON

The primary narrative of the Book of Mormon opens in Jerusalem ca. 600 B.C.E. A prophet named Lehi (not mentioned in the Old Testament), was instructed by God to warn the people of Jerusalem of the imminent Babylonian catastrophe, just as the Old Testament prophet Jeremiah was doing. In order to escape the destruction of Jerusalem and the enslavement of its inhabitants, Lehi was commanded by God to leave the city and take his family into the desert. After traveling through the desert for many years, they made their way to the coast of the Arabian Sea. Lehi's family built a boat and sailed for a land of promise, the then-unknown Americas.

Lehi died not long after their arrival in the promised land, and his children split into two groups, named after two of his sons, Nephi and Laman. The "Nephites" remained for the most part obedient to the commandments of God, and successions of prophets were chosen from among them to provide the people with continued revelations from God. The "Lamanites," on the other hand, were characteristically wicked and violent. The Nephites later met up with another group that had fled Israel at the same time as Lehi, called the Mulekites after their leader Mulek, a son of King Zedekiah of Jerusalem. The Nephites were also made aware of the records of another people, the Jaredites, who had fled Mesopotamia at the time of the Tower of Babel and arrived, also by ship, in roughly the same geographical area as the Nephites. The Jaredite record indicated that the entire nation was eventually destroyed by infighting resulting from their wickedness. The last prophet of the Book of Mormon, Moroni, included a condensed version of the Jaredite account on the plates obtained by Joseph Smith.

The Book of Mormon is an abridgement of the records kept on metal plates by the prophets of the Nephites, who wrote until roughly C.E. 420. Mormon, the second-to-last prophet, edited this abridgement and summarized the history and teachings contained on the records available to him. This abridgement included the history from the plates kept by Nephi, son of Lehi, and his descendants, and spanned nearly 1,000 years. The climax of the narrative is the appearance and ministry of Jesus Christ, following his crucifixion and resurrection in Jerusalem, to the Nephites in the Americas. In the Bible, Jesus says, "And other sheep I have, which are not of this fold: them also I must bring, and they shall hear my voice; and there shall be one fold, and one shepherd" (John 10:16 KJV). Jesus Christ's ministry to the Nephites is thus seen as a fulfillment of that biblical prophecy, the Nephites being among the other "sheep" that were not in Jerusalem during the time of Christ's ministry there.

The centuries immediately following Jesus Christ's appearance in the Americas were dominated by peace between the Nephites and Lamanites. However, this peace would not last, and ultimately the entire Nephite nation would be annihilated by the Lamanites in a great battle that occurred ca. C.E. 400. The last Nephite prophet to write on the plates, Moroni, buried the record to protect them from being destroyed by the Lamanites, and the records remained hidden until they were uncovered by Joseph Smith.

THE BOOK OF MORMON TODAY

While certain aspects of the emergence of the Book of Mormon undoubtedly seem fantastic, such as angelic visitations, buried plates of gold, and so on, there are other factors found in the book, like the complex literary features characteristic of Hebrew writing, largely unknown in Joseph Smith's day, that support its authenticity. Although the Church of Jesus Christ of Latter-Day Saints funds ongoing research into the historicity of the account through linguistic, historical, archaeological, and other analyses, it is not the academic witness that is paramount to members of the LDS Church. A promise written by the last prophet, Moroni, in the final pages of the book summarizes the place of the book in Mormon spirituality.

Speaking of the Book of Mormon, Moroni says, "And when ye shall receive these things, I would exhort you that ye would ask God, the Eternal Father, in the name of Christ, if these things are not true; and if ye shall ask with a sincere heart, with real intent, having faith in Christ, he will manifest the truth of it unto you by the power of the Holy Ghost. And by the power of the Holy Ghost ye may know the truth of all things" (Moroni 10:4–5). Readers of the Book of Mormon are encouraged by its authors, and by members of the Mormon Church, to make its authenticity and truthfulness a matter of spiritual reflection and meditation because of the central role that the Book of Mormon plays in LDS doctrine and practice.

In the introduction to the Book of Mormon, Joseph Smith is quoted saying that it is the "keystone" of the Mormon religion. If one were to believe in the authenticity of the Book of Mormon, he or she would also believe that its translator, Joseph Smith, was chosen as a prophet of God. Conversely, if one were to regard the Book of Mormon as inauthentic, he or she would necessarily disregard Joseph Smith as a true prophet of God and also the claims of the LDS church as the true church of Jesus Christ. The debate about these controversial doctrines of the LDS Church (i.e., modern-day prophets and Christian Scripture not found in the Bible), hinges on the authenticity of the Book of Mormon.

The powerful influence of the Book of Mormon on the worship of members of the LDS church can be seen in the way that the church proselytizes and how church services are conducted. Young LDS men and women, usually between the ages of 19 and 26, are encouraged by the church to serve full-time missions throughout the world. The message of these missionaries regards primarily the teachings of the Book of Mormon and how it compares to the Bible as another witness of the divinity of Jesus Christ. Little children who attend Sunday services at LDS meetinghouses hear stories from the Book of Mormon and are taught about the history of the Nephite and Lamanite people together with biblical stories and events. Mormon adolescents worldwide attend daily Church-sponsored classes called "seminary," in which they study the Book of Mormon, the Bible, and other doctrines of the LDS Church.

The Book of Mormon holds a unique place in contemporary discussion of religiosity and spirituality. For believers of the book's authenticity, the Book of Mormon serves as a foundation of faith in Jesus Christ as the son of God and the savior of the world, and in the Church of Jesus Christ of Latter-Day Saints as the "Lord's kingdom once again established on the earth" (Introduction to the Book of Mormon). For critics, it serves only as evidence of the imagination of Joseph Smith, that he was the literal author of the book (as opposed to its translator) and that all other doctrines of the LDS Church not found in the Bible are incorrect. Regardless of one's opinion of its authenticity, it must be recognized that the Book of Mormon has affected and continues to affect the spiritual and religious development of millions of people throughout the world, and stands as the centerpiece of one of the fastest-growing religions today.

—Peter Osborn and Cory Crawford

See also Mormonism

FURTHER READING

Benson, E. T. (1988). *A witness and a warning: A modern-day prophet testifies of the Book of Mormon.* Salt Lake City, UT: Desert Book Company.

Givens, T. (2002). *By the hand of Mormon: The American scripture that launched a New World religion.* Oxford: Oxford University Press.

Hardy, G. (Ed.). (2003). *The Book of Mormon: A reader's edition.* Urbana: University of Illinois Press.

Ludlow, D. H. (Ed.). (1992). *Encyclopedia of Mormonism.* New York: Macmillan.

BUBER, MARTIN

Martin Mordechai Buber (1878–1965) was born in Vienna and spent most of his childhood with his grandparents, who raised Buber after his parents' divorce. He later lived with his father and stepmother, but his separation from his mother had a profound impact on his life. In 1896, he studied philosophy at the University of Vienna, and two years later studied at the University of Leipzig where he encountered the Zionist movement and edited *Die Welt,* a popular Zionist publication. He also studied at Berlin and Zurich, and was a professor of religion at the University of Frankfurt from 1924 until 1933. He worked with Franz Rosenzweig on translating the Old Testament into German, and was appointed to the chair of social philosophy at Hebrew University where he taught until he retired in 1951. His work has influenced the spiritual and religious education and development of many who have studied his life and work.

In his early work, he was interested in Hasidic folk tales, and some of his early work, including *Daniel: Dialogues in Realization*, reflected an interest in mysticism. In the beginning, his involvement with the Zionist movement was more of an affirmation of Jewish culture, rather than Judaism, although his most important work *I and Thou* has been an important influence in religious studies. Buber's philosophical interests included Immanuel Kant's *Prolegomena* and Friedrich Nietzsche's *Thus Spoke Zarathustra.* Kant's distinction between perceiving an object (phenomena) and things-in-themselves (noumena) are problems mirrored in *I and Thou.* Buber was also interested in the broader humanities including the psychological work of Wilhelm Wundt, Carl Stumpf, and the hermeneutic theory of Wilhelm Dilthey.

I AND THOU

Buber's most well-known and engaging work, *I and Thou*, was originally published in 1923, but was not translated into English until 1937. Buber identified two ways in which humans relate to the world, each other, and the divine: "I–It" and "I–Thou." Both are necessary to human existence, but direct humanity to different ends. "I" never exists independently of relationships, and "It" and "Thou" reflect different aspects of humanity, nature, and God. His work had a large influence on

Jewish philosophy, and both Jewish and Christian theological studies, especially in his later writings such as *Good and Evil* and *The Eclipse of God. I and Thou* emphasized a dialogical view of humanity's relationship to God, and provided a metaphor that has influenced theologians and philosophers since its inception.

I–It indicates the relationship of a person to an object. The object is described in a language that categorizes it, impersonalizes it, and isolates it. The I–It relationship can be compared to a subject–object relationship where the subject is not relationally affected by the object; it is simply a relation of analysis and description. The primary limitation of the I–It relation is the one-way directionality of the relationship. The I is not moved or changed by its object; the relationship is already defined before there is any chance of reciprocal interaction. There is no sense of mutuality in the relationship; the "I" is denied any impact from the other. Although Buber showed the problematic aspects of this relationship, he also realized that both I–It and I–Thou were necessary aspects of humanity. Yet, Buber, felt that the I–It relationship had achieved a type of dominance that overshadowed the importance of I–Thou:

> In our age the I–It relation, gigantically swollen, has usurped, practically uncontested, the mastery and the rule. The I of this relation, an I that possesses all, makes all, succeeds with all, this I that is unable to say Thou . . . can naturally acknowledge neither God nor any genuine absolute which manifests itself to men as of non-human origin. It steps in between and shuts off from us the light of heaven.

In contrast to I–It, I–Thou describes a relationship that is reciprocal, mutual, and experiential. It is in the meeting between I and Thou that a person experiences her or his whole being and the being of the other. This is not an individual process, but a process of relation, the dialogue between one and another. In this relationship, one does not define or contain the other, but rather is affected by the other. No concepts or analyses are needed; the relation is simply experienced as each influences the other.

This relation can be understood as partially mystical, yet Buber wanted this relation to be about the present, not a mystical union separate from the physical world. The contrast between I–It and I–Thou reflects the difference between the mechanistic and objective world of science and the aesthetic, artistic, and religious world of Thou. Buber did not intend to remove the I–It relation, but argued that modern society has emphasized it too much at the expense of the creative impulse of the artist and the religious experience of the aesthetic. The I–It relation is not emotionally involved in what it describes, and it is not open to the change that it may encounter when confronted with Thou. It is content to define and remain distant, uninterested in the world around it.

Thou may be another person, nature, or the eternal Thou, God. In speaking of relating to nature, a tree may be classified and understood as an object or it may be experienced as Thou. The I–Thou relation focuses on how the experience of the tree affects and changes a person, rather than the tree simply becoming an object that is identified. Buber did not advocate for any type of dualism, but understood nature and God as part of the kingdom of God.

> There is not one realm of the spirit and another of nature; there is only the growing kingdom of God. God is not spirit, but what we call spirit and what we call nature hail equally from the God who is beyond and equally unconditioned by both, and whose kingdom reaches its fullness in the complete unity of spirit and nature. (1966: 28)

The importance of the I–Thou relation for spiritual development highlights the importance of relational engagement with the divine. This should not be seen as a mystical union that shuns nature, but rather an active engagement with God and his creation. Relating to God through the I–It relation transforms God into an object that is simply defined and abstracted but never experienced. When God is the eternal Thou, the person is able to open his or her self to being impacted by the divine, and the person is able to impact God. The relationship is mutual and reciprocal, focusing on how people allow their life and their person to be persuaded and moved in connection to the divine. This is not a relationship that occurs through having correct concepts or beliefs, but through openness and humility that allow two subjects to mutually interact with one another.

—James A. Van Slyke

FURTHER READING

Buber, M. (1913, 1964). *Daniel: Dialogues on realization.* M. Friedman (Trans.). New York: Holt.

Buber, M. (1937, 2000). *I and thou.* R. G. Smith (Trans.). New York: Scribner.

Buber, M. (1952, 1977). *Eclipse of God.* Westport, CT: Greenwood Press.

Buber, M. (1966). *The way of response: Martin Buber; selections from his writings.* In N. N. Glatzer (Ed.). New York: Schocken Books.

Buber, M. (1953). *Good and evil: Two interpretations.* R. G. Smith (Trans.). New York: Scribners.

BUDDHA

Buddha was born in Kapilavastu,
Became Enlightened in Magadha,
Taught in Varanasi,
Entered Nirvana in Kushinagara.
Now we set out Buddha's bowls;
May we, with all living beings,
realize the emptiness of the three wheels:
giver, receiver, and gift.

This verse, which is chanted before formal meals during Zen Buddhist retreats, sets out in abbreviated form the life and career of the man who has come to be known as the Buddha. The known facts of the Buddha's life do not fill much more space than that eight-line verse, and there is a certain irony in presenting a biography of the Buddha. Buddhism, as a set of religious practices, places little emphasis on the individual, and so is not inclined to concern itself with the life of its founder.

We do know that he was born in northern India around the year 600 B.C.E., the son of the ruler of the Shakya clan. His name was Siddhartha Gautama. We are told that prior to his birth his father received a prophecy that his son would be either a great religious leader or a mighty ruler. To ensure that his son would make what the father thought was the proper decision, he raised Siddhartha within the walls of the court, showering him with luxuries but not allowing him to venture outside. Siddhartha succeeded in slipping out of the palace and was confronted with a vision of a sick man, an old man, a corpse, and a wandering holy man. The realization that life involved suffering weighed heavily on Siddhartha's mind, leading him to abandon his previous life, leaving behind the palace, his wife, and his infant son, and setting out into the forest to pursue the life of a wandering monk.

Siddhartha studied with many of the holy men who wandered through the forests with their disciples seeking ways to come to terms with the unhappiness and dissatisfaction that people faced in their day-to-day lives. Despite his ability to master the various meditation techniques taught by the many schools of wandering monks, Siddhartha was unable to find answers to the question of why there was suffering. Following the ascetic practices prescribed by the various teachers left Siddhartha emaciated and weakened.

One day, a passing child from a nearby village offered him a bowl of rice cooked in milk. Siddhartha, in violation of what he had been taught, that the source of suffering lay in the body and that the path out of suffering required turning away from the body, understood that his own body was the vehicle through which he would reach enlightenment and that ignoring the needs of the body hindered his attainment of the Way.

Having revived himself with food, Siddhartha resolved to sit under a great bodhi tree until either he attained enlightenment or died. For six days he sat, and on the morning of the seventh, with the rising of the morning star, he came to the realization that all things are interconnected, that there is no distinction between self and other. He had reached enlightenment.

Siddhartha arose and sought out his former companions. While passing through the forest, Siddhartha met a man who stopped him and asked, "Are you a god?" Siddhartha smiled and said "No." "Are you a spirit?" asked the man. Again, Siddhartha smiled and said "No." " What are you then?" asked the man again. "I am awake," replied Siddhartha. This is the story which led to Siddhartha's more commonly known name. In Sanskrit, the word "Buddha" means the Awakened One.

In returning to his old companions, the Buddha began a teaching career that would continue until his death at the age of 80. His followers traveled with him from village to village, begging for their food and teaching villagers the path out of a world of suffering. During the rainy seasons, the Buddha and his disciples gathered in parks in shelters—given to them by wealthy followers. These became the early monasteries that formed the basis of the expansion of Buddhism.

From its beginning, Buddhism has been a technique or way to eliminate suffering. It takes no position on the existence or nonexistence of gods or an afterlife. The Buddha is supposed to have said to a philosopher who insisted on answers to metaphysical questions that insisting on answers to such questions is like a wounded man on the battlefield refusing treatment for his wounds until he is told the name of his assailant, his family background, what he had for breakfast, and the name of his pet dog.

The Buddha described his method using what he called the Four Noble Truths—that life is dissatisfaction, that dissatisfaction has a cause, that the cause has a cure, and that the cure is to follow the Eightfold Path. The Eightfold Path is simply having the right views and the right intention; engaging in right speech, right action, right livelihood, and right effort; and pursuing right mindfulness and right concentration. This path offered a way out of suffering that did not rely on metaphysics or a god. It is not that the Buddha denied the existence of a god, but rather that he considered God's existence to be beside the point.

From its origin in northeastern India, Buddhism extended to the southeast into what is now Burma, Cambodia, Thailand, and Vietnam. It moved south from India into Sri Lanka, and it followed the Silk Road through what is now Pakistan and Afghanistan and then Central Asia, on into China. From China, it spread to Korea and Japan. Sometime later, it moved north from India into Tibet. Today, it is practiced worldwide.

—*Edward C. Oberholtzer*

See also Buddhism

FURTHER READING

Conze, E. (1993). *A short history of Buddhism.* Oxford: Oneworld.

Goldstein, J. (2001). *Seeking the path of wisdom.* San Francisco: Shambhala Press.

Lopez, D. (2001). *The story of Buddhism.* San Fancisco: HarperCollins.

BUDDHISM

To the Westerner raised in a theocentric religious faith, Buddhism is striking for its not speaking of a personal god. Because it does not, many Westerners have mistakenly called Buddhism an atheistic philosophy rather than a religion. Doing so misses the essentially religious nature of Buddhism, the fact that it exists not for men and women to think about the nature of life, but for men and women to transform their lives into lives lived spiritually. Buddhism, like every other religious tradition, calls men and women to become faith-full. The main question, then, is not whether Buddhism is a religion, but what characteristics define its particular pattern of faith.

The central characteristics are surprisingly simple, although living out one's life as a Buddhist is hardly simple. Buddhists take their cue from the life of the Buddha, who described himself as the one who "woke up," who became enlightened. What did he wake up to, and what, in turn, are all of us encouraged to wake up to? The answer has to do first with understanding life as being askew, as full of suffering, as putting all of us in turmoil by there being constant change. Nothing is permanent—no matter how hard we try to create permanence.

From this seemingly pessimistic view of life as it really is, there is one conclusion to derive, namely, that we should not put our hopes in striving to live our lives the way we normally do, that is, in terms of our own selfish goals and desires. Doing so will only perpetuate the suffering.

At this point in the discussion, Buddhism changes from being pessimistic to being optimistic, to giving hope to all those who would follow. There is hope, says Buddhism, because there is Truth or Dharma. Amid all the impermanence and all the suffering, Dharma remains constant, and if we tap into Dharma, discover, and, most important, live according to Dharma, we will escape the sorry aspects of this world, escape the confines of our own little egos, and discover true happiness. Buddhists believe this not simply as a promise made but as a promise delivered, an experiment that has already been carried out and found to be true, as seen in the life of the Buddha.

But what, we may ask, does it mean to live a life according to the Truth, according to Dharma? Is this just another legalistic religion, one that calls us not to live lives passionately but to live lives anxiously and in fear of breaking this or that rule? The answer is, "Not at all."

The cosmic truth pointed to in the concept of Dharma is indeed about morality but not of a legalistic kind. Dharma is about the moral dimension of reality—the moral law that is written into the very fabric of existence and, as such, predates the Buddha and Buddhism. That moral dimension dictates that we focus our energies not on being righteous but on being *compassionate*, and on freeing ourselves from our petty goals and desires in order to unite with not only our fellow humans but with all of life. There is, then, an essentially mystical core to Buddhism, one not unlike the mystical core of Christianity, as many have observed. To live a Buddhist way of life is, then, to live a compassionate life, one that is committed to overcoming self-centeredness in order to dissolve the boundaries of the self that separate us from the world, and that are, in the final analysis, illusory. We are, say the Buddhists, separate selves in the sense that we have bodies and individual thoughts and feelings. But this is not the main point. The main point is that we are connected or, to be more precise, interconnected—so much so that what we take to be our definite and individual selves are, in fact, reflections of interconnectedness.

Nowhere is this Buddhist concept of interconnectedness better illustrated than in the concept of reincarnation. Reincarnation does not refer to the transmigration of souls or to the magical reappearance, following death, of the self in a different body or physical form. It refers to the fact that each of us has been influenced causally by those who have come before, even as we will influence causally those who follow us. We are, say the Buddhists, like candles standing in a row. When only the first candle is lit, it can light the second and then extinguish. The second can light the third and then extinguish, and so on down the line. The last candle lit is, then, a reincarnation of the first, even though the first and last appear to be totally separate. Just as the candles are connected (interconnected), so too are we all connected, whether we speak of those living or those who are dead.

Right living, that is, living according to the cosmic truth called Dharma, brings happiness. But what is meant here by happiness? To some extent it means the same here as it does to those following other faith traditions. Buddhists are no different from Hindus, Muslims, Jews, and Christians in claiming that there is peace and deep satisfaction in transcending the self and in leading a truly compassionate life that connects us positively to our fellow humans and to life in general. However, in the Buddhist case, there is a unique endpoint and emphasis. If petty, selfish desires are the problem, and if freeing oneself from the illusion of being a separate self is the solution, then the goal or endpoint is complete selflessness, complete dissolution of the self's boundaries. This is what Buddhists refer to as Nirvana. Nirvana is as close as Buddhists get to speaking of a godhead. The Buddha achieved Nirvana and returned to help others do the same. Those who later did the same are called Bodhisattvas. They are the Buddhist saints whose role it is to save others.

Nirvana may be the most dramatic and strange of all Buddhist concepts, at least to Western non-Buddhists. As such, it has attracted a great deal of curiosity among Westerners, often to the point of making Buddhists uncomfortable. Buddhists are uncomfortable with this Western curiosity because it often misses the main focus of Buddhism, which is on "right living" and Dharma. Buddhists know that Nirvana is not for us all, whereas working hard to live life "rightly" is for us all.

And so, in the final analysis, Buddhism, as one of the great faith traditions, is a call to do what it takes to live life "rightly" and according to what is true. To do so requires tremendous self-discipline. Buddhism is not about signing on to this or that belief. It is about rising early to meditate and get ready to live out the day in the right frame of mind. It is about reflecting constantly on one's thoughts and feelings and speech—so as to learn how to live more compassionately. It is, then, one of the great self-improvement programs known to humankind.

But to call Buddhism a self-improvement program is not quite right. Buddhism is not simply a program. It is, rather, a spiritual pathway. Buddhists are realists intent upon self-improvement, on becoming more compassionate and open to others. However, their realism and efforts at self-improvement are rooted in faith, faith that the nature of the universe is indeed essentially moral, and faith that in being compassionate, we tap into what is transcendent.

—*W. George Scarlett*

See also Buddha; Buddhist Scripture

FURTHER READING

Smith, H. (1961). *The world's religions.* San Francisco: Harper.

Smith, W. C. (1998a). *Patterns of faith around the world.* Boston, MA: Oneworld Publications.

Smith, W. C. (1998b). *Faith and belief: The difference between them.* Oxford, United Kingdom: Oneworld Publications.

BUDDHISM, SOCIALLY ENGAGED

Socially engaged Buddhists are Buddhists who are concerned with exploring the significance of the

Buddhist tradition in response to contemporary problems such as violence, poverty, discrimination, and ecological crisis. These persons and movements represent an important development within Buddhism and are contributing to new forms of Buddhist practice.

The term "engaged Buddhism" was first coined by the Vietnamese Buddhist monk Thich Nhat Hanh in the 1960s in the context of war in Vietnam. Not content simply to practice Buddhism in the monastery while remaining detached from the turmoil that his country was experiencing, he stressed instead the need to shine Buddhist insight upon the problems of war and injustice and to find ways to act to relieve suffering. During the war, Thich Nhat Hanh founded the "Order of Interbeing," a religious order made up of monks, nuns, and laypersons committed to engaging in Buddhist principles. He also founded the School of Youth for Social Service. The purpose of the School was to train young people in Buddhist spiritual disciplines and in the skills needed to engage in projects of education, health care, community organizing, and grassroots economic development.

As the war intensified, much of the attention of Thich Nhat Hanh and his followers shifted to relief work, caring for war orphans, and rebuilding villages destroyed by the war. Thich Nhat Hanh was eventually forced into exile. He lives today at Plum Village, a Buddhist community that he founded in rural France. Along with colleagues such as Sister Chan Khong, Thich Nhat Hanh continues to work on behalf of nonviolence, reconciliation, and healing through a worldwide ministry of teaching and retreats.

Another significant proponent of socially engaged Buddhism is Sulak Sivaraksa of Thailand/Siam. He is cofounder of the International Network of Engaged Buddhists (INEB), an organization of Buddhists from around the world who are committed to working for peace, social justice, and ecological sustainability both in the global community and in their local settings. Sivaraksa has been active in the quest for political and economic democracy in Thailand. His book *Seeds of Peace: A Buddhist Vision for Renewing Society* provides an excellent introduction to the central principles of engaged Buddhism.

One of the most well-known grassroots social movements based on engaged Buddhist principles is the Sarvodaya Shramadana movement of Sri Lanka. Founded in 1958 by A. T. Ariyaratne, Sarvodaya Shramadana is a village-based movement that is active in thousands of villages in Sri Lanka. The movement is centered on the activity of voluntary work camps in which persons join together to share their labor for the benefit of their village (digging a well, planting gardens, digging a latrine, etc.). During the work camp, the participants also take part in sessions in which Buddhist-inspired teachings are shared through song and drama and basic Buddhist practices such as lovingkindness meditation are taught. The goal of the movement is a dual one of both personal awakening and social uplift.

Other examples of engaged Buddhist action in Asia include the ongoing struggle against human rights abuses in Tibet and the struggle for democracy in Burma, led by Nobel Peace Prize winner Aung San Suu Kyi. In the United States, the activities of socially engaged Buddhists have taken a variety of forms. These have included involvement in the peace and environmental movements, efforts to aid the homeless, human rights advocacy, prison ministry, concern for welfare of animals, and the establishment of hospices for the dying.

Proponents of socially engaged Buddhism contend that concern for social justice follows naturally from the fundamental principles of Buddhism. Among these fundamental principles are the five ethical precepts to which all Buddhists are expected to adhere. Engaged Buddhists stress that these precepts have profound social implications. In discussing the first precept of not killing, for example, Thich Nhat Hanh highlights the need not only to make a personal commitment not to kill (including not to kill animals for food whenever alternatives are available), but also the need to confront the social manifestations of killing in the forms of militarism and structural injustice. When more than 30,000 children die each day due to hunger-related causes in a world of food abundance, then challenging the structures of the global economy that perpetuate this injustice becomes a necessary consequence of faithfulness to this precept. Similarly, Thich Nhat Hanh interprets the second precept of not stealing as not only forbidding personal theft and encouraging the virtue of generosity, but as also requiring a commitment to "prevent others from profiting from human suffering or the suffering of other species on Earth" (Nhat Hanh, 1993: 20). Thus, the second precept requires an active commitment to social and even interspecies justice.

With regard to the third precept forbidding the misuse of sexuality, Sulak Sivaraksa argues that this precept should include not only a personal commitment to sexual responsibility, but also a critique of male dominance/patriarchy in the very structures of society. The fourth precept concerning truthfulness Sivaraksa claims should lead not only to a personal commitment not to lie, but also to a critique of forms of advertising that stimulate false needs, as well as propaganda, bias in the news media, and other forms of false communication.

Lastly, with regard to the fifth precept against the use of intoxicants, Sivaraksa suggests that in addition to making a personal commitment to not use these products, attention must be given to overcoming the underlying factors that often contribute to substance abuse. Some of these factors that he highlights include economic inequality, unemployment, employment that lacks social value, and the destruction of communal bonds and spiritual traditions that he sees as resulting from a single-minded pursuit of economic growth.

Practitioners of socially engaged Buddhism tend to be very critical of the existing economic and political structures of the world. They highlight the need for alternatives based on spiritual values, the meeting of basic needs, more equitable distribution of wealth, popular participation in decision making, the use of appropriate technology, nonviolence, respect for the rights of women and minorities, and ecological sustainability.

—John Sniegocki

See also Buddhism; Thich Nhat Hanh

FURTHER READING

Nhat Hanh, T. (1993). *For a future to be possible.* Berkeley, CA: Parallax Press.

Sivaraksa, S. (1992). *Seeds of peace: A Buddhist vision for renewing society.* Berkeley, CA: Parallax Press.

Queen, C. (Ed.). (2000). *Engaged Buddhism in the West.* Boston: Wisdom Publications.

Queen, C., & King, S. (Eds.). (1996). *Engaged Buddhism: Buddhist liberation movements in Asia.* Albany: State University of New York Press.

BUDDHIST SCRIPTURE

After the Buddha died and entered into Nirvana, his followers formed a consensus about the Buddha's teachings. These teachings were memorized by his followers and then passed from one generation to the next by word of mouth until around the first century C.E. when they started to be written down. While the scriptures have been translated into modern languages to provide access to a broader segment of society, the original languages include Pali, Sanskrit, Chinese, and Japanese, among others. The scriptures have a significant influence on the religious and spiritual development of Buddhists throughout the world, and are also known to have a dramatic influence on the spiritual development of those who do not consider themselves Buddhist but are moved by, and even change their lives, according to the teachings of the Buddha found in the canon of Buddhist scripture. There are various canons of Buddhist scriptures, and each school of Buddhism identifies with a distinctive canon—although schools of Buddhism tend to have some scriptures in common with other schools. There are a vast number of Buddhist scriptures that deserve to be the focus of such an encyclopedic entry, but only a few will be touched upon here.

The three leading types of schools of Buddhism are Nikaya, Mahayana, and Vajrayana, each having their own scriptures. Nikaya uses only Theravada scriptures. Mahayana uses Theravada scriptures plus many additional sutras. Vajrayana uses Mahayana scriptures plus many tantric texts. The various schools and their specific scriptures teach of Buddhist practices and their aims, such as to be free of suffering (*dukkha*), to be awake to the realization of *anatta* (egolessness), and to achieve enlightenment and Nirvana. While some schools and their scriptures focus on cleansing the self of moral defilements of the "worldly self," other schools and their scriptures appeal to Bodhisattvas for a favorable rebirth, and/or encourage good and pure actions and know the value of abstaining from bad and impure actions.

THE THERAVADA SCHOOL OF NIKAYA BUDDHISM AND ITS SCRIPTURES

The Theravada school, whose name means "Doctrine of the Elders," is the only surviving school of Nikaya Buddhism, and is practiced natively in Sri Lanka, Burma, Laos, Thailand, Cambodia, and portions of Vietnam and Malaysia. The doctrine and practice of the Theravada school is completely based on the Pali Canon, which is considered to be the scripture closest to the authentic teachings of the Buddha. The Pali Canon was written on palm leaves in Pali, the liturgical language of Theravada Buddhism.

The Pali Canon consists of three categories of writings: the Vinaya Pitaka, the Sutta Pitaka, and the Abhidhamma Pitaka. These writings form the foundation of the doctrine of Theravada Buddhism. The Vinaya Pitaka, or the Book of Discipline, outlines the rules of conduct for monks and nuns, rules that were offered by the Buddha throughout his lifetime. The stories behind the rules are also supplied in the scriptures, providing believers with an understanding of how the Buddha resolved to bring harmony to a very diverse community of spiritual leaders. The Sutta Pitaka is a collection in five subdivisions that provide the Buddha's discourses and include all of the central teachings of Theravada Buddhism. The collection includes the essential teachings of the Buddha, details of his enlightenment, how to live morally, and how to meditate. The Abhidhamma Pitaka, or Higher Teachings, reframes the doctrines presented in the Sutta Pitaka to bring a framework of understanding to analyses of the nature of mental and physical existence.

THE MAHAYANA SCHOOL AND ITS SCRIPTURES

The Mahayana school of Buddhism focuses on universal compassion and the ideal of selflessness as exhibited by the Bodhisattva. Native Mahayana Buddhism is practiced today in China, Japan, Korea, and most of Vietnam. In addition to the Nikaya scriptures, which are the sole scriptures of Theravada Buddhism, Mahayana schools also recognize sutras (written in Sanskrit) that are concerned with the purpose of achieving Buddhahood. Buddhahood is achieved by following the path of the Bodhisattva over eons of time. However, given the large amount of time that this enlightenment is explained to take, many schools of Mahayana Buddhism allow for the concept of *working toward* enlightenment in a Pure Land or an environment that is highly conducive to the enlightenment process.

In addition to the Nikaya scriptures, the Mahayana scriptures consist of sutras, such as the Lotus Sutra, the Heart Sutra, and the Diamond Sutra. The Lotus Sutra, originally written in Sanskrit between 100 B.C.E. and 200 C.E., is considered one of the most influential Mahayana scriptures, and has as a key message the idea of *upaya* or skill-in-means. In the sutra, *upaya* is witnessed as the Buddha adapts his teachings to a specific audience of saints, monks, nuns, and Bodhisattvas.

The Heart Sutra, which is believed to have been written around the first century B.C.E., is only a page in length but is considered to be extremely influential, particularly in its teaching of *sunyata* or emptiness, referring here to an absence of the sense of self or essence of emptiness within all conditioned phenomena.

The Diamond Sutra represents a dialogue between the Buddha and the disciple Subhuti during which the Buddha teaches that both the self and the world around us are ultimately illusory.

THE VAJRAYANA SCHOOL AND ITS SCRIPTURES

Native Vajrayana is practiced today mainly in Tibet, Nepal, Bhutan, Mongolia, Kalmykia, and areas of India, China, and Japan. The Vajrayana school of Buddhism is framed on Theravada and Mahayana teachings, but also include the Buddhist tantras, which provide spiritual techniques aimed at refining Buddhist practice and supporting one's path toward enlightenment.

INFLUENCE ON SPIRITUAL DEVELOPMENT

There is a vast array of Buddhist scriptures (beyond what is described herein) that represent a wide diversity of teachings. As with any major religion or philosophy that is captured and sustained by the words within its leading texts, Buddhist scriptures provide adherents and those interested in learning more about the life and practice of the Buddha with the sustenance and guidance to promote religious and spiritual development. As the scriptures are shared with followers around the world, the beauty of the Buddha's life and his teachings will continue to have a positive impact on the lives of Buddhists and those who are touched by the beauty of his teachings.

—Elizabeth M. Dowling

See also Buddha; Buddhism; Religious texts

FURTHER READING

Hagen, S. (2003). *Buddhism is not what you think: Finding freedom beyond beliefs*. New York: HarperCollins.

Nhat Hanh, T. (1998). *The heart of Buddha's teachings*. Berkeley, CA: Thich Nhat Hanh.

Wikipedia. (2005). Buddhist scripture. Retrieved March 24, 2005 from www.en.wikipedia.org/wiki/Buddhist.

BUNYAN, JOHN

John Bunyan is one of the most popular religious writers in English. His most famous work, *The Pilgrim's Progress*, has been more widely read, and translated into more languages, than any other 17th-century text apart from the Authorized Version of the Bible. As a Puritan classic, *The Pilgrim's Progress* combines two aspects of spirituality that are rarely found together. The first is practical spirituality—the application of biblical doctrines and principles to the practical details of everyday social and domestic life. The book is written from a perspective of total Christian commitment and abounds with references and allusions to the Bible, and yet at the same time it is based on close observation and an intimate knowledge of ordinary people, their foibles, predicaments, and mundane lives. The second kind of spirituality is artistic, and involves the original, creative use of attributes and capacities like the imagination. Bunyan's achievement is to fuse these two dimensions of spirituality by representing Puritan virtues and values through allegory rather than through anecdote or direct description.

What is most remarkable is that this fusing of dimensions was achieved by a writer of humble origins with little formal education who spent many years of his adult life in prison. Bunyan was born near Bedford in England in 1628, the son of a tinker. He followed his father's trade intermittently, although he also spent 3 youthful years in the parliamentary army. A conversion experience in his mid-20s led him to lay preaching at a Free Church in Bedford, and he also began writing theological and evangelical texts. The restoration of Charles II to the English throne in 1660, however, curtailed the freedom of nonconformist preachers, and he was arrested for holding a "conventicle" (an illegal religious meeting). His absolute refusal to submit to the discipline of the Church of England meant that his prison sentence was drawn out from the original 3 months to a total of 12 years. The prison regime was fairly relaxed, however, and he was free to read and write, to preach inside and sometimes even outside the prison, and to support his family by making shoelaces. After 1672, he was less troubled by the religious authorities, and apart from one further brief imprisonment in 1677 he continued preaching as far away as London until his death in 1688.

The Pilgrim's Progress was begun in prison, but not published until 1678. It is an allegory describing the adventures of the hero Christian on his journey from the City of Destruction to the Celestial City. The symbolic names of characters (such as Faithful, the giant Despair, Mr. Worldly Wiseman and Little-faith) and places (the Slough of Despond, Vanity Fair, Doubting-Castle) point to the author's intention of identifying Christian vices and virtues, satirizing human vanity and hypocrisy, and drawing attention to the difficulties that beset anyone trying to live a truly Christian life. The purpose of the story is thus a spiritual and moral one, but its simple, homely style has made the story accessible to children, who (as with the stories of C. S. Lewis) may appreciate the adventures without fully understanding the spiritual symbolism until later. The second part of the story, published in 1684, tells how Christian's wife Christiana makes the same pilgrimage.

Altogether, Bunyan wrote some 60 works. Apart from *The Pilgrim's Progress*, the most famous is his autobiographical *Grace Abounding to the Chief of Sinners* (1666), which describes the long spiritual struggles he underwent in his 20s, leading to his career as a preacher. His influence on the development of English literature is significant, and can be detected particularly in Defoe and the early English novel. But his influence on the spiritual life of the country is arguably his most lasting achievement.

—J. Mark Halstead

FURTHER READING

Bacon, E. W. (1983). *John Bunyan: Pilgrim and dreamer.* Grand Rapids, MI: Baker Book House.

Bunyan, J. (1984). *The pilgrim's progress.* (Ed. N. H. Keeble). Oxford: Oxford University Press.

Bunyan, J. (2002). *Grace abounding to the chief of sinners.* New Kensington, PA: Whitaker House.

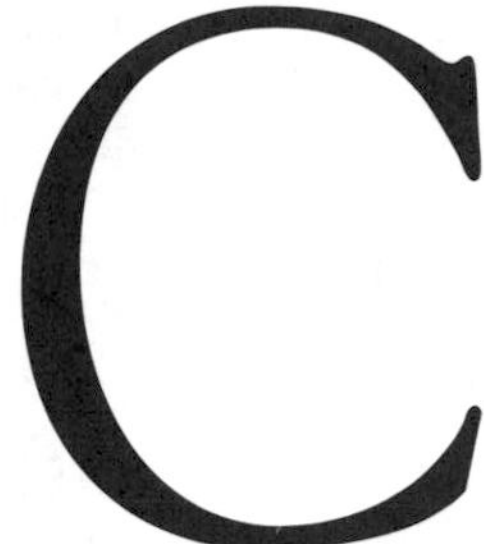

CATHOLICISM

All Catholics are Christian, but not all Christians are Catholics. So the confusion begins. Christians accept that Jesus of Nazareth is the Christ or Messiah of history, and is divine and rose from the dead; all Catholics believe this. Catholicism has been the decisive spiritual force in the history of Western civilization. Catholicism is not an island; rather, it is a continent, an entire world extending across 2,000 years and embracing more than 800 million people in every country on Earth. Catholicism is a way of being human, a way of being religious, and finally, a way of being Christian.

Catholicism touches every aspect of life and excludes none. But how does Catholicism differ from Christianity? First, Catholicism is about Catholic, which means universal. Catholicism is not about a national church, but rather a worldwide one. It is truly an international and multicultural institution. One of the first great councils of Church leaders met in Nicea in 325 and came up with the Nicean Creed. This prayer is prayed in every Catholic Church throughout the world. In it there are four "marks" of the Church: One, Holy, Catholic, and Apostolic. Prayers, worship, and ritual reflect the local church in language, music, and sacred art.

Catholicism today has a very optimistic view of creation and the human person. Creation and the human person are seen as fundamentally good. This has not always been the case. There have been points in history when the human person and the world were seen as being evil or corrupt. Only the spiritual was to be encouraged, not the body, worldliness, or sensuality. Thankfully, a more optimistic outlook eventually prevailed, which allowed Catholicism to underwrite sculpture, painting, stained glass windows, music, drama, plays, and scientific inquiry.

Catholicism is about holiness and wholeness. All people are to be holy every day, not just on Sunday at worship. Holiness recognizes that one needs a savior, and one cannot live in isolation. A community, the church, is needed. People are called to holiness as a group in holiness and wholeness, living up to their fullest potential. All people, every day. There is a fundamental dignity to all persons because they are all created in God's image and likeness. Catholicism attempts to hold on to the "and": faith and reason, grace and nature, spirit and soul. Yes, one is "saved," but one is not yet with God in heaven. There is a lifetime of trying to put one's faith into action.

There is a strong commitment in Catholicism to social transformation. One's relationship with God is in direct proportion to one's caring for those on the fringes of society. The early Church cared for widows, orphans, and the sick and dying. Throughout the history of the Church, leaders and common folk were always speaking up for those who were forgotten or neglected. In the United States, there was strong support for the early labor unions and workers' rights. A Roman Catholic priest, John Augustan Ryan, came up with the economic principles for a "just wage," which later became the reality of the minimum wage.

Catholicism has a profound sense of history, good and bad. Yes, there have been many sad and tragic times in the history of the Church. These should never be overlooked or whitewashed. But at these times men and women called by and inspired by God called the leadership and the entire Church back to foundational concepts.

Catholicism today has a profound respect for human knowledge. One needs to remember that after philosophy, theology is the oldest intellectual discipline. Theology is faith seeking understanding. There is a need to accept and study sacred texts and sacred tradition. There is a need to allow for the insights of reason and experience to show who and what the human person is. Science is not the enemy. Blind faith is not part of Catholicism.

There are 26 different branches of Catholicism, known as "rites." In the West, most are familiar with Roman Catholicism. But there are also the Armenian, Byzantine, Coptic, Ethiopian, Chaldean, Syrian, and Maronite rite Catholics, as well as the very large Eastern-rite Catholics who separated from Rome in 1054. Some Catholics accept the leadership of the Holy Father or the Pope in Rome; others would just see him as another bishop, or perhaps the first among equals.

Catholicism completely permeates the roots of European culture, art, and literature, from the beginnings of modern science in the 13th century to the foundations of nursing and mass education in the 19th century. Catholics have contributed to the arts, sciences, and humanities. In certain cases, they have brought with them a greater depth and vision precisely because of their faith. In the music of Palestrina, Elgar, or Messiaen, the poetry of Dante, the paintings of Giotto, Fra Angelico or Michelangelo, the plays of Shakespeare, the novels of Evelyn Waugh or Flannery O'Connor (the list could be extended indefinitely), one can clearly trace a Catholic spirit. One can see this also in other fields, in the contributions of E. F. Schumacher to environmental economics, of Mary Douglas and Rene Girard to anthropology, and of Alasdair MacIntyre and Charles Taylor to contemporary philosophy. The Catholic spirit exists not just in Europe, but on every continent. In fact, every country has its own expression of the faith, from the martyrs of Nagasaki to the apparitions of Our Lady of Guadalupe.

In the end, Catholicism is characterized by three main ideas: sacramentality, mediation, and communion. The special configuration of these ideas within Catholicism makes it unique. Catholicism is a tradition that sees God in all things (sacramentality), using the human, the material, and the finite (mediation) to bring about the unity of the human family (communion).

—Rev. David M. O'Leary

FURTHER READING

De Lubac, H. (1958). *Catholicism: A study of the corporate destiny of mankind.* New York: Sheed & Ward.

Dulles, A. (1985). *The catholicity of the Church.* Oxford: Clarendon Press.

McBrien, R. P. (1994). *Catholicism.* New York: Harper.

CHILD AND YOUTH CARE

Child and youth care (CYC) is a professional field focused on the care and nurture of children and youth, which currently includes concern for spiritual development in its approach to children and youth. The field, which is international in scope with strong European roots (where it is sometimes called psycho-education) combines concern for the both the educational and developmental needs of children. CYC work, which may be located in schools, hospitals, jails, youth centers and clubs, churches, care agencies, residential settings, and so on, focuses on the healthy development and best interests of children and youth. CYC draws on a number of operational principles:

1. The growth and development of children and youth is central to understanding them in the context of their life space or environment. Children and youth are always embedded in contexts that include their familial, social, cultural, and political circumstances and history which shape their lives.

2. Children and youth need to be viewed from a perspective of social competence rather than from a pathology-based orientation. They have skills, insight, and understanding based on a range of positive and negative experiences. They are always making choices and negotiating for the best outcomes for themselves, and need responsive care in the midst of their daily lives, and especially in the face of conflict, distress, and difficulty.

3. In order to meet children and youth in the midst of their lives, child and youth care workers develop therapeutic relationships with them and their families, engaging in direct day-to-day work with children and youth in their environments. Children live their days in family, personal, public and institutional settings and CYC professionals go into those environments to support and accompany children.

In the United Nations Convention on the Rights of the Child (UNCRC) (1989), spiritual development is acknowledged as an area of childhood development worthy of protection. Articles 17, 27, and 32 call for both standards of living that would allow, and legislation that would protect, children and youth from economic exploitation that would prevent them from experiencing healthy physical, mental, spiritual, moral, and social development. Note that religion is protected under separate articles that include other elements of education, cultural heritage, and practice (see Articles 14, 29, and 30).

As well, competency standards established in North America for CYC professionals reflect these assumptions and list spiritual development as one of seven areas of development that CYC workers are expected to be aware of as foundational knowledge for their practice.

It is clear that children and youth can and do have spiritual experiences, beginning in their younger years, often without the explicit awareness or support of adults, and that those experiences can and do affect their ways of perceiving the world and being in it. Because children live in families and cultures, they may also have particular religious traditions that shape them and their ways. They may have spiritual experiences and develop spiritually with or without a religious context. Some children's spiritual experiences may be private and internal, and not dependent on religious content, knowledge, or context. Other children may have a close relationship between their spiritual experience and their religious understanding of that experience.

This distinction is important for CYC workers who are employed in a wide range of settings where they must work with children and their families in culturally appropriate and sensitive ways that respect family traditions, including religious beliefs, while being concerned for the healthy spiritual development of children and youth. Professional ethics require that a particular religious or doctrinal position must not be presumed or imposed on the child, youth, or family, and that at the same time the CYC worker responds to the family respecting their existing religious or nonreligious position.

Attention to spiritual development in CYC is currently hindered by the lack of readily available materials and research to support a knowledge base for practice and in the training of CYC professionals. Only the most recent life-span development texts include references to spirituality or spiritual development, and confusion persists that tends to equate religion and spirituality.

Research in the field is beginning to show that children and youth, from early in their lives, have a wide range of intuitive and beyond-the-self experiences that can have significant impact on them. Because children are, for the most part, living in environments where those experiences are ignored, belittled, or denied, they have not been given the opportunity to express, interpret, and integrate those experiences into their developmental processes.

Questions are being raised about the impact of significant childhood life experiences that are not given space in a child's life. There is concern that suppression of these experiences may either sever children from confidence in their own perceptions and experience, or cut them off from a wider range of emotional experience rendering them less sensitive to others and perhaps to their own needs. The concern is that this may be making them vulnerable to a range of higher-risk behaviors harmful to either themselves or others. If healthy development requires attention to spiritual processes and experience, it is the responsibility of CYC professionals to broaden their understanding of the lives of children and youth to include spiritual development, and to create safe nurturing environments where children can explore and express their spiritual selves.

—Daniel G. Scott

FURTHER READING

Anglin, J. (1999). The uniqueness of child and youth care: A personal perspective. *Child and Youth Care Forum, 28*(2), 143–150.

Association for Child and Youth Care Practice. Retrieved from www.acycp.org/index.htm.

ChildSpirit Institute. Retrieved from www.childspirit.net.

The Children and WorldViews Project. Retrieved from www .cwvp.com/.

Fewster, G. (1990). Growing together: The personal relationship in child and youth care. In J. P. Anglin, C. J. Denholm, R. V. Ferguson, & A. R. Pence (Eds.), *Perspectives in professional child and youth care* (pp. 25–39). New York: Hawthorne Press.

The International Child and Youth Care Network. Retrieved from www.cyc-net.org/.

Maier, H.W. (1991). Developmental foundations of child and youth care work. In J. Beker & Z. Eisikovits (Eds.), *Knowledge utilization in residential child and youth care practice* (pp. 25–48). Washington, DC: Child Welfare League of America, Inc.

Mattingly, M.S.C., & VanderVen, K. (2001). Proposed competencies for professional child and youth care work personnel (March). International Child and Youth Care Network. Retrieved from www.cyc-net.org/pdf/competencies.pdf.

United Nations. 1989. *Convention on the rights of the child.* Geneva: United Nations.

CHILDHOOD EXPERIENCES

In reaction to the challenges posed by a 21st-century postmodern cultural context, religious communities are grappling with how to provide effective spiritual education for youth. The goal of these activities is to provide a firm foundation of childhood spiritual experience so that youth may subsequently take their place as committed adult members of the religious community.

Some methods employed are traditional in nature, while others evidence a willingness to experiment. These include cultivating knowledge and awareness of foundational sacred texts, modeling the faith for youth to observe it in action, encouraging youth to practice spiritual disciplines, including youth in religious ceremonies and services, and involving youth in mission and other cross-cultural experiences.

CULTIVATION OF AWARENESS OF FOUNDATIONAL SACRED TEXTS

Foundational sacred texts serve to ground youth in the spiritual beliefs, traditions, and ethical norms of the religious community. In Judaism, the tradition of passing on knowledge of God's law is as ancient as the religion itself (see Deuteronomy 6). Since the 19th century, Protestant Christianity has emphasized the importance of youthful study of the Bible through the now ubiquitous Sunday school program. Islam stresses the need for children to learn both the Qu'ran and Hadith. Beginning in 1988, the Gita Society embarked on an ambitious campaign to produce age-appropriate children's materials on the teachings of Hinduism's foundational text, the Bhagavad Gita.

Often, the teaching of a language accompanies the study of the sacred text. Examples of this practice include the study of Hebrew by Jewish children, Sanskrit by Hindu children, and Arabic by Muslim students.

ADULTS MODELING SPIRITUALITY FOR YOUTH

The interaction between youth and adults is a key component to spiritual development. In ancient Confucian philosophy, the subordination of youth to their elders exemplified this connection. Similarly, in contemporary practice of spiritual formation children and youth begins with the adults in their lives taking responsibility for living what they teach. Accordingly, adult leaders are expected to practice the religion's spiritual disciplines and model faithfulness to the precepts and values of their religious community.

For example, in the Youth Ministry and Spirituality Project coordinated by the San Francisco Seminary, adult leaders of local church youth ministries form a small supportive community dedicated to cultivating a contemplative life. Each member is asked to practice disciplines of *lectio divina* (a form of spiritual reading of Scripture) or silent contemplative prayer for at least 10 minutes a day, enter into a spiritual direction relationship in order to promote accountability, and engage in a monthly reflection exercise with other leaders to discover how God is moving in and through their ministry with youth. The leaders' lives communicate spirituality by example instead of by mere assertion.

This spirituality based model of youth education is notable for two features—a lack of dependence on a single paid professional youth pastor and the intentional inclusion of youth into the faith community's journey. Layperson teams that are accountable to pastoral staff often serve as their spiritual directors. The interaction between these lay leaders and children symbolizes the acceptance, caring and love of youth by the larger adult faith community. Wisdom and nurture are meant to flow through intergenerational interaction. Instead of segregating youth, this model encourages youth to interact with other generations as equal partners.

ENCOURAGING YOUTH TO PRACTICE SPIRITUAL DISCIPLINES

Youth are yearning for direct spiritual encounters of the divine presence and authentic practices which will facilitate such experience. As a result, they are very open to learning about and experimenting with classical spiritual disciplines. In Taiwan, for example, Chinese Buddhists are emulating Christian Protestants by sponsoring youth religious camps. Children gain experience in Buddhist meditation, chanting, and singing, and also receive instruction in the Four Noble Truths. In the United States, the Hindu community has initiated a youth meeting program called Bal Gokulam, which features prayer recitation, readings from Hindu texts, and opportunities for socialization with other Hindu youth.

Regarding Christian Bible study in both Roman Catholic and Protestant settings, *lectio divina* is being applied in youth group settings. Through repeated readings of a Biblical text, youth are encouraged to listen to their own hearts and the voice of the Spirit speaking through the passage. When practiced in a group setting, sharing takes place in an atmosphere of quiet attentiveness. The goal is to cultivate a spirit of contemplative reflection and awareness in each person, as opposed to teaching a preconceived lesson to the group.

Journal writing is another classical form of spiritual reflection that has gained a measure of acceptance among youth. Whether in a *blog* (an online journal that others are invited to read and even respond to by posting reactions) or a more traditional paper journal, contemporary youth seem comfortable with examining their daily experience as an act of spiritual exploration. This also corresponds with the postmodern emphasis on sharing one's narrative as an act of self-expression and truth sharing.

Not all contemporary Biblical exercises for youth hearken back to classical sources for their inspiration. Versions of the New Testament that are packaged in youth-oriented, magazine-style format are popular among older youth and teenagers. These modern-language Bibles focus on questions that are culturally relevant (such as how to get along with one's parents, dating Godly partners, and beauty secrets). If *lectio divina* seeks to foster the soul's desire to discern God's subtle presence, trendy texts for teens respond to the youthful need to respond to the loud and insistent voice of contemporary culture.

PARTICIPATING IN RELIGIOUS CEREMONIES AND SERVICES

Religious rites and ceremonies for children are characteristic of most religions. Hindu rituals are related to the conception, birth, naming, first feeding of the newborn child, and later on in childhood, his or her religious initiation (for boys born into the Brahmin caste, for example, at age 8), while Yoruba Muslims living in West Africa practice naming ceremonies for children upon their birth (see Carmody & Carmody). The Jewish practices of circumcision for male infants and the bar/bat mitzvah for teenagers are well-known rites of passage. In Eastern Orthodoxy, Roman Catholicism, and some Protestant denominations, infant baptism and confirmation are analogous to Jewish practices. In Protestant denominations that reserve baptism for those consciously embracing their faith, child/parent dedication ceremonies are now commonplace.

Many children and youth prefer to be active participants in the intergenerational religious ceremonies and worship experiences that their faith community offers. To be sure, there has always been a place for youth participation in the past (e.g., children's messages), but the current generation of youth desire to be leaders as well as congregants. They want to impact others and not just receive instruction. Inclusion and partnership with adults rather than passivity characterize their understanding of their place in worship services.

With the rise of contemporary praise worship in Protestant churches, youth can help direct worship service experiences by being part of the praise and worship team (which leads the singing) or the instrumental praise band. Variations on this theme include youth bell choirs and puppet ministries. Youth are involved in such innovative areas as liturgical dance and religious drama. In some settings, the traditional acolyte team is being retooled to include more youth in worship leadership roles (candle lighting, public Scripture reading, leading of responsive readings, and prayers). The rising use of multimedia presentations is also an acknowledgment that youthful expressions of devotion are informing the worship experiences of all generations.

Challenges also have emerged in this regard. Many children and youth who are visiting and attending youth groups come from home environments where religious teaching, training, and practice have been nonexistent or from families challenged by divorce and relational disruptions. Such youth often need to be oriented to the expectations and norms of the youth group setting in regards to acceptable behavior, dress, and use of language. It cannot be assumed that they will have even a cursory knowledge of the faith community's beliefs, religious ritual, or behavioral expectations. Meeting their psychological, social, and religious needs, while simultaneously serving the different needs of youth raised in the religious tradition, is often difficult. There is no consensus on how to address this challenge. Some youth groups create parallel tracks that tailor lessons according to the level of assimilation or spiritual maturity youth manifest, and provide social activities that include all youth. Other youth groups encourage core youth to be positive role models and mentors for new and less assimilated members.

EMBRACING MISSION AND CROSS-CULTURAL EXPERIENCES

Children in the 21st century live in a multicultural world. Diversity for them is not a theoretical idea, but a commonplace aspect of daily existence, whether in their neighborhood, school, or house of worship. In order to foster understanding and peaceful coexistence, many youth groups add a comparative religion component to their youth group experience. This may entail using a curriculum that examines other religions and compares their beliefs and practices to one's own, or visiting other houses of worship.

The familiar youth group trip is also being transformed by the desire to experience other cultures. Many youth groups are forsaking such time-worn activities as ski trip retreats for more adventurous undertakings, such as short-term trips to other countries. Although educational in nature, there is almost always some service component built into the cross-cultural encounter. A youth group from the heartland of the United States may visit a Mexican church and teach in a vacation Bible school. A youth choral or bell choir might organize a tour and visit several locations over a 2-week period. Or, teenagers might travel to the Caribbean to help build a church school wing. Increasingly, cross-cultural travel is becoming a two-way street. Countries that traditionally have hosted visitors are now sending youth delegations to other countries.

The benefits from these cross-cultural experiences are many. For the youth themselves, exposure to other cultures enlarges their worldview, increases their appreciation of their own culture, and gives them an opportunity to express and apply their faith. Congregations that sponsor the youth mission events also benefit from this exchange. Their adult members are given an opportunity to express support for their youth (financially as well as through prayer), and are often surprised by how the youth group's postmission trip presentation affects their own religious presuppositions and perceptions. The host congregations benefit as well. Resources for needed projects are received, supportive relationships and positive friendships are established, and follow-up opportunities for continuing interaction (such as ongoing sister church relationships) become possible.

—Lee B. Spitzer

FURTHER READING

Brooker, W. (1990). *Storyweaving: You and your faith journey.* Judson Church Membership Resources for Growing Disciples Series. Valley Forge, PA: Judson Press.

Carmody, D. L., & Carmody, J. T. (1993). *Ways to the center: an introduction to world religions* (4th ed.) Belmont, CA: Wadsworth.

The Gita Society. Retrieved from www.gita-society.com.

Huesser, D. B., & Huesser, P. (1985). *Children as partners in the church.* Valley Forge, PA: Judson Press.

Revolve: The complete New Testament. (2003). Nashville, TN: Thomas Nelson.

San Francisco Theological Seminary, Youth Ministry and Spirituality Project. Retrieved from www.sfts.edu/nc/resources/index.cfm/fuseaction/ ymsp/fuse/welcome/.

CHILD'S GOD

Against the backdrop of a long tradition of research emphasizing the anthropomorphic quality of children's concepts of God, recent research on children's representations of God have demonstrated how readily children may entertain strikingly nonhuman properties for God. In contrast to the popular view that children's concept of God begins as understanding God as a human who might live in the sky, even 3- to 6-year-olds seem to enjoy the requisite conceptual equipment to understand God as superknowing, superperceiving, the cosmic creator, and perhaps, immortal. Indeed, naturally occurring biases in how children conceptualize any intentional agent may encourage them to understand God in superhuman terms. In other words, children's agent concepts appear flexible enough and eager to accommodate superhuman properties.

As soon as children begin to demonstrate understanding of a particular dimension of human minds, they likewise discriminate to which minds that dimension applies, and readily apply superhuman properties to God. Thus, as children are learning that humans are fallible, they are resistant to including these features in their concept of God. This suggests that reasoning accurately (theologically speaking) about some of God's characteristics may come easier than reasoning accurately about the fallible form these characteristics take in humans.

GOD AS SUPERKNOWING

Developmental research in the theory of mind area over the past two decades converges on the conclusion that young children have an early bias to overestimate the knowledge and belief-accuracy of others. This bias to assume superknowledge of others renders young children (e.g., 3- to 4-year-olds) able to reason more accurately about God than about their parents, because unlike their parents, God is indeed superknowing. A series of experiments conducted by Barrett and Richert with 3- to 7-year-olds both in the United States and Mexico among the Yukatec Maya, has demonstrated that even when children begin to understand the fallible nature of beliefs and limitations on knowledge, they may continue to reason about God as superknowing. That is, they need not anthropomorphize. Some evidence suggests that even 3-year-olds begin to discriminate God's mind as more knowledgeable than other minds.

GOD AS SUPERPERCEIVING

Similar to their tendency to overestimate others' knowledge, 3-year-olds often have difficulty understanding that just because they perceive something a certain way, not anyone or everyone else perceives it the same way. Consequently, they might mistakenly assume that the book page that appears right-side up to them also appears right-side up to their mothers, for whom it is actually upside down. By age 5, children's ability to appreciate another's visual perspective approximates that of adults. Two sets of studies by Richert that investigated children's understanding of seeing, hearing, and smelling, support these findings. While the youngest children reported that a human would be able to see, smell, and hear things that were actually imperceptible, and the oldest children said that the human would not, a large majority of all children answered that God would perceive all. Even young children embraced decidedly different properties for God as compared with humans.

GOD AS CREATOR

Other lines of research have questioned the prevalence of what Piaget termed "childhood artificialism," or the notion that the natural world was created by humans, and suggests that very young children can also understand God as distinct from humans in creative capability. Petrovich has shown that British preschool-aged children are rather disinclined to credit people with the creation of natural things, and also that they are up to seven times as likely to attribute origins of natural objects to God instead of people. Other studies support the notion that children may have strong dispositions to understand the world as created, but not created by humans.

Evans asked American 5- to 10-year-old children to rate their agreement with various origin accounts. She found that regardless of whether parents taught evolution-based origins to their children, children vastly favored creationist accounts of origins for animals over evolutionist, artificialist, or emergentist accounts (that animals just appeared). Similarly, Kelemen found that young children have strong inclinations to understand both living and nonliving things as purposeful. They see living and nonliving things as possessing attributes purposefully designed to help them or serve themselves or other things. Kelemen has even raised the possibility that children naturally develop as "intuitive theists," and religious instruction merely fills in the forms that already exist in children's minds.

GOD AS IMMORTAL

Other research by Giminez, Guerrero, and Harris has tested when children understand that God is immortal, but that people are not. Three- to five-year-old children were interviewed about whether their friends and God (1) existed when there were dinosaurs in the world, (2) were a little baby at one time, (3) will get older and older, and (4) will die someday. Although the results may underestimate children's understanding of God's immortality because of nativity stories (God was once a baby), findings from this research are comparable to those of the research on children's theory of mind. The youngest children showed a tendency to underestimate human mortality, and by the age of any robust appreciation of human mortality, they already understood God as immortal. Immortality was, perhaps, easier for young children to understand than mortality.

CONCLUSION

Research on the divine attributes reviewed above suggests that young children seem to (1) have developmentally endowed cognitive predispositions to entertain these properties for intentional beings, and (2) have to pare back these properties as applied to humans. Human conceptual structures thereby help to explain why children are so willing to accept, and even seem to assume, that God is superknowing, superperceiving, has creative power, and is immortal. Hence, the development of God concepts, at least along these dimensions, may be characterized as simply adhering to assumptions that come naturally. It is human attributes such as limited knowledge and perception and mortality that must be learned. These predispositions help to explain the ease with which children seem to accept the possibility that God exists and is quite different from any other intentional being that they have encountered.

—Rebekah Richert and Justin L. Barrett

See also God

FURTHER READING

Barrett, J. L., & Richert, R. A. (2003). Anthropomorphism or preparedness? Exploring children's concept of God. *Review of Religious Research, 44,* 300–312.

Elkind, D. (1970). The origins of religion in the child. *Review of Religious Research, 12,* 35–42.

Evans, E. M. (2001). Cognitive and contextual factors in the emergence of diverse belief systems: Creation versus evolution. *Cognitive Psychology, 42,* 217–266.

Flavell, J. H. (1999). Cognitive development: Children's knowledge about the mind. *Annual Review of Psychology, 50,* 21–45.

Giminez, M., Guerrero, S., & Harris, P. L. (in press). *Understanding the impossible: Intimations of immortality and omniscience in early childhood.*

Goldman, R. G. (1964). *Religious thinking from childhood to adolescence.* London: Routledge and Kegan Paul.

Kelemen, D. (2004). Are children "intuitive theists"?: Reasoning about purpose and design in nature. *Psychological Science, 15*(5), 295–301.

Petrovich, O. (1999). Preschool children's understanding of the dichotomy between the natural and the artificial. *Psychological Reports, 84,* 3–27.

Piaget, J. (1929). *The child's conception of the world.* New York: Harcourt Brace.

Wellman, H., Cross, D., & Watson, J. (2001). Meta-analysis of theory of mind development: The truth about false-belief. *Child Development, 72,* 655–684.

CHRISTIANITY

Measured by the numbers of people who call themselves Christians, Christianity is by far the most successful religious tradition. By some accounts, almost a third of the world's population is Christian. However, if measured by its track record for whether members/believers have been faithful to their tradition and have treated others well, the Christian tradition has suffered serious problems. Christianity is no different from other faith traditions in having a history defined by both good and evil. However, because Christians have held great political and military power, the extremes seem to have been exaggerated. All too often, power has corrupted, either in the form of religious imperialism or in some other form, such as using religion to dominate others. As one critic put it, the Church (meaning the worldwide community of Christians) has always been an argument against becoming a Christian.

So, why has Christianity had such tremendous appeal and success? The answer points to one of the many ironies in the Christian tradition. This most dominant and powerful religion has as its central focus the life of a poor carpenter who preached in direct opposition to acquiring worldly rather than spiritual power. To understand Christianity, then, is to understand the life of Jesus and the experience of those who have felt they have known and been transformed by Jesus.

Historians have made much of the fact that by modern standards, what we know for sure about Jesus is not much. In fact, a century ago, some questioned whether Jesus ever existed. However, today, that view has been replaced with one stating we can be sure enough about a few essentials, and that these essentials are sufficient to tell the story.

The story is about a Jew in a politically oppressed backwater who was virtually unknown until, around the age of 30, he carried out a brief public ministry that ended in his being executed. He left no written record and no visible organization. His followers were common people without influence, political or otherwise. By this account, the life of Jesus was hardly a life to found a great religious tradition on.

However, what is missing in this account is Jesus, the man himself and his profound impact on all who came in contact with him. Jesus was a charismatic figure, meaning that he was more than just attractive. He seemed to have a special power. It was natural for the people of that time to think in terms of two worlds, the tangible world present to our senses and the invisible, spirit world. Jesus was charismatic inasmuch as he seemed filled with the power that comes from being connected to the spirit world.

Throughout history, there have been many charismatic religious leaders who now are largely forgotten.

Jesus was different. First, he was radically good, and in ways that made others want to be good as well. His concern was always with individuals, all individuals. He not only preached an egalitarian ethic of universal love, he lived it. Tax collectors, prostitutes, the rich, and the poor were all treated with the same loving concern, with perhaps only one exception. For those who took pride in their own righteousness and who preached a kind of righteousness that excluded compassion and love, Jesus expressed contempt. His loving nature was not, therefore, indiscriminate.

Jesus' impact on others had, then, much to do with his ethics and his character. However, ethics and character do not by themselves explain Jesus. History has shown us many good men and women who stood for truth, but none have come close to having the impact that Jesus has had. There is, then, more to the story of Jesus than his having charisma and character.

What makes the story of Jesus exceptional is the way that it has been experienced as a profound reconciliation between God and humankind. To understand Christianity is, then, to understand what Jesus was saying about God. It is also to understand how others experienced Jesus as offering not just a way to God, but also *the* way.

God is a symbol, a symbol with many meanings. Within the Christian faith tradition itself, there are many meanings. However, for Jesus, one meaning was all-important. For Jesus, God is not some impersonal force or power that set the universe in motion and then stepped back to simply watch. For Jesus, God is intensely personal, as evidenced in his referring to God as "Father." Furthermore, for Jesus, God is compassionate and loving—so much so that it would not be a distortion to say that, for Jesus, God *is* love. Finally, for Jesus, the love of God is powerful. It is a love that can bring about the seemingly impossible, including the saving of lost souls.

To understand Christianity, then, requires understanding what Jesus meant by salvation. Christianity has been so successful not because it has been aligned with political power, but because its followers have found in Jesus' life and words something profoundly true about the human condition.

The first truth is that, hard as we may try, we cannot save ourselves. Most of us backslide and fall short of living as we should. Most of us are anxious and doubting when we feel we should be calm and sure. Most of us never quite free ourselves of the tyranny of selfish desires, and of the one, great desire to promote, serve, and save ourselves. Most of us, then, have feelings that collectively add up to our feeling we are less than we should be, or, to use the Christian's metaphor, that we are less than what we were intended to be, namely, images of God.

This widespread, if not universal, experience of being less than we should be is also the experience of being cut off or separated from God—an experience that leads us to the second truth revealed in the Jesus story. Try as we might to connect to God, we are doomed to failure if we assume that we can take control. The essence of Christianity is, in a way, a terrifying essence, or at least one that creates anxiety when one fully realizes what is required.

What is required of the Christian is nothing less than giving oneself and one's control to God or, as the Quakers put it, "Let go and let God." This is terrifying, in part, because giving up control to another can in and of itself be terrifying. But for those realizing the true nature of the Christian call, it is terrifying mainly because the call is to a way of life so radically different from ordinary life as to seem, at times, otherworldly.

Here we come to perhaps the most important concept in Jesus' teaching, namely, the concept of the "Kingdom of God." Jesus' "Good News" for others was that the Kingdom of God is not some far away place or some afterlife residence. Jesus preached that the Kingdom of God is "among you," even if we cannot see or measure it.

In essence, Jesus was saying that the spirit and tangible worlds are connecting again, and that it is possible for each individual to be transformed or saved by reconnecting to that which He called the Kingdom of God. This spirit world is not a world of primitive magic, although to the outsider, Christianity has always seemed to have magic at its core. This spirit world is where (the word *where* functions here simply as a metaphor) God's will is done, where God and human unite, and where the community of humankind is itself united as members of a single spiritual body.

Salvation, then, is not from this or that individual sin, for sin is not to be thought of in the plural only or mainly (i.e., as a collection of sins). Sin is the one, great, original sin defined in the Adam and Eve myth, the sin of eternal separation between God and humankind. To Christians, Jesus has returned to us that state of being known before Adam and Eve's fall, that state of being in total communion with God, which gives power and contentment so great that we no longer fear anything, death included.

This brief summary suggests, then, that Christianity is, at its core, a radical faith, one calling for a renunciation of the old, this-world way of living, in order to live life as if in a spiritual world. Furthermore, it is radical in its emphasis on giving up control, on letting go and giving up the pretense that we can save ourselves.

The story of Christianity's essence might end here were it not for the fact that in so ending, we still would have no satisfying explanation of how the tradition spread so quickly to eventually take over the Western world. We need, then, to say a few words about the development of Christianity following Jesus' crucifixion.

The key figure in the early years was Saul of Tarsus, better known as St. Paul. St. Paul, a Jew and Roman citizen, lived after Jesus' death. At one time he actively participated in persecuting Christians, but, after a dramatic conversion experience, he became by far the most influential figure in establishing Christianity as a religion not just for Jews but for all. He did so by constantly traveling to energize and support the budding urban Christian communities dotting the Mediterranean world, but also by shaping Christian thought through his letters.

That thought had as its essence two main ideas. The first was the idea that Jesus lives not in the sense of still walking about, preaching and healing, but in the sense that he lives within those who have taken him into themselves, as Paul felt that he had taken Jesus into himself. The message of Paul was, then, a message not about theology but about personal experience, including his own and those of others as well. The other main idea was about love. While, as pointed out above, Jesus' own preaching and actions make clear that the mystery of God is bound up with the mystery of love, Paul led the community of Christians in a direction that, centuries later, culminated in the formulation of the Nicene and Apostles' creeds that, for many, define what Christians believe. We end this short summary, then, with reference to the doctrine of the Trinity, which states that the divine is best (although inadequately) defined as having three parts that are paradoxically one. Those parts are "The Father" (God), "Son" (Jesus), and "Holy Spirit." In the doctrine of the Trinity, the early Christian Church found a way to combat emerging heresies. However, the doctrine did much more. It provided a way to succinctly define the Christian experience.

To the outsider, the doctrine of the Trinity appears nonsensical, a product of illogical if not primitive magical thinking. However, to those who had experienced the transforming power of "letting go and letting God" and of living the life of faith, the doctrine of the Trinity made perfect sense. To the early Christians, their own experience was best defined as having a personal connection to Jesus, God, and a spirit felt in the fellowship of their Christian community.

The doctrine of the Trinity brings us back to perhaps the core message of the Christian faith tradition, or to what is known as its gospel or "Good News." That good news, according to Christians, is that God's true, loving nature was revealed in the life and death of Jesus; that Jesus is God, which makes his example binding on us all; and that Jesus is fully human, which makes his example relevant to all. In addition, the good news is that God and Jesus live as a Holy Spirit, which makes the Christian community into a community of diverse parts of the same "mystical body of Christ."

This, then, is a summary of the core meaning of what it means to be a Christian and what defines the Christian faith tradition. As any reader may infer, the cosmic picture painted by Christians is breathtaking—inspiring for many and appalling for others. Its breathtaking nature suggests clearly that to become a Christian or to call oneself a Christian is no small matter. It is, rather, a life-transforming matter, a radical reworking of life as ordinarily lived. It remains to be explained, then, why so many Christians, the vast majority it seems, are so ordinary.

A simple solution to this mystery has been, historically, to reserve the name "Christian" for only a few, that is, for those whose lives do indeed reflect the radical spiritual message found in the life of Jesus. However, making the judgment as to who is and who is not a Christian has, historically, been divisive, to say the least, so much so that some would rather adhere to the Biblical prescription to "judge not" and leave the answer to the question of who is a Christian up to God.

—W. George Scarlett

See also Kingdom of God

FURTHER READING

Latourette, K. (1953). *A history of Christianity.* New York: Harper & Row.

Smith, H. (1991). *The world's religions.* San Francisco: HarperSanFancisco.

CHRISTIANITY, ORTHODOX

The Orthodox Christian faith emerges from the Incarnation and earthly ministry of Jesus Christ, the immortal Son and Word of God, who became human in order to save humanity from the destruction of sin and death. It is historically based in the ministry of the apostles of Jesus Christ, who after Pentecost, were charged with bringing the saving message of Jesus to the world. Through the witness of Holy Scripture and the living tradition of the Church, the Orthodox Christian faith has remained a dynamic vessel of this saving message for two millennia.

Eastern Orthodox Christianity is oriented toward accomplishing a singular goal. It is a faith that brings the whole human being, body, mind, and soul, into communion with the Creator, the Giver of Life, the Source of all things, God the Trinity, Father, Son, and Holy Spirit. This communion, or relationship with God, is first and foremost a relationship of love, unconditional, unrelenting, and freely offered from Creator to created.

In practical, everyday ways, the Orthodox Christian Church provides a rhythmic cycle of daily, weekly, and seasonal sacramental worship that is geared toward reaching all human senses, both physical and spiritual. Worship life reaches out to the human sense of hearing through rich theological and narrative-oriented prayers, chanted in the sweetly haunting Byzantine style. It reaches out to the eyes through the use of vivid iconographic images of the Lord Jesus, His mother (the Theotokos or God-bearer), His disciples, and many of the saints and prophets who are part of Judeo-Christian history. Worship reaches out to the human sense of smell via the use of various kinds of incense, rising up like prayers in the midst of the congregation. Worship reaches out to the sense of taste through the Sacrament of the Eucharist, the feast of love, in which sweet wine and bread are transformed into the body and blood of the Lord. And finally, worship reaches out to the sense of touch, through the use of prayer ropes and the kiss of peace offered to one another during the Divine Liturgy.

The human being, in order to experience God's love, is created in a way which guides one toward answering two fundamental questions: Who (Whose) am I? and How do I deal with suffering?

The 2,000-year-old wisdom of the Eastern Orthodox Church directs human persons toward a number of different relationships, experiences, and images that are intended to bring to life very personal answers to these powerful questions. In the tradition of the Eastern Orthodox Church, there is no cookie-cutter approach to issues of identity, relationship, and healing. At the same time, ancient and practical wisdom offered by the Church highlights the necessity for loving relationships, sacramental worship, and Scriptural narratives and images as signposts for the human soul in search of its home, God's Kingdom, and heart.

WHO (WHOSE) AM I?

Orthodox Christianity insists that human beings are the creation of a loving God, created in the very image and likeness of God Himself. In the simplest terms, this means that human beings have been endowed with the power of living flesh and spirit, heart, and mind. The very purpose of our existence is to experience God's love by relating to Him and to other human beings through our unique gifts and personhood. We then are called to offer these imperfect gifts back to God (the Sacrament of Holy Eucharist) and direct them to a broken world in need of creativity and healing. Made in the image of the Creator and Life-giver, human beings are called to lovingly create and relate.

THE TRINITY

The theological belief that God exists as a Trinity of Persons, Father, Son, and Holy Spirit, is hardly a piece of abstract dogmatism or metaphysical theorizing for Orthodox Christians. God's existence as a Trinity of Persons speaks directly to the relational nature of all things, with the Creator of all things existing in constant and perfect relational union with Himself and with His creation, all bound together by love. As creatures made in the image and likeness of God, the Trinity, human beings are most human when embedded within a matrix of loving relationships, involving mutual self-sacrifice and the joy of shared life. Human beings are most themselves, and most God-like, when they are in communion with one another.

THE *NOUS*

The Eastern Orthodox Church sees the human being's ability to connect with the loving God as taking place through the *nous*. The *nous,* which is the Greek word for mind, is considered to be the part of the human that perceives plainly God's presence in all things, times, and circumstances. The *nous* is the eye of the soul, the organ that sees the Life-giver, sees the majesty of its Creator, and leaps for joy because of it. Unfortunately, we live in a world where there is much competition for the *nous*'s attention. There are powerful and seductive images that call the *nous* away from its home in the human heart, darkening it and distracting it as it attaches to temporary material gods.

Repentance—in Greek, *metanoia* (meta = change; *nous* = mind)—is the way in which the human being personally confronts the ways in which the *nous* has been darkened and distracted away from God. This is accomplished through both personal effort akin to athletic training (*askesis* = struggle) and collaboration with a spiritual elder or confessor (the Sacrament of Holy Confession). Prayer, fasting from meat and dairy products at certain times of the week and year, and alms giving are concrete ways in which the Orthodox Christian moves toward repentance. Seasonal rhythms attach this process to both the Church's cycle of feasts and fasts, as well as to the meteorological and seasonal changes of the earth.

THE POWERS OF THE SOUL

The human being also has been endowed with what St. Gregory of Sinai called the powers of the soul. These are the life energies that give human beings the fire of life, or the passion to create. When harnessed and tutored, they are a source of power, life, and light. When distracted and misdirected, they can be destructive forces of darkness, selfishness, and exploitation. The first power is called *thymos,* the Greek word for anger. It can be the source of human courage, motivation, and self-assertion, but it can also be the source of rage and violence. The second power is called *epithymia,* the Greek word for desire. It can be the source of creativity, devotion, and loving attraction, but it can also be the source of lust, destructive impulsivity, and betrayal. These powers of the soul work together with human intellect, reasoning, and imagination to fulfill the human destiny of reflecting God's love back into the world in unique and personal ways. Darkened and misdirected, however, they can be used in more selfish and deceptive ways.

HOW DO I DEAL WITH SUFFERING?

Two useful approaches to this second question, from an Orthodox Christian perspective, come from the Passion and Resurrection of Christ and from the simple but powerful Jesus prayer. These two icons are laden with meaning which direct human beings to their source of life, hope, and healing in the midst of brokenness, confusion, and distraction.

WE WORSHIP YOUR PASSION, O CHRIST

Embedded within the Holy Thursday evening service during Holy Week is the paradoxical hymn, "We worship Your Passion, O Christ." At the heart of this hymn is the acknowledgment that God is willingly taking on, in a fully human way, the greatest of all human tragedy and suffering, the reality of betrayal, violence, and brutal death, as well as the transient experience of hopelessness and separation from God. In doing this, God "tricks" death and the devil into opening the gates of Hades to receive the crucified Lord Jesus. It is then that God's ultimate action and message of hope reveals itself, with the Lord Jesus Christ going on a rampage of love and freedom, releasing all who were captive to death and the devil and returning them to loving communion with God.

Just as the above hymn ends with the call, "Show us also Your glorious Resurrection," the Good News (*Evangelion* = Gospel = Good News) of this reality in the immediacy of everyday life is the following: There is no human experience, no version of suffering, no bodily or spiritual condition that is outside God's loving, healing reach. This reality is embodied liturgically in the Sacrament of Holy Baptism, which is the death and resurrection of the human person into a new life as a Christian.

LORD JESUS CHRIST, HAVE MERCY ON ME

The Jesus Prayer, "Lord Jesus Christ, have mercy on me," has a special place as a way of experiencing and understanding the healing effects of living within a relationship with God. This is so because the Jesus Prayer focuses upon the reality that human beings are created as beings of depth, with a heart, soul, and spirit, or an inner life that goes beyond what one observes on the surface.

In order to understand the deep, healing meaning of this prayer, it is important to appreciate what constitutes the call for mercy. Often, a request or prayer for mercy conjures up images of small, sinful, cowering Christians begging a powerful and distant God to forestall punishment and destruction. This image significantly misses the mark of the true meaning of mercy from an Orthodox Christian perspective.

The Greek word for mercy is *eleison,* which comes from the root word, *elaion,* meaning olive or olive oil. This is no accident. The uses for olive oil in biblical times give an excellent perspective into the deeper meaning of the prayer, or the connection between mercy and the healing that comes in the midst of suffering. For example, olive oil was used for medicinal purposes in ancient times. In the parable of the Good Samaritan, when the stranger was left beaten and dying by the side of the road, the Good Samaritan cleaned his wounds with wine and olive oil. A second use of olive oil was as a source of sustenance and nourishment. It was then, as it is now, a healthy food. A third use of olive oil was to provide fuel to generate light. Finally, olive oil was used as to anoint honored guests, as well as to anoint royalty as part of their enthronement. The healing and anointing are brought to life liturgically through the Sacraments of Holy Unction and Holy Chrismation.

Far from being a call for release from punishment, the Jesus Prayer is a call for healing. When a human being cries out to his or her Creator for mercy, it is comparable to saying

> Lord, I am suffering and injured. Bathe my wounds with Your love so that I can be a vessel of that love. Feed me with Your love so that I can become a source of sustenance to others. Shine Your light of mercy on me and my path so that I don't lose my way into the passions of greed, selfishness, exploitation, and destructiveness. Anoint me as Your son or daughter, so that I can remember who I am.

CONCLUSION

The Eastern Orthodox Church is a vessel designed to direct its faithful members to experiences of healing connection with the Creator of all things, God the Father, Son, and Holy Spirit. Through a combination of loving relationships, sacramental worship and practice, and personal, disciplined prayer and spiritual exercise, the human person is guided toward the transformation of his or her God-given talents and power, in order to create and relate. This increased life of creativity and loving relationality then brings the human person more and more into a life that resonates with the purpose of life, from an Orthodox Christian perspective. That purpose is to join oneself in heart, mind, soul, word, and deed with the loving and healing presence of God.

—George Stavros

See also Christianity; Orthodox Christian Youth in Western Societies

FURTHER READING

Hopko, T. (1983). *The Lenten spring.* Crestwood, NY: Saint Vladimir's Seminary Press.

Schmemann, A. (1988). *The Eucharist.* Crestwood, NY: Saint Vladimir's Seminary Press.

Vlachos, H. (1994). *Orthodox psychotherapy: The science of the fathers.* Levadia, Greece: Birth of the Theotokos Monastery.

Ware, K. (1986). *The Orthodox way.* Crestwood, NY: Saint Vladimir's Seminary Press.

CHRISTIAN SPIRITUALITY

Christian spirituality describes a quality of life or a collection of practices that, according to Christian theology, fosters responsiveness to the Holy Spirit, the third person of the Christian Godhead. Christians believe that spirituality or spiritual practices, which range from prayer to seeking justice, not only cultivate their love for God, but they also foster love for neighbor and true selfhood—the optimum state of individual flourishing. While Christian spirituality, due to the early influence of Greek philosophy, has sometimes been identified with escaping or denying this life and body for a heavenly realm, in its fullest expression it is concerned with enhancing and completing embodied human life. Irenaeus, the second-century bishop of Lyons, proclaimed, "The glory of God is humanity fully alive," which identifies human flourishing with God's glory. Christians expect that connecting their lives to the Spirit's activity of embodying God's love in the world will culminate in the Kingdom of God, in which all creatures embody the purposes of God and their deepest yearnings. Christian understandings of spirituality have as sources the stories of God's work in the world, as contained in the Bible and elaborated by theologians, but also the concrete practical experiments of Christians throughout history. A more complete grasp of Christian spirituality requires an articulation of its Trinitarian theological context and its particular practices.

THE TRINITARIAN THEOLOGICAL CONTEXT OF CHRISTIAN SPIRITUALITY

According to Christian theology, spirituality is first a quality or practice of the inner life of God before it is a human quality or practice. The Biblical theological assertion that "God is love" describes the inner life of the Triune God, characterized by lively, interdependent, and mutually enhancing relationships among the Three-in-one, and approximated in Christian spiritual practices that engage practitioners in a similar dance of self-giving love with God and neighbor. This Trinitarian communion of mutual love is the primary condition for the flourishing of individual and corporate life, for diversity and unity within the inner life of God. Yet according to Christian Trinitarian theology, since God's nature is love, God's life cannot be contained within these internal Trinitarian relationships, but in order to be sustained as love must be extended. In creating the world, God extends this love. Indeed, God created a world in God's own image, in which love or mutually enhancing interrelationship—ranging from environmental ecosystems to human development—is a condition necessary for its flourishing.

The failure of humans to live in such lively, mutually enhancing, and loving relationships with each other, God, and all creation describes our brokenness or sin. Failing to live in loving mutuality means that humans cannot live into the fullness or glory for which we were created, nor can we support the general good of humankind and creation so that they too may be lifted into the glory for which they were created.

In addition to extending God's love through creation, God also extended love in the advent of Jesus Christ, whose reconciling ways of living and dying open us to the love that is internal to God and required by creation for its flourishing. After Jesus' ascension into heaven, Christians believe that the role of the Holy Spirit is to further God's love by awakening humans to God's love, empowering them into the fullness for which they were created and extending love to all creation.

The culmination of God's Kingdom as envisioned in Christian theology involves restoring all creation to the glory for which it was intended, including lively, mutually enhancing, loving interaction with all. In this eschatological vision, diversity does not involve isolation or fragmentation, but includes mutuality and complementarity among people, God, and all creatures. In this vision, unity does not involve obliterating or ignoring differences, but a harmony in which all are empowered in their uniqueness in and through their relationships with God and neighbor. This unity that the Spirit is knitting together, toward which all Christian spiritual practices are inclined, mirrors the inner life of God.

It is significant that Christian spirituality cannot rightly be understood as an individual endeavor, but the Christian Church provides a sacramental glimpse into the nature of God's own communion of unity and diversity. Christian theologians insist that not only does the Church point backward to the inner life of the Trinity, but forward as a glimpse of the Kingdom of God in which all creatures will be gathered in unity and love.

Christian spirituality involves practices that engage us in partnership with the Spirit, and awakening and empowering us for love of God, each other, and creation. A theological term for this partnership is "perichoresis" or "to dance with," which suggests the synergy of a dance in which partners are mutually transformed. Christian spiritual practices that foster this partnership fall into two general overlapping categories: way-of-life practices and contemplative practices.

WAY-OF-LIFE PRACTICES

Christians understand living in partnership with the Spirit as organizing their lives according to the vision of human life and relationships that Jesus illuminated. Christian spirituality involves deliberate attention to such mundane matters as how we eat, relate in community, make choices, create art, and seek justice, and how we treat strangers—in light of the story and vision of Jesus. Such practices often prompt ways of knowing and doing at variance from the dominant culture. For example, contemporary culture includes a hurried style of life that encourages us to drive through fast food establishments, greet the cashier as a functionary, and devour our food in isolation while we drive to our next appointment. Yet for Jesus, eating meals was an opportunity to offer gratitude to the Creator, to acknowledge those who grew and prepared the food, and to invite friends and enemies to share food with him. For Jesus, taking food was a reconciling act that encouraged love, mutuality, and unity.

All Christian practices have similar reconciling dimensions that counter habits of objectifying and using others for selfish purposes. Spiritual practices in the Christian tradition do not simply foster individual love of God, but also involve those that promote the reconciliation, completion, and glory of all creation. While some limit their discussion of spirituality to practices of prayer, the practices that connect us in partnership with the Spirit include a range of lifestyle practices, such as corporate worship, justice seeking, hospitality to strangers, Sabbath keeping, creative expression, theological reflection, feasting, fasting, discernment, and care of the earth. These lifestyle practices are among those that the Christian Church has historically embraced as able to keep us close to God's enlivening Spirit, enhance our love of God and neighbor, and draw forth the fullest expression of our individual and corporate humanity.

CONTEMPLATIVE PRACTICES

Of particular importance for Christians who seek to connect their lives to the Spirit's movement in the world are practices of prayer and contemplation, in which responsiveness to God, others, and self is strengthened. Practices of contemplation range from silent or centering prayer—the use of repeated phrases intended to draw the practitioner into their inner depths where God speaks, to lectio divina or "holy reading" of scripture intended not primarily for rational understanding, but to allow God to speak through the texts. Contemplative practice denotes a practice of focused attention or "deep gazing"—whether focused on God, self, or the stranger—and includes the core assumption that the highest act of love is not in doing, but in truly seeing the other. Seeing others "as they are" opens us to profound respect and compassion, through which we are transformed, but which also creates conditions for their transformation.

Those who cultivate habits of contemplation in prayer also extend these habits to perceive the goodness, holiness, or woundedness of each creature. Such compassion motivates many contemplatives to confront injustices of the world, and to celebrate and support life wherever it flourishes. While these themes—the importance of silence, encounter with the Holy, and appreciative and critical perception—of contemplative Christian spirituality run as a thread through history, their expressions have taken many forms ranging from Ignatian spirituality to Quaker clearness committees to Methodist holiness meetings to Latin American base communities.

In addition to the comparatively passive practice of prayer, the contemplative practice of "deep gazing" also creates a contemplative orientation to human action. In other words, the way of contemplation is not exhausted in prayer, but is enhanced when we mindfully engage and explore the concrete world to learn its secrets. Exploring the Spirit's life incarnate in the world is often a matter of trial, error, and keen observation. The biblical wisdom tradition, of which the Proverbs are characteristic, exemplifies this way of spirituality by urging confidence that this world belongs to God, and is therefore capable of whispering to us of God's truth. In the book of Proverbs, wisdom is not an abstract or otherworldly truth, but involves very practical maxims about priorities, relationships, and daily conduct, which are learned only through experience. This view of spirituality recognizes that anything that unveils the truth hidden in the world, including our active participation in the world, opens us to perceive the Spirit and invites us into partnership. It is therefore a mistake to make hard distinctions between contemplative spiritual practices and lifestyle practices in general or Christian activism in particular.

ASCETIC PRACTICES AND RESISTING SIN

We should not imagine that Christian spirituality involves a simple matter of drawing out the best of our humanity, that is, love of God and neighbor, and true selfhood. Christians have long acknowledged forces that inhibit the love and glory for which we are created. Humanity does not stand unequivocally ready to cooperate with the Spirit. Our hearts are often beset with ambiguity—by fear, hatred, mistrust, and ambition that throw us back on our individual projects and inhibit love of God and neighbor. Further, these fears and ambitions do not simply live in our hearts, but we create entire cultures that foster these fears and ambitions. As these fears become culturally validated, they impact our lives with double force—from inside and outside. In order to resist the power of fear and to cooperate with God's project of love, Christian spiritual practices engage Christians in shaping a world that supports life and love, but also encouraging close attention to one's inner life, and to how fears and ambitions overwhelm individuals and fragment our communities. Christian tradition has characterized as sin the failure to resist these fears and ambitions, and has emphasized the importance of resisting these inner and outer forces. A particular form of Christian spirituality concerned with resisting sin and its contexts is asceticism. Ascetic Christians have for centuries fasted from food, abstained from sex, lived in cloisters, and eschewed the temptations of sensationalism, thus seeking to limit the possibility of seduction to these lesser goods and focus their lives on greater goods—love of God and neighbor. While contemporary Christians, particularly feminist Christians, have correctly challenged the body-denying aspects of ascetic practices, nevertheless ascetic traditions remind us of the importance of dehabituating from patterns that distort our humanity and rehabituating around practices that foster love of God, neighbor, and true selfhood.

SPIRITUAL GIFTS

Another aspect of Christian spirituality involves the notion that the Spirit bestows special skills and capacities to Christians in order to further God's project of love in the world. This understanding is greatly influenced by the teachings of St. Paul (Rom. 12:6–8; Eph. 4:11; I Cor. 12:8–10, 28–30; 13:1–3; 14:6, 26) who elaborates various, apparently incomplete, lists of gifts or charismas of the Spirit—including prophecy, leading, teaching, governing, evangelizing, miracles, healing, tongues, alms giving, helping, serving, doing works of mercy, and administering material goods.

While in some Christian traditions the bestowal of spiritual gifts is thought to be interventions into nature while imparting some skill to which there has been no natural development, in other traditions spiritual gifts are seen to build on or complete some natural signature skill or capacity. In this latter view, all of nature, including human life, is seen to display a glimpse of God, however distorted, and to build on our natural capacities involves clarifying and completing these signature skills and mobilizing them on behalf of the Spirit's project of love and reconciliation.

Some have extended this understanding of spiritual gift to include the influence of social location—insisting, for example, that those in particular social positions, whether women, the poor, or ethnic minorities, provide unique wisdom and skills that can be mobilized by the Spirit. They suggest that the perceptions of those closest to social power and privilege can be distorted. Indeed, they conclude, all perspectives can only be partial and incomplete. Therefore, we require a range of alternate perspectives to complete our own. The perspectives and skills of those from various social locations may thus constitute gifts through which the Spirit works for our individual and corporate reconciliation and completion. This insight is echoed in Paul's articulation of the Body of Christ, requiring all parts—whether hands, feet, or head—in relation to each other and the whole.

This understanding of spiritual gifts can be focused in particular ways when reflecting on the social location of children and adolescents. A risk intrinsic to Western production-oriented society is that our push toward technical mastery may blind us to the Spirit's work in our midst. Often, this priority of mastery for the sake of production filters into the entire range of our values and institutions. Our inordinate priority of production often becomes too easily identified with a normative adulthood, since adults are most often productive as wage earners, and we interpret developmental theories through these priorities and emphasize older life stages as more advanced.

In viewing adulthood as normative or more important, we thereby undervalue the signature gifts of youth whose idealism, energy, or beauty is exhibited in important ways that are largely in recession among adults. Such a view ignores the possibility of God working in and through youth. The Pauline idea of spiritual gift or charisma brings the potential gifts of youth into focus in a way that values children and adolescents not as imperfect versions of adults, but as bearing important gifts to be energized for the Kingdom of God. They are not merely to be exploited by marketers, ignored or diminished by theorists, demonized by police, nor patronized by adults. Youth, by virtue of their social location as youth, have unique perspectives and gifts that Christians are called to help mobilize for God's Kingdom.

The signature gifts that young people offer their communities vary greatly, but typically include a keen sense for justice, beauty, physical prowess, intellectual curiosity, camaraderie, idealism, and hope. While contemporary structures that contain young people sometimes marginalize youth and obscure their gifts, historically the spirited gifts of young people have served their communities and the public good.

GIFTS OF YOUTH ENERGIZED BY THE SPIRIT

Throughout history young people have accepted roles in shaping a better world—including participation in every major justice movement, labor movement, civil rights movement, and environmental movement in modern history—as well as the various contemporary antiwar, antisweatshop, and antiglobalization movements. Before the middle of the 19th century, many young people engaged in serious work, held significant social roles, and contributed to social equilibrium. Prior to the 20th century, young people were anything but passive commodity consumers or recipients of education, roles to which they are now largely relegated. For example, David Farragut, the

U.S. Navy's first admiral, had his first commission as a midshipman at age 10, and his first command of a vessel at age 12. Thomas Edison ran his own printing business at age 12. The men who won the American Revolution were barely out of high school—Alexander Hamilton was 20, Aaron Burr, 21, and Lafayette, 19. What amounted to a college class rose up and struck down the British Empire. In France, Delacroix's painting of the French Revolution, *Lady Liberty Leads the People,* depicts Lady Liberty leading the people into freedom—herself led along by young people. French young people were among those who in 1789 fomented revolution in Paris cafes and died in numbers on the barricades, with cries of "liberty, fraternity, and equality," and marched alongside their elders in the early industrial era demanding lower bread prices and higher wages. The power of these young people to change the world included a keen social awareness and ability to comprehend and construct some of the most sophisticated political documents in history. Because the social roles embraced by youth engaged their signature gifts—of seeking justice, social renewal, beauty, and creativity—medieval myths also identified youth with spring, Easter, and the spirited rebirth of life.

In more recent times, young poets, musicians, and activists of the 1960s, like their premodern counterparts, broke open social codes that validated racism, sexism, militarism, and classism. Youthful revolutionaries and poets throughout history have held a sense of passion, curiosity, adventure, and creativity. And when the Spirit energizes these signature gifts of youth, they advance God's Kingdom of justice and joy. Christian spirituality at its best is not a device for alienating young people from themselves, but a resource for awakening the unique vocation and gifts of youth as youth. As Catholic mystic Thomas Merton insists, "[W]e give glory to God by living into God's purpose for creation." As observed by developmental theorist Erik Erikson, adolescence has its own virtue, and its own natural energy and telos apart from its trajectory toward adulthood. And when young people are empowered through spiritual practices to fully employ these gifts and to organize them around the Spirit's purpose of love, God is glorified and human life is vitalized.

—David F. White

See also Christiani]ty; Kingdom of God

FURTHER READING

Bass, D. (Ed.). (1998). *Practicing our faith: A way of life for a searching people.* San Francisco: Jossey-Bass.

Bass, D., & Richter, D. C. (2002). *Way to live: Christian practices for teens.* Nashville, TN: Upper Room Books.

DeMello, A. (1995). *The way to love: The last meditations of Anthony De Mello.* New York: Doubleday.

Merton, T. (1974). *New seeds of contemplation.* New York: New Directions Publishing.

Miles, M. (1990). *Practicing Christianity: Critical perspectives for an embodied spirituality.* New York: Crossroad/Herder & Herder.

Moltmann, J. (2003). *The spirit of life: A universal affirmation* (J. Kohl, Trans.). Minneapolis, MN: Fortress Press.

Palmer, P. (1999). *Let your life speak: Listening for the voice of vocation.* San Francisco: Jossey-Bass.

CHURCHES

The word "church" comes from the Greek word *ekklesia* for "belonging to the Lord," and with an understanding of holy people, especially people who are gathered for worship. *Ekklesia* in Greek had an original meaning of assembly of citizens who enjoyed full civil rights. Thus, the word "church" can mean the Lord's holy congregation. The idea of church is the abiding presence of God's definitive and fully articulated Word, who is Jesus, to the world. Since the Word was with God and in God, Jesus founded the church through his very reality. For many, the church is the central context of religious and spiritual influence.

In the Christian sacred scriptures, the New Testament, it is Jesus of Nazareth, the Christ or Messiah of history, who calls his followers into community. This is not a small secret church just for an elect few, but for all, especially sinners and those on the fringes of society. Jesus called people to belong to the Kingdom of God, and left behind the celebration of a memorial meal, the breaking of the bread. Many Christians see in the Gospel of Matthew (16:18), the foundation of the church with Peter as the first leader of this new community. It is Peter who is given the power to "bind and loose" and the keys of power to this new church.

The Pauline writings or letters in the New Testament show the meaning of church as a local community and a theological entity and not an organization. Paul had many difficulties spreading the early message of Jesus to the gentiles or non-Jewish people. But despite all these problems, Paul still stayed connected to the original community at Jerusalem. For the early believers, there were house churches where people gathered for the breaking of the bread. When Paul uses the term "church," he really means the universal church that is realized and represented in small local communities.

Most Christians would agree that Jesus did found a church, or that he laid the foundations for one. He gathered followers around himself, that is, apostles and disciples, for the purpose of preaching and proclaiming the Kingdom of God. It is clear that Jesus intended to pass on some type of leadership and power to Peter and others after his life, death, and resurrection. Finally, at the Last Supper Jesus intended for his followers to continue on and "do this in remembrance of me."

The early community of believers struggled with many issues for many centuries. One needs to remember that the early church was outlawed and underground until around the year 300. The Council of Nicea in 325 put down on paper many theological beliefs concerning God, Jesus, the Holy Spirit, and the idea of church. Nicea proclaimed that there are four marks of the church: One, Holy, Catholic, and Apostolic. Each of these marks has profound theological and historical meaning. Thus, the church becomes both a sign and instrument of the mission of Jesus, to establish the Kingdom of God. There is a strong missionary element to bring the message to all nations.

This mission of the church is to proclaim the word in evangelizing, while fostering the celebration of the sacraments and to be of service to those on the fringe of society. The mission of the church is to all and for all. The early believers had a difficult time understanding and living the full reality of what it meant to be a church. The subapostolic church (circa 65) and the postapostolic church (circa 95–100) were communities in transition. First, there was the purpose of missionary activity; eventually there was a need for pastoral ministry. There was the early tension of going from Jewish leadership and culture to Gentile leadership and culture.

Down through the centuries the notion of church is best understood by images. The church is the people of God, the Body of Christ, the temple of the Holy Spirit. Other centuries saw the church as a ship with Jesus at the center. Contemporary understandings focus on church as a political society, the church as a sacrament, the church as a pilgrim people, and the church as servant.

For Christians around the world, the church is a primary context of influence on religious and spiritual development. Individuals, families, and communities come together to worship within the walls of the church. It is within the church that blessed sacraments are witnessed and experienced. It is within the church that the Word of God is read, shared, and experienced. While each individual person who enters the church will have his or her own unique experience, each time he or she enters, the church is considered by all Christians to be a place of worship, wherein one's religious identity and development are enveloped and promoted. While each image or model of church takes on a specific direction or a major way of living out of the message, all Christian communities still struggle to be faithful to strive to be One, Holy, Catholic, and Apostolic.

—Rev. David O'Leary

FURTHER READING

Brown, R. (1985). *The churches the Apostles left behind: The New Testament cradles of Catholic Christianity.* New York: Paulist Press.

Harrington, D. (1980). *God's people in Christ: New Testament perspectives on the Church and Judaism.* Philadelphia, PA: Fortress Press.

Schnackenburg, R. (1961). *The Church in the New Testament.* London: SCM Press.

COLES, ROBERT

Robert Coles is a child psychiatrist, a professor of psychiatry, and the Agee Professor of Social Ethics at the Graduate School of Education at Duke University. He has been a visiting professor in the History Department at Duke University, is a founding member of the Center for Documentary Studies at Duke University, and is a coeditor of *Double Take Magazine,* published at the Center. He was also an advisor to President John F. Kennedy. A Pulitzer Prize–winning author, Coles has written sixty books and well over a thousand articles, reviews, and essays. He received the Medal of Freedom from President William Clinton, the highest honor awarded to a civilian in the United States, as well as being recognized as one of the nation's top creative geniuses by the MacArthur Foundation. With his most recent book, *A Call to Service,* Coles makes a case and an indirect plea for heightened levels of voluntary and community service. His work serves to educate its readers about child and adolescent spiritual and religious development and, as well, by calling for service to others, promotes heightened levels of spiritual and religious development in the lives of his readers.

Coles is recognized and applauded for his work with underprivileged children around the world and his insights into the way children develop, what children need to live happy and healthy lives, and how children understand the world around them. The spiritual and moral lives of children have been his primary interests. Those interested in studying and better understanding the moral and spiritual lives of children often start with readings by Coles, most notably *The Moral Life of Children, The Moral Intelligence of Children,* and *The Spiritual Lives of Children.* The stories he tells of young children and their experiences with the divine and that which they consider to be transcendent, as well as the stories of character development and moral questioning, offer the reader and student a comprehensive view of the varieties of moral, religious, and spiritual experiences in childhood. As a result of long-term observations of children, Coles offers stories of children's lives—as told by the children. He makes very little commentary or analysis of the stories told. He assumes the stories and the voices of children speak for themselves for the reader to decipher and enter into.

Coles offers in his books narrative dialogues shared between him and the children he interviews. The stories are intended to offer his readers a glimpse into the sensitivity that he finds in the lives of even very young children to moral issues, issues of character, and religious understanding. The story of Ruby Bridges, one of Coles's most well-known subjects, is a worthy example. Coles tells her story—the story of a 6-year-old African-American girl who was involved in the school desegregation movement in the Southern United States and who, despite facing abuse, hatred, and violence, found herself praying for the very mob of hateful adults and children who threatened her. In sharing this story, Coles not only educates the reader to the experiences of moral behavior, moral intelligence, and religiosity of young children, but challenges the reader to question the contexts that allowed/supported Ruby to be able to take the stance she did with such moral integrity and assurance.

Coles has been known to challenge the field of psychoanalysis and the theories of development that describe development as occurring in ages and stages. The stories that he provides, such as the story of Ruby Bridges, make clear that young children can pose questions about moral and religious significance that, while based in a different "moral notice" than that of adults, signify an awareness and understanding of issues of right and wrong and moral ideals that do not always fit into neat expectations of ages and stages.

Coles is very much a contextualist in his perspective, as the stories he chooses to share make clear that the multiple life contexts and historical time in which a child lives all have an impact on the moral and religious sensitivity and understanding of that child. As such, young children tend to develop their "moral compass" based on the different behaviors and reasoning of other children (i.e., peers), parents, religious leaders, and teachers that they meet throughout their young lives. Although preferring to distance himself from stage theory, Coles does recognize that as children age and become more abstract in their reasoning and more internalized in cultural practices, their cultural literacy elevates and their moral literacy declines.

In *The Spiritual Life of Children,* Coles shares results of his interviews, held over months and years, with children of different religious and spiritual traditions, including Hopi children in the Southwestern United States; Catholic, Protestant, and Jewish children in the Boston area of the United States; Christian children in Tennessee in the United States; and Pakistani children in London. Coles asks them simple questions, such as what God means to them. Coles hopes that the answers that the children respond with will provide the reader insight into the religiosity of children. The meaning behind the stories, without any analysis or judgment from Coles himself, is, again, left to the reader to consider. It is clear, however, that in the stories he chooses to share and the questions he asks in the interviews that Coles hopes to educate his readers and the broader adult society about the wisdom of young people and their understanding of and relationship with that which they consider to be divine. To assume young children cannot be religious or spiritual because they are too young, and therefore not within the appropriate cognitive or emotional stage, is to fail to listen to the stories children tell.

Coles's work with children and interest in their moral and spiritual lives can also be found in other works, such as the narratives he shares in *The Political Lives of Children.* He believes that children learn about politics much in the same way that they learn about morality—from their parents, friends, and teachers—and that the political lives of children merge with their moral lives. The stories shared in *The Political Life of Children* repeatedly display the dynamic between the moral and political consciousness of children, as children share their views on the relationship between issues related to freedom and those related to constraint.

In *A Call to Service,* Coles equates voluntary community service to a natural moral impulse that is part instinct and part the influence of religious tradition. As with moral literacy, Coles finds that one's natural instinct to give to others is increasingly silenced as the child becomes more highly immersed in a culture through education and peer influence.

Robert Coles inspires his readers to pay attention to the voices of children and to what they have to say about religion, spirituality, and moral issues. He asks his readers to listen to children, for within their stories lie their understandings of and relationships with that which they consider to be divine, transcendent, and right or wrong. While Coles defers from providing his own theory of spiritual/religious or moral development, his perspective can be found when his books and stories shared are read with care. Coles challenges his readers to identify within each story told by a child the particular contexts—both individual and contextual—that influenced the child's religious, spiritual, and/or moral development. By attending to the impact of the historical time on the child's development, Coles also brings attention to the role of time, in interaction with contextual influences, on a child's religious and spiritual development.

—Elizabeth M. Dowling

FURTHER READING

Coles, R. (1993). *The call of service: A witness to idealism.* Boston: Houghton Mifflin Company.

Coles, R. (1986a). *The moral life of children.* Boston: Atlantic Monthly Press.

Coles, R. (1986b). *The political life of children.* Boston: Atlantic Monthly Press.

Coles, R. (1990). *The spiritual life of children.* Boston: Houghton Mifflin Company.

Ronda, B. (1989). *Intellect and spirit: The life and work of Robert Coles.* New York: Continuum.

Woodruff, J., & Carew, S. (Eds.). (1992). *Conversations with Robert Coles.* Jackson: University Press of Mississippi.

COMMUNITIES, INTENTIONAL SPIRITUAL

There are thousands of intentional spiritual communities located around the world. Some are associated with a particular religious tradition, while others are ecumenical or interfaith in nature. These communities vary in size from a handful of people to several thousand. People are attracted to intentional communities for a variety of reasons. Most common is the belief that the sharing of one's daily life with others who have similar beliefs and values will contribute to a deepening of spiritual practice and faithfulness. In this entry, a selection of these communities, representing a variety of religious traditions, will be briefly discussed.

Among the most widespread intentional spiritual communities in the United States are the communities of the Catholic Worker movement. This movement was founded by Dorothy Day and Peter Maurin in New York in 1933 in the context of the Great Depression. Catholic Workers are committed to nonviolence, voluntary poverty, caring for persons in need, and working for social change. Most Catholic Worker communities are located in urban areas, providing hospitality to the homeless and food to the hungry through soup kitchens. Rural communities also exist, which care for the land, grow food for the urban houses, and serve as places of hospitality and spiritual retreat. More than 150 Catholic Worker houses and farms now exist in the United States and in several other countries. While rooted in the traditions of Catholicism, the movement is not officially affiliated with the Catholic Church. Persons of all religious traditions are welcome to be part of Catholic Worker communities.

Another widespread movement of spiritual communities is the L'Arche communities, initiated by Jean Vanier and Catholic priest Thomas Philippe in France in 1964. These communities are made up of persons with mental disabilities and others who choose to share life with disabled persons. L'Arche communities stress the unique value of each person in the eyes of God, especially those who have so often been marginalized by society. Great emphasis is placed on worship, service, forgiveness, and celebration as the bases of communal life. Today there are over 120 L'Arche communities in more than thirty countries, including numerous communities in the United States.

A different movement with a similar name is the Communauté de l'Arche (Community of the Ark) founded in France by Lanza del Vasto in 1948. Del Vasto was a Christian who went to India to live with and learn from Mohandas Gandhi. Gandhi gave him the name Shantidas, "Servant of Peace," and sent him back to France to spread the message of nonviolence there. The Community of the Ark is a family-centered movement that is committed to learning how to practice nonviolence in every aspect of life. Deep spiritual practice is seen as the foundation of nonviolence, and time is set apart each day for communal meditation and prayer. The largest Ark communities are located in a mountainous rural area in southern France, where they seek to be relatively self-sufficient through farming, with several smaller rural and urban communities in France and in other Western European countries. There is also a broader movement of Friends and Allies of the Ark. Members of the Ark movement often take part in public nonviolent actions. The Ark is an interfaith community that is open to persons of all religious traditions who are committed to nonviolence and to the deep practice of their own faith, and who are respectful of the faith of others.

One of the most well-known Buddhist communities in the world is Plum Village, a community in southern France that was founded by the Vietnamese Buddhist monk Thich Nhat Hanh in 1982. Thich Nhat Hanh, one of the most popular and respected Buddhist teachers in the world today, has lived in exile from Vietnam since the time of the Vietnam War. Plum Village is made up of Buddhist monks and nuns, Vietnamese refugees and their families, and members of the Order of Interbeing, an international religious order founded by Thich Nhat Hanh. Numerous visitors participate in the life of the community every year, including many persons from North America who come to take part in mindfulness retreats. These retreats focus on teaching people how to be fully present to the present moment, and in so doing to come to be more fully in touch with the wonders and joys of life and to be better able to work to relieve suffering in the world. While these practices are rooted in the Buddhist tradition, persons of all faiths are welcome to participate in the retreats.

Another spiritual community in France that attracts large numbers of visitors, especially young people, is the community of Taizé. Taizé is an ecumenical Christian monastic community that began in 1940. It is currently made up of about one hundred brothers from more than twenty countries and from a variety of Christian traditions, including the Roman Catholic, Anglican, Lutheran, and Reformed Christian traditions. Primary themes of the community include peace and reconciliation. For more than 30 years the community has welcomed tens of thousands of young people each summer to take part in worship, Bible study, discussion, and celebration. The young people live in large tents according to language, and join in worship and other activities together throughout the day. The music of Taizé, consisting of simple melodic chants, is internationally known, and is used in worship in many churches around the world.

One of the most popular nondenominational international spiritual communities is the Findhorn Community in Scotland. Findhorn is devoted to the cultivation of ecological responsibility and to the recognition of the presence of divinity within all beings. Findhorn espouses no particular creed or doctrine, but rather professes respect for all the world's major religious traditions and welcomes all spiritual seekers to take part in its activities. Thousands of people from around the world come to the community each year to take part in week-long courses focusing on themes of spirituality and ecological sustainability.

These are but a few samples of intentional spiritual communities that exist around the world. These examples represent well the many different contexts in which spirituality and religiosity develop and thrive, as well as the many different ways people come together to share and experience the spiritual and the divine.

—John Sniegocki

See also Thich Nhat Hanh

FURTHER READING

Day, D. (1997). *Loaves and fishes: The inspiring story of the Catholic Worker movement.* Maryknoll, NY: Orbis Books.

Del Vasto, L. (1974). *Make straight the way of the Lord.* New York: Knopf.

Fellowship for Intentional Community. (2000). *Communities directory.* Rutledge, MO: Author.

Janzen, D. (1996). *Fire, salt, and peace: Intentional Christian communities alive in North America.* Evanston, IL: Shalom Mission Communities.

Spink, K. (1986). *A universal heart: The life and vision of Brother Roger of Taizé.* San Francisco: Harper & Row.

Vanier, J. (1989). *Community and growth.* New York: Paulist Press.

CONFESSIONS OF ST. AUGUSTINE

The Confessions of St. Augustine, written by Christianity's single most influential leader since the Apostle Paul, is the foremost classic of Christian spirituality after the Bible. Written by Augustine of Hippo (354–430) around 400, the *Confessions* is a spiritual autobiography, the first and only such work of its kind in the first 1,500 years of Christian history. It is unsurpassed in Christian literature as a psychological and theological depiction of divine grace converting the perverted human heart to its original, blessed state. The most frequently quoted sentence from the *Confessions* is a prayer to God that expresses the primary premise of this work: "You arouse him [humanity] to take joy in praising you, for you have made us for yourself, and our heart is restless until it rests in you" (Book 1, chapter 1, verse 1). As is the case with other significant religious literary pieces, the *Confessions* serves as both a tool and trigger of spiritual and/or religious reflection and learning, and thereby has an impact on spiritual and/or religious development. The *Confessions* also offers a glimpse into and a model of a religious developmental journey.

The *Confessions* consists of 13 sections called "books." The first nine cover Augustine's life during the years 354 to 388, from his birth through his conversion to Christianity to the death of his mother, Monica. Book 10 deals with memory, Book 11 considers the nature of time, and Books 12 and 13 comprise a commentary on the biblical book of Genesis. Some scholars say that the first nine and last four books do not share a common theme, but the purpose of the last four books is probably best understood as the great thinker undergirding his personal recollections with their philosophical and theological context. God is at work through memory and in time revealing the mystery of divine purposes initiated in creation.

THE *CONFESSIONS* AND THE LIFE OF AUGUSTINE

The restless heart at the center of this work belongs to Augustine of Hippo, the religious genius who stood astride the great divide between two ages, the Early Church and the Middle Ages. Behind him were four centuries of formative Christian history, when orthodox Christian doctrines such as the Trinity and the true nature of Christ were hammered out, when the books of the Bible were settled upon, and when the essential means of public and private worship were given foundation. Before him were centuries of chaos and dissolution in the West, which would in large measure find preservation of orthodox Christianity's essentials dependent on work already done.

In his own life, Augustine faced most of the theological issues of his era and bequeathed to the Christians who followed him an unparalleled summary of the Christian faith as developed in the glory years of Roman Christian civilization. Augustine's perspective is a prototype of Western theology, and his fingerprints are found on its most characteristic and distinctive Christian motifs. One collection of Augustine's works consists of sixteen volumes of about 1,200, double-columned pages each. None has had more influence on Christian spiritual life than the *Confessions,* which also happens to provide great detail about the inner and outer life of its author.

The *Confessions* Years

Augustine was born in Thagaste, North Africa, to a Christian mother and a pagan father. As a child, Augustine pilfered from his parents and cheated at games with his friends. As a teenager, he and some friends stole some pears and threw them away.

Interpreted by some as a sign of Augustine's overactive conscience, such memories are better understood as keys to his ability to see, even in seemingly trivial wrongs, something of humanity's attraction to evil. In response to the suggestion that his preteen mischief was unimportant, he wrote: "Is this childhood innocence? It is not. . . . For these are the practices that pass from tutors and teachers, and from nuts and balls and birds, to governors and kings, and to money and estates and slaves." He saw in the theft of the pears, committed for no reason except the love of doing wrong, a clear sign that he loved neither his crimes nor their results, but rather the evil that motivated the crimes.

Even in the midst of these early, self-destructive days, Augustine reflected, God was at work. Naming the blessings of his own natural giftedness, family, friendship, and life itself, Augustine wrote: "Even then I existed, had life and feeling, had care for my own well-being, which is a trace of your [God's] own most mysterious unity from which I took my being" (1.20.31). These themes permeate the *Confessions:* humanity's irresistible leaning toward destructive ways and God's grace constantly at work to save and set right creation, including the man, Augustine.

Sexual conflict is another central spiritual issue in the *Confessions.* Augustine's mother, Monica, was a strictly moralistic Christian who considered his adolescent sexual passions a "present disease and a future danger" (2.3.8), while his proud pagan father joyfully recounted discovering signs of his 16-year-old son's maturing sexuality at the public baths. Both parents were more interested in their son's academic accomplishments than in helping deal with his promiscuity. Throughout his life, or at least until his conversion, Augustine struggled to integrate love and sexual longing in a healthy way. At age 30, he still prayed the prayer of his youth: "Give me chastity . . . , but not yet!" (8.7.17).

At age 16, Augustine left his small hometown to study rhetoric (part of language arts aimed at making effective arguments) in the city of Carthage. There he excelled as a student. He also joined the Manichaean sect, a dualistic religion that taught reason as the supreme guide to life, and the body's desires as a natural part of the evil created in nature, which must be transcended rather than integrated with the spiritual good.

After completing his Carthage studies, Augustine returned to teach school in Thagaste for a year. There, grief at the sudden death of his dearest friend undid his fragile sense of self, making him become "a great riddle" to himself (4.4.9). He found no relief for his "pierced and bloodied soul" (4.6.11). When he tried to rest in the religion and reason of his Carthage days, it "hurtled back upon [him] through the void" (4.7.12). Augustine tried the geographical solution, fleeing from the place of his unhappiness back to Carthage, but found that the source of his spiritual anguish was not in his circumstances, but in himself.

For 7 years, Augustine remained in Carthage, living with an unnamed woman who bore him a son, Adeodatus. During these years, he lost confidence in the Manichees, having discovered their shallow intellectual depths during a much anticipated interview with the Manichaean expert Faustus.

In an ambitious career move, Augustine, his woman friend, and Adeodatus moved to Rome, sneaking away at night after lying to his weeping mother to prevent her from going with him. Years later, Monica forced Adeodatus's mother to return to Africa so that Augustine might be eligible for a more suitable marriage, although said marriage never occurred. Augustine wrote that her parting "drew blood" from his wounded heart.

In Rome, Augustine learned the harsh truth that students do not always pay their tuition. Broke and disillusioned, he took a public position as a rhetorician in Milan, where he began to attend the sermons of the famous bishop of the city, Ambrose. From Ambrose, he learned that spiritual truth does not depend on the kind of rational certainty that proves "seven and three make ten" (6.4.6). Augustine also discovered in neo-Platonic philosophy some answers to the intellectual questions that troubled him, and found some honest friends with whom to discuss life and scripture.

After coming to an intellectual acceptance of Christian faith but still unable to live by his beliefs, Augustine heard from his friend Ponticianus the story of Antony, the Egyptian monk and founder of desert monasticism. This proof that the life he believed in could actually be lived, and lived by persons far less educated than himself, ended Augustine's self-denial about his failed spiritual state. He wrote that he felt as if Antony's story "took me from behind my own back, where I had placed myself because I did not wish to look upon myself" (8.7.16).

In a state of great inner turmoil, as he sat weeping and praying in a garden, he heard a child's voice repeatedly say, "Take up and read." Randomly opening Paul's letter to the Romans, Augustine read, "put you on the Lord Jesus Christ, and make not provision for the flesh. . . ." In that instant, he reports, he experienced a sudden conversion of life, after which he remained a steadfast Christian (8.12.29).

The young seeker had found in Milan an intellectually gifted preacher, conceptual help in philosophy education, biblical understanding with a circle of friends, and evidence of his beliefs actualized in the lives of committed Christians. These means led to an experience of the grace of God in his own life that never departed. He was baptized on Easter, 387, along with his friend Alypius, and his son Adeodatus.

Augustine determined to return to Africa to live out his life as a secluded scholar. Both the widowed Monica and Augustine's son died on his way home. The autobiographical part of the *Confessions* ends with the burial of Monica.

AUGUSTINE'S LATER YEARS

Augustine's biographer, Possidus, informs us that on a visit to the North African town of Hippo in 391, the church and its aged bishop persuaded a reluctant Augustine to become a priest among them. In a short time, he became their bishop, founded a priestly community according to a monastic lifestyle, and lived out his career there. No doubt his spiritual autobiography, which helped explain how God was working for good throughout all his life, even when he did not realize it, helped quell rumors about his checkered past.

As Augustine lay dying in 430, the churches of his homeland lay in smoking ruins. The siege engines of the Vandal barbarians, who had conquered Rome decades before, loomed outside the walls of Hippo. The spiritual lessons of the *Confessions* remained untouched, however: "Through prayerful reflection, the outer life, even when in disarray, may become a means to knowing the more expansive inner world of the self, and God is better known through clearer knowledge of the true Self, the untarnished image of the divine."

Augustine's life continues to serve as a model of religious development to this day.

—*Wm. Loyd Allen*

FURTHER READING

Ryan, J. K. (1960). *The confessions of St. Augustine.* New York: Image Books.

CONFUCIANISM

Confucianism is a Chinese religio-ethical tradition founded by Confucius (551–479 B.C.E). It is the leading component of the "Three Teachings," which also include Daoism and Buddhism, for their pervasive influence on the Chinese people's thought and behavior. As the mainstream tradition, it both reflects and reinforces the characteristic Chinese approach to life, emphasizing the relational aspects of human existence, this-worldliness, respect for tradition, self-cultivation through learning, action over doctrine, and harmony. Confucianism's influence lives on not only in China, but also in other East Asian societies.

Confucius lived in a period of social and political turmoil, when vassal states of the weakened Zhou approximately 1110–221 B.C.E.) government vied with each other for supremacy, providing fertile ground for innovative ideas on social order and effective government. Confucianism was one of the so-called "Hundred Schools" that arose in this period. Confucius believed that social order depends on people's ethical qualities, especially the ruler's. He set himself the task of restoring the declining tradition of the ancient sage-kings, and his genius lay in reinvigorating traditional concepts through creative exegesis, a practice often emulated by subsequent generations of Chinese reformers. For example, Confucius used the term *junzi,* which originally meant "nobleman," to refer to a virtuous person, thereby redefining nobleness as a virtuous achievement rather than a hereditary ascription. His own ambition was to convince the rulers to put his ideas into practice. After repeated frustrations, he settled down in his sixties to concentrate on educational activities. He is considered to be the first teacher in Chinese history to have broken the nobility's monopoly on education.

Posthumous official recognition came when the Han (206 B.C.E–220 C.E.) government of the unified empire declared Confucianism the state ideology. Numerous honors had been conferred on Confucius by emperors through the ages, including the title "Paragon and Master of the Ten Thousand Generations." Temples were dedicated to him, where rituals in his memory were performed. Traditionally, in every schoolroom there was an altar to Confucius, in front of which students would bow. The "Four Books," the core of the Confucian canon, became the syllabus for civil service examinations in the Yuan Dynasty (1260–1370 C.E.). Confucianism's status as state ideology ended only in the early 20th century with the overthrow of the imperial Qing government.

The Four Books are the *Analects,* a collection of conversations and anecdotes involving Confucius and his disciples; the *Book of Mencius,* a record of the conversations of Mencius (371–289 B.C.E.), a disciple of Confucius's grandson, and whose contribution to Confucianism's foundation is considered second only to that of Confucius himself; the *Great Learning* and the *Doctrine of the Mean,* two chapters singled out from the *Book of Rites* and grouped together with the other two works by the Song Dynasty neo-Confucian

Zhu Xi (1130–1200) so that, with Zhu's own annotations and commentaries, the four provide a systematic introduction to Confucian learning. Zhu's effort is part of neo-Confucianism, the movement from the Song Dynasty (960–1279) to the Qing Dynasty (1644–1911) that systematized and elaborated Confucian teachings and practices under the influences of Daoism and Buddhism.

The cardinal virtue highlighted in the *Analects* is *ren,* often translated as "human-heartedness." Etymologically, the character *ren* consists of two components that mean "two" and "person," reflecting the mutuality of human existence and the requirements that this imposes on one's dealings with others. Confucius advised helping others as one would like them to help one, and against doing to others what one does not wish for oneself, versions of the Golden Rule. Mainstream Confucians, following Mencius, believe in the innate goodness of people. However, for the seed of human-heartedness to flourish, nurture through proper conduct and reflection is required; hence, the importance of self-cultivation through learning. Internal human-heartedness needs to be given appropriate external expression in the form of proper conduct, which in turn provides the necessary scaffolding for the growth of human-heartedness, with each feeding on the other. Neither human-heartedness nor proper conduct alone suffices. This is an example of the Confucian way of dialectical thinking, which is aimed at a balanced perspective encompassing the two interpenetrating and mutually causative polarities of *yin* (the negative) and *yang* (the positive), in this case the internal substance and the external form. This dynamic and holistic way of thinking is most clearly expressed in the *Book of Changes,* another Confucian classic.

The practice of proper conduct that nurtures human-heartedness includes fulfilling the requirements of one's diverse social roles. Filial relationships provide the archetype for all other kinds of social relationships, because human-heartedness finds its first expression in the home. Rather than beginning with a set of abstract ethical principles, Confucians work with what is initially available—the child, with an innate incipient moral sense, in the family—and gradually extend the child's moral world and moral competence. More generally, living a genuinely human life is an art, involving the exercise of the virtues of human-heartedness, righteousness, propriety, wisdom, trustworthiness, sincerity, reverence, loyalty, and filial piety. As in all kinds of artful practice, learning through modeling is an effective method. Hence Confucianism's emphasis on the role of the sage as an exemplar of virtue and the consequent high esteem in which teachers are held. What is important is not what the sages said, but their exemplary actions that others can emulate and internalize as part of themselves. Tradition is to be valued for being the repository of practices constitutive of humanity.

Confucius warned that without human-heartedness, propriety is worse than nothing. For the practice of proper conduct to be an effective means of self-cultivation, mindfulness arising from sincerity and reverence, two other Confucian virtues, is essential. The same attitude applies to all actions. Thus, learning as a spiritual path involves dwelling in what is being learned until it becomes part of one's being and a guiding source of one's action. It is in this sense that Confucius held that learning is for the sake of oneself, not for others' sake. Confucius's description of his own lifelong spiritual development exemplifies this nicely. At 15, he devoted himself to learning. At 30, he was able to take his stand. At 40, he no longer harbored any doubts. At 50, he grasped the will of Heaven. At 60, his ear was attuned to truth. At 70, he could freely follow his heart's desires without transgressing what was right.

The ultimate goal of learning is to become one with Dao (the Way) and its embodiment. This allows one to realize one's authentic nature, which means that self-transcendence is at the same time a return to the source. However, from another perspective, it is also an outward movement in the sense that one's spiritual progression enables, and indeed requires, one to extend the harmony and order in oneself to one's community, both by providing an exemplar and by active service. The Great Learning expresses this ideal of "inward sageness and outward kingliness" by describing the progression from establishing a sincere will, through properly aligning the heart-mind, cultivating the self, regulating the family, and governing the state, to finally bringing peace to the world, with each step serving as the enabling condition for the next. This exemplifies on another level the holistic integration of the inner and the outer.

Although Confucius mentioned the will of Heaven, in practical matters he mostly held an agnostic attitude toward the supernatural domain. Confucianism's humanistic character is evident in its focus on human effort rather than supernatural intervention or guidance for achieving self-transformation. In fact, humans are thought to be interrelated to Heaven and Earth in a sort of spiritual resonance, because everything is made of the same primordial stuff—*qi,* a sort of matter-energy of dual spiritual and material nature—so that the ethical quality of human actions would have widespread ramifications, not only for human society, but also for nature. According to Mencius, through self-cultivation a person's *qi* is nurtured and strengthened, until it pervades all between Heaven and Earth.

This, and some of Mencius's other views, for example, that all things are complete within ourselves, are now interpreted as expressions of mystical experiences. Similar mystical utterances are frequently found in subsequent Confucian writings, especially after the introduction of the spiritual practice of "quiet-sitting" in the Song Dynasty under the influence of Buddhist meditation. Self-reflective journal keeping was another neo-Confucian practice, developed in response to the importance given to self-reflection in the *Analects.* These are not to be mistaken as hermitic practices. To Confucians, immortality is sought through bequeathing to posterity one's exemplary character, wisdom, or benevolent deeds.

—Ping Ho Wong

FURTHER READING

Confucius. (1997). *The Analects of Confucius* (S. Leys, Trans. and notes). New York: W. W. Norton.

Ching, J. (1986). What is Confucian spirituality? In I. Eber (Ed.), *Confucianism: The dynamics of tradition* (pp. 63–80). New York: Macmillan.

Tucker, M. E., & Berthrong, J. (Eds.). (1998). *Confucianism and ecology: The interrelation of heaven, earth, and humans.* Cambridge, MA: Harvard University Center for the Study of World Religions.

Yao, X. (2000). *An introduction to Confucianism.* New York: Cambridge University Press.

CONGREGATIONS

Congregations are understood to be intentional bodies of people, who gather in a specific place consistently with the commitment of spiritual and/or religious worship and practices. Congregations can refer to a church (also megachuch or home church), parish, cathedral (Christian), synagogue (Jewish), masjid/mosque (Muslim), temple (Buddhist, Hindu, Jewish), ward (Latter Day Saint), gurdwara (Sikh), assembly (Baha'i), or other group that represents a small, relatively autonomous membership unit with a religious organization. Congregations may be formally organized and institutionalized; or on the other hand, they may be loosely organized gatherings. While some number their participants in the thousands, most are quite small.

At its core, a congregation involves a body of people who adhere to a coherent belief system, set of values, and shared norms. It involves a regular, intentional assembly, and worship and the sacred. It has a particular place, and some form of ordained or lay leadership. In most religious traditions, people of faith regularly gather in congregations for worship, prayers, rituals, festivals, and rites of passage, spiritual nurture, transmitting doctrine and sacred texts, social support, fulfillment of obligation or disciplines, and charity or social action. For many people, congregations are also carriers of their culture's basic wisdom, traditions, and practices.

Although temples, mosques, churches, and other institutions in some cultures and traditions have historically been dedicated exclusively or primarily to religious rituals, prayer, and worship, these institutions tend to become multifaceted centers of community life when located in more religiously pluralistic, Westernized societies (and especially urban environments) or when the religious community faces oppression or persecution based on race, class, culture, or belief.

Congregations have been recognized to play an important role in society. They have been referred to as "mediating institutions," as institutions within culture that nurture a sense of character, morality, and civic engagement in young people. Congregations potentially impact their members through creating unique ideological, social, and spiritual environments. Religious institutions intentionally offer beliefs, moral codes, and values from which a young person can build a personal belief system. In addition, they provide an intergenerational body of believers to embody and exemplify these beliefs and values. In addition, congregations provide spiritual environments where young people can transcend their everyday concerns and experience connectedness with the divine and human others.

Religious congregations serve as what Garbarino refers to as spiritual anchors, or "institutions of the soul that connect children and teenagers to the deeper meanings of life and provide solid answers to the existential questions: Who am I? What is the meaning of life?" Youth need contexts in which to grapple with the spiritual issues of understanding their purpose in life, what they believe, and their place in the world. Congregations may provide a distinct context in which a young person can explore these issues that are critical to commitment to identity.

Sociologist Christian Smith suggests that religion or congregational involvement my influence young people in a variety of ways. He proposes three categories of influence. First, religion may influence young people through providing moral order. Religion provides moral directives, spiritual experiences, and role models that teach morals and may foster a commitment to them. Second, congregations provide the opportunity for learned competencies through religious practices, rituals, and service and leadership opportunities. Youth may gain community and leadership skills, coping skills, and cultural capital. Third, Smith suggests that through congregations, youth have access to unique social and organizational ties.

Research suggests that religious youth have access to unique social resources that are associated with positive developmental outcomes. For instance, Benson et al. showed that religious youth report having more developmental assets, including a network of supportive relationships and positive values. According to Wagener et al., participation in religious life seems to result in greater exposure to developmental assets, which in turn results in the reduction of risk-taking behaviors.

Another study demonstrated a congregation's potential impact in young people's lives by examining the influence of religious social context on adolescent moral development. King and Furrow used social capital theory as a conceptual model for understanding how positive developmental outcomes are mediated through congregations and other social settings. Social capital refers to the actual and potential resources that a person has access to through his or her network of affiliations and relationships. Through a study of urban youth, they found that religious youth reported more social capital or higher levels of trusting, mutual and interactive relationships. In turn, the presence of social capital was related to reporting higher levels of moral outcomes. Social structures, such as congregations or faith-based organizations, can facilitate social interaction, provide a trusting relational atmosphere, and promote a collective set of shared values and beliefs. Congregations not only provide beliefs and moral standards, but the members embody and enact them in community.

—*Pamela Ebstyne King*

FURTHER READING

Benson, P. L. (1990). *The troubled journey.* Minneapolis, MN: Search Institute.

Benson, P. L., Leffert, N., Scales, P. C., & Blyth, D. A. (1998). Beyond the "village" rhetoric: Creating healthy communities for children and adolescents. *Applied Developmental Science, 2*(3), 138–159.

Berger, B., & Berger, P. (1983). *The war over the family: Capturing the middle ground.* Garden City, NY: Anchor Press.

Billingsley, A. (1999). *Mighty like a river: The Black church and social reform.* New York: Oxford University Press.

Garbarino, J. (1995). *Raising children in a socially toxic environment.* San Francisco: Jossey-Bass.

King, P. E. (2003). Religion and identity: The role of ideological, social, and spiritual contexts. *Applied Developmental Sciences, 7*(3), 196–203.

King, P. E., & Furrow, J. L. (2004). Religion as a resource for positive youth development: religion, social capital, and moral outcomes. *Developmental Psychology, 40*(5), 703–713.

Orr, J. B., Miller, D. E., Roof, W. C., & Melton, J. G. (1995). *Politics of the spirit: Religion and multiethnicity in Los Angeles.* Los Angeles: Universtiy of Southern California.

Roehlkepartain, G. (2006). Congregations: Unexamined crucibles for spiritual development. In E. C. Roehlkepartain, P. E. King, L. M. Wagener, & P. Benson (Eds.), *The Handbook of Spiritual Development in Childhood and Adolescence.* Newbury Park, CA: Sage Publications.

Smith, C. (2003). Theorizing religious effects among American adolescents. *Journal for the Scientific Study of Religion, 42*(1), 17–30.

Stark, R., & Finke, R. (2000). *Acts of faith: Explaining the human side of religion.* Berkeley: University of California Press.

Wagener, L. M., Furrow, J. L., King, P. E., Leffert, N., & Benson, P. (2003). Religion and developmental resources. *Review of Religious Research, 44*(3), 271–284.

Wind, J. P., & Lewis, J. W. (Eds.). (1994). *American congregations* (Vol. 1). Chicago: University of Chicago Press.

CONVERSION

The term "conversion" can be defined in a variety of secular and religious ways. What is common to all definitions of the term is the notion of change.

Conversion can refer to anything that is changed from one use or function to another. In economic terms, it can refer to the exchange of one type of currency for another. It identifies a process in mathematics, and is also a word used to define the extra point or points scored after a touchdown during the game of football. Conversion also refers to the change that takes place when one adopts a new religion, faith expression, or belief system. This type of conversion is referred to as religious conversion.

The notion of conversion in terms of religion or religious cult may carry with it negative overtones when used in relation to a religious recruitment that manipulates people, especially the vulnerable, or "brainwashes" them as part of a conversion process. More positively, the word *conversion* is also used when referring to the sudden or dramatic or, most often, the gradual and developmental change of mind, heart, and behavior that is the substance of spiritual conversion. It is a deeply subjective change in the center of one's values that leads to a change in loyalties, life patterns, and the refocus of one's energies. It is quite possible to live a full life span with a spiritual sense of life and/or involvement in a religious tradition without necessarily personally claiming an experience of conversion. The issue of conversion in religious or spiritual terms can be a controversial topic precisely because the dynamics of conversion can be disruptive to people's lives. Change invariably disrupts the status quo.

The meaning of the term *conversion* from its Hebrew or Greek roots means to turn, turn again, and return. From the scriptural and spiritual point of view, conversion refers to the change—*metanoia*—that takes place in a person's thoughts, feelings, attitudes, and actions in connection to their personal spiritual self-awareness, relationship with the Divine, and sense of responsibility to others, even creation itself. For example, conversion points to the turning away from injustice toward justice, from inhumanity toward compassion, from contemporary forms of being in bondage toward false idols—such as money or power—to being embraced by a spiritual presence and/or spiritual community. Therefore, conversion involves the whole person in a radical reorientation to life, which includes a change in thinking, affect, attitudes, and, importantly, the actual way one chooses to live one's life as a member of the world community.

The disruption and disorientation that is often involved in conversion typically results in positive new self-perceptions, empowerment, and sense of redirection in life. In this regard, the ideas connected to the term conversion highlight a radical "turning around" of the whole person *and* a "return" to a more authentic self, which, in spiritual or religious terms, means a homecoming in God or the divine life. The story in the Christian Testament of the prodigal son found in the Gospel of Luke (15:11–32) is a good example of the process of conversion.

The very nature of religious or spiritual conversion is rooted in a conviction that God, the Divine-Other or Spiritual Presence, is an essential component in the conversion experience. The initiator of the "converting" experience is beyond the self, but requires the person to respond to the initiation for change. For example, grace in the Christian tradition is the ever-present gift of the ever-available offer of divine life, which is core to the experience of conversion.

One cannot be *forced* into a conversion if conversion is about a radical reorienting of one's mind and heart, attitudes, and behaviors. Authentic spiritual conversion is without external coercion and relies on the exercise of human freedom, desire, and will to respond to the graced invitation to change. Thus, some willingness within the person exists when the experience of conversion appears, whether the experience is sudden and in the high drama of a mystical vision, an extraordinary encounter, or human catastrophe.

While there are many stories that point to a lightning-bolt conversion suddenly redirecting someone's life, such as the first-century Saul being knocked off his horse, struck blind, repenting his persecution of the followers of Jesus, and then becoming the Apostle Paul, a follower of the very ones he had previously persecuted, most conversions are far more gradual in nature (Act of the Apostles 9). These more dramatic experiences of conversion, however, suggest a process and happen within a certain context and length of time, even if the conversion appears to be a single unexpected event. With most conversions, there is an unfolding life story that is the milieu for something new to break in and offer an alternative way of thinking, feeling, and acting.

While religious or spiritual conversion is possible in the life of a child, most children do not possess the developmental maturity to adequately negotiate and integrate an experience of conversion. It is important to note, however, that children possess an innate desire for attachment to love, and are quite susceptible to the spiritual dimension of life. The psychosocial developmental theories of Erik Erikson, the moral/faith developmental theories of Lawrence Kohlberg and James Fowler, and the work of child psychiatrist Robert Coles suggest that each phase of human development holds the potential, and even necessity, for critical change and growth, which can be viewed as connected to the processes of spiritual growth.

The premise of Coles's extensive observations and conversations with children from around the world is that children possess a vibrant inner life, are capable of contemplative prayer, experience the transcendent in nature, feel wonder, and engage in making sense of their life as a sacred journey. Fowler supports Coles and relies on Erikson's developmental stage theory in positing the experience of faith as the way each individual, from infancy to old age, finds coherence in and gives meaning to the multiple forces and relations that shape human life.

Fowler has developed a six-stage theory of faith development, which includes granting to young children, as early as 3 years of age, the intuitive capacity to engage the power of story, play, and build imagination. Adult nurturing of these capacities in children creates the seed bed for the more conscious and reflective experiences of growth in the inner realm that we call the spiritual life. Intuition is a powerful factor in sensing the kind of inner conflict or crisis that is pressing the person toward a new stage of growth. As children gain more sophisticated reasoning abilities, they also gain access to their own life narrative and begin to experience their lives as a pilgrimage of meaning, one with purpose and destiny.

The adolescent years—often portrayed as a phase of solidifying identity, separation from parental control, searching for intimacy, and struggling with conformity—are extremely ripe years for discovering the power of one's spiritual center or transcendent self. In this phase of life, it is quite possible for an adolescent to experience conversion in several ways. Adolescents may have gradually grown to a place of greater clarity with respect to their own commitment to a way of life, and find themselves ready and able to freely claim a chosen moral path. It is also possible for adolescents to experience a sharply defined event that opens them to new depths not previously understood or valued. This defining experience, which reorganizes their priorities and life direction, can be called conversion in the adolescent experience. Lastly, as adolescents realize the meaning of personal freedom and responsibility, they may discover a newfound ability to invest their love and loyalty in a faith community. Thus, the Jewish ritual of bar mitzvah or bat mitzvah and the sacrament of Confirmation in some Christian communities are examples of rites of passage for teenagers to exteriorize the interior reality of an adolescent's new season of maturing spiritual consciousness and transition into a new role within a community.

Most often conversion is a long process of psychosocial human development and spiritual change that has been active in the unconscious long before it breaks into consciousness. The "transforming moment" of conversion is actually embedded in the ongoing processes of growth and change that mark human maturation. One's actual life is the situational context in which transformation occurs. Just as there is that one moment when a baby takes a first step or a perplexing problem finds a solution, so too, in spiritual terms, there are decisive moments in life when a person becomes strikingly and unmistakably aware that she or he is being faced with a life-defining decision. In theological terms, such a moment is called a *kairos,* a Greek word for sacred time or the inbreaking of the holy unexpectedly into an ordinary moment in time. *Kairos* is about a fertile rich moment that holds the seeds of transformation.

The "crisis" that often precedes conversion is, as already noted, most often more gradual than traumatic and sudden. The following list identifies some of the common characteristics associated with an impending spiritual crisis-conversion:

- Restlessness
- Boredom or depression
- Lack of satisfaction with the current state of affairs in one's life
- Awareness that something is missing from life
- Vague and elusive agitation and struggle to name the source of a problem
- Desire for something new arising from questions about the meaning of life

Some of the outcomes of living through a *kairos* include becoming

- More organized in one's sense of priorities
- More aware of the importance of the intangibles in life, such as spirituality
- Possessing a clearer sense of direction in life
- More grateful, humble, open, generous, and compassionate

- Able to express and receive love more freely and genuinely
- Renewed in energy and enthusiasm for the gift of life
- Oriented beyond self to service of one's neighbor and the world

In short, the sense of "new being" associated with spiritual conversion includes an inner serenity that arises from anxiety, feelings of joy breaking through from depression, the emergence of hope beyond pessimism, the gesture of forgiveness instead of retaliation, and the discovery of courage in place of paralyzing fear—all of which are manifestations of the triumph of the dynamism of the human spirit. This kind of mature growth comes with change and change brings challenge as well as the hope found in new beginnings. Spiritual conversion is a psychodynamic process, or a breakthrough, whereby human beings experience greater depths of consciousness about the meaning and direction of life.

—Avis Clendenen

See also Grace; Retreats

FURTHER READING

Coles, R. (1990). *The spiritual life of children.* Boston: Houghton Mifflin.

Conn, J. (1989). *Spirituality and personal maturity.* Lanham, MD: University Press of America.

Fowler, J. (1981). *Stages of faith: The psychology of human developmentand the quest for meaning.* New York: Harper & Row.

Loder, J. E. (1981). *The transforming moment: Understanding convictional experiences.* San Francisco: Harper & Row.

Loder, J. E. (1998). *The logic of the spirit: human development in theological perspective.* San Francisco: Jossey-Bass.

Rambo, L. (1995). *Understanding religious conversion.* New Haven, CT: Yale University Press.

COPING IN YOUTH

Crisis situations are usually unexpected and virtually unpredictable, and therefore often linked with confusion. Their causes may be unpreventable—such as news of a family member's passing or heightened violence in the world—but religion, faith, and spirituality provide a framework for finding direction and meaning in the face of such dire situations. Enabling people to come to terms with loss, faith offers a connection to something beyond self, as it allows one to make sense of otherwise incomprehensible events. Such spiritual connections can be shared with children in order to calm and comfort them, and to aid them in their recovery from trauma.

Everyone responds differently to crises, regardless of whether the circumstances are deeply personal matters or universal situations. Some people are very vocal, vociferously expressing their state of emotional overdrive. Others internalize their emotional struggle, limiting their responses to the inquiries of concerned friends and relatives as they attempt to sort things out on their own. Nonetheless, everyone is affected by such events. In moments of crisis, adults can sometimes be too preoccupied with asserting control of a chaotic situation and maintaining composure. Such efforts, which can often drain every last bit of energy and focus, sometimes lead to greater uncertainty. Still, there is no question that when children are confronted with crisis, they turn to figures of authority for guidance; therefore, it is not entirely clear how adults should appropriately respond to children during crises.

Engaging children in discussions concerning matters of faith and God—or simply the sense that there is something larger at work in the world—can support children experiencing traumatic stress factors. It may also provide them with skills for coping with difficult matters in the future.

A child, like an adult, may express different emotions as a reaction to trauma: anxiety, depression, obsession, confusion, numbness, unfocused rage, denial, or difficulty finding meaning. Any or all of these reactions are possible. For example, it is not unusual for a 3- to 6-year-old to personalize crises, feeling as though his unrelated actions actually caused the catastrophe. In order to help the child work through such feelings, adults must convey that they can understand the child's response without judgment. Adults need to listen and provide an opportunity for the child to express his view.

Often a child coping with trauma will question the role of God and/or religion. Adults should try and speak openly about the questions children have about God and religion, so that children understand that their concerns can be talked about and addressed.

While young children often parrot what they've heard, they also generate a range of complex feelings of their own—sometimes expressing themselves in a manner that an adult may not understand or wish to condone. For example, a child may become "uncooperative" or "aggressive" during a crisis, and can often direct that anger toward God and/or religion. During crises, it is important to take a step back to appreciate and attend to feelings underlying children's behaviors. Aggression focused on God may veil fear or anger about God's perceived lapsed role in ensuring the child a sense of safety and constancy. In that case, emotional engagement is often more helpful than control, punishment, or suppression.

Listening to children's ideas and helping them recognize their feelings is much more useful than declaring what is "right" or "wrong." When adults talk about their own faith or tell stories about people who exhibited faith and admirable qualities during crises—qualities such as patience, hope, courage, and strength—they help guide the process of self-examination. Such reflections may support the young person in developing a healthy relationship with God.

When facing crises, some young people will encounter intense reactions, which serve as a means for coping. For example, both denial and shock may be reactions to a crisis. In denial, there is no acknowledgment that something very stressful has occurred and/or the intensity of the event is not fully experienced. Shock is a sudden and often intense disturbance that leads to a feeling of being stunned and dazed. While such reactions are usually temporary and may include feeling unpredictable, anxious, and nervous, preoccupation with the crisis—recurrent memories of the crisis, interference of these memories with everyday routine, and interruption in relationships—decreases gradually and subsides fairly soon after the crisis.

To facilitate recovery from crises, time to heal is needed, as are experiences with empathetic care. It is important that young people secure around them those familiar with a particular crisis and/or the emotions experienced with crises (such as specialized support groups) and to establish positive, healthy routines. Often faith-based groups and/or faith-based institutions can provide young people in crisis with a sense of security, belonging, and centeredness.

When such measures do not bring adequate adjustment, professional support should be considered. It is not unusual for those who experience crises to engage in counseling by specialists who understand such difficulties. These professionals are trained to provide constructive recommendations addressing thoughts, feelings, and behaviors that may seem impossible to manage. Pastoral counseling is often useful when young people are faced with crises, particularly when they face a crisis of identity with their own religion and God.

In the face of tragedy, many of us ask, "Can this tragedy also happen to me?" The foundations of our daily lives are shaken. Children need to feel secure; adults need to recognize how their own anxiety can challenge the child's sense of safety. In times of crisis, the notion of human fragility is dramatically amplified. Managing the struggle between opposing forces such as safety and vulnerability is one of life's basic challenges. Faith mediates the coexistence of such opposing forces, allowing a person peace of mind in the face of frightening events. Developing a connection with a spiritual reality provides the framework through which the meaning of such events can be understood and to which a response can be developed.

For example, family prayer may literally bring home the resources of our spiritual connection as the family joins together in one mind, connected in their beliefs despite the crisis. Catastrophic events give rise to the opportunity to discuss both the ability and inability to control life, and to understand how spirituality and a relationship with God can provide comfort in the face of life's challenges.

Tragedy is often abrupt and sudden. At such times it is common to ask: What is life about? Who am I? Why am I here? These authentic moments provide the opportunity to find meaningful answers to existentialist questions. Authentic moments help one bring control to life, to make changes, and discover the purpose of existence. Very often one's relationship with and understanding of that which is divine and/or spiritual influences one's perspective about and reflections on the crises experienced.

On a more scientific note, research suggests that a negative event may be reframed as an opportunity for spiritual growth and may increase religious meaning. While religion may have positive or negative effects, depending on how it factors into a crisis, positive interpretations bring both hope and a sense of control—a strengthening of purpose. In this way, spirituality offers a positive mechanism for coping with crisis.

Although crises often shatter one's sense of order and continuity, religion and spirituality provide clarification about direction, meaning, and purpose—stabilizing one's perceived place in the world. Faith and spirituality reveal how suffering and evil can be transformed through the Spirit—inviting one into personal transformation. Crises often lead to mourning of losses, but they can also serve as a reminder to be thankful for the many blessings received. In this way, crises invite self-examination. Through difficult trials, clarity about purpose in life often arises.

In the final analysis, responding to traumatic events confirms, yet again, the intangible resources on which people rely—the essential values of religion, faith, and trust in God. This faith gives direction to life—not only in the sense of a life struggling to survive but also a life demonstrating value and purpose.

—John T. Chirban

See also Faith; Crisis

FURTHER READING

Chirban, J. T. (2004). *True coming of age: A dynamic process that leads to emotional well-being, spiritual growth, and meaningful relationships.* New York: McGraw-Hill.

Moghaddam, F. M., & Marsells, A. J. (Eds.). (2004). *Understanding terrorism: Psychological roots, consequences, and interventions.* Washington, DC: American Psychological Association.

Park, C. L., & Cohen, L. H. (1993). Religious and nonreligious coping with the death of a friend. *Cognitive Therapy and Research, 17:* 561–577.

Schuster, M. A., Stein, B. D., Jaycox, L. H., Collins, R. L., Marshall, G. N., Elliott, M. N., Zhou, A. J., Kanouse, D. E., Morrison, J. L., & Berry, S. H. (2001). A national survey of stress reactions after the September 11, 2001, terrorist attacks. *New England Journal of Medicine, 345*(20): 505–520.

Weaver, A. J., Flannelly, L. T., Garbarino, J., Figley, C. R., & Flannelly, K. J. (2003). A systematic review of research on religion and spirituality in the Journal of Traumatic Stress: 1990–1999. *Mental Health, Religion & Culture, 6*(3): 215–228.

CRASHAW, RICHARD

Richard Crashaw was a 17th-century English devotional poet, but very different from his contemporaries John Donne and George Herbert in the way that he describes his spiritual experiences. He does not challenge his readers with intellectual ideas like Donne, or nurture them in more homely piety like Herbert, but rather seeks to stir their emotional responses through the rich sensuousness of his descriptions. For example, the awe with which he expresses Christ's sacrifice is inspired not so much by its doctrinal significance as the way to salvation, but by the rapture and wonder he feels at the worth and beauty of Jesus' blood (see the short poem "Upon the Body of our Blessed Lord, Naked and Bloody"). His poetry has much in common with the Italian poet Marino and with the Continental tradition of the religious mystics, and like them he expresses spiritual transcendence through intensely physical imagery.

Crashaw was born in London in 1612, the only son of a learned Puritan divine with strong anti-Catholic views. After his father's death, he studied at Pembroke College, Cambridge, later being elected to a fellowship at Peterhouse College in 1635. Both colleges were known for their High Church sympathies. In spite of his highly ascetic personal life, this was a time of great content for Crashaw, who divided his time among his academic work, preaching at Little St. Mary's Church, pastimes of poetry, music, and drawing, and his visits to the Anglican community at Little Gidding that had been established by George Herbert's friend Nicholas Ferrar. However, his happiness was short-lived, and before Cromwell's parliamentary forces smashed the statues in Peterhouse College and Little St. Mary's Church in 1643, he fled to Leyden and then Paris. By this time, he had converted to Catholicism, although he named his 1646 collection of poetry *Steps to the Temple* in honor of the Anglican George Herbert. He continued on to Rome where he remained virtually destitute for a year before being given a minor post. In 1649, he was eventually appointed subcanon in the Cathedral of Our Lady of Loreto, but died the same year.

Crashaw has been described as the chief exponent in English of the Baroque style. Underlying this style is the belief that the senses, emotions, and imagination can all combine in God's worship, and that an elaborate, decorative, overflowing style, and passionate, exotic imagery can best stimulate this response. In this view, religious art should appeal to the physical senses, while including symbolism that carries deeper spiritual meaning.

Crashaw's most important poems include meditations on incidents in the life of Jesus and many show his fascination with saintly women ("The Weeper," "On the Glorious Assumption of our Blessed Lady," "Sancta Maria Dolorosa," "A Hymn to the Name and Honour of the Admirable St. Teresa" and "The Flaming Heart"). Among his poetic techniques are a paradoxical fusion of binary opposites such as the sensuous and the spiritual, the secular and the divine, tears and ecstasy; a frequent appeal to the senses, particularly those of touch, taste and sound; the use of extravagant metaphors without any hint of irony, as when he compares Magdalene's eyes to "two walking baths, . . . portable and compendious oceans," and her tears to the cream above the Milky Way; and the use of erotic imagery to convey spiritual longing and spiritual experience. This last characteristic is seen in the sexual suggestiveness at the end of the "Letter to the Countess of Denbigh" and the description of St. Teresa pierced by the dart of the Angel of Love. The startlingly sensuous terms in which Crashaw depicts the spiritual world recall the sculpture of Gianlorenzo Bernini, and the earlier writing on divine love of such women mystics as Julian of Norwich.

—*J. Mark Halstead*

See also John Donne; George Herbert

FURTHER READING

Martin, L. C. (Ed.). (1957). *The poems, English, Latin and Greek, of Richard Crashaw.* Oxford: Clarendon Press.

Roberts, J. R. (Ed.). (1990). *New perspectives on the life and art of Richard Crashaw.* Columbia: University of Missouri Press.

CRISIS

Crises refer to experiences that challenge people to examine their values and beliefs. They prompt people to ask, "What matters? What do I believe, and why?" If crises are deliberately embraced and engaged, they can be opportunities for tremendous spiritual growth. Although the term "crisis" can refer to emotionally traumatic events, it usually does not. Used in this general sense, a crisis can include anything that challenges people to examine what they believe and why. Examples of crisis can range from something as simple as dialoguing with someone who holds a differing viewpoint on an important issue such as the death penalty, to something as serious as divorce of one's parents, physical or emotional abuse, or critical illness.

Spiritual growth develops in two ways: in dramatic spurts of rapid growth and in longer periods of slow, steady growth. The former, more dramatic type of growth, can result when persons who are in the middle of a life crisis do not try to avoid or escape from the challenges presented by the crisis, but intentionally respond to, and address, the salient issues. The latter, more gradual type of growth develops through regular and sustained practice of traditional spiritual disciplines (i.e., prayer, meditation, fasting, and the study of sacred scripture). Both ways typically complement one another and work together in tandem to eventually produce spiritual maturity.

Although crises can lead to deeper levels of spiritual maturity, crises are not pleasant to experience. Rather, they are fundamentally unsettling. Indeed, the Chinese word for crisis refers to both danger and opportunity. Crisis denotes struggling and wrestling with fundamental life issues. Because of this, many people try to avoid dealing with crises and only truly wrestle with hard questions when pressed by serious and unavoidable life circumstances. For example, people sometimes reorient their lives in terms of what is of lasting value after experiencing life-threatening illnesses such as cancer. Many who have reported near-death experiences often do the same. Such times of crisis offer unprecedented opportunities for profound growth in a variety of dimensions, including spiritual, emotional, cognitive, moral, and psychosocial identity development. Paradoxically, the times of greatest struggle can also be the times of greatest growth.

A classic example of crisis stimulating spiritual growth is found in Saint John of the Cross's classic work, *The Dark Night of the Soul.* In this work, the 16th-century Spanish mystic describes crises as times of spiritual desolation. Such "dark nights" of desolation are essential for the more profound levels of spiritual insight and maturity.

One need not experience the crisis personally. Often, crises occur through watching a friend or loved one go through a time of struggle. Similarly, reading classic works of literature can be powerful stimulants of growth. Readers have the opportunity of stepping into the shoes of persons from another time, place, or culture, and indirectly encountering the wide variety of dilemmas that people or literary characters have confronted.

The experience of crisis alone is not sufficient to stimulate growth. The crisis must be embraced and genuinely engaged. To do so requires virtues such as honesty, courage, and integrity. In order for development to occur, one must not only have been exposed to a crisis, but have actively wrestled with issues and ideas that are relevant to them, and ways of thinking that are different from their own. If spiritual growth is to occur, one cannot merely turn to religious belief for temporary relief (sometimes referred to as "foxhole" religion), but must deliberately and critically examine beliefs and values. In other words, in order to experience profound spiritual growth, one cannot compartmentalize one's spirituality from ordinary daily life. Instead, one must reorient and integrate spirituality, beliefs, values, behaviors, and lifestyle into a unified whole. In rare individuals, this can occur in a distinct moment of time. But for the majority of people, it is a lifelong journey.

This fact was the basis for the psychosocial theory of identity development proposed by Erik Erikson, a famous psychologist. Erikson identified eight stages of life. At each stage, a life crisis forces persons to wrestle with issues that are relevant or important to them. During such times of crisis, people may try on various roles and explore competing beliefs and ideologies. In this way one answers the question, "Who am I?" One's spiritual beliefs form a central part of their personal identity.

Crises also stimulate developmental growth by shaping the formation of cognitive schemas. Cognitive schemas are like mental scaffolding or mental templates that influence how information is perceived, processed, interpreted, evaluated, organized, stored, and retrieved. Religious beliefs (a specific type of schema) actively filter which data are stored, which are discarded, and how they are subsequently understood and interpreted. For example, a common childhood cognitive schema is that bad things happen to bad people, not to good people. Thus, if something bad happens to a person, that person deserved it because he or she was not a good person.

But what happens if something tragic happens to a person that they know is good and kind ("when bad things happen to good people")? In such a case, incoming data do not agree with an existing belief (schema) and the potential for a crisis is in the making. The result is cognitive dissonance—the tension that we experience when competing beliefs do not agree with one another. The person experiencing cognitive dissonance has two choices: either work the incoming data into existing beliefs or attempt to reconstruct the belief in order to accept the new data. Psychologists refer to these processes as assimilation (working the data into existing beliefs) and accommodation (reconstructing the belief in order to make sense of the new data). The more dramatic rates of spiritual development occur when accommodation occurs and existing beliefs are reconstructed.

Whether or not a person embraces and engages a life crisis (accommodates competing data by reconstructing an existing schema) depends on a number of factors. For example, environments that are perceived of as physically and emotionally safe (i.e., honest and genuine expressions of doubt and struggle are supported and encouraged as one wrestles with hard questions) foster this kind of growth. Opportunities for role taking (i.e., walking in another person's shoes via service learning, volunteer work, or reading great works of literature) stimulate growth and development. Having responsibility for others and for solving relevant moral dilemmas are powerful stimulants to growth and development. Culturally diverse environments provide opportunities to interact with persons holding differing viewpoints and values. And they provide challenges to one's own thinking. The availability of role models and the attitudes of one's peers and friends influence whether one will have the courage to honestly engage a crisis.

Crises are, by their very nature, difficult to experience. But the resulting benefits can be profound. Persons who work through a crisis emerge with an "owned" identity, rather than with a sense of self that has been "borrowed" from family and friends. They have a greater understanding of who they are, what they value, what they believe, and why they believe it. And they gain a greater appreciation for, and comfort with, the complexities and paradoxes of modern life. If and how one develops spiritually as the result of a crisis depends on the nature of the particular crisis, the individual (e.g., his or her history, temperament, and so on), and the context and conditions in which the crisis occurred and in which the individual responds to and recovers from the crisis.

—Gay L. Holcomb

See also Coping in Youth; Erikson, Erik

FURTHER READING

Dalton, J. C. (1985). Critical factors in the value development process. In J. C. Dalton (Ed.), *Promoting values development in college students* (NASPA Monograph Series, Vol. 4, pp. 47–61). Washington, DC: National Association of Student Personnel Administrators.

Droege, T. A. (1983). *Faith passages and patterns.* Philadelphia, PA: Fortress Press.

Hall, C. M. (1986). Crisis as opportunity for spiritual growth. *Journal of Religion and Health, 25*(1), 8–17.

CROP CIRCLES

Crop circles are large, geometric imprints in crop fields and other land areas in which the crops are flattened against the soil. The appearance of these mysterious imprints was first reported in the mainstream media in the early 1980s when they were found in agricultural fields in the south of England. Today, crop circles are reported in many countries all over the world at a rate of at least a hundred every year (and usually more). Their dimensions may vary from several square meters to larger than the size of a football field, whereas their geometrical complexity and intricacy are often breathtaking.

When the public interest in the crop circle phenomenon began to grow in the 1980s, some considered them the work of an extraterrestrial intelligence. At that time, the formations consisted of smooth, round circles with a well-defined border in which the flattened crop was neatly spiraled around the center of the circle. As the crop circles sometimes appeared in a very short time, without any sign of human involvement, and particularly without the presence of any apparent tracks leading to or from the circles, these imprints were interpreted by many as tracks of "flying saucers" that had landed in the fields.

In 1990, crop circles revealed a dramatic change. For example, instead of a circle, as usually found (sometimes with a thin ring around it), a much more complicated design appeared near the village of Alton Barnes, England. It consisted of several circles, connected by straight pathways and including elements similar to characters of the Roman alphabet. Rectangular bars of various lengths were found adjacent to it. It became clear that all those who had attributed the crop circle phenomenon to the result of a meteorological effect (e.g., created by a sort of whirlwind) had now been proven wrong. Many similar designs, of increasing complexity, would appear in fields around the world in subsequent years, and the simple expression *crop circles* started to be replaced by more advanced terms such as *crop formations, agroglyphs,* or *pictograms.* It was demonstrated by pioneers such as Gerald S. Hawkins, former chair of the Astronomy Department at Boston University, that the design of the patterns was not only intriguing, but also highly intelligent. Advanced mathematical theorems were found in the positions and proportions of the individual elements of the pictograms (e.g., the proportions of the areas of individual circles in one and the same pattern).

Today, the crop circle phenomenon has evolved to a phenomenon that nobody can deny. Over 10,000 formations have been reported worldwide (from all over Europe to China, and from the United States and Canada to Australia), and the pictograms have grown into very large, extremely complicated, and usually very beautiful pieces of landscape art.

As to the source of the crop circle phenomenon, opinions seem to vary. Many are convinced that they are all human-made, with the aid of simple tools to flatten the crop. And indeed, several self-acclaimed *landscape artists* have produced beautiful designs of flattened crops in farm fields, often secretly in the darkness of the night, but also as a well-paid job (e.g., for television commercials). Simple explanations provided in certain television shows and documentaries have convinced many that there is nothing mysterious about the appearance of circles and other patterns in farm fields or other land areas.

In contrast, many others are not willing to accept that all crop formations are made this way. They report repeated findings in some crop circles that cannot be explained as the result of simple mechanical flattening, such as remarkable cellular and chemical changes in the flattened crop or chemical changes in the soil. In fact, several peer-reviewed scientific articles have appeared that discuss these findings, and suggest the presence of high levels of electromagnetic energy during the creation of crop circles. In addition, many people report remarkable experiences in and around the crop circles, such as intense feelings of well-being (or the opposite), failure of electronic equipment, visions, and flying balls of bright light. At the least these balls of light seem to be a very real phenomenon, as they have not only been seen by many eyewitnesses, but have also been filmed on several occasions with video cameras. All in all, the crop circle community is clearly divided in two: those who believe the phenomenon has a very trivial explanation and those who believe there is more to it.

The crop circle "believers," as they are often called, usually interpret the crop circle phenomenon as a sign that planet Earth is going through a major transformation. The specific interpretations of this concept vary. For example, the Hopi Indians of North America see the circles as an expression of Mother Earth suffering from the bad use that humankind makes of her. Some Christians interpret the flying balls of light and the crop circles as the *signs in heaven and signs on earth,* as predicted in the Bible to appear before the

Apocalypse. Some see the signs as spiritual symbols that induce subconscious changes in the mind of people (in order to help them prepare for a dimensional shift that the Earth will be going through soon), whereas others assume that an extraterrestrial intelligence is trying to communicate with us, or is putting humans through a psychological exercise in order to prepare for their imminent arrival.

No matter which of these interpretations is correct, an interesting fact that nobody can deny is that even after at least 100 years of these phenomena (crop circles were reported in the early 20th century, and perhaps even in 1678), discussions about their origin are still ongoing. Another fact is that crop circles often seem to have very strong effects on the human mind, and many people claim that their lives have changed dramatically (mostly for the good) ever since they started to get interested in the phenomenon. One rational psychological explanation is that when people are confronted with a phenomenon that cannot be explained in simple terms and that seems to be a manifestation of a power that is beyond anything on Earth—and indeed, this is how many people feel when they are standing in a crop circle—it puts their lives in a different perspective, and makes everyday common worries all of a sudden seem small.

However, as mentioned earlier, some attribute this behavior as an effect of the symbols themselves, which act on the subconscious mind, whereas others simply believe that crop circles with their alleged mysterious characteristics make people think about other things than they usually think about, which opens up their minds and induces brand-new ideas that they never had before. In any case, the spiritual or psychological effects that crop circles have on people are usually very strong, and this is probably why many consider and treat crop circles as *temporary temples* that give them a place to meditate, relax, pray, or think.

A personal visit to a crop formation is likely required before one can develop a well-considered opinion about all of this. If you ever decide to do so (today there are even organized tours in the summer season, particularly in the south of England but also elsewhere), you will probably also experience that crop circles can have good effects on human mentality. It is surprising how in a world with still so much aggression, hatred, envy, and other negative emotions, a crop circle always seems to be a place of peace, love, loyalty, mutual respect, and friendship. People meet one another in a crop circle and behave like old friends, regardless of age, appearance, political preferences, gender, or skin color. Perfect strangers spend the entire day (or longer) inside the formations, and eat, talk, sing, and dance together. Regardless of their meaning and their origin, this fact is certainly an important aspect of the crop circle phenomenon that deserves our attention and appreciation, and should serve as a lesson for all of us.

—Eltjo H. Haselhoff

FURTHER READING

Haselhoff, E. H. (2002). *The deepening complexity of crop circles: Scientific research & urban legends.* Berkeley, CA: Frog.

Levengood, W. C. (1994). Anatomical anomalies in crop formation plants. *Physiologia Plantarum, 92:* 356–363.

Levengood, W. C., & Talbott, N. P. (1999). Dispersion of energies in worldwide crop formations. *Physiologia Plantarum, 105:* 615–624.

CULT FIGURES

Ancient apocalyptic beliefs have continued to exert influence in modern times. This is evident in the continual evolution of new cults that center their indoctrination on apocalyptic literature. At the core of their conviction is the end of this worldly existence, which is at hand. In most cults, members firmly believe that they are living in a world that is brimming with evil and chaos, and that the only escape is death. Cult leaders often prey on adolescents who are in the midst of deep identity development. Cults often provide young people with a sense of community and acceptance that they are unable to find in other places.

Throughout history, religious movements such as cults and sects have been an impetus to social change and spiritual expression. Cults gained attention in the late 1960s with the appearance of the Moonies, Solar Temple, Heaven's Gate, Wicca, Branch Davidians, and others that called attention to a new form of spirituality that was infiltrating society. These and other cult religions brought about alternative forms of Christian expression grounded in new beliefs and modernized interpretations of the Bible and other doctrines modeled to complement current societal issues.

New religious movements embody cultural integration and the transformation and globalization that have remodeled the essence of society. Religious cults focus on the individual's needs and present a new path to salvation led by a charismatic leader. The leaders impose new standards of service expected of the followers, and an element of sacrifice that ranges from breaking ties with friends and family outside the cult, to self-sacrifice and even suicide.

The leader's focus is typically directed toward apocalyptic beliefs, which demonstrate a rise of violence in the name of religion based on the belief that the followers are living in the last days. The followers live with serious expectations of an apocalypse, instilled by a level of enthusiasm that often blinds a person's judgment, and fosters often extreme behaviors resulting in death at the leader's command.

The relevance of the apocalyptic lore is directly linked to a prophet or a second messiah figure that the charismatic leader takes on, presenting himself as someone who can lead the cult to salvation. The rhetoric that such leaders use is full of apocalyptic imagery; often the Book of Revelations is read and preached to followers whose obedience and commitment to the cause are repeatedly reinforced. The leaders are passionate in their beliefs and cause, and personify the role of mother or father figure; followers become the obedient children turning to the leader for direction and strength.

The 1960s, an era of revolution and freedom within much of the world, saw the advent of a religious organization that came to be known as the People's Temple, led by the Reverend Jim Jones. Jones generated a mass following as a result of his orations on the topic of a "new truth" and the utopian dream. This megalomaniac leader was the focal point of the source of their salvation. Born on May 13, 1931, to a family of white supremacists, members of the Ku Klux Klan, Jones developed a fascination for church work at an early age. In 1963, he established the People's Temple Full Gospel Church in Indianapolis, an interracial congregation fostering a notion of a socialist utopian society.

During Jones's rise to religious notoriety, his mental stability was questionable; he reportedly suffered from frequent mysterious fainting episodes, and communicated with and heeded advice from extraterrestrials. Jones also practiced faith healing by claiming to heal with touch and prayer. One of the most intriguing attributes that comprised Jones's character profile was his visions of nuclear holocaust. These premonitory images served to fuel his paranoid behavior, and eventually became the foundation of the cult's subsequent conviction that the Apocalypse was indeed approaching. Jones became increasingly convinced and paranoid that Armageddon was imminent, and more to the point, that his hometown of Indianapolis was the point of origin. To further distance himself from imminent danger, he moved his Temple base and congregation to San Francisco, where Jones felt that he would be safe.

Jones became increasingly obsessed with nuclear holocaust, and convinced himself and his followers that the world had become riddled with evil and corruption. These fears that Jones used to instill in his followers paved the way for Jones to dream of his own utopian community rich with peace, love, and a righteous way of living. Jones made this idyllic fantasy into a distorted reality.

Rankled by his paranoia, Jones gathered patrons of the People's Temple movement and fled to Guyana, South America, to institute his version of utopia. However, once the followers were in "Jonestown" as it became to be known, Jones inevitably grew manipulative and controlling, while his paranoia worsened. New enemies threatened Jones and his followers, who drove Jones to later commit one of the most heinous acts of the 1970s. These new enemies that Jones would have to contend with were any and all U.S. government agencies and outside family members who threatened to weaken the fabric of the community.

Jones secured a remote location deep in the Guyana jungle to build his newfound community, where he felt safe from the repugnant and pervasive evils of the civilized world. Jones, a master manipulator, sought to establish complete dependence and infantilism among cult members as a technique of brainwashing. This goal was accomplished through the community's complete isolation.

In his last orders as leader of the People's Temple, Jones set up endurance trials for upcoming events. These trials were termed "white nights": sirens were set to sound off in the middle of the night, and followers were told that the jungle was swarming with the evils of outsiders and mercenaries. Once everyone in the community had gathered, they were given glasses of red liquid and told that it contained poison which would cause death in 45 minutes. These tests would occur randomly at Jones's will and without warning.

This ritualistic practice for the end of Jones's worldly kingdom became a reality on the eve of November 18, 1978. For reasons unknown to outsiders, Jones ordered that all 911 congregation members to commit their revolutionary deaths on that date. He laced a large quantity of fruit punch with generous doses of cyanide and Valium. Jones ordered all 276 children at Jonestown to drink the punch, followed by the adults. In the end, after members had carried out his orders, Jones shot himself in the head and Jonestown fell silent.

The phenomenon of Jim Jones and the People's Temple can be viewed as a cultural marking point. The cult itself represents an anomaly, and therefore a crack in the backbone of mid-20th-century Canadian and American culture. Jonestown and other such cults arose from a cultural climate in which members were products of their culture, and at the same time producers of a reactant culture. These cults search for a new reality, a new meaning, and a new purpose to escape from the corruption that was and is still evident in the modern world. Charismatic religious leaders such as Jim Jones provide this reality and reassurance to their followers, and they look to the Apocalypse for their new reality in this world and the next.

Another spectacular mass violence event took place 17 years later. This time the charismatic leader was David Koresh, a self-proclaimed Second Messiah.

Koresh was born in 1959 to a single mother in Houston, Texas; he never met his father. Koresh described his childhood as being very lonely, as he was often teased by other children, and suffered from dyslexia. At age 12, Koresh became fascinated by the Bible and memorized long passages. At age 20, he joined the Seventh Day Adventists; he was later excommunicated due to being a "bad influence" on the youth in the congregation.

In 1981, Koresh was welcomed into the Branch Davidians in Waco, Texas. Almost immediately, he attempted to assert himself in the cult as a leader. A power struggle between Koresh and George Roden for the role of leader ended in 1987, when Roden was killed during a shootout between the two men's followers. Koresh was put on trial for Roden's death; Koresh claimed that Roden was shot by mistake, as he (Koresh) was aiming at a tree.

In his role as the Second Messiah, Koresh was perceived as the deliverer of God's message, and revealer of the "truth." He often led 12-hour Bible studies preaching this newfound truth to his disciples. The Book of Revelations was at the core of his teachings, in which he emphasized the Seven Seals, and that he was the chosen ruler of the House of David to open the seal.

Death would allow Koresh's followers to reach salvation and live in God's Kingdom, for they would be following his law, as told by Koresh. Koresh became increasingly manipulative, and began to instill fear of an end time ushered in by the cult. Koresh moved his congregation to a complex in Waco that they named Mt. Carmel. Here he fostered a new enemy, the U.S. government, deemed to be the locus of evil in the world. His paranoia of the government fueled his teachings to take a different direction, one that involved preparation for death. All members acquired firearms and learned how to use them. Children who survived Waco recounted how at the age of 3, they knew the caliber of guns, and demonstrated for psychologists how they were to die, by taking a pistol in their mouth.

The children within the cult were never exposed to the outside world, were taught that the outside was evil and that they were the "good guys" who had to fight the evil outsiders. The children were also forced into obedience by use of the "Helper," a wooden paddle used to beat them, as adults were told by Koresh that God wanted them to do so.

Koresh also used sex as an instrument of control. Some of his twenty wives were spouses of his disciples. He ordered celibacy for the men, as only he could procreate with their wives, as ordered by God. This measure of control furthered his status as undisputed leader, and tested the obedience of his followers.

Koresh fueled the desire for his utopian community with the idea that history would evolve into an ideal human community, which is grounded in the Apocalypse from the Book of Revelation (20–22), The Assurance of the Second Coming (Rev 16:15/Acts 1:11), The Resurrection of the Dead (Rev 20:12/Dan 12:2), Last Judgment (Rev 20:12/Matt 25:31–33), and the Antichrist figure (1 John 2:18, 4:3–2/Rev13: 1–18). These Biblical passages were instrumental in Koresh's teachings to his disciples. His knowledge of the Bible and gift of rhetoric inspired his followers to support his cause and his beliefs that they were living in the time of the Apocalypse.

The FBI became wary of the Branch Davidians, mainly owing to reports of weapons caches and systematic child abuse, including Koresh's marriage to a 10-year-old. There was a 51-day siege, during which lists of demands were exchanged. On Wednesday, April 19, 1993, Koresh's waiting period ended. Members were calm but enthusiastic while awaiting their final act, their exodus to death. FBI agents raided the compound; gunshots were fired by both Koresh's disciples and the FBI, and cult members set the compound on fire, a fire that raged almost instantly.

Television viewers around the globe watched in horror as the compound burned. A total of eighty members died, including twenty children. Autopsy reports disclosed that many had died from asphyxiation from the intense fires that consumed the compound. Women and children who hid under wet blankets were killed by falling debris. Other members were shot to death in acts of suicide or apparent mercy killings. The pattern of death in Waco was one of hysteria, and not typical of the mass suicide as seen at Jonestown. In the end, Koresh died by shooting himself in the head, following through with the lesson that he had once taught his disciples.

The spectacular mass violence seen in Jonestown, Guyana and the Branch Davidian disaster in Waco, Texas are very rare. Violence, although on a smaller scale, has been associated with various cults in recent decades, including the Manson family, Synanon, Hare Krishna, London Group, Heaven's Gate, and Order of the Solar Temple. These religious organizations made their quest for a new spirituality, religious expression, and apocalyptic theory the focal points around which they shaped their belief systems and notions of the future.

The leaders of these cults shaped a new worldview of the cataclysmic end of the world based on themes of destruction and salvation in religious texts such as the books of Isaiah, Ezekiel, Daniel, and Revelations as a foundational tool to justify their predictions of future events and their own actions. Apocalyptic literature is a profoundly powerful collection of images, visions, and dialogues that has the ability to leave one in fear of both modern times and the coming end times. The inspirational battle of the forces of good and evil, and the rewarding of the righteous have led many to develop and follow a spiritual quest and their own path to salvation.

—Julie Wieland-Robbescheuten

See also Cults

CULTS

The term *cult* can apply to any small group dedicated to a common set of spiritually oriented beliefs or philosophies, but because of tragedies associated with cults, the term has taken on a decidedly negative meaning. For many, the term refers to a particular kind of group, one with a self-appointed, dogmatic, and charismatic leader who promotes deceptive-coercive recruitment practices to ensnare individuals to join a totalitarian community organized to solicit funds and secure favors that benefit neither the group's members nor society.

However, not all cults fit this negative description, and a good many do demonstrable good. Some cult experts prefer the terms "new religious movement" and "alternative religions" as ways to label these groups without negative bias. Among experts, then, there are roughly two groups generally referred to as "cult critics" and "cult sympathizers." Regardless of the type of expert, the most frequently posed research questions have been:

- Why do cults emerge?
- Who joins cults?
- Why do some cults become violent or lead to violent endings?

To some extent, cults emerge as reactions to social movements and societal change. For example, many of the cults that emerged in the 1970s were reactions to the social upheavals of the 1960s, particularly to the widespread rejection of white, middle-class values of the 1950s that included narrow conceptions of the role of women and a value system that was insensitive to diversity. Even before the civil rights movement and anti-Vietnam demonstrations, American youth in particular began to challenge conventions. The cults of the 1970s were, then, extensions of these efforts to challenge convention.

As for who joins cults, no single stereotype applies. Members of cults have at one time or another been described as young and idealistic and easily manipulated by authority figures. However, there is no distinct type of individual likely to join a cult or new religious movement—at least not according to the available research.

There are, however, conditions that support or encourage people to join cults. These conditions include mild depression; being in a transitional stage, and being dissatisfied with traditional, mainstream religious institutions. For example, young people entering college may feel unusually lonely and lost; so that joining a cult may help them feel connected and oriented. As another example, the members of Jim Jones's cult, the "People's Temple," were mostly poor African Americans who had suffered from racism and poverty. They found in the socialist and egalitarian philosophy of the People's Temple support that they could not find elsewhere. In short, cults serve important functions for members that have more to do with specific circumstances than with character traits.

The question of why some cults turn violent or lead to violent endings is central. The two most-discussed examples are the People's Temple and the Branch Davidians. In each of these cases, the majority of members died in a tragic ending. Many fault the leaders, Jim Jones and David Koresh, respectively. However, many also fault the poor judgment of outsiders (e.g., government officials) who exerted what some say was unnecessary pressure and force that precipitated the violence. In each of these cases, it was not the beliefs of the organizations that precipitated government intervention and led to their demise, but the suspected abuse of members.

Regardless of who is to blame for their tragic endings, these two cults have served as the main examples of "bad cults." The control that both Koresh and Jones had over their organizations did not allow for negative feedback or criticism, whether from inside or outside of the group. This lack of internal criticism created a dangerous level of conformity, which ultimately led to the tragic endings.

Cults such as the People's Temple and Branch Davidians have forced others to develop questions to evaluate whether a particular cult is "bad." The main questions are the following:

- Does an individual charismatic leader control the group?
- Are the members isolated from the outside world?
- Are the members restricted from criticizing their leader or questioning the beliefs of the group?
- Are extreme commitments demanded or excessive requests made for monetary contributions?
- Does manipulation, deception, or "brainwashing" occur?
- Does abuse occur, such as sexual abuse and corporal punishment of children that qualifies as child abuse?

Asking these questions helps to identify "bad" cults, but it also helps to distinguish bad cults from those that may be doing good. In many cases, the answers to all of these questions may be "no." For example, certain cult groups of young people have been described as "off-road religion" and age-appropriate insofar as they provide ways for young people to try out new identities to see what "fits." Other cult groups provide needed emotional support, as in the case of certain Wicca groups that attract women who have suffered from disappointments and discrimination.

In sum, there are bad and good cults, and the differences between the two are becoming increasingly clear. Furthermore, while there is no single type of person who tends to join a cult, there are common conditions encouraging people to join. Finally, we should remember that virtually all of the world's great faith traditions began as cults, so that we need to be especially thoughtful and avoid stereotyping when speaking about cults.

—Kevin Verni

FURTHER READING

Barrett, D. V. (2001). *The new believers: A survey of sects, cults and alternative religions.* London: Orion.

Dawson, L. L. (1998). *Comprehending cults: The sociology of new religious movements.* Toronto: Oxford University Press.

Robbins, T., & Zablocki, B. (2001). *Misunderstanding cults: Searching forobjectivity in a controversial field.* Toronto: University of Toronto Press.

Thaler, M. S., & Lalich, J. (1995). *Cults in our midst.* San Francisco: Jossey-Bass.

D

DALAI LAMA (TENZIN GYATSO)

The title *Dalai Lama* refers to an individual who serves as the spiritual and political leader of Tibetan people. In English, Dalai Lama roughly translates to "Ocean of Wisdom." Throughout history, each Dalai Lama has been recognized as the reincarnation of those before him. This belief is deeply rooted in the Tibetan Buddhist faith that an individual's spirit remains, even after the physical body dies. The 13th Dalai Lama of Tibet died in 1933. At that time, the Tibetan people began the search to identify his reincarnation, their future leader. In 1937, Lhamo Thondup, later named Tenzin Gyatso, was identified as the 14th Dalai Lama of Tibet.

Lhamo Thondup (translated to "Wish-Fulfilling Goddess") was born on July 6, 1935, to a poor family in the town of Taktser, situated in the Amdo region of northeastern Tibet. Just 2 years later, in 1937, the high lama Kyestang Rinpoche (a Tibetan Buddhist spiritual master) had a vision at Lhamo Lhatso, an oracle lake in southern Tibet, which directed a group of Tibetan monks to the home of Lhamo Thondup.

The monks arrived in full disguise, yet when Lhamo Dundrup saw one dressed as a servant, he immediately called him "Sera Lama." In fact, the man was a lama (teacher) from the Sera monastery in Tibet. Later, when the young boy was presented with various objects, he selected those that belonged to the 13th Dalai Lama, stating, "It's mine." The series of difficult tests that followed confirmed that Lhamo Thondup was the reincarnation of the 13th Dalai Lama.

The young boy was taken on a 3-month journey to Lhasa, the capital of Tibet. In 1940 the 14th Dalai Lama was installed on the Lion Throne at the Potala Palace, a 1,000-chamber winter home of the Dalai Lama, located on a mountainside overlooking the city of Lhasa. A regent governed the country while the 5-year-old Dalai Lama completed his rigorous religious education.

In 1950, 84,000 troops of the newly created People's Republic of China launched a major invasion of Tibet. The small Tibetan army was unable to handle such an invasion. As a result, the Dalai Lama was forced to finish his studies and assume full political rule of Tibet. The teenaged ruler struggled with his responsibilities, but he firmly grounded all his decisions and actions in Buddhist philosophy. Finally, on March 31, 1959, the Dalai Lama recognized he was no longer safe and that he could better serve the Tibetan people from outside Tibet. He fled the country and more than 80,000 Tibetans followed him into exile in India.

More than 1.2 million Tibetans (one fifth the population) have died as a result of China's occupation of Tibet. Tens of thousands have been arrested and tortured for their political views. Over 6,000 monasteries have been destroyed, ancient texts burned, and Buddhist followers prevented from becoming monks and nuns. Despite this abuse against his people, country, and religion, the Dalai Lama refuses to feel hatred toward China or its leaders. Continuing to adhere to a code of Buddhist morals, he recognizes that all people have endured suffering at some point in time. He maintains the Chinese, including their leaders, should be treated with compassion.

Now residing in Dharamsala, India, His Holiness the 14th Dalai Lama is one of the most recognized, well-traveled, and beloved leaders. In 1989 he was awarded the Nobel Peace Prize for numerous nonviolent teachings and peaceful efforts on behalf of Tibet. This honor led to tremendous international notoriety, and the Dalai Lama is now widely considered to be one of the greatest living spiritual exemplars.

The Dalai Lama has actively dedicated his life in exile to preserving all aspects of Tibetan culture. For example, he has established more than 50 agricultural settlements for exiled Tibetans and founded hundreds of Tibetan schools and monasteries in India, Nepal, and throughout the world. He has written more than three-dozen books, several of which are international best-sellers. Perhaps most notable are his continuous efforts to peacefully campaign for Tibetan independence and human rights in Tibet.

His Holiness the 14th Dalai Lama is the first Dalai Lama to live and control a government in exile. Questions remain over the identification of his reincarnation, as China continues to occupy Tibet. The Chinese government may either forbid future recognition of Dalai Lamas or control their selection. The 14th Dalai Lama has stated that the Tibetan people will ultimately decide what the future will hold. He explains that although recognition of Dalai Lamas may eventually cease, Tibetan Buddhist culture will remain as long as the Tibetan people exist.

—Lori Ellen Rutman

See also Buddhism

FURTHER READING

His Holiness the Dalai Lama of Tibet. (1997). *My land and my people: The original autobiography of His Holiness the Dalai Lama of Tibet.* New York: Warner Books.

Hunt, S. A. (2002). *The future of peace: On the front lines with the world's great peacemakers.* San Francisco, CA: HarperSanFrancisco.

Willis, C. (Ed.). (2002). *A lifetime of wisdom: Essential writings by and about the Dalai Lama.* New York: Marlowe & Company.

DANCE

Dance, in all of its myriad forms, has long held spiritual significance in the world's cultures. From Sufi whirling dervishes to modern Christian liturgical dance, religious communities the world over have and continue to explore the spiritual undertones of dance. In the United States, sacred dance takes a variety of forms, including ballet, jazz, and ethnic folk dances. A recent survey indicates churches in more than 23 denominations embrace dance as a form of worship, including Methodist, Lutheran, Catholic, Unitarian, Mennonite, Russian Orthodox, as well as some Jewish synagogues. The Sacred Dance Guild, an interfaith organization committed to dance as a catalyst for spiritual growth, sponsors events and workshops offering various dance forms from a unique blend of religious, ethnic, and cultural backgrounds.

To all appearances, American dance forms share little in common with their ancient ancestors. However, beneath the surface, there are many similarities. Dance as a spiritual practice has roots in the Paleolithic era. Ancient paintings and sculptures from the areas now known as Greece, Spain, India, Egypt, and a variety of other countries depict women dancing. Many scholars interpret these women as dancing priestesses.

The religious use of dance likely began as sympathetic mimicry of birth. Priestesses and midwives gathered around the birthing woman, miming her movements in an effort to support her and lend their energy to a successful birth. From these beginnings, early peoples set these movements to rhythms for use as a form of sympathetic magic for a variety of religious purposes.

In Ancient Egypt, for example, everyone danced, whether slave or king. While there were many nonreligious festival dances, the most prevalent dances were for religious purposes. The Ancient Egyptians danced in celebration of the gods, such as Hathor and Bastet, they offered harvest and fertility dances, and they danced at funerals to usher the spirit of the dead to the afterlife.

Cultures all over the world continue to use dance as a spiritual tool. In Morocco, dancers perform the *Guedra* as a ritual of blessing. The *zar* is another ritual dance used for emotional healing on behalf of someone who has been possessed. *Hadra,* which is part of a ceremony performed by the Sufi brotherhood called the *Aissawa,* is another exorcism ritual. Finally, the Mevlevi and Jerahi sects of Islam use whirling as a spiritual tool. Religious and spiritual dance rituals such as these are often used as intentional tools to promote healthy development. Many dance styles and practices have a particular appeal to young people and should be considered in attempts to better understand how religious and spiritual practices can impact healthy development in childhood and adolescence.

BELLY DANCE: CONNECTING THE SPIRITUAL DANCE WITH HEALTHY DEVELOPMENT

Belly dance, an Americanized synthesis of several different Middle Eastern dance forms, is growing in popularity as a spiritual practice. Once an underground phenomenon, belly dance has moved into the American mainstream due to its health benefits and use in popular music videos. These same videos have increased interest in learning the dance among adolescent girls. Like their adult counterparts, girls are finding that belly dance provides a moving spiritual outlet.

Although many believe belly dance to be Egyptian in origin, other theories suggest that traveling dancers brought the style to Egypt. Modern belly dance has many movements in common with the traditional dances of the Ghawazi of Egypt and the Ouled Nail of Algeria. Both groups have mysterious origins, but historical artifacts suggest that neither group originated in the country with which they are now associated. American belly dancers derive movements from these and many other forms of Middle Eastern dance. Though there are dozens of varied folk forms, belly dance isolates those movements that highlight the abdomen as the center of human creation or strength.

Belly dance came to America through the efforts of Sol Bloom at the 1893 World's Fair in Chicago. He brought together Middle Eastern folk dancers from several different countries, including Algeria and Tunisia, as "cultural expositions" for the fair. Unfortunately, the commercial burlesque stage soon picked up the movements of the dances, where they were twisted and vulgarized. American strippers and prostitutes adopted the costumes and movements of the dance for their own use. This adaptation gave belly dance the stigma it still bears today. However, rather than dehumanized sexuality, this dance should be considered an erotic celebration of life and the body. Those who shy away from the idea of the spirituality within belly dancing fail to appreciate the possibility of spiritual eroticism and refuse to acknowledge that eroticism and the celebration of the female body can be valid paths to spiritual growth.

Unlike other forms of modern dance, belly dance is wholly feminine and natural; it does not require extreme or unnatural contortions as do some common forms of dance. Belly dance brings girls back into union with the natural way their bodies move. It connects them with the primal force of feminine consciousness by connecting them to an ancient lineage of women who have done the same movements in dance, in birth, and in celebration of life and womanhood. This can be very healing in a physical, mental, emotional, psychological, and spiritual way.

The work of transpersonal psychotherapists Gay and Kathlyn Hendricks has shown that many emotional problems can be lessened by paying close attention to one's body and by treating one's emotions and sensations with the utmost respect. The spiritual and creative dimension of belly dance provides an opening through which girls can begin to explore the light and dark places of their own psyches, on their own terms, leading to a restoration of self.

Dancing also stimulates the unconscious, heightens life, and leads to a feeling of wholeness. It contains a spiritual dimension that is associated with the experience of ecstatic dance. Ecstatic dance involves a paradoxical melding with one's body while achieving a shift of focus and consciousness to the spiritual realm. This occurs when the dance becomes a spiritual discipline, a tool that teaches girls how to live inside, interact with, and grow through their bodies. For belly dancers, the body is not an obstacle to enlightenment or realization of spiritual truth. Rather, it is the key. Union with her body allows a girl to know herself, her essence, and her connection to all life in a way that mainstream American culture denies.

Belly dance as a spiritual practice is available within a wide variety of religious frameworks. For example, it has found an easy home within the modern-day pagan movement. Many pagans are also part of the belly dance community and bring their dance talents into their spiritual practices. In addition, some have studied the Middle Eastern rituals and incorporated modified versions into their own spiritual paths.

The dance can also play a role within the context of mainstream American religion. Some progressive Lutheran, Episcopalian, and Unitarian congregations have welcomed belly dance as liturgical dance during their services. Even some of the more conservative Christian denominations have accepted belly dance as part of special events, such as talent shows and celebratory dances during certain services. Consequently, even girls within mainstream religious institutions can experience the benefits of the dance.

Dance has long been used as an expression of cultural values, including the religious and spiritual rituals within different cultures. In addition to its historical functions for political advantage, celebration, and healing, dance is often (intentionally or unintentionally) a trigger of religious and/or spiritual development. Dance can also serve as a tool for promoting healthy emotional, physical, and mental development in young people. For example, with today's excessive emphasis on the shape of girl's and women's bodies, belly dance can provide a physical, emotional, and spiritual release from the pressures young people face. Belly dance celebrates the natural shapes and movements of a woman's body, a celebration that may go far toward combating the contemporary "thin-is-in" cultural message bombarding young girls. Rather than starving themselves for an unnatural slender figure, belly dance allows girls to rejoice in the natural curves of their bodies. This connection with the body provides a spiritual liberation that goes bone deep.

—Sandra R. Kirchner

FURTHER READING

Al-Rawi, R. (2003). *Grandmother's secrets: The ancient rituals and healing power of belly dance.* New York: Interlink Books.

Carlton, D. (1994). *Looking for Little Egypt.* Bloomington, IN: IDD Books.

Gioseffi, D. (1980). *Earth dancing: Mother nature's oldest rite.* Harrisburg, PA: Stackpole Books.

Richards, T. (2000). *The belly dance book: Rediscovering the oldest dance.* Concord, CA: Backbeat Press.

Stewart, I. J. (2000). *Sacred woman, sacred dance: Awakening spirituality through movement and ritual.* Rochester, VT: Inner Traditions.

DAOISM (TAOISM)

Daoism is a generic term covering various Chinese philosophical and religious traditions that trace their origins back to the possibly apocryphal figure Laozi from the sixth century BCE, after whom a small collection of mystico-poetic aphorisms is named, also called *Daodejing* (*Scripture [jing] of the Way [Dao] and Its Virtue [de]*). As its name implies, Daoism's cardinal concept is *Dao,* the primordial, creative source that gives rise to and nourishes all things and to which all things return. Human flourishing requires living with the grain of *Dao* in material and mental simplicity, in a state of tranquil freedom and active inaction.

Philosophical Daoism, emphasizing the fecundity of emptiness and the mutual definition and transformation of contrary qualities and states, provides the archetypical intellectual framework for diverse Chinese disciplines, such as aesthetics, medicine, and martial arts. Religious Daoism, which re-interpreted and developed the concepts of philosophical Daoism, addresses people's concerns with mortality and the supernatural, the former through alchemy and its extension in the form of "inner alchemy" involving cultivation of the body and the latter through various practices intended to influence spiritual beings. Both streams of Daoism, together with Confucianism, have shaped the basic outlook of the Chinese people for over 2,000 years, with their influences extending to China's East Asian neighbors.

The common version of *Daodejing* opens by stating bluntly that the communicable *Dao* is not the Absolute *Dao,* immediately putting the author's own effort into question and setting an ironic tone that permeates the entire work. A skepticism about language's fidelity also pervades *Zhuangzi,* named after Zhuangzi (ca. 369–ca. 286 B.C.E.), considered to be almost Laozi's equal as Daoism's twin founders. True to this skepticism, the language of *Daodejing* is poetic and paradoxical, while *Zhuangzi* employs parables to make its points. The results are two masterpieces, one of poetry, the other of prose, constituting two sources of the Chinese literary tradition.

The terse, enigmatic language of *Daodejing* makes it pregnant with interpretative possibilities, opening up immense imaginative space in the reader's mind, just as the primordial, empty *Dao* is the all-embracive mother of the whole creation. Considering also that the origins of this work on the elusive *Dao* are shrouded in mystery, *Daodejing* exemplifies what it preaches in more than one way.

The fact is that Daoism espouses very general principles discernible and applicable across diverse domains, even in modern physics, as Capra tries to show in *The Tao of Physics.* Because Laozi, thought to be Confucius's contemporary, lived in a politically volatile era with widespread suffering, *Daodejing* has been read both as political advice for the ruler and survival strategies for the ruled. For example, active inaction can be interpreted as laissez-faire government, Machiavellian machination, or self-preservation through withdrawal. Daoist political principles were actually part of the short-lived state-sanctioned Huang-Lao ideology in the early Han Dynasty (206 B.C.E.–220 C.E.)

before Confucianism's ascendance. Even after Daoism's official displacement by Confucianism, Daoist strategies, such as retreating before an advance, continued to inform many political intrigues behind the Confucian façade.

Elements of Daoist thought, with their aversion to bureaucratic imposition, and elevation of the lowly and the weak, were soon adopted by peasant groups rebelling against the Han government. They fashioned their religio-political regimes by combining these Daoist elements with egalitarianism, millenarian prophecies of an age of great peace, popular healing practices, and revelations from the deified Laozi now honored as the founder of their movements with titles like Lord Lao. This greatly advanced the development of religious Daoism, which was also stimulated by the arrival and spread of Buddhism in China around this time. The rebels eventually reconciled with successors of the Han government. Through official recognition and conferment of attendant privileges, religious Daoist sects were institutionalized, although rebels in subsequent ages continued to legitimate themselves with variations of Daoist religious beliefs.

With the establishment of Confucianism as state ideology and the domestication of rebellious Daoist movements, Daoism moved inward and developed its spiritual aspects. On the philosophical wing, this gave rise to Neo-Daoism, which elaborated the metaphysical nature of *Dao* and influenced various Chinese fine arts, such as calligraphy, painting, and poetry, by putting forth the ideal of spontaneous creativity, among other things, and emphasizing the meditative potential of artistic practices.

On the religious wing, esoteric practices pursuing personal well-being and immortality were developed. Soon mainstream Daoism became established as a spiritual path toward personal salvation. Since then Daoism and Confucianism have been two complementary, intertwining strands in the fabric of Chinese culture. Both traditions emphasize the complementary of contraries and the necessity of their harmonious integration, represented visually by the diagram of the Great Ultimate, showing a circle with two interpenetrating halves morphing into each other, an icon adopted by both traditions and now most frequently seen on the attire of religious Daoists.

Daoism and Confucianism themselves constitute just such a couple of contraries, with Confucianism guiding people's social behavior, exhorting intellectuals, for example, to pursue a career in public service, and Daoism providing them with inner solace and spiritual pursuits, especially in the face of frustration. Daoism and Confucianism have been likened to the *yin* (feminine aspect) and *yang* (masculine aspect) of Chinese culture, and *Daodejing* itself abounds in feminine imageries like "the gate of the mysterious female," described as the root of heaven and earth.

To simplify—the two streams are in fact not clear-cut—philosophical and religious Daoism hold different views of mortality, entailing divergent paths toward salvation. Philosophical Daoism takes a cosmic perspective, seeing all creation as equal, and life and death as an example of complementary natural processes with no difference in value, a view most clearly expressed in *Zhuangzi.* Salvation is to be achieved through indifference to death, enabling one to release the desperate hold on life, thus freeing one of all worries that inhibit one from plunging into life wholeheartedly. Self-actualization, the full development of the virtues or powers of the *Dao* in one's nature, is possible only if one forgets oneself—one of the Daoist paradoxes. One then can devote one's whole being to the task at hand and achieve oneness with *Dao* as instantiated in and guiding one's pursuit, even if the pursuit is as mundane as that of a cook cutting up cows.

Zhuangzi describes this marvelous state in numerous parables, emphasizing the importance of mindfulness for the progressive mastery of one's undertaking, whereby one gradually leaves the senses behind until one works wonders directly through one's spirit. For Zhuangzi's Perfect Man, death is overcome through freedom and transcendence, made possible by non-attachment to life. Human beings are decentered by philosophical Daoism's cosmocentric stand. *Dao,* which nourishes all things and effects their return to it without prejudice, provides the model for the enlightened one's actions.

On the other hand, religious Daoism retreats to a more anthropocentric stand, in the sense that it prizes human life and seeks literal immortality through various life-prolonging practices. The preparation of alchemical elixirs contributed to the development of science in ancient China, including the invention of gunpowder. Subsequently, the belief in the homology between the cosmos and the human body led to the internalization of alchemy. Inner alchemy, sometimes taking the form of sexual practices, is in effect the meditative practices involving visualizing the microcosm of one's body as providing variously the vessel, the fire, and the raw material for alchemical reactions, with one directing, concentrating, and transforming one's *qi* (airy matter–energy), *jing* (vital essence), and *shen* (spirit) in the formation of inner elixir. These self-cultivation practices involve simultaneously body and spirit and are believed to benefit both—which the Chinese do not distinguish sharply—ultimately enabling one to become immortal, just like many members of the Daoist pantheon who through self-cultivation had moved from the state of mortal beings to that of immortal spiritual beings.

These practices draw their theoretical inspiration from traditional principles such as the complementarity of *yin* and *yang,* the five interacting elements of earth, wood, metal, fire, and water in relationships of begetting and overcoming, and especially Laozi's idea that "returning" characterizes *Dao's* movement. Thus one's vital resources are to be conserved and nurtured, through forgetting and unlearning, until fully restored to their original undisturbed, bounteous, and pristine state as in the child. Striving and sensuous indulgences dissipate one's vital resources and are to be avoided. Instead active inaction is recommended.

Daoism esteems nature above artifice. It recommends frequent contacts with nature so that one may experience *Dao.* Chinese landscape paintings are a particularly well-developed genre. Technology is mistrusted, not only because it complicates life but, much more significantly, also because ingenuity promotes craftiness. Human nature being what it is, technology cannot but corrupt. *Dao* is a cosmic intelligence that one can tune into, but through the intuitive spiritual intelligence cultivated with one's body rather than through cerebral intelligence, which tends instead to alienate one from *Dao,* one's source.

—Ping Ho Wong

FURTHER READING

Girardot, N. J., Miller, J., & Liu, X. (Ed.). (2001). *Daoism and ecology: Ways within a cosmic landscape.* Cambridge, MA: Harvard University Center for the Study of World Religions.

Kohn, L. (Ed.). (1993). *The Taoist experience: an anthology.* Albany, NY: State University of New York Press.

Oldstone-Moore, J. (2003). *Taoism: Origins, beliefs, practices, holy texts, sacred places.* New York, NY: Oxford University Press.

Wong, E. (1997). *The Shambhala guide to Taoism.* Boston: Shambhala.

DAY, DOROTHY

The life of Dorothy Day serves as a model of religious and spiritual development across the human life span. Her life as a journalist, pacifist, and reformer makes her a role model to many—her involvement in social issues stretched from the women's suffrage movement to the Vietnam War. She is best known as a cofounder of the Catholic Worker Movement. Born on November 8, 1897 in Brooklyn, New York, she was the third of John and Grace Satterlee Day's five children. The family moved often due to John Day's work as a journalist and experienced spells of both poverty and moderate affluence. As a teenager, Day often found herself wandering the poorer neighborhoods of Chicago and New York, discovering her compassion for the plight of the poor and beauty in the midst of urban desolation. An avid reader, Day fueled her growing social conscience with books such as Upton Sinclair's novel *The Jungle.* Along with social concerns, organized religion intrigued Day. She was fascinated by the piety and spiritual discipline she witnessed in neighbors and roommates. While she disagreed with Church doctrines supporting charity over justice, she felt drawn to the Catholic Church because of its connection to immigrants and the poor.

In 1914 Day began attending the University of Illinois in Urbana, supporting herself with scholarships, domestic labor, and freelance writing. Her social outlook continued in a radical direction, and she dropped out of college after only 2 years. Soon after, she moved to New York and found a job covering labor strikes and demonstrations as a reporter for *The Call,* a socialist paper. After several months, she moved on to writing for *The Masses,* a socialist journal that was shut down for sedition within a few months of her arrival.

As a young woman, Day lived what she called a bohemian-like existence: moving from city to city, writing for different papers, living among the poor, and associating with young radicals. Day participated in, as well as wrote about, demonstrations and rallies regarding social conditions. In 1917 she went to prison for protesting in front of the White House about the exclusion of women from voting and holding public office. While in prison, she participated in a hunger strike to bring attention to the inhumane treatment of prisoners. Day and her suffragette companions were eventually freed by order of President Woodrow Wilson. She was jailed several more times in her life for acts of civil disobedience, including refusing to take part in civil defense drills in the 1950s and participating in a banned picket line when she was 75 years old.

Day's first novel, *The Eleventh Virgin,* published in 1924, included autobiographical information about a love affair she had had that resulted in pregnancy and an abortion. In 1924, with the money she obtained by selling the movie rights to the novel, Day bought a beach house on Staten Island where she sought emotional healing. She lived there for several years with her common-law husband, Forster Batterham, until the birth of their daughter, Tamar Therese, in 1927. Batterham shared Day's radical social views but opposed marriage and religion. As Day blossomed as a mother and seriously pursued her attraction to Catholicism, her relationship with Forster suffered. After Day and their daughter were baptized in 1928, Batterham left the family permanently. So began Day's concerted effort to reconcile her radical social views with her Catholic faith.

Day and her daughter eventually moved to New York City, and it was there, in 1932, that she met Peter Maurin. A French peasant and former Christian Brother who found his way to the United States, Maurin encouraged Day to use her journalistic skills to publicize Catholic social teaching and promote social transformation through peaceful means. In 1933 the first edition of *The Catholic Worker* was circulated in New York City for a penny a copy. Within a year, the eight-page newspaper grew from 2,500 to 10,000 copies a month. Day was the principal writer and editor, with Maurin frequently submitting short poems on faith and justice called *Easy Essays.*

The paper criticized industrialism and the accepted social order, and encouraged readers to take action based on the works of mercy outlined in Jesus' Sermon on the Mount. With the Depression in full swing and vast numbers of people in dire poverty, Day soon opened her apartment to practice what *The Catholic Worker* preached. Thus was born the first house of hospitality. Under Day's direction, it welcomed all and sought only to serve, not to evangelize. Eventually more apartments and then houses were acquired; by 1936 there were over 30 Catholic Worker houses across the country. In 2003, there were 185 worldwide.

The Catholic Worker Movement that Day inspired is known for its strong commitments to living in solidarity with the poor, acting on behalf of justice and practicing pacifism. These positions have drawn both criticism and praise throughout the years. During her lifetime, Day spoke and acted on every major social issue, including the Spanish Civil War in 1926, the Civil Rights movement of the 1950s and 1960s, the Catholic Church's Second Vatican Council, the Vietnam War, and the United Farm Workers' strikes in California. In addition to her public expressions of faith and justice, Day nurtured a deep prayer life, spending hours pondering scripture and the lives of saints.

By the end of her life, Day was embraced by her adopted church, but her name continues to spark debate in both Catholic and secular circles alike. She continued to write for *The Catholic Worker* and live in a house of hospitality until her death in 1980 at the age of 83. In 2000 Day was recommended for canonization as a saint, a process that typically takes several years.

—Elizabeth Mackenzie

FURTHER READING

Coles, R. (1987). *Dorothy Day: A radical devotion.* Reading, MA: Addison-Wesley.

Day, D. (1952). *The long loneliness: The autobiography of Dorothy Day.* New York: Harper Collins.

Forest, J. H. (1986). *Love is the measure: A biography of Dorothy Day.* Maryknoll, NY: Orbis.

DEAD SEA SCROLLS

Texts often provide the foundation and history of a religious tradition and are often a primary way in which devotees learn about and/or are trained in a religious tradition. The Dead Sea Scrolls represent one of many different religious texts that serve such a purpose. The term *Dead Sea Scrolls* refers to the collection of papyri and leather scrolls dated from the mid-third century B.C.E. to 68 C.E. that were found in 11 caves to the west of the Dead Sea, close to the ruins of Qumran, which date to the same period. Among the scrolls are the oldest existing manuscripts of the Hebrew Bible; all books of the Bible are represented, except Esther, and there are several copies of some books, such as the Psalms and Torah. Different versions of the Hebrew text and the inclusion of additional books, such as *Jubilees and Enoch,* suggest that the Bible had not yet reached its final form.

In addition to the biblical books, there are a number of sectarian documents that provide insight into the community that safeguarded them. Some tell their history, some give rules for membership in the community, some use the biblical prophets or psalms to explain current historical events, and some are psalmlike thanksgivings. One scroll describes a cosmic battle between the sons of light, led by a figure called the Teacher of Righteousness, and the sons of darkness. Their concerns focus on the correct priestly line, calendar, and purity laws, suggesting that the group defined itself against the Jewish hierarchy situated in Jerusalem. The manuscripts are written in Greek, Hebrew, or Aramaic.

These texts provide valuable information about Judaism in the Second Temple Period (from the third century B.C.E. to the first century C.E.). Most scholars believe that the texts were produced by a group identified by Jewish and Roman historians as the Essenes, a community-based group that was apparently wiped out by the Romans during the Jewish revolt in 66–70 C.E. They performed ritual cleansing (rock pools were found in the ruins, and the manuscripts refer to ritual washing) and shared a ritual common meal, not unlike the Christian Baptism and the Lord's Supper. They anticipated the presence of the messiah (or messiahs) and the final judgment. There is no evidence yet found that suggests the Essenes were related to early Christians, but some suggest that John the Baptist may have been associated with them. The scrolls testify to the diversity of Jewish traditions during that time.

The first scrolls were discovered in clay jars by a Bedouin shepherd in 1947; since then many caves in the area have been excavated, and fragments have been found in 11 of them. Of these, Cave 4 produced the most fragments. Amid a great deal of controversy over publication rights, an international team of scholars have worked hard to preserve, piece together, translate, identify, and publish their findings. Most have been initially published with commentary by Oxford University Press in *Discoveries of the Judean Desert.* Many of the scrolls are displayed in the Shrine of the Book at the Israel Museum, Jerusalem.

—Jane S. Webster

See also Baptism; Bible; John the Baptist; Judaism

FURTHER READING

Martínez, F. G. (1996). *The Dead Sea Scrolls translated: The Qumran texts in English* (2nd ed.). Leiden, NL: Brill.

VanderKam, J. C. (1994). *The Dead Sea Scrolls today.* Grand Rapids, MI: Eerdmans.

DELPHI

The world of ancient Greece was rich in spiritualism, faith, mythology, and the ever-present gods and goddesses. The Greeks believed that the gods governed every aspect of their lives. The gods and goddesses were immortal ancients of Greece and ruled on Mount Olympus. In the ancient world, it was believed that fate, destiny, or the gods determined a man's life. As people believed that their future could be revealed, oracles of every kind—personal and political—became a function of Greek society. The most famous being the Delphic Oracles, a site of pilgrimage for Greek and non-Greek alike in search of prophecies about the future.

In Greek mythology, the gods and their offspring created the world and make up the colorful Greek Pantheon, blessing humans with artistry, love, and other gifts. The gods, who were blessed with immortality, superhuman strength, and wisdom, were worshipped and adored by the Greeks. In times of trouble, and on specific days, offerings were made to the gods at their respected temples, which were spread throughout the Greek Empire. Priests and priestesses were in charge of proper ritual conduct, prayers, and libations offered to each assigned deity.

Zeus was considered king of the gods, good luck, and the avenger of murder. Along with Hera, his wife; Diana, the goddess of the hunt; Aphrodite, the goddess of Love; Dionysus, the god of wine; and others, Zeus filled the Greek Pantheon and governed humanity. In addition to being the parents and guardians of the Grecians, the Olympian deities were credited with the mythological tales that would assist children and adults in times of need or that would explain mysteries and set examples for correct moral conduct. The gods' main purpose was to be there to help humans in their lives and share with them a mystical and spiritual relationship.

The magnitude of the importance of gods in the lives of Greeks is demonstrated by the number of sacred precincts that the Greeks erected in dedication to the gods. Temples were where mortals could speak with the gods and appeal to them for help.

One of the most famous precincts or sites is the Delphi. At the Temple of Delphi, the god Apollo helped humankind by giving them the gift of foresight. This would be explained to the Greek pilgrims that made the journey to Delphi by Apollo's priestesses through oracles—the telling of the future events. Delphi is where the god Apollo's son, Asclepias, blessed with the gift to heal, would perform his miracles and heal the sick by divine intervention.

When the Olympian god Apollo came to the pre-Greek site of Delphi, a sacred female snake guarded it. Apollo, though magnificent and powerful, was never able to fully recover from the assault that the Pythoness launched on him. From that moment on, in order to preserve the person of the Pythoness, the servants in the Temple of Apollo were women. The fabled throne of prophecy within the sanctuary of Delphi has been called the "navel of the earth." From this seat, vapors were emitted causing enigmatic words that were recorded and interpreted as sayings of Apollo. While in trance, the priestess was believed to become the vehicle for the voice of Apollo, uttering prophecies capable of changing the history of the Greek people.

Aegeus and Jason from the myth of Jason and the Argonauts sought out the Delphic Oracle and had their lives changed. Jason inquired of the Oracle whether he should take on the task of retrieving the Golden Fleece to avenge the death of his father Aeson and take the throne from his uncle, Pelias. The Oracles also warned Pelias that a man only wearing one sandal would turn him off the throne of Iolcus—this man would be Jason. The Oracles encouraged Jason to do this task. Brutus, the founder of the Roman Republic traveled to Delphi to inquire of the Oracles about how he might take power away from Tarquinias and become the ruler of Rome. Oedipus consulted the Delphic Oracle to inquire about who his real father was and was told that he was destined to kill his real father and marry his mother. The Delphic Oracle was consulted as to why Thebes was plagued, revealing that Jocasta and her husband Oedipus were really mother and son.

As the Delphic Oracle was meant to reveal the future for humans as a gift to humans, angry gods and goddesses used the Oracle as a means to give false prophecies out of spite for the individual that had sparked their anger. The Greek gods had a reputation for not only loving their human children but for also intervening and toying with them in sometimes rather cruel and manipulative ways.

During the age of colonization in ancient Greece, in the eighth century B.C.E., there was a rebirth within Greek society. Specifically in the year 776 B.C.E., when the first Olympic games occurred, the flowering of one of the great Panhellenic sanctuaries at Delphi began where the athletes sought the oracles to foresee their outcome at the Games. The revival of these cults brought literature, art, sculpture, and more sacred buildings within the Greek Empire. The Greek religion was expanding and became fuller and more elaborate. Delphi and the oracles and devotion to Apollo began to increase during this period.

The stories of Greek mythology are a part of most Western educational experiences. The stories of the gods serve as cultural, historical, and anthropological lessons that reveal to their audiences the beliefs and practices of spiritualities past.

—Julie Wieland-Robbescheuten

DEVIL

The devil has been given numerous names that are synonymous for identifying the devil; Satan, Prince of Darkness, Lucifer, Mephistopheles, and the fallen angel. Regardless of which label one decides to use to identify the evil one, the devil, is without a doubt labeled as the cause of all evil, destruction, and suffering in the cosmos. The concept of the devil only exists in select religious traditions, namely the predominant monotheistic religious systems. Every religion has demons and evil antagonistic gods that persuade humans to commit evil deeds. But within the great religious world there exists only four religions (Zoroastrianism, Judaism, Christianity, Islam) that believe in one evil figure, the devil, as the cause of evil and suffering in the world. Belief in the devil and his home, the underworld or hell, can have differing influences on individual religious and/or spiritual development—from extreme to minimal to nonexistent. Whatever the impact, throughout human history, the devil has played and will continue to play an important role in the development of religiousness and spirituality throughout the world.

Zoroastrianism, the world's first monotheistic religion, was centered on the belief in a balanced world: light and darkness, good and evil. The all-powerful god of light and righteousness was Ahura Mazda, who was in constant battle with his demonic antagonistic match, Angra Mayu. This battle between the forces of good and evil laid the foundation for the additional monotheistic traditions focusing on this concept. Ancient

Hebrew, Christianity, and Islam are rich with narratives of Job, Jesus, and other biblical figures that wrestle with the devil and his incitements to do the opposite of what God wants.

Because the devil is described as chaos, he is designated, along with his many names, by a variety of symbols that represent evil and chaos. In the Hebrew text there is the serpent from Eden and the monster Leviathan. The crescent moon came to be interpreted as the horns of the devil, which are on ancient symbols of power, fertility, and luck. Therefore, the horns of the devil represent his princely power wrought with negativity.

The character of the devil was created through the meshing of pagan deities that came to be classified as demons by Christians linking Greco-Roman deities to attributes of the devil. The one mythological deity that has had the most influence in the creation of the image of the devil is the god Pan. Pan was associated with wilderness and hostility and was feared by the ancients. Pan was believed to be hairy and was similar in appearance to that of a goat with horns and cloven hooves. Christians took the myth of the god Pan and mixed his characteristics with another Greek deity, Hades, the god of the underworld, ruler of death. The final deity that was combined into creating the devil image was Charun, the Etruscan god of death. He was represented in Etruscan art with a huge beaked nose, shaggy beard and hair, pointed ears, wings, and smirking image. These three images were well-known in the ancient world and through fusing their physical and personality traits, the image of the devil emerged and is depicted in medieval and modern art as a goat or beastlike creature, a concoction of meshing three feared ancient deities into one figure, the devil.

There is a definite tension that exists within the world, the constant struggle that humans endure having to choose between good and evil. This sets the dynamic for the dualism, the power of God the righteous Lord against the source and concept of evil, the Lord of Darkness, the devil. The reality and problem of evil is constant in the world and is present within every world view.

The good and righteous God resides in heaven with his band of angels, seraphim and his servants, whose main objective is to protect humans, and through them God delivers His messages and works. In contrast, the devil presides in the underworld, beneath the earth, in a dark and dreary land. From the place of the devil's kingdom, emerges the myth of hell with its image of a land soaked in burning fire, the color of blood. This red fire led to the direct association that the devil himself was also red. As in direct contrast to God, the devil too has servants, demonic forces that work his will and tempt humans from righteous choices, attempting to steer them away from God.

During the apocalyptic period from 200 B.C.E. to 100 C.E., there were numerous books that were created, called the *pseudepigrapha,* a collection of false writing, telling of visions and revelations of the end of the world—connected with the problem of evil. In the apocalyptic period, the Jewish people were deeply concerned with evil, why it occurred, and why God allowed it to happen. One such text from the apocalyptic period was called the book of Enoch, in which the author writes in the words of Enoch (a great man from the book of Genesis who was lifted to heaven by God), who had a vision of Sheol (the underworld) and sees certain angels who lusted after the daughters of men and had left heaven in a fallen state. These fallen angels were now called *Watchers* for their interest in women defiled them before God and was done in direct defiance of God.

These fallen angels, Belial, Mastema, Azazel, Sammael, Satanail, and Semyaza, had one leader, Satan, who orchestrated their fall from heaven. Satan and his band of Watchers were punished by God for their evil actions and outright defiance and were banished for all eternity from heaven. This story explains the reasoning for the definite barriers between God and Satan, with God being righteous and the devil being evil.

The next evolution in building the devil's character is witnessed in the New Testament's Synoptic Gospels and the book of Revelations. In the New Testament there are numerous narratives of Jesus casting out people possessed with demons. In Matthew 4:1–11, Jesus is tempted in the desert by the devil himself; this depiction elevated the devil to a definite symbol of an evil tempter, and Jesus makes references to the devil and the coming age where the devil will tempt humans into taking his path (Mark 13: 1–31).

In the New Testament the devil becomes a central figure in the book of Revelations, which foretells the devil and his army of demonic servants battling with Jesus and his army of righteousness in a cosmic end-time battle between good and evil.

The devil, with his demonic and evil characteristics that were so graciously awarded to him through the centuries by humans out of fear and as a way to explain evil in their world, has maintained an element of fear through his powers even in the modern Western world. The devil was created from Pan and other figures that were well-known to the ancients. Through this process of taking what they know and putting a face to evil, the devil continues to be re-invented in modern times as new faces of evil emerge.

The image of the devil remains today a symbol of evil and is used to explain the divine balance of good and evil. The devil will continue to be the figure through which moral decisions are reconciled, ensuring that the world seeks a path toward righteousness, steering clear of this symbol of evil from ancient times to end times.

—*Julie Wieland-Robbescheuten*

See also Evil

FURTHER READING

Cohn, N. (1993). *Cosmos, chaos and the world to come.* New Haven: Yale University Press.

Collins, J. J. (1998). *The apocalyptic imagination.* Grand Rapids, MI: William B. Eerdmans.

Russell, J. B. (1988). *The prince of darkness.* Ithaca, NY: Cornell University Press.

DEWEY, JOHN

John Dewey was a philosopher and an educational innovator. He was also a poet who loved nature, children, and his fellow citizens. He was concerned with changing the course of moral ideas so as to overcome the dualisms between mind and world, soul and body, nature and God. For Dewey, nature represented the whole complex of human desires, hopes, memories, and knowledge, in their interactions with the world. Dewey noticed that to call somebody spiritual never meant to invoke some mysterious and unnatural entity outside of the real world. For Dewey a spiritual person possessed qualities of rich, coordinated, and sensitive participation in the many situations of life. Dewey's philosophy and teachings offer much to the student of spiritual and religious development.

According to Dewey, only spiritual people have souls, and soul and spirit are not to be considered as belonging to a mythic realm; just the opposite: they are embedded in real human experiences. The natural world displays continuity, that is, a harmonious unifying order. The unification of the self, however, can never be achieved just in terms of itself. Human doings and sufferings constitute a ceaseless experiential flux, in which the self transcends itself by means of a continuous integration of shifting experiences with the totality of the universe. Such integration represents a learning process described by Dewey as a readjustment in every form of human consciousness: spirit itself informs. This is what Dewey has called *learning from experience:* the ability to make multiple connections between what we do to things and what we can enjoy—or suffer—from things in return. Whatever people do cannot be reduced to an individual act but represents an experiment with the world outside—a transaction. To discover such a mutual connection means to learn.

For Dewey, the idea of God represented the active relation between the ideal and the actual. The human desire to unite the two belongs to what may be considered a spiritual act. Dewey distinguished between religion and the religious; the latter was not to be identified with the supernatural. He held another conception of that aspect of experience, one that was a qualitative category designated by an adjective, the religious, as opposed to religion. For Dewey, there is no such thing as a singular religion, but a multitude of different religions; therefore, religion is posited as a collective and not a universal term. People can make choices among many religions. Some values and functions in experience may also be selected. The emancipation of certain beliefs and practices from their institutional organization and developing attitudes that may be taken toward some ideal constitute, for Dewey, the religious quality of experience. As such, this quality signifies something that may belong to a variety of aesthetic, scientific, moral, or political experiences or experiences such as companionship and friendship. The religious reorientation brings forward the sense of security and stability by virtue of creating a better and more enduring adjustment to the real-life circumstances. New values are created so as to help in carrying one through the frequent moments of desperation or depression while not submitting to fatalistic resignation.

For Dewey, an experiential situation calls up something not present directly to sense perception. Dewey emphasized the role of imagination in the process of unifying the self with objective conditions, stressing that unity, as the idea of a whole, is to be understood as an imaginative, and not a literal, idea. Imagination expands the world only narrowly apprehended in knowledge or realized in reflective thinking. Imagination exceeds faith, the latter being based on the truth of the propositions solely by virtue of their supernatural author.

Because faith always has practical and moral import, Dewey stressed the difficulty embedded specifically in the moral component. The truly religious attitude is not limited to what is actually out there; it is inspired by belief in what is possible, even if only ideal in character. The realm of the possible is much broader than an intellectual assurance or rational belief can encompass. A human is never to be taken in isolation from the rest of the physical world—what Dewey called the *essentially unreligious attitude.* We are parts of a larger whole, and we have the capacity to intelligently and purposefully create conditions for a continuous inquiry into the mysteries of the natural world. The faith in intelligent inquiry—by means of natural interactions between people and their environment—becomes religious in quality.

Dewey's written works provide the reader and student with much to consider, particularly those who question and seek to understand a religious attitude as compared with dogma and to understand how ethics and our moral conduct play a very important role in common faith.

—Inna Semetsky

FURTHER READING

Dewey, J. (1916). *Democracy and education.* New York: Macmillan.

Dewey, J. (1934). *A common faith.* New Haven: Yale University Press.

Dewey, J. (1934). *Art as experience.* New York: Minton Balch.

DHAMMAPADA

Dating to the fifth century B.C.E., the *Dhammapada* is one of the most influential canonical texts in the Buddhist world. It is such a beloved classic that new translations of it appear regularly and novices, especially in Burma and Sri Lanka, recite the 26 chapters of verse from memory. The 423 stanzas are a distillation of hundreds of discourses that are attributed to the Buddha and appear in other scriptural works. These talks were delivered to all levels of society—to kings and queens as well as to merchants, laborers, mothers, and even criminals. Although the collection is based on the Buddha's teaching, people of other spiritual traditions will find its advice universal, for its aphorisms are conducive to living a harmonious life.

Various scholars suggest different translations of the title. *Dhamma* (in the ancient Pali language) or *Dharma* (in Sanskrit) is "the Truth," "the Law," or "the Norm"—what the Buddha discovered and proclaimed about the nature of existence. *Pada* is "sections," "parts," or "way." Thus, *Dhammapada* can be rendered as "The Way of Truth" or "Words of the Truth." Its verses serve two basic purposes: to imbue readers or listeners with a particular view of life, its difficulties, and their solution and to impart certain spiritual and ethical values.

As a primer of foundational Buddhism, the *Dhammapada* emphasizes the centrality of the mind in creating sorrow and happiness, the ephemeral nature of worldly or material pleasures, the role of personal responsibility, and the law of cause and effect (karma). It points to the Buddhist path as one that a wise person follows and a fool ignores. For example, the wise do not associate with low persons and bad friends, but with the best people and admirable friends.

The Buddha was radical in redefining nobility not as birth into the highest caste but as specific qualities of character and behavior (such as truthfulness, generosity, and patience), all earned through spiritual purification and self-mastery. Such noble development is not the result of repression, stringent asceticism, coercion by religious authorities, dependence on external forces or powers, or rites and rituals in worship of a deity. Instead, the Buddha highlighted conscious restraint from unwholesome mental, physical, and verbal action and conscious cultivation of a clear, steady, balanced mind and a heart filled with compassion and loving kindness. Through our own efforts, we can achieve peace of mind and inner freedom regardless of outer circumstances.

The verses of the *Dhammapada* suggest how to attain such peace. For example, Chapter 10 calls for nonviolence. It asks us to stand in someone else's shoes before acting. Knowing that everyone treasures life and trembles when threatened with a beating or death, would we kill or get others to kill for us? Similarly, if we speak harshly to anyone or cause conflict with our words, that verbal abuse will come back to haunt us in the pain of retaliation. The Buddha's message is that respect and sensitivity to others lead to harmony within and without. Even when someone verbally abused him, he always responded courteously and wisely.

The Buddha dispensed advice for how to attain that harmony. For instance, we easily notice and comment on the failings of others, yet remain oblivious to our own (verse 252). It would be better not to find fault with others and see what we do instead (verse 50). He also says that it is wiser to go alone and do no harm than to keep the company of fools who do ill (verses 207 and 330). Chapter 8 suggests that it is preferable to say one beneficial word or verse that upon hearing it brings peace than to utter thousands of useless words or verses. It is also better to act on our words and not merely say things that sound good (verses 51 and 52).

The Buddha promoted self-control for personal benefit and for the welfare of others. He stressed reining in anger and craving because otherwise there is no end to either unwholesome force. Unchecked anger can lead to intense hatred that results in violence. In Chapter 17 the Buddha exhorts the reader to abandon, conquer, and guard against anger to keep away suffering and misery. Frequently quoted, verse 5 contends that we will never banish hatred with hatred; only with goodwill and patience will we overcome hostility.

As in the case of anger, unchecked craving can lead to addiction that makes destruction possible. Chapter 24 describes a person whose craving is like a creeping vine that smothers the very support that holds it up. His sorrows spring up like wild grass after it rains. He runs around like a rabbit caught in a trap. He is like a spider that falls into its own web.

The Buddha used such simple similes so that everyone, of whatever educational level, could understand. As an itinerant teacher for 45 years, he addressed all ages, from children to the elderly. Although it is an introduction to the Buddhist perspective, the *Dhammapada* is not an abstract intellectual treatise but a practical guide to living well, to behaving ethically. The Buddha uttered these sayings to inspire those who heard him speak. Twenty-five hundred years later, millions of people are still reflecting on them and putting them into practice. Anyone can read them, but those who are unfamiliar with Buddhism would do well to select a translation with explanatory notes written by someone who does not interpret the Buddha's teaching through the lens of another religion.

—*Mirka Knaster*

See also Buddha, Buddhism

FURTHER READING

Buddharakkhita, A. (1985). *The Dhammapada: Buddha's Path to Wisdom*(Trans.). Kandy, Sri Lanka: Buddhist Publication Society. Retrieved July 24, 2005 from www.accesstoinsight .org/canon/sutta/khuddaka/dhp/abo

Carter, J.R., & Palihawadana, M. (2000). *The Dhammapada* (Trans.). New York: Oxford University Press.

Nārada Thera. (1954). *The Dhammapada* (Trans., 3rd Rev. ed.). London: John Murray.

DIALOGUE, INTERRELIGIOUS

It is far easier to determine cross-pollination in the realm of nature than in the world of religion. Scientists spend endless hours watching the process in the field and analyzing the evidence in laboratories. But how can theologians and other scholars ever be fully confident that the spiritual thinking of one group of people influenced the religious development of another? This is particularly problematic if the interpreters of history are blinded by their own religious persuasions and documentation is not only minimal but, in some cases, unreliable.

Nevertheless, in one way or another and often unconsciously, all religions have drawn on beliefs and practices of other traditions they have encountered. Sometimes the blending is the result of marriage between a woman of one spiritual community and a man of another. At other times it is the consequence of traders of different persuasions coming into contact, even settling down outside their own society. In addition, converts to one tradition carry with them ideas, beliefs, and stories from their own heritage. Close proximity of diverse neighbors can also lead to sharing practices. For example, although Jews do not have a history of asceticism, in medieval Germany there were pious Jews who incorporated severe austerities after having observed them among Christians. And some Jews living in the medieval Islamic societies of the Iberian Peninsula and North Africa studied with Sufi masters. The reverse is true as well: the development of both Christianity and Islam reflects borrowings from Judaism.

Whenever history has brought different peoples to live together, religions have modified each other, sometimes to their mutual benefit and sometimes not. In Latin America, Roman Catholicism was grafted onto indigenous spiritual systems. In China, where

Buddhism commingled with Taoism and Confucianism, it took on a different form than in Sri Lanka (Ceylon) or Myanmar (Burma).

Some of what happened many centuries ago is traceable, but much of it has disappeared in the mists of time. However, today, when it is clear that no religion is an island, as Rabbi Abraham Joshua Heschel (1907–1972) pointed out, there is the opportunity to experience a great range of religious life. We can consciously witness how interfaith exchanges take place and document them. One such active contemporary exchange is between Buddhism and Judaism.

Since the final decades of the 20th century, an unprecedented and disproportionate number of Jews have been drawn to practice in the different schools of Buddhism—Theravāda, Mahāyāna, and Vajrayāna. This phenomenon poses a curious question: Is it an anomaly, or has a Jewish-Buddhist dialogue occurred before?

While it is difficult to determine what actually transpired in the distant past, several writers suggest that Buddhists and Jews have known each other for at least 2 millennia and possibly much longer. Others are convinced that there was no early exchange or direct impact. Those who subscribe to linkages between the two groups in the ancient world point out that along with merchants, there were also ambassadors, emissaries, and missionaries who traveled the trade routes connecting India with regions to the west. For example, in the third century B.C.E., King Ashoka's deputy to Alexandria may have influenced the author of Ecclesiastes. One scholar notes that Jews were a trading connection between Christian Europe and Hindu-Buddhist India and Jewish settlements appeared in India in the first century. And the "silk road" between the Chinese and Roman empires passed through the Negev Desert of Israel.

There are references to India in early Jewish historical writings as well as in the Talmud, which includes some Sanskrit words. By the early medieval era, Jewish merchants made a whole body of Buddhist literature (the *Jātaka* tales) available to the Western world. Interestingly, one story in particular parallels the judgment tale of King Solomon in Kings 3:16–28. Thereafter, little to nothing is heard about a connection between Jews and Buddhists for many centuries.

In America, there was no public conversation about Buddhism until the mid- to late 1800s, and those who engaged in it were generally New England men of British and Protestant heritage. However, it was a Swiss-born Jewish businessman from New York City, Charles T. Strauss, who was both the first Jew and first westerner to publicly embrace the Buddha's teaching on American soil. At the World's Parliament of Religions of 1893 in Chicago, he performed the ceremony of taking refuge in the Buddha in front of an overflow crowd and remained devoted until his death.

Like the trade routes that opened relations between the Near East and Far East in ancient times, modern transportation and media have opened relations between Western Jews and Asian Buddhists. Austrian-born Israeli philosopher Martin Buber (1878–1965) received visits from Japanese *rōshi* (Zen master) Nyogen Senzaki (1876–1958) in Jerusalem and from Buddhist scholars D. T. Suzuki (1870–1966) and Masao Abe in New York. Israeli Prime Minister David Ben Gurion (1886–1973) discussed ties between Jews and Buddhists with Burmese Prime Minister U Nu (1907–1995) on TV in 1959.

During the "Zen boom" of the 1950s, beat poet Allen Ginsberg (1926–1997) proclaimed himself a "Buddhist Jew." Interest in Buddhism grew in the 1960s after some westerners who had practiced in Japanese temples in the 1950s returned and wrote about it. Foremost among them was Philip Kapleau (1912–2004), who became the first westerner ordained as *rōshi*. By the 1970s an estimated 50% of Zen people in San Francisco and 33% in Los Angeles were Jews, though the total Jewish population in the United States is estimated around 2%.

Through various levels of participation, Jews have been instrumental in the development of Western Buddhism. For example, they have helped establish some of the leading Buddhist teaching institutions in North America. After studying with Buddhist masters in India and Thailand, Joseph Goldstein, Jack Kornfield, Sharon Salzberg, and Jacqueline Schwartz founded the Theravāda-based Insight Meditation Society in Barre, Massachusetts, in 1975. Others have trained with Tibetan teachers and become Buddhist scholars, professors of Buddhist Studies, translators, and publishers. One of them, Sam Bercholz, started Shambhala Books, the first major publishing house to release Tibetan Buddhist works in the United States and later publish books about every school of Buddhism.

Still other Jews became popular dharma teachers themselves. Lama Surya Das, born Jeffrey Miller, is the first American Tibetan lama. Rôshi Bernard Tetsugen Glassman is the first American-born lineage holder in the Sōtō Zen sect of Japan. Ayya Khema (1923–1997), born Ilse Kussel in Berlin, was the first Western woman to be ordained as a Theravāda nun.

She founded a monastery ("Nun's Island") in Sri Lanka, and a Buddhist center in Germany, from which she had originally fled Nazi terrorism.

Academic or theological dialogue is another part of the Jewish–Buddhist encounter. However, while Christians have interacted with Buddhists through missionary activity as well as interfaith dialogue and have produced volumes of literature on the subject, there are far fewer Jewish–Buddhist dialogues or comparative research efforts on record. Unquestionably the most prominent of such dialogues resulted when the Dalai Lama invited a small delegation of diverse Jewish leaders to Dharamsala, India, in October 1990. Faced with the urgent need to preserve Tibetan culture, he sought to learn the "secret technique" that has enabled the Jews to keep their own tradition alive during 2,000 years of persecution and exile. It will be interesting to track whether their suggestions, based on Jewish practices, will inform the development of Tibetan Buddhism in modern times.

The area of Jewish–Buddhist encounter that has drawn the most attention and perhaps produced the most writing is personal experience. Dozens of magazine and newspaper articles, essays in anthologies, memoirs, other nonfiction, and even a novel recount variations on simultaneously being Jewish and engaging in Buddhist practice. These works reflect a different level of interfaith discourse. Instead of taking place between distinct representatives of the two traditions, the exchange is within practitioners themselves: Their very lives are the authentic dialogue. The various publications trace individual spiritual journeys. In some cases, Jews who took up Buddhist practice return fully to Judaism, even becoming rabbis. In other instances, they negotiate the paradox of integrating the two different religions.

As Jews participate in shaping Buddhism in the West, Buddhist practice is also reshaping Judaism. Engaging in Buddhist meditation has enabled some Jews to delve into the texts of their birth religion and discern ancient practices they could not previously recognize for lack of experiential understanding. In turn, this has helped open the door to Jewish mysticism. Additionally, The Spirituality Institute trains rabbis, cantors, educators, and social activists in the nonsectarian practice of mindfulness meditation that the Buddha first taught more than 2,500 years ago.

This phenomenon of "mixing and matching" Judaism and Buddhism is yielding academic fruit. There is increased interest in examining where the two converge and diverge. As Jewish practitioners of Buddhism explore the tradition from within, they can make research contributions that do not grow solely out of intellectual knowledge but also are informed by intimate experience, creating a marriage between theoretical and existential understanding. The present Jewish–Buddhist dialogue in the West may well be a modern-day version of the ferment that existed at the turn of the Common Era, when the Middle East was a crossroads where Eastern and Western ideas met.

This history of Jewish–Buddhist dialogue and interaction illustrates what happens when people of different religions interact with each other on more than a superficial level. It can have a profound effect on the development of personal practice as well as on the development of world peace. Instead of merely seeing each other as an outsider, even considering the other as wrong or misguided, individuals come to understand, on an experiential level, what the other one knows and does and are transformed by that knowledge. In such interfaith encounters lies the potential for followers of many kinds of spiritualities to live together in greater harmony and mutual respect.

—*Mirka Knaster*

See also Judaism, Buddhism

FURTHER READING

Boorstein, S. (1997). *That's funny, you don't look Buddhist: On being a faithful Jew and a passionate Buddhist.* New York: HarperSanFrancisco.

Kamenetz, R. (1994). *The Jew in the lotus: A poet's rediscovery of Jewish identity in Buddhist India.* New York: Harper SanFrancisco.

Kasimow, H., Keenan, J. P., & Keenan, L. K. (2003). *Beside still waters: Jews, Christians, and the way of the Buddha.* Boston: Wisdom Publications.

Lew, A., & Jaffe, S. (1999). *One God clapping: The spiritual path of a Zen rabbi.* New York: Kodansha International.

Linzer, J. (1996). *Torah and Dharma: Jewish seekers in Eastern religions.* Northvale, N.J.: Jason Aronson.

DIFFERENCES BETWEEN RELIGION AND SPIRITUALITY IN CHILDREN AND ADOLESCENTS

Spirituality and religion are, at least in part, overlapping concepts. They are highly complex and hard to define, and their exact relationship is difficult to describe. Today, they are used in a whole number of different academic disciplines (theology, religious and cultural studies, psychology, sociology, historical studies, etc.), in many different contexts, and in reference to different traditions or religions in different parts of the world. Yet their meaning and much of the scientific discussions about them in the past has been strongly influenced by European and Western Christianity and, in part, Judaism and Islam that accounts for some of the difficulties that currently are of central concern for many researchers in this increasingly international, multireligious, and open field of study. In addition to the broad long-term historical context that has shaped these concepts, there are contemporary social and cultural developments that have created a new interest in spirituality, which, more and more, is seen as clearly different from religion, in relationship to children and adolescents but also with adults.

The etymology of the concepts is telling but does not lead to consensual understandings or to clear definitions that can be relied upon in the present. Both terms go back to Latin roots. While the adjective *spiritual* may be traced back, as a translation, to the Greek (New Testament) *pneumatikos,* or *pneumatic*—relating to the pneuma or spirit (which again is rooted in the Hebrew bible's notion of ruach or spirit), the noun *spirituality* does not occur before the fifth century and becomes a common concept not before the 12th century. It is first used in a Christian context (baptism and Christian life after baptism), later in a more general sense to describe that which is different from body or matter and which is not subject to temporal limitations. The medieval connotations of the concept remain Christian in a broad sense, later, after the Reformation, more Roman Catholic than Protestant because of the special emphasis on spiritual discipline in Catholicism, for example, with the Jesuits. Today, the concept is used in all Christian denominations and also within Judaism, Islam, Buddhism, Hinduism, as well as in other traditions and religions in order to describe the spiritual aspects of these religions or traditions or to refer to special groups or orientations within these religions or traditions.

The origins and meaning of the term *religion* are doubtful, with Cicero connecting it to *relegere,* or to read over again, and other authors like Augustine to *religare,* or referring to binding obligation. Under the influence of early Christianity, the general concept of religion soon became identified with the Christian faith and was then used in opposition to what, from a Christian perspective, was seen as heathen idolatry and aberrations. It is only in modern times that the concept *religion* is applied, as a universal term, to all religions interchangeably and independently of different traditions, truth claims, and convictions, and religious practices.

In the contemporary literature, it is often stressed that there are no clear or consensual definitions of the two concepts. Most of the numerous definitions found in the literature are based on a certain normative understanding or on the wish to see a certain understanding prevail, not only in theory but also within the life of religious traditions or communities. The universal application of the concepts presupposes that their meaning is mostly independent of certain content but rather refers to general or universal functions or structures, like finding, expressing, or creating ultimate meaning, world coherence, cosmic order, foundations of ethical life, etc. According to this point of view, it is the specific function for the individual or for a group or community or society that defines the meaning of religion and spirituality. In contrast to this, the older literature also includes content-related features within the universal use of the concepts, for example, worship of a goddess or higher being. These kinds of content-related universals are now often criticized as illegitimate generalizations from Judaism, Christianity, and Islam to nontheistic or polytheistic religions. Comparative study of religion and spirituality is legitimate, but one must always be mindful of the origin of the concepts applied as well as of their being influenced and loaded by particular traditions and cultural settings. So-called indigenous religions or spiritual traditions, for example, in Africa or Asia cannot be adequately captured by making them fit into Western categories.

It is because of such self-critical insights and considerations concerning the limitations of one's concepts or terminology that some researchers have also called into question the concept of religion itself. The connotations of this concept—unity, shared convictions and creeds, institutional membership structures, etc.—may indeed be more in line with Western religions and especially with Christianity than with other kinds of religions in different parts of the world. Hinduism is a telling example. For westerners coming to India, it clearly was and is a religion that can be considered a parallel and competitor to Western religions. For the people living on the Indian subcontinent themselves, Hinduism may have never been a unified religious system at all. Moreover, the concept of religion is closely related to (Western) political history, and the connotations mentioned above must be understood against the background of political interests, among others, in political unity and national adherence. The conclusion from these etymological and definitional considerations must be that there should be no naive and uncritical use of the concepts of spirituality and religion.

The general observations concerning the two concepts must be kept in mind when we now turn to questions of their more specific use in reference to children and youth. When applied to today's children and youth, the understanding of spirituality is often supposed to be very broad and open. It is taken to be a purely formal concept that is not connected to any particular religious tradition or institution. Instead it refers to characteristics like interest in the divine, transcendence, ultimate meaning, etc., which can be filled in very different ways. In this sense, the reference to the spirituality of children and youth is in line with contemporary research that is trying to include a broad range of different spiritualities that, at least originally, were not connected to this term—like Native American spirituality, indigenous spirituality, ecological spirituality, women's spirituality, new age spirituality, etc. In the English language, the relationship between spirituality and religion is commonly defined by the different references to institutionalized religion that are characteristic of the two concepts. Religion then refers to institutionalized religion, to religious communities and hierarchies, most often with a fixed creedal and moral system in the sense of dogma. In contrast to this, spirituality means the individual and personal interest in transcendence, the ultimate, etc., often including the attempt of opening oneself up to spiritual experiences through the use of certain rites, practices, techniques, etc. Spirituality can also be or become communal but rarely in the sense of structured institutions.

It is this understanding of the difference between spirituality and religion that has made the concept of spirituality attractive for contemporary researchers. According to recent interview studies, more and more adolescents (and adults) in the Western world feel that they are not religious but that they are spiritual—that they can indeed have a deep interest in spirituality and in the spiritual dimensions of life without being religious. For obvious reasons, especially younger children are not included in such interview studies, but there also is a new and strong interest in the spirituality of children. What exactly does the difference between spirituality and religion mean in relation to children and adolescents?

Considering the present cultural and religious situation in many countries of the Western world, the difference between religion and spirituality clearly reflects the tensions between institutionalized forms of religion such as the churches, on the one hand, and the individual or personal interest or belief in transcendence, on the other. Many adolescents are especially critical of all institutions, including religious institutions. The traditional churches, for example, that are often referred to as *mainline churches,* strike them as dated institutions and as the embodiment of authoritarian doctrines that they do not find very convincing. Social and theological analysts have pointed out that such views are not only expressive of personal dissatisfaction with religious institutions but are also indicative of the broader cultural and social tendencies of religious pluralization and individualization that are characteristic of modern and postmodern societies. According to this view, modern individuals are not willing to accept traditional membership roles or the creedal and convictional or ethical obligations that come with such roles. Instead they insist on their own personal needs, experiences, insights, etc. "Everyone is a special case" is the telling title of a study on religion in Switzerland published in the 1990s.

The interest in personal or individual experience has also led to the uncovering of what has been called the *spiritual life of children.* It is quite difficult to come into immediate contact with the spiritual experiences of young children simply because children are often lacking the expressive means and especially the language to describe such experiences. Yet the narratives on childhood produced by adolescents or adults often allow—at least for some—a retrospective understanding of children's spirituality. Systematic collection and analysis of such narratives as well as refined interview techniques that permit respective dialogues with young children consistently support the understanding that children do have religious or spiritual experiences and that such experiences are not just due to the influence of a specific type of nurture to which they were exposed in their families. Rather, the ways in which children experience their social and natural environment seem to imply something like a transcendent overtone or dimension that accounts for the religious or spiritual interest of children.

What is most telling in relation to the difference between religion and spirituality in childhood is the observation that many narratives entail a conflict at the point when children, after a certain age, come in touch with institutionalized forms of religious instruction or worship. Even after several decades, people recall the deep disappointment that they suffered when their own religious or spiritual needs and experiences were not addressed by religious institutions or by religious education in school and when the religion presented to them there remained foreign, distant, cold, and meaningless for them. This kind of experience seems to create a permanent split between personal spirituality and official or institutional religion.

Researchers aptly describe the contemporary situation in Western countries as a "spiritual marketplace." Through popular culture and the media, children and adolescents are exposed to the influences of this marketplace from early on. Even television advertisement has come to include elements of spirituality, for example, by attaching the promise of deep personal fulfillment to products like cars or perfumes. Offers of psychological help and self-improvement are another case in point. The spiritual marketplace has many things to offer, new possibilities for personal development but also dangerous forms of addictive and exploitative practices. The varieties of spiritual offerings in the marketplace worry many people—not only the representatives of the traditional religions who observe the flourishing of nontraditional types of personal or spiritual life but also psychologists and social analysts who are concerned about the potential abuse of people's credulity. Not everything that toots itself spiritual has to do with spiritual interests—often it is a purely commercial and mundane matter. And not everything leads to personal growth and to the fulfillment of deeper needs but only fits the needs and interests of commercial enterprises.

Distinguishing between religion and spirituality in childhood and adolescence is helpful to the degree that this distinction allows for a new openness and appreciation in respect to young people's needs and longings, their creativity and independence that are not always addressed by the religious institutions in an adequate manner. The distinction becomes shallow, however, when it leads to the uncritical acceptance of whatever appears spiritual while everything religious is considered dated and meaningless. Both, theories of religion and of spirituality, must include a critical potential and critical attitude toward both, the abuse of religion and spirituality, especially concerning children and youth who may not yet be aware of the ambivalences to be encountered in this field full of fascinations.

—*Friedrich Schweitzer*

FURTHER READING

Ahn, G. (1997). Religion. In G. Müller *Theologische Realenzyklopädie, 28,* Berlin and New York.

Best, R. (1996). *Education, spirituality and the whole child.* London and New York: Cassell.

Coles, R. (1990). *The spiritual life of children.* Boston: Houghton Mifflin.

Fuller, R. C. (2001). *Spiritual, but not religious: Understanding unchurched America.* Oxford and New York: Oxford University Press.

Luckmann, T. (1967). *The invisible religion: The problem of religion in modern society.* New York and London: Macmillan.

Robinson, E. (1983). *The original vision: A study of the religious experience of childhood.* New York: Seabury Press.

Roof, W. C. (1999). *Spiritual marketplace: Baby boomers and the remaking of American religion.* Princeton and Oxford: Princeton University Press.

Schweitzer, F. (2004). *The post modern life cycle: Challenges for church and theology.* St. Louis: Chalice Press.

Waaijman, K. (2002). *Spirituality: Forms, foundations, methods.* Leuven: Peeters.

DISCERNMENT

Discernment is the ability to judge wisely and objectively. Discernment is an important and common trait of religious and spiritual tradition and education and, as such, is a key characteristic in discussions of religious and spiritual development. The concept of religious and spiritual discernment is most famously described and modeled by St. Ignatius in his *Spiritual Exercises* (1548/1997) in which he describes a unique method of prayer and meditation in which one carefully attends to or "discerns" one's feelings for the movement of the Holy Spirit. Ignatius taught principles of discernment to others by founding schools and directing silent, 30-day retreats. By the time of his death in 1556, Ignatius and his companions had founded 35 schools and had conducted hundreds of retreats. Today there are more than 20,000 members of the Society of Jesus, the religious order Ignatius founded, over 200 "Jesuit" schools worldwide, and 56 retreat centers in 24 U.S. states and 17 foreign countries.

Ignatius believed and shared with others that God establishes relationship in the human *heart,* the interior dimension of the person. In the heart, the person discovers God's purpose or *vocation* for his or her life. Each person is seen to have both a general and a specific vocation. At a general level, humans are called to "praise, reverence, and serve" God, but specifically how they are to do this is seen to vary from person to person. Ignatius discovered that when the call of God presents itself to the heart, it stirs the *emotions.* Thus, the way to know the will of God for one's own life is to discern with the *intellect* the various stirrings of the heart. The *will* then puts what the intellect has discerned into action in the world.

The overall goal of Ignatian spiritual development is to be able to "find God in all things." In order for this to occur, Ignatius believed that the whole person—body, intellect, and soul—must be educated. In particular, the body and the intellect must be freed from "inordinate attachments" that prevent them from being open to discerning the promptings of the Holy Spirit. Such attachments include physical passions and appetites, as well as psychological needs for esteem, power, and wealth. Ignatius guided others on the development of discernment. His teachings frame contemporary applied efforts to develop discernment in children and youth.

The ability to discern depends upon the commitment of parents, teachers, and the discerning individual. It is therefore impossible to articulate a series of invariant stages applicable to all individuals. However, given a familial and scholastic environment explicitly devoted to cultivating spiritual discernment in the young, it is possible to formulate a five-phase sequence of change based upon psychological capacities that emerge at particular periods in the life span. Ages, of course, are only approximations.

1. *Custodial Phase* (0–1½ years). By most accounts, the human intellect is only crudely developed in infancy. Since the ability to discern depends upon a differentiated intellect, the infant's *parents* are primarily responsible for the task of discernment during the first years of life. Parents' main task is to discern the infant's emotions and then reflect this information back to the infant in the form of gestures, facial expressions, sounds, and words, e.g., "You're frustrated because you can't reach that toy." These reflections are crucial because they are external tools of discernment the infant will later internalize and employ as a child.

2. *Transitional Phase* (1½–6 years). During this phase, the child begins to internalize and employ the reflected tools of discernment provided by parents and educational surrogates. The child teeters back and forth between being able to discern alone and needing the support of parents and teachers. This phenomenon is analogous to the "private speech" observed by Vygotsky (1986–1934) in which the child labors to make external linguistic tools his or her own. The child is also improving his or her ability to isolate and identify his or her emotions and to appreciate the connection between these effects and the will of God. This period of development is also one of great mental and physical activity. As such, it is an opportune time for the cultivation and practice of habits, for example, moral virtues, daily recitation of prayers, scripture readings, that will dispose the child to be open to the workings of the Holy Spirit.

3. *The Age of Reason* (6–13 years). While the previous phase was one of action, during this phase, the child is beginning to deal with the world primarily with his or her intellect. With the growing liberation of the intellect from the passions, logical error, and dependence on authority figures, comes an increased sense of self and presence to the heart. With these psychological achievements, the child is now in a position to perfect the skills of discernment so as to make decisions informed by spiritual guidance. This ability to discern enables the child to understand his or her general vocation to praise, reverence, and serve God, as well as how to concretely apply general moral norms to the decisions of everyday life.

4. *Spiritual Commitment* (13–17 years). If the previous phase is the period of the intellect, this phase is the period of the will. It is one thing for the child to understand his or her general vocation, it is quite another for him or her to make a commitment to live it out. Most religious congregations regard the young adolescent as a "spiritual adult" in the sense that he or she is regarded as capable of making mature decisions with respect to participating in the faith. Once

the adolescent has made a commitment to live a life guided by the Spirit, the task of parents and teachers is to help him or her identify and overcome internal and external obstacles that threaten to prevent the realization of his or her vocation.

5. *Lifestyle and Occupational Discernment* (17–21 years). Assuming a commitment has been made to the general vocation, during this phase, the young adult discerns his or her particular vocation. The particular vocation has two components: "lifestyle" and "occupational" vocation. With respect to lifestyle, some people are seen to be called to the "priestly" state of religious life, others to the married state, and still others to the lay celibate state. With respect to occupation, each person is believed to be called to perform a particular type of work in the world. In familial and educational settings, the young adult is given guidance and skills on how to make these crucial decisions about occupation and state of life. The thrust of these efforts is not "what do I want to do with my life?," but "what is God calling me to do with my life?"
6. *Incarnational Phase* (21–35 years). Assuming the identification of lifestyle and occupational vocation has taken place, during this phase, the young adult commits him or herself to living out or "incarnating" these vocations in the world. This may involve beginning a career, taking religious vows, or getting married. As most formal education ends during this time, it is important that the young adult begin to incorporate regular periods of prayer, reflection, and conscience examination into his or her daily life to ensure ongoing access to the spiritual guidance necessary for the full and proper realization of lifestyle and occupational commitments. Such "spiritual hygiene" may also involve devotional reading, retreats, and/or professional spiritual direction.

The development of discernment within an individual depends upon the back-and-forth movement between parents, culture, and religious tradition on one hand and the innate strivings of the individual on the other. Certainly context has an important influence on the development of discernment. As such, experience in religious and/or spiritual traditions, level of participation in religious and/or spiritual practices, the community of religious and/or spiritual adherents in which one is immersed, etc., all have an impact on the development of individual discernment. St. Ignatius has left us with a framework from which to model healthy discernment. It is of little surprise that his teachings remain key guideposts to those interested in and invested in the development and practice of discernment.

—*James Dillon*

See also St. Ignatius of Loyola

FURTHER READING

Ignatius. (1997). *The spiritual exercises of Saint Ignatius* (P. Wolff, Trans.). Liguori, MO: Liguori Publications. (Original work published 1548)

van Kaam, A. (1975). *In search of spiritual identity.* Denville, NJ: Dimension Books.

Vygotsky. L. S. (1986). *Thought and language* (A. Kozulin, Trans.). Cambridge, MA: MIT Press. (Original work published 1934)

DONNE, JOHN

John Donne's position as one of the greatest of English poets is unquestioned, but there is a much greater ambivalence about his religious and spiritual commitments. Some have seen his religious writing as deeply devotional and meditative, while others have found him to be 'not remarkable for any spiritual gifts and graces' and have dismissed his writing as "feigned devotion." Donne's life serves as a model of religious growth and how religiosity can impact and trigger devotions and passions in the rest of one's life. His poems have also been known to touch the spiritual and religious lives of many a reader.

Donne was born into a Catholic family in 1572 and was very familiar with contemporary prejudice against that faith. He went to Oxford at an early age but was unable to graduate because he was a Catholic. In due course he broke away from the faith and became an Anglican. He was ordained in 1615 and served as Dean of St. Paul's in London from 1621 until his death in 1631. Controversy remains as to whether he was simply a fair-weather convert to Anglicanism and whether he was really as tolerant of religious diversity in later life as some of his published sermons suggest. The controversy is compounded by the apparent gulf between the "worldliness" of his early life and the devotion to religion of his later years. As a young man, he trained in the law, served on military expeditions, traveled widely in Europe, became a Member of Parliament, and was described by a contemporary, Sir Richard Baker, as "a great visitor of ladies, a great frequenter of plays, a great writer of conceited verses." However, he ruined a promising career in 1601 by an injudicious marriage to his employer's niece, and it is sometimes suggested that he took Holy Orders only as a last resort after years of poverty and failure to win advancement at court. As Dean of St. Paul's he achieved some of the fame that had eluded him earlier, and his sermons drew large crowds.

Apart from some miscellaneous writings, Donne's poetry is usually categorized as either love poetry or religious poetry, and the assumption behind the categorization is that the love poetry belongs to his youth and the religious poetry to his more mature years. But this is an oversimplification, as the dating of the poems bears out. Both love and religious poems combine the same intellectual insight, emotional intensity, and spiritual significance, though they tend also to be arrogant and self-absorbed. Donne is profoundly (though not exclusively) interested in the spiritual dimensions of human love, as his poems "Aire and Angels" and "The Relic" indicate, as well as in divine love. One thing that binds the love poetry and the religious poetry into a unified body of work is the fact that erotic sexuality is often symbolic of religious experience, and vice versa. In "Holy Sonnet XIV"' he famously calls on God to ravish him, but in his erotic "Elegy XIX" he compares the "full nakedness" of his mistress once she has stripped off her last remaining garment to a soul free at last from the encumbrance of the body.

The movement from human to divine or from physical to spiritual lies at the heart of "Holy Sonnet XVII," in which the poet shows how his love for his wife Ann led him to seek God and how God's love has filled the vacuum left by her death. However, the link between the physical and spiritual worlds goes deeper than this. Donne's sermons demonstrate a profound interest in the theology of incarnation, and it is clear that for him it is through the body that the divine is revealed to us. Just as God is revealed in the person of Christ and just as the truth of the resurrection was brought home to doubting Thomas when he was able to touch the wounded hands and side of the risen Lord, so our understanding of the mysteries of spiritual love is extended through physical, human love (cf. "The Extasie"). Similarly, it is through the reunion of the parted lovers at the end of "A Valediction: Forbidding Mourning" that we gain an understanding of the eventual reunion of body and soul on the day of resurrection. The physical world in all its diversity is for Donne a mirror that reflects an image of spiritual reality.

—J. Mark Halstead

FURTHER READING

Donne, J. (1985). *The complete English poems* (C. A. Patrides, Ed.). London: Everyman.

Donne, J. (1953–1962). *The sermons, Vols. 1–10* (E. M. Simpson & G. R. Potter, Eds.). Berkeley: University of California Press.

Gardner, H. (Ed.). (1952). *John Donne: The divine poems.* Oxford: Clarendon.

Oliver, P. M. (1997). *Donne's religious writings: A discourse in feigned devotion.* London: Longman.

DOUBT

For many people—young and old alike—doubt is a frequent companion in our spiritual journeys. Adolescents often wonder if there is a God, if they can trust religious traditions and institutions, and if there is anything of transcendent value beyond the here and now. Is doubt the opposite of faith, or does doubt help faith grow? Surely in many cases, doubt can lead to genuine spiritual growth by challenging the individual and leading to new breakthroughs and deeper insights; in other cases, some individuals may expand their doubt to a wholesale rejection of faith. Doubt is part of the adolescent's personal experience, but it does not occur in a vacuum—adults can influence whether doubt derails faith or helps it grow. Different approaches can help illuminate adolescents' doubt and suggest ways to respond to it.

BIBLICAL APPROACHES

Scripture tells us that faith is "the assurance of things hoped for, the conviction of things not seen" (Heb. 11:1). The Wisdom tradition, especially Ecclesiastes and Job, offers a philosophical vantage on doubt, showing it to be a common and even natural aspect of living a faithful life. The New Testament also addresses doubt in many instances. One of the more famous ones is the "Doubting Thomas" incident

(John 20:29). Here, Thomas inserts his finger into the wound of Jesus, who responds, "Have you believed because you have seen me? Blessed are those who have not seen me and yet believe." Another crucial incident occurs when the man with a demon-possessed child asks if Jesus is able to help him (Mark 9:20–24). Jesus replies that "all things are possible to him who believes," and the father's famous retort is "I believe; help my unbelief!" This father feels the paradox and struggle inherent in faith, a predicament some youth find themselves in—wanting to believe, but reluctant to do so. As these excerpts illustrate, many organized religions recognize the impact of doubt and want to uphold individuals in their struggles with it.

THEORETICAL APPROACHES

Theologian Paul Tillich's (1957) classic, *Dynamics of Faith,* analyzes different kinds of doubt. The doubt integral to faith, Tillich claims, is existential doubt, the capacity to accept the uncertainty that comes with faith in the divine. Tillich insists that doubt is not the negation of faith but is always present in faith and that this faith has a distinct "in spite of," an uncertainty that goes hand-in-hand with faith. Tillich's view may also help the teenager (and adult) realize that courage is needed to face doubt. Every spiritual journey has its high seasons and low seasons, and faith is marked not by certainty but by trust.

Psychologist Gordon Allport suggests adolescent doubt may be due to skepticism—not about the deeper meaning and lasting commitments of faith but many of the concrete behavioral expressions of faith, such as worship styles, rituals such as communion or prayers, and so on. Adults could take on the important task of helping teenagers understand this crucial distinction between the ultimate object of faith and its worldly, concrete forms.

Another classic, *Stages of Faith* by James Fowler (1981), asserts that the opposite of faith is not doubt but nihilism—profound despair and inability to envision any transcendent relationships. Fowler describes how doubt emerges. In late childhood, youth notice discrepancies between major accounts of truth (e.g., science and religion) and wonder about which is "right." Children also detect hypocrisy in the gap between what adults preach and practice. Later in adolescence, youth develop an "individuative-reflective" faith that is marked by questioning whether their beliefs are actually their own or mere holdovers from others (parents, congregations, peers). Thus, doubt helps youth outgrow their earlier "absorbed" faith. This "demythologizing" or stripping away of prior beliefs can cause anxiety, but the result is that the teen feels a personal ownership of the faith. In some cases, this new faith may indeed be the teen's "old" faith (of family or congregation); the key difference is that the teenager now takes personal responsibility for believing and being committed to it.

EMPIRICAL APPROACHES

Several Canadian psychologists—Bruce Hunsberger, Michael Pratt, Mark Pancer, and others—have studied adolescent doubt. In one study of high school seniors, teens higher in religious doubt had parents low in warmth. Youth of such parents may feel alone and unsupported in their spiritual journey and thus be more inclined to doubt. In another study by Hunsberger and colleagues, teens and college students who had trouble forming a stable and committed identity were higher in doubt, whereas those with a foreclosed or premature identity had lower doubt. In the former groups, doubt seems linked to uncertainty over who they are; in the latter group, taking on an identity without sufficient exploration or questioning of beliefs seems to suppress doubting.

In another study, college students' doubt and fundamentalism were related in interesting ways: Doubters who were low in fundamentalism questioned the foundations of their religion, whereas doubters high in fundamentalism focused on the failure of others to live up to religious ideals. Overall, those higher in doubt scored lower in fundamentalism and right-wing authoritarianism.

In one study, the more complex and sophisticated students were in their thinking, the more young people also experienced doubt. Taking all this evidence together, adolescent doubt seems related to teenagers' identity maturity and complexity of thinking. However, some of these works were done on small samples of Canadian youth, so it is unclear whether these findings apply to youth in other cultures.

ADULTS' RESPONSE TO DOUBT

Will adults respond to adolescent doubts as inappropriate and heretical challenges or as genuine concerns that deserve genuine attention and response? Adults who live and work with youth may influence where teenagers' doubt leads and whether it feels like liberation or damnation. Adult responses to adolescent doubt may depend on adults' own feelings about doubt in one's spiritual journey. If adults see doubts as the "termites" of faith or think mature spirituality is about "having all the answers," they may respond to adolescents' doubt by ignoring or denying it or dissuading the youth out of it. If adults think doubt is healthy for spiritual growth and is the "ants in the pants" of faith that keeps us on our spiritual toes, they may welcome teens' doubts and discuss with them how to reconcile doubt with faith, questions with trust, uncertainty with commitment.

An adult's responses to youthful doubt may also reflect the adult's own faith traditions. There is surely wide diversity across denominations in their acceptance of doubt. Even within a single denomination, there are many positions. In mainline Protestant traditions, doubt is a normal essence of spiritual growth. Conservative or evangelical Christian traditions may view doubt as undermining young people's faith in the literal, inerrant word of God. In Judaism, the practice of Talmudic interrogation and disputation suggests an abiding respect for questioning as an integral component of mature faith, although the degree of acceptance of doubt may vary between and within different Jewish faith traditions.

Youth often think adults are uncomfortable with youths' doubts. In interviews with college students of many faiths, Hill found that virtually all said they had doubts about faith but they were told, directly or indirectly, that their doubts were not welcome at their place of worship. Allport asserted that parents and organized religions might do more to help doubting youth. Adults who work with youth must reconcile their own tensions about doubt to help youth with their struggles. Adults must also discern whether the teens' doubt is more or less healthy. When doubt moves a youth toward despair and a bleak feeling of "it just doesn't matter," adults could be compelled to organize a supportive response by family and community.

Adults must also gauge their response to the teen's personality. Doubting teens with a more analytic, intellectualized faith might respond best to philosophical or theological argument; those with a more emotional or intuitive faith may respond best to adults' warmth and acceptance. Perhaps all youth would benefit from hearing personal stories of adults close to them, many of whom have gone through their own dry seasons of doubt.

CONCLUSIONS

Let us return to some biblical exemplars of doubt. Rather than thinking of "doubting" Thomas as an oddball or obstinate skeptic, think of him as a poster-child for adolescent doubt. Teenagers are trying to figure out what to believe, and they, like Thomas, often want proof for the claims of their faith traditions. As Episcopal priest Fleming Rutledge (2000) noted in *Help My Unbelief,* it matters that Thomas' doubts were changed by seeing the wounds of Jesus. The experience of suffering and pain may accompany doubt and give rise to a deeper faith. Adults who work with youth may gain something if they look upon adolescents as contemporary doubting Thomases who are struggling amidst uncertainty and the "conviction of things not seen." Adults may help youth even more if they keep in mind the father of the demon-possessed child, saved by Jesus, whose lament captures the paradox and tensions of adolescent faith: "I believe; help my unbelief!" May all adults hear and answer the adolescent cry therein: "*Help* my unbelief!"

—Chris J. Boyatzis

FURTHER READING

Allport, G. W. (1950). *The individual and his religion.* New York: Macmillan.

Fowler, J. W. (1981). *Stages of faith: The psychology of human development and the quest for meaning.* New York: Harper & Row.

Hill, R. H. (1999). *When in doubt: The faith journeys of young adults.* Curriculum Publishing.

Hunsberger, B., Pratt, M., & Pancer, S. M. (2002). A longitudinal study of religious doubts in high school and beyond: Relationships, stability, and searching for answers. *Journal for the Scientific Study of Religion, 41,* 255–256.

Rutledge, F. (2000). *Help my unbelief.* Grand Rapids, MI: Eerdmans.

DRAMA

Drama can play a powerful role in facilitating spiritual development both in educational and community contexts. It has the potential to operate as an imaginative scaffold for spiritual development since the core constructs of drama involve both engagement and reflection, two essential features in cultivating spirituality. In improvisational process drama, children search for meaning and purpose, examine issues, and learn more about the real world from their improvised engagement in an imaginary one. The opportunity for "innerstanding" and inhabiting the lives of others enables young people to experience safe emotional engagement and take part in creative explorations of secular and faith tales. The creation of community, the opportunity to engage in open exploration and reflection through being as well as doing, the development of self-knowledge, and the chance to experience feelings of wonder and transcendence are all aspects of spirituality that can be fostered through drama. Drama, like spirituality, acknowledges that teaching and learning are not merely cognitive but are essentially emotional, aesthetic, and ethical.

The transformation of time and space is an essential part of drama and is often achieved through the creation of a community. Space and time are also central to spirituality. In drama a sense of the place and the people in the faith or secular tale is built, both fictionally and for real. For example, maps of a village may be drawn, people at work improvised, and different settings and related scenarios created. Through participation in the lives of others and through empathetic engagement in imaginary worlds, a sense of community can be experienced, although a balance needs to be struck between personal concerns and communal issues. Taking on a role is an act of authentic personal engagement, yet in drama more is demanded since participants operate together, responding to one another as members of the communal narrative.

Reflective connections too are central, to enable the learners to perceive links between the life of this community and their own lives. In the context of drama, time is taken to step out of the fictional frame, and imaginative connections are prompted in the form of text-to-life and life-to-text moves. In this way, the learners coauthor the text from the inside, making sense and constructing meaning together. In addition, through inventing possible scenarios and discovering the unknown, young people will be reasoning, moralizing, and imagining—some of the implicit strategies vital for a maturing spirituality. If young people write during drama, this often demonstrates their reflective tenor and emotionally positioned stance, fueling the processes of identification, connection, and transformation. They can also discuss parallel situations in the world and make freeze frames, for example, depicting similar situations both past and present in the world. If they are given the opportunity to explore these issues further, from within the relative safety of a distancing framework, then the young learners will not be made to feel personally vulnerable or exposed, even though they will be emotionally and psychologically involved. The drama and the reflective discussions provide a safety net and enable the learners to empathize whilst being given the space in which to reflect and quest for understanding within a communally shared context. Reflective engagement such as this can help young people handle ambiguity and uncertainty, explore different ways of seeing, and keep an open mind, all of which are responsibilities of spiritual education.

In the midst of the imagined community created, young people can discover their true nature, since the conflicts and tensions evident in drama are often experienced as real and begin to blur the distinction between being and becoming. In responding to the difficult situations in the unfolding drama, self-knowledge can be developed through relationships as decisions and moral choices are made. Spiritual development happens not only in the positive and warm relationships but through exploring relationships of pain and suffering as well, and in drama such difficult relationships are often to the fore. The dual process of finding oneself and losing oneself within the greater whole occur in drama, as children construct their own and others' narratives in order to explore their place in the world. The ascendancy of the collective is a significant feature of such drama, enabling both collaborative meanings to be wrought and individual insights to be accessed. Such drama can also encourage self-acceptance and increase trust in educational contexts.

Opportunities for feelings of transcendence exist in drama, particularly when ritual and symbols are used and when time is spent in silent contemplation, evoking a sense of timelessness or placelessness and creating an intense aesthetic experience. The children's exposure to awe, wonder, and fear through the engagement of their imaginations is central to this, for drama provides the chance to grapple with ultimate questions and deep dilemmas. Spirituality too addresses some fundamental human questions about the presence of a god, death, afterlife, grief, and loss for example. In opening up their awareness of such issues and responding to life experiences that are difficult to comprehend, drama enables young people to sense the mysterious, the possible, and the spiritual and helps them tangibly contemplate the essence of the human spirit. The ritual context can give increased access to spiritual insight.

The moral dilemmas, spiritual concerns, and ambiguous social issues that permeate faith tales make such stories very appropriate resources for exploratory classroom drama. Symbols, stories, parables, poems, and allegories can be brought to life and examined through the words, the movements, and the gestures of improvisational drama. In such drama, combined learning about religious narrative and spiritual awareness may be developed in a fluid and holistic manner. Such opportunities can empower children to become spiritually richer by releasing their human potential and recognizing their capacity to learn in an integrated manner. Through its emphasis on group cooperation and relationships, the significance of the feeling quality and the importance of the collective, drama can make an important contribution to spiritual development. By involving children in the action and moving constantly between engagement and reflection, children stand both within and outside themselves in dramatic contexts. This oscillation between affective engagement and emotional or cognitive distancing is the hallmark of drama and enables the learners to pause, to connect, and to consider the text they have created. This reflective space can deepen their sensitivity to moral and spiritual issues. Within the creative and reflective endeavors of drama, meaning and purpose are explored, and the chance to develop self-knowledge and increase insight abound. The symbiotic relationship between spirituality and drama, show how drama, as the art form of social encounters, can unlock a range of processes and strategies that enrich children's spiritual development.

—Teresa Grainger and Sue Kendall-Seatter

FURTHER READING

Grainger, T., & Kendall-Seatter, S. (2003). Drama and spirituality: some reflective connections. *International Journal of Children's Spirituality, 8*(1), 25–32.

Hay, D. (with Nye, R.). (1998). *The spirit of the child.* London: Fount.

Heathcote, D. (1995). Quoted in O'Neill, C. *Drama worlds: A framework for process drama.* Portsmouth, NH: Heinemann.

Winston, J. (1999). *Drama, narrative, and moral education: Exploring traditional tales in the primary years.* London: Falmer.

Winston J. (2002). Drama, spirituality and the curriculum. *International Journal of Children's Spirituality, 7*(3), 241–255.

DRUG AND ALCOHOL ABUSE

Research suggests that youth who participate in religious institutions, family religious rituals, and individual spiritual practices have lower rates of alcohol and drug use than do young people who have little or no connection to religion or spiritually based groups. In fact, religion and spritiutality appear to be among the most powerful immunizations against substance abuse. The reasons why remain unclear.

Social scientists find that the social support provided and values modeled by churches, synagogues, temples, and mosques create positive "moral communities" where internalized values, future orientation, a connection to ultimate meaning and positive self-concept, all can provide support and motivation to say no to drugs and alcohol.

Developmental psychologists bring a slightly different perspective when explaining how spirituality and religion immunize young people against substance abuse. From the point of view of developmental psychology, at each stage in life we are challenged with new tasks specific to that stage. For example, infants are challenged to use their attachments to caregivers to make themselves secure enough to explore their physical surroundings. Two-year-olds are challenged to become independent enough to occasionally want to "do it all by myself." Here we describe the normal developmental tasks of adolescence that place adolescents at risk for substance use and abuse. We then describe how these very same tasks can be addressed more positively when adolescents have involved themselves in faith traditions and taken on spiritual issues. Spirituality and religion can, therefore, provide the same developmental opportunities that substance use may seem to offer.

THREE DEVELOPMENTAL QUESTIONS: WHO AM I? WHERE DO I BELONG? WHAT AM I DOING HERE?

Establishing *autonomy* from one's family, finding a place where one *belongs,* and addressing questions of ultimate *meaning* are three central developmental tasks in adolescence. Furthermore, autonomy, belonging and meaning-making create vulnerability for substance use.

AUTONOMY: A DECLARATION OF INDEPENDENCE

Seemingly overnight, competent, communicative, self-confident children can turn into hip-hopping, moody, sloppy, secretive adolescents with purple hair, strange friends, and ever-present headphones. Who are these bigger-than-me young persons? Where did they come from? How can we protect and guide them when they are hardly ever around, and when present, don't listen?

Eric Erikson described the adolescent task of identity formation as one in which young adolescents begin to emotionally separate from their families of origin and establish a personal identity for themselves. The period of identity formation is a long period of "trying on" identities, styles, personalities, behaviors, and activities, a period when parents may experience their children as sullen and uncooperative. Young people, in turn, may experience their parents as being old-fashioned, intrusive, and controlling. Children who formerly accompanied their families to religious services now may refuse to do so and instead may be found sleeping late on weekends, scheduling alternate activities, and arguing endlessly about the hypocrisy of religious attendance in the absence of sincere belief. Family obligations such as attending religious services and eating supper at seven now may take a backseat to freely chosen peer and individual activities. What's wrong with doing homework from 2 to 4 a.m., lighting candles and incense in the bathroom, shaving one's head, and smoking marijuana and drinking at parties?

Experimental alcohol and drug use, then, can be a way of establishing an adolescent's identity and the right to choose. "I have a right to pierce my belly button, to eat nothing but mustard greens and French fries, and to drink alcohol and smoke marijuana, so long, of course, as nobody gets hurt and I get my schoolwork done."

In Fritz Oser's model of religious development, adolescents leave behind a conception of G-d as one who answers prayers, who rewards and punishes, and who negotiates with individuals in ways that allow individuals to get a better deal. For many adolescents, G-d has G-d's own domain and they have their own, separate domain where they are solely responsible for the actions. Furthermore, adolescents often start to question G-d, or, at least, their old childish conceptions of G-d. Adolescents question what is true and how they know what is true. The natural developmental questioning of old truths, that include truths about rules and norms for appropriate behavior, creates both a risk for substance abuse and an opportunity to build a deeper religious or spiritual core.

Although substance use, in moderation, is developmentally normal in adolescence, drug and alcohol use can move quickly from experimental use to risky use or even dependence. Here are some generally accepted warning signs: marked changes in habits including declines in school participation and grades, changes in sleeping and eating patterns, and changes in friendships. These indicators are the same for the beginning of substance *abuse* as they are for depression, though substance abuse and depression are often related. This is a reminder that while youth are trying on their new wings, they are also experiencing the loss of an old family nest. As much as they want to make independent decisions about smoking and drinking, they still want their lunch made for them and, in general, their daily needs met. They want autonomy, then, but without the responsibilities that accompany adult life.

BELONGING

Autonomy from family heightens the need to belong to some group outside the family. Finding a place "to hang out" with a group, a group where an adolescent feels he or she belongs, is critical for developing an independent identity. It is critical also for developing new ways of social participation, cooperation, collaboration, and taking responsibility. Informal peer groups, as well as activity groups such as sports teams, choirs, rock bands, rap groups, drama groups, and scouts, are typical forms of groups in which adolescents can find a new home. Finding a place where one belongs can mean a church/synagogue/mosque/temple youth group or it can mean a smoking, drinking, drug-using peer group.

Critical to a sense of belonging is feeling wanted and known for who you are. Equally critical is finding a place where adolescents can be their true selves—pimples, sagging pants, crazy thoughts, shaved head, bad grades (or good grades), dreams, doubts, hopes—that is, where adolescents can know that they will be accepted and included even when they are known. Too often, traditional religious institutions create an atmosphere where adolescents who are trying on alternative identities or who cannot seem to get their acts together feel put down, (mis)judged, and unknown so that they come to feel unwelcome. Too often, drug-using hang-outs provide the only places where adolescents do feel welcome.

A sense of belonging also means being able to contribute and participate by making the group happen in some way, by being a necessary part of the team, and by making the team one's own. If adolescents can provide the drinks, roll the joints, play the music, or provide the pot to smoke, then they are making a contribution to the group, however dysfunctional this contribution may be.

However, so too can adolescents find homes and sense of their contribution when they join faith-based, or spiritually based groups—especially when the leaders of these groups make themselves available, when they are emotionally open, and when they listen. Such religious and spiritually based groups are numerous and effective, especially in low-income and ethnic minority communities.

THE MEANING OF LIFE

For many young people, adolescence is a quest for meaning. The quest can be expressed in questions such as "How fast can I drive without going off the road? How drunk can I get and still drive home? How many hours can I study without sleeping? and How thin can I get?" However, the quest can also be expressed while lying beneath a tree and looking up at the heavens, in questions such as "Is there anything up there? Is all this random? Where did we come from? Where am I going? Is anybody up there in charge? What do you see when you look at the sky? Is it the same thing that I see? How do you know what's true? How do you know what's right?" And, "What's the purpose of life, anyway?"

Spiritual awakening, religious calling, and spiritual/religious commitment are perhaps more common in late adolescence than at any other time of life. Young people can become plagued by questions about the infinite, and often they find answers by following both traditional and nontraditional paths. "Twice-born souls" are likely to make radical changes in their life course. Likewise, young people with a religious or spiritual calling are likely to make life commitments before the age of twenty. Some young people, on the same spiritual quest, may seek answers through drug experiences, finding truth in visions induced by drugs. This quest for meaning, then, can be expressed in quite different spiritual and nonspiritual ways.

CONCLUSION: CREATING CONTEXTS FOR CONVERSATION

It is important to see adolescent drug and alcohol use in relation to developmental tasks for several reasons. When we understand the adolescent's own meaning for dysfunctional behavior such as alcohol and drug abuse, we can better distinguish developmentally normal from developmentally *abnormal* drug and alcohol use. Furthermore, we can better address underlying religious and spiritual questions that, left unaddressed, may contribute to drug and alcohol abuse.

Religion and spirituality offer immunity against problem drug and alcohol use because they offer a context and pathway to declare independence, to search for belonging and to find personal or ultimate meaning. But how can we help our children, our brothers and sisters, and our friends to choose a positive path over negative alternatives? How can religion help young people navigate the transition to adulthood?

One answer lies in creating contexts for conversation. Effective religious/spiritual programs (and families) share several features across denominations: They welcome young people. They make it possible, even "cool," for young people to raise and discuss questions of religion and spirituality. They provide adults and peers who listen to and honor young people's questions. And they make it safe to not have the answers.

But what about those young persons who got hooked, who became addicted? Being addicted means being stuck: stuck in a bad habit, stuck in a way of life that is a downward spiral. Being addicted means sometimes feeling like two people. It means thinking you want to stop using, that you are a good caring person, but going out and using again and again, cutting school, hanging out with friends you know are up to no good Being addicted, being hooked, means knowing better but not being able to stop yourself. When sober, you feel bad, sad, guilty. You want to get high again, to feel better. It works for a little while, until you sober up again.

In faith based recovery programs (including AA, NA, Ala-teen, and residential programs) people are encouraged by a fellowship of which they are a member to have faith that a Higher Power will restore them to sanity. Spiritual (faith-based) recovery programs often provoke both spiritual awakenings and a depression that is a natural part of abandoning old, dysfunctional ways.

—Ronnie Frankel Blakeney and
Charles David Blakeney

See also Erikson, Erik; Oser, Fritz

E

ECOLOGY

Planet Earth faces environmental issues of unprecedented severity: Acid rain is falling down, and garbage dumps are filling up. The ozone layer is thinning, and pollution is thickening. The rain forest is shrinking, and the human population is expanding. Oil spills are oozing everywhere, and toxic waste is headed anywhere that will accept it.

Does religion have anything to do with these environmental issues? For some, the answer is no: Religion has nothing to do with ecology, for religion is concerned about heaven as a destination and not concerned about the destiny of the earth. Religion focuses on the spiritual, not on the physical.

However, for others there has developed an awareness that religion not only has something to do with ecology but also that it *must* be involved: First, there is the religious mandate that human beings are to act as responsible stewards of the world that God has created. In the Hebrew Scriptures, it is proclaimed that God made everything that is and that all of this is intrinsically good (Gen. 1:10, 12, 18, 25, 31). Being created in God's image (Gen. 1:26–27), human beings are to care for and serve the creation (Gen. 2:15): Therefore, Noah is bidden to save the birds and beasts and reptiles no less than humans (Gen. 6:19–20). The covenant is subsequently made not only with Noah and his descendants, but also with all the creatures in nature (Gen. 9:10). Jonah is sent to Nineveh because of God's concern for the cattle as well as for the human beings there (Jonah 4:11). The Psalms declare God's concern for the welfare of animals such as wild donkeys, storks, cattle, wild goats, lions, and the creatures of the sea. Since they are important to God, they should also be important to humans (Psalm 104). Job gasps in amazement at the hippopotamus and the crocodile, which are of no conceivable utility to him, thus indicating that God did not create nature solely for human use (Job 40:15–24; 41:7–34).

Further, humans are to give themselves and nature "rest," symbolized by the weekly occurrence of the Sabbath day and in every seventh year, the sabbatical year, when the fields are to lie fallow (Leviticus 25:1–5). The land is a gift to be appreciated and protected, since everything on earth ultimately belongs to God (Psalm 24:1).

In the Christian Bible, it is proclaimed that God loves the world so much that God became incarnate in order to save a world that needed healing and restoration (John 3:16). God considers the lilies as more valuable than even the splendor of King Solomon (Matthew 6:28–29). The Apostle Paul views the whole of creation and nature groaning as a woman giving birth, but they will take part in redemption and fulfillment (Romans 8:19–23; cf. Isaiah 65:17f). Humans are to participate in this as their responsibility and special function, and not to do so is to be like the tenants in the vineyard who are punished for being irresponsible and wicked (Matthew 21:33–46).

Religion has something to do with ecology because this is a requirement for persons who take religion seriously. Stewardship is a responsibility for religious people.

Second, the ecological problems which beset planet earth are at their root, spiritual issues. Especially in Western culture, growth is valued as the means for establishing more markets for more products which will yield greater economic prosperity. However, growth without limits is not sustainable from a natural resources' point-of-view. If trees are cut down faster than they can be replaced in order to facilitate growth, then this action cannot be maintained forever. If pollutants are emitted into the atmosphere in a greater quantity and for a longer period of time than they can be naturally broken down, then the air humans breathe is unhealthy, acid rain falls down, and holes in the ozone layer of the stratosphere develop.

Western culture also advocates consumption as a personal lifestyle that promises happiness and meaning. The message which society sends is that the more persons have, the happier they will be, and that "enough" is always a little more than anyone has ever had. The drain which results on natural resources and the waste that is generated as a byproduct of this usage mean that nature is running out of resources and filling up with garbage.

Short-term benefits are also valued in Western culture over long-term repercussions. Gasoline is kept at an artificially, low price compared to the world market, and this encourages people to use it unreservedly in the short run, even though most scientists calculate that we have but 80 years of oil reserves left worldwide. Conservation of this resource and research and development of alternative energy sources are forgotten factors, even though these must be considered in the long run.

A final example, but perhaps most important of all, is that nature is regarded as a supply of resources to be exploited, rather than as a web of life of which the human species is a part. Nature is therefore seen as a commodity to be possessed rather than as a community with which to relate.

Environmentalists and ecologists insist that growth must be tempered by restraint; that consumption must give way to simpler living; that long-term consequences must have priority over short-term benefits; that nature must be viewed as a "subject" with which humans must relate positively rather than an "object" to be used and degraded.

This situation therefore involves a values dilemma and is a spiritual issue. Religion has its set of positive values, deep traditions, and scriptural wisdom to bring to bear on this values dilemma. As a result, religion (as well as science and technology) is crucial for responding to, and resolving, current ecological problems.

—Clifford Chalmers Cain

See also Environmental Ethics; Nature, the Sacred in

FURTHER READING

Cain, C. C. (1998, March). Stewardship. *American Baptist Quarterly,* 17(1).

Granberg-Michaelson, W. (1988). *Ecology and life: Accepting our environmental responsibility.* Waco, TX: Word Books.

Hall, D. J. (1990). *The steward: A biblical symbol come of age.* Grand Rapids: Eerdmans.

Hessel, D. T. (1985). *For creation's sake.* Philadelphia: Geneva Press.

Parham, R. (1991). *Loving neighbors across time: A Christian guide to protecting the earth.* Birmingham, AL: New Hope Press.

Rockefeller, S. C., & Elder, J. C. (1992). *Spirit and nature: Why the environment is a religious issue.* Boston: Beacon Press.

EDUCATION, HISTORY OF CHRISTIAN

THE EARLY CHURCH

Christian education began with Jesus himself who was educated in the religious life of Judaism. His teaching ministry is described in the New Testament Gospels where he is lauded as the master, and teacher of the New Torah, also known as the Sermon on the Mount. Jesus welcomed and taught many types of people, including the rich, the poor, the outcast, women, and children. Through parables, questions, and object lessons, he challenged traditional wisdom, inspired radical change, and recruited followers.

Christianity spread by the 12 disciples closest to Jesus as well as larger groups of disciples who were commanded by Jesus to teach others. Teaching and learning were crucial dimensions in the development of Christian communities as recorded in the New Testament book of Acts. Early church teachers and traveling prophets who instructed members of the Christian communities were gradually replaced during the first century by apostles, presbyters, and deacons.

As Christianity spread, the need for teachers to instruct about the Christian faith increased. This led to the beginning of the catechumenal schools in the first century. The purpose of the catechumenal schools was to prepare new adult converts for baptism. These candidates for baptism spent 2 to 3 years listening to sermons and instruction in Bible doctrine and the Christian disciplines of prayer, fasting, confession, exorcism, and Christian lifestyle. Following baptism, ongoing instruction in Christian living occurred through the bishop's sermons during weekly celebrations of the Eucharist. The catechumenate served as the major avenue for Christian education until the end of the fourth century.

THE MIDDLE AGES

By the middle of the fifth century, the catechumenate was no longer needed due to the emerging practice of infant baptism. The rise in infant baptism, due in part to the fourth century legalization of Christianity, and the decline of the catechumenate brought about the need for godparents who, along with parents, were responsible for teaching the faith. Since most adults and priests were poorly educated, church teaching centered on moral instruction, the Lord's Prayer, the Ten Commandments, and the Apostle's Creed.

Other formative forces of Christian culture included popular practices of piety such as holy days, processions, wayside shrines, pilgrimages, and adoration of saints. The Christian faith was also communicated through stained glass windows and other medieval visual art, referred to as "the Bible for the poor."

During the Middle Ages, schools of asceticism (the practice of self-denial or even self-punishment) and Christian life known as *monasteries* emerged to preserve and develop instruction in the Christian faith. Guided by moral and religious purposes, monks, priests, children of nobility, and sometimes children of the poor were instructed in reading, writing, arithmetic, singing, and the elements of Christian doctrine. Monastic training in the East was moral and ascetic, while monastic instruction in the West had a more intellectual focus emphasizing the necessity of reading and devotion to scripture. There were often two departments in monastic schools, one for interns, those intending to be monks, and one for externs, those intending to return to secular life after completing their education.

Charlemagne, emperor of the Roman Empire in the early years of the ninth century, ignited an educational renaissance through his efforts to improve the education of clergy and by insisting that every monastery and cathedral establish a school. Cathedral schools were intended for all people in the community and served as places of worship and social gatherings for young people. Instruction included Christian religion, grammar, rhetoric, dialectic, music, arithmetic, geometry, and astronomy.

Religious movements such as the Brethren of the Common Life promoted pious religion of the heart and made religious instruction a high priority. Educating schoolboys of the common people contributed to the gradual transition from medieval ecclesiasticism (church leadership) to scholasticism (school or educational leadership).

Church leaders brought about the scholastic movement by efforts to synthesize Christian theology and secular philosophy. The scholastic movement appealed to the intellectual interests of the time and influenced the development of medieval universities. Scholastic philosopher Peter Abelard (1079–1142) encouraged students to think for themselves through a process of questioning and doubt, and held that faith must be based on reason. Another leading scholastic thinker, Thomas Aquinas (1225–1274) developed the basic doctrinal framework of the Catholic Church through a masterful work, *Summa Theologica.* For Aquinas, faith was superior to reason.

THE RENAISSANCE AND REFORMATION

A revival of learning, known as the *Renaissance,* developed during the 14th century and took on a religious dimension as it spread throughout northern Europe. There was a renewed interest in the biblical languages of Greek and Hebrew, and the works of the early church fathers were published in a new form, the printed book. Biblical piety rather than scholastic theology became the mode for promoting the growth of the Christian faith. In some areas of Northern Europe, this revival of learning focused on reforming the church and Christian theology.

The educational efforts of Renaissance humanism (focus on human study) resulted in the establishment of secondary and preparatory schools. The curriculum combined secular and religious learning as well as the classical and medieval. Renaissance learning focused on the betterment of society and included traditional subjects of reading, speaking, writing, poetry, history, and moral philosophy. By the 15th century, the values of the Italian Renaissance on Scripture wedded with mystical philosophy had spread throughout Europe.

Desiderius Erasmus (1466–1536), the most influential Christian humanist in England, promoted a simpler and non-dogmatic version of the Christian faith, distinct from the abstract and theoretical nature of scholasticism. Erasmus promoted Christian piety based on knowledge of Scripture and the church fathers. He promoted learning through creative games and physical activity, and held that teachers should build knowledge and character in their students through love and understanding.

Renaissance humanism brought about cultural and political changes in Germany that enabled the Protestant Reformation. Martin Luther (1483–1546), a Roman Catholic priest and professor of theology at the University of Wittenberg, Germany, mobilized the Reformation when he publicly revolted against certain church teachings and practices. Luther argued that the Bible was the supreme authority in matters of Christian life and that everyone had the right and responsibility to access scripture. He also believed that every Christian could act as a priest for himself or herself and approach God directly.

A central concern of the 16th century Reformation was the reform of education, including early catechism training to graduate studies. Luther fought for the establishment of schools throughout Germany for all children, and he had a significant role in developing a national system of education in Europe. Luther communicated the ideals of his reform movement by developing educational systems for young children. The publication of Luther's *Large Catechism* for pastors and teachers and a *Small Catechism* for children marked his major contribution to Christian education. Through the catechisms, Luther sought to promote systematic education in Christian teachings.

In response to the Protestant Reformation, the Roman Catholic Church leaders met at the Council of Trent (three separate sessions between 1545–1563), giving serious attention to the education of the clergy and strengthening Catholic education by establishing schools. The Jesuits, a Roman Catholic order founded by Ignatius of Loyola, established many schools. The Jesuit system of education was thorough and effective, giving meticulous attention to educational principles, preparation of teachers, and a broad scope of learning. The Jesuit *Plan of Studies,* printed in 1599, guided Jesuit education without change for more than 200 years. The curriculum included creative and competitive learning strategies and encouraged positive teacher–student relationships.

THE BIRTH OF MODERN CHRISTIAN EDUCATION

Modern Christian education, rooted in the Renaissance and the Reformation, evolved from the influence of many major leaders and movements. The ideas of John Amos Comenius (1592–1670), a Moravian church bishop, demonstrated a break from the educational practices of the Middle Ages making a significant impact on European education of children. Comenius devised new methods of teaching Latin through pictures, and he believed that children should be taught according to their natural psychological development. Comenius also believed that people come to know truth through religious faith rather than secular studies.

In contrast to Comenius, Enlightenment (1680–1790) thinkers believed that human reason was the supreme authority for life rather than faith or church tradition. Enlightenment thought challenged traditional Christian theology, yet along with Comenius, it paved the way for the emergence of liberal and progressive approaches to education in the 19th century. Many of the Enlightenment ideas rejected by Christians were eventually incorporated into Christian education. For example, the revolt against children as small adults led by Enlightenment writer Jean Jacques Rousseau (1712–1778) was embraced by progressive Christian educators of the 20th century.

Catholic educators of the 19th century held to humanist tradition of liberal arts education, but condemned Enlightenment ideas as modern heresy. The papacy upheld the scholastic tradition of Thomas Aquinas, and rejected modern biblical scholarship. The ideals of Catholic education, such as the value of theological knowledge in liberal arts education, were articulated by John Cardinal Newman's 1852 work, *The Idea of a University.* In 1929, Pope Pius XI circulated a major letter on education that argued for the rights of the Catholic Church to maintain traditional Catholic education and attacked the modern progressive education in Europe and the United States.

Christian revivalism of the 18th and 19th centuries set the stage for new forms of Protestant Christian leadership and educational vision. John Wesley (1703–1791), founder of Methodism, provided educational instruction in the Christian faith through an elaborate system of small groups referred to as classes, bands, and societies. Those who responded to Wesley's preaching were organized into these groups in order to strengthen their Christian living. Concern for the spiritual nurture of children led Wesley to author teaching manuals and establish Methodist schools.

Robert Raikes, a publisher and social activist, gave birth to one of the most significant and far-reaching movements in the history of Protestant education. Due to the impact of 17th century industrialization, masses of poor children were subjected to harsh labor practices 6 days a week with no hope for education. In 1780, Raikes hired teachers to provide moral, spiritual, and literary education for poor children ages 6 to 14. Sunday school–related societies formed to support the movement, and the positive changes in the children led to phenomenal growth with over a million participants by 1831.

Although America borrowed the model of the Sunday charity schools from Britain, by the 1820s there were significant differences between them. While the Sunday Schools in Britain continued to focus on the needs of the poor, the Sunday schools in America included the rich as well as the poor. With the opening of public schools, the American Sunday School began to focus on religious instruction alone. Societies, such as the American Bible Society (1816), and the American Sunday School Union (1825) mobilized massive Bible distribution by Sunday School missionaries throughout America. Sunday Schools promoted memorization of Scripture, catechism, and hymns for the sake of self-discipline and self-respect, as well as religious and moral instruction.

In the 1960s a group of religious leaders from Illinois rallied for a unified Sunday School vision through an international convention system and corresponding uniform lessons. With the aid of 19th century revivals led by D. L. Moody and others, the renewed interdenominational Sunday school movement spread rapidly with millions of participants in the United States and abroad by 1890. The convention system de-emphasized theological themes for the sake of interdenominational harmony and promoted institutional networks for teacher training. Sunday School leaders focused on moral reform and a staged process of religious growth through the implementation of a regularized curriculum system.

The growing theological diversity at the turn of the century led to denominational control of the Sunday School by 1930. While Evangelical Christians expanded their educational efforts through mission projects, vacation Bible schools, Bible institutes, and Christian colleges, those in the liberal theological stream formed the Religious Education Association influencing the development of religious education programs in colleges, public schools, and churches.

The leading educators and theories that emerged throughout the 20th century supported three major Protestant groups. George A. Coe, Sophia Fahs, and H. Shelton Smith represented the liberal stream. Neo-orthodox educators included Iris Cully, Hulda Niebhur, James Smart, D. Campbell Wyckoff, and Lewis Sherrill. Lois LeBar, Henrietta Mears, and Larry Richards were a few of many evangelical educators. In spite of the theological distinctions, ongoing dialogue between and within each theological stream has led to a growing pluralism of approaches to Protestant Christian education.

Distinctions between traditionalists and reformers continue into the 21st century for both Catholics and Protestants. Yet, leading educators among the Catholics, such as James Michael Lee, Gabrial Moran, Mary Boys, and Thomas Groome, and among the Protestants, such as John Westerhoff, James Fowler, and Mary Elizabeth Moore, have enabled interfaith dialogue and vision appropriate to a postmodern ecumenical world.

—Beverly C. Johnson-Miller

FURTHER READING

Elias, J. L. (2002). *A history of Christian education: Protestant, Catholic, and Orthodox perspectives.* Malabar, FL: Krieger.

Reed, J. E., & Prevost, R. (1993). *A history of Christian education.* Nashville, TN: Broadman & Holman.

EDUCATIONAL ORGANIZATIONS IN WORLD RELIGIONS

The major religions of the world have evolved a wide array of formal and informal educational organizations to perform a variety of functions. They provide (1) information and points of entry for interested publics and possible new converts to the religion in question, (2) direct instruction via print, audio, and visual media for children, youth, and adults, and (3) diverse resources which adults and local organizational units can employ in formal and informal learning settings with their constituents. All major world religions have extensive and growing educational resources available online on the World Wide Web, some representing official positions and most representing the viewpoints of distinct subgroups within particular religions.

The Society for the Scientific Study of Religion (SSSR), Religious Research Association (RRA),

American Academy of Religion (AAR), and the Association of Professors and Researchers in Religious Education (APRRE) are umbrella international organizations for persons who study the educational dimensions of world religions and who share their findings in peer-reviewed publications and annual conferences. Members of these organizations produce the bulk of the research that informs the work of a much vaster set of educational organizations who create and distribute materials and provide services for intermediary organizations such as denominational groups, mosques, synagogues, temples, and churches and for practitioners and adherents, both young and old.

Christianity has spawned more educational organizations than any other major world religion, likely due to both its fractious doctrinal developments over time and its overwhelming presence within technologically advanced and economically robust countries. The World Council of Churches, an umbrella international organization for Christian denominations and groups, has the long-standing World Council of Christian Education. There has also been a recent surge of interest in adult theological education with an attendant Association of Centres of Adult Theological Education based in the United Kingdom.

Many countries with a large Christian presence have a plethora of national Christian education organizations. In the United States, for example, one can find organizations for private and parochial Christian schools (e.g., Association of Christian Schools International, National Catholic Education Association, Accelerated Christian Education), church-affiliated universities and colleges (e.g., Association of Jesuit Colleges and Universities, Association of Catholic Colleges and Universities, Council of Christian Colleges and Universities, American Association of Bible Colleges, Transnational Association of Christian Colleges and Schools Accrediting Commission), Sunday schools and church-based education (e.g., National Sunday School Association, Professional Association of Christian Educators, Commission on General Education of the National Council of Churches), informal Christian youth and children's groups that engage in education (e.g., Youth for Christ International, Catholic Youth Foundation, Campus Crusade for Christ, Intervarsity Christian Fellowship USA, Life Teen, Awana Clubs International, Pioneer Clubs, Navigators, Youth Ministry Network, Baptist Young People's Union, Child Evangelism Fellowship), seminaries (e.g., Association of Theological Schools of the United States and Canada), television networks and programs (e.g., Trinity Broadcast Network, Christian Broadcast Network), and the extremely large and active world of Christian publishing companies (e.g., Zondervan, Baker Book House, Group Publishing, Wm. B. Eerdmans, Thomas B. Nelson, Intervarsity Press, Hendrickson Publications, Our Sunday Visitor, Maryknoll, American Bible Society, and Gospel Light).

There are still other sources of religious education. Major mechanisms for the transmission of Christian beliefs and understandings to the next generation in the United States have been church rituals of confirmation and baptism, Sunday School or Sabbath school, parachurch and church-based youth groups, summer camps, Christian concerts, church services or masses, Bible studies, prayer meetings, and conferences and retreats for youth or adults.

Judaism, although much smaller in terms of the number of adherents, also has extensive networks at the global level and within particular countries where Jews are numerous. Global organizations include the World Union of Jewish Students, World Union of Jewish Studies, B'nai B'rith Youth Organization, European Association for Jewish Studies, and the European Union of Jewish Students. Sample Jewish educational organizations within the United States include those targeted to seminaries (Association of Advanced Rabbinical and Talmudic Schools), youth (North American Federation of Temple Youth, Young Judaea, United Synagogue Youth, Hillel, Bnei Akiva, Betar Likud, and the National Conference of Synagogue Youth), and the general public (e.g., the Jewish Publication Society). Sabbath schools or congregational religious schools have been a principle means for formal education in Judaism outside of the family unit since the mid-19th century in the United States, and organizations such as the Jewish Educators Assembly exist to share ideas among educators within this arena. They are increasingly common in Europe and elsewhere.

The role of educational organizations becomes somewhat less clear when considering Islam, Buddhism, Hinduism, and Shinto. This is likely due to the particular ways in which education historically was seen as related to the religious quest. The strongholds for these religions (e.g., the Arab world, Indian subcontinent, and Asia) generally have maintained practices linked more fully and explicitly to the historic bases of these religions. Most religious leaders have been reticent to make accommodations to modernity or to allow traditional religious practices to evolve.

Traditional Islamic education in the Middle East begins in the *masjid* (school) where instruction consists chiefly of memorizing the Qur'an and learning to read and write Arabic. Further study occurs at schools of higher study known as *madrasahs,* early Arabic precursors to the European universities of the Middle Ages. In some countries, the madrasahs are restricted to males only. Today, the curriculum still generally focuses on grammar, logic, rhetoric, law, early mathematics, Arabic literature and history, and Qur'anic studies and prayer. Occasionally medicine and agronomy are also taught, usually along traditional lines.

There is a growing feeling on the part of some leaders within the Muslim world (e.g., the International Institute of Islamic Thought & Civilization in Kuala Lumpur, Malaysia), and especially in the West, that there should be more of a focus on the Qur'anic concept of *tarbiyyah* (cultivating), which seeks to link modern concerns with the Qur'an and interpret its teachings in concert with issues and information facing youth and families today. Many mosques in the West that have adopted this philosophy have established Islamic schools consisting of four basic types: full-time, part-time, weekend, and home. A wide array of colorful, well-designed materials have been produced to support instruction including magazines, books, CDs, electronic games, and computer software that address such topics as Muslim history, Muslim science and scientists, Arabic and Urdu lessons, stories, biographies, instruction on hajj, the Qur'an, and prayer, as well as contemporary concerns such as sex education. This effort in the United States has received major support from the International Institute of Islamic Thought, the Islamic Society of North America (ISNA), the Islamic Circle of North America, and the Islamic Schools League of America. ISNA sponsors large annual conferences and printed proceedings. Two large Muslim youth organizations in the United States are the Young Muslims Brothers and Young Muslims Sisters who hold regional and national meetings.

Buddha advised (Samyuttanikaya V:29–31) that youth should acquire the seven auroras of a good life to become truly noble. They are (1) finding wisdom through the personal example of a friend, (2) developing discipline to one's life, (3) aspiring to learning and productive action, (4) realizing one's full potential through training, (5) recognizing cause and effect, (6) becoming self-aware (mindful), and (7) thinking wisely. While there have been Young Men's Buddhist Associations in many countries starting with the first in Yangon, Myanmar (Burma), in 1906, there are few organizations that would be viewed as "educational organizations" within Buddhism, except those that produce publications targeted principally to non-Buddhists. This appears to be due to the fact that *sikkha* (education) within Buddhism is largely a result of self-discipline, training, and personal enlightenment that does not lend itself to communal forms of learning. Some notable exceptions exist where instruction for children and youth is explicitly conducted, such as the Clear Vision Trust in the United Kingdom, the Nyima Dzong community in Alpes-de-Haute-Provence, France, and the increasing numbers of Dhamma schools linked to Vihara (Buddhist "churches") in the United States. These schools provide weekly sessions of 1 to 2 hours for children where Jataka stories (Buddhist parables and fables) are employed to teach about character. Buddhism as a formal part of the Religious Education curriculum has been required by law in Austria since 1983, and the Religious Education national curriculum within England prescribes the study of Buddhism as part of the Key Stage 2 Curriculum.

Hinduism also seems to lack significant educational organizations other than those engaged in reaching non-Hindus, although there are ways in which persons may study Hinduism, for example, obtaining a General Certificate of Secondary Education (GCSE) or Advanced/Secondary (A/S) level of educational qualification in Hinduism as part of Religious Studies within the formal English educational system. In recent years, Hindus in the United States and Great Britain have also generated Web sites and printed and media materials for children to learn about Hindu *dharma* and its origination in the land of Bharat (India), their motherland.

Shinto derives its name from a Chinese word for "ways of the gods." The Japanese people believe in *kami,* deities and noble people from history, including the ancestors of the Japanese people and Japanese ruling dynasties, and venerate them. There are four basic kinds of Shinto: state, shrine, sectarian, and folk. These kinds of Shinto are interrelated in the lives of most Japanese who honor kami who protect and advance the state of Japan, kami who are influential persons in Japanese history, and kami who are their family ancestors. Most homes have an altar (*kami-dana*, lit., "shelf of gods") and the family regularly worships there. This familial setting is where education about Shinto is first passed on and reinforced for children. The All Japan Shinto Youth Council exists for young Shinto priests, and there are general educational or social organizations in Japan including the All Japan Nursery School Association, the All Japan Ujiko Youth Council, and the All Japan Shinto Youth Conference.

—Dennis William Cheek

See also Buddhism; Christianity; Hinduism; Islam; Judaism

FURTHER READING

Anthony, M. J. (Ed.). (2001). *Evangelical dictionary of Christian education.* Grand Rapids, MI: Baker Book House.

Berkey, J. (2004). Education. In R. C. Martin (Ed.), *Encyclopedia of Islam and the Muslim world* (Vol. 1, pp. 202–206). New York: Macmillan.

Bukkyo Dendo Kyokai. (1991). *The teaching of Buddha.* Tokyo: Kosaido Printing Company.

Buson, M. (2003). *Our Sunday Visitor's 2003 Catholic almanac.* Huntingdon, IN: Our Sunday's Visitor Publishing Division.

Dalai Lama. (2001). *Dialogue on universal responsibility & education.* New Delhi, India: Paljor Publications.

Deegalle, M. (2004). Education. In R. E. Buswell, Jr. (Ed.), *Encyclopedia of Buddhism* (Vol. 1, pp. 247–248). New York: Macmillan.

Fox, S., Scheffler, I., & Marom, D. (Eds.). (2003). *Visions of Jewish education.* New York: Cambridge University Press.

Francis, L. J., Kay, W. K., & Campbell, W. S. (Eds.). (1996). *Research in religious education.* Macon, GA: Smyth & Helwys.

Glassé, C. (2001). *The new encyclopedia of Islam.* Lanham, MD: AltaMira Press.

ISNA Community Development Department. (2003). *Resource manual and program, April 18–20, 2003, The Westin O'Hare, Chicago, IL.* Plainville, IN: Islamic Society of North America.

Nimer, M. (2003). *The North American Muslim resource guide: Muslim community life in the United States and Canada.* New York: Routledge.

ELKIND, DAVID

To some extent, religious development rests on cognitive development or the development of thinking. Developmental psychologist David Elkind has explained this by showing that three key developments in children's thinking allow for key developments in their thinking about religion. Those three have to do with the ability to understand that objects and people do not cease to exist when they are out of sight (object permanence), the ability to not only represent or symbolize but understand what it means to symbolize, and the ability to give reasons and judgments using logic (i.e., conservation).

The first ability develops gradually during infancy. Around 3 or 4 years old it makes possible an appreciation for certain religious ideas, such as there are spiritual beings (e.g., God) that exist despite their not being visible and there is life after death. The second ability develops gradually during early childhood and makes possible school-age (around 6 or 7) children's appreciation for the many images and stories that define and make up their own religious tradition. The third ability develops gradually during late childhood and makes possible, around 11 or 12, an appreciation for different points of view about religion and religious issues. Developments associated with thinking, then, make possible the milestones in religious understanding and religious development.

Elkind also employs the familiar concrete-to-abstract and global-to-specific dimensions to explain how particular religious concepts develop throughout childhood. The concepts of prayer and religious denomination provide prime examples. For young school-age children, the meaning of prayer is often concretely tied to speech while being simultaneously over-generalized to apply to animals as well as to humans. Only gradually, then, do children come to think of prayer abstractly and specifically as conversation by humans with God, its content usually including requests, confessions, or expressions of thanks. Similarly, the meaning of religious denominations begins with references to concrete characteristics such as whether someone goes to a church or a synagogue. Religious holidays are not always clearly distinguished from secular holidays, e.g., Valentine's Day. Only much later do children understand that differences between religious denominations have to do with abstract differences in beliefs and patterns of faith.

In sum, David Elkind's research and similar research in what is sometimes called the *cognitive-developmental tradition* shows clearly that religious development rests on cognitive development and that one important aspect of religious development has to do with the development of new meanings.

—Taryn W. Morrissey

FURTHER READING

Elkind, D. (1967). The children's conception of prayer. *Journal for the Scientific Study of Religion, 6(1),* 101–109.

Elkind, D. (1978). Religious development. In D. Elkind (Ed.), *The child's reality: Three developmental themes* (pp. 1–45). Hillsdale, NJ: Erlbaum.

Elkind, D. (1997). The origins of religion in the child. In B. Spilka & D. N. McIntosh (Eds.), *The psychology of religion* (p. 97–104). Boulder, CO: Westview.

Piaget, J. (1969). *Judgment and reasoning in the child.* Malden, MA: Blackwell.

END OF LIFE, LIFE-SPAN APPROACH

The end of life is often a confusing and fearful time for the dying person and their loved ones. Spirituality and/or religion often come to the forefront during the dying process. Religious and spiritual beliefs, for instance, play an important role as a coping resource in the face of a life-threatening or terminal illness. Beliefs are often related to how a patient interprets the meaning and prognosis of a particular diagnosis. Strong religious or spiritual faith may cause negative life events, such as the diagnosis of a terminal illness, to be seen as opportunities for spiritual growth. By turning to a source larger than oneself, religious and spiritual beliefs can help reduce the discomfort and the anxiety caused by illness and the threat of death.

Patients who are more religious or spiritual are more likely to accept their illness and find some positive meaning in its diagnosis. Contrary to the popular understanding that religious and/or spiritual beliefs provide only a passive means of coping, such beliefs may actually empower an individual to take action (such as fighting against an illness). Furthermore, in situations in which death is imminent, giving up some control may in fact be a healthy form of coping. However, these are rarely isolated late life events but rather a continuation of a coping style that develops and is utilized across the life span, from childhood through old age.

It should also be noted that strong religious or spiritual beliefs may not always be beneficial as an individual faces death. Negative psychological outcomes are often linked to the ways in which people view their relationship to God. Patients coping with a terminal illness, for instance, might become angry with God and worsen their psychological health. Furthermore, certain religious doctrines may engender particular negative emotional states (such as guilt, shame, or anxiety) and negative attitudes and beliefs that may, in turn, impact negatively on physical and mental health. Religious or spiritual beliefs may create religious or spiritual turmoil in dying patients who perceive their illness as a punishment or abandonment by God and find themselves worrying and concerned about their eternal outcomes. Again, it is important to note that the positive and negative effects of religion and spirituality on psychological health may vary across the life span and may also vary by ecological factors, ranging from the self to the broader cultural context.

Older adults, among whom death is an expected and often planned-for occurrence, may have long grappled with the dual issues of spirituality and mortality. Thus, for such individuals, spirituality at the end of life is likely to provide comfort and acceptance. Children and adolescents faced with death, however, must address these issues prematurely. Due to many youth-oriented societies (such as in the United States) and the atypicality of childhood deaths, as well as adults' attempts to "protect" children from issues of death, many children confronted with their own mortality and/or the death of others may possess unrealistic and distorted views of the process.

The stress response of a child resulting from the news of a fatal illness is a transaction between the child (their age and/or cognitive and emotional developmental level) and the situation (family factors, type of illness, etc.). Very young children have some understanding of death. For example, many 4-year-olds think that dead things can become alive again spontaneously, for instance, by praying. Between the ages of 5 and 7, children transition from the Piagetian preoperational stage of thinking to the more advanced stage of concrete operational thinking; they begin to process abstract concepts but they need concrete examples to understand these concepts. Thus, their understanding of death also changes as they begin to understand the irreversibility, the nonfunctionality, and the universality of death. The family's religious beliefs may be a particularly salient situational factor that affects a child's cognitive understanding and emotional response to death. In order to make sense of what has happened to them, even children who are not from a religious home may use God as an all-purpose explanatory construct.

Issues of faith arise in even very young children. Slightly older e.g., (school-age) children may elaborate the concept of death with many religious and cultural meanings. Especially for those children who come from religious homes, these beliefs may offer comfort. Although some children might lose faith in God as they face death (either their own or the death of a loved one), most children from religious homes perceive God as a savior throughout their struggle with death. The efficacy of religious beliefs as a coping method in children can be seen in their interest and beliefs in life after death. It is interesting that although heaven is often mentioned among dying children, hell rarely is. On the other hand, while many school-age children may believe in and/or understand the concept of life after death, for some this idea may not be comforting if they fear facing this afterlife alone. Children experience less anxiety when allowed to openly acknowledge and discuss their fears and spiritual concerns.

Facing death in adolescence may present even more challenges. Due to the development of hypothetico-deductive reasoning in many adolescents, philosophical issues of life, death, and reality become more salient even among healthy adolescents. The acquisition of religious belief systems is an important component of the development of identity, which is a key task in adolescence. Adolescents facing mortality often experience intensified spiritual and religious concerns. The contemplation of a prognosis may force the adolescent to consider some aspects of religion, even if these aspects were rejected upon previous consideration. Like younger children, adolescents begin to consider life after death. Through spirituality and religion, adolescents also attempt to find answers to questions and meaning in suffering. Not only must these adolescents come to terms with death, but they must also make sense of dying young or before their time. Just as in childhood, if such cognitive searching and discussion is discouraged, emotional isolation may deepen.

In conclusion, many children and adolescents (as well as older adults) want and seek out formal religious and spiritual discussions as they near death or confront the death of loved ones. Especially in palliative care settings, spiritual care is vital to a holistic approach to caring for dying individuals and their families. In these settings, it is important to recognize and foster spirituality as well as to understand the importance of religious convictions and practices. Not only do different religions offer different views of death, but conceptions of death and dying change across the life span and vary on a range of cognitive and ecological factors, from the individual and family to society and culture.

—Toni C. Antonucci, Katherine L. Fiori, and Edna Brown

FURTHER READING

Bronfenbrenner, U. (1980). Ecology of childhood. *School Psychology Review, 9,* 294–297.

deVeber, L. L. (1995). The influence of spirituality on dying children's perceptions of death. In J. D. Morgan, (Series Ed.), D. W. Adams, & E. J. Deveau (Vol. Eds.), *Beyond the innocence of childhood: Vol. 2. Helping children and adolescents cope with life-threatening illness and dying* (pp. 295–316). New York: Baywood.

Holland, J., Passik, S., Kash, K., Russak, S., Groner, M., Sison, A., et al. (1999). The roles of religious and spiritual beliefs in coping with malignant melanoma. *Psycho-Oncology,* 8, 14–26.

Koenig, H. (2002). A commentary: The role of religion and spirituality at the end of life. *The Gerontologist,* 42, 24–25.

Pargament, K., & Hahn, J. (1986). God and the just world: Causal and coping attributions to God in health situations. *Journal for the Scientific Study of Religion, 25,* 193–207.

Piaget, J. (1971). The stages of the intellectual development of the child. *Bulletin of the Menninger Clinic, 26,* 120–128.

Sourkes, B. M. (1995). *Armfuls of time: The psychological experience of the child with a life-threatening illness.* Pittsburgh: University of Pittsburgh Press.

Speece, M. W., & Brent, S. B. (1984). Children's understanding of death: A review of three components of a death concept. *Child Development, 55,* 1671–1686.

Wenger, J. L. (2001). Children's theories of God: Explanations for difficult-to-explain phenomena. *Journal of Genetic Psychology: Special Issue, 162,* 41–55.

ENOCH, BOOK OF

The Book of Enoch was a major stimulus for the modern study of apocalyptic literature and how it describes the emergence of Satan, thc fallen angels, the Nephilim, and the end of time. The stories of Enoch provide moralistic teachings for the reader, demonstrating the religious piety that biblical figures possessed and serving as models for how the religious followers of the Bible should act. The apocalyptic genre within the Book of Enoch reveals divination in the decoding of mysterious signs that foretell the events that lead up to the end time and what the end of time will be like for humanity.

I Enoch, the story of the Watchers, is an apocalyptic work that focuses on the divinely appointed order and the evil forces at work that threaten it. The figure of Enoch himself is a mysterious figure of the Old Testament. Enoch appears in the book of Genesis (5:21–24) as the seventh patriarch in a genealogy from Abraham to Noah. Enoch was the father of Methuselah and a man of great piety. Enoch was said to have walked with God, and as a reward for his piety at the age of 365, God raised Enoch up to heaven. Some scholars have even suggested that this is the basis for the calendar with 365 days. God raised Enoch up to heaven giving Enoch divine knowledge and recognition, for he knows God. In Islam, Enoch is regarded as one of their many prophets.

The work of Enoch is not included in the Bible or the Apocrypha, yet Enoch and his work are widely known both before and after the time of Jesus and have enjoyed much prestige. Eleven manuscripts of Enoch's works were produced for the elusive Qumran community located in the Israeli desert, and it stretched into even greater circles and farther lands including Ethiopia. The original text of I Enoch was written in Aramaic, the common language of the time, and later was translated into Greek.

I Enoch was an apocalyptic text, and apocryphal writers of the time were well aquainted with Enoch's literature. References to the text can be seen in the New Testament and the Apocrypha. The cosmic journey of Enoch, the clear separation between good and evil, and the punishments and rewards that await humans become inlaid in further apocalyptic literature based on I Enoch. I Enoch carried the same authority of the canonical Bible under major Christian Fathers such as Clement of Alexandria and Tertullian until the third century C.E. In the fourth century, Jerome and Augustine demoted the authority of the text and its authority fell in the Western Church, while in the Eastern Church, I Enoch continued to be handled with great respect until the ninth century C.E.

The content of Enoch is not composed by Enoch himself, but by a collaboration of authors implementing a writing phenomenon of the time called *pseudepigraphy,* which presents ideas by putting oneself in the position of well-respected biblical primordial figures. By using Enoch's name, the writers anticipated well that the text would be read and respected.

I Enoch reflects the stresses and strains in ancient Palestine, the Antiochan persecutions, and the domination of foreign peoples. The narrative is richly interspersed with prophecies of the end of time—the final cataclysm. The Watchers provides a paradigm for the origin of evil and sin. The tendency to explain the human situation in mythic terms is characteristic of apocalyptic literature.

The visions of Enoch are of astronomical, cosmic, and divine nature, in his journeys to heaven and hell, to the realms of good and evil. Enoch is a mediator between God and the Watchers and speaks openly with God and the fallen angels, which further elevates the popularity of Enoch for having contact with God.

The text tells of a band of angels led by Lucifer who visited earth and consorted with women. The angels were involved in sexual relations with the women and taught them knowledge that was forbidden, such as crafting weapons. The offspring from the angels and the women were the Nephilim (Gen. 6:1–8), giantlike creatures that ravaged the earth and that are mentioned briefly in the Bible. The birth of the Nephilim gives explanation to the Flood to wipe out all things that were evil on the earth.

God punished Lucifer and the band of angels for disobeying his orders and sentenced them to meet their doom and to live in Sheol (hell). These angels introduced chaos into the ordered world, and they were banned from heaven and cast to remain in perpetual torment in a place that Enoch saw with colossal pillars of fire, a fiery abyss.

The Watchers is a prototype for all of humanity that those who fall from God's grace will be punished, just as God punished his angels. The good will be rewarded in paradise, in heaven, with God. The tension of good and evil, the evolution of how Satan came to be, is one of the most influential aspects of I Enoch, and this notion of the fallen angel has been the means to explain how Satan and evil came to be.

I Enoch still survives in its legend of Satan, the fallen angels, evil, and the end of time to come. The figure of Enoch has found a place within the Islamic faith as one of their prophets, for Enoch was so beloved by Allah (God) and the legends that spawned from the Watchers are still echoed in Christian churches on

Sunday mornings. Enoch, a silent figure in the Old Testament and model religious devotee to Yahweh, serves as a spiritual model for others to follow.

—Julie Wieland-Robbescheuten

ENVIRONMENTAL ETHICS

All the world's religions, faith traditions, and spiritualities pay respect to the concept of environmental ethics. While it is a commonly held belief that environmental ethics is a relatively new field, coming to life in the 1970s, the idea is present in Jewish and Christian sacred scriptures.

However, the early 1970s started the first celebration of Earth Day and the acknowledgement of environmental ethics as a separate field of study within philosophy and ethics. The field emerged almost simultaneously in three countries; Australia, the United States, and Norway. In the first two of these countries, direction and inspiration came largely from the earlier 20th century literature of the environment. The Scottish emigrant John Muir (founder of the Sierra Club and the "father of American conservation") and subsequently the forester Aldo Leopold had advocated an appreciation and conservation of things natural, wild, and free. There is now a linking of environmental ethics with the animal rights movement.

Caring for and being attuned to the environment, as promoted and practiced in environmental ethics, have long been key aspects of the religious and spiritual developmental trajectories of individuals and communities. Environmental ethics is taught in a variety of contexts—religious programs, schools, one-on-one interactions, and in personal revelations often gained through experiences in nature.

The book of Genesis in the Jewish sacred texts, which all Christians also accept, is the starting point for ethical environmental treatment. Chapter I verses 26–30 states,

> And God said, "let us make a human, in our image, according to our likeness, and let them dominate the fish of the sea and the birds of the skies and the domestic animals and all the earth and all the creeping things that creep on the earth." And God created the human in His image. He created it in the image of God; He created them male and female. And God blessed them, and God said to them, "Be fruitful and multiply and fill the earth and subdue it and dominate the fish of the sea and the birds of the skies and every animal that creeps on the earth." And God said, "Here, I have placed all the vegetation that produces seed that is on the face of all the earth for you and every tree, which has in it the fruit of a tree producing seed. It will be for you, and for all the wild animals of the earth and for all the birds of the skies and for all the creeping things on the earth, everything in which there is a living being: every plant of vegetation, for food." And it was so.

The prophets of the Jewish sacred texts teach about faith and justice. The quality of one's personal faith is dependent upon the quality of justice. Where one stands with one's Creator is dependent upon where one stands with those on the fringes of society, i.e., the poor, the widows, the aliens, those with illnesses. The dignity of the human person is always to be upheld, since the human person is created in God's image and likeness. Environmental ethics now links the concept of the dignity of the person to the dignity of creation. Some ethicists claim that one protects human dignity by rights and duties, and rights are a moral claim to a good that is essential to human dignity. Therefore, the environment is also essential to human dignity. To continue this line of thought, since the human person is sacred and social, one needs to be in community. There are many levels of community: family, civil society, region, or nation, but the most basic community is the community of the earth. This connection allows the linking of stewardship with the purpose of humanity.

Modern-day religious scholars and theologians would highlight the concept of stewardship as a critical aspect of environmental ethics and as an important way to live a life faithful to God's word. Each person is meant to be a cocreator with God in art, culture, science and in regards to the earth. Humans are entrusted with the earth. All the earth's goods are for all, all the time. The idea of stewardship now states that creation and nonhuman things are not the property of any one person, but each person is to care for and protect what was loaned to the human family by the Creator. Stewardship means one needs to give an accounting to the Creator of how one used the goods and materials of the earth.

Stewardship of the environment is also taught in schools and religious programs throughout the world. Young people are given the opportunity—through community service projects, classroom responsibilities, etc.—to become engaged in caring for the environment. Whereas some experiences are intentionally linked to a religious lesson, other intentional and nonintentional experiences, without being linked to a religious lesson, nurture and promote healthy spiritual development by engaging young people in activities that require them to transcend themselves. Stewardship of the environment also takes place on a daily basis around the world in one-on-one interactions between parents and children, teachers and students, peers, siblings, etc. Often individuals, just by immersing themselves in nature, are moved to become stewards. When stewards of the environment are thought about in this way, surely it is clear that environmental ethics has always been a part of religious and spiritual development.

Environmental ethics is an ever-expanding field of study. If one takes the stewardship model to heart, then one will treat the environment with respect and dignity at all times, thereby leaving the world a better place for the next generation.

—Rev. David M. O'Leary

See also Ecology; Nature, the Sacred in

FURTHER READING

Guha, R. (1999). Radical American environmentalism revisited. In N. Witoszek & A. Brennan (Eds.), *Philosophical dialogues: Arne Næss and the progress of ecophilosophy* (pp. 473–479). New York: Rowman and Littlefield.

International Association of Environmental Philosophy. Retrieved February 1, 2005, from www.environmentalphilosophy.org/

The International Society for Environmental Ethics. www.cep.unt.edu/ISEE.html

Nash, R. F. (1990). *American environmentalism: Readings in conservation history.* New York: McGraw Hill.

Varner, G. (1998). *In nature's interest? Interests animal rights and environmental ethics.* Oxford: Oxford University Press.

W. Maurice Young Centre for Applied Ethics. Retrieved February 1, 2005, from www.ethics.ubc.ca/

THE EPISCOPAL CHURCH

The Episcopal Church is the American branch of the Anglican Communion. The Anglican Communion is composed of 38 self-governing churches, located in 160 countries on five continents. The churches are linked by their common ground in scripture, tradition, and reason. Moreover, the Anglican Communion is connected by a recognition of the Eucharist as the central act of worship and the acceptance of the Apostles' Creed and the Nicene Creed as the statements of faith. The Eucharist and baptism are recognized as the central acts of worship and the Anglican Communion accepts the standards of worship set forth in the revised Book of Common Prayer, although separate congregations are permitted leeway in the observance of ritual.

The Church of England separated itself from the Roman Catholic Church mostly for political reasons. Consequently, it still has much in common in terms of doctrine with Roman Catholicism (in addition to commonalities with Eastern Orthodoxy). The Church was formally organized in the late 18th century when the American colonies proclaimed independence from Great Britain. Ties between the Church of the colonies and the Church of England were severed after the American Revolution. As a result, the Episcopal Church became a separate entity, dedicated to American ideals such as the separation of church and state but committed to preserving its Anglican heritage. Today, there are between 2 and 3 million baptized members throughout the world.

The basic unit of organization in the Episcopal Church is the diocese, a group of at least six parishes under the leadership of one bishop. Today, the Church comprises 100 domestic dioceses and 13 international dioceses. Within the United States, Massachusetts is the largest diocese with over 91,000 members, while Eau Claire, Wisconsin is the smallest, with just over 2,500 members. All of these dioceses are under the jurisdiction of a presiding bishop of the Episcopal Church.

The presiding bishop serves as the chief pastor of the church, president of the House of Bishops, president of the Domestic and Foreign Missionary Society, and president and chair of the Executive Council. The presiding bishop is elected by the House of Bishops and confirmed by the House of Deputies to fulfill such responsibilities as initiating and developing policy and strategy of the church, serving as the chief consecrator at ordinations of bishops, and representing the Episcopal Church to the world.

In addition to the presiding bishop, the Episcopal Church recognizes three orders of ordained ministers: bishops, priests, and deacons. Bishops preside over a diocese and priests are usually the primary ministers in local congregations, often assisted by deacons. Bishops ordain priests; priests are empowered to celebrate the Eucharist, pronounce absolution, and perform other sacraments. Deacons are ordained ministers charged with reading the gospel at the Eucharist and preparing the altar. Until the latter part of the 20th century, males were the only individuals eligible for ordination into the priesthood of the Episcopal Church. However, in 1974 the American Episcopal Church granted women ordination into the priesthood, and in 1988 the diocese of Massachusetts elected the first woman bishop. However, the decision to ordain women remains optional in each diocese. Today three dioceses in the United States continue to refuse to ordain or recognize the priesthood of women (Fort Worth, TX; Quincy, IL; and San Joaquin, CA).

The Church believes that the Bible is "The Word of God" and that all that is required for salvation is contained within it. However, they also believe that lessons in life can be learned outside of scripture and that scripture has to be interpreted according to tradition and reason. The standards of doctrine within the Episcopal Church are the Apostles' and Nicene Creeds, the Thirty-Nine Articles of 1801, and the Book of Common Prayer. Although these serve as the standard doctrines, the Episcopal Church has adopted an understanding of latitudinarianism and is therefore accommodating of alternative stances. As such, Episcopalians within the same church may be pulled more toward the practice of Calvinism, Catholicism, or Methodism. Regardless of particular stance, the Book of Common Prayer is held as a common framework that governs the worship of all Anglicans, with a varied commitment to the Thirty-Nine Articles.

At the essence of Anglican spirituality are three things: scripture, tradition, and reason. The faith of the Episcopal Church is grounded in a spirituality of grace. As such, those who worship in the Episcopal Church believe in a faith that is based upon the scriptures and thus interpret the scriptures in the light of the Church's tradition and reason.

—Pamela M. Anderson

FURTHER READING

Holmes, D. L. (1993). *A brief history of the Episcopal Church.* Valley Forge, PA: Trinity Press International.

Prichard, R. W. (1991). *A history of the Episcopal Church.* Harrisburg, PA: Morehouse.

Webber, C. L. (1999). *Welcome to the Episcopal Church: An introduction to its history, faith, and worship.* Harrisburg, PA: Morehouse.

ERIKSON, ERIK H.

The most prominent 20th century American psychologist of child and adolescent development, Erik H. Erikson (1902–1994), saw religion as important for supporting optimal human development. He is best known for establishing an eight-stage theory of the human life cycle and for instigating an upsurge in child and adolescent research in the latter half of that century. Part scientist and part artist, he originally trained in Freudian psychoanalytic theory but remodeled this heritage to fit his own observations. He accomplished this by incorporating a more holistic perspective that integrated both psychobiological and sociocultural factors in human development. In addition, unlike the predominantly critical approach to religion expressed by those who followed the psychoanalytic tradition, Erikson saw the positive value of religion in an individual's life. Erikson placed the concept of identity as the keystone of his model of human development, which spanned the entire life cycle. This emphasis paralleled his personal, lifelong concern with identity.

AGE PERIODS OF ERIKSON'S LIFE

Erik was born on June 15, 1902, in Frankfurt, Germany, to Karla Abrahamsen, a Jewish native of Denmark. Erik's original last name, Salomonsen, came from his mother's first husband who had separated from her 4 years before Erik's birth. Erik's biological father was a non-Jewish Dane who had left Karla before Erik was born. Karla reared young Erik as a single parent for the first 3 years of his life. She then married Theodor Homburger, a prominent children's physician and president of the local synagogue, who adopted Erik and changed his surname to Homburger. Theodor posed as Erik's biological father, and Erik only discovered the truth as an adolescent. Further complicating his sense of identity confusion, Erik Homburger's appearance (tall, blue-eyed, and blond) was unusual within his Jewish community. As an adult, Erik moved to the United States and eventually changed his name again, this time to Erik H. Erikson, that is, Erik's son.

MORATORIUM YEARS AND MONTESSORI INFLUENCES

After graduating from the German equivalent of high school, Erikson entered a state art school in

1921. Following a few years of formal art training, he lived a bohemian lifestyle as he wandered through Europe sketching, making woodcuts, painting, and visiting museums. After half a dozen years, he returned home, confused and exhausted.

In 1927, Erikson was interviewed for a job by Anna Freud, Sigmund Freud's daughter. Erikson began to teach art to children at the Hietzing School—an institution linked with Sigmund Freud and the Vienna Psychoanalytic Society. At the same time he also earned a teaching degree from the local Montessori teacher-training school. Some of Erikson's initial insights in child psychology came from these experiences as he taught children of different ages, observed their play, and began to analyze their behavior.

PSYCHOANALYTIC AND PSYCHOSOCIAL TRAINING YEARS

The experience of being psychoanalyzed by Anna Freud, coupled with the encouragement of many peers, led Erikson to decide to become a child analyst. He studied with Vienna's senior psychoanalysts, including the aging Sigmund Freud, and graduated from the Vienna Psychoanalytic Institute in 1933. Though Erikson's later theories were often at odds with psychoanalytic theory, he felt indebted to the field and was always respectful of Sigmund Freud.

An often overlooked ingredient in Erikson's intellectual development was his relationship with Joan M. Serson, who was teaching dance at the Hietzing School when they met and who became his wife in 1930. Joan was a trained sociologist and scholar, and her influence on Erik was significant, as she supported the development of his ideas and edited his writings. In effect, their relationship also wedded their two fields of psychology and sociology, therein giving birth to *psychosocial* theory. Furthermore, as a Protestant, Joan disagreed with Freud's largely negative thoughts on religion. Her support of religiosity was significant for Erik, who came to describe himself as most comfortable standing on the "shadowy borderline" between his German Jewish *and* Danish Protestant heritages.

As the Nazi regime began to threaten Vienna, Erik, Joan, and their two children moved to the United States in 1933. Erikson was accepted by the Boston Psychoanalytic Society and became the first child analyst in Boston. He also became a research assistant at the Harvard Psychological Clinic and conducted research on children and identity. In 1936, Erikson accepted a research position at Yale University where he began to work out his developmental stage theory, studying different forms of play carried out by children of different ages; he also traveled to South Dakota to study the Sioux Indians, in whom he saw the dramatic impact of cultural forces on child development.

The Berkeley Childhood-and-Society Years

In 1939, Erikson accepted a research position at the Institute of Child Welfare at the University of California–Berkeley. He later began teaching graduate seminars at Berkeley and opened a private practice in the San Francisco area. During this time his ideas regarding sociocultural factors in ego development were starting to crystallize. He developed the concept of *ego identity,* a consistent sense of one's own self in relation to one's culture. He also formulated the idea of *identity crisis,* a disruption or turning point in a person's ego development, which is most common during adolescence but can occur at any time. In 1949, he became a full professor in psychology at Berkeley. The book that would be his magnum opus soon followed.

The publication of *Childhood and Society* in 1950 established Erikson's scholarly reputation. The work consisted of a collection of earlier essays that Erikson retooled to appeal to a broader audience beyond specialists in psychoanalysis. Chapter seven, on the Eight Stages of Man, was a groundbreaking model of the life span that spanned from infancy through elder adulthood. This model, which will be described in more detail later, garnered him so much attention that he became a popular academic celebrity in America.

The Austen Riggs Clinician Years

At first, fame did not bring Erikson academic security. The rise of McCarthyism and anxiety about communism in the nation's universities troubled his sense of academic freedom. He refused to sign an oath at Berkeley and eventually resigned from his hard-earned tenured position. In 1951, he accepted a position as an analyst at the Austen Riggs Center, a mental health facility in Stockbridge, Massachusetts. The position provided valued time for writing, and he stayed there for a decade. During these years Erikson also became more vocal about the positive role of religious experience and began to take into account the role of religious traditions as a transmitter of values and psychological well-being across the life span.

Erikson was particularly inspired by one of his clinical patients, that of a seminary graduate who had been preparing for missionary work before having a psychotic episode. Erikson found a good bit of similarity between this clinical case and the identity crisis suffered by the father of the Protestant Reformation, Martin Luther, when he was a young man. He began preparing a new book that would integrate some of his clinical cases with a psychohistorical account of Martin Luther, centering on the central concept of identity diffusion or breakdown. Instead of portraying religion as an inherently pathological vice, Erikson saw in Luther's life a *homo religious* (Latin for "religious man"), who's personal developmental crisis was able to address larger sociological crises, such as religious and political freedom. Furthermore, Erikson's analysis offered a compatible link between Luther's theological revolution and Freud's psychoanalytic revolution and between religion and psychology in general. With the publication of *Young Man Luther* (1958), Erikson's acclaim expanded beyond the field of psychology.

The Harvard Professor Years

Erikson accepted an appointment as Professor of Human Development at Harvard University in 1960. He became very popular with students and a valued conversation partner with his peers, including Paul Tillich, a fellow German-born immigrant and Harvard theologian. In his first book from those years, *Insight and Responsibility* (1964), Erikson built upon his eight stages by adding specifically achieved "virtues" to each of the stages: hope, will, purpose, competence, fidelity, love, care, and wisdom. Each virtue represented an ego strength that would animate a person's morality and ethics. His model of human development was thus prized for attending to psychological strengths instead of only pathology and disease.

For several years, he worked on a psychohistory of Gandhi, which was concerned with the ethics of social identity and the negative ethical concept of *pseudo-speciation* (the tendency of human groups to isolate themselves from others, to regard themselves as the chosen people, and other groups as less worthy of respect). Emphasizing the life cycle's persistent movement toward an adult ethic of generative care, he likened Gandhi's concept of *Satyagraha* or "perseverance in truth" and nonviolent confrontation with Freud's psychoanalytic method of confronting the inner enemy. Additionally, Erikson's work with identity crises and the life cycle perfectly addressed the conflicts of the 1960s, when American youth rebelled against traditional institutions, embraced pluralism, and demanded their own meaningful identities. Erikson later received a Pulitzer Prize for *Gandhi's Truth* (1969).

Erikson became professor emeritus at Harvard University in 1970. During his retirement from teaching, he was able to flesh out his concepts of generativity and integrity with further detail. Having found Gandhi's life to exemplify generativity, Erikson examined the life of Thomas Jefferson with a continued focus on the moral ethic of care in *Dimensions of a New Identity* (1974). In the 1980s, turning his attention to the last stage of the life cycle, integrity versus despair, Erik and Joan worked together on *Vital Involvement in Old Age* (1986). Erikson generally emphasized the connected cycle of generations in his last works as he described linkages between the eighth stage and the first stage. Finally, Erikson considered the reality of death and how the sense of "I" was renegotiated at the end of life. Though the search for identity is most tangible during the adolescent age period, Erikson's life confirmed that the task of identity should never be seen as a completed project. Erik H. Erikson died in Harwich, Massachusetts, in 1994 at the age of 91.

ERIKSON'S CONTRIBUTIONS TO THE PSYCHOLOGY OF RELIGION

Erikson understood the importance of organized religious traditions and doctrines, but he never centered his work on them. Rather, in his studies of Luther, Gandhi, and Jesus, Erikson carefully examined religious experience as it related to identity formation, ethical choices, and the life cycle. In a sense, he was more interested in what many now call personal spiritual development, which he saw occurring at the complex intersection of individual life histories and the life histories of religious institutions. His intuitive approach, so helpful in psychoanalysis, proved to further his vigorous reflections on God, the "Ultimate Other," in relationship to one's vital inner core. Erikson saw different religions as social centers of meaning that aided people through the life cycle and helped them find identity and healing.

Many of Erikson's concepts lend themselves to the interpretation of religious experience, that is, to theological interpretation. Erikson's psychosocial theory embraces what many theologians value in seeing the individual in relationship to a larger social community. Added to this, Erikson's focus on generative care and the connectedness of generations is fruitful to religious constructions of personal and congregational values. Erikson noted, furthermore, that the primary "developmental virtues," which arise across the eight stages of life (e.g., *hope, fidelity,* and *care),* are not dissimilar to the primary "creedal values" of Christianity (e.g., *hope, faith,* and *love).*

Spiritual Development Grounded in Life-Cycle Stages

Overall, Erikson's greatest contribution to the study of religious development in childhood and adolescence is his life-cycle theory and its eight stages. His framework provides a foundation with which to better understand how it is that children and youth develop in their religious attitudes and behavior. With five of the eight stages occurring before young adulthood, Erikson skillfully delineated the psychosocial crises that each child and adolescent faces. Each of these stages has a biological base in an individual's physical maturing and cognitive development, as well as a sociological base in the society's role expectations. Erikson used the term *epigenesis* to describe the organic quality of this developmental model. Borrowed from embryology, the word describes the way in which fetal organs normally develop in a careful sequential priority with each other. Each stage of organic development is necessary for a good healthy life. Likewise, each of Erikson's psychosocial stages is built upon the other, as a resolution to a particular psychosocial crisis, and is, in turn, favorably balanced. Erikson's stages are described below, with particular attention to the first five, which occur during childhood and adolescence, and to their correlated spirituality.

1. *Trust Versus Mistrust* (infancy). Erikson relates psychosocial development during the first year of life to the infant's task of developing a favorable balance of *basic trust versus mistrust.* The infant's apparent question, "Can I trust again?" builds on the infant's biological preoccupation with, "Will I be fed again?" Consistent, trustworthy parental care enables infants to attain a favorable balance of trust over mistrust, which, in turn, helps ensure that the strength of *hope* will become a fundamental quality of the person in later stages of the life cycle. Parents who relate to their infants and children in a consistent and trustworthy manner promote their offspring's sense of faith in life itself. Such trust also undergirds religious faith.

2. *Autonomy Versus Doubt* (early childhood). Beginning around the second year of life, the child becomes preoccupied with *autonomy versus shame and doubt.* This tension is engendered by the toddler's growing motor control and ability to differentiate between self and others. Achieving a favorable balance of autonomy over shame at this stage enables the child to develop the strength that Erikson calls *will,* as in will power or courage. As children listen to stories of heroes of the faith, for instance, they are encouraged to become more willful and confident in their own early sense of God.

3. *Initiative Versus Guilt* (play age). In Stage 3 of Erikson's scheme, *initiative versus guilt,* new levels of physical and intellectual maturity allow children to broaden their social world beyond the family and to increase their curiosity and ability to explore this new world. If the preschool child completes this stage with a sense of initiative that outweighs his or her sense of guilt, *purposefulness* will be an enduring strength. This sense of purpose enables children to become religious actors as they embody their family's religious story.

4. *Industry Versus Inferiority* (school age). Around the age of 6, children generally join up with society and receive some systematic education. With a favorable balance of *industry over inferiority,* the child achieves the strength of *competence*—the enduring belief that one can begin a project and also complete it at an acceptable level of quality. Children explore their mastery of their community's religion during this time. They ask who is God, what does God do, and how does God do it. They delve into the stories of their tradition's sacred texts and the techniques of reading them with an uncritical acceptance of their religious tradition's teachings.

5. *Identity Versus Confusion* (adolescent age). As adolescents develop the cognitive ability to think

of infinite hypothetical possibilities, society requires that they learn to fill specific adult roles. These two changes are synchronized in an adolescent's psychosocial task of achieving a sense of identity and working out what he or she should do with their lives. Achieving a favorable balance of *identity over identity confusion,* according to Erikson, leads to the strength of *fidelity*—a sense of commitment to a self-chosen value system and the capacity to maintain loyalties freely made in spite of the unavoidable contradictions of value systems. Identity formation often socially takes the form of a search for a political, religious, or moral ideology that provides a durable set of values on which an inner coherence can be based. Conversion experiences often characterize religious development during this stage. Such experiences answer the question, "Who am I in relation to God?" and shift religious ideas to the center of the person's identity.

Each of the childhood and adolescent developmental stages and resulting virtues are reworked during the subsequent three stages of adulthood:

6. *Intimacy Versus Isolation* (young adulthood). For example, as young adults move to Stage 6, balancing intimacy versus isolation gives rise to the virtue of *love.* Those who lack a clear sense of their identity will find it difficult to realize an intimate relationship because they fear losing "who they are" as they fuse long-term relationships.
7. *Generativity Versus Stagnation* (middle adulthood). Adults at Stage 7, *generativity,* avoid excessive personal stagnation by creating and caring for the next generation. By parenting, mentoring, volunteering, and creating, they achieve the strength of *care.* Generative teachers of religious traditions support development through a genuine sense of concern and care. Generative adults take on the responsibility of the life cycle by bringing children through the first five stages of their lives.
8. *Integrity Versus Despair* (older adulthood). At Stage 8, which characterizes old age, the person's attainment of a greater ratio of integrity over isolation gives rise to the final strength of *wisdom.* A religious community's mature oldest adults often serve as wise elders, contributing to the stability of a congregation.

IDENTITY, VALUES, AND RELIGION

The concept of identity was central to Erikson's work. He coined the term, *identity crisis,* which became a prominent concept in adolescent studies. This crisis involves a renegotiating of one's values, as they are oriented around other individuals and society at large. Erikson's notion of identity is always framed by social values and norms. Each person's ethnicity, gender, physical characteristics, and social class all affect a young person's sense of identity.

As each person renegotiates his or her values in relation to society, personal religious affiliations and spiritual development are deeply affected. Erikson's essay on Jesus' teachings and his major work on Martin Luther both showed the way in which religious beliefs and actions are developed through the identity development of the individual. According to Erikson, Jesus' sayings in Galilee were spoken as he struggled through establishing his own sense of "I." He renegotiated the values of his given religion by reframing God as "Abba"—not a revengeful distant judge, but a gentle caring parent. With his strength of autonomy, Jesus reframed the notion of care to include all of humanity. Luther, suffering from a severe crisis of meaning and identity in the youthful years, used his autonomy and initiative to speak out against a religious tradition with which he could not identify. He trusted his faith in God and his own moral voice to break with the conventional values. In renegotiating his values and working out his identity, Luther enabled a society to speak out during its own crisis of meaning and identity. Just as Jesus' views on his identity spurred his society to a new religious identity, so were Luther's views the impetus for his generation's reformation.

SUMMARY

Erikson's life-cycle approach to personality development, particularly his charting of psychosocial and ethical development, is evidence of his own generativity. Erikson's writings also developed, over the years, an insightful understanding of the importance of religion for supporting development during each period of the life cycle. Further, the model has strong appeal to the virtue orientation of religious traditions. Erikson also showed how the life cycle of an individual and the life history of a society are held together by generative adults and religious communities, which provide the necessary developmental conditions for the next generation.

—*John Snarey and David Bell*

See also Freud, Anna; Freud, Sigmund

FURTHER READING

Aden, L. (1976). Faith and the developmental cycle. *Pastoral Psychology, 24*(3), 215-230.

Erikson, E. H. (1950). *Childhood and society.* New York: Norton.

Erikson, E. H. (1958). *Young man Luther.* New York: Norton.

Erikson, E. H. (1964). *Insight and responsibility.* New York: Norton.

Erikson, E. H. (1968). *Identity: Youth and crisis.* New York: Norton.

Erikson, E. H. (1981). The Galilean sayings and the sense of "I." *Yale Review, 70*(3), 321–362.

Erikson, E. H., & Erikson, J. M. (1981). On generativity and identity. *Harvard Educational Review, 51*(2), 249-269.

Erikson, E. H., & Erikson, J. M. (1997). *The life cycle completed: Extended version.* New York: Norton.

Friedman, L. (1999). *Identity's architect: A biography of Erik H. Erikson.* New York: Scribner.

Snarey, J. (1993). *How fathers care for the next generation: A four-decade study of generativity.* Cambridge, MA: Harvard University Press.

Wright, E. (1982). *Erikson: Identity and religion.* New York: Seabury.

Zock, H. (1990). *A psychology of ultimate concern: Erik H. Erikson's contribution to the psychology of religion.* Amsterdam: Rodopi.

ESCHATOLOGY

The world religions that are based on the Bible—Judaism, Christianity, and Islam—hold that the world had a definite beginning. Genesis describes that beginning as God bringing order out of chaos. Over time, when the world seemed to be reverting back to chaos, thinkers from these religions have speculated about the end (in Greek, *eschaton*) of God's creation. *Eschatology* is, then, a term coined by scholars to refer to speculating about the end of time. Central to all forms of eschatology is dissatisfaction with life in the present world. Eschatology calls for change and an end to the problems faced by the community. This change requires action from believers—whether by altering their own behavior, remaining steadfast in their faith, or working actively to reform their society. In most cases, however, God is taken to be the principal actor and the one who will transform this imperfect world into something better.

Though it is common to think that the *eschaton* always refers to a cataclysmic destruction of the world, eschatology takes several forms, most of which do not imagine the end this way. Scholars have subdivided eschatology into several subcategories.

Developmentally, the earliest of these is *prophetic eschatology.* The pre-exilic Hebrew prophets writing in the eighth to seventh century B.C.E.—particularly, Amos, Isaiah, and Zephaniah—criticized the Jews of Israel and Judah for failing to live up to their covenant with Yahweh (God). The people of Israel began celebrating a new holiday: the Day of the Lord, a New Year's festal day anticipating the great Day of Yahweh when the promises of the covenant would be fulfilled and Israel would be crowned with glory. But the prophets said such celebration was hypocritical, for the people were not following the moral and ethical demands of the covenant. So, the Day of Yahweh would be, in reality, a day of judgment, when the enemies of Israel and Judah would triumph and only the truly righteous would be saved from destruction. Soon after, these enemies did triumph, dispersing the northern tribes of Israel (in 721 B.C.E.) and sending the southern tribes of Judah into exile in Babylon (587–538 B.C.E.).

The situation of the Jews in Babylon led to a new form of eschatology, namely, *restoration eschatology.* Prophets in the time of the exile—particularly Ezekiel and Second Isaiah—wished to offer their people hope for a renewed Israel. They wrote of an end to Yahweh's punishment, an end to Israel's oppression by its enemies, and the beginning of a return to glory. Just as Yahweh once brought destruction in the form of invading armies, now he would bring salvation by gathering the dispersed Israelites like a shepherd rescuing lost sheep (as in Ezekiel) or by restoring the exiles to their land through raising up a righteous foreign ruler (for example, Cyrus, the Persian king who allowed the Judahite exiles to return to their homeland and who Second Isaiah called the Messiah).

Eschatology took another form in Hellenistic times when the conquests of Alexander the Great (356–323 B.C.E.) left many Judeans feeling anxious about their place in the cosmos. Yahweh now seemed more remote, apparently caring little about his people on earth.

When a Syrian prince attempted to force Hellenistic (Greek) culture on Jerusalem, *apocalyptic eschatology* was born—i.e., the belief that Yahweh's intervention in world events would take the form of a cosmic battle of good versus evil leading to the creation of a heaven on earth where the righteous would be rewarded for their steadfast faith. Apocalyptic eschatology can be observed in the canonical book of Daniel and in a variety of noncanonical Jewish literature, including the Enoch texts, *Jubilees,* and the Dead Sea Scrolls.

The chaos that came with Alexander's conquests led also to criticism of earthly forms of government. Jewish thinkers of the time wrote of an idealized "kingdom of God" that was free of the corruption and injustices of earthly kingdoms (Daniel 7:14; *Psalm of Solomon* 17:3; *Testament of Moses* 10:1; and 4Q246 and 4Q521 from the Dead Sea Scrolls). One day, they hoped, the kingdom of God would be realized upon earth.

The concept of the kingdom of God was used to great effect in the first century by John the Baptist and Jesus of Nazareth. Using the language of his apocalyptic predecessors, John proclaimed, "Repent, for the kingdom of God has come near" (Matt. 3:2 or Luke 3:3) and warned of a "wrath to come" (Matt. 3:7 or Luke 3:7). Jesus also spoke of a kingdom of God, but scholars are divided over whether Jesus was truly an apocalyptic prophet. John D. Crossan, a prominent historical Jesus scholar, characterizes the teaching of Jesus as eschatological but not apocalyptic. Defining eschatology more broadly as world negation, Crossan identifies several forms that eschatology may take: apocalyptic eschatology (which sees the world as overtaken by evil and in need of rescue by God), *ascetical eschatology* (withdrawal from the world through denial of luxuries such as rich food, sex, ostentatious clothing, property, and an occupation), and *ethical eschatology* (actively but nonviolently protesting against a system judged to be evil, unjust, or violent). While many scholars see continuity between the eschatological views of John the Baptist and Jesus, Crossan believes that John's eschatology was apocalyptic and Jesus' was ethical.

Whatever Jesus' particular views of the end time, the Christian movement that emerged after his death embraced a variety of eschatologies. Seeking to ingratiate itself with the Roman authorities who persecuted it, orthodox Christianity, distanced itself from apocalyptic eschatology as it made Christianity appear to be too subversive. Orthodox texts, particularly the Gospels of Luke and John, instead represent *realized eschatology*—the end of the evil powers' rule of the earth has begun with Jesus' ministry. This idea is expressed in a more spiritual way by Jesus in the Gospel of John: "Whoever believes in the Son has eternal life" (3:36)—eternal life here and now, not later.

Gnostic Christians embraced ascetical eschatology, believing that if they refused to have children, creation would, in effect, roll back. For Gnostics, the end was the beginning. Other Christians, such as the author of the book of Revelation, remained apocalyptic in their outlook.

Revelation's graphic description of the cataclysmic battle between good and evil was unsettling to many early Christians, and though the text was accepted as scripture, Christian leaders discouraged literal readings of the text. They said some day Jesus would return to usher in a new age, but not in the way described in the book of Revelation and not anytime soon.

In Islam, several forms of eschatology include the concept of the Day of Judgment. Muhammad, the founder of Islam, believed himself to be the last of a long line of prophets that stretched back through Christianity and into ancient Jewish history. Like the Hebrew prophets of old, Muhammad criticized his people for failing to follow established moral principles, which in this case meant the principles of *muruwwah* (manliness). He warned listeners of an impending doom, an apocalyptic day of destruction, when the deeds of every person would be weighed. On that day, the good would enter paradise, and the wicked would be condemned to hell. Islamic eschatology is, therefore, prophetic, and for the most part, it is apocalyptic though without being motivated by the threat of persecution.

The one major exception has been Shi'i Islam. As a result of discrimination from the majority Sunni, apocalyptic eschatology is more pronounced in Shi'i Islam. Shi'i Islam has evolved a doctrine that the true leader of Islam will one day come out of hiding, vindicate his followers, and establish just rule on earth.

In sum, biblically inspired eschatology has served as an important expression of dissatisfaction with the present and hope for the future. By our understanding the various forms that eschatology takes, we better understand world views and spiritual motives that serve as powerful forces of change. The subject of eschatology is, then, a subject to be taken seriously as it provides one key to understanding human behavior, historical change, and the spiritual lives of many.

—*Tony Chartrand-Burke*

See also Apocalypse; Jesus; Muhammad

FURTHER READING

Cohn, N. (1993). *Cosmos, chaos and the world to come.* New Haven: Yale University Press.

Collins, J. J. (1998). *The apocalyptic imagination: An introduction to the Jewish matrix of Christianity* (Rev. ed.) Grand Rapids, MI: Eerdmans.

Crossan, John D. (1998). *The birth of Christianity: Discovering what happened in the years immediately after the execution of Jesus.* San Francisco: Harper Collins.

Elliott, Mark A. (2000). *The survivors of Israel: A reconsideration of the theology of pre-Christian Judaism.* Grand Rapids, MI: Eerdmans.

EUCHARIST

The Eucharist is a sacrament or rite of the Christian church in which a congregation will use bread and wine to re-enact the last meal of Jesus before his crucifixion. It is also known as *Communion, Holy Communion* or *The Lord's Supper.*

WHAT IS THE EUCHARIST?

Christians usually celebrate the *Eucharist*—a Greek word that literally means "to give thanks"—in the context of a worship service. During the worship service, an ordained pastor or priest leads the congregation in a liturgy that usually includes a chance to confess sins. Most congregations also "pass the peace of Christ" by shaking hands, hugging, or kissing to show that there is no bad will between members of the congregation. The liturgy retells some of the story of God and God's people. While these liturgies may vary across Christian traditions, almost all include what are referred to as the *Words of Institution,* which are taken from 1 Corinthians 11:23–26, Matthew 26:26–28, Mark 14:22–24, and Luke 22:19–20. More prayers are offered, and people come up to receive the bread and wine.

How congregations receive the bread and wine varies a lot by congregation. Some receive a piece of bread to eat and then drink out of one big chalice or cup of wine. In other traditions, people receive a small, individual cup of wine. While some congregations kneel at an altar, others walk to the front of the church, receive the Eucharist, and return to their seats. In other churches, members pass the bread and wine to one another and help themselves. With the exception of a few denominations, how people take the bread and wine is more often than not a matter of congregational preference.

What determines how often a community practices the Eucharist is sometimes, but not always based on theology. Roman Catholics typically celebrate the Eucharist every week out of deference to their theological tradition that places tremendous importance on The Lord's Supper. Some Christian communities take communion four times a year or less. In their tradition, it is purely a symbolic meal that does not need to be celebrated very often. Most United Methodist and Presbyterian churches celebrate the Eucharist about once a month, despite the fact that their respective founders, John Wesley and John Calvin, believed that more frequent celebration was important.

WHAT DOES IT MEAN?

Christians partake of the Eucharist because, according to the gospels of Mark, Luke, and Matthew and to Paul's letter to the Corinthian church, Jesus commands them to do so in remembrance of him. On the night of the Passover feast, Jesus revealed that he knew one of his disciples was going to betray him. He then offered bread and wine from the table, saying "this is my body" and "this is my blood." He told the disciples that they were his blood and body as signs of a new covenant for the forgiveness of sins. He then commanded them to "do this in remembrance of me."

Since that event, the Christian church has spent nearly 2000 years debating the meaning of the word *is.* While some of the greatest divisions on the subject arose during the Reformation, there has always been debate within and between different Christian churches. Some theologians, including most Baptists, believe that Jesus' use of the word *is* was purely symbolic—that obviously the bread could not have been Jesus' body because his body was still in tact as he stood in front of the disciples. Others, such as Roman Catholic theologians, argue that Jesus was capable of any supernatural miracle: if Jesus said that bread "is" his body, then it *is* his body. This miracle can be repeated by ordained priests who use the words that it is believed Jesus used.

Just as different Christians have different beliefs about Jesus' use of the word *is,* different traditions have diverse opinions as to what "happens" in the Eucharist. Some take a more mystical approach that holds a more supernatural understanding of the sacrament. It is an especially powerful ritual for members of more sacramentally focused denominations such as the Eastern Orthodox, Roman Catholic, Anglican, Lutheran, and to some extent, Methodist, Presbyterian, and Reformed traditions. Although each denomination has its own perspective on what actually happens in the Eucharist, all of these traditions believe that Jesus is especially present in the meal.

Roman Catholics believe that the essence of the bread and wine actually turn into the body and blood of Jesus (this is called the *doctrine of transubstantiation*). Lutherans believe that Jesus is mystically integrated into the bread and wine but do not believe that the physical components themselves change (this is called the *doctrine of consubstantiation*). Other Protestant traditions hold that Jesus is mystically connected to the bread and wine through the Holy Spirit (another aspect or part of God) but that Jesus' body has ascended into heaven and cannot, therefore, be present in a church service. Regardless of these differences, all of these traditions maintain that whoever takes part in the Eucharistic ritual and believes in Jesus receives God's grace and experiences greater intimacy with the Christian community.

Other traditions, such as most Baptist churches, take a much more symbolic approach to the Eucharist (this approach is called *memorialism*). In this perspective, generally attributed to Zwingli, followers do not believe that anything supernatural occurs in the Eucharist. Rather it is a way of remembering Jesus that has been given to the church before he died. Because it is not as central to Christian living as it might be in a more sacramental tradition, Christians in these denominations tend not to celebrate Communion as often—celebrating four times a year or less. This is not to say that the Eucharist does have special meaning to Christians with this perspective. The bread and wine are still special because they are associated with Jesus—just as an old toy might be considered special to someone because it was given to them by a family member or loved one.

The Eucharist is a meal of contrasts that simultaneously observes joy and sorrow, death and life. That the first Eucharist took place at a Passover meal is significant. The Passover feast celebrates the night before the Israelites left slavery and began their journey into the promised land. This was seen as a great act of God's power, mercy, and love. Likewise, Christians see the death and resurrection that came after the Eucharistic meal to be an awesome act of God's love, power, and mercy. Therefore the Eucharist is not just a solemn memory of the sacrifice Jesus made. It is also a celebration of the great things that God did despite the pain of Jesus' crucifixion. Wine is simultaneously bitter and sweet. Some see this as a reflection of the Christian lifestyle that brings both joy and hardship. Eucharist comes from the Greek verb, *eucaristw* or "eucharisto," which means to celebrate. Ultimately, Christians remember that the bread and wine become or symbolize the body and blood of Jesus—a powerful reminder of the belief that their God loved them so much that God was willing to suffer for them (cf. Phil. 2).

That the Eucharist is a meal is also significant for Christian understanding. By sharing in a meal, communities become more like a family. Sharing in the same food symbolically represents the idea that Christians are all nourished from the same source and that they do so in community—not in isolation. Eucharist in the early church may have actually looked less like a worship service and more like a potluck supper in which members of the community brought food to share. Although there was certainly some liturgy in these gatherings, Paul makes it clear that the meal is intended to bring the community closer together and help people to settle their differences (cf. 1 Cor. 11–12). In fact, Christians are encouraged to do so before coming to the communion table. When a member of a Mennonite Christian community has an issue with another member, the two may be denied communion until they are able to resolve whatever it is that comes between them.

Regardless of different interpretations of exactly what happens in the Eucharist, it is universally agreed that it represents and reminds the Christian community of one of the most important nights in Christian history—the night in which Jesus, whom Christians believe to be God on earth, willingly decided to sacrifice his life for the good of God's creation.

—Rev. Michael J. Baughman

See also Grace, Sacraments

FURTHER READING

McGrath, A. E. (2001). *Christian theology* (3rd ed.). Malden, MA: Blackwell.

Schmemmann, A. (2000). *For the life of the world.* Crestwood, NY: St. Vladimir's Seminary Press.

Stamm, M. W. (2001). *Sacraments & discipleship.* Nashville: Discipleship Resources.

Stookey, L. H. (1993). *Eucharist.* Nashville, TN: Abingdon Press.

EVANGELISM

Most commonly associated with missionary work, evangelism is derived from a Greek term meaning "good news." The mission of evangelicals is to spread the good news of Jesus Christ and his ministry. Evangelism can be examined in four different stages: the time of Christ, missionary operations, the modern era, and the late 20th century to the present. Evangelism has a global objective in increasing faith in Jesus Christ. In the New Testament, Christ tells his disciples to "go make disciples of all nations." After the death of Christ, some interpreted this passage literally, and evangelism soon became a Christian mission enterprise.

Evangelism dates, then, all the way back to the first century C.E. Evangelism spread the word of Christ throughout the Roman Empire, Persia, and parts of India. Once Christianity became the dominant religion in Europe, missionaries were sent overseas in order to evangelize. Much of this missionary work was carried out in Africa and the Middle East.

Since the late 1800s, evangelism in America has been more commonly associated with animated preachers and, more recently, with conservative politics. Preachers such as Dwight L. Moody, Billy Sunday, Aimee Semple McPherson, and Billy Graham are examples.

The year 1954 marked the first television outreach by an evangelical preacher. Televangelism, as it came to be known, led to the creation of an "electronic church" that allowed worshippers and curious viewers to receive sermons while sitting in their living rooms. Popular televangelists include Oral Roberts, Pat Robertson (founder of the Christian Broadcasting Network), and Jim and Tammy Faye Bakker. Dedicated to the conversion of nonevangelists, televangelists Jerry Falwell and Jimmy Swaggart used their airtime to warn viewers of the evils of American society.

Several issues covered in television outreach stem from American society and the perilous consequences of everyday decisions. Homosexuality, divorce, interracial marriage, and financial responsibility are all frequent subjects in evangelist programs—as is finances. With regard to finances, viewers are often solicited to pay money to outreach programs or in some cases even to the preachers themselves. Several cases of fraud have surfaced regarding evangelist tithing.

While there are negative stereotypes associated with evangelism in the United States, much can be said about its positive contributions to society. Bob Jones Sr., one of the most popular evangelists, built Bob Jones University, which has been thriving for more than 80 years. Beginning in Florida in 1927 and moving to South Carolina in 1946, the university is known as the "citadel of biblical Christianity." Jones's vision was to establish a center for Christians from around the world that would be known for its academic excellence and what he referred to as "refined standards of behavior." Learning centers such as Bob Jones University advocate that Christ should be the center of all thought and conduct of students.

Evangelism is a broader term than *fundamentalism,* although often the two have been used interchangeably. However, it is possible to be a community or individual with a strong belief in the value of evangelizing, and yet not be identified with the central characteristics of fundamentalism. On the other hand, all Christian fundamentalists believe in and value evangelizing.

Today in America, evangelical churches are growing at a faster pace than other more "mainline" churches, especially in the South and Midwest. In doing so, they have become a major force in American politics and in shaping American culture.

—*Lula Lakeou*

EVIL

It is difficult to produce a single definition of evil—as if a string of words linked together could make the reality of evil comprehensible. In the Christian tradition, it is noted as the seventh petition in the "Lord's Prayer," when the gospel author places in the mouth of Jesus these words, "but deliver us from evil. . . ." In a very real sense, we have to see it and then say, "This is it. This is evil." This is it; this is evil: institutionalized slavery, apartheid, the

Holocaust, genocide, "9/11": these provide a few signposts that point to the reality of evil. Poet Maya Angelou once referred to the Holocaust—the mass murder of 6 million Jews during the Second World War—as the time when millions of ourselves killed millions of ourselves. This is evil. Evil is in opposition to life.

Evil can be referred to as a plight of and blight upon humankind to which there appears to be no solution. The world is riddled with an abundance of shaping traditions, political systems and social structures that have given birth to racial, sexual, social, and economic forms of prejudice and exploitation. Such is the stuff of which evil is made. For example, evil is made manifest through human inventions of thought and practice, which give prerogative to be arbitrarily cruel and punitive, for example, to those who are determined as intrinsically inferior. Many of the world systems or social orders are structured on a model of domination or subordination, meaning reality is skewed to established power relations where those who "naturally" are meant to dominate do so over those who are, supposedly by nature, meant to be dominated.

Institutionalized slavery is an example. The master or slave system is organized on the premise that there are those who "need" to be dominated by those empowered to dominate. It then becomes the privilege of those who perceive themselves masters to grant themselves permission to brutalize those whom they claim are theirs to control. Civilization in the 20th century through law and practice has confronted this system as evil. One race of people is not by nature superior to another.

Through history and across religious history humans have struggled to come to terms with the root cause of that which twists, knots, and gnarls human nature to such an extent as to produce suffering on a massive scale. The realization of the capacity for perversity in the exercise of free will is a common feature of virtually all the major religious traditions—Eastern and Western. How can evil be so predominant when most who live upon the face of the earth profess to adhere to the standard of the golden rule: "Do unto others as you would have them do unto you" (Matt. 7:12)? This guiding principle for right action exists in all major religions in some form.

The question of theodicy is fundamentally a philosophical and religious one: What kind of a God permits evil, especially innocent and undeserved suffering? Why would God permit evil, pain, destruction, and death when God is the epitome of absolute goodness, manifestation of grace, creator of life, and omnipotent eternal One? The attempt to reconcile the existence of God and the reality of evil is called *theodicy,* from two Greek words meaning God (*theos*) and righteousness (*dike*). Theodicy is the religious response to the problem of pain and suffering; an intelligible effort to bring together the unlimited goodness of an all-powerful God with the terrorizing reality of evil. The word was coined in the 18th century and has engaged theologians who explore the nature of the Divine in juxtaposition with the inconceivable horrors of death and destruction and the seemingly endless human propensity to cause harm and inflict suffering generation after generation.

Generally, the notion of evil is categorized in a twofold way: moral evil and natural evil. Moral evil refers to the exercise of human freedom and free will to deliberately inflict pain, cause harm, and destroy wholeness. For example, moral evil is the outcome of taking incredible human genius and using it to create weapons of mass destruction and then using those weapons upon human beings and the environment. Natural evil, on the other hand, refers to unpredictable phenomena beyond human control, such as earthquakes, tornados, floods, hurricanes, and all forms of "natural disasters," that result in catastrophes of epic proportions. There is argument that it is inappropriate to name such natural phenomena evil, as if the rain could stop itself from becoming a torrential flood or the winds control the direction of a hurricane to prevent a trail of destruction. The results of nature can be brutal, but uncontrollable nature is not evil. For some, the category of evil belongs exclusively to humankind's capacity to voluntarily perpetrate forms of inhumanity.

An ancient Western philosophy called *dualism* viewed reality as divided into hostile opposites, good and evil, due to an aberration of the good—original sin—that became the source of the entry of evil into created reality. Evil, then, is a by-product of the absence of the good. Evil is a contaminant of good and is always divisive. It is antilife. The reality of evil is not willed by God but arises from the exercise of human freedom by those who will to do evil. God "permits" but does not intend evil. This is the mainline construction of monotheistic theodicy. Other views, some part of Eastern philosophy and religion, include the notion that evil exists to serve a higher purpose. The realities of pain and suffering, intended or unintended, are necessary means for human and spiritual development. Without suffering and pain there is no growth in personhood to the deeper realms of human potential and altruistic love.

Popular culture uses slogans to motivate competition such as "no pain, no gain" or "no guts, no glory" in referring to the victory of endurance, such as in Olympic contests. Such slogans are used to motivate a "winning" attitude and unwittingly suggest a deeper, spiritual meaning. A Christian theology of the cross carries the vision that suffering can be meaningful and a source of spiritual growth. This notion is popularized by the phrase: "no cross, no crown." Behind these pop culture and religious slogans is the conviction that human beings possess great capacity for enduring enormous challenges and hardships without the need to capitulate to the easiest solution or compromise of integrity. Confronting the forces of evil pulls human beings out of the lures of excessive self-absorption, apathy, domination, and violence and toward love of neighbor, selflessness, strength of character, and care of the earth.

Those who succumb to the lures of egoism and self-destruction or whose character fails to develop in moral strength, empathy, and integrity are those whose early life experiences may have caused a separation from the development of a true self. Psychopathology riddles such a malformed psyche and sets the stage for the evolution of a destructive personality weak in emotional connectedness and mutuality with others. Such pathology left unaddressed leaves human personality in the grip of unregulated grandiosity, rage, hate, and narcissism. Through faulty exercise of human freedom, individuals gradually distort their innate direction toward the good and, in the process, actually become less free.

Empathy and mutuality in relationship evaporate from the repertoire of human exchange and social relations. A sense of accountability to others and one's citizenship in the world cease to matter to those caught in this compulsion. Persons exempt themselves from the norms that govern social relations and shared human responsibilities, what believers name *stewardship.* Such individuals exhibit unwillingness to undergo self-examination that might penetrate self-deception. These failings in human consciousness and conscience establish a pattern of attitude and action whose cumulative, progressive, and disastrous effects we can call evil. (These descriptions of deteriorations can be applied to institutions or social systems as well as individuals.)

The contemporary theology explored in the book *The Other Side of Sin: Woundedness from the Perspective of the Sinned-Against* (2001) question the accepted necessity that it is not possible for humans not to sin and thus perpetuate evil. Innocent suffering raises the question of the ultimate morality of the world and the goodness of God. What kind of a world do we sustain when the innocent suffer for the sins of others? Must it remain a permanent truth that each generation must be wounded all over again by the evil it inherits? In the end, each generation asks and answers the question, Who is God, in the midst of unrelenting evil? Ultimately, evil falls into the category of mystery, which comes from the Greek word *mysterion,* meaning something seemingly unsolvable but something about which there is always more to know.

—*Avis Clendenen*

See also Original Sin; Psychological Evil Sin

FURTHER READING

Evil. (1999). [Special issue.] *Parabola, 24*(4).

Jung, C. G. (1958). *Answer to Job.* Princeton, NJ: Princeton University Press.

Kelly, J. (2003). *Responding to evil.* Collegeville, MN: Liturgical Press.

Moore, Robert L. (2003). *Facing the dragon: Confronting personal and spiritual grandiosity.* Wilmette, IL: Chiron.

Park, A. S., & Nelson, S. (Eds.). (2001). *The other side of sin: Woundedness from the perspective of the sinned-against.* New York: State University of New York Press.

FAITH

Faith is one of the key concepts used to define and explain religious and spiritual development. For many, it is *the* key concept. Given its importance, then, faith might be expected to have a clear and agreed upon meaning. However, it does not. There are, in fact, many meanings, but each can be classified under one of two major traditions.

The first tradition defines faith in terms of *belief* or assent to supernatural, often "revealed" truth. This tradition was strong in the first centuries of Christianity, but today it can be found in discussions both within and outside the Christian tradition and within and outside religious groups. For example, a major topic among cognitive anthropologists and cognitive developmental psychologists today is the topic of how children acquire beliefs in the supernatural. Contrary to previous generations of researchers, today's researchers are emphasizing similarities in the religious beliefs of children and adults and demonstrating the complex mental operations involved in children's acquisition of religious beliefs. However, even a cursory analysis of this new literature suggests that in their focus on children's acquisition of religious beliefs, social scientists today are assuming that for all intents and purposes, belief and faith are the same. Likewise, in ordinary discourse about religion, it is common to find discussants equating faith and belief—as when individuals pose the question, "What religion are you?" and follow immediately with questions about what members of a particular religious group or faith are supposed to believe in.

The second tradition defines faith more in terms of trust, commitment, and an individual's response to a faith tradition. In this tradition, faith becomes an orientation toward life. In this tradition too, faith becomes a quality of persons rather than a single attribute or set of beliefs. In this tradition then, though belief is assumed to be one expression of faith, faith itself is far larger than belief.

In the second tradition, the meaning of faith as trust and commitment often leads to faith being discussed as a particular kind of response within a relationship. So, from the point of view of this second tradition, someone might say he believes in an evil person or power (e.g., Hitler, the devil) but has no faith in that person or power. In this tradition then, belief is neutral whereas faith is never neutral. In this tradition, most of the time faith is a virtue.

These two traditions and meanings of faith have important implications for defining and explaining religious and spiritual development. In adopting the first, intellectualistic meaning of faith as belief, religious and spiritual development become tied to whatever is considered to be revealed truth and the core beliefs of a particular religious group. In adopting the second, holistic meaning of faith as trust, commitment, and orientation toward life, religious and spiritual development become tied to how individuals and communities attempt to live their lives as expressions of what they take to be transcendent and sacred. In the first tradition then, faith (belief) development is a precursor to the development of the whole person. In the second tradition, faith development *is* the development of the whole person—or at least the core development that matters most.

In the last several decades, a number of scholars have argued that the first, intellectualistic tradition has led to a trivializing of religious and spiritual development. They argue that treating faith as belief provides a way for nonbelievers to dominate intellectually the study and explanation of religious individuals and communities. This same group also argues that the intellectualistic tradition continues a largely Western and biblical bias since in many non-Western faith traditions belief plays a relatively minor role in the religious lives of individuals and communities. Finally, those currently arguing for the second meaning of faith underscore its power for explaining not only individuals responding to religious faith traditions but individuals responding to secular "faith" traditions as well. For this group, one can have an entirely secular faith and live life trying to express some ideal or secular tradition such as the American democratic ideal or the scientific tradition. Indeed, more than a few have pointed out that science today has become a major, perhaps *the* major, faith tradition.

Finally with respect to the usefulness of defining faith as trust, commitment, and orientation to what is considered to be transcendent or sacred, faith can be usefully employed to define and explain narrow-minded, mean-spirited, even pathological faith. There are, after all, many examples of false prophets or individuals who come to see themselves as saviors of the world, individuals whose distorted faith leads them to commit evil acts motivated by their faith.

In sum, there are two main ways of defining faith and its development, one in terms of belief, the other in terms of trust, commitment, and orientation toward what is taken to be transcendent and sacred. The first way continues to be the most common way of defining faith, but there are good reasons for adopting the second way—reasons having to do with its capturing what is central and most significant about religious and spiritual development.

—*W. George Scarlett*

FAITH-BASED SERVICE ORGANIZATIONS

The term *faith-based service organizations* refers to organizations or programs that have a religious orientation and offer various forms of services to individuals or families. They can be church, synagogue, temple, or some other religious group or community-based programs that aim to help people and that involve religion in one way or another. For some faith-based service organizations, religion serves simply as motivation for their mission. For others, religion forms an integral part of the content of their program. In most faith-based service organizations, the staff and volunteers usually adhere to a specific faith or religious tradition, while participants may or may not share that faith or tradition.

The term *faith based* is inclusive and can refer to congregations and organizations of various religions and faith traditions. Additionally, it enables service organizations to designate religion or spirituality as an important part of their program, while communicating that proselytizing or evangelizing are not necessarily major goals.

By providing spiritual, religious, social, and/or practical support, faith-based service organizations can be important resources for youth, adults, and families. Furthermore, support can come in many forms, including tutoring, mentoring, programs for addiction recovery, providing legal assistance, and, in addition, religious education or programs specifically designed to nurture spiritual development. The focus of these organizations is usually on underprivileged populations.

The methods used by faith-based service organizations are varied. For example, Victory Outreach in Los Angeles is an extremely effective recovery program that helps men and women recover from addiction through faith conversion and spiritual growth. In contrast, Industrial Areas Foundation (IAF) organizes communities in a way that politically empowers underrepresented members of society, and in the South Bronx, the Urban Youth Alliance, a 30-year-old faith-based organization, provides after-school programs that include mentoring, counseling, recreation, and church and educational programming for neighborhood gang youth.

Although religious congregations have been at the heart of American public life since its inception, the terms *faith-based service organization* and *faith-based initiative* have gained increased prominence only in the past decade. For centuries service has always been central to the mission of religious institutions. They have fed and clothed the poor, offered guidance and counseling, and educated individuals. Today, their ability to effectively meet the complex issues facing youth and families has become identified as an important community asset within our society.

This is especially true in urban areas. Government officials, policy makers, foundations, and community organizations have begun to recognize that faith-based organizations are uniquely positioned within their neighborhoods to distribute social services to those in need. Congregations are often a natural resource for reaching their community. They are often highly trusted and regarded. They have a donor base, a committed core of volunteers, and their clergy have an intimate knowledge of the needs and habits of their neighbors.

Donald Miller and his colleagues at the Center for Religion and Civic Culture at the University of Southern California were among the first to document the important role faith-based organizations can play in addressing societal needs. They documented the central work done by faith-based organizations in rebuilding neighborhoods in south central Los Angeles after the Rodney King Riots in April 1992. After neighborhoods were devastated during the riots, faith-based organizations were among the first to provide resources for community redevelopment—by offering medical services, loans to start small businesses, and after-school programs for children.

To highlight the value of faith-based service organizations, President George W. Bush established a White House Task Force on Community and Faith-Based Organizations early on in his administration. The work of the task force led to the establishment of the U.S. Department of Health and Human Services Center for Faith and Community-Based Initiatives.

Significant controversy has surrounded the government's advocacy for legislation to provide federal funding for organizations with religious affiliations because some fear this kind of government support goes against the American democratic system of keeping church and state separate. Despite fears, in 2002 the U.S. Department of Health and Human Services established a Center on Faith and Community-Based Initiatives whose purpose is to fund local organizations that achieve valid public purposes such as decreasing violence, strengthening families, and improving neighborhoods.

Faith-based service organizations or initiatives can take on many shapes and sizes. They can refer to single congregations that offer particular services in its community, or they can refer to broad coalitions of congregations and government agencies—such as law enforcement agencies that offer alternative programs for juvenile offenders.

Faith-based service organizations appear to have much to offer for a variety of reasons. Their roots in the community provide opportunities to build strategic partnerships within the community, leverage resources, build financial and community support, recruit volunteers, attract participants, and implement programs. Furthermore, the fact that they are faith based serves to attract and engage certain participants as well as provide motivation and support for staff, volunteers, and the youth and adults who are served.

Faith-based organizations generally are faced with many legitimate needs including needs for food, clothing, and shelter. However, those that become effective service organizations usually are those that have a specific focus as to the services they provide. Having a specific focus sometimes provides a rallying point for congregations of different faiths. Although Muslims and Jews may not share the same doctrinal beliefs, and though in some parts of the world they may be enemies, when there is a faith-based service organization with a specific, needed focus, Muslims and Jews work together for the welfare of the children, adolescents, and adults in the neighborhood.

Faith-based programs intend to impact and transform the lives of their participants and their community. Sometimes the transformation intended is of a religious nature, and sometimes it is not. Although personal transformation through religious faith is often the ultimate goal, faith-based organizations recognize that there are many changes in the lives of their participants that are worth pursuing that are not necessarily religious in the narrow meaning of the term. In sum, regardless of their mission and size, faith-based service organizations are community-serving ministries that leverage faith or religion to be effective in the lives of individuals and in their communities.

—Pamela Ebstyne King

FURTHER READING

Berndt, J., & Miller, D. (2000). *Politics of the spirit: Portraits.* Los Angeles: Center for Religion and Civic Culture, University of Southern California.

Orr, J. B., Miller, D. E., Roof, W. C., & Melton, J. G. (1995). *Politics of the spirit: Religion and multi-ethnicity in Los Angeles.* Los Angeles: University of Southern California.

Trulear, H. D. (2000). *Faith-based institutions and high-risk youth: First report to the field.* Philadelphia: Public Private Ventures.

FAITH MATURITY

Numerous and diverse attempts have been made to measure religious and spiritual beliefs, practices, commitments, and attitudes. Each measure has a unique purpose, perspective, and operating assumptions and each contributes unique understanding to this rich and complex domain of life.

The Faith Maturity Scale (FMS), developed by Peter L. Benson and colleagues at Search Institute is a psychometrically robust construct that has been used in multiple studies of both adults and adolescents. Though primarily used with Catholic, Evangelical, and Protestant Christians in the United States and Canada, it has subsequently been utilized in and adapted for other religious traditions and cultures. In addition to its scientific validity with adolescents, college students, and adults across denominations and cultures, its grounding in the perspectives of congregational leaders and members also gives it particular value for reflection and planning.

Rather than measuring faith itself, FMS focuses on what Benson, Donahue, and Erickson describe as "the degree to which a person embodies the priorities, commitments, and perspectives characteristic of vibrant and life-transforming faith, as these have been understood in mainline Protestant traditions." Thus, in this model, faith is a way of living, not just knowledge of or adherence to doctrine, dogma, or tradition. This distinction sets this scale apart from most scales of personal religiosity, which emphasize orthodox beliefs and ritualistic practices, or the process of spiritual or faith development, not the substance of faith as manifested in daily life.

At the core of the FMS is an understanding of faith as having "vertical" and "horizontal" dimensions, with faith maturity being the integration of the two (*integrated faith*). The vertical dimension emphasizes the self and its relationship to God or the divine, or the inward journey. The horizontal dimension emphasizes obligation and action on the human plane through acts of service and justice, or the outward journey.

In addition, the FMS identifies eight core dimensions of faith that underscore the multidimensionality of faith. A person of mature faith has the following attributes (as developed for the original Protestant Christian sample):

1. Trusts God's saving grace and believes firmly in the humanity and divinity of Jesus.
2. Experiences a sense of personal well-being, security, and peace.
3. Integrates faith and life, seeing work, family, social relationships, and political choices as part of one's religious life.
4. Seeks spiritual growth through study, reflection, prayer, and discussion with others.
5. Seeks to be part of a community of believers in which people give witness to their faith and support and nourish one another.
6. Holds life-affirming values, including commitment to racial and gender equality, affirmation of cultural and religious diversity, and a personal sense of responsibility for the welfare of others.
7. Advocates social and global change to bring about greater social justice.
8. Serves humanity, consistently and passionately, through acts of love and justice.

The original FMS included 38 items that examined these eight dimensions as well as vertical and horizontal faith. Subsequent analyses and studies have developed shorter scales (between 11 and 13 items) that highly correlate with the original 38-item scale. Some of these alternate measures do not include the Christian-specific items, making them appropriate measures across monotheistic religious traditions. Various studies using these condensed measures have found faith maturity to be related to emotional maturity, personal meaning, and prosocial behavior (even after controlling for the effects of personality), secure attachment styles, and a nurturing family environment. These findings suggest that the FMS offers unique insight into human functioning, not just a repackaging or "religifying" of existing constructs.

The original study of U.S. mainline Protestant congregations found that 64% of youth (grades 6 through 12) had an undeveloped faith (low in both the horizontal and vertical dimensions), with only 11% of youth having an integrated faith (high on both dimensions). In addition, faith maturity tends to decline (cross-sectionally) during adolescence. Subsequent studies with Evangelical Christian youth (Seventh-Day Adventist and Lutheran Church–Missouri Synod) in the United States found somewhat higher levels of integrated faith (22% and 25%, respectively). Among mainline Protestant adults in the United States, levels of integrated faith were found to increase from 16% among young adults (ages 20–29) to as high as 57% for older adults (age 70+).

Just as important as mapping faith maturity among youth and adults, the FMS has been used widely as an outcome measure for understanding congregational effectiveness (instead of focusing only on financial strength or numerical growth as signs of health) and other contributing factors. Various studies point to the importance of family religious practices in nurturing faith maturity in both youth and adults. In addition, a wide range of congregational variables are associated with growth in faith maturity, including a caring climate, a climate that encourages thinking, and programming that engages both youth and adults in effective educational practices. Thus, several religious bodies and organizations from a wide range of Christian traditions have utilized the framework as a tool for designing their strategies for education and nurture with children and adolescents, guiding curriculum and program development as well as being utilized in seminary education of clergy and religious educators.

In addition, the scale offers a tool for meaningful dialogue among young people and adults about multiple dimensions of their spiritual journey that move beyond discussions of belief or dogma. In doing so, it helps young people internalize spiritual and religious practices that both engage them in cultivating their relationship with God (the "vertical" dimension) while actively engaging in acts of compassion and justice in the world (the "horizontal" dimension). Thus, by articulating a multidimensional understanding of faith and the spiritual life that resonates with scripture as well as human experience, the FMS has become a valuable tool for enriching the religious and spiritual lives of children, adolescents, and adults.

—Eugene C. Roehlkepartain

FURTHER READING

Benson, P. L., Donahue, M. J., & Erickson, J. A. (1993). The Faith Maturity Scale: Conceptualization, measurement, and empirical validation. *Research in the Social Scientific Study of Religion, 5*, 1–26.

Benson, P. L., & Eklin, C. H. (1990). *Effective Christian education: A national study of Protestant congregations: A summary on faith, loyalty, and congregational life*. Minneapolis, MN: Search Institute.

Erickson, J. A. (1992). Adolescent religious development and commitment: A structural equation model of the role of family, peer group, and educational influences. *Journal for the Scientific Study of Religion, 31*(2), 131–152.

Piedmont, R. L., & Nelson, R. (2001). A psychometric evaluation of the short form of the Faith Maturity Scale. *Research in the Social Scientific Study of Religion, 12,* 165–183.

Roehlkepartain, E. C. (1993). *The teaching church: Moving Christian education to center stage.* Nashville, TN: Abingdon Press.

Tisdale, T. C. (1999). Faith Maturity Scale. In P. C. Hill, & R. W. Hood, Jr. (Eds.), *Measures of religiosity* (pp. 171–174). Birmingham, AL: Religious Education Press.

FASTING

Fasting is refraining from bodily nourishment. Fasts vary according to degree, duration, and purpose. A complete fast is one in which all food and liquids are refused. More often, fasting is refraining from food, or limiting its amount, while continuing to drink water. A kind of selective fasting, sometimes called *abstinence* in technical religious terminology, is abstaining from only certain types of food or drink, such as meat or alcohol. Avoiding things other than food or drink is also sometimes called *fasting*, as in "fasting from television," but this usage goes beyond the typical definition of fasting.

The duration of a fast may extend from a single eating event to a few days to a lifetime. Fasts may be seasonal, such as Jewish Yom Kippur, Christian Lent's 40-day fast, or Muslim Ramadan's lunar month, or fasts may be tailored to more individual needs.

Fasting is an almost universal spiritual impulse usually tied to public or private religious observances. Of the ascetic spiritual practices, fasting is the most common and universal. Religions from all over the world, including Hinduism, Jainism, Buddhism, Native American religion, Judaism, Christianity, and Islam, practice fasting as an ascetic discipline of self-denial.

FASTING AS A SPIRITUAL PRACTICE

Most fasting worldwide has been and is practiced for spiritual reasons, but not all fasting is motivated by spiritual concerns. Dieters fast to lose weight or to purge the body of impurities. Persons go on hunger strikes to obtain political goals. Certain illnesses are associated with fasting, such as anorexia nervosa. As religious observance has declined in parts of the modern world, fasting for nonreligious goals has increased. Of course, fasts may include a combination of motives.

For Purification. Perhaps the most ancient purpose for fasting is purification through loosening the grip of physical matter on the spirit. Many religions, old and new, hold a dualistic view of reality. Spirit is good; matter is bad. Fasting within this context is a means to free the spirit from the body and the food and drink upon which it depends for nourishment.

In its most extreme form, the dualist purification motive may allow religiously sanctioned fatal fasting. In Hinduism, the rare and conditional practice of fasting to death is called *Prayopavesa*, salekhana is its counterpart in Jainism, and heretical Christian Albigenses of the Middle Ages practiced a life-ending fast called the *endura*.

The Abrahamic faiths—Judaism, Christianity, and Islam—are not dualistic in nature. In these faiths, fasting is a means of being purified from evil or wrongdoing, but not by separation from the body, a part of God's good creation to be purified as well.

For Protection and Self-Control. Another ancient reason for fasting is protection from evil. Mourning and fasting are closely related in many religious traditions. The origins of this connection lie in purification that comes from fasting, protecting from the evil spirits associated with death.

This protection motif in fasting applies as well to assistance against internal destructive passions. The fourth century Christian monk John the Dwarf compared the effects of fasting upon inner passions to a king cutting off food and water to his enemies through a siege. Such internal victories increase one's power and self-control.

For Penance. The practice of self-denial as punishment is penance. Fasting is used as penance to reestablish right relationships lost through disobedience. For example, the 11th chapter of the Hindu Laws of Mandu, a text from about 500 B.C.E., names various kinds of penance, including fasting, for certain violations of law. The penance for stealing wood, clothes, or molasses is a 3-day fast.

Christianity tied punishment for wrongdoing to repentance for sin, a necessity for justification under God. Third-century Christians practiced fasting as part of public penance. Forgiveness for sins against God and humanity is offered freely through grace, but the forgiven offered restitution through penance, often expressed as fasting. Though Protestant Christianity abandoned formal penance, the connection between fasting and repentance has remained strong in most Christian traditions.

Preparation for Divine Encounter. Fasting that purifies, protects, and justifies easily comes to be understood as a practice that prepares individuals or communities for contact with the divine. Fasting to prepare for worship is an example of self-denial creating space for encounter with the divine. The Jewish faith called for fasting on the Day of Atonement. Most Christian traditions encourage fasting before taking the Eucharist. Native Americans, such as the Lakotas, employ fasting in preparation for the Vision Quest, a search for a life and purpose through contact with the divine Source. The Islam's Qur'an gives as the main reason for fasting "so that you may attain taqwa or God-consciousness."

To Know the Self. Self-denial leads to self-knowledge. Fasting brings self-discovery as it stirs the inner passions. Irritability, impatience, anger, and anxiety as well as mental clarity, calmness, and empathy often arise during fasting. The fast becomes a solvent revealing underlying emotions and motives. Mahatma Gandhi said, "What the eyes are for the outer world, fasts are for the inner."

Voluntary separation from nourishment reminds those fasting of the conditional nature of their everyday existence. The spiritual counterpart of this realization is recognition of dependence upon divine resources.

This goes far toward explaining the intimate connection between fasting and prayer, so central to Judaism and Christianity, as well as some other faiths. Fasting leads to experience of dependence upon the Other for the most basic of needs; prayer issues naturally from this intimate awareness of divine necessity.

To Do Justice. Voluntary fasting, which awakens one to knowledge of the self's dependence upon the Other, often leads naturally to recognizing the needs of others. This fasting-induced empathy brings an ethical dimension to fasting in world religions that emphasize justice in the divine character. Jews, Christians, and Muslims encourage their followers to allow hunger pains arising during fasting to prompt them to remember the poor whose hunger is involuntary. Preaching on fasting, Augustine of Hippo wrote, "Let the voluntary want of the person who has plenty become the needed plenty of the person in want."

In Obedience and Imitation. The lives of certain exemplary figures, often called *saints*, reveal the benefits of fasting. Their disciples often fast in obedience to and imitation of such revered figures. Muhammad's example is codified in the dawn-to-dusk month-long fast of Ramadan, one of the Five Pillars (or duties) of Islam. Jesus, who never commanded fasting but seemed to assume it (Matt. 6:16–18), fasted for 40 days in the desert, and the Christian church institutionalized a 40-day fast in Lent, citing his example.

GENERAL CONSIDERATIONS

As a spiritual practice, fasting is typically a means of readying the self to encounter and serve the divine. Though fasting may be motivated by desire to increase personal power and perception, most world religions shun any ascetic practice that turns in upon itself rather than reaching out toward the divine and service to others.

Finally, fasting is a spiritual practice with clear physical consequences that must be given their due. Consideration of health conditions, such as diabetes, before fasting is important. Absolute fasts from both food and water are best limited to a few days at most, and lengthy fasts should be accompanied by a physician's advice. Many resources with common sense advice about the practical aspects of fasting are available and should be referred to by those who participate in this spiritual practice.

—*Wm. Loyd Allen*

FORGIVENESS

Transgressions violate people's psychological or physical boundaries. People can deal with transgressions by seeking to reestablish justice or redress the injustice. They may do this by enacting revenge (i.e., vigilante justice) or by appealing to some formal system to reestablish societal justice—such as judicial, criminal, political, or social justice. They may seek personal justice in the form of receiving an apology or restitution, or they might turn judgment over to a divine power to bring justice about.

People might also respond to transgressions by trying to control their emotions. They might forebear the transgression. Forebearing is withstanding and perhaps suppressing anger and hatred while controlling negative emotions. People might also simply accept the transgressions and the injustice and move on with their life. Acceptance acknowledges injustice and its ill effects but reduces the future importance of the event in governing one's behavior. It releases one from emotion by giving up one's expectations for the redress of injustice. People might reduce injustice through narrative approaches by excusing or justifying transgressions against themselves. Essentially, they tell a different story about the transgression.

Finally, people might deal with injustice by forgiving. *Emotional forgiveness* is the emotional replacement of negative unforgiving emotions (like bitterness, resentment, and anger) by positive other-oriented emotions such as empathy, sympathy, compassion, or love. When people forgive, their negative emotions subside. They are less motivated to get revenge or avoid the transgressor, and if forgiving is complete, they might feel love, compassion, sympathy, or empathy for the transgressor. Some people grant *decisional forgiveness*. They decide not to seek revenge or to avoid the transgressor even though they might not have emotionally forgiven him or her. Decisional forgiveness is a sincere statement about controlling one's future behavior. Forgiveness may be initiated by reasoning, simply experiencing positive other-oriented emotions toward the transgressor, acting kindly toward the transgressor, or having the transgressor act contritely or in a way that provokes empathy, sympathy, compassion, or love.

A child can be induced to grant decisional forgiveness at very early ages. Parents can model and instruct children to foreswear avoidance and revenge through decisional forgiveness. By controlling his or her negative behavior the child might even experience changed negative emotions and motivations, thus come to emotionally forgive. But the child also might not experience emotional forgiveness in tandem with decisional forgiveness.

Robert Enright and his colleagues have conducted substantial research on the development of reasoning about forgiveness. They identified six stages of development of how people reason about forgiveness. Enright's stages, which emphasize mercy, parallel Lawrence Kohlberg's six stages of reasoning about justice. The timetables of development of reasoning about justice and mercy are also parallel.

In Enright's model, very young children think that forgiveness will help them avoid punishment (Stage 1) or get rewards (Stage 2). As children progress into middle childhood and early adolescence, they learn to grant forgiveness and perhaps experience emotional forgiveness after reasoning that considers social disapproval and approval for their responses to transgressions. Only in adolescence and beyond are children thought to be capable of reasoning abstractly about forgiveness. In some ways, the consideration of how children develop the capacity to reason about forgiveness is less important than whether children actually *experience* forgiveness after a transgression. One's capacity to forgive (for instance) at Stage 5 does not imply that one will ever actually forgive. We all know brilliant adults who are spiteful, bitter, unforgiving, and vindictive.

Substantial research has shown that emotional unforgiveness has negative effects on people's mental health, physical health, and relationships and perhaps on their spiritual lives. Therefore, if people are to benefit from forgiving a transgressor, one important question is not When can children learn to grant decisional forgiveness? (Answer: Very young, if parents emphasize and enforce granting decisional forgiveness.) Nor is it When are children capable of mature reasoning about forgiveness? (Answer: Sophistication of reasoning changes with age.) Rather the important questions are

- When do children actually experience emotional forgiveness?
- How can parents and teachers facilitate their emotional experience?
- What factors determine how quickly the experience of emotional forgiveness develops?
- What factors affect whether children actually forgive emotionally when they are transgressed against?

Clearly, the capacity to reason in such a way that a child concludes that one *should* forgive can be important to whether he or she emotionally forgives. To reason that one should forgive for reasons more socially motivated than motivated by rewards and punishments will also affect how children and adolescents think about and try to experience forgiving. So, development of reasoning capacities is not unimportant to actually forgiving.

However, by understanding forgiveness as an emotional replacement of negative with positive emotions leads us to understand the development of forgiveness as being more complex than mere obedience or as being primarily a function of cognitive development. Other developmental considerations that are in line with the child's emotional development are important to understanding whether children actually forgive and at which ages.

First, temperament is important. Babies often develop easy, difficult, slow-to-warm-up, or mixed temperaments by 3 months. If emotional forgiveness is seen more as an emotional replacement than as a cognitive decision, we might note that babies with easy temperaments can legitimately be considered to be emotionally forgiving. The mother delays a diaper change: No problem. All is quickly forgiven by easy babies. In difficult babies the crankiness persists and may generalize. Obviously, there is no cognitive understanding of forgiveness, but emotional unforgiveness has been replaced with positive emotions toward the mother. Reasoning thusly, even infants emotionally forgive (in a primitive way), and some infants are more temperamentally geared for it than are other infants.

Second, childhood attachment to parental love objects should be expected to influence the degree to which children experience emotional forgiveness. Children who develop insecure attachment styles, which do not facilitate close relationships, are not expected to be heavily invested in experiencing forgiveness. Those with secure attachment styles are likely to value relationships more as they age. They thus try to preserve and restore them by emotionally (and decisionally) forgiving.

Third, from the early months of a child's life, emotion regulation occurs. Even babies at the youngest ages learn to emotionally down regulate negative emotions by self-soothing, calming, and distracting themselves from their frustrations. As children age, their repertoire of emotion-regulation strategies becomes more varied and sophisticated. The repertoire of emotion-regulation strategies that children develop differs across children. Those children who develop, even in their preschool years, an early sense of empathy, sympathy, compassion, and unselfish love for others are expected to be able to experience emotional forgiveness more quickly than are children who develop such capacities later or become impaired in those capacities.

Fourth, coaching from their parents can help children broaden and deepen their emotion-regulation strategies. Through emotion coaching, parents convey their meta-emotional philosophy to children. They directly and indirectly tell and show children what emotions are acceptable to experience and to express. They train children in how to deal with emotion-provoking experiences—notably (for our purposes) transgressions.

Fifth, people encounter stress throughout their lives. Stressors make demands for change. Children appraise the stressors and respond to their appraisals with stress reactions; or they respond to physical stressors, sometimes without appraisal. They try to cope with both situations and their own reactions. Some stress reactions are unpleasant and prompt children to employ problem-focused or emotion-focused coping strategies. Problem-focused coping strategies seek to solve the problem and deal directly with the stressor. Emotion-focused coping strategies seek to manage negative emotions. The development of a repertoire of emotion-focused coping strategies will facilitate or hamper forgiving depending on what types of coping strategies the child practices.

For example, a child who sees God as a hostile authority figure might be less likely to respond with forgiveness to someone who had offended him or her (especially to a parent, caregiver, or other authority figure) than would a child who perceives God to be nurturing and collaborative. Psychologist Kenneth Pargament (McCullough, Pargament, & Thoresen, 2000) has identified numerous religious and spiritual coping strategies. These religious and spiritual coping strategies—such as praying, meditating, and making positive attributions to God—can affect the capacity of the child to forgive. Prayer as a coping strategy might be more available to older children than to younger children, which demonstrates development as well.

Sixth, the religious and spiritual environment in the home will likely also affect the child's development of the experience of emotional forgiveness. Forgiveness (decisional or emotional), in response to a transgression, is valued by every major religion. It is generally considered to be the centerpiece of the Christian religion. Some religions firmly advocate decisional forgiveness and emphasize controlling one's negative behavior. Research scientists have found this to be most characteristic of Judaism and Islam. Other religions (notably Christianity) advocate emotional forgiveness in addition to decisional forgiveness. Buddhism promotes compassion and detachment from vengefulness, thus promoting emotional forgiveness (though most forms of Buddhism do not use the word *forgiveness*).

Religion and spirituality have been found to be correlated with forgiveness in adults. Membership in a religious denomination, which involves a belief system that values forgiveness more or less strongly, will determine some underlying cognitive, emotional, and behavioral structures of parents, which they transmit to and teach their children. Spirituality, the personal intensity with which parents adhere to their belief system involving the sacred, will affect the ways and frequency that children are exposed to demonstrations of forgiveness—decisional and emotional—as well as the importance they give it. Forgiveness has been shown to be related to religion in a variety of studies. Forgiveness has not yet been thoroughly investigated in terms of its relationship to spirituality.

Altogether then, we can see that children probably learn to grant forgiveness largely depending on the parents' belief system, their practice of encouraging and rewarding the child's expression of decisional forgiveness after being transgressed against, and their modeling of decisional forgiveness. However, the development of the experiencing of emotional forgiveness (in contrast to granting decisional forgiveness) is substantially less due to external demands from parents. Instead, it is highly related to the climate within the parent-child relationship, which affects the child's temperament, emotion-regulation capability, parental meta-emotional philosophy, cognitive development of the ability to reason about justice and forgiveness, repertoire of ways of coping with stress, and religious and spiritual environment.

—Everett L. Worthington, Jr.

See also Attachment

FURTHER READING

Enright, R. D., & Fitzgibbons, R. (2000). *Helping clients forgive.* Washington, D.C.: APA Books.

McCullough, M. E., Pargament, K. I., & Thoresen, C. E. (Eds.). (2000). *Forgiveness: Theory, research, and practice.* New York: Guilford.

Worthington, E. L., Jr. (2003). *Forgiving and reconciling: Bridges to wholeness and hope.* Downer's Grove, IL: InterVarsity Press.

FOWLER, JAMES

James Fowler is well-known in the United States and beyond for his faith development theory. His groundbreaking book of 1981, *Stages of Faith,* with its 35 printings and several translations has inspired theory and research in religious studies worldwide. More than 80 dissertations focusing on Fowler's theory and research, half of them using his research instrument or a variation thereof, are an indication of the growing attraction of faith-development theory. Two characteristics in particular make Fowler's theory interesting: its open and inclusive concept of faith as meaning making—which, while akin to the concept of spirituality, has the potential of qualifying spirituality—and its detailed analysis of changes of faith occurring during childhood, adolescence, and adulthood.

BIOGRAPHICAL INFORMATION

Fowler's background is theology. He earned his Ph.D. in 1971 at Harvard University in Religion and Society with a dissertation on the work of the theologian H. Richard Niebuhr. After teaching at Harvard Divinity School (1969–1975), postdoctoral research at Harvard's Center for Moral Development, and teaching at Boston College (1975–1976), Fowler joined the faculty of Candler School of Theology at Emory University in 1977. He was named a Candler Professor in 1987, and he established and directed the Center for Research on Faith and Moral Development and has served as Director of Emory's Center for Ethics and Public Policy since 1994. His winning the Oscar Pfister Award from the American Psychiatric Association (1994) and the William James Award from the American Psychological Association (1994) indicates Fowler's recognition in the field of psychology. The *honoris causa* doctor of divinity awarded from the University of Edinburgh in 1999 indicates again Fowler's worldwide recognition in theology.

FAITH IN INTERDISCIPLINARY PERSPECTIVE

Both theology and psychology come together in Fowler's thinking. This is obvious from the basic definitions in faith development theory. In terms of theology, the perspectives of Paul Tillich and H. Richard Niebuhr have influenced Fowler's concept of faith. Tillich and Niebuhr teach us to ask for faith by asking questions like the following: What is the ultimate value and power? To whom am I finally loyal? What am I ultimately concerned about? What gives my life meaning? The work of William Cantwell Smith, a great theorist of religion from a cross-cultural perspective, has also been important for Fowler in obtaining further clarification of this open concept of faith and its demarcation from belief and religion.

In terms of psychology, we see a strong impact from Erik H. Erikson's psychoanalytic view on religion and human development and of psychoanalyst Ana-Maria Rizzuto's developmental account of representations of God, especially in Fowler's 1996 book. However, most influential for Fowler's theory and research has been the theory and research of Lawrence Kohlberg, the well-known developmental psychologist at Harvard University who, influenced by the work of Jean Piaget, constructed a cognitive-structural theory of moral development. It is safe to conclude that Fowler owes his groundbreaking inspiration to envision a developmental schema of faith to his cooperation with Kohlberg. Fowler's concept of faith has, then, received its most characteristic imprint from the Piaget/Kohlberg tradition: Faith as meaning making is understood as a special type of knowing, namely *constitutive* knowing. Comparing Kohlberg's theory of moral development and Fowler's theory of faith development, one encounters striking parallels. The two theorists debated about whether moral development precedes faith development, or vice versa.

FAITH DEVELOPMENT

Faith, according to Fowler, undergoes several significant reconstructions during one's life and may proceed progressively through six distinct stages. Since Fowler has given these stages illustrative names, it is informative to attend to this terminology: Faith develops from an *intuitive-projective* style (Stage 1) in infancy and early childhood to the *mythic-literal* style (Stage 2), which we should not expect before the age of 6 or 7; the plasticity of a vivid and open imagination turns into a preoccupation with order, narrative realism, and literal truth. *Synthetic-conventional* faith (Stage 3) can be expected to emerge after age 11 for a majority of individuals. Here, the conventions of one's religious community and the distinction between *we* and *they* dominate, and the image of God is structured in terms of personal relations. Not before early adulthood—and not all individuals are expected to reach this stage—the *individuative-reflective* faith (Stage 4) may develop. In this stage, individuals construct an explicit system of knowledge about their religion and defend it even in opposition to their own groups and traditions.

According to Fowler's perspective, Stages 1 through 3 are in the foreground of spiritual development during childhood and adolescence. The stage transition from mythic-literal faith to synthetic-conventional faith is an especially major issue for children in primary and middle school age. The struggle with the emerging individuative-reflective style of faith has its primary time in middle and late adolescence.

FAITH DEVELOPMENT BEYOND THE INDIVIDUATIVE-REFLECTIVE STYLE

It is Fowler's central assumption that development must not come to an end with Stage 4. In *conjunctive* faith (Stage 5), structures of dialogue, a thinking style of complementarity, and the appreciation of the other and potentially strange religions have overcome and left behind the rigors of defending the autonomy and reflective absolutism of Stage 4. Finally, the examples of Martin Luther King, Mother Theresa, and Mahatma Gandhi illustrate the humility and total personal investment of sacrificing one's life for others and for the sake of humanity, which is characteristic of *universalizing* faith (Stage 6). Despite the fact that relatively few individuals develop a conjunctive style of faith—and universalizing faith in particular is extremely rare—these final stages are of crucial importance for Fowler's theory as they indicate the direction and the aim of faith development. In the profile of these final stages, faith development theory aims toward an answer to the predicament of modern religious culture in our Western societies between exclusive truth claims and careless relativism—an answer which, according to Fowler, corresponds to the theological vision expressed by the metaphor of the Kingdom of God.

FAITH DEVELOPMENT RESEARCH

Fowler is not only a theological and psychological theorist but also an empirical researcher. The empirical foundation of his major book, published in1981, consists of the considerable body of 359 faith development interviews. Research in faith development consists of an open-ended interview guided by a list of key questions about present and past relationships, about present values and commitments, and about religion. The answers are audio-recorded, transcribed, and then interpreted sentence by sentence to determine the stage of faith in each answer and finally in the entire interview.

THEOLOGICAL GROUNDING

The majority of Fowler's publications after *Stages of Faith* focus on a theological reinterpretation and grounding of faith development theory. This can be understood as a response to theological critics of faith development theory who diagnosed a lack of theological foundation in Fowler's 1981 book. Fowler's texts between 1984 and 1996 addressed themes such as vocation, the environment of the church, issues of religious and public education, questions of pastoral care in relation to faith development, and themes such as shame and guilt. In many of these contributions, however, we see the architect of faith development theory engage in correlations with psychological perspectives, among them Robert Keagan's theory of the *Evolving Self* and Ana-Maria Rizzuto's psychoanalytic view.

The inclusiveness of the concept of faith and of the theory of faith development point to a characteristic trait of Fowler's thinking which has attracted many colleagues in theology, religious studies, and psychology of religion and inspired them to welcome and advance theory and research in faith development.

—*Heinz Streib*

FURTHER READING

Fowler, J. W. (1981). *Stages of faith. The psychology of human development and the quest for meaning*. San Francisco: Harper&Row.

Fowler, J. W. (1996). *Faithful change. The personal and public challenges of postmodern life*. Nashville, TN: Abingdon Press.

Streib, H. (2003). Faith development research at twenty years. In R. R. Osmer & F. Schweitzer (Eds.), *Faith development and public life*. St. Louis, MO: Chalice Press.

FOX, GEORGE

George Fox was the founder of the Religious Society of Friends, commonly known as the Quakers because they were said to quake before the Lord. Always a seeker of wisdom, Fox finally discovered that true wisdom from God was to be found within rather than outside of oneself. His story is one of a seeker pursuing divine wisdom, only to discover wisdom was to be found within, in his own "Inner Light." Fox came from humble means, was imprisoned many times, but in the end left an important legacy in the history of Christianity.

Fox was born in 1624 in Leicestershire, England into very simple circumstances. His father was a weaver, and he himself eventually took up shoemaking. The church of his day left him unsatisfied and seeking more. He was a serious young man in his teens and was put off by any form of hypocrisy and/or deceit. In his *Journal* he tells of one episode at the age of 19 where he was at a party. The drunken behavior of these "nominal" Christians so disgusted him that he knew he needed to find something more. In 1643 he left home and traveled around England looking for enlightenment.

In 1646 Fox discovered what he called the "Inner Light of the Living Christ" already within him. In moments of stillness and contemplation that Inner Light would reveal itself to him, and to any others who sought after it. He believed that this inner enlightenment was a form of revelation, like the scriptures. Therefore he believed that God's revelation was not limited to the Bible but continued to come from the Holy Spirit to each believer. He argued that the Church of England did not have any special authority to mediate God's voice. Its ordained clergy had no special revelation from God and therefore were not necessary for knowing God. He was very critical of the professional ministry of his day and argued anyone can minister if God has illuminated his or her Inner Light. Likewise, he began to criticize the liturgical worship of the Church. He argued that if one was right with God on the inside and could hear that inner voice, then there was no need for such things as the Eucharist and baptism.

Fox began to travel around preaching this message in 1647, trying to persuade others that truth is found in the inner voice of God that speaks to each and every soul. Fox continued to discount the need for the clergy of his day and argued against what he called artificial titles and the swearing of oaths. Two very important points that distanced Fox from the other nonconformists of his day were his rejection of slavery and the declaration that war of any sort is unlawful for any Christian. These ideas did not sit well with the English authorities and the Church of England, and by 1649 he found himself thrown into prison in Nottingham.

It was in a courtroom that the name *Quaker* came into usage for the Friends. Fox and his followers had thought of themselves as the Society of Friends based on Jesus' words found in John 15:15 where Jesus said to his followers, "I have called you friends." While in court, a judge asked Fox if he was a part of the group known as Quakers. To this Fox was reported to have replied that all must tremble and quake at the Word of the Lord, and so yes, he was a Quaker in the sense that he quaked because of God's holiness. From this point forward The Society of Friends referred to themselves as Quakers as well as Friends.

Fox was eventually released and settled at Swarthmore Hall, home of Judge Thomas and Margaret Fell. Here Fox had a base to operate from, and spent time writing and traveling from there. In 1652 the Friends had their first community, or Meeting House as it was called, in Preston Patrick in northern England. By 1654, Quakers had spread to London, Bristol, and Norwich. By this time Swarthmore Hall had become the official headquarters for the preachers of the Religious Society of Friends. Fox continued to operate out of Swarthmore and after the death of Thomas Fell, Fox married his widow, Margaret, in 1669.

Quakers continued to face opposition both in England and in North America. By 1661 more than 3,000 Friends had been imprisoned, including Fox, who spent 8 months at the Launceston prison in 1656. In the end he spent eight different terms in various prisons during his lifetime. Quakers were always defiant, and unlike many of the other dissenting traditions of 17th century England, they refused to meet in secret.

Fox instilled a strong missionary spirit in the new movement. The movement sent missionaries to places like Jerusalem, The West Indies, Germany, Austria, and Holland. Fox himself traveled to Ireland in 1669, the West Indies and North America in 1671 and 1672, and to Holland in both 1677 and 1684. The Quaker influence became particularly strong in North America when William Penn, a Quaker, founded Pennsylvania in 1681 as an experiment in religious liberty and pacifism.

Fox died on January 13, 1691. While his influence might have seemed small at the time in terms of the number of adherents to Quakerism, his ideas have lived on. The world became more familiar with Fox when his *Journal* was published posthumously in 1694. Through the influence of his writings and his followers, slavery never had the same pervasive existence in England as it did in North America. His pacifistic message has always been a part of the Quakers and is still a distinguishing characteristic to this day. Other than Baptists, no other group to grow out of the unsettled times of 17th century England remain as organized, and much of this is due to the work of George Fox.

The ministries' of the Society of Friends today continue the work begun by Fox. Numbers are hard to determine with the fluidity of the beliefs and practices of the Society of Friends, but there are approximately 300,000 Friends worldwide. Of those, 17,000 are in Fox's home country of England, while about 93,000 are in the United States. These followers of Fox are divided into three main groups today, the Friends General Conference, The Friends United Meeting, and the Evangelical Friends International. These groups are involved in a variety of ministries around the world with Meeting Houses on every continent. They seek to provide spiritual growth through a variety of educational and retreat centers. They are especially devoted to social concerns. The Society of Friends seeks to alleviate poverty around the globe; they are also actively involved with orphanages. There is also a strong egalitarian emphasis by the Friends that stretches all the way back to Fox. Because of this the Society of Friends is involved in efforts to stop racism of all types. They are also involved in gender equality and supporting the rights of homosexuals. One of their key values has always been as peace activists and the Friends continue to lead all of Christianity in pacifistic efforts. While the Society of Friends is a small minority in Christianity in terms of the number of members, they continue to be an influential force with a worldwide impact.

—*Gary R. Poe*

See also Quaker Education

FURTHER READING

Fox, G. (1999). *The Journal.* New York: Penguin.

Jones, R. (2003). *George Fox: Seeker and friend.* New York: Kessinger.

Ingle, H. L. (1996). *First among friends: George Fox and the creation of Quakerism.* New York: Oxford University Press.

Steere, D. V. (Ed.). (1984). *Quaker spirituality: Selected writings. Classics of Western spirituality.* New York: Paulist Press.

FREUD, ANNA

Anna Freud (1895–1982) was the youngest of Sigmund Freud's six children and the only one among them who made her father's ideas into her own life work and mission. In 1918, Anna entered psychoanalysis with her father, published her first paper on psychoanalysis in 1922, and finally started practicing as a psychoanalyst in 1923. Being psychoanalyzed by one's own father would not be done today, but in those early days of psychoanalysis it was possible, while causing quite a few murmurs of disbelief. Becoming a psychoanalyst while having no formal education beyond high school would be unbelievable today, but it is to the credit of the public school system in Vienna in the early 20th century that Anna Freud was clearly a well-educated woman, displaying vast knowledge in various fields. Her own intellect, talent, and creativity are beyond dispute.

Sigmund Freud was diagnosed with cancer of the jaw in 1923, and during his 16 years of illness Anna tended her father, and took over many of his functions as he became less able to take care of things. She became General Secretary of the International Psychoanalytical Association and director of the Vienna Psychoanalytical Training Institute. The Freud family fled Austria for England in the summer of 1938, following the Nazi takeover of Austria. Anna lived for the rest of her life in London, where she became more and more involved in the psychological treatment of children. She was more of a practitioner than a theorist, and most of her contributions to the study of personality come out of her work with young children.

Anna Freud followed her father in regarding humans' long dependency in infancy and childhood as the setting that creates both the normal personality and pathology. The dependent child is exposed to the fear of object loss, love loss, and punishment. This creates the conscience and the capacity for compliance, but also neurosis. This long period of dependency, which characterizes humans, is responsible for the capacity for love and attachment to others. It makes the child human and social, and it also creates the capacity for religious and magical practices and beliefs. What the child experiences, together with dependence and helplessness, is love and care from adults, which can lead to the creation of religious ideas (e.g., heaven, salvation).

Anna Freud was among the pioneers of what has become known as *psychoanalytic ego psychology*. According to classical psychoanalytic theory, the structure known as *ego* is the executive center of the personality. It keeps in touch with reality and has to balance and control internal drives and reality constraints.

The ego-psychology theoretical orientation emphasizes not only sexual and aggressive drives but also adaptation and defense, i.e., personal adaptation to the environment and the defense of the ego from internal anxiety and external dangers. Successful adaptation to reality is achieved through both unconscious defense mechanisms and realistic actions. Defense mechanisms act by distorting the nature of a real threat or by avoiding it, thus reducing anxiety. Some ways of using defenses are successful, while others are maladaptive.

Important defense mechanisms are identification, i.e., the unconscious fantasy of internalizing the desired qualities of another; displacement, i.e., the redirection of drives toward more accessible goals; and reaction formation, i.e., the redirection of socially undesirable drives toward socially beneficial goals.

Turning against the self is a very special form of displacement, where the person becomes their own substitute target. It is normally used in reference to hatred, anger, and aggression rather than more positive impulses, and it is the Freudian explanation for many of our feelings of inferiority, guilt, and depression.

Defensive projection, which Anna Freud also called *displacement outward*, is almost the complete opposite of turning against the self. It involves the tendency to see your own unacceptable desires in other people. In other words, the desires are still there, but they are not one's own desires anymore.

According to the ego psychology approach, most human behavior is made up of reactions to anxiety and attempts to cope with them to the best of the ego's ability. Various rituals and magical practices are ways of providing the ego with relief from stressful situations. The ego has to find ways and devices to control anxiety, and religion can be such a way.

Defense mechanisms that play a major role in the development of religious activities include sublimation, i.e., the channeling of aggressive and sexual drives to socially approved activities. Unlike repression, which produces only neurotic symptoms whose meaning is unknown even to the sufferer, sublimation is a conflict-free resolution of repression, which leads to positively valued cultural works. The mechanism of undoing involves magical gestures or rituals that are meant to cancel out unpleasant thoughts or feelings after they have already occurred. It clearly has a major role in many traditional rituals.

According to Anna Freud, adolescent preoccupation with religious ideas is a way of coping with instincts. Sometimes, it is a reflection of adolescent rebellion and its resolution. Religious conversion may be a symptom of such an adolescent crisis and its resolution. At the height of the crisis, the adolescent is in danger of withdrawing from those around him and becoming totally narcissistic. He escapes this danger by convulsive efforts to make contact once more with external objects through passionate identifications.

Psychoanalytic ego psychology has suggested that there is a natural limit to rational reality testing and that the constant tension of keeping in touch with reality may be relieved by opportunities for regression in the service of the ego, e.g., controlled, limited regression from reality that is found in art and religion. This relatively new concept intends to remind us that not every regression is pathological, and this kind of limited regression may reflect flexibility and creativity. Regression in the service of the ego may play an important role in religious behavior.

—Benjamin Beit-Hallahmi

See also Freud, Sigmund; Object Relations Theory; Psychoanalytic Approaches

FURTHER READING

Freud, A. (1966). *The ego and the mechanisms of defense.* New York : International Universities Press.

FREUD, SIGMUND

Sigmund Freud (1856–1939) was a neurologist who developed an approach to human behavior known as *psychoanalysis*. Freud was a man of enormous learning and huge capacities and talents. His writings, which fill up about 30 volumes, cover all aspects of human experience, culture, and history.

The creation of psychoanalysis offered at once a theory of the human psyche, a therapy for the relief of its ills, and a method for the interpretation of culture and society. Despite repeated criticisms and qualifications of Freud's work, its influence remained powerful well after his death and in fields far removed from psychology as it is narrowly defined.

Sigmund Freud was trained as a physician and was drawn to neurology and psychiatry, but he was always more interested in theory than in practice. After starting his work with neurotic patients, he came to believe that many mental disorders are the product of unconscious conflicts. Freud suggested that humans are born with sexual and aggressive instincts, but starting early on in life, they must repress such desires, driving them away from conscious awareness. Some repressed desires do not disappear but unconsciously haunt our behavior and thoughts. Dreams, slips of the tongue, and neuroses are, Freud argued, distorted reflections of repressed desires that originate in childhood. Psychoanalytic practice aimed to uncover such hidden mental processes. Thus, dreams are the disguised expression of wish fulfillments. Like neurotic symptoms, they are the effects of compromises in the psyche between desires and prohibitions in conflict with their realization. Slips of the tongue and similar everyday errors, Freud claimed, had symptomatic and thus interpretable importance. But unlike dreams, they need not betray a repressed infantile wish, yet they can arise from more immediate hostile, jealous, or egoistic causes.

Another kind of everyday behavior Freud analyzed was humor. Seemingly innocent phenomena like puns are as open to interpretation as more obviously tendentious, obscene, or hostile jokes. The powerful and joyful response often produced by successful humor, Freud contended, owes its power to the release of unconscious impulses, aggressive as well as sexual.

Freud did not invent the idea of the conscious versus unconscious mind, but he certainly was responsible for making it popular. The conscious mind is what you are aware of at any particular moment, your present perceptions, memories, thoughts, fantasies, and feelings. Working closely with the conscious mind is what Freud called the *preconscious*, what we might today call *available memory*: anything that can easily be made conscious, the memories you are not at the moment thinking about but can readily bring to mind. No one has a problem with these two layers of consciousness. Freud suggested that these are the smallest.

The largest part by far is the unconscious. It includes all the things that are not easily available to awareness, including many things that have their origins there, such as our drives or instincts, and things that are put there because we cannot bear to look at them, such as the memories and emotions associated with trauma.

According to Freud, the source of our motivations is unconscious, whether they be simple desires for food or sex, neurotic compulsions, or the motives of an artist or scientist. And yet, we are often driven to deny or resist becoming conscious of these motives, and they are often available to us only in disguised form.

Our personality contains three structures: *id*, *ego*, and *superego*. The id is defined in terms of the most primitive urges for gratification in the infant, urges dominated by the desire for pleasure. Ruled by no laws of logic, indifferent to the demands of expediency, unconstrained by the resistance of external reality, the id is ruled by what Freud called the *primary process* directly expressing somatically generated instincts. Through the inevitable experience of frustration the infant learns to adapt itself to the reality.

The secondary process that results leads to the growth of the ego, which follows what Freud called the *reality principle* in contradistinction to the pleasure principle dominating the id. Here the need to delay gratification in the service of self-preservation is slowly learned in an effort to thwart the anxiety produced by unfulfilled desires. What Freud termed *defense mechanisms* are developed by the ego to deal with such conflicts. Repression is the most fundamental, but Freud also posited an entire repertoire of others, including reaction formation, isolation, undoing, denial, displacement, and rationalization.

The last structure to appear within the personality is the superego, developed from the internalization of society's moral commands through identification with parental dictates. The superego gains its punishing force by borrowing certain aggressive elements in the id, which are turned inward against the ego and produce feelings of guilt. These three structures are involved in the constant internal struggle, where innate instincts are always at war with society and reality. The best that can be hoped for is a temporary truce.

Freud devoted much attention to the development of sexuality in the individual. He described how this development is prone to troubling maladjustments if its various early stages are unsuccessfully negotiated. Confusion about sexual aims or objects can occur at any particular moment, caused either by an actual trauma or the blockage of a powerful urge. If this fixation is allowed to express itself directly at a later age, the result is what was then generally called a *perversion*. If, however, some part of the psyche prohibits such overt expression, then, Freud contended, the repressed and censored impulse produce neurotic symptoms. Neurotics repeat the desired act in repressed form, without conscious memory of its origin or the ability to confront and work it through in the present.

Focusing on the prevalence of human guilt and the impossibility of achieving unalloyed happiness, Freud contended that no social solution of the discontents of mankind is possible. The best to be hoped for is a life in which the repressive burdens of society are in rough balance with the realization of instinctual gratification and the sublimated love for mankind. But reconciliation of nature and culture is impossible, for the price of any civilization is the guilt produced by the necessary thwarting of man's instinctual drives.

Freud's writings are among the most ambitious attempts in history to present a comprehensive interpretation of religion. The topics Freud dealt with include, first of all, a developmental theory of religion, for humanity as a whole and for each individual. Freud also attempted to explain the functions and consequences of religion, for both society and the individual.

Freud's theoretical explanation for the origin and existence of religion is based on certain presumed universal psychological experiences and processes: the universal experience of helplessness, the tendency for compensation through fantasy, and the experience of early relations with protective figures. Every individual is psychologically prepared by these universal experiences to accept religious ideas that are obviously culturally transmitted. The question about the world of spirits is, Does this world exist "out there" and if it does not where is it? The psychological answer given by psychoanalysis, is that it exists within, in our own mental apparatus and our own mental abilities to fantasize and project. The world of spirits, the supernatural world unseen and somehow felt in religious experience, is a projection of the internal world. Psychoanalytic theory explains both the origin of supernaturalist ideas and their specific contents.

Freud's theory does not suggest that the individual creates his religion on his own, out of nothing, but that childhood experiences within the family prepare the individual for the cultural system of religion. Belief in omnipotent gods is a psychic reproduction of the universal state of helplessness in infancy. Like an idealized father, God is the projection of childish wishes for an omnipotent protector. If children can outgrow their dependence, he concluded with cautious optimism, then humanity may also hope to leave behind its prevalent and immature fantasies.

—Benjamin Beit-Hallahmi

See also Freud, Anna; Object Relations Theory; Psychoanalytic Approaches

FURTHER READING

Gay, P. (1995). *Freud: A life for our time.* London: Macmillan.

FUNDAMENTALISM

Fundamentalism originally referred to an American Protestant Christian movement occurring at the turn of the 20th century. Since then the term has been adopted by scholars to refer to a worldwide movement that includes various faith traditions. The usefulness of the term lies in its ability to capture the form and functions of a great many religious groups and to define the essence of their agendas. As used by scholars, the term is meant to describe, not evaluate.

At the heart of fundamentalist movements is their revolt against modernism and their call to return to the fundamentals of their faith traditions, fundamentals defined either in sacred texts such as the Bible and the Qur'an or in the practices of a faith tradition's founder or original community. Fundamentalism refers, then, to protests against developments associated with modernism, protests that are often energetic, sometimes aggressive, and occasionally violent.

Fundamentalists feel that certain developments associated with modernism undermine religious identity and their own religious worldview. They believe these developments undermine the ability to lead a morally pure life and, in some cases, a life that prepares for the afterlife. Their concern is not with developments in technology and science per se but only with those developments that challenge their religious worldview or have moral implications—as when Darwinian evolutionary theory challenged the creationist theory derived from a literal reading of Genesis.

In North America, the term *fundamentalism* has often been used interchangeably with the term *evangelism*—though more so at the beginning of the fundamentalist movement than in recent times. Evangelism refers to the winning or saving of souls. To evangelize, then, means to lead others to becoming saved. North American fundamentalists are, then, all about being saved and saving others—saved by believing in Jesus as the Lord and saved by accepting the Bible as the literal and inerrant word of God.

To be saved, it is not enough to attend church or to try hard to lead a good life. Being saved, say the fundamentalists and evangelicals, entails no less than a total commitment to Christ and a total belief in the Bible. To be a North American Protestant fundamentalist is, then, to embrace a biblical perspective that is clear, free from contradiction, and rejecting of alternative, nonfundamentalist worldviews. Being ecumenical is not, then, a part of the fundamentalist agenda. Therefore, North American Protestant fundamentalism, like other forms of fundamentalism around the world, runs counter to the dominant worldview in most societies today, a worldview that values pluralism and accepts there being multiple perspectives on what is true and valuable.

Nor is it a fundamentalist agenda to promote a separation of religion and state, a separation that has been central in North American and European democratic traditions. This is even more evident in Arab regions of the world where Islamic fundamentalism works to unite societies under Islamic law and under Islamic religious leadership.

Worldwide fundamentalism has, then, been both separatist in spirit and integrationist in political life. That is, while fundamentalists speak of the need to separate one's self from the unsaved and from this sinful or corrupt world; they also speak of the need for human kind to become a single, religious community.

Fundamentalism is not, then, simply about returning to a distant past or living in the present according to truths and prescriptions revealed in the distant past. It is also about working and waiting for an imagined future. In North American Christian fundamentalism, the imagined future is the second coming of Christ or *Parousia*, a time when sinners (nonbelievers) will be judged and the Kingdom of God will be established.

This theme of there being a cataclysmic future event or time when sinners will be judged and the righteous and true believers will prevail is not just a theme in North American Protestant Christian fundamentalism. It is also a theme in non-Christian, non-Western fundamentalist movements. The important point here is, then, not about the Parousia but about the general theme in all fundamentalist movements that today's secular, pluralistic society will be replaced by a monoreligious society.

One particularly controversial aspect of the focus on evangelism has been the recruiting efforts by a few fundamentalist groups on college campuses and in other places where youth gather. These groups have come under attack for their singling out vulnerable youth, for their sometimes using deception to recruit, and for their encouraging new members to separate themselves from the larger community. However, the fundamentalist movement is far broader than these youth-based groups, and so it is not clear whether any generalizations can be made with regard to fundamentalism and youth development.

Fundamentalism has and will continue to appeal to large segments of societies—especially in troubled times and in times of rapid transition. Its greatest appeal is in its offering clarity where there is doubt, order and continuity where there is disorder and discontinuity, and hope for being good and being saved where there is despair about being sinful and being lost.

On the other hand, fundamentalism will likely continue to be rejected by the majority and for several reasons. First, its appeal to return to previous ways runs counter to the majority's desire to develop new ways that reflect new conditions in modern life. Second, its appeal to adopt an uncompromising perspective, one that does not value alternative faith traditions and alternative worldviews, runs counter to the majority's desire to value cultural and religious diversity so as to live harmoniously in a pluralistic society. Third, its appeal to believe in the literal and inerrant truth of sacred texts runs counter to the philosophical and scientific ways of thinking that pervade modern academic and political institutions.

—W. George Scarlett

GAIA HYPOTHESIS

The Gaia hypothesis affirms that the earth is not just a place where life is found but that is itself a living organism ("Gaia"). It may be compared to the human body where billions of cells interact to make a single living being. The life forms on earth in all their diversity work together as a coherent, self-regulating living system. They interact with chemical, physical, biological, and geological forces and adapt and coevolve over time to maintain a balanced environment and to produce the optimal conditions for the growth and prosperity not of themselves but of the larger whole. Gaia may therefore be defined as a single yet complex living system involving the biosphere, atmosphere, oceans, and terrestrial crust. These interact to keep in balance the surface temperature of the earth and the oxygen levels of the atmosphere, just as our bodies regulate their own temperature and the oxygen levels in their arteries.

The hypothesis was formulated by the British scientist James Lovelock, while he was working for the U.S. NASA space program in the 1960s on experiments to detect the possibility of life on Mars. He realized that the atmosphere of a planet with life was fundamentally different from that of a dead planet like Venus or Mars. The name *Gaia* (the ancient Greek earth-mother goddess) was suggested to Lovelock by the novelist William Golding because of her dual role as a caring supporter and a ruthless annihilator. The name *Gaia* perhaps encourages a false tendency to view the earth anthropomorphically, with the equatorial rain forests functioning as the planet's lungs, the rivers and streams as its veins, the mountains as its bones, and living organisms as its senses. But the hypothesis does not imply that the earth actually is a goddess, or indeed any kind of sentient being with awareness, foresight, or intention. It is perhaps more helpful to view the earth as alive in the way a tree is alive—with much dead tissue, yet using sunlight, water, and minerals to grow and change over time.

The Gaia hypothesis has been criticized by scientists such as Richard Dawkins who argue that as Gaia cannot reproduce herself, she cannot be said to be alive in any meaningful way. However, while the hypothesis has by no means been substantiated (and indeed it is difficult to know how it could be), it has generated much scientific research. Lovelock has said himself that the hypothesis may just be a different way of viewing the facts we know about the earth. Some people find it easier to understand as a metaphor rather than a literal scientific statement, reflecting the interdependence of life and affecting the way we view the earth. As a metaphor, Gaia can be said to encourage cooperation rather than competition and the avoidance of damage through deforestation or carbon dioxide emission.

For Lovelock, Gaia is a religious as well as a scientific concept, though often the response to the hypothesis goes beyond his own view of humanity as peripheral, though dangerous, to the life systems of the planet. For many people, the Gaia hypothesis encourages a spiritual dimension in their relationship with the earth, and affirms the sacredness of what they have been conditioned to treat merely as resources to be exploited. Though it is claimed that the Gaia hypothesis does not conflict with any of the major world religions, it strikes a chord particularly with the beliefs of alternative communities and new forms of spiritual thinking in its emphasis on people's inner sense of connection with something larger than themselves. For some, too, it provides the motivation to live on a sustainable basis with other species and the earth's finite resources.

—*J. Mark Halstead*

FURTHER READING

Bunyard, P. (Ed.). (1996). *Gaia in action: Science of the living earth.* Edinburgh: Floris Books.

Lovelock, J. (1979). *Gaia: A new look at planet Earth.* Oxford: Oxford University Press.

Lovelock, J. (1988). *The ages of Gaia.* Oxford: Oxford University Press.

GANDHI, MOHANDAS K.

Mohandas K. Gandhi is better known as Mahatma (meaning, the "Great Soul") Gandhi. This title was given to him not just for his leading the early 20th century movement to free India from British rule. It was given to him also for the way he led and for his saintly character.

Gandhi began his career as a somewhat shy and undistinguished lawyer who no one could suspect would develop into a world leader. In 1891, after leaving India to work in South Africa, Gandhi's life changed dramatically after he was thrown off a train for refusing to give up his first-class ticket because a white man had refused to share the same compartment space with him. For the next 23 years Gandhi led social movements in South Africa to protest unfair laws and to win better living conditions for Indians working in South Africa. Furthermore, from about 1905 on, Gandhi committed himself to leading a spiritual life, one stressing simplicity, self-denial, and compassion for others. From 1905 on, then, Gandhi became both a political and a spiritual leader.

In 1914, after returning to his native India, Gandhi became the spokesperson for Indians yearning to free themselves from British rule. He developed a new method for nonviolent resistance, the method or practice of *satyagraha*.

Satyagraha combines the concepts of firm and truth to mean, literally, "standing firm for truth." For Gandhi, God is the truth element in Satyagraha, and to stand against social injustice is to stand for God. Unlike many spiritual leaders before him, Gandhi did not believe truth was revealed to him directly. Rather, he believed that truth comes through careful study, effort and experiment. Gandhi's resistance movements were, then, spiritual as well as scientific. Most important, they were nonviolent and designed so as to appeal both to the reasonableness of opponents and to their moral conscience. The latter was appealed to not just with arguments but with passive resistance by Gandhi and his followers, resistance that often resulted in their being beaten, jailed, even killed. The power of this method lay, then, in its showing the opponent (in this case, the British rulers of India), the unreasonableness and injustice of their position. No issue having to do with justice was too small or too large for Gandhi; for all such issues have to do with finding and serving God. So, Gandhi's Satyagrahas came in all sizes. They ranged from small labor strikes to nonviolent demonstrations to secure better sanitary conditions for entire cities. His most famous movement may well have been his 1930 march to the sea ending in his securing a pinch of salt from the sea in protest against a British law that gave the British a monopoly on the production of salt. The protest led, eventually, to brutal reactions on the part of the authorities which, in turn, elicited sympathy for Gandhi's cause, not only among Indians but also among the British. This was the effect that Satyagraha was designed to have. Satyagraha was, then, a powerful political tool even as it expressed the spirituality of its creator, Gandhi.

Gandhi's spirituality was also seen in his simplicity and self-denial. He dressed as a peasant and ate only meager vegetarian meals. He answered not to political pressures, not to his own desires, but to what he felt was true and just, namely, to God.

Gandhi's first priority was to find God and to live up to God's standards. For Gandhi, God is elusive, and the search for God can be never ending. However, God's elusiveness and the need to search indefinitely did not deter Gandhi, because he believed that searching for God is the only way to reach one's full potential.

Gandhi's image of a just and caring God led him to adopt a similar image of humans which, in turn, helped him care for everyone, regardless of their race, religion, or nationality. For Gandhi, all have value because all are made by God. To harm another is, then, to go against God.

However, Gandhi took his positive approach to others and to injustice a step further. He advocated returning good for evil. He tried to love everyone regardless of how others treated him and regardless of whether others were good or bad.

Gandhi believed, as did his mother, that animals too are beloved creatures of God and as such, are to be valued and respected. For most of his adult life he remained a strict vegetarian. Once even, he denied meat products for his sick son—against the advice of the family doctor.

Throughout his life Gandhi encountered and studied many faith traditions. He believed that God would always be with him, and so he was not worried about what faith he would eventually adopt as his own. Instead, he searched always for the best way to worship God. Gandhi probably spent more time studying Christianity than any other religion except Hinduism. He liked many of the messages and ideals expressed in Christianity, especially Jesus' message about turning the other cheek in response to insult. But he rejected the message that only Christians go to heaven. For Gandhi, God judges all people equally.

Gandhi's Hinduism was rooted in the value he found in Bracharya, the set of vows taken by certain Hindu holy men, vows that have to do with simplicity and self-denial. Later in his life, Gandhi stopped sexual relations, limited his meals to two a day, and wore the simple clothes of the lowest caste. Gandhi believed that by denying himself, he was opening himself up to God.

Gandhi was clearly a spiritual exemplar who spent the majority of his life crusading in the name of God. Both Gandhi and Satyagraha have become models of leadership, models rooted in spirituality.

—Ian McClellan

FURTHER READING

Gandhi, M. (1948). *Gandhi's autobiography.* Washington: Public Affairs Press.

Gandhi, M. (1951). *Satyagraha (nonviolent resistance).* Ahmadabad: Navajivan Publishing House.

Desai, N. (1980). *Handbook for satyagrahas: A manual for volunteers of total revolution.* Philadelphia: Movement for a New Society.

GNOSTIC GOSPELS

The Gnostic Gospels were discovered by peasants in 1945 near the town of Nag Hammadi in upper Egypt. The texts, written on papyrus and bound in leather, consisted of 13 separate books, known as *codices*. Scientific analysis of the writings indicated that they had originated around 350–400 C.E., but scholars concluded that they were copies of even earlier texts written in the first and second centuries after Christ. The texts were virtually all that remained of a body of early Christian writings from a religious movement known as *Gnosticism*. The texts and the movement of Gnosticism serve as good examples of the power of the written word and its influence in impacting religious ideas, practices, and understandings.

Gnosticism was one of many religious philosophies rooted in the newly formed Christian tradition that competed for respectability during the tumultuous early years of the Christian Church. When it emerged as a serious rival to orthodox Christianity, it was attacked as heretical, its texts were destroyed, and its teachers and adherents were denounced and even murdered.

In Greek, *gnostic* means knowing. Gnostic Christians took the name because they claimed to know God in a unique, intimate, and much deeper way than ordinary Christians. Gnostic churches had little formal structure, and the only qualification for membership was an assertion of direct, personal experience of the divine. In many Gnostic groups, men and women were equally eligible for leadership positions.

By contrast, the emerging orthodox Christian church organized itself around professional, all-male clergy who gained their authority through traceable, if increasingly distant, links to the apostles who had known Jesus. The Orthodox Church was hierarchical, and its members relied on the clergy for interpretations of scripture. Unlike the Gnostic groups, which held a multiplicity of sometimes conflicting beliefs, the Orthodox Church developed an authoritative written canon that established church doctrine and provided historical support for the church's claim of sole religious authority.

The codices discovered at Nag Hammadi contained 52 separate texts, many of them written in obscure and mystical language. Some of them claim to be "secret" writings based on first-hand knowledge not available to other Christians. Many of the writings offered alternative versions of stories familiar in the Bible, and some criticized foundational Christian beliefs such as the virgin birth and the literal resurrection of Christ.

Some Gnostics described the Creator as female or as a dyad consisting of feminine and masculine elements. This juxtaposition of opposing parts is found throughout

Gnostic thought and reflects the classic Gnostic view that the physical world was inherently evil while the spiritual one was inherently good. This dualistic philosophy was most forcefully articulated by the second century poet Valentinus, the most influential of the Gnostic teachers.

Perhaps the best known of the Gnostic texts is the Gospel of Thomas, purported to be a collection of Jesus' sayings. This book, thought to be as old as or even older than the four gospels that appear in the New Testament, presents Jesus as a spiritual teacher who, instead of preaching God's superiority over humans, preached humans' capacity for equality with God. "He who will drink from my mouth will become as I am," reads one quote attributed to Jesus. "I myself shall become he, and the things that are hidden will be revealed to him."

The notion that ordinary people were somehow themselves divine—or at least, with the enlightenment offered by Jesus, could become so—outraged orthodox Christian leaders, who countered with frequent, angry polemics charging the Gnostics with blasphemy. Scholars believe that the Orthodox Church was so consumed by its struggle against the Gnostics that its very structure and doctrines were affected by it. They point, for example, to New Testament texts such as Saint Paul's supposed letters to Timothy, which were actually written by orthodox leaders in Paul's name to discredit Gnostic ideas.

Other well-known Gnostic texts include the Gospel of Philip, the Book of James, the Secret Book of John, and the Gospel of Truth. All the texts discovered in Egypt have been translated from Coptic, and the entire collection of writings, known collectively as the Nag Hammadi Library, is now widely available. Though the Gnostic movement was effectively dead by the fifth century, the discovery of the ancient texts has rekindled contemporary interest in Gnosticism and prompted new debates about the origins of Christianity.

—*Melanie Wilson*

See also Dead Sea Scrolls

FURTHER READING

Meyer, M. (1986). *The secret teachings of Jesus: Four Gnostic Gospels*. New York: Vintage.

Pagels, E. (1979). *The Gnostic Gospels*. New York: Random House.

Robinson, J. (1990). *The Nag Hammadi library.* New York: HarperCollins.

GOD

To write about God is, of course, to write about what others have felt, thought, and said about God. In the end, God is a symbol pointing to that which cannot be contained in words. God is transcendence, power, and mystery that, from the beginning, humans have felt but never been able to define simply and for all time.

However, the history of how humans have struggled to define God has far more meaning than might be suggested when focusing only on the impossibility of defining God. This history has revealed that the struggle to define God has been nothing less than the struggle to define who we are as humans, both as individuals and as communities. In tracing the history of how God has been defined we are, then, tracing no less than our evolving identities.

There is in this history so much variation as to, at first, make the task of recounting the history impossibly complex. However, if we step back from the details, we start to see patterns that allow for basic distinctions, which, in turn, allow for an organization that helps to understand the nature of the struggle to define God. There are, it seems, three major distinctions to consider: that between gods and God, that between a personal and utterly transcendent God, and that between a transcendent and immanent God. We shall consider each of these distinctions in turn.

The idea of there being one God may well have been common from the beginning, but the more prevalent idea seems to have been that there are many gods. Indeed, even in early biblical times, many Jews understood their Yahweh to coexist with lesser gods.

The gods have usually been tied to functions and localities. In being tied to functions, humans must have felt more connected to the different powers that they depended upon: the god of the sky where rain comes from, the god of the earth out of which crops grow, and so forth. Gods with specific functions, then, provide a more manageable way to carry on transactions designed to influence—for example, sacrifices and petitionary prayers—than does one, single transcendent but distant and mysterious God.

The fact that gods were often tied to regions or specific localities also served a useful purpose. Having one's own, local gods provides added security and can ensure a tolerance for others' faith that is often undermined when there is faith in one, overarching, and jealous God. For example, the plurality of gods during the heyday of the Roman Empire is said to have been a mechanism by which Romans could hold together diverse groups under one political roof. A plurality of gods could, then, ensure a modicum of religious tolerance.

However, the plurality of gods left humans divided, not only divided in terms of there being communities and groups divided from one another, but also divided in terms of individuals having no single focus to provide a sense of personal integrity, identity, and purpose. The struggle to define and have faith in one God arose, then, as a struggle for integrity, identity, and ultimate moral or spiritual purpose.

Perhaps the most concrete example of this struggle for unity is that of Muhammad and the birth of Islam. Before Muhammad, the Arab world was defined in terms of tribal loyalties, which promoted violence between tribes and an inferior ethic within tribes. Muhammad's success in promoting faith in the one, all-powerful and just God overcame these petty tribal loyalties and promoted an ethic emphasizing justice for all and charity for those in need. Similar stories can be told about the experience of the ancient Jews and early Christians; however, again, the story of Muhammad provides the clearest example of how monotheism or faith in the one God can affect both individual and collective unity. The rise of monotheism can, therefore, be partially explained as meeting the need to integrate diverse groups and help individuals subordinate their selfish desires to what is the greater good of all.

However, monotheism presented its own problem or dilemma, namely, the dilemma of being faithful to God who is transcendent, all-powerful, and mysterious but still having to find a way to connect to God in a personal way. Forging a personal connection was easier in the old, pagan systems. In short, throughout history, the faithful have always struggled between keeping God almighty and transcendent at the expense of making God remote, on one hand, and making God personal and intimate at the expense of God's losing power and transcendence, on the other hand.

The solutions to this dilemma have been many. However, the early Christian solution can serve as a particularly noteworthy example. The early Christians expressed their faith in terms of their personal experience, not in terms of creeds or systematic theology. However, by the fourth century following Jesus' death, the Christian community needed a creed to address the various theological questions and heresies that were threatening to fracture and dissolve the community. The result was the doctrine of the Trinity, the doctrine that states that God is paradoxically "The Father," "The Son," and "The Holy Spirit" so that God is three in one. This creed was never intended as a logical formula. Instead, it was intended as a symbol to capture the essence of the Christian experience. It also provides a clear example of how humans work to solve this dilemma between preserving the power and transcendence of God, on one hand, and the need for personal connection, on the other. The Father points to power and transcendence while The Son and Holy Spirit point to personal connection.

The third major distinction helping us understand the history of how others have defined God is the distinction between transcendence and immanence. Here, we confront the dilemma between having faith in God and being scientific and rational. If God is totally other and transcendent, we would feel satisfied were we able to know God through evidence and reason. But God is a mystery, and while others have sought God's nature in God's actions, doing so has always led to conflicting interpretations. Furthermore, God's being defined as totally outside us has allowed for God to become a convenient means to project and use God for selfish purposes.

Throughout the history of monotheism, then, humans have searched to find God not simply outside but also (and for some, mainly) within. This search to find God within ourselves has sometimes been called *immanentism.* The great Swiss developmental psychologist Jean Piaget thought the transition from focusing on a transcendent God to focusing on an immanent God represented not only an historical achievement, but an achievement in the development of individuals as well.

Examples of immanentism can be found in all the great mystical traditions and especially in Eastern traditions. Here we see the faithful turning inward, so to speak, to find God or the divine spirit, to meditate and listen to "that still small voice," to experience the spiritual, and sometimes to dissolve the boundaries between self and other that effects a final resolution to this particular dilemma.

There are other distinctions and dilemmas that have defined how humans have struggled to define God and express God, but these three have been central. However, overriding all three has been one major dilemma for every religious tradition, regardless of whether or how God is defined.

That overarching dilemma has to do with defining the indefinable–whether it be God, Nirvana, or some other concept of the Ultimate. Initially this dilemma was not experienced as a dilemma. In the same way that children take myths and symbols to be factually true, so too did our distant ancestors take myths and symbols to be factually true. Even today, many insist on taking myths and symbols of God to be factually true. Religious myths and symbols have truth, but their truth is in their supporting "living life truly," that is, living life with spiritual and ethical meaning. Their truth is not, then, in their providing scientific evidence and logical proofs.

When the great religious myths and symbols for God have been taken literally, there have been problems, not the least of which has been the problems of prejudice and intolerance. After all, if my myth or symbol is true in a literal sense whereas yours is not, then I am likely to feel more knowledgeable, enlightened, and superior. Put another way, the struggle to define God has been a struggle for strong faith rooted in trust, conviction, and commitment while also being a struggle for a tolerant faith rooted in the humbling awareness that, at best, we can know God only "through a glass darkly."

—W. George Scarlett

See also Kingdom of God; Myth

FURTHER READING

Armstrong, K. (1991). *A history of God.* New York: Ballentine Books.

Cassirer, E. (1955). *The philosophy of symbolic forms, Vol. 2: Mythical thought.* New Haven, CT: Yale University Press.

GOD, HINDU VIEWS OF

At least three kinds of visions of God have arisen in the Hindu world.

Visualizable Representations. God as the Supreme principle has a triple aspect, each bearing a name: Brahma (Creator), Vishnu (Sustainer); and Shiva (Dissolver), and their consorts Sarasvati (Goddess of Learning), Lakshmi (Goddess of Prosperity), and Uma (Mountain Goddess).

Epic Personages. Certain heroes in major Hindu epics are regarded as manifestations of the Divine in human form. They are said to have appeared on earth during other eras (*yugas*) of human history. The most important of them are Rama, Krishna, and Murugan (among the Tamils of the south).

Abstract Principle. Divinity is also associated with an immanent principle that transcends human understanding and description, called *Brahman.* Brahman is abstract divinity beyond visualization and logical categories whose existence can be confirmed and experienced by the human spirit through spiritual exercises and self-surrendering devotion.

The Hindu concept of the Divine may be explained through an analogy: Consider a sumptuous dinner that you are enjoying through your perceptual channels of taste. The dinner became possible because of the cooking, which involves cutting the vegetables, boiling, frying, adding the right amounts of spices, etc. If these do not occur in precise and well-defined ways, the food will not appear in its delectable form. Finally, beyond the cooking and resulting products, there is the essence of the food itself: the proteins, the carbohydrates, the vitamins, the minerals, etc. These lie hidden from our normal view. Ultimately, it is the life-fueling energy implicit in the food that is responsible for our health and well-being. This energy is all too abstract to be visualized in its stark purity. It finds expression through a hundred different biochemical molecules. Thus there are three distinct dimensions of the food: the perceived level, the processes engendering it, and the basic invisible level, which is the ultimate source of it all.

According to the Hindu worldview, in the course of our everyday experience we become aware of things and events. A characteristic of all tangible constituents of the universe, whether of any life form or even of inanimate entities is transience: Sooner or later everything in the world transforms and dissolves. This transient dimension of the world is called *kshara:* that which is destructible. The perceptible universe consists of all these transient things.

Underlying the tangible material universe are immutable fundamental physical laws that are responsible for the functioning of the perceived world. These laws are not directly visible to us, but their nature and complexity can be grasped by the human mind. In the Hindu framework, the totality of natural laws is known as the *akshara,* or unerasable dimension. It gives rise to the *kshara.*

In the Hindu religious worldview, beyond the empirical and the intellectually grasped features, there is a third dimension. This is the ultimate substratum of the universe, somewhat like the essence of the food.

It is recognizable neither mentally nor perceptually because it does not manifest itself in any way. It is referred to as the *avyaya,* or unmanifest dimension. Its existence and essence can be apprehended by human consciousness by processes that transcend the perceptual-mental modes. This apprehension is what spiritual enlightenment is all about.

This unmanifest root of the cosmos is Brahman. Brahman is the equivalent of God in the Hindu framework. Brahman is beyond the constraints of space and time, of logic and causality. That is why verbal discourses on the nature of God always lead to contradictions and confusions. Brahman is to be apprehended, not comprehended; experienced, not described; vouched for, not proved. Those who have realized Brahman speak of ecstasy and bliss, not of belief or faith.

The material representations of the God symbols are called *mûrtis,* inappropriately referred to as *idols* by outsiders. A *mûrti* is a mapping on the visual plane of a transcendent principle that is too subtle for ordinary minds to grasp. It is not unlike a geometrical figure that a mathematician may draw to reach a result that he cannot as easily derive through reasoning alone. The *mûrti* enables the practitioner to engage in meaningful interactions with that for which it stands.

As to the question whether Hinduism is monotheistic or polytheistic, the answer would be: "There is but one God, and there are also many."

Again, to clarify the Hindu concept, an analogy may be considered. It is difficult to intellectually grasp what music is: Music is to be experienced, not defined. Is there one music or many? "Music" represents one entity, but its expressions are countless. Most people know "music" through its many expressions such as songs, sonatas, etc. Very few understand "music" at the intellectual and abstract level. They enjoy particular musical pieces and expressions and have no need to define it.

This, roughly, is the Hindu view of god. Like "music," there is one universal God, but, like "music," that God can only be experienced through one or more of the multiple manifestations.

—Varadaraja V. Raman

See also Hinduism; Hinduism: Supreme Being, the Hindu Trinity.

GOSPEL MUSIC

Gospel music suggests many things to different people. In its most general application, gospel music refers to religious music, regardless of age or origin. Congregational songs, ring shouts, quartets, sacred harp choirs, sanctified groups, and work songs all qualify. Less broadly, gospel refers to an innovative, popular style of music combining secular forms, particularly ragtime and blues, with religious texts. Although, there are many interpretations as well as different types of gospel music, to the African-American community, gospel music has historically been a significant source of hope and strength linking past, present, and future generations.

Gospel music is rooted in the religious songs of the late 19th century known as *Negro spirituals*. The lyrics of Negro spirituals were tightly linked with the lives of elders in the African-American community and heritage. The songs were anthems and testaments to the joys, pains, and hopes of the enslaved. It was out of the constant development of Negro spirituals that gospel music was inspired and introduced as another type of Christian song. Gospel music is utilized in a number of political, social, and educational settings to build solidarity and to express the joys, pains, and hopes of African Americans in a wide range of localities.

Gospel music was well established early in the 20th century with the late Thomas A. Dorsey (1899–1993) as one of the vanguards of this diverse genre of music. Dorsey's early career focused on the arrangement and composing of blues tunes; he later began writing gospel music that is considered some of the greatest gospel music ever written. Dorsey played a critical role in helping to shape this music that inspires, moves, and soothes the mind, body, and soul. Consummate musician by many standards, Dorsey is remembered as "The Father of Gospel Music." It was Dorsey who combined such genres as shape-note songs, spirituals, blues, and ragtime to create gospel music. His musical career afforded him many opportunities to accompany some of the most famous blues singers all over the world including Bessie Smith and Ma Rainey, who greatly influenced the creation and birth of gospel music. Dorsey's music can be heard today in African-American churches across the United States in neighborhoods, on street corners, through open windows, down alleys, in bars and restaurants.

America's premier gospel singer Mahalia Jackson, whose untrained but vibrant voice combines with the depths of true religious sincerity, brought the writing of lyrics and the performing of gospel music to national prominence. Her singing of Thomas Dorsey's most famous song "Precious Lord, Take My Hand" placed gospel music as a standard of American music and launched her musical career to national and international acclaim.

With its immense popularity, widespread appeal, and influence created and established by Dorsey and Jackson, gospel music became the center of urban social life in African-American churches as well as at many of historically Black colleges and universities (HBCUs) (e.g., Atlanta, Clark, Fisk, Hampton, Howard, Spelman, Morehouse) throughout the South. For example, the nationally and internationally known Fisk Jubilee Singers from Fisk University are known for their heart-wrenching, soul-stirring, hand-clapping, foot-stomping songs in celebration of the beginnings of Black freedom. Although, the choir is much larger today than when it was first established, the Fisk Jubilee singers continue their tradition of performing traditional Black sacred songs that reflect their advanced musical education and discipline sung in a nontraditional style to inspire Americans everywhere. Their early international tours helped introduce the world to a new genre of "spiritual singing," later to be recognized as gospel music.

Gospel music has in many ways influenced other forms of music such as soul, jazz, blues, and R&B. Some of America's greatest musical leaders from the past and present have been influenced or inspired by gospel and recognize it as a heritage. Some of these great leaders include Ray Charles, Stevie Wonder, James Brown, Aretha Franklin, Clara Ward, and Whitney Houston.. Contemporary gospel groups such as BeBe and CeCe Winans and Take 6, to name just a few, have found combining rhythmic tempos of jazz, blues, and R&B the reason for the diverse following of adults and children. Many musical artists mentioned above and new emerging artists began their musical careers in the Black church singing gospel music.

Like gospel music, the Black church has historically been a source of hope and strength for African Americans who might otherwise have been left out. It is in the Black church where some of gospel's greatest music was and is composed and performed. The space of the Black church, singing, and the interactions shared while singing, creates a sense of solidarity and congeniality that provides African Americans a great sense of self-esteem, self-worth, and enhanced empowerment. In a society where very often the voices of the Black community are muted, gospel music has been and continues to be the venue where African Americans from diverse localities are able to express freely their voices and be assured that their voices would be heard. Through the medium of gospel music, African Americans have been able to engage their young in positive experiences providing them with spiritual, educational, social, political, and economic access within diverse African-American communities and larger society.

Gospel music as a tool for empowering the African-American community can be traced as far back as slavery. Despite the apparent dangers associated with being Black during slavery in America, Blacks found solidarity and comfort in singing "old Negro spirituals" that became known as *gospel music*. Gospel music was considered by African Americans a productive way to ease their feelings of dejection given their plight in America. It was through gospel music that African Americans found the strength to surmount those difficult times in our nation's history.

Slavery was just one of the problems that gospel music supported African Americans in overcoming. Immediately following slavery other societal forces worked against African Americans in the United States. Discrimination in employment, education, and practically every aspect of American life for Blacks led to an even stronger push to maintain the quality and value of gospel music in the African-American community.

The Civil Rights Movement of the 1960s is yet another pivotal time in history whereby gospel music was utilized to bring together the African-American community in solidarity in great numbers. Similarly to the ways that Negro spirituals were used during slavery, African Americans during the 1960s also wrote gospel music to reflect the reality of the time period. As the Civil Rights Movement progressed, gospel music within the Black community made some permanent and temporary yet fundamental shifts. These shifts and changes in addition to reflecting the time sought to reach an even wider audience of Americans from diverse cultural and linguistic backgrounds. The changing of the tempos and extending of the lyrics serve to illustrate the deep frustrations and strong emotions as well as to demonstrate individuality and collectivism and cultural identity of the African-American community.

Gospel songs like "Move On Up a Little Higher," the first gospel recording by Mahalia Jackson to sell over a million copies, and "I Don't Feel No Ways Tied" and "Can't Nobody do me like Jesus" can be heard from African-American and other American communities as they assert their independence and freedom and their refusal to turn back considering all the educational, political, social, and economic gains made. Gospel music continues to provide African-American communities everywhere a language and voice to assert that "I am somebody, and because I know that I am somebody, I am not going to give up." Affirmations like these are the major reasons why gospel music has become such a powerful tool for communicating social injustices, inequalities in the African-American community, and the larger society. Stemming from traditions of the slave past, gospel music has increased its rhythms, drawing not only the sounds of ragtime, blues, and jazz into the church but also instruments such as drums, tambourines, triangles, guitars, saxophones, trumpets, and double basses, which have become central to bringing gospel music fully into the fabric of American life.

Today, gospel music in its more contemporary form is critical to the African-American community in guiding youth toward positive experiences that supports their growth and development and ultimately increases their life chances through the very poignant messages found in this genre of music. Although gospel music has undergone a number of changes, the messages of "We Shall Overcome" and "This Little Light of Mine" and "Never Turn Back" still resonate with African-American old and young when faced with difficult times and joy during happy times.

—*Brian L. Wright*

See also Spirituals, African American

FURTHER READING

Collins, C. M., & Cohen, D. (1993). *The African American.* New York: Penguin Studio Books.

Gates, H. L., & West C. (2000). *The African-American century: How Black Americans have shaped our country.* New York: A Touchstone Book, Simon & Schuster.

Grant, J. (1968). *Black protest: History, documents, and analyses.* New York: Fawcett Premier.

Kolchin, P. (1995). *American slavery.* New York: Penguin Books.

Lincoln, C. E., & Lawrence, H. (1990). *The Black church in the African–American experience.* Durham, NC: Duke University Press.

Lornell, K. (1989). Black gospel music. In W. Ferris and C. R. Wilson (Eds.), *Encyclopedia of Southern Culture.* Durham, NC: University of North Carolina Press.

Olson, D. (1999). *The father of gospel music remembered: Interview with Thelma Buckner.* Archive of Minnesota Public Radio.

Quarles, B. (1996). *The Negro in the making of America.* New York: Simon & Schuster.

Thernstrom, S., & Thernstrom, A. (1999). *America in black and white: One nation indivisible.* New York: A Touchstone Book, Simon & Schuster.

GRACE

In the broadest sense, *grace* means that Spiritual Presence is a given in human existence; it cannot be produced through human endeavor. Grace in Christian theology is understood as the present and future gift of God's favor, the universal and timeless offer of God's love into eternity, the power to change, and a participation in divine life here and now. Grace assists persons in meeting the challenges of growth that are part of each season of one's life. Each person bears the responsibility to shape his or her moral destiny, a destiny necessarily intertwined with others and the earth, even the cosmos, as the home humans share. Grace is the ever-available gift of God that holds the spiritual key to support human beings in transcending the flawed and very human tendencies toward self-absorption, selfishness, estrangement, domination, and hardness of heart. The painful realities of life do not always reflect the life God intended for humans in creation. In spite of the "fallenness" of the human condition, grace is given gratuitously; one doesn't need to "merit" it but rather to choose it.

The presence of grace is an essential ingredient in spiritual conversion. Without its reality and activity the deepest desires of the human soul and spirit for wholeness and inner and outer peace might not prevail against the forces that often overwhelm a person and lure them in a death-dealing, sinful, and damaging direction. Precisely because grace builds on nature and requires the exercise of personal freedom, a person can choose to change patterns of hurtful, destructive living and embrace, through grace, access to greater healing and new directions in living. Grace is not given to make up for something essentially lacking in human nature but is given as a free gift that is offered to widen and deepen access to human flourishing in the midst of the reality of human frailty.

The reality of grace means that God never ceases to give of God self to humans if people choose to be receptive. Openness to receiving the power and tenderness of grace can result in the ability to experience the change of mind and heart known as *spiritual conversion*. The ever-abundant presence of the ongoing gift of God's life, grace, is available in and through the actual and ordinary experiences of daily living. The time of grace is always at hand. All humans participate in God's life here and now to the degree that each freely and consciously chooses to engage the reality of the divine in humans' midst. Humans possess the divine spark—*imago dei*—residing in the human soul. Grace is God's free and enduring gift to enable each person to fully become the image of God that is already stamped into the essence of each human being. Informed by the work of Robert Coles (1991) and others, we are now much more aware of the vibrancy of the spiritual life of children and their unique quest to relate to a God of their experience. Adolescence reflects a prime developmental season where youth seek to claim for themselves a more personal and autonomous appropriation of meaning in life. This means that the task of self-realization, facing the responsibilities for one's own life—whether one is 8, 18, or 80 years of age—is challenging and cannot be avoided in any phase of life. Yet in spite of all the obstacles that enter the human experience that threaten one's growth to maturity in freedom, grace abounds.

—Avis Clendenen

See also Conversion; God; Sin

FURTHER READING

Clendenen, A., & Martin, T. (2002). *Forgiveness: Finding freedom through reconciliation.* New York: Crossroad.

Coles, R. (1991). *The spiritual life of children.* New York: Mariner Books.

McBrien, R. (1994). *Catholicism.* San Francisco: HarperCollins.

Tillich, P. (1963). *Systematic theology, Vol. 3.* Chicago: University of Chicago Press.

H

HAPPINESS

Happiness is an elusive but important concept both to psychologists and to theologians. For psychologists, a proper understanding of happiness is seen to stand at the heart of psychological well-being and optimal human functioning. For theologians, a proper understanding of happiness is the promise held out to those who are obedient to God's call. For example, in the Jewish scriptures, Psalm 1 proclaims, "Happy are those who reject the advice of evil men. Instead they find joy in obeying the law of the Lord."

A number of psychological traditions have set out to offer a definition of happiness and to develop sound measures to assess individuals' levels of happiness. A major contribution to this area has been made by Michael Argyle, who developed a psychological test known as the *Oxford Happiness Inventory.*

Argyle suggested that happiness comprises three key components: the frequency and degree of positive affect or joy, the average level of satisfaction over a period of time, and the absence of negative feelings, such as depression and anxiety. It was this definition that Argyle operationalized through the 29 items of the Oxford Happiness Inventory. Considerable literature has been developed that is concerned with mapping the predictors of happiness throughout life, giving attention both to personal factors (like age, sex, and personality) and to contextual factors (like participation in sport, watching television, and listening to music).

Using the Oxford Happiness Inventory, Leslie J. Francis conducted a series of studies designed to examine the relationship between different dimensions of religion and spirituality and perceived levels of happiness. These studies have consistently found that a positive attitude toward religion is associated with higher levels of happiness. For example, in one study Francis administered the Oxford Happiness Inventory to three different age groups of people alongside the Francis Scale of Attitude toward Christianity. The study included 944 pupils in their final year of compulsory schooling, 456 first-year undergraduate students, and 496 adults between the ages of 50 and 90. All three samples reported an association between a more positive religious attitude and a higher level of happiness. Similar findings have been reported among Hebrew-speaking Israeli students assessed by the Katz-Francis Scale of Attitude toward Judaism.

In conclusion, the available empirical evidence demonstrates that by contributing to a higher level of personal happiness and psychological well-being, religion makes a key contribution to positive youth and human development. It will be of interest to see if and how research related to happiness and religion continues to contribute to the field of positive youth development and what is known about religious and spiritual development.

—Leslie J. Francis

FURTHER READING

Argyle, M. (2001). *The psychology of happiness.* London, Routledge.

Francis, L. J., Kay, W. K., & Campbell, W. S. (Eds.). (1996). *Research in religious education.* Leominster, UK: Gracewing.

HEALING THE CHILDREN OF WAR

Armed conflict impacts religious and spiritual growth of children and youth and often serves as a trigger of potential change in the developmental trajectory of a child's religiosity and spirituality. Children victimized by armed conflict might question the existence of God or, alternatively, find God to be the only source of resiliency. Consequently, a child's religiosity and spirituality might have an impact on how a child responds to armed conflict. Some children might feel abandoned by God and adopt the role of helpless victims, while others might feel protected by God and find strength to survive even the worst acts of violence.

In the armed conflicts of recent years, children of all ages have increasingly been victimized as both targets and perpetrators of violence. Two million children are thought to have died in wars between 1990 and 2001, another six million have been wounded or disabled, and one million have been orphaned. The picture of the impact of the most recent war in Iraq on children has yet to emerge, but it will undoubtedly increase the number of casualties. Approximately 20 million children have been forced from their homes because of armed conflict and civil strife. Some seven million of those children have sought refuge in another country. Children constitute nearly half of the world's 38 million refugees and internally displaced persons (IDPs); the number of refugee children is increasing by 5,000 per day. An estimated 300,000 youngsters have been coerced into becoming fighters in civil wars across the globe and millions of adolescents are sold and trafficked into sexual slavery. Children in at least 68 countries live amidst the threat of 110 million landmines, and each year between 8,000 and 10,000 children are injured or killed by them.

Beyond these statistics are the haunting images of adolescent victims of rape, which has become as much a weapon of warfare as bullets and machetes; of child soldiers who are barely the height of the automatic weapons they carry; of children separated from their families in conditions of extreme deprivation; of youngsters forced to work under dangerous and harmful conditions; of school-aged children deprived of opportunities to learn; of children of all ages unable to find appropriate health care; and of children suffering various forms of trauma. Armed conflicts also increasingly serve as vectors for the human immunodeficiency virus (HIV)/acquired immune deficiency syndrome (AIDS) pandemic, which follows closely on the heels of armed troops and in the corridors of conflict. The statistics and images tell the same story: children and adolescents are the most vulnerable populations in armed conflict.

Although children of different ages, gender, and socioeconomic backgrounds experience the effects of armed conflict differently, war-affected adolescents are frequently worse off than other children. Adolescents are at a critical stage of development, transitioning out of childhood and on the threshold of adulthood. While they may not suffer the same rates of mortality and morbidity as very young children, they are at an increased risk to being recruited into military service, to being particularly vulnerable to economic exploitation, and to having fewer opportunities to attend school. In addition, adolescent girls are more likely to be sexually abused or held as sexual slaves, adolescent boys and girls are at a higher risk for HIV/AIDS and other sexually transmitted diseases (STDs), and adolescents may have to head households and assume adult responsibilities without sufficient support. Indeed, the importance of family to the well-being of children and adolescents in armed conflict cannot be overlooked. Studies dating back as far as World War II have documented lower rates of distress among children and adolescents who remained with their families in situations of armed conflict compared with other youngsters who lost parents in the conflict or were evacuated to children's centers located in more peaceful areas.

There is a growing literature on the impact of armed conflict on children, but the 1996 groundbreaking study prepared for the United Nations (UN) by Madame Graça Machel provides possibly the most complete picture of their situation. The central importance of this study is its attempt to reduce children's vulnerability to the conditions of violent conflict through the implementation of policies that would bind UN member states and parties involved in armed conflict to implement practices aimed at the protection of children and adolescents. Another significant contribution is its call for culturally appropriate forms of intervention and rehabilitation for child survivors. Indeed, considerations of culture—including religious and spiritual beliefs, rituals, and practices—must be at the heart of effective healing interventions.

There is evidence that religion and spirituality play a significant role in understanding and responding to the suffering of individuals and communities affected by armed conflict. In most major religions, including

Christianity, Judaism, Islam, Hinduism, and Buddhism, the experience of human misery, from sickness, natural disasters, armed conflict, violent death, atrocity, and genocide, is taken to be a vital condition of people's existential plight. Religious and spiritual beliefs provide meaning to the otherwise meaningless experience of human suffering. As a religious problem, the dilemma of suffering is not how to avoid suffering, but how to suffer—how to make physical pain, personal loss, or psychological trauma sufferable. Being a refugee—suffering in wartime; loss of homeland, parents, and family members; and the challenges of life in a new country—is for many forced migrants, a spiritual crisis of unparallel severity. Many of the basic spiritual needs, such as hope, meaning, relatedness, forgiveness or acceptance, and transcendence, are threatened in the forced migration process. Unmet spiritual needs put refugees' health at risk. Supporting refugees' faith is important in improving their mental health and facilitating their well-being.

Some people have difficulty imagining that children turn to religion in times of extreme suffering. During war it often seems that God has forsaken the suffering. Some severely traumatized war survivors seem to go through life with the cruel words of scripture, "My God, my God, why have you forsaken me?" (Matt. 27:46) on their lips. Many wonder how an omnipotent and all-loving God could allow people to suffer and how religious and spiritual beliefs can alleviate the suffering. Obviously, not everybody finds consolation in religion in the time of extreme suffering. Indeed, researchers note that violence has different effects for different children. Athey and Ahearn (1991) observe that for some, faith and belief in a higher power may provide strength and support. Others, however, may lose their faith or angrily reject their religious heritage in the face of the atrocities they have witnessed. Elie Weisel, writing about his experiences in concentration camps, said that after seeing innocent children burnt alive his faith was consumed by the flames and that the experience murdered his God and his soul. Since religion is part of identity development, questioning religious meaning might affect the identity development of a child or adolescent.

Numerous war survivors and some researchers, however, stress the importance of religion in coping with trauma. Many of the Sudanese "lost boys" who trekked hundreds of miles across hostile terrain to find safe haven have reported that faith was the main factor that helped them survive their ordeal, in which they experienced displacement by fierce fighting between the Islamic fundamentalist government in the Arab north and the guerrilla Sudanese People's Liberation Army, huts set ablaze, families murdered as they watched, and the excruciating hunger that followed. Documenting the experience of Cambodians who survived Pol Pot's "killing fields" and began new lives in America, Usha Welaratna underscores the importance of interpreting Cambodians' holocaust experiences within the context of Theravada Buddhism, while Neil Boothby describes the power of traditional religious rituals in promoting psychological healing among Cambodian refugee children in a Thai refugee camp. He notes that by creating opportunities for children to grieve and to honor family members killed by the Khmer Rouge, they were able to maintain a sense of continuity with the past and felt freer to move on with their lives.

Indeed, religious rituals play an instrumental role in trauma healing. One of the recognized effects of religious ritual is to create both sacred time and sacred space: a moment out of time and a place apart, nearer to the supernatural and the center of the universe than to the mundane places of everyday activities. Rituals renew the world by providing an opportunity to step outside of it; they renew time by combining the past, the present, and the future.

The spiritual power and healing of the *Jumah* prayer was apparent during Operation Provide Refugee at Fort Dix, New Jersey, a U.S. resettlement effort to assist Kosovar Albanians expelled by the Serbian authorities during the wave of violence that swept Kosovo in February and March 1998. The prayer was not only a religious ritual but also a very tangible exercise of freedom of religion. Many of the children and adolescents at Fort Dix, particularly those from Pristina where Serbian rule was enforced with the most rigor, participated in the Friday prayer for the first time in their young lives.

However, despite the diversity of religious and spiritual beliefs and practices that sustain many refugee and internally displaced children and adolescents in their processes of displacement, migration, reintegration into their own society, or integration into the resettlement country, religion and spirituality are virtually absent in policy debates and programming for refugee children and adults. It remains to be seen whether the federal faith-based initiatives spearheaded by the Bush administration in 2001 will change this situation in the United States, if not internationally. Researchers have also tended to neglect the role of religion and spirituality as a source of emotional and cognitive support, a form of social and political expression and mobilization, a vehicle for community building, and a factor contributing to individual and group identity. Most of the research and practical measures concerning the effects of political violence and armed conflict on children adhere to a biomedical framework, tend to secularize the suffering of refugee children, and shy away from interventions incorporating religious ritual and spiritual beliefs.

—Elżbieta M. Goździak

FURTHER READING

Athey, J., & Ahearn, F. (1991). The mental health of refugee children: an overview. In F. Ahearn and J. Athey (Eds.), *Refugee children theory, research, and services.* Baltimore: The Johns Hopkins University Press.

Boothby, N. (1988). Unaccompanied children from a psychological perspective. In E. Ressler, N. Boothby, & D. Steinbock (Eds.), *Unaccompanied children.* New York: Oxford University Press.

Garbarino, J., Kostelny, K., & Dubrow, N. (1991). *No place to be a child.* Lexington, MA: Lexington.

Gozdziak, E. M. (2002). Spiritual emergency room: The role of religion and spirituality in the resettlement of Kosovar Albanians. *Journal of Refugee Studies, 15(2),* 136–152.

United Nations. (1996). *Impact of armed conflict on children: Report of the expert of the Secretary-General Ms. Graça Machel* (Document A/51/306 & add.1). New York: Author.

Weisel, E. (1960). *Night.* New York: Hill and Wang.

Welaratna, U. (1993). *Beyond the killing fields: Voices of nine Cambodian survivors in America.* Stanford, CA: Stanford University Press.

Wessells, M. G. (1998). The changing nature of armed conflict and its implications for children: The Graça Machel/UN study. *Peace and Conflict: Journal of Peace Psychology, 4*(4), 321–334.

HEALTH

Young people find out more about who they are by discovering who and what they like and dislike. Under the best of circumstances they find out what they are good at, they establish significant relationships, they learn to think and act independently, and they discover what matters most to them. Through the relationships they develop with family members, peers, and intimate others, they find avenues of personal expression in school settings, personal interest groups, and work arenas. The totality of social relationships and arenas in which their explorations occur eventually leads to a more refined understanding of who they are and what they seek. For many young people, questions about spirituality and religiosity (and the contexts in which those questions arise) influence healthy identity development.

What happens when young people find a meaningful path for spiritual expression? Alternately, what happens when there is a dark, empty space that tells them life has no meaning, that there is only taking, getting, and doing whatever they need to do to get by? In the first example, a person with a feeling that life and living matter will tend to make choices that are healthier. In the second, a person will tend to make choices that may be damaging to them physically, emotionally, and spiritually.

The most powerful values are those that are forged through personal experiences. Spirituality may be linked to a specific religious path, or a particular spiritual teacher, or sometimes it is experienced as a sense that "there is something bigger than me, either within me or out there, and I want to get to know it." Divisions between various spiritual and religious traditions become less significant than the selection of a path that fits experientially for each young person. The most enduring spiritual values may have their roots in early family experience. The key to a spiritual path that helps young people feel connected and assists them in making wise and healthy choices lies in the universal truth of those values (love, compassion, and service to others) and the inspiration those values offer in a chosen life direction.

When spiritual values are self-chosen, personally experienced, and closely examined, they become a source of personal power and a way to relate to others. These values can help young people avoid risk-taking behaviors such as drug abuse, destructive dieting, and impulsive driving habits. The prevalence of homicide, accidents, and suicide in the age group from 16 to 25 suggests that deeply held spiritual values may help young people with their choices. They may begin to experience their bodies as more than physical objects to be used, but rather as a source of health, pleasure, and fulfillment toward their chosen goals. They may also learn that their feelings, thoughts, and spiritual values can guide them toward either healthy choices or destructive outcomes. Finally, as young people persist in developing spiritual values, they discover that body, mind, and spirit are not separate from each other. Rather, they are mutually interactive and represent an integrated whole. An action in one realm impacts the whole.

Most young people desire a fulfilling life. The means for achieving that precious goal are ongoing and based on social experimentation that eventually leads to certain conclusions. Physically and mentally healthy personal outcomes, guided by self-reflection, provide the feedback that helps the young seek a direction of integrity, personal integration, and spiritual fulfillment.

—*Evie Lindemann*

See also Health and Medicine

FURTHER READING

Baba, Meher. (1967). *Discourses.* South Carolina: Sheriar Press.

Blos, P. (1979). *The adolescent passage.* New York: International Universities Press.

Dalai Lama. (1998). *The art of happiness.* New York: Riverhead Books.

Pakaslahti, L., Karjalainen, A., & Keltikangas-Jarvinen, L. (2002). Relationships between adolescent prosocial problem solving strategies, prosocial behavior, and social acceptance. *International Journal of Behavioral Development,* 26, 137–144.

Spence, S. H., Sheffield, J. K., & Donovan, C. L., (2003). Preventing adolescent depression: An evaluation of the problem solving for life program. *Journal of Consulting and Clinical Psychology, 71,* 3–13.

Welwood, J. (1990). *Journey of the heart.* New York: HarperCollins.

HEALTH AND MEDICINE

Religion, spirituality, health, and medicine are fundamentally entwined in human life and well-being. Each is important to how we understand life, death, suffering, and healing and to how we make decisions about our health and health care. Historically, religious leaders healed bodies and minds as well as souls. Today in the United States, diverse religious and cultural healing systems interact with a dominant Western medical system in both complimentary and conflicted ways.

Religion and spirituality influence the health and health care of children and adolescents by various means. They shape how youth understand and engage their living and dying, how parents make health care decisions on behalf of their children, and how pediatricians perceive their patients' needs and thus how they practice medicine. Religion and spirituality affect how children and adolescents get sick, how they heal, as well as how they get sick and heal later on as adults.

This entry focuses on two subjects: religion's effects on physical health and medicine's growing attention to the spiritual dimensions of healing. The terms *religion* and *spirituality* are used interchangeably here because their meanings vary widely, often overlap, and because physicians and other clinical practitioners tend to use *spirituality* whereas health researchers tend to use *religion. Health* is understood primarily as a person's physical and mental well-being with a focus on the physical, and *medicine* (also known as *biomedicine*) refers to the treatment of disease through conventional Western medical practices.

HEALTH

Religion is increasingly recognized as one psychosocial factor affecting health and well-being much like other psychosocial factors such as age, gender, ethnicity, marital status, income, and occupation. As such, religion and health are the subject of a developing body of research being done by a wide array of medical, religious, and sociological researchers. Recent empirical data confirm what many have long assumed, that there is an overall positive relationship between religion and health.

Before examining this data, it is important to understand that relatively little research has focused on the effects of religion on children's or adolescents' health. Most research has studied adults, and often relatively religious adults at that, for example, the elderly and African Americans. Furthermore, many studies have limited their scope to a rather narrow range of religious traditions, most notably Christianity, and to a single medical tradition, i.e., Western biomedicine. The opportunities for future research are many.

Research to date finds largely beneficial associations between religion and health in both the short and the long term. More specifically, religion is found to have a positive influence on life expectancy (mortality) and on morbidity. In other words, greater religiosity is associated with living longer and with living with less disease.

Religious leaders, for example, white male Protestant ministers, tend to live longer than the general population.

Similarly, members of certain religious communities, for example, Seventh-Day Adventists, live longer than the general population. These lower mortality rates of Seventh-Day Adventists appear to be due in part to their belief-based healthy behaviors that include not using tobacco, alcohol, or caffeine. Religiosity is also inversely associated with heart disease, cholesterol, hypertension, suicide, and physical disability meaning that greater religiosity is associated with lower rates of these diseases.

ADOLESCENT BEHAVIORS RELATED TO HEALTH

Research on religiosity and the effects of religiosity on the physical and mental health of children and adolescents is scarce. The relatively few studies available concentrate primarily on specific health-related behaviors including the use of certain substances—alcohol, tobacco, and illicit drugs—on sexual activity, and on suicide. Given the significant influence of these behaviors on adolescent and, later, on adult health, this behavioral focal point is a fitting start.

Multiple studies, some of them large scale, have found that higher levels of adolescent religiosity are associated with lower levels of use and abuse of cigarettes, alcohol, marijuana, and illicit drugs. In other words, and generally speaking, youth who are more religious "do" fewer drugs. Not surprisingly, they also hold less permissive attitudes toward drug use. Thus adolescent religiosity appears to be a strong protective factor against drug use as well as against pro-use attitudes.

Adolescent religiosity is identified and measured in various ways across these studies. It can mean an adolescent's attendance at religious services, membership in or affiliation with a religious community, and/or participation in religious youth groups. It can also mean more private religious practices such as personal prayer or belief in the importance of religion. However measured, youth religiosity is associated with less involvement with drugs.

Most religious communities have identifiable beliefs and values related to sex and sexual activity, especially as they involve young people. These beliefs are often associated with particular directives, often proscriptions that are intended to influence youth behavior. In fact, religious youth do have notably distinct attitudes and behaviors about sex. Among adolescents and young adults, religious beliefs and practices are associated with lower rates of ever having had sex, with later initiation of sexual activity, with frequency of sexual activity, and with fewer sex partners. Not surprisingly, religiosity is also associated with less permissive attitudes toward sex.

Religious persons also tend to hold less tolerant views about suicide than their nonreligious peers. Moreover, adolescents and adults with religious involvement are less likely to commit suicide, to attempt to commit suicide, and to think about suicide.

While substances, sex, and suicide have been at the center of most research about religion and adolescent health, some researchers have branched out to learn about religion's possible wider role. John Wallace and Tyrone Forman analyzed questionnaires from nearly 5,000 high school seniors from across the United States that asked about their religiosity and a wide range of their health-related behaviors.

In this questionnaire religion was measured in three ways: by religion's importance to the student's life, by their attendance at religious services, and by their affiliation with a religious denomination or tradition. The behavioral risk factors they studied included cigarette, alcohol, and marijuana use, diet, exercise, sleep patterns, and injury-related behaviors including carrying a gun, knife, or club, engaging in interpersonal violence, seat belt use, drinking while driving, and riding while drinking.

Their findings regarding religiosity and substance use echoed the inverse relationship found in other studies: the more religious the youth, the less likely they were to use drugs. In parallel fashion, greater religiosity was associated with less involvement in injury-related behaviors. Also the more religious youth were more likely to have "healthy" diet, exercise, and sleep behaviors. In sum, religious youth were less likely than their peers to behave in ways that risked their health and more likely to behave in ways that could improve their health.

MECHANISMS OF INTERACTION

A large dose of caution is needed in interpreting these research findings. The presence of an association between religion and health does not necessarily imply a cause–effect relationship. We know that adults who attend religious services regularly tend to live longer. This may seem to suggest that attending services *causes* a person to live longer but such clear cause-and-effect relationships have yet to be established.

Precisely *how* religion shapes health and disease is hard to say with any degree of certainty. Three main mechanisms or pathways of interaction between religion and health have been proposed. The first mechanism, suggested already, is that religion, through its teachings for instance, promotes or inhibits healthy behaviors. A strongly held belief or value, such as the body should be treated with respect, may encourage religious persons to avoid risky behaviors and to practice health-promoting behaviors. These healthy behaviors in turn improve health and well-being and thus reduce the likelihood of disease.

Another way that religion may affect physical health is through its effects on mental health. High levels of religiosity is associated not only with less suicide, but also with less depression, greater optimism, and better coping skills in response to stress. Stress is known to have significant effects on the body's immune system. To the extent that religion mediates the effects of stress through, for example, its coping benefits, this may be another pathway by which religion affects physical health.

The third proposed mechanism for religion's influence on health is through religion's provision of social support, an important factor in health. The often rich social networks available in religious communities are proposed to be protective of health in various ways: by mediating stress and improving coping abilities, by providing health screenings for disease prevention and early disease detection, and by helping ill persons deal physically, emotionally, and socially with their conditions.

To further complicate this already complex picture, each of these three mechanisms appears to interact with one another. Careful research is needed to clarify these relationships.

RESEARCH CHALLENGES

Research on the relationships between religion and health is a relatively new field of inquiry. Many studies to date have significant limitations because of design flaws. Some studies use small unrepresentative samples; others consist of secondary analysis, meaning that the studies were done for some other purpose and then the data were used to consider religion and health. Still other studies inappropriately generalize their narrow findings to a larger population.

One challenge facing all research in this area is the problem of adequately measuring human religiosity and/or spirituality. Different measures can lead to different results, producing questionable findings. How can we best measure a person's religiosity? Given the varieties of human religiosity beyond the largely Christian experiences currently being studied, what measures appropriately reflect human religiosity?

Existing measures of religion are commonly distinguished by whether they represent public or private dimensions of religion. Public dimensions include measures such as whether a person is a member of a religious community, how frequently they attend religious services or religious youth groups, and how much time they spend in them. Examples of private dimensions include how important religion is to a person's life; whether a person holds specific beliefs, attitudes, or values (e.g., belief in the existence of God); and how often a person prays or meditates.

None of these measures alone captures the intricate nature of religion. This explains why some studies incorporate several dimensions into their measure of religion. The development of more sophisticated, multifactorial measures of religion is a high research design priority.

MEDICINE

Modern Western medicine focuses primarily on identifying and treating diseases of the physical body. The psychological dimensions of disease and health have received significantly less attention, and the spiritual dimensions have received even less so. But at the turn of the 21st century this is changing, and medical interest in religion and spirituality is thriving in ways that warrant hope for a deeper and more inclusive interest over time.

Medicine's growing interest in spirituality is due in part to the religion and health research described above, which has contributed significantly to an increased understanding of the effects of religious/spiritual practices, beliefs, and feelings on health and healing. Two other factors have played important roles: a greater recognition and appreciation of the diversity of medical and cultural worldviews present in the United States and a rising patient demand for whole person care that includes spirituality.

Patients as a group, that is to say, the general population, are more religious than physicians as a group. This fact suggests that medicine must be intentional about its inclusion of the spiritual into physical health matters. As such, the Association of American Medical

Colleges has established a set of learning objectives for medical students regarding spirituality. These objectives include being aware that spirituality is important to health and that spirituality ought to be incorporated into patient care as well as recognizing that medical students' spiritualities and cultural beliefs affect how they care for patients.

Medical education is changing and so too is clinical practice. A movement of physicians and others is underway to shift medical values and practices toward healing the whole person, not simply curing disease, toward recognizing that patients often suffer spiritually as well as physically and psychologically, and toward developing clinical practices that understand and incorporate spirituality and religion into health care. Pediatricians in particular will need to adapt their clinical practices in order to take seriously the spiritualities and religions of children's and adolescents' health, illness, and death.

SPIRITUAL HISTORIES

One way spirituality is being integrated into clinical practice is by means of the spiritual history. Physicians routinely ask patients a series of medical and social questions in order to learn the patient's history. Questions about spirituality are now more commonly included either as part of the social history or as a separate questionnaire.

Spiritual histories typically ask whether spirituality or religion is meaningful in a patient's life, where patients draw meaning and hope from, and whether they belong to a religious community. If the patient responds positively to these initial questions, further questions are appropriate regarding what spiritual beliefs they hold regarding their health, disease, or disability and how these beliefs might affect particular health care decisions they are facing. Other relevant questions ask about the patient's spiritual practices as a means to healing, for example, do they pray, meditate, do tai chi, read scripture, or attend religious services for health, and do they have spiritual resources, such as a spiritual leader, that the physician might support the patient in contacting, or would they like a referral to a chaplain.

Spiritual histories are particularly relevant in caring for severely and chronically ill or dying patients whose spiritual dilemmas are often most acute. The end of life frequently raises questions about the purpose and meaning of life, the need for hope, and feelings of despair. While physicians are not expected to be spiritual healers (nor are they trained to do so), they are in a unique position to support patients in a healing process that affirms not only the physical, but also the spiritual, social, and psychological aspects of their lives.

While many spiritual histories were first developed for adults, similar questions are important for children and adolescents. To the extent that parental spirituality influences the care of their children, it is appropriate for health care practitioners to learn also something of parental spiritual histories so as to come to an understanding of a family spiritual history. Given that parents routinely make critical health care decisions on behalf of their children, this understanding is particularly important for pediatricians and other practitioners working with children and adolescents.

HEALING CULTURES AND CULTURAL DIVERSITY

The parental responsibility for health care decision making is typically noncontroversial for parents within dominant Western religious traditions that largely accept and affirm conventional Western medical practices. However, controversy often arises when the beliefs, values, or practices of religious communities and those of biomedicine are at odds. Christian Science parents, for example, sometimes find themselves at the center of heated legal and moral debates about their children's health and healing. Biomedicine and Christian Science represent distinct healing cultures that are unlikely to be integrated into a single approach to care.

Religious healing, known also as *faith healing* or *spiritual healing,* is understood to be healing that occurs by non-scientifically observable means. While certain spiritual dimensions of human health are gaining acceptance in medical practice and research, medicine is a long way from recognizing the spiritual healing beliefs and practices central to dominant and nondominant cultures and religious communities in the United States. For example, many Christians believe that prayer can heal not only the soul but also the body and that prayer can heal not only one's own body but can also heal the bodies of family and friends for whom they have prayed.

Studies of "distant healing," that is, the healing of others through prayer, are exceedingly difficult to design and execute, but such studies are underway.

Interestingly, this research is somewhat controversial within religious as well as medical communities. Some religious practitioners reject the understandings of prayer and healing implied by researchers' attempts to measure the healing effectiveness of prayer. Prayer for these believers is primarily a means of communication with God, not a therapeutic intervention or a medical prescription. Furthermore, they believe that such studies misunderstand the nature of healing, which they understand to be ultimately a gift from God, not a predictable response to human prayer. Nonetheless, studies of prayer and other spiritual practices presumed to enhance health are proceeding and may offer important findings.

Medicine is challenged to recognize the diversity and depth of religious and spiritual contributions to human health and healing. Additional research on religion and health and improved medical education are important steps toward a fuller understanding of the constellation of connections between religion, spirituality, health, and medicine.

—Charlene A. Galarneau

See also Coping; Health; Meditation; Prayer

FURTHER READING

Association of American Medical Colleges. (1999). *Report III: Contemporary issues in medicine: communication in medicine.* Medical School Objectives Project (MSOP III). Washington: Association of Medical Colleges.

Barnes, L. L., Plotnikoff, G. A., Fox, K., & Pendelton, S. (2000). Spirituality, religion, and pediatrics: Intersecting worlds of healing. *Pediatrics, 106*, 899–908.

Cohen, C. B., Wheeler, S. E., Scott, D. A., Edwards, B. S., Lusk, P., and the Anglican Working Group in Bioethics. (2000). Prayer as therapy: A challenge to both religious belief and professional ethics. *Hastings Center Report, 30*, 40–47.

Donahue, M. J., & Benson, P. L. (1995). Religion and the well-being of adolescents. *Journal of Social Issues, 51*, 145–160.

Idler, E. L., Musick, M. A., Ellison, C. G., George, L. K., Krause, N., Ory, M. G., et al. (2003). Measuring multiple dimensions of religion and spirituality for health research. *Research on Aging, 25*, 327–365.

Koenig, H. G., McCullough, M. E., & Larson, D. B. (2001). *Handbook of religion and health.* Oxford: Oxford University Press.

Nonnemaker, J. M., McNeely, C. A., & Blum, R. W. (2003). Public and private domains of religiosity and adolescent health risk behaviors: Evidence from the National Longitudinal Study of Adolescent Health. *Social Science & Medicine, 27*, 2049–2054.

Pulchalski, C. M. (2001). The role of spirituality in health care. *Baylor University Medical Center Proceedings,* 14, 352–357.

Wallace, J. M., & Forman, T. A. (1998). Religion's role in promoting health and reducing risk among American youth. *Health Education & Behavior, 25*, 721–741.

HEAVEN

All of the monotheistic faith traditions (Jewish, Christian, and Islam) have a concept of the meaning of the term *heaven.* For some it is just the sky, for other traditions there is more theological insight placed on the term. A nonmonotheistic tradition such as Hinduism also has an idea of the afterlife, Moksha. One's understanding of the meaning of heaven is often reflective of one's stage of religious and spiritual development. Young children often see heaven as a physical place whereas others, more mature in thought, recognize heaven as a symbolic place.

In the Jewish sacred texts (the Old Testament) there is no clear evidence of belief in heaven, as a place of bliss or reward. The meaning of heaven is more a place in the cosmology. Heaven refers to the sky or the vault that seems to appear to arch over the earth. Generally, heaven is seen as a place reserved for God, i.e., a sanctuary. It is also the place of God's throne. But no place can contain God. The physical place of heaven serves as merely a symbol for the Divine transcendence. Later Jewish writings, or intertestament literature, develop the concept of heaven into a many tiered or leveled place, filled with spirits, and nine levels of angels.

It is in the Christian sacred texts (the New Testament) that the idea of heaven becomes a place of eternal bliss, where God's faithful people find their reward. Heaven is from where Jesus the Christ comes down from and, after his resurrection, ascends back to sit at God's right hand. The Christian scriptures continue to see heaven as a place of final reward, the Kingdom of God. Paul, in his writings, calls all believers "citizens of heaven" in Philippians 3:20. But with further reflection the early Christian community moves from a concept of heaven as a place to a concept that is more about the quality of human life in its full maturity and oneness in the presence of God.

The early church had a profound belief in eternal life thanks to Jesus' resurrection. This concept of eternal life became the idea of the beatific vision, that of beholding the Divine presence. The most recent statement from one Christian group, the Roman Catholic Sacred Congregation for the Doctrine of the Faith, issued a statement in 1979, "The Letter on Certain Questions Concerning Eschatology." The conclusions are very guarded in regards to heaven. The letter affirms the foundational belief in the resurrection of the body, the continuation of the human self after physical death, and the ultimate reward for the just that will one day be with the Christ. Then it warns against arbitrary imaginative representations since neither sacred scripture, sacred tradition, nor theology provide sufficient light for a proper picture of life after death.

This beatific vision, the full union of the human person with God, has been written about in literature and in elaborate paintings. Dante's *Divine Comedy,* the epic Italian poem, traces all the various levels of hell, purgatory, and heaven. Michelangelo's *The Last Judgment* also shows the various stages of those in torment and those believers arising to heavenly reward. The great Christian theologian Augustine prayed that "Our hearts are restless, oh God, until they rest in Thee."

The fulfillment symbolized by the idea of heaven does not mean the disappearance of the material world but its total transformation. Heaven is becoming one with God. There will be no trace of selfishness; we will cling to nothing of our own. Heaven for many in the Christian tradition is neither mythological nor simply the satisfaction of all human longings. Heaven is the goal of human existence, to be one with God. Heaven or the beatific vision is the full union of the human person with God and so also with one another in God.

For Muslims, the different heavens mentioned in the Holy Qur'an represent degrees of spirituality or domains. These levels are assigned to the different Holy Prophets. The origin of the concept of heaven is the planets that are visible to the naked eye. The "seventh heaven" marks the end of supra-formal creation and, in the symbolism of the seven directions of space, is in the center. The Holy Qur'an depicts the heavens as being cleft apart at the end of the world (82:1) or being rolled up like a scroll (21:24). The sky is the place where physical reality joins metaphysical reality. The sundering of the sky or the heaven is the eruption of the Divine into the created. This is also seen as the apocalyptic trumpet call of primordial sound. The dwellers of heaven for the Muslims are those who are being rewarded for leading a good life.

Hinduism, a polytheistic religious tradition, is all about conduct and not so much about beliefs or creeds. Moksha should not be seen as the Hindu version of heaven. Moksha is the final emancipation from rebirthing into many lives. Moksha is the breaking through and escaping forever from the impermanence that is the inescapable feature of mundane human existence. Moksha is sometimes confused with heaven because Hindus strive to become one with the Ultimate Reality.

How one thinks about and understands the concept of heaven reflects one's developmental trajectory. Ideally, at the end of life, one makes peace with one's life on earth and is ready to transcend to the divine kingdom.

—*Rev. David M. O'Leary*

FURTHER READING

Ratzinger, J. (1988). *Eschatology, death, and eternal life.* Washington, DC: Catholic University of America Press.

Viviano, B. (1988). *The kingdom of God in history.* Wilmington, DE: Glazier Press.

HELL

The term "hell" is derived from the North Germanic *hel,* meaning the realm of the dead. It is a popular expression for the place of failure of those souls who do not reach the reward of heaven with God. It is commonly thought of as place of punishment and final state of alienation from God. Hell is a common name for the dwelling place of devils and damned souls. How one conceives of hell in one's mind is reflective of one's individual religious development. Young children, in their concrete thinking, are more likely to think of hell as a physical place with red goblins walking around a world made of fire. Other, more mature thinkers are more apt to see hell in terms of symbolic concepts in relation to and comparison with life on earth and in the kingdom of heaven. Of course, one's understanding of hell is dependent upon the religious and/or spiritual traditions by which one has been influenced.

Since the earliest writings from various faith traditions, hell has always been thought of as located underground and also known as the underworld. The idea of hell is related to but not identical with Hades in nonbiblical literature such as in Greek mythology.

In the Jewish sacred writings, there is no clear and consistent idea of the fate of the dead. There is a notion of the underworld or Sheol. But this is not a place of suffering or punishment. It seems to be a place of shadowy existence having neither joy nor punishment. Here the dead neither thank nor praise God. There is no communication with God in the underworld (Isaiah 38:18 and Psalms 6:6). It is clear that no one can escape from the underworld.

Writers during the period between the Hebrew Bible or Old Testament and the Christian Scriptures, or New Testament, start to make a distinction between the fate of the good and that of the bad. Now the righteous enter into rest with God while the bad will live in pain. Now the idea of the underworld is not neutral but takes on the idea of a place of punishment for the wicked.

There is also the place of Gehenna, a real place which had been used as a site of cultic human sacrifices (see 2 Kings 23:10). This term, Gehenn,a is now thought of as a place of unquenchable fire and undying worms where the bodies of those who rebelled against God are on view (Isaiah 66:24). This prospect of eternal punishment now serves as motivation to strengthen people in their earthly suffering. A place of punishment is found very frequently in the apocalyptic literature and is given many details. This place of punishment is a place of darkness, eternal fire, chains, and a range of fitting punishments.

The New Testament uses the idea of Gehenna and adds to the concept. Gehenna is used many times in the Synoptic Gospels of Matthew, Mark, and Luke. The Pauline writings, or letters, also mention the idea of eternal punishment but without all the details found elsewhere in the New Testament. For Paul there will be eternal destruction and banishment from the face of God. There will tribulation and much distress for those who do evil.

Jesus' own "descent into hell," which is mentioned in the Apostles' Creed, should be seen as the underworld of Sheol, rather than the place of fire. The words "he descended into hell" therefore simply mean that he died and that he remained dead, at least for a short time. This is also seen as the time Christ preached to all the souls who died before his coming in order that they could now believe in him and leave Sheol.

Over the centuries, Christian churches have seen a development of the concept of hell based on the principle of retributive justice. Just as any society developed its concept of outlaws tried, judged, and punished, so too with the afterlife. There had to be a place of eternal punishment.

The most elaborate account of the idea of hell can be seen in Dante's *Divine Comedy.* Here hell is made up of nine circles or layers. One needs to remember this is not official Christian teaching but a literature that reflected popular opinion of its day. For Dante, the deeper one descends into hell, the greater the degree of wickedness and the more intense the punishment.

Modern Christian theological insight holds out for the possibility of hell. If people spend a lifetime denying God's call to relationship and living in a community of believers, then after the point of physical death that individual would have the choice or freedom to experience God's forgiveness and be purified from selfishness to enjoy God's presence or not. One could continue to choose isolation and be removed from the community of believers. Thus, hell is not so much punishment but isolation.

For Muslims there is also a concept of hell. Hell is a place of torment where the damned undergo suffering most often described as fire. The physical sufferings of hell are the consequences which come from the denial of God and God's will. When Muslims mention hell in conversation, they set off the idea with invocations of God's protection, for themselves and their listener. For the mere thought of hell is frightening, and its appearance in speech is seen as a dreadful omen that needs a word of prayer.

—Rev. David M. O'Leary

FURTHER READING

Michl, J. (1970). *Hell in sacramentum verbi.* New York: Herder & Herder.

Guardini, R. (1954). *The last things.* New York: Pantheon.

HERBERT, GEORGE

George Herbert is widely considered England's finest religious poet. Like John Donne, Richard Crashaw, Henry Vaughan, and Andrew Marvell, he belongs to a small group of 17th century poets (commonly known as the *metaphysical* poets), whose poetry combines powerful emotion, ingenious versification, witty imagery, intellectualism, and originality of thought. His admirers fall into two distinct groups—those for whom he is a model of simple faith and saintly devotion and those for whom his chief virtue is the complexity of his wit and poetic craftsmanship. A careful examination of his life helps to show how these disparate characteristics could be combined in a single individual.

Herbert was born into a distinguished family whose holdings included the Earldom of Pembroke. His mother Magdalen was a woman of great sensitivity and intelligence as well as piety, and she is known particularly as a friend and patroness to John Donne. His elder brother Edward achieved fame as a soldier, diplomat, philosopher, and writer, and it was only after their deaths that Edward was overshadowed by his younger brother. It appears that his mother had always intended the Church for George Herbert (his father had died when he was 3), but he made such a success of academic life both at Westminster School and then at Cambridge that he was tempted into an academic career. By the age of 21 he was a fellow of Trinity College Cambridge, and within a few years was appointed first as University Reader in Rhetoric and then as Public Orator for the University. This brought him to the attention of the royal court and also gave rise to political ambitions that culminated in his election to Parliament in 1624 as Member of Parliament (MP) for his home town of Montgomery. By the age of 32, however, he began to turn his back on worldly ambitions and decided to take Holy Orders. After an extended period of ill health (and perhaps soul-searching), he married Jane Danvers in 1629 and accepted the living of Bemerton near Salisbury a year later. For the remaining 3 years of his life, he was an exemplary priest, devoting himself to his duties and to his parishioners so completely that he was revered almost as a saint. Most of the 160 poems he wrote altogether in English were written during this time at Bemerton, though they were not published (in a collection called *The Temple*) until after his death. Within 50 years of his death, *The Temple* had passed through 13 editions and was widely venerated as a model of practical devotion.

Though he never wrote mystical verse, his poems exemplify a wide diversity of spiritual qualities and experiences. First, there are poems of simple praise and adoration of God; some of these, such as "Praise (II)" and "Antiphon (I)" have been set to music and are frequently found in hymnbooks even today. Secondly, there are poems of meditation, including the long poem "The Sacrifice," which highlights many of the ironies and paradoxes associated with the events of Passion Week. A third category consists of poetry whose subject is about the personal spiritual experience. This experience is wide-ranging, including an overwhelming sense of personal unworthiness ["Love (III)"], rebellion ("The Collar"), repentance ("Confession"), continuing spiritual conflicts ["Affliction (I)"], and the sense of calm which comes with reassurance of God's love ("The Flower"). Fourthly, some of his poetry is designed to strengthen the reader's faith ("The Quip") or moral character ("Vertue"). Finally, there is poetry that depends for its effect on other (perhaps less directly religious) spiritual qualities, like creativity and imagination. "Hope" is built around a sequence of complex symbols, while "Jordan (I)" provides a witty justification for his own verse by arguing for the equal status of religious and love poetry.

—J. Mark Halstead

FURTHER READING

Cope, W. (2003). *George Herbert—the golden age of spiritual writing.* London: SPCK.

Thomas, R. S. (Ed.). (1967). *A choice of George Herbert's verse.* London: Faber & Faber.

HESCHEL, ABRAHAM JOSHUA

Abraham Joshua Heschel (1907–1972) was born into a distinguished Hasidic family in Warsaw, Poland. As a child he was expected to become the spiritual leader of his group. From a very young age, Heschel immersed himself in the study of traditional sacred Jewish texts, including the Hebrew Bible, the Talmud, and the Zohar; and the classical Jewish commentaries, especially Rashi (Rabbi Shlomo ben Isaac 1040–1105), the outstanding commentator on the Bible and Talmud. In 1925 Heschel went to Vilna, now known in Lithuanian as Vilnius, to prepare himself for university study. Vilna was known as "the Jerusalem of Lithuania" because it was, at that time, the greatest center of Jewish learning.

Heschel was already an ordained rabbi when he arrived in Berlin in 1927. He received his Ph.D. in philosophy from the University of Berlin in 1933 for a dissertation on the Hebrew prophets. In 1938 the Nazis deported Heschel to Poland. He left Poland in 1939, just 6 weeks before the invasion of Poland.

In 1940 he arrived in the United States to teach at Hebrew Union College in Cincinnati, Ohio. From 1945 until his death in 1972, Heschel was professor of Jewish ethics and mysticism at the Jewish Theological Seminary in New York City.

Heschel is considered to be the foremost spiritual Jewish thinker and activist in the 20th century. Heschel, whose writings are authentically Jewish, has had a far-reaching impact not only on the Jewish community but also on Christians and members of other faith communities. Many Jews and Christians consider Heschel to be the Jewish saint of his generation.

Heschel wrote significant works on the Bible, on the Talmud, on the major medieval philosophers, including Judah Halevi and Moses Maimonides, and on some of the major Hasidic leaders, including the Baal Shem Tov (1690–1760), the founder of Hasidism. His best-known work, however, is his book entitled *God in Search of Man,* a book on his own philosophy of Judaism. It is devoted to showing three interrelated ways through which contemporary human beings can open themselves to God or, more precisely, through which they can respond to a God who is in search of human beings. The three ways are the way to God via the world, the way to God through the Bible, and the way to God through sacred deeds.

For Heschel the idea that God is in search of human beings, that God is a God of pathos who needs human beings and is affected by their actions, is the most fundamental idea of biblical thought. This idea, which lies at the core of Heschel's thinking, was already developed in his 1933 doctoral dissertation. Heschel returned to develop this idea more fully in his major work, *The Prophets,* published in 1962.

Heschel tells us that his own life was transformed by his deep immersion in the Hebrew prophets. After 1962 he left his study more and more frequently to become involved in a number of social and political issues. He opposed American involvement in the Vietnam War. He devoted a great deal of time to the Civil Rights Movement led by Martin Luther King, Jr., and he addressed himself to the plight of the Jews in the Soviet Union.

Heschel remains the most significant thinker to address the critical issue of the religious diversity of the world. In his essay "No Religion Is an Island," he presents a radical view of the world's religions. Heschel argues that no religion has a monopoly on truth or holiness and that the diversity of religions is the will of God. Heschel was the most important Jewish voice during the meeting of the Second Vatican Council (1962–1965). He played a major role in shaping the Church's view of Judaism. On several occasions Heschel met with Pope Paul VI and convinced him to remove a paragraph in the document that called for the conversion of the Jews.

A few weeks before he died, Heschel left the following message for young people: "And above all, remember that the meaning of life is to build a life as if it were a work of art. You're not a machine. And you are young. Start working on this great work of art called your own existence" (*Moral Grandeur and Spiritual Audacity,* 412).

—*Harold Kasimow*

FURTHER READING

Heschel, A. J. (1951). *The Sabbath: Its meaning for modern man.* New York: Farrar, Straus, and Young.

Heschel, A. J. (1951). *Man is not alone: A philosophy of religion.* New York: Farrar, Straus, and Young.

Heschel, A. J. (1955). *God in search of man: A philosophy of Judaism.* New York: Farrar, Straus and Cudahy.

Heschel, A. J. (1968). *Who is man?* Stanford, CA: Stanford University Press.

Heschel, A. J. (1973). *A passion for truth.* New York: Farrar, Straus, and Giroux.

Heschel, A. J. (1996). *Moral grandeur and spiritual audacity: Essays.* Susannah Heschel (Ed.). New York: Farrar, Straus, and Giroux.

Kasimow, H., & Sherwin, B. L. (Eds.). (1991). *No religion is an island: Abraham Joshua Heschel and interreligious dialogue.* Maryknoll, NY: Orbis Books.

HINDUISM

SOURCES

Hinduism is one of the most ancient religious systems of humankind. It does not have a historical beginning. Its origins are shrouded in the mists of antiquity. Scholars have connected it to the Indus civilization unearthed by archeology. Its founders were ancient sages, called *rshis,* who achieved enlightenment of spiritual truths, which they expressed in Sanskrit hymns known as the *Vedas.* Many Hindu insights and patterns of rituals are traced to these sacred texts of the tradition.

The doctrinal framework of Hinduism is in the *Upanishads,* which are elaborations and extrapolations of Vedic visions. Upanishadic rishis did not simply speculate about heaven, earth, and life. They penetrated into the core of human consciousness by spiritual exercises (*dhyâna*). For them, spirituality is not a metaphysical system but a recognition to be achieved by pursuing the path of the aspirant. Vedic utterances and Upanishadic aphorisms are the nuggets of a perennial worldview called *sanâtana dharma:* eternal code. Much of the metaphysical, moral, and spiritual framework of Hinduism is embodied in the *Bhagavad Gita* (Divine Song), which is regarded with reverence by many Hindus.

AFFILIATION AND MULTIPLE PATHS

Hinduism is a complex system of beliefs, ideals and practices. Affiliation does not result from proclamations of faith, but by birth. Hinduism does not recommend change of faith or conversion from one religion to another. It regards God and Truth as one, and leaves open the possibility that all people may call it by different names. The quest and effort to connect with the divine is what matters, not the paths and practices adopted for this. This insight that no approach can be considered best, implies an intrinsic respect for different religious modes. In this respect, Hinduism differs radically from religions whose goal is to convert others to their own visions of godhead and afterlife. Hindu doctrinal tolerance enables its practitioners to go into a mosque, church, or synagogue, and pray there in silence to their own vision of the divine principle.

A born Hindu may repudiate some doctrines but cannot be excommunicated. So there are atheist and agnostic Hindus as well as those who pray to personalized Gods and mystics who worship no god in temples. This unique feature of Hinduism stems from the principle that religious commitment should arise from the heart and that religious vision is an awakening.

THE HINDU PANTHEON

Divinity is conceived in the Hindu framework in complex metaphysical ways. The key idea here is one of a triple principle referred to as *Trimûrti* (pronounced trimoorthi). The *Trimurti* is a Hindu concept that stands for birth, existence, and dissolution of the cosmic cycle in grand time spans called *yugas.* These universal principles have also been deified in the mythopoesy of the tradition as Brahma, Vishnu, and Shiva. The elusive godhead is given form and substance here.

In traditional Hinduism, the metaphysical attributes of Shiva and Vishnu gave rise to two major branches of Hinduism, known as the *Shaiva* and the *Vaishnava* sects. A third branch, known as the *Shakta,* is dedicated to the worship of Shakti or the Female Principle governing the cosmos.

There are also other representations of the divine in Hinduism that serve to concretize the abstract divinity. These representations include Ganesha (the elephant-faced deity) and Murugan: the chief of the Tamil deities; Sarasvati, Pârvati, and Lakshmi—the goddesses associated with the Trimurti—and Rama and Krishna—incarnations of Vishnu, whose sagas are narrated in grand epics. Many in the Hindu fold also pay reverential homage to certain plants and animals. In Hinduism, the Divine is not only omnipresent and omnipotent, but also *omnimorphic,* i.e., taking on many forms. Hindu visions of God embody color and charm and have given rise to great art and poetry.

Esoteric meanings are associated with the forms and faces of the gods worshipped in Hindu temples, and there is symbolism in the genesis and doings of these gods. In the tales and epic allusions of the tradition we are reminded that Divinity transcends the constraints of space and time, of causality and conservation, even of ethical categories. In the vision of Hinduism, as narrated in its mythopoesy, gods may be good and bad, beautiful and ugly, merciful and cruel, majestically grand and dwarfishly small, handsome as a hero or plain as a tortoise. (A parallel worldview may be found in the lore of ancient Greece.) Hindu sages taught that compatibilities arise from narrow perspectives. In the cosmic grandeur they all dissolve. For example, the same vast sky can be pitch black at night and gloriously bright at noon. So it is with divinity.

Such were the inspirations behind the pantheon in the Hindu world. In our own times, physics teaches us that the same electron can be both particle and wave. These two seem to be contradictory but are, in fact, complementary. Similarly, the Hindu insight says that the world results not from contradictions but from complementarities. Our descriptions depend on our reference system. Life and Divinity are too complex to be reduced to a true or false answer.

Atman and Brahman

The Hindu view is that associated with every conscious being is an *atman* (pronounced aathman): the self. Atman infuses matter with life and consciousness.

The atman experiences and preserves its own identity. Every atman is regarded as a spark from the Supreme Being known as *Brahman.* Brahman is the spiritual undercurrent of the universe. Embodied atman is often unaware that its separateness from Brahman is temporary and illusory. Hinduism says that one purpose of religion is to enable us to experience this cosmic connection. It says in an Upanishad: *tat tvam asi—Thou art That.*

Thus, the Hindu spiritual vision regards individual consciousness from a cosmic perspective. It recognizes our transience as separate entities, yet incorporates us into the infinity surrounding us. There could be other manifestations of *Brahman* elsewhere in the universe. Most importantly, in the Hindu view, there is a subtle spirit at the core of everything. From this perspective, the religious expressions of humanity are echoes of the Universal Spirit, just as volcanic outbursts remind us of submerged forces of far greater magnitude.

Samsara and Karma

Reincarnation and *karma* are two key concepts associated with Hinduism. According to the Hindu view, physical death is the disembodiment of the Atman, which then encases itself in another body. This is the idea of the cycle of birth and death. This cycle is called *samsara* (pronounced samsaara) or reincarnation. Each of us is experiencing but one incarnation (embodied existence) in a series through which every atman goes. A related doctrine is the *law of karma.* Karma is consequential action. The law states that our current experiences, good and bad, are the fruits of what we did before in a past incarnation and that our current actions will result in new experiences in this or in a future incarnation.

The goal of spiritual evolution is to break away from the repetitious birth–death cycle. This is to be achieved through right action and spiritual effort. Such liberation is known as *moksha* or *nirvana.*

Dharma

The ethical and juridical component of Hinduism rests on the concept of *dharma:* it is sometimes defined as that which "holds in unity all the creatures of the world." Dharma is the ethical framework that keeps one at peace with oneself and with the world around.

There are 10 components of *dharma.* Three are for the development of spiritual potential: temperance, purity of body and mind, and control over one's senses. Three are for intellectual life: adherence to reason, pursuit of knowledge, and commitment to truth. Three relate to our impact on others: forgiveness, being without anger, and not coveting what belongs to others. The 10th item is perseverance.

Some behavior and values must change with place and time. What might have been conducive for a stable society at one time could be inappropriate at another time. What is polite in one society, such as hugging as a form of greeting, could be unacceptable in another. We need to modify dharma with time and place to maintain harmony. This leads to the notion of *yugadharma,* i.e., the *dharma* of the age, or *adyâtanadharma* (today's dharma). However, eternal values like caring, compassion, performance of prescribed duties, and respect for others are part of *sanâtanadharma:* the invariable and unchanging elements of dharma.

THE EPIC FOUNDATIONS

Hindu civilization rests on two grand epics that are reckoned among the masterpieces of world literature. They are called the *Râmâyana* and the *Mahâbhârata.* Unsurpassed in length and in their influence on a dynamic civilization, they are part of Hindu sacred history. They are also treasure chests of classical Hindu values and worldviews. In addition to numerous fascinating and colorful episodes, these epics inculcate the principles of justice, obedience to elders, sacredness of promise, the perennial struggle between the righteous and the wrong, and the ultimate victory of truth. This last principle is expressed in an ancient Sanskrit maxim *satyemva jayate* (truth alone triumphs) dating back several millennia. It is taught to children at an early stage, for they are told that those who adhere to what is morally right will triumph sooner or later. This is modern India's motto.

Fundamental Doctrines

Consider pools, ponds, and bottles of water everywhere in the world. Though located in different places in different containers, they all contain water as the oceans contain water. Likewise, in the Hindu view, Brahman, the substratum of the universe is like a spiritual ocean, and we are all like little bottles that contain a bit of that cosmic spirit. Every life in the world is a transitory manifestation of *Brahman.* Life is thus a conscious flicker that has the potential for realizing the link between this fleeting experience and the timeless, undifferentiated Brahman. Spiritual illumination involves the indescribable experience of the bond between the temporal and the eternal.

There is intrinsic respect in the Hindu world for anyone and any system that accepts the spiritual component of life and the world. According to the Hindu worldview, the Divine is not someone or something to be accepted simply because it is so stated in some holy books. Rather, the Divine is a nonmaterial dimension of the universe that is to be apprehended by direct effort and personal experience. Apprehension of this dimension is the goal of meditation, yoga, and other spiritual exercises.

The Caste System

Hinduism is as much a complex culture as an ancient religion. It has changed in many significant ways over the centuries, some of its features lingering much longer than others. One of these is known as *varnâshrama* or institution of social categories. Translated into English as the caste system, this is a hereditary profession-based classification of people into the priest class (*Brahmins*), administrating class (*kshatriyas*), mercantile class (*vaishyas*), laboring class (*shudras*), and those outside of this categorization (*avarnas*). In this matter Hindu society was not much different from similar stratification elsewhere in the world in premodern times. However, at some point this degenerated into a rigid system where endogamy (marriage of people belonging to the same group), class immobility (one cannot change one's caste), and noncommensality (one is not allowed to eat with people of a different caste) meant social inequality and marginalization of the lower classes. In spite of appeals from many sages and saints of the tradition, the caste system has persisted in the Hindu world for too many centuries. In recent years, with the rising of consciousness on human rights and equality, the system is beginning to break down, at least in urban centers. The constitution of modern India makes caste discrimination illegal.

Four Goals and Four Stages

Life is not mere existence; we do not live just to eat and drink every day, and eventually die. In the course of life we pass from stage to stage. In the Hindu framework, human life should be devoted to the attainment of four goals: righteous conduct (*dharma*), material resources (*artha*), enjoyment (*kâma*), and spiritual realization (*moksha*). No one goal is more or less important than another. A life without attaining all these would be incomplete because it is believed that for the full experience of life one must have a moral framework (dharma), economic independence to furnish our practical needs (artha), have family and friends to enjoy relationships (kâma), and also strive to attain spiritual fulfillment (moksha).

Likewise, in the ideal Hindu view, there are four stages in life, during each of which a specific responsibility is assigned. These stages are known as *âshramas.* In the first one, known as *brahmachârya,* one acquires knowledge and skills. In the second, called *grihastya,* the person is in the householder's stage during which one serves society by honest work, is loyal to one's spouse, and raises a family. The third stage is called *vânaprasthya.* A person enters this stage upon completing societal responsibilities, when children are established in life, and one's own retirement from work comes. The last ideal stage, known as *sannyâsa,* is when one is expected to renounce all worldly possessions and spend the remaining years of one's life in seeking ultimate liberation from life. This traditional model serves as a guide for life. It is not taken today as a rigid set of rules by which all Hindus live. This is an inevitable consequence of the transformations of culture and civilization resulting from technology, modernity, and urban lifestyles.

Commonalties Among Hindus

Some of the religious values, practices, and beliefs that all Hindus share are

- Worship of god in tangible forms to concretize unfathomable divinity.
- Sensitivity to the epics of the tradition: the *Râmâyana* and the *Mahâbhârata,* which provide the ethical framework of right and wrong, duty and responsibility.
- Reverence for the personified divinities of the sacred literatures, to give expression to devotion and love of god. Hindu centers of worship (temples) are described as the Home of the Gods, for here are housed the colorful *mûrtis* (icons) of the Hindu world, each associated

with episodes and histories and endowed with particular powers.

- Celebration of certain universal festivals, such as *dîpâvali* or Festival of Light, which marks the epic victory of good over evil, as told in the tradition.
- Performance of rituals in the presence of the sacred fire. Fire symbolizes the primordial and the eternal, that which was in the first moment of creation, which subsists in the cosmic void as stars, and which will arise as the all-consuming conflagration at the end of each cosmic cycle.
- Recitation of Sanskrit or Tamil hymns in prayers and in sacraments, to reflect the esoteric dimension of the religion and to affirm the tradition's cultural continuity. Sanskrit in the Hindu world is the sacred language of the Gods.
- Respect for the doctrines of *reincarnation* and the *law of karma.*
- Invocation of the Cosmic Principle for universal peace through the sacred syllables, *om shânti, shânti, shântihi!*

CONCLUDING REMARKS

Hinduism is one of the major world religions. Some of the more salient aspects of Hinduism are described in this entry. Hinduism has inspired magnificent music and grand poetry, sophisticated art and complex architecture, colorful dances, and profound philosophy.

Aside from philosophical insights, spiritual visions, and literary works, Hinduism's great message to the world is in the form of a simple prayer which says:

âkâsâd patitantoyam
yedâ gacchati sâgaram
sarva deva namaskârah
sri kesavam pradigacchadi.

As waters falling from the skies
Go back to the self-same sea,
Prostrations to all the gods that be
Reach the same Divinity.

HINDUISM BEYOND INDIA

Hinduism is generally associated with the vast majority of the inhabitants of India, but its influence on the thinking and practices of many other peoples has not been insignificant. China, Japan, Laos, Kampuchea, Tibet, and Sri Lanka have all felt the impact of Hindu thought directly or via its offshoot, Buddhism. Ever since Europeans began their contacts with India, travelers, thinkers, and writers have imbibed many elements of the Hindu spirit and spread these among their own people in many ways.

The current interest in the West in yoga and meditation, in Krishna consciousness and other elements of Hinduism are not of recent origin. Interest in such matters has always been there among many Western thinkers. Even some ancient Greek philosophers, such as Pythagoras and Plato, are believed to have been influenced by Hindu thought.

—Varadaraja V. Raman

See also Hinduism; Supreme Being, the Hindu Trinity

FURTHER READING

Gandhi, M. K. (1950). *Hindu Dharma.* Ahmedabad, India: Navajivan Publishing House.

Klostermaier, K. (1989). *A survey of Hinduism.* Albany, NY: State University of New York Press.

Radhakrishnan, S. (1927). *The Hindu view of life.* New York: Macmillan.

Raman, V. V. (1989). *Glimpses of Indian heritage.* Bombay, India: Popular Prakasha.

Sarma, D. S. (1962). *Hinduism through the ages.* Bombay, India: Bhartiya Vidya Bhavan.

Zimmer, H. (1951). *Philosophies of India.* New York: Pantheon.

HINDUISM: SUPREME BEING, THE HINDU TRINITY

The Supreme Being or God of the Hindu religion is the personal form of the Ultimate Reality. It is considered to have many characteristics, individual deities each representing a particular aspect of the Supreme Being. Each Hindu deity shares an existence with the Supreme Being and therefore Hindu worship is considered a monotheistic polytheism and not simple polytheism. Hindus believe there is only one Supreme Being and He is the God of all religions and that the cosmic activity of the Supreme Being involves creation, preservation, and dissolution and recreation. These three tasks are associated with the three deities, Brahma, Vishnu, and Shiva. They are called Sat-Tat-Aum, the Being, the Word, or the Holy Spirit. Lord Brahma brings creation and represents the creative principle of the Supreme

Being. Lord Vishnu maintains the universe and represents the eternal principle of preservation. Lord Shiva represents the principle of dissolution and recreation. Together, these three deities represent the trimutri (Hindu trinity). Brahma, Vishnu, and Shiva represent the same power (the Supreme Being), but in three different aspects—the Divine in its threefold nature and function. Each aspect of the trinity contains and includes the others. As such, the Supreme Being is called Brahma, Vishnu, or Shiva when performing the tasks of creation, preservation, and dissolution/recreation.

Hindus call Lord Brahma the Creator of the universe as He symbolizes creation. His divine consort is Saraswati, the Goddess of learning and knowledge, who provides Lord Brahma with knowledge necessary for the process of creation. As creation is the work of the mind and the intellect, Lord Brahma symbolizes the Universal Mind and the individual's own mind and intellect. Since most are born with a gift for intellect, not many feel the need to worship Brahma. Instead, Brahma is worshipped by seekers of knowledge, such as students, teachers, scholars, and scientists. Brahma is usually represented as a bearded, four-faced, four-armed deity. In popular images, He carries a rosary in the upper right hand, a book in the upper left hand, a kamandalu (water pot) in the lower left hand, and bestows grace with His lower right hand. The four faces represent the sacred knowledge of the four Vedas (Rig, Yajur, Sama, and Atharva) symbolizing that Brahma is the source of all knowledge necessary for the creation of the universe.

The four arms represent the four directions and thus represent the omnipresence and omnipotence of Lord Brahma. The four hands represent the four aspects of human personality, including the mind (back right hand), the intellect (back left hand), the ego (front right hand), and the empirical self or conditioned consciousness (front left hand). The rosary symbolizes time and the cycle through which the world moves from creation to sustenance, from sustenance to dissolution, and from dissolution to new creation. The rosary also represents the materials used in creation. The rosary's position in the back right hand suggests these materials are used in an intelligent way in creation. A book in the back hand represents that accurate information is important for any kind of creative work. A water pot (kamandalu) in the front left hand symbolizes the energy Lord Brahma uses to create the universe. The front right hand, symbolizing the ego, is shown in a pose bestowing grace, meaning that the Lord Brahma bestows grace and protects all true devotees.

In terms of the colors used to represent Lord Brahma, the golden face of Brahma indicates that the Lord is active when involved in the process of creation. The white beard represents wisdom, and the long beard represents the idea that creation is a process that goes on for eternity. The crown on the head of the Lord represents that Brahma has supreme power and authority over the process of creation. Brahma wears white clothes, representing the dual nature of creation (e.g., purity and impurity, happiness and unhappiness, vice and virtue, knowledge and ignorance). The lotus upon which Brahma stands or sits represents that Brahma symbolizes the creative power of the Supreme Reality. The swan upon which Brahma transports himself is a symbol of the power of discrimination and therefore represents the idea that although creation is pluralistic, there is only one Supreme Reality.

Lord Vishnu represents the part of the Supreme Reality that preserves and sustains the universe. His consort is Lakshmi, the Goddess of love, beauty, and delight. Vishnu is generally symbolized by a human body with four arms and in His hands He carries a conch (shankha), a mace (gada), and a discus (chakra). He also is commonly presented wearing a crown, two earrings, a garland (mala) of flowers, and a gem around His neck. He has a blue body and wears yellow clothes. Vishnu stands on a 1,000-headed snake (named *Shesha Nag*).

The four arms represent Vishnu's omnipresence and omnipotence, and the two arms in the front represent His activity in the physical world. The two arms in the back represent His activity in the spiritual world. The right side of the body represents the creative activities of the mind, and the left symbolizes the activities of the heart. The conch indicates that the Lord communicates with His devotees with love and understanding; the chakra in His upper right hand represents the idea that Vishnu protects His devotees from evil; and the mace signifies that Vishnu protects the world by the energy within Him. His front right hand is depicted bestowing grace on His devotees.

The snake denotes the mind and the thousand heads of the snake signify innumerable desires and passions of an individual. Just as a snake destroys its victim by its venom, an uncontrolled mind destroys the world by the venom of its possessiveness. The Lord has controlled all desires, and this is symbolized by showing Him seated on the two coils of the snake. When a sincere devotee of the Lord controls his desires, the Lord fulfills the devotee's genuine desires and helps him on his path. The blue sky represents that He pervades the entire universe and His blue body that He has infinite attributes. The yellow clothes Vishnu wears represent that He is on earth to uphold righteousness and destroy evil. The garland around His neck is a symbol of the devotee's adoration; the gem on His neck a symbol that Vishnu fulfills the desires and needs of His devotees; and, the crown a symbol of His supreme power and authority. The earrings represent the dual nature of creation (e.g., knowledge and ignorance, happiness and unhappiness, and pleasure and pain).

The worship of Lord Vishnu is very popular among Hindus, especially among the followers of the Vaishnava tradition (Vaishnavism). Lord Vishnu is also known by other names, such as Vasudeva and Narayana. Ten incarnations of Lord Vishnu that are popular among Hindus reveal God's help in various stages of human evolution from aquatic to human life. They include incarnations in the animal form (i.e., Matsya, the fish; Kurma, the tortoise; Varaha, the boar), incarnations in half-human and half-animal form (i.e., Narasimha, the man lion; Vamana, the dwarf), and incarnations in human form (i.e., Parasurama, the warrior; Rama; Sri Krishna; Buddha; and Kalkin).

Shiva is recognized as the third form of God. Due to His activity of dissolution and recreation, the words *destroyer* and *destruction* are often wrongly associated with Lord Shiva. When the process of creation is disturbed and life becomes impossible, Lord Shiva dissolves the universe to create the universe anew so that unliberated souls can have the opportunity to free themselves from bondage with the physical world. Lord Shiva protects souls from pain caused by an unbalanced or unhealthy universe and is therefore considered the Lord of mercy and compassion. He also protects devotees from the evil of lust, greed, and anger.

Shiva was originally considered a minor deity, known as *Rudra* in the Rig Veda, but eventually He gained more importance after absorbing some of the characteristics of an earlier fertility god. Shiva is attributed with many titles that signify His many strengths, including Mahabaleshwar (Great God of Strength), Tryambakam (Three-Eyed One), Mahakala (Great Time), and Nilkanth (the One with a Blue Throat). He is considered *anadi* (without beginning or birth) and *ananth* (without end or death). The five mantras that constitute Shiva's body are Sadyojaata or Mahadeva (earth), Vaamadeva or Uma (water), Aghora or Bhairava (fire), Tatpurusha or Nandi (air), and Eesaana or Sadasiva (space).

Shiva is often worshipped in an abstract manner, as God without form, because Hindus believe that God transcends all personal characteristics. Yet Hindus believe He can also have personal characteristics as long as the human devotee understands that God is not limited to a particular form. Shiva is represented in a variety of forms, most notably the lingam—an ovoid shape thought to signify the mystical experience of the absolute perfection of Shiva. The representation of the lingam comes from the story of Shiva rejecting samsara and smearing his body with ash, closing his eyes and performing austerities. Shiva generated so much heat that his body transformed into a pillar of fire—represented by a blazing lingam that threatened to destroy the world. Unable to control the fire, the gods did not know what to do when suddenly a yoni appeared—the divine vessel of the mother goddess, which contained the heat from the lingam and saved the cosmos from destruction. The nonanthropomorphic lingam form of Shiva is revered in temples throughout Asia. The lingam is a symbol of that which is invisible yet omnipresent—a visible symbol of the Ultimate Reality that is present in us.

Shiva is believed to live in Kailasa, immersed in deep meditation on Mount Kailash in the Himalayas with His wife, Parvati, and their sons—the six-headed Skanda (also known as *Karttikeya* or as *Murugan*) and the elephant-headed God of wisdom, Ganesh. Ganesh acquired his head due to the actions of Shiva, who decapitated him because Ganesh refused to allow him to enter the house while Parvati was bathing. Shiva had to give him the new head to placate his wife. In another version, Parvati showed the child off to Shiva, whose face burned his head to ashes, which Brahma told Shiva to replace with the first head he could find, an elephant. Skanda or Karttikeya is a six-headed god and was conceived to kill the demon Tarakasura, who had proven invincible against other minor gods. Shiva is often represented as being on His holy mount, the Bull Nandi, alongside His attendant Bhadra.

According to the Bhagavata Purana, Lord Shiva emerged from the forehead of Lord Brahma when Lord Brahma asked his sons to create children in the universe and they refused. This angered Lord Brahma and his anger caused a crying child to appear from his forehead. As the child was crying he was called *Rudra.* He later became Lord Shiva. Lord Shiva was also asked to go forth and create children in the universe, but when Lord Brahma observed the progeny shared the qualities of Lord Shiva, he asked Shiva to observe austerities instead of creating progeny. A slightly different version is told in the Shiva Purana. In the Shiva Purana, Shiva promises Brahma that an aspect of His Rudra will be born, and this aspect is identical to Him.

Hindus look to the Supreme Being and to the Lords of Brahma, Vishnu, and Shiva for knowledge, guidance, and protection. The Supreme Being is worshipped in its many incarnations in many different ways and through different practices. As such, the Supreme Being and the Hindu trinity described herein have a significant and leading role in the religious and spiritual development of Hindus around the world.

—*Elizabeth M. Dowling*

See also Hinduism

FURTHER READING

Hopkins, T. (1971). *Hindu religious tradition.* Encino, CA: Dickinson Publishing Co.

Jensen, E. R. (1993). *Hindu imagery: Gods, manifestations, and their meaning.* York Beach, ME: Samuel Weiser.

HUMAN RIGHTS

On December 10, 1948, the General Assembly of the United Nations adopted and proclaimed the Universal Declaration of Human Rights. The preamble to the declaration provides a foundation for modern-day human rights, based on the recognition that all humans have the right to freedom, justice, and peace in the world. The preamble goes on to explain that when inalienable human rights are ignored, "barbarous acts" have occurred. As the international legal implications of the original 30 articles are becoming ever more foundational to all aspects of the social and political life of nations, so too the influence of religion and culture has proliferated, and in ways arguably unexpected in a mid-20th century world increasingly dominated by secular and often militantly atheistic ideologies.

In abbreviated form the 30 articles from the Universal Declaration are as follows:

UN Universal Declaration of Human Rights

Article 1
All human beings are born free and equal in dignity and rights.

Article 2
Everyone is entitled to all the rights and freedoms set forth in this Declaration, without distinction of any kind, such as race, color, sex, language, religion, political or other opinion, national or social origin, property, birth, or other status.

Article 3
Everyone has the right to life, liberty, and security of person.

Article 4
No one shall be held in slavery or servitude; slavery and the slave trade shall be prohibited in all their forms.

Article 5
No one shall be subjected to torture or to cruel, inhuman, or degrading treatment or punishment.

Article 6
Everyone has the right to recognition everywhere as a person before the law.

Article 7
All are equal before the law and are entitled without any discrimination to equal protection of the law.

Article 8
Everyone has the right to an effective remedy by the competent national tribunals for acts violating the fundamental rights.

Article 9
No one shall be subjected to arbitrary arrest, detention, or exile.

Article 10
Everyone is entitled in full equality to a fair and public hearing by an independent and impartial tribunal.

Article 11
Everyone charged with a penal offence has the right to be presumed innocent until proved guilty according to law in a public trial.

Article 12
No one shall be subjected to arbitrary interference with privacy, family, home, or correspondence.

Article 13
Everyone has the right to freedom of movement and residence within the borders of each state.

Article 14
Everyone has the right to seek and to enjoy in other countries asylum from persecution.

Article 15
Everyone has the right to a nationality.

Article 16
Men and women of full age, without any limitation due to race, nationality, or religion, have the right to marry and to found a family.

Article 17
Everyone has the right to own property alone as well as in association with others.

Article 18
Everyone has the right to freedom of thought, conscience, and religion.

Article 19
Everyone has the right to freedom of opinion and expression.

Article 20
Everyone has the right to freedom of peaceful assembly and association.

Article 21
All have the right to take part in the government of their country.

Article 22
Everyone, as a member of society, has the right to social security.

Article 23
Everyone has the right to work.

Article 24
Everyone has the right to rest and leisure.

Article 25
Everyone has the right to a standard of living adequate for health and well-being.

Article 26
Everyone has the right to education.

Article 27
Everyone has the right freely to participate in the cultural life of the community.

Article 28
Everyone is entitled to a social and international order in which the rights and freedoms set forth in this Declaration can be fully realized.

Article 29
Everyone has duties to the community in which alone the free and full development of his personality is possible.

Article 30
Nothing in this Declaration may be interpreted as implying for any state, group or person any right to engage in any activity or to perform any act aimed at the destruction of any of the rights and freedoms set forth herein.

Given how wide-ranging the statement of human rights is—from basic civil and democratic political freedoms to rights of education, employment, health—it is not surprising that in an effort to make social progress through subsequent human rights work, the nature and extent of the rights' framework has become extremely complex, not to say controversial.

The most fundamental critique of the UN era of human rights is in terms of practical rather than theoretical terms. Human rights in the UN system imply universality. Yet human values are by their nature contested, and history reveals a tragically imperfect world where inequalities abound and justice is too often absent. At the 1993 World Conference on Human Rights in Vienna, expressions were made of the dismay and condemnation of the human rights' violations that continue to be implemented in certain parts of the world. It is this most fundamental sense of inequality in the geographical expressions of human rights' abuses that arguably presents the greatest cause of conflict the world over.

The UN today is far more representative than it was in 1948, with more than three times the number of nation states represented at the UN General Assembly. Ironically, the 1948 Universal Declaration is certainly the least democratically representative of all UN documents in human rights though remaining the most foundational. (The irony that two key signatories, Britain and France, retained at the time of the UN Declaration were exploitative vestiges of colonial empires in their overseas territories and dominions is not lost on many developing nations.) In general, this is why there are ongoing debates about whether the original 30 articles have universal status as an outline statement of moral intent, let alone as a system of detailed ethical guidance.

The United Nations has developed considerably since its foundation in 1945. So too have the structures for its maintenance and the nature and complexity of human rights. A common idea now is to see such development as "generation," with three interrelated generations of human rights: civil and political, or first-generation rights; economic, social, and cultural, or second-generation rights; and human solidarity, or third-generation rights. This crude measure recognizes that rights have evolved in modern times by a series of historical-social-political developments. The latest generation of human solidarity rights—relating to groups of individuals within a society such as women, children, minorities, or indigenous peoples—would have been refinements in thinking largely inconceivable to the writers of first-generation civil, political, and legal rights.

RELIGION, SPIRITUALITY, AND RIGHTS

The preamble to the 1981 UN Declaration on the Elimination of All Forms of Intolerance and Discrimination Based on Religion or Belief restates the wider context of the charter of the UN. Notably this reiterates the "dignity and equality inherent in all human beings," international commitment on the promotion of universal human rights and fundamental freedoms for all, "without distinction as to race, sex, language, or religion," and the principles of non-discrimination and equality before the law and the right to freedom of thought, conscience, religion, and belief.

As with the Convention on the International Rights of Correction, the UN Declaration on the Elimination of All Forms of Intolerance and Discrimination Based on Religion or Belief also emphasizes the role of such freedoms in the maintenance of a stable international order: "Considering that the disregard and infringement of human rights and fundamental freedoms, in particular of the right to freedom of thought, conscience, religion, or whatever belief, have brought, directly or indirectly, wars and great suffering to mankind, especially where they serve as a means of foreign interference in the internal affairs of other States and amount to kindling hatred between peoples and nations." Positively phrased, "freedom of religion and belief should also contribute to the attainment of the goals of world peace, social justice, and friendship among peoples and to the elimination of ideologies or practices of colonialism and racial discrimination."

Yet it is not simply past ills that are the concern of the UN, for the 1981 Declaration is also concerned about "manifestations of intolerance and . . . the existence of discrimination in matters of religion or belief still in evidence in some areas of the world." The 1981 Declaration also offers a commitment to adopt "all necessary measures for the speedy elimination of such intolerance in all its forms and manifestations and to prevent and combat discrimination on the ground of religion or belief."

What is significant here can be summarized in three points. First, after a long neglect (or low-level treatment) of religion explicitly, the UN system from the late 1970s and with the 1981 Declaration began to recognize the international significance of religion for a stable world order. Thus, during the 1990s, religion emerges explicitly in numerous international statements, gaining new and unprecedented prominence. For instance, there was the Cairo Declaration on Human Rights in Islam (1990), the Fundamental Agreement between the Holy See and the State of Israel (1993). The Vienna Declaration and Plan of Action (1993) and the follow-up to the World Conference on Human Rights UN High Commissioner on Human Rights (1998) also gave some prominence to religion, important in light of their respective post-Yugoslavia and post-Rwanda contexts. The new prominence given to religion culminated in the Oslo Declaration on Freedom of Religion and Belief (1998). Indicated by both the 1981 Declaration and the 1998 Oslo Declaration, the notion of freedom of religion was itself extended to freedom of religion and belief to allow for a wider interpretation of worldviews.

These developments have had the effect of linking in a fairly direct way the fundamental first- and second-generation rights of "freedom of thought, conscience, and religion" to third-generation rights of human solidarity, most notably in the linking of religious intolerance to the ending of racism, xenophobia, and discrimination more broadly. For example, the 1981 Declaration on the Elimination of All Forms of Intolerance and of Discrimination Based on Religion or Belief was followed just over a decade later by the UN Declaration on the Rights of Persons Belonging to National or Ethnic, Religious, and Linguistic Minorities, and the theme of unifying religious freedom with other forms of discrimination was highlighted by the World Conference Against Racism in 2001.

In this regard we need to remind ourselves that the Convention on the Prevention and Punishment of the Crime of Genocide was approved on December 9, 1948, the day before the signing of the Universal Declaration of Human Rights. Though increasingly contentious as a term, it was genocide that was on the mind of the newly formed United Nations when considering a Universal Declaration of Human Rights and when it finally made the Declaration in the form of 30 articles on December 10, 1948. Arguably, genocide defines the subsequent contours of the UN mandate in the all other areas of its operation, set to expand drastically in the coming decades, and it is genocide that is the foundational motivation behind all modern human rights legislation. In modern times this becomes highlighted through a lack of physical space, conflict over scarce resources, and the vested interests of those that share a different—often religious, ideological, or political—worldview.

We only have to look at history to see the relationship between bitter hatred of culture and the relationship between this and the excesses of violence we now call genocide. Amongst the first public acts of the Nazis in 1933 was the mass burning of books by authors and traditions hated by the Third Reich. Freedom of expression—whether religious, theological, or ideological—is being seen ever more prominently as a key barometer of an open society and a measure therefore of lived reality, that is, the politically embodied success, of all human rights discourse. Freedom of religious expression, belief, and practice are fundamental human rights that must be protected.

—Liam Gearon

See also United Nations

FURTHER READING

Forsythe, D. P. (2000). *Human rights in international relations.* Cambridge: Cambridge University Press.

Gearon, L. (Ed.). (2002). *Human rights and religion: A reader.* Brighton, UK: Sussex Academic Press.

Gearon, L. (2003). *The human rights handbook: A global perspective for education.* Stoke-on-Trent, UK: Trentham.

Ryan, S. (2000). *The United Nations and international politics.* London: Macmillan.

Sellar, K. (2002). *The rise and rise of human rights.* London: Sutton.

Wellman, C. (2000). *The proliferation of rights: Moral progress or empty rhetoric?* Oxford: Westview.

I

INTERVARSITY

Intervarsity or "IV" as its members affectionately call it, is a loosely connected federation of collegiate undergraduate and graduate students, faculty and staff, and chapters within national organizations found in many different countries of the world. The central focus of this global movement is for persons to have a personal relationship with Jesus Christ as Savior and Lord, placing IV squarely within evangelicalism. All members of IV affirm a written doctrinal statement that includes the Christian doctrines of the Trinity, divine inspiration and authority of the Bible, dignity of all people, sinfulness of humankind, deity of Jesus Christ and his resurrection, salvation through personal commitment of one's life to Christ, transforming power of the Holy Spirit, unity of all believers in Christ, need to reach others with the gospel and disciple new converts, the personal return of Jesus Christ, and a literal heaven and hell.

The origins of IV go back to university campuses in Great Britain in the 1600s where groups of Christian students met regularly for Bible study, prayer, mutual encouragement, and to be a witness to others of their personal faith. By the late 1800s, many of these campus groups were part of the Student Christian Movement (SCM) that organized activities both within and across campuses. As British theologians and churches in the late 19th century became more liberal in their views concerning traditional Christian doctrines, SCM chapters at many universities became increasingly disenchanted with this move toward liberalism and began to separate from the organization.

Two groups of these disaffected students at Oxford and Cambridge Universities decided to jointly meet at High Leigh, England during the annual "Inter-Varsity" rugby match between the two universities in 1919; the word "Inter" means "between" and "varsity" is the English term for students in college. The following year they invited student groups from other universities. By the tenth High Leigh conference in 1928, there were 14 participating university groups. Together they formed the "Inter-Varsity Fellowship of Evangelical Students" with the express purpose to "stimulate personal faith and further evangelistic work amongst students by upholding the fundamental truths of Christianity." This year also signaled the first missionary work of the group, as money was raised to support the journey of Howard Guinness, a recently graduated medical doctor and vice chairman of the British organization to help solidify emerging student groups among Canadian universities. After a year of decisive work in Canada that left behind a fledgling "Inter-Varsity Christian Fellowship of Canada," Guinness headed off to Australia for a year of similar work. Upon his return to Canada in 1930, he also established groups of students among Canadian high schools (the "Inter-School Christian Fellowship"), as well as supporting the formation of professional groups for working teachers and nurses.

The movement spread to the United States at the University of Michigan, when Stacey Woods, the Canadian IV director, helped students form a chapter in 1938. An InterVarsity Christian Fellowship/USA was organized in May of 1941 with Woods as its first secretary general. InterVarsity Press (IVP) was also formed shortly before the United States entered

World War II, and imported books from Britain's InterVarsity Press for U.S. chapters and students. IVP produced its first homegrown Bible study guide on the Gospel of Mark in 1943, and by 1947 had a formal publishing program underway using Fleming H. Revell Company as its distributor.

Leaders of these movements across ten countries (Australia, Canada, China, France, Great Britain, Netherlands, New Zealand, Norway, Switzerland, and the United States) met at Oxford, England in 1946 to seek stronger cooperation after the close of World War II. The following year, the International Fellowship of Evangelical Students (IFES) was formed at Harvard University to serve as an umbrella organization to "work and pray for a witness to Christ in every university in the world." Meetings of IFES have been held every 3 years since 1947, with 118 national groups formally registered at their 2003 meeting in the Netherlands.

All of these diverse student organizations are united in their commitment to colleges and universities as centers for Christian witness, discipleship in the Christian faith, Christian leadership development, and the integration of faith and rigorous academic pursuits and achievements. Many campus IV faculty advisors are tenured full professors who are nationally or internationally recognized in their respective fields. Throughout IV chapters worldwide, a strong focus is placed on student leaders with professional IV staff serving as mentors, and with many formal and informal educational and training opportunities being provided throughout the year. IV in the United States in particular, has also used some of its resources to support IFES work in various nations of the world, including the provision of over 65 current full-time staff. It is important to note that not all national organizations use the name "InterVarsity," including the British IV, which changed its name in 1974 to the College Christian Fellowship for Evangelical Unions, and more recently to the Universities and Colleges Christian Fellowship (UCCF). Many national organizations also work among high school students and their teachers.

Today, this global movement involves hundreds of thousands of students. In the United States alone in 2002–2003, there were over 1,000 full-time IV staff with 32,000 students and 2,000 faculty involved, organized into 810 undergraduate chapters on 565 campuses, as well as 141 additional chapters primarily geared toward graduate students and/or faculty. Over 4,000 students in IV-USA chapters participated in short- or long-term missions projects during the year, and more than 19,000 people attended one of four IV training centers in Colorado, Michigan, California, and New Hampshire. A student mission conference (which has been held since 1946) took place at the University of Illinois Urbana/Champaign campus during the winter break in 2003 and attracted more than 19,000 students to explore short-term and vocational mission opportunities with over 350 mission agencies and groups.

IVP publishes about 95 new books per year and carries over 800 titles in print, including many reference books that have won prestigious book awards for religious or academic textbooks/encyclopedias. Over 2 million books and booklets are sold per year, and copies of IVP titles have been translated into more than 60 languages including Chinese, Korean, Portuguese, Persian, Croatian, and Estonian. Annual revenues for IV-USA in 2003 totaled over $61 million, including $11 million from the sale of books.

—Dennis William Cheek

FURTHER READING

Anderson, P. M. (1998). *Professors who believe: The spiritual journeys of Christian faculty.* Downers Grove, IL: Intervarsity Press.

Barclay, O. R., & Horn, R. M. (2002). *From Cambridge to the world.* Nottingham, UK: InterVarsity Press UK.

Donald, M. V. (1991). *A spreading tree: A history of Inter-Varsity Christian fellowship of Canada, 1928–1989, sixty years.* Toronto, Ontario: Inter-Varsity Christian Fellowship of Canada.

Dunn, R. R. (2001). *Shaping the spiritual life of students.* Downers Grove, IL: Intervarsity Press.

Hunt, K., & Hunt, G. (1992). *For Christ and the university: The story of InterVarsity Christian Fellowship of the USA, 1940–1990.* Downers Grove, IL: Intervarsity Press.

Johnson, D. (1979). *Contending for the faith: A history of the evangelical movement in the universities and colleges.* Leicester, UK: InterVarsity Press UK.

ISLAM

Islam is the second largest religion in terms of numbers of members across the world today. Muslims account for roughly one-fifth of the world's population with over 1 billion adherents. The word *Islam* literally means submission. And the word *Muslim* derives from the same root, meaning "one who submits." The roots of the word Islam are also used to denote peace, soundness, and safety. Briefly, Muslims profess that there is no god but God, and embrace the message of the Prophet Muhammad, believing that he is the last messenger of God. Muslims across the world profess daily that "there is no god but God, and Muhammad is his prophet." This is the *shahadah,* or profession of belief, which, when proclaimed three times in front of a witness, is all that is needed to become a Muslim. But as with many religions, although it is easy to become a member, it is a much more involved matter to live a Muslim life.

Muslims believe Islam to be the final and most complete form of the family of religious traditions that includes Judaism and Christianity. Indeed, Muslims deeply revere many of the same figures found in the Jewish and Christian sacred scriptures. For Muslims, the most important people found in the Jewish and Christian scriptures are Noah, Abraham, Moses, and Jesus. These four along with the Prophet Muhammad are all regarded as prophets or God's messengers. Therefore, although Muslims believe that Islam is closer to what was intended by God to be communicated through all of God's true messengers, Muslims generally consider Judaism and Christianity to be part of their religious family, referring to Jews and Christians as "people of the Book."

Many non-Muslims in North America believe that Islam is primarily the religion of Arabic-speaking peoples. However, not all Arabs are Muslims, and not all Muslims are Arabs. There is a significant population of Christian, Jewish, and secular Arabs, and Arabs are in fact a minority ethnicity within the worldwide Muslim population. The greatest concentration of Muslims is actually found in Indonesia, and Muslims of South Asian descent, primarily from India and Pakistan, currently account for the majority of Muslims in North America overall.

THE PROPHET MUHAMMAD

The Prophet Muhammad was born in 570 C.E. in the city of Mecca in the Arabian Peninsula now known as Saudi Arabia. The Prophet Muhammad's parents died when he was very young, and he was raised by his uncle Abu Talib. Abu Talib was a poor but generous man, and because Muhammad had to earn his living from a very young age he never learned how to read or write. Muhammad learned to make his living as a trader and traveled with his uncle to Palestine and Syria. Muhammad came to be known in Mecca as a wise and honest man of great integrity. At the request of Abu Talib, Muhammad began to serve a wealthy 40-year-old widow named Khadijah by looking after her merchandise while she was traveling and trading with her caravan. Khadijah became very impressed with Muhammad as their relationship developed, and Muhammad, at the age of 25, and Khadijah, at the age of 40, were married.

In the year 611 C.E., on the 27th day of the month of Ramadan, Muhammad had retreated to the cave of Hira just outside Mecca as he customarily did in order to pray, meditate, and reflect on questions of great importance to him, such as the purpose of life and the struggle between good and evil. On this particular day, however, while he was in deep thought, the Prophet Muhammad heard a powerful voice call him. When he asked who was calling him the voice commanded him to "read." Muhammad replied that he could not read. Muhammad was then squeezed in the grip of a very strong hug for a moment and the voice commanded him a second time to read, to which Muhammad replied again that he could not read. Muhammad was squeezed once again, and a third time was commanded to read. This time Muhammad asked what it was he should read, and the voice replied "Read! In the name of your Lord who creates man from a clot! Read, for your Lord is most generous, who teaches by means of pen, teaches man what he does not know." Muhammad chose to obey this command, and became the Messenger of God. This event was the beginning of the revelation of the Muslim sacred scripture or writings known as the Qur'an. The Qur'an was revealed in segments to the Prophet Muhammad through the angel Gabriel over the course of the next 23 years.

When Muhammad returned to Khadijah after his experience in the cave of Hira, she believed in what Muhammad told her had happened, and she became the very first convert to Islam. Muhammad first spread the message he had been given by God to his close friends and soon began preaching openly in and around Mecca. But the Meccans were not pleased with Muhammad preaching that their idols were illegitimate gods and that God was the one and only true God. The early Muslims suffered terrible persecutions, and many died for their religion. During the most intense part of this persecution against Muslims, God granted Muhammad a special vision known as the Night Journey. Muhammad had a vision that he was led by a celestial guide from Mecca to Jerusalem, and then ascended through the seven heavens meeting earlier prophets from other places. He passed through a number of veils until reaching the veil of unity where he was able to look upon what human eyes cannot see and human minds cannot imagine. This Night Journey led to the institution of the five ritual daily prayers as a central part of the Islamic faith.

As a result of the persecutions against Muslims in Mecca, the new religious group moved to Medina, a town about 200 miles north of Mecca. This occurred in 622 C.E.; the move is known as the Hijra or migration, and marks the beginning of the Muslim calendar. The residents of Medina had invited Muhammad and the other Muslims to come to their town for protection, and Muhammad proceeded to set up a highly organized city-state there. Medina was a diverse town of Arabs, Jews, Christians, and others, and Muhammad set about drawing up a constitution for the city, one of the first in the world. The constitution set out the city's governing structure, recognized freedom of religion, outlined explicit ethical principles of defense and foreign policy, and arranged a system of social insurance.

But the Meccans were not about to let Muhammad and his followers go so easily. The inhabitants of Mecca organized three battles over 3 years beginning in 624 C.E. The Battle of Badr took place in the field of Badr outside Medina between 1,000 Meccan warriors and 313 ill-equipped Muslims. The Muslims quickly won the battle. Seventy Meccans were killed and 70 were later released from capture. One year later, 3,000 Meccans engaged 700 Muslims at the bottom of Mount Uhad in the Battle of Uhad. The Muslims almost lost this battle when a group of archers left their post on Mount Uhad disobeying strict orders not to move when they thought the battle was turning out to be an easy victory for the Muslims. The Battle of Uhad ended in truce, and the Meccans swore to return the following year. Finally, what is sometimes called the Battle of the Trench occurred the following year; it was not really a battle because none of the 10,000-strong force of Meccans and their allies could cross the defensive trench the Muslims had excavated around Medina. Ultimately, Muhammad persuaded the Meccans to sign a peace treaty, the Treaty of Hudaybia, after which Muhammad was able to devote time to spreading his message outside Medina, including in neighboring countries.

The Meccans continued to violate the treaty they had agreed to with the Muslims until 630 C.E. when Muhammad told them to choose to either respect the treaty or nullify it. The Meccans chose the latter, and woke up one morning to find 10,000 Muslims surrounding their city. The Meccans surrendered without incident, and Muhammad treated the people, including those who had committed heinous acts against members of his own family, with great mercy, leaving their ultimate fate to God.

Muhammad gave his farewell sermon 10 years after the Hijra, and after making the pilgrimage to Mecca in 631 C.E. In this sermon delivered to 124,000 Muslims, Muhammad reaffirmed the central practices of Islam and admonished them to follow God and adhere to his message spoken through his prophet. Muhammad died the next year at the age of 63.

After the Prophet Muhammad died, the next four elected leaders or Caliphs of the Muslim community are regarded by the vast majority of Muslims as the rightly guided Caliphs. These in order were Abu Bakr, Umar, Othman, and Ali. Unfortunately, both Othman and Ali were murdered because of dissension in the community. After Ali was killed, the Muslim community split and a number of various Muslim groups, schools, kingdoms, and countries were eventually formed and reformed.

THE QUR'AN

Muslims proclaim that the Qur'an is the message of God to all peoples revealed to the Prophet Muhammad through the angel Gabriel. The word *Qur'an* literally means "reading" or "recitation." The Qur'an was revealed to Muhammad over a period of 23 years, and is believed by Muslims to be the literal word-for-word message of God spoken in clear Arabic speech. Therefore, translations of the Qur'an into Arabic are not authoritative because they can never be precisely the same as that which was revealed in Arabic. There are 114 *surahs* or chapters in the Qur'an, arranged approximately from longest to shortest. The whole Qur'an is slightly shorter in length than the Christian New Testament. Although the Qur'an includes some narratives, it is not a story or a series of narratives but a complex interconnected text of rhythmic prose. Its language and style are inimitable, and indeed a number of skilled Arabic poets have failed in attempts to imitate the rhythmic prose of the Qur'an. The Qur'an has been systematically memorized and written down from the time of its revelation. The written fragments and oral memorizations were finally standardized and duplicated in their present form by a scholarly group commissioned to the task by Othman, the third rightly guided Caliph between 644 and 656 C.E. within 20 years of Muhammad's death. Muslims insist that these master copies have been painstakingly reproduced to this day.

In addition to the Qur'an, Muslims look to the Hadith for guidance. The Hadith are the recorded sayings, traditions, and actions of the Prophet Muhammad himself. The Hadith carry great authority for Muslims, but they are not as authoritative as the Qur'an because they are not the direct revelation of God.

ISLAMIC IDEAS AND PRACTICE

Islam is called a monotheistic religion by religious studies scholars, meaning that Muslims believe in one supreme divine being much like Jews and Christians. It is misleading to think of Islam as simply a "faith" or "belief," although these are convenient labels in North America for religions generally. But more importantly, Islam is a practice, the action of submitting one's life to God. More accurately, the practices of Islam are intimately bound up into the beliefs and ideas of Islam, and vice versa.

The five pillars or most important practices of Islam are the *shahadah* (profession of belief), *salat* (prayer), *sawm* (fasting), *zakat* (charity), and *hajj* (pilgrimage to Mecca). The *shahadah,* the profession Muslims make that there is no god but God and Muhammad is his prophet is the core practice and belief of Islam. To declare that there is no god but God is known as *tawheed.* This is the central worldview of Muslims, and from it derives all Muslim action and belief. *Salat* refers to the five ritual prayers commanded by God to pray every day at designated times throughout the day beginning before sunrise and ending well into the evening. *Sawm* is performed during the month of Ramadan. It does not only consist in physically declining food, drink, smoking, and sex, but also includes abstaining from evil thoughts, actions, and speech. *Zakat* is the command to give to those in need rather than merely a generic admonition to be generous. Often an annual percentage is offered from one's savings and income as *zakat. Zakat* aims to achieve a more equitable distribution of resources in accordance with God's original design.

Hajj to Mecca is a special honor in Islam. Muslims are required to perform at least one *hajj* in a lifetime if they are able to go. *Hajj* involves an entire ritual of meaningful submission to God in which a person suspends his or her normal everyday activities to converge with the Muslim community on the most holy places in the world for Muslims.

There is no notion of salvation in Islam, or of an original and unavoidable sin nature in humans. Rather, people have been designed and created by God to do good, but have forgotten and neglected their original design. This is why God has regularly sent prophets to remind people of their original design and purpose. Muslims believe that everything that exists has been created by God at the beginning of history, and that the conclusion of history will be marked by the Day of Judgment. On the Day of Judgment each person will account for what they have done and what they have not done and these will be weighed on a balance. If the person's right actions outweigh his or her wrong actions or inactions, then the person will go on to live eternally in paradise. And if the opposite is the case they will spend eternity in hell.

Shariah is a set of principles or guidelines for Islamic action. Although it is usually translated as Islamic law, technically it is not. Islamic law grows and changes with the situation that Muslims find themselves in, while the generic principles of Shariah are eternal. Shariah helps to guide Muslims on the right path.

Jihad literally means struggle or effort. It refers primarily to the struggle every Muslim makes to overcome his or her tendencies to forget God's message, and to commit wrong and instead to accomplish right action throughout one's life. This is known as the greater *jihad.* The lesser *jihad* refers to the allowance for Muslims to defend themselves against attack and to oppose injustice in the world. There are many ways to do this, and physical violence is a last resort, but if the situation deteriorates to the point of violence, then there are strict ethical guidelines governing the rules of engagement that Muslims must follow in event of war. The attacks on the World Trade Center towers in New York and the Pentagon building on September 11, 2001 violate numerous principles of *jihad.* Therefore, many Muslims agree that these actions are not condoned by any principles in Islam. Moreover, the phrase "holy war" is actually a phrase coined by Christians to describe their own quest during their Crusades on Muslims in the Middle Ages. The phrase "holy war" in Arabic does not appear anywhere in the Qur'an.

The two most important festivals on the Muslim calendar are the two *eid* festivals. *Eid* means feast. The Eid al-Adha is the Feast of Sacrifice that celebrates Ishmael's resistance of Satan's temptation to run away when God had commanded his father Abraham to sacrifice his son. God saw Ishmael's faithfulness and provided a sacrificial ram in his place. The Eid al-Fitr or Feast of Fast-breaking is celebrated on the first day after Ramadan, the month of fasting. Muslims often dress up in their best clothes, decorate their homes, and celebrate with elaborate feasts for up to 3 days for this holy occasion.

DIVERSITY WITHIN ISLAM

Islam is not monolithic; in other words, there are multiple versions of Islam. Although there may be enough agreement on the basic principles and history of Islam to observe continuity among most self-proclaimed Muslims worldwide, there is also a wide diversity of Muslim beliefs and practices among various Islamic groups.

Sunni Muslims comprise the largest group of Muslims in the world, and even among Sunnis there is great diversity. Generally they have no formal leadership hierarchy, such as that of the Catholic Church, and the leaders or *imams* are often simply respected members of the community who function as prayer leaders in the mosque and may be called upon to offer their educated advice on Muslim matters.

Shi'as are the second most common group of Muslim communities in the Muslim world, and there are a great variety of Shi'a groups. Shi'a communities generally are distinguished from Sunnis in their assertion of the privileged position of the Prophet Muhammad's family and descendants as leaders in the Muslim community. An imam in the Shi'a traditions then is not simply an appointed prayer leader, but a divinely instituted descendant of Muhammad. Ali, the fourth Caliph, is regarded as the first of 12 imams, and the 12th imam is believed to be in hiding until his apocalyptic return at the end of the age.

Sufis comprise a variety of groups of Muslims who engage in ascetic and moral practices in an attempt to achieve mystical union with God. There are many different groups of Sufis, and not all Muslims acknowledge that Sufis are real Muslims. However, Sufis self-identify as Muslims, and clearly build their practices on Islamic traditions.

MUSLIMS IN NORTH AMERICA TODAY

The first Muslims in North America were brought to America by force as slaves from Africa. Later, the first free Muslim immigrants were likely peddlers from Lebanon in the late 19th and early 20th centuries. There are currently approximately 600,000 Muslims in Canada according to the 2001 census, an estimated 6 million in the United States, and 15, 000 in Mexico. Muslims in North America are on the whole very organized and established enough to maintain their Islamic identity in the North American context, adding their rich cultural heritage to these societies.

Many Muslim children learn to recite the Qur'an at a very young age. Even in countries where Muslims do not speak or understand Arabic, children are taught to recite the Qur'an in Arabic. There are even contests in which very young Muslim children attempt to recite the entire Qur'an from memory in public. Children as young as 8 and 9 years of age have successfully memorized the entire Qur'an. Children are taught to proclaim the *shahadah* at a very young age, and Muslims continue to develop their understanding and practice of all the implications of that concise yet profound statement throughout their adolescence and adulthood. For children of Muslims who encourage observance of the daily prayers, *salat* marks out the sacred moments of every day when the *shahadah* is proclaimed, and one's body is prostrated in supreme humility and worship to Allah. Children are not required to fast during Ramadan, but many consider it a great honor when they reach the age they may participate in *sawm* during this sacred month. Neither are children required to pay *zakat,* and *hajj* too is something most Muslims do not participate in until they are adults. However, Muslim children of economically disadvantaged families and orphans are to benefit from *zakat* according to Islam, and all Muslim children likely look forward to participating in the *hajj* when they are old enough and able. Children make up a crucial part of the world's second-largest religion as they learn to embrace its ideas and participate in its practices.

—Christopher Cutting

See also Islam, Five Pillars of; Islam, Founding Fathers of; Islamic Sects, Sunni and Shi'a; Muhammad; Islamic Sects: Sunni and Shi'a

FURTHER READING

Ayoub, M. M. (2002). The Islamic tradition. In W. G. Oxtoby (Ed.), *World religions Western traditions.* Oxford: Oxford University Press.

British Broadcasting Corporation. (2004). Islam. Retrieved August 29, 2004, from www.bbc.co.uk/religion/religions/islam/index.shtml.

Eck, D. (2001). *A new religious America: How a "Christian country" has become the world's most religiously diverse nation.* San Francisco: Harper San Francisco.

Haddad, Y. Y. (Ed.). (2002). *Muslims in the West: From sojourners to citizens.* Oxford: Oxford University Press.

Haddad, Y. Y., & Smith, J. I. (Eds.). (2002). *Muslims minorities in the West: Visible and invisible.* Walnut Creek, CA: Altamira Press.

Ludwig, T. M. (2001). *The sacred paths: understanding the religions of the world.* Upper Saddle River, NJ: Prentice Hall.

Sardar, Z., & Malik, Z. A. (1994). *Introducing Islam.* Cambridge, UK: Icon Books.

ISLAM, FIVE PILLARS OF

The five pillars are the most important practices of Islam: the *shahadah* (profession), *salat* (prayer), *sawm* (fasting), *zakat* (charity), and *hajj* (pilgrimage to Mecca). The *shahadah,* the profession Muslims make that there is no god but God, and Muhammad is his prophet, constitutes the core practice and belief of Islam. Islam literally means "submission to God," and to fully submit oneself to God consists in submitting to God alone and embracing the message of his final and most important prophet. The Arabic word Allah is not a personal name of a particular God like Jesus, Buddha, or Krishna; rather, it designates for Muslims the one and only supreme divine creator being much like the English word "God." Indeed, Arabic Christians and Jews praying in their native language invoke Allah when they pray. And even Jesus Christ whose native tongue was Aramaic would have referred to God as Allahah in his own language. The five pillars represent the practices that are the most influential in religious and spiritual development of Muslims around the world.

To declare that there is no god but God is known as *tawheed.* This is the central worldview of Muslims, and from it derives all Muslim action and belief. God is absolutely unified. God has no partners, children, or various manifestations or forms. The unity of God is reflected in the unity of, and therefore absolute equality of all people. To recite the *shahadah* is to bear witness to the most important Muslim belief, and the *shahadah* is recited during individual prayer, communal prayers on Fridays, and sacred holy times such as the *eid* festivals and the sacred month of Ramadan. Reciting, proclaiming, and embracing the tenets of the *shahadah* are expressed by Muslim children and adolescents both during special occasions and in everyday practice, and it establishes the very foundation of their religion.

Salat or prayer refers to the five ritual prayers Muslims pray daily. The *shahadah* is repeated numerous times during each of the five daily prayers. Muslims also may pray generally for specific needs, issues, or just to spend time with God, but *salat* refers to the five ritual prayers commanded by God to be prayed every day at designated times beginning before sunrise and ending well into the evening. Each *salat* has a name and specific time of day or night when it is to be prayed. Each day begins with the *fajr* prayer at dawn. The *dhuhr* prayer takes place just after the midday sun has reached its zenith. The *asr* prayer is offered in the middle of the afternoon. Some Muslims believe this should take place when one's shadow is the same length as he or she is. Others believe the shadow should be twice one's length. As a result some Muslims will pray earlier in the afternoon than others. *Magrib* takes place at sunset, and *isha* is prayed after dark when the light of the sun can no longer be seen.

Many Muslims perform an ablution or purification before the ritual daily prayers known in Arabic as *wudu.* This ritual cleansing involves washing one's face including rinsing out the mouth and nose. Washing the hands and arms up to the elbows, then passing one's wet hands over the head, and washing one's feet completes the ritual. However, if one has been in contact with a dead body or human blood, engaged in sexual relations, or is menstruating, then a full-body wash known in Arabic as *ghusl* may be performed before prayer.

Muslim prayer is physical, verbal, and communal. Muslim prayer physically involves one's body in bowing, kneeling, prostration, and genuflection or ritual hand movements. The prayer begins as one cups hands behind the ears as if to listen more intently. The hands are then folded in front of the body with the right arm over the left, over one's chest or belly depending on his or her tradition. One then bows, hands on knees, and stands upright again. This is followed by a full prostration with legs folded underneath the body, and with one's forehead placed gently on the floor between the hands, which are also pressed down flat on the floor. The Muslim then sits up at the waist and prostrates again. Having kept one's toes in the same position as a kind of marker, the Muslim is then able to stand again in the same spot he or she was in before the prostration. Again the Muslim bows, stands upright, prostrates, sits up, prostrates, and this time sits up again (rather than standing). He or she then raises his or her right index finger either once or repeatedly depending on one's tradition, and turns his or her face to the right, and then to the left before standing again. During each of these movements and gestures a Muslim will recite phrases from the Qur'an and other ritual prayers.

This entire cycle is called a *rakah.* The morning prayer is prayed with two *rakahs;* the two afternoon prayers have four *rakahs,* the sunset prayer three, and the night time prayer four. Many Muslims will perform extra *rakahs,* especially on special occasions such as the 27th day of Ramadan, which is believed by many to be the night of power, when the Qur'an passed from a higher heaven to a lower heaven on its journey to earth, signifying Allah's decision to reveal the Qur'an to humanity. Although no one knows for sure which night is the night of power, it is believed that prayers offered on this night are worth more than a thousand prayers prayed on any other night.

The content of Muslim prayers is formalized, consisting mainly of the first *surah* (chapter) and other *ayat* (verses) of the Qur'an. These recitations are largely fixed and repeated in every prayer cycle. A helpful, albeit incomplete analogy, would be the Lord's Prayer for Christians. Often Muslims will offer personal prayers after the obligatory ones, holding one's palms open before one's face as if holding an open book.

Muslim prayer is always communal as well. For if he or she is not praying immediately with a group of Muslims, one always faces Mecca when praying, and is conscious that millions of Muslims around the world are praying while facing Mecca at the same time.

Sawm or fasting is performed during the month of Ramadan. *Sawm* does not only consist in physically declining food, drink, smoking, and sex, but also includes abstaining from evil thoughts, actions, and speech. For a full month Muslims will eat a small meal before sunrise, followed by a full day fast, including abstaining from drinking water. The fast is broken after sundown traditionally by eating a few dates. Muslims then pray before gathering for an evening meal of family or communal celebration called an *iftaar.* Because the Muslim calendar is lunar based, the month of Ramadan recedes a number of days each solar calendar year, and thus Ramadan will at times take place in winter, and at other times in the heat of summer. Winter fasts are relatively tolerable because of the short days, but Ramadan in the heat of summer can be quite a challenge. Muslims who live near the planetary poles where at times the sun never sets have had to make specific arrangements to account for the exceptional solar patterns. The month of fasting ends with one of the two greatest festivals of the Muslim calendar: Eid al-Fitr. During this 3-day celebration, people exchange gifts, spend time with family, friends, and loved ones, and share many feasts.

Zakat or charity is the divine command to give to those in need rather than merely a generic admonition to be generous. Often an annual percentage is offered from one's savings and income as *zakat.* Because of the unity of God and his creation, all people have equal right to the resources of this world. *Zakat* aims to achieve a more equitable distribution of resources in accordance with Allah's original design. The *zakat* is paid once annually and consists of 2.5% of one's accumulated wealth. This does not only include one's income, but savings, and many forms of personal assets. In a number of Muslim countries this is an obligatory tax, but in many immigrant communities it is a voluntary act of religious observance.

Hajj or pilgrimage to Mecca is a special honor in Islam. Muslims are required to perform at least one *hajj* in a lifetime if they are able. *Hajj* involves a series of ritual submissions to God in which a person suspends his or her normal everyday activities to converge with the Muslim community on the most holy Muslim places in the world. Muslims hold that Abraham instituted the *hajj* after Allah had commanded Abraham and his son Ishmael to build the *ka'bah.* The *ka'bah* is a large black stone housed in a cube brick structure in the center court of the great mosque of Mecca.

The pilgrimage begins as soon as one leaves one's home to journey to Mecca. Just outside the sacred city of Mecca, Muslims will trade their regular clothes for two pieces of unadorned white cloth, symbolic of burial clothes. These plain clothes symbolize the equality of all people regardless of class, wealth, race, or ethnicity. Pilgrims proceed to the grand mosque in Mecca where they ritually circle the *ka'bah* seven times. Pilgrims then travel to a long enclosed hall in the southern part of the great mosque where they walk briskly back and forth seven times, ritually reenacting the story of Hagar and Ishmael in which they had been turned out of their home by Abraham. In the story, Hagar ran back and forth between the two hills al-Safa and al-Marwa in search of water for her son Ishmael who was dying. After her seventh run, water began to gush up from the earth from what is regarded by Muslims as the sacred well of Zamzam. After pilgrims perform the running ritual they travel to the actual well of Zamzam for a drink from the sacred waters.

The main part of the pilgrimage begins on the eighth day of Dhu al-Hijjah, the month of pilgrimage. On this day Muslims venture out into the desert about 20 kilometers (13 miles) east of Mecca to the plain of Arafat. The Mount of Mercy is located on the plain of Arafat where pilgrims spend the afternoon standing together in solemn prayer. This ritual is analogous for Muslims to judgment day when they will stand before Allah to give an accounting of their lives. According to tradition, the Prophet Muhammad gave his farewell sermon here, and the last revelation of the Qur'an was revealed on this mount.

At sunset the pilgrims move on to Muzdalifa, a short distance from Arafat on the way back to Mecca. Here pilgrims celebrate and share their experiences together, as well as collect pebbles for the ritual stoning of stone columns to take place the following day. On the 10th day of the month of pilgrimage, the Muslim travelers move on to Mina where a single brick column represents Satan, and three other columns represent Satan's temptations. Pilgrims stone these columns, ritually reenacting the story of Abraham, who threw stones at Satan to drive him away when Satan was tempting Abraham to abandon Allah's command to sacrifice his son Ishmael. The entire pilgrimage ends with the other of the most important Muslim festivals: Eid al-Ahda, the festival of sacrifice, which echoes the sacrifice of the animal that Allah provided in place of Ishmael. These 4 days of celebration are often enjoyed in and around Mecca at the conclusion of the *hajj*. One who has performed to full *hajj* is ritually named a *hajji,* and is authorized to include an initial before one's name to signify this high honor.

Children are taught to proclaim the Shahadah at a very young age, and Muslims continue to develop their understanding and practice of all the implications of that concise yet profound statement throughout their adolescence and adulthood. For children of Muslims who encourage observance of the daily prayers, *salat* marks out the sacred moments of every day when the Shahadah is proclaimed, and one's body is prostrated in supreme humility and worship to Allah. Children are not required to fast during Ramadan, but many consider it a great honor when they reach the age that they may participate in *sawm* during this sacred month. Children are also not required to pay *zakat,* and *hajj* too is something most Muslims participate in as adults. However, Muslim children of economically disadvantaged families and orphans are to benefit from *zakat* according to Islam, and all Muslim children likely look forward to participating in the *hajj* when they are old enough and able.

—*Christopher Cutting*

See also Islam; Mecca; Muhammad

FURTHER READING

Ayoub, M. M. (2002). The Islamic tradition. In W. G. Oxtoby (Ed.), *World religions Western traditions.* Oxford: Oxford University Press.

British Broadcasting Corporation. (2004). Islam. Retrieved August 29, 2004, from www.bbc.co.uk/ religion/religions/ islam/index.shtml.

Eck, D. (2001). *A new religious America: How a "Christian country" has become the world's most religiously diverse nation.* San Francisco: Harper San Francisco.

Haddad, Y. Y. (Ed.). (2002). *Muslims in the West: From sojourners to citizens.* Oxford: Oxford University Press.

Haddad, Y. Y., & Smith, J. I. (Eds.). (2002). *Muslims minorities in the West: Visible and invisible.* Walnut Creek, CA: Altamira Press.

Ludwig, T. M. (2001). *The sacred paths: understanding the religions of the world.* Upper Saddle River, NJ: Prentice Hall.

Sardar, Z., & Malik, Z. A. (1994). *Introducing Islam.* Cambridge, UK: Icon Books.

ISLAM, FOUNDING FATHERS OF

The word *caliph,* from khalīfa in Arabic, means representative or steward. In the Qur'an the word is applied to Adam and to humankind in general, to refer to our responsibility and dominion over the earth and all God's creations. In the early days of Islam, the men who took up leadership responsibility following Muhammad's death were known as caliphs. The first four stand apart from those who followed and are collectively referred to by Sunni Muslims as "al-khulafā' ar-rāshidūn" or the "rightly guided" caliphs. They were among Muhammad's closest companions and so learned from him firsthand. However, unlike the Prophet, the caliphs did not receive divine revelation. Nevertheless, they were respected for their spiritual knowledge, though they did not have absolute authority in religious matters.

These first four caliphs were motivated by sincere faith, for they shunned the luxuries and riches that were emblematic of the kings of that era. They built upon the example of Muhammad, and their individual differences reflected different approaches and different interpretations of Islam. Confronted with new situations, they reacted with resourcefulness and good judgment. Like Muhammad, these first four caliphs had a unified, God-centered worldview that did not differentiate greatly between worldly and spiritual matters. They left a legacy not only in politics, but also in personal conduct, in spirituality, and even in mysticism. For future generations of Muslims, they set the standard of what leadership should mean. To understand these four, then, is to understand essentials about Islam and Islamic culture today.

Abu Bakr was the first of the rightly guided caliphs. During the pre-Islamic days, he was highly respected throughout Mecca for his friendly nature, his honesty, and his knowledge of tribal genealogies. As a wealthy merchant of noble lineage, he enjoyed great influence in class-conscious Meccan society.

Abu Bakr was the first adult man to convert to Islam, and, throughout Muhammad's life, he remained one of Muhammad's most devoted companions. He donated all of his wealth for the cause of Islam and for helping the needy. He paid for the freedom of at least seven slaves who, after accepting Islam, had been abused by their masters. He was Muhammad's right hand on the field of battle, but in peacetime, he was a tenderhearted and forbearing man. Nearing the end of his life, as Muhammad became too ill to lead the prayers, he insisted that Abu Bakr perform this duty, despite Abu Bakr's having a soft voice and despite his often breaking into tears while reciting the Quran.

Muhammad's death brought chaos and uncertainty, and many refused to believe that the prophet had died. Abu Bakr addressed the masses saying, "O people! Whoever has worshipped Muhammad, certainly Muhammad is dead, and whoever has worshipped God, God is Ever-living and He never dies." He then quoted from the Quran: "Muhammad is but a Messenger; and messengers before him have passed away. If he die or be slain, will you then turn upon your heels? Whoever turns on his heels will do no harm to God, and God will reward the thankful" (3:143). Abu Bakr's words, then, established a needed way of thinking to provide a successful transition following Muhammad's death, and so the Muslim people made him Muhammad's successor.

In his acceptance speech he laid out the principles that would define the ideals of government in Islam. "Help me if I am in the right," he said. "Set me right if I am in the wrong! The weak among you shall be strong in my eye until I have vindicated his just rights, and the strong among you shall be weak in my eye until I have made him fulfill the obligations due from him. . . . Obey me as long as I obey God and His prophet. In case I disobey God and His prophet, I have no right to obedience from you."

Abu Bakr's short rule was spent crushing rebellions and restoring order in Arabia. Perhaps his most important act was to establish clear rules for humane behavior during wartime. He commanded his followers not to kill women, children, and old men. He forbade them from harming monks or monasteries. Trees, crops, and houses were to be left unharmed, and the corpses of fallen foes were not to be disfigured. Treaties with other faiths were to be fulfilled, and those who surrendered were entitled to the rights and privileges of Muslim subjects. He died after only 2 years as caliph, and before his death, he appointed his friend, Omar ibn al-Khattab, to succeed him.

Omar was one of the most remarkable figures in the history of Islam. He was a fearless warrior with a fierce temper. At one time, he had persecuted Muslims. After his conversion to Islam, he turned his sword on Muhammad's enemies. When prisoners were captured in war, Abu Bakr advised the prophet to have mercy while Omar advised him to slaughter them. Often, Omar was frustrated by Muhammad's leniency towards enemies. He disagreed about what he saw as concessions made toward foes. However, under Muhammad's guidance, Omar replaced his vengeful nature with devotion to God. On many occasions when people used disrespectful language toward the prophet, Omar hastened to draw his sword but was stopped by Muhammad, and when Omar first learned of Muhammad's death, he thought it was a malicious lie. Many were fearful that when Abu Bakr appointed Omar as the next caliph, he would be hard on his enemies. However, Abu Bakr convinced them that Omar's becoming caliph would bring out his mercy. Abu Bakr was right.

By the beginning of Omar's rule, Islam was already at war with the Byzantine and Persian empires. By the end of his rule, Islam's dominion stretched across the Middle East and included areas populated by a variety of races, languages, and faiths. However, throughout this period of geographic expansion, Omar never sought riches, nor did he become a fanatic bent on Islamic world domination. For example, after the conquest of Iraq, one of Omar's generals asked permission to pursue the Persians into their homeland, but Omar replied, "I desire that between Mesopotamia and the countries beyond, the hills shall be a barrier so that the Persians shall not be able to get at us, nor we at them. The plain of al-Iraq suffices for our wants. I would prefer the safety of my people to thousands of spoils and further conquest."

When further conflict with the Persians ensued and some Muslims requested that Omar reverse his policy toward expansion into Persia, he replied, "What is the cause that these Persians persistently break faith and rebel against us? Maybe you treat them harshly." Eventually Omar conceded his position, and the entire Persian Empire fell before the Muslims. When the vast treasures of the conquests were brought before him, he wept, because he saw in these treasures seeds of destruction in the Islamic community.

As ruler of a mighty nation, Omar lived in hermitlike austerity, taking nothing for himself. He often acted as a commoner, working with his own hands to help the poor and hungry, and once, while traveling from Jerusalem to Arabia, he took turns riding his camel with the single servant who had accompanied him. Furthermore and despite his reputation for harshness, Omar maintained a policy of tolerance toward other faiths. In Jerusalem, for example, he established a treaty guaranteeing the life, property, and complete freedom of religion to the people of Jerusalem. And when invited to pray in Jerusalem's Church of the Resurrection, he politely declined, saying, "Should we say our prayers here, Muslims might someday claim the right to erect a mosque in this place."

Even at his death, Omar remained a spiritual exemplar. Omar was stabbed mortally during prayer, but he remained calm and peaceful. When told that the attacker was a Christian, he thanked God that his murderer was not a Muslim, for that would have shattered the unity of the community. He died, then, totally committed to Islam and to the establishment of an Islamic community.

Omar's successor did not share the same fate. Uthman bin Affan was chosen by an electoral council of six prominent companions to succeed Omar as the third caliph. Although he belonged to one of Mecca's most noble and wealthy clans, Uthman lived a simple and pious life, giving much of his wealth to charity. Although he held great stocks of goats and camels, in his last years he possessed only what he needed for pilgrimage.

Unlike Omar who was strict in enforcing austere standards, Uthman allowed his governors to amass wealth. For example, Mu'awiyah, who was the governor of Syria and a member of the Umayyad clan to which Uthman belonged, accumulated a fortune. Slowly accusations of nepotism and murmurs of discontent began to spread, leading, eventually, to angry mobs surrounding the caliph's house and trapping him inside. Uthman forbade his supporters to draw swords, as Muhammad had once warned that once the sword was drawn between his followers, it would never be sheathed until the Day of Judgment. The rebels stormed his house and slew him during his prayers, leaving the Islamic community irreparably divided.

During the dark period following Uthman's murder, Muhammad's cousin and son-in-law, Ali, ruled as the fourth and last of the "rightly guided" caliphs. Ali had been one of the first to convert to Islam. When Muhammad's kinsmen had rejected Muhammad, it was ten-year-old Ali who answered Muhammad's call. Many believe that Ali was the rightful heir to Muhammad and should have been the first caliph.

From the beginning of Ali's rule, he was pressed to avenge Uthman's death, in particular by Muhammad's widow, Aishah. Ali agreed that the murderers should be brought to justice, but he would not risk starting a war when the very existence of the nation and Islamic community was at stake. Instead he wisely moved to replace the old governors, rid his government of corruption, and thereby prevented accusations of corruption.

After Mu'awiyah refused to step down, a series of civil wars erupted, and the unity of the Islamic community was shattered. Ali was murdered by members of an extremist sect that had emerged during this period of civil war.

This period of civil war spawned the two major sects of Islam, the Sunni and Shi'a. The Shi'a believe that only members of the prophet's bloodline should have been caliphs. Of the four "rightly guided caliphs," they revere only Ali. Also, because of his simplicity, piety, and inner spiritual strength, Ali is also regarded as a founder of the Islamic mystic path, Sufism.

After the four "rightly guided caliphs," the Muslim world fell under the rule of Mu'awiyah. The caliphate became hereditary, and the Umayyad dynasty was established. The rulers of the Muslim world began, then, to live like traditional kings. The caliphs focused more on worldly wealth and luxury. The divide between Sunni and Shi'a grew and became a cause of bloodshed, a cause that has continued to the present day. However, the virtues of the first four caliphs survived, and Muslims today turn to these four as models of leadership and as spiritual exemplars.

—*Danyal Najmi*

See also Islam; Islamic Sects: Sunni and Shi'a

ISLAMIC SECTS: SUNNI AND SHI'A

In day-to-day religious practice and core beliefs, there is little difference between the two major Islamic denominations or sects: Sunni and Shi'a. Members of both sects believe in one God and in the Day of Judgment when every soul shall see the results of its deeds. Both believe in the same sacred text, the Qu'ran, which is the basis of their religion. Both follow similar practices with regard to prayer, worship, and charity. The similarities, then, outweigh the differences. It is history, then, not beliefs and practices, that divides them.

In the middle of the night, Muhammad often remained awake, bowing and kneeling in prayer to God. His eyes shed so many tears that his beard would become soaked. When asked what could cause such sadness to a man whose sins God had promised to forgive, Muhammad replied that he feared for the future of his community. Nations of the past had destroyed themselves through their mutual hatred and malice as well as through their pursuit of worldly riches. Unity was as essential to Islam's social structure as it was to Islam's theological doctrine. Despite his exhortations to his people to hold fast to brotherhood and unity, Muhammad's fears were realized only decades after his death.

The third leader or Caliph of Islam after Muhammad, Uthman bin Affan, was murdered by rebels within his own community. That murder heralded a political and religious conflict that has continued for over 13 centuries. Due to a series of misunderstandings, the fourth Caliph Ali, Muhammad's cousin and son-in-law, found himself fighting a battle against none other than Muhammad's widow, Aishah. Ever a true Muslim, Ali refused to speak ill of his adversaries. They were not his enemies, he said; they were his brothers. When Aishah was captured, he pardoned her and treated her with full respect.

The first true sect to split off from the general Muslim community was the Kharijites movement. This group believed that if the Caliph did not live up to their standards, it was their right to violently oppose him, despite any amount of bloodshed. Although the Kharijites as a sect have not endured, they are often seen as precursors of modern militant terrorist groups such as al-Qaeda. Members of the Kharijite sect murdered Ali, leaving the path clear for Mu'awiyah's victory.

A minority of the Muslim community believes that Muhammad specifically designated Ali to be his successor. They are called the Shi'a 'Ali, or partisans of Ali. The majority of Muslims, known as the Sunni, believe that Muhammad never clearly designated a successor to lead the community after his death. They believe in the legitimacy of the first four caliphs, who were endorsed by most of the early Muslim community.

After Ali's death, the Shi'a rallied behind his two sons Hasan and Hussein, who were also Muhammad's grandsons. Hasan renounced politics to live a peaceful life in Medina, where he died in 669 C.E./41 A.H. Meanwhile, Mu'awiyah ruled the vast Muslim world as fifth Caliph, and would publicly slander Ali in religious ceremonies. This outraged Ali's devoted followers, who were concentrated around Kufah in Iraq. Mu'awiyah departed from the proto-democratic practices of his predecessors and appointed his son Yazid as his successor, establishing the first hereditary monarchy in Islamic history.

Shi'a accounts describe Yazid as Satan personified, a cruel, tyrannical despot, and the antithesis to the ideals of Islam. Instead of giving allegiance to such a man, the people of Kufah offered their support to Ali's remaining son Husayn, promising to back him in a bid for the caliphate. Yazid demanded that Husayn acknowledge him as caliph and swear allegiance to him, but the latter refused. Husayn set off for Kufah with his most devoted followers, including men, women, and children. Yazid's generals intercepted him in the arid plain of Karbala. Against the thousands of Umayyad soldiers, Husayn's small company stood no chance. Husayn and his warriors resisted and were slaughtered, and the women and children were marched off in chains.

Husayn's martyrdom is extremely important to Shi'a Muslims; it is comparable to the martyrdom of Jesus in Christianity and reminiscent of the sacrifice offered by Abraham and his son, thousands of years earlier. The tragedy happened on the 10th day of the lunar month of Muharram on the Islamic calendar, the same day when Moses led the Israelites out of bondage and when Jews fast on their Day of Atonement. Muslims call the day Ashura, and Muhammad used to fast that day in accordance with the earlier Jewish tradition. For Shi'a Muslims, it is the holiest day of the year. The people of Kufah, under pressure from Yazid's forces did not come to Husayn's aid in his hour of need, and thus the Shi'a as a whole failed their leader. Ashura is a day of collective guilt and mourning, and some people participate in rather gruesome self-punishing rituals that are frowned upon by Sunni Muslims.

The story of Husayn's martyrdom is both history and legend at once, and it is impossible to separate the two. It is said that Husayn left for Iraq before completing his pilgrimage in Mecca. When asked about his strange decision, he replied that he would instead perform the pilgrimage in the desert of Karbala, where he would sacrifice not the traditional animal but instead sacrifice himself, his family, and his friends. When surrounded by 30,000 enemy soldiers in the burning desert of Iraq, he reminded his followers that they could escape, as it was he who the enemy was after. All of them refused, and stood by Husayn until each was slain. Husayn made several offers of peace, but all were rejected by his foes. When he was preparing to fight, Husayn saw his infant son dying of thirst and pleaded with the enemies for water. He was answered with a poisoned arrow that pinned the child's neck to the father's arm. In a final prayer, Husayn declared his absolute surrender to God, and proceeded to battle the forces of Yazid until he was slain and his head fixed upon the tip of a lance.

Indeed, any attempt to weed out imaginative embellishments from certain historical fact would bypass the beauty, valor, and tragedy of the tale. The impossible odds, the certain failure, the heroic struggle against the forces of tyranny, and the ultimate martyrdom have provided guidance and strength for the Shi'a in the many eras when they have suffered oppression.

A major legal difference between the Sunni and the Shi'a lies in the concept of the Imam in Shi'ism. Instead of Caliphs, the Shi'a revere a series of leaders called Imams, all of whom were members of Muhammad's family. The first Imam was Ali, who married Muhammad's daughter Fatimah. Their sons Hasan and Husayn were the second and third Imams, respectively. Ali, Fatimah, Hasan, and Husayn are referred to as the *ahl-ul-bayt* (people of Muhammad's house), and are sacred to the Shi'a. Only their descendants can become Imams. One of Husayn's sons survived the Karbala disaster to carry on the Imamate.

In Shi'ism, Muhammad and the Imams are believed to be infallible and sinless. Unlike the caliphs for the Sunni, the Imams were not only political leaders, but also religious and spiritual guides, believed to be divinely inspired. The teachings of the Imams constitute a source of law in Shi'ism—in addition to the Qur'an and the teachings of Muhammad.

Disagreement over Imams has led to several subdivisions within the Shi'a sect. The majority of Shi'a recognized Muhammad al-Baqir as the fifth Imam, but some followed Husayn's grandson Zayd instead and became known as the "fivers." Another minority disagreed about the seventh Imam, and became known as the Ismailis or "seveners." Several Ismaili chains of Imams have endured into the present day.

The majority of Shi'a Muslims are called "twelvers." The eleventh Imam, Hassan al Askari, died without an heir, causing a potential problem for his followers, since according to Shi'a belief there will never be an age without an Imam. Twelvers believe that his son, Mohammad al-Mahdi, the twelfth or "hidden" Imam who mysteriously disappeared as a child, will return near the end of time and lead his people to victory. The government of modern-day Iran is a twelver Shi'a theocracy.

The story behind the divide between Sunnis and Shi'as is, then, a story about leadership, and leaders' political authority, as well as religious and spiritual authority. This is not, then, a story unique to Islam. Rather, it is a story told in different ways in all the major world religions.

—Danyal Najmi

See also Islam; Islam, Five Pillars of; Islam, Founding Fathers of

J

JAINISM

The Jain tradition stems from Buddhism. The founder of Jainism, Mahavira, born around 599 B.C.E., was a senior contemporary of Gautama Buddha. He is considered by Jains to be the greatest religious leader and is called the *jina* (victor). The followers of Mahavira came to be called Jain(a)s, meaning followers of the Victorious One. Since the period of Mahavira's reformation within India, the tradition has continued to flourish in the Indian subcontinent, unlike the Buddhist tradition that faded out in India. There are about 4 million Jains today in India, the United Kingdom, Canada, and the United States.

Jain principles were taught by Mahavira, the final teacher in a series of enlightened individuals. The teachings of the Jain tradition are eternal, with no beginning and no end. The teachings are always there, and will continue to prosper and show people the path of their religion. No single Jain founding figure has been recorded, but there is a line of great teachers who reveal the teachings of Jainism to each successive era, with the greatest and most profound being Mahavira. The teachers of the Jain tradition are called Tirthankaras, meaning "crossing makers" who lead people to cross over into their new enlightened selves. The Tirths hold special status because they have achieved liberation or Kaivalya and are able then to teach the Jain path to others. Within Jainism there have been 24 Tirths; Mahavira being the last Tirth to appear in the current cycle of time. Through Mahavira, Jainism takes its present form. Mahavira is significant to the Jain tradition because he was a Tirthankara, he achieved Kaivalya, reestablished Jain teaching, and established the fourfold order of Jains (monks, nuns, laymen, laywomen).

Mahavira also established the three jewels of Jainism: (1) being right in faith (*samyak darsana*), which implies a moment of spiritual insight, the truth from a right viewpoint; (2) right knowledge (*samyak jnana*), which implies that one is led down the path by right knowledge and right conduct; and (3) right conduct (*samyak caritra*), which consists of the five vows or Mahavrata. The first vow is Ahimsa, which means the path of nonviolence; the second is Satya, which is truthful speech; the third is Asteya, which means no stealing; the fourth is Brohmacharya, which is avoiding sexual misconduct; and finally, Aparigraha is the detachment from worldly things.

Jains categorize all things into two categories: alive and not alive. *Jiv* means to be alive, and a person's soul is alive (humans, animals, plants, and vegetables are deemed Jivas). Ajiva is dead, such as matter, space, time, and motion. Together Jivas and Ajiva are eternal and coexist together in harmony. Dharma to Jains is the most important principle in the world. It is the main cause for all happiness. It comes from human beings, and through it human beings attain what is good. This principle coexists with the doctrine of Ahimsa, for humans are to enjoy and respect life not to pollute it through violence.

Karma to Jains literally means action or the fruits of one's actions. It is a substance that adheres to the soul of Jiva and obscures its truest nature. Karma as a substance binds the Jiva to this world at birth, released at death or through Kaivalya. One must work to remove the obscuring substance of karma from the

Jiva. Once the Jiva is freed from karmic bonds, it is liberated and becomes enlightened. Destroying karma is to cease karma-generating activities. There are many ways to do this, but the most often practiced way is through asceticism. Ascetics renounce their belongings, wealth, fame, and then can perform the austerities that are necessary for liberation. Annihilation of all of one's karma is the ultimate goal or Kaivalya.

The central teaching of Jains is belief in Ahimsa, or nonviolence. The phrase that can be found on Jain pamphlets and documents accurately details their belief in Ahimsa: *Ahimsa paramo dharmah*: "Nonviolence is the highest form of religious conduct." Their commitment to this belief is carried out to all forms of life here on earth. Dedication to belief, diet, manner and times of eating, movements, travel, choice of careers, and modes of conducting business are a reflection on how deeply Jains value the doctrine of Ahimsa.

The universe is viewed to be full of life in various forms, and any form of violence that is committed to these life forms through thought, deed, or word is said to stain one's Jiva. The Jain people have taken Ahimsa to the ultimate level, as can be seen with their diet. Jains are strict vegetarians and will not eat any root foods such as garlic, onions, or potatoes, for they might disturb and even kill the Jivas that live in the ground. Onions have layers, and are therefore believed by the Jains to house innumerable Jivas. Jain monks and nuns wear *mupatti*—a cloth over the mouth—so that no Jivas are injured while breathing.

There are two monastic orders within the Jain tradition. The first is called Svetambara, which include men and women. They wear white garments, and women are capable of achieving liberation within this order. The second order is called Digambara, and this order insists on nudity. They are reluctant to have nuns within this order for it may deter from their goal of Kaivalya, which is a lesser goal of liberation from the worldly cycle of rebirth.

There are sacred symbols and places where Jains are able to express their devotion to their religion. Worship and rituals are an integral part of Jain piety. Worship is done at a shrine in the home or at a temple to revere the Jinas and other liberated beings. Within the temples, the focal points are images of Tirths. Placing flowers within a temple is a demonstration of respect and honor toward the Tirths. Jains worship every day. The devotion of Jains is unlike worldly passion, as it is spiritual devotion and directed toward the Jinas. When devotion is stimulated through worldly desire, this is wrong action and damaging to the soul, but when it is prompted through a love of liberation it destroys karma and helps to free the soul.

Many Jains participate in pilgrimages to certain temples and other sacred sites. When at these holy places, the adherent is to express religious focus and spiritual reflection; participate in religious rites; interact with monks, nuns, and laypersons, and embrace the sense of community.

The role of children within the Jain tradition is one of great importance. Children are celebrated within Jainism, included in worship ceremonies, and taught at a very young age the practice of Ahimsa (nonviolence) as with their actions to others and their diet restrictions. Within the pilgrimages, religious development in children begins as they witness their parents' ritual conduct about the three jewels of Jainism, and listen to their prayers as well as services led by the religious leaders.

The swastika is a symbol of importance to the Jain people. The Sanskrit word "swastika" literally means well-being. The diagram of the swastika sees the human predicament and ways to overcome it. The four spokes represent the four stages of existence in the wheel of *samsara,* which is the cycle of life and death. The swastika appears on temples and households. This sacred symbol is used as a focal point for meditation practices among Jain members.

The practice of Ahimsa can be seen in modern times in the lives of important historical and religious figures. Gandhi welcomed the belief in nonviolence into his cause for independence from the British occupation in India. Later, in the United States, another prominent figure adopted the belief in nonviolence as seen through the teachings and practices of the Reverend Dr. Martin Luther King Jr. Ahimsa is attainable and can be extremely rewarding for the soul and for the individual. However, the individual must make the choice to devote his or her life to achieving Ahimsa.

—Julie Wieland-Robbescheuten

See also Buddhism

FURTHER READING

Oxtoby, W. G. (Ed.). (2002). *World religions: Western traditions.* Oxford: Oxford University Press.

JAMES, WILLIAM

William James (1842–1910), the father of American psychology and leading American philosopher, was also a pioneer in the psychological study of religion. A person of diverse talents, James distinguished himself in numerous fields related to religion and spiritual development. He is perhaps most famous for his seminal books in psychology—the two-volume work *The Principles of Psychology* (1890), and *The Varieties of Religious Experience* (1902). In the last decade of his life, he focused on the development of an American stream of philosophy, pragmatism. James's contributions are so substantial that several disciplines consider him a key historical figure.

STREAMS OF JAMES'S LIFE

Born on January 11, 1842, in New York City, William James was the eldest of five children. His father, Henry James Sr., had received a significant inheritance that allowed him to live as a man of leisure and a freelance free-thinking theologian, while his mother espoused a more conventional Christian path. Life in the James household was intellectually rich and unorthodox. James and his brother Henry Jr. (the future novelist) attended a succession of schools in Europe and the United States, and they benefited from a series of language tutors and diverse cultural experiences as the family lived in Dresden, Geneva, London, and Paris, and eventually settled in Cambridge, Massachusetts.

James's father was a gifted conversationalist, and the James children were encouraged to participate in family discussions. Other participants in those discussions regularly included visitors to the James home—Henry David Thoreau, Ralph Waldo Emerson, Nathaniel Hawthorne, Alfred Lord Tennyson, John Stuart Mill, and many others. William developed an eagerness for ongoing intellectual exploration, and a willingness to seriously engage with perspectives different from his own.

Art Student

The earliest identifiable vocational interests that James pursued were those of naturalist and artist. At the age of 18, he began formal studies with American painter William Morris Hunt in Newport, Rhode Island, but his vocation as art student lasted only 6 months. Nevertheless, the training James received as an artist continued to influence the ways that he focused his attention in other areas. He continued to sketch and draw and retained a keen observational eye for detail in his scientific pursuits. His observational abilities surfaced both in his empirical work and in his recognition of the importance of attention in human psychology.

Medical Student

In 1861 James began his lifetime association with Harvard University when he enrolled to study chemistry. His interest in chemistry soon paled, however, and he turned to physiology and medicine. James continued to combine his interests in science and nature, and in 1865, at the age of 23, James traveled to Brazil with Harvard naturalist Louis Agassiz. James was to serve as a field naturalist, collecting and marking species as they were added to Agassiz's collection. James's career as naturalist was cut short when he caught varioloid, a form of smallpox, and was hospitalized. Destabilized by illness, and deeply upset by the death of a favorite cousin, James returned to Boston to resume his medical studies. The following year, he began a clerkship at Massachusetts General Hospital, but by April he again fell ill and suspended his medical education. Periods of study alternated with periods of rest and travel until, in 1869, he completed training as a medical doctor at Harvard University.

Physiologist Stream

After completing his medical degree, James was still unclear about his vocational path. He experienced 3 years of ill health, and thus did not seriously pursue clinical practice. During these years, he remained interested in physiology and comparative anatomy, and when a friend, Henry Bowditch, decided to take a year's leave from teaching physiology at Harvard, he recommended James as a replacement. James was appointed instructor of physiology in 1872, and assistant professor of physiology in 1876. He taught physiology for 8 years.

During this time he became interested in physiological psychology. In 1875, James taught the first psychology course and established the first psychological laboratory in the United States, both at Harvard. Wilhelm Wundt, also in 1875, established the first psychological research laboratory in Europe. James's and Wundt's laboratories signaled that a "new" psychology was emerging. James himself clarified the link between the physiological and the psychological when he wrote to a colleague, "[A] union of the two 'disciplines' in one man seems then the most natural thing in the world, if not the most traditional." James's training in physiology influenced the way in which he approached future disciplinary endeavors. James's future writings would all be informed by his understanding of and the centrality he gave to the physical body.

Psychologist Stream

James began teaching psychology, as an assistant professor through the Department of Philosophy, in 1880. James's self-styled Darwinian approach to psychology became known as "functionalism" because the mind's stream of consciousness was understood as consisting of functional processes that allow people to adapt to their living environment. In contrast to James's functional psychology, Wundt's approach was known as "structuralism" because his structural analysis tried to break consciousness down into static elements and states. In addition, and in contrast to functionalists who studied individuals as they adapted to their everyday environment, structuralists studied people in laboratory settings.

James was appointed professor of psychology in 1889 and, in 1890, he published *The Principles of Psychology*, on which he had labored for 12 years. Its publication became a landmark event in psychology, brought James to prominence, and is still perhaps the best-known book in the field of psychology. The roles of physiologist and psychologist are intricately interwoven in *The Principles.* James considered the interconnectedness of mind and body a "general law." He believed no mental "modification" could occur without being accompanied by a corresponding "bodily change."

James's contributions were critical in helping psychology emerge as a separate discipline, distinct from philosophy. He was elected president of the American Psychological Association in 1894.

Psychologist of Religion Stream

After publication of *The Principles,* James began to study extraordinary states of consciousness. This intellectual stream led him to a closer study of religious experiences, which he defined as "the feelings, acts, and experiences of" individuals "in their solitude, so far as they apprehend themselves to stand in relation to whatever they may consider the divine." He studied the role that religion plays in people's lives, and emphasized that he was studying religion as an "essential organ of life" from a psychological perspective.

Focusing on individual religious experience instead of institutionalized religion, James believed that the most intense forms of religious experience could demonstrate normal processes of the human mind in high relief, and accordingly could be invaluable in its study. He presented his findings in The Gifford Lectures, delivered at the University of Edinburgh, and published them in book form as *The Varieties of Religious Experience* in 1902. *The Varieties* is widely regarded as the greatest classic in the psychological study of religion, and is the best known of his works among religious studies scholars. In *The Varieties,* James clarified the functions, dynamics, and integrity of personal religious encounters. Two years after its publication, James was elected president of the American Psychological Association for the second time.

Looking back, by the 2nd decade of the 20th century, the psychoanalytic movements of Sigmund Freud and Carl Jung had become the dominant psychological schools, although the work of James and G. Stanley Hall were foundational for the school of functionalist psychology that flourished under John Dewey and others in the 1920s. Subsequently, the "pure research" of the German laboratory model became foundational for the dominant school of behaviorism, while the person-centered work of James laid the foundations for contemporary personality psychology and humanistic psychology.

Philosopher Stream

James had always read philosophy, even during his medical school years, but it emerged as his primary preoccupation during the last decade of his life. During these years, his writings were primarily philosophical and, through them, he advanced the pragmatist movement.

Pragmatism (1907) is James's most well-known book among philosophers, some of whom have credited James's pragmatic philosophy with moving epistemology and ethics into the modern world. At the center of James's pragmatism is the idea that ideas are true because they work (i.e., help one to adapt to particular circumstances) instead of the other way around. James and his colleagues—Oliver Wendell Holmes, Jr. and Charles Sanders Peirce—viewed ideas as tools that individuals designed in order to better cope with demands of the world. They also believed that ideas were solidified socially, not simply individually. The growth of ideas depended on the interaction and exchange of their human "carriers." Ideas were provisional responses, and the ideas that would best survive over time were those that demonstrated adaptability to varying circumstances. Truth and value are no less constructed than discovered; this task carries with it an enormous ethical responsibility, and it is not coincidental that pragmatism arose in the wake of the Civil War.

The Civil War's atrocities taught James and his colleagues that those who are most certain are also those who most often resort to violence. The struggles of his day—between abolitionism and antiabolitionism, science and morality, evolution and theology—demanded solutions. Faced with such dichotomies, James's pragmatism sought a new way of thinking that would dissolve the apparent contradictions. In his 1906 lecture and 1910 essay, James pointed to the need for "The Moral Equivalent of War," a substitute for war's toughening and maturing functions, that would involve the conscription of each generation of youth for a couple of years to provide nonmilitary service for the common good. William James died in Chocorua, New Hampshire in 1910 at the age of 68. In his final ideas, however, is a forecast of the Civilian Conservation Corps, the Peace Corps, and similar forms of public morality and community service.

JAMES'S CONTRIBUTIONS TO THE PSYCHOLOGY OF RELIGION

Each intellectual stream in James's life allowed him to develop specific skills that enhanced his contributions to the study of religion. But it is through his second psychological masterpiece, *The Varieties of Religious Experience*, that James made his most vital and enduring contribution to the psychology of religion.

Neuropsychology of Religion

The Varieties opens with a chapter entitled "Religion and Neurology." While the beginning may seem unusual, it is consistent with James's understanding that psychology is grounded in human anatomy and biological temperament. James believed that every human phenomenon, including religious experience, was derived from natural antecedents, and that religious experiences have neural foundations, as do all human behaviors. In this sense, James believed religious phenomena originated in and were derived from nature. Thus, he explains that in *The Varieties* he draws his data from *documents humains,* the document of the living human organism.

James was also keenly aware, however, of the limitations of the biological sciences. The second purpose of his chapter on neurology and religion was to undermine the reductionistic claims of "medical materialism" that religious states of mind can be explained fully by the person's physical constitution. Thus, for example, a religious experience might be said to be "nothing but" the result of neural pathology, a poor digestive system, one's sex life, or epilepsy. James argues, in contrast, that religious experience cannot be *reduced* to mere biology and that the natural origins of religious experience are insufficient to determine their spiritual value.

James's contemporaries, such as G. Stanley Hall, questioned whether religious experience was better understood as purely physiological or secular and not religious. Believers debated whether such experiences were supernatural and subsequently not natural. Contemporary historians believe that James represented a mediating third tradition that asserted religious experience could be both natural and religious, that authentic religious experience and naturalistic accounts of an experience did not have to be mutually exclusive.

Person-Centered Psychology of Religion

The aim of James's psychology of religion was to focus on "interior" personal spiritual experience. His person-centered functional psychology allowed him to analyze the varieties of "firsthand" religious experience, which, in turn, highlighted religion's many functions in terms of meeting human needs. James argued that, when "judging of the value of religious phenomena," one must "insist on the distinction between religion as an individual personal function, and religion as an institutional, corporate, or tribal product." Ecclesiastical institutions were of little interest to James. The religious experience which he studied was "that which lives itself out within the private breast." Original, firsthand individual religious experiences, James observed, have "always appeared as a heretical sort of innovation to those who witnessed its birth." James was particularly interested in the experience of religious innovators, reformers, and founders who demonstrate extremes of religious intensity. In many ways, his work predated and predicted the American interest in "spirituality" as distinct from "religion."

In *The Varieties,* James sets up a continuum of religious personality orientations. At one end he places the "healthy minded," people for whom "happiness is congenital and irreclaimable." By healthy minded, James means "those, who, when unhappiness is offered or proposed to them, positively refuse to feel it, as if it were something mean and wrong." At the other end, he places the "sick souled," people who tend to maximize the evil they encounter in life, "based on the persuasion that the evil aspects of our life are of its very essence." The sick-souled individual has a divided sense of self that can only be unified through a transformative experience. James calls this transformation "conversion," which he links to a shift in attention and focus. One's focus "may come to lie permanently within a certain system; and then, if the change be a religious one, we call it a *conversion,* especially if it be by crisis, or sudden."

James was also fascinated by mystical experience. He hypothesized that "personal religious experience has its root and center in mystical states of consciousness." But he felt excluded from the full intensity of mystical experience. So he came to believe that while mystical experience is "absolutely authoritative" for those individuals who experience it, those without such experience should not feel compelled to accept mystical revelations uncritically. Although one cannot know the intensity or personal authority of another's mystical experience, what can be known is how that experience manifests itself in the "fruits" of religious charity, good works, and saintliness.

Morality and religion were interrelated for James because he believed religion could provide the energy to be moral when a purely "athletic" type of ethics "inevitably" weakens and disintegrates. James argued that a primary function of religion was not simply to supply moral prescriptions that allow one to accept the nature of the universe with fear or "stoic resignation," but rather to transcend "morality pure and simple" and accept the universe with "passionate happiness." Ultimately, James believed, we were dependent on the universe, and must inevitably face sacrifice and surrender. Religion thus makes attractive and genuine "what in any case is necessary."

James used the moral fruits of individual lives to gauge and understand the depth and intensity of the religious experience that precipitated them. By analogy, the importance of James's study of religious experience can be gauged by the profound influence it had on the subsequent history of the psychology of religion, including the work of Theodore Flournoy, Carl Jung, Gordon Allport, and Eugene Taylor.

Philosophical Psychology of Religion

James's lifetime interest in philosophy became his major mode of operation near the end of his career, and he devoted one of the last lectures in *The Varieties* to "Philosophy." James's contributions to the philosophical psychology of religious experience incorporated his dominant philosophical concepts—pluralism, radical empiricism, and pragmatism.

Pluralism

James held that the human condition is too varied to be accounted for by any single explanatory system. Rather, a plurality of powers (variables, gods, etc.) must be taken into account. James's open-mindedness led him to conclude that the study of religion should always emphasize the worthy-of-respect validity of multiple perspectives, traditions, and extremes in religious experience. He argued that different temperaments need different types of religious experiences. To James, religious pluralism was an ethical value that restrained one-sidedness and promoted tolerance.

Radical empiricism

James's method was *empirical* because all so-called facts and conclusions regarding the data are "hypotheses liable to modification in the course of future experience." His method was *radical* because he regarded the unity and order of the universe in itself as a hypothesis. James wanted to be loyal to all of the data, and not exclude any data, and to collect it "together without any special *a priori* theological system." Rational thought is to follow the data of our experience. Based on this method, for instance, he observed that mystical states were interpreted *post hoc.* Although mysticism itself is radically empirical in that it asks that we take religious experience seriously, James observed that how the mystic makes sense of an experience is not inherent in the experience itself, but is rather constructed after the fact as the person struggles to make sense of a profound experience. Thus, James argued that not only should religious thought follow from the empirical data of our religious experience, but it also should be defined in terms drawn from our experiences.

Pragmatism

James's pragmatic spirit is seen in his warm sensitivity to the observation that deep human needs are satisfied through religious experience. More specifically, James's attention centers on the pragmatic moral implications of religious experience and belief in God as known from the practical consequences that follow in people's personal lives after such experiences. Applying pragmatism to religious beliefs, the truth of a theological proposition is to be known by looking at the consequences of the idea. It is not known by its origin or roots but rather by its fruits—"the way in which it works on the whole." James's pragmatism, as a method of problem solving, also allowed him to lay aside dogmatic theologies concerned with the proofs of God and God's metaphysical attributes because they were of no practical significance. In contrast, James noted, God's moral qualities "positively determine fear and hope and expectation, and are foundations for the saintly life." James also believed that philosophy and theology will always have the important task of systematizing and drawing meaning from the ineffable religious experiences of individuals.

Judging James's philosophical psychology of religion by his own pragmatic criteria, one would probably conclude that it worked. It influenced, for instance, many religious-psychological innovators and the therapeutic practices they founded, including Elwood Worcester (founder of the Emmanuel movement), Anton Boisen (founder of clinical pastoral education), and Bill Wilson (founder of Alcoholics Anonymous).

CONCLUSION

While William James's diverse vocational pursuits during young adulthood may be viewed as a sign of uncertain identity, his explorations may also be fairly viewed as an indication of the complexity of his streams of thought. The waters of James's life reveal deeper and deeper levels of intricate connections, as new interests and areas of study flowed into existing currents. In William James, we find the most original mind in the study of American religion and spirituality. As a physiologist, James anticipated contemporary understandings of the interaction between feeling and emotion and the essential interconnectedness of mind and body. As a psychologist, he anticipated contemporary research findings from studies of consciousness, trauma, dissociation, and temperaments. As a philosopher, James and his colleagues launched what became the most American stream of philosophy, pragmatism. Perhaps what is most remarkable is that he drew upon each of these fields to empower his religious studies.

—John Snarey and Lynn Bridgers

See also Jung, Carl and Post-Jungians

FURTHER READING

Croce, P. J. (1995). *Science and religion in the era of William James*. Chapel Hill, NC: University of North Carolina Press.

Edie, J. M. (1987). *William James and phenomenology*. Bloomington: Indiana University Press.

Feinstein, H. (1984). *Becoming William James*. Ithaca, NY: Cornell University Press.

James, W. (1987). *Writings: 1878–1899*. New York: Library of America.

James, W. (1992). *Writings: 1902–1910*. New York: Library of America.

Levinson, H. (1981). *The religious investigations of William James*. Chapel Hill, NC: University of North Carolina Press.

Menand, L. (2001). *The metaphysical club*. New York: Farrar Straus and Giroux.

Perry, R. B. (1935–1936). *The thought and character of William James (Vols. 1—-2)*. Boston: Little, Brown.

Snarey, J. (Ed.). (2003). William James: the varieties of religious and moral formation [Special issue]. *Journal of Moral Education, 32*(4).

Taves, A. (1999). *Fits, trances & visions: experiencing religion and explaining experience from Wesley to James*. Princeton, NJ: Princeton University Press.

Taylor, E. (1996). *William James on consciousness beyond the margin*. Princeton, NJ: Princeton University Press.

JESUIT VOLUNTEER CORPS

Established in 1956, the Jesuit Volunteer Corps (JVC) is associated with the Roman Catholic Society of Jesus (Jesuits), and is an organization that aims to provide women and men an opportunity to spend 1 or 2 years of their lives working full-time for justice and peace. Jesuit volunteers see their mission as one of service to the poor. In keeping with this mission, they seek to become aware of the social structures that contribute to the oppression of low-income and marginalized persons. Since it was established in 1956, more than 7,000 members of the JVC have committed themselves to this endeavor, and there are currently 500 JVC volunteers in the United States and over 70 volunteers in other parts of the world.

In order to achieve this goal, the JVC has a wide variety of ministry opportunities both in the United States and internationally. Ministries vary from addiction recovery to education, legal services to prison ministry, and HIV/AIDS services to domestic abuse programs. At the core of each of these ministries is a concern for social justice, a need that involves numerous ministries across the United States and extends internationally to East Africa, Belize, Tanzania, the Pacific Islands of Micronesia, and Peru.

There are four main values promoted by the JVC. The first of these is the emphasis placed on community. All Jesuit volunteers are required to live in a community with other volunteers. Christian faith reminds the volunteers that God's will is to be found in the loving and respectful relationships among people; accordingly, these communities are joined by a shared vision and a common desire for justice. This idea of community extends beyond the volunteers' immediate living conditions and includes the people they serve: neighbors, co-workers, other volunteers, and members of local parishes who are encouraged to form relationships that challenge and support one another.

The JVC values a simple lifestyle. In light of this, each volunteer receives a small stipend each month, and the homes that each community occupies tend to be in low-income neighborhoods. The goal of such simple living is twofold. On the one hand, it encourages each volunteer to become conscious of the experience of the poor and marginalized, particularly the poor that they serve on a day-to-day basis in their ministries. On the other hand, it shifts the volunteers' focus away from financial concerns and encourages them to find value in activities that do not require large amounts of money.

The third value places an emphasis on social justice. The intent of each volunteer working among the poor is to encourage them to participate in the daily struggle for dignity, justice, and human rights. By living among and becoming friends with them, the volunteers forge relationships with those who are most easily forgotten by our society—relationships that challenge the volunteers to see the causes of poverty and oppression, and to understand the nature of the injustice that leads to their marginalization. Each volunteer's ministry placement places him or her in direct contact with the poor, and each ministry provides essential care that aims at empowering the poor to free themselves from the forces that oppress them.

The fourth value emphasized by the JVC is spirituality. Taken from the founder of the Jesuits, Ignatius of Loyola, Jesuit spirituality calls each volunteer to integrate a life of prayer with active work to further the reign of God. In keeping with this vision, the Jesuit volunteer seeks ways to use his or her unique talents in ways that take into account both where God will best be served, as well as where people will best be helped.

There is no such thing as a "typical" ministry: Each one is as unique as the volunteer. In general, however, each domestic placement involves the commitment of 1 year of service. Each year of service begins in August with an orientation. Following this orientation, the volunteers report to the cities in which they will do their ministry. The communities range in size, and many encompass a wide array of persons; recent college graduates, people reevaluating their lives, and married couples may all live together. Some may engage in education ministry while others work in a hospice or with AIDS patients. Food and other expenses are shared among the members of the community and meals are eaten together. There is also community time in which the entire community gathers together to engage in a common activity, such as a game of Frisbee in the park, a trip to a lake, or a board game. Prayer and reflection are important to the JVC experience, and they take the shape of liturgy, prayer services, and personal contemplation. Throughout the year, retreats and workshops are scheduled to afford each volunteer time to process and to reflect upon his or her experiences.

The motto of the JVC is that it leaves its participants "Ruined for Life." By this they mean to indicate that the year of service will challenge each person in unimaginable ways—demanding one to reevaluate social structures, materialistic tendencies, and the mechanisms that lead to the oppression and marginalization of the poor. Ultimately, in combining the emphases placed on community, simplicity, social justice, and spirituality, the "ruined" individual will have a year of experiences that have worked to open the heart and the mind to live always conscious of the poor and oppressed, a year that has "ruined" the person to such an extent that the personal mission of each volunteer is the promotion of justice in the service of faith.

—*Ryan Gerard Duns*

See also Loyola, Ignatius; Volunteerism

FURTHER READING

See http://jesuitvolunteers.org

JESUS

Non-Christian sources regarding Jesus are very limited, but these independent accounts do prove that in ancient times even the opponents of Christianity never doubted the historicity of Jesus.

Josephus, a Jewish historian of the court of Emperor Domitian, wrote about the events of the Jewish–Roman Wars (66–70 C.E.). Josephus Antiquities XX (200 C.E.), writes about the stoning (in 62 C.E.) of James, the brother of Jesus, who was the so-called Christ. Josephus uses the proper name "Jesus," for as a Jew he knows that "Christ" is a translation of Messiah, so he adds the qualifier "so-called" to the second name that was familiar in Rome.

Another Roman historian, Suetonius, writing on the life of Emperor Claudius, stated, "Claudius expelled the Jews, who had on the instigation of Chrestus continually been causing disturbances from Rome" (Vita Claudii 25:4). This no doubt refers to the problems of the Roman Jews being upset by the Christians in their midst. Suetonius mistakenly used the name Chrestus, instead of Christ.

The 1st- and 2nd-century Talmud writings of some rabbis also mention Jesus. The Talmud, a compendium of Jewish law, lore, commentary, apologetics, and polemics, reveals an acquaintance with the early Christian tradition. The picture offered in these writings may be summarized as follows: Jesus was born illegitimate, worked magic, mocked the wise, seduced and stirred up the people, and was crucified on the eve of the Passover. The writings of the Life of Jesus or The Toledot Yeshu were one such collection of assertions among the Jews of the Middle Ages.

Current Christian sources for Jesus are many, but have to be read as coming from a faith community who saw this Jesus of Nazareth as the Christ or Messiah of history. Christianity is the faith of those who recognize Jesus of Nazareth as the Christ, the Son of God, and accept him as their Lord and Savior. Christianity's beliefs and practices are the result of the experiences of those who knew Jesus during his earthly life, and of those since who know him through the grace of the Holy Spirit, given by God to those who put their trust in him. Most Christians believe in One God Creator, Jesus the Redeemer, and the Holy Spirit the Sanctifier—all of which is called One God the Trinity.

The main source for knowledge about Jesus is the Christian Scriptures, also called the New Testament, especially the Gospels of Matthew, Mark, Luke, and John. These writings were compiled between 70 and 100 C.E. All of them coming from an original faith community, first by way of eyewitness and oral tradition, and later being written down by the followers of the eyewitnesses.

The consensus among modern Scripture scholars designates Mark as the earliest of the Gospel writers around 65–70 C.E. Jesus in Mark's Gospel is a man with a purpose. In fact, the Gospel of Mark has been dramatized as a one-man play. There is no mention of Jesus' birth or childhood. Jesus' ministry begins with being baptized by John the Baptizer. Then he calls his disciples and announces the coming of the Kingdom of God. Mark's community comprised the Roman followers of Jesus.

The Gospel of Matthew (middle 80s C.E.) was written for the early Jewish followers of Jesus. Here Jesus is seen as the fulfillment of all beliefs from the Jewish Scriptures, also called the Old Testament. Jesus is like the new Moses, and Matthew shows the parallels between the two. Matthew establishes that, just as the Egyptian Pharaoh feared and loathed the Hebrews in Moses' time, so King Herod treated Jesus and his family with scorn. A collection of Jesus' most famous statements, the Sermon on the Mount or the Beatitudes, is in Matthew.

The Jesus of Luke's Gospel is a picture of compassion and forgiveness. The Gospel of Luke needs to be seen as the first part of a two-volume work. The Gospel of Luke and the Acts of the Apostles were written by and for the same person (ca. 85 C.E.). Luke shows Jesus as open to all believers, not just the Jews. He shows Jesus as the miracle worker, and the one who calls people to discipleship.

The first three Gospels show that Jesus' life and teachings have a certain similarity, resulting in their being called the Synoptic Gospels. The Gospel of John, written much later than the other three Gospels (ca. 95 C.E. or later), shows what happens when a believing community has the time to reflect on whom and what Jesus is. John's Gospel has Jesus as being awe inspiring right from the first verses. John shows Jesus as divine, coexisting with the Creator. John shows Jesus at the very beginning of creation.

The early church also had to struggle and reflect on who and what Jesus is. One needs to remember that the early church was underground for over 300 years. It was only after the Emperor Constantine became Christian that the serious task of theology could begin. The St. Anselm dictum that "theology is faith seeking understanding" is very true in regards to Jesus. Early councils of church leaders had to reflect and debate questions such as: Is Jesus human or divine? Is Jesus one person or two persons? Was Jesus created and born? All these questions were ironed out in early councils of church leaders.

The first great council was Nicea in 325, which produced the Nicene Creed that is still recited in most Christian churches. This council clearly stated that Jesus was divine, true God from true God, begotten not made, one in substance with the Father. The next great council was Ephesus in 431. This one had to be called because some were teaching that the Son of God in Heaven and the man Jesus on earth were two different persons. The Council of Ephesus in 413 declared that there is only one person in Jesus, although there is a difference between his divine and human natures. Thus, Jesus is one person, with two natures, human and divine.

The final council to tackle the question of Jesus' identity was the Council of Chalcedon in the year 451. Some were starting to teach that Jesus was only divine and not human. Jesus' divinity was so stressed that his humanity was being forgotten. The Council of Chalcedon proclaimed that both divine and human natures were present in the person of Jesus.

Every believer and each new generation needs to try to answer the "Who is Jesus" question. One is a Christian if one accepts that Jesus is divine. How one lives one's life should also be judged by the question "How ought a believer in Jesus the Christ live?" Throughout one's life, where one stands in relation to these questions has a significant effect on both religious and spiritual development.

—Rev. David M. O'Leary

FURTHER READING

Meier, J. P. (1991). *A marginal Jew: Rethinking the historical Jesus.* New York: Doubleday, 1991.

O'Carroll, M. (1992). *Verbum caro, an encyclopedia on Jesus, the Christ.* Collegeville, MN: Liturgical Press.

JOHN THE BAPTIST

John the Baptist, also known as John the Baptizer or the Baptist, was a Jewish prophet who lived in the 1st century C.E. in Palestine and is known as the forerunner of Jesus. Each of the four gospels in the New Testament begin the account of Jesus' adult life with a description of John and his preaching, although the specific details do not always agree. The lives of the prophets such as the Baptist serve as models of religious devotion to those who hear of their stories and lives.

According to the Gospel of Luke, John was set aside for great things even before his birth. John was the son of Zechariah, a righteous priest, and Elizabeth, a descendant of priests. When his parents were quite old and they thought they would never have any children, an angel appeared to Zechariah when he was serving in the temple. The angel—Gabriel—told him that Elizabeth was to have a son, and that they should name him John. The angel predicted that John would lead the people back to God. Because Zechariah questioned the angel, he was no longer able to speak. When Elizabeth was in her 6th month of pregnancy, Mary, her relative who was pregnant with Jesus at the time, came to visit. Elizabeth's child—who was filled with the Holy Spirit—recognized Jesus and leapt within the womb, causing his mother to bless Mary (these words are part of the "Hail Mary" recited by many Catholics). After the child was born, Zechariah named him John and was able to speak again.

As an adult, John the Baptist lived in the wilderness, eating only locusts and wild honey, and wearing a camel-hair cloak and a leather belt. He traveled around the area of the Jordan River warning people that God would punish them for acting unjustly; they should change their behavior (repent) and be baptized (immersed in water) as a sign that God forgave them. In this way, John prepared them for the coming "Kingdom of God." John baptized many people, including Jesus. (When Jesus came out of the water, the Holy Spirit came down on him in the form of a dove, and a voice from heaven identified him as God's beloved son.) John also taught a number of students, or disciples.

John the Baptist sharply criticized Herod Antipas, one of the Jewish rulers, for taking his brother's wife, Herodias. As a result, John the Baptist was put in prison. At Herod's birthday banquet, Herodias's daughter danced before his guests and so pleased the ruler that he granted her anything she requested. Prompted by her mother, the girl requested the head of John the Baptist "on a platter." Although Herod regretted his promise, he beheaded John.

Some people at the time thought that John might be the messiah (the mythological figure who was to free Israel from oppression), but the New Testament is clear in differentiating between the two. John was the prophet who proclaimed that the messiah was coming, and Jesus was the messiah. John baptized with water, Jesus with the Spirit.

Some historians speculate that John the Baptist was associated with the Qumran community (which produced the Dead Sea Scrolls), who like John lived in the wilderness near the Jordan River, practiced baptism, and preached a similar message.

John the Baptist is not to be confused with John the apostle, the son of Zebedee and brother of James, nor John the supposed author of the Gospel, Letters, or Apocalypse of John, nor John Mark. No writings are attributed to the Baptist.

—Jane S. Webster

See also Jesus; Judaism; Baptism; Dead Sea Scrolls

FURTHER READING

Matthew 3; 11:2–19; 14:1–12; Luke 1–3; 7:17–35; Mark 1:2–11; 6:14–29; John 1; 3:23–4:1.

JUDAISM.

See Specific Entries.

JUDAISM, CONSERVATIVE

Conservative Judaism attempts to follow the sacred Jewish teachings of the past while affirming openness to evolution of thought and practice. Conservative scholars and rabbis retain a deep commitment to the teachings of the Hebrew Bible, the Talmud, and subsequent Jewish teachings. Coupled with reverence for tradition is an acknowledgment that throughout history Judaism has continuously evolved to meet the changing religious needs of its community, and it should continue to do such. To that end, Conservative Judaism maintains the importance of traditional observance of *Shabbat* (The Sabbath), *kashrut* (dietary laws), and prayer, while incorporating more modern principles such as the equality of women. Like our coreligionists, Conservative Jews maintain a deep commitment to Hebrew, the language of the Jewish people, and Israel, their eternal homeland.

In North America, Conservative Judaism, along with Reform Judaism and Orthodoxy, represent the three major Jewish movements. While attempts to cultivate the movement abroad, particularly in Israel, are making progress, Conservative Judaism is most popular in America.

UNDERSTANDING OF GOD

Conservative Judaism affirms the existence of God and the centrality of God in Judaism but does not dictate theological dogmatism. Within the movement there is an acknowledgment that different life and spiritual experiences lead to different understandings of the divine. For example, many believe in a supernatural God that created the world and continues to exercise control over it. Others believe that God created the world and that, by gradually withdrawing from the world's affairs, God presents humanity with an opportunity to partner in creation by improving the condition of the world. A smaller group holds that the actual presence/existence of God is in a part a result of our experiences and conceptions of the divine.

Conservative Judaism celebrates its theological diversity. Consistent with the sacred texts (including the Bible and the Talmud), which present widely distinct and nuanced understandings of God, Conservative Judaism continues to explore the nature of God.

UNDERSTANDING OF THE JEWISH MISSION

Conservative Judaism affirms the Jewish people's special responsibility to advocate on behalf of those who are treated unjustly or marginalized by society. This responsibility defines their selection as the "chosen people." The Jewish people can only fulfill their special role by continuously seeking the creation of compassionate societies that ensure the welfare of the weak along with the powerful. The Conservative movement, with Reform and Orthodoxy, consistently teach the importance of providing *tzedakah* (mandatory charitable contributions) and engaging in volunteerism. Only through these means will Jews help steer humanity towards this lofty world vision.

UNDERSTANDING OF THE BIBLE

Conservative Jews believe that the Torah (The Five Books of Moses) records their ancestors' understandings of how God created the world, interacted with humanity, and revealed Godself to the Israelite nation. The most critical and celebrated of these revelations occurred at Mount Sinai. The clear presence of the human hand in recording the Torah and subsequent biblical texts prompts Conservative Judaism to reject fundamentalism and biblical literalism. The recognition of the central role of humanity in the formation of the biblical text does not detract from its holiness. Rather, Conservative Judaism maintains that the attempt of the human authors of the Bible to capture an understanding of God's essence, character, and will serves as the ultimate expression of holiness—the attempt to locate and enter into relationship with the divine.

UNDERSTANDING OF JEWISH LAW (*HALAKHAH*)

Conservative Judaism believes that Jewish law provides a meaningful common expression for the Jewsih community. Compliance with the laws of Shabbat (the Jewish day of rest), holidays, prayer, and *kashrut* (eating practices), among other areas of Jewish law, provide a communal language, experience, and distinctly Jewish way of living. Conservative Judaism affirms that compliance with Jewish law provides the opportunity to transform every moment into a sacred encounter. The observance of Jewish law highlights the importance of God in our lives, and a sense of obligation to humanity.

As Conservative Judaism recognizes that *halakhah* (Jewish law) is binding, the movement also ensures that the law consistently engages the Jewish people by evolving to meet the needs of the contemporary Jew. Throughout Jewish history, legal authorities grappled and molded the law as to ensure that it fairly guided the community. Conservative Judaism embraces this spirit. While carefully weighing traditional opinions and views, significant change is possible in Conservative Judaism's legal rulings. The rulings are largely left to the rabbis, who combine an understanding of classical sources with an awareness of modern developments.

When issues arise in which the pulls of modernity and traditionalism compete, the movement carefully weighs all possibilities before issuing a ruling. Therefore, when considering more controversial issues, the Conservative movement is often slower to respond than the Reform movement, which encourages progressivism, and quicker than Orthodoxy, which generally frowns upon change.

RELATIONSHIP WITH ISRAEL

The establishment of the modern state of Israel in 1948 is celebrated by Conservative Jews and viewed as miraculous. Israel is the Jewish people's eternal homeland—the geographic heart of their religious soul. Therefore, Conservative Judaism encourages all Jews to develop a special relationship with Israel by visiting, providing economic and moral support, and, for some, deciding to make *aliyah* (immigrating to Israel). Building a Jewish home in Israel is seen as an enormous contribution. Yet, this is not the only way to live a fulfilling Jewish life. Communities in the diaspora have consistently made significant contributions to Jewish life, and will continue to do such. The recognition of the importance of Isreal inspires the continuing efforts to build and expand uniquely Conservative institutions and communities in Israel. Furthermore, Conservative Jews feel a responsibility to ensure that Israel exists as a secure, democratic state, open to the presence of all people.

HISTORY OF THE MOVEMENT

The seeds of Conservative Judaism were sown in Europe at the dawn of the modern era. Beginning in the nineteenth century, Europe slowly began to cast aside the yoke of restrictions set upon the Jewish community. The Jews of Europe were gradually granted measures of freedom and access to European society. Medieval restrictions and persecution had traditionally plagued Jews. However, the traditionally imposed separation from greater society did serve to ensure that Jews remained a distinct, uncompromised entity. A more open world, where one had to choose to participate as a Jew, compelled the Jewish religious establishment to respond. The Reform Movement represented the most far-reaching response to modernity. A small group of more moderate reformers became disheartened by the perceived radical suggestions of the Reform Movement, and the aggressive pace at which it engaged this reformation. In 1854, the leader of this group, Zacharias Frankel, became the head of a new Jewish seminary, The Jewish Theological Seminary of Breslau. Affirming the importance of traditional Jewish learning and observance and modern scholarship, this institution served as a precursor to the development of the Conservative Movement in America. Frankel believed that the seminary should embrace the deliberate, disciplined manner through which change had historically occurred in Judaism as a means to confront modernity.

As an influx of Jewish immigrants from Europe arrived in America, the functioning of the religion in modernity became a topic of consideration and considerable importance for the emerging American Jewish community. Albeit almost thirty years later, the birth of Conservative Judaism in America closely mirrored the formation of Frankel's seminary in Breslau. In 1885, led by Isaac Mayer Wise, the Reform movement issued the Pittsburgh Platform, a document that provided the ideological foundation for the Reform Judaism in America. The rejection of Jewish ritual law, among other radical proclamations, defined this document. The Pittsburgh Platform successfully distinguished the Reform movement in America. Additionally, its sharp departure from tradition prompted the creation of a less radical brand of Judaism—a traditional Judaism suited for the modern mind and American lifestyle. In 1887, the Jewish Theological Seminary (then called the Jewish Theological Seminary Association) devoted to training a core of traditional American rabbis, opened. The establishment of the Seminary marked the institutional birth of Conservative Judaism.

The early seminary floundered; it ordained too few rabbis and was not successful in raising adequate funds. When a group of wealthy Reform Jews recognized that the influx of European Jews would not affiliate with Reform Judaism, they rescued the Jewish Theological Seminary from financial ruin. Their support of the seminary reflected their hope/anticipation that the school would produce a rabbinate, steeped in tradition and distinctly American that would serve the needs of the Eastern European immigrants. With its fiscal future secure, the seminary poised itself to assemble a faculty and leadership team worthy of distinction. The appointment of the renowned scholar Solomon Schechter as president of the institution in 1902 proved to be a major turning point in the fortunes of the nascent institution and the Conservative movement. Until his untimely death in 1913, Schechter ably directed the seminary and the movement. Under his leadership the school attracted skilled teachers and many students. In 1913, Schechter secured the formation of a network of congregations, named the United Synagogue of America, committed to supporting the seminary and espousing Conservative Judaism.

The growth of Conservative Judaism continued well after Schechter's death. From 1915 to 1970, Conservative Judaism experienced an era of tremendous growth. The Seminary, serving as the center of the movement, matured from a small rabbinical program to a major academy with multiple academic departments, close to five hundred students, and fifty full-time faculty members. The United Synagogue, which began as an association of twenty-two congregations, grew to almost eight hundred affiliated synagogues. The original alumni of the Seminary's rabbinical program developed into an international organization of Conservative rabbis with over thirteen hundred members. The strong institutional growth experienced within the movement directly benefited its constituents in many ways, including the formation of a United Synagogue Youth, a highly active youth movement, and Camp Ramah, a network of summer camps.

—*Rabbi Brian Schuldenfrei*

FURTHER READING

Dorff, E. N. (1998). *Conservative Judaism: Our Ancestors to Our Descendants.* National Youth Commission, United Synagogue of Conservative Judaism.

Gillman, N. (1993). *Conservative Judaism: A New Century.* Springfield, NH: Behrman House.

*Gordis, R. (Ed.). (1988). Emet Ve-Emunah: Statement of Pr*inciples of Conservative Judaism. New York: The Jewish Theological Seminary of America, The Rabbinical Assembly, The United Synagogue of America.

JUDAISM, ORTHODOX

Judaism is very old. Orthodox Judaism in particular claims loyalty to that which God revealed to the Jews and to Moses at Mt. Sinai more than 3,000 years ago. And yet, despite its age, worldwide Orthodoxy is currently a growing movement able to boast millions of active, observant, and devoted followers—people who live full and fulfilling lives while straddling both sides of the secular—-religious "divide."

What gives Judaism this vigor? While there is some dispute among Jews as to exactly what the Torah is, all agree that Jewish nationhood and faith are defined by Torah. Torah is the name sometimes given to the Five Books of Moses (also called Chumash, or Pentateuch). The five books are a faithful and exact record of the word of God to His prophet, Moses. These books describe the creation and social development of the world; the origins of the family that was to become the Jewish people, and their exile and slavery in Egypt; redemption; the revelation at Mt. Sinai; and some very limited details of Torah law.

Torah sometimes also refers to the whole Bible (Old Testament, Tanach). This collection includes the Five Books of Moses, 8 books of the prophets and 11 books of "writings" ("Ketuvim"). These 24 books (according to the traditional way of counting them) form the Scriptures (the part of Jewish literature that had always been written, as opposed to literature, as described below, that was originally oral). There are also times when the word Torah is used to cover the entire huge body of Jewish teaching. This includes the Tanach, the Mishna, the Talmud (the core of the "oral law" that began to appear in written form soon after the destruction of the Second Temple in Jerusalem), and tens of thousands of other books written as commentaries and analyses.

Finally, there is Torah a word used without reference to any specific book but to the sum of all the knowledge that is to be found in all of these works together. How to apply the principles of the Torah to a world forever changing has been the work of every generation's greatest scholars. The fruit of the untiring labor of these thousands of dedicated leaders is the Torah in its largest meaning, that is, one of the world's great libraries.

How has Torah life survived through millennia of exile, cruel persecution, drastically different social conditions, and the wondrous diversity of the human experience? It's been a combination of adherence to the Torah's morality, lifestyle, and study.

Judaism teaches that right and wrong are firm, permanent qualities that lie well within the reach of humans. The Torah is believed to be the inspired teaching of God; its values and laws are both true and eternal. However, as Torah literature is vast and complex, the trick is to figure out what that eternal truth actually is. Uncovering the truth is not such a simple process. In fact, there may be no document in all the world's libraries that has been the victim of such extremes of interpretation, misrepresentation, and critical abuse as the Bible. Even deeply religious people sometimes find themselves struggling with difficult Torah passages.

There are two ways to seek the Torah's moral message: approach the text with an agenda, that is, with a preexisting notion of what will be found, or leave the mind open for whatever the text might deliver. The second approach is the one much more likely to yield the Torah's true meaning. Since, however, this approach requires a high level of honesty and humility, success typically only follows constant and often painful self-analysis. In achieving these goals, experience has revealed no shortcuts. There would seem to be no alternative to intense, decades-long Torah study coupled with serious character development.

TORAH AS LIFESTYLE

There's no denying that Torah Judaism is a most demanding system. The sheer range of its commandments—addressing nearly every daily encounter and endeavor—requires a Jew to fundamentally adjust his work, family, and leisure life. The kosher laws can sometimes restrict her access to food, restaurants, and events such as professional conferences. Sabbath restrictions can hamper extensive travel, and limit the kinds of careers from which he can choose. Laws concerning honesty in business dealings make it all but impossible for an observant Jew to compete in certain fields. Tough restrictions on slander and needless criticism can severely restrict conversation. Some might find all that intimidating or even oppressive while others feel empowered, fulfilled, and elevated by these commandments. This is part of the eternal relevance of Torah life. For all the restrictions it may impose, decency is its own reward.

Let's examine, by way of example, the Sabbath laws. According to Rabbi S. R. Hirsch, working at any of the 39 categories of forbidden Sabbath activity demonstrates your feelings of dominance over the physical world by manipulating its resources (e.g., taking a tree, converting it first to paper, and then to a surface on which to store notes, or taking nuclear energy and converting it to an electrical current to power your telephone). In truth, this is a dominance that we have been allowed 6 days a week, but which we must relinquish to the world's true owner on that 7th day so as not to forget that it is really his world and we are only guests upon it.

By resting on Sabbath, therefore, one acknowledges (to himself or herself and to the rest of the world) both that God created this world (as in reciting "in memory of the creation") and that He is its active manager ("in memory of the exodus from Egypt"). Thus, by refraining from manipulative labor and celebrating the many joys of the Sabbath, one may develop a healthy humility in the face of the vastness of creation and intelligently internalize some of the most basic Jewish beliefs.

According to classical Jewish thought, even this is only part of the story. The Torah's commandments are actually means to a greater end. The 17th-century Italian thinker Rabbi Moshe Chaim Luzzato (in his brief, inspiring work, "The Path of the Just"), summarizes the message of Jewish tradition on man's ultimate goal. The greatest pleasure in God's universe, Luzzato writes, is "warming" oneself in the radiance of God's presence. God, who created humans with pure kindness, could have made the world in such a way that we would be immediately born to this radiance. But that would have been a hollow pleasure, a pleasure unearned (the "bread of shame"). Rather, continues Luzzato, humans were placed in this finite world with the task of refining ourselves so that, when we do depart for the next world, our souls will be pure and unblemished, receptive to Divine radiance. The tools needed to affect this refinement are the Torah's commandments. Each of us, standing alone before God, is responsible for our own perfection. No one else can do it for us.

TORAH STUDY

The seminal 19th-century German philosopher Rabbi S. R. Hirsch made this general observation about Torah: Man's purpose in this world is not to strive to see God, but to strive to see the world through God's eyes. God, in Hirsch's view, expects us to build homes, communities, and nations, where every act and function reflects His program of justice, kindness, and cheerful, uplifting spirituality. To achieve that harmonious goal, God gave a most complex and engaging Torah and the commandment to study it. This Torah, then, is the curriculum that will develop men and women whose eyes see things God's way. Both the content and the process of Torah study are singularly suited for personal and communal transformation (or, as some have phrased it, "up reach").

WHAT DO JEWS STUDY?

The Bible, in the Orthodox tradition, is nearly meaningless without its oral companion (which, according to the same tradition, was revealed side by side with the written text). Mishna and Talmud are the oral law's main components. The Mishna can be characterized as a highly focused outline of the oral law's principles, and the Talmud (also known as the Gemara) as the more accessible details and resolutions to countless apparent contradictions. Line by line, word by word, the rabbis of the Talmud analyze the Mishna and explain its intentions with the ultimate goal of arriving at the correct ruling (the *halacha*). The language (a flowing blend of Aramaic and Hebrew) is concise and technical, but somehow lively and very nearly musical.

It is not just legal discussion that fills the Talmud. The Talmud is a living portrait of a living nation. The diligent student is rewarded with a satisfying peek into the private lives of unusually great people. We see their brilliant minds, their pain, their struggles, their relationships and even their jokes. We also see the ordinary Jew of those centuries; his cares, problems, and often remarkable dedication to Torah. This glimpse at the very real people of that distant time guides readers to intelligently seek their own places within Jewish history.

There is purpose in every word of the Talmud. Every story contains an invaluable lesson on how to live as a Jew—how every aspect of Jewish life and not just the *halachic*, must be in service of God: How much money should a man spend on the "frivolous" needs of his wife? How should someone deal with bad-tempered kids? What kind of profit margin should he aim for in his business? It is all there—there is no area of the human condition left untouched by the words of the Talmud.

Torah study on all levels is very much alive and well in the 21st century. There are distinguished academies of Torah learning on five continents in which many thousands of students devote themselves to the goal of mastering Talmudic literature. Very few, despite eventually leaving the walls of their schools for other professional pursuits, ever consider themselves graduated.

In fact, intense Torah study remains a major life focus for countless thousands of Orthodox professionals.

The worldwide synchronized study of the Talmud, one difficult and demanding two-sided page every day (called "Daf Yomi"), completes the entire Babylonian Talmud every seven and a half years. The completion of the latest cycle (in March 2005) was marked by celebrations involving more than 70,000 people linked by satellite hookup to sports stadiums and concert halls around the world.

Yearning for greatness is the prerogative of every Jew, no matter her or his position, communal standing, or wealth. When the yearning (through Torah study) is accompanied by a long-term investment of disciplined effort, it is rewarded with experiences that often spill over into joy.

THIRTEEN PRINCIPLES

There are, wrote Rabbi Moshe ben Maimon (known as the Rambam, or, to the secular world, as Maimonides), certain things that every Jew has to believe. Just as God expects Jews to keep the commandments, so too are they required to believe thirteen basics. These, the beliefs of Jewish orthodoxy, stand sharply distinct from the teachings inspired by many of the ideological trends that Judaism has witnessed over the past 2 centuries. In fact, these beliefs go some distance to define orthodoxy.

The First Principle

A Jew must believe that the existence of the world or any part of it is impossible without the existence of the single, unique Creator, but that He, the Master of the world, requires nothing for His existence.

The Second Principle

A Jew must believe that there is only one God, and that He is unique and without any divisions. There is nothing in the universe with which this oneness can be compared. This aspect of God's existence is, according to the Rambam, clear from the verse "Shema Yisrael . . ." "Hear, O Israel, the Lord is our God, the Lord is one" (Deut. 6: 4).

The Third Principle

A Jew must believe that God has no body or any physical aspect, nor is His power the power of a physical body. This basic concept builds on the logic of the previous one: If God were to have a body, it would limit Him to the confines of that body, and therefore He would not be infinite and incomparable in the same way. The many places in where God is described as "stretching out His hand" or some similar physical action are, according to the Rambam, only figures of speech (anthropomorphisms) for sublime actions couched in words that humans can understand.

The Fourth Principle

A Jew must believe that God has always been in existence and always will be: He is eternal. Again, if this were not true, and God was limited (by time), then He would no longer be "infinite."

The Fifth Principle

A Jew must believe that there is no individual or power besides God whom it is fitting to worship or serve. To worship (or attribute independent power to) intermediaries (like angels, other human beings, or stars and planets) is forbidden. Such worship is in the category of idolatry. God created the universe and every single one of its parts; it is to Him that we owe all of our gratitude and subservience.

The Sixth Principle

A Jew must believe that God grants prophecy to people who have previously perfected their personal character and intellect and who follow all the commandments of the Torah. Prophecy does not come to simple, unlearned, and unprepared people.

The Seventh Principle

A Jew must believe that the prophecy of our teacher Moses (through whom the Torah was transmitted) was greater than all other prophecy in four ways: (1) it was not "heard" through any intermediary (i.e., an angel, a cloudy vision), but was direct; (2) it was always given while Moses was wide awake, in complete control of his faculties; (3) Moses was not overcome with shaking and dread as were other prophets, but was calm and alert; and (4) Moses had the ability to summon prophecy at will. Other prophets had to prepare and wait until God chose to appear. The Rambam also writes that Moses was different from any other human being before or since in that he was pure intellect. All of this is vital to belief in the validity of the Orthodox tradition, because it all comes through this one man. If there were any suspicion that he erred, then the entire Torah would come into question.

The Eighth Principle

A Jew must believe that the whole Torah is the true and completely accurate word of God as dictated by God to Moses. There is no difference between the verse "Shema Yisrael . . ." and any one of the (apparently trivial) lists of names and places that lie scattered throughout the Torah. They all come from God and there is great, limitless wisdom to be found in every word. This has implications concerning the oral Torah as well.

The Ninth Principle

A Jew must believe that since the entire Torah comes from God, one may not add to it or take away from it (i.e., add or subtract commandments, such as saying that there is no Sabbath commandment).

The Tenth Principle

A Jew must believe that God is aware of each of our actions.

The Eleventh Principle

A Jew must believe that there is reward and punishment for our actions.

The Twelfth Principle

A Jew must believe that the messiah, the descendant of King David and of King Solomon, will come and could come at any time, and that he will be for us a king greater than any other human king.

The Thirteenth Principle

A Jew must believe that in its proper time, there will be a revival of the dead—for those righteous individuals who deserve it.

—Rabbi Boruch Clinton

See also Judaism, Conservative; Judaism, Reconstructionist; Judaism, Reform; Torah

JUDAISM, RECONSTRUCTIONIST

Reconstructionist Judaism began as one man's passionate formulation of a solution to the ills of Jewish life as he saw them in the early decades of the 20th century. In the decades that followed, thanks to the work of devoted disciples, Rabbi Mordecai Kaplan's ideas became the basis for a new denomination within Judaism, taking its place alongside the Reform, Conservative, and Orthodox branches. The youngest and by far the smallest of the denominations, and the only one to be conceived and born in America, Reconstructionism continues to be an innovative and influential presence in Jewish life today through the work of its Rabbinical College, Rabbinical Assembly, and Reconstructionist Federation and through its congregations dotted across the United States and Canada. Current programs and activities include a summer camp and youth movement founded in 2002, a pandenominational program for teenage girls entitled "Rosh Hodesh: It's A Girl Thing!" and a diverse set of career options offered through the Rabbinical College.

MORDECAI M. KAPLAN AND THE CENTRAL IDEAS OF RECONSTRUCTIONISM

Mordecai M. Kaplan (1881–1983), the founding thinker of the Reconstructionist movement accomplished a lot during his 102 years. In addition to writing the many books and articles that embodied his ideas, Kaplan served "in the field" for most of his life as a congregational rabbi, teacher of teachers and rabbis, lecturer, and community organizer. Kaplan was also a man of many contradictions, whose strong opinions and commitment to honesty stirred up controversy. The Sabbath and festival prayer books he developed in the 1940s were so controversial that the Union of Orthodox Congregations of the United States and Canada pronounced a ban against them and went so far as to burn a copy of his prayer book. Such dramatic gestures did much to create misunderstanding as to what Kaplan was all about. Today however, thanks to ongoing scholarly work, Kaplan's place in the Jewish life of the 20th century is slowly being established. Many of the innovations that he championed or pioneered are commonly accepted today, including the bat mitzvah ceremony for girls and the idea of a Jewish Center (what some called *a shul with a school and a pool*) as a multi-dimensional community focus for study and leisure. The ideas he developed starting in the 1920s and expressed in his major work *Judaism as a Civilization* (Kaplan, 1934) remain fresh, challenging, and current in the 21st century.

Throughout his life, Kaplan fought against being bound by traditional practices that did not serve the well-being of Jews in the here and now. He fought as well for a way of life that included strong and joyous identification not just with America or only with the Jewish people but with both. It was his firm conviction that Jewish leaders should not compel people to follow traditional practices but that they should instead help to make Jewish life attractive, "interesting, significant, and beautiful" so people would *want* to be involved. This belief rested on an interconnected set of ideas that Kaplan worked his way through to ideas about God, about the sources of authority in society and about the importance of community and religion in making human life vibrant and meaningful.

Kaplan fiercely opposed what he called the *supernaturalistic* vision of God as a remote being sitting in judgment, rewarding, punishing, and changing the laws of nature at will, a conception that he saw as hopelessly out of touch with modern thinking. Furthermore, Kaplan believed that this view of God tended to render humans helpless and obedient or else arrogant in their presumption that their clan was party to a revealed truth denied other groups. Instead, Kaplan chose to seek the divine within human experience, in the power that impels and enables all of our best and highest achievements: ethical, cultural, religious, and artistic.

Closely related to Kaplan's idea of the divine was his view of religion and community. His study of the social sciences had shown him how crucial religions have always been among human communities, embodying their sacred values and articulating the rituals that foster depth, meaning, and a sense of belonging. Kaplan did not believe that religions originate in a realm detached from the human. Rather, he held that religions generally are a response to humanity's quest to meet its vital needs and that each particular religion is the product of a specific human group living in a particular time and place. In the matter closest to his heart, he concluded that the Jewish religion belonged to the Jewish people and was its creation. As a corollary, Kaplan insisted that it was arrogant and antidemocratic of the Jews to claim they were supernaturally chosen by God from among the nations of the world. He simply dropped the "chosen people" language from his prayer book, a choice that deeply upset most of the rest of the Jewish community in his time.

If Judaism was the central creation of the Jewish people, in Kaplan's view, it was not the only one. Rather, he saw Jewish life as a dynamic and evolving "religious civilization" involving land, language and literature, laws, folkways, arts, and social structures. Kaplan analyzed the span of Jewish history in terms of successive civilizations: the biblical, rabbinic, medieval, and modern (the curriculum of the Reconstructionist Rabbinical College today includes as the fifth civilization, the Contemporary). As time passed, the self-image of the Jewish people changed, as did their sense of their destiny. Each civilization, in its own time, had to be understood as an organic whole that was then transformed in the passage from one civilization to another. Such passages were precipitated when the conditions of life for Jews underwent drastic change, and demonstrated the incredible resilience of the Jewish people in overcoming potentially fatal challenges by creating renewed forms of thought and practice.

As engaged as he was by Jewish history, it was his own period, the modern, that was Kaplan's principal focus. For this period, he identified the double challenge of naturalism (vs. supernaturalism) and democratic nationalism as posing the newest and perhaps most serious challenge to the survival of the Jewish people, the challenge to which he responded with his life's work. Democratic nationalism in America offered Jews both the possibility of living as equal citizens, a right they had rarely if ever had as minorities before the modern period, and the opportunity—or temptation—of being part of the American national collectivity with its own quasireligious rites, its heroes, flag days, and family celebrations. From our vantage point in this postmodern, pluralist age, Kaplan's challenge to the Jews of his day remains relevant: the challenge to evolve the rich and complex identities that would allow them to live fully both as Americans and as Jews, an invitation to live vibrantly "in two civilizations."

Finally, Kaplan was a Zionist, convinced that the highest cultural and spiritual aspirations of the Jewish people would be lived out in Israel. Contrary to many of the Zionists of his day, however, but completely in accord with his approach to peoplehood and Jewish history, Kaplan did not devalue the lives and heritage of Jews living outside of Israel. Diaspora Jews also had rich, millennial histories and cultures to be proud of, to draw upon, and to renew in dialogue with the new Jewish society being constructed in Israel.

IRA EISENSTEIN AND THE BUILDING OF THE RECONSTRUCTIONIST MOVEMENT

Kaplan's hope and belief was that the power of his ideas would be enough to transform the thinking of Jewry the world over, but those in his circle saw that this was not about to happen. One man in particular, Ira Eisenstein, Kaplan's student, disciple, and later son-in-law, insisted that an institutional framework was essential if Reconstructionist ideas were to have an ongoing place in American Jewish life. Eisenstein's life and work constitute the bridge between Kaplan's ideas and the Reconstructionist movement as it is today.

It was Eisenstein's determination that eventually drove the construction of the Reconstructionist Rabbinical College, a move designed to disseminate Kaplan's ideas to succeeding generations of rabbis and to be the decisive gesture in establishing Reconstructionism as an official denomination rather than simply a school of thought or philosophy. As its first President, Eisenstein shepherded the College through the exciting and perilous years from when it opened its doors in 1968 through to 1981 and remained a commanding presence in the movement until his death on June 28, 2001, at the age of 94.

THE MOVEMENT TODAY

The Reconstructionist movement today is vital, engaged, and growing. It has continued to evolve and change, though it remains very much informed by Kaplan's central insights and values. The institutional structure of the movement consists of three bodies: The Reconstructionist Rabbinical Association (RRA), serving and supporting Reconstructionist rabbis and acting as their public voice; the Jewish Reconstructionist Federation (JRF), providing a range of services to the more than 100 affiliated Reconstructionist congregations; and the Reconstructionist Rabbinical College (RRC), which is home to a number of centers of excellence and innovation in addition to its training course for Reconstructionist rabbis. In addition, following the inauguration in 2002 of a summer camp and youth movement, Reconstructionism is paying increasing attention to young voices and young lives.

The work of the Jewish Reconstructionist Federation is supported by its more than 100 affiliated communities. Central to the work of the Federation are the values of belonging and community. These values are expressed in the characteristic informal, friendly, and welcoming style of Reconstructionist synagogues and havurot (smaller, informal groupings). Helping member groups to feel "comfortable, recognized, and supported" is also the Federation's goal in reaching out to its member congregations and in building community within the movement. It is characteristic of the Reconstructionist movement that the background work it does on issues of interest to its members, on matters such as homosexuality, the role of the non-Jew, disabilities, or the rabbi-congregational relationship are offered as *guidelines* rather than directives. The Reconstructionist style is not to offer "pronouncements, policies, procedures."

The Reconstructionist Rabbinical College trains rabbis through its regular 5-year civilization program of studies, with each year devoted to a different period: biblical, rabbinic, medieval, modern, and contemporary. Through the Lavy M. Becker Department of Practical Rabbinics, the curriculum also includes extensive preparation in practical rabbinics, covering skills that will be needed in the field such as counseling, group work, and administration. Ethics courses cover a wide range of topics of current concern including biomedical ethics, business and economic ethics, ethics of speech, and sexual ethics.

Echoing Kaplan's devotion to "Klal Yisrael," or the whole community of Jews, and in response to specific issues, a number of the activities at the Reconstructionist Rabbinical College are deliberately non- or pandenominational. This includes opportunities offered to students in the 5-year program to specialize in chaplaincy, including geriatric chaplaincy, or in campus work, education, or community organization. Alternatively, students may choose to pursue a joint masters degree in Jewish Education or Jewish Music through a cooperative arrangement with Gratz College.

The pandenominational work of the RRC includes a series of centers that offer opportunities for student internships as well as intellectual and programming resources for the broader Jewish world. The first of the centers to be founded is *Kolot,* The Center for Jewish Women's and Gender Studies. The intention of *Kolot* is to create new visions of gender roles in Jewish life by illuminating the traditions and texts of Judaism. Furthermore, *Kolot* aims to focus the best of contemporary scholarship on the real problems rabbis may encounter in the field, including domestic violence and breast cancer. Another highly successful, ongoing program developed by *Kolot* is called "Rosh Hodesh:

It's A Girl Thing!" This experiential program strengthens the Jewish identity and self-esteem of adolescent girls through monthly celebrations of the New Moon festival.

The Center for Jewish Ethics focuses research and teaching in the area of ethics across a range of issues of concern in society today. Work is being completed in 2004 toward a third center at the RRC, to focus on aging.

Launched in 2002 at a Reconstructionist Convention held in Montreal, Canada, the Noar Hadash (new youth) movement is being developed according to participatory Reconstructionist principles. Teenagers have been part of the planning process from the beginning and take pride in being the pioneers of a new movement and a new camp. The values of the movement include "spiritual peoplehood," the wisdom to be found in tradition, *tikkun olam* (repairing the world), the Hebrew language, involvement with Israel, and respect for the Earth. Honesty and questioning are encouraged, exploring how teenagers see God, both as Jews and as Americans or Canadians. At camp, the young people explore different historical periods on "Civilization Days" along with swimming, boating, canoeing, wall-climbing, artistic endeavors, and experiencing life in Jewish community full time.

Updated information on this and other programs and further background on Reconstructionism including audio resources, reading material, and bibliographies is available on the movement's excellent series of Web sites (see addresses in References and Further Reading).

—*Sharon Gubbay Helfer*

See also Judaism, Conservative; Judaism, Orthodox; Judaism, Reform;

FURTHER READING

Kaplan, M. M. (1934). *Judaism as a civilization.* New York: Reconstructionist Press.

Kaplan, M. M. (1994). *The meaning of God in modern Jewish Religion.* Detroit, MI: Wayne State University Press.

Scult, Mel. (1993). *Judaism faces the twentieth century: A biography of Mordecai M. Kaplan.* Detroit, MI: Wayne State University Press.

Staub, J. J., & Alpert, R. T. (1985). *Exploring Judaism: A Reconstructionist approach.* New York: The Reconstructionist Press.

Web site of the Reconstructionist Rabbinical College, including links to *Kolot:* The Center for Jewish Women's and Gender Studies and the Center for Jewish Ethics: www.rrc.edu/ [Retrieved May 17, 2004]

Web site for the Jewish Reconstructionist Federation, including links to audio resources, reading material and bibliographies: www.jrf.org/ [Retrieved May 17, 2004]

JUDAISM, REFORM

Reform Judaism originated in Germany in the 19th century. Jewish reformers were motivated by three great realities: a desire to take full advantage of newly granted rights, the Emancipation in Europe, and the Enlightenment. In response to these currents, and to the ideas of philosopher Moses Mendelsohn (1729–1786), Reform Judaism adopted a more liberal, flexible approach to religious activity than did traditional Judaism. Early reformers sought to do away with those rituals, customs, and prayers that were considered unenlightened and incompatible with modernity and rationality. Chief among the reforms instituted was to make the primary language of prayer in Reform services the vernacular or local native tongue, rather than Hebrew.

In Europe the movement toward reform stalled—in France over issues of doctrine and in Germany over issues of esthetic aspects of worship. It was imported readily into the United States, however, where it melded with earlier trends towards reform.

In the United States, Rabbi Isaac Mayer Wise became the leading reformer. In 1875, thanks to his efforts, the Hebrew Union College was established in Cincinnati for the training of Reform rabbis.

It was the Pittsburgh Platform, prepared in 1885 by a group of 15 rabbis that became the guiding principles of Reform Judaism in America. Some of the principles were:

> We accept as binding only the moral laws and maintain only such ceremonies as elevate and sanctify our lives, but reject all such as are not adapted to the views and habits of modern civilization.
>
> We hold that all mosaic and rabbinical laws as regulate diet, priestly purity, and dress originated in ages and under the influence of ideas altogether foreign to our present mental and spiritual state. They fail to impress the modern Jew with a spirit of priestly holiness; their observance in our days is apt rather to obstruct than to further spiritual elevation.

In the United States, the Reform movement is now the largest Jewish denomination. It is Reform Judaism which is most welcoming to intermarried couples and accepts patrilineal descent; meaning Reform Judaism recognizes as Jewish the child of a non-Jewish mother and a Jewish father, contrary to traditional Jewish law, which requires the mother to be Jewish. Reform Judaism, besides being the largest denomination, is also the youngest in ages of participants.

—Rev. David M. O'Leary

See also Judaism, Conservative; Judaism, Orthodox; Judaism, Reconstructionist

FURTHER READING

Frehof, S. (1944). *Reform Jewish practice and Its rabbinic background.* Cincinnati: Hebrew Union College Press.

Philipson, D. (1967). *The Reform movement in Judaism.* New York: Ktav.

JUNG, CARL AND POST-JUNGIANS

Carl Gustav Jung was a founder of analytical, or depth, psychology, which represents a huge achievement in our understanding of the physical world and the world of personal experience. The essential identity of human experiences reflected in worldwide myths and folklore led Jung to postulate the existence of the collective unconscious—or objective psyche shared at a deeper level by all members of humankind—that manifests itself through symbolic and latent images, called archetypes. Patients of Jungian therapy visit concepts of the spirit world through myth and archetype. Jung's psychology and particularly his ideas about archetypes contribute important concepts for the student of religious and spiritual development to consider.

In collaboration with Wolfgang Pauli, a physicist, Jung wrote an essay on an acausal connecting principle that he called *synchronicity*. Synchronicity explains the meaningful coincidence of events. According to Jung's theory, people are linked through the collective unconscious, and the psyche of a particular person interacts with the events of the world outside. A great mystery for Jung remained the realm of human consciousness and its profound relationship with the soul of the world, *anima mundi.* As in any relationship, subjective human experience is an important parameter. The human factor is a necessary condition of synchronicity, as without the former the events would not acquire meaning. An event has to make sense and be meaningful not because such-and-such cause brings about such-and-such effect, but because there is a correspondence between a person's individual mind and the collective unconscious. The true means of communication between consciousness and the unconscious mind is a language of symbols. Jung extended these ideas to practices in analytic therapy.

Jungian therapy, in its archetypal aspect, postulates that all products and expressions of the unconscious are symbolic, and thus carry certain messages. A symbolic approach creates a dialectical relationship between consciousness and the unconscious. Jung transcended the common meaning of consciousness as a merely intellectual and rational state of mind. To achieve emotional security and mental health means to continuously work on expanding the boundaries of one's consciousness. The life of such a person, for Jung, will have completeness, satisfaction, and emotional balance.

Jungian psychology posits typical situations in life as reflections of archetypal primordial patterns of instinctual behavior, which are practically engraved in the human mind or in our psychic constitution. Jung differentiated among various archetypes, such as an archetype of the Spirit, the Persona, the Trickster, the Shadow, or the Coniunctio. The latter is an archetype of the union. According to Jung, people should live in accordance with their own nature and should concentrate on self-knowledge, which is achieved through a process called individuation. Individuation consists of the integration of conscious and unconscious aspects of one's life for the purpose of achieving a greater personality: The culmination of individuation is represented by the actualized archetype of the self. Individuation, however, is a never-ending process toward wholeness, which remains an ideal goal.

Jung did not distinguish between psyche and matter—they represent two different aspects of the *unus mundus,* or one world. Respectively, he did not draw a line of great divide between the products of imagination and those of intellect in that both affect thinking, and all thinking aims at the creation of meanings. Archetypal ideas, according to contemporary post-Jungians, are considered to be both the structuring patterns of the psyche and the dynamical units of information. A key element in post-Jungian psychology is the balance between integration and fragmented complexes that constitute the individual's psyche. Individuation involves a conscious awareness about a possible conflict between many complementary opposites in an individual psyche rather than a simple elimination of a conflict.

James Hillman, a contemporary post-Jungian, sees individuation as a multiplicity because each one of us has not a single but many internal different personalities. Jung himself is viewed as a system theorist, and such an approach implies that the realms of both interpersonal and intrapsychic realities are connected by means of a seamless field of symbolic references. Symbolic experiences are numinous, that is, spiritual and mysterious; they are expressed in images and contain imagery.

According to Jung, symbols can hold together contents that intellect alone is incapable of, and such is a transcendent, symbolic function. Transcendence and symbols bring forward religion and creativity; for Jung, these elements are contained in a child's play. Jung afforded an important role to fantasy, which in its symbolic manifestation may trace out a line of one's anticipated psychological development. The unconscious therefore fulfills a prospective function. Because of the synthesizing nature of symbols, the meanings expressed in the multitude of unconscious images, such as in dreams, art, or active imagination, can be interpreted, elucidated, and integrated into consciousness. Analysts who practice Jungian therapy introduce their patients to this world of myth, symbol, and meaning and assist them in integrating these concepts into active consciousness. Jungian therapy continues to impact healthy psychological development, and welcomes patients into a more conscious relationship with the collective unconscious of the symbolic world.

—Inna Semetsky

FURTHER READING

Jung, C. G. (1959). *The archetypes and the collective unconscious.* Princaton, NJ: Bollingen Foundation.

Hopchke, R. H. (1992). *A guided tour of the collected works of C. G. Jung*. Boston: Shambhala.

Samuels, A. (1985). *Jung and the post-Jungians*. London and New York: Routledge.

KABBALAH.

SEE MYSTICISM, JEWISH.

KARMA, LAW OF

One of the perplexing questions facing religious systems relates to the uneven distribution of good and bad fortune in the world. Some are born healthy and some with poor health, some are born to wealthy parents and some to impoverished ones, some grow up in happy homes and some in dysfunctional families, and some succeed in life with little effort and some face only hurdles and accidents in life. All this seems incompatible with the vision of a God who is merciful, just, and compassionate.

Various traditions have come up with various explanations for this ancient and all too common feature of human societies. Hindu thinkers resolve the paradox in terms of what is known as the *law of karma.*

The word *karma* ordinarily means *action* in Sanskrit. In Vedic literature it generally meant ritualistic duties. In this context, however, it refers to any consequential action. Some of the acts that we do are inconsequential, while others have consequences. Scribbling on a piece of paper while waiting for a person may be inconsequential, but offering a helping hand to a person in need is a consequential action. A *karma* has some impact on others or on the world around us. The law of karma states that every karma has an experiential effect on the doer, that is, every individual will experience something as a result of his/her karma.

This experience (consequence on oneself) resulting from a karma may occur right away or at some future time. Furthermore, our current significant experiences are the results of our past karma. Indeed no one can escape the sweet fruits or the bitter berries arising from one's karma.

But what about little children who undergo pain? And how do we explain the fact that many people get away with all sorts of sins and crimes without ever apparently experiencing anything for their misdeeds? It is in this context that the notion of reincarnation becomes meaningful.

According to Hindu metaphysics, the âtman (soul) (pronounced aathman) migrates from body to body. The phenomenon of (physical) death is thus the disembodiment of the âtman that later encases itself in another body. One of the earliest expressions of this idea of the transmigration of the âtman is to be found in the Brhadaaranyaka Upanishad (IV.4.4).

Just as a leech that reaches the end of a blade of grass jumps over to another blade, so too the âtman, after leaving behind an unconscious body, enters another body. A famous passage in the Bhagavad Gita (11.22) propounds the doctrine of metempsychosis with this simile: Just as a man discards worn-out garments and puts on new ones, so too the souls abandon the old bodies and take on new ones.

Reincarnation or the cycle of birth and death is known as *samsâra* (pronounced samsaara). It is a basic tenet of Hinduism. Its fundamental thesis is the periodic reemergence of the âtman in physical encasements, that is, the continuity of the âtman on the temporal plane in association with different bodies. Consider the words in a book. We find that the same letter occurs over and over again in different contexts in different pages of the book. Likewise, the same soul appears in different bodies at different times. In other words, according to the notion of reincarnation, each of us has been on earth before in other bodies, and we will return again many more times in the future.

There are two positive effects of belief in reincarnation. First, the notion that the âtman is imperishable is a source of strength when death occurs. At that saddest of all moments in the course of a family's history, there is the assurance that all is not lost. The individual has literally departed, not died. Second, there is also the hope that the disembodied âtman will reappear in the family as a member of the generation yet to be born. It is not unusual for grandchildren to be named after their deceased grandparents for precisely this reason.

The idea of transmigration of the soul was accepted in many ancient cultures: in Mesopotamia, Egypt, Greece, and even medieval Europe. Plato referred to the Orphic tradition, according to which, for example, soul and body are united until death at which point they are liberated with a new birth. In the Hindu framework, the ultimate goal of spiritual evolution is to break away from samsâra, the repetitious birth–death cycle with its attendant woes and passing pleasures. This is to be achieved through right action and spiritual effort.

In the history of ideas, there have been two views as to our present condition and future prospects. One is fatalism, that is, everything was predetermined by an Almighty God, and we cannot change the course of events. The other is free will or that we have the choice to do good so as to ensure everlasting peace in heaven. The law of karma may be looked on as a blending of the two views in more earthly contexts. It accepts that our present condition was predetermined, not by God, but by our own previous actions. What this means is that we cannot point the finger at a merciless God for our sufferings. It also accepts free will in that it says we have the power to choose the good, and this will ensure our future happiness. Thus, the law does not imply a stoic acceptance of what has happened to us, for it leaves the future open. Recognizing the law of karma can inspire us to good and meritorious actions in the present life so as to ensure happier states in future incarnations. The law of karma is a wise blending of determinism and free will. It regards as unalterable what has already happened, yet as transformable what is yet to transpire. When something good occurs to you, you may give credit to yourself as having played a role in it at some time in the past. When something bad occurs, do not search for others or God to blame. Moreover, you have the potential to mold your future. And that future is not confined to this particular life.

Explanation in terms of the law of karma is as sound as any to reconcile assumed divine justice with observed social and hereditary nonuniformity. The law of karma and the associated belief in reincarnation are part of the religious worldview of people of the Hindu faith. To those outside the Hindu faith, it can be yet another interesting theory to explain the mystery of human existence.

—Varadaraja V. Raman

See also Hinduism

FURTHER READING

Radhakrishnan, S. (1971). *The Hindu view of life.* London: Unwin.

Rama Rao Pappu, S. S. (1987). *The dimensions of karma.* Delhi: Chanakya Publications.

KING, MARTIN LUTHER, JR.

Martin Luther King Jr. was an African American Baptist preacher and a prophet for racial equality. He was born just outside of Atlanta, Georgia, on January 15, 1929. His father was a minister and his mother was a schoolteacher. His parents believed that education would increase his knowledge and broaden his worldview, and that religion would shape his character, ethics, and faith in God. While religion and education helped Martin to see goodness in all people, he could not escape the impact that Atlanta's segregated bus system, harassment by white policemen, and inattentiveness by white store clerks would have on Southern black consciousness and identity. While Martin could have responded with anger to such situations, his religious upbringing taught him to believe in the power of brotherly love to redeem a world that might otherwise destroy itself. Thus, Martin's adult years were spent trying to end racial conflict and segregation. Martin Luther King's life is celebrated in the United States every year on his birthday, a day in which people remember and honor the positive changes he brought to individual lives, the country, and to the world. His life is a model of healthy religious and spiritual development; it is a life upon which many others model their own religious and spiritual development.

From the mid-1950s to the late 1960s, Martin Luther King Jr. was the most important leader of a nonviolent black freedom struggle that challenged racism and segregation in American society and paved the wave for equality for *all people.* During the 12 years that King was involved with the civil rights movement, blacks made more progress than in any other period in American history, overcoming the damaging psychological effects of generations of oppression, and acquiring a sense of unity and dignity.

King's method for effecting such change in America was known as nonviolent resistance. Nonviolent resistance called upon its participants to return love for evil and to display a nonviolent response in the face of indescribable violence. His philosophy of nonviolent resistance was a synthesis of the teachings of Jesus Christ and Mohandas Gandhi. Jesus' teachings from the Sermon on the Mount provided King with the motivating ideal of love, and Gandhi provided King with the method of mass nonviolent direct action.

The type of love advocated by Jesus was expressed by the Greek word *agape,* meaning an unconditional goodwill toward *all* people. Agape seeks "to preserve and create community."

This type of love was at the center of King's spirituality. Love of God had to be accompanied by love of humankind. Because the end cannot justify the means, hatred and violence were not acceptable. For King, nonviolent love was the discipline of the spiritual life.

From reading books on the life of Gandhi, King was impressed by the Indian leader's nonviolent tactics of boycotts, strikes, marches, and mass civil disobedience. Gandhi taught that nonviolence was an active form of resistance that confronted evil forcefully with love rather than violence and hatred. This philosophy helped to shape the character of the civil rights movement. For King, confronting injustice through nonviolent tactics was a way of putting feet to the prayers of the downtrodden. More specifically, he believed that a proper spirituality was one that combined the inner piety of prayer with the outer piety of social action.

As a result of such spirituality, civil rights marches and boycotts took on a spiritual dynamic. They were righteous demonstrations and acts of faith. Those who marched with Martin Luther King Jr. were hoping to build an integrated worldwide community where all God's children were welcome. Unfortunately, King's dream of an inclusive community was never achieved; he was assassinated in Memphis, Tennessee, on April 4, 1968. But his legacy includes a spirituality of unconditional love that was committed to confronting evil with nonviolence rather than hate. As a model of activism, King helped to shape the identity of the black church in the latter years of the 20th century. The faith of African Americans is not confined to the churches. Their faith has provided a prophetic voice that challenges injustice in the marketplace, political arena, and religious sector.

—Karen G. Massey

See also Gandhi, Mohandas K.

FURTHER READING

Colaiaco, J. (1988). *Martin Luther King, Jr.: Apostle of militant nonviolence.* New York: St. Martin's Press.

King, M. L., Jr. (1958). *Stride toward freedom: The Montgomery story.* New York: Harper.

KINGDOM OF GOD

The kingdom of God is a vital concept in the Scriptures of Israel (which Christians have called "the Old Testament"); it focuses on God as the king of the universe, the fundamental force behind all that is, and on God's role in shaping human experience. The promise of the kingdom is that people will finally come to realize divine justice and peace in all that they do. Jesus made the kingdom of God the center of his preaching as well as of his activity, and it remains the pivot of Christian theology. Within educational settings especially, views of the kingdom of God have shaped conceptions of ethical behavior, and have provided motivations to persist in the acts of teaching and learning.

Whether in present experience or in hope for the future, the kingdom of God was celebrated in ancient Israel in five different ways, all closely related to one another. They are all clearly represented in the books of Psalms.

First, the kingdom of God is behind the whole of created life, even as it is beyond the comprehension of any living thing. For that reason, the Psalms portray the kingdom as so near in time as to be present, and yet ultimate (the technical term is eschatological) from the point of view of full disclosure (Psalm 96:10):

> Say among the nations that the LORD reigns.
> The world is established, so as not to move:
> he shall judge the peoples with equity.

All the peoples are finally to know the truth that is now celebrated and sung in the Temple, but only in the future.

Second, the kingdom is transcendent in space as well as final in time. Although the usual setting of Israel's praise is in the Temple, every part of the creation will come to acknowledge what is known there (Psalm 145:10–13):

> All your creatures will give you thanks, LORD,
> and your faithful will bless you;
> they shall speak of the glory of your kingdom,
> and tell of your might,
> to make your mighty deeds known to the sons of men,
> and the glorious splendor of his kingdom.
> Your kingdom is an everlasting kingdom,
> and your rule in every generation.

All his creatures are to give thanks to the LORD, but it is his faithful in particular who are said to bless him. What is rehearsed in the Temple, the "strength of the fearful acts" of God, is to be acknowledged by humanity as a whole (Psalm 145:6).

Third, the kingdom is an insistent force of justice that will ultimately prevail. The kingdom is ever righteous, but attains to a consummation (see Psalm 10:15–16):

> Break the arm of the wicked, and evil;
> search out his wickedness until it cannot be found!
> The LORD is king forever and ever;
> the nations perish from his earth!

The punishment of the wicked is the dark side of the establishment of the poor. The vindication of the meek, the fatherless, and the oppressed (in verses 17, 18a) requires a reversal in the fortunes of those who do evil in order to be realized.

Fourth, human entry into the kingdom is contingent. Psalm 24 poses and answers a question which is central to the religion of Israel as reflected in the biblical tradition (Psalm 24:3–4):

> Who will ascend the mount of the LORD,
> and who will stand in his holy place?
> The innocent of hands and pure of heart,
> who has not lifted up his soul to vanity,
> and has not sworn deceitfully.

The point is that purity is affected by one's ethical behavior, as well as by the practices of purification (such as bathing and abstention from sexual intercourse) that were conventionally a part of ascending the mount of the Temple.

Fifth, Psalm 47 evokes how the recognition of God is to radiate from Zion, when it identifies "the people of the God of Abraham" as "the nobles of the peoples" (Psalm 47:9):

> The nobles of the peoples are gathered, the people of the God
> of Abraham;
> for the shields of the earth are God's.
> He is highly exalted!

Israel is the nucleus of the larger group of those who recognize the God of Jacob. From its center, the power of the kingdom is to radiate outward to include peoples beyond the usual range of Israel within its recognition.

Jesus articulated all five of these ways of seeing God's kingdom. He taught his disciples to pray to God, "Your kingdom will come" (Matthew 6; Luke 11), because he hoped for it to be fully present to all people. The dynamic quality of the kingdom's transcendence in Jesus' teaching is evident in a famous saying from "Q" (Matthew 12:28; Luke 11:20): "If I by the Spirit of God cast out demons, then the kingdom of God has arrived upon you." Entry into the kingdom is also the dominant image in Jesus' famous statement about wealth (Matthew 19:23–24; Mark 10:23–25; Luke 18:24): "Easier for a camel to wriggle through the eye of a needle than for a rich man to enter the kingdom of God." Jesus needed to cope with the issue of defilement as one member of Israel (with a certain set of practices) met with another member of Israel (with another set of practices). To deal with that question, a single aphorism of Jesus was precisely designed: "Nothing that is outside a person entering one can defile one, but the things coming from a person, these defile one" (Mark 7:15). Finally, in the course of Jesus' occupation of the Temple, Mark has Jesus say (Mark 11:17), "My house shall be called a house of prayer for all the nations, but you have made it a den of thieves."

In Jesus' teaching, the five coordinates of the kingdom become the dynamics of the kingdom, that is, the ways in which God is active with his people. Because God as kingdom is active, response to him is active, not merely cognitive. The kingdom of God is a matter of performing the hopeful dynamics of God's revelation to his people. For that reason, Jesus' teaching was not only a matter of making statements, however carefully crafted and remembered. He also engaged in characteristic activities, a conscious performance of the kingdom, which invited Israel to enter into the reality that he also portrayed in words.

Once experience and activity are taken to be the terms of reference of the kingdom, what one actually does is also an instrument of its revelation, an aspect of its radiance. Jesus' awareness of that caused him to act as programmatically as he spoke, to make of his total activity a parable of the kingdom. In a similar way, by emphasizing one or several of the coordinates of the kingdom (ultimacy, transcendence, judgment, purity, and radiance), Christian spiritualities have proven to evolve over time, and educational strategies have correspondingly varied.

—Bruce Chilton

See also Christianity

KOHLBERG, LAWRENCE

American developmental psychologist Lawrence Kohlberg (1927–1987) spent his life in pursuit of universal justice. He is best known for creating a stage model of moral development and a pedagogical model for moral education. He also developed a significant interest in religious faith, which he defined as the way that people find or construct ultimate meaning in their lives, and in how such faith might support moral reasoning and behavior. Kohlberg's joint pursuits originated in his life experiences as he responded to societal and personal tragedies.

STAGES OF KOHLBERG'S LIFE

Born in Bronxville, New York, on October 25, 1927, Laurence Kohlberg was the youngest of four children. His mother's background was Christian and his father was Jewish. His early years, despite his father's great wealth, were characterized by an unusual degree of family upheaval and dispersion. Perhaps it was this disorder that motivated a boyhood ritual, which he recalled as an adult to his friend, Jim Fowler, as follows: "I couldn't have been more than six. Alone, I took the Popsicle sticks I had been saving and placed them carefully in a stack meant to be a pyre. With a prayer to whatever indeterminate God there be, I took matches and lit the pyre in hopes of atonement and forgiveness." As a young boy, Kohlberg understood religion as a way of bartering with God, and thus, according to his own subsequent developmental research, was much like other similarly aged children.

As he entered adolescence, Kohlberg's peers recognized his intellectual and moral precociousness. When he graduated from junior high school, the class prophecy section of the yearbook forecasted that he would become known as "the great scientist and Nobel Prize winner." For high school, he attended an elite preparatory school in Massachusetts. His classmates there remembered him as a genuine intellectual who rebelled against arbitrary social conventions, such as rules against visiting girls on nearby campuses, and often found himself on probation. As a high school student during World War II, he knew of the plight of European Jewry and came to identify closely with his Jewish heritage.

MORATORIUM STAGE AND ZIONIST INFLUENCES

After finishing high school in 1945, Kohlberg became an ardent Zionist and joined the U.S. Merchant Marines. He traveled to Europe, where he witnessed the end of the war and met concentration camp survivors. After his tour of duty, he returned to Europe as a crew member on a ship, the *S. S. Redemption,* which was outfitted to smuggle European Jewish refugees through the British blockade and land them in Palestine, then a British-controlled territory. He willingly broke British laws, which he saw as unjust, to assist desperate refugees. While en route to Palestine in 1947, he and his fellow crew members, along with refugees, were captured by the British and taken to a refugee camp on Cyprus. Three months later, he escaped and made his way to Palestine where he lived on a kibbutz until he was able to return to the United States. When he arrived home, his family learned that he had changed his first name from Laurence to Lawrence and his nickname from Laurie to Larry.

THE CHICAGO STAGE

Larry Kohlberg took the questions raised by his wartime experiences to the University of Chicago where he enrolled in the fall of 1948. He studied the works of numerous psychologically inclined philosophers and philosophically inclined psychologists, including Socrates, Plato, John Locke, Immanuel Kant, Thomas Jefferson, Jean Piaget, and John Dewey. At that time it was possible to receive course credit by passing the final examination, and Kohlberg took exams for 4 years of courses and completed his B.A. degree in 1 year.

Torn between pursuing graduate work in law or clinical psychology, Kohlberg decided to do neither. He chose academic psychology and embarked on his quest for the cognitive-developmental foundations of universal moral principles. In 1958, at the age of 31, Kohlberg completed an extraordinary doctoral dissertation. It was based on interviews he conducted with 84 adolescent boys in Chicago about several moral dilemmas. The most famous dilemma concerns a man named Heinz, whose wife was dying. The boys were asked, "Should Heinz steal a life-saving drug or let his wife die for lack of the drug? Why or why not?" As Kohlberg examined the boys' reasons, he discovered distinct age-related differences in the complexity of the moral reasoning they used to arrive at and justify their answers. His dissertation laid out six stages of moral development, in contrast to Piaget's two. Kohlberg's theory eventually initiated a new field of study—the psychology of moral development and education.

Kohlberg went to Yale University as an assistant professor in 1958, and then returned to join the University of Chicago's faculty in 1962. At Chicago he continued to take a bold stand for the validity of universal moral principles, at a time when moral relativism seemed more defensible, and for psychology as an inherently moral science, at a time when the world had been shaken by the moral horrors of the Holocaust. Noting that the Holocaust incongruously occurred in a country noted for its citizens' high level of education, flourishing arts, and complex culture, Kohlberg wondered what factors promote the development of people's moral maturity. After 6 years at Chicago, he moved to Harvard.

The Harvard Stage

Kohlberg joined the faculty of Harvard University as a full professor within the Graduate School of Education in 1968. In 1974, he founded the Center for Moral Education and Development, which became a hub of research, training, and educational activities. As the Center's influence widened, a constant stream of scholars came from across the nation and around the world, seeking Kohlberg's advice and enjoying his kindness. His ideas, enthusiasm, and energy inspired many of these new colleagues, whom he challenged to develop the field he had founded in their unique way.

The 1980s were unusually generative years, as Kohlberg brought major projects to completion and reaped the rewards of his labor. In 1981, the first volume of his collected essays on moral development, *The Philosophy of Moral Development,* was published. In 1983, the empirical findings from his 20-year longitudinal study were published as a *Society for Research on Child Development Monograph.* The next year the second volume of his collected essays, *The Psychology of Moral Development,* was published. Also in 1984, with Ann Colby and several other colleagues, he published the long-awaited two-volume moral stage–scoring manual, *The Measurement of Moral Judgment.* With Clark Power and Ann Higgins, he completed the work for their volume on moral education, which was published in 1989 as *Lawrence Kohlberg's Approach to Moral Education.*

While his publishing successes soared, however, his physical health was declining. During a trip to Central America in late 1973, Kohlberg had contracted a particularly severe and painful form of giardiasis (a disease of the digestive system caused by the parasite, *Giardia lamblia*). The parasitic infection slowly weakened him physically over the next 13 years. His physical energy and emotional serenity were nourished, however, by the mystical perspective he derived from the experiences he had on Cape Cod during his summers. From his concurrent experiences of his own limits and his oneness with something more, Kohlberg became increasingly open to religious-like perspectives. Nearly all of his religious writings, which will be reviewed in the next section, date from this period (1974–1986). Suffering much physical pain and mental depression, Lawrence Kohlberg surrendered his life to the waters of the Atlantic on January 17, 1987.

KOHLBERG'S CONTRIBUTIONS TO THE PSYCHOLOGY OF RELIGION

Lawrence Kohlberg saw children and adolescents as moral philosophers, capable of forming their own moral judgments. As a developmental psychologist strongly influenced by Jean Piaget, Kohlberg delineated six stages of moral development from childhood through adulthood. He also recognized children and adolescents as being natural theologians, even if only tacitly. He viewed an individual's religion as his or her way of expressing and responding to the question of ultimate meaning in moral judgment and action. He did not advocate any particular faith tradition but, nevertheless, his search for universal morality and his articulation of moral stages depended on his belief in the existence of universal principles of moral justice—what some theologians call "natural law." Kohlberg believed that an ethic of justice was more mature within the natural order of things. He believed that the central function of religion was to affirm morality as being related to a transcendent being or infinite sense of the whole. In this way, moral and religious reflections were separable but related. These views allowed him to explore religion in relation to *moral development, moral education,* and *moral behavior.*

RELIGION AND MORAL DEVELOPMENT

Kohlberg's theory of moral development followed the characteristics of a Piagetian stage model. He claimed that stages of social moral reasoning are based on evolving mental structures or cognitive schemata within the developing brain. Each stage represents a qualitatively different way people resolve moral dilemmas. The six stages formed an invariant sequence—people do not skip stages or reverse their order. Similarly, Kohlberg theorized that the six stages were hierarchically integrated—higher stages are better in the sense that a person using a higher stage of reasoning can understand the moral reasoning used by lower stages, but the converse would not be true. Kohlberg also hypothesized that these six stages were universal—that they apply to all human beings at all times, even though many individuals do not progress through all of the stages.

Kohlberg and colleague Clark Power also theorized that social reasoning and religious moral reasoning have parallel structures. After a new stage or cognitive structure develops in the way a person thinks about social moral dilemmas, the person begins to generalize the changes to other areas, including religion. Thus, religious moral reasoning follows and parallels the six social moral reasoning stages.

Stages 1 and 2 are called the *preconventional stages* because people pass through them before entering the socially customary or conventional stages of moral reasoning. In Stage 1, which Kohlberg like Piaget called *heteronymous morality,* a child unquestioningly obeys authority figures. Children at Stage 1 avoid breaking rules set by parents, for instance, because they are afraid of punishment or external physical consequences. At this stage, God is understood in vague anthropomorphic terms, as being larger and more powerful than even adults. Young children are not yet able to ascribe intentionality to either adults or to God.

At Stage 2, termed *individualism, instrumental purpose, and exchange,* school-aged children follow rules only when it is in their immediate interest to do so. They assume others will also only follow rules when it is in their self-interest. What is moral is a reciprocal type of concrete exchange ("You scratch my back, I'll scratch yours"). Similarly, they appreciate that God, the rule giver, is also bound by quid pro quo reciprocity. If you give to God, through rituals or keeping your promises to him, you will receive what you pray for.

Stages 3 and 4 are known as the *conventional stages* because they are the stages in which most people spend most of their lives. People usually enter Stage 3, *mutual interpersonal expectations and conformity,* during preadolescence and adolescence. People at Stage 3 equate what is morally right with what is perceived to be "good" and "nice" by others; they conform to the rules and expectations of others so that others will like or approve of them. Similarly, God is now conceived of as a personal deity, and his moral expectations are understood as those of a caring friend or good parent. Not following God's moral guidelines can create a sense of personal shame.

Stage 4 is called *social system and conscience maintenance* because at Stage 4, people have a strong desire to maintain and be loyal to a social system within society such as a church, legal system, corporation, or educational institution. They determine what is morally right based on their allegiance to a particular social system and its policies. Stage 4 moral reasoning, for example, equates morality with what a legal system says is right or wrong, or with the moral rules of a religious institution such as a church, mosque, or synagogue. God is the supreme lawgiver and worship is a way of showing respect for God's preordained moral order.

Stages 5 and 6 are called *postconventional* because moral reasoning at these stages goes beyond the moral reasoning used by most people. Stage 5 is characterized by a focus on the *prior rights, human rights, and the social contract.* Moral reasoning at Stage 5 is motivated by the kind of thinking John Locke used to describe his contract theory of government. In Locke's theory and at Stage 5, people are viewed as having certain basic rights, such as rights to life and to property ownership, which are *prior* to society. Society was created to protect individuals' rights and to promote communal welfare. At Stage 5, God is viewed as promoting autonomous moral decisions and as a partner in human efforts to create a just society.

The hallmark of Stage 6 moral reasoning is the use of *universal ethical principles* to resolve moral dilemmas. Universal ethical principles differ from a rights perspective by viewing people as ends in themselves, as illustrated by Immanuel Kant's moral imperative, "Act in such a way that you treat humanity as an end and never only as a means." Justice at Stage 6 is understood as a universal ethical principle that views all human beings as free and autonomous. Persons at Stage 6 place themselves in the position of others who are being oppressed and aim to ensure their fair and principled treatment. To this end, Kohlberg suggested that Stage 6 religious moral reasoning generally adopts a cosmic, universal perspective. This perspective may include either a theistic or pantheistic conception of the ultimate order. Kohlberg considered Martin Luther King Jr. and Mahatma Gandhi as exemplars of the theistic version, and Spinoza and Marcus Aurelius to be examples of the pantheistic version.

RELIGION AND MORAL EDUCATION

Kohlberg saw religion and morality as separable and, thus, felt comfortable promoting moral education in public schools without engaging in religious education, which many saw as threatening the separation of church and state. Nevertheless, his methods of moral education had religious-like roots.

Kohlberg's approach to moral education included (1) moral dilemma discussions, (2) just community schools, and (3) public moral leadership. He credited his former student, Moshe Blatt, with conducting the first empirical study of a genuinely developmental moral education intervention. In Blatt's initial pilot study, he attempted to promote moral stage development among sixth-grade students in a Jewish Sunday School through weekly discussion of hypothetical moral dilemmas. He found that most of his students advanced in stage of moral development during the 3-month intervention. Encouraged by these findings and subsequent research, Kohlberg implemented this *dilemma discussion* model of moral education by integrating dilemma discussions into the curriculum of school classes in the humanities and social studies.

Kohlberg then broadened this view of moral education by drawing on the moral education practices he had observed at an Israeli kibbutz high school. This *just community* approach to moral education involved establishing classroom and school governance interventions based on direct participatory democracy. The teacher in a just community school was not merely a facilitator, but also a Socratic dialogue partner whose advocacy functioned within the constraints of students' democratic participation. Through these methods, Kohlberg's approach stressed group discussions and the democratic sharing of responsibility for group decisions regarding issues of fairness.

On a larger societal scale, Kohlberg pointed out that some religious leaders, like Martin Luther King Jr., functioned as public moral educators in that they created disequilibrium in their audiences to move them forward to more mature moral reasoning. Although King's *Letter from a Birmingham Jail* showed King as reasoning at *postconventional* Stage 6, Kohlberg observed, the letter also reached out to those at *conventional* stages of moral reasoning and offered them more adequate moral explanations, which could attract his readers to a higher stage of moral reasoning.

RELIGION AND MORAL BEHAVIOR

Although Kohlberg did not believe moral education should advocate a particular religious tradition, he thought that religion often played a key role in turning moral reasoning into moral action. Specifically, Kohlberg thought that religion dealt with questions that arise at the boundary of moral reasoning. He thought that the function of moral reflection was to resolve competing claims among individuals or peoples based on a social norm (such as keeping a promise) or ethical principle (justice). The function of religious reasoning was to affirm life and morality as related to a transcendent ground or sense of the whole. It addressed questions such as, "Why be moral in a world that is largely unjust?" A Judeo-Christian faith, for example, would affirm morality as being related to God and God's teachings to humanity.

How does moral stage development relate to moral action? How might religious faith impact moral action? To answer these questions, Kohlberg developed a model of the relationship of moral judgment to moral action. In this model, a person's moral stage influences and directs a person's moral judgment about what should be done in a given situation (deontic choice). This judgment is then filtered through a person's judgment about who is responsible for taking action in a given situation (aretaic judgment). If a person feels like she ought to act (deontic choice) and thinks she is responsible to act (aretaic judgment), then the person is much more likely to actually take moral action.

For Kohlberg, moral stage development directly affects a person's deontic choice, but other factors such as religion affect a person's aretaic judgment. For example, a person with strong religious commitments, which provide strong models of moral action, may not only decide that she ought to help a stranger in difficulty (a deontic choice driven by moral stage development), but she also will be more likely to make the decision to actually help the other person (an aretaic judgment driven by religion).

While Kohlberg viewed moral and religious education as separable, he understood that one's response to the ultimate questions of religion could bear heavily on one's moral development. Kohlberg discussed personal religious faith, including mystical spirituality, in connection with a hypothesized Stage 7. Kohlberg esteemed Spinoza as an exemplar of Stage 7 because Spinoza's *Ethics* displayed the ability to integrate his Stage 6 universal moral principles with a spiritual or metaphysical perspective on life's ultimate meaning. Spinoza's discovery of the union of the mind with the whole of Nature gave rise to his rational mysticism, an attitude toward nature similar to that of a theistic mystic toward God. Although Stage 7 was never formally incorporated into Kohlberg's theory, he discussed the possibility of a Stage 7 as a way of acknowledging the way in which people at higher stages of moral development often ground their moral reasoning in a cosmic or religious perspective.

CONCLUSIONS

Kohlberg's work in the psychology of morality was groundbreaking. He made morality a central concern in psychology, and he remains the person most often identified as the father of the field of the psychology of moral development and education. Although his theory and method of measuring moral development have not escaped criticism, particularly in terms of possible gender and racial-cultural bias, they continue to be relied upon for further research and work in moral development and education. In terms of religious and spiritual development, Kohlberg pioneered the position that moral maturity, beyond a person's stage of moral reasoning, rests upon the answers to ultimate questions of life, questions that lie in the domain of faith. Such moral maturity requires both the capacity for principled reasoning about conflicts in normative values, such as life versus law, as well as the faith conviction that one should and must live according to these larger principles. Moral reasoning alone is not sufficient for genuine moral maturity. Although Lawrence Kohlberg died at age 59, his voice remains vital to the ongoing study and pursuit of moral development.

—John Snarey and Charles Hooker

FURTHER READING

Brabeck, M. (2000). Lawrence Kohlberg. In A. Kazdin (Ed.), *Encyclopedia of psychology* (Vol. 4, pp. 453–454). Washington, DC: American Psychological Association.

Fowler, J., Snarey, J., & DeNicola, K. (1988). *Remembrances of Lawrence Kohlberg.* Atlanta, GA: Emory University.

Kohlberg, L. (1981). *Essays on moral development: Vol. I. The philosophy of moral development.* San Francisco: Harper & Row.

Kohlberg, L. (1984). *Essays on moral development: Vol. II. The psychology of moral development.* San Francisco: Harper & Row.

Kohlberg, L., & Ryncarz, R. (1990). Beyond justice reasoning. In C. Alexander, & E. Langer (Eds.), *Higher stages of human development* (pp. 191–207). New York: Oxford University Press.

Power, C., Higgins, A., & Kohlberg, L. (1989). *Lawrence Kohlberg's approach to moral education.* New York: Columbia University Press.

Siddle-Walker, V., & Snarey, J. (2004). *Race-ing moral formation: African American perspectives on care and justice.* New York: Teachers College Press.

KRISHNA

All the gods in the Hindu pantheon are representations of the divine, which give meaning, charm, and color to modes of worship. All representations are finite, and hence never perfect. A great many fascinating tales of miracles are told about baby Krishna. In the Hindu world, Krishna has become a hero to be remembered and revered. Lord Krishna is a divine personage in the Hindu world who is worshipped in temples. His life and deeds were first narrated in classical Sanskrit literature. He is regarded as one of the earthly manifestations or descents (*avatâras*) of the divine on earth. The name Krishna literally means "black."

According to tradition, King Ugrasena had a son Kamsa and daughter Devaki. Kamsa became a tyrant who imprisoned his own father. Devaki married Vâsudeva. A sage had predicted that Kamsa would be killed by Devaki's son. So the tyrant imprisoned Devaki and her husband, and killed every newborn child of his sister. Their seventh child was miraculously transferred elsewhere, and when the eighth child, Krishna, was born at midnight, he was stealthily taken away across a river and left with the wife of a cowherd named Nanda and his wife Yashoda. Nanda and Yashoda fled to a place called Gokula with the child and it was there on the meadows of the herd forest, Vrindâvana, that the boy was reared in the company of cowherds and milkmaids or *gopis.*

When Krishna played his magic flute, the gopis would throng around him and dance with joy. Each one of them would want to hold his hand. To satisfy them all, Krishna would transform himself into a thousand Krishnas. Sometimes he would steal their garments when they were still wading in water, and hide them high in a tree from where he would watch them. The symbolism is that the *gopis* are the individual soul, the cowherds are their physical bodies, and Krishna is the Supreme Soul who is beckoning them.

Many of Krishna's exploits are found in the Mahabharata, leading up to the last eventful war at Kurukshetra. Krishna is what the library is to the scholar, a vast storehouse of knowledge. At every juncture, kings and wise men ask Krishna for advice and counsel. He is also what nature is to the poet: an inspiration for song and dance. In the celebration of Krishna there is often happy music and colorful dance. Countless joyous songs and beautiful poetry have been composed in the name of Krishna. At the same time, Krishna is also what colorful toys are for children, an instrument for mirth and merriment. In the tales of Krishna, there is much merriment with the *gopis.* He is equally what the beloved is to the lover: the instigator of intense joy.

Krishna as a charming and youthful personage with a flute in his hand, and often portrayed near a cow, is one of the most universally recognized symbols in Hindu culture.

—Varadaraja V. Raman

See also Hinduism

L

L'ENGLE, MADELEINE

Madeleine L'Engle (b. 1918) is a prolific writer whose fictional works address spiritual questions in a manner that appeals to children of many ages. She is best known for her "Time Trilogy," especially *A Wrinkle in Time* (which won the esteemed Newbery Award in 1963) and for her series about the Austin family (*Meet the Austins, A Ring of Endless Light,* etc.). L'Engle has also written novels for adults, several autobiographical pieces, books on scripture, and collections of prayers—some sixty books in all. Most of her books have remained in print, and L'Engle has inspired love and devotion among millions of readers over the past four decades. Both adults and children regard her as a multitalented and prolific writer. She's also much loved as a teacher, having given many workshops and lecture tours. Perhaps her most significant contribution to children and adolescent spirituality is the way she explores the common ground between Christian belief and science.

L'Engle addresses spirituality through a blend of psychological realism and science fiction. Often her protagonists are awkward young people who are wrestling with important questions of belief and ethics, such as: What is my purpose in life? What does it mean to love well? Who is God? What is God? What happens after death? Why is there suffering in the world? How can I know God?

In their journeys to understanding, her protagonists undergo paranormal experiences. For example, Meg Murry (in *A Wrinkle in Time,* first book in the "Time Trilogy") is downcast because her father has disappeared for more than a year, presumably kidnapped. Then three eccentric women (possibly angels or witches in disguise) teach Meg how to time travel to another galaxy. This leads to many adventures and eventually to Meg's heroic rescue of her father and her little brother, Charles Wallace Murry.

Another example is Vicky Austin, the 16-year-old in *A Ring of Endless Light* who is wrestling with her own emerging sexuality and with the harsh reality of the deaths of several people she knows. When she discovers a talent for communicating with the dolphins that swim near her summer home (telepathy), they lead her to a deeper faith in God. Perhaps because she herself was an awkward, lonely child, L'Engle often portrays misfits and outsiders who grow into heroes.

L'Engle's work expresses her devotion to the Christian tradition and her deep love of, and delight in, the Bible. Her beliefs are orthodox, but often with an innovative, contemporary spin that affirms the common ground between science and Christianity. Christian themes include a loving, guiding God; the centrality of love and forgiveness; God's presence in the ordinary; the importance of moral choices; Christians as "light bearers"; the dignity of all people; and the importance of justice. Her work appeals to readers of many traditions, including Roman Catholics, Evangelicals, and many who are not Christian. Indeed, most of her fans probably do not think of her as a religious writer.

L'Engle also conveys a deep love of the arts and science. She believes that great artists, musicians, and scientists are as important to deepening spirituality as are great evangelists. Many of her characters are scientists, and scientific facts play important roles in her plots. For example, in writing *A Wrinkle in Time,* she researched quantum physics to accurately portray Meg Murry traveling through a tesseract or "time wrinkle" to another galaxy. Her theological ideas have been compared to those of Teilhard de Chardin. She sees God as the great Mystery and Creator, a source of endless fascination.

L'Engle's fiction also reflects her concerns for social justice. She is especially concerned about the environment, women's equality, and peace. She often shows a battle between good and evil on a cosmic scale, with children playing decisive moral roles. Personal spirituality naturally flows into political action.

L'Engle's concern about justice for women makes her books of special interest to girls and young women. Among science fiction novels, *A Wrinkle in Time* (1962) was ahead of its time in featuring a strong girl protagonist, Meg Murry. Meg's mother is well educated—with two doctorates and a Nobel Prize in science. In more recent years, L'Engle has written about her deepening concern for inclusive language for equal opportunities for women in church and society.

Another valuable aspect of L'Engle's novels is the fact that they feature intact loving families that young readers find appealing, families that include pets with distinct personalities. The Austin, Murry, and O'Keefe families each appear in several different works, so that readers can see characters grow into adulthood over decades. These families are exemplary yet realistic. Parents love their children and are also well-developed individuals in their own right. The children have chores, are loyal to siblings, enjoy family meals, and are well disciplined, even as they also disobey and bicker at times. L'Engle also portrays loving intergenerational relationships. For example, in the Austin series, Vicky Austin regards her grandfather as a mentor and confidant. He shares her love of language and her Christian faith, and treats her with deep respect, even though she is sixty years younger.

L'Engle has been described as a mystic, a "universe disturber," and a "boundary breaker." L'Engle believes that the imagination, story, myth, and even "magic" are essential avenues to understanding God. Her work has been censored by religious conservatives who object to her portrayal of imagination as a positive force, witches, and magic.

Born in 1918, Madeleine L'Engle has lived in New York or Connecticut most of her life. She was married for more than forty years to actor Hugh Franklin, who died in 1986. In addition to being a writer, she has spent many years at home raising her three children. In her eighties, she continues to write and speak to enthusiastic audiences of all ages. (She has also been known under the names Madeleine Franklin and Madeleine L'Engle Camp.)

Her most important works include "The Time Trilogy": *A Wrinkle in Time* (1962); *A Wind in the Door* (1973); and *A Swiftly Tilting Planet* (1978).

A more complete listing of her works can be found at these Web sites:

"The Tesseract: A Madeleine L'Engle Bibliography in Five Dimensions," http://members.aol.com/kfbofpgl/LEngl.html.

"Madeleine L'Engle Bibliography" (her own Web site), www.madeleine lengle.com/books/biblio_car.htm.

—Trudelle Thomas

FURTHER READING

Chase, C. (1998). *Suncatcher: A study of Madeleine L'Engle and her writing.* Philadelphia: Innisfree Press.

L'Engle, M. (1980). *Walking on water: Reflections on faith and art.* Wheaton, IL: Harold Shaw.

Smedman, M. S. (1986). Out of the depth to joy: Spirit/soul in juvenile novels. In F. Butler and R. Rotert (Eds.), *Triumphs of the spirit in children's literature* (pp. 191–197). Hamden, CT: Library Professional Publications, 1986.

LANGUAGE OF SPIRITUALITY

Just as mathematics education may be understood as progressive initiation into the distinctive language of mathematics ("square root," "quadratic equation," and so on) and moral education as initiation into the distinctive language of ethics ("ought," "virtue," "deontology"), so spirituality has its own distinctive language into which children need to be initiated if they are to grow spiritually. It is literacy—in other words proficiency in the distinctive language of the emotions, of computers, of spirituality or whatever—that empowers individuals to engage in thought, learning, and communication in these areas of life. But so little research has been done into the distinctive language of spirituality that it is not immediately clear what this phrase refers to, let alone how to initiate individuals into specifically spiritual discourses.

What distinguishes the language of spirituality from other languages is not a specialist vocabulary—indeed, the words used in spiritual discourse are generally commonplace ones, like "journey," "health," "hunger," "quest" or "struggle"—but a powerful reliance on metaphor. Metaphor provides the normal way of exploring and talking about areas of life that are not open to scientific investigation through the senses. The imagination uses readily understood social or physical experiences to explore more complex or abstract ideas. People's understanding of spiritual concepts and spiritual experiences is made possible through metaphor, and it is in this sense that metaphors actually structure the way that the spiritual domain is understood.

The use of embodied experience as a metaphor for spiritual experience has a long history. As early as Plato, the physical world was described as a shadow of the spiritual. In the Jewish scriptures, God is a caring shepherd leading his sheep out of danger, and the Song of Solomon celebrates God's love for his people through an extended metaphor of erotic love. In the New Testament, the human body is "the temple of the Holy Spirit," and the Church is the bride of Christ. Metaphors drawn from embodied experience are often the only way to explain spiritual realities. Our understanding is led upward from the familiar, and the human to the divine and the spiritual. Understanding and loving God (whom we cannot see) thus begins by understanding and loving our fellow human beings (whom we can see, and who show in tangible form something of God's nature). The conceptual systems through which we understand spirituality are constructed out of metaphors, and these conceptual systems in turn structure what we perceive, what we experience and the way we define spiritual reality.

One core metaphor in the spiritual domain that finds expression in a whole array of variations is "the spiritual life is a journey." The journey may involve persevering in the face of difficulties and temptations, overcoming obstacles, following the right signposts, discarding unnecessary baggage, passing through a particular landscape, focusing on the destination, helping others along the way, and refusing to turn back. Scott Peck uses a quotation from Robert Frost as the title of his bestseller on the spiritual life, *The Road Less Travelled* (1978), while Bunyan's *Pilgrim's Progress* (1678) builds the same core metaphor into a thoroughgoing allegory of the spiritual life. The same analogy is also found in the Gospels, where Jesus warns his followers to take the narrow path that leads to life, not the broad way that leads to destruction, and in Islam, where the normal term for Islamic law, *shari'ah,* literally means the main road or highway. Clearly the conceptualization of life as a journey is not restricted to the spiritual domain, but where it is used in this way it brings significant enrichment to the concept.

If spiritual language is primarily metaphorical, or is capable of carrying significance both literally and metaphorically at the same time, then spiritual meaning and spiritual truth must be different from other forms of meaning and truth. But this distancing of the spiritual domain from the level of ordinary literal meaning does not require us to conclude (as do Nietzsche and Derrida, for example) that the prevalence of metaphor undermines any search for timeless truth at all in relation to spirituality. Spirituality may well be an essentially contested concept, but not more so than aesthetics, and the language of spirituality may have something in common with the language of art and music. Metaphors do not only provide new insights into the spiritual life (and new insights that are thought-provoking because open to different interpretations and ways of thinking), but are the very bricks out of which the domain of the spiritual is constructed.

—J. Mark Halstead

LEWIS, C. S.

Probably most famous for his series of children's fantasy books, *The Chronicles of Narnia,* Clive Staples Lewis (1898–1963) was also well known as a writer of science fiction, Christian theology, literary criticism, and medieval scholarship. Because of the combination of Lewis's own childhood, his conversion to Christianity, his authorship of children's literature, and his work as a Christian *apologist* (someone who explains a religion to its critics), Lewis is an especially interesting figure for thinking about the role of the literary imagination in the spiritual and religious lives of children.

BRIEF BIOGRAPHY

Some of the details of Lewis's early life echo throughout the seven-volume work of *The Chronicles of Narnia.* For the first 9 years of his life, Lewis had a carefree and imagination-filled childhood. Lewis and his older brother invented a fictional land called Boxen and wrote many illustrated stories about it. He also spent a significant part of his childhood in a large house with many secret passages and plenty of attic space, a biographical detail that recalls both the games of Polly and Digory at the start of *The Magician's Nephew,* as well as the very concept of "traveling between worlds" around which *The Chronicles* are based.

Lewis was also a voracious reader in his youth (two of his favorites were *Treasure Island* and *The Secret Garden*), and he and his brother spent many rainy days telling adventure stories inside an old wardrobe. In *The Chronicles,* an old wardrobe becomes the magical means for travel to the land of Narnia. When he was 9 years old, Lewis's mother died after a long and difficult illness. Lewis was sent to a boarding school a few weeks after her death. Even this detail has poignant resonance with the ending of *The Magician's Nephew,* as the character Digory is able to heal his ailing mother with magical assistance from the land of Narnia.

Although Lewis had been raised a Christian by his parents, he abandoned Christianity in his teens, comfortable with declaring himself an atheist. It wasn't until his early 30s that his spiritual life began to turn again as his continuing meditations on religion led him to the point that he felt compelled to accept a basic belief in God: "In the Trinity Term of 1929 I gave in, and admitted that God was God, and knelt and prayed." Two years later, due in part to conversations with his friend J. R. R. Tolkien (author of *The Lord of the Rings*), Lewis came to believe that Jesus Christ was the Son of God. (For an allegorical account of his conversion, see *The Pilgrim's Regress* [1933].) Lewis died in 1963 after suffering from a variety of illnesses.

CHILDREN'S LITERATURE AND THE RELIGIOUS IMAGINATION

Lewis didn't consider writing children's literature until 1939. Because of the threat of German bombardment in London, Lewis had volunteered to take some children into his country home. His interactions with those children set his mind to work on story ideas. (Lewis did not have any children of his own, although he later gained two stepsons by marriage.) Lewis completed *The Lion, the Witch and the Wardrobe* in 1948. The entire set of *The Chronicles of Narnia* includes: *The Magician's Nephew* (1955); *The Lion, the Witch and the Wardrobe* (1950); *The Horse and His Boy* (1954); *Prince Caspian* (1951); *The Voyage of the "Dawn Treader"* (1952); *The Silver Chair* (1953); and *The Last Battle* (1956). (The books are listed in the order Lewis preferred that they be read.)

The Chronicles of Narnia is widely considered to be steeped in Christian imagination. And the writing of children's literature by a Christian like C. S. Lewis raises many interesting questions about the role of the imagination in the spiritual development of children. What does it mean to say that a set of fantasy stories spring from a Christian imagination? What is the relationship between the stories children hear and their religious beliefs? Do stories compete with religious beliefs or do they prepare children for them?

Lewis considers these types of questions in some of his own essays, found especially in *On Stories and Other Essays in Literature.* In "Sometimes Fairy Stories May Say Best What's to be Said," for example, Lewis observes that the stories he learned of Christ as a child *inhibited* his religious development because the stories would dictate in advance what a child should be feeling. Furthermore, he claims that he did not write his own stories with the goal of trying to say something about Christianity to children, insisting, rather, that the stories sprang from his own imagination, an imagination filled with Christian sentiment. The reader could ask, then, just what does it mean to say that the stories are Christian? Interested readers should also look particularly at "On Three Ways of Writing for Children" and "On Juvenile Taste."

Finally, Lewis took seriously the responsibility he had as an author to his many young readers, writing hundreds of letters of reply to young fans and inquirers (see *C. S. Lewis: Letters to Children*). He believed firmly that young people should be treated largely as equals and with intellectual respect.

EXCERPTS FROM THE CHRONICLES OF NARNIA

"Aren't you dead then, dear Aslan?" said Lucy.

"Not now," said Aslan.

"You're not—not a—?" asked Susan in a shaky voice. She couldn't bring herself to say the word *ghost.* Aslan stopped his golden head and licked her forehead. The warmth of his breath and a rich sort of smell that seemed to hang about his hair came all over her.

"Do I look it?" he said.

"Oh, you're real, you're real! Oh, Aslan!" cried Lucy, and both girls flung themselves upon him and covered him with kisses.

"But what does it all mean?" asked Susan when they were somewhat calmer.

"It means," said Aslan, "that though the Witch knew the Deep Magic, there is a magic deeper still which she did not know. Her knowledge goes back only to the dawn of time. But if she could have looked a little further back, into the stillness and the darkness before Time dawned, she would have read there a different incantation. She would have known that when a willing victim who had committed no treachery was killed in a traitor's stead, the Table would crack and Death itself would start working backward."

From *The Lion, the Witch and the Wardrobe*

"Don't you think it was bad luck to meet so many lions?" said Shasta.

"There was only one lion," said the Voice.

"What on earth do you mean? I've just told you there were at least two the first night, and—"

"There was only one: but he was swift of foot."

"How do you know?"

"I was the lion." And as Shasta gaped with open mouth and said nothing, the Voice continued. "I was the lion who forced you to join with Aravis. I was the cat who comforted you among the houses of the dead. I was the lion who drove the jackals from you while you slept. I was the lion who gave the Horses the new strength of fear for the last mile so that you should reach King Lune in time. And I was the lion you do not remember who pushed the boat in which you lay, a child near death, so that it came to shore where a man sat, wakeful at midnight, to receive you."

[. . .]

"Who are you?" asked Shasta.

"Myself," said the Voice, very deep and low so that the earth shook: and again "Myself," loud and clear and gay: and then the third time "Myself," whispered so softly you could hardly hear it, and yet it seemed to come from all round you as if the leaves rustled with it.

From *The Horse and His Boy*

In both excerpts above, we can see a certain resonance between the lion Aslan and the figure of Jesus. In the first case, Aslan offers himself as a sacrifice to the Witch in order to save someone else. He then resurrects, explaining to the children that there is a "deeper magic" that can undo Death itself, a magic that is accomplished when an innocent and willing victim is killed in the place of a traitor. In the second excerpt, it is revealed to Shasta that Aslan is always with him, protecting and guiding him. The passage concludes with the Old Testament formulation that God is God, Himself.

Lewis would always insist, however, that Aslan does not "represent" Jesus. Rather, he substitutes for "representation" the notion of "supposition," meaning the use of the imagination, as he puts it in a letter to a child: "I did not say to myself, 'Let us represent Jesus as He really is in our world by a Lion in Narnia': I said 'Let us *suppose* that there were a land like Narnia and that the Son of God, as He became a Man in our world, became a Lion there, and then imagine what would happen.' If you think about it, you will see that it is quite a different thing." At the same time, Lewis clearly thinks that the feelings produced by these stories are good preparation for coming to a deep understanding of the story of Jesus later in one's life. In another interesting letter to a mother who is concerned that her son loves Aslan more than Jesus, Lewis tries to reassure her that the thing the boy loves Aslan for doing and saying are simply the things that Jesus really did and said: "So that when Laurence [the son] thinks he is loving Aslan, he is really loving Jesus: and perhaps loving Him more than he ever did before."

But is this merging of a fictional character with the historical and religious significance of Jesus as uncomplicated as Lewis likes to think? Such questions make Lewis particularly interesting to think about regarding the emotional and imaginative lives of children who are of a particular religious faith.

—Greg Watkins

FURTHER READING

Arnott, A. (1975). *The secret country of C. S. Lewis.* Grand Rapids, MI: William B. Eerdmans Publishing Company. (A biography of C. S. Lewis written for young people.)

Dorsett, L. W., & Mead, M. L. (Eds.). (1985). *C. S. Lewis: Letters to Children.* New York: Touchstone.

Ford, P. F. (1980). *Companion to Narnia.* San Francisco: Harper & Row. (A dictionary style guide to the plot, characters, and themes of *The Chronicles of Narnia.*)

Lewis, C. S. (1956). *Surprised by joy: The shape of my early life.* New York: Harcourt, Brace & World. (Lewis's autobiography, including accounts of his childhood and conversion.)

Schultz, J. D., & West Jr., J. G. (Eds.). (1998). *The C. S. Lewis Readers' Encyclopedia.* Grand Rapids, MI: Zondervan. (A thorough guide to all things Lewis, and written in the form of encyclopedia entries.)

LINCOLN, ABRAHAM

Abraham Lincoln is best known for being the American president who held the country together during a long and bloody civil war and who engineered the end to American slavery. He is unique among American presidents, however, for also being considered a spiritual exemplar—not just by Americans but also by countless millions around the world. Lincoln is considered a spiritual exemplar for the virtues that defined his character, for his remarkable ability to make sound moral judgments about complex moral issues, and for his powerful faith in American democracy and in an all-powerful, just, caring, and mysterious God.

Lincoln had many virtues. Some were there from the beginning, while others developed later on under the stresses and strains of the presidency. His enduring virtues included honesty, self-discipline, simplicity, and compassion. His developed virtues included forbearance in the face of disrespect, and ridicule and steadfastness in the face of opposition and failure.

Moral judgment develops to the extent that it can handle increasingly complex and ambiguous moral dilemmas. Nowhere do we see this more clearly than in Lincoln's presidency. Lincoln faced several painful and complex moral dilemmas, but none more painful and complex than that between abolishing slavery and preserving the union.

Unlike the abolitionists of his time, Lincoln advocated going slow when opposing slavery. His slow and patient approach, what one biographer referred to as his "deadly moderation" toward ending slavery, won him disapproval and distrust. So, in managing the union–slavery dilemma, Lincoln's patient calculations constituted a spiritual achievement inasmuch as they were carried out at great personal sacrifice.

As for Lincoln's faith, early on in his political career, Lincoln expressed a strong faith in the American Constitution, in the legal system, and in the American way of government in general. However, in the 1850s when it was clear that the constitution, the legal system, and the government were upholding slavery, Lincoln's faith underwent a dramatic transformation.

What emerged in the late 1850s and especially during Lincoln's presidency was a powerful faith that fueled and guided Lincoln's leadership. That faith had two central ideas. The first was the idea expressed in the great democratic principle defined in the Declaration of Independence. The second was the idea of God being all-powerful, just, caring, and mysterious.

Faith is not the same as belief, so it would be wrong to say that these two ideas were important because they were Lincoln's beliefs. They were important, rather, because Lincoln took them to define who we are or should be, and because he worked tirelessly to help make that happen. His faith, then, showed as much in his acting (or more so) as in his believing.

Lincoln came to view the American Declaration of Independence's principle that all should have equal rights to life, liberty, and the pursuit of happiness as something sacred and as something to have faith in. He took this principle to be the cornerstone of American democracy and a spiritual guide for the nation. This was Lincoln's message in his moral battles against slavery, and this too was his message at Gettysburg.

But during his presidency and under the strains of prosecuting the bloodiest war in American history, Lincoln's faith became increasingly religious as it centered on a simple, yet powerful image of God. For Lincoln, God is almighty, just, caring and mysterious. For him, we "poor mortals" can never fathom God's intentions but can only place our hopes in God, trusting that He will bring good even out of tragedy.

This image of an almighty, just, caring, and mysterious God was there for Lincoln from the beginning to the end of the war—to sustain and guide him. Throughout the war, Lincoln expressed his anxieties about the future and his despair about the recent past. And often, his expressions of anxiety and despair were followed by reference to his image of God, which seemed to mollify his anxiety and despair. Because he believed God was in charge, Lincoln managed his anxieties and doubts enough to free him to find reasonable ways to act. Its other function was to help Lincoln act independently while remaining thoughtful and responsible, especially in the face of opposition by those with religious motives.

During the Civil War, then, Lincoln's faith sustained him in his trials, and kept him steadfast and able to make the many hard political and military decisions he had to make. But even more important, throughout the war, Lincoln's religious faith in a mysterious yet just and caring and all-powerful God kept him morally responsible, compassionate, and humble. For his character, his moral judgment, and his faith, then, Lincoln was indeed a spiritual exemplar.

—W. George Scarlett

LITERATURE, CHILDREN'S

The past 30 years have seen a tremendous outpouring of books aimed at children and adolescents. Never before in human history have so many good juvenile books been so widely available. Many of these books address spiritual questions relevant to young people: Is there a supernatural world? If so, what is it like? Does God exist? What happens when we die? How can I live a good life? How should humans relate to God and each other? Why is there so much suffering and evil in the world? In addressing enduring human questions, such books prepare children to make formative decisions about their futures. They can also foster imagination, a sense of roots, understanding of other cultures, and the ability to overcome obstacles. As such, literary works can often serve as a both a subtle and very significant trigger of religious and/or spiritual growth. All the books mentioned below are as valuable for adults as they are for children.

The vast quantity of spiritual literature can be divided into two overarching types: religious and what can be called "secular spiritual." Both types can stimulate thought and discussion about religious questions. This entry provides an overview of the types (and subcategories within each), suggest ways to locate such books, and provide examples of each—at least one suitable for reading aloud to younger children (age 10 and younger) and one for children over age 10 to read themselves. All the books mentioned for younger children have enough depth to appeal also to older children and adults. (*A to Zoo* is an invaluable reference tool that indexes children's books by theme.) While many of the literary works described are written in English, the categorization system applies as well to books written in all languages and from all cultures.

RELIGIOUS BOOKS

Religious books are explicitly concerned with religious beliefs and practices. This category includes at least four subcategories: (1) Bibles and other sacred texts geared to children; (2) stories based on the Bible but with an interpretive spin; (3) hero tales about various exemplary religious figures; and (4) nonfiction books about religious beliefs, traditions, and practices.

Bibles and Other Sacred Texts

In the Judeo-Christian tradition, Biblical stories include creation stories, accounts of the early Israelites, and events in the life of Jesus and the first Christians. Other major religions also have sacred texts, such as the Vedas and Bhagavad-Gita (for Hindus) and the Koran or Qur'an (for Muslims). Under the Dewey decimal classification system, all these are grouped with myth and folklore and are included in the genre of "traditional literature."

Suitable for very young children is *The Pilgrim Book of Bible Stories* (2003), which includes lively stories, accompanied by historical background information and realistic illustrations. An example suited to older children is *When the Beginning Began: Stories about God and the Creatures and Us* (Lester, 1999).

Midrash

Midrash is a Jewish term for retelling of biblical stories with an interpretive spin. Midrash takes an interesting character or detail from the original story and spins a provocative tale about it to emphasize an important idea. Rabbi Sandy Eisenberg Sasso has written *But God Remembered: Stories of Women from Creation to the Promised Land,* all from the Hebrew Bible. (Sasso has written several picture books of interest to both Jews and Christians. These can be used with adults as well as children to spur reflection.) A collection of *midrashim* suited for older children is *Does God Have a Big Toe?* (Gellman, 1989). *Midrashim* stimulate children's imaginations, helping them see the relevance of biblical texts.

Hero Tales

Hero tales are true stories of exemplary individuals with religious motivations. These include both short narratives and longer biographies of biblical figures, saints, and other figures. Examples for young children are *Queen Esther Saves Her People* (Gelman) and *The True Tale of Johnny Appleseed* (Hodges, 1997).

Hero tales for older children include *The Diary of Anne Frank* (1952), *Buddha* (Demi, 1996), and *Martin Luther King* (Bray, 1995). Most such books can be found with other biographies (Dewey Number 921). Collections of hero stories have been published, such as *The Hero's Trail* (aimed at teenagers; Barron, 1998) and *The Children's Book of America* (Bennett, 1998).

Religious Traditions

Books in this category shed light on religious beliefs, customs, and personal practices. This category also includes cookbooks, books about religious holidays, and prayer books. One example for young children is Gerstein's *The Mountains of Tibet,* a picture book about reincarnation in Tibetan Buddhism told from the point of view of a child about to be reborn (1987). A book of prayers from many different world traditions is *In Every Tiny Grain of Sand* (Lindbergh, 2000). Its illustrations show humans doing everyday things in a way that emphasizes their commonalities.

An example aimed at an older child is *The Remembering Box* (Clifford, 1985). This short novel tells of a Jewish boy's many Sabbath visits alone with his grandmother during which she reminisces about traditions from her earlier years. This category also includes books that introduce children to unfamiliar religious traditions, such as *My Friends' Beliefs: A Young Reader's Guide to World Religions* (Ward, 1988). It provides a respectful overview of all major world religions and many different Christian sects, as well as a profile of a young believer from each group. *The Koran for Dummies* written by a young adult (Sultan) is a good introduction to Islam.

"SECULAR SPIRITUAL" BOOKS

The second large category is so-called secular literature, and it includes a wide range of genres, ranging from picture books to nonfiction, realistic fiction, fantasy, and more. This category encompasses books from several different genres (mostly fictional) that address spiritual questions. For the sake of brevity, this entry will be limited to five important themes: (1) unseen worlds, (2) death and the afterlife, (3) solitude and the inner journey, (4) evil and the issue of forgiveness, and (5) appreciating religious difference.

Unseen Worlds

Many different kinds of books address questions such as: "Does God exist? Are there supernatural realms? Are we alone in the universe? Can we communicate with other beings?" One such book directed toward younger children is *Somewhere in the World Right Now* (Schuett, 1995). This picture book takes the reader around the world, touching down in many different places at the same moment in time. In Africa elephants sleep standing up, in India dawn is breaking, and in Siberia people are preparing their mid-day meal, even as a child in America is settling into bed. This book helps a child to realize that no human is at the center of the universe, and that each person is a part of a much greater whole, mostly unseen by us.

For older children, fantasy and science fiction are especially rich resources for considering questions about the supernatural. The best known of these is the Harry Potter series by British author J. K. Rowling (six books to date, beginning with *Harry Potter and the Sorcerer's Stone*). This series is the most widely read in the history of publishing and has enticed children to read other fantasy books. Harry has been living with callous relatives, when, on his 11th birthday, he learns that he is in fact a wizard and is being summoned to another world to battle the diabolical Lord Voldemort. The series chronicles Harry's gradual transformation from a lonely self-doubting orphan to a mature leader who is capable of fulfilling his noble vocation.

Other fantasy authors also write of quests into formerly unseen worlds: C. S. Lewis (*Chronicles of Narnia*), Madeleine L'Engle ("The Time Quartet," beginning with *A Wrinkle in Time*), and A. K. Applegate (the Animorph series of 60-plus novels). Such series have in common a child's invitation to an unseen world, followed by heroic action in a cosmic battle between good and evil. Along the way, the child characters learn courage, compassion, loyalty, and other virtues.

Death and the Afterlife

By school age most children have had been touched by death, eliciting questions such as "Why do people die? Where do they go?" *Badger's Parting Gifts* (Varley, 1984) is a picture book that tells of old Badger, beloved by all the animals. When he dies, he finds himself running down a very long tunnel, "as if he had fallen out of his body." His friends gradually come to terms with their grief by reflecting on the gifts that Badger gave each during life (he helped one learn to skate, gave another his favorite gingerbread recipe, and so on). *Charlotte's Web* (White, 1952) addresses the issue of how to live and die well.

A realistic chapter book aimed at older children is Katherine Paterson's *Bridge to Terabithia* (1977), which tells of an 11-year-old mountain boy's "best friendship" with an imaginative new girl in his class. When she dies in a flash flood, he gradually lets his grief open him to "the shining world."

Solitude and the Inner Journey

By ages 9 to 11, most children begin to wrestle with concerns over loneliness, belonging, and peer pressure. They may sometimes struggle to find a sense of value and identity as friendships change. A book suitable for young children is the classic, *The Velveteen Rabbit* by Williams, which tells of a stuffed rabbit who feels a rivalry with fancier toys. Freedom comes as the rabbit gradually "becomes real" by loving, being loved, and living well with the boy.

Also addressing solitude is L'Engle's *A Ring of Endless Light* (1970), a realistic novel about 16-year-old Vicky Austin. She wrestles with feelings of loss as she assists her mother in providing home hospice care for her beloved grandfather. The same summer she deals with her first boyfriends, and also discovers an uncanny ability to communicate by telepathy with dolphins. Vicky digs deep (often praying or meditating) to find her own spiritual center in the midst of these changing relationships. "Who am I? Can I stand alone? Will God help me?" are questions Vicky faces as she searches for her own path as a "light bearer."

Sin and Forgiveness

Early in childhood children start to become aware of the existence of hurt, pain, suffering, and sin. Preschoolers often experience this in the form of sibling rivalry. The picture book *When Sophie Gets Angry—Really, Really Angry* (Bang, 1999) helps young children deal with antisocial impulses; it tells of little Sophie who is vexed beyond endurance by a sister who grabs her toys. After a tantrum, she bolts outdoors, runs as far as she can, then climbs a tree. Aloft, "the world comforts her," and Sophie can release her anger and return home with a peaceful spirit.

A more complex book about sin and forgiveness is aimed at older children: *Words by Heart* (Sebestyen, 1979). Set in 1910, this novel tells of a family who courageously survives as the only black family in their Texas community. When the father is murdered by racial bigots, daughter Lena must come to terms with the atrocity and with her father's legacy of forgiveness and love of God.

Appreciating Religious Difference

There is also a growing body of literature that helps children to learn about religious traditions beside their own, and the dark side of religious belief. One such book geared to young children is *Old Turtle* (Wood, 1992). This is a fable about the various creatures of the Earth who bitterly argue about all manner of things, especially about God. Eventually an ancient turtle rises from the depths of the sea and helps them find God in each other and the beauty of the Earth. (See also its sequel, *Old Turtle and the Broken Truth.*)

For older children a book that addresses religious differences is Yolen's *Armageddon Summer,* which tells of teenagers caught up in an apocalyptic Christian cult that predicts the exact date of the world's end. The two protagonists eventually reject the cult's extremism even as they recognize their own spiritual needs. *Rebels in the Heavenly Kingdom* (Paterson), set in China, also shows the tension between authentic faith and religion gone awry.

CONCLUSION

In addition to these five themes, many contemporary books address social issues with spiritual dimensions, including environmental damage, war, and poverty. Moreover, a huge body of traditional fables, folk tales, proverbs, and fairy tales also touch on moral and spiritual concerns. Poetry for children is often filled with wonder, whimsy, humor, and fantasy, which are often spiritual expressions. Teachers may be more willing to use "secular spiritual" books than those that are explicitly religious. The literary themes and works described often serve as triggers of religious and spiritual reflection and development to the reader.

—Trudelle Thomas

See also Narrative

FURTHER READING

Bang, M. (1999). When Sophie gets angry . . . really really angry. Troy, MI: Blue Sky Press.

Barron, T. A. (1998). *The hero's trail: A guide for heroic life.* New York: Putnam/Philomel.

Bennett, W. J. (1998). *The children's book of America.* New York: Simon & Schuster.

Bray, R. (1995). *Martin Luther King.* New York: Greenwillow Books.

Clifford, E. (1985). *The remembering box.* Boston: Houghton Mifflin.

Demi. (1996). *Buddha.* New York: Henry Holt.

Frank, A. (1952). *The diary of a young girl.* Garden City, NY: Doubleday.

Gelman, R. G. (1998). *Queen Esther saves her people.* New York: Scholastic.

Gellman, M. (1989). *Does God have a big toe?: Stories about stories in the Bible.* New York: HarperTrophy.

Gerstein, M. (1987). *The mountains of Tibet.* San Francisco: Harper & Row.

Hodges, M. (1997). *The true tale of Johnny Appleseed.* New York: Holiday House.

L'Engle, M. (1962). *A wrinkle in time.* New York: Ariel Books.

L'Engle, M. (1980). *A ring of endless light.* New York: Dell.

Lester, J. (1999). *When the beginning began: Stories about God, the creatures, and us.* San Diego: Silver Whistle.

Lewis, C. S. (1994). *The chronicles of Narnia boxed set.* New York: HarperTrophy.

Lima, C. W., & Lima, J. A. (2001). *A to zoo: Subject access to children's picture books,* (6th ed.). Westport, CT: Libraries Unlimited.

Lindbergh, R. (2000). *In every tiny grain of sand: A child's book of prayers and praise.* Cambridge, MA: Candlewick.

Paterson, K. (1977). *Bridge to Terabithia.* New York: HarperCollins.

Paterson, K. (1983). *Rebels of the heavenly kingdom.* New York: Lodestar.

Rowling, J. K. (1998). *Harry Potter and the Sorcerer's Stone.* New York: Arthur A. Levine Books.

Sasso, S. E. (1995). *But God remembered: Stories of women from creation to the promised land.* Woodstock, VT: Jewish Lights.

Schuett, S. (1997). *Somewhere in the world right now.* New York: Knopf.

Sebestyen, O. (1968). *Words by heart.* New York: Atlantic Monthly Press.

Trelease, J. (2001). *The read-aloud handbook* (5th ed.). New York: Penguin.

Varley, S. (1984). *Badger's parting gifts.* New York: HarperTrophy.

Ward, H. (1998). *My friend's beliefs: A young reader's Guide to world religions.* London: Walker.

Water, M. (2003). *Pilgrim book of Bible stories.* Cleveland, OH: Pilgrim Press.

White, E. B. (1974). *Charlotte's web.* New York: HarperTrophy.

Williams, M. (1958). *The velveteen rabbit.* New York: Doubleday.

Wood, D. (1992). *Old turtle.* New York: Scholastic.

Wood, D. (2003). *Old turtle and the broken truth.* New York: Scholastic.

Yolen, J., & Coville, B. (1999). *Armageddon summer.* New York: Harcourt Brace.

LITERATURE, MORAL DEVELOPMENT IN

Many high school students wonder why English has to be such a large part of their curriculum. They think that at first glance it does not offer any concrete tools for the future, but, in reality, an understanding of literature is essential in developing the self, and many of the texts taught at the high school level are taught to enrich the student's understanding of how moral struggles are met by characters in a variety of situations. In a way, in secular education these works of literature stand in for sacred texts. They provide a base of narratives from which to draw inspiration, ideas, and moral standards; furthermore, they often address spiritual concerns head on. The universality of the texts' themes explains why these texts are taught in a wide range of high schools public and private, religious and secular.

Throughout the canon of English literature taught at the high school level, issues of morality, moral crisis, and *moral identity* are frequently addressed in profound ways. Many of the texts in the classic canon (the texts chosen as appropriate and necessary for general literary education) are chosen because they demonstrate the path to an independent moral understanding often through crisis, death, and hardship. From the very beginnings of the English literary tradition to contemporary literature, this pattern still defines what is included in the canon of acceptable texts for high school students.

Shakespeare's play *Hamlet,* for instance, shows the transformation of a privileged prince into a grieving figure questioning his own moral identity through the moral struggle of death. Wavering through various philosophical options and reactions, the title character, Hamlet, is swallowed up in his own search for revenge and autonomy. Although his end is tragic, Hamlet manages to gain both revenge against his uncle, the murderer of his father, and an understanding of how destructive this revenge truly is. Thus, the reader is left to undergo the moral transformation that the play's title character cannot. The questions of revenge, mortality, and the struggle for *self-identity* that dominate the play are exactly what makes it so appealing for the high school classroom.

The Holy Sonnets of John Donne, although a complicated example, are frequently used to show one's struggle to understand death through a Christian lens. *Holy Sonnet X* and *Holy Sonnet XIV* are the most frequently read because they deal directly, and in sophisticated ways, with the human struggle with death and salvation. In both of these texts, the poet presents a paradox, the most sophisticated of literary tropes, to make their complex moral point. In *Holy Sonnet X* (Death be not proud . . .), the poet meditates on the idea that death itself will die so that all shall live, and in *Holy Sonnet XIV* (Batter my heart . . .), the poet claims that he must be enslaved and enthralled by God in order to be set free. The complexity of this moral journey and the sophistication of how it is explained make it a prime example of the moral journey and development of a moral compass as being a necessity for acceptance into the literary canon of high school texts.

Also from the 17th century, John Milton's poetry meditates on the promise of salvation and the human response to this promise. His early poem, "On the Morning of Christ's Nativity," juxtaposes the gentility of the baby Jesus with the profound demands that his birth and resurrection placed on humanity. The poet suggests that when celebrating the birth of Christ, one must also celebrate the search for human salvation through Christ, and is struck by how demanding this search is. Two poems that offer different, yet complementary, options are his twin poems "L'Allegro" and "Il Penseroso," which present a lighthearted, mirthful approach against and in conjunction with devotion to contemplation and melancholy. His poem "Lycidas" shows a struggle to understand our ability to fulfill our vocations under the constant threat of our mortality, while his great epic *Paradise Lost* deals with humanity's fallen nature. Many of his poems seek to answer the call to God's vocation and moral demands in an individualized personal way, but some assert that they are also somewhat filled with Milton's own pride.

In the 18th century, Alexander Pope and Jonathan Swift, the two great satirists of the century, presented responses to the era's crisis of morality—the search to survive against the onslaught of colonialism, mercantilism, and capitalism. Pope's mock epic "Rape of the Lock" shows the foolishness of vanity, while "Eloisa to Abelard" shows the pain of a love denied by rigid religious regulations. In the span of his work, the moral and autonomous self struggles against the greater systems that would oppress it. These systems range from vanity-driven economic policies to rigid medieval moralities.

Jonathan Swift in a similar light seeks to put all of humanity under the same moral guidelines, showing in his famous novel *Gulliver's Travels* that all societies are equally corruptible, equally racist, and so on. In many of his poems, he shows the hidden corruption of the impersonal, urban world of 18th-century England. These works, too, underline the importance of creating an independent morality within a larger economic and political system.

Nineteenth-century American literature is full of moral texts that call the reader to an elevated moral state. Placed against the struggle to abolish slavery, many of the abolitionist texts, mainly *Uncle Tom's Cabin,* seek to portray slavery as a corrupt institution oppressing thoroughly moral slaves who want nothing more than what they own by God's creation. The homespun morality of the slaves, based in biblical teaching, is presented as more just than the socially influenced corrupt morality of the slave system. This text, like many others mentioned here, shows the struggle of an individual morality against a corrupting system.

Into the 20th century, texts like *Twelve Angry Men* and *To Kill a Mockingbird* highlight a similar individualized moral struggle against society. Other texts like *The Great Gatsby* and *Native Son* show morally ambiguous characters involved in similar struggles to assert an autonomous identity. The struggle for identity is also represented well in James Joyce's short story "The Dead" in which a colonial, culturally self-hating Irishman comes to terms with his identity and morality through the landscapes and powerful personal stories and struggles of his own people. The 20th-century text, so concerned with the struggle for individual identity, is full of self-defining moral crises. Moral crises and the struggles to resolve them are the centerpieces of texts like the ones mentioned here, and relate to the development of spirituality and morality as the greatest way to respond to a greater system in which we all live.

—Timothy John Duffy

FURTHER READING

Abrams, M. H., & Greenblatt, S. (Eds.). (1999). *The Norton anthology of English literature: Vol. 1 B, The sixteenth century/the early seventeenth century* (7th ed.). New York: W.W. Norton.

Abrams, M. H., & Greenblatt, S. (Eds.). (1999). *The Norton anthology of English literature: Vol. 1 C, Restoration and the eighteenth century* (7th ed.). New York: W.W. Norton.

Baym, N., & Tanka, J. (Eds.). (2002). *The Norton anthology of American literature: Package 1* (6th ed.). New York: W. W. Norton.

LORD'S PRAYER, THE

There are two versions of the Lord's Prayer in the New Testament. Of the two versions (Matthew 6:9–15; Luke 11:2–4), Luke's is widely considered the earlier in form, and it does seem plain that Matthew presents what is, in effect, a commentary woven together with the prayer. The relative sparseness of Luke has won it virtually unanimous recognition among scholars as the nearest to the form of an outline which Jesus recommended.

Matthew	**Luke**
Our father, who is in the heavens, your name will be sanctified, your kingdom will come, your will happen as in heaven, even on earth. Our bread that is coming, give us today, and forgive us our debts, as we also have forgiven our debtors, And do not bring us to the test, but deliver us from the evil one.	Father, your name will be sanctified, your kingdom will come. Our bread that is coming, be giving us each day, and release us our sins, because we also ourselves release everyone who is indebted us, And do not bring us to the test.

The same basic prayer of Jesus is reflected in both these versions. The differences between them show that early Christians allowed themselves considerable freedom in how they put their prayers into words. They understood that true prayer was not a matter of literal repetition, and Jesus specifically warned against mechanical and ostentatious prayer (Matthew 6:5–8). Matthew gives us the version of the prayer most often used in its community, just as Luke provides us with the received view in its community.

The different versions of the prayer present the same meaning behind Jesus' teachings, but in different styles and wordings. The basic model or outline of the Lord's Prayer upon which both versions are based consists of calling God father, confessing that his name should be sanctified and that his kingdom should come, and then asking for the bread God will provide that day, forgiveness, and not to be brought to the test (i.e., not to be forced into disloyalty to God).

Assessed by its individual elements, the Lord's Prayer may be characterized as a fairly typical instance of the Judaic piety of its period. To call God "father" was—as such—nothing radical, and the association of his fatherly care with his actual provision for prayerful Israel is attested in Psalm 68:5. The same passage shows that the connection of God's holiness to his fatherhood was seen as natural, and the importance of sanctifying God's name within the earliest of Rabbinic texts of prayer—such as the Kaddish, which means "Sanctified [be God's name]"—is well known. That his holiness is consistent with people being forgiven and accepted by him is also unexceptionable. Finally, the idea that God's being king amounts to a "kingdom" that was about to be revealed is amply precedented within the Aramaic paraphrases of the Hebrew Bible known as the Targumim, and they insist upon the loyal response of God's people to that revelation.

According to the prayer, God is to be approached as father, his name sanctified, and his kingdom welcomed. The act of prayer along those lines, with great variety over time and from place to place and tradition to tradition, has been a hallmark of Christianity.

To address God as one's father, and yet to sanctify his name, acknowledges the ambivalence that might permeate attitudes toward God. He approaches us freely and without restraint, and yet is unapproachable, as holy as we are ordinary. The welcoming of his kingdom, of his comprehensive rule within the terms of reference of our world, wills away our ambivalence. His intimate holiness is to invade the ordinary, so that any ambivalence is overcome by the force of God itself. The kingdom is dynamically ingressive, and is welcomed in the act of prayer, however others might react to the kingdom.

The three elements that open the prayer, then, characterize a relationship and an attitude toward God which the one who prays makes his or her own. The distinctiveness of the prayer is nothing other than that consciousness of God and of one's relationship to him which is implied, and which is recapitulated whenever one prays in that way. Such an awareness of God and of oneself is what Christians kindle when they pray the Lord's Prayer. And at the same time, the prayer is nothing other than the Lord's; whatever the merits of such a consciousness, it is only ours because it was Christ's first. That is why the filial consciousness of praying in this manner is as strong as it is: one is God's child, and Jesus' sister or brother in the same instant.

This prayer reveals how Jesus conceived living spiritually on a daily basis. He taught his followers to turn to God as intimately as they would to their parents, asking their heavenly father for their needs as they would ask a father for bread. This prayer also stresses that God is holy so that the person who prays welcomes this divine sanctity into his or her life, and can experience forgiveness on that basis. Just as remembering God's holiness addresses human sin, so Jesus taught that welcoming God's Kingdom addresses human despair. Disciples who embrace God's Kingdom in the world perform the hopeful dynamics of God's revelation to his people just as Jesus did, and remain constant witnesses to divine presence in the world.

The Lord's Prayer is commonly recited in Christian worship, and people often first learn it as a form of words. But it was framed by Jesus for a much deeper purpose than that. This prayer is designed for constant use so that prayer helps a person become continually conscious of God's presence with us as an intimate friend, a source of holiness, and the most important force in the world. That, Jesus taught, makes us confident that the needs we encounter will be met, our faults dealt with, and any despair transformed into hope.

—*Bruce Chilton*

See also Prayer

LUTHER, MARTIN

Martin Luther (1483–1546) is known the world over as the German priest who in the 16th century set the Protestant Reformation in motion. In 1516, Luther composed his now infamous set of 95 theses with the sole intention of proposing a number of Church reforms. To his surprise, his 95 theses met with tremendous popular support, and at the same time, caused great controversy. As a result, he was promptly ordered by the Papal Court to recant his statements.

Refusing to compromise his beliefs, Luther found himself the leader of a movement that eventually led to a radical break with the Catholic Church, which, at the time, was the prevailing religious, political, and social institution. The result of this split, or what is now referred to as the Reformation, gave rise to Protestantism, one of the major denominations that makes up Christianity today.

Luther was born on November 10, 1483 in Eisleben, Saxony into particularly tumultuous times. The Holy Roman Empire of Germany was under constant political turmoil. All of Europe too was adjusting to changes brought about by the Renaissance, the transition from the Middle to the Modern Age, as well as trying to cope with the devastating effects of the black plague. These turbulent times formed a fitting background for Luther's movement, the Reformation.

At the time of his birth, Luther's parents were lowly peasants, but after the family moved to Mansfeld to mine copper, they became one of the most respected families in the area. As a child, young Martin distinguished himself as one of the brightest in his school, and his parents planned for him to pursue a future as a lawyer. Even as a child, Luther was known for his recurrent bouts of melancholy, a characteristic that would remain part of his identity throughout his life.

In 1505, Luther received his master's degree from the University of Erfurt, but his plans to continue on to law school were interrupted. On a return trip to school after visiting his parents, he was caught in the middle of a thunderstorm. After being thrown to the ground by a sudden flash of lightning, Luther, cried out, "Saint Anne, help me! I will become a monk!" Luther's parents, especially his father Hans, were incensed. Nevertheless, he joined an Augustinian monastery in Erfurt 15 days later.

Once in the monastery, Luther sought to appease God by obsessively and excessively performing certain religious duties; he confessed daily, even up to 6 hours at a time, and often fasted for days on end. Despite the fact that his efforts did not earn him peace with God, Luther was ordained a priest in 1507. He then began studying theology at the University of Erfurt where he was influenced by the humanist slogan "back to the source." As a result, Luther often studied the Scriptures in their original Hebrew and Greek forms. After receiving his doctorate in 1512, Luther became a professor at Wittenberg University and a priest of Wittenberg's City Church 2 years later.

As Luther pored over the Scriptures in preparation for his lectures, he came to understand God's justice not as centered on punishment, but rather, on mercy. Now often referred to as "the Tower experience,"

Luther himself claimed that this moment of revelation took place in his study room as he read Paul's Epistle to the Romans. However, other scholars have suggested that Luther's understanding was more a result of cumulative study. Regardless, adopting the notion of justification by faith, not works, was a turning point in Luther's spiritual development and life.

As Luther delved further into his studies, he found that his biblical interpretations differed significantly from those of the Church. In 1517, Luther wrote a letter to his superiors asking for an end to the sale of indulgences, a Church practice that claimed its members could decrease their time spent in purgatory in exchange for money. Luther also included in his letter 95 theses concerning other issues he had with the Church. Popular myth purports that Luther nailed these theses to the door of Wittenberg's Castle Church, but most scholars agree that this report is pure legend.

Although Luther never intended to break with the Church and could hardly have imagined that copies of his theses would quickly circulate throughout the country, he refused papal orders to recant his views. As the Church declared Luther a heretic and began an inquisition in Rome, Luther produced what are considered his three greatest works: *Address to the Christian Nobility of the German Nation, The Babylonian Captivity,* and *The Freedom of the Christian Man.*

In 1521, Luther appeared before Emperor Charles V at the Imperial Diet of Worms, where he was again ordered to renounce his teachings. Although his journey to Worms could have resulted in arrest or death, along the way he was greeted more as a hero than as a heretic. After Luther refused to retract his beliefs, he was condemned as an outlaw. However, prince and elector Frederick the Wise of Saxony staged a kidnapping that enabled Luther to be brought to Wartburg Castle. Here, Luther hid in safety as the Reformation recouped itself.

Alone in the castle except for a warden and two servants, Luther fell into a deep depression. During this time, he was also plagued by a number of physical ills, including acute constipation and insomnia. However, Luther remained active, writing a number of treatises as well as translating the New Testament from Greek to German. By 1534, Luther finished a translation of the entire Bible, which set a new standard for the German language as a whole.

Although many reforms were effectively put in place during his absence, Luther returned to Wittenberg to deal with some of the more radical members of the movement. He soon found himself caught in the midst of the bloody Peasants' War, which lasted from 1524 to 1526.

During this time, several monks and priests found themselves wives as a protest against celibacy, and as a testament to his own take on this issue, in 1525, Luther wed Katharina von Bora, a former nun who had found refuge in Wittenberg. Luther and Katherina eventually had six children.

Although Luther had originally considered marriage as merely a remedy for lust, he began to write of the many beneficial lessons to be found in family life. However, just 2 years into his marriage, he fell into the most depressive state of his life. Indeed, Luther's last 20 years, from 1526 up until his death in 1546, are most notable for frequent outbursts of rage that were, for him, part of his ongoing depression.

The aging reformer's anger and depression stemmed in part from the fact that he took on the near impossible task of keeping in order an increasingly fragmenting movement. In addition, the Reformation was beset with the martyring of many of its followers and the religious indifference of the majority of the populace. Despite the added physical discomforts of heart congestion, fainting spells, an ulcer on his leg, and acid stones, to name a few, Luther refused to give up.

As early as 1523, Luther had added to his already full plate the task of trying to convert the Jews to Christianity. When his amiable efforts to win over Jewish believers failed, his writings resorted to using vulgar obscenities, and he even proposed such extreme measures as the burning of Jewish synagogues. The title of Luther's 1543 treatise, *On the Jews and Their Lies,* offers a hint of Luther's overly harsh stance. However, some scholars have pointed out that Luther also treated other groups whom he considered to be hindrances to the Gospel with equal ferocity. For instance, Luther viewed Anabaptists, papists, and Turks as Satan's tools.

While Luther's life was characterized by his fervor, his last lecture at Wittenberg University ended with the words, "I am weak. I cannot go on." Shortly thereafter, he traveled back to his birthplace of Eisleben to settle a dispute, and passed away without incident on February 18, 1546.

Luther's influence lies in a number of spheres across a number of centuries, from his expertise in the arenas of writing and music to his effects on larger societal institutions such as religion and politics. While often hailed as an icon, Luther never claimed to be a model of piety. Luther's theology remained rooted in his own deeply personal, and often turbulent, relationship with God. Luther openly admitted that he often struggled to feel and practice what he preached, even after he arrived at the pivotal moment of his spiritual life—Luther's discovery of justification by faith and the subsequent change in his rigid image of God as bearer of punishment to arbiter of mercy.

While Luther's doctrinal impact is evident even in present-day Christianity's emphasis on salvation by faith, a human touch still remains throughout his life and work. Thus, another of Luther's legacies is the melding of the personal and the theological into a modern vision of faith in a God who is both intimate and authoritative.

—Pamela Chu

See also Catholicism; Christianity

FURTHER READING

Bainton, R. H. (1950). *Here I stand.* New York: Abingdon.

Marius, R. (1999). *Martin Luther: The Christian between God and death.* Cambridge, MA: Belknap Press of Harvard University Press.

Wittenberg, K. D. G. (1997). *A mighty fortress is our God: Martin Luther.* Retrieved from www.luther.de/en.

M

MAGIC

At first glance, "magic" and "spirituality" hardly appear to belong together. The words "magic" or "magician" in the modern world are widely employed to refer to entertainers at children's birthday parties, colorful antics of the clown and card shark, splendid moments in life, and beliefs both good and bad. Modern thinking about magic conjures up images of smoke and mirrors, masters of illusion and the sleight of hand of nimble-fingered performers that have little connection with spirituality. In order to flesh out an understanding of magic that permits spirituality, these modern expectations must be set aside, and the world of ancient magic and spirituality must be entered. Before doing so, however, it is important to note that a spirituality informed by magic is practiced by young and old in almost all religions of the world. From the Dionysian cults of ancient Rome to Haitian voodoo, Christian, Sufi, Jewish, and Buddhist mysticism to shamanic ritual, the continuing significance and vitality of magic and spirituality is alive and well in the modern world.

Historically, cultures have universally recognized the power inherent in magic with fear and ambivalence, but also mindful that its power must be harnessed for their benefit. Not surprisingly, ancient Greek and Roman literature record some ambivalence and credulity toward magic and its practitioners, but both were nevertheless required because of the open-ended nature of life at the whim of forces beyond human control. Credulity was registered not because magic was perceived the trade of fraudulent tricksters and cunning performers, but because the art was dangerous and powerful. Magic worked and had serious consequences if incorrectly employed. The Acts of the Apostles in the New Testament offer an example of the early world of magic and its connection to the religious/spiritual, recording the story of the seven sons of Sceva who, as itinerant exorcists, invoke the name of Jesus to drive a demon out of a possessed person. Summoning the name of Jesus backfires on them, and the evil spirit "leaps on them, masters them all, and so overpowers them that they flee out of the house naked and wounded" (Acts 19:13–16). These human practitioners had tried to gain control over the demon but were overcome themselves.

In the ancient world of the Babylonians, Egyptians, Greeks, Romans, Judeans, and early Christians, magic was the very fabric through which the universe was perceived and magicians were the mediators between the mundane and celestial powers that made up the fabric. Definitions of magic abound, but one that holds up defines magic as rituals of power and practitioners as mediators of that power. Rituals of power empower humans by giving them a measure of control over various hostile forces operating in the universe, both mundane and heavenly, and with knowledge to secure access to these powers. In other words, these rituals help people gain control of a variety of good and bad celestial energies, and the forces of death that impinge on their daily lives. Sicknesses, personal disasters, memory loss, baldness, death, and being possessed were thought to be the result of these forces directly interfering in the lives of humans. Similarly, knowledge of the future, acquisition of love, wealth, health, fame, and union with the gods was also thought to be in the purview of these heavenly forces.

These invisible energies sometimes were hostile and created difficulties for humans and at other times were friendly and showered kind gifts upon them. The question for humans then was of how best to manipulate and tap into the power that these hidden forces represented. Not only was gaining control an issue but also appealing to them for help when disasters struck. As such, these rituals of magic were deeply spiritual for people of antiquity. It involved humans actively seeking to achieve personal communication or union with divine beings who were central to the ongoing success of their lives. Magic, as a form of religious expression and piety, was about humans taking seriously their dependence on the invisible energies of the universe capable of either harming or helping them.

It was clear to ancients that experiencing success or failure in life was the result of Chance (Tyche) or Fortune (Fortuna). In the Greek and Roman world, the highly regarded goddesses Tyche and Fortuna were worshipped and honored as patron deities of luck or fortune. It was in their hands that human destiny, good fortune, and long life rested. In addition, to improve the odds for success, humans also negotiated with underworld deities, the demons and spirits of the dead and the star deities, the constellation of the Bear, and gods such as Apollo Helios, and abstract deities such as the All (Aion), Time (Chronos), Destiny (Moirai), and Nature (Physis). Popular Egyptian deities (Isis and Osiris) and the god of the Jewish people (Iao, Adonai) and early Christians were similarly invoked to achieve life's goals. Given that humans were blown about by the invisible winds of the universe, where security, hope, comfort, and stability were tenuous at best, summoning these powerful forces for help was a necessity.

A multiplicity of religious groups, guilds, associations, and ritual experts made use of these rituals of power. For example, the Therapeutae of Upper Egypt were renowned for their healing arts and knowledge of medicinal plants and herbs. Magicians, healers, diviners, exorcists, wise women, prophetesses, shamans, holy people, priests, prophets, pharaohs, emperors, kings, and conjure doctors appealed to the divine powers on behalf of their human clients. Indeed, these ritual experts worked within communities familiar to them, often inheriting their powers from previous family members of the community. These specialists claimed to be acquainted with and comprehend the multiplicity of religious traditions around them. They knew the secret words and rituals required to communicate with the demons, deities, spirits, and the dead across a broad spectrum of religions. At their disposal were mysteries that had been handed on from generation to generation that permitted them to regulate, control, and manipulate these invisible forces.

A Jewish book of mysteries (*Sefer Ha-Rezim*) recounts how Noah was the recipient of mysteries he was unable to master but that he and successive generations passed on until received by Solomon, who mastered them. These experts had in hand remedies for the many ailments that inflicted human beings: from spells for binding a lover and charms for direct vision and winning at dice to healing fevers, coughs, scorpion stings, and discharge from the eyes. Wondering sages such as Moses, Apostle Paul, Jesus, Apollonius of Tyana, Honi the Circle Drawer, and Plotinus, among numerous others, were endowed with power to exorcise demons, heal the sick, raise the dead, and bring an end to drought. These ritual experts had been gifted from on high and given access to a higher spirituality. Because they were powerful, ordinary mortals sought them out so as to receive from them what they desired most—a hedge against a hostile environment and union with the gods.

Magic was not the exclusive reserve of the specialist but was inclusive of all who wished to avail themselves of it. The literature of antiquity is extensive and documents an astonishing array of techniques and rituals designed to assist humans in their quest to communicate with divine beings. Recitation of prayers, fasting, meditation, abstention from certain kinds of foods, staring at fixed points, hyperventilating, bellowing, and using the body to achieve altered states of consciousness were just a few of them. A common desire of mortals was to seek union with the gods in order to achieve direct vision, heightened awareness, foreknowledge, and memory. On other occasions, mortals yearned to ascend into heaven as an enquirer and behold the secrets of the universe. Or, they longed for encounters with the divine for the purpose of being imbued with a god-like nature. Remarkable prayers were part of the repertoire for encounters with the divine. Prayers guided and protected the initiate from the advance of hostile gods angered by mere mortals daring to trespass on their territory. Proper preparation was absolutely essential because direct encounters with deities were fraught with danger.

As in the ancient world, success and health are important for many in today's world. So also is mediating the celestial powers for the benefit of humans. In many parts of the world today, ritual performances to achieve success are alive and well. Powerful patrons of the supernatural, such as voodoo priests, shamans, witch doctors, medicine men, clairvoyants, preachers, and priests continue to ply the trade of mediating the sacred for anxious and troubled human beings. These ritual experts of sacred power are common in Eurasia, the Americas, and Australia. Shamans worldwide engage in vision quests and seek internal transformation, cleansing, and reconnection with the spirits of the earth and universe in order to facilitate the healing of body, mind, and spirit. Moreover, rituals integral to spiritual magic, such as meditating, praying, reciting mantras, staring at fixed points, abstaining from food, and centering the self, continue to be of significance to humans. These rituals frequently trigger ecstatic states in which one becomes possessed by the spirit and enters into a mystical union with the gods. States of spirit possession and mystical union with the gods are found in almost all known religions of the world and sought by both old and young.

A resurgence of interest in ancient and modern spiritualities is particularly noticeable among young people. Without the religious inhibitions and habits of adults, along with a healthy dose of curiosity, tolerance, and imagination, they are willing to experiment with spiritualities that depart from the traditional paths of religious expression. The New Age movement, Wicca, and Neopaganism with their focus on spiritual magic are but a few examples of current religious expression appealing to the youth of today.

It is during the transition from adolescence to early adulthood that a self-defined spirituality in youth begins to emerge. With the influence of family and extended kinship waning, and the influence of peers rising along with a clearly developing sense of autonomy, religious expression in adolescents takes on new shape. No longer obligated to hold on to the religious values and sentiments of the family, they favor a renewed spiritual vitality that suits them individually. Organized religion with its dogmatic formulations and staid expressions of piety during this period of increasing independence is exchanged for an interconnectedness with the universe in which other expressions of spirituality are actively sought. They are attracted to the multidimensional character of spiritual magic because it helps not only to cement a firm sense of self and identity but also to mold a spirituality that is in character with what that redefined self and identity is coming to be. Consequently, expressions of spirituality that focus on rituals of empowerment, self-expression, autonomy, and a connectedness with the universe are highly attractive to adolescents.

—Dietmar Neufeld

FURTHER READING

Betz, H. D. (Ed.). (1986). *The Greek magical papyri in translation.* Chicago and London: University of Chicago Press.

Dickie, M. W. (2001). *Magic and magicians in the Greco-Roman world.* London and New York: Routledge.

Janowitz, N. (2001). *Magic in the Roman world.* London and New York: Routledge.

Meyer, M., & Mirecki, P. (Eds.). (1995). *Ancient magic and ritual power.* Leiden, Netherlands: E. J. Brill.

MARY

Mary of Nazareth, biological mother of Jesus believed by Christendom to be the Messiah, Savior, and Son of God, is indisputably historical. She is, as well, a complex tapestry of history, legend, cult, theology, spirituality, liturgical feasts, piety, and artistic imagination. Mary has been the subject of intense devotion and dispute for millennia. In a universal way she can be considered part of the ancient goddess tradition of the archetypal Great Mother, like the Indian goddess Kali, the eternal feminine principle of life.

By the 2nd century in the Christian Church East and West, Mariology, the study of Mary, produced traditions in which the Church fathers idealized Mary. Mary—the New Eve—was viewed as the obedient female who reversed the disobedience of the first Eve, and makes possible the coming into the world the New Adam, Christ, or Emmanuel. History is replete with scholarly writings and Marian iconography, including paintings by great masters, Michelangelo's *Pieta,* popular devotions such as the 13th-century Angelus, the 15th-century Litany of Loreto, Hail Mary, and Rosary. The granting to Mary in 431 C.E. the title of Theotokos, meaning Mother of God, at the Council of Ephesus is but one of the many Church councils to theologically advance the importance of Mary.

There is a long history of Marian apparitions or visions of Mary appearing to ordinary people, such as the vision of Mary at Guadalupe, Mexico, in 1531 or Bernadette's visions at Lourdes in 1858 to the later 20th-century phenomena of apparitions of Mary reported in Medjugorje, Yugoslavia. The titles of Mary—Queen of Peace, Mirror of Justice, Mother of the Disappeared—reveal an enduring influence across generations, races, and cultures.

Contemporary critiques, articulated by feminists, find the patriarchal and misogynist influences in Western culture and religious tradition often provided a distorted vision of Mary. Passive female characteristics of submission, humility, and docility were projected onto Mary, and in turn, onto all women. Such representations offer an incomplete interpretation of both the historical Mary and the symbol that Mary is as a timeless model of courage, faith, and discipleship. Renewed interest in Mary, explored across religious and ancient spiritual traditions alike, is best exemplified in the title of the book *Mary Is for Everyone* (1997), a publication of the Ecumenical Society of the Blessed Virgin Mary established in 1967 for the purpose of enhancing understanding of Mary across faith traditions.

BIBLICAL ROOTS AND ROUTES

The search for the historical Mary takes its beginning point in the New Testament or Christian Scriptures. Little quantitatively exists in the books of the New Testament relative to biographical material on Mary. The Gospel of Luke provides most of the biblical material on Mary. The first chapter contains the story of the Annunciation when the angel Gabriel announces the news to the young teenager Mary that she is "blessed among women," having found "favor" with God. She is to conceive and bear a son and his name will be Jesus, Emmanuel, meaning "God-with-us" (Luke 1:26–38). The Gospel of Luke also contains the universally famous prayer of Mary called the Magnificat, a prayer of praise attributed to Mary in accepting the angel's message to her (Luke 1:46–55).

The birth at Bethlehem, the customary presentation of the child Jesus by Mary and Joseph in Jerusalem, cautionary words to Mary foreshadowing her suffering, references to Mary "pondering" what she hears in her heart, the story of Jesus being lost and then found preaching in the Temple, and the scene where Mary is seemingly ignored by Jesus (Luke 3:31–35) provide brief windows of insight into the mother of Jesus. She is either "near the cross" as Jesus dies (John 19:25), or, in the synoptic gospels—Matthew, Mark, and Luke—"at a distance" and not mentioned by name (Matt. 27:55, Mark 15:40, Luke 23:49). Luke, also the author of the Acts of the Apostles, places Mary in the Upper Room after the Ascension (Acts 1:14). There is a vast field of research open on Mary, and modern biblical scholarship has been engaged in renewed attention to Marian texts in the New Testament, such as those previously identified along with the infancy narratives in Matthew and the Woman in the Apocalypse.

The primacy of various texts and their interpretation divide Roman Catholic and Protestant views on Mary. Scripture scholar Raymond Brown has suggested that Protestants take their starting point on Mary from Mark 3:31–35, and Catholics begin with the Annunciation in Luke 1:39–46. In short, mainline biblically based Protestant traditions believe Mary's miraculous conception of Jesus through the action of the Holy Spirit and accept her revered position in being the mother of the promised redeemer. They consider that after the birth of Jesus, Mary and Joseph produced other biological children. Most Protestant traditions shy away from the kind of Mariology that marks Catholicism.

Catholic tradition builds from and beyond the biblical texts to hold the singularity of Mary as perpetual virgin and mother solely of Jesus, a chaste relationship with Joseph, substantive doctrinal and dogmatic teachings on Mary, and much popular piety and ritual surrounding devotion to and veneration of Mary. For example, the Catholic Church holds as dogma—a permanent article of faith—the Immaculate Conception and the Assumption of Mary into heaven. The Immaculate Conception was declared dogmatic teaching in 1854, highlighting Mary's singularity as "blessed among women," which enabled her to escape the claims of original sin at the time of her conception in her mother's womb. In 1950, Pope Pius XII defined the dogma of the Virgin Mother's Assumption, which teaches that at the time of her death Mary was assumed—taken up body and soul—into the glory of heaven.

Both these dogmatic promulgations were the climax of centuries of belief and provided post-Reformation clarifications about Mary that intentionally distinguished Protestantism from Catholicism. Since the renewals in theology and practice inaugurated by the Second Vatican Council (1962–1965), dialogue across Christian denominations and with other faith traditions, the development of feminist interpretation, appreciation for Marian devotion across cultures, resurgence of interest in the intersections of depth psychology and feminine spirituality, Mary, as the feminine face of the divine, continues to be the subject of intense devotion and dialogue.

—*Avis Clendenen*

See also Jesus

FURTHER READING

Carr, A. (1988). *Transforming grace: Christian tradition and women's experience.* San Francisco: Harper & Row.

McLoughlin, W., & Pinnock, J. (1997). *Mary is for everyone.* Herefordshire, England: Gracewing/Fowler Wright Books.

Richo, D. (2001). *Mary within: A Jungian contemplation of her titles and powers.* New York: Crossroad.

Warner, M. (1976). *Alone of all her sex: The myth and the cult of the virgin Mary.* New York: Knopf.

MEAD, GEORGE HERBERT

George Herbert Mead was a social psychologist who taught philosophy at the University of Chicago from 1894 until his unexpected death at age 68. Mead never published a book and wrote few major papers. Thus, most of what we know of him was pulled together after his death by students from collected notes.

Mead theorized that the mind and the self were developed as people interact with each other, sharing meaning through language and gestures. However, because any particular person might interpret the meaning of words or gestures differently, people might internalize different perceptions and meanings. This capacity to understand the symbol or meaning behind a word or a gesture made humans distinct from the animals. It also posed an understanding of humans and their behavior that ran counter to existing explanations where a particular action automatically caused a predictable reaction regardless of how the action was understood.

To explain further, Mead has one consider the game of chess. When the first player moves a game piece, it calls out a response from another person and the two players come to share some common meaning of what the act means. In order for the second player to move wisely, she must then take on the perspective or assume the role of the first player, while simultaneously considering what her own next move might be. Thus, the second person has the capacity to become an object to her self. By so doing, the anticipated response of the first person now becomes a stimulus for controlling one's own action, and the meaning of the first person's act has in some way become internalized as one's own experience.

The equivalent of the chess game may involve a much more complex exchange of words and acts. Still, the intent is to arouse in others either the same or an antagonistic response to that which they have aroused in themselves. Thus, Mead believed that each person in the game had to carry within themselves the attitude of everyone else playing the game, a concept that he called the "generalized other."

From this understanding, Mead developed his notion of the self-concept. Through identification with others and role taking whereby we see through another person's perspective, we come to carry within ourselves the attitudes of others. On the one hand, these shared meanings allow us to participate meaningfully in society. On the other hand, they create in us thoughts and feelings by which we evaluate ourselves according to the social expectations of these various groups. Mead described the self as an ongoing dialogue between the "me" and the "I." The "me" represented the internalizations of the generalized other, or to say it another way, the thoughts and feelings one had about oneself that came from the way she believed people in particular groups regarded her. The "I" represented the ability that a person had to select, create, or choose an individual response to these "me" representations.

Mead's social psychology thus provides a way of understanding how religion, ritual, and symbolism, as components of the "me," may become internalized and play a defining role in one's self-concept. However, since the "I" interprets the messages from the "me," a person exercises some choice in how or if to develop spiritually and in the meaning he gives to religious acts or thoughts. For example, two teenagers may be raised in the same religious home. Through identification with parents, one of them may internalize their parents' faith without really ever examining her beliefs. The other teen may rebel against their parents, develop a role different than the compliant child and come to a very different set of religious beliefs and associations. From Mead's perspective, religion serves us best not by providing clearly marked theology by which to deal with God, but rather by extending the social attitude of everyone belonging to the same group to the universe at large.

The end result is a society built on something like perfect neighborliness.

—*Chris Kiesling*

FURTHER READING

Secord, C. F., & Backman, C. W. (1964). *Social psychology.* New York: McGraw-Hill.

Strauss, A. (Ed.). (1964). *George Herbert Mead on social psychology: Selected papers.* Chicago: Phoenix Books.

Mead, G. H. (1934). *Mind, self & society from the standpoint of a social behaviorist.* Chicago: University of Chicago Press.

MECCA

Pronounced "Makkah," also called "Om Al-Qura" in Arabic, which means the mother of all cities, the holy city of Mecca is located in the west of the Arabian Peninsula between Mount Sarawat and the Red Sea. It is the most important city for Muslims since it is the birthplace of Prophet Mohammed, the founder of Islam, and home to the Ka'bah (the cube), the holiest Islamic shrine. Five times a day, millions of Muslims turn toward Ka'bah while performing their prayers.

Each year, more than 2 million Muslim come to Mecca for *hajj* (pilgrimage). It is essential for each Muslim who can, to participate in the *hajj* at least once in his or her lifetime. A much larger number visit Mecca throughout the year to perform *umra.* While not obligatory, *umra* is nevertheless considered a highly regarded ritual in Islam.

The history of Mecca goes back long before the birth of Islam in the 7th century. According to ancient tradition, Adam and Eve, after they were cast away from heaven and after 200 years of lonely wandering, came together to Jaba Arafat (the mount of recognition), near the city of Mecca. It is also believed that Adam was instructed by God to build the Ka'bah as the first house of worship on Earth. Later, the Ka'bah was rebuilt by Abraham and his son Ishmael. Once the construction was completed, God commanded Abraham to climb a nearby mountain and call on mankind to pilgrimage to the ancient house "Al-Bayt al- Atiq," a call that is answered to the present.

Historians have also noted the commercial importance of Mecca throughout history. Strategically located at the crossroads of the Mediterranean, Africa, and the east, Mecca became a center where caravans carrying goods met and trade agreements were consummated. The Koran mentions "the summer caravan and the winter caravan" with thousands of camels carrying the goods of Yemen through Mecca. The Quraysh tribe, which inhabited Mecca for several centuries before the revelation of Islam, played a central role in economic activities, facilitating agreements, and financing caravans. These roles gave the tribe wealth and prestige among Arab tribes in the Arabian Peninsula. Yet, it was neither wealth nor prestige that explains the Quraysh legacy that lives today. Rather, it was the birth of Muhammad, Islam's prophet, that made the name Quraysh the most honorable of all Arabs.

Muhammad was born in Mecca in 570. At the age of 40, Muhammad received a divine message from God through Gabriel, as he was sitting in a cave (*ghar hir'a*) in a fountain of light (*jebel innor*) on the outskirts of Mecca. There, he was declared the messenger of God to all mankind.

Muhammad started preaching monotheism to his own people; only a small number of Meccans followed him, as the overwhelming majority opposed him. More than a decade later, Muhammad and his followers migrated (*hijra*) to Medina, a city located 200 miles north of Mecca, where they formed the center of the Islamic state. The Islamic calendar begins with this event, and is thus named the *hijri* calendar. Eventually, Muhammad and his followers captured Mecca. Muhammad performed *hajj,* died, and was then buried in Medina, making Medina the second holiest site for Muslims. Mecca today is home to more than 1.5 million Muslims descended from people who migrated from countries as far away as China and Russia. The Ka'bah remains the focal point of the city, surrounded by the holy mosque. The height of Ka'bah is 13 meters, while its dimensions follow: northeast wall, 12.63 meters; eastern wall, 11.22; western wall, 13.10 meters; and northwestern wall, 11.03 meters. It is covered in black material woven in golden Koranic calligraphy. Worshippers are seen circling the Ka'bah 24 hours a day, 7 days a week throughout the year. Approximately 1.3 billion Muslims turn to the Ka'bah for prayers every day. However, the Ka'bah itself is not the object of worship. The object of worship is Allah or God.

—*Lamis Al-Solaim*

See also Islam; Qur'an; Muhammad; Mosque

FURTHER READING

Epistino, J. (Ed.). (1999). *The Oxford history of Islam.* Oxford: Oxford University Press.

Nomachi, A. K., Nasr, S. H., & Nomachi, K. (1997). *Mecca the blessed, Medina the radiant: The holiest cities of Islam.* New York: Aperture.

Robinson, F. (1996). *Cambridge illustrated history, Islamic world.* Cambridge: Cambridge University Press.

Wolfe, M. (1997). *One thousand roads to Mecca: Ten centuries of travellers writing about Muslim pilgrimage.* New York: Grove Press.

MEDICINE

Religion, spirituality, and medicine share a long and eventful history. For millennia, virtually all cultures have turned to spiritual leaders to heal the sick and comfort people who are suffering. Since health, illness, and death were often viewed as the workings of gods and other spirits, it was natural to seek out the ministrations of those in the community with access to these mysterious forces. For vast stretches of human history, it was the priests, shamans, and mystics who were the practitioners of "medicine." In fact, it was not until 17th-century Europe when the Church formally relinquished its intellectual hold over the human body, that medicine became the subject of science. It then took another 200 years or more for biological principles to advance enough for the concept of disease to even exist. And it was not until well into the 20th century that the scientific medicine started to show convincing results.

A RELIGIOUS NATION

Despite the enormous and undeniable successes of modern medicine since then, the majority of Americans steadfastly cling to the notion that their religious convictions have a serious role to play in their own health. Medicine's rational explanations, devoid of any need for spiritual influences, are well known and widely respected, particularly in a country with the most technologically advanced health care in the world. Nevertheless, research indicates that most Americans turn to their religious faith or spiritual sensibilities when they or their loved ones fall ill. What accounts for this apparent contradiction? And, how do doctors and other health professionals—who have replaced the priests and shamans as the healers of society—cope with their patients' persistent faith in the healing powers of religion?

It is important to emphasize that most Americans do not choose medicine over religion or vice versa. To be sure, there are small minorities who completely reject the conventional sciences and embrace an exclusively spiritual resolution to all their problems, medical and otherwise. Conversely, there are those who subscribe to no religious faith or spiritual aspirations, and take a purely scientific approach to all their affairs. Most, however, choose both paths, sometimes simultaneously and sometimes in succession, often beginning with their faith in science before turning to their faith in God.

TAKING BOTH PATHS

When faced with an illness, usually a serious one, most people are drawn to both medicine and religion for a variety of reasons. First, despite medicine's numerous accomplishments there remain many conditions for which doctors have little or nothing to offer. Mortality from cardiovascular diseases like heart attacks and strokes, for example, has been steadily declining for the past 40 years or so. Even though there are many explanations for this trend, there is little doubt that steady advancements in modern medicine have saved many of these lives. Success in this area, however, has led to new challenges elsewhere. As fewer people die from heart disease, they are living long enough to develop other conditions associated with old age.

Alzheimer's disease is a prime example. As the population ages, increasing numbers of older adults must face this devastating illness, which robs its victims of their thoughts, memories, and personalities. While physicians have a few medications that they can try, none have proven to be very effective. Patients, and especially their families, are left to deal with an inevitable downhill course with little help from the "miracle" of medicine. It is no wonder that many turn to other more spiritual sources of support, particularly for a condition like Alzheimer's, which strikes at the very end of life.

Second, despite its scientific power, biomedicine has only begun to explain many of life's observable phenomena. Returning to the example of Alzheimer's, researchers have made great strides in discovering what goes wrong in the brains of patients with this disease. The hope is that this understanding will one day lead to a cure. Many people, however, suffer from illnesses that doctors cannot explain, let alone treat. This is because the scientific method favored by physicians, which reduces complex systems like the human body into its smallest components, is not well suited to the task. Doctors often have a difficult time with patients who suffer from chronic headaches, backaches, exhaustion, mood swings, insomnia, and other ailments that go undiagnosed and inadequately treated because their pattern of suffering is inconsistent with the reductionist approach. Under the circumstances, many patients suffering like this would naturally turn to methods offering a more holistic, and perhaps spiritual, perspective on the problem.

Finally, medicine and religion can actually be viewed as two ways of achieving the same goal. A uniquely human attribute is the capacity to appreciate the concept of destiny. We are not satisfied simply living for today, but spend a great deal of time and effort thinking about our future and attempting to control it. One attraction of a religious life is that it provides a sort of roadmap to guide us toward what otherwise could be a terrifying journey into the unknown. Rather than a series of chance events tumbling along without direction, our spiritual lives give us a sense of purpose and meaning through which we gain a handle on our future.

In many respects, medicine accomplishes the same end, but through very different means. One of the main reasons we seek the services of doctors is to allay our fears of the future. Using the scientific method, doctors collect information about our lives and use it to predict future risks. Moreover, if the future looks less than bright, they will intervene in an effort to improve our prospects. Put simply, both medicine and religion have the capacity to instill within us that quintessentially human necessity: hope. And for most of us, each alone is insufficient. Science, no matter how concrete and persuasive, cannot address all our insecurities. And, neither can religion, despite its profound meaning and inspirational reassurances.

GOD AT THE BEDSIDE

With so many patients drawing on their own spiritual resources, how do doctors see the connection between religion and the services they provide? It probably comes as no surprise that doctors, as a group, are generally skeptical about God's active role in the affairs of humans. While many physicians feel that they are "doing God's work," most believe they are doing so without the aid of divine intervention. This is not to suggest, however, that doctors have no appreciation for the considerable effect that religion and spirituality have on the health of their patients. A sizable and growing volume of scientific evidence supports the observation that spiritual lives tend to be longer and healthier than nonspiritual ones. Since there are many plausible scientific explanations for such an association, few physicians find cause to dispute this connection.

Disagreement comes not from the role that religion plays in the health of their patients, but from the role that religion plays in the health *care* of their patients. Physicians usually raise the issue of religion with their patients only when death is near and the services of a clergy member may be helpful. It is the uncommon physician who actively takes advantage of a patient's religious convictions in the course of her or his treatment and recovery. This is despite the fact that a majority of seriously ill patients, according to surveys, would welcome the addition of a spiritual component to their medical care.

Advocates supporting the routine integration of religion into patient care raise a number of points. First, if there truly is a well-founded connection between a person's religious faith and his or her health, it would be irresponsible for physicians to ignore this valuable piece of information. Everyone would quickly find fault with a physician, for example, who did not ask every one of his or her patients if they smoked, drank alcohol, took drugs, or practiced unsafe sex, all of which have a direct impact on health and safety. Why should a patient's religious beliefs and practices be viewed any differently? Second, even if there were no convincing association between religion and health, it is unreasonable, and even arrogant, to expect medical science to effectively handle all the existential issues raised by a serious illness. Ignoring such spiritual crises would be tantamount to abandoning patients at their most vulnerable moments. Asking a member of the clergy to fulfill this role is certainly appropriate, but it does not abrogate the responsibility of physicians to be there for their patients. Finally, even if an illness is not life threatening, what is the harm of praying with a patient who requests it?

Conscientious physicians do many things for their patients, even if they do not directly contribute to a health outcome. Listening to patients well beyond what is necessary to make a diagnosis, for example, is a standard part of the compassionate practice of medicine. Physicians endeavor to do this (if given the time) because it serves the patient in the end by fostering a more therapeutic patient–physician relationship, among other benefits. Why would engaging patients' spiritual lives—even just politely acknowledging their prayers—be any different?

Physicians reluctant to incorporate religion into their practices counter with a variety of concerns. First, even if they would like to provide spiritual support, they lack the expertise to do so. Medical students receive no formal training in religious or spiritual counseling, and therefore, are not competent to discuss such issues with their patients. Just as a pastor or rabbi would never consider removing a gallbladder or setting a fracture, it would be dangerously irresponsible for physicians to minister to their patients' spiritual needs. Second, these physicians are extremely reluctant to give even the impression of a legitimate connection between a patient's condition and his or her religious views.

Unless done with utmost sensitivity, a policy of interjecting religion in the context of an illness risks blaming patients for their current misfortune. Patients may wrongfully assume that had they been more religiously faithful, they would have remained in good health. Even more alarming, a religiously zealous physician may send subtle signals that membership in his or her particular denomination would have benefited the patient. Finally, there is the issue of integrity. Many physicians pride themselves on being honest and forthright with all their patients, and feel uncomfortable compromising their own values or beliefs. They may find it ethically objectionable to feign a mutual interest in their patient's religious life when in fact they subscribe to a different religion or no religion at all.

Religion and medicine, whose pursuits were once indistinguishable, have long since endured an uneasy relationship. Even additional research further solidifying a connection between spirituality and health will not be enough to bring the two sides back together in the unified service of patients. Many other issues must be addressed before physicians willingly invite God to join them on their hospital rounds. Despite this reticence, Americans are, and will likely remain, one of the most religious people on Earth, and we should not expect medical science alone to ever address the most vexing aspects of being sick. For all its remarkable accomplishments, modern medicine has yet to inspire enough faith to sustain our hope for the future.

—Richard Glickman-Simon

FURTHER READING

Kaptchuk, T. J., & Eisenberg, D. M. (1998). The persuasive appeal of alternative medicine. *Annals of Internal Medicine, 129*(12), 1061–1065.

Koenig, H. G., McCullough, M. E, & Larson, D. B. (2001). *Handbook of religion and health.* Oxford, UK: Oxford University Press.

Matthews, D. A., McCullough, M. E., Larson, D. B., Koenig, H. G., Swyers, J. P., & Milano, M. G. (1998). Religious commitment and health status: a review of the research and implications for family medicine. *Archives of Family Medicine, 7*(2), 118–124.

Mueller, P. S., Plevak, D. J., & Rummans, T. A. (2001). Religious involvement, spirituality, and medicine: implications for clinical practice. *Mayo Clinic Proceedings 76*(12), 1225–1235.

Post, S. G., Puchalski, C. M., & Larson, D. B. (2000). Physicians and patient spirituality: professional boundaries, competency, and ethics. *Annals of Internal Medicine, 132*(7), 578–583.

MEDITATION

There is a story about a young Hindu man named Ratnadatta who grew up in a city in Northern India. Ratnadatta's father, a wealthy merchant, was a Buddhist devotee. Ratnadatta was ashamed of his father's religion and criticized it on many occasions. His father objected that both Hinduism and Buddhism teach the importance of compassion and controlling the mind, so his son's criticisms were unwarranted. Ratnadatta would not listen. The father eventually told the king of the ongoing argument with his son. The king, who supported the religions of all his subjects, hatched a plan. He informed the son that he had been judged guilty of a crime and would be executed in 1 month. Ratnadatta spent the next 2 months worrying about his impending doom and could neither eat nor sleep. At the end of 2 months, he was brought before the king. The king told him that he would not be executed, and that he had pronounced the sentence so that Ratnadatta would learn fear of death. Ratnadatta thanked him, and then asked about the path leading toward liberation from death. The king gave him a bowl full of oil and told him to walk around the city with it. He ordered a contingent of soldiers to follow Ratnadatta, giving them orders to behead him if any oil spilled. Now, at that time there was a festival in the city, but Ratnadatta was so focused on the oil that he did not notice any of it. The king said, "You should practice religion with the same concentration. A man who withdraws from outward distractions realizes the truth and will never again be caught in the web of actions. Thus, I have taught you the essence of the doctrine of liberation" (Somadeva, 1994: 68–69).

This story serves to illustrate two points. The first concerns the centrality of disciplining the mind for the spiritual quest. The second point is that techniques to discipline the mind are not the sole possession of any one religion, but are important to different degrees within all religious traditions. "Meditation" is nothing other than a set of techniques designed to discipline the mind. While this definition may seem simple, the variety of techniques and goals of meditation found across religious traditions vary widely. The following will shed some light on the major varieties of meditation commonly encountered.

When people commonly refer to meditation, they are usually thinking of a formal, usually seated, meditation in which the meditator attempts to transcend the ordinary world and attain a state that defies any attempt to put into words. The meditation techniques found in religions are actually broader in scope than this common definition would suggest. Meditation techniques fall into roughly two groups: meditations that attempt to transcend language and rational deliberation in order to calm the mind, and those that embrace language and deliberation in order to discern what is true according to the principles of religious teaching. In either case, the meditation techniques taught by a religion will always be a product of the doctrines taught by that religion.

TECHNIQUES TRANSCENDING LANGUAGE AND DELIBERATION

Meditations of the first category can be found in most of the world's religions. In most cases, this is the preferred spiritual practice for those who believe that the ultimate reality (whatever that may be) transcends all language. In many of these traditions, the approach to the ultimate state is broken down into stages. While the ultimate goal may be equally indescribable across traditions, the stages of meditation leading to the ultimate goal reflect the doctrinal specificities of the tradition from which the meditation springs.

Certain branches of Hindu yoga hold that the only reality is the Self (*atman*), which, it turns out, is none other than God. This "Self" is not, however, the self that we are normally familiar with. Rather, it is the unmanifested source of everything that we think and perceive. The self that we are normally aware of is actually an illusion. In these systems of yoga, meditation aims at cutting through the thoughts that lead to the false understanding of the self in order to arrive at the true Self. Since this true Self cannot be captured with words, the closer the mind can come to a wordless state devoid of any representation, the closer it will be to being aware of the true Self. The approach to this self can be taken in stages. An early model for the stages of the path can be found in the "four stages of consciousness" of the Mandukya Upanishad. In that text the path to the Ultimate is likened to four states of consciousness. The first stage is waking consciousness in which subject and object both exist. The next stage is the dream state, in which subject and object appear to exist, but are revealed to be illusions upon awakening. The third stage corresponds to the state of dreamless sleep, in which there are no subjects or objects represented to consciousness. The fourth stage goes beyond the subtlety of the third and is experienced only by practiced *yogis*. It is a state of consciousness in which no mental representation occurs at all, and is the state in which the Self/God manifests in its true nature.

Buddhists also have meditations that aim at reducing mental activity. In the story of Ratnadatta above, Ratnadatta begins to learn to meditate by focusing on a bowl of oil. By focusing hard on one thing, he is not distracted by the festival that goes on around him. Meditation on physical objects is a common starting point for Buddhist "calming" (*samatha*) meditation. The stages of Buddhist meditation, like that of Hindu meditation, will step by step remove more and more distractions until a state of one-pointedness and equanimity is reached. Buddhists, for the most part, do not believe in a true Self in the same way that Hindus do. They do, however, use very similar meditations to calm the mind and cut off its discursive activity. The goal of these practices is to stop the mental processes that ultimately lead to sinful actions and to see that there is no Self.

Similarly, Taoists held that the Tao (the "Way") is the source of all things, and that all things are in some way manifestations of the Tao. The Tao Te Ching encourages the practitioner to "embrace the One"—a statement that has been interpreted in many ways through the centuries. One early form of Taoist meditation sought to mentally withdraw from all manifestations in order to merge with the original Tao.

In Christianity, there have been several saints who have maintained that God or Christ is completely transcendent to the point that we cannot say anything about God. This aspect of Christian mysticism is usually referred to as the "via negativa" (the negative way) or "apophatic theology" (theology by way of denial). Examples can be found in the works of Dionysius the Areopagite, Saint John of the Cross, and Theresa of Avila. There are times, especially during prayer, in which the silence of God is experienced. Christian mystics will often refer to this wordless state of mind as "contemplation" as opposed to "meditation" which is more of a reasoned analysis. It is these saints (usually called "mystics") who describe a progressive path to attain union with that source.

In Judaism, the progressive approach to the indescribable is best represented in the literature of Kabbalah. The Sefer Yetzirah presents nine stages (called "spheres") and 22 paths that one may traverse in meditation to the indescribable Ain Soph (Kether).

TECHNIQUES EMBRACING LANGUAGE AND RATIONAL DELIBERATION

If we limit our definition of meditation only to those techniques that avoid language and calm the mind, then we will miss many of the other ways in which religions discipline the mind toward religious ends. The majority of meditations used by religions involve or even embrace language as a means of attaining the goal. Here it will be helpful to remember that the English word "meditation" itself comes from the Latin stem *meditor,* meaning simply "to reflect, muse, consider, meditate, give attention." The same holds for the Sanskrit word *dhyana,* which also means "attending to" or "thinking about something." *Dhyana* is the root from which the Japanese word "Zen" is ultimately derived. As noted above, Christian mystics used "contemplation" for mental calming meditations, and reserved the word "meditation" for meditations using language. So, what are some of the different ways that religions use language to discipline the mind toward religious ends?

Meditation as Principled Discernment

Meditation techniques that embrace language aim at cultivating a principled discernment of the world. That is to say that the meditations are to transform the way that we ordinarily see the world so that we learn to see all things through the lens of the religious doctrine. Perhaps the most basic of such disciplines consists of accurate self-reflection and evaluation. A good example of this can be found in Buddhism. A Buddhist practitioner who engages in *vipassana* ("seeing with discernment") or "mindfulness" training will systematically go through all parts of daily experience to see each thing as impermanent, suffering, and without a soul. Other meditations of this category serve as remedies for specific mental afflictions. For example, if someone is distracted by sexual desire, they are to meditate on the body as disgusting. After the meditator has mentally enumerated all of the tissues, fluids, and waste products of the body and mentally labeled each of them "disgusting," the desire for someone else's body wanes. By the same token, if the meditator is distracted by anger, she is to meditate on the feeling of compassion toward someone that she likes and then extend that feeling to all sentient beings. Unlike meditations aimed at stopping deliberative thought, mindfulness meditation is meant to be performed as one goes about his daily business. It is not reserved exclusively for seated meditation.

Similar meditations are also found in Christianity and Judaism. For example, for some varieties of Christianity, the awareness of one's sin is crucial to spiritual progress. Ignatius of Loyola describes the enumeration of sins as a formal meditation technique in his *Spiritual Exercises.* Even beyond such formal meditations, Christians are to reflect on their lives and are to discern and catalogue certain actions as sinful more generally. In this respect, the sacrament of confession not only serves as an opportunity for forgiveness, but it serves as an occasion for mindful self-reflection on the details of one's behavior. As a spiritual discipline, Christian reflections on sin differ from nonreligious types of self-awareness insofar as the identification of sin is guided by Church teachings on what is and is not a sin. Similar reflections on one's sins can be found in virtually every religion. In Judaism, the time of Rosh Hashanah is a time of reflection and penitence. Awareness of sins is also important in Buddhism, and plays a large role in Pure Land Buddhism (especially in Japanese Jodo Shinshu Buddhism).

It should be noted at this point that techniques employing language and rational deliberation are not necessarily the opposite of techniques that transcend language and rationality. Two examples will suffice. The first example can be found in Zen Buddhism.

In certain forms of Zen (especially forms taught in Korea and that taught by the Japanese master Hakuin), one is to meditate on a kind of spiritual riddle called a *koan.* The typical example of a koan is the question, "What did your face look like before your mother and father met?" This kind of question does not have a rational solution and yet the practitioner is to meditate on the question as if it had an answer. The strenuous application of deliberation on the koan produces doubt. The practitioner is to cultivate and hold onto this doubt until it becomes an all-consuming "great doubt." Finally, when it seems that all hope is gone, the practitioner somehow breaks through to the other side of the question and achieves a standpoint in which all things appear as they really are. The final experience may be "beyond words and letters," but the path to that experience was paved with words.

A similar process can be found in Christianity and Pure Land Buddhism. The meditations on sin have two purposes. The first, of course, is to become aware that one has done wrong and to generate a resolve not to sin again. The second purpose, which receives greater or lesser emphasis depending on tradition, is to prepare the soul for the experience of grace. When one realizes the magnitude and pervasiveness of one's own sinfulness, one stops trying to deserve grace. Only then does the true experience and meaning of grace become apparent. In Protestant forms of Christianity, the experience of grace after having realized the extent of one's sin is called the "conversion experience." In Pure Land Buddhism, this is called the experience of the "other power" (*tariki*) of Amitabha Buddha.

FOCUS ON THE DIVINE

Visualization

Other meditation techniques that involve the constructive activities of the mind include visualization. We all dream, daydream, and fantasize. Visualization uses the same mental function that produces fantasies and turns it toward a productive end. Instead of letting the mind wander wherever it will, the meditator uses visualization to construct a particular image, usually strictly guided by tradition. For example, Pure Land Buddhism holds that there is a Buddha named Amitabha who lives in a faraway Western Paradise. The meditator is to mentally create a picture of that paradise in detail, starting from its outer rim and proceeding to the center where Amitabha teaches. If the meditator works long enough at this visualization, then she may either go to that paradise in a dream or Amitabha will visit her in a dream. Furthermore, if one does this practice for long enough, Amitabha will come to the meditator at the time of death to take him or her away.

There are similar visualizations in Christianity. A good example of Christian visualization techniques can be found in St. Ignatius of Loyola's *Spiritual Exercises.* Just like the Buddhist practitioner, Loyola teaches the Christian practitioner to visualize Christ in a certain setting, such as at the resurrection, in the synagogue, and so on, and to put himself in the picture.

Names and the Power of Words

For many religious traditions, the words of scripture or the names of divine beings become the objects of meditation. The classical Hindu tradition held that gods have at least three bodies. The first body is what the god is in itself. Only rare humans can have any knowledge of this. The second body of the god is a body made of sound. This sound is not the temporary sound that we hear for a moment and is gone. Rather, it is a transcendent sound that is heard with the mind. This sound is made more concrete as it becomes embodied in the Sanskrit alphabet. The sound is finally made physical when one utters it with the physical mouth as a *mantra.* The more times that one utters the mantra, the more manifest the god associated with the sound becomes. In Hinduism, the practice of repeating the mantra of a particular deity is called *jappam.*

The belief that the essence of a deity is somehow contained in a mantra or in the name of that deity is also found in Buddhism. The most striking example of this can be found in Pure Land Buddhism, in which Amitabha Buddha offers his name to all sentient beings, so that all they have to do is to utter his name with a pure heart in order to be reborn in his paradise.

Western religions also employ meditations on the name or names of God. For Christians, the name of Christ is especially powerful, while Muslims will recite the 1,001 names of God. For Jews, the Tetragrammaton is especially important. In certain Kabbalah texts such as the Sepher Yetzirah, just as in Hinduism, it is the very alphabet itself that emanates from God and forms creation.

When it comes to meditations using language, it is sometimes difficult to distinguish the phenomenon of meditation from that of prayer, especially in Western religions. A primary example of this is the Rosary or the Twenty-first Psalm ("The Lord is my Shepard, I shall not want . . ."). Many people will recite the Twenty-first Psalm as a kind of prayer, with the exception that it is not a prayer insofar as it does not ask for anything. It is rather a statement of fact that the meditator reflects upon as she or he recites it.

Music and Emotion

Related to the meditations that use language are meditations that use music. Here it should be remembered that a meditation is a technique that disciplines the mind toward a religious goal. Here again, there are two ways in which music is used as an aid to disciplining the mind.

There are some religious traditions which hold that certain notes and harmonies actually produce effects on the mind. Pythagoras believed that all things in the universe moved according to certain harmonics. Confucianists held that music was a vehicle through which the gentleman could cultivate his virtues. Some Indian Tantric traditions hold that certain notes can actually awaken the spiritual centers in a yoga practitioner.

More importantly, music connects with our emotions. When we go to the movies, the visual image and the dialogue tell us what is happening, but it is the musical score that tells us how to feel about what we are watching. As human beings we all have emotions. For many traditions, what separates a sinner from a saint is not that the sinner has emotions and the saint does not. The main difference lies in the fact that the saint's emotions are directed toward the ultimate, while the sinner's emotions are directed toward the common. As such, religious music will often try to cultivate certain common emotions (usually love), and direct them toward the uncommon, namely the Divine.

Examples abound. Medieval Christian mystics are well known to have written beautiful love poetry with God or Christ as the lover and the singer as the beloved. The Song of Solomon is often interpreted in this light. Love songs are put to similar use in the Ghazzals in Islam and in the many Kirtans and Bhajans dedicated to Hindu gods.

Some traditions combine the belief in the power of the name of the God with the power of music to produce devotion. Some Christian sects will use hymns both to produce the emotions of joy and devotion as well as to utter the name of Jesus. In a similar fashion, Hindus of the Gaudiya sect founded by Caitanya in the 16th century (often referred to as Hari Krishnas) sing the name of God ("Hari Krishna") repeatedly to music, drumming, and sometimes dancing in order to produce a similar feeling of devotion.

—Joseph Walser

FURTHER READING

Somadeva. (1994). *Tales from the Kathasaritsagara* (Arisha Sattar, Trans.). New Delhi: Penguin Books India.

MEHER BABA

Merwan Sheriar Irani (1894–1969), who was known to his many followers around the world as Meher Baba (literally Compassionate Father), never sought the limelight. Most of his life was spent working with the sick, poor, and mentally imbalanced in India. However, his teachings and his service to humanity have attracted the attention of many Westerners since the 1930s. Meher Baba made three trips out of India in the 1930s and two trips in the 1950s. Although he gave discourses about spirituality and was always ready to answer questions from those who met him, he did not consider himself primarily a teacher. In what he called his Universal Message, Meher Baba declared: "I have come not to teach but to awaken." Many of his teachings were about love. "I have come to sow the seed of love in your hearts so that, in spite of all superficial diversity which your life in illusion must experience and endure, the feeling of oneness, through love, is brought about amongst all the nations, creeds, sects and castes of the world."

While in college at Deccan College in Poona, India, he experienced profound personal spiritual transformations. Instead of completing his studies, he began to teach the people who were drawn by his growing reputation as a sadguru (spiritual teacher). Several years after he began teaching, Meher Baba declared that spoken words were not what people needed in order to understand how to live a spiritual life. As a result, he began to observe a vow of silence. When he began keeping silence, he indicated that he would not speak for a period of 1 year. However from July 10, 1925, when he began his silence, he did not utter a spoken word right up until his death in 1969. At first, Meher Baba communicated by means of written notes, and then began to spell out messages on an

English alphabet board. On December 31, 1926, he wrote his last message, and in 1954, he stopped using the alphabet board entirely and relied on a unique system of hand gestures to communicate. Although he did not speak audible words, his followers felt that he communicated directly to their hearts. Meher Baba's real message was not given in words, but through an inner experience of love. Meher Baba said, "Things that are real are given and received in silence. . . . I am never silent. I speak eternally. The voice that is heard deep within the soul is my voice."

The central message that he communicated was that the meaning of life is that God is love, and the purpose of life is to experience oneness with God. Love is the force that produced the world and that maintains the world as we know it. He asserted "that God is the only Reality, the true Self of every finite self." Although this sounds a bit abstract, it boils down to the concept that every individual has an inner core that is divine (an inner spark of the Divine Flame or a drop of the Infinite Ocean of Love that is God). Other statements he made about love included: "It is for the sake of Love that the whole universe sprang into existence, and for the sake of Love that it is kept going." "God is love. And love must love." "Life and Love are inseparable. Where there is life, there is love."

Meher Baba's personal spiritual experiences gave him the knowledge and understanding of his own divine nature so that he could declare that he was God in human form or the avatar. He also declared that the only difference between him and the rest of humanity was that he realized his divine nature while other people did not realize their true nature because they remained veiled in ignorance.

He declared that his life's work was for the purpose of giving a spiritual push to mankind through his example and through the inner help that he could provide. "I am not come to establish any cult, society or organization; nor even to establish a new religion. The religion that I shall teach gives the Knowledge of life of the One behind the many. The book that I shall make people read is the book of the heart that holds the key to the mystery of life. I shall bring about a happy blending of the head and the heart. I shall revitalize all religions and cults and bring them together like beads on a string."

Meher Baba did not require any particular spiritual practices from his followers. Although his writings include information about meditation, prayer, and other spiritual practices, his main recommendation for achieving the oneness with God about which he taught was through remembrance of God and love for God. He described religious rituals of the major religions as being empty and not spiritually helpful. He did not advocate any individual religion over any other. He told his followers to follow the teachings and precepts of whatever religion appealed to them but to do it wholeheartedly and sincerely.

Meher Baba's own words sum up his teachings: "The only Real Knowledge is the knowledge that God is the inner dweller in good people and so-called bad, in saint and so-called sinner. This knowledge requires you to help all equally as circumstances demand, without expectation of reward, and when compelled to take place in a dispute, to act without the slightest trace of enmity or hatred; to try to make others happy with brotherly or sisterly feeling for each one; to harm no one in thought, word, or deed, not even those who harm you." "Start learning to love God by loving those whom you cannot love. The more you remember others with kindness and generosity, the more you forget yourself, you find God."

—Hugh M. Flick, Jr.

FURTHER READING

Davy, K. (1981). *Love alone prevails.* North Myrtle Beach, SC: Sheriar Press.

Haynes, C. (1989). *Meher Baba: The awakener.* North Myrtle Beach, SC: Avatar Foundation, Inc.

Hopkinson, T., & Hopkinson, D. (1974). *Much silence—Meher Baba: His life and work.* Bombay: B.I. Publications.

Kalchuri, B. (1973). *Lord Meher: The biography of the avatar of the age, Meher Baba in twenty volumes.* North Myrtle Beach, SC: Manifestation, Inc.

Meher Baba. (1971). *The everything and the nothing.* Berkeley, CA: Beguine Library.

Meher Baba. (1971). *Sparks from Meher Baba.* North Myrtle Beach, SC: Sheriar Press.

Meher Baba. (1973). *God speaks.* New York: Dodd, Mead, and Co.

Meher Baba. (1987). *Discourses.* Myrtle Beach, SC: Sheriar Press.

Naosherwan Anzar. (1974). *The beloved: The life and work of Meher Baba.* North Myrtle Beach, SC: Sheriar Press.

Natu, B. (1977). *Glimpses of the god-man* (Vols. I–VI). Walnut Creek, CA: Sufism Reoriented.

Purdom, C. B. (1971). *The god-man: The life, journeys and work of Meher Baba with an interpretation of his silence and spiritual teaching.* Crescent Beach, SC: Sheriar Press.

Purdom, C. B. (Ed.). (1981). *Meher Baba: God to man and man to God.* North Myrtle Beach, SC: Sheriar Press.

Reiter, Lawrence. (Ed.). (1982). *Love personified: photographs of Avatar Meher Baba.* North Myrtle Beach, SC: Manifestation, Inc.

Stevens, D.E. (Ed.). (1967). *Listen humanity.* New York: Dodd, Mead & Company.

MEHERABAD

In April 1923, Merwan Saheriar Irani, who was called Meher Baba by his followers, led a group of his followers about 6 miles out the Dhond Road from the city of Ahmednagar to a remote location near the small farming village of Arangaon. He stopped near a small shrine to the Muslim saint Gilori Shah that was situated near an old British outpost from World War I which had fallen into disrepair. Arangaon had been a regionally important place of pilgrimage as far back as the 9th or 10th century when a Hindu holy man named Vithoba had lived there, and where a small temple in his honor had been constructed. Several centuries later in the 17th century, a saint named Buaji Bua, who is credited with a number of miraculous actions, also lived in Arangaon. According to legend, Buaji Bua buried himself alive in Vithoba's temple. Even to the present day, pilgrims visit the temple in Arangaon for blessings.

Without revealing his reasons, Meher Baba decided to stay at the old British outpost with a few of his followers. The owner later donated the land to Meher Baba for his use, and the settlement became known as Meherabad, or, literally, the "flourishing place of compassion."

When Meher Baba arrived on the Meherabad site, there was a stone water tank on the top of a small hill (Upper Meherabad), and several small stone buildings at the foot of the hill across some railroad tracks (Lower Meherabad). The water tank was used originally by Meher Baba for periods of seclusion, meditation, and fasting. Over the years, other structures were added. In 1924, a small hut was constructed for Meher Baba's use in Lower Meherabad that became known as the Jhopdi. Meher Baba slept and often spent periods of seclusion in the Jhopdi. On June 26, 1925, Meher Baba declared to his followers that he would observe silence, beginning July 10. At that time, he said he would remain silent for a period of 1 year, but from the point he emerged from the Jhopdi on July 10, 1925, he did not utter a spoken word right up until his death in 1969. At first, Meher Baba communicated by means of written notes but also began to spell out messages on an English alphabet board. Later he dispensed with the alphabet board, and communicated exclusively by means of a unique set of hand gestures.

In 1927, Meher Baba had a pit excavated near the original water tank building. He continued his periods of seclusion in this pit. Eventually stone walls and a tin roof were added, and in 1938 the tin was removed and the structure was covered with a dome. At that time, Meher Baba declared that this building would be his tomb or *samadhi.* On the four corners at the base of the dome there were symbols of four great religious traditions, including a Christian cross, an Islamic crescent moon, a Zoroastrian firepot, and a replica of a Hindu temple. Over the door is inscribed one of Meher Baba's well-known teachings: "Mastery Through Servitude."

In Lower Meherabad, a free clinic was built, which continues to operate for the benefit of the local villagers and pilgrims. In 1927, the Meher Ashram School for Boys and the Hazrat Babajan Girl's School were opened. Some of the boys who preferred meditation to the formal academic curriculum were taught separately in what became known as the Prem Ashram. These schools continued until 1929. In 1937, Meher Baba opened an ashram for what he called "God-intoxicated souls" or Masts. Many of these Masts were not conscious of the world around them and incapable of caring for themselves. Meher Baba would wash them and feed them personally. In addition, Meher Baba often had programs at Meherabad and around India in which he would wash the feet of lepers and bow down to them.

Despite Meher Baba's dislike of publicity of any kind, he attracted followers from around the world during his lifetime. Since his death in 1969, many pilgrims from around the world have visited his samadhi at Meherabad. Large annual gatherings are held at Meherabad on Meher Baba's birthday (February 25), on Silence Day (July 10), and on the day he died (January 31). At Meherabad, there is currently a pilgrim center that can house 52 people, but because of the huge increase in the numbers of visitors from all over the world, a new pilgrim center is under construction that will house 600 visitors to the tomb of Meher Baba once it is opened in 2006.

—Hugh M. Flick, Jr.

See also Meher Baba

FURTHER READING

Davy, K. (1981). *Love alone prevails.* North Myrtle Beach, SC: Sheriar Press.

Haynes, C. (1989). *Meher Baba: The awakener.* North Myrtle Beach, SC: Avatar Foundation, Inc.

Hopkinson, T., & Hopkinson, D. (1974). *Much silence–Meher Baba: His life and work.* Bombay: B.I. Publications.

Kalchuri, B. (1973). *Lord Meher: The biography of the avatar of the age, Meher Baba in twenty volumes.* North Myrtle Beach, SC: Manifestation, Inc.

Naosherwan, A. (1974). *The beloved: the life and work of Meher Baba.* North Myrtle Beach, SC: Sheriar Press.

Natu, B. (1977). *Glimpses of the God-man Meher Baba* (Vols. I–VI). Walnut Creek, CA: Sufism Reoriented.

Purdom, C. B. (1971). *The God-man: The life, journeys and work of Meher Baba with an interpretation of his silence and spiritual teaching.* Crescent Beach, SC: Sheriar Press.

Purdom, C. B. (Ed.). (1981). *Meher Baba: God to man and man to God.* North Myrtle Beach, SC: Sheriar Press.

Reiter, L. (Ed.). (1982). *Love personified: Photographs of avatar Meher Baba.* North Myrtle Beach, SC: Manifestation, Inc.

Stevens, D. E. (Ed.). (1967). *Listen humanity.* New York: Dodd, Mead.

MEXICAN AMERICAN RELIGION AND SPIRITUALITY

Religious practices infuse the daily life of Mexican Americans. Including the foreign- and U.S.-born, Mexican Americans (also referred to as Chicanos) are the largest Hispanic group in the United States. Although their customs vary widely from generation to generation, 70% of Mexican Americans are followers of Catholicism, but in recent years, many have looked toward Protestantism for spiritual nourishment. Mexican Americans figure significantly in several Protestant faiths, including the Latter-Day Saints (Mormons) and the Presbyterian Church. Over the past 10 years, however, Chicano membership has greatly increased in evangelical denominations such as the Seventh-Day Adventists, Jehovah's Witnesses, and Pentecostals. Despite these trends, the religious beliefs of Mexican Americans remain predominately influenced by Catholic traditions rooted in Mexico.

When the Spanish conquistador Hernán Cortés landed on the coast of Mexico in 1521, he imposed Catholicism on the indigenous population. Priests accompanied Cortés into New Spain, the name given to Mexico under Spanish dominion. Once under the cross and crown of Spain, indigenous people struggled to maintain their polytheist religious practices in the face of fierce pressure to convert to Catholicism. The Spanish clergy, demanding that the indigenous people acknowledge only one god, viewed the worship of Quetzalcoatl (the feathered serpent) and Tezcatlipoca (the smoking mirror) as acts of heresy. While priests forbade indigenous religious practices, they also placed restrictions against the exercise of Protestantism and Judaism. As a result, the Mexican population remained largely Catholic, although Catholicism varied considerably among its indigenous rural followers. These differences occurred because local priests and bishops tolerated the combination of native religious practices with the rites of Catholicism. Today, the Mexican American laity adheres to a multidimensional brand of Catholicism that is both tightly and loosely connected to traditional practices. The changing image of La Virgen de Guadalupe (Virgin of Guadalupe, also known as The Virgin Mary) reflects this dynamism.

La Virgen de Guadalupe is the most sacred figure of Mexican Catholics. The popular story of how Guadalupe came to Mexico begins on December 12, 1531. According to Roman Catholic belief, the Virgin Mary miraculously appeared on four occasions to a Christian Aztec, Juan Diego, on the hill of Tepeyac, just north of Mexico City. La Virgen spoke to Juan Diego in the Aztec language of Náhuatl and identified herself as the compassionate, entirely and ever virgin, Guadalupe. Juan Diego sought out Bishop Juan de Zumárraga to convey the miraculous sighting and to inform him of La Virgen's desire to have a basilica built in her honor. After thrice dismissing the humble peasant's apparition as imaginary, Bishop Zumárraga urged Juan Diego to request from La Virgen an infallible sign of her presence.

Juan Diego's fourth encounter with La Virgen proved the last, as the Blessed Mother provided the humble peasant with proof of Her identity. Five-petal, bi-colored Castilian roses adorned a portrait of La Virgen on Juan Diego's *tilma,* a cloak made of cactus fibers. As Juan Diego unwrapped his tilma for Bishop Zumárraga, roses tumbled to the clergyman's feet and suddenly the sacred portrait of the Ever Virgin Holy Mary appeared. Nearly 200 years after the miraculous event, the Basílica de Guadalupe was dedicated in 1709 in Mexico City. Five hundred years later, Pope John Paul II canonized Juan Diego acknowledging the humble peasant's wondrous witnessing of La Virgen. Mexicans in the United States and Mexico commemorate the apparition of the Blessed Mother with feasts, pilgrimages, and prayers on December 12.

The image of La Virgen de Guadalupe remains significant in the religious and spiritual life of Mexican Americans. However, the portrait of the Blessed Mother has changed from her original likeness. Chicana artists reimaged La Virgen as a feminist symbol of womanhood. Inspired by the Chicano and feminist social movements of the 1960s and 1970s, artist Yolanda López fashioned the Virgin Mary as an independent Mexican American woman. López's most famous painting of the Blessed Mother, "Portrait of the Artist as the Virgin of Guadalupe," represents La Virgen as a powerful and virtuous role model for Chicanas. Most recently, digital artist Alma López recast the image of the sacred Virgin and the angel Gabriel as two modern Chicanas uninhibited by nudity and religious convention in her work, "Our Lady." Nonetheless, the López renderings of La Virgen de Guadalupe remind us that the Chicano experience is a constant interplay between American and Mexican cultural dynamics.

Mexican American Catholics celebrate a multitude of holidays throughout the year. Las Posadas marks the beginning of the Christmas season with 9 days of celebrations, called the "novena" or 9 days before the Nativity. From December 16 to December 24, *posada* (the inn) observances reenact Mary and Joseph's difficult sojourn from Nazareth to Bethlehem in search of shelter. Children figure prominently in these rituals. At dusk, a small child dressed as an angel leads a procession of *peregrinos* (pilgrims) in a search for the posada. Small statues of Joseph and Mary usually carried by teenagers accompany the house-to-house quest for refuge. While the pilgrims request lodging in three different houses, only one will provide shelter. Each observance ends in prayer and song at a Nativity scene. The last posada signifies the beginning of Jesus' birth. Christmas Eve or *la nochebuena* commonly includes the gathering of family and friends, the opening of gifts, and the attending a *misa de gallo* (rooster's mass). This mass's name is in honor of a rooster that crowed to announce the birth of Jesus. After mass, all enjoy *tamales, buñuelos, churros,* and *chocolate caliente* into the early morning of Christmas day or El Día de Navidad.

Mexican Americans continue their observance of Christ's life into the New Year. The end of the calendar year on December 31 is marked with a mass to give thanks for God's grace, while prayers beseech blessings for the New Year. On January 6, the Day of the Wise Men or El Día de los Reyes, children reflect on the virtues of gratitude while learning about compassion toward animals. Traditionally, Mexican children also receive Christmas gifts on January 6 just as the Three Wise Men brought gifts to the baby Jesus. The evening prior, children place straw in their shoes for the Wise Men's camels only to awaken to them filled with candy and toys.

Spring observances of the resurrection of Christ begin with Miércoles de Cenizas or Ash Wednesday. On this holy day of obligation, parishioners attend mass and receive ashes on their forehead in the shape of a cross as a symbol of repentance for past sins. Ash Wednesday also marks the first day of Lent or Cuaresma, a 40-day period before Easter devoted to foregoing an earthly enjoyment in a show of devotion to God. Semana Santa commemorates the final week of Lent, and is a period set aside to observe the slaying of Jesus. The observance of Holy Saturday and Easter Sunday highlight the life of Jesus with a procession of Christ's resurrection.

Throughout the year, Mexican Americans commemorate the life of Christ on Earth while celebrating those people who have passed into heaven. The Day of the Dead marks the Mexican American observance of death in life, a custom rooted in Aztec celebrations of the departed. Five hundred years ago, the Aztec month of Miccailhuitontli recognized the deaths of children. Today, El Día de los Muertos celebrations vary greatly in custom, but all ceremonies mark the passing of the deceased with colorful altars of remembrance on November 1 and 2. The first day of the celebration, which falls on All Saints Day, recounts the memory of departed infants and children, often referred to as *angelitos* or little angels. All Souls Day or November 2 is a time of remembrance for those who have passed away as adults. During these two days, relatives visit, clean, and adorn gravesites or build altars to the memory of the dead. Altars and gravesites, decorated with *papel picado* (perforated paper), candles, photographs, and marigold or chrysanthemum flowers, accompany the favorite foods and beverages of the deceased. Artists' use of the *calavera* or skull in life-like animation reflects the playfulness of the dead and their frolic among the living. The observances of El Día de los Muertos in the United States remind us that religious practices and art expression, like the Mexican American people themselves, are transnational in nature.

Forces in both the United States and Mexico have shaped the religious practices of Chicanos. While the steady stream of Mexican immigrants remains 88% Catholic, 23% of all Mexican Americans are Protestant. When second- and third-generation Chicanos leave the Catholic Church, many choose to worship at evangelical churches, especially the Pentecostal faith. The history of Mexican American Pentecostals goes back to early 20th-century Texas where Francisco Olazábal (1886–1937) began to hold revival campaigns in 1917. In 1918, Olazábal founded his own church in El Paso as more Spanish-speaking people converted to Pentecostalism. Although there is a wide spectrum in practice and doctrine, in general Pentecostals believe in the gifts of the Holy Spirit (charismata) and the Spirit baptism. Pentecostal denominations with large Hispanic memberships include the Assemblies of God, the Church of God in Christ, and the United Pentecostal Church. These churches attract many Mexican Americans into membership because of the high rate of Latino clerical leadership, an emphasis on Hispanic culture, and programs that serve the needs of immigrants, youth, and women.

Church participation makes up the core of Mexican family and community life in the United States. Despite their theological differences, Protestants and Catholics share similar philosophical and moral opinions that may serve as the basis for national political participation. Issues such as immigrant rights, the debate on abortion, and clerical reform of the Roman Catholic Church highlight the role of religion in the shaping of the Mexican American civic voice.

—Grace Peña Delgado

See also Catholicism

FURTHER READING

Andersson, D. (2001). *The Virgin and the dead: The Virgin of Guadalupe and the Day of the Dead in the construction of Mexican identities.* Göteborg, Sweden: Institutionen för religionsvetenskap, Göteborgs universitet.

Castillo, A. (1997). *Goddess of the Americas: Writings on the Virgin of Guadalupe.* New York: Riverhead Books.

Dolan, J. P., & Hinojosa, G. M. (1994). *Mexican Americans and the Catholic Church, 1900–1965.* South Bend, IN: University of Notre Dame Press.

Dunnington, J. O. (1997). *Viva Guadalupe! The Virgin in New Mexican popular art.* Santa Fe: Museum of New Mexico Press.

Espinosa, G., Elizonda, V., & Miranda, J. (2003). Hispanic churches in American public life: summary and findings. *Interim Reports, 2,* 1–29.

Maldonado, D. (2001). *Crossing Guadalupe Street: Growing up Hispanic and Protestant.* Albuquerque: University of New Mexico Press.

Matovina, T., & Poyo, G. E. (Eds.). (2000). *Presente! U.S. Latino Catholics from colonial origins to the present.* Maryknoll, NY: Orbis Books.

Ochoa, M. (2003). *Creative collectives: Chicana painters working in community.* Albuquerque: University of New Mexico Press.

Pulido, A. L. (2000). *The sacred world of the Penitentes.* Washington, DC: Smithsonian Press.

Sanchez-Walsh, A. (2003). *Latino Pentecostal identity: Evangelical faith, self, and society.* New York: Columbia University Press.

U.S. Census Bureau. (2000). Hispanic population in the United States: March 2000. *Current Population Reports.* Washington, DC.

MINDFULNESS

Mindfulness refers to the energy inherent in all people to bring their full awareness to any particular thing. Some people are led to develop their mindfulness in order to live more centered, less stressful lives. For others, mindfulness is a spiritual practice, a means of seeing more deeply into themselves and into all of life.

The Buddha (560 B.C.E.–480 B.C.) gave many discourses describing how mindfulness could be cultivated through various practices. Today, mindfulness (or meditation) practices are taught by ordained clergy of many spiritual traditions, by lay meditation practitioners, and by educators and health professionals. These practices have become important activators of spiritual and religious development for many who practice them.

Vietnamese Zen master Thich Nhat Hanh, author of the influential work on mindfulness, *The Miracle of Mindfulness,* equates mindfulness with living fully in the present moment. To do so, individuals must do two things—in essence, stop and smell the roses. That is, first people need to stop their mind's tendency to constantly review the past and anticipate the future, and simply rest in the here and now. Second, they need to smell, look, listen, or simply be fully with whatever it is that is present in their particular here and now. Through meditation, mindfulness practitioners train themselves to concentrate their attention on a single thing, to develop "one-pointed attention." This special kind of attention is nondiscursive in nature, that is, observing something without creating concepts about it.

In his Satipatthana Sutra or Discourse on the Four Establishments of Mindfulness, the Buddha described methods for doing just this, being mindful of the body in the body, mindful of feelings in the feelings, mindful of the mind in the mind, and mindful of objects of mind in the objects of mind. Mindfulness of the body in the body denotes experiencing the body directly as opposed to thinking about it, thus the phrase "in the body." In a similar way, feelings are experienced directly, and mind or awareness itself is experienced simply by watching what is going on in one's consciousness (e.g., planning, judging, etc.). Finally, one can learn to watch the particular contents of one's awareness (e.g., plans, judgments, or sensory input like the smell of a rose) as they arise, change, and pass away.

Mindfulness is always mindfulness of something. In Zen and Vipassana (or Insight) seated meditation, practitioners use mindfulness of breath to support the development of states of pure awareness. Other forms of formal, body-focused mindfulness practices include walking meditation, yoga, Eastern movement practices such as tai chi and qi gong, and ritual dance including the Hawaiian hula and the whirling of Sufi Dervishes. In Buddhist walking meditation, the practitioner breathes in, taking a step, then breathes out, taking a step, maintaining awareness of each step and breath. In the West, labyrinth walking is a Christian form of walking meditation. Meditative walking differs from ordinary walking in that its objective is the walk itself, each step itself, and not a final destination. In yoga, probably the best-known form of meditation on the body, awareness is focused on both moving in and out of and holding particular physical poses while maintaining breath awareness. Yoga is used as a preparation for formal, seated meditation and as a meditation in its own right.

The mental discipline required to maintain awareness of the present moment over any length of time is significant. Most people find the support of others doing a common practice to be important. Courses and retreats often provide starting points for mindfulness practice. Eventually, individuals tend to seek out groups that practice the kind of meditation they are drawn to, or they start new groups. Groups are usually guided by the teachings and practices associated with a particular teacher or school of practice and may or may not have a religious affiliation. Having the support of a group and a strong mindfulness practice are particularly valuable when individuals experience strong emotions. These conditions make it easier for practitioners to embrace their feelings with the energy of mindfulness. This allows them to be with their feelings in a nonreactive way, to learn from them, and begin to transform them.

Mindfulness is not only a practice for the temple or yoga studio. It is a practice for all of one's daily life. Eating, washing dishes, driving to work, or any other act can be done with mindfulness, with full attention. There are Jewish prayers to be recited before eating bread, before washing hands, before taking the first step of the day, which elevate these mundane acts to the level of the sacred. Similarly, there are *gathas*, or mindfulness verses, recited by Buddhists of some traditions on commencing many daily activities, that serve to bring the mind into full contact with the activity.

Buddhists understand the world as having two dimensions, the historical and the ultimate. When eating a meal to satisfy hunger, one is hardly aware of what is being eaten. One is absorbed in conversation or in thought about the next task needing attention. One is living life in the historical dimension, caught up in one's personal story. By way of contrast, eating in silence, attending to the sacredness of each bite and each sip, as in Holy Communion, one may experience the interconnection of all creation that has manifested in this food and drink, experiencing the same activity in the ultimate dimension.

However practitioners strengthen their ability to be mindful, as they spend time attending to their own field of awareness, they begin to relate to the world and to themselves in a different way. Becoming more aware of negative mental states as they arise, mindfulness practitioners can receive them with more ease, even regarding them as opportunities for learning. Seeing how their experiences of the world and of themselves are ever changing mental constructions, practitioners may begin to see the interdependence of these constructions, and their sense of a permanent, separate self may begin to loosen. All the while, there are other insights to be had like the discovery of the full fragrance of a rose. Mindfulness and the practice of mindfulness and meditation can be significant activators in one's spiritual, religious, and life journey.

—Richard Brady

See also Buddhism; Meditation

FURTHER READING

Gunaratana, H. (1991). *Mindfulness in plain English.* Boston: Wisdom Publications.

Nhat Hanh, T. (1975). *The miracle of mindfulness.* Boston: Beacon Press.

Nhat Hanh, T. (1998). *The heart of the Buddha's teaching.* Berkeley, CA: Parallax Press.

Suzuki, S. (1970). *Zen mind, beginner's mind.* New York and Tokyo: Weatherhill.

MONASTICISM

Monasticism refers to the lifestyle of people who live in a religious community as they seek to mature spiritually and serve others. The origins of the term itself came from both Greek and Syrian forms of *monos* or *monachos,* which indicate singularity. In its earliest usage, the connotation was of a solitary ascetic life of religious devotion. In many circles, it was associated with those living a solitary life in a community of others seeking a similar solitary life. The primary example of this was the medieval monk who, while living in the community of a monastery, still had his own cell where he spent a good deal of time alone in prayer, meditation, and study. In Christian history, monastics were committed to what were known as the three counsels of perfection: poverty, chastity, and obedience. Both men and women pursue the monastic lifestyle, with the men usually known as monks or brothers, and the women as nuns or sisters.

There are monastics in most major religious traditions. One of the most famous monks is the Dalai Lama, the head of Tibetan Buddhist monasticism. Buddha himself drew up a set of rules, or a lifestyle guide for those followers living together in religious communities over 2,500 years ago. According to Buddha, one could not be fully enlightened without embracing the monastic life, known as the Sangha. The rule or guide for Buddhist monasticism is known as the Patimokkha, which is comprised of 227 rules for monks and 311 rules for nuns. These monastic communities were intended to interact with the rest of their community by providing spiritual counsel and teaching for the community at large. This service to community beyond the walls of the monastery is a component of most monastic traditions. There are various expressions of Buddhist monasticism, often reflecting the geographical context. Beyond the Tibetan monks, the second most prominent Buddhist monastics would be the Shaolin priests of China. This form of Buddhist monasticism also became the form in Korea and Japan where it is also known as Zen Buddhism.

In the Hindu religion, Manu, the founder of Hinduism, taught that males of the three upper castes could retire to a life of reflection after rearing his family. These monks are known as *sadhus,* and are noticeable because of their saffron robes. The monastic life in Hinduism is much more solitary, and involves extreme renunciation by which the monk gives up almost all personal belongings, any contact with women (including eye contact), any money or valuables, and all personal relationships. By its nature, Hindu monasticism is almost exclusively a male practice.

Christian monastics are more familiar to those living in the West. Monasticism began in Christianity in the 4th century C.E. in Egypt and Asia Minor. The first monks and nuns were hermits, but very quickly Christian ascetics began to gather in monastic communities. In Egypt, Pachomius started one of the first Christian monastic communities on the Nile River around 320 C.E. In Asia Minor, Basil, the Bishop of Caesarea, started a monastic community in the mid-4th century in the city to minister to the people there. From that point forward, monasticism became a very important feature in Christian spirituality.

In Western Europe, Benedict of Nursia introduced monasticism. In the early 6th century (529 C.E.), Benedict founded the monastery at Monte Cassino, which became the model for most of Western Christianity. To create a community of discipline and order, he authored his *Rule,* which became the foundation for all monastic orders to follow. In Benedict's *Rule,* he spelled out how the monk or nun would spend each and every day. He set aside seven times a day for prayer, which he considered the primary work of the monks. The *Rule* also spells out how monasteries should organize themselves, divide up the work, and relate to the rest of the world. In the West, monks and nuns were affiliated with various orders of monastics, each with unique ministries and ideals. The followers of Benedict came to be known as the Benedictines.

Other groups developed in the Middle Ages based on Benedict's *Rule,* but in the 13th century a new model for monasticism arose in Western Europe. The growing population and struggle to survive left increasing numbers of the people in poverty. In Northern Italy, Francis of Assisi felt a call to minister to these people. Francis initiated what is known as mendicant monasticism. *Mendicant*, in this sense, refers to begging. The Franciscans were known as a begging order in that they begged for their daily sustenance and that of the impoverished they lived with. Mendicants did not believe in owning property and so they did not live in a monastery as such. Instead they lived out in the world, and were known as friars instead of monks. They worked hard at trying to alleviate the suffering faced by the poorest inhabitants of Europe of their time.

Another mendicant group was born in the 13th century as well. The Dominicans were founded by a Spaniard named Dominic in 1220. The Dominicans are known as the Order of Preachers, as Dominic traveled the countryside preaching and begging. He also became involved with the Church's suppression of those deemed heretical, especially in southern France. Because of this emphasis on preaching and teaching, the Dominic order became the predominant source of professors in the first universities of Europe.

Monastic orders continued to develop throughout Europe. Currently there are well over 75 different orders in the Catholic Church. These include such groups as the Cistercians, Capuchins, Augustinians, Trappists, and Jesuits along with a number of women's orders such as the Carmelites and the Sisters of Mercy, which began as an order of nurses.

Eastern Orthodox monasticism played a very significant role in the culture of the Byzantine Empire. Eastern Orthodox monks provided both spiritual and legal counsel throughout the Empire. There was always a very close bond between the leaders of the monasteries and the secular rulers in places like Constantinople. Monasticism in Eastern Christianity was never as divided as that found in Western Christianity. Distinctions separating orders were less important than in the West. Monks were free to roam and settle in monasteries wherever they might find themselves. Most monastic centers of Eastern Christianity were organized around the rule of Basil written in the mid-4th century. To this day, Eastern Orthodox monks still visit the most famous of their monasteries on top of Mount Athos in Greece.

Monasticism has played key roles throughout history. Most importantly, monks and nuns have been responsible for education and the preservation of ancient texts, nursing and hospitals, orphanages, and other social ministries throughout the world. Although overall numbers have dwindled, monasticism continues to have a vibrant and active ministry throughout the world in such places as Calcutta, India, and in the work of Mother Teresa's followers.

—Gary R. Poe

See also Asceticism; Buddha; Buddhism; Dalai Lama; Hinduism; Catholicism

FURTHER READING

Benedict. (1998). *The Rule of Saint Benedict.* New York: Vintage Spiritual Classics.

Creel, A. B., & Narayanan, V. (1990). *Monastic life in the Christian and Hindu traditions: A comparative study.* New York: Edwin Mellen.

Dunn, M. (2003). *The emergence of monasticism: From the desert fathers to the early Middle Ages.* New York: Blackwells.

Gutschow, K. (2004). *Being a Buddhist nun: The struggle for enlightenment in the Himalayas.* Cambridge, MA: Harvard University Press.

Harmless, W. (2004). *Desert Christians: An introduction to the literature of early monasticism.* Oxford: Oxford University Press.

Henry, P. G., & Swearer, D. K. (1989). *For the sake of the world: The spirit of Buddhist and Christian monasticism.* Minneapolis, MN: Fortress.

Johnston, W. M., & Renkin, C. (2000). *Encyclopedia of monasticism.* Chicago: Fitzroy Dearborn.

Judge, E. A. (1977). The earliest use of the word "monachos" for monk and the origins of monasticism. *Jahrbuch fur Antike und Christentum, 20,* 72–89.

Laboa, J. M., et al. (2003). *The historical atlas of Eastern and Western Christian monasticism.* Collegeville, MN: Liturgical Press.

Lawrence, C. H. (2000). *Medieval monasticism: Forms of religious life in Western Europe in the Middle Ages.* New York: Longman.

Tsirpanlis, C. N. (1986). The origin, nature and spirit of Christian monasticism. *Orthodox Thought and Life, 3,* 81–95.

Wijayaratna, M., & Collins, S. (1990). *Buddhist monastic life: According to the texts of the Theravada tradition.* Cambridge: Cambridge University Press.

MORMONISM

THE ARTICLES OF FAITH

In March 1841, Joseph Smith—the founder of the Church of Jesus Christ of Latter-Day Saints—wrote a short statement in reply to a newspaper's request that he explain Mormonism. Part of his reply outlined 13 of the church's core tenets, which are now known as The Articles of Faith. While The Articles of Faith are best understood when considered as a whole, two in particular capture the essence of Mormonism: first, belief in Jesus Christ as the literal and atoning Son of God; and, second, belief in the modern-day restoration of the church that Christ organized during His mortal ministry.

THE ATONEMENT OF JESUS CHRIST

> *We believe that through the Atonement of Christ, all mankind may be saved, by obedience to the laws and ordinances of the Gospel.*
>
> *Third Article of Faith*
> (Intellectual Reserve, 1981)

At the very core of Mormonism, one finds belief in Jesus Christ as the Redeemer and Savior of mankind. However, in order to fully understand the Mormon conception of Christ's role and its centrality to Mormonism, one must first understand Mormons' "Plan of Salvation."

The Plan of Salvation is a summary of the origin, purpose, and final destiny of mankind. Mormons believe that all human beings are God's children, and that they lived in His presence before their birth into this world. In this pre-Earth life, certain differences distinguished God from His children. First, His children existed as spiritual beings who lacked a physical body. Because of this, spiritual progression would be impeded, as they would not have the opportunity to learn to let spiritual desires override carnal desires. Second, they lacked the knowledge gained by experiencing mortality and learning to choose good over evil.

Because of God's love for His children, He implemented a plan that would allow them to gain a physical body and experience mortality. This would, in turn, provide an opportunity for God's children to grow and progress further than if they had remained in the premortal world. This plan was taught to all of God's children in the pre-Earth life, and all were given the opportunity to accept or reject it.

Knowledge of the premortal life would be withheld from God's children as they entered mortality so that each could learn to distinguish between good and evil without the aid of a clear memory of their divine origin. However, in learning to choose good, it was inevitable that mistakes would be made. Sin would make God's children unworthy to return to His presence unless they were first cleansed.

The introduction of mortality into the world and the consequence of sin are illustrated in the Genesis account of Adam and Eve. By eating the forbidden fruit, Adam and Eve transgressed against one of God's laws, and were consequently cast out of the Garden. Thus they became mortal, and physical death entered the world. In addition, they were separated from the presence of God—a separation that Mormons describe as a "spiritual death."

It is important to understand the relationship between Adam's transgression and its effect on his posterity in Mormon theology. The second article of faith states, "We believe that men will be punished for their own sins and not for Adam's transgression" (Intellectual Reserve, 1981). Therefore, the fault for Adam's action is not shared with his posterity. However, the effects that Adam introduced into the world are.

The need for a Savior is now clear. As imperfect fallen beings, neither Adam nor his descendants could overcome physical and spiritual death. The only way for mankind to overcome its fall would be for a divine being to make intercession on behalf of humanity. Furthermore, because Adam's fall was infinite in its effect on humanity, this intercession would likewise need to be infinite in its influence. As Paul wrote in his letter to the Corinthians, "For since by man came death, by man came also the resurrection of the dead. For as in Adam all die, even so in Christ shall all be made alive" (1 Cor. 15:20–22).

Jesus Christ, being the Son of God and a perfect being, took upon himself the sins of the world. He thereby satisfied the demands of justice, clearing the way for God's children to be forgiven of their sins insofar as they believed in Him and obeyed His teachings. Thus, he attained the power to cleanse God's children and make them worthy to return to God's presence. Furthermore, because Christ was the Son of God through a mortal woman—in other words, both fully human and fully divine—He had the power both to die and to overcome death (John 5:26). As a result of Christ's resurrection, all of God's children will likewise be resurrected, their spirits reuniting with their physical bodies.

By overcoming both sin and death, then, Christ provided the means for Adam's descendants to be redeemed from physical and spiritual death. It is Christ's mission that makes God's plan of salvation possible, and for this reason faith in Christ is the foundation of Mormon belief.

CHRIST'S PRIMITIVE CHURCH RESTORED

The Sixth Article of Faith articulates the second central tenet of Mormonism:

> "We believe in the same organization that existed in the Primitive Church, namely, apostles, prophets, pastors, teachers, evangelists, and so forth." (Intellectual Reserve, 1981)

During Christ's mortal ministry in Jerusalem, He organized a church to ensure that His truths would be taught after His departure from the Earth. He called 12 apostles and gave them priesthood authority—or the authority to act in God's name—to conduct the affairs of His church (Mark 3:14–19; John 15:16). He also called an additional 70 disciples and gave them authority to preach His doctrine (Luke 10:1). Finally, Christ established ordinances, such as baptism, that were to be performed in a specific manner within His church.

The New Testament is a record of Christ's ministry in Jerusalem. Mormons, while accepting the Bible, also believe that Christ ministered to the peoples of the ancient Americas. The Book of Mormon is a record of this ministry. It covers a span of time from roughly 600 B.C.E. to 424 C.E., and its central event is Christ's personal ministry in the Americas shortly after his resurrection in Jerusalem. Just as in Jerusalem, Christ called 12 disciples and gave them the priesthood authority to act in His name (3 Nephi 12:1; 3 Nephi 28:36–37), instituted ordinances such as baptism (3 Nephi 11:23–28, 3 Nephi 18:1–11), and established His church with the mandate that it be called after His name (3 Nephi 27:1–5, 8).

A short while after the establishment of Christ's church in both Jerusalem and the Americas, Christ's teachings were rejected, His followers persecuted, and His church ultimately corrupted. Eventually, the church lost its priesthood authority, and, consequently the true church of Christ was lost from the Earth. Mormons refer to this period of history as the Apostasy.

In this way, Christ's church followed the biblical pattern established by Adam, Noah, Abraham, and Moses. Each of these prophets taught Christ's truth and was accepted for a time. Eventually, though, the prophets were rejected and the truth they taught was lost. However, it is important to note that after each rejection of truth, God called another prophet to restore that truth. Mormons believe this Apostasy was overcome, and Christ's true church restored through the modern-day prophet Joseph Smith.

This restoration began in the spring of 1820 in upstate New York. At the age of 14, Joseph Smith found himself confused by the contradictory teachings of different religions. One morning he went to a secluded grove of trees and knelt in prayer, asking for divine guidance as to which church he should join. In response to his prayer, God and Christ appeared to him and counseled him not to join any church. Rather, they explained that he would play a role in restoring Christ's church to the Earth (Intellectual Reserve, 2004).

In September 1827, an angelic messenger revealed to Joseph Smith the location of ancient records containing the Book of Mormon and commissioned Smith to translate them. In May 1829, John the Baptist, and later the apostles Peter, James, and John, appeared to Smith and gave him priesthood authority to act in Christ's behalf. Finally, on April 6, 1830, the Church of Jesus Christ of Latter-Day Saints was officially organized in Fayette Township, New York.

After Smith's death in 1844, Brigham Young followed as the second prophet and president of the church. From that time forward, the death of one prophet has always been followed by the calling of another, each of whom has possessed the same priesthood authority given to Joseph Smith, and has received divine revelation as to the leadership of the church and the instruction of its members. Mormons believe that, in this way, Christ continues to guide His church and communicate with His followers. In Mormonism, then, the church becomes a "living" entity. Simply put, the heavens are very much open, and God is in constant communication with His children through His chosen prophet. This belief is, perhaps, best summarized in the ninth article of faith which reads, "We believe all that God has revealed, all that He does now reveal, and we believe that he will yet reveal many great and important things pertaining to the Kingdom of God" (Intellectual Reserve, 1981).

—Mitchael C. Steorts

See also Book of Mormon

FURTHER READING

Intellectual Reserve, Inc. (1979). *The Holy Bible.* Salt Lake City, UT: Church of Jesus Christ of Latter-Day Saints.

Intellectual Reserve, Inc. (1981). *The pearl of great price.* Salt Lake City, UT: Church of Jesus Christ of Latter-Day Saints.

Intellectual Reserve, Inc. (2004). *True to the faith: A gospel reference.* Salt Lake City, UT: Church of Jesus Christ of Latter-Day Saints.
Smith, J. Jr. (Trans.). (2004). *The Book of Mormon.* New York: Doubleday.
Talmage, J. E. (1984). *Articles of faith.* Salt Lake City, UT: Deseret.

MOSES

Moses led the people of Israel out of slavery in Egypt and through the Sinai Peninsula to the doorstep of their entry into Canaan and the fountainhead of Israelite law. Jewish and Christian traditions say that God revealed the law (found in the Bible in Exodus 20–Deuteronomy 30) to him at Mount Sinai and on a plain in the country of Moab, now part of the modern state of Jordan. Indeed, tradition ascribes authorship of Genesis through Deuteronomy (except for the account of his death in Deuteronomy 34) to him. His leadership of the escapees in their travels and the high morality of the teachings ascribed to him make him a dominant figure of the Hebrew Bible/Old Testament.

Narratives about Moses include that of his birth to a priestly family in servitude in Egypt (Exodus 2–3). It offers a twist on the typical story of abandonment. His life was threatened by a governmental edict to slay all Hebrew male babies as a means of population control, but his family concealed him as long as possible, and then placed him in a small watertight boat where Pharaoh's daughter went to bathe. His sister Miriam stayed close by, and offered to find a Hebrew wet nurse (his own mother) for the child when the princess found him. When he was old enough to be weaned, he was taken to the Pharaoh's daughter to live among the royalty.

Moses broke from Pharaoh's house after killing an Egyptian who he saw abusing an Israelite. He married into the family of a Midianite priest, and assumed the life of a shepherd until God summoned him to the task of leading Israel from Egypt. En route to begin that task, Moses had another experience in which God commanded Moses' wife, Zipporah, to circumcise him (Exodus 4:24–26), thus reinstituting a rite that God commanded Abraham to begin. Jewish males were to be circumcised on the 8th day of their life as a permanent, visible sign of their covenantal relationship to God.

The most mysterious event prior to Israel's escape from Egypt was the Passover, during which the firstborn sons of the Egyptians died, but the sons of Israelites survived who had followed Moses' instructions to touch blood from sacrificial lambs to the lintel and doorposts of their homes (Exodus 12:22). The Passover observance features children asking about the significance of the meal and receiving instruction from the parents.

Moses, at times aided and at times opposed by Aaron, his brother, and Miriam, his sister, led the people not only out of Egypt, but—according to tradition—for 40 years in the Sinai, perhaps in the northern region around Kadesh-barnea, before leading them to an area east of the Jordan River, where they were poised to enter it under new, younger leadership. He died after seeing the promised land of Canaan from a mountain.

Moses' other contribution was the mediation of God's law on Mount Sinai. Many modern scholars debate the extent to which that law derived from Moses himself, but many would agree that he was responsible for some or much of the law (particularly the Ten Commandments) and came to be seen as the fountainhead of all law or *torah* (instruction).

The Commandments may be divided into two parts. The first four deal with how all people, children and adults, are to relate themselves to God: worship God only, make no idols, not blaspheme God by acting badly in the name of God, and take regular times for rest and worship. The observance of Sabbath, at home or in groups, characterized Israelite life, and may have been unique to Israel in the ancient Middle East. The other six deal with how to relate to other people: Honor parents, respect the life and property of others, abstain from sexual relationships outside of marriage, do not lie, and do not covet. It is difficult to imagine six rules more basic to human development and community life.

The most important commandment for the religious development of the young is the command to honor one's parents. Modern readers often understand it to be aimed at children, and it surely was. It was also aimed at adults. Under this law, people never outlive their obligations to honor and respect their parents. This lesson, learned young, is to last throughout one's life as adult children might end up as primary caregivers to their parents.

Tradition teaches that Moses received from God the rest of the laws in Exodus through Deuteronomy. In those four books, other laws pertaining to relationships between children and parents include prohibitions against striking or cursing one's parents (Exodus

21:17, 17) and against incest (Leviticus 18:12–18). Children are to receive regular instruction and play an active role in religious observance. They are to memorize and recite laws, and along with their parents bind small representations of those laws on the doors of their houses and to their bodies (forehead and arm) to remind them to obey (Deuteronomy 6:7–9).

In the absence of formal schools, almost all instruction, behavioral and occupational, is meant to come from within the family. The Mosaic law was and still is intended both to help shape the character of the children and to regulate family life in the community and before God as a people consecrated for life before God. Dietary regulations (Leviticus 11) also shape the home and bind together the community as places of covenantal sharing, distinguishing in groups from outsiders, and preserving cultural identity.

To this day, Moses' life serves as a role model to young people. For example, a typical curriculum of a Jewish primary day school might have grade-appropriate instruction taking Moses as a role model for everything from behaving with humility to keeping the commandments, staying physically fit, and making charitable contributions. He is also venerated in Christianity, although Jesus is seen as the new Moses, the new lawgiver. In Islam, the Qur'an portrays Moses as having received the same message as Muhammad (Sura 2:81; 3:78–79), but thc Jewish people did not follow it (Sura 6:83–89). Both traditions, however, look upon Moses as God's spokesperson.

—Paul L. Redditt

See also Judaism

FURTHER READING

Hermann, S. (1981). *A History of Israel in Old Testament times*. Philadelphia: Fortress.

Rowley, H. H. (1950). *From Joseph to Joshua*. The Schweich Lectures of the British Academy, 1948. London: British Academy.

Thompson, T. L. (1987). *The origin tradition of ancient Israel*. Journal for the Study of the Old Testament Supplement Series 55. Sheffield, England: Sheffield Academic Press.

MOSQUE

For an individual who observes a religion, ritual is the most indicative sign of the character, existence, and foundation in that faith. Ritual activities and their attendant buildings, clothes, and other ritual paraphernalia are emblems of each religion and for each member of a religion. Through creating shared symbolic expression, ritual symbols unify the faithful. In Islam, a religion deeply embedded in ritual, the mosque is not only central to Muslim ritual, but clearly identifies the Muslim faith worldwide.

To be Muslim means to be part of a worldwide community, as in the global participation by Muslims in daily prayers and attendance at the mosque. Although the Muslim ritual of praying five times a day (*miqat*) at daybreak (*salat al'asr*), noon (*salat al-zubr),* midafternoon (*salat al-asr*), sunset (*salat al-maghrib*), and evening (*salat al-'isha'*) does not have to be done within a single designated building (for Muslims are to pray wherever they are), the mosque has become the central physical element manifesting the presence of Muslims at any given place in the world.

Before prayers can be started, there must be purification of the attendant through ritual washing of the arms up to the elbows, the mouth, nostrils, feet, and ankles three times in succession. Within the mosque there are water tanks, urns, or fountains for this purpose. Muslims are required to remove their shoes upon entering the inner core of the mosque, for it is believed to be sacred ground. As Moses removed his sandals when seeing God at the Burning Bush, Muslims also practice this ritual as a submission and honor paid to God. In the mosque, the floors are laid with carpets or mats end to end, for Muslims are to pray in a clean place, free of defilement. Both men and women are to be moderately dressed. For women, this means that their hair and body are to be covered, exposing only their face and hands. In various countries around the world, Muslim women are allowed to enter the mosques; however, their placement within the mosque may differ. In Egypt, a barrier divides the men from the women. In Canada, there are separate rooms for women to pray in. The reasoning for the separation is so that the women will not distract the men from complete devotion to Allah. Once these rituals are completed, the attendant is purified in body and in spirit and is ready to offer prayer to Allah.

The *muezzin,* the man who chants thc call to prayer from the highest tower in the mosque, can be heard at the beginning of each designated time of prayer. The muezzin calls out to the community of Muslim faithful to worship together. In modern times, the muezzin uses electronic amplifiers, as cities and

Muslim populations have grown. The muezzin enunciates the following:

> *La ilah illa Allah* (There is no God but God)
> *Muhammad rasul Allah* (And Muhammad is the messenger of God)

The mosque is the ideal location for congregational prayers. Friday noon prayers, the Sabbath for Muslims, are generally well attended by the faithful who seek to engage with their community in worshipping Allah. The *imam,* a learned teacher retained by the mosque, leads the service in the mosque for all five daily prayers.

The architectural blueprint of the mosque is based on the same design as an Arab home, complete with spacious courtyards. The courtyard is a gathering place before and after prayer services for friends and families to socialize. The mosque has undergone minimal transformations from its original form, imposing a sense of majesty and the spirit of Islam.

The minarets that are located at the top of the highest tower on the mosque are the first eye-catching adornment. The star and moon crescent, the universal symbols of Islam, commemorate the moon and single star that guided the Prophet Muhammad on his *hijra* (night flight) from Mecca to Medina in 622 C.E., and marks the date from which the Muslim calendar begins.

In addition to sites of worship, mosques have also been used as libraries, schools, gathering places for armies, and as courts of justice. These additional uses of the mosque further emphasize the alliance of Islam with the religious, educational, and political aspects of Muslim life.

Moving to the interior of the mosque, one witnesses the cool, spacious ambiance in which nonrepresentational ornamentation adds a bit of decoration in an otherwise plain decor. There are no graven images or paintings of Muhammad or any of the prophets of Islam, as Muslims believe these to be a form of idolatry. The ceilings and walls are ornate with stunning arabesque motifs, while in some mosques surfaces contain a series of calligraphic verses from the Qur'an; both types of adornment derive their power and Islamic validity from their capacity to reveal the secret that the power and sovereignty of God are everywhere, as are truth and beauty.

Besides the rosettes, calligraphy, and other powerful art, the mosque is meant to be a place of worship or submission to Allah, and must contain nothing that will detract from devotion to Allah. There is no furniture within the inner sanctum of the mosque. There is only the *minbar,* which is a seat at the top of steps and is used as a pulpit for the *imam* to speak from. The most important area of the mosque is the *mihrab,* a small niche in the wall of the mosque. It points in the direction of Mecca and directs the way for Muslims to pray—toward the holy city of Mecca, the center of Muslim life and ritual activity.

Mosques around the world are the loci of religious development. Young children accompany their parents to participate in the daily prayers, as well as religious schools in the mosques. The mosque is also home to the religious interpreters of the Shari'a (law), who determine how to apply ancient knowledge to modern situations.

The mosque unites Muslims, as there is always someone of the Islamic faith praying in a mosque at all times of the day. It also is a place for community development, as after the prayers, Muslims gather for food in the courtyard, reconnect with friends, and talk about daily life.

Visitors may enter most mosques throughout the day; some people stay in the mosque all day. Families are generally encouraged to attend services and worship together, generating a warm and inviting ambiance. This atmosphere further projects the mosque as an emblem of Islam and the Muslim community.

—Julie Wieland-Robbescheuten

See also Islam; Prayer

FURTHER READING

Oxtoby, W. G. (2002). *World religions: Western traditions.* Oxford, UK: Oxford University Press.

MOTHER TERESA

Mother Teresa's life serves as a model of spiritual and religious development, and represents well how giving to others allows some to transcend self and achieve a heightened level of religious and/or spiritual development. Her life has had an immense impact on the spiritual and religious development of thousands of people around the world.

Mother Teresa was born in 1910 in Skopje, Macedonia. Her birth name was Agnes Gonxha Bojaxhiu. She was raised Catholic by parents who cared for the poor and the less fortunate. Her family's generosity was to have a significant impact on her life. She became engaged in religious communities as a teenager, becoming a member of Sodality, a youth group in her local parish. Her participation in this group and her interactions with Jesuits sparked an interest in missionary work. By age 17, Agnes was called to her first vocation as a Catholic nun, joining the Sisters of Loreto, an Irish order that did a significant amount of work in India. It was when she took her vows as a Sister of Loreto that young Agnes took the name Teresa after Saint Thérèse of Avila. She chose the Sisters of Loreto because of their vocation to provide education for girls.

Mother Teresa was sent to India where she taught geography and catechism in a local Catholic high school. By the time she was in her early forties, she became principal of this school. During her time as principal, Teresa caught tuberculosis and was sent away for treatment. On a train ride to Darjeeling, where she was to recuperate, Mother Teresa received her calling to leave the convent and dedicate her life to the extreme poor. She soon came across a woman dying in the street directly in front of a hospital. She stayed with the woman until she died and from then on dedicated her life to serving the poorest of the poor. She received permission from the Pope via the Archbishop of Calcutta to live as an independent nun. After a short training period with the Medical Mission Sisters in Patna, she returned to Calcutta and found temporary lodging with the Little Sisters of the Poor.

Her work with the extreme poor started in a slum school. She would also visit sick people at their homes to nurse them. Shortly after starting this work, former students of hers joined her in dedicating their lives to caring for the destitute and sick, particularly those who were turned away by the hospitals. She soon received Vatican permission to start her own order whose mission was to serve "the crippled, the blind, the lepers, all those people who feel unwanted, unloved, uncared for throughout society, people that have become a burden to the society and are shunned by everyone." This group of missionaries was recognized as the Missionaries of Charity by the Calcutta Diocese. To identify herself with the poor she wore a plain white sari with a blue border and a simple cross pinned to her left shoulder.

After almost 50 years of work, the Missionaries of Charity had grown from 12 sisters in India to over 3,000 in 517 missions throughout 100 countries around the world. Mother Teresa's work inspired other Catholics to affiliate themselves with her order. The Missionaries of Charity Brothers was founded in 1963, and a contemplative branch of the Sisters followed in 1976. Lay Catholics and non-Catholics began to enroll themselves in the Co-Workers of Mother Teresa, the Sick and Suffering Co-Workers, and the Lay Missionaries of Charity. In answer to the requests of many priests, Mother Teresa also began the Corpus Christi Movement for Priests. Mother Teresa's goodness affected thousands of people. She was one of the first leading figures to advocate and care for victims of leprosy and HIV/AIDs.

For her work on behalf of the world's neediest people, Mother Teresa received many awards, including the Pope John XXIII Peace Prize, India's Jawaharlal Nehru Award for International Understanding, the Koruna Dut angel of charity award from the president of India, the Nobel Peace Prize in 1979, and the Medal of Freedom, the highest award given to a civilian in the United States.

Mother Teresa was an active lobbyist and advocate for human rights around the world. Her dedication to protect the rights of the world's most vulnerable was made clear when, at the 1994 National Prayer Breakfast sponsored by the leading political figures of the United States, Mother Teresa challenged the audience to fight against abortion and, rather than abort babies, to give all the unwanted children to her care. Not surprisingly, Teresa received the criticism of many pro-choice and family-planning advocates.

Mother Teresa had suffered from heart problems and had two rather severe heart attacks in the 1980s. Later in life, she contracted malaria and was treated for a chest infection. She was hospitalized in the United States with pneumonia, and later hospitalized in Mexico for congestive heart failure. Mother Teresa died of cardiac arrest at the age of 87 in her convent in India. Her Order of Charity continues to serve the poorest of the poor in five continents.

Following her death, the Pope began the process of beatification of Teresa, which is the first step toward sainthood. Beatification requires evidence of a miracle occurring at the hands of the person in question. The Vatican recognized a miracle at the hands of Teresa in 2002 for the curing of a tumor in an Indian woman's stomach. Although there was some controversy behind the accuracy of the story, Teresa was formally beatified by Pope John Paul II in 2003 with the title Blessed Teresa of Calcutta. Evidence of a second miracle is needed for her to be canonized.

Mother Teresa's gifts to the world live on in her missions. Her life and work will continue to serve as a role model to people throughout the world, and as a leading example of heightened levels of spiritual and religious development.

—*Elizabeth M. Dowling*

FURTHER READING

Gonzalez-Balado, J. L. (1997). *Mother Teresa: Her life, her work, her message.* Ligouri, MD: Ligouri Publications.

New Advent Catholic Encyclopedia. (2004). Mother Teresa. *New Advent Catholic Encyclopedia, 2004.* Retrieved December 28, 2004, from www.newadvent.org/cathen/.

Wikipedia Online Encyclopedia. (2004). "Mother Teresa." *Wikipedia Online Encyclopedia, 2004.* Retrieved December 27, 2004, from http://en.wikipedia.org/wiki/Mother_Teresa.

MUHAMMAD

Muhammad (born ca. 570 C.E. in Mecca, Arabia; died there in 632 C.E.) is known in history for receiving the messages that comprise the Qur'an and for founding Islam. Both his life and his teachings serve as essential guides of behavior to Muslims and Muslim practices, which punctuate the daily life of the individual and the community with observances significant to the religious and spiritual development of children. These practices include in particular the fivefold daily prayers, charity, fasting, and religious festivals. While it is perhaps too much to claim that Muhammad taught overall equality between men and women, he did grant to women full human dignity, and advocated and displayed kind treatment for children, including orphans.

THE LIFE OF MUHAMMAD

According to tradition, Muhammad was born after the death of his father into a family of the Hashemite clan of the Quraysh tribe in Mecca, that is, into the tribe responsible for the care of the traditional Black Stone and its shelter the Ka'bah, the site of annual pilgrimages. He went to live first with his grandfather, who died when Muhammad was about 8, or 2 years after his mother died. The orphan was then reared by an uncle, a caravan driver. Muhammad was hired as a young man as an advisor and assistant to a widow named Khadijah, whom he married at the age of 25. He traveled on her behalf, encountering along the way Jews and Christians who influenced his religious thinking. He and Khadijah produced two sons who died in infancy and four daughters, only one of whom outlived him.

Becoming dissatisfied with the polytheism of his culture, he began seeking one God. In a dream or trance one night, he saw the angel Gabriel, who gave him the first of Allah's messages. These revelations continued, and soon Khadijah converted to his new way of thinking. He began his public career by going to the Ka'bah and reciting his messages. He first convert outside his family was Abu Bakr, a businessman. Since Muhammad's messages were fiercely monotheistic, the Prophet was not well received. He preached for a decade gaining a few other converts, but ultimately (in 622 C.E.) he had to flee from the leaders of the city to Medina, whose leading citizens had invited him to come as their political leader.

Revelations continued during his 8 years in Medina, but his relations with the city of Mecca deteriorated, culminating in armed conflict. Mecca capitulated, and Muhammad became its ruler as well. He died unexpectedly at the peak of his power in 632 C.E. without having named a successor. Sunni Muslims accept Abu Bakr as his successor, while Shiites accept Muhammad's kinsman Ali, son of the uncle who reared him, as successor.

Muhammad's life became the model for Muslim piety. (Sura 33:21, presumably not by Muhammad, reads: "Verily, in the messenger of Allah you have a good example for anyone who looks to Allah and the final judgment.") Hence, traditions (*Hadith*) about him developed to flesh out the lifestyle of a good Muslim. For example, in his home life, Muhammad was said to have acted as the servant of family members and servants, setting an example for his own children. Another tradition claimed that he was affectionate toward children, and a blessing he authored praised the man of modest means and a father of children as a champion of Allah, provided that he exercised restraint in dealing with his wife and children and laughed in their company.

TYPICAL MIDDLE EASTERN FAMILY PATTERNS

Middle Eastern culture emphasizes the importance of the family, which traditionally exhibited six basic features. First, families have tended to be extended, that is, headed by an older man who managed the common property; the extended family consisted of his wife, unmarried daughters, and his sons, daughters-in-law, and their children. In such a family, children would be taught and disciplined by all adults in the extended family. Second, families were patrilineal, tracing children's ancestry through the men only. Third, families also tended to be patrilocal—when possible, new families headed by sons lived with or near their fathers. Fourth, families were also patriarchal—fathers were heads of nuclear families, just as the oldest man headed the entire extended family. Fifth, families were endogamous, exhibiting a strong preference for marrying cousins (the father's brother's children) or occasionally half-siblings. The Qur'an limits marriage to other Muslims or people of the book (i.e., the Bible). Some interpreters have argued that *perhaps* non-Muslims who were virgins were acceptable. With both parents Muslim, the home would be the place where children would receive their primary religious instruction. Finally, Middle Eastern families have occasionally been polygamous. Muhammad allowed marrying as many as four wives, but required equal treatment of them all. (This practice has been defended recently on the grounds that some secondary wives were widows, who might have had no other means of support except prostitution.)

Modern life, of course, makes following some of these practices difficult, but Muslim families remain close knit and patriarchal. Polygamy, in particular, is frowned upon, but not forbidden, and the pilgrimage to Mecca is but a dim hope for many. Still, the Muslim home remains the primary locus for the religious and spiritual development of children.

THE TEACHINGS OF MUHAMMAD

Muhammad's teachings may be divided for convenience into two categories: theological and behavioral. Muhammad's theology, influenced by the Bible, was monotheistic, offering a stark contrast to the polytheism of many of his contemporary Arabs. The Prophet was the ultimate spokesman for Allah on Earth. One feature of his theology important for religious development was accountability. Muhammad taught that Allah would judge humans for their conduct. He denied that human nature is sinful. Hence, spiritual development consists of eliciting the moral behavior most natural to human beings.

In light of this theology, Muhammad instituted the Five Pillars (or duties) of Muslim life. The first was the confession of faith: "There is no Allah but Allah, and Muhammad is the Prophet of Allah." This confession requires the submission to Allah that the word "Muslim" (one who submits) denotes. Thus, Muslim children learn from their earliest days that they are dependent on Allah for their life and should obey Allah's commands. While some Muslims hold that merely repeating the confession makes one a Muslim, many leaders list conditions for making one a Muslim. One such condition is that the confession must be perfectly understood by the person making it. Small children might be able to repeat the confession by memory, but would be expected to learn well its meaning.

The second pillar is the need for prayer five times daily: at dawn, midday, afternoon, evening, and before retiring to bed. These prayers are not extemporaneous, but feature recitations from the Qur'an and provide children with daily reinforcement of the basic confessions and obligations of Islam.

The third pillar is almsgiving, which may take the form of contributions to places of worship, but also of help to needy individuals or families, sometimes made anonymously so that the recipients do not feel inferior to their benefactors. Such charity today may take the form of free or inexpensive medical clinics for the poor, especially mothers and children.

The fourth pillar is fasting. Since Islam follows a lunar calendar, the month of fasting (called Ramadan) may fall at any time during the year. It requires abstention from food and drink from dawn to dusk, as a means of disciplining oneself in Islam. While small children and sick people are exempted from this observance, adolescent children will be reminded during Ramadan of their need to submit to Allah's moral will.

The fifth pillar is the obligation to a make a pilgrimage to Mecca once in a lifetime, but for most children fulfillment of that pillar is remote. Recognizing that fact, Muslim tradition excuses those not yet of age from the obligation. Still, infants and small children occasionally participate with their parents, experiencing for themselves the blending of nationalities into a single community that is central to Islam. Pilgrims repeat the actions of the prophet by marching around the Ka'bah in the middle of Mecca's sacred mosque, and remember the foundational event of Islam, the flight of Muhammad from Mecca to Medina in 622 C.E.

The Muslim calendar is marked by festivals that point to the significance of Mohammed and the influence of his religion upon the culture and daily life of Muslim children. The first, 'Id al-Fitr, concludes the month-long fast of Ramadan; it is observed on the first day of the next month. It reminds everyone, including children, of the bounty of God. The second, 'Id al-Adha, usually follows 70 days later, and coincides with the events during the pilgrimage to Mecca, so that all Muslims at least theoretically are observing that basic ritual. This festival is as close as most children come to making the pilgrimage, but it gives them a sense of participation. The third, Muharram, is the Muslim New Year's Day. The fourth, Mawlid an-Nabi, commemorates the Prophet's birthday, while the fifth, Lailat al-Mi'raj, celebrates his ascension. These last two festivals provide excellent opportunities for teaching children about Muhammad and his teachings.

The Qur'an also includes specific injunctions of Muhammad about the treatment of children. Loyal Muslims are to aid the needy, beggars, slaves, and orphans. He specifically forbade taking financial or other advantage of orphans. Muslims are to be respectful and humble to their aged parents and protective of their children. Such instructions probably presuppose living in extended families where a man's parents and children were in proximity, but they retain their force in contemporary Muslim life.

Finally, one should note that the obligation to recite the Qur'an in Arabic has led Muslims to institute schools where the reading and memorizing of the Qur'an is at least a top priority, if not the only one. Consequently, the obligation has promoted both literacy and institutionalized instruction by teachers steeped in the Qur'an for Muslim young people, particularly for males. In these many ways (e.g., through the practice of the five pillars, the reading of the Qur'an, Islamic teaching and education, and participation in festivals), Muhammad's life has influenced and will continue to influence the spiritual and religious lives of Muslims around the world.

—*Paul L. Redditt*

See also Islam

MUIR, JOHN

John Muir is regarded today as an influential conservationists who fought tirelessly to preserve wilderness areas and wildlife from commercial exploitation and destruction. His deep understanding of and affinity toward the wilderness helped to establish several national parks across the country. He formed the Sierra Club in 1892 to protect the parks and served as the first president of the organization. In his honor, several natural sites have been named after him, including Muir Woods National Monument, an area of pristine redwoods, in Marin County, California. Muir's contributions to wilderness preservation has impacted the lives of many who turn to the wilderness for spiritual fulfillment and renewal.

THE DEVELOPMENT OF MUIR'S WILDERNESS IDEOLOGY

Born April 21, 1838, in Dunbar, Scotland, John Muir was the first of seven children born into a middle-class family who immigrated to Wisconsin when Muir was 11. His father Daniel practiced a hard and humorless Campbellite religion, which took a rational, simple, and straightforward approach to, and interpretation of, the Bible. While his father dismissed anything but religious or practical books as frivolous and impious, Muir's intellectual horizons were opened during early adolescence when he was introduced to Romantic poets from the neighborhood boys. Muir's interest in Byron, Poe, and Wordsworth expanded into travel essays, novels, biographies, history, mathematics, and philosophy. He became consumed with images of the wilderness set forth by the Romantics. From his intellectual curiosity (especially in the areas of science and mathematics) arose a desire to apply his newly acquired knowledge. At the age of 22, Muir was admitted into the University of Wisconsin, although he never graduated.

MUIR'S IMAGES OF NATURE

Muir arrived in Yosemite Valley in 1868 and immediately saw himself in spiritual partnership with nature. To Muir, all beings have spiritual strivings and he believed that it was in nature that the longings of the soul could be consummated. Muir was transformed by the majesty of the Sierra Nevada, which was the spark that drove his experiences, moving him into a life of passionate environmentalism and preservation.

Muir saw value in all of creation and the ecological interconnectedness of all things. For him, studying the wilderness was not a means to discover how to best exploit the natural resources available for use by humans, but, rather, was a religious activity. He would explore the mountains in ways he likened to devout Christians who read their Bibles. Like his father, he rejected orthodox religion and preached the Gospel according to his own beliefs; for his father, it was the Campbellite gospel, and for Muir, the gospel of the wilderness. Moreover, while his father believed that only God had the ability to redeem our sins through God's own divine will, so did Muir believe that human nature would resort to sin if one's spiritual education was neglected. Muir's solution to this issue was to get people into nature and away from civilization so that they could experience God as he experienced Him. It was through his prolific writings that Muir let the rest of the world into his spiritual life.

CONSERVATION AND PRESERVATION

Muir's conservation and preservation activities unfolded as a natural consequence of his divine images of nature. Having seen the effects of overgrazing by sheep and cattle in the early 1880s, he wrote that it could be estimated that nine-tenths of the Sierra hillsides looked more like the inside of a dusty corral than a wondrous mountain range. Additionally, loggers began cutting down trees for profit. Before Muir's eyes, his wilderness was being destroyed. In 1896, the federal government authorized a mandate that regulated the amount of timber being seized from public lands. Congress responded by appropriating $25,000 for the inauguration of a national policy for forested lands in the United States. However, still angered and outraged, Muir asserted that if the wilderness was not to be ruined for the benefit of a few, then the people must be organized to stop it. He wrote prolifically about the values of the wilderness to inspire people to take action against loggers. He filled more than 60 volumes of personal journals, published more than 300 articles and 10 major books—all of which recounted his travels and elaborated on his spiritual images of nature. His writings reached people all over the country and, in fact, moved them to action.

His unflagging commitment to the wilderness helped to establish Yosemite Valley as a national park in 1890. While Muir feared that businessmen and others would undoubtedly seek to limit the boundaries of the park, he formed an association to protect Yosemite. As a consequence, the Sierra Club was established in 1892. During his tenure as president of the organization, he personally helped in the creation of several other national parks (Sequoia, 1890; Mount Rainier, 1897; Petrified Forest, 1906; and Grand Canyon, 1919), which earned him the title of the "father of the national parks."

John Muir single-handedly changed the thinking of an entire country with respect to protecting the wilderness. Although he did not create the concept of conservation, he did radicalize the notion of land use and introduced the concept of wilderness protection. Nature, he said, was not just a means to connect with our spirituality and our own sense of the divine, but we had to protect it if humanity was to continue to thrive. While Muir was first motivated into action because of the destruction he saw to the natural environment due to shepherding of sheep, Muir's greatest environmental battle ended in defeat in 1913 when the Hetch Hetchy Valley was to become a reservoir for the city of San Francisco. That fight today still serves as a reminder to the Sierra Club of the passion that a single man and a group of concerned citizens had for the protection of the wilderness. The Sierra Club remains a nonprofit conservation and outdoor organization dedicated to the exploration and preservation of American wilderness and wildlife.

Muir's passion for the wilds and his commitment to live in an environmentally sensitive fashion is his enduring legacy. Arguably the most passionate and influential naturalist and conservationist this world has ever met, Muir was a spiritual exemplar in his unyielding resolve to protect the mountains and the wilderness, which he believed were God's creations. He inspired and motivated a nation of people into action. He became the voice of the wilderness, speaking on behalf of the oceans, mountains, nonhuman animals, and trees whose voices could not be heard.

—Pamela M. Anderson

See also Sierra Club

FURTHER READING

Muir, J. (1912). *Story of my boyhood and youth.* Boston: Houghton Mifflin Company.

Muir, J. (1988). *The mountains of California.* San Francisco: Sierra Club Books.

Stoll, M. (1993). A psychological interpretation of John Muir's journey from the Campbellites to the "range of light." In S. M. Miller (Ed.), *John Muir: Life and work.* Albuquerque: University of New Mexico Press.

MUSIC

Music has great power to move the human spirit. It can mediate our relationship with God and become an integral part of religious and spiritual ceremonies. Music is customarily part of the rituals of every group of people and it often has a significant role in the major events of human life (birth, union, death), as well as in regularized ritual and worship.

Sacred music usually has a text, which may be from traditional writings such as the Bible or Qur'an, or from spiritual texts such as the poetry of Henry Vaughan. Much of sacred music is notated but some is still transmitted through an aural tradition. Depending on the tradition, it may be sung by a soloist, choir, congregation, priests, or laypeople. In religions that worship in a church, an organ often accompanies the singers since it is the instrument capable of the most diversity of sound (volume and timbre). In other cultures, the singers may be unaccompanied (a cappella) or sing with instrumental accompaniment of various sorts.

THE BUDDHIST TRADITION

Chant is the principal sacred music of Buddhism. Buddhist chants vary according to region and beliefs. The chants, learned largely by rote, are complex and may include recitations of sacred texts, usually in Tibetan or Sanskrit. Yang chanting is performed without metrical timing, and is accompanied by resonant drums and low, sustained vocal pitches. Throat singing (or overtone singing), typical of Buddhist chant, is a type of singing that manipulates the harmonic resonances of air in the throat. One regional example is Shomyo, a style of Japanese Buddhist chant found mainly in the Tendai and Shingon sects that has two styles, called *ryokyoku* and *rikkyoku.* According to Tibetan Buddhist theory, the orchestration, rhythm, tempo, and repertory of ritual music must be suited to the deity to which it is offered. Performance of Buddhist music is almost exclusively done by monks and occurs regularly throughout the day at monastic hours.

THE CHRISTIAN TRADITION

The earliest form of sacred music for the Christian Church is Gregorian chant (or plainsong), for which large numbers of melodies were composed and then codified toward the end of the 1st millennium. Over many centuries, a tradition arose in which music was offered to God on behalf of the congregation by a choir. This has produced complex and innovative music in a wide variety of styles and genres. Examples of Christian liturgical and nonliturgical music can be found in every period of music history from the medieval era to the present. The most common forms of Christian music are the anthem, antiphon, cantata, canticle, carol, chorale, hymn, motet, and requiem. Not all Christian music is intended for liturgical performance; an example is the oratorio (e.g., Handel's *Messiah*). The hymn has a long tradition of being the primary form of congregational music. Hymns and carols are usually divided into verses (strophic) that are sung to a tune that is repeated.

Within the Christian Church, there are large variations in the type and use of music. In the Catholic tradition and following the Reformation, much of the music is sung by the congregation and, since the Second Vatican Council (1962–1965), the traditional use of Latin has been replaced by texts in the vernacular. In the Orthodox Christian tradition, most singing is done by priests and is unaccompanied or accompanied by bells. In the Protestant tradition, certain distinct musical styles have evolved, notably the spiritual (a type of folksong that originated in the African-American community in the mid-18th century) and gospel music (American religious songs that developed from black evangelical groups). Contemporary Christian music, or CCM, is influenced by secular popular music of the late 20th century. CCM has become enormously popular, and is the principal music played on Christian radio.

THE HINDU TRADITION

Bhajan is the general term for popular Hindu religious music associated with *bhakti,* an approach to union with God. The *bhajan* literature is extensive and diverse, comprising thousands of songs in many languages. *Bhajans* may be performed anywhere, alone or in groups, and may take from an hour to many days to perform. Musical instruments are used to accompany most *bhajan* songs and rituals; drums and cymbals are common, although many different instruments are used, including the well-known string instrument called the sitar.

Like other non-Western musical systems, Indian music divides the octave into multiple segments called *srutis,* which are roughly equal to one quarter of a whole tone of Western music. Indian sacred and secular music uses thousands of melody types called *ragas,* each of which is ascribed certain ethical and emotional properties, and is associated with a certain season and a certain time of day. Ragas are used with rhythmic patterns, called *talas,* and form the basis for improvisation.

THE ISLAMIC TRADITION

The Islamic tradition has several musical elements in regular use, such as the Adhan, the call to prayer, performed by a *muezzin* (singer) from a *minaret* (tower); the Salat, the prayers recited five times daily; and recitation of the Qur'an. Music for public religious celebrations includes Mawlid, music performed for the birthday of Muhammad, and Ashurah, music performed during the mourning period commemorating the death of the spiritual leader Imam Hussein. In Islamic religious music, there is great diversity in the use of instruments. There are also many regional variations to the music. Some Muslims believe that only vocal music is permissible (*halal*) and that instruments are forbidden (*haram*). South Asian Muslim religious music falls into two broad categories: *talhīn* (cantillation), which is scriptural or liturgical, and *inshād* (plural *nashā'id,* invocations), which is nonscriptural or nonliturgical.

THE JEWISH TRADITION

Jewish liturgical regulations call for the regular chanting of scripture in a florid style of cantillation. This requires great skill, so it is performed by a professional called a *ba'al qeriah* or *ba'al qore* who uses specific modes (scales) and melodies. The traditional manner of singing prayers in the synagogue is known as *hazzanut,* "the art of being a *hazzan*" (cantor).

Another important part of the Jewish liturgy is the sequence of benedictions or blessings (*berakhot*) known as the Amidah (or standing prayer). Jewish devotional music is almost entirely vocal. As a special call to prayer and repentance on certain High Holidays such as Rosh Hashanah (the Jewish New Year), a *shofar* (ram's horn) may be used. Liturgical music is an important part of events marking the passage of life, such as bar-mitzvahs and bat-mitzvahs and at weddings.

—Andrew Shenton

FURTHER READING

Sadie, S., & Tyrrell, J. (Eds.). (2001). *The new Grove dictionary of music and musicians* (2nd ed.). New York: Oxford University Press. [Also available online, through subscription at: www.grovemusic.com.]

Westermeyer, P. (1997). *The church musician.* Minneapolis, MN: Augsburg Fortress Publishers.

Wilson-Dickson, A. (2003). *The story of Christian music: From Gregorian chant to black gospel, an authoritative illustrated guide to all the major traditions of music for worship.* Minneapolis, MN: Augsburg Fortress Publishers.

MYSTICISM

Saint Augustine once remarked with respect to "time" that on one level he knows what it is, but if pressed to give a more exact definition, he finds himself a bit at a loss. Mysticism is like time. Some of the difficulties encountered in defining time appear in any attempt to be more precise about mysticism. The etymology of "mysticism" implies a connection to mystery, which in theological language further implies that we can never fathom it entirely. A general definition that has the virtue of covering traditions as diverse as Buddhism, Christianity, Hinduism, Islam, and Judaism is the attempt by humans to attain the ultimate reality of things and experience communion with the Highest.

In *The Varieties of Religious Experience,* William James identified four "marks" of mystical experience that are reflected in much of his subsequent writing, both as elements of definitions and in the course of discussions of mysticism: ineffability, noetic quality, transiency, and passivity.

Ineffability: Since no adequate report of this kind of experience can be given in words, it follows that it must be directly experienced. In this respect, it is said to resemble feelings more than intellectual states. For example, you can tell someone about the experience of being in love, but there is no substitute for the firsthand experience. The mystic after the mystical experience is invariably incapable of describing what happened or even, it would seem, of remembering anything at all except that something did happen. The mystic often lacks the power to reflect articulately on the experience or to express it in apt forms of communication.

Noetic quality: The comparison with feeling does not mean to suggest that mystical states are devoid of knowledge content. For example, you can know a person by being given a short biographical sketch of them, but you know them in a different way through the experience of loving them. Mystical theology is knowledge of God by experience, arrived at through the embrace of unifying love. The mystical experience is a vision of the world that is free, to a very unusual extent, from the interposition of concepts. There is obviously something nonmental, alogical, paradoxical, and unpredictable about the mystical phenomenon, but it is not, therefore, irrational or antirational or religion without thought. Rather, as Zen masters say, it is knowledge of the most adequate kind, only it cannot be expressed in words. Mysticism may be defined as belief in a third kind of knowledge, the other two being sense knowledge and knowledge by inference. The dominant aspects of this third type of knowledge are intuition and love.

Transiency: The feelings and aspects cannot be sustained for a long period of time. The mystical experience admits of various degrees, from short and rare divine or sacred "touches" to the practically permanent union with the One in the so-called mystical marriage.

Passivity: Although one can take the initiative to more readily dispose oneself to receive mystical experience, the experience itself is experienced as independent of one's own efforts. Sometimes the mystical feels as if one were grasped and held by a superior power. For example, you can do things to be a more loving person, and one more capable of receiving love. But the decision by another to love cannot be coerced; it must come freely from them.

The emphasis placed on mysticism and the psychic phenomena of mysticism has varied according to time and place. In late 19th-century France, for example, great stress was placed on mystics, and they were regarded as defining criteria of genuine mysticism. Christian mysticism today, as formed by the works of Saint John of the Cross, is by no means composed of ecstasies, visions, and other extraordinary psychological phenomena. They are not essential to the mystical experience, and indeed are considered to be sometimes hindrances to its proper realization. In the higher states of spiritual marriage, they normally cease.

The union of contemplative and active elements in mysticism is of special note. The passivity associated with mystical experience does not preclude mystics from being persons of great initiative and energy. Mysticism need not be world destroying. Holiness does not mean a retreat from or rejection of the world. To be a mystic is not the same thing as being a spectator on the fence. On the other hand, over-involvement with the world can mean that the potential for contemplation either goes uncultivated or can be lost. Both East and West have cultivated monastic traditions for the development of contemplation.

The many religious traditions differ on the degree of involvement with the world that is correlated with mystical contemplation. But all would agree that running away from the world is not the mystical way; the challenge is to make the mystical experience interfused with daily life and religious observance. Mysticism is the art of union with reality. The mystic is a person who has attained that union in greater or less degree, or who aims at and believes in such attainment. A mystic is one who recognizes that prayer is a dialogue. It involves a give-and-take, a listening and speaking. The One speaks to us, we listen. We speak to the One, One listens. Prayer begins with the One, not with us. The One does not need prayer, we do. The listening element in prayer is usually the most important. Perseverance in prayer can consist in simply starting over once again, today and every day. Joy comes from being in the presence of the Other. Mysticism and mystical are simply about immediacy. A mystic is one who seeks an immediate union with the One without interference or mediation of objects, images, doctrines, thoughts, or ideas.

—Rev. David O'Leary

FURTHER READING

HarperCollins Spiritual Classics. (2004). *The cloud of unknowing.* San Francisco: HarperCollins.

Harvey, A. (1997). *The essential mystics: Selections from the world's great wisdom traditions.* New York: Harper.

James, W. (1985). *The varieties of religious experience.* Cambridge, MA: Harvard University Press.

Meninger, W. (1989). *1012 Monastery Road: A spiritual journey.* Petersham, MA: St. Bede's Publications.

MYSTICISM, JEWISH

Jewish mysticism involves a personal encounter with God upon his throne, known as the Merkavah, "the Chariot." The throne of God is not perceived in a literal way, but as the generative point of all creation.

It was called the Chariot because this vortex of creative energy was conceived of as movable, so that it might be experienced in any place and at any time. The Chariot was the source of God's energy and intelligence, the origin of his power to create and destroy. By focusing one's mind on the Chariot in meditation, sages of the Merkavah sought knowledge and experience of God. This divine reality determines the significance behind any time and place that people might live in. Sensitivity to the presence of God as the Chariot that makes his presence known was a powerful force in the religion of the prophets, which influenced the conception of the spiritual life in both Judaism and Christianity. The chain of tradition that teaches how to become aware of this presence is called the Kabbalah, an ancient term that resonates with mystical meaning to this day.

In its origins, the tradition of thinking of God in this way is more ancient than Israel itself. From Mesopotamia, from the 23rd century B.C.E. and the 15th century C.E., stories are told of kings and courtiers entering the palace of heaven and receiving visions and empowerment there. Israel learned these royal traditions from Babylonia, and converted them into prophetic authorization, especially during the time of Ezekiel (during the 6th century C.E.). Ezekiel himself related his classic vision of the throne of God as a chariot, a Merkabah, and what is usually called Merkabah mysticism derives from his vision (in Ezekiel 1).

The chariots of Israel's enemies might have been impressive, but in Ezekiel's mind the greatest Chariot of them all rolled through the heavens. The steeds of heaven were surreal: "Every one had four faces, and every one of them had four wings, and their legs were straight legs and the sole of their feet was as the sole of a calf's foot, and they sparkled like burnished brass. They had the hands of a man under their wings on their four sides" (Ezekiel 1:6–8). The four faces Ezekiel saw on each beast were those of a man, lion, ox, and eagle (Ezekiel 1:10). (These faces were to become the symbols of the four Evangelists during the 2nd century.) Magnificent wheels supported the four monsters, which propelled the Chariot at the speed of lightning. After Ezekiel, the book of Daniel (chapter 7) detailed this vision even further (during the 2nd century B.C.E.). In the time of Jesus, the book of Enoch, found in fragments in Aramaic at Qumran, took that tradition further.

The book of Genesis says of Enoch only that "he walked with God, and he was not" (Genesis 5:22). This disappearance is taken as a sign that Enoch enjoyed a vision by ascent into the multiple heavens above the Earth, and was authorized to relate its wisdom to Israel, indeed to act as an intermediary to the angels who had disobeyed God. From Ezekiel, through Daniel and Enoch and on to John and Jesus, there is a growing tradition, a *kabbalah* (something received), which reflects a deep commitment to the disciplined practice of the vision of God's throne. The fragments of Enoch at Qumran are found in Aramaic, which suggests that the book was used not just by the Essenes (who tended to guard their sectarian documents in Hebrew) but also by a wider audience. In fact, the book of Enoch is also quoted at a later stage in the New Testament, so that there can be no doubt of its widespread use. Another work found in Hebrew at Qumran and widely attested elsewhere, the book of Jubilees, also presents Enoch as a figure of revelation: He himself knows the Torah later communicated to Moses by angelic communication.

Focus on the Merkabah is also evident in the experience of Jesus. Traces of that are perhaps plainest in the story of Jesus' baptism. That takes us back to Jesus' association with John "the Baptist," which means "the immerser" (*baptistes* in Greek, from the verb *baptizomai,* "immerse"). Many people came to John for this immersion, most often on the way to the temple along the well-established path of pilgrimage that followed the Jordan Valley. John offered them purification in God's own water, and the assurance that this was the sign of Israel's true purity. For the followers of John, this continual immersion was more than a matter of simple repentance; there was also an esoteric meaning. John conveyed a definite understanding of the final significance that his purification for Israel offered. As John himself expressed it, immersing oneself in water prepared one to receive the spirit of God, which was to drench all Israel with its sanctification. The key to John's preparation lies in the wording attributed to him, "I immerse you in water, but he himself will immerse you in holy spirit" (Mark 1:8; see Matthew 3:11; Luke 3:16). The link between purification with water and the vindicating presence of God's spirit is explicitly made in the book of Ezekiel, the same book that provides the meaning of the Merkavah (Ezekiel 36:22–27). After all, God's spirit proceeded from his throne, the source of all true judgment.

Jesus' skill in this vision made him one of John's most prominent disciples. The Gospels relate the particular vision of Jesus (Matthew 3:13–17; Mark 1:9–13

Luke 3:21–22). As Jesus was immersed for purification, he came to have an increasingly vivid vision of the heavens splitting open and God's spirit coming upon him. And a voice: "You are my son, beloved; in you I take pleasure." Each of these elements is resonant with the Israelite *kabbalah* of the divine throne.

The heavens are conceived of in the story of Jesus' baptism (as in the Judaism of the time) as multiple hard shells above the Earth, so that any real disclosure of the divine must represent a rending of those firmaments. But once opened, Jesus' vision is not of ascending through the heavens, as in the case of Enoch, but of the spirit, as a dove, hovering over him and descending. That image is a vivid realization that the spirit of God at creation once hovered over the face of the primeval waters (Genesis 1:2) as a bird. The bird was identified as a dove in Rabbinic tradition, and a fragment from Qumran supports the association. The spirit, which would one day come to Israel in Jesus' vision was already upon him, and God took pleasure in him as a "son." The term "son" itself appears extremely frequently in the Old Testament, in order to speak of the special relationship between God and others. Angels can be called "sons of God," Israel is referred to as a divine son (most famously in Hosea 11:1), and the Davidic king can be assured by divine voice, "You are my son, this day have I begotten you!" (Psalm 2:7). All these are expressions, not of a biological relationship, but of the direct revelation that God extends to certain people and angels. Jesus claims that he is of their spiritual lineage within his embrace of John's *kabbalah.*

Practitioners of divine presence in both Christianity and Judaism embraced these traditions long after Jesus. Jewish mysticism, however, is better attested than its Christian counterpart, because after the Church was embraced as the religion of state during the 4th century, Christian writings as a whole became less personal and intense than their Judaic counterparts. By the Middle Ages, a highly literate form of Jewish mysticism emerged fully, especially in the enriching mix of Judaic, Muslim, and neo-Platonic cultures in Spain and the south of France during the 13th century C.E.

By this time two foci of meditation were prevalent. One was on the *shiur komah,* the "measure of the body." This referred to God's corporeal reality, of which the human body—in the divine image and likeness—provided a reflection. The other focus involved discerning the Sefiroth, the emanations that vibrated outward from God and made all that is, and resonated with the formations of the body. The Kabbalah at this stage represented the highest accomplishment of Judaic mysticism as a philosophical and personal discipline.

Conventional scholarship long sidelined the Kabbalah; even worse, commercial exploitation has trivialized its subtle teaching. But no mystical tradition better explores the intersecting mysteries of human character and divine presence than the medieval Kabbalah.

—Bruce Chilton

See also Enoch; Judaism, Orthodox

MYTH

Every ancient culture created its own unique collection of myths, which are legends that recount the exploits of dynamic characters who struggled with antagonistic opponents, lost loves, and experienced personal triumph over common life obstacles. These characters, whether heroic or tragic, offer ancient and modern readers a method for understanding life, and provide comfort for those who suffer, knowing that great heroes suffered in life as well. The interest in mythology continues to exist in both ancient and modern legends, with universal themes that have evolved in every culture. Mythology from all cultures shares a common element that unites the purpose of myths, which is that each culture and religion draws on myths as the essential truths that dominate humanity and create reason and alleviate anxieties in this world.

The ancients recognized stronger powers than those present in their world; they had theories about the creation of the world, death, the sun, rain, floods, drought, and evil elements. Recognition of the power behind these events and entities, led early cultures to create myths that provided answers to make sense of their universe and all that it entailed. Mythology is a compilation of legends with recurring themes such as oracles, prophecies, enchantment, voyagers, heroes, sorcery, and magic. Mythology evolved from the Egyptians, Iranians, Sumerians, Central Asia, Babylonians, Indus Valley, Nepal, and shamanistic practices of Siberia, the Middle East, and the Mesopotamian world, creating a cradle of legends that dominated the lives and religious beliefs of the people in these civilizations.

Surviving legends are fragmented, and in some cases can only be partially translated. Many of the dominant legends that have survived come from Greece and Egypt, recounting the gods, heroes, creation, and belief in the afterlife. These mythological influences continue in modern civilizations, as their many themes and heroes are reenacted in the visual arts and are reformatted in literature, such as Shakespeare's Marc Antony and Cleopatra, and the many tales of Herakles, Cyclops, Ulysses, and the Buddha. Mythology also continues in modern religious cults such as the cargo cults, Millerites, Jehovah's Witnesses, and many others that have used the power of literature to create legends that explain their world, their position in it, and the world to come.

The power of mythology is most evident in the dynamic response to the legends of these myths, religious ideals and beliefs that arose from myths, and methods of worship. New religious and spiritual practices were the direct result of mythology, and gave to the ancients a new level of control in which they ensured their destiny in this world and the next through actions of worshipping and honoring their gods. Mythology also revealed the reality of why situations that plagued people such as drought, death, and suffering were the result of meddlesome gods; the myths that surround nuisance gods provided new deities with a humanistic and entertaining quality.

Some myths served as warnings, instructing people on how not to anger the gods and to appreciate blessings from the gods. In another ancient myth, Arachne was a very gifted woman, but arrogant and lacking in humility. The myth tells of Arachne's great skill in weaving, which she flaunts in the presence of the goddess Athene, who turns the young girl into a spider, thereby providing a lesson about humility.

Mythology in all its forms touches on issues of diversity and continuity in human nature, human existence, moral standards, death, the afterlife, and the path that one is to take to achieve a prosperous and fruitful life. Legends offer stories of heroes who suffered at the hands of mortals and immortals, such as Odysseus, Ajax, and Bota Ili, the wild, demonic woman of the Kedang people of east Indonesia, and others who were favored by the gods, such as Aeneas the Trojan hero and the favorite of the Romans, Hercules, Horatius who defended Rome against the Etruscan army, Feridun the ancient Iranian hero, and Yoshitsure the Japanese hero who overpowered the giant. The figures who were favored and who suffered provide guides for how to live a good life, as well as its opposite.

Mythology also includes sorcery, such as the magic spells in the myths of Merlin, and mythical creatures such as the Sphinx, Medusa, and Centaurs. Whether or not the reader believes in the people and events captured in myths, the stories provide action, mystery, and wonder that ensure their popularity and survival.

—Julie Wieland-Robbescheuten

NARRATIVE

Down through the ages great spiritual teachers have understood the power of story. This we can see in the ancestral tales of the Hebrew Bible, in the stories of Job and Esther, in the parables of Jesus, and in the Jataka tales told by the Buddha. It has been through story that human beings have come to understand who they are; to determine how they are to relate to one another and to the world about them; and to contemplate the nature of the Divine—all of which are concerns arising from the spiritual aspects of our being.

A BRIEF HISTORY OF STORY

Ruth Sawyer traces the beginnings of storytelling back to prehistoric times, and through her work, we can speculate that an early hunter may have given us a first narrative in the form of an impromptu chant exulting in his act of bravery and accomplishment. Gradually these chants may have developed into prose narratives, and the focus on the storytellers' actions may have broadened to include family, tribe, and others—until the third-person narrative came into being. Over time, the quest for understanding beyond immediate, concrete experience may have developed: wonderings about patterns in nature and whether there is a force beyond what one can see that shapes the world. Stories were created to explain these forces, and the ancient myths came to be.

In early cultures the storytellers were teachers: bards, troubadours, minstrels, seanachies, and ollahms. It was the storytellers' work to pass down the epics, myths, sagas, and legends that expressed the history, wisdom, and values of their societies. Following the invention of the printing press, print became the dominant medium for storytelling, and today we see stories told across the airwaves, through film, and through electronic media. Yet the power and appeal of story is in no way diminished. Indeed, despite modernism's attempt to devalue narrative as a way of knowing, the human need for story may be stronger than ever.

STORY IN SPIRITUAL TRADITIONS

The Hebrew Bible begins with a story—two stories, actually, from two different oral traditions—about how the world came to be. What follows is story after story: of how God caused humankind to multiply and spread over the face of the earth, of God's interactions with the matriarchs and patriarchs of the Hebrew people, including fictional stories such as the stories of Job and Jonah. These stories, interspersed with commands and regulations for living, were passed down from generation to generation, reflecting and shaping the Hebrew people's sense of their own identity and their understanding of God.

The first four books of the Christian Testament are stories of the life of Jesus of Nazareth. In them we learn that Jesus himself was a storyteller. He told stories to answer people's questions about how to relate to God and to fellow human beings. When Jesus came to the core of his message, the proclamation of the Kingdom of God, the best way Jesus knew to describe the Kingdom was through story: "The Kingdom of God is like a merchant who . . ." the Kingdom of God is like a householder who. . . ."

Buddha was likewise a storyteller. He told his Jataka tales as stories from his former lives; they were told to illustrate moral points. There are more than a thousand such tales recorded in the Buddhist scriptures—many that were added by the Buddha's followers.

THE NATURE AND APPEAL OF STORY

According to Jerome Bruner, narrative is one of two primary modes of human thought, one of two "distinctive ways of ordering experience, of constructing reality" (Bruner, 1986, p. 11). The other is the logico-scientific mode, which deals in general causes and is concerned with verifiable, empirical truth. The narrative mode seeks not so much to establish formal and empirical truths as to establish verisimilitude and lifelikeness. Bruner says that narrative "is built upon concern for the human condition," in contrast to the "heartlessness" of logical thought (Bruner, 1986, p. 14).

Mikhail Bakhtin describes two kinds of discourse: authoritative discourse, which strives to determine behavior or "ideological interrelations with the world" and discourse as having an interior persuasiveness (Bakhtin, 1981, p. 342). Authoritative discourse is characterized by distance from oneself and an absence of dialogic possibilities. It is static, with its own single calcified meaning. Discourse having interior persuasiveness is flexible, with malleable borders. It does not appeal to any external authority but is contextualized and can be related to one's own life. This second type of discourse offers further creative interaction; it is open, unfinished, capable of further representation. Harold Rosen describes narrative discourse as having this interior persuasiveness.

We can see the interplay of both types of discourse in both Eastern and Western spiritual traditions. But the passages of authoritative discourse, the laws and commandments, the insights into spiritual principles, are set in the context of story. The teachings are authoritative to us in large part because of the witness of the lives of the people who proclaim them, what we know of their life stories. The narratives that accompany the teachings ground them to our understanding. As Roy Heller asks, "Do I not kill because the law says 'Do not kill' or because when I hear stories about killing I understand, 'This is what it means to kill'?"

Storytelling has been called *indirect teaching*. There will always be a place for direct teaching to support spiritual development, but it is narrative that has the power to engage the heart, to capture the imagination, to transform understanding, to invite the "yes": yes, that is true; yes, that is who I am; yes, that is what I want to become.

USING LITERATURE FOR SPIRITUAL DEVELOPMENT

In the past children's literature was often characterized by a heavily didactic tone—authoritative discourse disguising itself as fiction. Over time, however, the tone and content of children's literature have changed. Today, children's literature that focuses on spiritual matters is more apt to raise important questions that children themselves may be considering rather than to provide answers to them. This development is consonant with what research is showing us about children's cognitive and spiritual development; children are not born "blank slates" upon which knowledge is to be inscribed; they are constantly constructing meaning from the environment about them. Recent research (Robert Coles, 1990; Tobin Hart, 2003; David Hay with Rebecca Nye, 1998; Daniel Scott, 2004) indicates that children have an innate spiritual capacity which their environment may either nourish or inhibit. Reading and discussing stories that raise spiritual questions is a natural, time-proven way to nurture children's spiritual development.

In the late 20th century literary theorists began to question the idea that works of literature hold one static meaning that the reader ideally is to "get." According to Louise Rosenblatt, the meaning of a literary work resides not in the pages of a text but in the transaction that occurs between reader and text. The literary experience is a synthesis of what the reader already thinks or knows or feels and what the text offers. What the reader brings to the literary encounter—one's life experiences, present preoccupations, inner needs, purpose for reading, even the setting in which the reading event occurs—affect the meaning the reader will make of the text. The text both guides the reader's interpretation and constrains it, but multiple interpretations are to be expected; each literary encounter is unique to the reader, the text, the time, and the place.

Wolfgang Iser points out that writers of literary works leave gaps, or blanks, in the text when information is not made explicit. The reader is drawn into the text by filling in the gaps, by supplying what is meant by what is not said. The text continues to guide, to confirm, or correct the reader's inferences, as the reader continually casts forward toward a future horizon of possibilities, while retaining the "past horizon that is already filled" (Iser, 1978, p. 111). An asymmetry between the reader and the text is occasioned by the gaps. Because this imbalance is undefined, a variety of communications is possible.

These insights suggest that the most fruitful way to share books with children is to discuss them in an open-ended way, not expecting children to arrive at a particular interpretation. There are many outstanding children's books that lend themselves to such discussion, including picture books, realistic fiction, fantasy, biography, historical fiction, traditional literature, and poetry.

Whether in book or oral form, storytelling remains an indispensable support for spiritual development. This applies to children as well as to adults.

—Ann M. Trousdale

See also Literature, Children's

FURTHER READING

Bakhtin, M. M. (1981). *The dialogic imagination.* (C. Emerson & M. Holquist, Trans.) Austin, TX: University of Texas Press.

Bruner, J. (1986). *Actual minds, possible worlds.* Cambridge, MA: Harvard University Press.

Coles, R. (1990). *The spiritual life of children.* Boston: Houghton Mifflin.

Hart, T. (2003). *The secret spiritual world of children.* Makawao, HI: Inner Ocean.

Hay, D. (with Nye, R.). (1998). *The spirit of the child.* London: Fount.

Heller, R. C. (2001). *Old Testament II.* Houston, TX: Perkins School of Theology.

Iser, W. (1978). *The act of reading: A theory of aesthetic response.* Baltimore, MD: Johns Hopkins University Press.

Rosen, H. (1986). The importance of story, *Language Art, 63*(3), 226–237.

Rosenblatt, L. (1978). *The reader, the text, the poem.* Carbondale, IL: Southern Illinois University Press.

Sawyer, R. (1962). *The way of the storyteller.* New York: Penguin Books.

Scott, D. G. (2004). Retrospective spiritual narratives: Exploring recalled childhood and adolescent spiritual experiences. *International Journal of Children's Spirituality, 9*(1), 67–79.

NATIVE AMERICAN INDIAN SPIRITUALITY

In explaining Native American spirituality, the 1969 Pulitzer Prize winner N. Scott Momaday, a Kiowa Indian, tells the story of an old Indian man who every morning of his adult life got up before dawn, painted his face, and prayed the sun up out of the ground. To understand American Indian spirituality, one must attempt to understand and, above all, respect the relationship between that old man and the creation.

There is no monolithic or all-encompassing definition or explanation of Native American spirituality. Prior to European contact in the present-day United States, there were more than 500 Indian nations; some were related, most were not; some shared the same concepts of spirituality, many did not. What is true of one Indian nation may have been totally unrecognized by another. For the most part, however, spirituality was a personal relationship that connected the individual's spirit to the creation, to the present world, to a sense of place, a relationship with other humans and the animals and for some, a gateway into another life after the present.

Creation came about in many different ways, at different times, and in different places for the ancestors of today's Native American Indian people. It is perhaps most telling that these creation histories have for the most part been called *creation myths* by the uninformed, carrying with those words the pejorative connotation that they are untrue or just a fanciful story to be told around a campfire or in a teepee somewhere on the Great Plains. For Native people these histories are their sacred truths of creation and are as historically informative and timeless as the Bible, the Koran, the Torah, or any other creation history. In anthropological words, in most Western religions, creation reflects a concept of monogenesis, or one beginning in one place at one time. Native spirituality, however, comes from a polygenesis beginning, or many beginnings in many places at different times where life could be supported. Two examples follow.

Frank Fools Crow, a Lakota holy man and Ceremonial Chief of the Sioux, when asked where the Lakota came from, stooped down and picked up a handful of South Dakota dirt and stated, "We Indian people go way back to ancient times, when Great Grandfather, the Great Spirit, molded us from the ground and gave this land to us. He placed us here, and told us that it is our land. We are part of it and one in spirit with it. That is why we seek harmony with all creation. We share the same Creator and heritage." The Lakota creation as told by Fools Crow is perhaps the shortest and most direct. Other sacred truths of creation are longer and more complex.

The Cherokee people believe that before this world their ancestors lived in a sky world, which although beautiful and filled with all that they needed, became crowded over time. In search of a new home, they looked below their sky world and saw that all below was water. They asked the great buzzard (at a time when people could speak with animals and birds) to fly down below and see what he could see. The great buzzard returned from an extended flight and told them that all that existed was water, water as far as the eye could see. A plan was developed whereby the great buzzard would again fly below, this time with a water beetle on his back. When the great buzzard flew above the water, the water beetle was to dive into the water, swim below, and see if there was anything upon which to build a new world. The plan was set, and the water beetle did as told, coming up and reporting that he had been unable to find anything. Water beetle was requested to do this again, and on the third try he returned to the surface with a ball of mud in his pincher. He sat the mud upon the surface of the water, and it began to expand out on the surface forming a landmass. Pleased with the results, buzzard and beetle returned to the sky world.

After a period of time the great buzzard was asked to fly back down to the new surface and see if it was a good place for The People. The great buzzard returned from his flight stating that the land was large but soft and muddy. There were no plants and no animal life. Over a period of time the great buzzard made additional trips, each time reporting that things were improving. The land was firming up; trees and plants were beginning to grow. The great buzzard flew close to the ground, and as his wings went up, the mountains were formed; as his wings went down, the valleys were formed. Soon the new world would be ready for The People.

When the time finally arrived for the move to the below world, the Cherokee people got upon the back of the great buzzard and he transported them to the surface. As they approached they saw what a beautiful place the creator had provided. There was ample room for both "two-leggeds" and the "four-leggeds." The climate was favorable and crops would grow well. The people disembarked from upon the great buzzard and settled themselves into their sacred lands in parts of present-day Kentucky, Tennessee, North and South Carolina, Georgia, Alabama, and Arkansas.

Even though the great majority of the Cherokee were removed from their sacred lands during the Removal Era of the 1830s and 1840s, they still retain a spiritual connection to the land that their ancestors were given and where many of them were buried.

These truths of creation are only the beginning point in understanding Indian spirituality just as a child's birth is only the beginning point for his or her later life. Indian children were raised in a spiritual world where every place and every thing around them was interwoven and interconnected. Tribal elders and family members inculcated the spiritual into the daily rhythm of the child's life and instructed the child in the cycle of the world and his or her part and place in it. The child was taught that all things were spiritual and that spirits and or spirit power was present in most everything whether it be natural phenomenon such as wind, rain, thunder, steam, or in trees, rocks, sacred sites, and unexplained events. Animals too had spirits, and through rituals such as a vision quest, or perhaps as the result of a dream, a spirit helper or helpers could be attained to assist the child as he or she prepared for adult life. Additional spirit helpers might be added to a person's repertory as they became older, and these spirit helpers could be called upon in time of crisis or whenever needed.

For the Native American man, woman, and child, the spiritual world was not separate from the everyday experiences of life. From sunrise to sunset, and while they slept, they lived in a spiritual world. Spiritual leaders, only men in some Native societies, both men and women in others, negotiated the distance and relationship between the human and the sacred. These people, often called *Shamans,* interpreted dreams, assisted in the vision quest experience, and/or carried out rituals designed to keep peace (and prosperity) between the spiritual world and the Native people. In some Native Nations healing societies represented the connection between the spiritual and physical world. Among the Iroquois League, the False Face Society healed the sick while wearing hand-carved masks, the design of which had come to them in a dream vision from the spiritual side of the universe. Among the Dene (Navajo) some healing ceremonies were, and continue to be, conducted on a sand painting that consisted of an intricate spiritual ceremonial design made by a traditional Navajo chanter (medicine person) trickling fine colored sand, crushed minerals, pollen, or powder onto a neutral sand base. This connection between spiritual design, natural elements, and healing also serve to show the connectedness of Native people to what many Native people call "Mother Earth."

Many people have misinterpreted the concept of Mother Earth as a sort of Native American environmental concept. While the natural environment is a part of Native spirituality, Mother Earth is better envisioned as the cosmological and spiritual world within which Native people live, work, marry, raise families, conduct ceremony, and pay respect to the Creator. Some Indian people refer to this as "the sacred hoop." In its most simple definition it can be viewed as a set of concentric circles each overlapping and woven around the other. These various weavings taken together make up the whole of Native American spirituality. The center circle is Mother Earth; the circles that are woven around and interconnected are concepts such as time, history, family, ceremony, place, culture, government, and law. Early European settlers failed to recognize this complicated sense of cosmology and claimed that Indian people were without religion, history, or culture.

When the European colonists and later U.S. citizens set out to expand across the American continent under the guise of manifest destiny, cultural and spiritual myopia resulted in the destruction of Indian Nations, their cultures, their religions and caused severe damage to the complicated system of beliefs that were embodied in and made up the totality of Native spiritual cosmology. Early explorers and European settlers who followed in their footsteps expected Native American people to either be converted to the Catholic or Protestant religions voluntarily (or in the case of the Spanish) by force of coercion. Failure to convert often resulted in death or being sold into slavery in the West Indies or in Malaga, Spain.

For both the Catholic and Protestant religions, the worship service, the focal point of their spirituality, was the cathedral or church building. Huge ornate buildings were built with spires reaching into the heavens. Sermons were preached in languages foreign to the Native tongue and the practice of Native religions was denounced as devil worship. For Native people the world was their church. Where early Europeans saw the forests as dark and foreboding, filled with evil spirits, Native People saw these forests as places where spirits resided, where they could be at one with nature and their creator. Native people revered the natural world and all that was in it. They did not need a church building; the universe was that building. They did not need priests to intercede with the Creator; they spoke with the creator daily as they went about their lives. Europeans failed to understand this sophisticated level of spirituality and carried out a relentless religious warfare against Native religions and Native people deemed to be worshipers of Satan.

In the 21st century, at a time when more than 50% of Native Americans live in urban areas, Indian spirituality still exists within the heart and soul of many Native people. Apache families still return to their reservations to celebrate the coming of age of their daughters in the *NJA NJLEESH,* "She is painted," ceremony that tests the young woman's suitability to be recognized as a woman among the Apache people. Among the Dene (Navajo), service men and women returning from war will participate in the Enemy Way Chant that exorcises the ghosts of death, violence, and ugliness that they have seen and experienced. The Apache and Dene are examples of the many Native people from many Native Nations that return yearly to their reservations to participate in ceremonies and to renew their spiritual relationship with the Creator.

Among the Serrano Indians of Southern California the last girl's puberty ceremony was practiced some 140 years ago; however, the ceremony serves to demonstrate the spiritual connection between the past and present as young Indian girls "came of age." At the onset of puberty a "waxen" ceremony was held. A shallow pit was dug and lined with heated stones. The stones were covered by leaves, and the young girl was laid in the shallow grave. This symbolized the death of childhood and entrance into womanhood. Sacred songs were sang, food was offered to the creator and those in attendance, and the young woman (no longer a child) was raised from the grave and was now eligible for marriage. Many factors have contributed to the decline of Indian culture in southern California; however, the failure to observe native religious rites such as the girl's puberty ceremony is intrinsically connected.

Spiritual practice, tradition, and faith have been and continue to be at the center of the lives of Native Americans. As such, it is impossible to separate the spiritual lives of young people from the rest of their development. Promoting and preserving the spiritual practices of Native American traditions is therefore an important aspect of healthy development.

—Troy Johnson

See also Native American Spirituality, Practices of

FURTHER READING

Beck, P. V., Walters, A. L., & Francisco, N. (1990). *The sacred: Ways of knowledge, sources of life.* Flagstaff, AZ: Navajo Community College Press.

Eagle Man, McGaa, E. (1990). *Mother earth spirituality.* New York: Harper and Row.

Gill, S. D. (1982). *Native American religions: An introduction.* Belmont, CA: Wadsworth.

Johnson, T. R. (2002). *Distinguished Native American spiritual practitioners and healers.* Westport, CT: Oryx.

NATIVE AMERICAN SPIRITUALITY, PRACTICES OF

Native American spirituality encompasses the diverse cultures and lifestyles of native peoples living in all parts of the western hemisphere. The diversity is connected to the main ways that tribes have survived physically. There are, then, hunting tribes, fishing tribes, and agriculture tribes, all with their unique and special traditions. Indeed, the diversity has created a variety of spiritual needs leading to there being a variety of ways that spiritual needs get expressed. For example, in tribes where hunting is essential, the emphasis is on animals being spiritual, while in agriculturally based tribes, the emphasis is on crops and the land having a sacred identity. However, in many ways, the similarities outweigh the differences; for throughout Native American societies, the core meaning of spirituality is essentially the same.

One of the main similarities has to do with spirituality being different from religion. In most Western cultures, the meaning of spirituality is tied to organized religion—not so for Native American peoples. For Native American peoples, spirituality is expressed in all aspects of life. Indeed, in many Native American languages, there is no word for religion. For Native Americans, as for other peoples, spirituality fulfills emotional needs and the need to provide meaning beyond that provided by science and practical reasoning. However, for Native Americans, spirituality, much like science, provides a way of understanding the world and how it operates.

Gaining self-understanding is also a spiritual need. For many Native Americans, spirituality defines who they are and what their relation is to the world. Each individual is seen in a spiritual context that is complex and contrary to how the individual is seen in most Western cultures. For Native Americans, humans have a special but not superior place in the world. That is, for Native Americans, no living thing has power or dominion over another. Different species, the human species included, form a web rather than a hierarchy. This web-of-life view is reflected in the role that animals play in Native American creation stories. For instance, in the Iroquois tradition, the world was created on the back of a turtle, and in the Ottawa tradition, men were created from the parts of dead animals.

Native American animism also reflects the web-of-life view—as all living things are seen as being spirits or having consciousness. This view creates a special kind of reverence for life, and when adopting it, the world becomes a spiritual stage on which humans play but a limited role. One important example of this is the reverence accorded to the land. For many Native Americans, the land is alive and spiritual, and in some tribes, the sacred and personal status of the land is expressed by referring to the land as a mother.

Native American spirituality also shapes the lifestyles and values of Native Americans. The role of the individual is that of maintaining the balance of life by fulfilling one's role, and one's role is both in the world at large as well as in one's community. For example, for Native Americans, it is essential to revere the land and respect life as well as to fulfill obligations to one's community.

In Native American spirituality, life is a spiritual journey, and the growth of the individual is understood as spiritual growth. This growth is marked by rites of passage, so that for Native Americans, ceremonies play an integral part of their spiritual development. The "vision quest" is one such ceremony.

The vision quest is a time when youths go into isolation to fast and become aware of their spiritual connection to the earth. In some cases, the vision "question" is also to discover their spiritual guardian. Among the Sioux, the Navajo, and other tribes in the southwest, the sweat lodge ceremony also marks and promotes spiritual development. Steam heat is used to produce sweating, which, in turn, intensifies the experience of prayer and reflection.

However, prayer and reflection occur not only in ceremonies but also in everyday behavior, including the telling of stories. For Native Americans, storytelling can be sacred acts—especially when stories are means of defining the community, its history, and its traditions. Native American spirituality is, then, a means for understanding Native American culture and what it means to be Native American.

—Genevie Gold

See also Native American Indian Spirituality

FURTHER READING

Axtell, J. (Ed.). (1981). *The Indian peoples of Eastern America.* New York: Oxford University Press.

Deloria, V. (1973). *God is red.* New York: Grosset & Dunlap.

Gill, S. D. (1943). *Native American religions: An introduction.* Belmont, CA: Wadsworth.

Gill, S. D. (1981). *Native American religious action: A performance approach to religion.* Columbia, SC: University of South Carolina Press.

NATURALISM

The term *naturalism* is usually contrasted with supernaturalism to emphasize that things and occurrences in the world can be understood in terms of the laws of nature, without invoking supernatural entities as do most traditional religions. Many philosophers, both ancient and modern, have subscribed to a naturalist philosophy, as do a great many professional scientists. Most naturalists are either atheists, that is, they deny the existence of any God; or they are pantheists, that is they picture a God who pervades all of Nature.

Much of the inanimate world, and even many features of living creatures, including human beings, may be adequately explained in terms of the physical entities and principles discovered by science. Traditional religions speak about the human condition as something special, with characteristics that are too unique and subtle to be reduced to the basic ingredients of matter. They insist that there are human attributes such as thought and feeling, formulations of right and wrong, the sense of justice and the quest for truth, the capacity to reason and to create poetry, that we may bracket into the notion of the human spirit. And the human spirit, say most religions, transcends matter and energy, atoms and photons. It is not within the scope of science to analyze it to its ultimate material components.

Until the rise of Darwinian evolution in the latter half of the nineteenth century, even biologists kept religion and God as separate from science. However, the theory of evolution brought in two elements that blatantly contradicted traditional religious belief systems. First, the theory of evolution explains that Man did not appear fully constituted on the planet; rather, he emerged ever so slowly from lower forms of life. Secondl, the variety of organisms in the world resulted from chance factors which instigate the emergence of different plants and animals. The success of Darwinism led some biologists to imagine that some day science would replace all of the symbols and artifacts of religion.

The goal of science is to explore every aspect of the natural world. Science strives to account for all of the richness and variety in the phenomenal world in terms of fundamental entities, immutable laws, and universal principles. Naturalism is characterized by complete faith in the potential and total success of the methodology of science in efforts to understand every aspect of the phenomenal.

Naturalism is characterized by a confidence in science's potential to understand such aspects of the phenomenal world as are important to our existence; or at least that through the methods of science, we can understand them better than through any other mode. This confidence arises from the proven successes of the scientific methodology during the past four centuries.

To some, the extraordinary successes of the sciences have lowered confidence in some of the tenets of traditional religions. Insofar as these pertain to explanations of the phenomena in the physical world, science has replaced most religious claims. However, the religious framework also includes other elements besides explanations of phenomena, such as feelings of reverence, a sense of sacredness, profound gratitude, and an ethical framework. These do not arise from scientific discoveries, theories, and explanations, but they are no less important for individual serenity and collective sanity.

It is in this context that religious naturalism arises. Religious naturalism holds that all the positive values, experiences, and attitudes that ensue from traditional religions are accessible via a purely naturalistic view of the world. Furthermore, it also shields one from features of traditional religions such as superstition, bigotry, and unscientific explanations of natural phenomena. It insists that there is no need to assume the existence of the supernatural, or of a God endowed with the characteristics of omnipotence, omniscience, compassion, mercy, and the like. Thus, religious naturalism denies the existence of heaven, hell, and transcendent beings. It maintains that the physical world in all its complexity is the only reality. In the terrestrial context, a plethora of living organisms have arisen, of which *Homo sapiens* is perhaps the most sophisticated. From the complexity of the human brain have emerged capacities such as thoughts, values, and abstract concepts.

Religious naturalism holds that all of the cultural, conceptual, and historical aspects of humanity can also be explained from the naturalistic framework. Furthermore, religious naturalism regards naturalism as the only valid approach to reaching any rational and coherent understanding of the world. By this view, when the naturalistic worldview is wisely adopted, it can add meaning, purpose, and fulfillment to life as effectively as any religion.

Religious naturalists fully appreciate the element of community building. The idea of people being bound together in a common worldview is implicit in the word religion. (The word has been traced to the Latin *ligare,* to bind.) Religious naturalists discuss their framework from mildly varying perspectives. Some are not very different from secular humanists in that they separate themselves from anything religious. Some are avowed atheists who are against all organized religions. Some have suggested that our universe is just one of many—one species of universe within a multiverse (in the Darwinian sense). By this view, our universe has evolved over time, has grown by adaptation, and is destined to annihilation. Some religious naturalists argue that religions are inevitable cultural delusions to which most humans are subject. But there are also religious naturalists who take the values of traditional religions seriously, and even adopt some terminologies of traditional religions, such as mystery, gratitude, and reverence, giving these terms new interpretations.

What unites all religious naturalists is the conviction that gods and religions are not, as the traditions claim, revelations of the transcendent to a chosen few, but natural products of cultural evolution. As to heaven and hell, religious naturalism holds that the transcendental realities enunciated by traditional religions can be more meaningfully conceptualized in other ways. Religious naturalists try to understand the nature and origin of belief in God; they seek its roots within the brain, neurons, and genes. In their view, religions have emerged, not unlike organisms, from the contingencies of survival and adaptation. Religious naturalists exert to build a theology based on biology and neurology, relate mysticism to molecules, and probe into the sacred depths of nature.

Religious naturalists seek meaning from within the natural world, trusting science and art, traditional wisdom and poetry. They do not separate humanity from the rest of the natural phenomena. They are deeply interested in issues of peace and justice. As with religious adherents, religious naturalists also experience feelings of deep joy and reverence

Religious naturalists write books, exchange views, and organize meetings in which they explore the countless implications of their worldview in the modern context. Religious naturalism, however, is not an organized system of thought or philosophy, but a movement in which many scholars, thinkers, and scientists participate.

—Varadaraja V. Raman

FURTHER READING

Cavanaugh, M. (1995). *Biotheology: A new synthesis of science and religion.* Lanham, Maryland: University Press of America.

Drees, W. B. (1996). *Religion, science, and naturalism.* Cambridge: Cambridge University Press.

Goodenough, U. (1998). *The sacred depths of nature.* New York: Oxford University Press.

Gould, S. J. (1999). *Rocks of ages: Science and religion in the fullness of fife.* New York: Ballantine.

Griffen, D. R. (2000). *Religion and scientific naturalism: Overcoming the conflicts.* Albany, NY: SUNY Press.

Rue, L. (2000). *Everybody's story: Wising up to the epic of evolution.* Albany, NY: SUNY Press.

Sagan, C. (1994). *Pale blue dot: A vision of the human future in space.* New York: Random House.

Swimme, B., & Berry, T. (1992). *The universe story.* San Francisco: Harper.

NATURE, THE SACRED IN

The natural world is obviously important, even essential. We rely on nature for our very existence. Therefore, it might be assumed that nature holds the same significance, value, or meaning for everyone. However, this is not the case. In fact, for different people, nature holds very different meanings.

Two different meanings divide people roughly into two main groups. The first group views nature as primarily valuable for producing wood for houses, oil for heating, crops for food, that is, products that sustain our physical existence. The second group views nature as being primarily valuable for its beauty, its fascinating complexity, and for how it can effect us spiritually. We might refer to these two groups as differing as to whether they see nature primarily in terms of nature's *instrumental* or of its *intrinsic* value.

Within the group emphasizing nature's intrinsic value, there are further divisions—between those who emphasize the sacred in nature and those who do not. It might be assumed that most religious people emphasize the sacred in nature, but that has not always been the case. Through the centuries, there have been many religious people who have treated nature as simply ours to exploit.

Furthermore, those who find the sacred in nature also constitute a diverse and complex group. There are religious as well as nonreligious people in this group. There are those who feel we humans are a part of nature (that we are "human animals") and those who feel we are not (who admire nature from afar, so to speak). However, the common bond of finding the sacred in nature outweighs the differences.

An example of someone who, early on, found the sacred in nature is the world-renowned biologist, Jane Goodall. Jane Goodall is famous for her studies of chimpanzees.

Throughout most of her life, Goodall has used religious and spiritual language to describe her experience of nature. For example, in *Reason for Hope, A Spiritual Journey,* she says, "the forest—any forest—is, for me, the most spiritual place" (Goodall, 1998, p. 268) and then goes on to compare a forest to a cathedral. She says that when she walks through a forest, she feels a spiritual presence and feels that everything is connected through the power of God.

Early on, Jane Goodall was encouraged to form a personal connection with nature—by her mother especially. She used to climb up into her favorite tree, which she called "Beech," and "feel the lifeblood of Beech, coursing below the rough bark." It was this early connection with nature, coupled with her family's relaxed but strong religious faith that led to Goodall's developing a spiritual connection to nature.

Goodall's finding the sacred in nature makes her one among many. Among those many are those who see nature as sacred because a sacred hand made it. That is, they feel that nature is sacred because God made it. Trees and flowers are, for them, works of God, and so, for them, to cultivate a connection to a tree or a flower is to cultivate a connection to God.

Others feel, in nature, something spiritual but not especially religious. They may feel so because, in nature, they feel most at home. Much of today's talk among conservationists (as when the earth is referred to as *Mother Earth*) has this quality of speaking about nature as a spiritual home.

In summary, there are two main ways of viewing nature and its value or meaning. There is the view that emphasizes nature being primarily an instrumental value, something that benefits all of us by meeting our physical needs. Then there is the view that emphasizes nature being primarily an intrinsic value, something that can benefit us by meeting our spiritual needs.

Throughout history, the first view has been the dominant view. However, recently, and partly as a result of the ecological crisis, there has been a shift toward the second view of nature as an intrinsic value, one emphasizing that in nature we can find the sacred.

—Amelia Sinkin

See also Ecology; Environmental Ethics

FURTHER READING

Goodall, J. (1999). *Reason for hope: A spiritual journey.* New York: Warner Books.

NEO-PAGANISM

Many recent reports name Neo-paganism as one of the fastest growing religious populations in the world, but to speak of Neo-paganism as a single religious expression is misleading. Rather, *Neo-paganism* is an umbrella term for a variety of loosely connected contemporary Western religious systems. Key elements such as reverence for the earth and a focus on mystery teachings tie these systems together.

Many Neo-pagans follow a philosophy much akin to the Gaia hypothesis, a scientific theory from the mid-1970s that held that the earth behaves as a single organism. Therefore, spiritual expression in Neo-pagan religions is often channeled through environmentalism, outdoor worship, and natural crafts, such as herbalism and working with gems and crystals. Neo-pagan holidays are based around natural solar and lunar cycles.

Mystery teachings represent the inner beliefs associated with pre-Christian European religions and are focused on the three great mysteries: birth, life, and death. In essence, mystery teachings trace the journey of the soul as it moves through the material world and prepares to pass into the spiritual realms beyond. These teachings often focus on natural processes as parallels for the soul's journey and use stories to illustrate its path. The various forms of Neo-paganism incorporate the myths and legends of the mystery teachings from whichever culture they are based upon.

The theological foundations of the Neo-pagan religions are diverse. Many are polytheistic, meaning that they believe in multiple gods. Asatru, for example, is a form of Neo-paganism based on the Norse pantheon of gods, including Odin and Freya. Other polytheistic forms of Neo-paganism include the Hellenists (based on Greek mythology) and those who follow Egyptian gods. As can be seen, many Neo-pagan religions are built around historical interpretations of various cultural gods and goddesses, while others are more general by placing two universal deities, the god and goddess, at the foreground.

While polytheism is probably the most common religious philosophy amongst Neo-pagans, some subscribe to more pantheistic or panentheistic philosophies. Pantheism is the belief that everything, the totality of reality, is god. That is, only god exists and all that exists is god. Panentheism, on the other hand, is the belief that a god interpenetrates every part of nature but is nevertheless *fully distinct* from nature. While not completely exclusive from polytheism, these philosophies are much more common in the feminist goddess worship circles that comprise a segment of Neo-paganism.

While the ideals discussed above serve to tie the Neo-pagan religions together, the most similar thing about them is their diversity. Neo-pagans do share the idea that no one path is right for every person. In other words, each person must find his or her own way. For that reason, even within a distinct and well-formed Neo-pagan tradition, the differences in the beliefs and practices of its members are likely to be vast. Add to this the immense number of traditions, coupled with the millions of practitioners who do not belong to any formal tradition, and it is nearly impossible to generate an overview of Neo-paganism that is general enough to be factual but detailed enough to be informative.

WICCA: WESTERN MYSTERY TRADITION

An easier task is to provide a more detailed description of a smaller subset of Neo-paganism. The most common Neo-pagan religion is known as *Wicca,* a word with etymological connection to the word *witch.* Many followers of Wicca see themselves as continuing the practice of a pre-Christian nature religion that went into hiding during the Inquisition, while others see their religion as a revival of those pre-Christian beliefs and point to the work of Gerald Gardner as the origin of their current practice.

Wiccan religious practice is based around a series of solar and lunar holidays. The solar holidays, called the *Wheel of the Year,* are Samhain (October 31), Yule (winter solstice, approximately December 21), Imbolc (February 2), Ostara (spring equinox, approximately March 21), Beltane (April 30), Litha (summer solstice, approximately June 21), Lammas (August 2), and Mabon (fall equinox, approximately September 21). The symbolism of these holidays is steeped in the Mystery Teachings, and they are often viewed as the life cycle of the God, who is born at Yule, begins to court the Goddess at Imbolc, mates with the Goddess at Beltane, begins to fade at Litha, dies at Samhain, and is reborn the following Yule. The lunar holidays, called *Esbats,* mark the phases of the moon and are tied to the life cycle of the Goddess. She is the Maiden as the moon waxes, the Mother at the Full Moon and ages to the Crone at the New Moon.

Spell casting and divination are among the most well-known and misunderstood practices of Wiccans. For many Wiccans, magic is a form of ritualized prayer, aimed at creating changes in the world by focusing the practitioner's will. It is governed by two basic religious tenets, the Wiccan Rede and the Law of Return. The Rede can be summed up in the statement "Harm none," and the Law of Return states that any energy sent out, returns to the sender. Together, they are an ethos of self-responsibility for one's actions.

CHILDREN AND ADOLESCENTS IN NEO-PAGAN RELIGIONS

Until recently, Neo-pagan religions have been composed mostly of adult converts. Now, however, the number of Neo-pagan children and adolescents has skyrocketed. This increase comes from two sources. First, many Neo-pagans have begun to raise children in their religious traditions. In addition, the number of teenagers converting to Neo-paganism has been steadily on the rise in recent years. These two groups, children raised in the tradition and teenagers who have converted, must be treated as distinct cohorts when discussing the spiritual and religious development of Neo-pagan children.

Children raised in Neo-pagan traditions are often exposed to a wide variety of religious and spiritual ideas. In addition to the holidays and values of mainstream Christian culture, children are introduced to Native American, Eastern, and Caribbean religions and ideas. As a result, the god images that Neo-pagan children are raised with are very diverse. Some children are familiar with gods and goddesses from a variety of cultures and mythologies, while others know only the more general God and Goddess.

Discretion has come to be a very important skill for young Neo-pagan children to learn. Extended family, school personnel, and friends are often misinformed or even hostile to the beliefs practiced by the family. As a result, children must learn to keep their religious beliefs private. This is often very hard for children who are engaged and excited about their religion and want to share it with their friends and family.

The path is very different for adolescents who convert to Neo-pagan religions. Most of them were raised in Judeo–Christian households, and the beliefs and practices of Neo-pagan religions are very different from those of their families. Unlike children raised in the tradition, these teens often face opposition from their parents. Owing to fear of legal reprisals, few Neo-pagan groups will teach under-age seekers without express parental consent. Therefore, most teens must learn about the religion from books and the Internet, with no direct adult supervision or guidance. This results in a very different understanding from those children raised and guided on the path by their parents.

Though there are many difficulties for both Neo-pagan-born and converted children and teens, the opportunities for personal exploration and spiritual growth are vast. Children and teens are encouraged to directly interact with nature and engage in spiritual practices, such as meditation, to enhance their spiritual development. The deity images they are introduced to are usually from a variety of civilizations, encouraging multicultural understanding and appreciation. Most importantly, Neo-pagan children and teens are encouraged to explore spiritual ideals for themselves, creating a personal spiritual identity that can serve as a foundation for understanding psychological, emotional, and physical development.

SUMMARY

Neo-pagan religions offer children and adolescents a diverse religious and spiritual environment. They are encouraged to find their own path, while being schooled in respect for the earth and appreciation for life's mysteries. While being members of a misunderstood minority religion is often difficult, the avenues for religious and spiritual expression are vast.

—Sandra R. Kirchner

FURTHER READING

Adler, M. (1997). *Drawing down the moon: Witches, druids, goddess-worshippers, and other pagans in America today.* New York: Penguin/Arkana

Campanelli, P. (1997). *Ancient ways: Reclaiming pagan traditions.* St. Paul, MN: Llewellyn.

Grimassi, R. (2000). *Encyclopedia of Wicca & witchcraft.* St. Paul, MN: Llewellyn.

Monaghan, P. (2001). *Wild girls: The path of the young goddess.* St. Paul, MN: Llewellyn.

Starhawk. (1999). *The spiral dance: A rebirth of the ancient religion of the great goddess.* San Francisco: HarperCollins.

NIEBUHR, REINHOLD

Reinhold Niebuhr (1892–1971) was born the son of Gustav and Lydia Niebuhr on June 21, 1892, in Wright City, Missouri. He had three siblings, one of whom also became a famous theologian and ethicist, Helmut Richard Niebuhr. Reinhold's first introduction to the Christian faith came through the German Evangelical Synod where his father was a minister, and Elmhurst College, a small denominational high school. He began his formal theological studies at Eden Seminary and completed a master's degree at Yale Divinity School. From Yale, he moved to Detroit, where he was the pastor of a middle-class congregation for 13 years before he accepted an academic position at the interdenominational Union Theological Seminary from 1930 to 1960. Niebuhr was married to Ursula M. Keppel-Compton, and they had two children together, Christopher and Elisabeth. Ursula, a professor of religion at Barnard College, was an intellectually challenging colleague as well as an excellent editor of Niebuhr's work. Reinhold Niebuhr's life and work have influenced the religious and spiritual lives and development of those who study him and his teachings.

PESSIMISTIC OPTIMIST

The apparently contradictory phrase "pessimistic optimist" that Robert Brown uses to describe Niebuhr alludes to two important aspects of his theology. In *An Interpretation of Christian Ethics,* he looks at both the possibility of love in the Christian Church as well as the need to realize the limitations of humanity in living it out. Pessimism refers to Niebuhr's emphasis on the sinful nature of humans, so much so that Reinhold resurrected the term "original sin," which led to severe criticism from both philosophers and theologians. Although he later regretted using the term, hc intended it not as a reference to Eden or ultimate depravity, but to the simple acknowledgment that sin limits all human endeavors through pride and rebellion against God.

In the Gifford lecture series *The Nature and Destiny of Man,* Niebuhr describes sin as rebellion against God and humanity's place in the universe. Sin is not just a part of the individual person, but also a part of the institutions, communities, and nations of humanity. He believed that democracy was an important part of modern living and the checks and balances of the constitution held back any particular group from gaining too much power. In *The Children of Light and the Children of Darkness,* Niebuhr described the ability and the need for democracy due to man's "inclination to injustice."

The key to Niebuhr's optimism is his belief that although sin is present in humanity, the connection to the transcendence of God provides a different perspective. Humanity is a part of nature, and thus subject to a limited perspective, but each religion attempts to transcend this limit through a connection to an ultimate source of meaning and value. For the Christian, Biblical faith provides this transcendent view and allows humanity to see beyond itself.

PUBLIC THEOLOGIAN

In addition to being an active pastor and academic, Niebuhr was also actively involved in politics and social activism. Niebuhr joined with many Jewish leaders and their concerns with poverty and social justice in Detroit. Earlier in his career, he was taken with Marxist thought and was a critic of contemporary American capitalism. He later moved away from some of his socialist ideals, although he never fully gave up on pointing out different social ills and the problems they created for society both in communism and capitalism. His theology made him keenly aware that any type of social structure had the possibility of becoming corrupt, yet these same systems were necessary in controlling the sin inherent in humanity. He published in theological journals, but also in secular political journals as well, and gained support from atheists such as Arthur Schlesinger and Hans Morgenthau who agreed with his social and political views while disagreeing with his theology.

Niebuhr witnessed several important historical events, including the Great Depression, world war, and cold war, and commented on each as a theologian who actively explored the philosophical and political ideas of his day. Although he held to traditional biblical faith, he did not settle for easy answers to the complex problems of his lifetime. For Niebuhr, the Church must be a witness for secular society while remaining self-conscious of its own propensity toward sin. Niebuhr drew from several aspects of the Christian tradition, including the prophets of the Old Testament, the writings of the Apostle Paul, and the work of Christ. He attempted to be faithful to the message of the Christian Church, while making it relevant and understandable to a modern audience.

SPIRITUAL DEVELOPMENT

Niebuhr highlights some important aspects of spiritual development, especially for those in the Christian tradition. First is the importance of looking at sin both in individuals and social structures, especially in regards to pride and power. This reflects the importance of being self-critical and realizing one's limitations; each person has the same capacity for sin in any type of situation. Second, although awareness of sin is important, this concept must be connected with an understanding of the ability of the Church to show the love of God to the world. God brought redemption to humanity through the work of Christ, which has brought a new world and a new understanding of humanity's relationship to the divine and to each other. Third, one's faith and theological concerns should be actively involved in public life, both in the questioning of current cultural and societal norms and issues of social justice and poverty. Spiritual maturity requires being actively involved in facilitating social change and witnessing the love of to God nations.

—James A. Van Slyke

FURTHER READING

Niebuhr, R. (1932). *Moral man and immoral society: A study in ethics and politics.* New York: Charles Scribner's Sons.

Niebuhr, R. (1935). *An interpretation of Christian ethics.* New York: Harper & Bros.

Niebuhr, R. (1945). *The children of light and the children of darkness: A vindication of democracy and a critique of its traditional defense.* New York: Charles Scribner's Sons.

Niebuhr, R. (1949). *The nature and destiny of man: A Christian interpretation.* New York: Charles Scribner's Sons.

Niebuhr, R. (1952). *The irony of American history.* New York: Charles Scribner's Sons.

Niebuhr, R. (1986). *The essential Reinhold Niebuhr: Selected essays and addresses.* R. M. Brown (Ed.). New Haven, CT: Yale University Press.

NODDINGS, NEL

Nel Noddings is a contemporary philosopher of education. She teaches at Stanford University and Teachers College, Columbia University. She is world famous for her innovative approach to moral education, which she calls *caring.* She suggests that a caring attitude is necessary to enable changes in our schools and the whole educational system. In her many books she describes concrete examples of caring at a variety of levels: for others, for plants and animals, for our environment, and for the spiritual self. Her work inspires many educators, parents, as well as others interested in creating and nurturing environments that care for the spirit.

Noddings's approach is an ethical and educational model to be implemented in school classrooms. She calls for introducing spiritual questions into our curriculum. Even math classes may be relevant to a religious or spiritual problematic because such figures in the math curriculum as Descartes or Pascal struggled with the difficulties involved in trying to prove the existence of God. Noddings argues that the modern liberal education is devoid of feeling and caring dimensions and does not enrich the human mind and spirit but tends to narrow its scope. A caring, feminine approach to education is not limited to logical reasoning but draws attention to human passions, concerns, and ethical responsibilities. Noddings's vision includes schools designed as the centers of care where youth can work in a collaborative manner. A caring education, she argues, will enable children to develop into adults capable of caring for others in this world.

A central concept in Noddings's ethics is *relation.* A caring relation is an encounter between two human beings that creates a sense of connection. Both the caregiver and the care receiver contribute to this relationship. A caregiver has a specific state of consciousness described by Noddings as receptive and full of desire to help a stranger in need. This desire constitutes a motivational displacement. A care receiver must necessarily be responsive as otherwise a caring relation would not be mutual and reciprocal. The desire to be cared for represents a universal human characteristic. Noddings contrasts the standard model of religious moral education with the idea of confirmation, which represents an act of affirming and encouraging the very best in somebody's action even if such a better self is only potentially present. Contrary to moral judgment, confirmation sustains a continuous connection between the two people.

Addressing questions of children's belief or unbelief in God, Noddings stresses that they should be the subject of intelligent inquiry. Noddings reminds us of John Dewey's view on democracy that should include a common truth on the encounter of God in people in all departments of action. The existential and metaphysical questions should be raised in an ordinary classroom and during regular high school classes. Noddings's discussions focus on the nature of God and many gods; the possibility of spiritual progress and the danger of religious intolerance; human desire to experience a sense of belonging; feminism and the politics of religion; immortality, salvation, and humanistic aspirations; science, mathematics, and religion; human dependence on God; and secular ethics. The question of the meaning and purpose of life is of equal importance to children and adults alike. Teenagers often succumb to pessimism. Rather than denying this feeling, Noddings suggests a life-oriented education, capable of assisting students in realistic self-evaluation and creating a caring environment.

Noddings stresses a moral life in the community and its specific importance for students who are especially proud of group loyalty. The hard questions of self-understanding and learning to apply the compassionate rules of the group in relation to treating strangers should become part of students' own ethical and social responsibility. Noddings thinks that students should begin to understand the fragility of facts devoid of context and speaker. She points that value education should not be dogmatic. She calls fundamentalism the biggest stumbling block to educating for pluralistic values. She insists that a critical and appreciative examination of religion belongs in schools and students would benefit from it.

Noddings presents feminist spirituality as an alternative to traditional patriarchal religion noticing that women have long suffered inferiority under the prevailing theological and philosophical theories. She suggests that students should be exposed to both the story of the Fall and to its feminist critique with the emphasis on the Goddess religions, in which the biblical serpent brings knowledge and healing. Students should have an opportunity to study the plurality of positions and become aware of many alternative and often controversial religious beliefs. Noddings is interested in the problem of evil. The deep exploration of this and other questions contributes to an enhanced capacity for all people to make intelligent connections to the spiritual realm.

—*Inna Semetsky*

FURTHER READING

Noddings, N. (1984). *Caring: A feminine approach to moral education.* Berkeley: University of California Press.

Noddings, N. (1993). *Educating for intelligent belief or unbelief.* New York and London: Teachers College, Columbia University.

OBJECTIVISM

Objectivism refers to a philosophy developed by the Russian-American author Ayn Rand. Literally, objectivism means "to be objective." Thus, Objectivists assert that truth exists in the external world and is not relative to each individual. Rationality is the tool by which individuals apprehend truth. In objectivist philosophy, then, there is always a "right" and "wrong" answer. When two people have conflicting perspectives, for example, objectivists do not dismiss the argument as a "difference of opinion." They insist either that only one is correct or that both are incorrect. There can only be one truth, and it is the person with a greater command of rationality who perceives truth.

The most controversial aspect of objectivism is its implications for ethics. Much of Rand's philosophy rebelled against the religious and communist institutions of her time. Rand felt that both these institutions wrongly stressed self-sacrifice and altruism over the needs of the individual. Doing so, she argued, promoted a "moral crisis" because a functioning society can only exist if its individuals take their own survival and vitality as their primary moral concern. However, for Rand, *survival* did not refer to just the bare essentials needed to exist. Survival also referred to the development of personal values and the achievement of personal goals. While communism and religion wished to subjugate personal values and goals under "greater" societal values and goals, Rand believed that societal goals and values are oppressive unless individuals make them their own. However, irrespective of whether they are societal or personal, from the objectivist perspective, goals and values must be rationally attained. Thus, if two people have conflicting personal values, one must have the correct values and the other incorrect values or both have incorrect values. While she agreed society cannot tell one what goals and values to adopt, Rand did believe that all rational people adopt the same values.

Rand wrote not only about the attainment of values but also about the content of rational values themselves. In particular, Randian ethics distinguishes between the values by which one leads one's life and the virtues that allow one to preserve personal those values. Rand identified three cardinal values, reason, purpose, and self-esteem, and three corresponding virtues, rationality, productiveness, and pride. Self-esteem and pride give objectivism its egoistic tinge. Whereas in other ethical systems, pride is seen as corrosive, in objectivism self-pride and self-love are seen as central sources of meaning.

But does objectivism constitute a philosophy or a dogma with religious overtones? This is a highly debated question about objectivism. Rand, herself, vehemently opposed the idea that objectivism is a dogma or a religion. However, many in the objectivist community behave like they are in a religious group. For example, objectivists often treat Rand's writings as if they are sacred texts, and Leonard Peikoff, Rand's successor and head of the Ayn Rand Institute, now acts like an objectivist version of a religious leader who denounces "heretical" interpretations of Randian thought.

Today objectivism seems to have lost its critical edge that made it a popular philosophy during Rand's lifetime. Because objectivists do not believe rational thought can have several different conclusions, rational criticisms of Rand's work are dismissed. As a result, the beliefs of objectivists have become dogmas rather than sources of critical philosophical thought. For this reason, objectivism seems to have changed from a philosophy to a dogmatic form of thought not dissimilar to dogmatic religion.

—*Jed Daniel Forman*

FURTHER READING

Rand, A. (1964). *The virtue of selfishness.* New York: Signet.

Sciabarra, C. M. (1995). *Ayn Rand: The Russian radical.* University Park: The Pennsylvania State University Press.

Robbins, J. W. (1974). *Answer to Ayn Rand.* Washington, DC: Mount Vernon Publishing Company.

OBJECT-RELATIONS THEORY

The concept of *object relations* in psychoanalytic writings means relations with significant others and their internal representations, starting with infancy and the mother (*object* in psychoanalytic writings always refers to another person). Primitive, early, object relations are the starting point for personality development. Whereas, for Freud, the drive-based quest for sensuous gratification conditions the structure of the personality, these theorists argue that the individual seeks relationships before seeking gratification. The pattern taken by the individual's relationship with others, internalized during early childhood, structures the adult personality as well as adult spirituality.

What is known as *psychoanalytic object-relations* theory represents the psychoanalytic study of the nature and origins of interpersonal relations and of the nature and origins of internal, unconscious structures deriving from interpersonal contacts and experiences. Present interpersonal relationships are regarded as the reactivation of past internalized relations with others. Psychoanalytic object-relations theory focuses upon the internalization of interpersonal relations, their contribution to normal and pathological personality development, and the mutual influences of internal fantasies and the reality of interpersonal relations.

Individual personality is formed through object-relations patterns that are set up in early childhood, become stable in later childhood and adolescence, and then are fixed during adult life. The functioning of the adult personality depends on the maturity of one's object relations. Object-relations theorists propose that the ego, which is the center of the personality, seeks objects, and this is the basic drive animating the human personality. The role played by the mother's constant presence during the first stages of life makes it the factor around which personality is organized. The mode by which one manages one's dependence on and differentiation from the mother is the structuring force of the individual mind. Psychoses and neuroses are accounted for by the complications of parental care rather than by eruptions of repressed desire.

Motivations experienced by the individual's body alone are thus de-emphasized, and correspondingly, the formative significance of relating to others is played up. Sexuality is demoted to a secondary role. It may complicate the relationship with the object, but it does not by itself constitute that relationship. Body sensations carry messages but are not equivalent to the contents of these messages. Communication is channeled through the surface of the body, the sensitivity of which intensifies with the child's age. At all stages, bodily sensation is a means rather than an end of communication.

While classical psychoanalytic theory viewed the personality as an information-processing system in touch (or out of touch) with reality, in object-relations theory the emphasis is on internalized and projected ideas, leading to a total distortion of reality. Compared to classical approaches, object-relations theory is even more pessimistic. It views personality as less reality oriented, and its structure as determined earlier in life. While in Freud's version the "critical period" in personality development is the Oedipal stage, years 3 to 6 of life; it is during the first year that object-relations patterns are determined.

The common core of classical psychoanalytic theory and object-relations theory can be summarized in the two concepts of desire (for an object or for instinctual gratification), and separation from the object. Both approaches agree that it all starts with the young child and its understanding of sex, birth, and family relations, with the resulting confused ideas that stay with us forever. Object-relations theory says that the process all starts very early, which means that the cognitive confusion is greater and deeper.

Winnicott asserted that at the original point from which all humans start there is already a relationship. The baby is an aggregate of sensations and body parts without an organizing principle. This may only be provided by the parent "who is holding the child" physically and whose presence functions as an external perimeter that contains the various stimuli and so orders them into a meaningful whole. Thus, relationship precedes individuality. There is no such thing as a baby, because there is always attached to it someone caring for the baby. The lack of individual separateness in the initial stages of life goes beyond the fact of physical dependence. It involves the absence of inner cohesion.

At this point the child creates what Donald W. Winnicott calls the *transitional object.* This object appears when the reassuring internal representation of the mother is projected onto a tangible item, such as a blanket or a soft toy, which the child invests with special meaning and identity. The transitional object helps the child bridge the frustration of parental unavailability. That object is simultaneously internal and external: it carries a subjective meaning, but being tangible, it is also objectively perceived. In later life the soft toy or blanket is substituted by games, artistic creativity, and intellectual discussion. Such activities provide individuals with spaces where they can externalize their internal images.

The rise of object-relations theory and the attention given to pre-Oedipal experiences (preceding the age of 3) have broadened the scope of the basic psychoanalytic view of personal and cultural phenomena. This theory in particular provides a good basis for understanding the world of spirits in relation to the internal world of objects.

Regarding religious beliefs, object-relations theorists follow Sigmund Freud in viewing any religious belief system as based on projections. While Freud emphasized the projection of the father, the so-called Oedipal object, object-relations theory suggests that what is projected is the maternal image, formed earlier in the child's development. The objective existence of the caring figure, without whom the infant would not survive, is the source of fantasies about caring spirits, who promise eternal love and boundless happiness. As the developing child internalizes hope and trust, he comes to live within an inner psychic universe of unseen but providential presences. When he is subsequently introduced to supernaturalist beliefs through cultural experience (God, the angels), he takes to it naturally.

Cultural fantasies expressed in so-called mystical experiences reflect an attempt to recreate the mother–child symbiotic encounter. The early experience of creating a substitute for the mother, known as the *transitional object*, is the model for cultural rituals and beliefs. This experience is one case of transitional states, where a real stimulus near the person starts a fantasy process in which object relations are projected on it. This "substance of illusion," as Winnicott described it, is the starting point for the creation of art and religion.

The behavior in an individual of turning to "spiritual search" is most likely to be caused by a loss of a significant other or a significant relationship. This search makes possible an imaginary contact with the lost object. Loss or absence in the child's relations with parental figures may lead to the appearance of religious experiences.

—Benjamin Beit-Hallahmi

See also Freud, Sigmund; Psychoanalytic Approaches

FURTHER READING

Faber, M. D. (2002). *The magic of prayer: An introduction to the psychology of faith.* Westport, CT: Praeger. .

Winnicott, D. W. (1971). *Playing and reality.* London and New York: Routledge.

ORIGINAL SIN

All human beings have rights to food, clothing, shelter, personal dignity, and safety rights that have to be honored if the human community is to be humane. Earth is populated with billions of people, millions of whom are malnourished, homeless, poor, oppressed, illiterate, exploited, dying from treatable diseases, living the social and economic consequences of the debilitating cycles of poverty, domestic violence, autocratic political regimes, racism, colonialism and militarism. Humans participate in the genocide of other humans. It is sometimes referred to as *ethnic cleansing,* whereby one group of people from one ethnic or cultural background insists on its natural superiority over another and justifies its violence in attempting to eradicate some humans from the face of the earth. These realities dehumanize human existence and leave the human community anything but humane.

Then there are decisions made by industrialized nations about the use and abuse of the environment, decisions that have long-term consequences for the whole world with respect to air, water, and land. Environmental theory says we may all live by robbing nature, but some standards of living demand that the robbery continue excessively and indifferently.

As a result of excessiveness and indifference, innocent people suffer. At times, the guilty go free and injustice prevails. Such injustice is often passed on from generation to generation. Fear, guilt, despair, estrangement, anxiety, and violence seem, then, to be as much part of the human saga as the experience of loving relationships, joy, interpersonal and social harmony, respect, creativity, physical and emotional security, and hope.

Intelligibly explaining this complex and often contradictory human condition into which we are born is the challenge for those attempting to support the psychosocial and spiritual development of children and adolescents. Those who study and write about children, such as the psychiatrist Robert Coles, report that at an early age, children start wondering about the nature, complexity, and destiny of their lives. Furthermore, awareness of anxiety begins early in life and focuses on why bad things happen to good people or simply on why things are the way they are in a seemingly unjust world. It is quite common in the early years of religious training for children to realize that the world as they know it is not the world intended by the God of their religious tradition. Such moral and spiritual sensibilities take shape in the early formative years. Children can be aware that some of the entanglements they experience in their young lives do not arise from their personal choice, desire, or will. Original sin is a Christian doctrine or faith-based teaching that attempts to make sense of this experience that there is something terribly awry with the world.

The Creation stories in the Hebrew Scriptures in Genesis 1 and 2, while distinct from each other and written over 500 years apart (Genesis 2 being older than Genesis 1), reveal a Creator God active in designing the features of the universe with creation's centerpiece being humans, male and female, made in God's own image to share with God the stewardship of all creation. As the Genesis story unfolds, the tale of Adam and Eve in the garden describes a decisive moment that damages the covenantal relationship between God and humans. The choice to disobey God turns paradise to predicament. Adam, Eve, the Garden of Eden, the cunning serpent, fruit trees, fig leaves, egoism, terror, shame, and banishment, all are symbols in this powerful story of The Fall. Christian theology teaches that with Adam's "fall" all humanity sinned. This original sin ruptured the primal flow between Creator and creatures albeit without severing God's unconditional love for His creatures and creation.

The stories that follow in the Book of Genesis are illustrative of the predicaments humans encounter following Adam and Eve's disastrous choice to disobey God. Cain and Abel are brothers, yet Cain hates and murders his own brother (Gen. 3:1–26). There is the story of Noah and the great flood; a story of God's desperation with human wickedness and God's decision to keep covenant with Noah and future generations (Gen. 5–9). The Tower of Babel story in Genesis 11 is yet one more example of the residue of original sin in the curse of human miscommunication and failures to understand.

The award-winning author of books for children of all faiths, Rabbi Sandy Eisenberg Sasso, takes such biblical tales and recasts them as means to explore themes of jealousy, anger, fear, and violence. In a number of her children's books, including *Cain and Abel: Finding the Fruits of Peace,* she teaches that as much as we might wish, we cannot shield children from the hurt and rejection that exists all around them. These mythically truth-telling stories explain how sinfulness interrupted God's original plan.

While many of the world's religions explore the fallen state of human nature, Christianity has done most to develop the doctrine of original sin. From a biblical perspective, Adam's sin has been interpreted as one of hubris, meaning great pride, believing he could chart his own course without God. His prideful display inaugurated an inseparable breach between God and humanity. In this breach is born shame, guilt, suffering, death, and the desire for salvation that is a never-ending consequence for himself and his descendants. While the figure and symbol of Adam is prominent in the development of this Christian doctrine, the woman Eve has carried the primary blame for the origin of sin. For millennia, her indictment as Adam's temptress has been used to reinforce the subordination of women in Western patriarchy and religion. It is from a literal interpretation of the Genesis story of The Fall that women have been collectively branded "Eve, the devil's gateway."

Although such patristic theologians as Irenaeus, Tertullian, and Origen espoused original sin as inescapable universal sinfulness, no one has been more influential on the topic than the father of Western

Christian theology, Augustine (354–430 C.E.). Augustine claimed that the fall of Adam was so great a misuse of human freedom and so great a sin that human nature itself became "fallen." Furthermore, human nature became not only sinful but also "a breeder of sinners." According to classical Augustinian theology, the inbred human propensity to sin leads to its actual inevitability because the tendency of Adam's sin, hubris, is transmitted through procreation and not primarily through bad example or personal decision. Thus, for Augustine, the first step in gaining help to limit the effects or remove the stain of original sin was to take an infant to receive the grace of the sacrament of baptism. While guilt over inherited or original sin was countered by the grace of baptism, the weakness to sin remained.

Doctrine develops with the new insights that each era brings to the central teachings of the Christian faith. While the basic notions of original sin from the classical tradition remain operative, other areas of the teaching have changed and developed. For example, the transmission of original sin by sexual intercourse is no longer a part of the contemporary understanding of original sin. Mainline Christian theologies today promote the essential goodness of human nature, including the sexual/relational dimension. Modern Protestant theologian Paul Tillich understood original sin as estrangement from one's essence that is an inevitable fact of birth. Tillich suggested that threats to self-actualization or realization are so tied to daily existence that the human birthright, so to speak, is riddled with anxiety. Twentieth-century liberation theologies, including feminist theology, have probed new theological territory in questioning hubris or pride as the sole denominator of original sin.

Today, original sin is described as a universal fact, a source of our collective guilt, universality and historicity of finitude, a disruption of essential unity, an estrangement from true being, a tendency toward narcissism, and the unhealed structures of society, all of which result in the potential failure to make human life in all of its manifestations, truly human.

—*Avis Clendenen*

See also Augustine, Evil, Myth, Sin

FURTHER READING

Clark, E. & Richardson, H. (1996). *Women and religion: The original sourcebook of women in Christian thought.* San Francisco: HarperCollins.

Pagel, E. (1988). *Adam, Eve, and the serpent.* New York: Random House.

Saiving, V. (1979). The human situation: A feminine view. In C. Christ & J. Plaskow (Eds.), *Womanspirit rising.* San Francisco: Harper and Row.

Sasso, S. E. (2001). *Cain and Abel: Finding the fruits of peace.* Woodstock, VT: Jewish Lights.

Suchocki, M. (1994). *The fall to violence: Original sin in relational theory.* New York: Continuum.

Schoonenberg, P. (1965). *Man and sin: A theological view.* Notre Dame, IN: University of Notre Dame.

ORTHODOX CHRISTIAN YOUTH IN WESTERN SOCIETIES

Orthodox Christians are defined here as those who belong to Churches arising from the ancient Patriarchal Sees of Constantinople, Alexandria, and Antioch. This definition encompasses both Eastern Orthodox groups and Oriental Orthodox traditions such as the Coptic Orthodox Church. The historical roots of these communities lie in the Middle East and Eastern Mediterranean but in recent times many Orthodox communities have been established in countries such as France, England, the United Stated, and Australia. A key factor in understanding the challenges facing Orthodox youth in Western countries is to recognize that they are not, comparatively speaking, large communities.

The first issue that these Christians face is that their churches are usually identified with a particular ethnic group. This is often expressed in the group's self-description such as Greek Orthodox, Serbian Orthodox, or Macedonian Orthodox. Maintaining ethnic identity with emphasis on language and other salient social features can be quite difficult, but these issues are compounded when religious beliefs are also included in cultural identity. When an Orthodox youth attends a community event, for example, is this an affirmation of his or her ethnic or religious identity? Undoubtedly the influence of both factors are difficult to distinguish, but a number of writers have pointed out that religious beliefs and practices suffer if they are made subordinate to a more general expression of ethnic origin.

A second issue can be given the general heading of difficulties living an Orthodox life in a culture that, whilst not openly hostile, does not support traditional beliefs and practice of Orthodox Christians. A critical point is that many of the social and moral expectations placed on Orthodox youth, especially women, are not in accord with Western norms, and tensions can arise from what are seen as burdensome regulations. These tensions are most pronounced in those communities that are the most integrated into the wider community. In general, more integrated communities are those that have been established in Western countries the longest and are of European origin as opposed to those that have arrived more recently usually from the Middle East. Many of the ritualized practices that form an important and sustaining part of Orthodox life are also foreign, or even at odds with, norms in Western cultures. For example, many Orthodox communities have extensive and elaborate fasting rituals, which in countries of origin are more readily accepted than in lands of recent settlement where even most mainline Christians have abandoned or curtailed traditional fasting practices. In a similar vein, the liturgy, which is at the heart of the communal life of Orthodox traditions, is a long and elaborate ritual that can be difficult to fit into a busy weekend schedule with many competing demands.

In comparison to both Catholic and Protestant traditions, Orthodox communities lack a comparable level of institutional support. Orthodox youth and young adults are often without the benefit of specific educational initiatives, such as schools and universities that cater to their needs. In Australia and elsewhere, for example, many Orthodox youth attend Catholic schools in the absence of ones for their particular community. As a result, the local Orthodox Church becomes an important focus for a wide range of activities that must cater to a range of ages. Without proper planning and support, local communities can struggle to develop these services leaving youth to feel that they have been neglected or excluded. A sign, however, of the increasing prominence of Orthodox communities in many countries is their willingness to address these structural deficiencies with a new emphasis on establishing an instructional presence. One example of this is programs designed especially for young adults that run during holiday periods in purpose-built facilities.

Lastly, many of the core beliefs of Orthodox Christians flow from rich and complex theological positions. Whilst these dogmas are tenaciously adhered to, they can be difficult to pass on to younger generations who are influenced by the highly secular discourse of Western societies and have not benefited from targeted educational programs. An example of this is the pivotal nature of Trinitarian statements to many aspects of Orthodox belief and practice. These beliefs derive from the common experience of the Patristic period but involve technical and precise language that is often difficult to convey even to young people who have a high level of secular education. This can lead to cognitive dissonance between the professional knowledge of the young adult and their religious beliefs. In such circumstances the side with the weaker cognitive basis tends to be overwhelmed by the stronger. In the case of Orthodox youth this can lead to their worldviews becoming more secular and akin to that of the prevailing culture.

—Richard Rymarz

See also Christianity, Orthodox

FURTHER READING

Clendenin, D. (1995). *Eastern Orthodox theology.* Grand Rapids, MI: Baker.

Cross, L. (1988). *Eastern Christianity: The Byzantine tradition.* Sydney, Australia: E. J. Dwyer.

Elias, J. (2002). *A history of Christian education.* Malabar, FL: Krieger.

Ware, K. (1979). *The Orthodox way.* London: Mowbray.

OSER, FRITZ K.

Fritz K. Oser is best known for his work in the fields of religious and moral development, educational psychology, and political education. This entry highlights his contributions in the fields of spiritual and moral development.

Born in1937 in Switzerland, Fritz Oser studied philosophy at the University of Basel under Karl Jaspers and educational psychology, developmental psychology, and systematic pedagogy at the University of Zurich where he received his Ph.D. in 1975. His postdoctoral work with Lawrence Kohlberg at Harvard University prepared the way for the construction of his theory of religious development.

Oser's theory argues that religious development is universal and occurs in stages. Each stage represents an integration of the stages below and is a qualitatively different way to think about religious questions. Religious development usually happens due to a confrontation with a problem that cannot be solved using one's current stage of religious judgment. This development happens independently of the content of a specific religion. The theory is similar to James Fowler's theory of faith development but has a stronger focus on how people define their relationship to God or what they take to be Ultimate (God).

Oser (together with Paul Gmünder) also developed a stage theory of religious judgment. This theory identified patterns of judgment used in concrete situations, particularly in situations calling into question one's relationship with God or what one takes to be Ultimate–such as when tragedy strikes or when there is a momentous decision to be made. These patterns are defined by bipolar dimensions needing to be coordinated—such as transcendence versus immanence, holy versus profane, trust versus absurdity, and freedom versus dependency. At lower stages, people see only one polar dimension at a time. At higher stages, people connect polar dimensions such that, for example, the Ultimate is seen as both transcendent and immanent.

Using information about how people differentiate and coordinate polar dimensions central to making religious judgments, Oser constructed five stages of religious judgment to capture overall development: In stage one, the orientation is toward religious heteronomy. God is understood as active but intervening unexpectedly in the world. Humans merely react to God's interventions. In stage two, the orientation emphasizes reciprocity. Even though the Ultimate is seen as being all powerful, individuals are seen as being able to influence God, for example, through prayer and by making promises. In stage three, the orientation emphasizes autonomy of the self. Here, the influence of the Ultimate Being is considerably reduced as individuals stress their own personal autonomy and responsibility in making decisions. People in stage four perceive the Ultimate in ways reminiscent of Tillich's phrase "The ground of all being." At stage four, an indirect, mediated relationship with God emerges. Finally, at stage five, the orientation emphasizes religious intersubjectivity and autonomy. The higher the stage, then, the more individuals experience themselves as autonomous and free while also experiencing themselves as dependent upon and connected to God or whatever is taken to be Ultimate. Oser's related line of research has been on moral development. Oser and his associates (e.g., Wolfgang Althof) have written several books and articles in which they critically evaluate Kohlberg's theory and address such central issues as whether moral development can be captured by structural analysis only and whether there are gender differences in moral reasoning.

The work on moral development has made its most important contribution by distinguishing two processes by which moral development proceeds. According to Oser, moral development can result from wrestling with moral dilemmas, hypothetical or real, and/or from living in a just and democratic environment. In the second case, individuals (children) develop morally as they learn to deal with the many naturally occurring conflicts between themselves and others.

Fritz Oser's contributions to our thinking about religious and moral development have been considerable. But like so many other major researchers, his additional contribution has been to support the development of other researchers and to help establish a community of researchers dedicated to better defining the field. Oser's contribution, then, cannot be measured simply in terms of his articles, books, and theories. It needs also to be measured in terms of his being a community builder.

—Ines Wenger Jindra

FURTHER READING

Oser, F. K. (1994). Moral perspectives on teaching. *Review of Research in Education, 20,* 57–127.

Oser, F. K., & Althof, W. (1992): *Moralische Selbstbestimmung. Modelle der Entwicklung und Erziehung im Wertebereich. Ein Lehrbuch.* [Moral autonomy: Developmental and educational models.] Stuttgart: Klett.

Oser, F. K., & Baeriswyl, F. (2001). Choreographies of teaching: Bridging instruction to learning. In V. Richardson (Ed.), *Handbook of research on teaching.* (4th ed.) Washington, D.C.: American Educational Research Association.

Oser, F. K., & Biedermann, H. (Eds.). (2003). *Jugend ohne Politik: Ergebnisse der IEA-Studie zu politischem Wissen, Demokratieverständnis und gesellschaftlichem Engagement von Jugendlichen in der Schweiz im Vergleich mit 27 anderen Ländern.* [Youth without politics: Results from the IEA-study of political knowledge, understanding of democracy and social engagement of youth in Switzerland in comparison with 27 other countries]. Zürich: Rügger.

Oser F. K., & Gmünder, P. (1991). *Religious judgment. A developmental approach.* Birmingham, AL: Religious Education Press.

OUTCOMES, ADOLESCENT

Within the social sciences the study of religion among adolescents has increased significantly in the past 10 years. One of the areas of research that has grown the most is the study of how religion impacts the lives of youth—or how religion impacts adolescent development. Specifically, scholars have looked at how religion is associated with the presence of positive outcomes in adolescents. Secondly, researchers have also examined how religion is related to the lack of risk taking or dangerous or delinquent behaviors in young people. Findings to date suggest that religious involvement often acts as a source of support, resiliency, encouragement, coping, meaning, satisfaction, values, moral development, and behavioral prescriptives.

Religious affiliation not only seems to protect adolescents from problem behavior and maintain youth in times of stress, but it also enables them to thrive by fostering positive developmental outcomes and prosocial behavior. This entry summarizes the research on religion and adolescent well-being and risk-taking behaviors. In addition, it provides an overview of theoretical explanations describing these positive associations.

RELIGION AND WELL-BEING AND THRIVING

A growing body of research documents a positive relationship between religion and adolescent well-being or thriving (see Roehlkepartain, King, Wagener, & Benson, 2005). In these studies religiousness is measured in many ways. Most researchers ask youth how frequently they attend religious services or activities. They also frequently ask how important being religious or spiritual is in their lives. In addition, sometimes they ask about religious commitment, religious values, and what religious beliefs they might have.

When scholars have examined the relationships between religion, spirituality, and thriving, they find a complex pattern of associations. In one case analysis of the Search Institute's Youth and Their Parents dataset (N = 8,165 youth and 10,467 parents), researchers found that spirituality (defined as experiencing transcendence and defining self in relationship to others and having genuine concern for others) and religion (defined as institutional affiliation and participation with a religious tradition and doctrine) both had direct effects on thriving (defined as a concept incorporating the absence of problem behaviors and the presence of healthy development). In addition, religion mediated the effects of spirituality on thriving. These findings suggest that spirituality and religiousness may both play unique roles in the development of thriving. Although most existing research confirms the positive role of religion, this study demonstrated that spirituality may have an influence on youth thriving beyond that of religion.

A number of studies suggest that religion is a constructive resource for enabling youth, who are either physically ill or healthy, to cope with problems. For example, when examining children, early adolescence, and late adolescents, attending church seems to help young people cope with academic achievement. In addition, at-risk youth who attend church are less likely to drop out of school. Church attendance has been found to be a key factor in promoting health-enhancing behaviors, such as exercise, diet, dental hygiene, and seatbelt use. Another study demonstrated that religious youth are more likely to take care of themselves and less likely to engage in health-compromising behaviors—even after controlling for other relevant factors (Wallace & Forman, 1998).

Several studies indicate a positive relationship with religion and such indicators as community service and altruism (see Roehlkepartain et al., 2005). At Catholic University, James Youniss and his colleagues have been studying the relationship between religion and different forms of civic engagement in the past 10 years. They have found that religious youth were more involved in community service compared to those adolescents reporting little religious activity. In fact, when looking at a nationally representative database called *Monitoring the Future*, Youniss and his colleagues reported that students who believe that religion is important in their lives were almost three times more likely to participate in service than those who do not believe that religion is important. Other researchers have shown that believing that religion is important in your life and having religious values have both shown to be associated with various forms of civic engagement. A team at Fuller Theological Seminary has shown that youth who view themselves as being religious also report an elevated concern for others, and religious youth report higher levels of altruism and empathy than their less religious peers.

Studies of individuals nominated for moral excellence also note religious themes as distinctive among many nominees. Colby and Damon (1992) found that most of the moral exemplars in their study of 23 adults who were nominated for their extraordinary moral commitments claimed that faith commitments played a significant role as a foundation for their moral action. The authors suggested that religion acts as a unifying construct in the lives of those with a salient moral identity, promoting the integration of personal goals and moral concerns. Hart and Fegley (1995) made a similar observation noting the positive role of religion in the lives of youth recognized for their remarkable commitment to caring and contributions to others. An important finding in these studies is the unique relationships between identity, religion, and prosocial commitments. For many, caring values, attitudes, and behaviors were not independent of their spirituality; rather all aspects of their morality were governed by their religious beliefs and experience, which informed their goals of service and care and closely related to their identity.

Having a sense of meaning and purpose in life is an important part of thriving or well-being. Religion has been recognized to provide a set of beliefs and values that can give purpose to a young person. For example, young people often explain that it is their religious beliefs that motivate them to care for those in need. In addition, religious congregations provide communities of people who can help interpret life events and help give meaning to everyday and extraordinary occurrences. Several studies have shown that religion has been shown to have a positive impact on personal meaning. Another study found that youth participating in religious communities are more likely to report having a sense of purpose indicative of a commitment to a personal philosophy.

REDUCTION OF RISK

In addition to being associated with factors that contribute to adolescent well-being and thriving, religion is consistently negatively related to a wide range of risk-taking behaviors [see Smith & Faris (2003) for review]. Several studies have found various religious measures (in particular religious attendance and religious salience) to be inversely related to juvenile drug, alcohol, and tobacco use. After reviewing the existing research on substance use and abuse and religious values, one team of researchers concluded that religious commitment may be a powerful component of abstinence decisions among religious youth, particularly minority youth. Higher levels of religiousness are related to lower levels of crime, violence, and delinquency. In addition, research demonstrates inverse associations between adolescent religiousness and youth having had sex, the number of sexual partners, recent occurrence of intercourse, and teenage pregnancy. Religion is associated with less frequent thought of suicide, attempted suicide, and actual suicide. Studies confirm that religiousness is associated with lower levels of depression and hopelessness.

THEORETICAL EXPLANATIONS

Although research demonstrates the relationship between religion and positive developmental outcomes, scholars have just begun to explore why this relationship might be the case. Researchers are beginning to ask many questions. Do religious youth have access to more developmental resources that make a positive difference in their lives? Does religion help nurture a strong identity in young people? Do the religious beliefs and moral codes of religions influence the decisions that young people make?

One explanation that has been proposed is that religion provides access to a developmental infrastructure rich in social and values-oriented resources. From this perspective positive benefits of religion result from an increased access and exposure to components of a network of family and community resources that support healthy development. It is reasoned that an adolescent's religious participation embeds the youth in a community that surrounds and exposes him or her to multiple social support resources including supportive parents, adults, and peers. Studies have shown that religious youth report higher levels of developmental assets (such things as supportive adults outside the family, boundaries, and expectations from parents) than their less religious peers. Additionally, youth who are more active participants in religious institutions or who value being religious or spiritual report lower levels of risk behaviors, such as substance abuse and violence (Wagener, Furrow, King, Leffert, & Benson, 2003).

Research findings explain that these developmental resources mediate the effects of religion on risk outcomes. Another study showed that religion alone did not explain the relationship between adolescent moral outcomes, but it was the relationships to which religious youth had access (i.e., having parents, peers, and adults who youth interacted with, trusted, and shared values) that made the majority of difference predicting the moral outcomes (King & Furrow, 2004). In other words for the youth in this study, it was not just being religious or going to a religious congregation that made a difference in their moral lives, but rather it was the presence of trusting, interactive, and mutual relationships that made a significant difference.

Another potential explanation for religion making a difference in the life of youth is that religion and spirituality also directly influence identity development, which is crucial for developmental success. Religion creates a potentially rich context in which identity can take shape by offering unique ideological, social, and spiritual environments. Religious institutions intentionally offer beliefs, moral codes, and values from which a young person can build a personal belief system. In addition, they provide an intergenerational body of believers to embody and exemplify these beliefs and values. In addition, congregations provide spiritual environments where young people can transcend their everyday concerns and experience connectedness with the divine and human others.

Several studies [see King (2003)] provide support for the argument that religion and spirituality can function as resources in positive identity development among youth. One found that religious youth reported higher levels of commitment and purpose when compared with nonreligious youth. Another noted that intrinsic forms of religiousness were more likely linked to identity achievement. The distinction between intrinsic and extrinsic religiousness was used to differentiate a more utilitarian religiosity from an intrinsic or internalized response. Another study examined the relationship of religious participation to Marcia's identity commitments. Although they found that identity commitments of foreclosure and achievement were related to church attendance, later studies have not always replicated these findings. Other researchers found only weak associations between identity achievement and religious commitment. In turn, identity diffusion has also been associated with lower levels of importance of church or temple participation, orthodoxy of Christian beliefs, and intrinsic religious commitment.

Research suggests that religion offers youth unique developmental assets as well as a rich environment for identity development. Having access to an explicit worldview, a community of support, and experiences of transcendence provide many youth with resources that enable them to develop in positive ways and to protect them from getting involved in dangerous behaviors. Although this is not always the case and at times religion when taken to extremes can cause deleterious effects for young people, it is often a positive resource for development. The review of existing theoretical and empirical literature suggests that there are places of developmental leverage within congregations and faith-based organizations. That being the case, parents, youth practitioners, therapists, and community leaders can turn to religious communities as resources of positive development for their youth.

—Pamela Ebstyne King

FURTHER READING

Colby, A., & Damon, W. (1992). *Some do care: Contemporary lives of moral commitment.* New York: Free Press.

Donahue, M. J., & Benson, P. L. (1995). Religion and the well-being of adolescents. *Journal of Social Issues, 51*(2), 145–160.

Hart, D., & Fegley, S. (1995). Prosocial behavior and caring in adolescence: Relations to self-understanding and social judgment. *Child Development, 66*(5), 1346–1359.

King, P. E. (2003). Religion and identity: The role of ideological, social, and spiritual contexts. *Applied Developmental Sciences, 7*(3), 196–203.

King, P. E., & Boyatzis, C. J. (2004). Editors' introduction: Exploring adolescent spiritual and religious development: Current and future theoretical and empirical perspectives. *Applied Developmental Science, 8*(1), 2–6.

King, P. E., & Furrow, J. L. (2004). Religion as a resource for positive youth development: Religion, social capital, and moral outcomes. *Developmental Psychology, 40*(5), 703–713.

Roehlkepartain, E. C., King, P. E., Wagener, L. M., & Benson, P. L. (2005). *The handbook of spiritual development in childhood and adolescence.* Newbury Park, CA: Sage Publications.

Smith, C. (2003). Theorizing religious effects among American adolescents. *Journal for the Scientific Study of Religion, 42*(1), 17–30.

Smith, C., & Faris, R. (2003). *Religion and American adolescent delinquency, risk behaviors and constructive social activities.* Chapel Hill, NC: National Study of Youth and Religion.

Wagener, L. M., Furrow, J. L., King, P. E., Leffert, N., & Benson, P. (2003). Religion and developmental resources. *Review of Religious Research, 44*(3), 271–284.

Wallace, J. M., Jr., & Forman, T. A. (1998). Religion's role in promoting health and reducing risk among American youth. *Health Education & Behavior, 25*(6), 721–741.

P

PARENTAL INFLUENCE ON ADOLESCENT RELIGIOSITY

As the primary caretakers and overseers of a child's life, parents play a strong role in the childhood development of spirituality and religiosity. Indeed, a number of studies have shown that parental religious beliefs and practices are predictive of child and adolescent religiosity. What is more, the influence of parents appears to have an even greater effect on childhood religiosity than does that of the peers with whom children spend so much of their time. Given the degree to which parents shape the religiosity of their children, parental religious influence, or *religious socialization,* appears to be a critical area of investigation. Despite this great need, relatively little empirical research has been directed toward increasing our understanding of parents' role in children's religious development.

What little theoretical and empirical work has been done presents a complex picture of parental religious socialization. Clearly, childhood spiritual and religious development is a multifaceted enterprise, occurring within the domains of cognition, affect, interpersonal relationships, private behavior, and others. Similarly, the role of parents appears to have a complex influence upon the spiritual and religious development of their children. While in the psychological community there are a large number of clinical theories regarding how parents influence children's beliefs in God and religion, few of these theories have been tested empirically. For instance, psychologists such as Freud and those of the larger psychodynamic school of thought suggest that early childhood impressions of parental figures factor greatly into one's eventual understanding of God. However, the specific nature of this relationship is debated between schools of thought, and few controlled studies have tested their hypotheses, which tend to rely for support on individual case studies and personal observations.

Recently, two different lines of empirical research have attempted to more closely examine parental religious socialization. The first is called *spiritual modeling* and is based on the larger psychological theory of *observational learning,* which has received a great degree of empirical support in the social psychological literature. Proponents of the spiritual modeling theory include Bandura, Oman, and Thoresen, among others. They suggest that children learn spiritually relevant beliefs and behaviors by observing the religious behavior of others. This approach emphasizes the role of what are called *spiritual exemplars,* those whose behaviors exemplify a certain religious or spiritual approach to life.

Spiritual exemplars function as role models, whose religious or spiritual behaviors can be perceived, imitated, and then eventually acquired as personal habits and beliefs. When applied to parents, this theory would suggest that the greater a parent's religiousness and the more observable are his/her behaviors, the greater will be the religiousness of the child. Studies that exemplify this approach are those that focus on the relationship between parental religious importance and religious participation and their children's religious outcomes. Findings from such studies suggest that, as predicted, parents who hold strong spiritual/religious beliefs and who participate in observable religious activities are more likely to have children who report religious beliefs themselves.

A second theory that has been proposed to account for the influence of parents is called *spiritual capital.* This theory is based on the *social capital* theory of Furstenberg and others, which suggests that interpersonal relationships, social networks, and other social structures represent an important resource to children (and others) and allow for greater access to a variety of benefits. It suggests that the stronger and more robust the relationship, the greater its capacity to channel such benefits to the individual. Social capital theory has received a fair degree of recent empirical support. The concept of spiritual capital builds upon the assumptions of social capital theory, and posits that the parent-child relationship and shared parent-child activities play an important role in religious socialization. This theory would predict that spiritual or religious parent-child interactions (spiritual capital) contribute significantly to child religious development. Such interactions may include shared religious rituals, family prayer, or conversations about religious and spiritual issues. In this theory, religious *interactions* take the place of religious *example* in predicting child religious development. This theory is supported by the finding that increased youth participation in religious family rituals is related to higher levels of such children's overall religious participation, as well as to other religious outcomes. Further support comes from the finding that child religiousness is higher in children whose families are closer and whose parents are more supportive.

A recent study that investigated the claims of spiritual modeling and spiritual capital found some support for both theories. Results suggest that when parents are perceived as spiritual role models, children are more likely to report both a greater importance of religion and a positive experience of God. Consistent with spiritual-modeling theory, the findings confirm that some degree of religiousness and spirituality can be learned through the observation and imitation of spiritual role models or exemplars. The study also found that religious interactions between parents and children made a significant contribution to adolescent religiousness, beyond what can be explained by parental role modeling alone. Indeed, the findings suggest that when adolescents participate in family conversations about faith, and in family religious activities, they are more likely to see religion as important to themselves and are more likely to have positive spiritual experiences of God.

The theories of spiritual modeling and spiritual capital make clear some of the ways in which parents influence the religious development of their children. Not only do parents serve as observable spiritual role models for children to observe and imitate, but they constitute vital spiritual resources in their role as interactive partners who participate in shared parent–child religious activities. These shared activities make available to children a variety of spiritual and religious benefits that would otherwise be unavailable to them. However, continued research and theoretical development is necessary to better understand the specific activities and relational qualities that are most important in parent–child religious socialization.

—Ross A. Mueller and Pamela Ebsytne King

FURTHER READING

Bandura, A. (2003). On the psychosocial impact and mechanisms of spiritual modeling: Comment. *International Journal for the Psychology of Religion, 13*(3), 167–173.

Bao, W. N., Whitbeck, L. B., Hoyt, D. R., & Conger, R. D. (1999). Perceived parental acceptance as a moderator of religious transmission among adolescent boys and girls. *Journal of Marriage and the Family, 61,* 362–374.

Cornwall, M. (1988). The influence of three agents of religious socialization: Family, church, and peers. In D. L. Thomas (Ed.), *The religion & family connection: Social science perspectives* (pp. 207–231). Provo, UT: Brigham Young University Religious Studies Center.

Erickson, J. A. (1992). Adolescent religious development and commitment: A structural equation model of the role of family, peer group, and educational influences. *Journal for the Scientific Study of Religion, 31*(2), 131–152.

King, P. E., & Mueller, R. A. (2004). Parents' influence on adolescent religiousness: Spiritual modeling and spiritual capital. *Marriage and Family: A Christian Journal, 6*(3), 413–425.

Oman, D., & Thoresen, C. E. (2003). Spiritual modeling: A key to spiritual and religious growth? *International Journal for the Psychology of Religion, 13*(3), 149–165.

Ozorak, E. W. (1989). Social and cognitive influences on the development of religious beliefs and commitment in adolescence. *Journal for the Scientific Study of Religion, 23*(4), 448–463.

Tamminen, K. (1994). Religious experiences in childhood and adolescence: A viewpoint of religious development between the ages of 7 and 20. *The International Journal for the Psychology of Religion, 4*(2), 61–85.

PEER AND FRIEND INFLUENCES ON ADOLESCENT FAITH DEVELOPMENT

Research into the roles of peer and friend relationships has been an active area of inquiry for developmental scientists, particularly those studies investigating their role in promoting healthy adolescent development. Strong relationships with peers have been linked to perceived self-worth, high levels of perspective-taking and prosocial behavior, and decreased risk of emotional and behavioral problems. Only recently, however, has intentional discussion ensued as to the role of peers and friends in more domain-specific areas of adolescent development, particularly as it pertains to religious *faith development.*

Theories of adolescent development give central importance to the change in the nature of adolescents' relationships with parents and the rising prominence and presence of relationships with peers, especially friends. Important structural and functional differences separate peer relationships from adolescent-parent relationships. For example, an adolescent can relate on restricted levels to a parent (e.g., son or daughter), but the same adolescent must relate to age-level associates according to the dimensions of the peer group and on a dyadic level with particular friends.

There is a distinct structure to adolescent interpersonal relationships. For example, friendship is the experience of having a close, dyadic relation that provides opportunities for loyalty, affection, and intimacy. Alternatively, participation within a peer group is the experience of being liked or accepted more widely by the members of one's peer groups, offering a sense of inclusion. Thus, although friendship and peer groups are conceptually and empirically related, the literature suggests that they each contribute uniquely to an adolescent's social adjustment and development. The resulting discussion will not make qualitative distinctions between *peers* and *friends,* but it is noted that influences on adolescent faith development likely do differ according to the nature and structure of the relational system.

As one moves from childhood to adolescence, most developmental and social scientists articulate agreement on the enlargement of one's social contexts beyond the family to include that of peers and friends. During adolescence one becomes immersed in an environment that is defined largely in interpersonal terms, of which its unifying value and power derive from the qualities experienced in personal relationships. As a result, the adolescent becomes acutely aware of the expectations and judgments of significant others. For example, the views of one's peers notably inform both the experience and expression of faith for the youth. For most adolescents, bridging the gap between the parental indoctrination and personal revelation of faith experience are the important contributions made by peers and friends.

Although religious scholars theorize that adolescent peer groups should be expected to play an increasing role in the development of religious faith (especially during the early and middle adolescent stages), conclusions regarding the role of peers and/or friends in adolescent faith development are tenuous at best and completely neglected at worst. Theory and research that do exist focus quite heavily on the transmission model of interpersonal relationships on religiosity; that is, the religious behavior of peers and friends (e.g., peer church attendance) have been found to have at least moderate positive influence on religious practice (e.g., participation in the church youth group and enjoyment of that participation) but less substantial influence on adolescents' religious belief. Thus, peer and friend influence limited to that of providing religious behavior modeling appears to have marginal influence on an adolescent's faith development, and only then in the direction of concurrent religious behavior itself.

In addition to the transmission model of peer influence, at least two other models have been proposed to describe the nature of peer and friend relationships on adolescent faith development, the transaction model and the transformation model. In the first case, the transaction model states that peers and friends not only have the potential to shape an adolescent's own religious behavior and participation, but they also impact the more intrinsic nature of religiosity by way of their reciprocal interaction and religious communication. More than one study has demonstrated that the extent to which one's faith journey is actively shared (i.e., via interaction and dialogue) with and between friends and peers impacts adolescents' experience of God and maturing of faith. Thus, the adolescent seems to be influenced not only by their friends' and peers' modeling of religious behavior but also by the sharing of faith experiences (e.g., frustrations, successes, mutual goals) between an adolescent and his or her friends and peers.

A third model, the transformation model, attempts to put into perspective the dynamic nature of both parent and friend relationships and its affect on adolescent faith development. In general, the transformation model suggests that although time spent with parents during the adolescent years steadily declines, the role and influence of peers and friends does not eliminate that of the adolescent's parents. Instead, with specific reference to adolescent faith development, important friendships seem to add to the strength of faith modeling and faith dialogue already initiated and still present within the parent–adolescent relationship. Thus, the transformation is represented by both the widening and deepening in the adolescents' relationship system to include similar-age relationships in addition to those already present with the parent(s).

There is growing support for the suggestion that parental modeling and support provide a foundation upon which the adolescent can begin his or her search for meaning through faith. In most cases, however, an adolescent's experience of faith does not normally end with the acceptance of his or her parents' faith. Rather, parents may provide the "necessary" modeling and motivation for the development of faith, but they are rarely "sufficient" in bringing the adolescent to his or her potential in religious belief and commitment. It is more likely that the internalization of beliefs that was initially nurtured by parents evolves to include and be represented by meaningful and deepening friend relationships with which the adolescent can share faith journeys on a more symmetrical and truly reciprocal level. The relationship with "faith-full" friends becomes, then, useful to the adolescent not only as a place to be comfortable with shared beliefs but also as a forum that legitimates the adolescent's own search for individual belief and commitment that was started many years earlier within the context of the parent–child relationship.

—*Kelly Dean Schwartz*

See also Faith Maturity

FURTHER READING

Bukowski, W. M., Newcomb, A. F., & Hartup, W. W. (Eds.). (1996). *The company they keep. Friendship in childhood and adolescence.* Cambridge, UK: Cambridge University Press.

Fowler, J. W. (1981). *Stages of faith: The psychology of human development and the quest for meaning.* New York: HarperCollins Publishers.

Parke, R. D., & Ladd, G. W. (Eds.). (1992). *Family-peer relationships: Modes of linkages.* Hillsdale, NJ: Erlbaum.

Schwartz, K. D., Bukowski, W. D., & Aoki, W. (2005). Friends, mentors, and gurus: Peer and nonparent adult influences on spiritual development. In E. C. Roehlkepartain, P. Ebstyne King, L. Wagener, and P. L. Benson, (Eds.). *The handbook of spiritual development in childhood and adolescence.* Thousand Oaks, CA: Sage Publications.

PLURALISM

Humanity is heir to many religions. Since ancient times, every culture and people has had its religious visions. Through the ages, the major religions split into different sects and subsects, often competing with one another in the matter of their doctrinal truths. When people of one religion encountered those of another, conflicts and controversies often ensued, occasionally even bloodshed. The history of interreligious wars is among the sad pages of human history.

There were (and still are) societies where all members belong to the same sect or faith while those of other religions were persecuted or expelled. But there are also societies where people of different faiths live together in peace. One of the hallmarks of modern nations is that they ensure that this can be the case.

In the modern world the notion of diversity and tolerance of different ideas was propagated by thinkers of the European Enlightenment in the 18th century. According to the *Barnhart Concise Dictionary of Etymology* (HarperCollins, 1988, p. 578), in the 19th century the word *pluralism* was used to refer to "the holding of two or more church benefices at one time." Today we use the term *religious pluralism* to denote a state of affairs within a society in which a variety of religious beliefs and practices are allowed and where efforts are made to understand and appreciate one another.

In 1893, the first Parliament of World Religions was held in Chicago. It was perhaps the first time in modern history that people of different religions came together under a single roof and spoke to one another about their respective faiths. And it was the first major step toward what today we call religious pluralism. It was an eye-opener for some in the Christian world when they came to realize that there is mature religious wisdom in cultural settings that were foreign to them. Understanding and sympathy for religions to which one is not attuned are both a consequence of and a requirement for religious pluralism. Indeed, one who is committed to the principle of religious freedom can gain a deeper understanding of one's religion even while appreciating that which is good in the religion of others.

TWENTIETH CENTURY AND LATER

In the spirit of the 1893 Parliament there have been efforts to establish understanding among the religions of humankind in the century since the Chicago meeting. The International Association for Religious Freedom (IARF) was founded in 1900; a Religions of the Empire Conference was held in London in 1924, and the World Congress of Faiths (WCF) was held in 1936. The WCF expresses the conviction that "understanding between people of different religions is important for good community relations, for moral and spiritual renewal and for world peace." This organization publishes the journal *Interreligious Insight.* It also served as an inspiration for the establishment of the International Interfaith Centre at Oxford in 1993.

More recently, the concept of religious pluralism has been given further boost in the context of an America where immigrants of different denominations build places of worship in accordance with their own traditions. Though each group could preach and follow its own religious system, all of them remained relatively isolated. In due course, some thinkers began to feel that all the religions represented in a community must be recognized in public, and so arose a movement to recognize the existence of other religions and understand the various religions that are represented in the country. An expression of this growing awareness is the emergence of numerous interfaith groups in many Western countries, which organize meetings, symposia, and other events in which scholars and practitioners representing various religious traditions expound and exchange their respective religious traditions.

TWO APPROACHES TO RELIGIONS

There are two radically different views of looking upon religious beliefs. According to the first, religious beliefs are inculcated convictions about God and related matters. They have historical, cultural, and psychological origins. They are appealing and meaningful to people, but they have only relative validity; that is to say, their relevance is to specific groups. Therefore, in so far as they do no harm to others, all the religions of the world are essentially equivalent. This view is held generally by people who do not subscribe to any particular religion. This does not mean that they do not attach any value to religions or that they do not respect any religion. We may call this the secularist view of religion. It is easier to accept the notion of religious pluralism from this perspective, because it attaches only relative truth value to any religious tradition. Indeed, most people who subscribe wholeheartedly to religious pluralism tend not to take any religion seriously.

According to the second view, religions embody profound truths with long-range implications. The sources of religion are superhuman, and the truths enunciated by them are revelations of the Absolute. From this perspective again, though there are many religious systems in the world, there is only one right religion. All the others, however well-intentioned and ethically commendable they may be, are flawed in their doctrines. In other words, they are essentially mistaken in their understanding of God and the hereafter. As this view is generally held by people who take their own religion very seriously, we may call it the religionist view. From this point of view, practicing religious pluralism may seem tantamount to rejecting the absolute validity of one's own religion, for it concedes implicitly that the other religion might be just as true in its doctrines as one's own.

No matter who is right about religion, the secularist or the religionist, the fact remains that the vast majority of the people in the world subscribe to the latter view. That is to say, most people believe that their own religion is the one and only one correct religion. They hope and wish for all humankind to become converts, by confession or by conviction, to the spiritual framework of their own particular religion. Ironically, this very attitude is what makes religious pluralism extremely important for the modern world.

OPTIONS

Two possibilities are open for the religionist. One may enforce one's own religion on others by whatever means. For example, the laws of a nation might prohibit any religion other than the one proclaimed by the (religionist) state. In today's world this is the case in some Islamic and Communist countries. Alternatively, one might grant to others the right to have the same conviction about their religions as one entertains about one's own. The laws of nations that subscribe to this approach permit the practice of all religions to their citizens. This is the case in the so-called secular democracies of the world.

In the view of many, such religious tolerance sanctioned by the laws of a land marks a major step forward in the history of civilization. In a sense this fundamental difference in perspectives is at the root of some political confrontations in today's world. Whatever it is, in countries where there are people of more than one faith, it is difficult in the modern world to openly ban other religions. Such a move is only one small step away from religious persecution. It is not surprising that religious pluralism has become the hallmark of enlightened democracies.

However, it must be realized in this context that there is a difference between the laws of the land and the attitudes of its citizens. As noted earlier, the question of religious pluralism becomes relevant to individuals who have deep faith in their own religious world-views. It is difficult for them to reconcile this with the notion that other faiths must be given equal validity.

This leads us to the recognition that there are two levels from which one might subscribe to religious pluralism. One is at the *philosophical level.* Here we accept that one group has as much right to believing in the absoluteness of its religious framework as another group, and that therefore we must give all religions equal weight. No one religious group has greater claims to religious truths than another. This view is adopted by religious secularists.

The second is at the *pragmatic level.* Here one recognizes that in this day and age in an enlightened heterogeneous society or even in the global context, it is impossible for the members of one religious community to openly reject or disparage another religion. At this level, therefore, one is more or less obliged to accept religious pluralism because one does not have another choice.

At the philosophical level, one considers loyalty to one's own faith as very similar to the love one feels for one's own parents. Such love need not deter others from experiencing a very similar love to their various families. Indeed, it would be unrealistic to ask everybody to love our own parents with the same intensity as we do. Nor does respect for the love that others feel diminish in any way respect for one's family. These considerations must be valid at the pragmatic level of religious pluralism also.

SOCIETAL AND PERSONAL IMPACT OF RELIGIOUS PLURALISM

Whether from philosophical or pragmatic considerations, the practice of religious pluralism can have two significant consequences. The first is *societal.* If every group in a society adopts religious pluralism as a way of life, it will lessen the conflicts and mutual arrogance that come from a parochial religiosity that denies others the feelings of commitment and loyalty one feels for one's own religious tradition. Those who refuse to adopt the perspective of religious pluralism in a heterogeneous nation and in a multicultural world, add much to the pain and hate that are already dividing human beings into so many fragmented groups.

At the personal level, religious pluralism enables one to recognize that there is beauty, truth, and wisdom in every religious tradition of the human family and tends to enhance and enrich one's own vision and commitment to one's religion. The following poem expresses a view that reflects what religious pluralism is all about.

Grand Religion
Some say it was Krishna
Who came to save and please us.
Some think it was Buddha,
Yet others that it was Jesus.
To some, the Laws of Conduct,
To Moses God did speak
But to Prophet Mohammed.
Like the frog which was so certain
That its pond was all the sea,
Every one is slightly right
As far as one does see.
Our sun is surely brilliant:
None can this deny.
But does it make much sense to say
There's naught else in the sky?
If religious frogs just jump out
Into the big, big sea,
They'll know there's much more
To religious ecstasy!
Religions are volcanoes:
Powerful sure they are.
But they come from a deeper Source
That's grander, oh by far.

—*Varadaraja V. Raman*

PLURALISM, HINDU APPROACH

Religious pluralism is an important goal of modern societies. It embodies the principle that in a civil society, people of all faiths must be accommodated and respected and must enjoy freedom to worship and follow their chosen tradition. Though this sounds reasonable to people who have grown up and been educated in modern democratic nations, it was/is not always a universal practice. One obstacle for this has been the doctrinal conviction that one's own religious mode is the only correct one and, therefore, must be universally accepted. The notion that there is only one way of apprehending the divine arises from the belief that there is but one individual with whom God ever communicated, that there has been only one savior or one prophet in all of human history.

In this matter, the Hindu approach is very different. The notion of religious pluralism is implicit in the Hindu doctrinal framework. It is explicitly stated in the Vedas, which are the scriptural roots of the Hindu tradition. An often quoted phrase in the Rig Veda is,

> ekam satt viprâ bahudâ vadanti
> God (Truth) is one; the learned call it by different names.

This is an affirmation of monotheism, but with a twist. Underlying this statement is the idea that Divinity is one, but that it is perceived differently by different people. This is what religious pluralism is all about: not only to allow for different ways of describing and worshipping God, but also to recognize that human beings respond to and describe the transcendent in different ways.

In the Hindu framework, practically every individual can communicate directly with God who may be reached by following many different paths.

Because of this worldview, there have been many spiritual leaders in the Hindu world, each interpreting their spiritual insights in their own particular ways and gathering around them numerous followers. As a result, there are numerous sects and subsects among Hindus. Many of which are anchored to particular historical personages, but all of them subscribe to one God who has countless manifestations. This conviction enables the practitioners to respect the views and symbols of all sects. It enables most Hindus to bow in reverence to the religious modes of every religion in the world.

During the spiritual initiation that is reserved to male members of the upper castes who are expected to be the guardians of the spiritual wisdom of the tradition, one is taught to recite the following verse:

> âkâst paditantoyam
> yadâ gachchadi sâgaram
> sarva deva namaskâra
> srî kesavam pradigachchadi.
>
> As waters falling from the skies
> Return to the self-same sea,
> So homage to all the gods
> Return to the same Divinity.

When adopted, this guiding principle makes interreligious conflict less likely, as one of the main catalysts for interreligious conflict is the different stance religions hold on monotheism and religious pluralism. By the pluralistic view, even while retaining loyalty to one's own tradition and religion, people can still respect the religions of others.

In the complex and diverse world in which we live, where nations harbor people of various faiths, the Hindu perspective on the matter can be very helpful for interreligious harmony and doctrinal peace.

—Varadaraja V. Raman

See also Hinduism; Pluralism

POLITICS AND RELIGION IN THE AMERICAN PRESIDENCY

God has played an important role in the American presidency, from the revolutionary era to the present. Presidents from Thomas Jefferson to George W. Bush have invoked God's name in the service of presidential politics. The consistency of these invocations is testimony to their political and cultural significance.

God's influence on the American presidency reflects, in part, in each president's political motivations and strategies for invoking God. More specifically, presidents have had different political purposes for calling upon God.

However, God's influence on the presidency also reflects characteristics of American culture, in particular, its history, which is rooted in religion. American presidents have incorporated God into their public statements to achieve a wide range of political objectives. For instance, presidents commonly structure their references to God as supplications for God's guidance, solemn vows to act according to God's will, and thanksgivings for God's grace. These presidential expressions of faith in God help religious Americans to identify with their president and support his policies—because they foster the belief that the president is driven by the same moral force that motivates them.

Therefore, in lending moral credibility to their public personas by invoking God, presidents hope to increase support for their political agendas. For example, when promoting a more activist role for America in world affairs, Woodrow Wilson said, "I pray (that) God may give me the wisdom and the prudence to do my duty in the true spirit of this great people." Establishing himself as a moral and religious man led many to believe his political agendas were enlightened. Wilson and his advisors expected, then, that a portion of Americans would agree with their president on religious grounds and agree with his mission to "Make the world safe for democracy."

Given the religiosity of the American populace, it is not surprising that Americans use their impressions of presidents' personal morality and religious beliefs to assess their presidents' policies. This behavior has political significance because it suggests religion's influence on American government is greater than might be expected if considering only the somewhat paradoxical commitment of Americans to a separation of church and state.

American presidents have traditionally upheld the Calvinist image of a just, omnipotent, and mysterious God. They have done so to encourage solidarity and to lift morale during divisive and challenging times. For example, in Abraham Lincoln's second inaugural address and for the purpose of uniting a divided nation, Lincoln used a Calvinist image of God when saying, "The Almighty has his own purposes" and "The judgments of the Lord are true and righteous all together."

This Calvinist image is used today and for the same purpose. For example, at a National Prayer Breakfast and for the purpose of winning solidarity while leading the country during a controversial war, George W. Bush suggested, "We can be confident in the ways of Providence. Behind all of life and all of history, there's a dedication and purpose, set by the hand of a just and faithful God." American presidents clearly understand that people depend upon their religious faith to have faith in their president.

Just as the broader American religious populace acts publicly on the basis of privately held religious beliefs, the broadly defined religious beliefs shared in public by many American presidents have often reflected their private faith as well—although not always directly. For example, President Jefferson, in public expressions of faith, did not directly reflect his personal religious beliefs. However, in his publicly advocating for religious pluralism, he was expressing his personal and private faith as an enlightened deist, someone whose faith is expressed in its emphasis on reason and considering the variety of perspectives.

On the other hand, Woodrow Wilson's religious beliefs were consistent both on and off the political stage. Wilson was a Presbyterian who read the Bible daily and attended religious services regularly. His religious faith led him to believe that nothing in the world happened without divine participation, and he was convinced that he was an instrument of God. Thus, he communicated his public policies to the American people with a self-confidence borne of faith in the will of a higher power. Wilson, in public as well as in private, often referred to God as his guide.

Similarly, Abraham Lincoln's personal and public expressions of faith were consistent with one another. For example, in his personal notes as well as in his public speeches, he expressed his belief that the Civil War might well have been God's plan.

As for the presidency today, George W. Bush's personal spirituality is ostensibly mirrored in his public policy. Bush acknowledges that prayer and religion sustain him and, like Wilson, he believes himself to be an instrument of God whose duty it is to promote American involvement in world affairs. For example, in his September 20th, 2001 speech to Congress, he remarked, "Freedom and fear, justice and cruelty, have always been at war, and we know that God is not neutral between them"—which reflects his stated belief that God mediates in world affairs and that America's involvement in world affairs has a religious dimension.

The spiritual lives of American presidents reflect not simply the spiritual lives of these men. They also reflect the broadly religious foundation of the American populace. Like its presidents, the American public finds ways to express its private religious values in public, such as through charitable giving and volunteerism. Surveys indicate the average religious person is 23% more likely to make financial contributions to charities and 26% more likely to volunteer time doing community service than is the average nonreligious person.

America's preoccupation with religion is puzzling to most western European countries, because they do not claim religious foundations for political thinking and action. Therefore, leaders in these countries are much less likely to invoke God in public forums, and the average citizen may be less likely to engage in charitable giving and community service.

Clearly, positive social outcomes have sprung from Americans' sense of religious belonging and mission, and just as clearly, American presidents will continue to solicit support by making use of religious language. However, using religious language in public political discourse carries a risk because such language can be used to support a pernicious agenda. Perhaps the clearest example is Nazi Germany and Hitler invoking God's name to promote his evil agenda.

Notwithstanding the dangers, God will always play an important role in American presidential politics, both because of America's religious heritage and because America is a democracy. In the words of the famous French political philosopher and observer of American culture, Alexis de Tocqueville, "Religion is much more necessary in democratic republics than in any others. How is it possible that society should escape destruction if the moral tie is not strengthened in proportion as the political tie is relaxed?"

—*Annie Berndtson*

See also Lincoln, Abraham

FURTHER READING

Brands, H. W. (2003). *Woodrow Wilson.* New York: Henry Holt.

Goodstein, L. (2004, October 26). Personal and political, Bush's faith blurs the lines. *The New York Times.* p. A20.

Hunt, J. G. (1997). *Inaugural addresses of the Presidents of the United States: Revised and updated.* New York: Gramercy.

Reich, K., Oser, F., & Scarlett, W. G. (Eds.). (1999). *Psychological studies on spiritual and religious development.* Langerich, Germany: Pabst Science Publishers.

Stout, J. (2004). *Democracy and tradition.* New Jersey: Princeton University Press.

THE POPE

The title Pope is the name given to the Bishop of Rome, the chief pastor of the Roman Catholic Church. Although the pope's powers as bishop of the Church came from a sacramental act of ordination, the pope is elected. Since 1179 the papacy has been filled by the Sacred College of Cardinals from whom the elected pope receives the titles of Bishop of Rome, vicar of Jesus Christ, successor of the prince of the apostles, supreme pontiff of the universal Church, patriarch of the West, primate of Italy, archbishop of the Roman province, sovereign of the state of Vatican City, and servant of the servants of God. The pope's jurisdiction over the faithful of the Church and his supreme authority in all questions related to faith and morality were originally defined in the Vatican Council's Constitution *Pastor Aeternus.*

The position of the pope, as leader of the Church, has direct and indirect influences on the spiritual and religious development of individuals, families, communities, and nations. While the jurisdiction of the Pope has changed little throughout the centuries, different individual popes have certainly had differing effects on people throughout history. Therefore, the influence of a particular pope and the influence of the office of the papacy must both be considered in understanding impact on religious and spiritual development. In addition, the influence of the pope and the papacy must be considered in accordance with historical time and the specific societal circumstances that existed in communities and nations around the world and how the pope and the office of the papacy became involved—or refrained from involvement. The pope impacts more than those within the Roman Catholic Church. By papal decree and encouragement, the Catholic Church is highly involved in social service and human development work, thereby touching the lives—religious/spiritual and nonreligious/nonspiritual—of billions of people around the world.

ORIGIN OF THE PAPACY

The institutional role of head of the Church originated when Jesus named Peter to this position. In Matthew 16:17–19, Christ promises the office to Peter and no other Apostle through this personal blessing:

> Blessed art thou, Simon Bar-Jona: because flesh and blood hath not revealed it to thee, but my Father who is in heaven. And I say to thee: That thou art Peter; and upon this rock I will build my church, and the gates of hell shall not prevail against it. And I will give to thee the keys of the kingdom of heaven. And whatsoever thou shalt bind on earth it shall be bound also in heaven: and whatsoever thou shalt loose on earth, it shall be loosed also in heaven.

Peter is made the foundation and house of the Church, and through its relationship with Peter, the Church will always overcome forces of Evil. In the Old Testament prophecy (Isaiah 28:16) and in Christ's own words (Matt. 7:24), Christ bestows authority of the Church to Peter, an authority that was His own. By this promise, Christ associates Peter to Himself. In Matthew 16:19, Christ offers the keys to the kingdom of Heaven to Peter, thereby conferring on him supreme power over the Church. Peter was given this role after the resurrection, described in John 21, wherein the Lord makes Peter shepherd of the lambs and the sheep before His leaving of the earth. Peter thereby takes His place as the Good Shepherd.

Christ intended the Church to be governed by one single authority, an authority position that was to be and is eternal to give the Church strength against its perpetual enemies—i.e., those within the gates of hell. As such, the office of Peter became a permanent feature within the life of the Church.

While there is little doubt that Peter visited Rome and was martyred there, there is doubt that he was ever bishop of Rome. However, references to his bishopric are frequent (e.g., Eph. 55:8; cf. 59:14) as are testimonies that from the very earliest times the papacy has held supreme authority over the universal Church. The understanding of the papacy being the successor of St. Peter is held to be a truth revealed by the Holy Spirit to the Apostles and by them transmitted to the Church.

THE POPE'S JURISDICTION

With the words, "Whatsoever thou shalt bind on earth, it shall be bound also in heaven; and whatsoever thou shalt loose on earth, it shall be loosed in heaven," Christ made clear that the legislative authority he had within the Church also necessarily entails judicial authority. Peter and his future successors of the head of the Church were thereby given the power to impose laws (and determine when offenses are made to those laws), grant dispensation from these laws (and impose penalties and to pardon sins, John 20:23), and, if need be, to annul laws. Granted to Peter and his successors is supreme magisterium—the ability and right to declare doctrines and prescribe a rule of faith that all must follow. The pope's rule is supreme to all but Christ, and his jurisdiction extends only to the ends of the kingdom and not to matters extrinsic to the Church. When a pope legislates, he does so through powers given to him by Christ and not from government rulers, and he legislates over the faithful in spiritual and nonspiritual matters, including canon law, which oversees possessions such as schools, seminaries, and churches and the materials needed to successfully run and protect those possessions. Although the pope does have wide jurisdictional powers, for some time, as more nations saw Catholic populations diminish in representation, civil governments gained higher and wider legislative power.

The office of the pope has seen changes throughout the centuries in doctrine, legislative powers, and even in where it is housed. In the 20th century and today, popes have generally been incredibly active in moral and doctrinal teaching as well as human development and political debates and activities. The influence of the papacy within the Church has always shaped the Catholic faithful. That influence does not seem to be waning at all. In fact, faithful from around the world look to the pope for guidance—in that which is spiritual and nonspiritual—as much if not more than they ever have. As head of the Church, the pope will always maintain a role in the religious and spiritual development of millions of people around the world, and due to his wide and impressive jurisdiction and legislative powers within the Church, the pope will always be a controversial figure on the world political and sociocultural stage.

—Elizabeth M. Dowling

FURTHER READING

Barraclough, G. (1968). *The medieval papacy.* NY: Harcourt, Brace & World.

Coppa, F. J. (2002). Dictionary of popes and the papacy. *The Catholic Historical Review, 88*(3), 556–557.

Meyendorff, J. (1992). *The primacy of Peter.* New York: St. Vladimir's Seminary Press.

Pope. www.newadvent.org/cathen/12260a.htm. (January, 2005).

POSITIVE YOUTH DEVELOPMENT

In these early years of the 21st century a new vision and vocabulary for discussing America's young people has emerged. Propelled by the increasingly more collaborative contributions of scholars, practitioners, and policy, youth are viewed as resources to be developed [see Benson (2003), Damon and Gregory (2003), and Lerner (2004), for reviews]. The new vocabulary emphasizes the strengths present within all young people and involves concepts such as developmental assets, positive youth development, moral development, civic engagement, well-being, and thriving (see Benson, 2003, Damon & Gregory, 2003; Lerner, 2004, for reviews).

A key theoretical basis of the emergence of this new conceptualization of, and vocabulary about, adolescence may be found in contemporary developmental theories that stress that human development is a product of the systemic relations among variables from the multiple levels of organization—ranging from biology through culture and history—that comprise the ecology of human development (Lerner, 2002). Past concepts of development were predicated on cartesian philosophical ideas about the character of reality that separated, or "split," what was regarded as real from what was relegated to the "unreal" or epiphenomenal (Overton, 1998). In human development, major instances of such splitting involved classic debates about nature versus nurture as *the* source of development, continuity versus discontinuity as an appropriate depiction of the character of the human developmental trajectory, and stability versus instability as an adequate means to describe developmental change. However, today, most major developmental theories eschew such splits and use concepts drawn from developmental systems theories [e.g., Lerner (2002) and Overton (1998)] to depict the basic developmental process as involving relations—or "fusions" (Tobach & Greenberg, 1984)—among variables from the multiple levels of organization that comprise the ecology of human development [e.g., see Bronfenbrenner (2005)].

In short, in contemporary developmental science, the basic process of development involves mutually influential (that is, bidirectional) relations between levels of organization ranging from biology through individual and social functioning to societal, cultural, physical, ecological, and ultimately, historical levels of organization (Lerner, 2002). The relational character of development means that some degree of change is always possible within the developmental system, as the temporality of history imbues each of the other levels of organization within the developmental system with the potential for change. Temporality means that at least relative *plasticity* (the potential for systematic change) exists within the integrated (fused) developmental system and that changes in the relations between individuals and their context (which may be represented as changes in individual ←→ context relations) may be instituted by entering the ecology of human development at any of its levels of organization.

Relative plasticity constitutes a basic strength of the developing individual and provides a theoretical rationale for adopting both an optimistic orientation about enhancing the course of human life and, in reference to the adolescent portion of the life span, for adopting the new, positive, and strength-based vision and vocabulary regarding the potential of youth to thrive (Lerner, 2004). Simply, given the presence of plasticity in human development, a potential for change predicated on bidirectional, individual ←→ context relations, it is possible to assert that *every* young person has the potential for successful, healthy development and that *all* youth possess the capacity for positive development.

BIDIRECTIONAL INDIVIDUAL ←→ CONTEXT RELATIONS AND THE CONCEPT OF TRANSCENDENCE

At the same time, however, the individual ←→ context relations instantiating the potential for plasticity in any adolescent requires that the young person act to support the positive functioning of the context that is supporting him or her. Humans' evolutionary heritage established mutually supportive individual ←→ context relations as integral for human survival (Gould, 1977). At an ontogenetic level, individuals must then transcend complete self-interest or "zero sum game" orientations if they are to contribute to positive structure and change in their proximal and distal settings. Simply, human survival as a species and individual thriving across the life course depend on transcending the self, on making contributions beyond the self in time and place (Lerner, 2004).

In other words, in human development, successful (adaptive, health promoting) regulations at the level of individual functioning involve changing the self to support the context and altering the context to support the self. Such efforts require the individual to remain committed to contributing to the context and to possess, or to strive to develop, the skills for making such contributions. Such a commitment to maintaining the social institutions that, in turn, provide the person with the opportunity to flourish as a healthy individual is the essence of adaptive developmental regulation, that is, of exchanges between individuals and their social worlds that are mutually beneficial. Such regulation provides a developmental basis, one underscored by the neotenous phylogenetic history of humans (Gould, 1977), for postulating that young people develop a sense of self (an identity) that involves the belief that one *should* contribute to civil society. In other words, in youth who manifest exemplary, positive development, that is, who are thriving, there should be an integration of moral and civic identity that promotes adolescents' contributions to mutually beneficial relations between themselves and their social worlds.

Through civic engagement, then, thriving youth enter onto a life path marked by what are termed the *Five Cs* of positive youth development, that is, character, competence, confidence, connection, and caring (or compassion). Such youth will pursue the noble purpose of becoming a productive adult member of their community (Damon, Menon, & Bronk, 2003), a person contributing positively to self, others, and the institutions of civil society. In other words, such youth will develop the "Sixth C" of contribution—to self, family, community, and ultimately, civil society. A commitment to contribution rests on defining behavior in support of mutually beneficial individual context exchanges as morally necessary. Individuals' moral duty to contribute exists because, as citizens receiving benefits from a social system supporting their individual functioning, it is necessary to be actively engaged in maintaining and, ideally, enhancing that social system (Youniss, McLellan, & Yates, 1999).

This type of developmental regulation—between thriving individuals and their civil society—is the essence of a system marked by liberty (Lerner, 2004). Figure 1 provides an illustration of the model of thriving that we have developed (e.g., Lerner, 2004).

In short, adaptive developmental regulation results in the emergence among young people of an orientation to transcend self-interest and place value on, and commitments to, actions supportive of a social system promoting equity, democracy, social justice, and personal freedoms. The integration of individual and ecological assets (Benson, 2003) through adaptive developmental regulation provides the developmental "nutrients" (resources) requisite for thriving. We hypothesize that spirituality is the emotional "fuel" energizing the thriving process.

THRIVING AND SPIRITUAL DEVELOPMENT

The sense of transcendence of self and of zero-sum-game self-interest that accrues as integrated moral and civic self-definitions (identities) develop may be interpreted as a growing spiritual sense (Benson, 2003; Dowling, Gestsdottir, Anderson, von Eye, & Lerner, 2003; Dowling et al., 2004). Erikson (1959) discussed the emotional "virtues" that were coupled with successful resolution of each of the eight psychosocial crises he included in his theory of ego development. He specified that fidelity, defined as unflagging commitment to abstract ideas (e.g., ideologies) beyond the self, was the virtue associated with adaptive resolution of the identity crisis of adolescence, and thus with the attainment of a socially prescribed, positive role (cf. Youniss and Yates, 1999). Commitment to a role was regarded by Erikson (1959) as a means for the behaviors of youth to serve the maintenance and perpetuation of society; fidelity to an ideology coupled with a role meant that the young person would gain emotional satisfaction—which, to Erikson (1959) meant enhanced self-esteem—through contributing to society by the enactment of role behaviors (Lerner, 2002).

One need not focus only on crisis resolution to suggest that behaviors attained during adolescence in the service of identity development may be coupled with an ideological "virtue," that is, with a sensibility about the meaningfulness of abstract ideas that transcend the self (Youniss & Yates, 1999). From a perspective that focuses on adaptive developmental regulation within the developmental system, it is possible to suggest that spirituality is the transcendent virtue that is coupled with the behaviors (roles) reflecting an integrated moral and civic identity.

Contemporary researchers (e.g., Youniss and Yates, 1999) show increasing interest in addressing the impact of community contributions and service activities on healthy identity development. Erikson (1959) proposed that, when young people identify with ideologies and histories of faith-based institutions, identities can be placed within a social-historical framework that connect youth to traditions and communities that transcend the immediate moment, thereby providing young people with a sense of continuity and coherence with the past, present, and future.

Consistent with Erikson's prescription, youth-service programs sponsored by faith-based institutions such as the Catholic Church are embedded in interpretive values and historical meaning. For example, a parish that sponsors a highway cleanup activity for its youth will likely rely upon a moral and value-laden framework to explain its involvement, describing that involvement in religious traditions and stories (Youniss & Yates, 1999). Youth who take part in service activities are likely to "reflect on these justifications as potential meanings for their (own) actions. These established meanings, with their historical richness and picturing of an ideal future may readily be seen as nourishment for youths' identity development" (Youniss & Yates, 1999, p. 244).

As such, youth whose exchanges with their contexts (whose developmental regulations) are marked by functionally valued behaviors should develop integrated moral and civic identities and a transcendent, or spiritual, sensibility (Benson, 2003; Youniss & Yates, 1999). There is in fact evidence that adolescents' sense of spirituality is linked to thriving.

In two studies that used an archival data set from Search Institute (1984), entitled "Young Adolescents and their Parents" (YAP) data set, Dowling et al. (2003, 2004) studied the links among spirituality, religiosity, and thriving among a subsample of 1,000 adolescents randomly selected from among the larger cross-sectional group of 8,165 youth, ranging from fifth through ninth grades, present within the YAP.

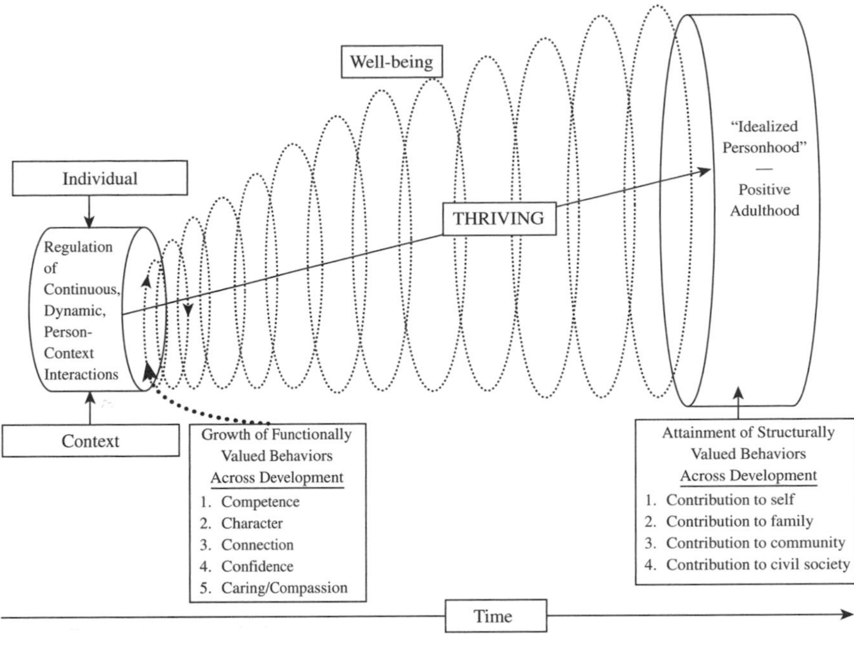

Figure 1 A developmental contextual view of the thriving process

This research used Reich, Oser, and Scarlett's (1999) conceptualization of spirituality and of religiosity. In Reich et al.'s view, spirituality is the commitment to ideas or institutions that transcend the self in time and place, that is, as viewing life in new and better ways, adopting some conception as transcendent or of great value, and defining one's self and one's relation to others in a manner that goes beyond provincialism or materialism to express authentic concerns about others. In turn, the subordination of self to institutions that are believed to have relations to the divine is the essence of religiosity, which Reich et al. (1999) operationalize as involving a relationship with a particular institutionalized doctrine about a supernatural power, a relationship that occurs through affiliation with an organized faith and participation in its prescribed rituals. Finally, thriving was conceptualized through the use of the terms that, as noted above, are involved in the new, positive conceptualization of adolescence see also Lerner, 2004).

Accordingly, using these operationalizations, Dowling et al. (2003) reviewed the set of 319 items in the survey to which the YAP adolescents responded and identified 91 items that pertained to religiosity, spirituality, and positive youth development or thriving (e.g., social competence, self-esteem, and respect for diversity). Using several statistical procedures, three spirituality factors, four religiosity factors, and nine thriving factors were identified as existing among these items.

In turn, Dowling et al. (2004) explored the role of spirituality in thriving by using the 1,000 adolescents from the YAP data set studied by Dowling et al. (2003). A conceptual model that included paths from spirituality to religiosity, from religiosity to thriving, *and* from spirituality to thriving was a better fit to the data set than models that either lacked the direct effect of spirituality on thriving or the mediating effect of spirituality on thriving through religiosity. In short, more so than a path from spirituality to thriving that involved the mediation of religiosity, among the YAP youth the strongest influence on their thriving was a path directly from spirituality.

CONCLUSIONS AND DIRECTIONS FOR FUTURE RESEARCH

Contemporary scholars of adolescent development are pointing to the implications of spirituality on positive youth development (see, for example, Lerner, 2004 and Youniss and Yates, 1999) and are conceptually differentiating the role of spirituality from the role of religiosity in such development. However, there has been no attempt to date to longitudinally establish the differential links in adolescence among spiritual development, religious development, and thriving, particularly in a data set having sufficient statistical power and measurement quality to assess the neuropsychological, cognitive, affective, moral, and contextual bases of this developmental process. Clearly, this is a key direction that should be taken in future research.

In addition, future research should be attentive to cultural, racial, ethnic, religious, and socioeconomic diversity. For instance, in different societies there is variation in what a person must do to manifest structural values of productive and healthy personhood. That is, how a person must function to manifest structurally valued regulation will vary from social or cultural setting to setting and across historical (and ecological) conditions (Elder, Modell, & Parke, 1993; Erikson, 1959). For example, in some societies regulations that support inter-individually invariant belief in and/or obedience to religious dictums may be of superordinate value. In turn, in the United States, regulations that support individual freedom, equity, and democracy are highly valued, and attributes such as the Five Cs of positive youth development are often regarded as healthy outcomes of functionally appropriate developmental regulations. In turn, attributes antithetical to these five attributes (for example, attributes such as negative self-regard, abusive or manipulative social relationships, and the absence of integrity) are instances of unfavorable individual outcomes that (we presume) derive from inadequate developmental regulations.

In all cases, however, each society will show variation within a given historical moment in what behaviors are judged as valuable in (consistent with) supporting the universal structural value of maintaining or perpetuating person-context regulations subserving mutually beneficial individual and institutional relations (Elder, Modell, & Parke, 1993). As a consequence, the markers or indices of what an individual must manifest as he or she develops from infancy to adult personhood may vary across place and time (Elder et al., 1993). Accordingly, there may be variation across different societies and points in time within the same society in definitions of person-context relations that comprise positive youth development, and thus in the specific behaviors that move a young person along a life path wherein he or she will possess the functional values of society and attain structurally valued personhood. Simply, there may be both historical and cultural variation in the specific, functionally valued components of the thriving process.

In sum, developmentally emergent and contextually mediated successful regulations of positive person-context relations ensure that individuals will have the nurturance and support needed for healthy development. Simultaneously, such regulation provides society with people having the mental and behavioral capacities—the inner and outer lives—requisite to maintain, perpetuate, and enhance their social world.

To sustain the individual and societal benefits of these person-context relations, socialization must promote (1) a moral orientation among youth that good is created through contributions to positive person-context relations and, as a derivative of this orientation, (2) a commitment to build the institutions of civil society by constructing the ecological "space" for individual citizens to promote in their communities the culturally specific institutions of civil society. Thus, when young people understand themselves as morally committed to and behaviorally engaged in building civil society, and when they as a consequence possess a transcendent sense of the importance in life of a commitment to an enduring nature or being beyond the limits of their own existence, they are able to be agents both in their own, healthy development and in the positive enhancement of other people and of society.

—Richard M. Lerner, Pamela M. Anderson, and Amy E. Alberts

FURTHER READING

Benson, P. L. (2003). Developmental assets and asset-building community: Conceptual and empirical foundations. In R. M. Lerner & P. L. Benson (Eds.), *Developmental assets and asset building communities: Implications for research, policy, and practice.* (pp. 19–46). New York: Kluwer Academic Press.

Bronfenbrenner, U. (2005). *Making human beings human.* Thousand Oaks, CA: Sage Publications.

Damon, W., & Gregory, A. (2003). Bringing in a new era in the field of youth development. In. R. M. Lerner, F. Jacobs, & D. Wertlieb (Eds.), *Applying developmental science for youth and families: Historical and theoretical foundations.* Volume 1 of *Handbook of applied developmental science: Promoting positive child, adolescent, and family development through research, policies, and programs* (pp. 407–420). Thousand Oaks, CA: Sage.

Damon, W., Menon, J., & Bronk, K. C. (2003). The development of purpose during adolescence. *Applied Developmental Science, 7,* 119–128.

Dowling, E. M., Gestsdottir, S., Anderson, P. M., von Eye, A., & Lerner, R. M. (2003). Spirituality, religiosity, and thriving among adolescents: Identification and confirmation of factor structures. *Applied Developmental Science, 7,* 253–260.

Dowling, E. M., Gestsdottir, S., Anderson, P. M., von Eye, A., Almerigi, J., & Lerner, R. M. (2004). Structural relations among spirituality, religiosity, and thriving in adolescence. *Applied Developmental Science, 8,* 7–16.

Elder, G. H., Jr. (1998). The life course and human development. In W. Damon (Series Ed.) & R. M. Lerner (Vol. Ed.), *Handbook of child psychology: Vol. 1 Theoretical models of human development* (5th ed., pp. 939–991). New York: Wiley.

Elder, G. H., Modell, J., & Parke, R. D. (1993). Studying children in a changing world. In G. H. Elder, J. Modell, & R. D. Parke (Eds.), *Children in time and place: Developmental and historical insights* (pp. 3–21). New York: Cambridge University Press.

Erikson, E. H. (1959). Identity and the life-cycle. *Psychological Issues, 1,* 18–164.

Gould, S. (1977). *Ontogeny and phylogeny.* Cambridge, MA: Harvard University Press.

Lerner, R. M. (2002). *Concepts and theories of human development* (3rd ed.). Mahwah, NJ: Erlbaum.

Lerner, R. M. (2004). *Liberty: Thriving and civic engagement among America's youth.* Thousand Oaks, CA: Sage Publications.

Lerner, R. M., Anderson, P. M., Alberts, A. E., & Dowling, E. M. (2004, March). *On making humans human: Spirituality and the promotion of positive youth development.* Invited presentation to the Mid-Winter Meetings of Division 36 (The Psychology of Religion) of the American Psychological Association. Loyola College, Columbia MD.

Overton, W. F. (1998). Developmental psychology: Philosophy, concepts, and methodology. In W. Damon (Series Ed.) & R. M. Lerner (Ed.), *Handbook of child psychology: Vol. 1 Theoretical models of human development* (5th ed., pp. 107–187). New York: Wiley.

Reich, H., Oser, F., & Scarlett, W. G. (1999). Spiritual and religious development: Transcendence and transformations of the self. In K. H. Reich, F. K. Oser, & W. G. Scarlett (Eds.), *Psychological studies on spiritual and religious development: Being human: The case of religion, Vol. 2.* (pp. 57–82). Scottsdale, AZ: Pabst Science Publishers.

Tobach, E. & Greenberg, G. (1984). The significance of T. C. Schneirla's contribution to the concept of levels of integration. In G. Greenberg & E. Tobach (Eds.), *Behavioral evolution and integrative levels* (pp. 1–7). Hillsdale, N. J.: Erlbaum.

Youniss, J., & Yates, M. (1999). Youth service and moral-civic identity. A case for everyday morality. *Educational Psychology Review, 11,* 361–376.

PRAYER

Prayer has been called the heart and soul of religion. Without prayer, religion would be stripped of its main means for connecting individuals to God, the gods, saints, ancestors, or whatever is taken to be a divine or spiritual source of power. Prayer, then, is connection via communion. As such, prayer is what establishes a relationship between individuals and a spiritual power or the Divine.

To simplify matters, is to focus here on individual, petitionary prayers directed to God. Public, institutional prayers serve their purposes; however, it is the individual, personal prayers that are most significant for the process of connecting and establishing a relationship. The focus on petitionery prayers (prayers where specific requests are made and wishes are shared) is justified given that this is by far the most common type of prayer. As for the focus on prayers directed to God, such prayers have a similar, if not identical form to prayers directed to gods, saints, and ancestors—so we may assume that there is carryover with respect to what prayer means for these other prayer contexts.

Prayer as a form of communion and relating follows similar patterns to those found in relationships between persons. Therefore, we gain a better understanding of prayer if we see prayer from the point of view of how human relationships develop. One of the most striking features of children's ways of communicating and relating to others has to do with the difficulty they have in distinguishing their own perspective or point of view from that of others. This difficulty has been referred to as children's natural egocentricity. Here, then, *egocentricity* refers not to selfishness but to relative inability to distinguish and coordinate perspectives.

We see this egocentricity in the way prayers develop. Children's prayers are striking for the charming way they assume that God is there to answer their wishes. That is, children who have an active prayer life usually demonstrate a naive faith that their will and God's will are one in the same.

Contrast this childlike faith with that of a spiritual exemplar. For example, during the American civil war, one of Lincoln's generals once said to him, "Let us pray that God is on our side"—to which Lincoln responded, "No, let us pray that we are on God's side." The contrast being drawn here is, then, a contrast in general attitude. For children, the attitude is that God exists to hear and answer our wishes and requests. For spiritually mature adults, however, the attitude is that we exist to figure out and respond to God's wishes and requests—not our will, then, but " . . . thine be done."

Prayer develops also as a shift away from taking a passive to taking an active stance toward life's problems. For example, the great 19th-century abolitionist, Frederick Douglass, who was raised a slave, said, as a child, he prayed asking God to free him. Later on, he said, "Prayer got down in my feet, and I ran away."

This passive-to-active shift in prayer is most commonly seen in the shift away from asking God to change external reality (e.g., "Make my grandmother get well") to asking God for support needed for the praying individual to have the hope, courage, wisdom, or whatever to act more responsively or effectively. Praying for strength, then, marks a significant shift away from the more passive type when it is God's strength, not the individual's, which is the focus of the prayer.

A third distinction defining prayer's functions and development has to do with feeling God's presence. In all faith traditions with a concept of God, there is the dilemma of keeping God transcendent and powerful but not at the expense of feeling disconnected from God. That is, in being kept "on high," God is always in danger of becoming so remote as to be irrelevant. Prayer serves to manage this dilemma by insuring a sense of God's presence, for people do not pray so much because they believe in God but, rather, people believe in God (feel His reality and presence) because they pray. In sum, prayer functions and develops to make God's reality and presence felt because that feeling can empower.

This last statement, that prayer can empower, brings us to the last major issue defining prayer and its development, namely, the issue of prayer's efficacy or effectiveness. For children, there is no puzzling about this issue because for children, God always answers prayers or if he doesn't, children assume it is because there is something wrong with the person or with the way the person prayed.

Only later on do individuals puzzle about this issue of efficacy. Furthermore, the way older individuals puzzle reveals the fact that they have overcome their childish egocentricity. Prayers work, they say, not so much because their own wills have been served but because they have found ways to serve God's will. Furthermore, prayers work not solely or even mainly in terms of mere appearances (e.g., a sick relative becomes miraculously cured) but in terms of deeper, more spiritually meaningful transformations occurring (e.g., a family comes together around a relative's illness and becomes stronger spiritually). Older, more mature individuals make, then, a distinction between appearance and a deeper spiritual meaning or reality.

In sum, prayer begins as an effort to bend God to our will. It functions first and foremost to change the reality outside of ourselves. It begins as a talking at rather than with God. But with age and development, prayer becomes a way to discover and mold ourselves to what is felt to be God's will, to feel connected to God in order to cope with or change troublesome feelings, and to experience closeness with and the presence of God and thereby become empowered.

—*W. George Scarlett*

FURTHER READING

James, W. (1902). *The varieties of religious experience.* New York: Longmans, Green, and Co.

Scarlett, W. G., & Perriello, L. (1991). The development of prayer in adolescence. In F. Oswer, & W. G. Scarlett (Eds.), *Religious development in childhood and adolescence,* (pp.63–76). San Francisco, CA: Jossey-Bass.

PRAYER IN PSYCHOLOGICAL PERSPECTIVES

Prayer is close to the heart of many religious traditions. Prayer represents the human side of the hypothesized two-way communication between people and their God or gods. What people think they are doing when they are praying and what effect prayer has on the people who are doing the praying or on the people for whom prayer is offered are questions which have occupied psychologists and other empirical scientists of religion for well over a century.

The gauntlet was first thrown down for a proper scientific investigation of prayer by the 19th-century statistician Sir Francis Galton in two influential publications in 1872 and 1883. Galton argued that questions about the nature and effectiveness of prayer were not merely matters for philosophical and theological speculation, but were properly matters for empirical enquiry. The key research since Galton's pioneering challenge can best be summarized within three research categories concerned with the understanding of prayer, with the subjective effects of prayer, and with the objective effects of prayer.

Key research into the development of an understanding of prayer during childhood and adolescence was pioneered during the 1960s by Robert Thouless and Laurence Brown. In one of his studies, grounded in developmental psychology, Brown explored the responses of 398 boys and 703 girls between the ages of 12 and 17 to seven situations: success in a football match, safety during battle, avoidance of detection of theft, repayment of a debt, fine weather for a church fête, escape from a shark, and recovery of a sick grandmother. In relation to each situation he addressed two questions: Is it right to pray in this situation? Are the prayers likely to have any effect? The data demonstrated a consistent age-related trend away from belief in the causal efficacy of petitionery prayer.

A second classic study grounded in developmental psychology and concerned with age-related stages in religious thinking during childhood and adolescence was reported by Ronald Goldman in the 1960s. Goldman employed projective picture tests to uncover the thinking of 200 young people between the ages of 8 and 16. He concluded that young people's concepts of prayer changed according to a fixed stage developmental sequence in accordance with Jean Piaget's model of intellectual development from preoperational thinking, through concrete operational thinking, to abstract operational thinking.

A very different theoretical framework was taken by Brown in two studies published in the 1990s grounded in social psychology. This time Brown examined the influence of home, church, and denominational identity on an attitudinal predisposition to pray and the practice of prayer among 4,948 11-year-olds and 711 16-year-olds. He demonstrated that among 16-year-olds the influence of church was stronger and the influence of parents weaker than among 11-year-olds. From these data he concluded that children and adolescents who pray were more likely to do so as a consequence of explicit teaching or implicit example from their family and church community than as a spontaneous consequence of developmental dynamics or needs.

The first study concerned with assessing the subjective effects of prayer on those who were doing the praying was reported by Francis Galton in his 1872 paper. Galton argued that clergy were a more prayerful group of people than either doctors or lawyers, and that if their prayers were effective, clergy should be expected to live longer than the other two groups. His first set of data, based on 945 clergy, 294 lawyers, and 244 medical men indeed demonstrated a higher life expectancy among clergy, but Galton dismissed this finding as evidence of the effectiveness of prayer on the grounds that their greater longevity might more readily be accounted for by their "easy country life and family repose."

In recent years a great deal of serious research has been invested in monitoring the subjective effects of prayer on those who were doing the praying. Such studies have been conducted among the general population and among groups that merit special attention, especially among the sick and among the elderly. The general consensus is that prayer is associated with a wide range of positive psychological benefits.

Building on this tradition of research, Leslie J. Francis published four papers in the 1990s and 2000s examining the relationship between prayer and purpose in life among different samples of young people between the ages of 12 and 15. He found that increased levels of prayer were associated with higher levels of purpose in life, irrespective of whether the young people attended church. One of the studies was based on young people who never attended church; those who prayed in this sample recorded a higher sense of purpose in life. Another study was based on young people who attended church weekly; those who prayed in this sample recorded a higher sense of purpose in life.

Francis advances the following theory to account for these findings. He argues that young people who pray are, consciously or unconsciously, acknowledging and relating to transcendence beyond themselves. Acknowledging such transcendence and relating to that transcendence through prayer places the whole of life into a wider context of meaning and purpose. The following psychological mechanism proposes a causal model according to which prayer may influence purpose in life. The practice of prayer implies both a cognitive and an affective component. The cognitive component assumes, at least, the possibility of a transcendent power. Such a belief system is likely to support a purposive view of the nature of the universe. The affective component assumes, at least, the possibility of that transcendent power being aware of and taking an interest in the individual engaged in prayer. Such an affective system is likely to support a sense of value for the individual.

The first study concerned with assessing the objective effects of prayer on those for whom others were praying was also reported by Francis Galton. This time Galton argued that members of royal families were the most prayed for group of people and that if prayers for royal families were effective, royalty should be expected to live longer than comparable groups. His set of data, based on 97 members of royal houses, 1,632 gentry, 1,179 English aristocracy, 945 clergy, 569 officers of the army, and several other groups demonstrated that far from being the longest lived, the royalty were the shortest lived of all the groups he studied. He concluded that prayer has no efficacy.

In recent years a great deal of serious research has been invested in monitoring the objective effects of prayer on those for whom others were praying. The best known of these studies, by Randolph C. Byrd, was published in the *Southern Medical Journal* in 1988. Byrd's study was concerned with the therapeutic effects of intercessory prayer in a coronary care unit. Over a 10-month period, 393 patients admitted to the unit were randomized, after signing informed consent, to an intercessory prayer group or to a control group. The patients, staff, doctors, and Byrd himself were all unaware which patients had been targeted for prayer. The prayer treatment was supplied by "born again" Christians. The intercessory prayer was done outside the hospital daily until the patient was discharged from the hospital. Under the direction of the coordinator, each intercessor was asked to pray daily for rapid recovery and for prevention of complications and death. Although there were no differences between the prayer group and the control group at the time of entry to the unit, a significantly better rate of recovery was experienced by the prayer group.

In 1999, in the *Archives of Internal Medicine,* William S. Harris published a replication and extension of Byrd's pioneering study. This study involved 1,013 patients randomized at the time of admission to receive remote intercessory prayer (prayer group) or not (usual care group). The data demonstrated that compared with the usual care group, the prayer group experienced a significantly better outcome.

The important point is that both of these studies were conducted to the scientific standards employed in medical research to assess the effectiveness of different medical procedures, treatments, and drugs. It is odd that such studies are not better known by and taken more seriously by those properly concerned with the value of religious and spiritual development.

In conclusion, the empirical evidence demonstrates that prayer makes a positive contribution to the youth and human development of those who pray and may also carry beneficial consequences among those for whom prayer is offered.

—*Leslie J. Francis*

See also Prayer

FURTHER READING

Brown, L. B. (1994). *The human side of prayer: The psychology of praying.* Birmingham: Alabama, Religious Education Press.

Francis, L. J., & Astley, J. (Eds.). (2001). *Psychological perspectives on prayer: A reader.* Leominster: Gracewing.

Goldman, R. J. (1964). *Religious thinking from childhood to adolescence.* London: Routledge and Kegan Paul.

PRESBYTERIAN

Presbyterian refers to several Protestant denominations in the United States of America. All of these denominations trace their history back to the Protestant Reformation in the 16th century. Two distinctions of Presbyterians are (1) they follow a pattern of religious thought known as *Reformed theology* and (2) their form of polity, or church government, stresses representational leadership of both ministers and church members.

Much of what Presbyterians believe is based on the writings of the French lawyer John Calvin (1509–1564), who trained as a priest in the Catholic Church. After leaving the Catholic Church, Calvin served as a pastor in Geneva, Switzerland, in exile. His writings crystallized much of the Reformed thinking that preceded him. From Geneva, the Reformed movement spread to other parts of Europe and the British Isles. Many of the early Presbyterians in America came from England, Scotland, and Ireland. The first Presbytery in America was organized in Philadelphia in 1706. The first General Assembly was also held in Philadelphia in 1789. That Assembly was convened by the Rev. John Witherspoon, the only minister to sign the Declaration of Independence.

DIFFERENT PRESBYTERIAN DENOMINATIONS

The Presbyterian Church in the United States has changed several times. Parts of the church have split and parts have reunited over the years. The largest division occurred in 1861 during the Civil War. The two branches established by that division were reunited in 1983 to create the Presbyterian Church (U.S.A.), currently the largest Presbyterian group in the country with national offices in Louisville, Kentucky. Other Presbyterian churches in the United States include the Presbyterian Church in America, the Cumberland Presbyterian Church, and the Associate Reformed Presbyterian Church.

REFORMED THEOLOGY

Reformed theology emphasizes God's supremacy over everything and that humanity's main purpose in life is to bring glory to and enjoy God forever. Central to this tradition is the recognition of the majesty, holiness, and providence of God who creates, sustains, rules, and redeems the world in the freedom of sovereign righteousness and love. Along with recognizing the sovereignty of God, Presbyterians also emphasize the authority of the Bible, justification by grace through faith, and the priesthood of all believers. This means that God is the supreme authority throughout the universe.

Humankind's knowledge of God and God's purpose for humanity comes from the Bible, particularly what is taught in the New Testament through the life of Jesus Christ. Salvation (justification) through Jesus is God's generous gift to humankind and not the result of humanity's accomplishments. The priesthood of believers refers to the belief that all people, ministers and lay people alike, are to share God's love with the whole world. That is also why the Presbyterian Church (U.S.A.) is governed at all levels by a combination of clergy and laity, men and women alike.

PRESBYTERIAN POLITY

Calvin developed the *Presbyterian* pattern of church government, which puts governing authority primarily in elected laypersons known as *elders.* The word *Presbyterian* comes from the Greek word for elder. Elders are elected by the people to lead and serve the congregation. Together with ministers, they exercise leadership government, and discipline and have responsibilities for the life of their congregation as well as the church at large (*Book of Order,* G-10.0102). When elected, commissioners to higher governing bodies, or elders, participate and vote with the same authority as ministers of the Word and Sacrament, and they are eligible for any office (*Book of Order* G-6.0302).

The body of elders elected to govern a particular congregation is called a *session.* Elders are elected by the members of a congregation and serve to represent the other members of the congregation. Their primary role is to seek to discover and represent the will of Christ as they govern. Presbyterian elders are both elected and *ordained.* Through ordination they are officially set apart for service. Ministers who serve the congregation are also part of the session. Session is the smallest, most local governing body. The other governing bodies are *presbyteries,* which are composed of several churches in a geographic region; *synods,* which are composed of several presbyteries; and the *General Assembly,* which represents the entire denomination. Elders and ministers who serve on these governing bodies are also called *presbyters.*

PRESBYTERIAN CHURCH (U.S.A.)

As far back as 1837 the Presbyterian Church declared that it was a missionary society whose purpose is to share the love of God in Jesus Christ in word and deed and with the entire world. Still, to this day, the church aims to be a witness to the good news of Jesus Christ throughout the world, engage in mission activities, seek to alleviate hunger, foster self-development, respond to disasters, preach the gospel, heal the sick, and educate new generations for the future. In partnership with more than 150 other churches and Christian organizations around the world, the missionary efforts of the Presbyterian Church (U.S.A.) involve approximately 1,000 volunteers and compensated personnel. The church has a membership of more than 2.5 million in all 50 states and Puerto Rico. Currently there are 11,260 congregations, 20,940 ordained ministers, 1,255 candidates for ministry, and 108,532 elders.

Young people are an important part of the Presbyterian Church (U.S.A.). Youth usually are confirmed into the church during their 8th or 9th grades when they become members of their congregation. Sunday school is offered to children and adolescents to provide young people the opportunity to learn Bible stories and Christian traditions in an age-appropriate manner. Most Presbyterian churches have youth ministry programs that focus on nurturing the spiritual lives of junior and senior high school students. These programs usually meet one evening a week and offer teaching, discipleship, worship, and social activities. Youth ministry programs also offer periodic retreats, camping, service, and mission opportunities.

Presbyterian Youth Connection is a national Presbyterian Church (U.S.A.) initiative that seeks to provide young people (ages 12 to 18) with an identity as believers in Jesus Christ, a sense of belonging in the church, and skills as leaders. The Presbyterian Youth Connection offers resources and events for youth and youth leaders at the local level. The goals of the initiative are to nurture young people to be disciples of Jesus Christ; to respond to the needs and the interests of young people; to work together, youth and adults, in partnership; to connect youth with the whole church, community, and the world; and to include all young people, reaching out and inviting them to belong to the community of faith.

—Pamela Ebstyne King

FURTHER READING

http://www.pcusa.org/

Presbyterian Church (U.S.A.). (2002). *Book of confessions.* Louisville, KY: Office of the General Assembly.

Presbyterian Church (U.S.A.). (2004). *Book of order.* Louisville, KY: Office of the General Assembly.

Rogers, J. (1985). *Presbyterian creeds: A guide to the book of confessions.* Louisville, KY: Westminster/John Knox Press.

PROPHETS OF THE HEBREW BIBLE

The word *prophet* comes from the Greek word *prophetes,* which means a link between the divine and human. The prophets are distinct figures in the Bible who are known for their apocalyptic messages, visions, and delivering God's messages to the Israelites. God sent prophets as a corrective to the leaders and community of Israel. The prophets were to ensure that the people did not falter from God and that the king ruled wisely and within God's laws. Stories of the prophets of Israel fill the Bible with tales of their fiery passion. Their enigmatic stories recount their names, miracles, sayings, and deeds. The words and deeds of the prophets have had a profound impact on humanity. The sayings and deeds of the prophets of Israel are enshrined in 16 books of the Hebrew Bible, otherwise known as the Old Testament.

At Mount Sinai, God bestowed to the Israelites his gift to them, a code of law written by him for his people. These laws stated what the Israelites had to do in order to maintain their covenant (promise) to God. Moses was called upon by God to mediate between God and the Israelites. This calling of Moses by God lays the foundation within the tradition of prophets; God spoke to Moses directly, but as God says in the Book of Numbers 12:6 that "Moses is not a prophet, for I speak to Moses face to face and not in riddles or visions." All future prophets would stand in the shadow of Moses.

The rules of prophecy dictate that God will never talk to them directly as he did with Moses but will speak to them through visions, riddles, and dreams. In the Book of Deuteronomy 18:21, the Hebrew people laid the criteria for determining the false and true prophet. One sign that a person is a real prophet is when a person predicts something and it is fulfilled, for truly the Lord has spoken to them.

The personal lives of prophets are not mentioned in the Bible so scholars know little of the prophets personal stories. What is known about prophets is from their deeds—confronting their leaders directly, challenging their actions under God. Some prophets were nearly killed for voicing their predictions and visions, such as Daniel who was thrown into a den of lions and Jonah who was plunged into the belly of a whale. Yet, in spite of the imminent dangers that surrounded being a prophet, they continued to spread the word of God.

The Hebrew Bible tells of prophets that emerged within roughly a 400-year span between 1200 B.C.E. and 800 B.C.E. The prophets all had their own unique qualities but shared one commonality—the belief that the spirit of God was upon them allowing them to reveal God's message to his people. While there are a number of prophets in the Hebrew Bible that played a significant part in moral and ethical teaching, six are considered to be truly great prophets: Samuel, Elijah, Amos, Isaiah, Jeremiah, and Ezekiel.

In the year 1050 the first traditional prophet, Samuel, is called upon by God to shepherd Israel into the age of monarchy. Samuel anoints Israel's first King, Saul, sealing a tension that would remain for centuries between prophet and king. With the beginning of the age of prophecy, ushered in by Samuel, there is a definite split in Jewish history where one person (the king) took on the political aspect of ruling Israel and the other person (the prophet) managed the spiritual aspect.

Prophets did not always work alone; they often worked in groups. Some prophets had elaborate rituals, driving themselves into a frenzy dancing, singing, and playing instruments. Their goal was to come into a state where they could get closer to God. It is out of this group of prophets that the great prophet Elijah emerged. In the year 886 B.C.E., Elijah is called by God to prophesy his words to Israel. Elijah's voice rallied the political opinion of King Ahab who was Jewish but participated in both Jewish and pagan rituals. Ahab's pagan wife, a Phoenician princess, Queen Jezebel, performed public acts of paganism rather than Judaism. The two along with their followers and priests worshipped pagan deities of Baal and Ashara. Elijah soon found himself with an enemy, and his task was to keep King Ahab honest and faithful to God and the laws of Israel.

When Elijah witnesses Queen Jezebel constructing altars to her gods and ordering the murder of several prophets who speak out against her and her priests, Elijah confronts the King to gather all the people and the prophets of Baal and Ashara to Mount Carmel. On the summit of Mount Carmel, Elijah openly challenges 450 prophets of Baal to see who would send down fire first, the God of the Hebrew people or Baal. The prophets engaged in the spiritual challenge, but Baal sent no fire and God did. Victorious, Elijah thus defeats paganism and orders that all of the pagan priests and prophets be slain.

Elijah learned many things about God and his work. As in 1 Kings 19:11, God reveals to Elijah that he is not in fire, wind, or earthquakes but that he speaks quietly to people's hearts. Elijah matured as a prophet and his great time came when he ascended into heaven on a fiery chariot. As Elijah ascended to heaven his cloak fell to earth, to his successor, Elishah, giving him the strength of prophetic power and ensuring prophetic continuity.

The golden age of prophecy in the 8th century B.C.E. was a tumultuous time for the Hebrew people. It is during this time that, in the year 792 B.C.E., the prophet Amos appeared. Amos, a simple herdsman, heard tales and witnessed the social and moral decay of the nation. As a proclaimed prophet, Amos called for a change.

Amos's oracles are full of divine judgments against those in high places in society such as the priests and kings. In the book of Amos 10:11, through visions Amos predicts that the king will die by the sword and that Israel will go into exile and the Temple will be destroyed. Amos is considered to be a traitor and is kicked out of Bethel for his fiery predictions. Amos was indeed a true prophet for the King was killed, the Northern Kingdom did fall, the children of Israel were exiled, and the Temple destroyed.

In the year 742 B.C.E., Isaiah became a prophet through a vision he had where he saw God and his angels. Seraphim came to Isaiah and touched his lips healing him from all inequity and sins. This event solidified Isaiah's status as an angelic being, chosen by God to speak to his people. During the time of Isaiah, the Assyrian superpower ravaged and annihilated city after city, and the Israelites were trapped in a dangerous time. One of Isaiah's tasks was to encourage and guide the Israelites through this time. Isaiah's text is the longest prophetic text in the Bible, and his voice is that for peace and tolerance. Isaiah is optimistic in his text, that there will be a period in the future of Israel where the nations will be at peace with each other. Isaiah saw that God would protect the Jewish people if only they were to uphold their end of the covenant with God and remain faithful and obedient.

In one of the strangest acts in the Bible, the Prophet Isaiah strips naked and wanders the streets of Israel for 3 years, as a method to dramatically foretell to the people of Israel that the King of Assyria will strip away the captives from Israel after he defeats them (Isaiah 20:2). Isaiah, along with his messages of optimism, also has clear warning for the Israelites and even goes to the king and pleads with him not to align with a foreign alliance. The prophet predicts that these things are going come to pass shortly. But again in his optimistic tone, Isaiah also tells the Hebrews that God's wrath will not last forever and that he will return them from exile and will spare their Temple in Jerusalem. Fulfilling the prophecy of Amos and Isaiah, the Northern Kingdom fell as predicted. Only Jerusalem was spared. The prophet Isaiah is also profoundly important for his words that would change the course of human history, words that later reverberated in the New Testament in the Book of Matthew 1:23, with the telling of the birth of Jesus.

Nearly 100 years after Isaiah, in the year 626 B.C.E., the next great prophet, Jeremiah, emerged. Jeremiah was not unlike any other prophet, for he is called to prophesy before his birth, and there is never a time when Jeremiah is not under the obligation of God. Jeremiah is ordered to forego marriage and children and is to dedicate his life to God and to delivering his word. Jeremiah is commanded by God to wander the streets of Jerusalem relentlessly preaching a message of repentance.

The time of Jeremiah lays witness to the Babylonians invading the northern land, paganism penetrating again in the Promised Land, and the nation itself crumbling. Jeremiah lashes out against idolatry, false prophets, and breaking God's laws. Jeremiah was in constant conflict with the people of Israel and his own family who threatened to kill him. Jeremiah was dismissed as a fool and hated as a traitor for his predictions. Jeremiah was imprisoned for issuing a prophecy of the impending demise of Jerusalem. Jeremiah pleaded to God for assistance, but God instructed Jeremiah to continue his work. After numerous attempts to reach the king and the children of Israel, Jeremiah attempted one dramatic attempt to deliver his message. Wearing a wooden yoke, Jeremiah wandered the streets to symbolize the impending fate of captivity by Babylon. This act had him branded as a traitor, imprisoned, and left to die. Jeremiah was rescued and smuggled to Egypt never again to return to Jerusalem. The prophet's predictions came true, and Jerusalem and the temple were destroyed by Babylon. The Jews were exiled to Babylon and became slaves to Babylon. With Jeremiah, the connection of prophecy and politics comes to an end. Jeremiah's inability to gain objective proof for the Hebrews that his message was true was fatal to the prophetic enterprise. The movement remained spiritual but not political.

The last of the great prophets was Ezekiel, a prophet who was nonpolitical in his message but whose message and contribution to Judaism was unlike his predecessors. In Babylon in the year 593 B.C.E., when the Israelites were held captive in Babylon, Ezekiel got his call to prophesy from God. Ezekiel's message was not of repentance or warning, but of comfort. Ezekiel is not a prophet of doom, but of hope. Ezekiel foretold the return of the Jews to their homeland; a prophecy that was eventually fulfilled. Ezekiel's stories are filled with trances, apocalyptic dreams, and a bizarre act in which Ezekiel ingests a scroll as a dramatic gesture to show that the word of God is truly within him. When Ezekiel speaks, he is indeed speaking the word of God.

The uniqueness of Ezekiel is seen early in his text, with his details of a chariot vision, with the wheels having heads of creatures spinning around and around. Some contemporary scholars have interpreted Ezekiel's chariot vision to be the first sighting of a flying saucer. Just as Jewish mystics attempted to decipher the true nature of Ezekiel's vision, modern scholars have added their own such interpretations.

In addition to Ezekiel's chariot vision, his text addresses Jews in the Diaspora. After the destruction of Jerusalem, Jews were scattered from one end of the world to the other. Ezekiel wanted to show the Israelites that God called to him in a foreign land, in Babylon, not in Jerusalem, and that if God could appear to him in a foreign land, then he could appear anywhere. With this example, emerged a new Jewish thought, that God can be worshipped anywhere. This marks a major turning point in Judaic history, for this realization creates the way for modern Judaism, a time when the Israelites created a new identity as Jews.

After the prophet Ezekiel, the age of prophecy begins to wane and eventually disappears completely. It is not known why prophecy ended or even why it began. By the time of Alexander the Great in the year 300 B.C.E., it is clear that prophesy was dead. The prophetic phenomenon had served its purpose of revealing the word of God to teach the children of Israel that they are to follow God's laws and uphold the covenant.

There was a general consensus by the Jewish community that God was not speaking through people anymore, that this was not the way Judaism would evolve. God had said everything that was necessary to humanity. What the people needed now were reminders. These reminders came in the forms of sages and rabbis whose main task is to remind the children of Israel of God's message in the prophetic texts that these great prophets left behind.

—Julie Wieland-Robbescheuten

See also Judaism; Bible, Jewish

PSYCHOANALYTIC APPROACHES

Psychoanalytic ideas have been immensely influential in Western thought for the past 100 years, since the inception of this intellectual movement by Sigmund Freud.

How does one decide whether an idea or an explanation is psychoanalytic? Psychoanalytic writings can be recognized through their use of a common vocabulary that has become, over the years, part of everyday intellectual discourse: conscious and unconscious, id, ego, superego, primary process, projection, object relations, identification, and defense mechanisms.

There is a large body of literature, created by a large group of authors who share common assumptions about personality dynamics. Psychoanalysis is known today as a personality theory, as a theory (and a practice) of psychotherapy, and then as a psychological theory of culture. Here we are going to deal with psychoanalysis as a general theory of human behavior, leading to applications in the analysis of culture. We are interested in the treatment of religion as one variety of the latter.

Two assumptions were suggested by Sigmund Freud to characterize his approach. The first states that all psychic processes are strictly determined (no accidents, chance events, or miracles can be referred to as explanations); the second states that unconscious mental processes exist and exert significant influences on behavior. These unconscious forces shape much of the individual's emotional and interpersonal experiences.

We all are ready to admit momentary, fleeting, childish, irrational thoughts, but we consider these experiences marginal. Psychoanalysis claims that they may be much more than trivial or marginal and that unconscious processes are possibly the main determinants of observable behavior.

The emphasis on unconscious processes in personality can be summed up as follows:

1. Large parts of the personality are unconscious, and these are the more important ones.
2. Unconscious memory is the repository of significant early experience.
3. In an adult, unconscious ideas are projected, creating severe distortions of reality, especially interpersonal reality.

Psychoanalysis is a theory of struggle, conflict, and compromise, assuming the dynamic nature of human behavior, always resulting from conflict and change. Additional assumptions reflect the idea of overdetermination and the multiple functions of behavior. The overdetermination assumption states that any segment of behavior may have many preceding causes. This is tied to a developmental, or historical, emphasis, leading us to seek first causes in any individual's personal history and unique experiences.

Psychoanalysis proposes a universal sequence of psychological development, which becomes a basic epistemological ordering of the world and of individual personality, culture, and humanity. The universal experience of the human infant includes a developing awareness of three realms, always in the following order: first, one's body and its experienced needs; second, awareness of the existence of another human; third, knowledge and emotional investment in relations between itself and other humans. All further experiences must be based on these early experiences, acquired in that order, and will be assimilated into that order. The existence of such a universal sequence cannot be challenged, and therein lies the attraction of psychoanalysis for those wanting to understand not only the human personality but also human society and culture.

The psychoanalytic view of human motivation is often regarded as utterly pessimistic, but we have to admit that it is realistic. Judging by their conscious and unconscious drives, humans are undeniably nasty and brutish, aggressive, and infantile. However, beyond this bleak picture of immorality and perversity lies the capacity for sublimation, love, and cultural creativity.

The problem of childhood is a central issue defining psychoanalysis. The infant's unrealistic drive for wish fulfillment is supposed to be left behind by the adult, but childhood is always alive behind the adulthood facade. The legacy of childhood is far from marginal, and it is coexistent with adult functioning. We can observe it on both the individual and the cultural levels.

Freud's ideas about development focus on what has come to be called *psychosexual development,* that is, the transformation, molding, and sometimes perversion of biologically determined erotic drives in early childhood. The focal point of psychosexual development is the Oedipus complex, woven around the child's attachment to its parents as love objects or identification models occurring between the ages of 3 and 6. Early childhood experiences serve as historical precedents in every individual's life and in the life of every human culture.

The psychoanalytic view of maladaptive behavior emphasizes its continuity with adaptive behavior and leads to viewing pathology as a useful analogy of cultural structures. Moreover, maladaptive behavior is analyzed through the detailed recognition of defensive sequences, that is, not only the final outcome—symptoms—but also the internal sequences leading to it are carefully outlined.

The theory presents us with an ideal of flexibility and moderation, as opposed to rigidity, which is pathological but inevitable. Rigidity in the form of rituals and ritualized defenses become one of the sources of analogies for religion. The analytic starting point of symptom and syndrome, and their unconscious background, serves as the model for looking at religion.

Psychoanalysis assumes the psychic unity of mankind, which is significant when we deal with cultural traditions. Universality is found at the most basic level of body, birth, sex, and death. This working assumption has a particular relevance to the phenomenon of religion. Universal themes in religious mythology are the result and reflection of the psychic unity of mankind, which in turn is the consequence of common psychological structures and common early experiences shared by all mankind. The same basic psychological processes and complexes are expressed in individual products (dreams, stories, daydreams) and in cultural products (art, literature, folklore, wit, religion, law, science), because these complexes are basic and central to human experience.

Psychoanalysis has had more to say about religious actions than any of the various traditions in academic psychology. It is the one psychological approach to the understanding of religion that has had a major effect on both religion as an institution and on the study of religion. Psychoanalytic approaches to the question of culture and religion, and to the question of individual integration in society, have affected all social science disciplines. The psychoanalytic study of religious beliefs and institutions has drawn considerable attention on the part of scholars in the fields of religion, history, sociology, and anthropology. Psychoanalysis is the only major psychological theory that offers an explanation of religion as part of a comprehensive theory of human behavior, in which religion is presented as an instance of general psychological forces in action.

In this area, as in many others, Sigmund Freud's writings offer a rich variety of hypotheses regarding various religious beliefs and practices. Some of the better known hypotheses derived from psychoanalytic theory are the father-projection hypotheses, i.e., the idea that the images of the gods are derived from childhood experiences with paternal (and maternal) figures, and the superego projection hypothesis, i.e., the idea that the gods are a reflection and echo of the unconscious and severe conscience that all humans share.

Judging by their immense influence in all the academic fields that study religion, psychoanalytic ideas seem to be of truly enduring value for the psychological understanding of religion. We really have no other theory that matches the scope of psychoanalytic interpretations of culture and religion. Enlightening—that is the greatest compliment we can pay psychoanalytic ideas and that is exactly what psychoanalytic approaches wish to be. They represent the continuation of enlightenment tradition in regard to human activities around ideas of spirituality and the sacred.

—Benjamin Beit-Hallahmi

See also Freud, Anna; Freud, Sigmund; Object Relations Theory

FURTHER READING

Beit-Hallahmi, B. (1989). *Prolegomena to the psychological study of religion.* Lewisburg, PA: Bucknell University Press.

Beit-Hallahmi, B. (1996). *Psychoanalytic studies of religion: Critical assessment and annotated bibliography.* Westport, CT: Greenwood Press.

La Barre, W. (1970). *The ghost dance : The origins of religion.* New York: Doubleday.

PSYCHOLOGICAL CORRELATES OF RELIGION

Correlation is a mathematical term concerned with examining and expressing the observed relationship between two factors. Among young people there is an observed positive correlation between age and height. As young people grow older they tend to grow taller. There is a clear correlation, but the correlation is not perfect. Some 8-year-olds may be taller than some 12-year-olds.

There is a well-established scientific research tradition in the psychology of religion that is concerned with testing and mapping the correlates of religion during childhood and adolescence. Such a scientific approach is able to adjudicate between conflicting theories and opposing points of view. Typically, studies of this nature attempt to measure at least two variables (say, sex and frequency of church attendance or religious beliefs and attitude toward abortion) among a well-defined group of people. The correlation coefficient is a measure of the strength with which the two variables are or are not related.

Correlations vary between 0 and 1. A correlation of 0 demonstrates that there is no association between the two variables, while a correlation of 1 demonstrates a perfect relationship. In the social scientific study of religion a number of important relationships between religion and other variables are reported around the level of 0.2, expressed as follows, $r = +0.2$ or $r = -0.2$. The positive correlation shows that as one variable increases (say, frequency of church attendance), another variable increases (say, altruistic behavior). The negative correlation shows that as one variable increases (say, frequency of church attendance), another variable decreases (say, acceptance of substance use). Correlations between religious variables (say, prayer and church attendance) are often reported at around, $r = +0.5$. This means that frequency of prayer increases in line with frequency of church attendance but that the relationship is not perfect. Some people who pray never go to church, while some people who go to church never pray.

Correlation coefficients also need to be tested against probability levels, expressed in studies as *p*. The probability level checks whether the relationship could have occurred by chance or whether it is "statistically significant." The three key levels of significance are expressed as $p < .05$ (the relationship could have occurred by chance 5 times in a 100), $p < .01$ (the relationship could have occurred by chance just once in 100 times), and $p < .001$ (the relationship could have occurred by chance just once in 1,000 times). The lower the probability of the relationship occurring by chance, the greater is the level of confidence that can be placed in the findings.

Correlational studies cannot of themselves determine the direction of causality in a relationship. Often, however, there are good theoretical reasons for postulation of a direction. For example, if religious beliefs were found to go hand in hand with attitudes toward abortion, it is more plausible to suggest that religious beliefs influence attitudes toward abortion than to suggest that attitude toward abortion influences religious beliefs. Current research is able, on the basis of such theories, to distinguish between two kinds of correlates of religion: the factors that help to shape religiosity and the factors that are, in part, shaped by religiosity.

According to the research findings, there are three well-established predictors of the religious and spiritual development of young people in Western Christian societies (where the majority of the research has been conducted): sex, age, and parental influence. Consistently females are found to be more religious than males. Religiosity declines during the years of schooling. Parental influence is a determining factor on whether children and adolescents show an interest in religion and spirituality. Other significant predictors include personality, type of school attended, and the peer group.

According to the research findings there are also well-established consequences of young people being religious. These include a less permissive attitude toward drugs, alcohol, and tobacco, a greater sense of empathy for others and prosocial behavior, a clearer sense of purpose in life, and often a greater sense of personal happiness.

Correlational studies also have to be aware that some apparent relationship may in fact be caused by a third factor. For example, sometimes the correlation between church attendance and another variable may be a consequence of sex differences between males and females, caused by the simple fact that women are more likely than men to attend church. For that reason it is wise to take sex differences into account, either by computing correlations for males and for females separately or by using "partial correlation" procedures, which are able to "partial out the influence of sex differences before computing the correlation coefficient.

In conclusion, the empirical evidence demonstrates that there are verifiable and scientifically grounded patterns of relationships that predict and can be used to promote positive religious development and positive youth and human development.

—Leslie J. Francis

FURTHER READING

Argyle, M. (2000). *Psychology and religion: An introduction.* London: Routledge.

Loewenthal, K. M. (2002). *The psychology of religion: A short introduction.* Oxford: One World.

PSYCHOLOGICAL EVIL

Psychological evil is a term most often used synonymously with moral evil. Moral evil refers to the exercise of human freedom and free will to deliberately inflict pain, cause harm, and destroy wholeness with respect to self, other, and creation. The scope of violence in the later part of the 20th and the beginning of the 21st century has prompted interest in exploring the causes at the root of the distortions to the human psyche, which results in the capacity of some individuals to behave in incredibly cruel and destructive ways, often beginning at an increasingly young age. Gradually, psychological evil is becoming a category of its own as a distinctive subset of moral evil. The study of pronounced socially destructive behaviors is gaining currency in psychotherapeutic as well as theological circles.

In 1983, M. Scott Peck, the psychiatrist and best-selling author of many books, first released the ground-breaking text *People of the Lie: The Hope for Healing Human Evil.* Peck pushed the limits in suggesting that the problem of evil cannot be solely relegated to the moral domain of theologians and philosophers. It is simply no longer enough to discuss evil exclusively in terms of the fallen dimension of human nature and, in turn, relegate its reality to the religious world of sinful human nature and the tempting wiles of Satan. With the advent of developments in the personality and biological sciences in the late 20th century, the study of human destructiveness has crossed into previously uncharted territory by exploring what distinguishes those who are evil from the mentally ill and emotionally disturbed.

In Europe, the work of psychotherapist Alice Miller has received worldwide attention on the causes and effects of childhood trauma. The titles of her books reveal the kind of challenging thought that discloses the harm being done to children in childhood: *For Your Own Good; Breaking Down the Walls of Silence; Thou Shalt Not Be Aware;* and *Banished Knowledge.* In Miller's *The Drama of the Gifted Child: The Search for the True Self,* she turns her attention to analyzing the effects of parental failures in nurture, which result in childhood trauma and subsequently produce emotionally underdeveloped adults, who, in turn, parent others in a vicious cycle of emotional deprivation generation after generation. Neurobiological research into the human brain has established that children deprived of access to the emotional world of love and caring can become incapable of having such feelings, losing the power to develop the reciprocal and mutually enhancing relationships that make human life worth living.

Miller's work, based on extensive clinical practice, is intersecting with neurobiology in exploring the connections between early childhood failures to thrive emotionally and the underdevelopment of those sections of the brain that enable us to care for ourselves and others. Clinical findings and case studies seem to confirm the hypothesis, but more research needs to be done in order to understand how to turn the tide on so many abused and neglected children growing into adulthood with a repressed range of emotional responses, which too often leads to lives of pathological destructiveness toward themselves and others.

In 1996 and 2000, respectively, award-winning author and notable psychoanalyst Carl Goldberg produced two salient books on the subject of psychological evil, *Speaking With the Devil: Exploring Senseless Acts of Evil* (1996) and *The Evil We Do: The Psychoanalysis of Destructive People* (2000).

Based on four decades of clinical experience, Goldberg explores the complex of psychodynamics at the root of destructive behavior.

These researchers, along with a host of others, recognize that the behavioral and biological sciences have an essential role to play in exploring and explaining the origins and development of the unrelenting and senseless acts of cruelty and destructiveness that have become endemic to contemporary life. Serial killers, genocide, and the complex origins of the events of 9/11 are definitive illustrations of the need to become more adept at the psychoanalysis of destructiveness in human personality.

Originally, scientific resistance to making evil a focus of psychological inquiry was tied to the moral objection that evil is not an appropriate subject of scientific study. There was a concern that if such study ensued, malevolent motivations would be reduced to psychiatric categories that would result in the abnegation of responsibility for individual acts of harm. Mass murderers, terrorists, those enmeshed in clinical narcissism, to name a few, would find scientific and legal defense for diminished responsibility for their devastatingly abusive and violent behaviors.

Clinicians, like Goldberg, are working to develop theories about the developmental sequence that produces destructive and dangerous personalities so that psychological evil can be addressed and ultimately treated through psychoanalysis, as well as the many forms of spiritual healing offered through religion. Relying on the analyses of extensive case studies, Goldberg has identified five factors as the primary factors that impede the ability and desire to lead a decent life: (1) shame vulnerability, (2) benign neglect, (3) inability to mourn, (4) linguistic difficulties in expressing feelings, and (5) witnessing significant people who behave as if rage-filled anger is a legitimate means for dealing with frustration and conflict.

Like Miller and Peck, Goldberg advances the thesis that the roots of destructively pathological personality are found in developmental failures in childhood, which seriously limit the child's capacity for emotional connectedness and mutuality with others. According to Goldberg, the more prominent the presence of these factors, the more distorting the impact on the child, with the consequent inclination toward destructive attitudes and actions.

In short, *shame vulnerability* refers to the depleted sense of the child's self-worth and the negative reinforcing of inadequacy. Benign neglect arises from having caretakers who are emotionally and/or physically unavailable to provide the child with needed attention, security, guidance, and compassion. The inability to mourn is a condition that is imposed upon a child who is consistently discouraged from grieving the inevitable disappointments and losses in life. Studies show that children who cannot express their painful emotions often grow into adolescents and adults who become masters of pretense and denial. Language is part of what mediates understanding and intimacy between people. Linguistic difficulties, the use of language to convey feeling and meaning, are frequently found in people who commit violent crimes. Lastly, the attitudes and actions of parents and adult models within the world of the child have a powerful shaping influence on what become acceptable ways of negotiating people, places, and things and the inherent tensions of living.

Human behavior is a product not only of environmental challenges but also of the free exercise of choices humans make in dealing with the reality of the burdens and blessings of their unique individual life. Research into destructive personalities helps to illumine the factors and conditions that create the developmental milieu for such aberrations of acceptable behavior but does not completely exonerate a person from responsibility for the consequences of their behavior.

Psychological evil is quickly becoming a specific category of study and practice in the hope of gaining greater insight into predicting those predisposed to destructive behaviors, and thus offering a coherent understanding of signs and symptoms that will aid in early detection and treatment. Experts in the field of medicine, theology, personality and social sciences are now carefully studying the distorted relational-social systems and malformation of personality of those from whom evil emanates—those who exhibit the capacity for extreme brutality and atrocity.

—Avis Clendenen

See also Evil

FURTHER READING

Goldberg, C. (2000). *The evil we do: The psychoanalysis of destructive people.* New York: Prometheus Books.

Goldberg, C. (1996). *Speaking with the devil: Exploring senseless acts of evil.* New York: Viking Press.

Miller, Alice. (1997). *The drama of the gifted child: The search for the true self.* New York: Basic Books.

Peck, M. S. (1983). *People of the lie: The hope for healing human evil.* New York: Touchstone Books.

PSYCHOLOGICAL TYPE AND RELIGION

Psychological type is the term given to the highly distinctive way of describing personality differences among people developed by Carl Gustav Jung (1875–1961). Psychological type is concerned with deep-seated differences among people and is not to be confused with character. Character is concerned with how people develop and grow (good or bad). Psychological type is concerned with how people are made.

According to Jung's theory, psychological type is as much a part of our basic makeup as being male or female, having brown eyes or blue eyes, being born with blond hair or black hair. The two questions of interest for religious and spiritual development concern whether some psychological types may be more inclined to religion and spirituality than others and whether different psychological types may be more attracted to different ways of being religious and spiritual.

Jung was attracted to the opposites and contrasts in people. For example, most people have two hands, and we might expect them to be able to use their two hands with equal skill. However, most people develop their preferred handedness early in life. They seem naturally to prefer one hand over the other, and as a positive consequence they develop the potential of that hand. The other inevitable and less positive consequence is that they neglect the full potential of the other hand. It is often only when accident and misadventure fall and we harm the preferred hand that we regret the adequate development of the less preferred hand. Most people are either right-handed or left-handed. Jung conceived of psychological qualities in similar ways.

Jung's theory of psychological type distinguishes between four sets of bipolar psychological opposites. The first set of opposites is described as our preferred *orientation,* the choice between introversion (I) and extraversion (E). The second set of opposites is described as our preferred *perceiving* process the choice between sensing (S) and intuition (N). The third set of opposites is described as our preferred *judging* process, the choice between thinking (T) and feeling (F). The fourth set of opposites is described as our *attitude toward the outer world,* the choice between judging (J) and perceiving (P).

Jung's ideas about psychological type have become well-known through psychological tests that set out to measure these types. The two best-known tests are the Keirsey Temperament Sorter and the Myers-Briggs Type Indicator. The use of these tests in church-related contexts has led to a body of theory and evidence regarding the relationship between psychological type and religious development, as summarized by Leslie J. Francis in *Faith and Psychology: Personality, Religion, and the Individual* (2004).

Orientation (the choice between introversion and extraversion) is related to our preferred source of psychological energy. The extravert is energized by the outer world, while the introvert is energized by the inner world. Extraverts enjoy communicating with others. They thrive in stimulating and exciting environments. They are usually open people, are easy to get to know, and enjoy having many friends. When extraverts are tired, they reenergize by being with others. Introverts enjoy solitude, silence, and contemplation, as they tend to focus their attention on what is happening in their inner life. They may prefer a small circle of intimate friends rather than many acquaintances. When introverts are tired, they reenergize by being alone. Extraverts learn best by working in groups, while introverts learn best by working alone.

Such qualities of introversion and extraversion suggest very different paths of religious and spiritual development. Extraverts feel at home in the church that has a strong emphasis on group solidarity and social activities. In such an environment the introvert longs to escape and is quickly drained of energy. Introverts feel at home in the church that has a strong emphasis on individual spirituality and affirms individuals in their solitude. In such an environment the extravert longs to escape and is quickly drained of energy. For the extravert, spiritual refreshment is found in the house party and the summer camp. For the introvert, spiritual refreshment is found in the silent retreat and in individualized programs.

During the periods of childhood and adolescence many religious groups make the mistake of treating all young people as extraverts. In later life a higher proportion of introverts stay with their faith community.

The perceiving process (the choice between sensing and intuition) has to do with our preferred way of perceiving the world and our preferred way of taking in information. Sensing types start with the raw data and gradually build up the bigger picture, while intuitive types start with the bigger picture and gradually make sense of the data. Sensing types focus on the realities of the situation as perceived by the senses. They are concerned with the actual, the real, and the practical. They tend to be down to earth and matter of fact. Intuitive types focus on the possibilities of a situation, perceiving meanings and relationships. They are interested in exploring new and untested ways of doing things. They tend to be up in the air and sometimes impractical. Sensing types like to stick to what they know. Intuitive types get quickly bored with what they have experienced before.

Such qualities of sensing and intuition suggest very different paths of religious and spiritual development. Sensing types are at home in the church that has attachment to a strong tradition and a set way of doing things. They welcome solid and straightforward teaching, and studying the texts of their scriptures. They tend to prefer a certain and conservative faith. In such an environment intuitive types feel constrained and cramped in their spiritual development. Intuitive types are at home in the church that welcomes experimentation, innovation, and change. They welcome imaginative teaching that approaches the topic from novel and oblique perspectives. They tend to prefer a questioning and liberal faith. In such an environment sensing types feel unsupported and overchallenged in their spiritual development.

The judging process (the choice between thinking and feeling) has to do with our preferred way of making judgments or of coming to decisions. Thinking types start with a commitment to objective impersonal logic, while feeling types start with a commitment to subjective personal values. Both thinking and feeling are rational processes, but what counts most heavily in the two forms of rationality differs one from the other.

Thinking types value integrity and justice. They are known for their truthfulness and for their desire for fairness. They consider conforming to principles to be of more importance than cultivating harmony. Feeling types value compassion and mercy. They are known for their desire for peace. They are more concerned to promote harmony then to adhere to abstract principles. Thinking types are guided by their head. Feeling types are guided by their heart.

Such qualities of thinking and feeling suggest very different paths of religious and spiritual development. Thinking types are at home in churches that proclaim the justice of God and are concerned with the objective truths of the faith. Thinking types want to test others' understanding of God. In such an environment feeling types can feel uncomfortable, especially when their heads are opened up as muddled and confused by the thinkers' logic. Feeling types are at home in churches that proclaim the mercy of God and are concerned with the needs of others. Feeling types want to warm others' love for God. In such an environment thinking types can feel uncomfortable, especially when their hearts are revealed as cold by the feelers' concern that they too should display the same kind of comparison and sensitivity for others.

The attitude toward the outer world (the choice between judging and perceiving) has to do with our preferred way of operating in the outer world. The judging types use a judging process in the outer world (either thinking or feeling), and as a consequence their outer world is well organized and structured. Perceiving types use a perceiving process in the outer world (either sensing or intuition), and as a consequence their outer world is spontaneous and flexible. Judging types enjoy routine and established patterns. They prefer to follow schedules in order to reach an established goal and may make use of lists. They tend to be punctual, organized, and tidy. They prefer to make decisions quickly and to stick to conclusions once made. Perceiving types have a flexible, open-ended approach to life. They enjoy change and spontaneity. They prefer to leave projects open in order to adapt and improve them. Their behavior may seem impulsive and unplanned.

Such qualities of judging and perceiving suggest very different paths of religious and spiritual development. Judging types are at home in churches that are highly organized, structured, and predictable. Services are planned well in advance and run to schedule. In such an environment perceiving types can feel frustrated by the lack of room for spontaneity and flexibility. For them the environment is too uptight. Perceiving types are at home in churches that are flexible, adaptable, and unpredictable. Services are subject to spontaneous inspiration and change. No one quite knows whether they will begin on time or when they will end. In such an environment judging types can feel frustrated by the lack of planning and preparation. For them the environment is too messy and chaotic.

When Christian churches are compared with the population as a whole, among adults there tends to be an overrepresentation of introverts, intuitive types, feeling types, and judging types (ISFJ). Similar research has not been conducted among other faith groups.

Psychological type theory is of considerable practical benefit to practitioners concerned with youth development and with religious and spiritual development. The theory enables practitioners to recognize the types of people among whom their programs and strategies work most effectively and the types of people who are less likely to benefit from such provisions.

—Leslie J. Francis

See also Jung, Carl and Post-Jungians; Psychopathology, Personality, and Religion

FURTHER READING

Baab, L. M. (1998). *Personality type in congregations: How to work with others more effectively.* Washington, DC: Alban Institute.

Francis, L. J. (2004). *Faith and psychology: Personality, religion, and the individual.* London: Darton, Longman and Todd.

Francis, L. J., & Atkins, P. (2002). *Exploring Mark's gospel (Personality Type and Scripture Series).* London: Continuum.

Goldsmith, M. (1994). *Knowing me knowing God.* London: SPCK.

PSYCHOPATHOLOGY, PERSONALITY, AND RELIGION

The psychology of personality is concerned with describing fundamental ways in which people differ. The scientific study of personality looks for the patterns in individual differences, classifies these patterns, and seeks to give explanations for them. There are two main groups of personality theories.

One group concentrates wholly on differences within the "normal" population. The other group is concerned with those differences that lead to "abnormal" behavior, to poor psychological health, and to mental illness. This second group is concerned with psychopathology.

Both groups of personality theories are relevant to understanding religious and spiritual development in childhood and adolescence. The first group of theories helps to address the question whether there is a link between personality and religion or spirituality. Are some personality profiles more conducive to religious and spiritual development than other personality profiles? The second group of theories helps to address the question whether there is a link between psychopathology and religious or spiritual development. Is religion and spirituality associated with better or with poorer mental health?

Before examining these questions further, it is crucial to distinguish between two similar but very different terms, namely, *personality* and *character.* Character is concerned with how people develop and grow (good or bad). Character can change and be changed. Personality is concerned with the much deeper concept of how people are made. Most personality theorists try to delve below the surface. According to this, personality is as much of our basic makeup as being male or female, having brown eyes or blue eyes, being born with blond hair or black hair. Many religious traditions are concerned with reshaping peoples' character, but they need at the same time to accept and to work with peoples' personality. Expecting people to change their basic personality in response to religious conversation may be as mistaken as to expect them to change the color of their eyes or to change their sex.

From a theoretical point of view, over the years the psychology of religion has advanced very different theoretical perspectives regarding the relationship between Christianity and psychological health. One position has taken the negative view that religion is associated with lower levels of psychological health, while the other position has taken the positive view that religion is associated with higher levels of psychological health. The negative view is exemplified in the classic writings of Sigmund Freud, who sees the Judeo-Christian tradition as capturing the human psyche in a state of infantile immaturity, leading to psychological vulnerability and neuroses. The opposite psychological view is exemplified in the classic writings of Gordon Allport, who sees the religious images of the Judaic-Christian tradition as providing powerful developmental tools promoting and leading to psychological health.

A particularly interesting and powerful model of personality used in studies of religion and spirituality is the three-dimensional model developed by Hans Eysenck. Eysenck's three-dimensional model of personality has been employed in a large number of studies since the late 1970s to attempt to adjudicate between these two conflicting theoretical positions on the relationship between religion and mental health. The strength of Eysenck's model of personality resides in the way in which he unites perspectives from abnormal psychology and normal psychology. Eysenck argues that psychological disorder or abnormality is not categorically discrete from normal personality. For Eysenck, psychological disorder is located at one extreme end of normal personality and remains continuous with normal personality. The Eysenck Personality Questionnaire distinguishes between two psychopathologies, neurotic disorders and psychotic disorders.

In Eysenck's model, neurotic disorders lie at one extreme of a dimension of normal personality, ranging from emotional stability, through emotional lability, to neurotic disorders at the extreme end. Eysenck characterizes people who score high on the neuroticism scale but who fall short of neurotic disorder in the following way. They are anxious, worrying individuals, who are moody and frequently depressed. They are likely to sleep badly and to suffer from various psychosomatic disorders. They tend to be preoccupied with things that might go wrong and with a strong emotional reaction of anxiety to these thoughts.

In Eysenck's model, psychotic disorders lie at one extreme of another dimension of normal personality, ranging from tender-mindedness, through tough-mindedness, to psychotic disorders at the extreme end. Eysenck characterizes people who score high on the psychoticism scale but who fall short of psychotic disorder in the following way. They are described as cold, impersonal, hostile, lacking in sympathy, unfriendly, untruthful, odd, unemotional, unhelpful, lacking in insight, strange, and with paranoid ideas that people are against them.

According to Eysenck's theory, neuroticism and psychoticism are totally unrelated to each other. To know where individuals score on one of these dimensions of personality does not help you to predict where they score on the other dimensions. In other words, these two dimensions are orthogonal to each other.

Eysenck's dimensional model of personality adds a third orthogonal dimension to these two dimensions of neuroticism and psychoticism. The third dimension, which is not itself concerned with psychopathology, ranges from introversion, through ambiversion, to extraversion. Extraverts are characterized as sociable introverts who like parties, have many friends, need to have people with them to talk, and prefer meeting people to reading or studying alone.

Within a Christian context, studies using Eysenck's model have been reported in Australia, Canada, France, Germany, Hong Kong, the Netherlands, Norway, and South Africa, as well as in the United States of America and the United Kingdom. Studies have also been reported in a Jewish context in Israel. The evidence from these studies is consistent and conclusive. Using Eysenck's scales, there is no evidence to support either a positive or a negative relationship between religion and neuroticism. Using Eysenck's scales, there is wide evidence to support a negative relationship between religion and psychoticism. In other words, religion is associated with *lower* psychoticism scores. Using Eysenck's scales, there is no relationship between religion and either extraversion or introversion.

Looked at from another perspective, there is, on the basis of these studies, a recognized link between personality and religion. Although the two personality dimensions of extraversion and neuroticism are independent of religion and spirituality, the third personality dimension of psychoticism is related to religion and spirituality. Those who record lower scores on this dimension of personality (those who are tender-minded rather than tough-minded) are more likely to be drawn to religion and to spirituality.

There are two main conclusions that can be drawn from this research tradition regarding the relationship between religious and spiritual development and positive development. The first conclusion is that a clear link exists between at least one major personality dimension and religion. The second conclusion is that there is no empirical evidence to link psychopathology and religion within general population studies.

—Leslie J. Francis

FURTHER READING

Eysenck, H. J., & Eysenck, M. W. (1985). *Personality and individual differences: A natural science approach.* New York: Plenum Press.

Francis, L. J. (2004). Faith and psychology: *Personality, religion, and the individual.* London: Darton, Longman and Todd.

Funder, D. C. (1997). *The personality puzzle.* New York: W. W. Norton.

PUBLIC EDUCATION, SPIRITUAL DEVELOPMENT IN, A CHARTER SCHOOL CASE STUDY

Charter schools are independent public schools designed and operated by educators, community leaders, education entrepreneurs, and others and are open to all students. Each charter school has a distinct mission and vision and, therefore, has the opportunity to focus on aspects of education that they believe are essential to educating children. Increasingly more charter schools are beginning to incorporate a focus on spiritual development into their missions, interactions with children, staff, and families, and curricula.

KEY FEATURES AND STRATEGIES IN MORAL AND SPIRITUAL EDUCATION

While each school that intentionally incorporates spirituality into its school environment likely has its own unique approach and philosophy, common features and strategies found in moral and spiritual education include the following:

Pluralism. Pluralism is seen in the school as a gift or strength that helps the student appreciate his own or her own tradition, ethnicity, race and appreciate the same in others.

Inclusiveness. Starting with common ground, likeness—"She's my friend, she's like me"—the strategy is to build from this bond toward appreciating difference as something that stirs delight and wonder, and not as a threat.

Awareness. Students are aware of the spiritual core within themselves, and the above elements are designed to make this core more clearly present in their emerging self-understanding.

Respect. This is a process that includes, in order, (1) self-respect, without it one is not ready to engage the other; from this (2) respect for others becomes a possibility. Building on this respect in the classroom there follows (3) respect for the environment (which includes the classroom and school buildings, the surrounding natural environment). Finally, once these local features have been understood, there enters the inculcation of (4) respect for society. This is the issue of citizenship.

These features and strategies imply that there is an experiential logic to the way we grow habits and virtues and that this can be practiced in school life if there is sufficient training to facilitate it. One begins with the immediate and local and then extends outward.

The East Bay Conservation Corps (EBCC) Charter School in Oakland, California, serves as a case study of schools that effectively put these features and strategies into practice. The EBCC Charter School was created out of the belief that public schools in the United States must prepare children for the challenges, opportunities, and responsibilities of life in a democratic, pluralistic society. Through service learning, the curriculum and culture of the school integrates spiritual development, creative expression, and service across a full range of academic subjects.

ABOUT THE EBCC CHARTER SCHOOL

In September 2001, the EBCC Charter School opened its doors to equip young students with academic, artistic, and civic literacy in a learning environment that fosters their intellectual, physical, and spiritual development. Students at the EBCC Charter School learn through serving their school and neighborhoods and then by extending this service to stewardship of the broader San Francisco Bay Area community and environment.

As a public school, the EBCC Charter School cannot narrowly advocate any particular religious tradition but endeavors to help each student find a personal spiritual center that can be carried over to lifelong practices in a culturally diverse world. As the school was planned, the key founders recognized that we live in a world where too often information and data overshadow the place of wisdom and virtue. The goal and challenge in planning for the school was, therefore, to create opportunities for silence and reflection, along with learning and acting, in order to realize a more complete understanding of what it means to educate children.

The five guiding principles of the school are (1) academic and artistic excellence; (2) values, ethics, and spiritual development necessary for thoughtful citizenship in a pluralistic, democratic society; (3) service as a way of learning; (4) participation in the life of the school and the community through stewardship of the environment; and (5) creative partnerships in sustaining public education. Now entering its fourth year, the school is a thriving model of the school's vision, mission, and guiding principles and currently serves 180 students in grades K through 5.

INTENTIONAL SPIRITUAL EDUCATION

By intentionally incorporating spiritual education into the school experience of all who attend and are touched by EBCC, the school honors the discovery and pursuit of the core meaning and purpose of one's life; the pursuit of a vision of life that offers meaning and connection to others; the recognition that a spiritual vision becomes a center from which a person interprets and finds meaning in experiences of every kind; the development of a moral compass to guide one's behavior; and the capacity for experiencing wonder and humility in the face of mysteries.

The major tenets of the school consist in finding ways to encourage and foster the spiritual development of each child, to assist each child in understanding the historical community and family elements that have shaped him or her in this respect, and to be cognizant of the way this is modeled in the lives of faculty, staff, and parents. In a pluralistic, urban culture, students and faculty bring to the school community a rich variety of spiritual and moral traditions, some broadly shared and some not. The school seeks to build upon this richness, finding ways to engender core values basic to the school community: honesty, caring, courage, pursuit of truth, ability to listen with respect and empathy to those from different backgrounds. The school finds these to be common virtues for the flourishing of the school community and public life. Working to nurture these virtues and helping students to appreciate and practice still others constitutes the ethical dimension.

The premise of nurturing these virtues is that to be a human being is to have moral propensities and a core spiritual vision. If one is not aware of developing and integrating this vision, if one is not clear and articulate about it, then one is not fully empowered as a person. The school is dedicated to bringing this type of spiritual literacy to the surface and seeing it as something essential to well-being and about which we become educated.

ESTABLISHING SCHOOL ROUTINES AND RITUALS

The task of the EBCC Charter School has been to develop a school culture—a balance of structure, discipline, and caring—that helps carry the vision and mission forward. Procedures and ground rules guide students in the hallways, the playground, and the classrooms. Routines and rituals engender a spiritual dimension and bring students, teachers, and families closer together. These include morning gatherings in silence, service-learning projects from reading with senior residents to planting neighborhood gardens, and weekly assemblies to honor the accomplishments of the whole school community.

The spiritual and ethical aspects of school life are embedded in the daily life routines of the school. As examples, the curriculum is integrated across academic disciplines; periods of silence center on important goals of the day; oral expressions of personal family stories and interests are shared; the stories of others and of various traditions are shared; play and creative activity are built into the school life through arts, physical activities, and special projects; and learning through service occurs in the broader community. In addition, students develop a clear understanding of their values and priorities; they build habits that support the community values of truth seeking, courage, caring, honesty, and respect; they gain knowledge of histories and stories from many cultures; they develop in writing and participation in music and the arts; and they gain knowledge and respect for the environment.

SPEAKING FROM THE HEART, PRACTICING THANKS

As the EBCC Charter School journey continues, putting the mission of spiritual development within the context of service learning and a solid, yet creative academic program into concrete practice will be the "ultimate test" of its success. Now in its fourth year, the EBCC Charter School is striving to fully realize its vision of spiritual development for all its students. What is clear is that the school is moving in the right direction and provides a compelling example for other public schools. In the end, perhaps this is the heart of the EBCC Charter School's vision for all students—a simple sense of spirituality that is carried throughout their lives.

—Richard Lodish and Cathleen Michaels

FURTHER READING

Coles, R. (1990). *The spiritual life of children.* Boston: Houghton Mifflin Company.

Educational Leadership. (1998/1999). The Spirit of education. *Educational Leadership, 56,* 4.

Kessler, R. (2000). *The soul of education: Helping students find connection, compassion, and character at school.* Alexandria, VA: Association for Supervision and Curriculum Development.

Livsey, R. C., & Palmer, P. J. (1999). *The courage to teach: A guide for reflection and renewal.* (1st ed.). San Francisco: Jossey-Bass.

Tanenbaum Center for Interreligious Understanding. (1999). *Building blocks for democracy curriculum.* New York: Tanenbaum Center for Interreligious Understanding.

PURPOSE IN LIFE

Purpose in life has become a key construct in positive psychology. From a theoretical perspective, psychologists like Victor Frankl postulated that the sense of purpose and meaning in life is crucial for optimal human functioning. Purpose in life is understood to be central to the meaning-making system that counters meaninglessness. As such, purpose in life is a central component of psychological well-being. According to this view, it is purpose in life that makes living worthwhile and which helps to prevent despair from leading to negative outcomes, such as suicide. Various attempts have been made by psychologists to measure and assess the extent to which purpose in life varies from one person to another. Recent research has suggested a significant link between purpose in life and religion.

Early research concerning purpose in life focused largely on the relation between this construct and various psychopathologies. Lower levels of purpose in life were found to predict higher substance use, greater levels of stress, depression and suicidal ideation, and higher levels of general anxiety. More recent research has demonstrated how higher levels of purpose in life predict various aspects of positive psychological adjustment and well-being, including positive affect, life satisfaction, self-image, self-esteem, and better health. There is every reason, therefore, to take the development of purpose in life seriously during childhood and adolescence.

The idea of purpose in life is also central to many religious traditions and theological perspectives, as discussed, for example, by Paul Tillich. According to this tradition, the God whom we meet in the ground of our being gives meaning and purpose to existence and provides a strong counter to existential anxiety and existential meaninglessness. Against this kind of theological background, it is reasonable to hypothesize that optimal religious and spiritual development should be associated with a higher sense of purpose in life.

In a series of recent studies, Leslie J. Francis has developed a psychologically based theory to account for such a hypothesized link between religion and purpose in life. This theory focuses specifically on the religious aspect of prayer and suggests that young people who pray are, consciously or unconsciously, acknowledging and relating to transcendence beyond themselves. Acknowledging such transcendence and relating to that transcendence through prayer places the whole of life into a wider context of meaning and purpose.

The evidence from the empirical studies conducted by Leslie J. Francis confirms the hypothesized link between personal prayer and purpose in life among young people during childhood and adolescence. These studies have controlled for other variables that might contaminate the relationship between prayer and purpose in life. The finding has always been the same: young people who pray also enjoy a higher sense of purpose in life. This is even true for young people who never attend church, but nevertheless pray.

—Leslie J. Francis

FURTHER READING

Francis, L. J. (2005). Prayer, personality, and purpose in life among churchgoing and nonchurchgoing adolescents. In L. J. Francis, M. Robbins, & J. Astley (Eds.), *Religion, education, and adolescence: International empirical perspectives.* Cardiff: University of Wales Press.

QUAKER EDUCATION

Quakerism began in England around 1650. Seeking a more direct and authentic spiritual experience without the intermediary of a hierarchical clergy, George Fox and other founding Quakers were drawn to worship in silence. Embracing the belief that there is that of God in each person, these early Quakers held that through patient listening the Spirit of Truth and Light could illuminate and transform them. This belief in spiritual equality led the Society of Friends to embrace each man *and* woman's message spoken from the silence and to respect differences.

Given the reliance on each and every person's role as a minister, Friends soon recognized the importance of establishing schools. The founders of early Friends Schools sought to minister to the needs of body, mind, and spirit and to the divine light within each student.

Today, over 325 years later, this same seeking for a balanced education that honors body, mind, and spirit serves as the core philosophy of more than 80 Friends schools in the United States and many more across the world. The Friends Council of Education nurtures the spiritual life of these schools by strengthening the connections among them and fostering Quaker practices.

Meeting for Worship lies at the heart of Quakerism and at the heart of Friends' Schools. The silent meeting operates without a minister and without program or prearrangement. Waiting in the silence in weekly Meetings for Worship, students and teachers alike listen for spiritual awakenings and inspiration from within or from others. Although this is an activity for which discipline is required, spontaneity and freedom are also vital. Anyone, child or adult, can express a concern, share an insight or make an observation. This simple corporate searching in silence can provide both mental refreshment and spiritual democracy. Young children in Friends' schools learn to swim in this pool of silence and reflection, strengthening their skills over time.

Children and parents also become increasingly aware of the testimonies that guide the Society of Friends. The idea that there is that of God in everyone is a guiding belief of Quakerism and serves as the foundation of the testimonies of equality, simplicity, peaceful resolution of conflict, social justice, and stewardship of the environment. Quaker schools trust and believe in the essential goodness of each member of the community and strive to nurture a respect for self and others to enable the development of responsible, independent, empathetic individuals. Children will learn to manage their own behavior appropriately and do so for the good of the community. Quaker schools encourage children to believe they can make a difference in the world and solve conflicts peacefully.

At Quaker Schools the values and beliefs of the Society of Friends are integrated into every part of the community and provide the foundation for the spiritual growth of students. They are not a separate curriculum relegated to a particular day or period.

At Quaker elementary schools there are, however, many special projects that nurture the growth of spirituality as part of a sound education. For example, at Sidwell Friends School, third and fourth graders study conflict resolution and are trained to be playground mediators. They explain to 6- and 7-year-olds how to resolve differences by listening carefully to what other people are saying, restating the problem in their own words, and quietly agreeing to solve the problem together. They have class discussions, preceded by silence, when problems arise and book clubs where spiritual values in literature are studied.

At Sidwell Friends School, as at most other Friends schools, students are involved in creating guidelines for behavior that promote respect. These "Respectful Reminders" are posted throughout the classrooms. A common occurrence at many Friends schools is for classes to take turns carefully formulating a query, a thought-provoking question used by Friends to seek the Truth and deepen understanding. Each month the entire school would consider and reflect upon the query created by a class. Often these queries relate to spiritual and ethical issues: "When we have different opinions and beliefs from others, how can we stay true to ourselves without bruising the feelings of others?" "Do I stand up for someone who has been called a hurtful name, or do I stand by? Do I speak or remain silent?" "In this New Year, how can we make peace in our world, resist peer pressure, and not hurt others?" "When we feel frustrated or angry, what can we do so that we don't take out our frustration and anger on others?" "How can we learn to appreciate and use the quiet time we spend in Quaker Meeting?"

One of the key Quaker tenets is to "Let your life speak." Quaker schools struggle daily to impart spiritual values to children that will help them to become persons of integrity, intelligence, and compassion. By helping children see the world in its complexity and to respond sincerely and generously as caring members of a greater community, they are helped to develop and refine the most human of sensibilities.

Service learning gives Quaker schools an ideal opportunity to help children connect in a productive and positive way to the larger community in which we all live. Schools must continue to ask at what age and in what ways young children are ready to learn the painful truths about the gap between the haves and have nots, the gap between our ideals and realities. And as part of this, educators must ask how elementary school can make service learning an important part of the spiritual life of young children—long before they reach adolescence, when most service programs begin.

For the past 25 years at Sidwell Friends, every Wednesday during the school year the Lower School classes have worked together to make a 50-gallon pot of soup for Martha's Table, a soup kitchen and family center in the heart of Washington, D.C. Every Lower School child trudges off to school on those mornings with a vegetable in his backpack—and some degree of awareness that his carrot or potato will wind up as part of a weekly offering to those in need. The growing empathy of the spirit that the Martha's Table program has provided is an important part of the Quaker education of the children.

The most important aspect of the Martha's Table program is the involvement of the parents. On scheduled Saturdays, 20 or 30 members of school families—fathers, mothers, children, and grandparents—meet at Martha's Table to prepare food. Approximately 3,000 sandwiches are made. In this association with the school, families and teachers foster an ethical attitude and a spiritual grounding that appreciates service as a lifelong obligation. These activities at Lower School also teach young children the values of helpfulness and responsibility in the context of a community of people. They push youngsters to ask the question, "What do we want our society to be like?" At Quaker Middle and Upper Schools service is also integrated into the culture of the school and the larger community. Service learning projects can vary from supporting a local Special Olympics program to establishing an irrigation system in Costa Rica.

The service projects, discussions, queries, Quaker testimonies, meeting for worship, and a focus on cherishing each individual are important parts of the spiritual puzzle. But to integrate these and other programs into the daily life of school requires consistent action and deed from adults, from how to respond to one child's excluding another on the playground to issues as broad as service and diversity. In Quaker schools, spiritual life is more sea than island. For a spiritually sound climate to prevail, adults make space for quiet and the opportunity for reflection. Adults also address how they treat each other, how they react to other's behavior, how they make decisions, how they deal with disagreements and tensions, how they hold themselves accountable, how they treat others above and below them on the economic ladder, and how they treat people who are different from them. When all is said and done, children aren't going to grow up having a sound spiritual foundation if they don't see adults modeling clear, consistent, and good values. As someone quipped, "Children may close their ears to advice, but they open their eyes to example."

—Richard Lodish and Christine Fernsler

FURTHER READING

Jones, R. M. (1997). *The faith and practice of the Quakers.* Richmond, IN: Friends United Press.

Lacey, P. A. (1998). *Growing into goodness: Essays on Quaker education.* Philadelphia: Friends Council on Education.

Lodish, R. (1995). *A Child in the principal's office: Laughing and learning in the schoolhouse.* Thousand Oaks, California: Corwin Press.

Smith, R. L. (1998). *A Quaker book of wisdom: Life lessons in simplicity, service, and common sense.* New York: William Morrow and Company.

QUR'AN

Muslims proclaim that the Qur'an is the spoken and recorded message of God to all peoples revealed to the Prophet Muhammad through the angel Gabriel. The word *Qur'an* literally means "reading or recitation." The Qur'an was revealed to Muhammad over a period of 23 years and is believed by Muslims to be the literal word-for-word message of God spoken in clear Arabic speech. Therefore translations of the Qur'an are not authoritative because they can never be precisely the same as that which was revealed in Arabic. The Qur'an serves as the guiding text in the religious and spiritual development of Muslims around the world.

There are 114 *surahs* or chapters in the Qur'an arranged approximately from longest to shortest, and there are 6,236 *ayahs* or verses. The Qur'an is slightly shorter in written length than the Christian New Testament. Although the Qur'an includes some narratives, it is not a story or a series of narratives but a complex interconnected text of rhythmic prose. Its language and style are inimitable, and indeed a number of skilled Arabic poets have apparently tried in futility to imitate the rhythmic prose of the Qur'an. The Qur'an has been systematically memorized, recited, and written down from the time of its revelation. The written fragments and oral memorizations were finally standardized and recorded in their present form by a scholarly group commissioned by Othman, the third Caliph between 644 and 656 C.E. within 20 years of Muhammad's death. Muslims insist that these master copies have been painstakingly reproduced in reliable textual succession to this day.

THE QUR'AN REVEALED

In the year 611 C.E., on the 27th day of the month of Ramadan, the Prophet Muhammad had retreated to the cave of *Hira* just outside Mecca as he was accustomed to doing in order to pray, meditate, and reflect on questions of great importance to him such as the purpose of life and the struggle between good and evil.

On this particular day however, while he was in deep thought, the Prophet Muhammad heard a powerful voice call him. When he asked who was calling him, the voice commanded "read." Muhammad replied that he could not read. Muhammad was then squeezed in the grip of a very strong hug for a moment, and the voice commanded him a second time to read, to which Muhammad replied again that he could not read. Muhammad was squeezed again and a third time was commanded "read." This time Muhammad asked what it was that he should read and the voice replied, "Read! In the name of your Lord who creates man from a clot!, Read, for your Lord is most generous, who teaches by means of pen, teaches man what he does not know."

Muhammad chose to obey this command and became the Messenger of God. This event was the beginning of the revelation of the Muslim sacred scripture or writings known as the Qur'an. At first the Qur'an was revealed in short concise *ayahs,* and later it was revealed in longer *ayahs* and *surahs,* over a period of 23 years.

COMPILATION AND TRANSMISSION

The compilation of the Qur'an took place within 20 years of the Prophet Muhammad's death. The primary method of recording and transmitting the Qur'an was through systematic recitation. The Qur'an remains today the most memorized book in all of human history. Memorization was not an individual or haphazard occurrence, but a communal and systematic skill constantly under the correction of a community of reciters. In addition, the entire text of the Qur'an was written down by the time of the Prophet's death on any material that could be used for writing: fragments of paper, leather, papyrus, pieces of wood, thin white stones, shoulder blade bones, and palm-leaf stalks. But these pieces of writing had not been compiled into one organized and standardized text during the life of the Prophet.

The first leader or Caliph of the Muslim community elected after the death of the Prophet Muhammad was Abu Bakr. The Battle of Yamana in 633 C.E. during Abu Bakr's rule killed a large number of skilled Qur'anic reciters. Alarmed by this loss, Abu Bakr instructed a scholar by the name of Zaid to carefully collect and authenticate all existing written collections of the Qur'an together in one place. This collection was kept in safekeeping and passed down to Umar the second Caliph, then to Umar's daughter who also had been a wife of Muhammad, then to Othman the third Caliph. Othman finally instructed a scholarly group of Muslims to carefully assemble the written fragments of the Qur'an into a single standardized text of which six copies were painstakingly made. The Qur'an is not arranged chronologically in the sequence it was revealed, nor does it form a single narrative story. One of the most widely used editions of the Qur'an in print today is the so-called Egyptian edition first printed in Cairo in 1925.

THE QUR'AN IN MUSLIM LIFE

First and foremost, the Qur'an is spoken. The most direct experience of the Qur'anic revelation is through recitation in the original Arabic. *Tajweed* is the art of singing recitation, and one who has memorized the entire Qur'an is known as *hafiz. Tartil* is also a form of recitation that proceeds as a slow methodical chant. The *salat* or ritual prayers to be prayed five specific times a day are mostly recitations of Qur'anic *ayahs.* The Qur'anic text has been divided into *juz'* or 30 divisions for recitation over a 1-month period. Many Muslims use the *juz'* divisions to aid in reciting the entire Qur'an during the sacred month of Ramadan.

Muslims observe ritual washings and purifications before handling the Qur'an or reciting its contents. The Qur'an is often whispered in a Muslim baby's ear soon after birth. It is recited as a part of Muslim weddings. And it is ritually spoken at Muslim funerals. New ventures in public or private life are marked with the recitation of blessings from the Qur'an. Public meetings in some Muslim countries are even begun with a reading from the Qur'an. Muslims create one of the only forms of art they are allowed, because of the Qur'anic injunction against any form of representational art, by drawing elaborate and beautiful calligraphy of Qur'anic verse. And the principles and message of the Qur'an resonate like an eternal divine voice through the lives and actions of Muslims from birth to eternity.

Many Muslim children learn to recite the Qur'an at a very young age. Even in countries where Muslims do not read or understand Arabic, children are taught to recite the Qur'an in Arabic. But translations of the Qur'an are often provided in order to understand approximately what one is reciting. There are even contests in which very young Muslim children attempt to recite the entire Qur'an from memory in public. Children as young as 8 and 9 years of age have successfully memorized the entire Qur'an. When children and adolescents take part in the ritual of praying five times daily or attend the Friday communal prayer, *ayas* from the Qur'an are recited by heart during the prayers. Children and adolescents also participate in community prayers during the *Eid* festivals, and the entire Qur'an is recited in *masjids* throughout the world during the sacred month of Ramadan. The content of the Qur'an plays an essential role in the prayer, devotional, and communal life of millions of Muslim children and adolescents around the world today.

INTERPRETATION OF THE QUR'AN

It is essential to understand that a translation is already an interpretation of the translator, and therefore the Qur'an can only be directly and truly understood in the original language in which it was revealed. Some Muslims have even been concerned that some Western scholars have colored their translations of the Qur'an in a certain way. One particular *ayah* has been translated by a Western translator "Idolatry is worse than carnage," where the meaning of the Qur'an is closer to "oppression is worse than killing." And another *ayah* referring to Islamic paradise has been translated "men to be wedded to chaste virgins," where the Qur'anic meaning is closer to "there for them shall be spouses purified." Therefore, some Muslims for good reason are concerned that Western scholars at times produce translations of the Qur'an that are colored with violent and sexual nuances not intended in the original text. This is a major concern because the vast majority of Muslims are dependent on translations of the Qur'an or at least Arabic-speaking leaders. For although most Muslims learn to recite the Qur'an and even memorize it as a child, few who do not actually speak Arabic understand what they are reciting.

The first textual source Muslims consult to help them interpret the Qur'an is the Qur'an itself. What may not be clear in the Qur'anic passage in question may be clarified in passages elsewhere in the Qur'an that address the same event or concern. The second source now preserved and transmitted in texts is the history of the Prophet Muhammad's life, called *sira,* as well as the example and traditions of the prophet known as *hadith.* Together, the *sira* and the *hadith* form the *sunnah,* which means example, path, or method. Muslims look to the example of the Prophet's life and actions to help clarify the meaning of the Qur'an on many matters. The *hadith,* however, are not as authoritative as the Qur'an itself, because they are not word-for-word divine revelation.

The science of collecting authentic and reliable *hadith* developed into a full-fledged and elaborate scholarly system for categorizing and measuring the reliability of a particular reported *hadith,* which included evaluating the personal reliability of the source person, the plausibility that the people in the chain of *hadith* transmitters could have actually met, the logical and rational consistency of the report itself, its agreement with the rest of the Qur'an, and many other careful indicators of reliability. One of the earliest and certainly one of the most widely used and respected collections of *hadith* was that collated by Imam Bukhari who died in 870 C.E. Finally, there have been a number of respected commentaries that attempt to accomplish *tafsir,* that is, exegesis or careful and systematic interpretation of the original intent of the Qur'anic text. These began to be assembled near the end of the ninth century, and there are six specific collections that comprise the most widely used commentaries still in use today.

CONTENT OF THE QUR'AN

The Qur'an addresses itself to all people of all times. The essential message of the Qur'an is contained in its first seven *ayahs,* "In the name of God, the most Gracious, the Dispenser of Grace: All praise is due to God alone, the Sustainer of all the worlds, the Most Gracious, Lord of the Day of Judgment. Thee alone do we worship; and unto Thee alone we turn for aid. Guide us to the straight way—The way of those upon whom Thou hast bestowed Thy blessings, not of those who have been condemned (by Thee), nor of those who go astray." This *surah* is repeated 17 or more times a day by Muslims during the five daily prayers and is known as the *Umm al-Kitab* or Mother of the Book.

The major themes of the Qur'an comprise the nature and character of God's transcendence and absolutely unique and eternal existence, as well as the appropriate response to and worship of God. The Qur'an also proclaims the true created nature of people and intention of God for human lives as a reminder to people to fulfill their God-given purpose and destiny, as well as the responsibility of people to care for and be responsible trustees of this world. The nature of human societies is addressed in practical discussions and examples of how to form an orderly and ethical Muslim social order or *ummah.* Two hundred and fifty *ayahs* are devoted to a discussion of rules for social behavior, economic issues, and criminal and international law. Nature is also described as God's creation that submits to God by its very design. And the value of reasoning and rationality is celebrated in the Qur'an in some 750 *ayahs,* almost one-eighth of the Qur'an.

Qur'anic scholars have identified what they believe to be the Meccan and Medinan *surahs* of the Qur'an. The Meccan *surahs* are generally made up of short, concise chapters of powerful *ayahs* admonishing listeners to accept the one and true God, to turn from their sinful practices, and to avoid the impending divine judgment. Because of the short length of the Meccan *surahs,* they are to be found for the most part toward the back of the Qur'an. The Medinan *surahs* are best described as those revelations that occurred after the *hijra* or migration of the Muslim community from Mecca to Medina in 622 C.E. For although the Muslim community came back to Mecca eventually and the Qur'an continued to be revealed at this time, the revelations after the *hijra* possess a similar style and themes. The Medinan *surahs* are on the whole larger with longer *ayahs* more characteristic of a teaching style. These *surahs* are concerned with guiding the Muslim community in Medina through narratives of earlier prophets and their communities, stories, parables, legal principles, and exhortations on how to live together as an organized Muslim *ummah.*

Ultimately, the Qur'an provides humanity with *hudud* or signals of the limits of human behavior, leaving it to Muslims to work out how these guidelines are to be applied in everyday life. For example, the Qur'an instructs Muslims to avoid the use of interest on loans of any kind, to be modest in all facets of their life, and to ever balance justice with mercy. But it is up to individuals and communities of Muslims to work out precisely how these principles will be lived out in everyday existence.

—Christopher Cutting

See also Islam; Islam, Five Pillars of; Islam, Founding Fathers of; Muhammad

FURTHER READING

Ayoub, M. M. (2002). The Islamic tradition. In W. G. Oxtoby (Ed.), *World religions Western traditions.* Oxford: Oxford University Press.

British Broadcasting Corporation. (2004). Islam. Available from www.bbc.co.uk/religion/religions/islam/index.shtml (August 29, 2004).

Denffer, A. V. (1983). *Ulum Al-Qur'an: An introduction to the sciences of the Qur'an.* Leicester, UK: The Islamic Foundation.

Sardar, Z., & Malik, Z. A. (1994). *Introducing Islam.* Cambridge, UK: Icon Books.

R

RELATIONAL CONSCIOUSNESS

Relational consciousness is a psychosocial term that has recently gained attention in the field of religious and spiritual development. It refers to an awareness of our interdependence with other beings, including God, animals, and other humans. It suggests a nuanced sensitivity to the complexity and connection of all creatures. More specifically, the phrase refers to an intuitive, *experiential* awareness, a *felt sense,* rather than a mere intellectual awareness. The term was popularized by David Hay in the 1990s through his research into the spirituality of English school children. From interviews with children, Hay came to the conclusion that much of what has been seen as spirituality or religion is actually this awareness of being in relationship with some larger reality.

Hay's work bears many similarities to *Varieties of Religious Experience,* published in 1902 by William James who also sought to discover the range and commonalities of paranormal experiences, or what he called an awareness of "the more." James concluded that religious experience cut across all cultures and could be an invigorating force for good. Hay carries James' work further by contributing insights into childhood spirituality. Hay argues that children are born with relational consciousness and that it persists throughout early childhood. However, in the west this sensitivity is suppressed by age 7 to 9. According to Hay, this suppression tends to lead to a societal deterioration of values and loss of social coherence.

The term *relational consciousness* provides educators (especially those in public schools) a way to talk about spirituality without equating it with a single religious tradition. It is a step toward finding common terminologies among those who lack a common tradition yet want to work together to promote spiritual growth in children. Hay would like to see educators and others protect relational consciousness in children, especially through stories. Re-telling, reading, and discussing stories help children to name familiar experiences (such as flow or point awareness, defined below).

Relational consciousness is an alternative to the "possessive individualism" that has become the norm in the Western world. Possessive individualism holds that

1. The only reliable way of knowing the world is through the physical senses, especially through science.

2. A human being's primary identity is as an individual who defines himself in opposition to other beings (i.e., at odds with other humans and nature).

3. Possession (of things, power, and property) is the most important way of expressing one's value.

In contrast, relational consciousness holds that

1. What can be known extends beyond the physical world and includes supernatural, spiritual, or nonmaterial realities; these can be accessed through other forms of consciousness besides the scientific and rational.

2. A human being's primary identity is *in relationship* with other beings (intentional connection with God, people, nature).
3. In the large picture, possessions are fleeting and unimportant measures of value.

According to Hay, relational consciousness manifests itself in relationships, specifically four key relationships, including

1. *Self and God* include concerns about ultimate reality, the transcendent realm, the presence of God, and love of God.
2. *Self and people* refer to awareness of interpersonal relations.
3. *Self and world* refer to sensitivity to beauty and nature, including landscapes, plants, and animals.
4. *Self and self* refer to identity, self-worth, concern about "the real me," and belief in life after death of the body.

Research on relational consciousness grew out of questions about how ordinary children talk about spirituality. During a 3-year qualitative study during the 1990s, Hay, Nye, and others interviewed numerous English school children, most of them irreligious. Hay was especially interested in nonreligious language for articulating *felt experiences* of interdependence with God or nature. He found that most children could clearly recall memories of relational consciousness from early childhood, but as they matured, they began to discount them, so that by puberty most suppressed relational consciousness altogether. Adults and peers seemed to conspire to convince children that spiritual experiences and beliefs were trivial and misleading.

Even for those children who were part of a religious tradition, once they reached a certain age, the experiential component of religion was often supplanted by dogma. As children lost touch with relational consciousness, most accepted a rationalist, materialist worldview. Results of Hay's research were published in *The Spirit of the Child* in 1998. Although his research methodology has been criticized, many educators have embraced his ideas.

Hay's relational consciousness challenges the dominant view of religious development in childhood (based on the views of Jean Piaget and James Fowler), which holds that children between birth and age 7 are "pre-religious" and thus unable to grasp spiritual reality. Fowler argues that children's spirituality must advance through *literalist* and *conventional* stages that necessitate identifying with one belief system; beliefs rather than experience become the most important way of supporting spiritual growth. Fowler also argues that only exceptional individuals grow into a sense of connectedness to all other beings, and then only later in life.

In contrast, Hay argues that children, especially under age 7, have access to important kinds of knowing, even when they lack a belief system that validates such knowing. Hay would like to see schools as well as religious institutions focus upon the experiential aspect of spirituality rather than upon teaching creeds. In this way, relational consciousness could be kept alive and deepened throughout the life cycle. For this to occur, adults should focus children's attention daily toward spiritual awareness (through silence, contemplation, prayer, mantras, etc.) and provide a cultural expression of spirituality (through ritual, stories, and social teachings). These activities need not be aligned with a particular religious tradition. Instead of discounting children's innate spirituality, educators should regard it as a source of insight.

The loss of relational consciousness has had disastrous consequences for human societies, according to Hay. Those who lose relational consciousness lose a sense of their own value and purpose, and they lose respect for other creatures. They cease to respect or believe in God. Children grow up alienated from nature and society. Such losses can lead to narcissism, rampant consumerism, aggression, sexual promiscuity, drug abuse, and despair. Hay links the loss of relational consciousness to widespread social disintegration, violence, and degradation of the natural environment.

Hay developed a set of categories for three different aspects of relational consciousness: awareness sensing, mystery sensing, and value sensing. These categories provide a framework for cultivating children's innate spirituality. Hay and his colleagues would like to see these different kinds of awareness integrated into school curricula so that children can develop fully as spiritual beings (see Spiritual Formation and Mystagogy). These aspects of relational consciousness are briefly described below.

Awareness sensing refers to alternative ways of knowing or modes of perceiving the spiritual world.

For example "here and now" awareness (also called *point awareness*) involves focusing attention on the present moment, as in Buddhist mindfulness meditation. Another example is "flow," the experience of being caught up in an all-absorbing experience. Activities such as meditation, prayer, silence, and periodic withdrawal are ways to cultivate awareness.

Mystery sensing concerns ultimate questions about reality and the purpose of the universe. It includes emotions such as wonder, awe, delight, and amazement. It also suggests an awareness of human limitations and the danger of arrogance. A strong sense of mystery leads to self-forgetfulness and union with God (or the spiritual world). It can also lead to a sense of purpose and right livelihood. Activities such as worship, ritual, and "philosophizing" (asking questions with children, listening to them, discussing what is unknown) can enhance a sense of mystery. The arts also play a part.

Value sensing refers the ability to discern good from evil, hopefully in order to cultivate the good. What is worthy? What is enduring? What is true? What is the best way to treat others? These are the questions addressed as one develops a sense of value. Perhaps this category is the one most developed in American religious life, with a strong emphasis on character development and the cultivation of personal virtue.

Hay believes that people in the Western world lack an adequate language and discourse for relational consciousness. They are blinded by their rational, secular, individualist worldview and thus see human beings primarily as isolated individualists. Educators can provide language and discourse for relational consciousness through the use of various kinds of stories.

In the past, shared religious stories fostered relational consciousness and prosocial values. Handed down from one generation to the next, religious stories included Creation stories, biblical narratives (parting of the Red Sea, Jesus' birth), and lives of the saints and other religious heroes (Moses, David, Martin Luther King, or Mary Baker Eddy).

In the West, religious stories no longer dominate the imagination the way they once did. Hay argues that other kinds of stories can be used in school to foster relational consciousness. He mentions specifically autobiography, fiction, the language of play and games, and the language of science and technology. For example, many children have embraced science fiction, the language of technology, and fantasy to talk about moral and spiritual issues. For many, this has become an accepted way to speak of other worlds. Children's reading (or listening to stories) can help them imagine traveling through time and space, encountering parallel universes, morphing into other states or being, and fighting battles with cosmic significance. Hay suggests that such narratives are a spiritually important alternative to the overemphasis on empirical science as the only source of truth.

Hay's work is significant for the way he enables educators from many traditions to work together to preserve and promote children's spirituality. By emphasizing a discourse of *experience,* they allow children themselves to put their spirituality into words. Shared terminology (such as Hay provides) and shared stories help adults to provide children with scaffolding for spiritual experiences. Because religious discourse is not useful for all people, children can benefit from access to other kinds of discourse and stories. There is also the potential for other discourses to enrich religious discourse.

Relational consciousness is especially useful for those concerned about the natural environment because of the way it links relating to the earth with relating to God. It is also of great value for those who want to promote dialogue among adherents of various faiths and between the religious and secular realms.

Several criticisms have been leveled against Hay's work. He has been criticized for not adequately addressing evil and sin. Hay focuses upon the positive aspects of spiritual awareness; for him, what James calls "the more" is always positive. Adherents of particular religions may object to Hay's efforts to find a common ground and a common language to be shared by all humans. Hay leaves it to others to take into account gender and ethnicity as important factors in relational consciousness.

Despite these possible objections, the concept of relational consciousness provides a way to explore spiritual development that is both pragmatic and innovative.

—Trudelle Thomas

FURTHER READING

Hay, D., & Nye, R. (1998). *The spirit of the child.* London: Fount/HarperCollins.

James, W. (1902). *Varieties of religious experience.* New York and London: Longmans, Green.

Vygotsky, L. (1962). *Thought and language.* Cambridge, MA: MIT Press.

RELIGIOUS DIVERSITY IN NORTH AMERICA

The three countries that make up North America are primarily countries of immigrants. Following the explorers of the 15th and 16th centuries, European immigrants began to increasingly colonize North America in the 17th and 18th centuries. These immigrant peoples were primarily made up of diverse Christian and some Jewish communities and began to form their own states, constitutions, and countries in the 18th and 19th centuries beginning in the Eastern areas of the continent and finally consolidating their western boundaries in the 19th and early 20th centuries. The matter of cultural, ethnic, racial, and religious diversity has been a major issue confronting Canada, the United States, and Mexico from their beginnings. The question of whether and how to assimilate, integrate, tolerate, or embrace diversity remains a crucial issue today, exponentially heightened as immigration laws have largely opened up since the mid-1960s massively increasing the number and diversity of cultural and religious communities present today in North America. Addressing issues and concerns raised by First Nations Native Peoples, African Americans, and a host of national, ethnic, and religious minority peoples in North American countries has become a major challenge in these societies for both the common citizen and public policy makers.

Judeo-Christian religious diversity has played a crucial role in the history of North American countries and, despite the advent of modernity characterized by secularism and the scientific revolution, continues to play a significant role in popular culture, politics, and cultural knowledge today. Furthermore, religious diversity is a crucial facet of North American immigrant, cultural, and ethnic diversity. Especially apparent among immigrant groups is the role of religious communities in integrating new immigrants into North American societies. Not only do numerous religious institutions provide basic settlement services, but they also play a crucial role in providing a social network of relationships and a sustainable settlement community. Especially prevalent among immigrants is the tendency to express, preserve, and live out their cultural and ethnic identities through their religious communities and traditions. This double function of immigrant and ethnic religious communities together with the long-established historical and continuing importance of religion in North American culture dramatically highlights the importance of religious communities and of being genuinely educated about North America's religiocultural diversity.

Historically, the countries of North America have endeavored to protect religious diversity by establishing and preserving the freedom of religion. The United States even went as far as to attempt to separate religion from state institutions at a very early stage in its history. In 1786, the Virginia Statute for Religious Freedom was passed and became a model legislating for the freedom of religion in the 1791 Bill of Rights. The first amendment consists of the statement, "Congress shall make no law respecting an establishment of religion or prohibiting the free exercise thereof." This article was intended not only to protect state institutions from religious interests but to protect religious institutions from state domination. And Alexis de Tocqueville, a well-known French visitor to America in the 1820s, observed on his travels, that the separation of religion and state has in many cases served to increase religious participation and diversity rather than subtract from it.

Canada on the other hand, although it guards religious freedom as well, has never officially embraced a policy of separating church and state. Rather, Canada has historically endeavored to protect religious freedoms by enshrining the liberties of minority religions in the constitution. For example, the Canadian constitution includes a protection for fully funded Catholic separate schools in those provinces that possessed them at confederation in 1867. Because of this legislation the province of Ontario still funds Catholic schools with public funds to this day. Moreover, Canada's official multicultural policy has led to the public funding of activities for immigrant religious communities such as language classes, citizenship classes, leadership training sessions for youth, teacher training, and conferences.

North American countries are addressing the issue of dramatically increased religious diversity in a plethora of ways since this issue has gained in importance exponentially as immigrant religious diversity has multiplied since the opening of immigration laws in the United States in 1965, and in Canada in 1967. One group of religious communities that has gained increasing prominence, and is facing increasingly challenging issues in North America because of its incredible growth, and also because of the repercussions of the September 11, 2001 attacks, is the Muslim communities of North America. A closer look at Muslim communities here will help to unearth the complexity and extent of the challenge and incredible potential of North America's religious diversity for both everyday citizens residing in North American countries and for their public policy makers.

ISLAM AND RELIGIOUS DIVERSITY IN NORTH AMERICA

Historically, states have attempted to address the issue of diversity in any number of ways from exclusion and outright elimination, to assimilation and versions of integration and tolerance, to accommodation, preservation, and support for cultural difference. Although the United States allows every individual the rights and freedoms to pursue and preserve any legal form of culture he or she chooses to engage in, the United States is popularly known as a cultural melting pot of assimilation. However, not only does this perception ignore the incredible success with which diverse and distinct immigrant and ethnic religious communities have survived here, it renders the recent so-called multicultural wars in the United States inconceivable. Indeed, America has begun to struggle with multicultural voices that have made significant headway in educational institutions and the mass media that may have implications for religious and specifically Muslim diversity.

Many non-Muslims in North America believe that Islam is primarily the religion of Arabic speaking peoples. However, not all Arabs are Muslims and not all Muslims are Arabs. There is a significant population of Christian, Jewish, and secular Arabs, and Arabs are in fact a minority ethnicity within the worldwide Muslim population. The greatest concentration of Muslims is actually found in Indonesia, and Muslims of South Asian descent, primarily from India and Pakistan, currently account for the majority of Muslims in North America overall.

The first Muslims in North America were brought to America by force as slaves from Africa. The first immigrants likely came from Lebanon in the late 19th and early 20th centuries working as peddlers. There are currently an estimated 600,000 Muslims in Canada, 6 million in the United States, and 15,000 in Mexico. Muslims in North America are on the whole very organized and established enough to maintain their Islamic identity in the North American context, adding their rich cultural heritage to the countries of North America.

But Muslim diversity in North America has not just included immigrant minorities but has become increasingly prevalent among ethnic or racial minorities as well. And here a possible connection between multiculturalism in America and Muslim diversity may be seen. A significant number of African Americans have converted to Islam during the 20th century. A reasonable estimate places African Americans at 30% of the total American Muslim population, which would register them at an estimated membership of approximately 2 million. The largest African American Muslim group today is known as the Nation of Islam. The most important figure in this group historically has been Elijah Muhammad, and the present leader of the group is Elijah's son W. D. Muhammad. Significant personalities and leaders in this movement include Muhammad Ali and Malcolm X.

The Nation of Islam is significant because the shape of multiculturalism in the United States has taken on a highly racialized tone. Multiculturalism in America is a counterdominant movement that intends to represent America's ethnic and racial diversity more accurately and fairly in United States's institutions. To date, most efforts have been limited to education practices and the mass media, but there is great potential for this political discourse to address the concerns of not only racial and ethnic minorities but also immigrant and religious minority groups as well.

Even though the United States is well-known for its stringent separation between church and state and thus continues to affirm that the publicly funded school is no place for religious education, some schools have taken advantage of the American court's affirmation that the public school is indeed a place to teach about religious traditions. And some private or charter schools are beginning to receive some public funding as long as they uphold certain curriculum standards, but otherwise they are free to include some religious education in their programs. And just as multiculturalism in America has tried to more accurately represent African Americans in the mass media, so too Muslims can benefit greatly with more accurate representations of their religion in the presses. There has also been some effort to accommodate Muslim minorities in issues relating to employment. In 1989 the District of Columbia passed legislation requiring all employers to allow Muslims leave to attend Friday prayers. President Bush recently pushed the boundary between church and state by offering some funding to religious institutions to provide social services. But unfortunately these funds have been primarily limited to Christian institutions and have not addressed the needs of diverse immigrant and minority religious communities.

There are of course numerous other historic, ethnic, and immigrant religious communities throughout North America, and Diana Eck's Pluralism Project is an invaluable and exhaustive project that is seeking to document and understand the incredible new religious diversity present in America. The Web site for this project and the CD-ROM published by this project is full of useful information on this subject.

Canada too has begun to address the issue of religion in public schools and religious accommodation. Karim H. Karim reports that one Muslim's attempt to procure time off work to attend Friday prayers at his mosque led to the termination of his employment. However, this Muslim successfully won his case in court and was reinstated in his job with the right to attend Friday prayers without pay. Separate Catholic schools continue to be fully funded with public dollars in the province of Ontario. And the province of Alberta has recently decided to fully fund any religious separate school that requests government funding provided that they meet certain curriculum and policy guidelines. Canadian public schools are also trying to include optional courses about religious traditions into their curriculums. Karim H. Karim reports that Muslim communities in Canada have been successful in garnering public monies to support programs in organizational development, Muslim conferences, classes in citizenship enhancement, development of youth leadership, Muslim exhibitions, classes in teacher training, and minority language classes including Farsi, Urdu, and Arabic.

Canada has also very recently been looking seriously at the question of allowing some Muslim groups to institute parts of Sharia law in their communities. This is not a proposal to institute the worst of penal law in some Muslim countries that has been broadcast by the popular media but rather is a proposal to include a purely optional and limited portion of civil law in areas such as legal separation, divorce, and the custody of children. Similar options are already available through approved programs to some Christian and Jewish communities, and on the whole have worked surprisingly well because of their orientation toward reconciliation and restoration, rather than the confrontational winner-take-all approach of many state legal institutions. However, a strong national Muslim women's organization is very concerned about this development's impact on the real legal choices of Muslim women in Canada. This question is as yet wide open, but Canada has decided that it is preferable to ask and struggle with these questions of accommodation rather than simply ignore its religious diversity and legislate for the dominance of the majority culture across all minority communities.

—Christopher Cutting

FURTHER READING

Eck, D. (2001). *A new religious America: How a "Christian country" has become the world's most religiously diverse nation.* San Francisco, CA: Harper SanFrancisco.

Fleras, A., & Elliot, J. (Eds.). (2001). *Engaging diversity: Multiculturalism in Canada.* Scarborough, ON: Nelson Thomson Learning.

Haddad, Y. Y. (Ed.). (2002). *Muslims in the West: From sojourners to citizens.* Oxford: Oxford University Press.

Haddad, Y. Y., & Smith J. I. (Eds.). (2002). *Muslims minorities in the West: Visible and invisible.* Walnut Creek, CA: AltaMira Press.

Karim, K. H. (2002). Crescent dawn in the Great White North: Muslim participation in the Canadian public sphere. In Y. Y. Haddad (Ed.). *Muslims in the West: From sojourners to citizens* (pp. 262–277). Oxford: Oxford University Press.

President and Fellows of Harvard College & Eck, D. (2004). *The Pluralism project.* www.fas.harvard.edu/~pluralism/ [September 20, 2004]

RELIGIOUS THEORY, DEVELOPMENTAL SYSTEMS VIEW

The focus of a developmental systems theory of religious development describes and explains the changing nature of one's perceived relationship with the divine across the life span as defined by the unique, dynamic interaction of characteristics of the individual and characteristics of the individual's context across time. All developmental systems theories describe and explain development as a *relational* process involving the integration of variables from multiple levels of the human ecology (i.e., from biology through cultural and historical levels). Recognition in developmental systems theory of multiple contexts and their interactive relationship with variables of the self necessitates much more than a singular conception of religious development, both in terms of quantitatively measured growth (e.g., growth in amount of knowledge about religious tradition) and in terms of qualitative growth (e.g., change in the subjective experience of the sacred). In addition, domains of knowledge, such as religious knowledge, can show growth at different times throughout the life span.

In this developmental systems perspective, the notion of temporality indicates that there are multiple meanings of time affecting religious development, and all are embedded within historical changes. For instance, normative age-related and normative historical (i.e., period in history) changes may impact individual and contextual variables in their structure and function, and nonnormative historical events (e.g., wars, economic depressions) may also impact religious development across the life span. In turn, there can be distinctions among individual, family (generational), and historical time. To understand religious development across the life span, it is necessary to consider how all components of temporality interact.

In assessing religious development, it is therefore important to consider the age of the person in question to determine, for example, his or her probable cognitive level (impacting the ability to think abstractly about purposefulness and connectedness) and if and how the individual is influenced by the historical time in which he or she is embedded. In terms of nonnormative events, as an example, September 11th challenged Americans' individual and collective identities and will likely influence (in both positive and negative ways) the religious identities of many, particularly those most highly affected. As a result of the interconnectedness of all other variables, no human variable is protected from the influence of time.

Given that developmental system theories acknowledge the temporal (historical) embeddedness of all levels of the ecology of human development, it therefore also recognizes change as a ubiquitous component of religious development. As such, these theories see the potential for plasticity (i.e., systematic change) in religious development, and this potential affords an optimistic view wherein planned actions (interventions) can be undertaken to promote positive developmental change.

IDENTIFYING THE INDIVIDUAL AND CONTEXTUAL VARIABLES THAT INFLUENCE RELIGIOUS DEVELOPMENT

Variables of the person that impact the person-context relation and thereby influence religious development include one's cognitive developmental level and, more specifically, the ability to think about issues related to self and other (e.g., the divine or sacred)—issues that are religious in nature. The ability to manipulate oneself physically within the world also might play an important role in the development of religiosity (e.g., in one's ability to participate in religious rituals and/or attend religious services), as does socioemotional competency, such as the ability to develop healthy interpersonal and intrapersonal relationships. The separate and interrelated influences of cognitive, motor, and social competencies on religious development differ for each individual and change throughout each individual's life span.

Recognizing the broad diversity of religious traditions and practice, it would be difficult to delineate all of the possible variables related to the religious. Certainly, contexts such as faith-based institutions, faith-based activities such as youth programs, and religiously devoted families are common contexts of influence. Whereas there are a great number of common contexts of influence, the religious contexts that are less common (e.g., personal places of prayer and meditation, personal resources such as scripture, psalm, and art) are innumerable, and internal characteristics such as cognitive capacity vary widely between and within individuals across time. As such, religious contexts can be diversely described both between and among individuals and between and among groups. In addition, for each individual and group, the influence of multiple levels of the context on religious development changes across time.

Whereas some well-known theories of development (i.e., Piaget's theory of cognitive development) provide developmental systems theory with knowledge about the role of individual characteristics such as cognitive competency in religious development, King provides a categorical system that accounts for a wide range of potential contextual influences on religious development. The contextual categories she names are (1) the ideological, (2) the social, and (3) the spiritual. For their breadth of contextual identification and description, these three contexts are considered in a developmental systems theory of religious development.

The ideological construct is provided by the religious tradition that intentionally promotes certain moral codes and values. Smith explains that the major world religions offer wisdom in the form of an ideology for the human race about how life should be lived. This wisdom or ideology is, according to Smith, presented in the form of (1) religious ethics (e.g., avoid crimes against humanity), (2) virtues (e.g., humility, charity, and veracity), and (3) vision (i.e., a sense of belonging to the whole of the human race, a sense of a grand design that is bigger than the human mind can comprehend, and a sense of the mysteries that no human mind can resolve). Cognitive capabilities and characteristics of ego identity and physical maturation that develop throughout the life span all dynamically interact with each other and with the ideology promoted by one's religion differentially across time.

How does the interaction between individual and religious ideological characteristics influence development? While James and Kwilecki provide many descriptive cases of individual developmental trajectories of change as a function of the interaction between person characteristics and religious ideology, King describes group differences among adolescents who self-identify themselves as religiously active versus those who do not so self-identify. Religiously active adolescents report a higher level of shared beliefs, values, and goals with their parents, peers, and other adults than adolescents who are not religiously active. King explains that religiously active youth are embedded in a religious community of relationships that offer them a consistent ideological framework. A social context of peers, family, and other adults is, then, another environmental influence on developing religiosity.

Similar to King's analysis, and as also described by Erikson, religious traditions place devotees into a specific religious social context—a family of adherents from the past, present, and future. Participation in religious tradition therefore unites the individual with a history of past believers, embedding the individual in the ethics, values, and vision (i.e., ideology) of a historically established religious family. Identifying with history provides the opportunity to transcend the present and feel connected to and dependent upon the past, present, and future. In addition, religious institutions provide the rare opportunity for adherents to be in an intergenerational environment wherein members have multiple opportunities to witness the ideology of the religion being activated. Bandura's social cognitive theory on religious development explains well the impact of spiritual models on religious development and, in this way, is useful to theory construction of a developmental systems view of religious development.

In terms of the role of the spiritual context, King explains that religious traditions and ritual offer the individual intentional doorways for developing a connection or relationship with the divine. Participation in religious ritual, as Erikson described, enables the individual to feel a part of a historical religious family, a feeling that summons a heightened consciousness of others (that) often triggers an understanding of self that is intertwined and somehow responsible to the other. James's perspective adds to this discussion that there are three things that represent religious experience in "most books on religion," and these three things certainly provide experiential opportunities for relationships with the divine to develop. These experiences include sacrifice, confession, and prayer. Ritual and experience embedded within religious tradition embed the individual and group of adherents in a context of spirituality.

What, in terms of unique variance, do these contexts, when dynamically interacting with core processes of human development, add to religious development? The answer lies partly in the inherently relational nature of these specific contexts with developing characteristics of the individual. What is unique about these religious contexts is the multiplicative influences of a specific ideology and worldview that intentionally promotes a religion's ethics, values, and vision: the social context of past and present religious adherents—the intergenerational family of religious devotees—and the opportunity to have the specific religious ideology and family couched in a spiritual framework, which provides the individual with both a developing relationship and understanding of the divine and a growing understanding of the self in relation to other, providing the individual with a sense of purpose and meaning that transcends his or her immediate concerns.

In a developmental systems view, the differences or changes in religiosity between individuals and within individuals (i.e., in terms of the qualitative and quantitative changes in religiosity that occur throughout one's lifetime) are, in part, dependent upon the interactive influence of individual variables and variables of the context such as the particular church, synagogue, or temple with which the individual identifies, the amount of participation by the individual in religious services and tradition, age and cognitive and psychological competencies, the religiousness of one's parents and peers, and so on.

For example, different religious institutions can provide youth with different beliefs, values, and worldviews—impressions and understandings that impact a young person's identity development differently across the individual's life span. This potential impact of religious institution on identity development is true not only in terms of different religious denominations (e.g., Mormon vs. Muslim) but also in terms of different institutions within the same faith (e.g., two different mosques within the same town). As another example, level of religious participation has been found to affect identity development. King found that youth who are active participants in their religion have a higher sense of a shared worldview as well as shared values and goals with their parents, peers, and other adults than youth who are not religiously active.

These examples make evident the fact that there is an indefinite number of individual and contextual contexts that affect religiousness. Taken together (and when placed within a developmental systems perspective), these core processes and unique characteristics provide a more comprehensive definition and explanation of the religious development process than has been previously offered. As such, for those interested in understanding religious and spiritual development and/or for those invested in promoting healthy religiosity and spirituality within themselves and/or others, developmental systems theory provides a useful framework that explains why, across the human life span, the unique relation between one's contexts and individual characteristics are important to consider.

—Elizabeth M. Dowling

FURTHER READING

Bandura, A. (2003). On the psychological impact and mechanisms of spiritual modeling. *International Journal for the Psychology of Religion, 13,* 167–173.

Erikson, E. (1959/1980). Identity and the life cycle [Monograph]. *Psychological Issues, 1,* 50–100.

Fowler, J. (1981). *Stages of faith: The psychology of human development and the quest for meaning.* San Francisco, CA: Harper & Row.

James, W. (1902/1961). *The varieties of religious experience.* New York: Modern Library.

King, P. (2003). Religion and identity: The role of ideological, social, and spiritual contexts. *Special Issue Applied Developmental Science,* 7(3), 197–204.

Kwilecki, S. (1999). *Becoming religious: Understanding devotion to the unseen.* Lewisburg, PA: Bucknell University Press.

Lerner, R. M. (2002). *Concept and theories in human development,* 3rd ed. Mahwah, NJ: Lawrence Erlbaum.

Piaget, J. (1970). *Genetic epistemology.* New York: Colombia University Press.

Smith, H. (1991). *The world's religions: Our great wisdom traditions.* New York: HarperCollins.

RETREATS

The word *retreat* is used as both a verb and a noun. As a verb, retreat means to pull back as in an action of withdrawing, particularly for reasons of safety, security and well-being. As a noun, retreat refers to a place of refuge, seclusion, or privacy. In all religious traditions, as well as increasingly being adapted to the corporate world, the notion of retreats primarily refers to an individual or group engaging, alone or with others, in a process of rest, renewal, and recreation.

Retreats include the component of rest, meaning a withdrawal from and suspension of regular daily activities for the purposes of renewal and recreation. Renewal implies recuperation of energies—physical, emotional, and spiritual—in order to experience a rejuvenation of body, mind, and spirit. Retreats generally embody a withdrawal-and-return motif. Retreating, in this sense, is the change of pace that enables an individual immersed in solitude and silence or with others in a community atmosphere to experience restoration or revitalization of creativity and purpose through various practices, disciplines, meditation, and contemplation. This purposeful withdrawal from workaday life is temporary and leads to a return to daily living with renewed vigor, enthusiasm, and sense of direction.

Western religious understandings of the notion of retreats have their source in Jewish and Christian conceptions of the Sabbath. Most likely, the Sabbath is a prebiblical notion that holds the day of rest as a literal and metaphorical command of the importance of hallowing the gift of time and releasing men and women from the tyranny of production-oriented tasks to remember to make holy a day of rest, prayer, and fellowship. Therefore, Sabbath celebrated in Jewish homes from Friday sunset to Saturday sunset is an illustration of the retreat theme of withdrawal from labor and return to labor after Sabbath.

The B'nai B'rith Youth Organization (BBYO) is an example of the variety of retreat experiences available to Jewish youth. BBYO is the largest Jewish youth organization in the world with over 20,000 members worldwide. A diverse range of opportunities provides Jewish youth with a deeper appreciation of their religion and culture, as well as community service known as the practice of *tzedekah.*

Observant Muslims—those who practice Islam and follow the teaching of the Koran—similarly to the practice in Jewish households, celebrate the home as the primary venue for faith formation. It is not uncommon for Muslim families in the United States to have a room in the home dedicated as a sacred space where prayer can take place five times a day as believers face Mecca. The two principle elements of Islamic religious practice takes place in the home: prayer and the fast associated with Ramadan, an annual season of prayer, fasting, family unity, and pilgrimage. Beyond the strong influence of the home on the faith formation of children and adolescents, the Muslim day school, Sunday school at the Mosque, Muslim youth camps, and the extensive opportunity to attend Muslim "conferences" are the principle means for deepening the faith for Muslim youth.

Making an annual retreat is a common spiritual practice among vowed religious, clergy, and many laypersons in Catholicism and various other Christian denominations. There are a variety of styles and formats to these retreats. Most people will withdraw from home and go to a retreat or spirituality center to experience this kind of interior renewal. Some retreats are done on an individual basis, whereby the "retreatant" is guided by a spiritual director and follows a certain pattern of spiritual practices for a weekend, 8 days, or 30 days, which is a particular kind of retreat based on the *Spiritual Exercises* of St. Ignatius. The patterns of prayer and ritual used on a retreat vary greatly and are influenced in both the West and the East by the spiritual legacy of the specific religious tradition as well as the great spiritual masters.

With over 340 ecumenical and interfaith retreat centers in the United States and Canada and the emergence of youth ministry as a vocation and career path, spiritual growth opportunities for children and youth have expanded beyond the traditional Saturday or Sunday religious school, youth camps, or summer vacation faith-based programs found in Judaism, Islam, and Christianity.

Young people across faith traditions now have extensive options for retreat-type experiences that provide developmentally appropriate, enjoyable, and challenging opportunities to experience supportive communities, explore new relationships with those of like values, broaden perspectives by meeting peers from differing ethnic and faith traditions, and make the connections between faith, service, and justice. The Catholic Church sponsors youth retreats called *Kairos* and *Koinonia*. Summer Bible camps and the Solo Cons form annual offerings in various Protestant denominations. Jewish "Midrasha" and "Rites of Passage" retreats, as well as an array of "conferences" in Islam are but a few examples of the scope of retreats that create the occasion for personal, spiritual, religious, and social development.

Retreats are often experienced in the context of a community of persons, including families and faith communities, deciding together to engage in reflection and rejuvenation. Family retreats, often called *conferences* in Islam, provide focused time for family members to reconnect, spend time relaxing together, talking about serious matters of family life and issues, and share some form of faith-based activity. Other group retreats are specifically designed to respond to interest groups, such as retreats called "Adventures in Nature," "Earth Wisdom," or "Canadian Wilderness Retreats," which are geared to youth and provide opportunity for young people to experience the rugged natural outdoors, build community, share the beauties of creation, and learn about ecological spirituality. There are retreat programs that provide respite for caregivers of chronically or terminally ill children or those without sight or hearing. Such retreats are often free of charge to the children living and dying with tremendous physical and emotional challenges. Teens and young adults often staff such retreat experiences, such as the "Believe in Tomorrow" or the annual retreat for children burn victims, which depend on the volunteerism of adolescents and young adults to share their health and strength with others.

Yoga or Zen retreats offer insights into and experience of the spiritual practices associated with Eastern spirituality. These forms of body movement, meditation, silence, and emptying of self appeal to youth seeking access to ways of developing greater emotional and spiritual balance in life. In Buddhist countries of Southeast Asia, boys, following their formal schooling years and prior to beginning a more independent life away from home, live as a Buddhist monk in spiritual retreat for a few months or full year. Traditional Hinduism outline stages that lead to the mature Hindu life (like Buddhism, this is the exclusive domain of males), which includes the initiation time when a male youth lives with his guru for study and prayer. In North America, adaptations of these practices can be found in retreats with an Eastern focus for both young men and women.

The 21st century reveals that many religious as well as holistic health organizations offer the retreat experience online so that one can stay home and still create an opportunity to find rest and recreation through guided meditation and practices aimed at restoring the human spirit.

—*Avis Clendenen*

See also Conversion; Meditation; Prayer; Spiritual Exercises of St. Ignatius

FURTHER READING

Hunter, R. (Ed.). (1990). *Dictionary of pastoral care and counseling.* Nashville, TN: Abingdon Press.

Connecting users and provider of retreats and retreat-related services around the world: www.retreatsonline.com [Retrieved April 17, 2004]

Oldest Muslim youth group information: www.jaannah.org/myrna/ [Retrieved April 17, 2004]

Largest Jewish youth organization: www.thisisfederation.org/alliance/teens/trf/groups/bbyo.htm [Retrieved April 17, 2004]

REVELATION

Revelation refers to something or someone being hidden and then uncovered or made known. Among religious traditions, revelation usually refers to supernatural truth that cannot be grasped through perception and reason alone—such as when certain faith traditions speak of God's justice and care for the faithful being revealed in the Bible's exodus story. Revelation has been a central concept in discussions of religious and spiritual development—especially when faith is considered as a response to revelation.

Throughout history, revelation has referred to a passive experience, that is, to something that happens to an individual rather than to something an individual initiates and actively pursues. Revelation is, then, closely tied to the concept of grace, which refers to God's actions, not to the actions of individuals.

The notion that knowledge can be passively received by an individual or implanted into an individual by another runs counter to current philosophical and scientific understandings of what is involved when individuals come to know reality. By and large, modern philosophy and modern science view the process of knowing as dependent on how individuals actively image and interpret reality and how they coordinate their own limited perspectives on reality with those of others. For the most part, then, modern philosophy and science have opposed the classical concept of revelation on the grounds that it runs counter to what we know about how individuals gain knowledge and come to understand reality.

The concept of revelation has also been attacked on the grounds that claims about what is revealed often have contradicted one another, promoted self-serving ends, and led to disaster. For example, throughout history there have been claims by false prophets about truths revealed to them; claims that these prophets have used to cause great harm.

Despite these attacks on the concept of revelation, a good many find themselves caught in a dilemma. On one hand, the insights provided by modern philosophy and modern science cannot be ignored. Nor too can history's lessons concerning the misuse of the concept of revelation. On the other hand, without some concept of revelation, faith can falter for not having anything to build on—no firm foundation on which to grow.

As a way out of this dilemma, several modern thinkers—theologians mostly—have adopted a different concept of revelation from the traditional, authoritarian concept. Traditionally, God, the church, a sacred text, or someone in authority does the revealing or dictates what has been revealed. As mentioned, the traditional concept of revelation leaves the individual in a passive-responsive role only. This has been true regardless of whether the presumed revelation has been a proposition for establishing dogma, a historical event revealing something about God's nature, or an individual's mystical experience of God.

The newer concept of revelation rejects these older, authoritarian meanings and replaces them by linking revelation to the concepts of development and consciousness. The newer concept views spiritual development as a dynamic interplay between individuals and life, an interplay that can push or lead to higher stages of spiritual consciousness. With this newer concept then, revelation becomes not revelation of something new but of something that has been there from the beginning. Revelation in this newer sense is, then, close in meaning to the psychological term *insight.* In other words, when we gain insights into what is most important or meaningful, we may experience those insights as revelations.

The advantage of this newer concept of revelation is that it aligns the concept of revelation with modern philosophical and scientific thinking. The disadvantage is that it creates a split with how religion and spirituality have been experienced historically.

It remains to be seen whether the advantages outweigh the disadvantages. It may be that the newer concept of revelation renders the term *revelation* superfluous. The terms *development, insight,* and *consciousness* may suffice. But if this is the case, then one might well ask on what basis can individuals have faith?

More likely some notion of revelation will continue to be used in order to establish the grounds for having faith. In the future, the concept of revelation is apt to help individuals hold onto the power of older notions for engendering commitment and conviction while also helping individuals to remain intellectually honest. The concept of revelation is, then, likely to remain a useful, even necessary concept for defining and supporting religious and spiritual development.

—W. George Scarlett

RITUAL

In searching for appropriate educational models to enhance the spiritual development of children and youth, it is helpful to consider the learning model embedded in traditional ritual practices, particularly those that were used in coming-of-age ceremonies and other rites of passage in religious and traditional cultural settings. Rites of passage are cultural and spiritual ceremonies and practices used to mark changes in the station or status of persons in communities. They include ceremonies such as marriage, funeral rites, birth and naming, as well as coming-of-age rituals. They can include investiture or membership ceremonies, graduation rituals, and so on. In religious communities, ceremonies like confirmations, baptisms and their variations are combined rites of passage and investiture rites.

Ritual practices serve a variety of functions in a community, and are based on an educational or pedagogical model that assumes learning takes place through participation. Rites of passage are designed to make clear that one or more members of a community are changing their status or place in the community. The ceremony serves to make a public declaration of the change of status in order to affirm it for the participants, whose new status is ceremonialized, and to inform the rest of the community so that the new status is accepted and respected. A marriage ritual, for example, makes clear that two individuals have become a couple and that their choice is being acknowledged communally. The community is being told, through ceremony, that these two are no longer single and available. They will now be treated in light of their new status as a couple, assured that their choices and intentions are known and honored by the community. The ceremony also acts to remind others in the community of the commitments or promises that they have made in the past. The promises being made in the ceremony recall and renew the vows they made in the past.

Communal rituals usually include spiritual components that connect the participants and the community to powers beyond themselves and across time. There are often deliberate religious practices including prayer, singing, chanting, or drumming, invocation of the Divine, and a recall of traditional stories, teachings, texts, and ancestors. There is cultural wisdom in ritual practices that marks clear borders for people's lives that function, at the same time, as a conserving and renewing force within a community.

COMING OF AGE

The implications for spiritual development and education of children and youth can be better understood with an explanation of a rite of passage: coming of age. Many cultures have practiced specific ceremonial and ritualistic processes to mark the move from childhood into the beginning of adult life. During the years of puberty, the time of coming of age, there is an awareness that the physical, emotional, intellectual, spiritual, and social changes happening to boys and girls made them open to being influenced by the world around them. In this time of transition, they are pliable, amenable to being shaped by their context. In leaving childhood and its assurances, children enter a period of uncertainty and questioning in which they are seeking to form adult identities. In response, cultures develop deliberate experiential learning practices and rituals that shape these youth into a form that is appropriate and necessary for their culture. The aim is to imprint on the lives of these youth the adult form or shape of the culture's way of thinking, its values and meanings, as well as its spiritual and religious assumptions. The goal is to produce from boys and girls successful adult men and women who can sustain and build their community and its ways of life, its values, its beliefs, and its meanings.

RITES-OF-PASSAGE STRUCTURE

In any rite of passage there are three stages. The first is leaving. Children leave behind their childhood and its context, relationships, and ways as they take up the responsibilities and roles of adult life. The departure means that what they are will not be sufficient for the next stage of life. In some way their childhood self dies, and they take up a new self through the process.

The middle or liminal stage is the time of transition, now called *adolescence,* and is the critical time in a rite of passage as it is the time of change. The *liminal time* (meaning the in-the-doorway space) is considered by some to be a dangerous place (and time) because it is an in-between state in which the youth in passage are open, vulnerable, and pliable. They are no longer rooted or located in the past of childhood, and they are not yet anchored in the new stage. Current culture acknowledges that children change developmentally. In contrast, past cultures believed that the character was naturally transformed and lives were consequently molded into a shape that would last into the future. A coming-of-age rite is designed to provide a way through or a passage for this journey.

It is necessary to guide a young person through matters of vocation, sexual identity, mortality, values, and meaning so that they became adults for their culture, aware of responsibilities, able to negotiate difficulty and take up a role that contributed to community life. The intentional cultural practices provided by elders assume that young people are vulnerable because they are in transition. Therefore, an educational process, complete with mentors and elders and a deliberate communal process full of theatre and ritual, is necessary.

The final stage of coming of age is the reentry or integration into the next phase of life. The actual rite of passage is usually concluded with a ceremony that declares the task complete. Whatever is needed to be learned has been learned, and the children are now ready to be publicly declared adults and will henceforth be treated as adults. The communal celebration marks the end of a process that can be up to several years in length. After it is complete, the new adult is expected to be and act as an adult and is expected to be treated as an adult. There is a clear borderline that is crossed by the whole community. The culture surrounding the ceremony has built-in practices to ensure the success of the new adults in the community. The mentoring of elders and guides confirms and supports the new adult to meet the expectations of the community.

THE EDUCATIONAL MODEL

Step One. Part of the success of rites of passage is the educational approach embedded in ritual life that assumes humans are shaped or given form primarily by participation. By taking part in a cultural activity a person begins to acquire the shape or molding embedded in that activity, being formed like a piece of pottery. Children, for example, acquire a language by living in it. Their minds are shaped to the structure and assumptions of the language they are learning because they live in the world of that language. They learn the thinking and perspective inherent in their language along with the language. They are being shaped to a way of speaking and a way of thinking. Similarly, participants in rites of passage are involved in a series of actions that shape them in a form appropriate for their community. The shape being given includes a way of thinking that contains spiritual awareness and assumptions. The spiritual values and perspective of a culture are already there, inside its actions and rituals, and are best learned through participation, experientially.

This educational practice reverses the school-based approach that assumes one must be instructed in structure and content in order to acquire knowledge. Participation is a different kind of learning: learning through practice. It is an immersion experience and does not require understanding to precede learning. One takes part in an experience that contains ideas and assumptions that shape a participant to a way of life. They are implanted in the learner experientially and made familiar through activity.

Step Two. In order to integrate and understand the thinking being experienced, the second stage of learning in the participatory model is a process of reflection or consideration. It requires guidance and the presence of elders or mentors who can assist learners in reflecting on what they have experienced, exploring its meaning for them, and beginning to surface the implicit values inside the activities. It requires taking time to reflect on what shape is being given, to consider what that form might mean, and to become aware of personal values, roles, responsibilities, and place in the community. Understanding grows out of the experience in a deliberate guided and supported process of reflection.

Step Three. The process of formational learning is not complete without the third stage in which there is a deliberate acquisition of skills and content appropriate to the shape that has been taken. The focus shifts to acquiring the knowledge and skills necessary to pursue a way of life as a contributing adult member of the community. There is an acknowledged need to identify what skills or content someone must have for who they are becoming in order to pursue their direction and to meet the community needs of survival and development. Elders or teachers are needed to provide support, encouragement, and skills training. This stage of education may move slowly as the learners become aware of their interests through reflection, which directs them to a vocation or career leading to an acknowledgment of needed skills and content. There is a remarkable economy of learning in the participatory approach as the learner is shaped or formed to receive specific knowledge through participation and is enthusiastic to acquire skills and content, and consequently, the learning is directed and contained. The content to be taught has a container prepared to receive it and hold it.

THE WISDOM OF RITUAL

The learning process of rites of passage has been used in many cultures and religious communities for centuries with consistent success. It recognizes that

1. Interest and engagement happen most easily through participation.
2. In taking part, the learner is already invested in an outcome.
3. Through participation the values and assumptions of the context are learned indirectly.

The process does not begin with information or content but with immersion in events and activity. It is not about filling minds with content but engaging lives through participation in forms of activity. Ritual life also assumes there will be community involvement in learning with elders or mentors who supervise the process. These elders must also be watchful, noting the habits and character of the participants, steering them to appropriate activities and eventually to appropriate teachers and instructors.

The educational model in ritual also assumes that the learner must be reflective in order to discover, from within, what draws them. It assumes that life has purpose and meaning and that only in an inner or spiritual process can a person come to know his or her own place and calling and the value for them. Further it insists that content and skills come at the point in the educational process when shape has been given and the learner is committed to learning and formed to acquire and retain the content and skills. It acknowledges that there is a significant role for teachers, mentors, and elders in the process. Wisdom must be passed on in thoughtful and guided ways. Risk is inherent in learning and a process that protects learners acknowledges that a spiritual danger exists in how the learner is being formed or shaped.

IMPLICATIONS

The foundational knowledge that in the coming-of-age period of life a formational process is happening helps us recognize that shape making *is* going on. It is not a question of being or not being shaped but rather what kind of shape taking is happening. The challenge for any culture, then, is to consider what influences are giving shape to a person's life through participation.

If a successful learning process requires that the steps of reflection and skills acquisition are completed, there must be mentors, guides, and elders who can and will enter the difficult space of reflection to assist in the values being passed on by the culture and have them acknowledged, clarified, and affirmed. These guides also serve as role models, that is, individuals who are well formed and who can be copied for their "shape." It is critical for cultures to make explicit who the role models are and what their shape or form inspires.

Skills will be learned one way or the other, but the nature of those skills and the way they are used are dependent on an effective reflective process, at an appropriate time in the process, being part of the learning. Skills and content will be valued if they make sense and have a life container that can hold them.

Rites of passage, especially coming of age, continue to go on in every culture. The formational experience is happening but is often not an intentional process. The cultural agency required to produce effective adults for a culture may be abandoned to agendas that are not interested in maturity or reflective practice. It may be that the cultural agency for formation has been turned over to impersonal processes that cannot provide the attentive and watchful guidance of a local, invested community. If young people, during their coming-of-age process, are being formed by participation, it is worth considering what sense of meaning they gain and what they learn from the values connected to the repetitive or ritualistic participation in which they engage.

Being steeped in images and repetitions of images is a type of participation that forms those who participate in the images offered. This is the knowledge that permeates traditional rituals and ceremonies. Images are steeped in meaning and values. A reflective and critical assessment of those images must happen if the shape they are giving to lives is to be understood and directed to the benefit of all. However, if the flow of participatory action never stops and there are no sites of reflection, there can be no real coming of age. There may be a lack of elders to guide the process. It is wise to consider who acts as mentors during any reflection on values and equally wise to wonder about the character of the humans being formed in any cultural process.

If the result of formational practices in a culture is adults who live with a degree of uncertainty, vulnerability, and insecurity, as well as with unclear values and meaning, there are implications for the culture and for the young being raised within. It is important to analyze cultural rituals and their embedded meanings to see what is actually being taught through participation and a formational process. It is necessary to consider whose ends are being served and what spiritual values are being offered by a culture. Cultures that are deliberate about rites of passage, especially coming of age, know that formation of lives is significant and transmits values. Rites of passage need to be intentional, deliberate, and the work of the whole community.

—Daniel G. Scott

FURTHER READING

Anglin, J. P., Artz, S., & Scott, D. G. (1998). Special issue: Rites of passage in the postmodern age: Implications for child and youth care workers. *Child & Youth Care Forum, 27*(5), 317–335

Eliade, M. (1958). *Rites and symbols of initiation.* (W. R. Trask, Trans.) New York: Harper & Row.

Mahdi, L. C., Foster, S., & Little, M. (Eds.). (1987). *Betwixt & between: Patterns of masculine and feminine initiation.* La Salle, IL: Open Court.

Turner, V. (1967). *The forest of symbols.* Ithaca: Cornell University Press.

ROSICRUCIANISM

The Rosicrucians are members of a mystical fellowship or brotherhood that came to prominence in Europe in the early 17th century. The emblem of the fellowship is an open-petalled red rose at the center of a golden cross, perhaps symbolizing blood and sacrifice, beauty and purity, as well as the binary oppositions of male and female, suffering and glory. The fellowship appears to draw its teachings from a range of esoteric movements including alchemy, magic, Gnosticism, and Jewish and Egyptian mysticism. It is neither a religion nor an order of Freemasons, though it has some of the features of both of these, but is more concerned with the discovery of spiritual truth and the hidden meaning in things.

Though its roots are sometimes traced as far back as first century Egypt, the origins of the fellowship are traditionally thought to lie with a German scholar, Christian Rosenkreutz, whose dates are said to be 1378–1484. He is described as having learned mystic secrets from the Arabs while traveling in the Holy Land, Egypt, and Morocco. It is not clear whether Rosenkreutz is a historical figure, a mythological or allegorical personage, or an assumed name.

Key figures in the history of Rosicrucianism include the Swiss alchemist Paracelsus (1493–1541), the English scholar, magician, and traveler John Dee (1527–1608), the German alchemist Michael Maier (1568–1622), the English doctor and scholar Robert Fludd (1574–1637), the German theologian Johann Valentin Andrea (1586–1654), and possibly the scientist and writer Francis Bacon (1561–1626). Three important publications in the early 17th century were the *Fama Fraternitatis* (1614), the *Confessio Rosae Crucis* (1615), and the *Chymische Hochzeit Christiani Rosenkreutz* (1616). As well as telling the story of Christian Rosenkreutz, these texts spoke of the dawning of a new age, a secret brotherhood whose members had special healing powers and a new knowledge that was to solve the world's problems. They excited the popular imagination, and by 1620 more than an additional 400 pamphlets had been published discussing Rosicrucian ideas.

Rosicrucianism remained very much in the public eye for the next hundred years, and references to it abound in the literature of the time, including, for example, one in Pope's dedication to his famous poem "The Rape of the Lock." In 1714, issue no. 379 of the *Spectator* contains a description of the tomb of Rosenkreutz, and issue no. 574 contains an account of Addison's conversation with a Rosicrucian, which he describes as a mixture of "unintelligible cant" and "natural and moral ideas." His conclusion is that the Rosicrucian's "great secret was nothing else but content." Perhaps it was the rationalization of Rosicrucianism in the 18th century and the identification of the Philosopher's

Stone with spiritual contentment that led to a loss of interest in its ideas. But the Rosicrucian message has always been the advancement of humanity through spiritual enlightenment accompanied by such values as tolerance, compassion, and selflessness.

Various groups calling themselves Rosicrucian and claiming to be a continuation of the genuine Rosicrucian tradition still exist in the 21st century, the biggest of which is probably Antiquus Mysticusque Ordo Rosae Crucis (the Ancient and Mystical Order of the Rosy Cross [AMORC]), with its headquarters in San Jose, California. They see it as their role to bring an ancient spiritual tradition to modern consciousness, but their influence is insignificant compared to the great days of Rosicrucianism.

—J. Mark Halstead

FURTHER READING

Yates, F. (1972). *The Rosicrucian enlightenment.* London: Routledge and Kegan Paul.

S

SACRAMENTS

Saint Augustine defined *sacrament* as a visible sign of invisible grace. Later, the definition expanded to a sacrament being an outward sign instituted by Christ to give grace. An even more elaborate definition is that sacraments are perceptible signs, words, and actions, accessible to our human nature. By the action of Christ and the power of the Holy Spirit they make present efficaciously the grace that they signify. Truly the sacraments are efficacious signs of grace, instituted by Christ and entrusted to the Church, by which divine life is dispensed to the believers. The visible rites by which the sacraments are celebrated signify and make present the graces proper to each sacrament. They bear fruit in those who receive them with the required dispositions.The actual number of sacraments has differed over the course of Church history. Most of the main line Christian churches would accept the Sacraments of Initiation, Baptism, Confirmation, and Eucharist. Baptism is the sacrament that one receives as an infant or as an adult, if unbaptized. Baptism is recognized by all the Christian churches that use the ritual formula of "I baptize you (name) in the Name of the Father and of the Son and of the Holy Spirit." Baptism incorporates the individual into a believing community of the church and makes one a member. Baptism is received only once in a lifetime.

The sacrament of Confirmation is a continuation, a ratification or sealing of Baptism. If an individual was baptized as an infant, the individual now speaks for him or herself in preparing for the sacrament of Confirmation. Confirmation helps the individual focus on the missionary dimensions of the baptismal commitment. This sacrament is received by teenagers and adults. Confirmation is only received once in a lifetime.

The third and most important Sacrament of Initiation is Eucharist. This is the preeminent sacrament from which all others have meaning. It is when the community of believers gathers around the table (altar) for the breaking of the bread. The Eucharist is the celebration of Jesus' last supper, when he took bread and wine and gave them to the church as his Body and Blood. This Eucharist is celebrated weekly in some Christian churches.

Some Christian churches have the sacraments of vocation, of which there are two: the Sacrament of Matrimony and the Sacrament of Holy Orders. The Sacrament of Marriage celebrates the free giving of one person to another person, for a lifetime. This is also a reflection of the love of Christ for the church. Sometimes the church is called the bride of Christ. Matrimony celebrates and witnesses the covenant of love between two people. A covenant is always understood as freely given and unearned. The Sacrament of Matrimony should only be celebrated once unless there is a death of a partner. Some Christian churches do allow for a second marriage.

The Sacrament of Holy Orders is for the ordained clergy of a Christian church. It should be seen as a sacrament of service by which some are called by God, through the church, to be the spiritual leaders. Some Christian churches also have the fulfillment of Holy Orders and Deacons, which is the step before being ordained a full clergy person. The Sacrament of Holy Orders is only received once in a lifetime.

Some Christian churches also have the sacraments of healing, of which there are two: the Sacrament of Reconciliation or Confession and the Sacrament of the Anointing of the Sick. The Sacrament of Reconciliation or Confession focuses on forgiveness in our life and on our acceptance of that forgiveness, which brings the believer back to spiritual health in the family of God and the community after the individual turned away from God's will. The Sacrament of Reconciliation in some Christian churches can be celebrated weekly. Most would suggest it be received before Christmas and before Easter. Some Christian Churches do not believe an individual needs to celebrate this sacrament with a clergy person but can ask forgiveness directly from God.

The Sacrament of the Anointing of the Sick takes place as the community gathers in faith to pray over and lay hands on those who are sick, because the church, like Christ, desires the health of the whole person. Some Christian churches would celebrate this sacrament once a month or a couple of times a year. Other Christian churches would just have the clergy person anoint the sick person either before going into a hospital or any time a sick person wants to receive this sacrament. Not all Christian churches have the Sacrament of Anointing of the Sick.

Over the course of church history, the exact number of sacraments has changed, depending on the particular insights of the believers and the church leadership. In some centuries the sacrament of Holy Orders was three in number: Deacon, Priest, and Bishop. In other centuries the Church itself was considered a sacrament.

Sacraments are more than just a magical number of ritual acts that give grace. They are profound opportunities for people already in God's grace to gather and celebrate that fact through symbolic action and ritual. Sacraments do not happen in church so much as they happen in people who come together as "Church" to celebrate what has already been happening to them. Most of the Christian churches would say that Jesus Christ gave or instituted the sacraments for the people of God, that is, members of the Church.

Sacraments do not begin or end with church leaders or liturgical celebrations. They begin with God's love and care through Jesus Christ to believers. Over time the exact style and method of celebrating a sacrament may indeed change. Because the Church is always changing, sacraments do not end. As long as the Church continues to live and celebrate the sacraments, sacraments will be ongoing symbols of God's loving care.

Yes, sacraments are the visible signs of invisible grace. They are outward signs instituted by Christ to give grace. They are the life of the Church and much more.

—Rev. David M. O'Leary

See also Baptism; Eucharist

FURTHER READING

Osborne, K. (1988). *Sacramental theology: A general introduction.* New York: Paulist Press.

Schillebeeckx, E. (1963). *Christ the sacrament of encounter with God.* New York: Sheed & Ward.

SACRIFICE

Sacrifice is a basic activity at the foundation of the world's religions, often involving huge expense, monumental building, and the service of dedicated priests. For both practitioners of religion and those who study religion, sacrifice is difficult to fathom. Modern society does not present any direct equivalent of sacrifice, and for that reason attempts have perennially been made to explain sacrifice in terms of more familiar social relationships. This entry surveys the basic presentations of sacrifice within the Bible and then assesses modern attempts to understand sacrifice.

SACRIFICE IN BIBLICAL PERSPECTIVE

The book of Leviticus describes sacrifice in the particular case of an offering called *sacrifice of sharings* (Lev. 3:1), where participation in a meal is basic. The notion that a sacrifice might involve worshippers in a feast is commonplace in ethnographic studies, and it is specifically attested to in patriarchal and Mosaic narratives. Jacob formalizes his treaty with Laban on that basis (Gen. 31:51–54), and Jethro celebrates both the Lord's greatness and the presence of Aaron and the elders thereby (Exod. 18:9–12).

In 1 Samuel 1:3–5, it is recounted as a matter of course that Elkanah should distribute sacrificial portions in his own household. At the time of the sacrifice to solemnize the covenant, Moses, Aaron, Nadab, Abihu, and the 70 elders are said to have beheld God eat and drink. That festive communion is an example of a sacrifice of sharings (Exod. 24:4–11). The association is persistent in royal provision for feasts together with sacrifices, whether the king involved be David (2 Sam. 6:17–19), Solomon (1 Kings 3:15; 8:62–65), or Hezekiah (2 Chronicles 30:22).

In Leviticus 3, the animals offered are the focus: they must be unblemished cattle, sheep, or goats, male or female (vv. 1, 6, 12). The offerer lays his hand on the animal and kills it in front of the tent of meeting (vv. 2, 8, 13). The priests take up their duties of throwing the blood and receiving the fat of the entrails, the kidneys with their fat, and the remainder of the liver which comes off with them (vv. 3, 4, 9, 10, 14, 15). Following the logic that the fat belongs to God as well as blood, the lamb is also taken (v. 9). The priests offer these fatty portions for "an odor of pleasantness to the Lord" (v. 5, cf. vv. 3, 16), or God's "food" (vv. 11, 16).

God's desire is to consume a part of what is pure with his people and sacrifice was and is a way to offer life in the way that God pleases so that life can be intensified. Hence, the Temple occupied a dominant place in Judaism as the single placc where sacrifice could be offered. The Temple in Jerusalem was conceived of as the intersection between heaven and earth for prophets and teachers in Israel until its destruction by the Romans in 70 C.E.

Like many of the prophets before him and many other rabbis in his own time, Jesus keenly interested himself in how sacrifice was offered in the Temple (Matt. 21:12–13, Mark 11:15–17, Luke 19:45–46, John 2:13–17). He objected to the presence of merchants who had been given permission to sell sacrificial animals in the vast, outer court of the Temple. His objection was based on his own, peasant's view of purity: he felt that Israelites should offer what they produced themselves, not things they had just bought from priests. He believed so vehemently what he taught that he and his followers drove the animals and the sellers out of the great court, no doubt with the use of force.

Jesus' interference in the ordinary worship of the Temple might have been sufficient by itself to bring about his execution. Roman officials were so interested in its smooth functioning at the hands of the priests whom they appointed that they sanctioned the penalty of death for sacrilege. Yet there is no indication that Jesus was arrested immediately. Instead, he remained at liberty for some time, and he was finally taken into custody after one of his meals, the Last Supper.

Jesus could not simply be dispatched as a cultic criminal. He was not attempting an onslaught upon the Temple as such; his dispute with the authorities concerned purity within the Temple. Other rabbis of his period also engaged in forceful demonstrations of the purity they required in the conduct of worship.

The meaning Jesus gave his meals after what he did in the Temple brought about his arrest. Jesus had long celebrated fellowship during meals as a foretaste of the kingdom. But now he also added a new and scandalous dimension of meaning. His occupation of the Temple having failed, Jesus said of the wine, "This is my blood," and of the bread, "This is my flesh" (Matt 26:26, 28; Mark 14:22, 24; Luke 22:19–20; 1 Corinthians 11:24–25; Justin, *1 Apology* 66.3).

In Jesus' context, the context of his confrontation with the authorities of the Temple, his words can have had only one meaning. He cannot have meant, "Here are my personal body and blood"; that is an interpretation which only makes sense at a later stage. Jesus' point was rather that, in the absence of a Temple that permitted his view of purity to be practiced, wine was his blood of sacrifice, and bread was his flesh of sacrifice. In Aramaic, "blood" and "flesh" (which may also be rendered as "body") can carry such a sacrificial meaning, and in Jesus' context, that is the most natural meaning. The meaning of "the last supper," then, actually evolved during a series of meals after Jesus' occupation of the Temple. During that period, Jesus claimed that wine and bread were a better sacrifice than what was offered in the Temple: at least wine and bread were Israel's own, not tokens of priestly dominance. No wonder the opposition to him, even among the Twelve (in the shape of Judas, according to the Gospels), became deadly. In essence, Jesus made his meals into a rival altar, and we may call such a reading of his words a ritual or sacrificial interpretation.

The sacrificial interpretation has two advantages over the traditional, autobiographical interpretation as the meaning Jesus attributed to his own final meals. The first advantage is contextual: the sacrificial interpretation places Jesus firmly with the Judaism of his period and at the same time accounts for the opposition of the authorities to him. The second advantage is its explanatory power: the sacrificial interpretation enables us to explain subsequent developments in the understanding of Eucharist within early Christianity and to appreciate the ongoing importance of sacrificial thinking within modern culture.

CURRENT THEORIES OF SACRIFICE

Four views of sacrifice that appear frequently in scholarly and popular literature and that represent sacrifice as a primitive and mistaken notion are important to consider because they point to a more comprehensive perspective on what sacrifice truly involves.

Sacrifice has been seen as a gift, given in the hope that a god might be bought off, so that evil might be warded off and good produced. That critique of sacrifice is ancient, the expression *do ut des* ("I give that you might give") is in the stock and trade of the Greco-Roman disaffection with anthropomorphism—the idea that the gods are really human in their form and in their motivations. In the 19th century, Edward Burnett Tylor spelled out the alleged mistake of the theory: sacrifice is a bribe offered to a deity. Tylor was willing to admit that sacrifices might be offered and accepted in a symbolic sense, but he only concerned himself with the examples he could find of people giving so that deities might give in return. Yet the majority of known instances of sacrifice, which are far more routine, are simply not explained by this theory.

Before there were gifts, there was food, and William Robertson Smith attempted to explain the consistent link between sacrifice and eating. He found that in the most ancient Hebrew sacrifice, in which the animal victim was presented at the altar and devoted by the imposition of hands, the greater part of the flesh was returned to the worshipper, so that God and worshipper were joined in the communion of eating the same flesh. Robertson Smith understood sacrifice as a communal act, and he did so with such emphasis that the earlier, unreflective emphasis upon the individual in religious life was overcome within the study of sacrificial activity. Moreover, he correctly recognized the social dimension of sacrifice, its celebration and consumption of the fruits of common labor. Sadly, however, Robinson Smith concluded that the god was in some sense eaten in sacrifice, and evidence for this theory is very thin. As a result, in biblical study, the theory of sacrifice as a gift has all but eclipsed the model of communal eating that Robertson Smith developed.

James George Frazer's *The Golden Bough* was first published in 1890, just after the posthumous appearance of Robertson Smith's lectures and has been through many incarnations. Frazer believed that the purpose of sacrifice was to free immortal spirit from the impairment and inevitable decay of being tied to a mortal being. Sacrifice is a form of liberating violence (from the point of view of the preservation of spirit) or of destructive violence (from the point of view of the victim destroyed). More recently, René Girard has argued an interesting variant of this theory. He maintains the central problem of society is how to diffuse envy, which is as endemic as it is potentially violent. The answer is to find a scapegoat, to whom social problems are attributed. The victim is then lynched, and the release of envy results in a replication of this sacrifice.

Two French sociologists, Henri Hubert and Marcel Mauss, contended that sacrifice is intended to maintain a balance between the divine world and the human world. The rite as a whole is one of either *sacralization,* where the purpose is to increase the sanctity of the sacrificer, or of *desacralization,* where the purpose is to transfer the sanctity of the sacrificer to the victim. The purpose of the sacrifice is to protect or empower those who offer sacrifice.

For Tylor, sacrifice is tribute; for Robertson Smith, it is a communal consumption of deity. Frazer sees the death of the victim as the destruction of an envelope of power, in order to release that power. Hubert and Mauss portray sacrifice as the knife's edge that balances the sacred and the profane. None of the paradigms sketched above is negligible: the simple fact is that they are based upon some evidence. The problem is that no single one of them explains the others, nor can it account for the wide range of sacrificial activities in which worshipers do not deploy any particular theory of sacrifice.

Fundamental within all these theories, however, is the understanding that in sacrifice life is offered, consumed, and revived, after the paradigm of the book of Leviticus and the practice of Jesus. The continuing power of sacrificial thinking is rooted in its practical dedication to the pattern of human renewal as accomplished by sharing the products of human work in the presence of the divine.

From this perspective, sacrifice is not in the least an exotic or primitive activity. Whenever human beings share the products of their own labor with an awareness that this sharing occurs with God's approval and in God's presence, it is a sacrificial act. The character of this activity is determined by a community's discernment of what should be shared, with whom, where, and when. Both ancient and modern societies frame basic ethical concerns when they decide how they sacrifice.

—Bruce Chilton

SAINTS

Saint is a Christian concept. However, if we follow its various meanings from the Middle Ages to the present, we discover that it applies to faith traditions everywhere. There are, in other words, holy men and women in all faith traditions who conform to one or more of the meanings given to the concept of a saint. Anneke Mulder-Bakker has identified four meanings of saint—with different meanings being emphasized differently at different times in history.

In the Middle Ages, it was more common to experience certain objects, places, and persons as being intimately connected to the power and mystery of God, so that wearing a relic, kneeling in a Cathedral, or being in the presence of a holy person was, in effect, tapping into the great power in the universe that we collectively refer to as God. In the Middle Ages especially, saints had about themselves a numinous quality, and this was their main meaning. However, even today, one finds certain modern-day figures such as Gandhi and Mother Teresa evoking in others this same feeling of reverence and feeling of being in the presence of the divine.

Since the Middle Ages, saints have also taken on the role and meaning of *intercessor,* especially for those who experience tremendous distance between themselves and God. In the Catholic Church, saints became specialists with regard to intercession—so that the faithful came to pray to St. Anthony to help them find lost articles or prevent shipwrecks and to St. Francis for the care of animals.

Saints, Mulder-Bakker reminds us, also serve occasionally as the logos for particular towns, communities, and geographic regions. For example, St. Patrick is the patron saint of Ireland, and so ceremonies having to do with St. Patrick also have to do with being Irish.

However, in modern times, by far the most important meaning of being a saint is that of being a moral exemplar. Saints are good, extraordinarily good. Their goodness is so extraordinary as to be a mystery, a mystery explained, in part, as an expression of something essentially spiritual, not moral. This is how William James (1902) explained the saint's virtue and how present-day social scientists are beginning to explain moral exemplars.

James and present-day social scientists have found that for the moral exemplar, there often is a deep and abiding religious or spiritual faith underlying and sustaining the exemplar's extraordinarily virtuous way of life. For James, the saint is one who continuously feels himself or herself in touch with that unseen and benevolent power we refer to as God—and it is this constant experience of being connected that sustains a loving, compassionate, and just way of behaving, even in evil times. For the saint, then, faith and morality are not separate.

It is no wonder, then, that saints play a special role in the spiritual lives of many. They provide us with vivid, concrete models of who we should struggle to become. However, beyond struggling, we find in saints the comfort and hope that comes from realizing that there are those among us who have shown us humans who we really are—reflections of the sacred or divine.

—W. George Scarlett

See also Gandhi, Mohandas K.; James, William; Mother Teresa

FURTHER READING

James, W. (1902). *The varieties of religious experience.* New York: Longmans Green.

Mulder-Bakker, A. (2002). The invention of saintliness: texts and contexts. In A. Mulder-Bakker (Ed.), *The invention of saintliness.* New York, Routledge.

SALVATION

The term *salvation* refers to freedom of the human race and/or the individual from evil. It is a term that is often connected to conversion experiences and to experiences that trigger healthy spiritual and/or religious development. Salvation is most often connected to religious experience; however, as within the New Age Movement, salvation is increasingly sought out and found in secular experiences.

As described in scripture, Jesus Christ saved humankind from sin and its consequences by establishing the reign of truth and thereby showing humans the way to overcome ignorance, offering strength to his human subjects in their struggle against evil, and serving as the liaison between humans and God and reconciling humans with God through atonement of sins. In terms of individual human salvation, the process is described in the Council of Trent in which the grace of God calls the sinner to repent. The sinner can accept this grace or turn away from it. By accepting the call, the individual sinner is "disposed for salvation," meaning he or she puts faith in the power of God, trusts in and loves God, and begins to hate all of his or her own individual sinfulness.

Following this disposition for salvation, the individual accepts God's grace and justifies that grace through a changed personhood—a personhood of goodness and charity. Salvation is a process that develops at different paces within and between individuals. There are endless contexts and experiences that may trigger the process of salvation—from an act of charity offered by a stranger to a religious ritual such as penance or baptism. Whether one is able to accept God's grace, therefore, often depends on the dynamic interrelation between individual and contextual characteristics and timing.

Of discussion among Catholic theologians is the nature of the relationship between grace and salvation. That is, there is some disagreement as to the way in which grace and free will work in the process of salvation, to what degree and in what quality fear and love play a role in being disposed for salvation, and what role the sacraments play in salvation.

Within Christian traditions different conceptualizations of salvation are understood to be true. For example, in the Pentecostal tradition, salvation is often linked to the baptism of the Holy Spirit and the ability to speak in tongues. In more liberal Christian traditions the concept of the need for salvation is rejected as is the concept of eternal damnation in hell as they trust in the loving kindness, forgiveness, and goodness of God.

Within Orthodox and Conservative Judaism, salvation is achieved by following God's Law as delivered to Moses. However, given that Judaism interprets the Hebrew Scriptures differently, Judaism has no concept of original sin or of the human race being condemned or therefore saved from eternal damnation.

Salvation is also considered by Eastern religious traditions to be part of the process that prepares one for death. To be free of worry from death and to be free of the material enticements available on earth is to have achieved salvation. Salvation is a concept that is also used to describe spiritual secular experiences. However the meaning is largely the same, expressing a release from that which is evil, sinful, and unhealthy to that which is good and healthy. Those who are saved and perceive themselves as being saved often believe they have transcended a former negative human state to a more positive human state. As such, salvation plays a key role in the spiritual and religious developmental trajectories of many individuals and, according to some beliefs, the entire human race.

—Elizabeth M. Dowling

FURTHER READING

Maas, A. J. (2003). *Salvation.* Retrieved February 10, 2005 from http://www.newadvent.org/cathen/13407a.htm.

Robinson, B. A. (2003). *Teachings on salvation by a variety of religious groups.* Retrieved February 10, 2005 from http://www.religioustolerance.org.

SAVE THE CHILDREN

Eglantyne Jebb established the Save the Children Fund in England in 1919, in the aftermath of the First World War. Today's Save the Children organization often cites their founder with the saying: "All wars, disastrous or victorious, are waged against children." In the early years of the Fund, Eglantyne Jebb perceived a need for the welfare of children and young people that extended beyond the acute problems of wartime and postconflict situation. In 1923 Eglantyne Jebb wrote the Children's Charter. This was adopted by the United Nations' Declaration of the Rights of the Child in the 1950s. This in turn led to arguably one of the United Nations' most successful pieces of international legislation, the UN Convention on the Rights of the Child (1989), ratified by the vast majority of the world's countries.

Those articles of direct relevance to the spiritual and religious development of young people are highlighted here.

PART I: Children's Rights

Article 1 defines a *child* as "every human being below the age of eighteen years unless under the law applicable to the child, majority is attained earlier."

Article 2 presents states' responsibilities to "respect and ensure the rights set forth in the present Convention to each child within their jurisdiction without discrimination of any kind, irrespective of the child's or his or her parent's or legal guardian's race, color, sex, language, religion, political or other opinion, national, ethnic or social origin, property, disability, birth or other status."

Article 3 states that "In all actions concerning children, whether undertaken by public or private social welfare institutions, courts of law, administrative authorities or legislative bodies, the best interests of the child shall be a primary consideration."

Article 4 presents states' responsibilities to "undertake all appropriate legislative, administrative, and other measures for the implementation of the rights recognized in the present Convention. With regard to economic, social and cultural rights, States Parties shall undertake such measures to the maximum extent of their available resources and, where needed, within the framework of international cooperation."

Article 5 presents the responsibilities of states to "respect the responsibilities, rights and duties of parents or, where applicable, the members of the extended family or community as provided for by local custom, legal guardians or other persons legally responsible for the child, to provide, in a manner consistent with the evolving capacities of the child."

Article 6 states that "Every child has the inherent right to life." It presents the responsibilities of States to ensure "the maximum extent possible the survival and development of the child."

Article 7 outlines the need for the child's birth to be registered immediately: "the right from birth to a name, the right to acquire a nationality and, as far as possible, the right to know and be cared for by his or her parents."

Article 8 presents the responsibilities of states to "undertake to respect the right of the child to preserve his or her identity, including nationality, name, and family relations as recognized by law without unlawful interference."

Article 9 presents the responsibilities of states to "ensure that a child shall not be separated from his or her parents against their will, except when competent authorities subject to judicial review determine, in accordance with applicable law and procedures, that such separation is necessary for the best interests of the child."

Article 10 deals with "applications by a child or his or her parents to enter or leave a State," especially "for the purpose of family reunification" and the need for states to deal with such applications "in a positive, humane and expeditious manner."

Article 11 outlines the responsibilities of states to take all measure "to combat the illicit transfer and non-return of children abroad."

Article 12 outlines the responsibilities of states to "assure to the child who is capable of forming his or her own views the right to express those views freely in all matters affecting the child, the views of the child being given due weight in accordance with the age and maturity of the child."

Article 13 states that "The child shall have the right to freedom of expression; this right shall include freedom to seek, receive and impart information and ideas of all kinds, regardless of frontiers, either orally, in writing or in print, in the form of art, or through any other media of the child's choice."

Article 14 states the rights of the child "to freedom of thought, conscience, and religion."

Article 15 states the rights of the child "to freedom of association and to freedom of peaceful assembly."

Article 16 states that "No child shall be subjected to arbitrary or unlawful interference with his or her privacy, family, home or correspondence, nor to unlawful attacks on his or her honor and reputation."

Article 17 presents the responsibilities of states to "recognize the important function performed by the mass media and shall ensure that the child has access to information and material from a diversity of national and international sources, especially those aimed at the promotion of his or her social, spiritual, and moral well-being and physical and mental health."

Article 18 presents the responsibilities of states to "use their best efforts to ensure recognition of the principle that both parents have common responsibilities for the upbringing and development of the child. Parents or, as the case may be, legal guardians, have the primary responsibility for the upbringing and development of the child. The best interests of the child will be their basic concern."

Article 19 presents the responsibilities of states to "take all appropriate legislative, administrative, social and educational measures to protect the child from all forms of physical or mental violence, injury or abuse, neglect or negligent treatment, maltreatment or exploitation, including sexual abuse."

Article 20 states that "A child temporarily or permanently deprived of his or her family environment, or in whose own best interests cannot be allowed to remain in that environment, shall be entitled to special protection and assistance provided by the State."

Article 21 presents the responsibilities of states to "recognize and/or permit the system of adoption shall ensure that the best interests of the child shall be the paramount consideration."

Article 22 presents the responsibilities of states to take appropriate measures to protect refugee children.

Article 23 presents the responsibilities of states to "recognize that a mentally or physically disabled child should enjoy a full and decent life, in conditions which ensure dignity, promote self-reliance and facilitate the child's active participation in the community."

Article 24 presents the responsibilities of states to "recognize the right of the child to the enjoyment of the highest attainable standard of health and to facilities for the treatment of illness and rehabilitation of health."

Article 25 presents the responsibilities of states to "recognize the right of a child who has been placed by the competent authorities for the purposes of care, protection or treatment of his or her physical or mental health, to a periodic review of the treatment provided to the child and all other circumstances relevant to his or her placement."

Article 26 presents the responsibilities of states to "recognize for every child the right to benefit from social security, including social insurance, and shall take the necessary measures to achieve the full realization of this right in accordance with their national law."

Article 27 presents the responsibilities of states to "recognize the right of every child to a standard of living adequate for the child's physical, mental, spiritual, moral and social development." The Article also recognizes that the parent(s) or others responsible for the child have the primary responsibility to secure, within their abilities and financial capacities, the conditions of living necessary for the child's development."

Article 28 presents the responsibilities of states to "recognize the right of the child to education, and with a view to achieving this right progressively and on the basis of equal opportunity." In particular, this involves making "primary education compulsory and available free to all," the encouragement of secondary education and making higher education "accessible to all on the basis of capacity by every appropriate means."

Article 29 outlines some general comments on the implementation of Article 28.

Article 30 states, "In those States in which ethnic, religious or linguistic minorities or persons of indigenous origin exist, a child belonging to such a minority or who is indigenous shall not be denied the right, in community with other members of his or her group, to enjoy his or her own culture, to profess and practice his or her own religion, or to use his or her own language."

Article 31 presents the responsibilities of states to "recognize the right of the child to rest and leisure, to engage in play and recreational activities appropriate to the age of the child and to participate freely in cultural life and the arts."

Article 32 presents the responsibilities of states to "recognize the right of the child to be protected from economic exploitation and from performing any work that is likely to be hazardous or to interfere with the child's education, or to be harmful to the child's health or physical, mental, spiritual, moral or social development."

Article 33 presents the responsibilities of states to "take all appropriate measures, including legislative, administrative, social and educational measures, to protect children from the illicit use of narcotic drugs and psychotropic substances."

Article 34 presents the responsibilities of states to "undertake to protect the child from all forms of sexual exploitation and sexual abuse."

Article 35 presents the responsibilities of states to "take all appropriate national, bilateral and multilateral measures to prevent the abduction of, the sale of or traffic in children for any purpose or in any form."

Article 36 presents the responsibilities of states to "protect the child against all other forms of exploitation prejudicial to any aspects of the child's welfare."

Article 37 states that "No child shall be subjected to torture or other cruel, inhuman or degrading treatment or punishment. Neither capital punishment nor life imprisonment without possibility of release shall be imposed for offences committed by persons below 18 years of age."

Article 38 presents the responsibilities of states to "undertake to respect and to ensure respect for rules of international humanitarian law applicable to them in armed conflicts which are relevant to the child."

Article 39 presents the responsibilities of states to "take all appropriate measures to promote physical and psychological recovery and social reintegration of a child victim of any form of neglect, exploitation, or abuse; torture or any other form of cruel, inhuman or degrading treatment or punishment; or armed conflicts. Such recovery and reintegration shall take place in an environment which fosters the health, self-respect and dignity of the child."

Article 40 presents the responsibilities of states to "recognize the right of every child alleged as, accused of, or recognized as having infringed the penal law to be treated in a manner consistent with the promotion of the child's sense of dignity and worth."

Article 41 states that "Nothing in the present Convention shall affect any provisions which are more conducive to the realization of the rights of the child and which may be contained in the law of a State party or international law in force for that State."

SOURCE: Convention on the Rights of the Child (20 November 1989, entry into force 2 September 1990). PARTS II-III (Articles 42–54) refer to procedural matters. For a full text of this document, follow links at http://www.unhchr.ch/html/menu3/b/k2crc.htm.

Save the Children is one of the world's foremost nongovernmental organizations for the care of young people in need. Although its origins are from the carnage of war, the Save the Children Foundation that emerged in the 1920s from the Save the Children Fund developed a remit extending well beyond. In 1932, Save the Children (United States) was founded by John Voris moved by the plight of hunger and deprivation of Appalachian children, a concern for basic welfare programs such as the "Hot School Lunch" that extended through the United States. By the time of the Second World War the organization had emerged as a mature organization operating through many countries in war-ravaged Europe. By the 1960s, operations had extended to Latin America, the Middle East, and Africa. The 1979 United Nations "Year of the Child" significantly extended awareness of children's issues and helped facilitate a massive expansion of Save the Children's operations. It was there to respond to the cataclysmic Ethiopian famine in 1984.

Today's Save the Children works across a wide range of social issues, including early childhood development, primary education, youth development, and adult literacy. One of its major campaigns has been on involving corporate sponsors to get involved in their work, shrewdly selling the positive benefits to corporate image for doing so. And much of its work continues—for example the "Every Mother, Every

Child" initiative—to highlight the inextricable link between children and their mothers.

—*Liam Gearon*

See also United Nations

FURTHER READING

Beigbeder, Y. (2001). *New challenges for UNICEF: Children, women, and human rights.* Basingstoke, UK: Palgrave.

Landsdown, G. (2001). *Children's rights: A second chance.* London: Save the Children.

Landsdown, G. (2001). *Promoting children's participation in democratic decision making.* Florence, Italy: UNICEF.

Seabrook, J. (2001). *Children of other worlds: Exploitation in the global market.* London: Pluto Press.

United Nations. (2002). *The rights of the child, fact sheet 10.* New York: United Nations.

SCIENCE AND RELIGION

There is a new spirit and attitude regarding the relationship between science and religion. Today, more and more scholars, including leading scientists, theologians, and philosophers are characterizing the relationship as complementary and interactive. This positive, complementary, and interactive view has not always been the dominant view. In fact, throughout most of history, two alternative views have prevailed. The first view, more ancient, conflated science and religion such that the two were indistinguishable. We see this in the medieval designation of theology as the "queen of the sciences." We see this even more clearly in primal and ancient religions, which provided religious explanations for natural events—such as the ancient Greeks' explanation that the sun moves across the sky because it is pulled by Apollo and his team of horses.

The Enlightenment Era and the development of modern science during the 18th and 19th centuries brought a new dominant view of the relationship between science and religion, one that saw science as replacing religion and one that promoted a secular faith in reason and in a scientific approach to reality. This new dominant view was reinforced by the dazzling array of explanations that developed out of scientific inquiry, explanations of everything from how leaves make use of light to how spiders spin webs, to how babies learn a language, to how stars are born and die. The enormous power of modern science both to explain the universe and to support the development of new technology made religion seem obsolete—a holdover from primitive times, a crutch for those who need comfort, and a poor and childish substitute for scientific reasoning.

However, a number of 20th-century developments both within science and within the philosophy of science changed our view of science—by emphasizing that science and religion have much in common. The newer view shows just how much science, like religion, is influenced and defined by worldviews and frameworks for thinking, by faith in what cannot be observed, and by value judgments.

Nowhere is this newer view of science shown more clearly than in the current talk of paradigms, models, and metaphors. Philosophers of science have shown that modern science has developed not so much by adding new facts as by replacing old paradigms. For example, the universe viewed as a giant machine worked well as a paradigm, model, and root metaphor during Newton's time and long thereafter. However, when physicists turned their attention to explaining the structure of light and other incredibly fast-moving phenomena, a different paradigm, model, and root metaphor were needed.

In a similar vein, scientists and philosophers of science have come to stress how science, like religion, relies on faith in what cannot be directly observed. For example, without directly observing electrons, scientists have used the atomic model as an invaluable conceptual tool for explaining reality.

Finally, scientists and philosophers of science have shown how much values and value judgments influence what questions are asked as well as influence how scientists observe, categorize, measure, and explain. Perhaps the most infamous example is that of the scientific racism that developed during the 19th century and continued to develop well into the 20th century. Thinking they were merely describing the facts and measuring objectively, 19th- and 20th-century biologists and social scientists defined and measured human intelligence in ways that overvalued how they themselves thought and undervalued how groups different from themselves thought. Values, not facts and objectivity, guided their research on intelligence to produce a distorted and damaging view of human diversity.

In summary, the old view that science can replace religion because only science is objective is no longer the dominant view. Within the scientific community as well as within the community of philosophers studying science, the dominant view now is that science, like religion, is inevitably dependent on paradigms, models, and metaphors, dependent on faith in what cannot be seen directly, and dependent on making value judgments.

Because science and religion are now seen as having much in common, does this mean that today we are reverting back to when science and religion were conflated and treated as a single, undifferentiated enterprise? Not at all. The emerging view today suggests that science and religion have complementary and interactive roles. On one hand, science must explain the material universe and in so doing, foster in us a spiritual and ethical relationship with the universe. On the other hand, religion must take the lead in defining our individual and collective responsibilities for living in our universe. Nowhere do we see this complementary and interactive view of science and religion more clearly than in current discussions of the ecological crisis.

By most accounts, there has been a serious degradation of our natural environment. Urban sprawl has replaced scenic countryside. Rivers that once provided drinking and bathing water now offer neither. Air that once was clean is now polluted, and valuable species of wildlife that once appeared in abundance are now extinct. These and other negative developments having to do with the natural environment have, on one hand, raised complex questions about the use of technology and science to exploit the natural environment, and on the other hand, raised equally complex questions about traditional religious views of our relationship with nature. Today, then, there are fascinating conversations going on between scientists, theologians, and moral philosophers regarding how best to conceptualize this ecological crisis.

These conversations have led to changes on both sides of the science–religion relationship. On science's side, we see a marked increase in the use of the term *spiritual* to capture the feelings and attitude that scientists have and want all of us to have toward that which they are explaining. That is, scientists now speak of their finding intrinsic spiritual meaning in understanding how nature and the universe work. Rather than opposing religion, then, scientists now see their work as a way to deepen our spiritual sense of how all of life is interconnected.

On religion's side, we see theologians and moral philosophers questioning traditional dominion views of the human–nature relationship. Dominion views often have humans located above nature and below God—with nature existing for the pleasure and good of humans. Whatever the nuances might be in any given dominion view, all dominion views imply that humans can justify their actions solely on the basis of what is best for humans.

With the ecological crisis, many are questioning dominion views and substituting for them a view that gives nature rights and treats humans as co-inhabitants of the universe alongside nonhuman life forms. That is, today, in the ecology movement, human animals are accepting their place in the world as fellow creatures alongside nonhuman animals and learning from nature about what might be a deeper, more spiritual ethic stressing the intrinsic value of biodiversity. Today, then, around certain issues such as how to prevent further degradation of our natural environment, science and religion have become partners, not adversaries, in order to help better define our relationship with the universe so that we live more meaningful, more responsible, and more spiritual lives.

—*W. George Scarlett*

SEARCH INSTITUTE

Search Institute is unique among child and youth development research institutions not only for its consistent commitment to understanding and valuing the spiritual and religious domain of individual and community life but also in its emphasis on ensuring that the knowledge generated is both useful and accessible to leaders, practitioners, and parents.

Headquartered in Minneapolis, Minnesota, Search Institute is an independent, nonprofit organization with a mission to provide leadership, knowledge, and resources to promote healthy children, youth, and communities. Within this broad learning and application mission, the institute has developed and maintained a rich history of exploring and strengthening the understanding of religious and spiritual development among children and adolescents and of strengthening the people and places that influence young people's lives.

Founded in 1958 by Dr. Merton P. Strommen as the Church Youth Research Center, the institute pioneered national, survey-based studies of adolescents affiliated with Protestant denominations. These portraits shaped educational and Christian youth ministry programs in thousands of congregations. These efforts became some of the earliest attempts in the United States to use the social sciences as tools for learning and improvement in religious organizations.

The innovativeness, quality, and usefulness to practitioners and leaders of these early research efforts soon led to broadened interest in the organization's work among youth-serving organizations, schools, and colleges, and the name was changed to Youth Research Center (1969) and then to Search Institute (1977). Dr. Peter L. Benson became president of Search Institute in 1985, after previously serving for 7 years as the institute's research director.

In 1990, the institute premiered the concept of developmental assets—a framework of positive relationships, opportunities, experiences, and personal qualities that help young people thrive and avoid risky behaviors. This line of inquiry catapulted the institute to international prominence and is now one part of a multifaceted program of theory and research.

In addition to this broad research agenda, Search Institute has particular expertise in the scientific study of religion and spirituality, religious institutions, and religious youth work. Early work focused primarily in Protestant Christian denominations and congregations, but it has expanded to include all faith traditions through an intentional interfaith focus. A notable study was done in 1990 with 11,000 youth and adults in six Protestant denominations in the United States, which premiered Search Institute's Faith Maturity Scale (Benson & Eklin, 1990; Roehlkepartain, 1993).

These two strands of work—developmental assets and religious and spiritual development—have been linked through a number of initiatives focused on equipping congregations of all faiths to play an important role in youth development. These have included field research (Roehlkepartain, 2003), practical tools (e.g., Roehlkepartain [1998]), training, and an online self-study survey for congregations (Search Institute, 2003).

With support from the John Templeton Foundation, in 2003 the institute launched a major initiative on the science and theology of spiritual development in childhood and adolescence. This initiative seeks to map the state of spiritual development in childhood and adolescence around the world, then to stimulate new research and dialogue that will not only advance knowledge and understanding, but also improve practice in families, congregations, and other settings. An early contribution of this initiative is *The Handbook of Spiritual Development in Childhood and Adolescence* (Roehlkepartain, King, Wagener, & Benson, in preparation).

Because of its commitment to making research relevant to practitioners, the institute sponsors an annual conference of practitioners that focuses on asset building in communities, offers a comprehensive line of practical resources, makes training and technical assistance available to a wide range of communities and organizations, and forms alliances with state-level networks and national organizations.

—Eugene C. Roehlkepartain

See also Benson, Peter; Assets, Developmental

FURTHER READING

Benson, P. L., Donahue, M. J., & Erickson, J. A. (1989). Adolescence and religion: A review of the literature from 1970 to 1986. *Research in the Social Scientific Study of Religion, 1,* 153–181.

Benson, P. L., & Eklin, C E. (1990). *Effective Christian education: A national study of Protestant congregations: Summary report.* Minneapolis, MN: Search Institute. Available for download at www.search-institute.org/congregations/ResearchReportsArticles.html.

Roehlkepartain, E. C. (1993). *The teaching church: Moving Christian education to center stage.* Nashville, TN: Abingdon Press.

Roehlkepartain, E. C. (1998). *Building assets in congregations: A practical guide for helping youth grow up healthy.* Minneapolis: Search Institute.

Roehlkepartain, E. C. (2003). Making room at the table for everyone: Interfaith engagement in positive child and adolescent development. In R. M., Lerner, F. Jacobs, & D. Wertlieb, (Eds.). *Handbook of applied developmental science,* vol. 3: *Promoting positive youth and family development* (pp. 535–563). Thousand Oaks, CA: Sage.

Roehlkepartain, E. C., King, P. E., Wagener, L. M., & Benson, P. L. (Eds.). (2005). *The handbook of spiritual development in childhood and adolescence.* Thousand Oaks, CA: Sage.

Search Institute (2003). *Building assets, strengthening faith: An intergenerational survey for congregations.* Minneapolis, MN: Author. (www.search-institute.org/congregations/BASF).

Strommen, M. P. (Ed.) (1971). *Research on religious development: A comprehensive handbook.* New York: Hawthorn Books.

SEDONA, ARIZONA

Sedona is a small town in north-central Arizona, 110 miles south of the Grand Canyon. Sedona's spiritual significance is enhanced by its location near many Native American communities and ample lore about energy sites in the earth. Sedona is known for its stunning natural setting, especially its breathtaking red-rock formations. The rocks' signature red hue comes from hematite, an iron oxide abundant in the sedimentary formations. At 4,500-ft elevation, Sedona has a biodiversity of desert and forest flora and fauna, with a widespread juniper–pinyon pine ecosystem and a lovely combination of desert cacti and succulents and forest vegetation, all dotting the red-rock formations.

Sedona was "put on the map" in the early 1900s by businessman and farmer Carl Schnebly. Schnebly named it Oak Creek Canyon, for the large creek flowing through the area, but the government told him the name was too long to fit on a cancellation postmark. Schnebly then honored his wife—Sedona—a Mennonite woman from Pennsylvania, and thus this lovely town received its lovely name.

Almost a thousand years earlier, the area was home to Sinagua and Anasazi Indians. Settlements preserved to this day include Tuzigoot and Montezuma's Castle, the latter a cliff-face dwelling. Both sites were home to 12th- and 13th-century Indians, though these sites are shrouded in mystery as the Native Americans disappeared suddenly from this region leaving few clues behind.

Today, Sedona shows Native American influence. Large Navajo and Hopi reservations cover much of Arizona and neighboring states, and Sedona's atmosphere is enriched by authentic Native culture. But in addition to, for example, the rug trade based on local Navajo women's rich tradition of rug weaving, the area is also littered with kitschy gift shops selling dream catchers and other popularized Native American artifacts, many manufactured overseas.

As well as its natural beauty and Navajo flavorings, Sedona's local lore has it that a spiritual energy arises from so-called vortexes in the earth. Some sources point to the 1970s as when local talk of such sites began. These geospiritual locations are said to induce in visitors a deeply meditative spiritual experience. The formations of Cathedral Rock and Bell Rock are said to be home to such energy sites. Some vortexes are said to have upflow energy, others an inflow energy. Upflow sites are common near mountains and mesas and enhance a sense of contemplation or prayer; inflow sites are common around canyons and valleys and promote the search for life's deeper truths. The vortex "business" is part of contemporary Sedona. Local merchants and spiritual centers offer vortex "tours," some promising to take the visitor "deep within the Mother Earth energies"; other spiritual centers offer "total bliss in sacred space."

Such claims of spiritual energy emanating from the rocks are laughed off by some yet sworn to by others. Though it is difficult to know whether these claims are grounded in geologic science, Native American traditions, or the musings of the area's many "New Agers," with its dramatic beauty and Native essence Sedona creates an indelible spiritual experience. This place surely evokes spiritual contemplation, deep reflections on one's inner being alongside feelings of genuine connectedness to what is beyond.

—Chris J. Boyatzis

SELF-ESTEEM

Self-esteem and self-concept have been important ideas in the psychology of adolescence since the 1960s. Particularly important at that stage were the writings of S. Coopersmith and M. Rosenberg. Both of these psychologists devised ways of measuring self-esteem or self-concept, and both began to demonstrate the key part played by these constructs in the development of healthy life styles, positive attitudes, and educational attainment. Some research traditions have established a clear link between religious beliefs and self-concept or self-esteem.

According to Coopersmith, young people with a positive self-concept and good self-esteem are likely to feel that they can make up their mind without too much trouble, that they are popular with others of their own age, that things usually do not bother them, and that, when they have something to say, they usually say it. Young people with a poor self-concept and low self-esteem are likely to feel that there are lots of things about themselves they would change if only they could, that they are not as nice looking as most people, that they get upset easily, and that most people are better liked than they are.

Empirical research into the relationship between religious and spiritual development during childhood, adolescence, and adulthood and self-esteem has produced a mixed set of results. Some studies demonstrated a positive relationship between religion and self-esteem, while other studies demonstrated a negative relationship between religion and self-esteem. Put simply, the issue seems to be concerned not so much with whether young people believe in God but with the kind of God in whom they believe. The research tradition that has made the most significant contribution to this issue is concerned with *God images.*

The research evidence suggests, on the one hand, a link between affirming God images and positive self-esteem and, on the other hand, a link between rejecting God images and poor self-esteem. According to this tradition, those who hold a positive God image construe God as saving, accepting, loving, freeing, forgiving, approving, and lenient. Those who hold a negative God image construe God as damning, rejecting, demanding, restricting, unforgiving, disapproving, and strict.

Two very different psychological theories have been advanced to account for the linkage between God image and self-esteem. The first theory sees God images influencing self-image. This theory argues that individual self-evaluation is, at least partly, derived from the individual's view of how he or she is evaluated by others. Parents and parent figures play a particularly important part in such formation. By extension, if the primary emphasis in religion is thought to be a God who views individuals as unconditionally acceptable and accepted, it is reasonable to hypothesize a positive effect on self-esteem. However, if the primary emphasis in religion is thought to be a God who views individuals as unworthy and miserable sinners, it is reasonable to hypothesize a negative effect on self-esteem.

The second theory sees self-concept influencing God images and was advanced by P. L. Benson and B. P. Spilka in the 1970s drawing on cognitive consistency theory. According to their account, consistency theory suggests that information that implies the reverse of one's usual level of self-regard tends to create dissonance. To avoid the discomfort caused by cognitive dissonance, techniques like selective perception and denial can be used to keep information consonant with one's self-image. This theory suggests that individuals with low self-esteem will be disinclined to believe in a loving God who accepts them, while individuals with high self-esteem will be disinclined to believe in a strict God who rejects and judges them.

In conclusion, the empirical evidence demonstrates a clear link between theological beliefs about the nature of God and the development of self-esteem in youth and human development.

—Leslie J. Francis

FURTHER READING

Francis, L. J., Kay, W.K., & Campbell, W. S. (Eds.). (1996). *Research in religious education.* Leominster, UK: Gracewing.

SEMIOTICS

Semiotics is a study of signs and their signification, or meaning. It belongs to an interdisciplinary science. The word *semiotics* is derived from Greek words for "sign" and "signal." As a separate science, semiotics studies things that function as signs. Semiotics is also a metalanguage that serves to describe human behavior because people are sign users. In ancient times semiotics was a branch of medical science, in which signs were taken to describe medical symptoms for the purpose of diagnosis. Later it became a branch of philosophy where verbal and nonverbal signs were taken to be representations of the true nature of things. Those who study semiotics are deeply immersed in religion and spirituality wherein sign and symbol use are so prominently integrated.

The scholastic tradition posited a sign to be something that we can not only directly perceive but also connect with something else, by virtue of our or somebody's else experience. Sign therefore is an instrument of human knowledge, learning, and development. Symbol is generally a synonym of sign, which has a conventional meaning. But signs can be polysomic, that is, they may connote more than one meaning. Therefore, symbolic meanings are characterized by their surplus. A symbolic connotation may demonstrate a deeper layer of meanings, sometimes with complex emotional associations or having a cryptic character as pointing to something beyond itself.

Semiotics exceeds linguistics; the latter limited to words and sentences as verbal signs. Based on the relationship to spoken language, three types of general semiotic systems may be distinguished: (1) language substitutes, such as writing, whistles, and Morse code; (2) language transforms, or formal scientific terminology; and (3) idiomorphic systems, such as music or gestures. A sign not only represents but also causes other signs to come to mind as a consequence of itself: this relation is expressed in the medieval formula *aliquid stat pro aliguo,* which is translated as "something stands for something else." An interpreter of signs connects the antecedent with its consequent by means of a specific inferential sign relation.

Charles Sanders Peirce, a famous American philosopher (1839–1914), has held a pansemiotic perspective on the whole universe, that is, a view that the world may be composed exclusively of signs. The whole world is considered to be a semiotic sphere.

In contrast to the immediate sense data of the surrounding world, the human mind uses mediation when, within experience, it crosses what Alfred North Whitehead called the *semiotic threshold.* All thinking proceeds in signs, and the continuous process of *semiosis* can never be stopped; thus human development is potentially unlimited.

A key concept in semiotics is communication, or the flow of information and the exchange of signs. Semiosis is a communicative process, that is, a mutual interaction between any two systems. Semiotically, communication as information sharing is considered to be an organizing principle of nature. Magic is also a form of semiotics, because it operates by means of signs, such as charms, names, or speech acts. Mental images belong to a category of signs, and from a semiotic point of view a mental image is an icon, or representation, of the real world. An internal image serves as a semiotic tool, called the *interpretant,* so as to bring to knowledge something that has been directly perceived. An intentional interpretative act gives a sign its meaning: without a lived experience signs remain lifeless and mute.

Religious texts are primary resources wherein semiotics is studied. The sign is a key concept in the Bible. The Old Testament speaks of the signs of the covenant between the people of Israel and God. In Genesis, the natural phenomenon of a rainbow is interpreted as a sign. In the Gospel of Saint John of the New Testament, sign is a central concept because the miracles performed by Christ are presented as signs of God's glory and power. The universe contains natural signs. In this theological interpretation of nature, all physical objects, even rocks, can be subject to interpretation and therefore have spiritual meanings.

Cultural artifacts are also capable of communicative potential, that is, different objects in our life may carry cultural and psychological significance. All objects are relational and belong to a semiotic triad of subject, object, and referent. Even commodities become signs within the process of exchange and consumption. The pictorial signs and images are of particular importance. Traffic signs or playing cards form their own codes with their respective meanings. In applied semiotics, advertising plays a significant role by virtue of being an exchange of messages. Many people look forward to discovering hidden, or subliminal, meanings in advertisements as being supplementary to their overt meanings.

Semiotics is a study that will surely flourish and develop as humans are continually looking for meaning and purpose in the signs and symbols around them. Semiotics has much to offer those interested in diving more deeply into spiritual and religious meaning and to finding answers to spiritual and religious questions.

—Inna Semetsky

FURTHER READING

Noth, W. (1955). *Handbook of semiotics.* Bloomington/ Indianapolis, IN: Indiana University Press.

Sebeok, T. (Ed.). (1986). *Encyclopedic dictionary of semiotics.* Berlin: Mouton de Gruyter.

SERVICE

Virtually every religious tradition emphasizes compassion, generosity, service, and justice as priorities—even obligations—for people of faith. For example, in Jewish traditions, *tzedakah* (giving, or more literally, acts of justice) and *gemilut chasadim* (acts of loving kindness or service to others) are considered *mitzvot*—divine commandments that Jews have an obligation to observe. Christians point to numerous passages in the Gospels where Jesus emphasized compassion and justice as being central to faith, including the Great Commandment: "You shall love the Lord your God with all your heart, and with all your soul, and with all your mind. . . . You shall love your neighbor as yourself" (Matt. 22:37, 39, NRSV). Charity, or *Zakat,* is one of the Five Pillars of Islam. Sympathy and compassion for the benefit and welfare of all beings is at the center of Buddhism. And compassion is one of the Three Jewels in Taoism.

This faith commitment—combined with growing evidence of the power of serving others for both nurturing faith and giving young people opportunities to contribute to the life of the faith community (while also contributing to overall positive development and thriving)—has led congregations of many faiths to engage young people in service as a core theme in their youth work. Youth service takes many different forms and uses many different terms, depending on the emphasis and tradition. It may include, for example, social action, activism, volunteerism, service learning, or missions.

Serving others through volunteer activities, service learning, and other forms of service has become a widespread emphasis in positive youth development and citizenship education in the United States since the 1980s. It is also growing internationally, with various forms of service and civic engagement formally operating in every major region of the world, though the concept of volunteering or service is less formalized in developing countries. A growing body of research in positive youth development and thriving shows consistently positive relationships between a prosocial orientation and service to others and a wide range of thriving behaviors, including a positive orientation to schoolwork, being seen as a leader, valuing diversity, and overcoming adversity. In addition, serving others is negatively related to a wide range of high-risk behaviors, including problem alcohol use, use of illicit drugs, use of tobacco, gambling, antisocial behavior, and violence.

Despite the increases in youth service to others through schools (with about two thirds of K-12 public schools in the United States offering community service opportunities for students), congregations remain a primary institution for engaging young people in service to others in the United States. According to *Independent Sector,* 53% of youth volunteers first learned about volunteer activities through their congregation. This pattern attests to the strong links between service to others and religious or spiritual commitments. Religious youth are almost twice as likely to engage in service as those who are not active in a faith community.

Search Institute surveys of 217,000 6th- to 12th-grade youth in public schools in the United States found that 60% of young people who attend services, programs, or other activities in a "church, synagogue, mosque, or other religious or spiritual place" at least 1 hour per week also say they serve in the community at least an hour a week. In contrast, only 36% of young people who are not active in a faith community are engaged in service to others at that same level. These findings are consistent with analyses of *Monitoring the Future* data on 12th-grade youth in the United States that show significant positive correlations between service and religious participation, even controlling for race, age, gender, rural or urban residence, region, parental education, number of siblings, and presence of father or male guardian in the household.

In addition, *Independent Sector* has found that only 40% of American young people with no religious affiliation volunteer. However, 60% of Protestant Christian youth volunteered, compared to 63% of Catholic youth and 74% of youth affiliated with other religious traditions, including Judaism. Some of this service occurs within the institutional context of the faith community (which provides a wide variety of services to the community), while some of it occurs in the broader community, schools, and other settings. In each case, there are strong links between faith or spirituality and a commitment to serving others—links that transcend particular religious traditions and beliefs.

For many people, serving others is not only related to religion or spirituality, it is integral or core to this domain of life. Indeed, many definitions of spiritual development emphasize issues of contribution and self-transcendence on behalf of others as an integral dimension. One study found that spirituality includes two significantly related but distinct factors: participation in activities of self-interest and an orientation to help other people. Finally, models of faith or religiosity, such as the Faith Maturity Scale—developed as a result of a study conducted by the Search Institute assessing the maturity of faith of 11,000 youth and adults in six Protestant denominations in the United States—include a "horizontal" dimension (or an "outward journey") in which faith and spirituality are expressed through a commitment to serving others through compassion and justice.

A growing number of religious communities are recognizing the important role that serving others plays in young people's identity formation and spiritual and civic development. However, not all service experiences have equal impact, and poorly designed projects can have a negative impact. The field of service learning suggests best practices for engaging young people in serving others that include designing service projects that address authentic community needs, engaging young people as leaders throughout the process, and utilizing an intentional process for debriefing or reflecting upon the experience. Engaging young people in intentionally designed service-learning experiences has significant potential not only to ensure that young people make a real contribution to community life, but also triggers processes that facilitate their civic, spiritual, and religious development.

—Eugene C. Roehlkepartain

See also Positive Youth Development

FURTHER READING

Benson, P. L., & Eklin, C E. (1990). *Effective Christian education: A national study of Protestant congregations: Summary report*. Minneapolis, MN: Search Institute.

Available for download at www.search-institute.org/congregations/ResearchReportsArticles.html.

Benson, P. L., & Roehlkepartain, E. C. (1993). *Beyond leaf raking: Learning to serve/serving to learn.* Nashville, TN: Abingdon Press.

Dowling, E. M., Gestsdottir, S., Anderson, P. M., von Eye, A., & Lerner, R. M. (2003). Spirituality, religiosity, and thriving among adolescents: Identification and confirmation of factor structures. *Applied Developmental Science, 7,* 253–260.

Hodgkinson, V. A., & Weitzman, M. S. (1997). *Volunteering and giving among teenagers 12 to 17 years of age: Findings from a national survey.* Washington, DC: Independent Sector.

McBride, A. M., Benítez, C., & Sherraden, M. (2003). *The forms and nature of civic service: A global assessment.* St. Louis, MO: Global Service Institute, Center for Social Development, Washington University.

Roehlkepartain, E. C. (2003). Faith communities: Untapped allies in service learning. *NYLC Generator 21*(3), 20–24.

Roehlkepartain, E. C., Bright, T., & Margolis-Rupp, B. (2000). *An asset builder's guide to service-learning.* Minneapolis, MN: Search Institute.

Roehlkepartain, E. C., Naftali, E. D., & Musegades, L. (2000). *Growing up generous: Engaging youth in giving and serving.* Bethesda, MD; Alban Institute.

Scales, P. C., & Benson, P. L. (2005). Prosocial orientation and community service. In K. A. Moore & L. Lippman (Eds.), *Positive youth development: Establishing indicators for child and adolescent development.* New York: Springer.

Smith, C., & Faris, R. (2002). *Religion and adolescent delinquency, risk behaviors, and constructive social activities.* Chapel Hill: National Study of Youth and Religion, University of North Carolina at Chapel Hill.

Youniss, J., & Yates, M. (1997). *Community service and social responsibility in youth.* Chicago, IL: University of Chicago Press.

Youniss, J., McLellan, J. A., & Yates, M. (1999). Religion, community service, and identity in American youth, *Journal of Adolescence, 22,* 243–253.

SHAMANISM

Shamanism may be classified as a magic-religious or earth-based spiritual practice, which is deeply rooted in the everyday life of a society. Shamanism is most often associated with hunting and gathering societies or primitive cultures of the past. A traditional form of Shamanism is said to have been the first form of spiritual practice more than 30,000 years ago, but by no means is it unsophisticated or simple. The principals and techniques within Shamanism provide a sense of social order between the world of the spirits, plants, animals and humans. Societies where Shamanism was and is practiced believe that there are different worlds or realities, which are interconnected and interdependent. These worlds may be that of the animals, plants, or elements such as water, air, and fire, which are believed to have humanlike qualities and characteristics. These worlds work together to bring healing and harmony to universal order. There also exist different forces within the worlds that may be positive or negative. These forces are often associated with good or evil in other religious practices. Shamanism therefore serves to bring balance and harmony between the different worlds and positive and negative forces.

Many primitive communities in the past and present had to face environmental threats and uncertainty and saw these crises as a sign of disorder or unbalance between the worlds. The practice of Shamanism provides a way to resolve these crises such as famine, disease, and infertility within a given society. Today, as in the past, different forms of Shamanism are found around the world, with the largest concentration of its practices in north and central Asia, as well as in the circumpolar regions.

Shamanism is based on the central belief that the material world in which we live is influenced and pervaded by the world of spirits or invisible forces. Shamanistic practices and techniques are performed by the central figure known as the *shaman.* The word *shaman* meaning "one who knows" comes from the Tungus people of Siberia. Mircea Eliade, a religious scholar, defines Shamanism as a practice in the "technique of ecstasy," a form of transformation where the shaman through trance (an altered state of consciousness) is able to access the world of the spirits, communicate with them, and relay the knowledge and information to the community.

The role of the shaman may be held by a man or woman and is dependent on the social order of a given culture. While the shamans of the Amazon are primarily men, women hold the position of the shaman in Korean societies. The shaman is the key communicator with the invisible forces or spirits. Unlike priests, shamans are not organized into full-time ritual or spiritual associations. Although the shaman is the primary communicator and healer within the community, he or she must also fulfill other more mundane responsibilities to their family and community. In many ways the shaman serve the community in their ability to communicate, heal, and guide the community on a part-time basis. In general, a shaman may be identified as the communicator and master of spiritual influences, a ritualist of complex methods, assuming a special position within a society, which justifies his or her practices.

In some societies shamans inherit their powers from their ancestors, whereas in others they are "called" or "chosen" through prophetic dreams or near-death experiences. A fundamental experience of the shaman is that of death and rebirth, which reflects this transformation process. A shaman must undergo the death of his or her personal ego in order to break down the internal psychological structures that would hinder his or her ability to communicate with the spiritual forces in the other worlds. While some shaman may acquire special skills and talents through their illness experiences, most must spend years to learn the knowledge of medicinal plants, ritual songs or dances, healing rites, and trance techniques.

Trance or altered states of consciousness are induced in a variety of ways, depending on the social environment and cultural practices. Hallucinogenic drugs or alcohol, fasting, dancing, and drumming may be used to reach a level of trance that provides the altered state needed by the shaman to communicate with the spirits. Three levels of trance states have been identified by anthropologists who have spent many years studying the techniques of shamans. The first level is a "light" trance where the shaman still has partial awareness of the exterior forces and may easily come out of the trance state. The second level is associated with nightly "dreaming," where the shaman is able to receive messages and knowledge from the spirit helpers in their dream state. This knowledge is used to bring harmony, balance, and healing to the community. The third level of trance is a "deep" trance state where the shaman often appears to be dead. In this deep trance the shaman is able to journey to the land of the dead as part of a healing ritual. Shamans are assisted into these trance states in the presence and often with the help of community believers. The believers also serve as judges or evaluators of the shaman's ability and healing power.

Along with being the communicator between the worlds, the role of the shaman is also that of healer. Many illnesses and crises are associated with sorcery or evil influences within several cultures. The shaman engages in a struggle with the dark forces in order to free the patient and promote healing. The promotion of healing is brought on by the shaman's ability to resolve an unbalanced relationship between the patient and the dark forces, whether resulting from sorcery or other external influences, and establishing an integration of balanced energies within the patient. The same principles apply when the shaman is attempting to address a crisis in the community. The shaman is able to bring a communal understanding to the distress and bring forth a meaningful resolution. In other words, the shaman is able to manipulate the symbols from his or her trance state and provide a coherent solution to a specific problem.

Shamans are sometimes feared due to their powerful abilities and may at times be blamed for the sickness and death by other communities, yet they are not sorcerers. Unlike sorcerers, shamans practice and engage in their spiritual rituals in the public sphere. The shaman is also different from the magician as they use their skills and abilities on behalf of the community and not for personal gain.

Although our world has changed drastically and our way of life is far different than it was during hunting and gathering cultures, there still exist societies, especially in Asia, that engage in the practices and techniques of traditional Shamanism.

NEO-SHAMANISM

Neo-shamanism refers to spiritual practice that reflects traditional Shamanism practice on a very fundamental level yet is contemporary in nature. Neo-shamanism is often referred to as the "rebirth" of Shamanism because it strives to address the human quest for meaning in its attempt to understand our spiritual experiences. Many Neo-shamanic spiritual practices today, as in the past, deal with the communication with spirits and the worlds of animals, plants, minerals, and humans.

The practice of Neo-shamanism as a spiritual discipline is diverse and may be found in many parts of the world, from California to Germany to Australia. What most Neo-shamanic groups have in common is the way in which these groups have emerged within our modern society. Unlike traditional Shamanism, which is linked to traditional and cultural ties founded in history, Neo-shamanism has emerged out of an era of individual freedom and exploration. At the height of the 1960s, many people were exploring different forms of spirituality, which revolved around altered states of consciousness and techniques that would allow them to reach higher levels of consciousness through deep states of ecstasy. Those who pursued the quest for individual meaning amidst the secular Western world came to be called *seekers*.

The study of Neo-shamanism and its renewed interest in the 20th century can be attributed to three academic scholars: Mircea Eliade, a historian of world religions, and two anthropologists, Carlos Castaneda and Michael Harner. It was these scholars who introduced the general population to the techniques and practices of Neo-shamanism. Eliade has been called the "grandfather" of Neo-shamanism because it was his initial work on traditional Shamanism in Asia, the Americas, and ancient Europe that brought forth the founding definition of Shamanism, a practice in the "techniques of ecstasy." Eliade concluded that Shamanism was a universal practice manifested in virtually all cultures. This definition set the stage for Shamanism and Neo-shamanism to be viewed as universal and undifferentiated in nature.

Carlos Castaneda, an American anthropologist, and his many popular books describing his personal experiences with the Yaqui medicine man Don Juan, inspired a larger portion of the American population in the early 1970s to seek Shamanic experiences. These Neo-shamanic experiences were first explored in the spaces of the imagination as seekers read *The Teachings of Don Juan* and the books that followed.

Another anthropologist, Michael Harner, introduced his book *The Way of the Shaman* in 1980 and provided the seekers tangible techniques and skill development in Neo-shamanic practices. Harner began teaching what he has described as "core Shamanism" and founded the Foundation for Shamanic Studies. Core Shamanism perpetuated the universal belief, as initiated by Eliade more than 30 years ago, that Shamanic practices and techniques were common to many cultures past and present. Seekers were able to initiate themselves into Shamanic practices within a weekend workshop taught by Harner.

The main focus of Neo-shamanic practices and spiritual techniques is that of transformation, to change or shift the mental, emotional, and physical aspects that have caused the seeker pain and move them toward, healing. Unlike the traditional shamans who performed their practices for and in the presence of the community, many neo-shaman practices and spiritual techniques are conducted in private, where one focuses on their individual needs and personal healing. While in traditional Shamanism the novice learned his or her techniques from an older shaman, Neo-shamanic novices learn their techniques and skills in a workshop setting. On some level these weekend gatherings create pseudo-communities where people of like mind can share their experiences.

The techniques and practices are more often learned from reading books such as *The Way of the Shaman* or *Way of Shamanism,* which are available at popular New Age bookstores and shops. The path of the neo-shaman is an easy path compared with the dangerous and uncertain process of the traditional shaman. For some Neo-shamanic groups there is no demand to become an apprentice, making a commitment to serve the community. Others such as the Deer Tribe Metis Medicine Society protect the teachings and techniques from those who are not committed to their own healing and the healing of their community.

Once the techniques and skills have been taught and practiced within the workshop setting, the neo-shaman explores the trance states brought on by drumming or fasting within their own personal ritual. Psychedelic drugs are discouraged and many practices resemble meditative techniques. The focus of the trancestate is the same as with traditional Shamanism. In trance, the neo-shaman attempts to reach the world of spirits and engage in communication with the spirits in order to bring a sense of awareness and understanding to a particular concern or crisis. This awareness and understanding helps the neo-shaman, whether for themselves or others, to facilitate healing and balance. In addition, the techniques and skills that the neo-shaman learns promote their sense of personal power and self-mastery. The process of death and rebirth of the personality psyche is also pronounced in Neo-shamanism as in traditional Shamanism. The death of the ego allows the neo-shaman to reach a higher level of awareness, an awareness of one's the spiritual side.

It is believed within many Neo-shamanic groups that promoting spiritual awareness and knowledge facilitated through Neo-shamanic techniques of trance states elevates healing, increasing the person's wellness. The neo-shaman's main concern is that of healing, incorporating the healing of spiritual causes of illness and disease with more scientific and biomedical causes. In the modern world today spiritual causes of illness are not well-received within the health care field, and therefore, Neo-shamanism is often interpreted as a form of therapy.

Many of the Neo-shamanic techniques and practices resemble Native American practices such as the sweat lodge or vision quest. Many Native American people are upset about the "borrowing" of their cultural spiritual practices and actively oppose the teachings of Neo-shamanism. Neo-shamanism, while aware of the opposition, strives to portray itself as a diverse, nonreligious, and universal spiritual movement, which aims to bring healing and spirituality to the modern world.

Although Shamanic techniques have been said to exist for thousands of years in many different cultures, Neo-shamanism is still a recent phenomenon. The lines are often blurred between Shamanism and Neo-shamanism, and tensions remain between what is appropriate to borrow from a culture that one is not one's own. But in many ways Neo-shamanism is an attempt by those who feel that they have lost their cultural spirituality in this modern secular era to revitalize a fundamental human desire to communicate with the world of spirits and heal themselves and their community.

—Olga Nikolajev

FURTHER READING

Eliade, M. (1964). *Shamanism: Archaic techniques of ecstasy.* New York: Pantheon.

Halifax, J. (1982). *Shaman: The wounded healer.* New York: Crossroads.

Harner, M. (1980). *The way of the shaman.* New York: HarperSanFrancisco.

Jakobsen, M. D. (1999). *Shamanism: Traditional and contemporary approaches to the mastery of spirits and healing.* New York: Berghahn.

Noel, D. C. (1999). *The soul of shamanism: Western fantasies, imaginal realities.* New York: Continuum.

Rutherford, L. (1996). *Way of shamanism.* London: Thorsons.

SIERRA CLUB

The Sierra Club is the nation's oldest and largest grassroots nonprofit conservation and preservation organization. The club was founded in 1892 by John Muir and a group of passionate outdoor enthusiasts to protect Yosemite Valley National Park from waste and destruction and to promote the preservation of America's natural forests. Muir served as the first president of the Sierra Club until his death in 1914. The Sierra Club is dedicated to educating people about conserving global ecosystems and lobbies for legislation to preserve the environment. Moreover, the club organizes wilderness outings both domestically and internationally. For more than a century, the Sierra Club has played a pivotal role in securing millions of acres of wilderness for recreation, education, and conservation. In protecting the wilderness and bringing people in closer contact with nature, the work of the Sierra Club has been known to positively impact the spiritual lives of many.

EARLY PROTECTION AND CONSERVATION

In the early years of the Sierra Club, the organization lobbied for the continued establishment of national parks and opposed efforts to construct dams in protected areas. The most well-known debate led by the Sierra Club in the history of the United States over the use of wilderness was the proposal to dam the Hetch Hetchy Valley in the Tuolumne area of Yosemite National Park. After the earthquake of 1906 that destroyed most of the city of San Francisco, Mayor James D. Phelan proposed to dam the Hetch Hetchy Valley to create a reservoir to transport fresh water and hydroelectric power to the city of San Francisco. While Muir testified before Congress in 1908 that he thought that Hetch Hetchy's broad, spacious meadows were more beautiful and picturesque than Yosemite and, therefore needed to be protected as a national park, in 1913 the city of San Francisco won the long-fought battle to turn this wilderness valley into a reservoir.

While the damming of Hetch Hetchy was a major defeat for the Sierra Club, it garnered national attention to the conservation efforts of the organization. In the years following 1913, the Sierra Club continued to push for the establishment of additional national parks. Accordingly, Olympia National Park in Washington State was established in 1938, and 2 years later Kings Canyon was designated as a national park. During the 10-year period between 1940 and 1950 the Sierra Club was responsible for stopping the construction of dams in Glacier, Dinosaur, and Kings Canyon National Parks.

INTERNATIONAL ENVIRONMENTAL PRESERVATION AND CONSERVATION

Although during the early years of the Sierra Club's history the focus on protecting and preserving natural land was primarily a domestic issue, in 1971 the organization expanded its mission to protect the *global* environment. The Sierra Club International Program was created in an effort to assemble governmental agencies, corporations, and other institutions to work together to educate the world about natural resources and ecosystems, focusing specifically on global population, human rights policies to protect activists, and free trade. The commitment of the Sierra

Club to protect the earth's ecosystems is coupled by its commitment to protect the rights of the people who do this preservation and conservation work worldwide. However, in order to advocate on behalf of an issue, one must be dedicated to the cause.

SIERRA CLUB OUTINGS

John Muir's passion to protect the wildlife and natural resources from needless destruction was born out of his love of nature's pristine beauty. He believed that taking people out of the city and into the wilderness would inspire a similar passion to conserve and fight to protect the natural world. As such, in 1901 the Board of the Directors determined that an annual summer outing would be a significant addition to the Club's regular activities. The first outing served as a model for what is now known as the High Trip. These excursions have evolved over the course of the past century to include new and more sophisticated techniques for wilderness recreation. However, due to the popularity in wilderness recreation in the postwar years, the High Trip outings paid greater attention to "minimum impact" camping such that the presence of visitors in the backcountry would leave the least effect on the environment. Moreover, as the interests in conservation grew among the High Trip participants, the trips extended beyond California and into parts of Washington State, Wyoming, and Idaho. Today, there are more than 350 trips offered by the Sierra Club that will take people throughout the world to participate in activities ranging from activist trips and service trips to kayaking, backpacking, and skiing trips. Muir's passion for the wilderness was one that he wished to share with all human beings including those who ordinarily cannot get into the wilderness (i.e., urban youth, seniors, and physically challenged).

Inner-City Outings

The Inner-City Outings (ICO) was first established in 1971 by the San Francisco Bay chapter of the Sierra Club as a community outreach program to provide wilderness experiences for young people who otherwise might not have them. Youth who participate in these trips come from diverse ethnic and racial backgrounds; some are visual and/or hearing impaired, and some are physically disabled. They are led by a group of dedicated volunteers into the backcountry where they learn survival and interpersonal skills and develop abilities to face challenges outside their neighborhoods, in addition to discovering the vast wilderness in a manner that protects and preserves the environment. The ICO seeks to promote a greater appreciation and understanding of diverse cultures and to foster respect of self and others while simultaneously developing a conservation ethic among its participants through outdoor exploration, education, sharing, and spiritual growth.

Since its inception in 1892, the Sierra Club has been the most effective advocate for the environment locally and globally. Today, there are over 700,000 active members in the Club who are committed to resolving pressing global concerns such as ensuring clean water, ending commercial logging, stopping global warming, and protecting our wildlands. In the true spirit of John Muir's vision, the Sierra Club has been instrumental in organizing concerned citizens to preserve nature's most splendid wild places so that its beauty can be experienced, protected, and appreciated by generations to come. By valuing and preserving the environment, the Sierra Club will continue to play a role in the spiritual lives of those touched by the beauty of nature for many years to come.

—Pamela M. Anderson

See also Muir, John; Wilderness

FURTHER READING

Cohen, M. P. (1988). *The history of the Sierra Club, 1892–1970.* San Francisco: Sierra Club Books.

Turner, T. (1991). *Sierra Club, 100 years of protecting nature.* New York: Abrams.

Carr, P. (1989). *The Sierra Club, a guide.* San Francisco: Sierra Club Books.

SIN

The language of sin may appear outdated in the 21st century, yet it is a relevant concept that can assist human beings in their quest for greater meaning and purpose in life by identifying those personal and institutionalized attitudes and actions that negatively impact the quality of human living. In many mainline Christian traditions sin has been viewed personalistically and legalistically. Sin is a personal infraction of an external and objective law that results in separation from God and neighbor. A focus on personal guilt and degrees of culpability for specific actions is assessed either by a priest or minister. Heartfelt contrition ideally follows for the offense. The repentant sinner confesses and promises to live a better life by not falling prey to repeating the offending behavior again. Grace assists a sinner toward conversion of heart. Forgiveness is the antidote to contritely repented sin.

In this understanding of individual transgression or act-centered sin there is little room for consideration of a person's motives, life context, the needs of the victim or victims of the sinner's behavior, the social implications of sin, or the ways in which an institution or social system is complicit in sin. Theologians and the Christian churches owe much to the personality or human sciences along with the range of social sciences in contributing to the development of the theological doctrine of personal and social sin. In short, without losing the stress on individual acts of destructive transgression, developments in an understanding of sin now explore the motives or patterns of behavior that result in ruptures of trust and love between and among persons. More in-depth examination of the choices that produce suffering encourage people to explore their own complicity in sheltering themselves from taking responsibility for the consequences of their behavior. The Christian understanding of sin now extends beyond the accumulation of personal guilt to the interpersonal, social, and systemic realization of accommodation to and complicity with forms of inhumanity or crimes against the earth, such as racism or ecological destruction. Exploring a vision of being human provides entry for a theological understanding of sin.

Christian theologian Letty Russell suggests that while born human, humans are engaged in a lifelong process of "becoming human." Her perspectives reflect a global experience of sin. Humans cannot escape the challenge that human life is not a given but must be created as life unfolds within the continuum of a biological life span. Humans can be authentically understood as beings in relationship. Context and history shape what it means to be human. Through interaction with one's environment, which includes many components such as culture, family, values, religion, and country, to name a few, one learns how to orient oneself to life, to function, to look at the world and name it, to exert influence on the quest for meaning and purpose; in a sense, to be an agent of one's own destiny. Russell suggests three ingredients in keeping human life human: (1) all human beings possess inherent dignity, (2) all persons participate in the shaping of their own futures, and (3) as beings in relationship, all humans are naturally drawn to community where care, nurturance, support, and challenge are constituent elements that necessarily contribute to human growth.

Other forces exerted by humans intentionally or unintentionally can thwart human flourishing and thus counter each of the previously identified essential human ingredients in the following ways: (1) it is a violation of human dignity to objectify or belittle a person, (2) it is a violation of a person's innate right to be moral agents of their own destiny through means of domination and control, and (3) it is a violation of the primary need for human community to create systems and situations that isolate persons and subsequently generate cycles of debilitation that breed the failure of human beings to thrive. The realities of forces exerted by humans to intentionally or unintentionally thwart human flourishing raise questions regarding the human capacity to do harm.

The human capacity to cause harm leads directly to the theological notion of sin. An understanding of sin is to be found firstly in the situation humans find themselves in before God and each other. That situation is one constituted by freedom. According to the major religions of the "book," meaning Judaism, Christianity and Islam, human beings are created essentially free to respond or not respond to the Divine, make choices, and author their own lives. God's will and gift of human free will can work in mutual cooperation. This must be so because one must be free in order to love. There is no coercion in God's nature; therefore, it is contrary to the Divine nature to manipulate human response.

Individual self-determination and realization in community, then, are fundamental to human nature. This means that each person is primarily responsible for growth in becoming and developing their unique potential as a being in relationship, specifically as this is understood within one's own cultural milieu. Humans live this primary responsibility within the sphere of their relational and social worlds, which is a mix of shared obligations and entitlements. Ideally, human beings possess the power (agency) and responsibility to share the direction and destiny of their own lives.

At the same time, all human beings find they are dealing with the reality of human limitation. No one escapes the claims of sickness; physical, mental, and moral weaknesses, aging; suffering of all stripes; the experience of anxiety and fear; and ultimately, death.

Theologically speaking, humans, personally and corporately, are situated in a multidimensional world where they manifest the gift of freedom through the panoply of decisions made every day.

An important caveat here includes an ever-growing awareness that severe debilitating environmental situations, such as child abuse, untreated acute mental illness, racism, or other forms of physical and psychic neglect, often result in a distorted sense of one's capacity to author one's own life in relationship, coupled with the possible inability on the part of such persons or groups to access the means to achieve their full potential. These persons neither bear the primary responsibility for their failure to thrive nor the same moral culpability and capacities as others reared in healthier, freer, and more nurturing environments. These individuals are the victims of the cycles of abuse and dehumanization that distort Russell's vision of the human person as previously cited.

A theological vision of the human person includes the conviction of God's predilection for the poor and the notion of grace, God's eternal self-gift of life. It is the *anawim,* the poor of the world, to whom God directs abundant grace to assist those most downtrodden with the almost miraculous capacity to transcend undeserved extreme hardship and live authentically rich human lives *in spite of* severe restrictions placed on their freedom and destiny.

As previously noted, the innocent suffer. Injustice abounds in a world populated by billions of people who do not necessarily live peaceably with each other or equitably share the material resources needed for survival. Starvation remains a reason why thousands of people, mostly children, die each day in poverty-stricken areas of the world. Institutional slavery, the Holocaust, and 9/11 are but three examples of historical realities that mark and mar the human story; in each case these realities are human inventions, arise from complex situations, devised and perpetrated by the free exercise of human minds, hearts, and hands.

The long sweep of religious tradition has sought an explanation as to the nature of human nature and what kind of a God, Divine Benevolent Being, or Creator of the Universe would permit such atrocities in a world of God's own creation? In Christian theology, the category used to contain and explain these aberrations of human nature is sin and original sin. Christian doctrine or faith-based teaching on the matter is quite clear: precisely because it is not in God's nature to manipulate human free will, the possibility for evil exists within human capacity. There was, however, original blessing before original sin. The Creation myths in chapters 1 and 2 of the Hebrew Scripture's book of Genesis are the bases for a creation theology that arises from the hymn that recounts God's blessing in the design of the created world and includes the capstone of the creation of man and woman in God's own image. The nature of human nature in its totality is essentially good and oriented toward goodness. Joy, pleasure, laughter, and love reflect God's original intention in sharing partnership with human beings in partnership with each other in caring for the earth and all God's creatures, great and small.

The great truth-telling myth of The Fall is the scripturally based lesson that human freedom exercised through Adam and Eve resulted in a tragic choice to presume that the decision to disobey the Creator would have no consequences (Gen. 3). Classical theology has named the first sin as one of hubris, meaning pride. In relation to the Genesis story of The Fall, the hubris attributed to Adam is understood as his decision to replace a God centeredness with ego centeredness and dismiss God's claim upon him. Adam and Eve and the fall symbolize the illusion that someone other than God is god. The choice of the mythic first parents turned paradise into the human predicament that is now part of the unavoidable painful realities that impact every human life. Original sin is the universal fact of human existence into which every human person is born.

Probing questions as to what the origin of sin says about the nature of God or of the Divine remain central to the theological enterprise, which reflects on the meaning of human experience in light of the reality of a God whose presence remains active in the world. Theologian Carol Frances Jegen suggests that the root of our misunderstanding about personal and social sinfulness is a distorted image of God. Far too often, persons carry an image of a demanding, vengeful deity who sends suffering to punish or test. This image of God supports the notion that human nature became essentially "fallen" as a result of the mythic Fall, thereby changing the innate human disposition toward goodness and right relationship to an innately self-centered disposition prone toward selfishness at the expense of others.

Ultimately this kind of reasoning results in a pessimistic vision of human nature not grounded in the creation theology of Genesis. It also leads one to imagine that God requires the painful challenges of human life as retributive payback for Adam and Eve's original mistake. Even more dramatic, God demanded the death of Jesus—the New Adam—as recompense for Adam's sin. Of course, various Christian denominations, as well as other religious traditions, offer different points of view on these matters.

Islam's view on the history of human–divine relations is comparable to that of Judaism. That is, the Qur'an, like the Hebrew Bible, recognizes human infidelities, while simultaneously holding the conviction of the unlimited forgiving capacity of Allah or Yahweh to call forth humans from ignorance and ingratitude toward right relation with the Divine and each other. There is little in Islam and Judaism by way of formal doctrine on humanity's inherent disposition to sin, which is parallel to Christianity's notion of original sin. There is, however, a story within Islamic tradition in which angels remove the heart of Muhammad and wash away any stain of sin from it, thus symbolizing the Prophet's special status as the sinless, ideally suited Messenger of Allah.

Buddhism and Hinduism recognize the deep-seated nature of the fallen state of humanity, but this is conceived as the product of thousands of lifetimes of human habit. In these Eastern religious traditions, a human life span is but one in a potentially infinite number of rebirths. This is the meaning of reincarnation. Any given life span produces moral and physical decay as human beings find themselves combating the powerful forces of evil and delusion. Such habits can only be purified and redeemed through the processes of reincarnation. A common saying is that Buddhism teaches the ultimate perfectibility of human nature, but it does so in a historical framework that recognizes that we are unlikely to make much progress in just one life span.

Sin might best be placed in the theological category of mystery, *mystery* meaning something about which there is always more to know. In his Letter to the Romans, St. Paul captures the mysterious dilemma that confounds many human beings, irrespective of religious tradition: "I do not understand my own actions. For I do not do what I want, but I do the very thing I hate. Now if I do what I do not want, I agree that the law is good. So it is no longer I that do it, but sin which dwells within me . . . I can will what is right, but I cannot do it. For I do not do the good I want, but the evil I do not want I do . . ." (Rom. 7:15–20). This condition of our own inability, at times, to choose and do the better, nobler thing is a transcultural phenomenon of human experience that is part and parcel of everyone's life.

Modern depth psychologist Carl Jung helped illumine this mysterious human condition by exploring the reality of the "shadow" in human personality. The shadow is that which is hidden from the individual's consciousness and resides in the unconscious, unavailable until the person takes responsibility for the whole of their lives. Far too often people flee from the claims of the shadow since it holds the undesirable parts of one's personality; those ways of being we prefer not to own or examine and therefore repress. Eventually the desire for growth and impulse toward individuation urge the individual to pay attention to the shadow and bring its contents to light. The shadow in human personality is not in and of itself sinful; refusal to deal with the reality of the shadow often results, however, in the sinful situations of egocentric patterns, excessive self-righteousness, intolerance, interpersonal strife, and violent behaviors—all by-products of the unattended shadow in human personality.

Sin is basically understood as the inevitable human frailty of not being continuously perfect. Sin is seen as consciously or unconsciously falling into patterns that "miss the mark" (the words for sin in the New Testament) and cause the runner in faith to stumble. Sin is living in estrangement from one's essence, seriously disorients right relations, and always has interpersonal and social consequences. Becoming entangled in sinful patterns of living necessarily result in a dislocation from loving, right, just, and reciprocal relationships. Those entrapped by sin experience a hardness of heart. Tendencies toward self-justification abound, often preventing sinners from seeing the light of critical self-examination that might lead to repentance, which happens under the power of grace. Sin pushes a person egocentrically inward, spiritually backward, and ultimately deathward, which is the real meaning of the term *mortal sin.*

—Avis Clendenen

See also Evil; Forgiveness; Grace; Original Sin

FURTHER READING

Clendenen, A., & Martin, T. (2002). *Forgiveness: Finding freedom through reconciliation.* New York: Crossroad.

Jegen, C. (1989). *Restoring our friendship with God: The mystery of redemption from sin and suffering.* Wilmington, DE: Michael Glazier.

Park Sung, A., & Nelson, S. (Eds.). (2001). *The other side of sin: Woundedness from the perspective of the sinned against.* Albany: State University of New York.

Russell, L. (1982). *Becoming human.* Philadelphia: Westminster Press.

SIQUEIROS, DAVID ALFARO

In Mexico, early in the 20th century, a few well-known artists became convinced that art should no longer be for the wealthy only. They began to create art meant for the poor, who were struggling under the oppression of dictator Porfirio Diaz. Instead of painting to sell their works in galleries, these artists painted larger-than-life murals—on the walls of schools, churches, and other buildings and public areas where all could see.

One of the most prominent of these muralists was the political activist David Alfaro Siqueiros (1896?–1974). Siqueiros created murals to raise the hopes and spirits of the poor and to instill nationalism in those he considered to be the "real people of Mexico." His murals portrayed the oppressed Mexican people and inspired social reform. In recognition of his courage and personal sacrifices for the common good, Siguieros has been acknowledged as a spiritual exemplar.

Born in Chihuahua, Mexico, to a bourgeois family, Siqueiros went as a teenager in 1910 to Mexico City to study art and architecture. This time also marked the beginning of the Mexican revolution. Siqueiros quickly became involved in student strikes and, at age 18, joined the Mexican Revolutionary Army. He later joined the Communist Party and was jailed and exiled several times for his radical views and harsh criticisms of the Mexican government.

Even so, the government commissioned large-scale murals by Siqueiros and his fellow muralists, Diego Rivera and José Clemente Orozco, who shared his revolutionary outlook. These commissions gave him the opportunity to make his living educating the public about social injustice.

Siquieros's communist political views focused on distributing power and wealth among all of the people of Mexico. He spoke out against those artists who paid little attention to Mexico's working class. In his "Declaration of Social, Political, and Aesthetic Principles," written in 1922, Siqueiros said, "We repudiate so-called easel painting and every kind of art favored by the ultra-intellectual circles, because it is aristocratic, and we praise monumental art in all its forms, because it is public property. . . . Art must no longer be the expression of individual satisfaction, but should aim to become a fighting, educative art for all."

In creating his art, Siqueiros stood out from his contemporaries by using techniques that gave his murals vividness and three-dimensionality. With the centuries-old technique known as fresco, the paint is applied to a freshly plastered wall. He also used the modern technique of airbrushing, which helped him cover large areas more quickly, along with stencils to create sharp edges.

In order to communicate his message about injustice, Siqueiros incorporated powerful emotion in his work, with the intent of moving viewers to become more deeply connected to the subject matter. For example, the painting "Peasant Mother" portrays an indigenous Mexican mother cradling her baby surrounded by a vast, empty desert landscape. By eliminating all life except the woman, her baby, and three cacti from the landscape, Siqueiros intensifies the bond between the woman and her baby—and raises the question of whether her surroundings are supportive of both. In another mural, titled "Echo of a Scream," viewers witness the pain of a young, malnourished child left alone to scream in silence amidst the ruins of war. The image of the child's screaming face is enlarged and superimposed in the center of the painting in such a way that viewers cannot avoid witnessing the child's torment.

By playing on human emotions in such a way, Siqueiros forces viewers to form a connection to the painting's subject and in doing so, to feel and fully realize something intensely spiritual. He used this technique to gain support for the revolution that he became so much a part of.

"La Nueva Democracia" is another example of the powerful way Siqueiros connected art and social reform and, at the same time, expressed something deeply spiritual. In this mural, a nude woman thrusts her shackled arms out towards the viewer in an attempt to break free from the ominous forces that keep her a prisoner. With the use of the fresco technique, the figure seems to reach out of the wall in such a way that no passerby can ignore her and her desperate cry for freedom.

In 1933, Siqueiros wrote, "The painters and sculptors of today cannot remain indifferent in the struggle to free humanity and art from oppression." Throughout his life Siqueiros held true to his ideals and fought tirelessly to free his country from oppression by exploring the spiritual connection between art and sociopolitical freedom.

—Jake Jurkowitz Brotter

FURTHER READING

Ades, D. (1989). *Art in Latin America.* New Haven and London: Yale University Press.

SISTINE CHAPEL

ROME AND THE POPES

Constantine, Rome's first Christian Emperor, erected and dedicated a basilica to St. Peter, Christ's first representative on earth, above the apostle's tomb. The basilica became home to the popes, Peter's successors, who required their own chapel. Several Renaissance popes undertook construction and decoration of the *capella papalis,* notably Sixtus IV, the Franciscan friar Francesco della Rovere (1414–1484), who reigned as pope from 1471 to 1484, and Sixtus's nephew, Julius II, the Franciscan Giuliano della Rovere (1443–1513), who reigned from 1503 to 1513. Sixtus and Julius were clerics, generals, and patrons of culture and the arts. Sixtus had the purpose-built chapel abut the original St. Peter's. Julius laid the cornerstone of the present-day St. Peter's and worked to complete decoration of his uncle's chapel.

THE SISTINE CHAPEL

The brick Sistine Chapel (*Sistina*) was designed by the Florentine architect Gionvani de Dolci and built between 1475 and 1483 by Baccio Pontelli proportionate to the Temple of Solomon in Jerusalem: 130 ft long by 43 ft wide by 65 ft high. The Chapel was consecrated in August 1483, the anniversary of Sixtus's election, and dedicated to the Virgin of the Assumption.

Structure and Decoration. The Sistina consists of four stories. The basement and mezzanine below the chapel are each divided into nine rooms, the latter occupied by the offices of the Masters of Ceremonies (one of whom, Paris de Grassis in 1518 declared the Sistina the first chapel in the world, both for its majesty and for its structure). The attic above housed the Pope's guards, for the Sistina was originally a chapel and a fortified bastion of the Vatican Palaces.

Art was used to illuminate stories for the illiterate and recall doctrinal messages for the literate, for services were long and filled with meandering eyes and minds. The frescoes adorning the Sistina's walls and ceiling portray biblical and papal history and spirituality as well as the story of humanity as intended by God from the creation on the first day to judgment on the last day, encompassing *ante legem, sub legem, sub gratia* in the ancient formula. In 15th-century fresco, cartoons or full-scale drawings of a composition were first executed on large sheets of heavy paper. They were then cut into sections, whose shapes coincided with areas to be painted. In the technique of *buon fresco,* a 3/4-inch layer of rough plaster (*arriccio*) was applied to the surface. Just before painting, a finishing smooth 9/16-inch layer of finer plaster *(intonachino)* was applied. Actual fresco painting, which must take place in a window of about 6 hours before the *intonachino* dries, leaves little time for rethinking and little space for error. The cartoon was perforated along key contours, mounted, and then dusted (*spolvero*) or incised *(incisione)* along its contours to transfer the outline of the design to the fresco.

Walls. The interior walls of the Sistina are divided into three zones. Leo X (Giovanni de Medici, 1475–1521, the Franciscan who succeeded Julius II and reigned from 1513 to 1521) commissioned Raphael in 1515 to design 10 scenes from the lives of Saints Peter and Paul to decorate the lowest zone with trompe l'oeil curtains. From Raphael's cartoons Pieter van Aelst (in Brussels) wove tapestries of gold and silver thread that were hung in the lowest zone. (These Leonine tapestries were stolen in 1527 but later recovered. They were hung again in the Raphael Anniversary Year, 1983.) A 12-chorister *cantoria* overhangs the chapel floor at this level.

The iconographic program conceived by Sixtus IV for the middle zone of the walls compares the Old and New Covenants. Corresponding events in chronological cycles of the lives of Moses and Christ appear in 12 (11 × 18 ft) parallel en face frescoes. The thematic subtext is the evolution of the Evangelical Law of Christ over the Written Law of Moses. This zone was frescoed (July 1481 to May 1482) by the 15th century's greatest artists: Sandro Botticelli, Piero di Cosimo, Bartolomeo della Gatta, Domenico Ghirlandaio, Francesco Granacci, Pietro Perugino, Bernardino Betti Pinturicchio, Cosimo Rosselli, and Luca Signorelli. (The frescoes by Signorelli and Ghirlandaio were replaced with frescoes by Matteo da Lecce and Hendrik van den Broeck.) To promote unity and harmony, frescoes on opposite walls depicting corresponding chronological scenes were awarded to the same atelier.

In the highest zone are 14 windows and false niches with scallop-shell backs about 8 feet high each portraying the full-length standing effigy of a pope in colorful gowns. This gallery of 28 pontiffs is arranged in chronological order based on the papal history of Bartolomeo Platina, Sixtus' librarian.

Last Judgment. While Clement VII (Giulio de Medici, 1478–1534, reigned from 1523 to 1534) commissioned Michelangelo to execute a *Last Judgment* on the altar wall, in 1536 Paul III (Alessandro Farnese, 1468–1549, reigned from 1534 to 1549) forced him to execute the fresco. This was 25 years after Michelangelo had completed the chapel ceiling (see below). In 1541, Michelangelo unveiled his 45- by 40-foot picture of the last act of human history. Michelangelo adopted the iconographic tradition of symmetry around a central dynamic Christ the Judge with the heavenly zone above and a terrestrial zone below, dividing the Blessed, raised to Paradise on Christ's right, from the Damned, destined for hell on his left. No other architectural structure organizes the composition; rather, Michelangelo reinvents the cosmic moment, presciently rendering psychological individuation of elect and damned alike. The *Last Judgment* is the last word on spirituality in this chapel that contrasts good with evil (note that the Book of the Damned held by angels beneath Christ is much larger than the Book of the Blessed). Michelangelo painted nearly 400 (mostly nude) figures, but following accusations of obscenity ("One man's virtuosity in representation is another's anatomical exhibitionism"), Daniele de Volterra censored the painting. In a sardonic signature, at least one Michelangelo self-portrait appears in the flayed skin of St. Bartholomew, suspended over the abyss of the Dantesque inferno.

Vault. The original ceiling of Sixtus's time was a starry Vault of Heaven in gold and lapis lazuli attributed to Pier Matteo d'Amelia. The walls of the chapel attracted attention, but the ceiling disappointed. On May 10, 1508, Julius II wrote a 3,000-ducat contract to Michelangelo to refresco the Sistine vault. Although Julius initially commissioned a particular design in oils, he relented to let Michelangelo *aquello che io volevo*. Michelangelo was an unwilling and complaining participant throughout the ordeal, considering himself a sculptor in Rome to fashion Julius's tomb (only his *Moses* was completed) not paint a ceiling. Michelangelo's charge was to build a scaffold 50 feet above the chapel floor so as not to obstruct ongoing liturgy and ceremony; to cut away the existing fresco and lay on a new undercoat *arriccio,* and to fresco the ceiling with a fresh coat of painted *intonachino.*

The vault of the Sistine Chapel (12,000 square feet) is also divided into three zones. In a garland of 14 (originally 16) semicircular lunettes and 8 triangular spandrels above the gallery of popes (the Successors of Christ), Michelangelo frescoed the Ancestors of Christ in single figures in the lunettes and in the spandrels (mostly) balanced pairs and triplets. This full chronological genealogy of 14 generations begins with Abraham, Isaac, Jacob, and David (according to Matt. 1:1–17), although the earliest were replaced by *The Last Judgment.* These ancestors remain today, as Michelangelo depicted them half a millennium ago, in postures of intent waiting and preparation for the second coming.

The outer *fasciae* are occupied with figures of ancient seers and depictions of incidents of salvation of the Chosen People. Four pendentative scenes at the corners include David and Goliath, the Punishment of Haman, Judith and Holofernes, and the story of the Brazen Serpent. Notably, Michelangelo highlighted David, Judith, and Esther—a boy and two women—as deliverers of the Hebrews. Sibyls and prophets were thought to foresee the coming of the Savior. Sibyls, the pagan prophetesses of antiquity, linked Christianity to pre-Christian classical tradition. The Delphian, Erythrean, Cumaean, Persian, and Libyan Sibyls also represent the known continents, then coming into consciousness at the start of the age of exploration and foretelling the worldwide spread of Christianity. Each pagan diviner is rendered in an expressive rotary movement of the body. The seven Old Testament prophets—Zechariah, Joel, Isaiah, Ezekiel, Daniel, Jeremiah, and Jonah—appear in geometrical compartments of an illusionist architectural schema accompanied by spirit pairs who intermediate with God.

The latitudinal spine of the chapel ceiling is occupied by nine panels representing key episodes from Genesis. Moving from the laity entrance (in the order he painted them) come the Drunkenness of Noah (man in a state of unconsciousness of God); the Flood; the Sacrifice of Noah; Original Sin and Expulsion from Earthly Paradise; Creation of Eve; Creation of Adam; Separation of Land and Water; Creation of the Sun, Moon, and Plants; and Separation of Light and Darkness (God's initial act) over the altar. Michelangelo increasingly adopted colossal dimensions to match the epic character of his narrative subjects.

Michelangelo's design called for more than 150 pictorial units and more than 300 individual figures including 40 ancestors of Christ, 5 mythological sibyls, 7 Old Testament prophets, and 9 episodes from Genesis (plus *genii, putti, ignudi,* etc.). Before setting to this work, Michelangelo Buonarroti (1475–1564) had not frescoed since his apprenticeship with Ghirlandaio. Frescoing required diverse techniques, including extreme foreshortening *(di sotto in su)*, which Michelangelo was not expert in, and at the beginning he made errors that had to be painted over (so-called pentimenti, or repentances). Michelangelo divided his work by measures of what could be accomplished in a day (*giornata*); *The Last Judgment* required 450 *giornata.* He executed the vault and altar wall largely by his saturnine, solitary, and superstitious self, although he also enlisted assistants in seeing these works completely through. Although Michelangelo sometimes quoted designs and poses from classical sources, by and large the vault and altar were autograph painting ("in his own hand") and of his own invention. Along the way, Michelangelo also invented new iconographies of God and the creation of Adam. Michelangelo made dramatic use of pigment and color in the service of form, composition, clarity, and legibility, at first relying on cartoon designs, either pounced or incised. Later in the program (under Julius's constant pressure to finish), Michelangelo worked, in an economy of effort, freehand. This somber colorist structured his pictures with little graphic design and succeeded to paint massive novel figures that could be read and appreciated from the chapel floor far below. Not yet finished, Michelangelo's vault already received notoriety in Albertini's 1509 Rome guidebook. Michelangelo completed the vault work between 1508 and 1512 in two campaigns separated in September 1510 and August 1511 by an enforced hiatus. He unveiled the vault on October 31, 1512, one spectator calling it "the language of the Gods." Nonetheless, Hadrian VI (reigned from 1522 to 1523) wanted to destroy the chapel because of Michelangelo's stew of nudes a mere 10 years after the ceiling was finished.

The entire history of humankind is represented in the decoration of the Sistine Chapel from the original act of creation, where God is shown separating light from darkness, through to the seven Angels trumpeting the end of time in *The Last Judgment.* Goethe, who visited the Chapel in 1787, observed: "The era of the Renaissance is encapsulated within its walls. Without having seen the Sistine Chapel one can form no appreciable idea of what one man is capable of achieving."

So many necks are craned for so long during a visit to the Sistina (as was Michelangelo's during his painting) that hardly anyone notices the pavement is an exquisite geometric polychrome marble mosaic of Cosmati work specifically designed to conduct processional currents during mass and precisely arrange the celebrants. A marble choir screen separates the presbytery reserved for unaccredited laity from the clergy's nave.

CONTEMPORARY FUNCTION

The Sistine Chapel is one of the most important places in Christian faith and in art history. Today, the chapel serves the College of Cardinals as a conclave (*cum clavi* or "behind locked doors") to elect a new pope. In the 500 years intervening since its decoration, the frescoes were obfuscated somewhat by varnish, animal glue, and the famously white or black smoke signals of conclave decision making. The chapel underwent an extensive 10-year-long restoration during the 1990s. Thousands of visitors enjoy the Sistine Chapel daily.

—Marc H. Bornstein

FURTHER READING

de Vecchi, P. (Ed.). (1994). *The Sistine Chapel: A glorious restoration.* New York: H. N. Abrams. http://www.kfki.hu/~arthp/tours/sistina/

Gilbert, C. (1994). *Michelangelo: On and off the Sistine ceiling.* New York: George Braziller.

Giudici, V. (1998). *The Sistine Chapel: Its history and masterpieces.* New York: Peter Bedrick.

King, R. (2003). *Michelangelo & the Pope's ceiling.* New York: Walker.

Pietrangeli, C., Chastel, A., Sherman, J., O'Malley, J., de Vecchi, P., Hirst, & M., et al. (1986). *The Sistine Chapel: The art, the history, and the restoration.* New York: Harmony.

SOUL

The notion of *soul* is often evoked in discussions of spirituality. A stirring piece of music or an exceptional artwork can "touch one's soul" with the sense that an unmistakably spiritual experience has taken place. While soul is commonly called upon in spiritual discussions, there are few clear-cut distinctions concerning its meaning. The word *soul* has been religionized in Western culture, and most people associate the soul with theology and religion. In this common usage, soul is often a noun. It is something one has, or a quality one possesses. Soul is the seat of consciousness and awareness, which moves through this life and into the next, whether that is another life, heaven, or oblivion, relatively intact.

Soul has not always been viewed in this way. By contrast, the ancient Greek word for soul, *psyche,* referred to the deepest passions of the human being. The English word *soul* derives from the Old English *sawol* and the Anglo-Saxon *sawal,* words that have to do with breath or life force. Therefore, another way of thinking about soul refers to a human and universal way that we view the world. We experience life through its mythological and metaphorical lens.

Since Descartes set forth the maxim "I think, therefore I am" more than 300 years ago, Western society has elevated rational thought and paid little attention to the soul. But to understand the soul, we have to seek soul out personally and experientially. Soul can be felt when moved by a poem, stirred by music, or touched by a ceremony or symbol. Soul is the deep, empathic resonance that vibrates within us at such moments. The catch of the breath, the lump in the throat, or the tears in the eyes are signs of the soul's presence. Thus the soul can be felt, touched, and known, but it forever resists a Western need for abstract, operational definitions.

Spirit and soul are sometimes seen as being at odds. Spirit is associated with the soaring, limitless experience of heights and expansiveness. It is impersonal and timeless, concerned with the afterlife, cosmic issues, idealistic values and hopes, and universal truths. Soul, on the other hand, is about depth. It is the wondrous approach to daily life that involves us in history and cannot be separated from the body, family, immediate context or mortality. Spirit and soul cannot exist without each other. They are two sides to the same coin of human experience. Most important is a critical view that does not elevate one over the other.

CARING FOR THE SOUL

Thomas Moore focuses on the sacred in his work with soul. Care of the soul is concerned with attending to the small details of everyday life. Unfortunately, soul has been neglected in our fast-paced, superficial culture, leading to "loss of soul." When soul is neglected, it does not just vanish. Instead, it makes its absence known as obsessions, addictions, violence, and loss of meaning.

An important part of spirituality, then, is concerned with caring for soul by becoming attuned to the ways that soul manifests in everyday life. Because soul speaks through images and myth rather than logic and abstraction, it requires one to be aware of its style of communicating. This involves becoming aware of the qualities of soul in one's life, such as subtlety, complexity, ambiguity, and wonder.

Soul making is a term used by many writers throughout history. It implies that soul does not simply exist in stasis must be cultivated in our inner life through imagination. By focusing on the dreams, images, symbols and fantasies produced by soul, we weave meaning through the everyday events of our lives.

There are many ways to nourish the soul. Meditation is popular spiritual practice that crosses numerous religious boundaries. Soul speaks through those quiet moments when the blaring and rushing of the world are set aside. The act of meditation, then, forces a person to quiet their mind and, focus on the soul and listen.

Another way to feed the soul is for people to slow down and look for messages from the soul everywhere, not just in the quiet moments of meditation. This requires one to view the world through symbols, fantasies, and dreams. Every event or detail is mined for the images beyond the literal meaning. This can be encouraged by surrounding oneself with things that are reminiscent of soul, such as artwork, music, or scents.

The creation of rituals also aids in experiencing soul. Rituals use symbolic gestures and patterns to separate the current moment from the bustle of everyday life, allowing soul to be present. Simple acts, such as saying a blessing at mealtime or celebrating rites of passage, make room for soul.

While the richness and meaning provided to life by soul are often positive things, the search for soul is not always peaceful or easy. Often, seeking the soul leads to a Dark Night of the Soul. At some point, a person realizes that life can no longer be lived as it has been.

By enduring times of painful and destructive change, he or she seeks to rediscover inner fire through transformation of body and mind. Many people find direction and comfort in images and rituals taken from religious traditions, such as the death and resurrection of Christ. Others move through the Dark Night with the aid of modern psychotherapy. However, the person is guided, he or she must be willing to move into the dark parts of the soul, where pain, violence, and destruction live. Only then, can he or she learn how to reemerge and live life in a more soulful way.

SUMMARY

Soul is slippery and amorphous. It is felt only in those brief moments when we feel its power or note its absence. Spirituality, however, would lack passion and depth without the touch of soul. It provides the ground from which spirit soars and transcends. The search for soul can be enjoyable or painful, but it is always profoundly moving.

—Sandra R. Kirchner

FURTHER READING

Hillman, J. (1975). *Revisioning psychology.* New York: HarperPerennial.

Lesser, E. (1999). *The new American spirituality: A seeker's guide.* New York: Random House.

Moore, T. (1992). *The care of the soul: A guide for cultivating depth and sacredness in everyday life.* New York: HarperPerennial.

Sardello, R. (1992). *Facing the world with soul.* Hudson, NY: Lindisfarne Press.

SPEECH, ETHICAL

Praying, observing holy days, and engaging in various rites and rituals are obvious components of religious practice, but ethical speech or speech ethics is also a prime arena for expressing a tradition's core beliefs. The ancient teachings of the world's spiritual communities reflect a universal understanding regarding verbal conduct: It can promote well-being, or it can inflict harm. It can lead to the loftiest attainments or make a person fall off the path.

The foundation of ethical speech in any spiritual tradition is the absence of an intention to harm others. The old ditty that sticks and stones may break the bones but words can never hurt is not true. If it were, religious leaders would not exhort their followers to refrain from harsh, malicious, false, or frivolous speech. Although the tongue is soft, it can be sharp as a sword plunged into someone's heart. Sacred texts recognize that words destroy more people than weapons do. While we need to be fairly close by to be shot or knifed, gossip and slander can devastate a person from far away. To paraphrase the Talmud in modern terms, a gossiper in New York can kill someone in New Delhi. The Bible concludes that "Death and life are in the power of the tongue" (Prov. 18:21).

When informed by wisdom and compassion, ethical speech is decent, kind, and respectful as well as beneficial, truthful, and timely. It is also balanced by attentive and open listening. Because the opposite occurs too easily and too often, there are precepts, guidelines, and advice about "guarding the tongue." In general, the preference is for brevity over verbosity. For example, the Buddha counseled that it is better to say a single word that induces peace than to utter a thousand useless words. A Sufi expression recommends that we not say anything until we see that it is worth saying. The Daoist sage Lao-tzu wrote that those who know do not talk whereas those who talk do not know. The Baha'i consider excess speech a deadly poison. Chief Joseph of the Nez Perce said that we do not need many words to speak the truth. Others have recommended that our words not be empty: we should do what we say and say what we mean.

Clear prescriptions about proper and improper use of the mouth, tongue, lips, and ears include speaking the truth. One of the five Buddhist precepts is abstaining from falsehood. One of the 10 biblical commandments is not bearing false witness, for the Lord hates "a lying tongue" (Prov. 6: 16–17). Psalm 34 suggests that if we want to live a life of good fortune, we should keep our lips from deceitful speech. There is also the recognition that lying is a dangerous activity because once a person tells a deliberate untruth, any other misdeed is likely.

Additional guidelines indicate that even if something is true, it is important to consider whether saying it is useful. If it will hurt someone, then expressing it would not be in keeping with spiritual ideals. For instance, those who believe in a Creator God assume that each individual is created in God's image. Therefore, everyone deserves to be treated accordingly: Who would intentionally injure God's creation?

Another criterion for wise speech is choosing the right time. If the truth will fall on deaf ears, there is no point in sharing it. The manner in which we communicate is equally important. No matter how violently someone speaks to us, the Buddha and other spiritual masters have said we should not let that pervert our own speech. Ideally, our voice should be gentle, pleasant, and polite, and our heart should be filled with compassion and friendliness.

Precepts of speech not only help society run more smoothly but also help develop a character based in spiritual values. By avoiding false speech, a person becomes trustworthy and reliable. By eliminating hateful words, she is not divisive but instead promotes friendship, harmony, and concord among others. By not speaking harshly, she is considered courteous, agreeable, and lovable.

Religious "laws" take into account that unwise or unkind speech has a multiple impact. Generally, we think slander affects only the object of it by damaging that person's reputation, livelihood, and maybe even marriage. But Jewish sages conclude that bad-mouthing actually "kills" at least three people. The slanderer demeans not only another but also himself and proves to be untrustworthy. The listener who accepts the slander reaps consequences as well. By making himself a party to evil or unwholesome verbal behavior, he cheapens his own character. Thus ethical speech entails more than what we say; it also includes what we voluntarily listen to. The Talmud teaches that fingers have a pointed shape so that we can put them into the ears to shut out malevolent speech. Spiritual teachers discourage being a party to idle talk because it encourages "tale bearers" and "mischief mongers" that disturb the peace of a community. As the Bible says, "For lack of wood the fire goes out; and where there is no whisperer, quarreling ceases" (Prov. 26:20).

All the major religious traditions agree that everyday speech tends to be inconsequential, superficial, and unrefined chatter or troublemaking, misleading, and spiteful gossip. Christian mystics Meister Eckhart and St. Teresa found talk about anything other than God a waste of a person's precious time and energy. The Buddha similarly instructed his disciples to avoid topics of conversation that do not support attaining enlightenment and instead to engage in discussions about the Dharma (the "Truth").

Ethical speech or speech ethics is a practice that crosses all religious boundaries. It reflects each tradition's teaching on the importance of self-control in developing a virtuous character and learning wisdom. Unrestrained speech is often connected with anger, and anger, with unleashing injustice. It prevents us from fulfilling the highest aspirations of the religion we follow. But, according to James in the New Testament, if we can control the tongue, we are "perfect."

A story in the Talmud, the authoritative body of Jewish tradition, highlights this inherent potential in speech. One day, Rabbi Shimon ben Gamliel asked his servant Tobi to go to the market and buy the best dish he could find. Tobi came home with a tongue. Then the rabbi told him to go and buy the worst dish. Again, Tobi brought back a tongue. When the rabbi asked him why he had bought a tongue both times, he replied that a tongue could be both good and bad. When it is good, it is unsurpassable, but when it is bad, there is nothing worse than an evil tongue (*Vayikra Rabbah* 33).

—Mirka Knaster

FURTHER READING

Baker, W. R. (1995). *Personal speech: Ethics in the Epistle of James.* Wissenschaftliche Untersuchungen zum Neuen Testament: 2. Reihe: 68. Tübingen: J. C. B. Mohr (Paul Siebeck).

Baker, W. R. (1996). *Sticks and stones: The discipleship of our speech.* Downers Grove, IL: InterVarsity Press.

Gunaratana, B. H. (2001). Skillful Speech. In *Eight mindful steps to happiness: Walking the Buddha's path* (pp. 91–108). Boston: Wisdom Publications.

Pliskin, Z. (1975). *Guard your tongue: A practical guide to the laws of Loshon Hora, based on Chofetz Chaim.* Brooklyn, NY: Bnay Yakov Publications.

Right Speech (*sammā vācā*). http://www.accesstoinsight.org/ptf/samma-vaca.html (revised 10 Oct 2003).

Telushkin, J. (1996). *Words that hurt, words that heal: How to choose words wisely and well.* New York: Quill/William Morrow.

SPIRITUAL DEVELOPMENT OF CHILDREN AND YOUTH: BIBLICAL DESCRIPTIONS

Though few in number, there are enough biblical accounts of child and adolescent experiences to formulate a biblical perspective on the spiritual development of children and youth. In particular, the accounts of Joseph, Samuel, David, Mary, John the Baptist, and

Jesus show us that the biblical chroniclers considered preadult experiences to be significant and instructive for future generations—particularly for their showing God to be active in the lives of young people. The message of the biblical chroniclers seems to be that the spiritual experiences of the young prepare them for the challenges and responsibilities of adulthood and that adults have a responsibility to nurture and direct youth so that youth respond to God's call. Three examples of childhood experiences and three of experiences in adolescence will suffice to make this message clear.

THE CHILDHOOD EXPERIENCES OF SAMUEL, JOHN THE BAPTIST, AND JESUS

The childhood experiences of Samuel in the Old Testament and John the Baptist and Jesus in the New Testament affirm that youth are called to respond to the divine presence as it is revealed in and through their formative years:

"And the boy Samuel continued to grow in stature and in favor with the Lord and with men" (1 Sam. 2:26).

"And the child (John) grew and became strong in spirit; and he lived in the desert until he appeared publicly to Israel" (Luke 1:80).

"And Jesus grew in wisdom and stature and in favor with God and men" (Luke 2:52).

The accounts of the childhood experiences of Samuel, John the Baptist, and Jesus depict spiritual experience not as an end in itself but as preparation for full adult participation in the community of faith and society. Also, and as the preceding quotes make clear, these stories suggest that for the biblical chroniclers, *growth* refers not to physical growth but to spiritual growth or development. Samuel grows in stature, John the Baptist in strength, and Jesus in wisdom—but all three (stature, strength, and wisdom) have a central spiritual meaning.

The biblical accounts also make clear that parents and adult mentors play central roles in nurturing the spiritual development of the young. Hannah, Elkanah, and Eli superintend young Samuel's spiritual development. Elizabeth and Zechariah promote John's intense relationship with God, and Mary, Joseph, and a number of teachers set the stage for Jesus' adult life as a servant of God.

These accounts, though similar in important respects, offer different and complementary principles regarding the support needed for children to develop spiritually. In the case of Samuel, the message is that formative religious observance and activity can set the stage for children's ability to receive divine revelation, guidance, and direction. The message is that mystical experience can come to children provided they have prepared themselves or been prepared to receive the divine call.

Samuel's childhood is spent in the Temple where he serves as an apprentice to Eli the high priest (1 Sam. 1:18). In both Jewish and Christian traditions, children are to be encouraged to participate in religious observances and worship. The practical experience gained enables the testing and development of a child's gifts and skills. Accordingly, Samuel is permitted to serve as a "boy wearing a linen ephod" even before he experiences the voice of God.

In the famous account of Samuel's hearing God's call (1 Sam. 3:1–18), the chronicler indicates that "Samuel did not yet know the Lord: the word of the Lord had not yet been revealed to him" (1 Sam. 3:7). Acting as a spiritual director, Eli counsels Samuel on how to respond to God's call—showing that adult mentors provide needed support in the spiritual development of the young by helping them understand and respond to God's call.

The biblical account of Samuel's childhood also confirms the Jewish and Christian conviction that God seeks to bless the development of children who dedicate their lives to fulfilling the divine purpose. 1 Samuel's depiction of Samuel's development concludes thusly, "The Lord was with Samuel as he grew up, and he let none of his words fall to the ground" (1 Sam. 3:19).

The New Testament's account of Jesus' development illustrates additional biblical principles of spirituality in childhood. The gospel of Matthew, in seeking to promote the Christian claim that Jesus is the fulfillment of Jewish Messianic expectations (Matt. 1:22–23; 2:5–23), locates Jesus' spiritual development in childhood within the larger development of Israel as the people of God. The events during Jesus' infancy recapitulate Israel's formative Genesis and Exodus experience—both in the nativity event and in the flight from Egypt in response to the threat of being killed by King Herod (Matt. 2:13–23). The message here is that a child's spiritual development takes place within the context of the spiritual development of a child's family, community, or people. Developmental themes are, then, bequeathed to children by parents, extended family, ancestors, and whole cultures and nations. As a result, children are provided the possibility of living these themes out in new and creative ways.

Luke's account of Jesus' childhood development focuses on two experiences at the Temple in Jerusalem–the epicenter for Israel's spirituality. In the first (Luke 2:21–40), Jesus undergoes ritualistic purification according to his family and community's religious tradition–so that he might identify with his people and prepare himself for a lifetime of consecrated service. The role of the elder Simeon is highlighted. Simeon prophesizes that "This child is destined to cause the falling and rising of many in Israel, and to be a sign that will be spoken against, so that the thoughts of many hearts will be revealed" (Luke 2:34–35).

Twelve years later, in the second Temple episode, Jesus is no longer a passive character. Years of study in his faith have made it possible for Jesus to actively participate in the rigorous give and take typical of rabbinic study of scripture. According to Luke, the spiritual development of Jesus was, then, supported by his having been schooled. The boy Jesus remains behind in Jerusalem and is later found by his parents "in the temple courts, sitting among the teachers, listening to them and asking them questions" (Luke 2:46). As an adult, Jesus would be at odds with most of his fellow Jewish teachers and leaders, but in this account, he willingly submits to his teachers' authority. They mentor him by answering his questions—which in Jewish tradition is a pathway toward wisdom. They also critique his grasp of the faith (Luke 2:47).

This second Temple story also eludes to yet another biblical message about childhood spirituality, namely, a message about obedience. From a biblical perspective, obedience is a precondition for spiritual development. Lest we think that Jesus' staying behind in Jerusalem was an act of disobedience, the biblical account states that Jesus returned to Nazareth with his parents and "was obedient to them" (Luke 2:51). This message about the importance of children being obedient is found throughout the Old and New Testaments (see Hebrews 4:6, for example). Through being obedient to parents and elders children and youth manifest humility and a desire to learn from those who are further along in their spiritual development. Accordingly, Jesus' willingness to obey his parents indicates his acceptance of personal responsibility for his spiritual development. Later on, as an adult, his willingness to obey God constituted a central indicator of his spiritual maturity.

> And being found in appearance as a man, he humbled himself and became obedient to death—even death on a cross! Therefore God exalted him to the highest place and gave him the name that is above every name, that at the name of Jesus every knee should bow, in heaven and on earth and under the earth, and every tongue confess that Jesus Christ is Lord, to the glory of God the Father" (Phil. 2:8–11).

> During the days of Jesus' life on earth, he offered up prayers and petitions with loud cries and tears to the one who could save him from death, and he was heard because of his reverent submission. Although he was a son, he learned obedience from what he suffered and, once made perfect, he became the source of eternal salvation for all who obey him. (Heb. 5:7–9)

ADOLESCENT SPIRITUAL DEVELOPMENT: LESSONS FROM THE ACCOUNTS OF JOSEPH, DAVID, AND MARY

Adolescence as a discreet stage in which young people engage in formal education and seek to define who they are in relation to others is largely a construct of modern derivation. However, three biblical accounts of adolescents are consistent with the modern view. As in the accounts of Samuel, John the Baptist, and Jesus, these additional biblical accounts embody principles inherent in the Jewish and Christian understanding of spirituality in youth.

The Genesis account of Joseph's development commences with the observation that he is a "young man of seventeen" (Gen. 37:2). His being his father's favorite child provokes jealousy among his siblings, and this jealousy is exacerbated by Joseph's sharing his dreams (Gen. 37:3–11).

Three observations regarding the biblical perspective on adolescent spiritual development can be gleaned from this account. First, the fact that Joseph received dreams from God is significant. In ancient Israel, dreams constituted one way to hear the divine voice. In this account, then, we find once again that the biblical perspective sees God relating to youth in the same way God relates to adults.

The second observation is that the forces that propel adolescents' spiritual development are often beyond their understanding and control. Joseph's faith in God enables him to negotiate his brothers' betrayal and its aftermath, even though he will not understand the dynamics underlying the betrayal, until he is much older (see Gen. 45:5–8; 50:19–21).

The third observation is about the naïveté of youth. The interplay between Joseph's naïveté and his spiritual experience deserves special attention. What if Joseph had been more reticent about sharing his dreams? What if he had shared his dreams only with his father—whom the story indicates would have considered his experience in a positive light? If this had happened, Joseph's spiritual development would undoubtedly have looked quite different from what it was.

The story of David gives us yet another window on the biblical perspective on youth's spirituality. According to biblical tradition, David was only 30 when he assumed the throne of Israel (2 Sam. 5:4), but years before he had been tested when he faced the awesome challenge of confronting the Philistine warrior, Goliath. At the time of this challenge, David's exact age is unknown, but it is likely that he was in his late teens—old enough that he could assume authority over others in military service (1 Sam. 18:5) but still youthful enough to be considered "only a boy" by both Saul (1 Sam. 17:35) and Goliath (1 Sam. 17:42). Furthermore, although he is old enough to oversee his father's flocks, he is not old enough to officially join the Israelite army (1 Sam. 17: 12–14).

Unlike in the case of Joseph, there is no indication that God communicated directly to the youthful David. Although he experienced himself as being anointed by God, through Samuel (1 Sam. 16:13), David does not appeal to this anointment or to any other mystical experience when he responds to Saul's skepticism by saying he can face Goliath. Instead, David appeals to past events in which God empowered him to succeed. "The Lord who delivered me from the paw of the lion and the paw of the bear will deliver me from the hand of this Philistine," he says, and Saul responds, "Go, and the Lord be with you" (1 Sam. 17:37).

In preparation for facing Goliath, David shuns offers of military garb designed for adult warriors. He relies instead on the clothing and weapons appropriate to his age and experience (1 Sam. 17:38–40). The message here may be that youth need to equip themselves for spiritual tasks in ways appropriate to their age.

A third biblical example of the spirituality of youth occurs with Jesus' mother, Mary. Most New Testament scholars believe that Mary was a teenager when she became pregnant with Jesus. Her youthfulness stands in contrast to Elizabeth's being past the normal age for childbearing (Luke 1:7). If we assume this to be the case, then hers is the most prominent New Testament account of youthful spirituality—with the exception of Jesus' Temple experience when he was 12.

In the Christian tradition, Mary has long been acknowledged as offering a profoundly positive role model for those wishing to be faithful to God's call. This is shown particularly in her response to the angel Gabriel who announces the news of Jesus' impending birth. In spite of her natural fear, Mary willingly processes Gabriel's message. In fact, she demonstrates incredible poise and maturity as she questions the angel (Luke 1:26–37). Furthermore, she humbly submits to God's will even though it must have been, at the time, mystifying. She says, "I am the Lord's servant. May it be as you have said" (Luke 1:38).

In the Bible, then, we find children and youth depicted as developing spiritually inasmuch as they respond to or are led to respond to God's call and inasmuch as they are obedient to parents and teachers. In the Bible, we see children and youth capable of having significant spiritual experiences that help them develop into adults who can face life with courage, compassion, wisdom, and humility and who can continue to develop spiritually.

—Rev. Dr. Lee B. Spitzer

SPIRITUALITY, CONTEMPORARY APPROACHES TO DEFINING

An examination of research on spirituality yields three distinct approaches to the relationship between spirituality and religiosity. There are researchers who view spirituality as an integral part of religiosity; those who view spirituality as separate from religiosity; and those who view spirituality as synonymous with religiosity. Among other reasons, such as epistemological and ontological changes that Western culture and civilization are undergoing in the postmodern era, the recent increase in articles and studies on spirituality may well be a consequence of diffuse and one-dimensional definitions of religious and secular concepts in the modern world. The existence of these diverse trends and definitions epitomizes the bewilderment around the concept of spirituality and attests to the need to widen the scope of the definitions of spirituality.

Spirituality is largely associated with religiosity, as it addresses the connection between the human and the sublime, between the concrete and the abstract, and between man and God. As such, spirituality is typically connected with conventional measures of religiosity like closeness to God, institutional beliefs, and religious practices. However, spirituality is also recognized as an expression of human longing to approach a supreme entity or power situated beyond human control and grasp, thereby expressing the existential uniqueness of humans over animals. Spirituality is realized in abstract aspects of human life that constitute part of one's existential secular or religious being.

Studies that deal with religiosity have mainly focused on behavioral aspects of its manifestations. Focus on behavior clearly limits the scope of religiosity as a concept, leaving uncharted territory in the human spiritual world that defies positivistic definition. Moreover, it gives rise to a monolithic system of dichotomous definitions in which one who does not conform to the behavioral patterns labeled "religious" is defined as "secular" and vice versa. Modern society, however, endorses differentiation. Spirituality may be manifested among religious and secular people alike, thereby demanding a redefinition of the concept of secularity, not as the absence of religion but rather as an independent entity that embodies various realms of spirituality.

Spirituality is one of the ways in which people construct knowledge and meaning; spiritual identity is regarded as the framework within which the ultimate questions of life are meditated. Indeed, spirituality is regarded in the literature as a universal human capacity that is mainly related to well-being. This takes on a broader meaning when spirituality is examined in the context of the relatively new branch in psychology known as *positive psychology.* The aim of positive psychology is to transform psychology from a preoccupation with repairing the bad things in life, to an emphasis on a salutogenic—health-promoting—perspective of human existence. Spirituality is related to hope and happiness and, therefore, can be seen as an integral part of positive psychology.

Most research on spirituality has been conducted in the fields of psychology and sociology of religion and is based on empirical studies. Only a small part of this research addresses the philosophical aspect or contributes to the construction of a conceptual theoretical framework. Much of this research is based on Fowler's (1981) stage theory of faith development, which rests on cognitive psychology. Fowler's theory was intended to describe religious development, but it was subsequently adopted by researchers in the field of spirituality because no other theories were available. However, adopting a theory from research on religiosity again assumes that religiosity is identical to spirituality. Several scholars found that the most spiritual are, by a variety of measures, those who are also the most religious. In contrast, other scholars found that most of those who view themselves as spiritual do so by default; they are less religious rather than more spiritual.

A discussion of spirituality needs to be based on the premise that spirituality epitomizes postmodernity. In a postmodernist era, where sorrow, despair, alienation, and depression dominate, spirituality can shed new light and convey a new message. What characterizes the postmodern era is the disappointment with rationalism and the preference for the contextual cultural factor over the rational. The expansion of research on spirituality seems to be a direct outcome of the secularization process in the postmodern era, accompanied by the revival of the privatization and individualization of religiosity. Scholars have found that spirituality is connected to the affective, the rational, the cognitive, and the unconscious symbolic domains.

The spirituality movement is often viewed as part of a sociocultural trend defined by both deinstitutionalization and individualization. The deconstructionist trend of the meta-narrative and differentiation processes creates fundamental changes in the scope of religiosity. The trend toward spirituality seems to challenge the coherence of religiosity and creates anxiety among researchers and educators, especially in America. Peter Berger (1979) has stated that pluralism is a threat to religiosity. Pargament claims that the spiritual movement may be seen as a sign that "something is missing in the way religion is currently defined and practiced" (1999, pp. 6–7).

If secular people define themselves also as spiritual and if secularism is viewed as the opposite pole to religiosity on a continuum (i.e., less religious means more secular), then additional dimensions (beyond an absence of religiosity) are needed to conceptualize secularity. Moreover, perhaps if attention is given to the parameters for measuring secularity and religiosity from a more broad and diverse perspective, this will open a new way to better understanding spirituality in the modern era.

—Zehavit Gross

FURTHER READING

Ahmadi Lewin, F. (2001). Investigating the religious and spiritually oriented coping strategies in the Swedish context: A review of literature and directions for future research. *Illness, Crisis & Loss, 9*(4), 336–356.

Alexander, H. A. (2001). *Reclaiming goodness: Education and the spiritual quest.* Notre Dame, IN: University of Notre Dame Press.

Bellah, R. N., Madsen, R., Sullivan, W. M., Swidler, A., & Tipton, S. M. (1985). *Habits of the heart: Individualism and commitment in American life.* Berkeley, CA: University of California Press.

Benson, P. L. (1997). Spirituality and the adolescent journey: Reclaiming children and youth. *Journal of Emotional & Behavioral Problems, 5*(4), 206–209.

Berger, P. L. (1979). *The heretical imperative: Contemporary possibilities of religious affirmation.* Garden City, NY: Anchor Press.

Bridges, L. J., & Anderson Moore, K. (2002). Religious involvement and children's well-being: What research tells us (and what it doesn't). *Child Trends Research Brief.*

Bruce, S. (2002). *God is dead: Secularization in the west.* Oxford: Blackwell.

Cimino, R., & Lattin, D. (1998). *Shopping for faith: American religion in the new millennium.* San Francisco: Jossey-Bass.

Fowler, J. W. (1981). *Stages of faith: The psychology of human development and the quest for meaning.* New York: Harper & Row.

Gordon, P. A., Feldman, D., Crose, R., Schoen, E., Griffing, G., & Shankar, J. (2002). The role of religious beliefs in coping with chronic illness. *Counseling and Values, 46*(3), 162–174.

Gross, Z. (2001). My mind is my God—Images of God and self definition. In H.-G. Ziebertz (Ed.), *Imagining God: Empirical explorations from an international perspective.* Munster: Lit Verlag.

Halford, J. M. (1999). Longing for the sacred in schools: A conversation with Nel Noddings. *Educational Leadership, 56*(4), 28–32.

Hill, P. C., & Pargament, K. I. (2003). Advances in the conceptualization and measurement of religion and spirituality: Implications for physical and mental health research. *American Psychologist, 58*(1), 64–74.

Marler, P. L., & Hadaway, C. K. (2002). "Being religious" or "being spiritual" in America: A zero-sum proposition? *Journal for the Scientific Study of Religion, 41*(2), 289–300.

Pargament, K. I. (1999). The psychology of religion and spirituality? Yes and no. *The International Journal for the Psychology of Religion, 9*(1), 3–16.

Poll, J. B., & Smith, T. B. (2003). The spiritual self: Toward a conceptualization of spiritual identity development. *Journal of Psychology and Theology, 31*(2), 129–142.

Roof, W. C. (2000). *Contemporary American religion.* New York: Macmillan.

Scott, R. O. (2001). Are you religious or are you spiritual?: A look in the mirror. *Spirituality and Health* (Spring), 26–28.

Seligman, M. E. P., & Csikszentmihalyi, M. (2002). Positive psychology: An introduction. *American Psychologist, 55*(1), 5–14.

Sheridan, D. P. (1986). Discerning difference: A taxonomy of culture, spirituality, and religion. *The Journal of Religion, 66*(1), 37–45.

Smith, C. (2003). Theorizing religious effects among American adolescents. *Journal for the Scientific Study of Religion, 42*(1), 17–30.

Smith, C., Denton, M. L., Faris, R., & Regnerus, M. (2002). Mapping American adolescent religious participation. *Journal for the Scientific Study of Religion, 41*(4), 597–612.

Stewart, D. L. (2002). The role of faith in the development of an integrated identity: A qualitative study of Black students at a white college. *Journal of College Student Development, 43*(4), 579–596.

Tisdell, E. J. (2000). Spirituality and emancipatory adult education in women adult educators for social change. *Adult Education Quarterly, 50*(4), 308–335.

Weber, L. J., & Cummings, A. L. (2003). Relationships among spirituality, social support, and childhood maltreatment in university students. *Counseling and Values, 47*(2), 82–95.

Wong-McDonald, A., & Gorsuch, R. L. (2000). Christianity or superstition? Effects on locus of control and well-being. (ERIC no: ED473725).

Zinnbauer, B. J., Pargament, K. I., Cole, B., Rye, M. S., Butter, E. M., Belavich, T. G., et al. (1997). Religion and spirituality: Unfuzzying the fuzzy. *Journal of the Scientific Study of Religion, 36*(4) 549–564.

SPIRITUALS, AFRICAN AMERICAN

The roots of the Black religious experience can be found in the undeniable musical art form commonly called *the spiritual.* The best estimate of the earliest appearance of the spiritual is 1760. Prior to this date, slaves created and sang early forms of American folk music. The first religious music of the antebellum slaves was the spiritual. The spirituals helped to unite the descendants of various African tribes by singing about their common experience as slaves. The spirituals gave them a sense of identity and stirred in them a hope for freedom. The spirituals were also significant for young slaves because they could not read. By listening to the songs, children learned about the stories of the Bible and the faith experiences of the adults. For the young slaves, singing spirituals was their first introduction to the life of faith. Spirituals are still sung throughout African-American churches, homes, and communities.

Spirituals are meant to be communicative. Some emphasize the coded meaning of spirituals while others note the other-worldly emphasis communicated in spirituals. Whatever interpretations may be given to the message and meaning of spirituals, it is important to remember that the music of spirituals was a means of survival, and a cultural and theological cry of a people. Spirituals express the social and theological beliefs of the slaves. The songs nurtured a sense of faith and hope in an oppressed people, which were passed on to subsequent generations. To understand the significant role spirituals played in the social and religious life of the slave community, it is necessary to investigate the characteristics and nature of the music.

Rhythmic. Just as rhythm is the fundamental trait of African music, so is rhythm the fundamental trait of the African-American spiritual. Rhythm varies across the extensive range of spiritual types. Some are slow and deliberate, others are driving and pulsating, and others possess the beat of elation and celebration. The rhythm helps to express the range of emotions felt by the persons singing the spiritual.

Antiphonal. There is a "call and response" mode found in most spirituals. The authentic spiritual form is not given to solo performance; spirituals are mainly choral in form and structure. There is frequently a soloist that establishes the melody or lead line. The soloist is then responsible for cueing the group into various points of the song. The group takes over with blending voices and improvised harmony.

Participatory. Because of the choral and antiphonal nature of the spiritual, singing is a community event. Everyone is expected to participate. The flexible, improvisational structure of the spirituals gave them the capacity to fit an individual slave's specific experience into the consciousness of the group. One slave's sorrow or joy became everyone's through song. Singing the spirituals was both an intensely personal and vividly communal experience in which an individual received consolation for sorrow and gained a heightening of joy because his or her experience was shared.

Given to Improvisation. The spirituals had easy, repetitive melodies that allowed for spontaneity in the lyrics. The lyrics for the spirituals would change, based upon the daily life experiences of the slaves. The spirituals communicated the slaves' feelings about their plight.

One famous slave spiritual was, "Don' Let Nobody Turn You Round."

During the racial confrontations in Birmingham in 1963, the Blacks interspersed such verses as "Don' let segregation," etc., or "Don' let no jailhouse," etc., which reflected in modern times how easily the spiritual form is given to spontaneity and situational creation of new lyrics.

Repetitive. In most spirituals, the melodic lines and lyric lines repeat with only slight variation. In the slave community, this melodic and lyric repetition helped to enhance the life expectancy of the spiritual because it served as a built-in memory facility for those who could not read. Most slaves could not read, so the stories of their faith, common experience, and heritage had to be learned through memorization.

Deep Biblicism. The lyrics for the majority of spirituals are drawn directly from the Bible, with considerable attention given to Old Testament imagery. In many instances, one may find Old Testament and New Testament references within the same song. In the spirituals, a sense of sacred time operates in which the present is extended backward so that characters, scenes, and events from the Bible become dramatically alive and present. When no direct Bible reference is identifiable, the substance of the truth proclaimed in a spiritual is at least biblical in implication. Needless to say, the spiritual is the primary source for communicating the stories of the Bible to the members of the community.

Eternality of Message. One of the most profound traits of the spirituals is that many of them carry a timeless message that fits the contemporary human circumstance. The message speaks not only to the slave condition out of which it was born, but also to the human condition at many points in history, giving it a quality of universality. The message of the spirituals connects the experiences of people across time and place.

All of these characteristics obviously contributed to the unique nature of the Black spiritual which, in turn, became the root for all subsequent Black music. But the greatest contributions of the spirituals can be found in the purpose they served to give identity and dignity to the African-American slave community, to pass on the stories of faith and heritage to future generations, and to give hope that there was a better life awaiting those who suffered injustice.

Today the spirituals are still being sung in African-American churches because they are such an integral part of African-American history. The children who hear these songs connect with the experiences of people across time and place—from the captivity to the Jews to the bondage of the slaves—and are inspired by their courage, faith, and hope. Children also learn significant lessons about life from the spirituals. They learn how to treat others, and they learn how to cope with the difficulties of life.

—*Karen G. Massey*

See also Gospel Music

FURTHER READING

Lovell, J. (1972). *Black song: The forge and the flame.* New York: Macmillan.

McCall, E. (1986). *Black church lifestyles.* Nashville, TN: Broadman Press.

Mapson, W. (1984). *The ministry of music in the Black Church.* Valley Forge, PA: Judson Press.

Raboteau, A. (1978). *Slave religion.* New York: Oxford University Press.

Walker, W. T. (1979). *Somebody's calling my name.* Valley Forge, PA: Judson Press.

ST. AUGUSTINE.

See Confessions of St. Augustine

ST. BONAVENTURE

A classic figure in Western Christianity, St. Bonaventure was born in Italy in 1221. The period of Bonaventure's life, 1221–1274, spans the time in history known as the high Middle Ages. He entered the Order of Friars Minor, also known as the *Franciscans,* in 1238 or 1243; the exact date is uncertain. He gained the title of the "Second Founder" of the Franciscan community because of the scope and depth of his commitment to the vision of the first founder, St. Francis of Assisi. Bonaventure's spiritual leadership within the Franciscan community, spiritual teachings, and intellectual contributions on the relationship of philosophy to Christian theology eventually led to his canonization as a saint of the Catholic Church in 1482 and his being named in 1588 by Pope Sixtus V a Doctor of the Church. Bonaventure's ability to give the mystical movement begun by St. Francis of Assisi a solid theological and psychological basis gave rise to the additional names of the Seraphic Doctor and Doctor Devotus.

Bonaventure's baptismal name was John, after his father Giovanni de Fidanza. While there is no formal biography of St. Bonaventure and limited details of his youth have been preserved, there is a significant legend, which offers an explanation as to why John became Bonaventure. Aspects of the legend appear in Bonaventure's own writings, which tell the story that while yet a child, John was preserved from death due to the intercession of St. Francis of Assisi. When presented to St. Francis for the healing blessing, Francis is said to have exclaimed, *O buona ventura,* meaning "oh, good fortune." There is no evidence that this event actually occurred, but the change in name foreshadowed the good fortune St. Bonaventure's legacy has been to Franciscan spirituality and Christian theology.

Three major trends impacted the 13th century, the time in which Bonaventure lived. First, the Crusades brought Christianity into contact with Islamic culture causing Christianity to reflect on itself as it encountered other worldviews. Second, the recovery of the complete works of the great philosopher Aristotle offered a scientific philosophical system perceived by some as superior to that of the great father of Western Christianity, St. Augustine (354–430 C.E.). Third, the rise of new types of monastic orders, preaching and mendicant—meaning living a life of radical poverty—generated tensions between the religious and secular professors at the famous University of Paris, where Dominican Thomas Aquinas (1225–1274) and Franciscan Bonaventure (1221–1274) studied and taught side by side as scholars and friends. These factors brought a new worldview and culture to Europe that had to be addressed by university scholars and theologians such as Bonaventure.

In the Middle Ages it was believed that reason and faith existed to interpret each other. Christian theologians and philosophers followed the motto: *credo ut intelligam,* I believe in order to know. The interplay between reason and faith, intellect and will, has been called "the eternal conversation." This was a debate that absorbed the great minds of Bonaventure's time. There were those at Paris questing for a self-sufficient philosophy without concerns for the claims of faith. Intelligence, for Bonaventure, was always at the service of devotion. God acts in the midst of human history and experience. The gift of reason is meant to help interpret God's ongoing revelation for the purpose of giving meaning to human living.

Bonaventure's public teaching at the University of Paris ended in 1257 when he was elected at 36 as Minister General of the Franciscans. His call away from university life removed his distinctive influence on Christian scholasticism and thus enabled Thomas Aquinas's favored reliance on the metaphysical system of Aristotle to overshadow Bonaventure's more experiential convictions about knowledge as the journey into God.

Beginning in the late 20th century, Bonaventure's writings have experienced resurgence. Interest in existentialism, process theology, creation-centered theology, Franciscan spirituality, and new approaches to a spiritual vision of the human person have brought St. Bonaventure to the fore in the contemporary quest for meaning.

—Avis Clendenen

FURTHER READING

Cousins, E. (Trans.). (1978). *Bonaventure.* New York: Paulist Press.

Etzkorn, G. (Trans). (2000). *St. Bonaventure: Selected writings of theology and spirituality.* St. Bonaventure, NY: Franciscan Institute Press.

Hayes, Z. (1977). *The hidden center: Spirituality and speculative Christology in St. Bonaventure.* Chicago: Franciscan Herald Press.

ST. IGNATIUS OF LOYOLA

Ignatius of Loyola was a 16th-century Spanish spiritual visionary who founded one of the largest Roman Catholic religious orders of men in the Catholic Church known as the *Society of Jesus* (*Societas Jesu*) in 1540. Members of the Society of Jesus are often referred to as *Jesuits* (initials S. J.), a term of 15th century origin, which means one who frequently uses the name of Jesus. This worldwide religious order continues into the present day with more than 20,000 men serving in 112 countries on six continents. The priests and brothers who profess religious vows of celibacy, poverty, obedience, and service to God's people carry on Ignatius's apostolic and spiritual work in almost every country of the world. Ignatius made one of the most distinguishing contributions to Christian spirituality through the development of the *Spiritual Exercises,* an organized method of prayer and practice aimed at deeper self-understanding and relationship with God. He was canonized a saint of the Catholic Church by Pope Gregory XV in 1662 and ever since has had a lasting influence on religious thought and spiritual practice.

Ignatius was born in 1491 in the castle of Loyola to a wealthy family from a Basque province in Spain. He was the youngest son of 13 children. Raised as a nobleman, Ignatius was extravagant and consumed with a desire for personal glory. He was fond of gambling, swordplay, and all the activities of the knighthood of his time. He experienced a turning point in his life in 1521. Ignatius was a 30-year-old soldier defending the fortress of the town of Pamplona against the French, who claimed the territory as their own against Spain, when he was seriously wounded in both legs by a cannonball. He was forced to convalesce in the castle of Loyola, where he underwent several operations without anesthetic to repair his serious and disfiguring wounds. It was an injury from which he never fully recovered. The lengthy recuperation forced the active nobleman and warrior Ignatius to rest and reflect. The only books available in the castle were a four-volume life of Christ and the lives of the saints. Serious reading was new to Ignatius and with it he experienced a journey into his previously unexplored interior life. He took notes in a little book about his inner experiences. This was the beginning of his religious conversion, and eventually the little notebook would become *The Spiritual Exercises of St. Ignatius.*

The drama of his conversion led Ignatius to abandon his old desires for conquest, romance, and worldly power. Recovered from his wounds, though limping, Ignatius decided to make a pilgrimage to Jerusalem to walk along the way that Jesus walked. His journey took him toward Barcelona, the point of embarkation for Rome, where pilgrims sought permission to visit the Holy Land. Ignatius stopped first, however, in Manressa where he stayed in a cave outside of the town. While intending to stay only a short time, Ignatius was drawn into the deeper caverns of his own interior life. He experienced an encounter with God—a vision—that would direct him to embrace the truth that life is the journey of "finding God in all things." This grace, finding God in all things, remains a core virtue of Jesuit spirituality. It was in the literal and metaphorical cave at Manressa that Ignatius began to detail his own experience of spiritual awakening and conversion, and he drew on these in articulating the *Spiritual Exercises* that became the heart of Ignatian spirituality and mission.

After completing his pilgrimage to the Holy Land, Ignatius set his mind to a serious study of theology and philosophy. He continued to share his insights with those who were open to experiencing the ways of spiritual growth he directed. Twice he was investigated by the Spanish Inquisition and even imprisoned for a time. He eventually made his way to the University of Paris where he met Francis Xavier and Peter Faber. Under the influence of Ignatius's spiritual exercises, they were drawn into Ignatius's vision and eventually assisted him in founding the Society of Jesus.

In 1537, at the age of 45, Ignatius was ordained a priest. Two years later, the Society of Jesus was founded. Ignatius and his two companions decided to go to Rome and place themselves at the disposal of the pope. Pope Paul III approved the formation of the *Societas Jesu* and the wounded warrior mystic Ignatius watched his small company grow to a thousand members before his death in 1556.

Centuries later, people continue to find meaning in following the spiritual path known as the *Spiritual Exercises of St. Ignatius.* The structure of the Ignatian exercises facilitates spiritual growth by helping people to develop prayerful, self-reflective attitudes and skills to discern the workings of the creative and destructive forces busy within each human heart. Ignatius grew to view each human being as a spiritual seeker on the pilgrimage called life.

—Avis Clendenen

See also Mysticism; St. Ignatius, Spiritual Exercises of

FURTHER READING

Dugan, I., & Clendenen, A. (2004). *Love is all around in disguise: Meditations for spiritual seekers.* New York: Chiron Publications.

O'Neal, N. (2002). A biography of Ignatius Loyola. http://www.luc.edu/jesuit/ignatius.bio.html

Patterson, M. (2001). Chivalry inspired a courtier saint, *National Catholic Reporter, 37*(24), 13–16.

ST. IGNATIUS, SPIRITUAL EXERCISES OF

Ignatius was born at the castle of Loyola in Spain in 1491. He founded the Society of Jesus, one of the largest religious orders in the Catholic Church in 1540. Ignatius of Loyola has had a lasting influence on Christian spirituality and was canonized a saint by Pope Gregory XV in 1662. Members of the Society of Jesus are commonly known as the *Jesuits.* Today there are more than 20,000 Jesuits ministering in 112 countries. Their formation as Jesuit priests and brothers, as well as their distinctive spiritual ministry is rooted in the *Spiritual Exercises* of St. Ignatius.

Ignatius had little spiritual inclination in his early life. He was raised a nobleman and warrior and enjoyed a rather self-indulgent life of an aristocrat of his time. When he was 30 years old and engaged in a battle defending the fortress of his town of Pamplona, Spain, against the French, he was seriously wounded by a cannonball. Both his legs were injured in the assault and surgeries without the benefit of anesthesia did not produce a complete healing. He was forced into a long recovery in the castle of Loyola where his only activity was reading. The only books available to him in the castle were a four-volume life of Christ and the lives of the saints. Serious reading was new to Ignatius and with it he experienced a journey into previously unexplored regions of his imagination. In place of his former dreams of being a victorious warrior and courtier of princesses, he found himself identifying with the stories of Holy Scripture and imaging himself in the gospel stories or taking on the spiritual quests of one of the saints, which he was reading about during his long convalescence. This was the beginning of his religious conversion, initial experiences of contemplation, and his discovery of spiritual discernment, or discernment of spirits, which is at the heart of his *Spiritual Exercises.*

Gradually Ignatius felt called to abandon his former ways and old desires for fame and fortune. When he was sufficiently recovered from his wounds, though limping, Ignatius decided to make a pilgrimage to Jerusalem to walk the way that Jesus walked. His journey took him toward Barcelona, the point of embarkation for Rome, where pilgrims sought permission to visit the Holy Land. Ignatius stopped first, however, in Manressa where he stayed in a cave outside of town. While intending to stay only a short time, Ignatius was drawn into the deeper caverns of his own interior life. He experienced an encounter with God—a vision—that would direct him to embrace the truth that life is the journey of "finding God in all things." This grace, finding God in all things, has remained a core virtue in Jesuit spirituality for 450 years.

It was in the literal and metaphorical cave at Manressa that Ignatius began to detail his own experience of spiritual awakening and conversion. The little notebook that he carried from his healing time in the castle of Loyola began to expand to become a book, *Spiritual Exercises,* which is the heart of Ignatian spirituality.

Ignatius composed and revised the spiritual exercises over a 25-year period prior to its first publication in 1548. The *Spiritual Exercises* of St. Ignatius contain instructions, admonitions, annotations, examinations, warnings, methods, prayers, meditations, and other "exercises" designed to lead one to virtue, discernment of good and evil spirits operating in one's life, deeper renewal in faith, clearer sense of direction in life, and personal and social transformation through love.

Ordinarily, the *Spiritual Exercises* are experienced in the context of a 30-day retreat, although there are now many variations of experiencing the *Exercises.* For example, Jesuit Creighton University in Omaha, Nebraska provides an online Ignatian retreat. In all instances, following the spiritual path laid out by St. Ignatius through involvement in a series of exercises is meant to assist people in following a path, which leads them to greater self-awareness, a felt appreciation for God's loving design in their lives, and a pattern of prayer that enters the daily rhythm of one seeking greater union with God.

Each day of the week is divided into five exercises. There is a pattern to each exercise, each day and each week of the 30-day retreat. The five periods of prayer are spaced throughout the day and evening. Prior to the beginning of each meditation period, the retreatant, guided by a director, is invited to focus on a theme, such as God's creative goodness or one's own struggle between the forces of good and evil. One begins by praying for the true desire to be open to interiorly exploring the workings of God in the now of one's life. Scripture reading is part of each exercise, and a retreatant is asked to experience the scriptural story as being personally addressed to her or himself. The retreatant, through quiet listening and patient waiting, gains access to the inner realm and attends to the spiritual stirrings and the experience of communing with God (spiritual consolation) or, as sometimes happens, to the felt sense of God's absence (spiritual desolation). Keeping a journal, like Ignatius's own notebook, is often part of each prayer session so that one can record the inner happenings and reflect on these periods of prayer with the spiritual director who helps interpret the movement of God's Spirit and acts as a guide day by day through each of the themes of the Ignatian Exercises.

The retreat programs, spiritual growth opportunities, and social service outreaches connected to any Jesuit educational institution or spiritual life center is founded on principles of the *Spiritual Exercises* of St. Ignatius. The men and women who are trained in Ignatian and Jesuit spirituality give retreats to youth in parishes and are retreat team leaders for Jesuit high schools in and beyond the United States. No adolescent or young adult would graduate from a Jesuit institution without experiencing an encounter with Ignatian spirituality.

In brief, Ignatian spirituality is engaging and adapts itself to each particular person wherever one is on life's journey. The flexible disciplines of the *Spiritual Exercises* create the interior condition for spiritual awakening and deeper self-knowledge.

—Avis Clendenen

See also Conversion; Prayer; Retreats; St. Ignatius of Loyola

FURTHER READING

Fleming, D. (1996). *Draw me into your friendship: A literal translation and contemporary reading of the spiritual exercises.* St. Louis, MO: The Institute of Jesuit Sources.

Ganss, G., Divakar, P., & Malastesta, E. (1991). *Ignatius of Loyola: The spiritual exercises and selected works* (Classics of Western Spirituality Series). New York: Paulist Press.

An online retreat. Creighton University. http://www.creighton.edu/CollaborativeMinistry/cmo-retreat.html.

STAGE-STRUCTURAL APPROACH TO RELIGIOUS DEVELOPMENT

Most theorists describing religious development using a structural approach assume that all humans are alike. From this perspective, a single theory of human development applies to all. This assumption does not deny that individual differences exist. However, as will be shown, the assumption of basic likeness is supported empirically.

A child's thoughts and feelings, ways of acting in the world and seeing it differ from the corresponding state of affairs for an adolescent and even more so for an adult. However, this development of one's religiosity and spirituality is not like reaching a destination by driving a car on an even road. It is more like climbing a mountain hidden in fog on a narrow path, sometimes needing to backtrack, sometimes needing to rest, sometimes needing to find anew an ascending trail.

Given the difficulties of the ascent, it is best to do the "climbing" as a member of a team, that is, to pursue religious development as a member of a religious community. If circumstances do not permit this, it is still helpful to share one's experience with other religious seekers: for instance, to discuss the last advance, to bring out what was different from previous experiences, and to inquire about what to expect and observe on the next leg "up."

In Eastern spirituality, development is presented metaphorically by a series of ox-herding pictures. In the ox-herding pictures, the ox stands for an initial aim of religious or spiritual development. The developmental sequence is presented as (1) seeking the ox; (2) finding the tracks; (3) finding the ox; (4) catching the ox; (5) taming the ox; (6) riding the ox home; (7) forgetting the ox and being alone again; (8) forgetting both ox and one's self; (9) returning to the source; and (10) entering the marketplace with helping hands.

Jews (and others) can take the cue for a possible next step in their religious development from Job, who recognizes and confesses after much suffering: "I know that you [the Lord] can do all things and that no purpose of yours can be thwarted. 'Who is this that hides counsel without knowledge?' [asked God, Job 38:2]. Therefore, I have uttered what I did not understand, things too wonderful for me, which I did not know. 'Hear, I will speak; I will question you, and you declare to me' [said God, Job 38:3]. I heard of you by the hearing of the ear, but now my eye sees you; therefore I despise myself, and repent in dust and ashes" (Job 42:2–6, NRSV).

Christians (and others) may follow the lead of the apostle Paul: "When I was a child, I spoke like a child, I thought like a child, I reasoned like a child; when I became an adult, I put an end to my childish ways" (1 Corinthians, 13:11, NRSV). Again, not only for Christians, the life of Jesus may serve as an exemplar. When the hungry Jesus was tempted by the devil in succession about food, power, riches, and glory (Matt. 4:3–10; Luke 4:3–12), he explained why each time he declined the devil's invitation. In the "dark night" in Gethsemane (Matt. 26:36–46, Mark 14:32–42, Luke 22:39–46) Jesus struggled to accept God's will, which involved his painful death on the cross, but finally did so. Mohammed plays a similar role in the development of Islamic spirituality (as noted in the Qur'an, surahs *Al-Ahzab* 33:21 or *Al-Qalam* 68:4).

How can one understand the developmental changes involved? As it often happens when dealing with complex occurrences that are not fully open to inspection by the senses, several explanations are advanced. Regarding psychological development, they come in three broad types of theories:

1. This kind of change simply develops inside humans as part of growing up, just like a plant grows from a seed.
2. We are born with a blank slate inside of us, and socialization from family, school, church, synagogue, mosque, or temple (and so forth) makes us what we have become.
3. We have a (structured) natural endowment, but it only develops according to its own "laws" through interaction with our physical and human surroundings (our family, culture, etc.).

Each of these theories is valid in a particular area. The first type of theory applies specifically to the body, for instance, to its brain size (and its height). A contrasting example follows: In the Middle Ages, the European Emperor Frederick II wanted to find out which language is the "natural" one and so forbade caretakers to talk to their babies; the fact that these babies never spoke supports the second type of theories.

In the end, the babies in Frederick II's heartless experiment died—thus validating the third type of theory, which will be the focus for the rest of this entry. We shall discuss the stage-structural theories of Ronald Goldman, James W. Fowler, and Fritz K. Oser and Paul Gmünder.

ALL HUMANS ARE ALIKE, SOME ARE ALIKE, NONE ARE ALIKE

To repeat, most theorists describing religious development using a stage-structural approach assume that all humans are alike. With this perspective, a single theory of human development applies to all. Stage-structural theorists provide evidence for their theories by, for example, explaining that in learning to speak, children always go through the same sequence of stages: babbling, uttering syllables, pronouncing words, and forming sentences, and this irrespective of which specific language is under discussion. Similarly, developing logicomathematical thinking always proceeds from arbitrarily manipulating things and observing what happens, to solving problems by manipulating concrete things in a logical manner, to solving problems in the head and in the process inventing and assessing all sorts of (hypothetical) solutions to a given problem.

Analyzing these two examples shows that an inherent "developmental logic" is at work. That is, the reversed order does not seem likely. Can one imagine any healthy person born with the ability to form full sentences who next becomes restricted to speech in disjointed words, followed by uttering syllables only, and then for the longest part of his or her life, to babbling? Or can anybody imagine that somebody just born solves all sorts of problems creatively in the head, then moves on to only look for solutions through manipulating concrete things, and finally spends the longest part of his or her life simply playing with things and observing what happens? Perhaps we can image such sequences, but we recognize they are mostly absurd. The indicated *developmental logic* seen in structural stage sequences presumably has to do with a developing, more powerful brain and the accumulation of experiences acquired in various interactions. A conclusion drawn from this state of affairs is that stages are (1) qualitatively different, (2) follow an invariant "logical" sequence, and (3) are ordered in a way that their order is irreversible.

Of course, we all share features such as physical bodily changes, metabolism, adaptation to circumstances, and dying. In these ways, all humans are alike. Humans differ from other species, for instance, on account of the sophistication of our communication skills, imitation skills, record-keeping skills, and planning. However, some individuals are more like certain people than they are to others. For example, adolescents may share commonalities in cognitive or social development that infants and the elderly may not share. As individuals, we all differ from each other as a result of our individual, unique capabilities, experiences, interests, and views. As a result of our unique characteristics and experiences, no two humans are alike. It is, then, a matter of choice to focus on similarities that define the structural stage approach.

EARLY STAGE THEORIES OF ST. AUGUSTINE AND OTHERS

Stage theories of religious or spiritual development have historical models. The Christian church father Saint Augustine (Aurelius Augustinus, 354–430), Bishop of Hippo, described six degrees of inner growth, which were later taken up by others, such as Meister Eckhart and Margerite Porete (at the end of the 13th and beginning of the 14th century). The gist of Augustine's degrees of religious and spiritual maturation is as follows:

Degree 1: The novice (whatever his or her age) develops best through spiritual nourishment from helpful narratives about role models such as saints, loving persons, and Jesus.

Degree 2: The path leads away from human authority and toward divine authority with its unchangeable commandments.

Degrees 3 to 6: The good sense of what is real and matters most has pacified bodily needs, and the soul and mind unite. Henceforth, the individual increasingly does the right things of his or her own accord so that temptations and negative occurrences no longer have an impact. The concerns of earthly life fall away as the individual strives to honor the privilege of having been created in the image of God.

The developmental path, then, goes from getting to know role models, to internalizing critical attributes, to transforming the self thereby, and finally, to live in peace.

In a similar vein, St. Bonaventure (1221–1271), St. Ignatius of Loyola (1491–1556), St. Teresa of Avila (1515–1582), all provided stages to describe the spiritual journey having the comparable outcome of inner peace and equilibrium between worldly aims and activity on one hand, and spiritual aims and activities, on the other. Resulting as they do from their authors' praxis as spiritual counselors, these stage descriptions have their usefulness, and the corresponding exercises are still practiced today.

However, the underlying assumptions correspond more to the second type of developmental theory (starting from an empty slate) than to the third type (starting from a structured natural endowment): at least at degrees 1 and 2, the emphasis is more on socialization than on the development of an "autonomous" psychic structure by way of appropriate interactions with the outside world and one's own reflections. We now turn to more recent type 3 theories that involve empirically researched structural changes.

RELIGIOUS UNDERSTANDING

How does the forgoing relate more closely to a structural approach to religious development by stages? First, all depends on what is understood by *religious development.* If religious development is restricted to an understanding of sacred texts and the like, then one theory fits all to some extent.

Ronald Goldman, a British educator, offers a theory that models well the structural stage approach to describing an evolving religious understanding based on Piaget's stages of logicomathematical thinking. Goldman (1968, pp. 52–64) interviewed children and adolescents about the Burning Bush story in Exodus 3:2–6. He questioned "Why was Moses afraid to look at God?" The youngest children gave answers such as "God had a funny face," "Moses was frightened of the rough voice," and "It was because he hadn't spoken politely to God." Clearly, the children introduced their own knowledge and possibly their experience into the biblical context. Similarly, the question "Why do you think that the ground on which Moses stood was holy?" elicited "Because there was grass on it," or "He was standing on a ho" (the first part of holy, described by the child as nice, hard ground), or "It was hot ground. It would burn his shoes." Goldman gives further examples concerning the bush burning without being burnt, the parting of the Red Sea (Exod. 14:21), and the temptation of Jesus (Matt. 4:3–10, Luke 4:2–11). While the answers differ as to their *content,* they all reflect a particular *structure* of the mind, which Goldman labels "Intuitive religious thinking." At this stage, children fail to provide explanations in terms of what is relevant for understanding the meaning of the biblical story.

The next stage is "concrete religious thinking," which according to Goldman represents a different structure of the mind. Now the question, asking why Moses was afraid to look at God, is answered quite differently by older children: "Moses thought that God would chase him out of the holy ground, because Moses had not taken off his shoes," and equally the question why the ground was holy: "Because the holy would go down through God's feet into the ground, and make it holy." Now the elements of the answers are taken from the biblical text, and a *concrete* situation is worked out using inductive and deductive logic.

Goldman's final stage is represented by "Abstract religious thinking." The same questions are now answered: "The awesomeness and almightiness of God would make Moses feel like a worm in comparison," respectively, "The presence of God would hallow it [the ground] like a magnetic field. The magnetic field is everywhere but the pole is in one spot. God is concentrated there." As is apparent from these answers, the mode of thinking has changed from concrete situations to verbal propositions that take into account the psychology and spiritual experience depicted in the biblical story.

Goldman's theory of religious understanding, then, illustrates the stage-structural approach: Whatever the religious content, it is the developing mental structure that makes for a quite different understanding according to the developmental stage reached. And this is posited to apply the world over. Yet the domain of applicability is restricted, and we have to look for developmental stage theories that cover more of religious (and spiritual) development than just religious understanding.

OSER AND GMÜNDER'S THEORY OF RELIGIOUS JUDGMENT

Science never portrays "reality" in its entirety but rather concentrates on a restricted domain. This is to keep the resulting theory manageable and meaningful, and ensure that it can be tested stringently in a reasonable time, using "normally available" means.

Fritz Oser (a Swiss educator and psychologist) and Paul Gmünder (a Swiss theologian) have concentrated on the development of the relation between an individual and what represents for him or her an Ultimate Being, God for religious believers. Analogous to Kohlberg's theory of *moral judgment,* they call their theory a theory of religious judgment (RJ). A core assumption of RJ is that the religious structure of the psyche is sui generis, in a class of its own, and hence differs from moral structure, logicomathematical structure, and other structures. The RJ of a person conceptually refers to a religiousness, which may not necessarily be contextualized within an existing religion. RJ is not identical with religious knowledge or a simple religious emotion. Whereas a person acquires religious knowledge from socialization into a religious culture, from a particular religion, or conceptually from commonalties of various religions, in contrast, religious judgment involves one's processing of particular events, especially events that cannot be controlled by human beings, such as one's own accidental near death or the unexpected death of a loved one.

Mainly on account of their unexpectedness, unusualness, and emotional impact, such events raise questions: Does the event come from inside (my imagination, lack of understanding of what is going on) or from outside (a rather rare yet real "coincidence")? Does it make me feel free to follow my inclinations and pursue my personal aims, or does it make me dependent on a set of unchangeable circumstances? Is it part of the sacred, or part of the profane? Does it give hope for the future, or does it lead to despair? Are there any long-term implications, or should it be forgotten soon? Did some "eternal will" bring it about, or did it result by chance?

Therefore, according to Oser and Gmünder another characteristic of RJ is the incorporation of eight polar pairs:

1. Transcendence versus immanence
2. Freedom versus dependency
3. Trust versus fear
4. Holy versus profane
5. Hope versus absurdity
6. Eternity versus ephemeral
7. Functional transparency versus opaqueness
8. Divine providence versus (good or bad) luck.

RJ development cannot be characterized only by the changes in the person–Ultimate Being relationship; there is also the changing relationship between the poles of each pair: from being far apart and excluding each other (typically a child, at one point in time is full of hope, at another time full of despair) to finally their natures being recognized as linked, as enabling each other's existence. For example, fully developed RJ understands that only because I depend on God, experience God's love, and follow God's commandments am I really free (within a space thereby defined). Thus, each stage of RJ development is characterized by a change in the person–Ultimate Being (God) relationship itself and that between the poles of each pair.

This state of affairs is not assessed directly in RJ interviews but inferred by Oser and Gmünder (and their associates) via questions about specific dilemmas put before the respondents. Questions dealt with in such dilemmas are, for instance, whether a promise made to God in a stressful situation must be kept and, if not kept, whether God will punish. Some prototypical answers are reproduced in the following stages.

The RJ stages resulting from and being confirmed by (multicultural) empirical research can be described as follows:

DEVELOPMENTAL STAGES OF RELIGIOUS JUDGMENT ACCORDING TO OSER AND GMÜNDER

Stage 1. There is an Ultimate Being (God) who protects you or sends you something hurtful and dispenses health or illness, joy or despair. The Ultimate Being influences you (and all other living beings) directly. The Ultimate Being's will must always be fulfilled. Otherwise, the relationship is broken. ("God will punish if one does not keep one's promise.")

Stage 2. The Ultimate Being (God) can be influenced by prayers, offerings, the following of religious rules, etc. If one cares about the Ultimate Being and passes His tests, He will act like a trusting and loving father, and you will be happy, healthy, successful, etc. An individual can influence the Ultimate Being, or he or she can fail to do so, depending on his or her needs and free will. ("If someone breaks his or her promise, he or she should do something to make it up to God.")

Stage 3. The individual assumes responsibility for his or her own life and for matters of the world. Freedom, meaning, and hope are linked to one's own decisions. The Ultimate Being (God) is apart. He has His own field of action; we have ours. The Ultimate Being's wholeness encompasses a freedom, hope, and meaning that are different from the human ones. Transcendence is outside the individual but represents a basic order of world and life. ("An accident has nothing to do with God even if someone breaks his or her promise; he or she is responsible for what happens to him or her.")

Stage 4. Now an indirect, mediated relationship with an Ultimate Being (God) has come into existence. The individual continues to assume responsibility, but he or she wonders about the conditions for the mere possibility of being responsible. He or she sees his or her commitment as a way to overcome lack of meaning and hope, as well as absurdity. Transcendence is now partly inside (immanence): the Ultimate Being becomes the condition for the possibility of human freedom, independence, etc., via a divine plan. ("We should reflect and follow our conscience").

Stage 5. The Ultimate Being (God) appears in every human commitment, yet transcends it at the same time. The Ultimate Being becomes apparent in history and in revelation. Transcendence and immanence interact completely. This total integration renders possible universal solidarity with all human beings. The "realm of God" becomes a cipher for a peaceful and fully committed human potential, which creates meaning not in options detached from the world but rather in a truly social perspective.

Apart from meeting the stage definitions stated earlier (stages are qualitatively different, follow an invariant "logical" sequence, and are ordered in a way that is irreversible), these structural stage descriptions also illustrate the difference between psychic *structure* (which is supposedly shared by "all persons") and actual *content.* (mostly different for different persons). The Ultimate Being (God), and its role in the relationship with individuals, figures as an abstract *structure* that develops through "universal" stages. According to stage theory, this is in principle true irrespective of specific attributes of the Ultimate Being (such as being all-powerful, present everywhere, just, loving, etc.), which are not indicated directly and explicitly in the stage descriptions. Likewise, the human person concerned is pictured as an abstract structure without individual differences such as differences in temperament, cognitive style, or emotionality. Therefore, RJ does not describe every individual path to the fog-covered top of the mountain but refers to way stations many wanderers will reach sooner or later.

RJ theory is used specifically in religious education and pastoral counseling: it is helpful to explain why everybody does not have the same religious views (because of stage differences) and where religious development is headed. However, not all of religious "development" is covered (for instance, conversion or change of denomination). Also, Oser emphasizes that accumulating religious knowledge and experience is equally part of religious development, not just changes in RJ stages (which new religious knowledge and experience may trigger).

Compared to Goldman's theory, the theory of Oser and Gmünder covers a wider area of religious development; Fowler enlarged that area even further.

FOWLER'S FAITH DEVELOPMENT THEORY

The origins of faith development theory (FDT) lie in the praxis of counseling. From the beginning, FDT aimed at illuminating a path persons follow from the origins and awakenings of faith through the interactive process of forming and reforming frames of meaning, in and between communities of shared traditions and practices. In addition to other inputs, the American theologian James W. Fowler has taken his cue also from Kohlberg's (and thence Piaget's) theory, but Fowler's FDT is based more broadly (too broad some say) than RJ theory.

Fowler defines *faith* as a composition, a dynamic and holistic construction of relations that include self to others, self to world, and self to self, all construed as being related to an ultimate environment. Faith is here seen as a multifaceted, central form of human action and personal construction. It is said to involve both conscious and unconscious processes, both thinking and (strong) emotions. Making use of both religious and nonreligious directions and forms, faith is the result of grappling personally with the relationships evoked.

Fowler emphasizes that selfhood and faith develop together as a gradual and difficult sequence of constructions. Selfhood and faith concern the following eight dimensions:

1. Form of logic
2. Role taking
3. Form of moral judgment
4. Bounds of social awareness
5. Locus of authority
6. Form of world coherence
7. Symbolic functioning
8. Developmental level of self.

Fowler's seven faith stages are labeled (0) primal faith, (1) intuitive projective faith, (2) mythic-literal faith, (3) synthetic-conventional faith, (4) individuative (keep as is)-reflective faith, (5) conjunctive faith, and (6) universalizing faith.

It would vastly exceed the scope of this entry to describe in detail what happens at each stage and what is constructed with each dimension (1) to (8) (For further reading, see the "References and Further Reading" section.) To give a sense: The impact of dimension (1) is close to that described by the Goldman theory as far as Fowler's Stages 2, 3, and 4 are concerned. More complex, "post-Piagetian" forms of thinking permit a deeper religious understanding to evolve at Fowler's Stages 5 and 6. Similarly, the other dimensions develop from a basic, egocentric, literal view of role-taking, moral judgment, social awareness, of who is in control, whether and how the world coheres, the meaning and significance of symbols (such as the cross, water, etc.), and one's personal characteristics to a more differentiated and integrated abstract and more encompassing view of aspects (2) to (8). Each dimension contributes in its specificity to the construction of Fowler's overall faith stages.

Fowler's stages are assessed from intensive interviews about one's life tapestry, and hence an account of one's religious and spiritual development. A detailed scoring manual permits translation of the results of such an interview into FDT stages.

As with RJ theory, FDT is used specifically in religious education and pastoral counseling: in its way it is helpful to explain why not everybody has the same faith (because of stage differences) and where faith development is headed.

CONCLUSIONS

As was pointed out, there are limitations to the stage-structural approach. To summarize, all structural theories emphasize commonalities of religious and spiritual development but do not address personal differences, at least not explicitly. Nor does the specific content of a given religion (rituals, holy scriptures, etc.) matter. Nevertheless, the stage-structural approach describing religious development in terms of stages offers a potential help for situating one's own development and for facilitating religious education and pastoral counseling.

Let us visualize much of what was said in this entry via three verses from a song ("Who Am I?" by Leonard Bernstein).

> Who am I?
> Was it all planned in advance?
> Or was I just born by chance
> In July?
> Oh, who on earth am I?
> Did I ever live before
> As a mountain lion
> Or as a fly?
> My friends only think of fun;
> They're all such incurable tots!
> Can I be the only one
> Who thinks these mysterious thoughts?

Having read these verses, what thoughts may come to mind? There is here not only the helicopter view of one's entire life but also the search for what was before birth, issues at the core of many religions. A "family relation" with various animals is implied, on the one hand, and a difference with certain human friends, on the other. So, the songwriter, in his own way, makes the point that "All humans are alike, some are alike, none are alike" and thereby underlines the message of this entry.

—K. Helmut Reich

FURTHER READING

Goldman, R. (1968). *Religious thinking from childhood to adolescence.* New York: Seabury Press.

Fowler, J. W., Nipkow, K. E., & Schweitzer, F. (1991). *Stages of faith and religious development. Implications for church, education, and society.* New York: Crossroad.

STEIN, EDITH

Edith Stein's story is an example of the different development paths one's religiosity can take and the multiple reasons that can influence that path. Interest in the life and writings of Edith Stein has continued to grow since her death in a Nazi concentration camp during World War Two. She is one of the most influential figures in contemporary Catholicism, especially amongst younger generations who are striving to find meaning in a world that is indifferent to many of the certainties of early times. Stein was born in Breslau (Wroclaw) in what was then German Silesia. Edith was reared in a large devout Jewish family headed by her widowed mother. The family's religious observances are noteworthy because of the trend amongst many German Jews of the day to become secularized. Stein was greatly influenced by her mother, who was a matriarchal figure with enormous energy. She lavished attention on her children and also kept a watchful eye on her business.

As a young girl Stein lost her religious convictions. She was a brilliant student and was supported in her intellectual endeavors by her family. At university she studied under the renowned phenomenologist Edmund Husserl. So impressed was Husserl that he made her his assistant, a position of some importance within the culture of German universities where the assistant to a professor is seen as the apprentice or even heir apparent to that particular school of thought.

It was through Husserl's former pupil Max Scheler that Stein came to the serious study of Catholicism, a path that would eventually lead to her conversion. Her interest was further aroused by her encounter with the writings of St. Teresa of Avila. So profound was the impact of these writings that Stein was baptized on New Year's Day in 1922. She maintained her academic interests and wrote on a variety of themes. Her most ambitious project was an attempt to synthesize the philosophical realism of Aquinas with the phenomenological insights that she was expert in. This process began with her translation of Aquinas's *On Truth* and culminated in the publication of one of her major works, *Finite and Eternal Being*.

From the 1930s two quite opposite forces dominated Edith's life. Rising antisemitism in Germany made it difficult for Jews to maintain a public life. By 1933 she had to relinquish all university teaching posts and for the rest of her life struggled to keep one step ahead of her Nazi tormentors. Edith's interest in the contemplative life was so strong that she entered the Carmelite monastery in Cologne in 1933 making her final profession in 1938. With the situation for Jews in Germany becoming unbearable she transferred to a convent in Echt in the Netherlands. Here she almost completed her major treatise on suffering and the human condition, *The Science of the Cross*. In a Gestapo crackdown of Christians of Jewish origin she was arrested on August 2, 1942 and died about a week later later in Auschwitz.

For many Christians today Stein's thought represents an approach that is especially relevant to those living in Western postindustrial societies. Stein's expertise in phenomenology provides a way of examining human experience without assumptions or preconditions. This close observation of the world leads Stein, and many of her followers, to a deeper contemplation of the order and system in the universe—the God waiting to be discovered. By understanding the human and the created world the human intellect naturally seeks to explore the domain in which all striving and longings find meaning.

—Richard Rymarz

FURTHER READING

Baseheart, M. (1997). *Person in the world: Introduction to the philosophy of Edith Stein.* Dordrecht, The Netherlands: Kluwer.

Koeppel, J. (1992). *Edith Stein: Philosopher and mystic.* Collegeville, MN: Liturgical Press.

Stein, E. (1986). *The collected works of Edith Stein. Vols. 1–6.* Washington, DC: ICS Publications.

STONEHENGE

On Salisbury plain in southern England stands an awesome testament of time and mystery—an arrangement of stones that has been the subject of endless poems, studies, legends, and speculations that date as far back as King Arthur and his court. Stonehenge presents a unique cryptic puzzle about the lives of a prehistoric people. Interest in the beauty and mystery of Stonehenge did not surface until the Dark Ages when people began to wonder about the purpose behind the stone structure and about the people that lived in the Stone Age on the Salisbury plains. The decoding of the mystery of Stonehenge unlocks centuries of theories about the somber stones of the Druids. The rugged stones are blank with no words of dedication, no constructional notation, and no readable clues. As the mystery behind the stone structure begins to unfold, a door of history stands ajar. By the 21st century the mystery behind the positioning of the stones (a master plan of architecture) was revealed.

Stonehenge was built between the years 1900 and 1600 B.C.E., a thousand years after the pyramids of Egypt and a few hundred years before the fall of Troy. Its creation corresponded with the flourishing of the Minoan civilization of Crete. In Mesopotamia, Abraham was living at Harran and the Israelites had not yet come into bondage in Egypt.

Within the circular walls of Stonehenge there are pairings of trilithons making a horseshoe shape. These are three stones that are rectangular in shape. Two "heel" stones are anchored into the ground and the third stone rests on top, creating a houselike image. The structure of Stonehenge, seems at first glance nothing more then large stones randomly laid out on Salisbury Plain; however, after much investigation, these stones turn out to provide more information that reveals Stonehenge to be a monumental temple. Stonehenge is decorated with intricate celestial alignments in complete simplicity and symmetry of design so that the rays of the sun shine through specific areas at certain times of the day and year, showing that the engineers who constructed Stonehenge possessed intelligence of a high order.

There have been numerous theories devised by anthropologists and archaeologists about what took place within the stone structures, such as that the Stonehenge sun–moon alignments were created and elaborated to make a calendar to tell time for planting crops and that the structure allowed priests to maintain priestly power, as they were able to call out to the multitude to see the spectacular rising and setting of the moon and sun and their union in an eclipse.

One of the most interesting recordings of the people of Stonehenge comes from the transcripts of the Greek historian Diodorus, who wrote in 1 B.C.E. that Stonehenge was a "Temple in the land of the Celts" and that the God Apollo visited the Celtic island every 19 years and danced the night through the vernal equinox. The writings of Diodorus echo the religion of the Greeks, for the veneration of the sun and moon was also an important element within Greek religion. The writings of Diodorus are richly suggestive and provide clues into the lives of the people of Wessex. They held the sun and moon in highest regard, objects of holiness enough to build an elaborate monument to honor these two celestial bodies.

It seems that every historical era has created its own interpretation of the meaning behind Stonehenge. During the Middle Ages, the presence of the grim stones invited the explanation that the magician Merlin produced them through the use of his wand. This theory had died out by the 17th century when Inigo Jones, an architect, concluded that Stonehenge was much too elegant for the early Britons, who were a savage and barbarous people. Jones proposed that the stones were constructed by the Druids, a more highly intelligent group. Another scholar, Jon Aubrey, agreed with Jones that the Druids used the structure as a temple, a sacrificial high place, ceremonial grounds, or a place where weekly libations were made to their gods. Classic literature abounds in reference to the Druids, elevating them to a mysterious and fascinating people.

This being said, no modern scholar gives credence to the theory of the Druids and their Celtic cult as being responsible for the masterpiece of Stonehenge. In 1961, new theories that incorporated advanced technology in the areas of computers and science shed new light on the mystery of Stonehenge. It was within this time that a new group of Stonehenge decoders emerged called the *proto-Newtons of Stonehenge.* They were confronted by three wonders in the firmament: sun, moon, and *x* being the unseen force. Was *x* the God of the Bible? Did the three coordinates symbolize the Trinity of the Christian tradition, or did the engineers behind Stonehenge believe in another unnamed force that governed their world? The elements of sun and moon were undeniable to the proto-Newtons as being the two major areas of Stonehenge worship. Professor Fred Hoyle, an astronomer, tested out this theory and determined that Stonehenge was a sanctuary to pay reverence to the celestial bodies, which made up the religion of the people of Wessex.

Astronomer Gerald S. Hawkins made the most advances in proving the theory of celestial alignments through his endless testing and retesting of the exterior and interior of the stones. Based on Hawkins's work, Stonehenge is understood to be an early computer that tested and measured the movement and happenings in the skies—specifically the positioning of the sun and moon (considered prehistoric deities) over Stonehenge. Through the testing and retesting of the correlation of the rise of the sun and moon, and their positioning with the celestial bodies, Dr. Hawkins's theory was proven accurate. The trilithon pairings that make up the horseshoe within the circle point to the sun and the moon. By this positioning, the Stone Age viewer saw the solstice rising sun—the disk—and the rising moon. Standing within the horseshoe, the individual viewer is forced to look through the paired archways toward the sun and the moon.

The theory of Stonehenge will continue to fascinate scholars and scientists alike for generations to come. One fact that has proven undeniable by all generations that have come to know Stonehenge is that it remains a supreme emblem of a proximate craft and a mystery that welcomes all those who wish to attempt to unlock her secrets.

—Julie Wieland-Robbescheuten

FURTHER READING

Hawkins, G. S. (1965). *Stonehenge decoded.* New York: Doubleday.

SUICIDE AND NATIVE AMERICAN SPIRITUALITY

The shadow of youth suicide hangs heavy over today's Indian Reservations and among urban Indian people. As in all societies there is no treasure as precious as that of the lives of the children. Suicide is the second leading cause of death among American Indian youth with a crude death rate of 37.1 per 100,000 (2.7 times that of youth of all races in the United States). Suicide is the fourth leading cause of death among American Indian youth ages 5 through 14. Within the Indian youth suicide group, American Indian children placed in non-Indian homes for adoptive or foster care suffer a rate of 70 suicides per 100,000, a rate that is six times higher than that of youth in the United States. Alaska Natives had the highest suicide rate in the nation in 2000, averaging 42.9 suicides per 100,000 people; over six times the national average. While suicide rates for youth 14 through 19 years old have decreased somewhat, rates for 10- and 14-year-olds are approximately four times higher than that for the general U.S. population and have continued to increase steadily.

Scholars and researchers point to important aspects of human behavior that can be applied to Indian youth. This set of relationships is composed of underlying causes that are generally circumstances in the individual's environment, precipitating stress events, personal feelings such as alienation, anomie, helplessness, hopelessness, and despair. These personal feelings are placed into motion by stressful events that are manifested by the development of suicidal thoughts and gestures, the culmination being the successful suicide act. Additionally, circumstances in the environment represent underlying factors such as economic and social conditions that contribute to suicide rates among Indian youth. What these scholars and researchers miss, however, is the interconnectedness of the American Indian spiritual world (spirituality) and the everyday process of life. For American Indians the spiritual is ever present in their world, from the time of awakening to the time of sleep. In some cases even the process of sleep, or dreaming, also has deep spiritual meaning. For American Indian youth one cannot separate the spiritual from the physical or emotional realities without causing severe trauma.

American Indians in general have high rates of depression. Overwhelming stress from rapid acculturation and loss of spiritual and additional identity leads to a state of chronic depression. The unemployment rate for Indian people continues to be higher than national averages, and on some reservations unemployment is more than 60%. According to Census Bureau data for 1990, the median income of Indian families in the United States was $21,750—considerably lower than the national average of $35,225, and more than twice as many Indian people (51%) were living below the poverty level. The educational attainment of Indian people is also below national averages. While 20% of those 25 years and older in the general population have completed 4 years of college, only 9% of American Indian people have done so. Finally, alcoholism is a major threat to the survival of Indian culture as fewer traditional values and life ways are passed on to the youth in the society.

Environmental circumstances and coupled stress events place Indian youth on a dangerous path toward suicidal behavior. Stress events may include a death among the immediate or extended family members, failure in school or job, or conflict between white social values and deep-seated cultural beliefs. While most youth in America are faced with the problems associated with making the transition into adulthood, Indian youth face even greater conflicts than most other American youth, particularly due to their minority status, fewer economic and educational opportunities, and cultural differences. Indian adolescents must choose from at least two, not totally clear paths: traditional life on an Indian reservation or assimilation into an urban environment. Assimilation most often includes the abandoning of the spiritual world that provides a basis for who they are as an Indian person. Faced with this pressure, some—particularly those with little support who have suffered the consequences of prejudice, discrimination, and unclear and seemingly hostile values—turn to various forms of self-destructive behavior, including suicide.

Alienation appears as an early symptom of fear and confusion, resulting from stress. This is often accompanied by dramatic changes in behavior patterns such as decline in school performance or in self-destructive acts such as alcohol or drug abuse. Helplessness furthers feelings of alienation and has been defined as a desire to escape from what one considers being an insoluble problem and having no hope that relief is possible in the future. It is at this point that the Indian youth begin to visualize thoughts of powerlessness over his or her environment. Events seem insurmountable, and the person now feels alone. These feelings often overshadow all others and quickly turn to a feeling of hopelessness. Socioeconomic factors as well as alcoholism can have a severe impact on family discord and dysfunction, which also contributes to the feeling of hopelessness and self-destructive behavior. It is at this point that the Indian youth is most vulnerable.

Often human resources are few and Indian youth have a limited number of people with whom to consult.

Many schools that serve American Indian students are unsupportive of the academic, social, cultural, and spiritual needs of Native students. Indian youth may face racism from their fellow students as well as inaccurate portrayals of Native Americans in American history. These events may further lower their self-esteem. According to the Group for the Advancement of Psychiatry, pathways to assimilation to dominant society norms are often blocked due to racism, and as a result, Indian youth slip into cultural marginalization. They have at this point lost many essential values of traditional culture and have not been able to replace them by active participation in American society in ways that are conducive to enhanced cultural and psychological self-esteem. Without the help of friends and relatives, or if those are removed or fail, finality is near. Anomie is the next step when the Indian youth loses his or her sense of purpose in life and their personal identity. Anomie is followed rapidly by despair.

When the Indian youth enters the final stage of despair, he or she falters between thoughts of life and death that is usually accompanied by severe withdrawal symptoms. Often subtle clues to suicide are given, while behavior usually changes dramatically. Talking about wanting to join dead relatives or having an experience of being visited by the dead may provide a clue to an impending suicide attempt. The individual seemingly will break the depression cycle, which may appear promising. However, it may simply mean that all options have been exhausted and that a plan for suicide has been developed. Intervention and planning are critical at this point because counseling may generate thinking around activities of life to detract from thoughts about death. Planned intervention must reconnect the at-risk person with a human resource that fits his or her particular need. This reconnection is often with members of the extended family, peers, or teachers. Another critical point of reconnection is with the Indian culture from which Native American people often draw their strength.

—*Troy Johnson*

See also Native American Indian Spirituality; Native American Spirituality, Practice of

FURTHER READING

Group for Advancement of Psychiatry. (1989). Suicide among American Indians and Alaskan natives. *Suicide and ethnicity in the United States* (pp. 30–57). New York: Brunner/Mazel Publishers.

Johnson, D. (1994). Stress, depression, substance abuse, and racism. *American Indian and Alaskan Native Mental Health Research, 6*(1), 29–33.

Johnson, T., & Tomren, H. (2001). Helplessness, hopelessness, and despair: Identifying the precursors to Indian Youth Suicide. In C. E. Trafzer & D. Weiner (Eds.), *Medicine ways: Disease, health, and survival among Native Americans.* Walnut Creek, CA: Rowman & Littlefield.

May, P. A. (1987). Suicide and self-destruction among American Indian youths. *American Indian and Alaska Native Mental Health Research, 1*(1), 52–69.

Shore, J. M., Manson, S. M., Bloom, J. D., Keepers, G., & Neligh, G. (1987). A pilot study of depression among American Indian patients with research diagnostic criteria. *American Indian and Alaska Native Mental Health Research, 1*(2), 4–15.

U. S. Department of Health and Human Services, Public Health Service, Indian Health Service. (1996). *Trends In Indian Health,* 67. pp?

T

TAROT

A Tarot deck consists of 78 pictorial cards. The pictures on the cards resemble illustrations from a fairy tale or an adventure story that symbolize an individual's journey through life with its many events and experiences. Each card represents a moral lesson that a human soul must learn in order to be fruitful and creative in experiential endeavors.

Throughout life, each of us has to often leave behind some illusions and dependencies that are counterproductive to human growth and spiritual development. These situations are also symbolically represented in Tarot cards. Nearly every one of the cards has an image of a living being, a human figure situated in different contexts. This figure represents not just a physical body but the mind, soul, and spirit as well. And while a body goes through life and accomplishes different tasks, the human psyche too goes through transformations, as life itself calls for the constant renewal and enlargement of our consciousness. The journey through the cards' imagery is therapeutic, as each new life experience contributes to self-understanding and, ultimately, spiritual rebirth. In the Tarot deck, rebirth is signified by the Sun card, with its image of a small child warming in the sunshine, the psychic energy of a child enriched by the solar energy of the whole universe.

There is no proven origin of Tarot cards. Various sources mention different geographical and historical roots. The only factual information about Tarot's genesis is a set of 17 elaborately painted cards now located in the Bibliotheque Nationale in Paris and documented as dating back to 1392. The collection in the Pierpont Morgan Library in New York contains 35 cards from a full deck whose origins go back to around the middle of the 15th century.

Tarot has been traditionally used as a divinatory tool, although Tarot has also been related to a family of card games that are integral to certain cultures. Each card in the deck carries a strong humanistic aspect in terms of the dominant personality drive being an instinct to grow, develop, differentiate, and nurture our spiritual feelings. Tarot readings, despite being considered by some to be irrational, nonetheless are thought by others to help achieve a wider scope of awareness than rational thinking alone can provide.

Tarot brings to awareness many initially unperceived meanings, thereby contributing to human learning based on one's own experience, both actual and potential. The cards may be considered to project subconscious human desires, wishes, beliefs, and hopes, and the power of Tarot symbolism is such that the images may transcend existing blocks and defenses. The Tarot images cannot be reduced to merely arbitrary symbols; according to the Hermetic tradition they constitute, in a coded format, an ordered system of esoteric knowledge, and the *memoria.* The Tarot symbols can be considered to represent the universal language that is structured in accord with a certain syntax and semantics. A Tarot reader translates the nonverbal, pictorial language of symbols and signs into spoken words. Many typical life experiences are represented in the patterns that appear when the cards are being spread in a certain layout. As themes emerge in the course of a reading, therapeutic material is being gathered. This material contributes to the healing of one's psyche as it provides some guidance toward solving a variety of problems or clarifying an ambiguous situation. People learn from their many experiences when Tarot pictures are narrated. This narrative knowledge represents a path toward spiritual development. No card is taken as an impending fate; instead, Tarot pictures provide a means for developing one's ability to reason critically and to enable self-reflection, so crucial for youth.

The four suits in the Tarot are connected to four ancient elements: pentacles to earth, wands to fire, swords to air, and cups to water. One of the most popular spreads is called the Celtic Cross: it comprises ten positions that are said to be combined together to provide information illuminating a particular question. Some positions in a spread signify the dimension of time, which is why there can be a peculiar feeling of gazing into the future and revisiting the past during readings. Philosophically, a spread reflects a four-dimensional view of time in which past, present, and future events coexist. David Bohm, a physicist, has posited all events as enfolded in the timeless implicate order. In the physical world, they unfold into explicate order, thereby creating time in our customary three-dimensional reality. Perhaps Tarot readings enable us to access the implicate order in its past and future aspects. Moving along the levels of order, human consciousness undergoes evolution: It grows and expands as it reaches the spiritual realm. The spiritual quest becomes quite literally associated with personal growth as an individual acquires greater knowledge and awareness along his/her developmental path.

—Inna Semetsky

FURTHER READING

Bohm, D. (1980). *Wholeness and the implicate order*. London and New York: Routledge.

Dummett, M. (1980). *The game of Tarot: From Ferrara to Salt Lake City*. London: Duckworth.

Semetsky, I. (1998). *On the nature of Tarot. Frontier Perspectives* 7(1), 58–66.

TEEN CHALLENGE

Teen Challenge (TC) is a global ministry of the General Council of the Assemblies of God, USA, focused primarily on individuals' life-controlling problems, especially substance abuse. TC dates its origin to 1960, when the Reverend David Wilkerson, a Pentecostal preacher from rural Pennsylvania, opened the first Teen Challenge Center in Brooklyn, New York. He read a newspaper account of a highly publicized murder trial in New York City in 1958 where all seven defendants were teenagers, members of a street gang, and accused of a brutal crime. Wilkerson drove 8 hours to New York City with a strong determination to speak to these "boys" about their need of a personal relationship with Jesus Christ who loved them. Nearly arrested by the judge when interrupting the courtroom to request to see the teens (subsequently denied), he began to meet with other gang members in Brooklyn. The evident needs of these teens to find a way out of their lives of daily substance abuse and ongoing gang warfare, led Wilkerson to establish what would be the first of many TC Centers. The demand for these Centers and the fundraising necessary to support them proved too much of a task, so Wilkerson turned over the ministry in 1963 to the Division of Home Missions of the General Council of the Assemblies of God, USA, with his brother, Don Wilkerson, as the first national director.

The treatment program of TC today is similar to when it was founded. Its central focus is for each resident having a relationship with Jesus Christ and developing a deep personal spirituality. The formal treatment program runs for a year and includes a regimented schedule that includes times for personal and group Bible study, personal and group prayer, recreation, work (both within and external to the Center), counseling, education (both GED and limited vocational training is offered), and church services. Each Center is locally owned and operated with training and support provided by the national office. Local Centers have a local operating or advisory board comprised of community and religious leaders. Many volunteers from churches in the areas surrounding a Center provide countless hours of donated services, including building upkeep and repair, cooking, recreational competition, "buddy" systems, and educational services. Many Center directors and staff are themselves graduates of the TC program. Since the 1980s, there have been accreditation standards for Centers that cover fiscal management, program implementation, staff training, and residents' rights issues. Inspections by the national office occur every 4 years.

The ministry has grown steadily over the years. In 2001, more than 3,300 year-long clients were served through its U.S. network of more than 160 adult male centers, adult female centers, adolescent female centers, adolescent male centers, prison ministries, reentry programs, TC Ministry Institutes, Crisis and Referral centers, and administrative offices. Combined annual income in 2001 was $68 million in cash and an equivalent amount in donated goods and services. There are an additional 250 centers in over 70 foreign countries. Indigenous church groups support some Centers; others are part of mission outreach from the United States.

A series of studies have focused on the efficacy of the TC approach to drug and alcohol rehabilitation. These include studies commissioned by the National Institute on Drug Abuse and researchers associated with the Universities of Southern California, Indiana, Tennessee, and Pennsylvania, and Northwestern University. Studies to date all indicate very positive effects from the program, although the exact nature of these effects, their long-term benefits, and their comparability to effectiveness of other programs remain unclear.

TC is one of many faith-based initiatives in the United States that has come under public scrutiny as the White House seeks to promote federal dollars in direct support of these types of programs. Besides perennial issues of the separation of church and state, other issues that remain to be addressed include federal regulations regarding drug abuse rehabilitation facilities (most TC Centers could only meet these standards at enormous cost), suitable outcome measures, and the manner in which TC can control its intake (currently persons admitted to the program must be open to using principles derived from the Bible to change their lives).

TC has evolved over the years to meet challenges presented by adolescents and adults who engage in continual substance abuse. It has established its global reputation as a program that is quite effective for persons willing to engage with its spiritual orientation to the problems of substance abuse.

—Dennis William Cheek

See also Alcohol and Drug Abuse; Faith-Based Organizations

FURTHER READING

Bicknese, A. T. (1999). *The Teen Challenge drug treatment program in comparative perspective.* Unpublished doctoral dissertation, Northwestern University.

Reynolds, F. M. (2002). Teen Challenge. In S. M. Burgess & E. M. Van Der Maas (Eds.), *The new international dictionary of Pentecostal and charismatic movements* (pp. 1116–1118). Grand Rapids, MI: Zondervan.

Sherrill, E., & Sherrill, J. (1984). *Cross and the switchblade.* Grand Rapids, MI: Chosen Books.

Wilkerson, D. (1997). *The Cross is still mightier than the switchblade.* Shippensburg, PA: Destiny Image.

TEMPLETON, SIR JOHN

Sir John Marks Templeton was born in Tennessee more than 90 years ago. He is known for his pioneering work in international investment as well as spiritual and religious study and practice—two interests that are not naturally found within the same individual. He has led a life marked by a quest for open-mindedness and understanding of the possibilities of life as well as those possibilities beyond those experienced on Earth. For his great contributions and capabilities, Queen Elizabeth II knighted him Sir John in 1987. He now lives an active and yet peaceful life as a British citizen in Nassau, the Bahamas. While his success in the financial arena warrants a graduate-level course of study on its own, the focus of this entry is his interest in the study of science, religion, and spirituality.

With the impressive sums of money that Sir John acquired as a result of his outstanding success in international investment work, he was able to begin to focus and direct his money to philanthropic causes, most notably, by creating the Templeton Prize for Progress Toward Research or Discoveries about Spiritual Realities. The award exceeds $1 million and has been given annually since the early 1970s. The first recipient of the award was Mother Teresa of Calcutta. Other winners include the evangelist Billy Graham, author Aleksandr Solzhenitsyn, and theoretical physicist Paul Davies. Through the John Templeton Foundation, Sir John also gives away close to $40 million a year, mostly to efforts aimed at the study of the cooperation between science and religion. Sir John does not claim to be a theologian himself, but will allow that his life experiences have given him the opportunity to support research that pursues the study of God. He is a man who is constantly questioning tradition and challenging believers and nonbelievers alike to wonder what else might be true within and outside their respective traditions and beliefs, as well as what other practices might be (more) effective. To Sir John, the study of religion and of God is never-ending, and cannot be fully captured in the sacred texts upon which most major world religions are framed.

Influenced primarily by the Presbyterian tradition and New Thought traditions such as Christian Science, Unity and Religious Science, Sir John takes what he considers a "humble approach" to theology, given, as he declares, that very little is actually known or understood about God. While many in the fields of theology and science find themselves standing on opposing sides of the fence, Sir John believes that it will be scientific study that will reveal greater understanding about religion, and that science will, in fact, be a revitalizing source for religion in this century. While the theory of evolution and the idea of God the Creator seem incompatible to many, Sir John sees them as compatible notions.

Sir John is himself a prolific author. His works include *Wisdom from World Religions,* which serves as a collection of spiritual principles from the sacred writings of leading world religions and spiritual traditions. Other notable works include *Discovering the Laws of Life* (1994); *Evidence of Purpose* (1994); *The Humble Approach* (1998); *Agape Love: A Tradition Found in Eight World Religions* (1999); and *Pure Unlimited Love* (2000). Throughout his writings, Sir John focuses on the importance of humility and on the power of agape—which he sees as universal to religious traditions.

Through the John Templeton Foundation and The Templeton Foundation Press, Sir John's spirit and quest for open-mindedness will make an impact on the study of science and religion for years to come.

—*Elizabeth M. Dowling*

FURTHER READING

Templeton, J. (1994.). *Discovering the laws of life.* Conshohocken, PA: Templeton Foundation Press.

Templeton, J. (1994.). *Evidence of purpose.* Conshohocken, PA: Templeton Foundation Press.

Templeton, J. (1998). *The humble approach.* Conshohocken, PA: Templeton Foundation Press.

Templeton, J. (1999). *Agape love: A tradition found in eight world religions.* Conshohocken, PA: Templeton Foundation Press.

Templeton, J. (2000). *Pure unlimited love.* Conshohocken, PA: Templeton Foundation Press.

Templeton Foundation. (2005). Retrieved April 27, 2005, from www.Templeton.org/sir_john_templeton_/index.asp.

THEODICY: GOD AND EVIL

Theodicy refers to attempts to explain how it is possible that evil and pain and suffering exist along with a God who is good and loving and powerful. The issue has often been phrased in this way: If God is all-powerful and evil exists, then God must not be good and loving, or else God would have used God's power to prevent evil from occurring; or, if God is good and loving and evil exists, then God must not be very powerful, for God in God's goodness and love would have wanted to prevent evil from occurring. In a shorthand way, the question that captures the issue is this: Why do bad things happen to good people? This is a question that most humans are confronted with and struggle with. At different developmental stages through a person's life and depending on different life experiences, an individual's position on theodicy may change.

Various responses (theodicies) have been put forth to address this issue. One response is to assert that human beings simply do not know why God and evil simultaneously exist. The reason simply lies beyond humans' comprehension and ability to know. After all, humans are limited in their intelligence and restricted in their perspective. As a result, they cannot fathom how it could be the case that a good and powerful God and pain and suffering exist.

This theodicy is customarily termed "mystery," and it accents the tremendous dissimilarity between finite human beings and an infinite God. This theodicy also often appeals to the biblical figure Job, who continued to believe and have faith even though he did not understand why the terrible things that happened to him did in fact occur. This theodicy argues that God alone knows the answer or the reason. Humans do not know because they *cannot* know.

The strength of this theodicy is that it preserves the almightiness and goodness of God by reminding humans that they are human and not gods themselves. It encourages humility. At the same time, its weakness lies in its more modest estimate of human beings' ability to question, to think, and to arrive at answers. If human intelligence is a God-given gift, then ought it not to be directed toward all areas of life and to all questions that arise?

Another response is to suggest that God is not immediately responsible for evil in the world. Rather, God is the source of good things that occur, and the Devil (the demonic, Satan, the Evil One, Lucifer) is responsible for the bad things that happen. As a result, persons ought not to blame God for the things that the Devil does.

This theodicy is often called "cosmic dualism," and it draws on the sense in various religions that there is a negative force in life and the world that causes and promotes evil, as well as a positive force in life and the world that encourages and promotes goodness. This theodicy sometimes appeals to the figure Jesus, who wrestled with temptation from the Devil in the wilderness and emerged victoriously (Luke 4:1–13).

The strength of this theodicy is that it makes God responsible for the good things that occur and thereby preserves God's goodness by accounting for the bad things that occur by pointing to the Devil as the culprit. The weakness of this theodicy is that it brings God's power into question: With another cosmic force competing with God, it would seem that God is not all-powerful in the world because God must share power with another agent of action. Further, this theodicy does not let God ultimately off the hook; for, though God is spared immediate responsibility, God holds final accountability as the ultimately more powerful force, unless it is argued that the Devil and God are equally powerful.

Another response is to point to human beings as the source of evil in the world. Individuals are free to choose how they will live their lives and how they will relate to one another. Often times, humans misuse their freedom and choose unwisely. This, in turn, produces pain and suffering, sometimes for the individuals themselves and often times for others.

This theodicy suggests that people need look no further than themselves to explain why evil occurs. It appeals to the biblical figures Adam and Eve, who were placed in the Garden of Eden and given choices. Their failure to make good choices resulted in the pain and suffering of their expulsion from the Garden.

This theodicy is often called "bad choices," and has as its strength the location of evil in the abuse of human freedom. Each person knows that he/she is not perfect, and extrapolating from this, the individual has a sense of the enormity and gravity of suffering and pain that can result from this imperfection and unwise choices. This theodicy also preserves the goodness and power of God, because humans are the source of evil and because God self-limits God's power in such a way as to preserve human freedom as genuine and not just delusional.

The weakness of this theodicy is that, although it does account for moral evil coming out of the context of the abuse of human freedom, it does not account for natural evil that occurs as a result of earthquakes, floods, tornadoes, epidemic diseases, hurricanes, and tidal waves. And further, it does not ultimately spare God responsibility, since, although God reduced or bracketed God's power in order to create space for human freedom, God could have intervened at any time, and in certain extreme cases of the abuse of human freedom, in order to make things right and set things straight. The Holocaust with its annihilation of 6 million Jews is one specific example.

Another response is to regard pain as a trial or a test. That is, suffering is a means to an end, an end being moral improvement or a demonstration of the strength of a person's faith. Just as fire can temper metal, making it more durable and improving its quality, so the heat of pain and suffering can temper a person's soul, strengthening it and raising its level of maturity. This theodicy is sometimes termed "soul strengthening" and applies to the figure Job, whose trials and tribulations are understood to be a test in which he demonstrates the power and perseverance of his faith.

The strength of this theodicy is that it takes evil and regards it as providing a potential for positive results. Thus, whether pain and suffering is either caused or allowed by God, it can have a good result. As people sometimes say, "Something good can come from something bad."

The weakness of this theodicy is that the amount of pain and suffering may be greater than the benefit to be derived. That is, the extent of evil may outweigh the positive results to be obtained. For example, if someone is tortured and dies at the hands of a barbaric oppressor, the good that comes from this evil may either not be obvious or commensurate with the amount of suffering endured.

A final response is to reconfigure the power that God possesses. According to this theodicy, God has tremendous power, but God does not have unlimited power. This does not mean that God does not influence the world, but it does mean that everything that happens in the world is not determined by God.

This theodicy is called "God's limited power," and it appeals to the biblical record when God acts as an agent of persuasion to influence persons to do the right thing, but not as an agent of determination to *make* persons do the right thing. According to this theodicy, not everything that happens is in accord with God's will, for God's power is neither unlimited nor coercive.

The strength of this theodicy is that it preserves God's goodness and love. The evil in the world is not something that God has the power to change but unfortunately does not have the disposition or will to do so. Rather, evil is something that happens in the world for whatever reason, and God is not in a position either to keep it from happening or to receive the blame for causing it to happen. The weakness of this theodicy is that it makes God's power limited rather than unlimited. Consequently, the traditional understanding of God's majesty and sovereignty is at stake.

Some creative thinkers have tried to combine two or more of these various theodicies in order to form new ones and better ones. But, as is the case with all theodicies, there are strengths in each that deserve to be noted and weaknesses that cannot be overlooked. In a final sense, it comes down to what the individual person finds most appealing or convincing, given that no theodicy is completely watertight.

—Clifford Chalmers Cain

See also Evil; God

FURTHER READING

Griffin, D. R. (1976). *God, power, and evil.* Philadelphia: Westminster Press.

Hick, J. (1963). *Philosophy of religion.* Englewood Cliffs, NJ: Prentice-Hall.

Kushner, H. S. (1989). *When bad things happen to good people.* New York: Schocken.

Lewis, C. S. (1948). *The problem of pain.* New York: Macmillan.

Tremmel, W. C. (1997). *Religion: What is it?* (3rd ed.). Orlando, FL: Harcourt Brace.

THEOLOGIAN, ADOLESCENT AS

Describing contemporary adolescents by the term "theologian" would hardly achieve widespread consensus within developmental or social psychological communities. In describing the religious and spiritual experiences of youth around the globe, one is just as likely to hear adjectives like pluralistic, undeclared, or "agnostic" (i.e., no knowledge that God can or does exist). Adolescence, however, continues to be the period of life when many individuals seek and find answers to their spiritual and religious questions. Before describing three areas of experience prominent during adolescence that illustrates that adolescents are both intentionally and developmentally active in their theological exploration, the term "theologian" is explored as a construct to inform this discussion. As will be demonstrated, the maturational cognitive, social, and behavioral changes that are unique to adolescence contribute quite holistically to the spiritual and religious development of the young person.

WHAT IS A THEOLOGIAN, AND CAN AN ADOLESCENT BE ONE?

Social scientists working in the area of religious and spiritual development seem hesitant to explore a field of study—theology—that has historically been left to seminaries and other religious disciplines. Simply stated, theology is nothing more or less than the study of God; more specifically, it is the ongoing process of seeking, critiquing, and refining an increasing knowledge of God. Thus, a theologian is anyone who speculates about theology, and/or the prominence, nature, and knowledge of God. Implied in this definition is the acknowledgment that, for reasoned exploration to take place, God does indeed exist. That most adolescents believe in the existence of God has been overwhelmingly supported in numerous surveys. What remains to be explored, however, is the nature of how the adolescent experiences, understands, and generally wrestles with the processes critical to acts of theological inquiry, critique, and refinement.

The course of developing one's theological understanding during adolescence is not scripted, nor is there any certainty that all or even most adolescents will come to favorably embrace their understanding of God. Support for this proposition comes from studies looking at a developing theologian's supposed antithesis—atheism—wherein at least four types of atheists have been identified. First, developmental atheists are those who designate themselves as atheists when they claim not to believe in what they believed at earlier ages. Second, social or ecclesiastical atheists are those who have quit as members of a church or other religious institutions. Third, philosophical atheists are those who have thoroughly worked through their former beliefs, and hence denied any existence of a divine Ultimate Being. Finally, easy atheists are those who are characterized by an absolute absence of interest in religious affairs.

For all but the easy atheist, then, even adolescents who reject God, the church, and/or its principles appear to expend considerable cognitive energy and social commitment to the consideration of and decisions about religious faith and God. Theologians are not defined by the results of their searching and refining, only by the fact that they extend effort and resources in attempts to increase their understanding of religious faith and God. In this way, is every individual who has some reason for his or her atheism a theologian, too? Atheists who intentionally and objectively examine their faith, and consequently come to deny His existence, usually know very well what they are rejecting or have lost—sometimes even better than believers who more or less let God be God. Whether the adolescent accepts or rejects this understanding does not disqualify her or him as a theologian. There are at least three processes prominent within most adolescents' experience—religious doubt, theological dissonance, and identity formation—that contribute to the essence of theological inquiry.

DOUBT, ATTRIBUTIONS, AND THE ADOLESCENT THEOLOGIAN

Religious and theological understanding for children in their primary school years is largely imitative in nature. Learning religious practice rather than developing religious belief is the primary experience for the child. As children become adolescents, their cognitive abilities and social environments expand and allow for more abstract questioning and consequent understanding of religious ideas. Such developmental change is certainly one of the reasons why most religious decision making, including conversion and apostasy (i.e., the renunciation of a religious faith), takes place before the age of 19.

Rather than becoming increasingly engaged in religious pursuits, however, religious awareness and understanding appears to stutter during the transition from childhood into adolescence. The theory is that as children move into adolescence, experiences that were once interpreted as evidence of God's nearness or guidance are now given a more secular interpretation. Cognitive attributions of God also change during adolescence, in that school-age children tend to experience God more in situations of fear, loneliness, and emergencies, while adolescents identify more internal difficulties as the source of their experiencing God. Thus, children progress from a concrete, separate, and external experience of God to a more abstract, general, and internalized experience during adolescence.

Adolescents' conceptualizations of God are also qualitatively different from those of children. Descriptions of God tend to include more symbolism, suggesting that there exists a progression of cognitive abilities that allow children to use such representations more freely with age. As children get older, the way they talk about God tends to change from the concrete mode of thinking to reflect more abstraction, conceptualization, and symbolization. This transformation in thinking allows adolescents to cognitively process "things spiritual" in a way that differs from childhood. Such qualitative change in thinking, however, often leaves the adolescent consumed with *doubt;* doubt about the authenticity and/or origins of their faith (e.g., church, parents), and about their capacity to come to their own conclusions about faith and God without the guidance of these foundations.

Empirical studies on the function of religious doubt further inform the proposition of the adolescent as theologian. For example, although religious doubt during adolescence is not accurately defined by the presence of consistent internal (e.g., cognitive maturation) or external (e.g., peer influence) factors, there is some indication that doubts tend to hang together in a general "doubt syndrome." Furthermore, there is some correlation between the extent of one's religious doubts and the integrative complexity of thinking about those doubts. The questions remain as to whether the adolescent theologian extends the psychological energy necessary for both deep and complex doubt, and whether such doubt always results in disengagement from religious faith. In most cases, the religious doubt expressed by the typical adolescent is not so much a denial of a specific teaching or spiritual leadership as it is an expression of a more general tendency to question and wonder about things.

The presence of doubt related to religious beliefs during adolescence is not purely an intellectual exercise. Estimates are that upward of one-half of children in North America under 12 years of age attend religious gatherings at least once a month (the majority being weekly attendees), while only one in three 13- to 18-year-olds attend with the same regularity. Such privatization of belief among youth around the world may be linked to a decrease in the social prominence of religion in pluralistic societies (e.g., Australia). Thus, although adolescents have the potential to experience God and their religious faith in ways that are qualitatively more complex and dynamic than that of their childhood counterparts, many adolescents consider their theological options from a distance. It may be that many young theologians make intentional use of a prodigal experience, a religious running away, that includes exercising the freedom to abandon behavioral elements of their faith (e.g., church attendance) as part of their theological journey.

DISSONANCE AND RELIGIOUS DECISION MAKING

Taken together, the considerations above on atheism, religious doubt, and temporary abandonment support the proposition that the period of adolescence is ripe for both religious embracing *and/or* religious rebellion, risks that all theologians must be willing to take as they seek to increase their understanding of God. Most transitions in religious development are also facilitated by a *dissonance* that exists between belief and disbelief or between their religious attitudes and behavior. Some would state that this cognitive discomfort represents the perceived contradictions between religious authorities (e.g., church, parents) and disconfirming experiences (e.g., identity confusion) that force the adolescent to introspectively reflect on certain unavoidable tensions. One of the ways of resolving such dissonance is via overt (e.g., at-risk behavior) or covert (e.g., intellectual exploration) rejection of authoritative religious values; this is commonly known as rebellion within most religious communities. The debate continues as to whether such rebellion contributes to religious development or is more characteristic of disengagement from religion. What is known is that the cognitive dissonance involving the tension between the offering of unconstrained spiritual opportunities and those more traditional attempts at religious development (e.g., church, parochial schooling) becomes palatable for the adolescent.

One factor contributing to the resolution of this dissonance (and the concomitant rebellion) may be the response from those within the adolescent's social and interpersonal milieu. Whether such dissonance is viewed as "backsliding" or as potentially growth producing is significantly informed by the perceived support (or lack thereof) of the adolescent's social environment (e.g., church, family, peers). In many cases, if significant others approach such questioning with overtures of support and encouragement, the adolescent is more likely to complete this reconsolidation and internalization of his or her religiosity or spirituality. This resonates well with the notion that one's capacity for mature relationships with others is a predictor of one's capacity for a mature relationship with God, which is a core component of spiritual development. Alternatively, for young theologians who are forced to comply with a faith that is not their own, the result is likely to be either a foreclosed and defensive faith or outright rejection of religious faith or spirituality.

SEEKING SELF, SEEKING GOD

The dissonance, doubt, and decision making that permeate many an adolescent theologian's experience take place within the larger domain of identity formation. Developmental psychology has taught us that if we gain nothing else from adolescence, we must obtain a coherent sense of self-identity that will assist us in successfully navigating future life stages. Although most would endorse the importance of identity formation, and despite the presence of religion as one of the stated ideological components of identity development, there are relatively few published empirical studies on the religious correlates of identity. Those that do explore such terrain find predictable results; adolescents who find themselves in psychological spaces where identity exploration is either discouraged or undervalued are often also uncommitted or extrinsic in their religious orientation, while those who are actively exploring or have achieved a reliable identity status (e.g., have both explored and committed to an identity) are also associated with intrinsic, personally invested religious orientations.

Although the directionality of the identity—-religiosity association is not elucidated by research to date, it is clear that those adolescents who have intentionally sought answers to two important questions, "Who am I?" and "Who is God?" seem to come to favorable conclusions in both regards. It may be that the doubt and dissonance associated with the search for self and God culminates in an experience of fidelity (a resolving virtue of identity development) and intimacy that can only be found when the young theologian devotes him or herself fully to both inquiries. Indeed, research indicates that adolescents who actively engage in activities (e.g., youth service programs) sponsored by faith-based institutions are likely to increase their integrated moral and civic identities in addition to that of transcendent or spiritual sensibility. Thus, it matters little whether the adolescent theologian seeks God and finds self or seeks self and finds God. More importantly, adolescents are capable of extraordinary commitment to the complementary processes of testing the consistency and meaningfulness of their beliefs about self and about

God, criteria that designate them most appropriately as adolescent theologians.

—Kelly Dean Schwartz

See also Doubt

FURTHER READING

Altemeyer, B., & Hunsberger, B. (1997). *Amazing conversions: Why some turn to faith and others abandon religion.* Amherst, NY: Prometheus Books.

Lerner, R. M., Dowling, E. M., & Anderson, P. M. (2003). Positive youth development: Thriving as the basis for personhood and civil society. *Applied Developmental Science, 7*(3), 172–180.

Parks, S. (1991). *The critical years: Young adults and the search for meaning, faith, and commitment.* San Francisco: HarperCollins Publishers.

Shelton, C. M. (1983). *Adolescent spirituality: Pastoral ministry for high school and college youth.* New York: Crossroads.

THICH NHAT HANH

Thich Nhat Hanh (pronounced *tick-not-hawn*) is one of the most well-known Buddhists in the world today. He is regarded as the founder of "socially engaged Buddhism," and was nominated by Martin Luther King, Jr. for the Nobel Peace Prize in 1967 in recognition of his work to end the war in Vietnam. He is the author of more than 100 books, which have been translated into more than 20 languages. These books include works on Buddhist philosophy and practice, history, fiction, and poetry.

Thich Nhat Hanh was born in Vietnam in 1926. His given name was Nguyen Xuan Bao. Thich Nhat Hanh is the name he received after becoming a monk. "Thich" is a title of respect given to all Buddhist monks and nuns in the Vietnamese tradition. "Nhat Hanh" means "One Action." Thich Nhat Hanh is most commonly referred to by his followers as "Thây," which means "Teacher."

Thich Nhat Hanh became a Buddhist novice at the age of 16 and received full ordination as a monk at the age of 23. A Buddhist revival was taking place in his homeland during this time, as the Vietnamese people sought to revitalize their own culture and traditions in response to French colonial rule. After World War II, Vietnam declared its independence, which led to a decade-long war with the French. After the Vietnamese defeated the French in 1954, a war with the United States began. This war would result in the deaths of nearly 3 million people. Throughout his life in Vietnam, Thich Nhat Hanh lived in the context of war, and it was in response to injustice and war that his understanding of Buddhism developed. Dissatisfied with simply finding a path to personal peace, he stressed that Buddhists must be socially engaged and must seek ways to actively address problems such as war and poverty. This social engagement, he argued, was required by the Buddhist vow to relieve the suffering of others.

In the midst of war in Vietnam, Thich Nhat Hanh helped to found several institutes for Buddhist studies and a Buddhist publication house, assisted in the formation of the Unified Buddhist Church of Vietnam, founded the Order of Interbeing, and established the School of Youth for Social Service. The School of Youth for Social Service trained young people and sent them out into the villages to engage in projects of education, health care, community organizing, and grassroots economic development. As the war escalated and many villages were destroyed, much of the effort of the School turned to relief and reconstruction projects. Many students and colleagues of Thich Nhat Hanh were killed during the war. Thich Nhat Hanh and his followers sought to foster reconciliation, and were committed to nonviolence, refusing to support any armed group. This position of neutrality led them to be viewed suspiciously by all of the armed parties, and they suffered violence from all sides.

In 1966, Thich Nhat Hanh left Vietnam to visit the United States. He had previously spent 2 years living in the United States as a student of comparative religion at Princeton University and as a professor at Columbia University. This time he came with a mission to call upon the American people to put an end to the war in Vietnam. He met with members of Congress, peace groups, and with people such as Martin Luther King, Jr. and Thomas Merton, the famous Catholic monk and author.

After his visit to the United States in 1966, Thich Nhat Hanh was refused entry back into Vietnam. He has lived in exile from Vietnam ever since. Currently he lives in Plum Village, a community that he founded in southern France. The community is made up of monks, nuns, and other members of the Order of Interbeing, refugee families, and many visitors who come each year for retreats. Thich Nhat Hanh also regularly travels throughout the world to speak and lead retreats, including trips to the United States every other year. Many of the retreats that he gives in the United States are for veterans of the Vietnam War, trying to help these veterans to heal from their spiritual and psychological wounds of the war.

The religious teachings of Thich Nhat Hanh center upon the practices of mindfulness and meditation. Mindfulness involves being fully present to the present moment, and in so doing coming into touch with the joys and wonders of life. Being in touch with the joys and wonders of life does not, however, mean overlooking life's suffering. Rather, through mindfulness and meditation one is able to look honestly at the negative realities of life without being overcome by grief, anger, or despair. Practices of mindfulness and meditation enable one to transform these negative emotions such as anger into positive action for reconciliation, healing, and social justice.

For Thich Nhat Hanh, as for Buddhists in general, the central virtue is compassion. By "looking deeply" through meditation, one comes to understand that those who cause harm do so as a result of their own brokenness and suffering. Rather than seeking to destroy them, the appropriate response is to seek ways to bring about healing.

At the heart of Buddhism are five ethical precepts. Thich Nhat Hanh refers to them as the five "mindfulness trainings." These include commitments to (1) foster compassion for all living beings/don't kill; (2) foster generosity/don't steal or exploit; (3) foster responsible sexuality/don't engage in sexual activity without love and a long-term commitment; (4) foster loving and truthful speech/don't lie, gossip, or slander; and (5) practice mindful consumption/don't use substances that cloud the mind such as drugs and alcohol.

Thich Nhat Hanh stresses that these practices of mindfulness, meditation, and commitment to the ethical precepts are not of value only to Buddhists. They are practices that persons of all religious traditions can benefit from. Thich Nhat Hanh's life serves as a model for how life experiences can influence the direction of one's religious development and in what ways one's religious life can impact the lives of others.

—John Sniegocki

See also Buddhism; Buddhism, Socially Engaged

FURTHER READING

Nhat Hanh, T. (1987). *The miracle of mindfulness: An introduction to the practice of meditation*. Boston: Beacon Press.

Nhat Hanh, T. (2001). *Essential writings*. Maryknoll, NY: Orbis Books.

Nhat Hanh, T. (1995). *Living Buddha, living Christ*. New York: Riverhead Books.

TORAH

In the narrowest sense, the Hebrew word *Torah* refers to the first five books of the Bible. They are also called the Five Books of Moses (and from the Greek, the Pentateuch), because historically Judaism accepted that not just the Ten Commandments, but the entire Torah was revealed to Moses and to the Jewish people at Mount Sinai. The Torah contains the laws of Judaism (including 603 *mitzvot* or commandments) and provides an ethical framework for the Jewish people. It also contains the history of the Jewish people from the creation of the world until their arrival at Canaan after the exodus from Egypt. The Torah is of central influence to the religious and spiritual development of Jews around the world.

The Pentateuch is made up of five books: Genesis, Exodus, Leviticus, Numbers, and Deuteronomy. Genesis (or "In the beginning") tells the story of the creation of the world, and Adam and Eve's exile from the Garden of Eden, as well as the story of Noah and the great flood that destroyed the world. It also tells the story of the fathers (or Patriarchs) of Judaism, and of great importance, it tells of the covenant between God and Abraham, in which God selects Abraham and his descendents as the "chosen" people. Exodus (or "Going out") tells the story of Moses and of the Jews' delivery from slavery in Egypt. It also tells the story of Moses receiving the Torah from God on Mount Sinai. Leviticus (or "Then he called") is a book of laws and instructions, specifically relating to rituals and practices associated with worshiping God. Numbers (or "In the wilderness") tells the story of the Jews wandering in the desert for 40 years after the Jews left Egypt. Finally, Deuteronomy (or "Words") consists of the last teachings of Moses before his death. It is a summary of the laws by which the Jews are to live. Its purpose is to promote purity and unity among the Jews.

The Jewish holiday of Shavuot, which occurs in the spring, celebrates the giving of the Torah at Mt. Sinai. On the eve of Shavuot, it is traditional to stay up all night to study Torah. Many synagogues hold study sessions so that congregates can learn together as a community.

In a broader sense, Torah can refer to the entire Jewish Bible (or Tanakh), which in addition to the Five Books of Moses, includes the Prophets (Nevi'im) and the Writings (Kethuvim). The Prophets consists of 21 books. The first 9 are Joshua, Judges, I Samuel, II Samuel, I Kings, II Kings, Isaiah, Jeremiah, and Ezekiel. There are an additional 12 books of Minor Prophets: Hosea, Joel, Amos, Obadiah, Jonah, Michah, Nahum, Habakkuk, Zephaniah, Haggai, Zechariah, and Malachi. The Writings consist of 13 books: Psalms, Proverbs, Job, Song of Songs, Ruth, Lamentations, Ecclesiastes, Esther, Daniel, Ezra, Nehemiah, and I Chronicles, and II Chronicles.

Beyond the Bible is the Oral Torah, which came to be the Talmud. Traditionally, Judaism asserts that the Oral Torah is the oral instructions God gave to Moses on Mount Sinai along with the Written Torah. These instructions involved how to interpret the written scriptures. In the 2nd century C.E., owing to fears that the Oral Torah would be forgotten, a basic outline called the *Mishnah* was written. This outline did not include in-depth explanations of the laws (or Gemara) of Judaism. In 5th century C.E. (about 300 years after the Mishnah was completed), the Mishnah and the Gemara were compiled into a complete work called the *Talmud*. The Talmud thus contains all of the oral instructions and laws of Judaism. (There are actually two Talmuds, one written in Jerusalem and one in Babylonia. The Babylonian Talmud became the authoritative version.)

The Talmud is made up of six sections called *sedarim* (or "orders"), which are further divided into 63 *masekhot* (or "tractates"). The six Seders are Seeds, Season, Women, Damages, Holy Things, and Purities. Seeds deals with the laws of agriculture, prayer, and blessings. Season deals with the laws of the Sabbath and holidays. Women deals with the laws of marriage, divorce, and contracts. Damages deals with civil law, financial law, and ethics. Holy Things deals with sacrifices and the Temple. Purities deals with the laws of ritual purity.

The Torah used for services in Judaism is written on a parchment scroll. The scrolls are handwritten in Hebrew calligraphy by a *sofer* or ritual scribe and are scrolled from right to left, just as the words are written right to left. One is never supposed to touch the parchment of the Torah, and thus when reading from it, a pointer is used. The scrolls are covered with fabric, often ornamented with crowns on the handles and a breastplate on the front. These scrolls are kept in a cabinet in the Temple called an "ark."

Each week in synagogue, a passage of the Torah, called a *parshah*, is chanted. In addition, a passage from one of the Prophets, called a Haftorah is chanted. (A specific Haftorah is assigned to each *parshah.*) In addition, on holy days and holidays, special readings from the Torah and Haftorah are chanted. The Torah is divided into 54 passages, and the entire Torah (from Genesis to Deuteronomy) is read in 1 year. The final portion of the Torah is read on a holiday called Simchat Torah (or "Rejoicing the Law"), which occurs in the autumn a few weeks after Rosh Hashanah (the Jewish New Year). On Simchat Torah, the final passage of the Torah is read and then immediately, the first few paragraphs of Genesis are read in order to demonstrate the wholeness of the Torah—it is a never-ending circle.

Before chanting from the Torah, the Torah is paraded around the synagogue. The chanting is divided into portions and members of the congregation are given the honor of having an *aliyah* (or "ascension"), which is reciting a blessing over the portion of the reading about to be chanted. In many synagogues, either before or after services, members of the congregation gather to study and discuss that week's portion in more depth.

In the broadest sense, Torah is a Hebrew word that can mean teaching, instruction, or law. Thus, any Jewish study, whether history, philosophy, law, or tradition, can be referred to as Torah study, because ultimately it is derived from what is contained in the Five Books of Moses. Whether defined narrowly or broadly, Torah (both its study and the living out of its precepts) is central to the faith and practice of Judaism.

—Penny F. Altman and Deborah L. Bobek

See also Bible, Jewish

FURTHER READING

Jewish Publication Society. (1985). *Tanakh, a new translation of the Holy Scriptures according to the traditional Hebrew text.* Philadelphia: Jewish Publication Society.

TOWER OF DAVID

The Tower of David is quite literally where Jerusalem began—from historical, religious, and geographical perspectives. To the east of the Tower are historical sites spanning 4,000 years of the city's history including the Exodus, conquests led by Joshua to reach the Promised Land, and construction of the city by King David. To the west of the Tower lies the city of Jerusalem where prophets preached the word of God, foreign invaders penetrated and conquered the land, and where "radicals" emerged such as Jesus. The oldest remains of the city wall are buried in the bedrock of the hill underlying the Tower, which archaeologists have dated back to King Hezekiah in 8th century B.C.E., who built a wall and towers after the Assyrian invasion of Judah documented in 2 Chronicles 32:5. The wall was damaged during the Babylonian invasion, which led to the exile of the Jews in 586—587 B.C.E.

The Tower of David is located atop Mount Zion ridge in the Citadel at the Jaffa Gate entrance to the Old City. The Tower is one of the three surviving towers and surrounding fortresses built by King Herod to defend Jerusalem. Herod built this tower at the West Gate entrance of Jaffa because that location of the city was considered to be a weak link in the city's defense against foreign invaders. The Citadel is known as the Tower of David because it is thought that King Herod built it on the site of an earlier fortress constructed by Kind David. The Tower of David has formed part of the defense structures of Jerusalem for 2,700 years without interruption.

The historian Josephus in his book *The Jewish Wars* details the architectural work of King Herod. King Herod was a great architect who built numerous structures in Caesaria and within Jerusalem. One of Herod's building projects that Josephus describes was his palace, which stretched within the Citadel to the south. Josephus comments that Herod's palace was wondrous beyond words. Herod constructed three defense towers, naming one after his wife Mariamme, his friend Hippicus, and the third after his brother Phasael, which is now the Tower of David renamed by the Byzantines.

According to the New Testament, Jesus was judged at King Herod's palace. The historian Josephus accounts that Jewish "rebels" were summoned before the Roman ruler, and were scourged and then crucified. In 6 B.C.E., the Roman procurator came to Jerusalem to govern, and he resided in the Herodian palace. This is where men of the Roman governing body would stay in Jerusalem. The palace and Citadel have remained sites of importance in Jerusalem.

The treatment of Jewish rebels by the Imperial Cult and Roman forces led to a band of rebels who led numerous attacks against the Romans. The Emperor Vespasian and his son Tacitus led a war against those who rebelled against Roman law. The great fire of 66 C.E. led to the burning of the Herodian palace and a large number of architectural structures within the Citadel.

During the Arabic period, the Fatimids lost the Citadel and Jerusalem to the Crusaders. In centuries to come, the Citadel was destroyed and built up numerous times by a variety of foreign occupations. On the top of the Tower of David is a mosque whose presence marks the Islamic presence in the city of Jerusalem. The minaret of the mosque hangs above the pleated tower top, reminding visitors of Islamic rule in Jerusalem after the Jews were exiled many years before. The Tower and mosque bring together the new and old Jerusalem in a part of history that can never be forgotten. In 1310 C.E., King Bin-Qalawoon built the mosque on the top of the Tower as a religious symbol for all to witness that Islam was the new order in Jerusalem. The Mamluk Sultan Muhammad in the 14th century built the final form of the Citadel. During the Mamluk period, Jerusalem became neglected and the Citadel barely survived.

The Ottoman victory led by Sultan Suliman the Magnificent in the 16th century marks the major renovation project of cleaning the Citadel and constructing the Jaffa Gate entrance to the western wall of the city. After the city became part of the Jewish state in the 20th century, history was made. This was the first time that the Citadel was not used for strategic purposes.

Art and architecture are mirrors of a society. They reflect the state of its values, especially in times of crisis or transition. In the past 10 years, the interior of the Tower of David has been remodeled, transforming this witness of history into a museum. The museum lies within the Citadel, and serves as a testament of the Tower's years of service as part of the city's defense and now educational center. The museum of the Tower of David recounts the history of Jerusalem from its earliest Canaanite days evolving to its periods of glory and defeat, and countless episodes of bloodshed. The museum has the ability to bring 4,000 years of Jerusalem's history to life.

Nowhere in Jerusalem can another site like the Tower of David be found where archaeological finds coexist in situ side by side. The contents within the Tower of David are considered to be an illustrative, rather than a historical, museum. There are no objects of authenticity, but rather the museum uses exhibits that display each period of history to recount the history of Jerusalem.

The history displayed in the museum is neither limited to the city of Jerusalem, nor to the culture of a single people. The displays parallel the history of Jerusalem with the evolution of the Western world, including the earliest developments of Western civilization in the Fertile Crescent, the conquest of Alexander the Great, and the intrusion of numerous empires such as the Greek, Roman, and Ottoman. The birthplace of Christianity and the growth of Islam up until the Industrial Revolution can also be traced through the contents of the Tower of David museum.

The presentation of history within the Tower of David focuses in a symmetrical fashion on the periods of the city's history that tap into different religious systems, including Egyptians (now the Coptic faith that shares the beginning of the Exodus to the Promised Land); Zoroastrianism (which marks the intrusion of Babylon into the city, and the exile of the Jews in 586/587 B.C.E.), and the practices of the many monotheistic (Judaism, Christianity, Islam) and polytheistic (Hinduism, Babylonian, Imperial Cult) faiths.

The Citadel has proven to be a wonderland of priceless finds for archaeologists. The excavation records detail finds unlike any other site, including potsherds, Byzantine wares, Islamic glass, and oil lamps from the Greek and Roman periods. The periods of occupation can be traced through these finds from the Hasmonean period (the time of the Crusades) to the domination of the Ottoman Empire. Below the Tower of David, the visitor can see a medieval moat that was filled in the late 19th century for defense purposes.

The Tower of David continues to inspire research and theories about the city of Jerusalem, and the people who roamed the site of the birthplace of numerous religions that exist today, and attempts to tap into the previous world to provide answers to eternal questions, such as the purpose of life. Scholars speculate about the type of warfare that predominated during the city's numerous periods of conflict, as well as who was attacking the city from the Jaffa entrance and why the attacks took place from this side. The Tower of David has intrigued those who have witnessed the silent stone structure that holds the secrets of time within its bricks. Archaeologists and scholars alike continue to visit the Tower to excavate the remains of the past, and thereby shed light on more details about the history of Jerusalem.

—Julie Wieland-Robbescheuten

TRANSFORMATION, RELIGIOUS

Religious transformation is a change in the forms or structures of one's religious being. This could include changes in a person's religious worldview, beliefs, practices, and/or lifestyle. Many factors contribute to religious change such as the discovery of other religions, or disappointment in one's religion due to suffering or other difficulties and contradictions. However, religious change also results from natural human development as it occurs throughout the life span.

Change in religious faith and morality parallels the development of the personality. Although human development does not equal religious transformation, religious change corresponds with, and is enabled by, the natural forces of human growth. Religious transformation, as it occurs throughout the life span, must be described in relation to stages of human development.

INFANCY

The relationship between human growth and religious life begins at birth and is transformed with each new stage of development. The capacity to deal with absent objects (such as a parent who leaves the sight of an infant) develops during infancy, leading to a lifelong search for permanence in a world of change. The concept of God is a universal religious solution to this search.

CHILDHOOD

Children apply their normal cognitive (thinking) processes to religious ideas and concepts, and their cognitive developmental level sets the limits for their level of religious thinking. During the early years (ages 2 to 6), stable patterns of knowing are not yet developed, and a child's ability to reason is controlled more by the imagination than by logical thought. Children at this stage of development are, at times, unconcerned with reality, and learn through free experimentation and intuition. Young children do not yet distinguish between fantasy and reality, and tend to think of God in magical terms or concrete terms such as God's being a kind and generous old man with a beard. Such views are often reinforced, and even introduced, by adults, so it is often difficult to say for sure what part of children's beliefs comes from adults, and what part comes from their own minds.

At about age 7, a dramatic shift occurs in a child's reasoning abilities from intuition and imagination to thinking that is concrete (tangible, practical) and based on reality. Children at this stage of development can clearly distinguish between dreams and reality, but cannot yet distinguish between a hypothesis and a fact. At this developmental stage, a child's concept of God/sacred would be based on concrete images or objects such as pictures, icons, and religious books such as the Torah or the Bible.

Older children (ages 7 to 12) understand and embrace concrete images and expressions of religious life because they are only capable of applying their logical reasoning to present concrete objects or events. A religious statue would be an example of a concrete image, and a worship practice such as prayer would be an example of a concrete expression of religious life. Older children also establish a sense of belonging to their religious communities by acceptance of the religious stories, beliefs, symbols, and moral rules that are taken literally (real, based on actual facts).

ADOLESCENCE

As a child enters adolescence (age 12), the limitations of concrete thinking are altered and the beginning of formal operational thinking is attained. The cognitive growth to formal thinking includes the capacity to construct hypotheses, form generalizations, and demonstrate abstract thinking. While the concrete thinking of childhood focuses on objects, the formal thinking of adolescence involves thinking about concepts and their relationships. Formal thinking is thinking about thinking.

Although there is a big difference in the religious thinking of those entering adolescence, and the older adolescent, both early and late adolescents share freedom from the limitations of concrete thinking. By age 13, most adolescents are able to begin thinking in terms of propositions (belief statements) that coincide with their ability to understand God through symbolic and abstract ideas. In other words with this new level of thinking, adolescents are capable of understanding their religion through statements of belief such as "God is love," and symbols such as a dove that stands for peace or a cross that stands for Christianity.

The transition to formal thought allows the adolescent to explore questions regarding the meaning of life that would include questions of beliefs and values. Although formal thinking in early adolescence is undeveloped, it may still lead the young adolescent to ask complex questions and look for answers that are beyond the young adolescent's ability to understand. As the adolescent develops deeper levels of hypothetical reasoning and intellectual abstraction, the adolescent may deal with complex questions of faith and meaning.

The ability to think beyond the present and to think about thinking enables the adolescent to form theories and ideas about the state of the world. This reflective ability then leads to the construction of personal values and beliefs needed to reform the world. Although adolescents are capable of living and defending their ideals, they are not yet capable of reflecting critically upon their ideals.

ADULTHOOD

The thinking capacity that develops during adolescence remains throughout adulthood, providing ongoing potential for growth in every dimension of life. Religious development continues to correspond with the natural forces of cognitive and emotional growth and can be described according to the three distinctive phases of adulthood: early, middle, and older.

Whereas children and adolescents rely on others such as religious leaders and parents to provide and support their religious beliefs and way of life, young adults rely more on their own judgment. As individuals transition to early adulthood, they begin taking self-conscious responsibility for religious commitments and moral actions. Intellectual development during early adulthood involves ambivalence and a discovery of relativism that result in spiritual searching and wariness.

While young adults clearly choose one set of ideals or values over another, middle-aged adults are more open to accepting opposite or contradictory views. Religion during middle adulthood is often marked by complexity, ambiguity, and respect for other religious beliefs and traditions. Although middle-aged adults may firmly maintain commitment to one particular religion, they can do so while realizing that their perspective on life and faith is not the final fullness of truth.

As people age, their perspective on life and faith continues to expand, because older adults are able to look at the world through the perspectives of others. Religion for older adults involves commitment to the values that give meaning and worth to their lives, and they often join causes or institutions that promise to maintain their values into the future.

—Beverly C. Johnson-Miller

FURTHER READING

Fowler, J. (1981). *Stages of faith: The psychology of human development and the quest for meaning*. San Francisco: Harper and Row.

Goldman, R. (1968). *Religious thinking from childhood to adolescence*. New York: Seabury Press.

Johnson-Miller, B. C. (2000). The complexity of religious transformation. Ann Arbor, MI: UMI Dissertation Services.

Parks, S. (1986). *The critical years: The young adult search for a faith to live by*. San Francisco: Harper & Row.

TROELTSCH, ERNST

Ernst Peter Wilhelm Troeltsch (1865–1923) was a German Protestant theologian and philosopher of history and culture. He taught theology at the Universities of Göttingen (1891–1892), Bonn (1892–1894), and Heidelberg (1894–1915) before taking up his final post as professor of the study of culture at the University of Berlin (1915–1923). Troeltsch is well-known for the way he used the concepts church, sect, and mysticism to characterize types of Christian groups as well as for his discussions of the proper Christian attitude toward other religions.

In his most famous published work, *The Social Teaching of the Christian Churches* (1912), Troeltsch details how, throughout Christian history, Christians have fallen into three main categories or "types" of social groups, which he designates church, sect, and mysticism. The church type, which seeks to accommodate itself to the wider society as much as it can, represents Christian society in its most highly organized and institutional form. Thanks to Christ's death and resurrection, the church possesses divine grace, and is therefore able to offer salvation to its members. There are no demanding entrance or membership requirements in the church type; it is open to the masses, to people of widely varying degrees of religious commitment and moral integrity.

By way of contrast, the sect type is more a voluntary society than an institution. Rather than seeking to accommodate itself to the wider society, the sect tends to view itself as being in an adversarial relationship with society. Indeed, part of the sect's witness is to pass judgment on the evils of "the world." Membership in the sect is open only to "true believers," those who have had strong personal experiences of being "reborn." Members must maintain high standards of religious practice and ethical uprightness, or risk being expelled from the sect.

Mysticism emphasizes personal, inward religious, or spiritual experience over doctrines and public worship, and is therefore the least formally organized type of Christian association. Small numbers of like-minded Christians band together to share their mystical experiences, and encourage each other in their spiritual endeavors. Such groups tend to be temporary, rather than permanent.

Troeltsch's categories of church, sect, and mysticism can be viewed as an anticipation of more recent theories related to spiritual personality types, in which there is a recognition that "one size does not fit all" in the realms of religion and spirituality. People are fundamentally different, so different people will naturally seek different ways of forming religious or spiritual associations. Young people may want to begin the soul-searching process that leads to the discovery of which sort of religious society, or which type of spiritual association, best fits their own spiritual personality.

Troeltsch's other important contribution concerns his view of the proper Christian attitude toward other religions. Very significantly, his attitude toward other religions changed as he matured. Earlier in his life, Troeltsch was convinced that Christianity was the world's one and only "supremely valid" or "absolutely valid" religion—that its superiority over other religions could actually be demonstrated. He articulated this position in *The Absoluteness of Christianity and the History of Religions* (1902).

Upon further reflection, Troeltsch changed his mind on this crucial issue. In his *Christian Thought: Its History and Application* (1923), he concluded that Buddhism is just as "absolutely valid" for the Buddhist, Islam just as "absolutely valid" for the Muslim, and so on, as is Christianity for the Christian. This later position is a form of relativism, insofar as it recognizes that one's view of what is religiously or spiritually true "relates to," or emerges "in relationship with," the religious or spiritual tradition to which one is committed.

Today more than ever, the survival and well-being of the world depend on interreligious understanding and tolerance. This question that Troeltsch struggled with through much of his life—"What is my stance toward the religious other?"—is a question all serious religious and spiritual people need to ponder, preferably beginning when they are still young.

—Joseph Molleur

See also Mysticism

FURTHER READING

Drescher, H. G. (1993). *Ernst Troeltsch: His life and work* (J. Bowden, Trans.). Minneapolis: Fortress.

Troeltsch, E. (1923, 1979). *Christian thought: Its history and application* (F. von Hügel, Ed.). London: University of London Press; reprint, Westport, CT: Hyperion.

Troeltsch, E. (1960). *The social teaching of the Christian churches*. (O. Wyon, Trans.). New York: Harper & Row.

TUTU, ARCHBISHOP DESMOND, AND THE SOUTH AFRICAN TRUTH AND RECONCILIATION COMMISSION

Throughout most of the 20th century the nonwhite population of South Africa suffered from discrimination. This included legislation that prevented nonwhites from voting in elections. One fervent campaigner against this discrimination was Archbishop Desmond Tutu. Tutu, who retired as the Anglican archbishop of Cape Town in 1996, had been a long-time campaigner for equal rights for nonwhites because he believed that the racist political system in South Africa did not measure up to the standards of the Christian religion. Tutu argued that the Bible teaches that all men are equal; the South African political system taught that nonwhites were second-class citizens. In 1984, he won the Nobel Peace Prize for his campaigning.

Tutu was born in 1931, and began his career as a teacher. After studying theology, he became a Church of England minister in 1960. Having completed a master's degree at King's College in London, he returned to South Africa to teach theology. In 1975, he was the first black minister to be appointed dean of St. Mary's Cathedral in Johannesburg. He was appointed bishop of Lesotho in 1978 and archbishop in 1986. He is a lively and energetic character, always full of fun. As Archbishop, he would often get up at 4 o'clock in the morning to pray for up to an hour. It was his spirituality and his religious faith that led him into the field of politics. For Tutu, being a Christian meant opposing prejudice and racism in South Africa.

By the mid-1990s, the racist political system known as apartheid had been demolished, and in 1994 nonwhites were able to vote for the first time in a democratic election. Nelson Mandela, who became the nation's president, set up a Truth and Reconciliation Commission with Desmond Tutu as its chair. The Commission began its work in 1996, and presented a five-volume report to President Mandela in 1998.

For much of the 20th century, South Africa practiced apartheid. This meant that whites and nonwhites developed and lived separately. There were separate schools for white children; if families went to visit the beach, the whites enjoyed the best areas while the nonwhites bathed together at separate beaches. In the event of a road accident, two ambulances would be called, one for the white victims and one for the nonwhites. Shops had separate entrances; the whites would enter by the front entrance while the nonwhites would enter elsewhere. Nonwhites were not generally permitted in areas where the white population lived. They had to carry a pass that indicated which areas they were allowed to visit. Many of the nonwhites lived in townships or slum areas outside the major cities.

The injustice of apartheid led to hate, violence, and killing. This was not only between the white and nonwhite communities, but sometimes also within various nonwhite communities themselves, as different political parties and individuals argued for different ways to end the apartheid system. In 1960, black South Africans organized a peaceful protest against the injustice of apartheid at Sharpeville. The white South African police killed 69 protesters. Many were shot in the back—they clearly represented no threat to the police at all. In 1976, a group of unarmed schoolchildren were shot and killed as they demonstrated against the fact that they were not allowed to be educated in their own language, but had to receive their schooling in Afrikaans, the language of the whites. Blacks would often be arrested by the police, and some would die while in police detention.

In 1994, the apartheid system came to an end. Nonwhites were allowed to vote, and they were no longer treated as second-class citizens. Nelson Mandela's government had to decide what to do with all the people, white and nonwhite, who had caused so much suffering and death in previous years. Three options were available. First, it could set up courts to try those who were alleged to have carried out crimes. This option would be very costly, and in many cases it would be difficult to find people who had witnessed incidents. It was therefore rejected. Second, the government could offer amnesty—it could say that crimes that had taken place under the apartheid system were to be forgotten, and that no one could bring criminal proceedings against anyone. That seemed to be unfair to those who had suffered, so Nelson Mandela recommended to the South African Parliament that it should set up a Truth and Reconciliation Commission.

The act of Parliament that set up the Truth and Reconciliation Commission said that people who had committed politically motivated crimes would be granted amnesty—they would be forgiven—provided that they made a full confession to the Commission. In addition, anyone who had been a victim was offered a hearing at one of the Commission's meetings—their story would be listened to and recorded.

What Mandela and Tutu wanted was for people to forgive rather than to seek revenge. They were asking blacks to forgive what the whites had done to them. They were asking blacks to forgive what other blacks had done to them. They were asking the whites to forgive what the blacks had done to them. For Desmond Tutu, this idea of forgiveness was at the center of his Christian faith.

The South African Truth and Reconciliation Commission held meetings around the country. One of its meetings took place not far from Bisho, where in 1992 a demonstration had taken place. The demonstration for free political activity had been organized by the African National Congress. The march had ended with 28 unarmed protesters being killed by a group of soldiers. The commission hearing took place in a hall that was filled with those who had been injured or who had lost loved ones in the massacre. As the soldiers told what had happened, the blacks became very angry. The audience became hostile. Tutu reports how the senior army officer then turned to the audience and asked for forgiveness. He said that his soldiers were sorry. He said that the massacre was something his soldiers would have to live with for the rest of their lives. He asked the relatives and friends in the audience to forgive what they had done. The crowd, which up till then had been hostile and very near to lynching the soldiers, applauded. The soldiers had been honest and had openly told their story; through their senior officer, they had asked for forgiveness. The black audience, having been asked to forgive, did so.

Another hearing of the Commission dealt with a bomb blast that had taken place in 1983. Twenty-one people had been killed and 219 people injured. The bomb had been planted at the headquarters of the South African Air Force by a black South African. Neville Clarence, one of the 219 people injured, attended the hearing. He had been blinded by the bomb blast. The man applying for an amnesty, Abooker Ismail, apologized for planting the bomb. During the course of the hearing, Clarence went over to Ismail and shook hands with him, saying that he was ready to offer forgiveness. The two men shook hands. Their long handshake appeared on the front pages of many South African newspapers. As at the Bisho massacre hearing, there was no revenge or retribution, only reconciliation between people and forgiveness.

In the hearings of the Truth and Reconciliation Commission, Tutu saw forgiveness and reconciliation again and again. This for him was the route demanded by his Christian faith—he felt that in following this path, he was following the example of Jesus. Desmond Tutu says that people,

> despite the awfulness of their deeds, remain children of God with the capacity to repent and to be able to change. . . . This is a moral universe. . . . [T]here is no way that evil and injustice and oppression and lies can have the last word. . . . It is in our best interest that we become forgiving, repentant, reconciling and reconciled people because without forgiveness, without reconciliation, we have no future.

Tutu hopes that other countries might follow the same path as South Africa and its Truth and Reconciliation Commission. He suggests that God wants others to look at what happened in South Africa and to follow its example. He suggests that God wants to use South Africa as a symbol of hope for other countries caught up in violence and turmoil. He often says that what happened in South Africa could act as a model for what could happen in Israel/Palestine.

Desmond Tutu and the South African Truth and Reconciliation Commission show how Christian teaching of forgiveness can be put into action at a political level. Tutu would argue that Christianity is not just something that one lives as an individual, but that it also has consequences for how we live in society. The pain and suffering of the nonwhite South Africans and their subsequent response to the call to forgive is seen by many as a shining reflection of the Christian gospel.

—David G. Kibble

See also Forgiveness

FURTHER READING

Botman, H. R. & Petersen, R. (Eds.). (1996). *To remember and to heal: Theological and psychological reflections on truth and reconciliation.* Cape Town, Human and Rousseau.

Bronkhorst, D. (1995). *Truth and reconciliation: Obstacles and opportunities for human rights*. Amsterdam: Amnesty International (Dutch section).

Graybill, L. S. (2002). *Truth and reconciliation in South Africa: Miracle or model*? Boulder, CO: Lynne Riener.

Tutu, D. (1996). *No future without forgiveness*. New York: Doubleday.

TYRANTS

Tyrants have played a special role in the spiritual history of Judaism and Christianity. In stories about evil tyrants, Jews and Christians alike have found messages about faith and about the superior power of good when faced with evil. In both the Hebrew and Christian Bibles, we find tyrants first stimulating announcements about the old world order's imminent demise and then apocalyptic visions of the messiah ushering in a new millennium with good triumphing over evil. The Old and New Testaments, then, have provided a lens with which to view tyrants, both old and new.

Tyrants have often been cast as a type of antichrist due to their evil acts toward followers of God. This was the case with Assur, Amalech, and Holofernes, who brutalized the Israelites. It was also the case with Abimilech (Judges 8–9), the son of Gideon, who led the killings of his 70 brothers. Added to this list is Doeg Idumaneus, who slaughtered 85 priests by order of King Saul (1 Samuel 22:7–23). In Exodus 1:15–22, on hearing that an infant had been born who would one day take away his glory, the Pharaoh of Egypt ordered his men to kill the male children of the Hebrew slaves—thereby securing him a special place on the long list of Old Testament tyrants.

However, of all the Old Testament tyrants, Antiochus Ephiphanes (215-164 B.C.E.) may have been the worst. Antiochus Ephipanes has been regarded by many to be the antichrist who will battle with the coming Messiah. In 1 Maccabees, Antiochus attacks worship on the Sabbath by sacking the Golden Altar and holy cups and bowls. In 2 Maccabees 5:15–27, he has his men slaughter the grown men in the Judean wilderness and sells the women and children into slavery.

Antiochus's contempt for the Jews extends into 2 Maccabees 6:1–11, when he issues an edict stating that Jews were to forsake the laws of their ancestors and of God, by calling their temple the Temple of Zeus. Antiochus then proceeds to fill the Holy Temple with statues of Zeus, Apollo, and other Greek gods. This led to the Maccabean revolt, which is still celebrated today in the festival of Chanukah.

The antichrist and evil tyrants are the most fascinating figures of Christian apocalypticism. In medieval times, the term *antichrist* was regularly applied to the evil tyrants of the New Testament. There have been numerous interpretations throughout the ages of who and what this figure of the antichrist might be. Since the Middle Ages, scholars have examined the New Testament, uncovering evil tyrants who persecuted Christians and Christ. These tyrants were opponents of God and his church. The Roman emperors Diocletian, Domitian, and Julian all persecuted the early Christians, and as a result, became types of antichrist.

The peculiar fascination with evil tyrants that led to the compilation of the antichrist figure is due to the horrific actions that these individuals inflicted on the righteous. King Herod is one of the most noteworthy, as he ruled the land of Judea in a corrupt and unholy manner. He was a man of great ability, albeit a madman, who was reviled as the king responsible for killing countless priests, courtiers, and families, and who had babies slaughtered in an attempt to murder the Christ child.

In 40 B.C.E., Rome awarded Herod the crown of Israel, and as his first act of defiance to Jewish law, Herod ascended the Capitoline Hill in Rome to make an offering to the Roman gods. This breaks the first two commandments of Jewish law: Thou shalt have no other god but God, and Thou shalt not bow down to idols. Later, Herod defeated the Jewish forces in battle, and took his place on the throne of Israel as king. His first act as king was to put to death the old members of the regime and create a new aristocracy whose members were loyal to him.

In the New Testament, only Nero may have outdone Herod. The interpretations of Nero (Roman emperor, 54–68 C.E.) are interesting, for they join the apocalyptic antichrist to an original pagan belief in the return of Nero. Christians identified Nero with the evil power that the Apostle Paul wrote about in 2 Thessalonians 2:7. Nero's persecutions of the Disciples, the church, and the people of Christ were seen as the work of the devil.

Nero became the worst tyrant of the Christian Bible and later, the full embodiment of the antichrist. The historian Tacitus reported that in the first century, rumors of Nero's return were common among the people of Achaia and Asia after his death. The historian Suentonius wrote that although there was much joy and celebration when Nero died, many expected him to return and destroy his enemies.

The tyrants who populate the Hebrew and Christian Bibles provide clear pictures of the sufferings inflicted on God's people. Yet, without these evil tyrants, there would be fewer moral lessons and fewer examples of the triumph of good over evil. Thus, the stories of tyrants have been about more than just suffering. They have been about the strength and faith of the early Jews and Christians, thus making them models for generations to come. In the end, then, the main message has been that if one has faith in God, good will triumph over evil.

—Julie Wieland-Robbescheuten

FURTHER READING

Elliot, J. K. (1993). *The apocalypse of Peter: From the apocryphal New Testament*. Oxford: Clarendon Press.

Emmerson, R. K. (1981). *Antichrist in the Middle Ages*. Seattle, WA: University of Washington Press.

Hillerbrand, H. (Ed.). (1979). *The Reformation: A narrative history related by contemporary observers and participants*. Grand Rapids, MI: Baker Book House.

Williamson, G. A. (1966). *The history of the church from Christ to Constantine*. New York: New York University Press.

U

UNESCO

The United Nations Educational, Scientific and Cultural Organization (UNESCO)—based in Paris (www.unesco.org)—was formed in the postwar period to cater to the immediate social and cultural needs of the worst affected by the global conflict. As with many other organizations formed at the time, its scope and range of activity rapidly expanded. Technically a key organ of the United Nations machinery, UNESCO has a strong national and regional focus with many offices based in and named after the constituent countries, such as UNESCO UK. Today, UNESCO defines its "forms of action" across the following wide spectrum:

- Establishment of international standards: conventions, agreements, recommendations
- Declarations
- Conferences and meetings
- Studies and research
- Publications: books, periodicals, reports, and documents
- Technical and advisory services to member-states: staff missions, consultants, supplies, and equipment
- Training courses, seminars, and workshops
- Subventions to nongovernmental organizations (NGOs)
- Financial contributions: fellowships, study grants, and travel grants

Two major UNESCO conferences in 1990 and 2000 demonstrate UNESCO's commitment to educational development in the broadest contexts:

- 1990 World Conference of Education for All, Jomtien, Thailand (with UN Development Programme, United Nations International Children's Emergency Fund [UNICEF], and World Bank)
- 2000 World Education Forum, Dakar

The immense scope and range of UNESCO's work are illustrated by the links that the organization has to many aspects of human rights, such as education and working for democracy and pluralism. More information is available at www.unesco.org.

United Nations Educational, Scientific, and Cultural Organization (UNESCO)—Paris: Links

Division of Human Rights, Democracy, Peace and Tolerance

Management of Social Transformations Programme (MOST):

- Multiculturalism
- Linguistic rights
- Religious rights
- Cultural heritage

Intercultural dialogue and pluralism

World Intellectual Property Organization (WIPO), Geneva, Switzerland

Traditional knowledge

Universal Declaration on Linguistic Rights

Child rights

The State of the World's Children 2000

World Education Forum, Dakar 2000

Since 1946, UNESCO has published more than 10,000 titles across the full range of its activities, including book-length reports, scholarly research, and newsletters. Two major UNESCO databases provide the serious researcher with numerous national and global sources of information, many of which have direct relevance to the educational and especially cultural development of young people in a religiously diverse world, notably the UNESDOC database on the Internet, which contains full text of all official UNESCO documents since the end of 1995; and the UNESBIB database of more than 100,000 bibliographical references to UNESCO documents, publications, and its library collection (www.unesco.org).

UNESCO has a special brief for the implementation of international legal standards focusing on or of relevance to freedom of religious and cultural modes of expression. Through its famous World Heritage site label, UNESCO quietly protects many of the planet's most precious natural and human resources. UNESCO's approach to the denial of basic religious and cultural freedoms by oppressive regimes is through encouragement of dialogue, sympathetically envisioned by its Declaration of the Principles of International Cultural Co-operation (UNESCO, 4 November 1966). This must, however, be contextualized by the wider United Nations setting of international legal standards that defend freedom of expression.

International Legal Standards: Defending Freedom of Expression

Convention on the International Right of Correction (16 December 1952, effective 24 August 1962)

Covenant on Civil and Political Rights (1966)

International Covenant on Social, Economic and Cultural Rights (1966)

Declaration of the Principles of International Cultural Co-operation (UNESCO) (4 November 1966)

Recommendation concerning Education for International Understanding, Cooperation and Peace and Education relating to Human Rights and Fundamental Freedoms (UNESCO) (19 November 1974)

For full texts of the documents, follow links at www.unhchr.org.

More widely still, UNESCO's work must be set in the broader remit of the United Nations under the heading of the "right to development," obviously of both direct and indirect relevance to spiritual and religious development, but set within a wider sociocultural and political context.

The right to development is arguably among the most complex of all human rights, partly because development is so broad and thus so difficult a term to define. Several articles of the Universal Declaration are relevant. Examples are Article 23, "Everyone has the right to work"; Article 25, "Everyone has the right to a standard of living adequate for health and well-being"; Article 26, "Everyone has the right to education"; and Article 27, "Everyone has the right to freely participate in the cultural life of the community." All of these directly impinge on personal and social development. Interestingly, Article 29, "Everyone has duties to the community in which alone the free and full development of his personality is possible," is the only article to mention the idea of *duty* or *responsibility* in which the word *development* appears most prominently.

The right to development can be seen as a second-generation right (relating economic, social, and cultural development) or a third-generation right (relating to questions of "human solidarity"). In terms of UN human rights policy, it fits both second- and third-generation thinking. On one hand, notions of development are fundamental to the International Covenant on Economic, Social and Cultural Development (1966). Yet, on the other, the specific UN Declaration on Development appears only in 1986, 20 years after the covenant was written. There are increasing moves to integrate development and human rights discourse together within international legislation. This is evidenced by the following UN conferences and summits to discuss development issues where human rights discourse increasingly came to the fore. The preamble to the Declaration on the Right to Development thus highlights the notion of the indivisibility of all rights. It recognizes that "development is a comprehensive economic, social, cultural and political process, which aims at the constant improvement of the well-being of the entire population and of all individuals on the basis of their active, free and meaningful participation in development and in the fair distribution of benefits resulting therefrom."

Indeed, it recalls the provisions of both the International Covenant on Economic, Social and Cultural Rights and the International Covenant on Civil and Political Rights, and in so doing "the right of peoples to self-determination, by virtue of which they have the right freely to determine their political status and to pursue their economic, social and cultural development." It also recognizes "the right of peoples to exercise, subject to the relevant provisions of both International Covenants on Human Rights, full and complete sovereignty over all their natural wealth and resources." What would have been unthinkable in 1948, and increasingly inevitable in 1966, was the sense of historical injustice done by the presently wealthy and former colonial powers so instrumental in drawing up the Universal Declaration of Human Rights.

The range of post-1948 standards of relevance to the right to development is presented below.

International Legal Standards: Defending the Right to Development

Universal Declaration on the Eradication of Hunger and Malnutrition (16 November 1964)

Declaration on Social Progress and Development (11 December 1969)

Declaration on the Rights of Mentally Retarded Persons (20 December 1971)

Declaration on the Use of Scientific and Technological Progress in the Interests of Peace and for the Benefit of Mankind (10 November 1975)

Declaration on the Rights of Disabled Persons (9 December 1975)

Declaration on the Right of Peoples to Peace (12 November 1984)

Declaration on the Right to Development (4 December 1986)

Guidelines for the Regulation of Computerized Personal Data Files (14 December 1990)

International Convention on the Protection of the Rights of All Migrant Workers and Members of Their Families (18 December 1990)

Principles for the Protection of Persons with Mental Illness and the Improvement of Mental Health Care (17 December 1991)

Universal Declaration on the Human Genome and Human Rights (UNESCO) (11 November 1997)

Right to Enjoy Culture, International Cultural Development and Co-operation Declaration of the Principles of International Cultural Co-operation (UNESCO) (4 November 1966)

Recommendation Concerning Education for International Understanding, Co-operation and Peace and Education Relating to Human Rights and Fundamental Freedoms (UNESCO) (19 November 1974)

For full texts, follow links at www.unhchr.org.

In the final analysis, despite talk of the integrated nature of (economic, social, and cultural; civil and political) rights, the right to development is crucially dependent in one way or another on finance. Thus, the Declaration recognizes that the "creation of conditions favourable to the development of peoples and individuals is the primary responsibility of their States," with hopes that on a global level there might be "a new international economic order."

—*Liam Gearon*

See also Human Rights

FURTHER READING

Bendell, J. (Ed.). (2000). *Terms for endearment: Business, NGOs and sustainable development.* Sheffieldm, UK: Greenleaf.

Gearon, L. (2003). *The human rights handbook: A global perspective for education.* Stoke-on-Trent, UK: Trentham.

Organisation for Economic Co-operation and Development. (2000). *The creative society of the 21st century.* Paris: OECD.

Roddick, A. (2001). *Take it personally: How globalisation affects you and how to fight back.* London: Thorsons.

Schechter, M. G. (2001). *United Nations-sponsored world conferences: Focus on impact and follow-up.* Tokyo: United Nations University Press.

United Nations. (2002). *The Committee on Economic, Social and Cultural Rights.* New York: United Nations.

Webb, W. L., & Bell, R. (1997). *An embarrassment of tyrannies: Twenty-five years of index on censorship.* London: Victor Gollancz.

UNICEF

The United Nations International Children's Emergency Fund (UNICEF) was created by the United Nations General Assembly in 1946 to help children after World War II in Europe. As in many postwar situations affecting civilians, immediate needs included basic needs for survival such as health care, food, and shelter. Over the years, UNICEF's importance in these areas of welfare remains, but the organization has significantly broadened in scope in subsequent decades. In partnership with national governments, nongovernmental organizations, and other United Nations agencies, UNICEF monitors, assists, and facilitates state welfare provision, and is a powerful force for the protection of children's interests, including health and education, as well as those aspects of children's lives that might otherwise be overlooked such as spiritual or religious and cultural identity.

In 1953, UNICEF became a formal part of the United Nations system, with its humanitarian focus on children extended from Europe to the developing world. Its name was shortened to the United Nations Children's Fund, but the acronym UNICEF was somehow retained.

Based in New York City, UNICEF (www.unicef.org) defines its mission as "Changing the world with children," emphasizing both that children are citizens, and therefore partners in the struggle for the fulfillment of their basic human rights. According to its self-defined mission, "UNICEF helps children get the care and stimulation they need in the early years of life and encourages families to educate girls as well as boys. It strives to reduce childhood death and illness and to protect children in the midst of war and natural disaster. UNICEF supports young people, wherever they are, in making informed decisions about their own lives, and strives to build a world in which all children live in dignity and security. Working with national governments, NGOs, other UN agencies and private-sector partners, UNICEF protects children and their rights by providing services and supplies and by helping shape policy agendas and budgets in the best interests of children." The timeline summarized below indicates how this mission has developed since 1946.

1946: Food to Europe

After World War II, children in Europe faced famine and disease. UNICEF was created by the UN to provide emergency aid.

1950: For all the world's children
As Europe recovers after the war, some countries believe that UNICEF's job is over, but the United Nations General Assembly extends UNICEF's task to include working with children and families throughout the developing world.

1953: UNICEF becomes permanent part of the United Nations
The beginning of UNICEF's international campaign against yaws, a disfiguring disease affecting millions of children that could be cured with penicillin.

1959: Rights of the child
The UN General Assembly adopts the Declaration of the Rights of the Child, focusing on children's rights to education, health care, and good nutrition.

1962: Education
In the newly independent African countries, UNICEF supports teacher training and supplies classroom equipment. By 1965, education accounts for 43% of UNICEF's assistance to Africa.

1965: Nobel Peace Prize
UNICEF is awarded the 1965 Nobel Peace Prize in Oslo, Norway, "for the promotion of brotherhood among nations."

1979: International Year of the Child
During this year, marked by celebrations around the world, people and organizations reaffirm their commitment to children's rights.

1981: Breastfeeding Code Approved
The World Health Assembly adopts the International Code of Marketing of Breast Milk Substitutes to stop a decline in breastfeeding.

1983: Child Survival and Development Revolution
UNICEF launches drive to save the lives of millions of children each year through programs that control dehydration, immunize children, and support breastfeeding and good nutrition.

1989: Convention on the Rights of the Child
The Convention is adopted by the UN General Assembly. It enters into force in September 1990. It becomes the most widely accepted human rights treaty in history.

1990: World Summit for Children
An unprecedented summit of heads of state and government at the United Nations in New York City sets 10-year goals for children's health, nutrition, and education.

1996: Children and conflict
Report of the expert of the secretary-general, Graça Machel: "The Impact of Armed Conflict on Children," a study supported by UNICEF.

1998: United Nations Security Council debates children and conflict
The Council's first open debate on the subject reflects the magnitude of international concern for the impact of war on children.

2001: Say Yes for Children campaign launched
The Global Movement for Children begins mobilizing every citizen of every nation to change the world with children. The Say Yes for Children Campaign builds on this momentum, with millions of children and adults around the world pledging their support for critical actions to improve children's lives.

Further details are available at www.unicef.org.

The Summit for Children, with the World Declaration and Plan of Action, held 8–10 May 2002, was a meeting of the UN General Assembly dedicated to the children and adolescents of the world. Providing an opportunity to review progress in the lives of children in the decade since the 1990 World Conference on Children, it brought together government leaders and heads of state, NGOs, and representatives of major UN bodies, as well as children themselves, at the United Nations in New York.

One of the statements arising from the Conference was the World Declaration on the Survival, Protection and Development of Children (see www.unicef.org/wsc/declare/htm). The adopted plan of action related to this Declaration committed participants to carefully timed targets for achieving improvements in the lives of children around the globe. The Global Movement for Children that resulted from the Conference is designed to be a platform for action that "will work to provide a united voice for all those throughout the world working to improve the lives of children." Nelson Mandela and Graça Machel (who wrote an important report in 1996 on children and armed conflict) were among those calling for a partnership between governments, civil society, and the private sector to form a global movement "committed to ending discrimination against children and adolescents." The aim of this partnership has the high ideals of changing the world for children in order to "ensure that every child, without exception, is assured the right to dignity, security and self-fulfillment."

The range of conventions and declarations outlined here reiterate the notion that children's rights are human rights, but that their vulnerability makes it necessary for many more general or seemingly unrelated international legal standards to make particular reference to the specific rights of the child or the context of childhood.

International Legal Standards: Defending Children's Rights

Declaration on the Rights of the Child (20 November 1959)

Declaration on Social and Legal Principles Relating to the Protection and Welfare of Children, with Special Reference to Foster Placement and Adoption Nationally and Internationally (3 December 1986)

Convention on the Rights of the Child (20 November 1989, effective September 1990)

United Nations Rules for the Protection of Juveniles Deprived of the Liberty (14 December 1990)

United Nations Guidelines for the Prevention of Juvenile Delinquency (The Riyadh Guidelines) (14 December 1990)

Optional Protocol to the Convention on the Rights of the Child on the Involvement of Children in Armed Conflict (25 May 2000, effective 12 February 2002)

Optional Protocol to the Convention on the Rights of the Child on the Sale of Children, Child Prostitution and Child Pornography (25 May 2000, effective 18 January 2002)

For full texts of these documents, follow links at www.un.hchr.org.

In the context of children's rights, the 1989 Convention on the Rights of the Child remains the most single ratified of all such UN conventions (see Save the Children and the Rights of the Child).

As recognized at the World Conference in Vienna, there have been many failures in the implementation of many human rights, the years following the adoption of the Convention on the Rights of the Child have been marked by some significant advances on behalf of children.

> Many countries have used the convention as the basis to revise domestic legislation and improve protections for children, or have appointed special ombudspersons or envoys for children. As the Committee on the Rights of the Child, the body that monitors compliance of government parties to the convention, has evaluated country reports under the convention, it has developed new standards of protection and pressed governments for specific reforms. (Strand & Nowrojee 2001)

The World Summit for Children demonstrates at least goodwill in the global community to achieve a better world for children, including protecting and promoting healthy religious and spiritual development, even if reality often falls far short of high ideals.

—Liam Gearon

See also Human Rights; United Nations

FURTHER READING

Beigbeder, Y. (2001). *New challenges for UNICEF: Children, women and human rights.* Basingstoke, UK: Palgrave.

Gearon, L. (2003). *The human rights handbook: A global perspective for education.* Stoke-on-Trent, UK: Trentham.

Landsdown, G. (2001). *Promoting children's participation in democratic decision making.* Florence, Italy: UNICEF.

Strand, R. M., & Nowrojee, B. (2001). Refugees still at risk: Continuing refugee protection concerns in Guinea. *Human Rights Watch (HRW), 13(5A).* http://www.hrw.org/reports/2001/guinea/

UNICEF. (2000). *The UN Convention on the Rights of the Child.* London: UK Committee for UNICEF.

United Nations. (2002). *The rights of the child.* Fact Sheet 10. New York: United Nations.

UNITED NATIONS

In the aftermath of World War I, the international community established the League of Nations to curtail some of the worst excesses of mass slaughter. That the League of Nations was powerless to prevent the genocide and slaughter on a genuinely global scale during World War II did not deter the international community from starting again after that war with the construction of another, not dissimilar organization. Thus, the United Nations (UN) was born with grand aims of world peace and freedom in a tolerant world that worked by consensus but respected the diversity of cultures. The Charter of the UN was signed on 26 June 1945, in San Francisco, at the conclusion of the UN Conference on International Organization, and came into force on 24 October 1945.

It was a world seemingly weary of war. The Preamble to the Charter sets forth a context critical for all aspects of development in any society and determination to:

- Save succeeding generations from the scourge of war, which twice in our lifetime has brought untold sorrow to mankind
- Reaffirm faith in fundamental human rights, in the dignity and worth of the human person, in the equal rights of men and women and of nations large and small
- Establish conditions under which justice and respect for the obligations arising from treaties and other sources of international law can be maintained
- Promote social progress and better standards of life in larger freedom

For these ends, the Charter outlines a code of behavior:

- To practice tolerance and live together in peace with one another as good neighbors
- To unite our strength to maintain international peace and security
- To ensure, by the acceptance of principles, and the institution of methods, that armed force shall not be used, save in the common interest
- To employ international machinery for the promotion of the economic and social advancement of all peoples

Article 1 states that the purposes of the United Nations are:

1. To maintain international peace and security, and to that end: to take effective collective measures for the prevention and removal of threats to the peace, and for the suppression of acts of aggression or other breaches of the peace, and to bring about by peaceful means, and in conformity with the principles of justice and international law, adjustment or settlement of international disputes or situations which might lead to a breach of the peace
2. To develop friendly relations among nations based on respect for the principle of equal rights and self-determination of peoples, and to take other appropriate measures to strengthen universal peace
3. To achieve international co-operation in solving international problems of an economic, social, cultural, or humanitarian character, and in promoting and encouraging respect for human rights and fundamental freedoms for all without distinction as to race, sex, language, or religion
4. To be a center for harmonizing the actions of nations in the attainment of these common ends (For full text of the Charter, follow links at www.un.org.)

The discrepancy between moral ideal and historical/political reality was as evident at the time of the UN Charter as it is now, perhaps more so. The timing, for example, of the first signatures on the Charter on 26 June 1945 is chilling. These signatures appeared—with their commitment to peace amongst nations—less than 2 months before the atomic bombs were dropped on Hiroshima (August 6, 1945) and Nagasaki (August 8, 1945).

The timeline of the United Nations since its inception shows how the organization has developed exponentially into a truly global and far-reaching one. In relation to human rights and humanitarian work in particular, the UN Universal Declaration of Human Rights (1948), signed 3 years after the Charter, has proliferated into a complex of other declarations, covenants, conventions, and world conferences.

The United Nations: A Timeline

1940s

26 June 1945: Signing of the Charter of the United Nations (San Francisco)
9 December 1945: Convention on the Prevention and Punishment of the Crime of Genocide
10 December 1945: Universal Declaration of Human Rights

1950s

4 November 1950: European Convention on Human Rights (Council of Europe)
28 July 1951: Convention relating to the Status of Refugees
20 December 1952: Convention on the Political Rights of Women
23 October 1953: Protocol Amending the Slavery Convention (originally signed in Geneva, Switzerland, 25 September 1926)
28 September 1954: Convention Relating to the Status of Stateless Persons
7 September 1956: Convention on the Abolition of Slavery, the Slave Trade, and Institutions and Practices Similar to Slavery
25 June 1957: Convention on the Abolition of Forced Labor
20 November 1959: Declaration of the Rights of the Child

1960s

14 December 1960: Declaration on the Granting of Independence to Colonial Countries and Peoples
20 November 1963: Declaration on the Elimination of All Forms of Racial Discrimination
21 December 1965: International Convention on the Elimination of All Forms of Racial Discrimination
Committee on the Elimination of All Forms of Racial Discrimination established
16 December 1966: International Covenant on Civil and Political Rights
International Covenant on Economic, Social and Cultural Rights
Human Rights Committee established
7 November 1967: Declaration on the Elimination of Discrimination Against Women
Proclamation of Teheran—International Conference on Human Rights
26 November 1968: Convention on the Non-Applicability of Statutory Limitations to War Crimes Against Humanity

1970s

30 November 1973: International Convention on the Suppression and Punishment of the Crime of Apartheid
9 December 1975: Declaration on the Protection of All Persons from Being Subjected to Torture and Other Cruel, Inhuman or Degrading Treatment or Punishment
18 December 1979: Convention on the Elimination of All Forms of Discrimination Against Women
Committee on the Elimination of All Forms of Discrimination Against Women established

1980s

27 June 1981: African Charter on Human and Peoples' Rights (Organization of African Unity)
25 November 1981: Declaration on the Elimination of All Forms of Intolerance and of Discrimination Based on Religion or Belief
10 December 1984: Convention Against Torture and Other Cruel, Inhuman or Degrading Treatment or Punishment
28 May 1985: Committee on Economic, Social and Cultural Rights established to monitor implementation of International Covenant on Economic, Social and Cultural Rights
4 December 1986: Declaration on the Right to Development
20 November 1989: Convention on the Rights of the Child
Committee on the Rights of the Child established
15 December 1989: Second Optional Protocol to the International Covenant on Civil and Political Rights, aimed at abolition of the death penalty

1990s

14 December 1990: Basic Principles for the Treatment of Principles
18 December 1990: International Convention on the Protection of the Rights of All Migrant Workers and Members of their Families
18 December 1992: Declaration on the Protection of All Persons from Enforced Disappearance
Declaration on the Rights of Persons Belonging to National or Ethnic, Religious or Linguistic Minorities
14 June 1993: World Conference on Human Rights (Vienna) opens
25 June 1993: Vienna Declaration and Plan of Action

20 December 1993: Declaration on the Elimination of Violence Against Women
Third Decade to Combat Racism and Racial Discrimination proclaimed (1995–2004)
Post of United Nations High Commissioner for Human Rights established
21 December 1993: International Decade of the World's Indigenous Peoples proclaimed
23 December 1994: United Nations Decade for Human Rights Education proclaimed (1995–2004)
1995: World Conference on Women's Rights (Beijing)
10 December 1998: Fiftieth anniversary of the Universal Declaration of Human Rights

2001

4–8 September 2001: World Conference against Racism, Xenophobia and All Forms of Discrimination (Durban, South Africa)

Further details are available at www.un.org.

In the context of its historical development, the United Nations has always considered children's issues to be important through work by bodies such as UNICEF and UNESCO. During the 1980s, specific attention to the rights of children as citizens came to the forefront of international legislation through the 1989 Convention on the Rights of the Child.

Unfortunately, in the UN era reality often falls far short of ideals. Of the goals set by such global conferences and UN conventions, one area of failure is in education. Education is a critical factor in eliminating poverty and deprivation. The Global Campaign for Education is an alliance of NGOs—Action Aid, Oxfam, and a number of agencies from the developing world—who have challenged the failure to fulfill the promise of "education for all," which has been central to the UN's mandate since the Universal Declaration. The Global Campaign for Education particularly challenges the declaration made at the World Education Summit in Dakar in 1990, that no country seriously committed to education for all would be prevented from implementing this through lack of resources. In a paper entitled "Broken Promises," the Campaign for Global Education summarizes the crisis:

> Education is a basic right. It is also the keystone of poverty eradication efforts. Yet more than half a century after this right was enshrined in the UN Declaration, education is in crisis in the world's poorest countries. 125 million children—nearly 60 percent of them girls—are out of primary school. Many times that number of children receive an education that is so curtailed, or of such low quality, that they acquire few of the tools needed to escape poverty. Nearly one billion adults are unable to read and write.

The following is a summary statement of the key areas of concern raised by the Global Campaign for Education, including major promises made at the Millennium Summit in 2000 and reaffirmed at the Special Session on Children (May 2002) and the World Summit on Sustainable Development (August 2002), notably:

- Gender equality in primary and secondary schools by 2005
- Universal completion of primary education, and a 50% reduction in adult illiteracy, by 2015

Yet the Campaign for Global Education suggests that "without concerted action by both donors and developing countries' governments, these promises will be broken. On current trends, the goal of universal primary education will be missed in 88 countries, and 75 million children will remain out of school in 2015. Already, the 2005 goal of gender equity in education appears beyond reach." The achievement of such goals remains fundamental to the most basic capacity of children and young people's spiritual and religious development.

—Liam Gearon

See also Human Rights; Save the Children: UNICEF

FURTHER READING

Forsythe, D. P. (2000). *Human rights in international relations.* Cambridge: Cambridge University Press.

Gearon, L. (2003). *The human rights handbook: A global perspective for education.* Stoke-on-Trent, UK: Trentham.

Ryan, S. (2000). *The United Nations and international politics.* London: Macmillan.

Sellar, K. (2002). *The rise and rise of human rights.* London: Sutton.

Wellman, C. (2000). *The proliferation of rights: Moral progress or empty rhetoric?* Boulder, CO: Westview Press.

VAUGHAN, HENRY

Henry Vaughan is a member of that small band of 17th-century poets known as the metaphysicals, whose poetry combines wit, reason, and powerful emotion. In fact, Vaughan wrote in conscious imitation of George Herbert, and in the preface to his most famous collection of poems, *Silex Scintillans* (1650; enlarged edition 1655), he acknowledged both a poetic and a spiritual indebtedness to the author of *The Temple.* It is surprising therefore that those poems which show the most spiritual imagination are those in which the influence of his mentor is least apparent. Vaughan's work and that of his metaphysical cohort represent well the instillation of that which is spiritual and religious into art—art which itself serves to inspire and trigger the spiritual lives of its viewers and readers.

Henry Vaughan and his twin Thomas were born in Llansantffraed in the Welsh county of Breconshire, in 1621. He spent 2 years at Jesus College, Oxford, and 2 years at the Inns of Court in London before returning home at the start of the Civil War to work as secretary to the Chief Justice of the Brecon Circuit. By the age of 25, he was married and had published his first volume of secular verse. As a Royalist, however, he was subject to serious persecution and this, combined with illness and family misfortunes, led to a personal crisis and conversion experience. His best religious verse was written during this period. He wrote little after the age of 35, but began to practice as a doctor and kept up this occupation for the remainder of his long life. After the death of his first wife, he married her younger sister, and had four children from each marriage. He lived the last 50 years of his life in Breconshire, his later life being marked by a series of lawsuits, and was buried in Llansantffraed churchyard in 1695.

Vaughan's spiritual worldview was undoubtedly influenced by his twin brother, Thomas, himself a minor poet. The latter took Holy Orders after his time at Oxford, and held the living of Llansantffraed until he was evicted from it in 1650 as a Royalist. Thereafter, until his death in 1666 he devoted himself to science, medicine, and mystic philosophy, and became one of the most famous British alchemists of the 17th century.

Under Herbert's influence, Vaughan links spiritual understanding to simple beauty and commonplace affairs (as in "Peace"), and like him he describes the spiritual upheavals that he experiences on his journey through life ("Regeneration"). But he draws far more on the sights and sounds of nature than Herbert, as in contrasting human restlessness with the acceptance of the divine will by animals, birds, and flowers in "Man," and glorying ecstatically in nature's beauty in "The Morning Watch." Vaughan's faith also has more of a mystical dimension, and recurring themes in his poetry include the spiritual symbolism of light, love, life, and humans' relationship with the eternal and the unseen. The famous opening lines of "The World" convey something of this mystical symbolism:

> I saw eternity the other night
> Like a great ring of pure and endless light.

In "The Retreate," Vaughan not only recalls the purity and the innocence of childhood, but seems to imply that childhood is a time when the soul is closer to God and nature—a thought that clearly foreshadows Wordsworth's "Intimations of Immortality."

—*J. Mark Halstead*

See also Herbert, George

FURTHER READING

Davies, S. (1995). *Henry Vaughan.* Bridgend, Wales: Seren Books.

Martin, L. C. (Ed.). (1957). *The works of Henry Vaughan.* Oxford: Clarendon Press.

VODUN (VOODOO)

The name *Vodun* can be traced back to the African word meaning spirit, which is central to the Vodun tradition. West African religion has gone through a series of transitions since the arrival of Europeans and their Christian beliefs to the Ivory Coast. The old religion of West Africa was not forgotten, but made way for a union with Christianity forming the new Vodun religion that is practiced today in most parts of the world. The roots of Vodun go back nearly 6,000 years on the African continent in parts of Togo, Benin, and Nigeria, where Vodun evolved and spread to the Yorubans who elevated this practice beginning in the 18th century. Vodun is sometimes referred to as voodoo, vodoun, and vodou.

During colonial times, the import of slaves from the West African region to Haiti began a new episode in the history of Vodun practice when the new land brought challenges to the old religious and cultural practices. The slave masters that ruled over the newly conquered people of West Africa actively suppressed many aspects of Vodun practice. Many Vodun priests were tortured, killed, or imprisoned for their religious beliefs and practices.

The Roman Catholic Church, upon the arrival of West African people in Haiti and other West Indian islands, baptized slaves. Many Vodun believers, fearing the same fate as their priests and other members, created an underground society in order to continue the veneration of their spirits and gods. Those who practiced Vodun adapted some of the Christian saints into Vodun practice and culture; the saints were given Haitian Creole names, thereby syncretizing Christian and African-based religious traditions.

Similar to Christianity, Vodun is a religion of many traditions and practices. As each path (denomination) of Christianity has a different method of worshipping and interpreting biblical texts, so does Vodun have different paths that the devout take to worship. Each Vodun group worships a slightly different pantheon of gods and spirits known as the Loa (*lwa*), which literally means "mystery" in the Yoruba language. The almighty God called Olorum is unknowable to the Vodun believers. He governs the lesser God Obatala who he commissioned to create the earth and all the creatures and other life forms that inhabit the Earth. Adherents and scholars of Vodun interpret these two beings as representations of God and Jesus in their position of being knowable and unknowable.

Both Christianity and Vodun share belief in a supreme being. The Loa resemble Christian saints in that they were once people who led exceptional lives and were given a single responsibility in life. Both share a belief in an afterlife; the centerpiece of religious ceremonies (mass) in both practices is a ritual sacrifice and consumption of flesh and blood. As Jesus said to take his body and drink his blood in memory of him, the Vodun offer animal blood and flesh to the Loa. The two traditions also share a belief in the existence of invisible evil spirits or demons that attempt to steer humans off their path of goodness. Followers of Vodun believe that each person has a *met-tet* (master of the head), which corresponds to a Christian's patron saint. Each person has a soul composed of parts, including *gros bon ange* (big guardian) and a *ti bon ange* (small guardian angel). This concept is also known in Christianity as the belief in angels who are God's servants and protectors of humans.

The rituals of the Vodun have the distinct purpose of making contact with a spirit to gain favor through offerings of animal sacrifices and other gifts to gain a higher standard of living or improved health. Humans and the Loa have a symbiotic relationship, each depending on the other. Humans give the Loa food and gifts, and in exchange the Loa give rewards. Rituals are also done to celebrate events in a person's life such as birth, death, and marriage.

Each ritual of the Vodun is carried out in a structured fashion beginning with the feast that is conducted before the main ceremony. Next there is the creation of the *veve,* the pattern of cornmeal or flour on the floor, which is unique to the Loa for which the ritual is being performed. The participants in the ritual chant and use rattles and drums that are purified, and together these instruments provide a very powerful part of the ritual. While some participants are conducting the instruments and chanting, the *houngan* or *mambo* dance escalates with intensity until the Loa possesses them. The *ti bon ange* of the priest has his or her body, and the spirit of the Loa has taken control. The possessed priest now behaves like the Loa. Both the *houngan* and *mambo* confine their activities and powers of Vodun to "white magic," which is used to bring forth fortune and healing to members of the Vodun tradition. People known as *caplatas* perform acts of evil sorcery called "black magic," which has also been called "left-handed Voodoo."

Animal sacrifices are performed at Vodun rituals. The animals are purified, and a goat, sheep, chicken, or dog is sacrificed for the Loa. The blood of the sacrificed animal is collected in a vessel, and the priest drinks some of the blood, which satisfies the hunger of the Loa. The slaughtered animal is then cooked and eaten by participants in the ritual.

Vodun priests can be male (*houngan*) or female (*mambo*) and hold the same status of importance within the religion. The Vodun place of worship is a temple called a *hounfour,* which is adorned with a *poteau-mitan,* which is the main aspect of the temple. The *poteau-mitan* is the place where God, spirits, and ancestors can communicate with people. The altar in the temple is elaborately decorated with candles, pictures of Christian saints, and items that are of importance to the Loa.

Cemeteries are an important part of Vodun rituals. The first male buried in a cemetery is called a *baron,* and will protect the other family members that come to be buried in the same cemetery. A cross at the entrance of the cemetery called the *kwa baron* is a site where food, candles, and other gifts are offered at the base. This offering is an important ritual for veneration of the Loa, since the cemetery defines the spatial contact between the living and the dead. The key time for contact with ancestors for the Vodun is the Christian Eve of All Saints or Halloween. The ritual calendar of the Vodun corresponds to Roman Catholic feast days. The calendar indicates which Loa will be venerated, or to which Christian site a pilgrimage will be made by adherents.

What stands out as unique to the Vodun people is the belief that a dead person can be revived after burial. The raised persons are called zombies, and they have no will of their own and are subject to control by others. In reality, a zombie is a person who is not dead, but who is under the influence of powerful drugs administered by an evil sorcerer. Few Voduns have ever seen a true zombie, but they maintain strong beliefs in the raising of the dead.

The misconceptions of Vodun can be directly linked to a book written in 1884 by S. St. John titled *Haiti or the Black Republic.* S. St. John described the Vodun tradition as very dark and evil, including such horrific acts as human sacrifice and cannibalism. Having no concrete knowledge about Africa or the peoples of Africa, many people in the West received this book as reliable instead of as an inaccurate and sensationalized fictional account. Hollywood quickly devoured the mystery and dark aspects that St. John wrote about, which provided countless horror movie plots.

Finally, in the 1950s, anthropologists and other scholars shed light on the true nature and mystery behind Vodun. However, the dark legends of Vodun continue to spark intrigue and fascination among many in the Western world.

Vodun has thrived in various denominations in Brazil, Haiti, Cuba, Dominican Republic, Canada, and the United States (mainly in New Orleans). The Vodun tradition exemplifies an old religion that has survived through combining new practices with old beliefs.

—Julie Wieland-Robbescheuten

FURTHER READING

Oxtoby, W. G. (2002). *World religions: Western traditions.* Oxford, UK: Oxford University Press.

VOLUNTEERISM

Volunteerism is a dynamic institution whose definition or appearance varies according to time period and culture. Generally, volunteerism refers to the institution or tradition marked by one's (either individual or group) voluntary action in response to a recognized need or set of needs. It typically involves the giving of time, energy, service, and on some occasions, resources, materials, and/or even one's body, as is the case in voluntary donations of blood or organs to the Red Cross or alternative organizations and institutions. Religious traditions and practices often engage individuals in volunteer activities and, in turn, volunteerism often triggers heightened levels of religious and/or spiritual development.

There are at least four different organizational settings associated with volunteerism: mutual aid and the self-help arena; philanthropic service aimed at others; participation; and lastly, advocacy, lobbying, or campaigning. One might encounter each of these settings in all regions of the world, although again, they may differ according to varying structures of economics, societies, cultures, and political systems. Volunteerism is as widespread as the issues that it attempts to address, and as varied as its host cultural settings. It is important to note that these four settings, in all their variety and diversity, need not be mutually exclusive—that is, one might be involved in more than one arena at once.

Despite the range of possibilities and vast room for differences, volunteerism, in general, fittingly shares some fundamental characteristics or core elements. First, the act of volunteering is done out of one's own initiative, and is free from any authoritative dictum. Further, it is not done in the spirit of financial profit—one does not look to gain fiscally from volunteer activities. And while it may not be done fully in the spirit of exchange, volunteerism can benefit both the recipient(s) and the volunteer(s) in many ways. Volunteers typically experience an extensive desire to bless others, and through their act(s) of compassion, sharing, and caring, to be blessed themselves.

Considerable professionalization of volunteerism has occurred in recent times. Certain volunteer activities require a particular skill base and limit their opportunities to only those volunteers who possess the ever-increasing specialized skills demanded. One need only think of Doctors Without Borders or Volunteers for Prosperity, each of which involves voluntary medical and/or health professional services. It seems apparent that these organizations would accept only the most qualified of volunteers to administer healthcare practices in and among the circumstances they find themselves in, whether it be the most complex, lifesaving, surgical procedure, or efforts in meeting the most basic of healthcare needs.

While opportunities for volunteers lacking specific training and/or skills continue to diminish in conjunction with the rising need for volunteers with specific professional grounding, statistics show that the volunteer rate in the United States grew from 59.8 million (27.4%) for the 12-month period ending in September 2002, to 63.8 million (28.8%) for the 12-month period ending in September 2003. Of this figure, 34.6% worked principally in volunteering for a religious organization or institution; 27.4% for an educational or youth-services-related organization or institution; 11.8% for a social or community service organization or institution; and 8.2% for hospitals or other healthcare organizations or institutions.

As conservative approximations estimate a decline in church service and church-related group participation by nearly one-sixth since the 1960s, the viability of the religious volunteer organization remains. It seems that great consideration must be afforded to religiously inspired, although ecumenical, voluntary organizations that typically engage in public aims and objectives. However, any attempt to number, let alone identify, all of these religiously inspired volunteer organizations would be utterly impractical, given the wide variety that exists in their respective objectives and institutional settings. A few notable examples include Habitat for Humanity International, the Saint Vincent DePaul Society, Bread for the World, Pax Christi, and Dignity USA.

There are, additionally, groups that flank the paradenominational organization at both ends—the explicitly religious affiliated volunteer organization and the volunteer organizations lacking any explicit ties to religion. Regarding the explicitly religious organizations, many are foundational or evangelical branches of particular faith traditions or communities that often look to Scriptural sources and God's love as a motivating foundation. These groups typically seek to meet a variety of human needs while, at the same time, introducing their beneficiaries and the surrounding community to specific religious messages and teachings that they hold dear. Notable examples from this group include the Salvation Army, Jesuit Volunteer Corps, Mercy Corps, Maryknoll Missionaries, and Catholic Charities.

At the other end of the field are those public and private groups who attempt to meet particular human needs without any explicit affiliation to a particular faith community. However, it is important to note that these groups engage in activities and with spirits that are not, necessarily, in contradiction to those of more faith-centered organizations or activities. Further, many faith communities or individuals of faith volunteer their efforts in conjunction with many of these organizations. Thus, while ties to religion might not be explicit, they are often implicit. Examples of this kind include the United Way of America, Big Brothers and Big Sisters of America, the Peace Corps, and United Nations Volunteers.

Additionally, it is crucial to understand that volunteerism can manifest itself in numerous ways beyond participation in one of these more formal organizations. Individuals regularly volunteer their time and skills to various causes such as school or church functions and activities, as athletic coaches and/or officials, toward political or social agendas, volunteer fire departments, and so on.

For many, the act of volunteering is a concrete expression of one's own religious or spiritual convictions. These acts typically transcend one's own self-interests and seek to bring about a better life and improved world for others. In fact, volunteerism can move beyond individual acts to become a lived pattern that expresses one's awareness and appreciation of something which transcends the self. All the while, the self can be informed and transformed by these acts or this lived pattern. Through volunteering, one recognizes his or her own abilities as a political and moral agent often functioning within a specific value-bearing tradition. Through these acts, one might arrive at an awareness of the potential of the holy and creative spirit in themselves and others—this certainly holds the potential for cultivating a closer connectedness and identity with others and with the divine.

While space and time permits only a cursory examination of volunteerism in which, inevitably, many (perhaps most) groups do not get the attention they so appropriately deserve, a treatment like this does allow one to grasp the broad diversity encompassed by the institution of volunteerism and, hopefully, how it can be a win-win situation for the volunteer(s), recipient(s), and community at large. Given that volunteerism often serves to trigger heightened levels of religious and/or spiritual development, those interested in promoting the healthy development of young people should provide young people with opportunities for volunteerism and should consider encouraging their participation in volunteer activities.

—Eric N. Abercrombie

FURTHER READING

Baggett, J. P. (2001). *Habitat for humanity: Building private homes, building public religion.* Philadelphia: Temple University Press.

E-Volunteerism: The Electronic Journal of the Volunteer Community. Retrieved from http://e-vonlunteerism.com.

Kipps, H. C. (Ed.). (1997). *Volunteer America: A comprehensive national guide to opportunities for service, training, and work experience.* Chicago: J. G. Ferguson.

McGuckin, F. (Ed.). (1998). *Volunteerism.* New York: W. H. Wilson.

United Nations Volunteers. Retrieved from www.unv.org.

WESLEY, JOHN

John Wesley (1703–1791) lived in England for the majority of his life. He was an Anglican priest, evangelist, theologian, and church reformer. His unique perspectives on grace have made him the object of significant study in recent times. Due in part to his influence, British Methodism developed as its own entity in English culture. John Wesley is generally considered to be the primary founder of Methodism in America—a movement that led to the development of several denominations including the United Methodist Church, African Methodist Episcopal Church, Free Methodist, Nazarene, and others. His life serves as a model and example of religious development and of the influence of the context and historical time on religious development across an individual's life span. His work and theology have framed and impacted the religious and spiritual development of many adherents throughout the world.

The second son of Susanna and Samuel Wesley, John spent his childhood in the town of Epworth, England, where his father served as an Anglican priest. His mother, Susanna, played an important role in his faith development and learning. She was very strict and insisted that all of her children not only were well learned but also practiced acts of piety such as prayer and bible study. John Wesley entered Oxford in 1720. While at Oxford, he received his bachelor's degree and doctorate, was ordained in the Anglican Church, and became a Fellow of Oxford—guaranteeing him a lifetime salary, regardless of where he worked. Although this learning was crucial to Wesley's development, his most important experiences may have been serving as the advisor to a group of Oxford students—including his brother, Charles Wesley—who worked together to live "holier" lives. They practiced regimented schedules of prayer, fasting, study, service, and worship. Students began to mock them with the title "Methodist"—a title that the group soon adopted with pride as more people began to practice their method for holy living.

Beginning a new chapter in his life, John Wesley left Oxford and endured the difficult journey to the "new world" so that he could minister to the colonists and "Indians" of a new colony, Georgia. During a particularly rough storm on the Atlantic, Wesley marveled at the faith of a group of Moravians—a sect devoted to personal practices of holiness—who were so sure of their salvation that they sang hymns of praise while the ship threatened to sink. Despite being a clergyperson who had helped others embrace faith, the young priest was not confident in his own salvation. This haunted him during both his short (and unsuccessful) ministry in Georgia and his more successful ministry upon returning to England. He was counseled by a Moravian friend to preach faith until he had a faith that gave him the confidence he was lacking. He took the advice to heart and continued to preach.

Wesley preached not only in churches but also in fields and town squares—something with which he was uncomfortable, but he did because it helped people claim their faith. Wesley continued to question his own salvation until May 24, 1738. On that day he attended a reading of Luther's interpretation of Romans, a book in the New Testament, and experienced the assurance for which he had been looking. He felt his heart "strangely warmed" and knew that God would forgive his sins. This encounter, known as Wesley's *Aldersgate experience,* led the priest to consider himself a true Christian.

Wesley and the other early Methodists spent the remaining years of their lives continuing to preach repentance and holy living. They established elaborate systems of small groups—called *societies* and *bands*—that supported individual Christians as they struggled to live holier lives. Throughout his life Wesley continued in his zeal for the sacraments, evangelism, holy living, and acts of service. Although some animosity did develop between practicing Methodists and Anglicans, early Methodism is best understood as a sect within the Anglican Church.

After the American Revolution, the Anglican Church had a dwindling presence in the newly independent United States of America. Growing numbers of Methodists were left without clergy to provide them with the sacraments. Rather than have so many go without the Eucharist, Wesley ordained a small number of English preachers and sent them to America to establish a new church. Through the remainder of his life, Wesley continued to write and publish sermons, a complete commentary on the Bible, many hymns, and several theological tracts. He died in 1791.

In many ways, Wesley's theology was a product of his Anglican upbringing. As he crafted his theology, he relied primarily upon scripture, but he also took into consideration reason and the tradition of the church. While this was consistent with the theological tradition of the Anglican Church, Wesley also relied upon the role of experience as a further way of distilling God's will and understanding the Bible.

While Wesley never detailed a system for doing theology, a 20th-century theologian and historian named Albert Outler distilled from Wesley's writing a means of constructing theology. Termed the *Wesleyan quadrilateral,* Outler suggests that one should examine scripture and then understand it through the lenses of tradition, reason, and experience. This approach to theology has gained widespread acceptance among the United Methodist Church and other Wesleyan denominations.

Wesley is regarded for his ability to bring together aspects of different traditions or contradicting theologies. He stressed the therapeutic or healing aspect of the faith that was generally associated with Eastern Christianity while still attending to the role of grace in Christian development that typifies Western Christianity. He also developed the concept of *prevenient grace* as a way to delicately balance the accountability for one's actions, found in the free-will traditions, and the emphasis on original sin that pervades predestination traditions.

Another distinctive aspect of Wesley's theology comes out of his attention to "holiness" or Christian living. Relying upon Matthew 5:48, he believed it was the duty of all Christians to work toward and attain perfect love for God and perfect love for neighbor. Christians would still sin by making mistakes, but their intent and devotion to God could become perfect.

—Rev. Michael J. Baughman

See also Methodist

FURTHER READING

Heitzenrater, R. P. (1995). *Wesley and the people called Methodists.* Nashville: Abingdon Press.

Maddox, R. L. (1994). *Responsible grace.* Nashville, TN: Kingswood Books.

Outler, A. C. (Ed.). (1980). *John Wesley.* New York: Oxford University Press.

Weems, L. H. (1982). *John Wesley's message today.* Abingdon Press.

WESTERN WALL

Every culture and religion is unique in its own way, possessing distinct rituals, practices, and places of significant spiritual importance. One such place for Judaism is the Western Wall, or *Kotel HaMa'arawi* in Hebrew, also known to the world by its other name the Wailing Wall, or *Al-Buraq* in Arabic. It remains one of the most important places of Judaic pilgrimage and the site where Shabbat (Sabbath) ritual is held in Israel and where Friday night prayers, singing, and worship are shared amongst the different denominations in the Judaic tradition from the Hasidic to the Reform Jew, at the holy site where God still remains.

The Western Wall was first constructed under the direction of King Solomon and was finished in approximately the year 515 B.C.E. under the direction of two overseers, Zerubbal and Haggal. At that time Jerusalem was seen as the center of the world, the hub of humanity. The Temple that was constructed was the center of power—a place where God would come to worshippers on the Day of Atonement (Yom Kippur) and a place where Jews could feel God's presence daily.

The first profanation of the Holy Temple occurred when the Babylonians desecrated the holy sanctuary and exiled the Jewish people as slaves to the Babylonian Empire. In the year 538 B.C.E., King Cyrus (who in Isaiah 45:1 is called the *anointed,* a term that was used in the Hebrew Bible to address both priestly and kingly figures) freed the Hebrews and allowed them to return to their holy land of Israel. Once the Hebrews returned, they began an immediate mission to rebuild Jewish society, and the center of that society was the Temple. In the book of Ezra, in approximately the year 444 B.C.E., the second Temple was reconstructed. Both the first and second Temple existed for a span of 400 years before they were destroyed.

The second wave of destruction to the Temple occurred in the year 66 C.E., under the Roman legions that marched in Jerusalem under the order of the Roman emperor Vespasian. The Jewish wars, as recorded in the writings of the historian Josephus, was a reaction to increasing tensions between the Roman authorities and Jewish people. The numerous minirevolts led by zealots increased and finally reached the end of the emperor's tolerance. Under Vespasian's command, Jerusalem was besieged, and the second Temple was destroyed.

What remains today of the second Temple is the outer courtyard of the Holy Temple of Jerusalem. It is located on the Temple Mount, the original location of the first and second Temples, spanning 800 years of existence. The Wailing Wall continues to inspire belief by many religious the Jews that the Wall is a fulfillment of God's promise to his chosen people and that no matter what catastrophe should befall Jerusalem, He would leave some remainder of the Temple as an eternal sign of the unbreakable bond between God and His chosen people.

The Temple Mount serves as a holy site for Christians, Muslims, and Jews, for this is the site where God showed the patriarch Abraham the land in which he would be the father of a great nation, and the same area in which the *Akeda*, or the binding of Isaac, occurred in Genesis, where Abraham was to sacrifice Isaac to God. Where the Dome of the Rock sits today is the site where the holiest center of the Temple sat, called the Holy of Holies, or *Kodesh HaKodashim* in Hebrew. Only the high priests on the Day of Atonement (Yom Kippur) were permitted to enter the innermost holy sanctuary on this day.

The wall has been the focal point for much heated political and religious debate in Israel for the past 50 years, for the Temple Mount is built on Mount Moriah, the foundation from which God is said to have created the universe. It is also the home to the Islamic holy sanctuary of the Dome of the Rock, which is located directly behind the wall. Close by the wall is the Al-Aqsa Mosque, which is the third holiest site to Muslims next to Mecca and Medina and is the place from which, according to tradition, Mohammed ascended into heaven. Contention over this area is at the heart of Arab–Israeli struggles. For in order for the third Temple to be built, the Dome of the Rock must be destroyed. Ownership and declarations of the true "owners" of the Temple Mount have resulted in bloodshed and a seemingly unending stalemate.

Jews have prayed at the wall for thousands of years, with a fervent belief that God will return to Israel to rebuild the third Temple, which will usher in the Messianic Era. Today, the wall is a religious pilgrimage site, a place of spiritual development for Jews and people of varying religious traditions. It is impossible to escape being captivated by the flurry of activity that surrounds the wall. One unique aspect of the wall is that there is a barrier to separate men from women. Men of non-Jewish descent are permitted to go to the wall only if they are wearing a *kippa,* or head covering, in keeping with the Jewish practice out of humility and respect toward God.

There is a tradition that continues today, and for any visitor to the wall, Jew, Muslim, Buddhist, and Christian alike, a prayer written on a piece of paper is rolled and inserted into the cracks in the wall, to be answered by God. This belief is important to newlyweds who, after their ceremony, will come to the wall to say a prayer and insert their own written prayers into the cracks. The wall is also a place where 13-year-old boys have their bar mitzvah ceremony, and is the final destination of the Israeli army's new recruits, who march 100 miles to the wall for final prayer and an oath before God. The wall serves as a reminder of God's connection to and covenant with the Jewish people, with the hope of God's return for the third Temple to be rebuilt. Sanctity is found in the wall, a sanctity that has emanated from it since its construction so many thousands of years ago and that will continue for years to come.

—Julie Wieland-Robbescheuten

WICCA AND WITCHCRAFT

Wicca and witchcraft are part of a larger contemporary religious movement called *paganism* (or sometimes *neo-paganism*). There can be some confusion when using the terms *witchcraft* or *Wicca* because not all practitioners agree about what these mean. For some, the terms are synonymous. For others, Wicca is but one version of witchcraft referring to those structured traditions that are directly associated with the British traditions begun by Gerald Gardner and Alex Sanders.

Witchcraft and Wicca, as pagan religions, draw on myths and traditions attributed to pre-Christian Europe. Of particular influence are nature-based practices (cyclical festivals based on agriculture, moon cycles, herbal healing), occult practices (divination and magic), and mythology about ancient deities with a focus on the goddess (or goddesses) as primary in a pairing with a less emphasized god (or gods). Deity is also immanent, rather than transcendent. This means that the goddess is right here within the natural world. In fact, the earth is said to be the body of the goddess. What is meant by the natural world is everything on and in the earth—including humanity. The goddess is not understood as some otherworldly being, inaccessible and distant. She is believed to be within each and every one of us—as is the god—in our very physical bodies. This idea implies that all of the natural world—including humanity—is sacred and needs to be treated as such. Thus, many witches tend to be involved in ecological movements and political action against racism, homophobia, sexism, and such.

The largest pagan group today is Wicca, which began in Britain in the 1940s and 1950s when civil servant Gerald Gardner began reviving what he believed to be an ancient religious system maintained in secret from the Stone Age until the present. As part of the modern pagan movement, Wicca was influenced and shaped by a Western magical or mystery tradition that has spanned Western history.

One of the highly significant influences on modern paganism in general, and the development of Wicca in particular, is the Romantic Movement of the 1800s. It was during this time that many Europeans and Americans turned to exalting nature, the irrational, and the feminine as understood and admired in ancient Greece. It was during the Romantic period that the classical goddesses of Greece and Rome were transformed from goddesses of civilization (the city, learning, justice, etc.) to aspects of one great goddess of nature.

Along with the romanticizing of nature and the goddess, came a popularization of occultism, which was due largely to the French scholar Eliphas Levi's work beginning in the 1850s. Levi blended mystical traditions such as the Kabbala, Tarot, and ancient Egyptian systems of magic, along with the traditions of the Knights Templar and the mysteries of the Holy Grail.

Gardner's construction of Wicca in the 1940s and 1950s brought together these existing traditions and practices to create a new religion. This new religion has new members go through various initiation rituals through which they gain secret knowledge at each of three levels. Those at the top levels, high priestesses and high priests, have authority over those below them and are charged with the spiritual guidance of those in their coven (ritual group). With the help of Doreen Valiente, one of Gardner's high priestesses, Gardner's new religion became increasingly popular in Britain as a revived "indigenous" magical tradition.

Though there were pagan groups early on in the history of the United States, paganism and witchcraft began gaining popularity there when Wicca traveled from Great Britain to the United States. In the United States and Canada, witchcraft became more eclectic (that is drawing from multiple and varied ancient and occult traditions) and less structured than it had been in Britain. This is not to say that there are not traditional Wiccan covens operating in North America. However, Wicca and paganism in general gained popularity largely in countercultural groups that disdained hierarchy and structure. These groups, such as environmentalists, anarchists, feminists, and pacifists, took the principles, mythologies, and ritual practices of Wicca and removed the hierarchical, initiatory structure to create new traditions and nontradition-affiliated covens, often claiming the name witchcraft rather than Wicca. It is also in North America where solitary witchcraft (practicing without a coven) gained numbers.

In North America, witchcraft has often been closely associated with contemporary goddess spirituality, which grew out of the feminist critique of the Judeo-Christian, Western religious tradition. The main criticism of this tradition was that it is patriarchal and, as such, perpetuates social systems which devalue women. The Judeo-Christian tradition is based on dualisms that posit an essential opposition between male and female, spirit and earth, mind and body, and light and dark and rank these opposites so that male, spirit, mind, and light are considered to be superior to female, earth, body, and dark. This is evident, it is said, in the figure of the "Father God"—the masculine divine. It also shows up in practices such as keeping women from positions of authority within churches and synagogues. Many feminists who make this criticism choose to look for examples of female divinity from various traditions and incorporate these images into new religious traditions to fit North American (mostly urban) contexts—religions that focus on the female.

The term *witch* is often used as a symbol of defiance in the face of the deliberate destruction by mostly Christian officials and state authorities of women of power, women who had knowledge of the earth and the body, and women who were midwives and herbalists. To use the term *witch* as a positive image is, then, to take the history of the mistreatment and subjugation of women and turn it on its head. It is to proclaim loudly that, yes, women do have power and, no, it is not evil.

Because of this female focus, many think witchcraft is only for women. Contrary to this opinion, there are many men involved in witchcraft who find the need for a shift in the power dynamics of Western society. Many of these men realize that fighting the subjugation of women is not just a "women's issue," that all are affected when women and men are set in opposition to one another.

Witchcraft and Wicca have become increasingly popular in North America through television, movies, and popular press. Teenage girls are particularly attracted to these traditions, largely because they allow for a female self-identity that is strong, powerful, and holding spiritual authority, an identity that many girls do not find elsewhere.

—Chris Klassen

See also Witches in Popular Culture

FURTHER READING

Eilberg-Schwartz, H. (1989). Witches of the West: Neopaganism and goddess worship as enlightenment religion. *Journal of Feminist Studies in Religion, 5*(1), 77–95.

Greenwood, S. (2000). *Magic, witchcraft and the otherworld.* Oxford and New York: Berg.

Harvey, G. (1997). *Contemporary paganism: Listening people, speaking earth.* Washington Square: New York University Press.

Hutton, R. (1999). *Triumph of the moon: A history of modern pagan witchcraft.* Oxford: Oxford University Press.

WILDERNESS

Retreat into wilderness in search of a spiritual vision is an old practice. It is familiar from the vision quest practiced by many Native Americans, from the Buddha's years in the wilderness, from Jesus' confrontation with temptation in the wilderness of Sinai, and from the 40-year wanderings of Moses and the Israelites. In this tradition wilderness has been thought of as a place where humans can encounter divinity directly, uncluttered by the distracting overlay of civilization. It represents a place for spiritual challenge and growth, a place where the soul can be found wanting or worthy, a place to find inner peace and communion with the divine. As such, the wilderness can be considered a trigger and/or context of both spiritual and religious development.

The tradition of seeking spiritual experience in wilderness remains alive in the modern world both for individuals and groups. Some groups promoting wilderness experience explicitly offer vision quests. Others offer only adventure or self-exploration, yet it seems certain that much of their success depends on the same characteristics of wilderness experience that have long been sought for their spiritual value.

It is possible to analyze at least some of the spiritual benefits that a person may garner from a sojourn in wild nature. These benefits are available, but not inevitable, since favorable conditions and a receptive state of mind are required. There are at least six interrelated spiritual benefits to be found in wilderness experience: enduring, sublime, beauty, competence, inner peace, and self-forgetting.

THE ENDURING

The great spiritual traditions all come to terms with the transience of all things human. No moment of happiness lasts, and decay and death await every earthly object of our love and concern. In Buddhism this transience is an element of *duhkha*, or the unsatisfactory nature of human existence to which the Buddha offered a remedy. Islam and Christianity also promise a very different remedy in the form of an eternal, changeless God and eternal afterlife, of reunification with those we have known and loved.

Wilderness, too, offers experience of the enduring, if not the eternal. Though modern science tells us that in time all species will become extinct and mountains will erode to the sea, by comparison with human things, stones and hills are nearly eternal, and the cycle of seasons seemingly endless in their repetition.

In this life we never experience God in his eternity, so ancient landscapes and the starry skies are as close as we may ever come to earthly experience of eternity. In wilderness one may encounter the enduring, coming face to face with ancient things and timeless cycles, and this direct encounter is part of what makes sojourn in wilderness a moving spiritual experience.

THE SUBLIME

In wilderness one often experiences the sublime, that is, things and processes that are immense, powerful, even threatening and intimidating. Towering mountains, vast landscapes, the power of a raging river are all reminders of one's insignificance and vulnerability. This effect is much stronger when, as is typical in wilderness travel, one has been stripped of modern comforts and technology and must confront these features unaided. A mountain is immense even when seen from the comfort of an automobile, but the experience of its immensity is multiplied when one must climb it or go around it on foot.

The sublime is godlike in its power and capacity to awe. It is no accident that mountain tops have so frequently been thought of as the abode of the gods, that volcanoes have been worshipped, that the sea has been a god, for people have always associated the sublime and the divine.

A person need not think that the mountain is a god in order be humbled by it, reminded of one's insignificance, and struck with wonder about the meaning of life and one's own importance. What is puzzling is not that this can be a powerful experience, readily available through experience of wilderness, but that we find comfort in it, that experience of the sublime face of wild nature provides a spiritual benefit.

The explanation may be that wild nature humbles not only individuals, but humankind and all of its ambitions. To be insignificant in a human crowd is often painful, for it reminds us that we have not achieved the fame and fortune that others have. To be insignificant in wild nature, by contrast, can be comforting, for wilderness dwarfs not only ourselves, but fame and fortune too.

BEAUTY

The beauty of wilderness is a cliché, apparent in countless calendars and coffee table books. Since humankind originated in wild nature, its beauty seems apt to be the prototype for all beauty not derived from the human form. The beauty of calendars and books is exclusively visual beauty, but this is only a small part of the beauty experienced by a person living in the wilderness. That person experiences beauty with all of the senses. She smells the fragrances on the air; feels the wind, sun, and rain on her skin; hears the birdsong, the wind song, the chatter of insects; feels her own bodily response to the contours of the land. A sojourn in wilderness is not a distant contemplation of beauty by sight alone, but an immersion in multisensory beauty. The spiritual effect is likely to be a profound feeling of peace and joy and of gratitude for one's existence.

COMPETENCE

The beauty one can experience in wilderness is not, of course, guaranteed. One can also experience hardship, discomfort, and danger. In fact some degree of this is practically guaranteed, since to live in wilderness is necessarily to give up most of the comforts of civilization and to rely upon one's own powers in unaccustomed ways. Oddly, though, this is often felt to be an intensely empowering experience. The exertions needed to travel in wilderness may engender feelings of peace and well-being in purely biochemical ways by stimulating the release of endorphins in the brain. But they also give one a feeling of competence and of self-worth.

Wilderness experience is especially suited to do this because the challenges it provides typically involve self-overcoming rather than competition against others. Where competition is against other people, there must be winners and losers; but where one strives only to overcome one's own fears and limits, no one need lose. This is especially true because failure of one kind can be a success from another point of view. Failure to climb the mountain, for instance, can reveal one's wisdom in knowing to turn back and one's stamina in making it back safely despite exhaustion.

PEACE

All of the elements described thus far contribute to the sense of inner peace that wilderness experience provides, but at least one more aspect of wilderness experience does so as well. Mihaly Csikszentmihalyi has described the characteristics of experiences that people find so enjoyable that they seek them for their own sake and not for external reward. The pleasurable, restorative state of mind these experiences provide he calls flow. The experience of flow is promoted by activities that involve risk and challenge near the limit, but within the participant's ability, that provide relatively swift and unambiguous information about success or failure, that provide opportunities for improvement of performance, and that thus focus the participant's attention, driving ordinary cares and anxieties from one's awareness.

The challenges encountered in wilderness frequently have these characteristics. Living and traveling under one's own power in wilderness provides obvious challenges to one's skill and stamina; success and failure are immediately obvious; opportunities for improvement are ample. As a result, the cares and worries of everyday life in civilization are driven out of mind by one's physical removal from them, by the urgency of the immediate concerns of life in the wild, and by one's focus on the tasks at hand. This leads in turn to relief from one's usual nagging concerns, a feeling of inner peace and greater openness to the spiritual feelings already described, each of which makes its own contribution to the feeling of inner peace.

SELF-FORGETTING

Every spiritual tradition extols the loss of excessive self-concern as among its major goals. All the elements described so far contribute to this self-forgetting for the wilderness traveler. The wilderness traveler is removed from the scene of everyday social and economic anxieties. She is in direct contact with the enduring and sublime, both of which diminish the importance of those everyday concerns. Her attention is almost certainly focused on the immediate demands of her challenging life and not on the concerns of her life in civilization. The intense beauty of her environment is comforting. She is apt to feel competent, secure, and at peace with herself. As a result, she is likely to give less attention to her insecure ego and to lose herself in her surroundings and in the demands of her immediate life.

The spiritual dimension of wild nature has been felt in many diverse spiritual traditions. No doubt it is felt somewhat differently in each. A monotheist, for instance, would see the wilderness landscape as God's creation, might feel God's helping presence when facing challenges, and might think of her peace and joy as gifts from God and signs of his near presence. How our distant forbearers felt the spiritual dimensions of wilderness is less certain than how the spiritual power of wilderness remains for us today It is therefore of little surprise that people of all ages seek out nature and wilderness experiences for opportunities for spiritual and/or religious reflection and growth.

—Baylor Johnson

See also Nature, the Sacred in; Sierra Club

FURTHER READING

Csikszentmihalyi, M. (1990). *Flow: The psychology of optimal experience.* New York: Harper & Row.

Johnson, B. L. (2002). On the spiritual benefits of wilderness. *International Journal of Wilderness, 8*(3), 28–32.

Muir, J. (1911). *My first summer in the Sierra.* Boston and New York: Houghton Mifflin.

Nash, R. (1973). *Wilderness and the American mind* (Rev. ed.). New Haven, CT: Yale University Press.

Oelschlager, M. (1991). *The idea of wilderness: From prehistory to the age of ecology.* New Haven, CT: Yale University Press.

Thoreau, H. D. (1972). *The Maine woods.* J. J. Moldenhauer (Ed.). Princeton, NJ: Princeton University Press.

WITCHES IN POPULAR CULTURE

Hollywood has had a long history of using the figure of the witch to entertain. In the past this figure has largely been one of strangeness, suspicion, and fear. The stereotypical image of the Wicked Witch of the West from the film version of *The Wizard of Oz* has shaped popular notions of the witch in children's fantasy and Halloween revelry. Many people continue to think of a witch as a negative, scary character who corrupts innocent youth. In North American popular culture an interesting trend, however, has developed over the past 10 years or so that has drastically reshaped the image of the witch. Where once witches were stereotypically evil, ugly old women with warts and a predilection for corrupting innocence, more and more we are now seeing young women of relatively benign or even benevolent power trying to save the innocent and integrate with "normal" society. Some notable examples in movies and TV are *Practical Magic; Sabrina, the Teenage Witch; Buffy, the Vampire Slayer;* and *Charmed.* In each of these examples the witches are regular women (in the very limited sense of Hollywood normal) who have access to power that is generally not available to others.

It is this access to power that makes popular-culture witches so appealing, particularly to young girls and women. In a society in which women and girls are denied power, the popular culture image of the good witch can be empowering. Not only are TV and Hollywood witches able to be relatively successful in everyday life, they can defeat demons, oppose patriarchy, and look good doing it. These characters provide an outlet for young women to share their anger and frustration with a world that still does not fully allow them agency and to dream of a reality in which the tables are turned.

Popular culture versions of witchcraft not only allow young girls and women to associate femaleness with power, they have also led many young girls and women to turn to pagan witchcraft and Wicca as a way to access this power in real life. That said, it is important to point out that the witchcraft found in popular culture does not resemble witchcraft and Wicca in any real way. None of the witches in current TV or movies are practicing a form of pagan religion. However, their use of magic, mythology, and occult practice resemble some of the sources pagans also draw on. Whether popular cultural representations of witches influence many to become involved with witchcraft and Wicca long term remains to be seen.

—*Chris Klassen*

See also Wicca and Witchcraft

FURTHER READING

Krzywinska, T. (2002). Hubble-bubble, herbs, and grimoires: Magic, Manichaeanism, and witchcraft in *Buffy.* In R. V. Wilcox & D. Lavery (Eds.), *Fighting the forces: What's at stake in Buffy the vampire slayer* (pp. 178–194). Lanham: Rowman & Littlefield.

Levine, M. (2000). Charmed and dangerous: The so-called power of celluloid witches. *Bitch: Feminist response to pop culture, 12,* 58–63, 80.

WORLD YOUTH DAY

Since 1985, a key feature of the pontificate of Pope John Paul II has been the staging of World Youth Days (WYD). These events, held every 2 or 3 years, are amongst the largest international gatherings of young people. In the millennium year of 2000, The WYD in Rome attracted more than 2.5 million pilgrims. In 1995 the gathering in Manila recorded an attendance in excess of 4 million. Simply for attracting so many recipients, WYD has become a significant social phenomenon. Participants are mainly Catholics although the invitation to take part is extended to all.

Venue and Date of World Youth Days

Year	*Venue*
1984–1985	Rome
1987	Buenos Aires
1989	Santiago de Compostela, Spain
1991	Czestochowa, Poland
1993	Denver
1995	Manila
1997	Paris
2000	Rome
2002	Toronto
2005	Cologne

The target WYD audience is between 16 and 35 years of age. WYD has a deliberate emphasis on pilgrimage, and hence each has had a strong international flavor with representative participation from all continents. The emphasis on pilgrimage is reinforced by the selection of traditional pilgrimage sites, such as Rome, Santiago de Compostela, and Czestochowa as venues. The format of WYD has a characteristic structure. Prior to a WYD, those planning to be participants attend a series of planned talks (catechesis) arranged around the city in which the event is taking place. These are designed as a preparation for the specific day. Talks are usually given to national groups or, in the case of the host country, regional groups and are typically given by bishops or other leadership figures. This reinforces the idea that WYD is an activity, which comes with the sanction and sponsorship of the Catholic Church. In the evening, events are planned that are intended to introduce participants to the breadth of Catholic culture. Part of this is the deliberate mixing of pilgrims from different countries. On WYD the highlight is the Papal Mass. The mass is often on the outskirts of the city in order to accommodate the large numbers involved.

World Youth Day has provided one of the clearest indicators of John Paul's emphasis on the New Evangelization. Implicit here is the concern that wider culture has either drifted from or not been sufficiently influenced by the Christian message. The Pope explicitly has called on youth to be the agents of a new proclamation of the gospel to those who have never heard it or have neglected it. Participation in WYD is intended to provide youth with a heightened sense of religiosity by providing a peak religious experience of the universality and strength of the Catholic tradition. It is anticipated that youth will develop their spirituality by sharing their experiences with disparate groups, of similar ages, all within the atmosphere of communal expression of religious faith.

The involvement of John Paul II has given WYD both its impetuous and its on-going strength. The ability of John Paul II to attract such a high level of interest in focused specific events and in a variety of settings is seen as one of the features of his pontificate. Some have commented that the emphasis on the Pope has provided too narrow a focus, and whilst providing a peak religious experience for many of those who attend, the long-term effects on both individuals and society are much more difficult to ascertain.

—Richard Rymarz

FURTHER READING

Harris, B. M. (1982). *Portraits of youth ministry.* New York: Paulist Press.

Benson, P. (1996). *Developmental assets among youth.* Minneapolis, MN: Search Institute.

WORSHIP

Worship is a complex phenomenon that is difficult to capture within a definition. Worship has a meaning to honor or revere a supernatural being or power or to regard or approach a holy thing with veneration, to give adoration to it, with the appropriate acts, rites, or ceremonies. Mostly, it is understood as an act of reverence and honor shown to the Creator. Worship expresses and mediates the divine–human relationship. Worship has been described as a response of adoration evoked in one who has encountered the presence of the Creator. Worship has also been depicted as the grateful rejoicing of those who have experienced the Creator's action in their lives. The possibility of worship implies human subjects who want a relationship with the Creator and a Creator who fulfills that desire. It may be expressed in formal prayer (liturgical and nonliturgical, communal and private) or in the ordinary deeds of everyday human life that flow from an inner attitude of reverence and honor of the Creator.

Worship is ritualistic, which means that it follows a prescribed routine. Worship is never left to improvisation. Historically, religion has included ritual practiced by a society. The general history of religions shows that there is a constant tendency toward rigorous uniformity in worship that increases as the religion grows older. Although there is the possibility of a purely personal and internal religion with no ritual performance and no association with other persons, worship has been a part of all cultures that have a structured, ritualistic, public method of prayer and devotions. As such, while worship is most commonly thought of in terms of religious practice and as an act that promotes religious development, worship is also very much a part of nonreligious, yet spiritual traditions.

In worship, what originally were spontaneous acts becomes the model that must be followed in detail. The worshipping group is not free to tamper with the details of a rite that has such a sacred origin. Worship when it is a public ritual becomes liturgy or the officially sanctioned action of a community of believers. Worship is not merely the recitation of words but also the performance of actions; and the symbol of the action is not as self-evident as the symbol of the word. Each new generation of believers tends to reclaim the main points of worship, action and word that connect the common believers to the higher power or Creator.

Worship at times needs to be explained. The worship action, by definition, achieves contact with the Creator in some way, and only a symbolic action can achieve this. It is precisely through its symbolism that the action is effective, and therefore the symbolism must remain unaltered.

Ritual worship is social, performed in a group for a group. The general history of religions shows that the worshipping group commits the act of worship to one or several authorized members. An official representative is always acting as a servant for the larger worshipping or believing group members. The act of worship in certain faith traditions can be expanded to liturgy, prayer, meditation, and private devotions.

Identifying liturgical worship as a form of ritual action calls attention to the fact that it is a symbolic process. Worship is a dynamic symbolic activity in which space, objects, words, time, and relationship all play a significant role in shaping meaning.

—Rev. David M. O'Leary

Y

YMCA

As an organization that views development as the integration of spirit, mind, and body over the life course, a progressive exposure to skills development is at the heart of the YMCA's program philosophy. You learn to walk before you run and to respect and relate to peers as equals before you assume leadership roles, in life and in organizations. The YMCA considers spiritual and religious development in childhood and adolescence to be a process that is integral to maturation. As such, without being their primary purpose or intent, spiritual and religious development occur through programs and relationships of the YMCA.

While at its founding in 1844 the central focus may have been an evangelical and proselytizing interest in young men moving into the industrial centers of England, the YMCA has survived more than 150 years and spread to more than 130 countries because the scope of its work has expanded and its evangelical goals contracted. The motivation of YMCA work has always had a thread of Christian witness with the underlying principles of the work representing mostly Christian values. But the work is never directed solely to service to Christians and the program does not serve evangelism or orthodoxy of faith.

The YMCA is not intended to serve as a substitute for a church or faith community in the religious and spiritual development of an individual. The YMCA does not offer a catechism or confession as the content or a condition of membership and participation. The YMCA does, to the extent that aspirations can be attributed to institutions, hope to support individuals in their exploration of questions and emotions that become the definitions and practices of beliefs and faith in their lives. It is an explicit part of its stated mission to build a healthy spirit (and mind and body) for all.

There is no definition of the spirit, however, within the YMCA. Broadly speaking, it is understood to correspond to that innate, native, human predisposition to seek the transcendent, and to find meaning and purpose in life, which perhaps is grounded in some higher power. Recent research appears to affirm that the attraction and success of YMCA programs for children and adolescents is due in part because they embody and respect the desire and need to seek a life of purpose. This can be a very powerful need for youth, and a very rewarding area for service to youth by adults.

YMCA staff have virtually no formal training, little experience, and few expectations that they will be confessional mentors to youth in any way except as role models, demonstrating their own continuing spiritual journeys and exhibiting high moral and ethical values. Listening with respect to youth as they seek to define those values for themselves and speak about their life purpose and dreams can be a sufficient basis of powerful relationships with youth.

The YMCA collapses a range of ethical values into a consensually accepted set of four: caring, honesty, respect, and responsibility. The focus on values within the YMCA is part of an orientation to youth work called character development. The YMCA is one of many youth-serving organizations that have selected a subset of a larger universe of values as a way of defining the core precepts of their communities and, in one sense, as definitions of spirit for their members.

The most common programs within the YMCA for children and adolescents are almost self-evidently not religious or spiritual in intent by their titles: Youth Sports, Youth & Government, Leaders Club, Earth Service Corps, Black and Minority Achievers, and Resident Camping. But because each is delivered in the context of a deeper foundation as an exercise in developing character or philanthropic citizenship, there is at least a discernable element of maturation in integrity, authenticity, and service that has religious content in most faith traditions, and spiritual value in most reflective traditions.

Partnering with researchers who study developmental issues at the levels of individual, institution, and community, has enriched and informed the YMCA about program philosophies and organizational goals that appear to support youth development in successful transitions to adulthood and citizenship. The work of Peter Benson and the Search Institute has identified 40 developmental assets that can be used to examine, assess, and inform work with youth by organizations such as the YMCA.

John McKnight and Jody Kretzmann at the Asset Based Community Development Program at Northwestern University bring a slightly different perspective to development issues, leading the YMCA to examine how it works with other institutions in a larger community (both formal and informal) to provide opportunities and support youth as they integrate developmental experience into a construction or identity for themselves.

When viewed through the lens of a still larger literature of research on human development, which begins at the biogenetic level of brain chemistry and structure, and includes investigations of the role of family, school, peers, and religious institutions, the YMCA has access to very rich models to design and evaluate its work with children and adolescents. This is a dynamic system, which means that continuing work constantly leads to change and refinement in existing programs and to the introduction of new programs.

At the organizational level, the YMCA is a federation of nearly 1,000 independent, autonomous local associations. These 1,000 associations operate nearly 2,500 branches and camps, and they also deliver programs in thousands of schools, community centers, religious facilities, public parks, hospitals, and so on. It is estimated that the YMCA serves over 10,000 communities in the United States alone. Respecting local autonomy means that there is also significant regional diversity in program offerings and emphases. As an organization that seeks to reflect the communities it serves in staff, lay leadership, and membership, communities with differing levels of diversity, economic, racial, and religious pluralism, the local YMCA is likely to mirror that diversity.

To the extent that the identification of a spiritual path of development is free of common labels of religious particularity (character development, practices of reflection from meditation to yoga, service learning, and other expressions of altruism), they can be a part of YMCA programs in many settings. Some settings, however, raise a higher bar of secular definition so that programs are more narrowly defined as recreational or academic. Programs in public schools, for example, are least likely to reflect an appreciation of the interest and need of youth to explore the spirit. Programs in environments that are completely defined by the YMCA, such as residence camps, and programs that are more explicitly spirit centered, such as Rags & Leathers, are important parts of the camp tradition.

The dialogues about the role of spiritual and religious development of children and adolescents take place in a number of different contexts for the YMCA. Within the profession, there is a lively discussion about the continuity of current programs and practices in an organization with a historically rich Christian heritage. Among lay leaders (board members, policy volunteers), there is a dialogue about the way in which an organization adapts to a changing society, and in particular one in which religious diversity continues to increase. Even quite external to the organization, there are discussions about the role and place of organizations that have moved, as a reflection of changes in society, away from a more religious or spiritual orientation to a more secular presentation, some bemoaning the loss, others admiring flexibility or adaptability, with neither particularly aware of internal dialogues.

The YMCA is embedded in American society in a number of ways. At a time when definitions of charitable organizations and the accountability and transparency of philanthropic organizations are under scrutiny by business and political sectors, the place of support of the spirit in charity and philanthropy is important. At a time when responsibility for community development and human services is increasingly shared between the government and the private sector, motivations of and relationships to faith traditions are important. In addition to delivering programs to children and youth that respect and support their growth in spirit, mind, and body, the YMCA has an important role to play in defining the debate and developing a consensus as a matter of social and public policy on why such service is important and how it is to be provided.

—*Mark C. Johnson*

FURTHER READING

Hinding, A. (2001). *Proud heritage: A history in pictures of the YMCA in the United States.* 150th anniversary edition. Virginia Beach, VA: Donning Company.

Hopkins, H. (1979). *John R. Mott, 1865–1955: A biography.* Grand Rapids, MI: Eerdmans.

Limbert, P. M. (1997). *Reliving a century: An autobiography.* Asheville, NC: Biltmore Press.

YOGA

Yoga is a spiritual discipline that developed in India more than 5,000 years ago. It has influenced, and been influenced by, the religious traditions of Hinduism, Buddhism, and Jainism, but is not a religion itself. Indeed it is practiced by millions of people throughout the world of various religious faiths and backgrounds, and in the United States and other Western countries, it is often regarded, despite its antiquity, as a form of "new age" spiritual expression.

There are more than 100 forms of yoga, but almost all derive from one of several main branches, each of which is characterized by distinct philosophical underpinnings and techniques. All forms of yoga, however, share the same ultimate goal: the integration of mind and body, self-transcendence, and enlightenment. The word "yoga," in fact, derives from the Sanskrit for "unity," suggesting the convergence of various facets of the self.

Of the principal branches of yoga, the most familiar to Westerners is Hatha yoga, which seeks to create a sense of well-being and transcendence through physical routines that include body poses, or *asanas,* and particular breathing techniques. Other branches include Guru yoga, Bhakti yoga, Jnana yoga, and Raja, or Classical, yoga. Practitioners of Raja yoga dedicate themselves to following the well-known "eightfold path," which lays out discrete steps (such as restraint from negative acts, withdrawal of the mind from the senses, and mental concentration) meant to lead to enlightenment. Other branches of yoga stress chanting, dedication to a guru, and acts of devotion to one's own conception of a supreme being.

Hatha yoga, translatable as the "yoga of force," is a particularly diversified branch, and has given rise to the forms of yoga most popular in the United States. These include Viniyoga, Ashtanga, Kripalu, Bikram, Ananda, Sivananda, and, perhaps best known, Iyengar yoga. Although they vary in physical intensity, all work in some way to integrate body poses, breathing, relaxation, meditation, and visualization.

Yoga is an ancient discipline that predates the cultural traditions with which it is usually associated. Archaeologists working in the Indus Valley have discovered soapstone carvings dating from 3,000 B.C.E. depicting people in yoga poses. Yoga evolved as part of a complex system of early Indian, or Vedic, thought that sought to solve the metaphysical riddles of existence through the unification of mind and body. As the discipline spread, it became interwoven with spiritual traditions such as Hinduism that were beginning to emerge on the Indian subcontinent. The Yoga-Sutra, compiled by Patanjali sometime in the 2nd century B.C.E., is one of the earliest writings describing yoga as a philosophical system, and to this day it remains a foundational text for yoga students and scholars.

Yoga was introduced to the West by Swami Vivekananda, a spiritual leader from India who represented Hinduism at Chicago's Parliament of Religions in 1893 and went on to teach for several years in the United States. His lectures, which among other things explained the philosophy and practice of yoga, ignited a genuine interest in Eastern philosophy among audiences who had previously considered Indian cultural traditions to be primitive. Despite the blossoming of interest in Eastern thought, however, yoga became widely popular in the United States only in the 1960s, when Americans once more became fascinated by Indian spiritual traditions. Great Indian popularizers of yoga in mid-century America were Sri Krishnamacharya, who developed Viniyoga; Shrila Prabhupada, who founded the worldwide Krishna movement based on Bhakti yoga; and Maharishi Mahesh Yogi, who drew on yoga techniques to develop transcendental meditation.

Yoga in Western countries has become associated with health and fitness, and it has indeed been shown by researchers to have positive impacts on arthritis, anxiety, back pain, premenstrual syndrome, and a variety of other chronic medical conditions. Ironically, however, yoga is not meant to focus practitioners on the physical or the emotional self, but to help them transcend the self entirely. This fact has led many yoga masters to criticize the American tendency to view yoga as just another form of exercise. Others take the opposite view, claiming that it is perfectly appropriate for Westerners to modify yoga to suit contemporary tastes. The debate between traditionalists and modernizers will no doubt continue.

What is certain is that for a variety of reasons—be it an abundance of readily accessible yoga classes, the relatively low cost of instruction, or the plethora of books and videos on the topic—yoga was enjoying unprecedented levels of popularity in the United States and other Western countries by the 1990s. Given the enthusiasm of its devotees, who in recent years have included older baby-boomers seeking to counter the effects of aging, and teenagers encountering the discipline for the first time, the trend seems likely to continue.

—*Melanie Wilson*

FURTHER READING

McAfee, J. (2001). *The secret of the Yamas: A spiritual guide to yoga.* Woodland Park, CO: Woodland.

Feuerstein, G. (1997). *The Shambhala encyclopedia of yoga.* Boston: Shambhala.

Sivananda Yoga Vedanta Center. (1998). *Yoga mind & body.* New York: DK Publishing.

YOUNG LIFE

Young Life is an international nonprofit, nondenominational Christian organization that uses a relational approach between adults and young people as the principal means by which youth are brought to a transformative spiritual encounter with Jesus Christ. This evangelical movement started in Gainesville, Texas with a part-time Presbyterian youth minister, Jim Rayburn. Rayburn was challenged by his church in 1938 to develop a ministry to unchurched youth at the local public high school. He began to build personal relationships with selected youth at the high school, and then bridged these relationships into a weekly club for students. Determined to not make the event like "church," Rayburn pioneered a format that included games, skits, singing, and food.

After graduating from Dallas Theological Seminary, Rayburn and four fellow graduates launched Young Life in Dallas, Texas, in October 1941. Within the space of four years, they had student clubs all across Texas, and in 1946 moved their headquarters to Colorado Springs, Colorado; by that point they had 20 full-time staff working across several western and mid-western states. A chapter at Wheaton College began in this period to make heavy use of volunteers rather than paid staff. This innovation became a hallmark attribute for the explosive growth that Young Life was to subsequently experience.

From the 1940s through the 1960s, Young Life was principally working with suburban high school students and by the end of the 1960s, clubs were found in virtually every state. In the early 1970s, Young Life turned its attention to multiethnic and urban areas, and subsequently to isolated rural areas and other nations. The early focus on clubs broadened over time to encompass weekend and summer camps located on 25 premier properties in the United States and Canada, weekly discussion and Bible study groups called Campaigners, a ministry to youth with disabilities (Capernaum), a ministry to junior high and middle school youth (WyldLife), Young Life "schools" that train adult staff for youth ministry, Military Communities Youth Ministries (U.S. military bases and ten nations in Europe and Asia), and the Amicus International Student Exchange. A total of eight seminaries in the United States offer specialized programs to Young Life staffers as part of their ongoing professional development. Total Young Life staff in 2002 included 3,288 paid staff, and 26,767 volunteers (United States) and 981 volunteers (internationally). All staff members, paid or volunteer, sign an evangelical statement of faith concerning the Bible, the Trinity, the death and resurrection of Jesus Christ, personal salvation in Christ, eternal life for the "saved," and eternal judgment for others. A board of 23 trustees, drawn from across the United States, guides the ministry.

As of May 2003, Young Life was in more than 4,073 schools and other outreach locations around the world. Total participants in the 2002–2003 school year included over 180,000 kids in weekly activities and an estimated total of over 800,000 students participating in at least one activity in more than 800 communities in the United States. Over 40,000 adolescents attended summer camps, and another 36,000 participated in weekend camps during the school year. Young Life is present in 49 countries outside the United States, with 393 ministries to nationals, international school students, or adolescent dependents of the U.S. military. Total revenues in 2002 were over $185 million, along with more than $10 million in capital contributions related to the various properties owned in North America. Denny Rydberg, the first executive hired from outside the organization, was named the fifth president of Young Life in 1993.

Young Life continues to provide dynamic and life-changing experiences for youth through its multifaceted program offerings around the globe. True to the focus of its founder, Young Life takes a decidedly nontraditional approach to youth ministry within the context of evangelical Christianity.

—*Dennis William Cheek*

FURTHER READING

Burns, J., Devries, M., & Fields, D. (2002). *The youth builder: Today's resource for relational youth ministry.* Ventura, CA: Gospel Light.

Rayburn, J., III. (2000). *From bondage to liberty: Dance, children, dance.* Charlotte, NC: Morningstar.

Senter, M. H., III. (2000). "Young life." In M. J. Anthony, W. S. Benson, D. Eldridge, & J. Gorman (Eds.), *Evangelical dictionary of Christian education* (pp. 736–737). Grand Rapids, MI: Baker.

Woodruff, M. (2000). *Managing youth ministry chaos.* Loveland, CO: Group Publishing.

YOUTHBUILD

Human beings have a universal desire to be cared about, to care about others, and to belong to a community in which people care about each other. In our society, we have put a religious label on, and religions have given voice to, this need to care and belong. However, this is a deep spiritual need that transcends religion, social class, nationality, and all forms of identity. If we do not fulfill this fundamental spiritual need, we will not fulfill the deepest aspirations of humanity. When we do fulfill it, we liberate the best in the human psyche. If we want to raise children and youth who are good citizens, who fulfill their potential, and who take leadership for a better world, they need to belong to something that allows them to explicitly define their desire to serve and care and make a difference.

This is a spiritual need that exists independent of religion as well as within religion. It needs to be understood by secular humanists, named, spoken to, and welcomed within our programs of social change and human development.

The importance of this need is particularly apparent among disconnected youth. There are 5.4 million 16- to 24-year-old young people in America who are unemployed and not in school. More than 2 million of them are poor, and an additional 365,000 are in prison. These young people have fallen off the edge of society. For most of them, their academic, employment, social, and spiritual development are stalled, or in reverse, moving toward powerless despair, antisocial withdrawal, or acting out. They are at serious risk of becoming permanently disconnected from positive community and productive lifestyles.

Yet they are fairly easily reclaimed. The right combination of opportunities within a caring community can awaken an enormous desire to build a positive life and give back to families and communities. Having experienced profoundly difficult life crises and family problems, many of these young people hold just under the surface a passionate desire to help make the world a better place. They have seen the underside of society, and if given a chance, they would like to change it.

YouthBuild is an example of a program for young people that produces inspiring results for thousands of out-of-school and out-of-work youth and young adults. In it young people build housing for homeless and low-income people while attending a YouthBuild alternative school. It has been authorized and funded as a program of the U.S. Department of Housing and Urban Development since 1993. There are now 200 YouthBuild programs in 44 states. About 55,000 youth have participated since the first YouthBuild was started in 1978 in East Harlem.

YouthBuild is not a religious organization, yet its directors consider the program "faith based" in the secular sense, given that it espouses faith in humanity, faith in the power of love and opportunity as change agents, and faith in the sacred value of every human being no matter how damaged the person may have been by past experiences. The program believes in collective ventures to enhance the well-being of communities and society.

The adults who come to work in YouthBuild programs have faith in the value of caring about other human beings. They believe caring about others makes a difference in the world; indeed, it is the cause to which the adults in YouthBuild have given their lives. The primary motivation of those who work with YouthBuild is not materialistic, nor is it religious. It is humanistic: They care about the welfare of communities, fellow human beings, and the planet. They work very hard to make the world a better place, especially for people who have been born poor and live in an oppressed community.

YouthBuild does not deliberately recruit staff members from any religious group, and does not ask people about their religious faith or their spiritual practices, although people with strong religious backgrounds gravitate to YouthBuild. Among the people who have emerged as local leaders are a Jesuit priest, Catholic nun, Buddhist monk, Muslim imam, and many highly engaged members of numerous specific faiths. To the extent that employees and participants experience YouthBuild as a spiritual community, it is because leaders welcome and embrace the spiritual needs of members. These needs are not usually identified as "spiritual," but rather as universal human needs.

The need to love and be loved is fundamental. The need to be useful, to give, to belong, and to see the value of one's contribution to the community and the world, is universal. Simply recognizing that—within a society that is profoundly materialistic and individualistic—unleashes spiritual energy.

When youth or directors are gathered together from around the country to share their experiences and learn from each other, or when young people are given a chance to express their deepest feelings of connectedness and their highest aspirations for becoming somebody who can make a difference, what often emerges spontaneously is prayer. When people feel supported, connected, inspired, and liberated to pursue their best selves and contribute to something larger than themselves, they are moved to give thanks to whatever higher power that they have learned to talk to. This takes the connection deeper, as people feel another level of their own consciousness and identity being accepted. Soon tears may flow as young people speak freely from their hearts about their personal change, inspiration, gratitude, and vision. The role, then, of leadership is to accept the spontaneous expression of religious expression and guide the group toward ecumenical prayer that welcomes diverse faiths.

When YouthBuild held a nationwide rap contest, explicitly prohibiting lyrics that were violent, sexist, or materialistic, what developed was a wonderful array of songs about God and revolution. Deep religious energy and a desire for profound social change infused the passionate release that comes through rap.

At one national conference, when the young leaders had taken a pledge to commit themselves to the well-being of their communities, to take leadership with a spirit of love and justice, they spontaneously called for saying the Pledge of Allegiance, drawing on another early source of a sense of belonging.

When the attacks of September 11 occurred, YouthBuild students in New York City spontaneously asked to go to Ground Zero to help. YouthBuild students in other communities held bake sales and sent money to the victims. The outpouring of their sympathy was another expression of a spiritual connection to other human beings in their larger community.

When people feel cared about, they feel grateful. They want to give back. They feel connected, and the urge to give love surfaces naturally.

In most YouthBuild programs, the students say a pledge that goes something like the following (each program modifies and writes their own pledge if they so choose):

We, the Brothers and Sisters of YouthBuild, pledge before God and all Mankind:

- The love and loyalty of our hearts,
- The wisdom and courage of our minds,
- The strength and vigor of our bodies,
- In the service of our fellow citizens.

We dedicate ourselves to bring about unity in our community. We promise to stand up for justice, brotherhood, sisterhood, and peace, and

- To work diligently and creatively, and
- To think generously and honestly.

All this we do out of profound respect for our community and ourselves.

Such a pledge gives direction and commonality to something the young people are yearning for: belonging to something larger than themselves with positive values and a vision of the life we can lead and the community we can create. This is an essential spiritual experience.

—Dorothy Stoneman and Anne Leslie

FURTHER READING

Duke University, Fuqua School of Business, Center for the Advancement of Social Entrepreneurship. (2004). *The growth of YouthBuild: A case study.* Retrieved January 14, 2005, from www.fuqua.duke.edu/centers/case/faculty/publications.html.

Stoneman, D. (2000). *Leadership development.* Somerville, MA: YouthBuild USA. Retrieved January 14, 2005, from www.YouthBuildUSA.org.

Z

ZOROASTRIANISM

Zoroastrianism emerged more than 1,000 years before the rise of Islam, in the remote desert of Babylon (today Iran). This religious tradition professes belief in one all-powerful and supreme god, and is rich with moral codes and apocalyptic notions. The historical development of Zoroastrianism is problematic, for there are numerous gaps in recorded works and many of the texts are not datable. However, the direct influence that this tradition had on the ancient Israelites, and on later Christian and Islamic religious practices and belief systems, cannot be questioned. Zoroastrianism is alive today in small remnant communities in both India and Iran. These communities have preserved the tradition for the past 14 centuries. Although there are only about 100,000 adherents to the Zoroastrian tradition living today, Zoroastrianism is considered a great religious tradition because of the structure of its religious ideas and its contribution to the history of Judaism, Christianity, and Islam.

The religious beliefs of Zoroastrians are grounded on belief in the supreme creator god Ahura Mazda, meaning "Wise Lord." In ancient times, these people were referred to as Mazda worshippers who practiced the highest moral standards of the "Good Religion." The ethical component of Zoroastrianism emphasizes morality as both an ideal and as an achievement. Zoroastrians claim their vocation in goodness in thought, word, and deed. They have lived this vocation throughout the centuries, and have earned a solid reputation for trustworthiness in both the social and business worlds of ancient and modern times.

The name Zoroastrian refers to the traditions and the prophetic founder and teacher of the faith, Zarathushtra, whose name among the Greeks came to be known as Zoroaster. As a prophet, meaning one who speaks to god, Zoroaster revealed the secrets and will of Ahura Mazda, proper religious conduct, practices, and beliefs. Zoroaster, a great son of Persia, flourished 258 years before Alexander the Great, making him active in about 558 B.C.E.

Zoroaster's life followed a unique path. As an infant and youth, legends indicate that Zoroaster was protected from an attack by wild beasts. As a man he was given the gift of healing, and he performed miraculous cures such as reviving a horse near death. Zoroaster continued to develop into his role as a prophet, and entered into a spiritual odyssey testing his faith against demonic forces that attempted to steer him toward the path of evil via temptation.

It was at this time when Zoroaster began the first stages of Zoroastrianism that he had a vision of Ahura Mazda, the one supreme creator god. In his vision, Zoroaster saw this good god in his heavenly realm, surrounded by six Amesha Spentas—holy immortals or angels. This moment helped Zoroaster understand that religion reflects an ongoing universal battle. In his vision from Ahura Mazda, Zoroaster was made aware that the forces of light (good) are in constant combat with the demonic counterpart, Angra Mainyu. Angra Mainyu is the dark antagonist to the god of light, Ahura Mazda. Angra Mainyu is surrounded by his evil spirits called the Lie, who serve his every command. Zoroaster called this dark army the *daeva,* which is a polytheistic term meaning "many gods."

The history of how Zoroastrianism was created comes from the legend describing a great battle between Ahura Mazda, the god of truth, and Angra Mainyu, the god of the lie. This notion of the constant battle between truth and lies was most satisfactory to Zoroaster when he witnessed all the evil around him, and he believed that Ahura Mazda was only good, and through him humans could be good. This belief led Zoroaster to preach the news of one supreme creator god, and to choose a path of goodness over evil.

The evolution of the Zoroastrian religion is based on secrets and ethical teachings that Ahura Mazda shared with Zoroaster. Zoroaster began a new religious movement of believing in one god in the Babylonian region.

The Zoroastrian tradition includes a strong belief in sacred texts called the Avestan Scriptures. They are deemed the holiest of Zoroastrian literature because they are believed to be delivered by the god Ahura Mazda to Zoroaster who compiled the Avestan Scriptures himself. The Avestan Scriptures are written in their original form of old Persian, which is the oldest form of the Persian language dating back to the Achaemenian era (559–331 B.C.E.). The Avestan Scriptures are divided into major and minor sections. The major section of the Scriptures focuses on right worship, laws, sayings, and the resurrection of Zoroaster. The religious worship for Zoroastrians is done through the sayings of a collection of hymns that are recited daily. These are called the "Five Gathas," and are written by Zoroaster himself as a personal address to Ahura Mazda, praying to God for righteousness. All Zoroastrians are to worship Ahura Mazda as the one and only supreme god.

The second section of the Avestan Scriptures contains the Laws (Videvdat) that dictate how Zoroastrians can defend themselves against demons and live good and holy lives. The Laws of the Scriptures are a collection of texts that counter the forces of evil through purity laws, defining how to avoid evil and purify oneself for God, and describing the end times.

Another important section of the Avestan Scriptures consists of the Hadhokht Nask, which are sayings that describe the soul's fate after death. Zoroastrians have a firm belief in final judgment and the resurrection of all peoples. After death on the fourth day, a deceased person crosses the bridge called Chinvat, which connects humanity with the unseen world. The righteous will find the bridge as broad as a highway, and they will take it to the House of Song where they will await the Last Day. For the wicked, the bridge will seem narrow as a razor, and they will fall off of it into hell.

Belief in the resurrection of Zoroaster to fight against Angra Mainyu and his dark army of *daevas* comes through in this compilation written by Zoroaster, as he attested that it was shown to him by Ahura Mazda himself. Just before the Last Day, Zoroaster will return in the form of a prophet conceived by a virgin by his own seed stored in a mountain lake. A prophet would appear in this way at 1,000-year intervals during the 3,000 years between Zoroaster and the renovation of the world.

These and other beliefs can be seen within the three monotheistic faiths of Judaism, Christianity, and Islam. The influence of Zoroastrianism in the development of Judaism is dated to the exile of the Israelites in 586 B.C.E. to Babylon (Iran). Here the Israelites lived as slaves and were thrust into the religious practices of the Babylonians. These teachings and beliefs influenced the Judaic faith as seen in the Book of Daniel, which is the first apocalyptic book of the Old Testament. The teachings of Satan as God's rival, life after death, final judgment, and redemption appear in the Book of Daniel and later works, and were not elaborated until the exile.

Many symbols are central to the Zoroastrian tradition. The first is fire—the central symbol of divine presence is in fire. Zoroastrians have been called fire worshippers, but they do not worship the fire. Instead, fire represents a sign of the power of light, which is Ahura Mazda. Another important religious image for Zoroastrianism is the symbol of Ahura Mazda, which is crafted into a disk called the *farohar,* which has wings, a tail, and a pair of long, curved legs. A male figure is depicted on this *farohar* from the waist up in a profile above it. The figure is bearded, wears a robe, and holds a ring in the left hand. This symbol is found in the households of most Zoroastrian adherents.

There are no portraits of Zoroaster himself, but later centuries have developed an iconographic tradition depicting him. Zoroaster is portrayed with long wavy hair, under a white turban, full beard, dressed in white loose trousers and a robe. Behind him are sunrays and a halo, and he carries a staff in his right hand. This icon can also be found in many Zoroastrian homes.

Congregational worship is not a typical feature of Zoroastrian ritual. It is more individualistic, where the individual shows his or her own devotion to God through recitation of hymns and prayers at any time, in addition to the Five Gathas that are recited at specific times during the day.

The place of worship for Zoroastrians is a sanctuary, or fire temple, known as the *agiari,* or fireplace. A large metal urn with sand and ash on which the sacred fire burns continuously is placed on a stone platform in a chamber. Priests or *magi*, who add wood and say five prayers (*gahs*), during the day maintain the fire.

The Zoroastrian calendar is an ancient solar version of 12 months of 30 days each, plus 5 remaining days that do not form part of any month but are set aside for time of special ritual called the Gatha Days, meaning five in number. On these days, the community comes together as a whole and feasts and prays.

Within the calendar, there is a cycle of devotion outlining in great detail the appropriate forms of worship on specific days. The 9th day of the month is sacred to fire. This is the day most favored for visiting the fire temple and making an offering of wood or other goods. The 9th month is also devoted to the worship of fire (i.e., light or God).

The 10th day of the 8th month is dedicated to water. This is a time when Zoroastrians stand at the edge of a body of water and offer individual prayers to God. Four days each month are dedicated to Ahura Mazda and to his creations. The year-end period relates to the origin of the agricultural seasons. This is called the Muktad period, when Zoroastrians come together to offer a community prayer and feast.

Zoroaster's emphasis on ethics calls to mind the step-by-step moral teachings in other religions that form humans' moral code. The accomplishments of Zoroaster as a prophet and a reformer can be seen not only in Islam, Judaism, and Christianity, but also in the modern usage of Zoroastrians themselves. A small community that survives and lives according to the Avestan Scriptures and continuing the battles of good versus evil, Zoroastrians have contributed much to monotheistic traditions.

—Julie Wieland-Robbescheuten

FURTHER READING

Oxtoby, W. G. (Ed.). (2002). *World religions: Western traditions.* Oxford: Oxford University Press.

Index